The Best Recipes in the World

ALSO BY MARK BITTMAN

How to Cook Everything: Bittman Takes On America's Chefs

The Minimalist Entertains

The Minimalist Cooks at Home

The Minimalist Cooks Dinner

Simple to Spectacular

Jean-Georges: Cooking at Home with a Four-Star Chef

How to Cook Everything

Leafy Greens

Fish

THE BEST RECIPES IN THE WORLD

MORE THAN 1,000 INTERNATIONAL DISHES TO COOK AT HOME

Mark Bittman

BROADWAY BOOKS ■ NEW YORK

PRINTED IN THE UNITED STATES OF AMERICA

BROADWAY BOOKS and its logo, a letter B bisected on the diagonal, are trademarks of Random House, Inc.

Visit our Web site at www.broadwaybooks.com

First edition published 2005

Book design by Elizabeth Rendfleisch
Illustrations by Fritz Dumville

Library of Congress Cataloging-in-Publication Data
Bittman, Mark.
    The best recipes in the world : more than 1,000 international dishes to cook at home /
Mark Bittman.—1st ed.
        p.   cm.
    1. Cookery, International.   I. Title.
TX725.A1B525 2004
641.59—dc22   2003069714

ISBN 0-7679-0672-1

10   9   8   7   6   5   4   3   2   1

To home cooks everywhere,

and to the memory of Craig, Julia, Phil, Max, and Helen

ACKNOWLEDGMENTS

I dreamed about writing an international cookbook for thirty years, and I'm grateful to everyone who allowed me to convert my fantasies into reality. It's literally impossible, however, for me to mention everyone who helped me, kind cooks worldwide who invited me into their homes and shared their skills, their warmth, and their families' food. How similar we all are when cooking and eating never ceases to amaze me.

I had plenty of help at home, too. Genevieve Ko Sweet worked hard and long in helping me determine the ultimate versions of the recipes you see here; Kate Bittman and Peter Meehan also played key roles in getting the manuscript into shape.

At Broadway Books, my editor, Jennifer Josephy, managed the project (and me) in stunningly efficient fashion. Copy editor Chris Benton caught more gaffes than I care to admit, smoothed my not-always-brilliant prose, and helped me reorganize the book into the (I hope user-friendly) shape in which you see it. I'm happy to count Doubleday/Broadway publisher and president Steve Rubin among my friends, and I remain grateful for his professionalism as well.

The other staff at Broadway Books were also terrific. I worked most closely with Elena Park, Ada Yonenaka, Elizabeth Rendfleisch, Luisa Francavilla, Catherine Pollock, and Nicole Dewey. Many others—outstanding professionals all—worked hard on this massive project.

Some of the ideas that were spawned by this book found a home in stories that ran in the *New York Times,* where I happily work with Kathleen McElroy and Nick Fox. Pat Gurosky and Kris Ensminger have been terrific colleagues for years, and Barbara Graustark is inspiring, understanding, and supportive. Sam Sifton was my editor during much of the period I was working on this book, and there is no better. Other people to whom I will remain thankful forever are Linda Giuca, Louise Kennedy, Trish Hall, Rick Flaste, and Chris Kimball. My debt to Jean-Georges Vongerichten is equally enormous, though the rumors that he taught me how to cook are unfounded.

There was a period of researching this book—a rather intense five or six years—that was especially challenging. I relied heavily on the support of many, many relatives and dear friends: Karen Baar, John Ringwald, David Paskin, Pamela Hart, Sherry Slade, Fred Zolna,

Semeon Tsalbins, Bob and Mary Newhouse, Shari and Harry Sucheki, Joe and Kim McGrath, Jack Hitt, and Lisa Sanders. Special mention: the Baldinos, for being ideal neighbors.

To Angela Miller, Charlie Pinsky, and John H. Willoughby, people who are there for me every day, my love and thanks. To Alisa X. Smith, who spent more time with me (and this book) than anyone else, I add my eternal gratitude. And to my parents, Murray and Gertrude, and my kids, Emma and Kate—I just consider myself lucky. xxx guys.

CONTENTS

Introduction Home cooking has never been easier, more exciting, or filled with as much potential. A mere generation ago—in many parts of the country a mere ten years ago—if you wanted soy sauce or miso, you went to an Asian market; if you wanted decent olive oil or mozzarella, you went to an Italian market; and if you wanted bulgur or phyllo, you went to a Middle Eastern market. Now all those ingredients, and many more, are routinely available at supermarkets throughout North America. Creating a well-stocked international pantry may still require some time and work—your supermarket may not carry miso, curry paste, or chipotles (though many do)—but lots of formerly exotic items are widely available. And the international pantry—which requires only occasional replenishment—enables the home cook to vary his or her cuisine with almost no work.

Every bit as important as ingredients, however, is knowledge: what do we do with this miso, these chipotles, this curry paste? Here again we're in luck. More information about the cooking of other lands is available than ever before, and the planet becomes smaller every year. With or without this cookbook, if you had never cooked Vietnamese food before and wanted to do so tonight, you could dig up a few recipes, head over to the supermarket, spend a couple of hours in the kitchen, and be wolfing down that caramelized shrimp before dark.

So. We have the ingredients and we have the knowledge. My goal in this book is to help you become familiar with the ingredients, to distill the knowledge, and to make the recipes as accessible as possible and as "American" as I can, without robbing them of their souls.

THE TECHNIQUES OF INTERNATIONAL COOKING

This is not as challenging as it sounds. In my other boldly titled book, *How to Cook Everything*, I focused on the techniques of basic cooking. I recognized that there was a crying need for a book that covered the basics—one written primarily for the couple of generations of cooks that we had lost to so-called fast and convenience foods, to the lure of restaurants, to lack of interest and the family of two wage earners. (In fact, there are a dozen reasons why many Americans began to stop cooking in the fifties and sixties and have only recently resumed or taken it up for the first time.)

But the voyages I took for this book convinced me of something I'd already known: ingredients change, but technique does not. It's all basic. I have traveled consistently for three decades, always with food as the focus, but beginning in 1999 I began to travel internationally with increasing frequency, with the aim of making the recipes included in this book as authentic as possible at home. As I said, my trips confirmed that cooking techniques simply don't vary from one place to the next.

At least not much. Some techniques, of course, are unique to a given culture, and others are tweaked from one culture to the next. One might wrap food in banana leaves before steaming; another might use corn husks or paper (or, for that matter, aluminum foil)—but this hardly makes a difference. In the broad scheme of things, for home cooks who are not looking to become expert at any given cuisine, these differences are irrelevant. It turns out that the techniques of cooking—applying heat to food with the goal of making it more digestible, palatable, and, ultimately, delicious—are pretty much the same wherever you go. (Think about it; how many ways can you actually cook?) It's the flavors that change.

The world's cuisines have far more in common than not. Think about bits of food wrapped in pastry and baked, fried, or steamed. You might call them dumplings, pot stickers, ravioli, or empanadas, gyoza, manti, or pierogi (I could go on). They're universal. I recently held a dumpling up in front of a class of students at a local community college, where the ethnic groups were as diverse as they are at the JFK International Arrivals Terminal. I asked whether anyone came from a country where such a thing didn't exist. No hands were raised. The differences are more about whether you season them with parsley and Parmesan or garlic and soy sauce and ginger than about how you put them together.

The same is true of basic soups and stews; the same is true of salads; the same is true, largely, of grilled dishes. These things are universal; the techniques are simple, and the differences among them are subtle. This does not mean the differences in flavors are subtle—far from it! You make an egg drop soup with Parmesan and parsley, then you make one with soy sauce and cilantro, and the tastes are completely different. But the techniques are identical.

I'm not saying that technique doesn't matter. Because of differences in fuel supply, weather, and history, different cultures favor different methods. Stir-frying, which developed in regions where wood is hard to come by, uses much less fuel than grilling, which is popular where wood is plentiful. Many cultures do not bother with ovens (and therefore leavened bread), either because it's just too hot or, again, because ovens require lots of cooking fuel. But these are not issues for the American home cook.

In fact, it's safe to say that if you know the basics of cooking—by which I mean if you know how to use a burner, an oven, a broiler, and a grill, and you know a little about buying food, storing it, cleaning and trimming it, and chopping it—you know the basics of international cooking. If you consider yourself at all adept at any one cuisine, be it "American" (a meaningless term if ever there was one), French, Italian, Mexican, or Indonesian, you are already adept at the basic techniques of every cuisine. All you need do is become familiar with the groups of ingredients that make a cuisine distinctive, and you're well on your way.

Though I can make a decent meal out of almost any ingredients you give me, my own technique is not much more advanced than was my grandmother's. The difference between her and me is simply the difference in our times: we are fortunately exposed to unprecedented amounts of both ingredients and information from all over the world. And the difference between me and a chef—which I most definitely am not—is that I am neither trying to impress anyone nor trying to make a profit on the food I cook. I'm just trying to prepare great-tasting food that can be replicated by anyone who uses my recipes.

WHAT IS INTERNATIONAL COOKING?

Every cookbook makes choices, and obviously international cooking is a broad topic. (Only a cookbook about a very specific slice of cooking, say Majorcan cuisine, could even begin to claim to be comprehensive, and still it would have to be a very good cookbook about Majorcan cuisine.) It would be fair,

therefore, for you to wonder what kinds of international dishes are included here. So let me explain my goals about cooking and cookbook writing in general and international cuisine in particular.

Like everyone else, I love to eat in restaurants, and I'm terribly impressed by what great chefs can do. But I have become, in effect, a recipe hunter: I look for dishes I can cook for myself and friends, those that might eventually wind up in my *New York Times* column or my cookbooks. Recipes like these rarely come from the "best" restaurant in town but from neighborhood restaurants or home cooks.

When I research, I am invariably referred to the "best" restaurant in whatever city I visit, a place that might ignore local cooking entirely, focusing instead on French or what might be called "contemporary international" cuisine; or a place that would try to gussy up the local cuisine, almost inevitably making it worse, not better.

Sometimes the places and people I have the greatest success with are those I find under protest. Someone might say, "The food is very good there, but it's a family place, with only locals—not in an interesting neighborhood and not the kind of place for a visitor." Comments like these have led me to spectacular eating experiences in Stockholm, Rome, Istanbul, the Mekong Delta, the Yucatán, and countless other places.

When I'd look for a home cook, the experience was similar. I'd hear "She"—almost always "she," of course—"cooks only the local things; it's really not very special." To me this was a dead giveaway that I'd found the right person.

As in local handicrafts, what's ordinary and traditional in the cooking of other cultures is exactly what's special to the curious traveler—and cook. Because what's not special to the people who belong to any culture other than yours may well be special to you.

The culture that defines much of the world is

American. What's exotic to families in Vietnam and Turkey is exactly what is common to us—Hollywood; cheap, hip fashion; McDonald's; and Chili's. What's special to those of us who visit these countries may be what is boring to them: the daily herb-, noodle-, and meat-rich soup called pho or the skewered ground meat with eggplant.

Those are the kinds of dishes on which I have focused here: the daily cooking and eating of the people of much of the rest of the world. This is a very personal (more on this in a minute) compilation of the simplest, best-tasting food I have experienced in my travels. In fact, you can think of this book as a printed version of all the meals I've truly loved in good bars, little joints, mom-and-pop operations, and home kitchens.

Though it's all close to my heart, it's not exactly my food. But that's the point. (There's a quote from Montaigne I like: "I have only made up a bunch of other men's flowers, providing of my own only the string that ties them together.") It is the historical and traditional food of cooks from around the world.

REALITY AND AUTHENTICITY

Do I make changes? Of course. Remember that all cuisines originated in subsistence cultures, when the preparation of food was not an option and the amount of time it took was less of an issue. We are freed not only from the burden of raising chickens, for example, but of raising the food needed to feed them and even of cutting them up. We neither pick olives nor brine them. We neither grow corn nor dry and grind it for meal. Nor do we need to think about any of these things months or years in advance or worry—much—about whether it rains.

All of this may be obvious, but my point is that when you take into account all the work that goes into planning, growing, harvesting, slaughtering, and butchering food, coupled with the fact that the kitchen appliances on which we rely most are just about a century old (imagine if all recipes began "build a fire in your stove"), it's not surprising that many traditional recipes remain complex, and more time-consuming than they need be.

Some of the recipes I publish are streamlined, modernized, or updated versions of absolute classics. For us, scarcity is all about time; we have, if anything, too many ingredients. So a dish like shrimp lo mein borrows from an ancient and international tradition of combining noodles with whatever bits of protein and vegetables can be found and codifies it in a way that works for today's cooks. Similarly, shrimp in green sauce, an Iberian dish, can be made in almost no time, thanks to the now-ubiquitous food processor.

In fact, what strikes me as most surprising is that many of the dishes included here are little changed from their traditional versions. Jook—also known as congee and little more than rice porridge—is a perfect example. I was told to look for it when I first visited Hong Kong and have eaten it in Chinese communities all over the world since then. Only last year did it occur to me that it was a dead-easy creation, one that could be made at home in just as many guises as I'd seen in restaurants and one that—despite its odd name—had wide-ranging appeal; it's become one of my favorites.

Similarly, xec—a Mayan citrus salsa—could not be more straightforward, nor could it be made with more common ingredients, yet what it does to plain grilled meat is truly remarkable. And sweet black pepper fish, a Vietnamese classic, relies for most of its flavor on two condiments you have sitting right on your counter: sugar and pepper. Though the preparation is unusual (the sugar is used to make a slightly bitter caramel sauce) and the results are spectacular (people really love this one), you can't possibly begin with anything more ordinary.

It's my job to make recipes like these useful. This is not a scholarly work, not an intellectual survey of world cuisine, but a practical one. It's also a personal one; the recipes I've omitted are those I've never experienced—and believe me, there are plenty—those I don't believe translate well to the home kitchen, or those I plain don't like.

There is always the question of authenticity. I have almost no culinary roots other than the ones I've put down myself; needless to say, I am not Lebanese and Vietnamese and Mexican and French. Everything I have learned I have learned as an adult, from other people, and from other people's cookbooks. So what makes my food "authentic"?

There are two approaches to bringing back recipes from abroad: One is to find the absolute "true" version (which of course doesn't exist) and to re-create it as closely as possible, in painstaking detail. My approach is to find a common, good-tasting version of an authentic dish and to re-create it in ways that do not rob it of its integrity but make it accessible.

I approach every dish I encounter with an open mind. I try to enjoy it to its fullest and understand it as deeply as I can. And I've learned this: every cook has her or his own way of doing things. Even the most codified cuisine—French—leaves plenty of room for interpretation. And even the simplest dish in the world—lentils and rice, for example—can be prepared literally hundreds of ways. (If you don't believe me, try cooking Dal, page 433, followed by Lentils and Rice, page 439—you'll quickly understand just how widely different recipes using the same main ingredients can be.)

So I believe if my intentions are true, if I understand a dish—its meaning, even soul, if you will—and I try to keep its flavors intact, authenticity will follow. Undoubtedly I fail at times, but I do believe those are the exceptions.

A NOTE ON FRANCE AND ITALY VS. EVERYWHERE ELSE

My goal here was not to find the most esoteric recipes I could. On the contrary, it was to find the most common recipes in the countries that are underrepresented in most cookbooks. I've always been fascinated by the cooking of Asia (I learned the basics of Indian and Japanese cuisines before tackling those of French or Italian), and I like to think this book acknowledges how much the world of food has changed: Asian food is now—finally—considered the equal of European food, something that was definitely not true thirty years ago. At that time even Italian food was considered exotic, and, for the most part "international" meant "French." French food was the epitome of good cooking, and Asian food was something most Americans experienced at their local Chinese restaurant.

In the eyes of many epicures, French food remains the ne plus ultra of cuisine; Italian food is a close second. To these people, the food of other countries may taste good, but it doesn't embody the subtlety, the skill, the complex synthesis of flavors. (It's true that Western European cooking is the world's most wine friendly, and many epicures believe that wine is integral to good eating, so, for them, they're right. It's equally true that much of the most-heralded Western European cooking is overthought and overworked.)

But anyone who has enjoyed a nicely prepared Jook (page 123), Lamb Pilaf with Cinnamon (page 412), Fish Fillets Poached in Caramel Sauce (page 232), or Red-Cooked Chicken (page 280) has quickly recognized the beauty of these dishes. No one would call them "haute cuisine," but they're all fabulous, authentic, and extremely easy to prepare. Furthermore, they represent their countries of origin—China, Turkey, Vietnam, and India, respectively—quite admirably. It takes an open mind and a broad palate to appreciate this food, but not much more.

I don't mean for this to become a shouting match.

I love French food, real French food, the stuff that French people—as opposed to French chefs—cook for themselves, and I've included some of it here. Besides, the fact that you have read this far probably means I'm preaching to the converted: you're sold on the idea that global cuisine goes far beyond that of Western Europe.

For that reason, I have intentionally downplayed the number of both French and Italian recipes in these pages. That does not mean I don't include them; indeed, there are plenty of winners. It just means that they do not comprise, as has so often been the case in "international" cookbooks, the majority of recipes. Both of these cuisines have received sufficient attention—both in my own books and in many others—to satisfy any home cook who cares to look.

USING *THE BEST RECIPES IN THE WORLD*

Like all cookbooks, this one is personal, which means at its heart it is a reflection of me. So it will help you to know that I'm a thoughtful but essentially lazy cook. Therefore:

• I don't use two ingredients where one will do.
• I don't mind spending a long time cooking a single dish as long as I don't have to pay much attention to what's going on (which is why I love baking bread and braising).
• I'll rarely use an ingredient not sold at my local supermarket. (The most time-consuming part of my style of cooking is often shopping, and I don't want it to take longer than it has to.)
• I think one great dish—one prepared thoughtfully and with love—is the basis of a great meal. When people ask me for serving suggestions, my most common answers are "bread and salad" and

"rice and a steamed vegetable." You can go beyond this, of course, but that's your choice. (I also find that many serving suggestions are overly specific; I want to expand your possibilities, not limit them.)

The chapter-by-chapter organization of *The Best Recipes in the World* is traditional and familiar to anyone who uses cookbooks. But inside each chapter, things are a little different. I have tried to think of each chapter as a separate entity and, rather than organize them by ingredient or by country, I've tried to organize them by categories that make sense in the kitchen. For example, the appetizers chapter is organized by how amenable each recipe is to advance preparation; when you're entertaining (which is when most people serve appetizers), the most important thing to know is whether a dish can be cooked a day or an hour ahead of time.

The meat chapter is organized by cooking technique. This is because most braised recipes, for example, can be made with almost any meat; the fact that you're braising (and again, the flavoring you're using) is more important than whether you choose lamb or pork as a meat.

Obviously, I think this kind of intrachapter organization makes sense. But the idea is to make it transparent to you, to make *The Best Recipes in the World* as useful as possible without extra work on your part.

It's all pretty simple; basically, the cooking of other cultures is the same as that of your own, with a little tweaking. The amazing thing is that few people realized this, and the few defining ingredients of each culture rarely left their own countries, even as recently as fifty years ago, making this realm of cooking unavailable to most of the world's citizens. Now it's open to everyone, at least in the United States and Canada. To get started you might need a leap of faith, but not much more. Take it.

THE INTERNATIONAL PANTRY

The focus of this book is on the straightforward dishes that comprise the repertoire of the world's home cooks. Many of these dishes are simple, basic, and easily accomplished using a variety of on-hand ingredients along with one or two things brought home from the market. With this approach, anyone can cook almost anything.

It's all a lot easier if you maintain a well-stocked pantry—and this means more than a couple of cans of tuna fish, a jar of mayo, a bag of chips, and a bottle of salsa. A couple dozen ingredients belong in every kitchen all the time, and a few dozen more will allow you to expand your horizons to the ends of the earth. Fortunately, most of these ingredients keep nearly indefinitely. Even better, taken together, these ingredients can take you a long way toward preparing literally hundreds of different dishes in thirty minutes or less. The basic list is far from arcane:

Anchovies. Packed in olive oil, best bought in resealable glass jars rather than cans.

Baking soda, baking powder, yeast (SAF or other brand "instant" yeast), and sugar.

Canned beans. Dried beans are preferable, but canned beans are undeniably convenient. If you think of it, cook dried beans ahead of time and freeze them in their cooking liquid.

Canned stock. A compromise, but a necessary one. If you get into Southeast Asian cooking, coconut milk is almost as important.

Canned tomatoes. Those from California are usually fine.

Capers. Packed in vinegar.

Chiles, dried. Except for northern Europe, these are nearly universal. Heat itself is easy to come by: just get the long, straight dried chiles or any other of a variety of (usually bright or brick red) chiles. But be sure to stock some mild anchos (dried poblanos) and smoky chipotles (dried or canned in adobo) as well. For more information, see page 588.

Dried mushrooms. Especially cèpes (porcini) and shiitakes. See page 112.

Flour, cornmeal, and the like. Store in the fridge if you have the room, to prevent the oils in them from turning rancid. Flour should be unbleached, and in the recipes it's all-purpose unless specified otherwise.

Olive oil. Extra virgin, please; extra virgin oil is the result of the first pressing of the olives—the "cold" pressing, meaning that the olives haven't been heated or treated with chemicals to coax out a second batch. It's infinitely less expensive than it once was and worth every penny. Country of origin doesn't matter much, though the Italophiles will hate me for saying so. And even if you start tasting and find a brand you like, it will taste different the next time you buy it. You might, as many home cooks do, have one "good" bottle on hand—an oil whose taste you really love—for finishing dishes and making salad dressing and a second "everyday" bottle—the kind of extra virgin oil that costs $20 a gallon or so—to cook with.

Onions, potatoes, garlic, and other long-keeping vegetables. When I call for chopped onion, garlic, or shallot, I mean peeled too.

Pasta. If you're focusing on Italian pasta, start with that. Rice noodles from Asia are good to have around as well, as are udon (from Japan) and Chinese wheat noodles.

Rice. See page 505. Start with a long-grain and a short-grain variety.

Soy sauce. Look for brands (Kikkoman is pretty good) that contain no more than soy, wheat, salt, water, and bacteria.

Spices. Ideally, spices should be ground just before use (sometimes after toasting) but few people (self included) do this consistently. But even whole spices, you should know, do *not* keep eternally. I try to replace my spices anually—buying new ones from Penzey's (see Sources) or the like—it's a small investment for big flavor.

Vinegar. Good red or white wine vinegar, rice vinegar, and balsamic or sherry vinegar (see page 170).

To stock your pantry with the basics of other countries is really not much more challenging, and the lists give me an opportunity to try to explain briefly what sets each region's cuisine apart from others.

First of all, it's worth reiterating that this is not a comprehensive book (I don't believe such a book could exist, but if it could, this isn't it). There are subtleties of Cambodian and Turkish cuisines, for example, that I will never understand. And to lump each of them under a broader category—like Southeast Asian or Middle Eastern—is, to some extent, insulting.

But for my practical purposes, and for the purposes of this book, it's safe to say that there are fewer than a dozen culinary regions in the world. Of course you can spend your life exploring the cooking of the French or Cambodian countryside, but that's not my intent. For my purposes, France is a region; so is Italy; so is China; another region is Iberia, which comprises not one but two countries; Scandinavia, North Africa, and Southeast Asia each contain more than two countries.

Ethnocentric as it may be, it is a reflection of the development of each region's cuisine that some are broken down further than others. France's cooking really is more extensive than Vietnam's. That doesn't mean French food is "better"—you may prefer Vietnamese cuisine, which certainly provides us with plenty of great recipes—but that Vietnamese is more limited than French.

In any case, here we go, on my whirlwind tour of the world's most interesting cuisines and what you need to stock to tackle their recipes without much further ado. You'll note that there are regions missing, but their ingredients are covered by other lists; for example, if you have the ingredients lists in the Middle Eastern/North African pantry and the French pantry, you are set for Spanish cooking—in fact, you're set for European cooking in general.

JAPAN AND KOREA

Best characterized not by sushi but by soy, Japanese cuisine developed, like so many others, based largely on geography. Meat is not a big part of the country's culinary history; fish, rice, and soy are. Both the products of the sea (not only fish, but seaweed) and the bounty of soy (in the form of soy sauce, miso, and a few more esoteric products) are the defining flavors of Japanese cooking. In fact, a basic preparation, dashi—a quickly made stock whose flavor underlies countless dishes and lingers in the air everywhere—is a combination of seaweed (specifically kelp) and shaved dried bonito (a tunalike fish); dishes made with dashi are often finished with soy sauce.

Much Japanese food is quite subtle (it reminds me, oddly enough, of Scandinavian food, with its reliance on spanking-fresh fish, simply prepared and very simply seasoned). And at the introductory level—which is what we're dealing with here—it's very simple. You learn a few recipes, you learn how to handle a few ingredients, and you're ready to impress people.

Korean food, to me, is Japanese food with guts (I know I'm going to make both friends and enemies with statements like that). Generally, Koreans use more chiles and loads more garlic. They also eat more meat and more cold-weather food in general (Korea is farther north than Japan). Their reliance on fermented soy, sesame seeds, and seaweed marks their cuisine as closely related to that of Japan; not surprisingly, since it shares a border with China, there are heavy influences from that food also.

Dried bonito flakes. These paper-thin shavings from a dried fish in the tuna family are sold in small or large packages and keep forever (and smell great in the pantry). Used almost exclusively for dashi (page 162), the basis of many Japanese dishes; if you don't plan to cook much Japanese food from this book, you can skip these.

Dried red chiles. Korean food relies heavily on these.

Dried shiitake mushrooms. Always handy, useful in many cuisines. See page 112.

Go chu jang. Wonderful Korean chili paste (see page 591). Hold off on buying this until you need it.

Mirin. Sweet cooking wine with a distinctive and lovely flavor.

Miso. See page 123. Truly one of the world's great ingredients.

Panko bread crumbs. For whatever reason, the Japanese make the best packaged bread crumbs. You'll use these all the time, in many different cuisines, and they're stocked at a lot of supermarkets, in the Asian aisle, these days.

Preserved plums (umeboshi). Totally optional but nice.

Rice vinegar. Good not only here but for light vinaigrettes across the board.

Sake. Optional. Great to drink and good in cooking.

Seaweed, especially kombu (kelp) and nori (laver). For making dashi and seaweed salad. See page 483.

Sesame oil. Dark, roasted, and used often in most East Asian cuisines.

Sesame seeds. Color doesn't matter; you will usually toast these (see page 596) and sometimes grind them. (You can also buy toasted sesame seeds, ground or whole.)

Soy sauce. Called shoyu in Japan. Wherever you buy it, whatever type you buy, it should contain no more than water, soy, wheat, salt, and a culture. Anything else is not only unnecessary but detrimental. Also see page 275.

CHINA

Large volumes have been written about Chinese cooking, and only a small handful can be considered even marginally comprehensive. Not surprising, given that this is among the three or four most extensive cuisines in the world. (It's also the most dynamic, changing now more dramatically and rapidly than any cuisine except for American.) My goal is to provide a few representative recipes that outline the basics.

Chinese food relies heavily on stir-frying, though braising is common enough and roasting makes an occasional appearance, and on every fresh ingredient you can name. No cuisine makes better use of animals and vegetables; there is hardly an ingredient in the world that isn't cooked in some way and in some place in China.

And the fact that these ingredients are often handled similarly—stir-fried—and that the seasonings used with them are limited in number makes Chinese cooking extremely approachable.

Black rice vinegar. Not essential, but a complex (and cheap!) cousin of balsamic vinegar.

Dried black mushrooms. These are the same as shiitakes; wood ear mushrooms and other fungi are also nice to have. See page 112.

Fermented black beans. See page 207. These keep forever.

Fresh ginger. Not exactly a pantry item but, with garlic, used so frequently that if you become a fan of Chinese cooking you will want to have it around. (Dried ginger is useful too.)

Fresh scallions. Ditto. Unless a recipe says otherwise, use both the white and green parts after trimming off the rough ends.

Hoisin sauce. Made from fermented soybeans, sugar, and chiles. Look for a brand with not much more than those ingredients and keep it refrigerated; it will last for months if not longer.

Oyster sauce. Unfortunately, most oyster sauce contains MSG and a host of other additives. Optional.

Sesame oil. See Japan.

Sesame seeds. See Japan.

Shaoxing wine. Cooking wine with a distinctive flavor. See page 274.

Soy sauce. See Japan. Most soy sauce made in China—at least that exported to the States—is inferior. Use the Japanese stuff (some of which is made in America and is quite good).

Star anise. Great spice, essential here.

Szechwan peppercorns. Once illegal, these are legitimate again—a good thing. Great flavor, with a tongue-numbing quality that can make eating chiles easier. See page 369.

SOUTHEAST ASIA

Increasingly popular, and understandably, because much of this region's food is to Asia what Italian cooking is to Western Europe: lighter, fresher, and more vegetable oriented.

But part of the appeal of Southeast Asian food must be attributed to its near-standard combination of flavors, one of which is not often found in savory dishes in the rest of the world: sugar. Southeast Asian food is often sweet, whether from palm or regular sugar or from coconut milk, which is used as often here as stock is in France.

Of the other flavors most closely and readily associated with the region's cooking, several stand out: nam pla, lime, and chile, whose presence can easily be (and often is) overpowering. Lemongrass is fairly common also, as, of course, are ginger (and its close cousin, the difficult-to-find galangal) and garlic. Many, many dishes—especially in Thai food—are hot, sweet, sour, and salty.

Black pepper. Very big in Vietnam; see India.

Cilantro. Key, but keeps for only a few days.

Coconut milk. Easily made fresh (page 584), this is undeniably more convenient when canned. Most brands contain a single preservative (sodium metabisulfite), so that's almost unavoidable. The flavor is good despite this.

Curry powder. A variable blend of spices, which can be bought almost anywhere or made to suit your taste (pages 592–593).

Curry paste. Canned, and handy, but you can make a similar mixture pretty easily, in the pan (see page 328). Still, it doesn't hurt to have some around.

Dried shrimp, shrimp paste. An acquired taste. You won't use it often, but shelf life is infinite, so pick some up. Also sold in paste form (shrimp paste), which is convenient.

Fish sauce. Goes by the names of nam pla, nuoc mam, and others; see page 500. Essential and keeps forever.

Galangal. Hard-to-find root; ginger almost always is a suitable substitute.

Ginger. Keeps, refrigerated, for a couple of weeks.

Lemongrass. Ditto. To trim, see page 143.

Lime. Essential. Usually far less expensive at Asian markets than "normal" supermarkets.

Lime leaves. Best fresh, these are acceptable dried and keep far longer. But buy the fresh when you see them.

Mint. Another key Southeast Asian herb.

Palm sugar. Authentic, but if you can taste the difference in cooking between this and brown sugar, you should be a professional taster. Also called jaggery.

Rice noodles. Like all dried pasta, keeps indefinitely. See page 537.

Shallots. Used in much of the world's cooking, shallots are the luxury version of onions. Always peel them if chopped or sliced. Fabulous in stir-fries and stews. Keep for weeks refrigerated or even at room temperature.

Soy sauce. See Japan.

Tamarind paste. You can make your own tamarind paste (see page 585) or buy it. Its sourness is not duplicated by the sourness of substitutes, but lime juice will work in a pinch.

Thai basil. Not easy to find (easy to grow, however), and quite perishable, but distinctive. Great if you can find it.

Thai chiles. These are hot and fiery, easily substituted for but nice to have around if you can find them fresh.

INDIA

I'm convinced that the sole reason Indian cuisine intimidates people is that many (if not most) recipes from India have long—sometimes inordinately long—ingredients lists. But what is on those lists? Mostly spices. Stock up on spices once a year or so, and you will be prepared to cook many Indian recipes without much further ado. They're easy to find, not only online and at Indian markets but also at most health food stores. (Admittedly, a few, like amchoor and asafetida, are more difficult to find, but you can cook without these if necessary.)

The cuisine of India, like that of China, is grand and varied. There are more voluntary vegetarians in India than anywhere else in the world, so it's a cuisine filled with opportunity for people who don't eat meat of any kind (I've tried to include a good proportion of vegetarian Indian recipes here). The breads, too, are comparable to the best of Europe, though completely different in style.

Many, many—perhaps the majority—of Indian dishes are braised or stewed. This makes them ideal for cooking in advance (and, therefore, for entertaining). It also gives you plenty of time to experiment and learn. This is a cuisine that is unfamiliar to most Americans but deserves exploration and will reward it.

Amchoor powder. Dried mango. Provides intense sourness; good but not essential.

Asafetida (hing). One of the world's most unusual spices, this is actually a dried resin. Its flavor is unique and, in some instances, indispensable. These instances are rare; on the other hand hing keeps forever, especially if you buy it in chunk form and grate a little each time you need it.

Black pepper. Americans don't think much of this as a spice. Obviously we use it quite a bit, but it's used more in India and sometimes takes center stage (as it does in Vietnam). I'm not obsessed with "freshly ground black pepper," but when it's used as a primary spice, it's good to start with whole black peppercorns and crack them coarsely. In the recipes I list it with salt merely as *black pepper* and leave the choice to you.

Cardamom. Native to India, cardamom is a member of the ginger family and one of the most flowery, sweet smelling of all spices. It can be purchased either in the pod or ground, but commercially ground cardamom quickly loses its flavor, and pods last a long, long time. Each pod contains a dozen or so of the bumpy seeds, which can be used whole or ground with a mortar and pestle. You can also cook the pods whole, especially in braised dishes, and they're not bad to eat, either, although to the uninitiated they will come as a surprise, a little like eating a peppercorn (but without the heat).

There are two important varieties of cardamom: green, which is the more sweetly aromatic of the two and is, after saffron and vanilla, one of the most expensive spices in the world; and brown or black, which is larger and has a more pungent camphorlike aroma. White cardamom is green cardamom that has been bleached instead of sun dried. You can substitute its seeds for those of green cardamom, but its pod is virtually flavorless and therefore contributes nothing in dishes where whole pods are used.

Cayenne. Much Indian food needs a source of heat, whether dried chiles, hot red pepper flakes, or ground cayenne.

Coriander. The leaves of fresh coriander (cilantro) are often used to garnish Indian dishes, but more important are coriander seeds, which are toasted, ground (or sometimes left whole), and added to many dishes. Preground coriander is acceptable but not as fragrant.

Cumin. Ditto—cumin is an important spice here, usually toasted before grinding. You can use preground cumin of course.

Curry powder. A mix of different spices, defined variously. See pages 592–593.

Fennel seeds. Distinctive anise flavor; may be used whole or ground.

Fenugreek. Widely used in Indian cooking, fenugreek seeds come ground and whole; the whole seeds are yellow and flat. They are bitter and very lightly aromatic; use sparingly. Fenugreek itself is a legume, and the greens are cooked in India; they're delicious, but I've seen them in this country only a couple of times.

Garam masala. The "real" name for curry powder. See page 594.

Lentils, chickpeas, and other legumes. Used big time, more than in other cuisines. You can successfully cook with common lentils and beans, but you may eventually want to get into the more unusual orange lentils (which cook very quickly) and red and black beans from India. They're easy enough to find, but also easy enough to substitute for.

Saffron. One of the world's most treasured spices, for its rich, mellow, but distinctive flavor and outrageous color. Expensive but worth it. Buy large quantities—an ounce at a time makes sense—because it's much cheaper that way, you're more likely to get real saffron, and it keeps well for years.

Turmeric. A bitter spice that is rarely used on its own. Gives a brilliant yellow color to anything with which it's cooked. Often used as a substitute for saffron.

GREECE, THE MIDDLE EAST, AND NORTH AFRICA

I tend to think of this as the land of cumin, coriander, and chickpeas, but of course it goes much deeper than that. Turkey and the surrounding countries are the world's leaders in cooking with eggplant, lamb, and yogurt (sometimes in the same dish). Vegetable stews and meat stews containing loads of vegetables—and sometimes dried fruits—are more common here than elsewhere. Sesame seeds are important as well.

These are cuisines whose influences are profound elsewhere in the world but that have not become as popular in the States as they deserve. This is perhaps because much of the food is better cooked at home, or at least in modest restaurants, than it is in the kinds of restaurants that gain national attention. (In the more than twenty years I've spent writing about food, I can think of exactly two Greek restaurants that have had national reputations and none from Turkey, the Middle East, or North Africa.)

Yet many dishes from this region—which you might think of as the Mediterranean sans Italy, France, and Spain—are deservedly popular throughout the world. Think of baklava, falafel, and couscous, and you've only scratched the surface.

And it's a good style of cooking for many home cooks, simple, with big flavors and loads of flexibility both in timing and in ingredients. Nor is it especially unfamiliar to most people.

Cayenne. Often replaced in this area by hot paprika, simply another form of ground chiles.

Chickpeas. Among the world's most important legumes, these belong in every pantry. They are not at all bad canned, so it makes sense to keep a couple of cans around, but cooked dried chickpeas are better, so whenever you have the time or forethought it's a good idea to cook a batch; see page 431. You can freeze them in their own cooking liquid, which makes them almost as convenient as canned.

Coriander. Leaves (cilantro), seeds, and roots are all used. See India.

Cumin. See India.

Dried fruit. Used more extensively here than elsewhere, and wonderfully. You have many choices in buying dried fruit, but the big question is usually whether it has been sulphured. Sulphur, to which some people are allergic (but is otherwise harmless), preserves color and texture. Unsulphured fruit can be tough, though this doesn't matter much in cooking, just snacking.

Honey.

Hot and sweet paprika. Like cayenne, a form of dried ground chiles. Unlike cayenne, paprika comes in a range of heat, from completely mild to bitter and mildly hot to almost as hot as cayenne. Paprika, like many ground spices, does not keep forever; try to use it up within a year. See, too, pimentón (Spain).

Nuts. Like dried fruit, nuts are used extensively in both sweet and savory cooking; walnuts primarily. See page 29.

Phyllo (or warka, or brik). Thin sheets of dough, virtually impossible to make at home, quite easy to buy (and store) frozen. For baklava (page 628) and many savory pastries.

Saffron. See India.

Sesame seeds. See Japan.

Tahini. Ground sesame seeds—think of it as peanut butter made from sesame seeds—used primarily as a seasoning. Essential in hummus (page 19).

FRANCE (AND EUROPE IN GENERAL)

French cooking was once thought of as all butter and cream, but my how that has changed. Though the cuisine of the northern part of the country—and much of northern and central Europe—still relies heavily on dairy for the flavor of its dishes, we've learned that southern France is olive oil country, as is just about every region that borders on the Mediterranean.

France's cuisine, in fact, is about as misunderstood as any. What most people tend to think of as "French" cuisine is the haute cuisine of restaurants, but France—like Italy, Mexico, China, India, and the other grand cooking countries—is made up of dozens of small regions, each with its own preferences and its own dishes.

Most of these dishes are cooked at home and in small restaurants, and few make it to the world's "important" French restaurants or even those in Paris. And though France is a leading country in Europe in generating these kinds of dishes, other neighboring or nearby countries have their own specialties as well (though most are clearly influenced by the cooking of France, which was and remains an agricultural powerhouse and an exporter of culture).

Anchovies. You can buy whole salted anchovies, then rinse, fillet, and pack them in oil yourself, but if you get a good brand of anchovies packed in oil, you'll save time. I buy 1.1-pound (half-kilo) jars from Italy; usually they cost about $15 and last me a year or so (unless I go on a binge, which does happen from time to time). Stored in the refrigerator, they're perfect.

Bacon. There is so much you can do with bacon, pancetta, prosciutto, and other long-keeping cured meats that it's worth having a piece around. A well-wrapped hunk of slab bacon or prosciutto will keep in the refrigerator for weeks if not longer.

Bay leaves. An ounce will last you a long time, so get some good ones. The best, in theory, are from

Turkey, but most dried bay leaves from the Mediterranean are good. These are the best option and are becoming easier to find. California bay (laurel) is not a great substitute.

Capers. Most commonly sold packed in vinegar—which makes people think that capers are vinegary—these keep, refrigerated, for a long time and are useful when simply tossed into a variety of dishes. Salt-cured capers, which are a little harder to find, are definitely worth trying; rinse them in one or two changes of water before using to remove excess saltiness.

Cornichons. Little pickles from France. You can live without these, but they make a good addition to vinaigrettes, mayonnaises, and cold platters of meats and pâtés.

Horseradish. Fresh horseradish is best, but the prepared stuff is fine. Only problem is, it loses intensity once opened, so replace it periodically.

Legumes. See page 430. There are some French varieties of lentils and white and pale green beans, known as flageolets, that are especially good.

Parsley. Especially for those of us who live in colder climes, fresh parsley is among the most important things you can stock in your refrigerator. It adds freshness, color, and flavor to almost every dish with European flavors. Buy it weekly and get used to using it, not by the pinch but by the handful.

Red and white wine. If you don't drink, you can almost always substitute water or stock, with maybe a teaspoon of vinegar for acidity. But if you do, the quality of wine you drink is about the same quality you should cook with.

Rosemary. Fresh is a luxury for everyone except those who live in mild climates, but dried is very good. It's also easy to grow indoors, in a pot, and the aroma is beguiling.

Saffron. See India.

Sage. Easy enough to grow, and wonderful fresh, it's not bad dried either.

Shallots. See Southeast Asia.

Sour cream or crème fraîche. Every culture has a soured cream or milk, or mild cheese; good thick yogurt, fromage blanc, and queso fresco all belong to the same family. It's worth having one of these around, but it's not critically important.

Thyme. Like rosemary and sage, great fresh. Unlike them, not so good dried. Worth buying occasionally at the supermarket if you can't grow it yourself.

ITALY

Despite all the fuss made about it in the last couple of decades, Italian food is among the world's simplest, akin to Japanese food in its reliance on just a few important flavor combinations and (usually) quick, uncomplicated cooking methods. If you get into making fresh pasta, you have a world of great eating in front of you, and it can be a challenging one; but if you eschew that pleasure, you'll be looking at a cuisine that is as straightforward as any other.

The great thing is that even lousy supermarkets now carry decent olive oil—used not only for cooking but as a flavoring—and real Parmesan (Parmigiano-Reggiano), two of the real keystones of cooking in Italy. Almost everything else is common to the rest of the world.

Anchovies. See France.

Basil. Whenever you can find fresh basil (usually in the summer), it's worth having. And commercial dried basil is useless. Useless.

Extra virgin olive oil. See page 6.

Marjoram. Better, in many cases, than oregano, especially when dried.

Oregano. Greek rather than Mexican if you have a choice.

Parmesan cheese. Parmigiano-Reggiano is the real thing; grana di padano is a decent substitute, though harder to find and not much less expensive. Well wrapped, it keeps for months and months. It's good to have some pecorino Romano as well.

Wine. See France.

SPAIN

A handful of pantry items helps distinguish Spanish food from that of its neighbors. The influence of North Africa, the combination of Mediterranean and Atlantic cultures (shared only by France), and the often blazingly hot climate sets Spain apart from the rest of Europe.

Almonds. See page 29. Almonds are grown in Andalusia and elsewhere throughout southern Spain and are used in many Spanish desserts (see page 632, for example). Tossed with oil and salt, the especially delicious Marcona almonds are great for snacking.

Chorizo. Spanish chorizo is a dry-cured sausage, a kind of salami made with pork, garlic, cumin, and lots of pimentón (see next column). It's sold in both sweet and spicy versions, though unless you're truly sensitive to chile heat, I think the two are interchangeable—the "hot" is not blazing. Do not substitute fresh Mexican-style chorizo in Spanish recipes; the two are worlds apart. Chorizo keeps for a month or more and is easy to find online if you can't get it locally—www.latienda.com is a great site for this.

Garlic. The Spanish have an almost unnatural affinity for it. (So do the cooks of most other great cuisines.)

Olive oil. See page 6 for a description of styles. Spanish olive oils are typically lighter and less bitter than the much heralded Tuscan varieties, but it seems to me that the key with Spanish food is not so much the oil itself but the copious amounts of it Spaniards use, not only for cooking, but as a seasoning, almost a sauce.

Pimentón. Pimentón is a distinctively flavored type of Spanish paprika made from peppers dried over smoldering oak ashes. The drying process, which can last for days, imparts the pimentón with its characteristically smoky, sweet flavor. A lot of the pimentón produced in Spain goes into flavoring chorizo (it gives the sausage its reddish brown color and smoky flavor); much of the rest is packaged in cute little tins and sold as dulce (sweet), agridulce (bittersweet), and picante (hot). I've seen the three varieties used interchangeably and together, so buy what sounds best to you, but do look for Pimentón de la Vera if you can find it. It is supposed to be the best Spanish paprika on the market and was the first European chile product to earn a Denominacíon de Origen, or name-controlled status, which restricts the use of names like Parmigiano-Reggiano, Champagne, and Roquefort to mean specific products from specific areas.

Piquillo peppers. See page 47.

Saffron. See India, but know that most of the world's saffron comes from Spain. It gives paella its trademark golden hue.

Salt cod. See page 245.

MEXICO AND LATIN AMERICA

In their authentic forms, perhaps the world's last great unexploited group of cuisines, ironic because they are geographically the closest to us. But—and I'm not talking only about Mexico here—these are among the world's original "fusion" cuisines, existing indigenous American cuisines that were affected greatly by trade with the Europeans, the importation of slaves from Africa, the immigration of the Chinese, and so on.

Though Brazil, Peru, Argentina, and Chile all have interesting culinary features, and the cuisines of the Caribbean offer some great recipes, it is Mexican food that is the most interesting and complicated in this hemisphere. ("American" cuisine is the most difficult to define; if you allow that it contains most of the world's food, it's sensational; if you limit it to traditional WASP cooking, it's about the least interesting on the planet.)

Mexican cooking can be quite involved; as you might expect, I limit my selections to the simpler dishes, but even these are light-years away from the offerings of 90 percent of the "Mexican" restaurants in this country.

Most of the ingredients you need for recipes from Mexican and other Latin cuisines are covered elsewhere, but there are a few specialties:

Beans. For Mexican dishes you want mostly red and black beans.

Chiles. See page 588. Critically important in Mexican cooking. Stock a variety of dried chiles, especially chipotle and ancho. Fresh chiles are good too, of course—if you live west of the Mississippi, or near a really good supermarket or Mexican market, you'll often find fresh jalapeño, poblano, serrano, and Anaheim.

Cilantro. See India.

Cumin. See India.

Lime. See Southeast Asia.

Oregano. In this case Mexican.

Pepitas. Hulled pumpkin seeds. Sold salted, as a snack, or unsalted (which is what you want for cooking). Also sold toasted or raw, but easy enough to toast yourself (see page 612). They are sometimes ground and used as a thickening and flavoring agent or even as a coating, in the manner of bread crumbs. They'll keep in your pantry for a month or two, longer in your freezer (though they'll lose flavor as they age).

Appetizers and Snacks Just because we call something an appetizer doesn't mean it must be served that way. In fact, the concept belongs more to restaurants, which have the staff and the time to serve meals in stages; at home we tend to put everything on the table at once.

The exceptions, of course, are dinner or cocktail parties, holidays, and other special occasions. For those, the dishes in this chapter become extremely important.

But if you think of them as light dishes, or those you can prepare in advance, or serve at lunch or late at night, or use as side dishes, everything in this chapter has value beyond the meal-starter. So it's a section well worth browsing.

COLD APPETIZERS REQUIRING NO COOKING

This first group comprises cold, uncooked starters. Some—marinated olives, for example—are as simple as can be and are great for stand-up tidbits. But not all of them are little nibbles; some are quite elegant and actually require forethought. Some can be (or must be) made ahead and some are last-minute preparations. But they're all perfect for making on a hot day when you don't want to use the stove.

Spicy Cold Celery CHINA ■ ▦

MAKES **4 SERVINGS AS A STARTER OR SIDE DISH**

TIME **10 MINUTES, PLUS 3 HOURS TO MARINATE**

Northern Chinese and Taiwanese meals—especially in restaurants—often begin with a little nibble, dishes of savory snacks that are set on the table with tea. They are generally items that you can pick up with your chopsticks and pop in your mouth in one motion. This cold celery dish is a perfect example, with just the right gentle crunch and bite to whet your appetite.

> 1 pound celery stalks
>
> 1 teaspoon salt
>
> 1 tablespoon plus 1 teaspoon sugar
>
> 3 tablespoons dark sesame oil
>
> 1 tablespoon soy sauce
>
> 2 teaspoons vinegar, preferably rice or cider
>
> 1 garlic clove, minced
>
> 1 teaspoon chili oil, optional

1. Cut the celery into 2-inch lengths. Mix with the salt and 1 teaspoon of the sugar and set aside for 10 minutes while you whisk together the remaining ingredients.

2. Rinse, drain, and pat dry the celery, then toss with the dressing. Let stand in the refrigerator for at least 3 hours and up to a day. Serve chilled.

Marinated Olives ITALY ■ ▦

MAKES **ABOUT 8 SERVINGS**

TIME **1 HOUR, LARGELY UNATTENDED**

Throughout the Mediterranean, you'll find olives already on the table when you sit down to a meal. But they're far different from the canned olives (usually Mission) routinely—and unfortunately—sold in supermarkets here. Not only are they a variety of different types; they're simply but wonderfully seasoned. This easy treatment is so effective that most people are shocked at the results.

Use an assortment of olives if at all possible—Kalamatas, some of the good green type, tiny Niçoises, and so on—and the olives will be not only beautiful but varied. You can make this recipe in any quantity, using the same proportions.

> 2 cups assorted olives
>
> 2 garlic cloves, peeled and lightly crushed
>
> 2 tablespoons extra virgin olive oil
>
> 1 teaspoon fresh rosemary leaves
>
> ½ lemon, cut in half and segmented as for a grapefruit

Toss all the ingredients together in a bowl. Marinate for an hour or longer at room temperature. Toss again just before serving. If you are not serving them the same day you make them, refrigerate, then remove from the refrigerator an hour or two before serving.

Olives

Olives are among the oldest and most symbolic foods, the tree and its branches ancient symbols of life, prosperity, and peace. And the oil—the most easily extracted, most useful, delicious, and healthiest of all cooking oils—has been treasured as long as there has been "cuisine."

The Mediterranean is the birthplace of the olive tree and continues to be the world's largest olive producer, yielding more than 90 percent of the crop. There are nearly a billion olive trees in the world, and almost all of them are in the Mediterranean, but traders and missionaries spread olive trees to wherever there are mild winters and hot, dry summers.

Many varieties of cured olives are available, but all olives begin just about the same. Green olives are unripe; darker olives are fully ripened (and contain more oil). Olives cannot be eaten directly off the tree because their skin contains a bitter chemical called oleuropin. To make them palatable, olives are cured in oil, saltwater, lye, or simply salt. The various methods determine the olives' ultimate flavor and texture (as, of course, will any herbs or spices added during the curing process).

The most common olives include:

Black or Mission. Picked when ripe or green; cured in lye, then oxygenated.

Kalamata. Picked when ripe or nearly so; dark brown, purple, or black; cured in brine.

Niçoise. Picked when ripe and dark red or brown; salted, with a slightly sour flavor.

Picholine. Picked when ripe; cured in lime and wood ashes, then seasoned with salt.

Spanish. Usually picked young; cured in lye, then fermented in brine for half a year to a year; packed in a weak brine; sometimes stuffed with pimientos.

Portobello Spread ITALY ■ ▥

MAKES **4 TO 8 SERVINGS**

TIME **10 MINUTES, PLUS RESTING TIME**

It's not entirely clear that this preparation originated in Italy, since portobellos pretty much surfaced (no pun intended) at the same time throughout most of the Western world; but at least it's an Italian-style preparation. In any case, while we are accustomed to eating these large, dark, meaty mushrooms grilled or sautéed, they are also excellent served raw, as they are here, on Crostini (page 41) or in a salad.

1 pound portobello mushrooms, stems discarded and caps cleaned

1 pound ripe tomatoes, preferably plum, cored, seeded, and chopped

2 garlic cloves, minced

1 teaspoon fresh rosemary leaves or $^1/_2$ teaspoon dried

3 tablespoons fresh lemon juice, or to taste

$^1/_4$ cup extra virgin olive oil

Salt and black pepper to taste

1. Cut the mushroom caps into small dice, then toss them with the tomatoes, garlic, rosemary, lemon juice, and oil. Cover and let rest, for up to an hour at room temperature or overnight, refrigerated. Bring back to room temperature before serving.

2. Season with salt and pepper and spoon onto crostini or eat with a fork.

Diced Tomato Spread. Omit the mushrooms. Use about a pound of ripe tomatoes, cut in half through their equators, then squeezed and shaken over the sink to remove as many seeds as possible. Dice and proceed as above, adding about ½ cup minced red onion to the mix.

White Bean Dip MIDDLE EAST ■ ▦ ▨

MAKES **8 SERVINGS**

TIME **10 MINUTES (WITH PRECOOKED BEANS)**

Fantastic in emergencies and reason enough to stock canned beans in your pantry. Serve as a dip for breadsticks, pita or other bread, or raw vegetables.

> 2 cups drained cooked or canned cannellini or other white beans, still moist and liquid reserved
>
> 2 garlic cloves, peeled, or to taste
>
> ¼ cup extra virgin olive oil, plus oil for drizzling
>
> Salt and black pepper to taste
>
> 2 teaspoons ground cumin, or to taste
>
> Fresh lemon juice to taste
>
> ¼ cup chopped shallot, red onion, or scallion for garnish, optional

1. Put the beans in a food processor with the garlic, olive oil, salt, pepper, and cumin. Turn the machine on and process until the mixture is smooth, stopping and scraping down the sides if necessary and adding a bit more bean liquid or olive oil if necessary.

2. Taste and adjust the seasoning—add more garlic, salt, pepper, or cumin if you like—then transfer to a bowl. Add lemon juice a tablespoon at a time, until quite tart, then garnish with the chopped shallot if you like. Use immediately or refrigerate for a day or two. Bring back to room temperature

before serving. Drizzle with a little olive oil and sprinkle with a little more cumin (or some paprika) before serving.

Hummus EASTERN MEDITERRANEAN ■ ▦ ▨

MAKES **8 OR MORE SERVINGS**

TIME **20 MINUTES (WITH PRECOOKED CHICKPEAS)**

Chickpeas are among the best legumes, and this is among the best recipes you can prepare with them, an eons-old Middle Eastern classic. Generally, I'm not a big fan of canned beans, but for whatever reason canned chickpeas are not bad at all, and I always keep some on hand so I can make a batch of this at the last minute, to use as a dip or a spread. You can make hummus without tahini; it will be a little looser and less complex tasting but still good.

> 2 cups drained well-cooked (page 431) or canned chickpeas, liquid reserved
>
> ½ cup tahini, optional, with some of its oil
>
> ¼ cup extra virgin olive oil, plus oil for drizzling
>
> 2 garlic cloves, peeled, or to taste
>
> Salt and black pepper to taste
>
> 1 tablespoon ground cumin or paprika, or to taste, plus a sprinkling for garnish
>
> Juice of 1 lemon, plus more as needed
>
> Chopped fresh parsley leaves for garnish

1. Put everything except the parsley in a food processor and begin to process; add the chickpea liquid or water as needed to allow the machine to produce a smooth puree.

2. Taste and adjust the seasoning (I often find I like to add much more lemon juice). Serve, drizzled with the olive oil and sprinkled with a bit more cumin or paprika and some parsley.

Yogurt Cheese EASTERN MEDITERRANEAN ■ ▨

MAKES **8 OR MORE SERVINGS**

TIME **OVERNIGHT, LARGELY UNATTENDED**

This might be a new, unexpected way to use yogurt, yet it's probably as old as yogurt itself. It's the easiest cheese you can possibly make, since it needs no special equipment or curdling agents—basically, it's yogurt with the excess liquid removed.

There is, however, a key here: you must start with good whole-milk yogurt. Thick, locally made Greek or Turkish yogurt is the ideal (well, the ideal is yogurt you make yourself), but any high-quality yogurt will produce a nice cheese.

Serve with crackers, chips, and/or raw vegetables.

1 pound plain yogurt

Salt to taste

1 tablespoon paprika

1 tablespoon extra virgin olive oil

1. Line a strainer with a sheet of cheesecloth; hang over a mixing bowl so the bottom of the strainer clears the bowl by at least an inch. Dump the yogurt into the center of the cheesecloth. Allow the whey to strain out of the yogurt at least overnight or up to 24 hours; this should happen in a cool place—the refrigerator is fine.
2. After this initial straining, squeeze out any remaining whey by pulling tightly on the ends of the cheesecloth. Store in the refrigerator in an airtight container until you are ready to use (it will keep for several days). Before serving, add salt, then garnish with paprika and olive oil to serve.

YOGURT CHEESE

Herbed Cheese Dip FRANCE ■ ▨

MAKES **6 OR MORE SERVINGS**

TIME **10 MINUTES, PLUS ABOUT 30 MINUTES TO REST**

We have all eaten herbed cheese, but most of it is store-bought and contains who-knows-what. This is a traditional herb cheese with almost nothing in it; you can also make it with fresh goat cheese or with Yogurt Cheese (preceding recipe).

Serve with crackers, lightly toasted pita, and/or raw vegetable sticks.

½ pound cold farmer cheese or cream cheese

¼ cup sour cream

1 tablespoon fresh thyme leaves

"Raw" Fish

Long before refrigeration, fish was a mainstay of the world's coastal communities. And before people could count on refrigeration to help preserve fish, they used what they had on hand: salt, sugar, vinegar, lemon or lime juice, smoke, deep holes in the ground, papaya leaves—and, of course, freezing-cold temperatures. Necessity, then, was responsible for those seafood recipes prepared without heat, including gravlax and ceviche. These, like salt cod (page 245) and pickled herring (page 37), are seafood dishes that rely on techniques like pickling, salting, and marinating, rather than heat, for "cooking."

Ceviche, a specialty of Central and South America, is made by bathing raw seafood in lemon or lime juice, flavored with herbs, chiles, and aromatics. The fish is allowed to marinate for anywhere from a couple of minutes to several hours. The acid in the marinade tenderizes the fish, chemically softening the connective tissue, while turning the raw, translucent flesh white and opaque, giving it the appearance and appeal of cooked fish. While ceviche looks and tastes a lot like cooked fish, strictly speaking the fish isn't cooked.

Gravlax, among the simplest of cured dishes, is a specialty of Sweden. Traditionally, the salmon would be buried underground and allowed to ferment (*grav* means "buried," and *lax* means "salmon"). Now, to make gravlax, we "bury" raw salmon fillets in a mixture of salt, sugar, and usually dill—there are many flavor variations—and then refrigerate it under a light weight for a couple of days. Like ceviche, gravlax is a recipe for curing fish—a way of preserving it—not cooking it. The salt creates an inhospitable environment for bacterial growth, preserving the fish by drawing moisture out and depriving bacteria of the "free" water molecules they need to thrive.

Most food, and certainly all (edible) fish, is safe to eat raw, as long as it's fresh, disease free, and parasite free. And while eating ceviche or gravlax is generally safe, if you're cautious you will want to use finfish that has been frozen to -4°F for 7 days or 31°F for 15 or more hours (this will take a commercial freezer), which will kill parasites like tapeworms and roundworms. And because salt and lime or lemon juice won't kill bacteria the way heat does, be sure to buy only the freshest and most meticulously handled fish you can find. (Or see the Mock Ceviche—which is actually cooked—on page 35.)

---

1 garlic clove, peeled, or more to taste

Salt and black pepper to taste

1. Combine all the ingredients in a food processor and blend until smooth. (Alternatively, mince the garlic and mash all the ingredients with a potato masher or fork until fairly smooth, then beat for a few moments with a wire whisk.) Taste and adjust the seasoning as necessary.
2. Scrape into a bowl and refrigerate until stiffened slightly. Serve cold.

Ceviche Marinated Scallops MEXICO ■ ■ ▨
MAKES **4 TO 8 SERVINGS**
TIME **30 MINUTES**

In any coastal region where you find limes, you'll find ceviche, going by one name or another. In Mexico, it's frequently made with a combination of scallops, shrimp, conch, and octopus (the last two usually precooked to the point of tenderness), and those are all good fish for the mix. If you can find spanking-fresh fillets of your local white fish, you can use that here too, although scallops alone are easy and fabulous.

(They're also the safest shellfish to eat raw, but if the whole thing makes you nervous, see Mock Ceviche, page 35.) If you happen to have a couple of different colors of bell peppers, mix them; it'll make the dish really sparkle.

1 pound perfectly fresh sea scallops or a mixture of fish, cut into ¼-inch dice

½ cup minced bell pepper

1 teaspoon minced lime zest

¼ cup fresh lime juice

Salt to taste

Cayenne to taste

Chopped fresh cilantro leaves for garnish

1. Toss together all the ingredients except the cilantro and let sit at room temperature for 15 minutes.
2. Taste, adjust the seasoning, and serve, garnished with the cilantro.

Guacamole MEXICO ■ ■ ▨

MAKES **4 SERVINGS**

TIME **10 MINUTES**

In Mexico, guacamole is traditionally made in a molcajete, a mortar made from volcanic rock. It's a lovely tradition, but since you probably don't have a molcajete, use a bowl and fork or a potato masher.

The admittedly more complicated variation that follows is superior but not nearly as quick.

1 lime

1 garlic clove, minced

1 scallion, 1 shallot, or bit of red onion, trimmed and chopped

1 serrano or jalapeño chile, stemmed, seeded, and minced, pure chile powder, like ancho or New Mexico, to taste, or a few pinches of cayenne

½ teaspoon coarse salt, or more to taste

2 tablespoons chopped fresh cilantro leaves

3 medium-ripe avocados

1. Grate the lime zest and reserve; cut the lime into wedges. Put the lime zest, garlic, scallion, chile, and salt into a bowl and mash until the mixture is well combined. Add the cilantro and mash a few more times.
2. Cut the avocados in half and reserve the pits if you will not be serving the guacamole right away. Scoop the pulp into the bowl and mash, leaving a few chunks of avocado. Squeeze in the lime juice from the reserved lime wedges to taste.
3. Season with more salt and serve or tuck the pits back into the mixture, cover with plastic wrap, and refrigerate for up to 4 hours (the pits will keep the guacamole from turning brown). Remove the pits before serving.

Guacamole with Roasted Chiles. Substitute 2 fresh poblano chiles for the serranos. Prepare a charcoal or gas grill or broiler; the fire should be quite hot. Roast the chiles until the skin is blackened and blistery, then cool, peel, stem, seed, and mince. Proceed as directed, substituting the roast chile for the serrano or jalapeño.

Platanitos Plantain Chips CARIBBEAN ■ ▨

MAKES **4 SERVINGS**

TIME **20 MINUTES**

A popular snack in the Caribbean, these wafer-thin crisps are best eaten right away, and though this amount technically makes 4 servings, you may be tempted to eat all of them alone. The plantains' inherent sweetness is countered nicely with a little heat from the cayenne. These are best as an accompaniment to mojitos or other Caribbean cocktails, or use as a garnish for any Caribbean dish. They will stay crisp for a few hours if you store them in an airtight container as soon as they cool.

> 1 teaspoon salt
> ¼ teaspoon cayenne, or to taste
> Lard (traditional) or corn, grapeseed, or other neutral oil for deep-frying
> 2 medium-ripe plantains (yellow-green, not green, yellow, or yellow-black), peeled (page 472)
> Lime wedges

1. Mix together the salt and cayenne. Set aside.
2. Put at least 1 inch of lard or oil in a large, deep skillet or saucepan. The broader the vessel, the more of these you can cook at once, but the more oil you will use. (They cook very quickly, so don't worry if your pan is narrow.) Turn the heat to medium-high; you want the temperature to be at 350°F (on a deep-fat thermometer) when you start cooking.
3. While the fat is heating, shave the plantains, using a vegetable peeler, a sharp knife, or a mandoline set to just about the thinnest setting. If you are using a peeler, press down with some pressure so that the slices are not too thin. Traditionally, they're cut the long way (a mandoline makes this easy), but you can make round chips if you find it easier.
4. Fry as many slices at once as will fit without crowding, turning if necessary. Total cooking time will be about 2 minutes; the chips should not brown but turn a deeper yellow. Remove with tongs or a slotted spoon and drain on paper towels or paper bags. Sprinkle with the salt-cayenne mixture and lime juice and serve immediately.

Mariquitas de Yucca Yucca Chips. Substitute 2 yuccas, peeled and halved crosswise, for the plantains. Put in a medium saucepan, cover with water, and cook until tender but not mushy, about 15 minutes.

Drain, cool, then slice as thin as possible and fry as directed.

Gravlax Salt- and Sugar-Cured Salmon
SCANDINAVIA ■ ▨
MAKES **16 OR MORE SERVINGS**
TIME **24 TO 36 HOURS, LARGELY UNATTENDED**

One of the simplest and most impressive cured dishes and certainly the king of cured fish. Speaking of king, if you can find wild Pacific salmon (usually spring through fall), especially king or sockeye, use it; if not, farm-raised salmon is quite good when treated this way. In fact, farm-raised salmon is a pretty good option—because it is harvested and shipped to stores daily it's usually perfectly fresh, a requisite for all salmon you'd consider using for gravlax.

Generally, gravlax is ready within 24 hours, but it's better after a little longer than that, and you can hold it for another couple of days before serving if you like; it will become increasingly dry and strong flavored, not a bad thing. In any case, treat finished gravlax as a fresh food and use it within a few days.

GRAVLAX

1 cup salt

2 cups sugar

1 bunch of dill, stems and all, chopped

2 bay leaves, crumbled

$^{1}/_{2}$ cup minced shallot

1 teaspoon cracked black pepper

Grated zest of 2 lemons

One 2- to 3-pound salmon fillet, pin bones removed with
    tweezers or pliers

1. Mix together all the ingredients except the salmon.
    Place the salmon, skin side down, on a large sheet
    of plastic wrap. Cover the flesh side of the salmon
    with the salt mixture, being sure to coat it com-
    pletely (there will be lots of salt mix; just pile it
    on).
2. Wrap the fish well in plastic. Refrigerate for at least
    24 hours and preferably 36.
3. Unwrap the salmon and rinse off the cure. Dry,
    then slice on the bias. Serve plain, with lemon
    wedges, or with Mustard Dill Sauce (page 608),
    thinned with a little sour cream.

Boquerones Marinated Fresh Anchovies
SPAIN ■ ■

MAKES **6 OR MORE SERVINGS**

TIME **24 HOURS, LARGELY UNATTENDED**

Along with Spanish food in general, these have become increasingly popular in the States, and they're
fun, rewarding, and easy to make at home. Of course,
the key is to begin with superfresh anchovies, and we
are finally seeing more of these. (You can use the same
method with fresh thin fillets of mackerel, a more
common fish, or with smelts, which can be handled
the same way as the anchovies.) These are good
served on buttered toast or crackers and passed as a
snack.

You might wonder why your boquerones are not
as white as those sold in restaurants; it's because
you're not using a bleaching agent.

1 to 1$^{1}/_{2}$ pounds fresh anchovies

1 cup white wine vinegar

Salt

$^{1}/_{4}$ cup extra virgin olive oil

1 teaspoon minced garlic, optional

Chopped fresh parsley leaves for garnish

Lemon wedges

1. To fillet the anchovies, grasp the body just behind
    the head and pull down on the head; most of the
    innards will come out along with it. Run your
    thumb along the belly flap, tearing the fish open all
    the way to the tail and removing any remaining in-
    nards. Then grab the backbone between your
    thumb and forefinger and gently pull it out. Re-
    move any spiny fin material and drop the fillet
    into a bowl of ice water.
2. Rinse and dry the anchovies, then place them in a
    narrow bowl. Add the vinegar and a large pinch of
    salt and stir. Cover and marinate for about 24
    hours. Drain, then sprinkle with salt, oil, garlic if
    you like, and parsley. You can refrigerate them at
    this point for up to a few days. Serve with lemon
    wedges.

Taramasalata Fish Roe Puree
GREECE ■ ■ ■

MAKES **6 TO 8 SERVINGS**

TIME **ABOUT 15 MINUTES**

This creamy dip is made from tarama, the salted (and
sometimes smoked) roe of mullet or other fish (we
usually see it made from cod or salmon roe). Serve
it with strips of fresh vegetables, like cucumber,

Anchovies

Anchovy is the name given to various herringlike fishes, native to warm waters worldwide. Most Americans think of them as European, and indeed they show up in many Mediterranean and even Nordic cuisines regularly, because they have been caught and preserved there for millennia; the ancient Roman sauce, garum, was anchovy based. But Asians, too, have used anchovies forever, and the Thai nam pla and related fish sauces of other Southeast Asian countries—all of which you'll find in various recipes throughout this book—also employ anchovies.

Anchovies, as everyone knows, have a distinctively strong flavor, but part of this comes from the preserving process. They are usually filleted, cured in salt, and packed in oil. They're perfect pantry items: If you buy those packed in glass jars, you can simply open and close the container at will, and they'll keep for a long,

long time in the refrigerator. If you buy tinned anchovies, transfer any you don't use to a glass or plastic container and refrigerate. If you buy salted anchovies (sold in bulk at Italian and other markets), you must rinse and fillet them yourself: once you do that, you can dry them and pack them in oil, but why you'd want to go through this trouble I don't know.

Boquerones (page 24), the Spanish tapa of marinated anchovies on toast, begin with fresh anchovies. They are increasingly easy to find in fish markets, but they do not keep well, so look carefully for bright eyes and a fresh sea smell. Filleting them is a chore but far from impossible.

Finally, there are the dried anchovies of Asia. In Korea, these are seasoned in a sticky spicy sweet sauce and served as a side dish (page 52). They are also used in Southeast Asian dishes for a unique salty flavor.

red pepper, carrot, and celery, toasted pita bread, or both.

3 or 4 slices good white bread, preferably stale

2 or 3 garlic cloves, to taste, peeled

One 7- or 8-ounce jar tarama

Juice of 2 lemons, or to taste

About 1/2 cup extra virgin olive oil

Salt and black pepper, if necessary

1. Soak the bread in water to cover while you prepare the other ingredients. When it's soft, squeeze the water from it and put it in a food processor with the garlic, tarama, and a couple tablespoons of lemon juice.
2. Turn the machine on and add olive oil in a steady stream until the mixture is smooth and creamy. Taste and add more lemon juice, oil, or garlic if you like; you may also add a little salt and pepper.

Serve immediately or cover tightly and refrigerate for up to a couple of days before serving.

Carne Cruda   Marinated Beef   ITALY ■ ■
MAKES **4 SERVINGS**
TIME **10 MINUTES**

Carpaccio, now a staple at many high-end restaurants, even non-Italian ones, is a glorified version of this Piemontese specialty (in Tuscany and other parts of central Italy, an even simpler plate of cured meats is served routinely), which will provide a vibrant beginning to any dinner party. This dish depends on the flavor of olive oil, so break out the good stuff.

The meat will be easier to cut into small pieces if you put it in the freezer for about half an hour first to firm it up a bit.

Raw Meat

Raw meat dishes have both rustic and sophisticated roots. Steak (or beef) tartare has various mythic origins. Did the Tartars shred raw meat with their knives and eat it hurriedly? Did Attila and his men ride and fight all day long with raw meat under their saddles—thereby tenderizing the meat—and then quickly chop it, spice it, and eat it?

Or—my guess—steak tartare evolved in various parts of the world (a similar dish exists in Korea, and there are raw versions of kofte and kibbe), because good raw beef is delicious and can take a huge variety of seasonings.

Unlike tartare, carpaccio—the Italian version of raw beef—is a recent phenomenon, created in 1961 in Venice (at Harry's Bar) and named after the Italian painter Vittore Carpaccio, who was well known for using red in his paintings. Carpaccio was originally made by searing the beef, then slicing off the seared portion of the meat and thinly slicing the raw interior; the searing part may be skipped.

About safety: if you buy good meat—not preground—and handle it carefully, the risk of salmonella (which is a contaminant not present in the meat itself) is just about nil. Raw, rare, whatever; it will be fine.

---

1 pound beef tenderloin, trimmed, cut into ¹/₂-inch or smaller cubes, and chilled

1 cup arugula, chopped

¹/₄ cup chopped fresh parsley leaves

¹/₃ cup extra virgin olive oil

1 tablespoon fresh lemon juice, or more to taste

Salt and black pepper to taste

1. Toss the beef in a bowl with the arugula, parsley, oil, and lemon juice.
2. Season with salt and pepper, add more lemon juice if necessary, and serve immediately.

Carpaccio. For a time, the darling of pricey restaurants: Omit the parsley. Shave about 12 slices of Parmesan with a vegetable peeler. Instead of dicing the beef, slice it as thinly as possible (this will be easiest if you freeze it about halfway to solid first). Place the beef slices on a chilled plate and top with arugula and Parmesan. Drizzle with the olive oil and lemon juice and season with salt and pepper. Serve immediately.

Cig Kofte Raw Meatballs TURKEY ■ ▪

MAKES **4 TO 8 SERVINGS**

TIME **40 MINUTES**

Especially when made with lamb, this is incomparably delicious; serve it with good bread or toast.

There was a time when this meat was chopped, then pounded and kneaded by hand, for longer than you or I have the patience to do. The food processor makes quick work of the process, and if you buy good fresh meat from a reliable source and handle it carefully, it's as safe as a rare hamburger.

¹/₂ pound bulgur, preferably fine grain (#1)

¹/₂ to ³/₄ pound boneless fresh lamb (from the leg or loin) or beef (preferably tenderloin)

1 teaspoon not-too-hot pure chile powder, like New Mexico, or a pinch or two of cayenne, or to taste

1 medium onion, finely chopped

1 teaspoon ground cumin, or to taste

1 tablespoon tomato paste

1 cup finely chopped fresh parsley or cilantro leaves

Salt and black pepper to taste
Lemon wedges for serving

1. Put the bulgur in a bowl and cover with boiling water; put a plate on the bowl and let the bulgur sit until fairly tender, about 30 minutes. Drain, then squeeze dry. Meanwhile, cut the meat into chunks and pulverize it in a food processor, stopping the machine to scrape down the sides occasionally; process until it will not become any finer.
2. Combine the meat and bulgur in a bowl and knead for a minute with your hands. Add the remaining ingredients except the lemon and knead a little more. Taste and adjust the seasoning.
3. Form the mixture into small balls or logs and serve immediately (or refrigerate, covered, for up to a couple of hours) with the lemon.

COOKED APPETIZERS THAT CAN BE PREPARED IN ADVANCE

The value of these appetizers—cooked, but served warm, at room temperature, or even cold—cannot be overstated. These are dishes that can be prepared in advance—sometimes a day in advance or even more, but usually several hours—yet their quality does not diminish before serving.

In fact, it may improve; throughout the world, there are many countries where serving food straight from the oven, grill, or pan while it's piping hot is not a high priority. Throughout the Mediterranean, especially, food is cooked in the cool temperatures of the morning and allowed to mellow for a couple of hours before serving.

The advantages of dishes like this for entertaining are obvious. In fact, I would argue that at least one preparation from this group be included at every dinner party.

Fried Peanuts CHINA ■ ▨ ▨
MAKES **2 CUPS, ENOUGH FOR 8 AS A SNACK**
TIME **10 MINUTES, PLUS COOLING TIME**

Fried peanuts will amaze your guests with their crunch and fresh, distinctive flavor. Add different kinds of nuts if you like, as long as they are "raw" to begin with (the industrial shelling process uses enough heat to cook the nuts, at least a little bit). The best raw peanuts are usually found in the fall (peanuts are an exception; the best season for other nuts is spring), when they are fresh and tender. Like any nuts, these are great with drinks, especially beer.

Peanut or neutral oil, like corn or grapeseed, as needed
2 cups shelled raw peanuts, with skins
Coarse salt to taste

1. Put at least 1 inch of oil in a deep, fairly narrow saucepan and turn the heat to medium-high. When the oil reaches 300°F (this is on the cool side for frying; be careful not to overheat), add the peanuts and cook, stirring occasionally, until they are a rich golden brown, about 5 minutes.
2. Remove the peanuts with a slotted spoon, drain on paper towels, and sprinkle with salt. Strain and save the oil (covered and refrigerated) for another use; it will be great for using in stir-fries. Serve at room temperature.

Fried Peanuts, Mexican Style. Cook the peanuts with 6 unpeeled garlic cloves and 4 small dried red chiles. Drain and season with salt and fresh lime juice to taste.

Fried Peanuts, Southeast Asian Style. Combine 1 teaspoon curry powder (pages 592–593), ½ teaspoon superfine sugar, and salt and cayenne to taste. Cook the peanuts as directed and sprinkle on the spice mixture. Taste and adjust the seasoning.

Fried Peanuts, Indian Style. Combine 1 teaspoon garam masala (page 594) with salt and cayenne to taste. Cook the peanuts as directed and sprinkle on the spice mixture. Taste and adjust the seasoning.

Roasted Walnuts EASTERN EUROPE ■ ▪ ▫

MAKES **2 CUPS, ENOUGH FOR 8 AS A SNACK**

TIME **15 MINUTES, PLUS COOLING TIME**

Salted nuts are made wherever they're grown and are infinitely better than nuts from a jar or can. Note that these are not fried—there is no additional oil—but roasted. This basic, easy recipe can also be used for whole almonds or hazelnuts.

> **2 cups walnut halves**
>
> **2 teaspoons coarse salt**

1. Preheat the oven to 350°F. Run cold water over the walnuts and, without drying, put them in one layer on a baking sheet. Sprinkle the salt over them and bake, without stirring, until light brown and fragrant, 10 to 15 minutes.
2. Remove from the oven, cool slightly, and serve, or hold at room temperature for up to a few hours.

Spicy Fried Almonds SPAIN ■ ▪ ▫

MAKES **2 CUPS, ENOUGH FOR 8 AS A SNACK**

TIME **10 MINUTES, PLUS COOLING TIME**

This is a standard at tapas bars in Spain and a perfect addition to any cocktail party. The salt will adhere to the nuts better if you grind it for a few moments in a food processor or spice or coffee grinder; this gives it a more irregular surface than it usually has.

> **3 tablespoons extra virgin olive oil, or as needed**
>
> **2 cups whole almonds, with skins**
>
> **1 teaspoon ground cumin, optional**
>
> **1/2 teaspoon cayenne, or to taste, optional**
>
> **Coarse salt**

1. Coat the bottom of a wide saucepan with oil and turn the heat to medium-high. When it is hot but not smoking, add the almonds and cook, stirring occasionally, for just a few minutes, until they are toasted and browned lightly.
2. Remove the almonds with a slotted spoon, drain on paper towels, and sprinkle with cumin if you like, cayenne, and salt to taste. Serve at room temperature, within a few hours.

Channa Crunchy Chickpeas

CARIBBEAN ■ ▪ ▫

MAKES **6 OR MORE SERVINGS**

TIME **10 MINUTES (WITH PRECOOKED CHICKPEAS)**

This delicious snack from Trinidad and Guyana is the perfect accompaniment to any cold cocktail, and if you think of it while you're cooking chickpeas for another recipe, it's incredibly easy. If you're curious about Old World origins of New World foods, you'll be interested to know that, in India, one of the many words for chickpeas is chana.

> **One 16-ounce can chickpeas, or at least 2 cups cooked chickpeas (page 431), drained**
>
> **Corn, grapeseed, or other neutral oil as needed**
>
> **Salt and cayenne to taste**

1. Preheat the broiler. Drain, rinse, and lightly dry the chickpeas. Lightly grease a rimmed baking sheet with the oil and spread the chickpeas on it.

Nuts

Nuts vary almost as much as fruits. Not only flavors but growing habits differ wildly: Peanuts are actually legumes, and almonds are related to stone fruits—they're very similar to the pit of an apricot. Some nuts grow on trees, others on shrubs, still others underground.

Like fruits, nuts are among the human race's oldest foods; there's evidence of them as a food source for primitive peoples on almost every continent. They remain among the simplest and best of snacks but have made their way into great recipes as well.

Although nuts may be labeled raw, technically speaking the industrial shelling process uses enough heat to toast them slightly. Further toasting always brings out more flavor. You can toast nuts on the stovetop, in the oven, even in a toaster oven. A few words about them individually:

Almonds. Probably Middle Eastern in origin, and once valued for trade on the Silk Road. Mentioned in the Bible and long made into marzipan. A symbol of fertility for the ancient Romans, found in cooking throughout Europe. See, for example, Braised Lamb with Honey and Almonds (page 406).

Walnuts. The oldest known nut, probably from Persia. Historically used from southeastern Europe through the Middle East, all the way into the mountains of India.

Valued by ancient Greeks and Romans, pressed for oil in the Middle Ages, and now used extensively in the Middle East and North Africa. See Skordalia (page 600).

Peanuts. From the Andean lowlands of Bolivia and Peru. Brought to Europe by the Spaniards, then to Africa, India, Macao (and thus China) by the Portuguese. Arrived in the States (and Caribbean) via Africa. Today the most widely used nut internationally, for oil, in stews, as a stand-alone snack, and as peanut butter. See Nketia Fla (page 296).

Hazelnuts. Also known as filberts because they ripen around St. Philbert's Day in Europe. Especially popular in European pastries.

Cashews. South American in origin, now grown more in India than elsewhere.

Pistachios. Originally from Turkey and elsewhere in the Middle East, now widely grown in California. (The Turkish and Iranian varieties are far superior, however, and are often found in Middle Eastern markets.)

Pecans. Indigenous to the U.S. Valued by Native Americans, now a staple in American southern cuisine and rarely seen elsewhere in the world.

Broil until golden brown and crunchy, about 5 minutes.

2. Season with salt and cayenne and serve or store in an airtight container for up to a week.

Red or Black Bean Dip MEXICO ■ ▨ ▨
MAKES **ABOUT 8 SERVINGS**
TIME **30 MINUTES (WITH PRECOOKED BEANS)**

Like most other bean preparations, this is far better with beans you cook yourself than with canned (frozen beans, now available at many supermarkets, fall somewhere in the middle). But even with canned beans, it is so much better than commercially made bean dip you may never go back.

If you cook the beans yourself, start with the recipe for Black Beans with Garlic and Cumin (you can cook red beans this way too), page 438, and cook them until they are quite soft. Reserve the cooking liquid. Serve with tortilla chips, toasted pita bread (not a traditional combination but a good one), or raw vegetables.

¼ cup lard (preferred) or neutral oil, like corn or
   grapeseed
1 teaspoon minced garlic
2 cups well-cooked red or black beans
1 tablespoon ground cumin, or more to taste
1 medium onion, peeled and cut into chunks
Pinch of cayenne, or more to taste
Salt and black pepper to taste
Bean cooking liquid or chicken stock as needed

1. Put the lard or oil in a medium skillet, preferably nonstick, and turn the heat to medium. When the lard melts or the oil is hot, add the garlic and cook until it begins to sizzle. Add the beans and cook, stirring and tossing, until warm. Set aside about ½ cup of the beans and put the rest in a food processor.
2. Add the cumin, onion, cayenne, salt, and pepper, along with a bit of the liquid. Process until smooth, adding more liquid if necessary to allow the machine to do its work. Taste and adjust the seasoning, adding more cumin, salt, pepper, or cayenne if you like, along with the reserved beans. Serve immediately or cover and refrigerate for up to a couple of days; bring back to room temperature before serving.

Imam Bayildi Stuffed Eggplants TURKEY ■ ▨
MAKES **4 OR MORE SERVINGS**
TIME **1 HOUR, PLUS RESTING TIME**

You are served this everywhere in Istanbul and everywhere told this story: the dish is so delicious that the imam or priest to whom it was served simply fainted—"bayildi." (Some people say he was so very thrifty that he fainted at the profligate amount of olive oil used, but since olive oil is no longer especially expensive—and a half cup is not that much, after all—you can enjoy this dish without guilt.)

As is almost always the case, the small, light-skinned "Japanese" eggplants work best because they lack the bitterness common to larger eggplants. If you cannot get those, use the smallest eggplants you can find. This dish is always served at room temperature (or cold), so make it ahead of time.

½ cup extra virgin olive oil
4 small eggplants, about 1 pound or a little more total,
   trimmed and peeled
2 medium onions, sliced
4 garlic cloves, sliced
2 ripe tomatoes, cored and diced (drained canned
   are fine)
½ cup chopped fresh parsley leaves
1 tablespoon sugar
Salt and black pepper to taste
1 lemon, cut into wedges

1. Preheat the oven to 375°F. Heat half the oil in a large skillet over medium-high heat. Add the eggplants and brown on all sides, adjusting the heat and turning as necessary; drain on paper towels. Cut a slit lengthwise in each eggplant, taking care not to cut all the way through, then assemble them in a baking dish that will hold them snugly.
2. Add the remaining oil to the skillet and turn the heat to medium-low; cook the onions and garlic,

stirring occasionally, until very soft and fragrant, about 10 minutes. Add the tomatoes and cook until softened, about 5 minutes more, then stir in the parsley, sugar, and salt and pepper. Remove from the heat.

3. Stuff the onion-tomato mixture into the slits in the eggplants. Pour any remaining pan juices and 3 tablespoons water over the eggplants, cover loosely with foil, and bake for 30 minutes. Remove from the oven, cool to room temperature, squeeze the lemon juice on top, and serve.

Eggplant Caviar FRANCE ■ ▪

MAKES **8 OR MORE SERVINGS**

TIME **1 HOUR**

Its flavor bears no resemblance to real caviar, its ingredients (except for the salt) have nothing to do with caviar, but its texture—supposedly—is akin to that of caviar. If there are enough seeds in your eggplant—not necessarily a good thing—I suppose you could argue that its graininess is like that of caviar. In any case, it's a wonderful spread for Crostini (page 41), as a dip for fresh vegetables, or as a stuffing for roasted peppers or tomatoes (pages 492).

> 2 medium or 4 small eggplants, about 1 pound total
>
> ¼ cup extra virgin olive oil, plus a little more for rubbing the eggplants
>
> ¼ cup fresh lemon juice
>
> ½ teaspoon minced garlic, or to taste
>
> Salt and black pepper to taste
>
> Minced fresh parsley leaves for garnish

1. Preheat the oven to 500°F. Pierce the eggplants in several places with a thin knife or skewer, then rub them with a little olive oil. Place on a baking sheet or roasting pan and roast, turning occasionally,

until they collapse, 15 to 30 minutes, depending on size. Remove and cool.

2. When the eggplants are cool enough to handle, scoop out the flesh. Place it in a food processor with the lemon juice, ¼ cup oil, the garlic, and salt and pepper. Pulse until chopped but not quite pureed; taste and adjust the seasonings. Garnish with the parsley and serve or cover and refrigerate for up to a few hours (bring back to room temperature before serving).

Roasted Eggplant Caviar MIDDLE EAST. Better, because of the added smokiness: Start a charcoal or wood fire. Pierce the eggplants and rub them with olive oil as directed. Grill, turning occasionally, until the eggplants collapse and their skin blackens, 15 to 30 minutes, depending on size. Remove and cool. When the eggplant is cool enough to handle, proceed with the recipe.

Creamy Eggplant Caviar. Omit the oil and lemon juice. While the eggplant cooks, heat ½ cup heavy cream with the garlic in a saucepan over low heat, until steam rises from its surface. Cool and process with the eggplant pulp, salt, and pepper. Taste and adjust the seasoning, garnish, and serve.

Baba Ghanoush MIDDLE EAST. Like Hummus (page 19), this can be served as a dip or a spread; toasted pita is the traditional accompaniment. Omit the oil. While the eggplant is roasting, toast ½ cup pine nuts by heating them in a dry skillet over medium heat, shaking occasionally, just until they begin to brown. When the eggplant is cool, put it in a food processor with the pine nuts, lemon juice, garlic, pepper, and ⅓ cup tahini (sesame paste). Process until very smooth, adding a few teaspoons of water or olive oil if necessary. Taste and add salt and/or more lemon juice or garlic if necessary. Garnish with minced parsley and serve.

Beet Caviar RUSSIA ■ ■

MAKES **6 OR MORE SERVINGS**

TIME **5 MINUTES (WITH PREROASTED BEETS)**

This brilliantly colored starter is an unusual and extremely elegant way of using beets. Serve it with chips, bread, or toast or as an accompaniment to any roast poultry dish. Make this ahead of time if you can; it's best after marinating overnight.

> 4 fresh beets, about 1 1/2 pounds, washed,
> roasted, and peeled (page 442)
> 2 tablespoons extra virgin olive oil
> 2 tablespoons fresh lemon juice
> Tabasco sauce to taste
> Salt and black pepper to taste
> Chopped fresh parsley leaves for garnish,
> optional

1. Place the beets, oil, and lemon juice in a food processor. Pulse until the mixture is finely minced.
2. Season with Tabasco, salt, and pepper and serve or cover and refrigerate for up to a day. Garnish with parsley if you like before serving.

Beet Caviar with Walnuts. Chop 1/2 cup shelled walnuts, not too fine (you want pieces, not powder). Toast them in a small dry skillet over medium heat, shaking the pan frequently, until they become fragrant. Stir them into the beets just before serving.

Spicy Beet Caviar. Add to the mix 1 shallot, roughly chopped (do not process); 1/4 teaspoon cayenne or Tabasco sauce, or to taste; and 1/4 cup minced capers.

Roast Pepper Spread with Walnuts and Garlic MIDDLE EAST ■ ■

MAKES **ABOUT 2 CUPS, ENOUGH FOR 8**

TIME **15 MINUTES (WITH PREROASTED PEPPERS)**

This stuff is great, and I have never tasted it in this country except in my own kitchen. I first had it in Turkey, where it was quite spicy, but have since learned that it's equally acceptable milder. Dried urpa or aleppo pepper, or hot paprika, is the ideal seasoning—a bit of bite but not overwhelming—but judicious use of hot red pepper flakes is also good. You can also omit the heat entirely.

This spread can be made hours or even a day in advance. Always, however, serve it at room temperature, never cold. Serve with bread or vegetable sticks; it makes a great sandwich ingredient too.

> 3 or 4 red peppers, roasted (page 470), or about 1 1/2 cups
> canned or jarred red peppers (preferably piquillos, but
> pimientos are okay too)
> 1 cup walnuts
> 1 tablespoon roughly chopped garlic
> 2 tablespoons extra virgin olive oil
> 1 lemon
> 1 teaspoon ground cumin
> Hot red pepper flakes, hot paprika, or any small dried chile
> to taste
> Salt to taste

1. Make sure the peppers are without seeds. Combine them in a food processor with the walnuts, garlic, oil, the grated zest of the lemon, and the cumin. Process, turning the machine on and off, so the ingredients are pulverized but not pureed; you want a paste, but one with a little texture. (You could use a mortar and pestle if you have one, plus the energy.)
2. Transfer the paste to a bowl and add the hot red pepper flakes, salt, and juice of the lemon. Taste

and adjust the seasoning. Serve or cover and refrigerate for up to a day or two (bring back to room temperature before serving).

Sautéed Spinach with Sesame
KOREA ■ ■ ▨

MAKES **4 OR MORE SERVINGS**

TIME **20 MINUTES**

Compare this recipe, which is usually served cold as a panchan (small appetizer or side dish), with the Japanese version on page 184, and you'll have a vision of the difference between Japanese and Korean cooking, which are closely linked and starkly different at the same time.

  3 tablespoons dark sesame oil

  1 tablespoon minced garlic

  1 pound spinach, large stems removed, roughly chopped

  1 tablespoon sugar

  1 tablespoon soy sauce

  Salt to taste

  1 tablespoon toasted sesame seeds (page 596) for garnish

1. Put 2 tablespoons of the oil in a large skillet over medium heat; a minute later, add the garlic. The instant it begins to sizzle, add the spinach and cook, stirring occasionally, until it is completely wilted. Turn the heat to low.
2. Stir in the sugar and soy sauce and cook for a few more moments. Turn off the heat; taste and add salt (or more soy sauce if you prefer) if necessary. Serve hot, warm, at room temperature, or cold, drizzled with the remaining sesame oil and sprinkled with the sesame seeds.

Miang Gung Green Leaf Wraps THAILAND ■ ▨ ▨

MAKES **4 SERVINGS**

TIME **30 MINUTES**

I first had this appetizer as street food, near a market in Bangkok. The combination of raw ingredients normally used as flavoring agents for cooked dishes was intriguing and refreshing. The betel leaf used to hold everything together gave an additional bite to the dish. Betel leaves are impossible to find here, but the dish remains delicious with spinach leaves or even lettuce. If you're not familiar with Thai fish sauce (nam pla), see page 500. You put it all together at the table, so it's kind of fun.

Serve this as the start to any meal featuring other food from Southeast Asia.

  One 1$\frac{1}{2}$-inch piece fresh ginger, peeled and chopped

  1 tablespoon shrimp paste (page 9) or dried bay shrimp

  $\frac{1}{4}$ cup palm or brown sugar

  2 tablespoons nam pla

  $\frac{3}{4}$ cup unsweetened shredded coconut

  $\frac{1}{4}$ pound medium to large shrimp, peeled

  4 shallots, minced

  One 1-inch piece fresh galangal or more ginger, peeled and minced

  4 fresh chiles, preferably Thai, stemmed, seeded, and minced

  1 lemongrass stalk, trimmed, smashed, and minced (page 143)

  $\frac{1}{4}$ cup chopped roasted peanuts

  8 betel, spinach, butter, or Bibb lettuce leaves

  2 limes, cut into wedges

1. Put the first four ingredients and $\frac{1}{2}$ cup of the coconut in a blender. Blend until smooth, keeping the blender running and adding just enough water, about $\frac{1}{2}$ cup, to produce a saucelike consistency. Set aside.

2. Bring a small pot of water to a boil. Add the shrimp and cook until pink, 2 to 5 minutes. Drain, rinse under cold water, drain again, and chop into small dice.

3. Serve at the table. Each guest should put a bit of the shrimp, shallots, galangal, chiles, lemongrass, peanuts, and remaining coconut in the center of the betel or other leaf. Spoon some of the sauce and squeeze some of the lime onto the filling, wrap loosely, and eat.

Shrimp Deviled Eggs SPAIN ■ ▣ ▨

MAKES **4 SERVINGS**

TIME **20 MINUTES**

Unlike common deviled eggs, these, usually served as a tapa, have both texture and more flavor. The shrimp and olives bring a nice saltiness to the dish, which is ideal for a picnic.

 ¼ **pound medium to large shrimp, peeled**

 4 hard-cooked eggs (page 338)

 6 pimiento-stuffed olives, chopped

 1 tablespoon minced onion

 2 tablespoons chopped fresh parsley leaves, plus more parsley for garnish

 1 teaspoon Worcestershire sauce

 1 teaspoon extra virgin olive oil

 Salt and black pepper to taste

 2 tablespoons mayonnaise, preferably homemade (page 602)

1. Bring a small pot of water to a boil. Add the shrimp and cook until pink, 2 to 5 minutes. Drain, rinse under cold water, drain again, and chop into small dice.

2. Peel the eggs, halve them lengthwise, and remove the yolks. Mash 2 of the yolks in a medium bowl and set aside the remaining yolks. Add the shrimp, olives, onion, parsley, Worcestershire sauce, and oil and mix well. Season with salt and pepper.

3. Mound this mixture into the egg whites. Top with a little dollop of mayonnaise and crumble the remaining yolks on top. Garnish with parsley and serve or cover with plastic wrap and refrigerate for up to a day; bring back to room temperature before serving.

Salmon Deviled Eggs. Substitute ¼ pound cooked, shredded salmon or chopped smoked salmon for the shrimp.

Tea Eggs CHINA ■ ▣

MAKES **12 EGGS**

TIME **2 HOURS, LARGELY UNATTENDED**

This is special-occasion food for many Chinese, served as part of large meals. The eggs simmer in their special dark liquid, and eager hands reach in to retrieve an egg, peel it, and devour it. The smoky flavor and pretty patterns on the eggs are mysterious looking but easy to create. By all means, make these ahead of time, as you would any hard-cooked eggs.

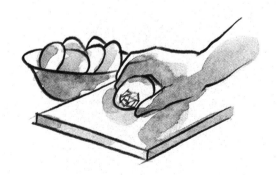

CRACKING A TEA EGG

12 eggs

¹/₂ cup loose black tea leaves, preferably keemun
   or lapsang souchong

2 tablespoons soy sauce

2 tablespoons Shaoxing wine or dry sherry

Four ¹/₂-inch-thick slices fresh ginger

2 star anise

1 cinnamon stick

1. Put the eggs in a saucepan with water to cover and turn the heat to medium-high. Bring to a boil, then turn off the heat and cover. Let sit for 9 minutes. Drain and rinse under cold water, then lightly tap the eggs on a hard surface to create a web of fine cracks. Do not peel or allow the shell to come off.

2. Meanwhile, put the remaining ingredients in a saucepan (it can be the same one) with about 3 inches of water and bring to a boil over high heat; reduce the heat to low. Gently lower the eggs into the liquid and simmer, uncovered, for an hour, stirring occasionally. Remove from the heat and let sit until the liquid cools. Peel the eggs and serve warm or refrigerate in the liquid and serve chilled. They will keep in the refrigerator for several days.

Cheese Mantecaos NORTH AFRICA ■ ▓ ▒

MAKES **4 SERVINGS**

TIME **20 MINUTES**

These are the Platonic ideal of our packaged cheese puffs, with the texture of macaroons and the flavors of fresh cheese and fragrant spices. Serve as a snack or stand-up food. You can prepare the dough ahead of time and refrigerate it until you are ready to bake or make the biscuits themselves ahead of time and store them in an airtight container for up to a day.

8 tablespoons (1 stick) cold butter, cubed

2 cups grated Emmental (Swiss), Gruyère, Cantal,
   or good-quality Cheddar cheese

1¹/₂ cups flour

1 egg, lightly beaten

¹/₂ teaspoon salt

¹/₂ teaspoon cayenne

3 teaspoons cumin seeds, lightly toasted in a dry skillet
   until fragrant

1 tablespoon paprika, optional

1. Preheat the oven to 400°F. Put the butter, cheese, flour, egg, salt, cayenne, and cumin into the bowl of a food processor and pulse, just until the mixture resembles coarse meal; do not overprocess. (You can also use a pastry cutter or a fork to cut the mixture to the same consistency.)

2. Form the mixture into 1-inch balls. Line the balls on a nonstick or lightly greased baking sheet, leaving 2 inches between them. Slightly flatten each ball with your fingers.

3. Bake until the pastries puff and become golden brown, about 10 minutes. Cool completely on a wire rack, then garnish with paprika if you like and serve within a few hours.

Spicy Cheese Straws INDIA Omit the cumin and paprika; increase the cayenne to 1 teaspoon, or to taste.

Mock Ceviche PERU ■ ▓ ▒

MAKES **6 OR MORE SERVINGS AS A STARTER,**
   4 SERVINGS AS A LIGHT LUNCH

TIME **30 MINUTES OR LESS**

True Ceviche (page 21) "cooks" fish by marinating it in an acidic dressing. But there is a similar dish in which the fish is simmered in boiling water first; it's used most frequently with seafood that is tough when raw, but it's also used—at least in this country—as a form of reassurance. It's a bit of a cheat, but so what? There is little difference between the texture or quality of fish that has been marinated in lime and that of fish that has been cooked quickly (which is why marinating in lime is perfectly acceptable in the first place).

Like all ceviche, this is a great starter.

Salt and black pepper to taste

½ pound shrimp, any size

½ pound sea scallops

½ pound cleaned squid, cut into rings (tentacles left whole)

2 tablespoons extra virgin olive oil

1 small fresh chile, stemmed, seeded, and finely minced, or hot red pepper flakes or cayenne to taste

½ cup minced red onion

1 small garlic clove, minced, optional

¼ cup minced red or yellow bell pepper, optional

¼ cup diced tomato, optional

¼ cup diced avocado, optional

¼ cup fresh lime juice

½ cup fresh cilantro leaves, roughly chopped

1. Bring about 2 quarts of water to a boil and salt it. Add the shrimp, reduce the heat to medium, and cook for 2 to 5 minutes, or until they are pink and firm. Remove with a slotted spoon and run under cold water to chill. Peel and set aside.

2. Cook the scallops and squid together in the same water for 2 minutes, or until the scallops are firm and not quite cooked through and the squid is fairly tender. Remove with a slotted spoon (reserve the cooking water) and run under cold water to chill, then combine with the shrimp.

3. Toss the fish with the olive oil and, if you like, cover and refrigerate until ready to serve (up to 24

hours). Toss with all the remaining ingredients except the cilantro, then taste and add more salt and pepper if necessary. If the mixture is dry, add a little more olive oil or lime juice or some of the cooking water. Stir in most of the cilantro, then garnish with the remainder and serve.

Gefilte Fish EASTERN EUROPE ■ ■

MAKES **8 TO 12 SERVINGS**

TIME **ABOUT 2½ HOURS, LARGELY UNATTENDED, PLUS CHILLING TIME**

Traditionally made with freshwater fish—carp, whitefish, and pike—this is just as good with fish from the sea. You can even mix in some darker fish, like bluefish and salmon, although it is not traditional. Equally untraditional is the food processor, which makes this formerly formidable job a snap. Good, strong horseradish is the essential accompaniment. Make this a day before you want to serve it.

3 pounds whitefish scraps—skeletons, heads (gills removed), and skin

2 large onions

2 celery stalks, roughly chopped

2 bay leaves

1 tablespoon peppercorns

3 pounds fillets of assorted fish, preferably freshwater, like carp, whitefish, and pike, rinsed and patted dry

3 eggs, lightly beaten

3 tablespoons matzo or cracker meal

Salt and white (preferred) or black pepper to taste

About 3 cups carrot chunks

About ½ cup Creamy Horseradish Sauce (page 608), Sharp Horseradish Sauce (page 607), or prepared horseradish to taste

1. Put the fish scraps in a large pot with 1 onion, the celery, bay leaves, peppercorns, and water to cover; bring to a boil, then reduce the heat to low.

2. Peel the other onion, quarter it, and combine it with the fish fillets in a food processor. Pulse until coarsely chopped; do not overprocess. (You may have to do this in batches.) Add the eggs, one at a time, pulsing after each addition. Add the matzo meal and about $1/2$ cup water and process for a few seconds; the mixture should be light, smooth, and almost fluffy. Add a little more water if it seems too dry. Season with salt and pepper.

3. Drop the carrots into the simmering stock. With wet hands, shape the fish mixture into small ovals, about the size of eggs. Lower each one of them into the simmering stock; don't worry about crowding. Cover and adjust the heat so the mixture simmers; cook for about $1/2$ hours, then turn off the heat and let the fish cool in the liquid.

4. Use a slotted spoon to transfer the fish balls and the carrots to a platter. Raise the heat to high and reduce the stock, if necessary, to about 2 cups. Strain it over the fish balls, cover the platter, and refrigerate. Remove the fish from the refrigerator about 30 minutes before serving. Serve with a bit of the jelly, a few carrot pieces, and plenty of horseradish.

Pickled Herring SWEDEN ■ ▩

MAKES **4 SERVINGS**

TIME **ABOUT 24 HOURS, LARGELY UNATTENDED**

The hardest part of this dish, these days, is finding fresh herring—which is astonishing, because a large percentage of the world's supply is caught off our shores and shipped elsewhere. In the countries bordering the North Sea, however, it is celebrated, and if you can find it here—it's in fish markets from time to time—this is a great treatment, an essential part of any smorgasbord, but also wonderful served with sour cream ("creamed herring") and boiled potatoes. If the herring is whole, ask your fishmonger to fillet it for you.

¼ cup salt

1½ pounds fresh herring fillets, boned

½ cup white vinegar

½ cup sugar

1 tablespoon allspice berries

1 tablespoon white peppercorns

2 bay leaves

1 red onion, thinly sliced

1. Dissolve 3 tablespoons of the salt in 3 cups cold water. Place the herring fillets in the saltwater, cover, and refrigerate for about 12 hours.

2. Place the remaining salt, the vinegar, sugar, allspice berries, peppercorns, and bay leaves in a small saucepan with 1 cup water. Stir over medium-high heat until the sugar dissolves, then remove from the heat and cool.

3. Remove the herring from the saltwater and place in a shallow baking dish. Lay the onion on top of the fish, then pour on the pickling mixture. Cover and refrigerate overnight. Serve directly from the dish.

ALLSPICE BERRIES

Goi Cuon Rice Paper Spring Rolls VIETNAM ■ ▪

MAKES **8 ROLLS, ENOUGH FOR 4 TO 8 APPETIZER**
 SERVINGS

TIME **40 MINUTES**

I learned how to make "summer rolls" in a tiny village in the Mekong Delta. I was not only the only non-Vietnamese at the table; I was also the only male. My pathetic technique was laughable to my co-workers, but I quickly got the hang of it. So will you.

Rice paper wrappers, sold in Asian markets, keep forever. Their flexibility is truly amazing, and the simple variation will give you an idea of the different directions in which you can go. This is just a basic outline; these rolls can be filled with infinite variations of vegetables, meat, and even fruit, so don't worry if you don't have one or two of the ingredients here. You can cover these with a moist towel or plastic wrap and keep them for about an hour, no longer, before serving.

8 rice paper sheets, 10 or 12 inches in diameter

1/2 pound cooked pork or chicken, cut into thin strips

**12 medium shrimp, cooked, peeled, and split in half
 lengthwise**

**One 4-ounce bundle dried rice vermicelli, soaked in
 hot water until softened (about 10 minutes) and
 drained**

1/2 cup fresh mint leaves, roughly chopped

1/2 cup fresh cilantro leaves, roughly chopped

**1/2 cup fresh basil leaves (preferably Thai), roughly
 chopped**

**2 scallions, trimmed, cut into 2-inch pieces, and sliced
 lengthwise**

2 carrots, grated or shredded

4 red-leaf lettuce leaves, thinly sliced crosswise

1/2 cup chopped roasted peanuts

**Peanut Sauce (page 586), Nam Prik (page 586),
 or lime wedges**

SPRING ROLLS

1. Set up a workstation: lay out a damp kitchen or paper towel on the counter and a large bowl of hot water (110–120°F, which is about what it measures from most taps). Dip a sheet of the rice paper in the hot water, turning once, until soft, about 10 seconds. Lay it flat on the towel.

2. On the bottom third of the rice paper, spread an eighth of each of the remaining ingredients, except the sauce, in a line. Fold in the bottom edge and

both sides and then roll tightly into a cylinder. The rice paper will adhere to itself. Repeat this process with the remaining ingredients.

3. Serve with either of the dipping sauces or the lime wedges.

Warm Vegetarian Spring Rolls. Omit the meat, shrimp, and vermicelli. Heat 2 tablespoons corn, grapeseed, canola, or other neutral oil in a large skillet over medium heat. Scramble 2 eggs, remove, and then brown one 3-ounce block of tofu on all sides. Cut the tofu into thin strips. Wrap the spring rolls as directed, using the egg, tofu, and remaining ingredients, substituting more Thai basil for the mint and cilantro. Serve warm with Hoisin Chili Sauce (page 584).

Tropical Spring Rolls. This is an authentic variation, not some fusion concoction. Omit the pork, vermicelli, carrots, and peanuts. Use shrimp, lobster, or crabmeat and add one peeled and sliced mango. Roll as directed and serve with Sweet Nam Pla Dipping Sauce (page 586).

Cold Cut Beef Shank CHINA ■ ■

MAKES **8 SERVINGS AS A STARTER OR IN SANDWICHES**
TIME **ABOUT 4 HOURS, LARGELY UNATTENDED**

Thin, cold slices of beef in a flavorful soy sauce make a popular starter at Chinese banquets. The dish is usually served alongside other chilled meats, like Soy-Poached Chicken (page 274) and Barbecued Pork (page 373). You can also use it as a sandwich stuffing or snack on it at any time. For information on Szechwan peppercorns, see page 369.

About 2 pounds boneless beef shank or brisket
$\frac{1}{2}$ cup soy sauce

$\frac{1}{2}$ cup rice wine or white wine
3 scallions, trimmed
One 1-inch piece fresh ginger, peeled and sliced
2 star anise
1 teaspoon Szechwan peppercorns
1 teaspoon sugar
$\frac{1}{2}$ teaspoon five-spice powder or 2 cloves plus
    5 coriander seeds and 1 cinnamon stick
Fresh cilantro sprigs for garnish

1. Put all of the ingredients except the cilantro in a large saucepan with a lid; add just enough water to cover the beef, about $1\frac{1}{2}$ cups. Bring the mixture to a boil, lower the heat, cover, and simmer for about 4 hours, adding more water if necessary. The meat is done when very, very tender.

2. Use a slotted spoon to remove the beef from the braising liquid (reserve the liquid), and let it cool to room temperature; cover and refrigerate until cold. Strain the reserved liquid and refrigerate.

3. To serve, use a sharp knife to cut the beef into $\frac{1}{4}$-inch slices across the grain. Garnish with the cilantro and serve with the braising liquid as a dipping sauce.

Pashtet Calf (or Chicken) Liver Pâté RUSSIA ■ ■

MAKES **4 SERVINGS**
TIME **30 MINUTES, PLUS CHILLING TIME**

This is a popular item throughout Eastern Europe and is often formed into fanciful shapes (as is its close cousin, chopped chicken liver, at many American bar and bat mitzvahs). It tastes just as good served from a bowl and spread on crackers or toast.

3 tablespoons butter, softened
2 ounces slab bacon, chopped
1 medium onion, chopped

1 pound calf liver or chicken livers, picked over for veins
   and chopped
1 teaspoon freshly grated nutmeg
1 tablespoon brandy or dry vermouth, plus more to taste
Salt and black pepper to taste

1. Melt half the butter in a large skillet over medium heat. Add the bacon and cook, stirring occasionally, until the fat melts, about 5 minutes. Add the onion and cook until softened, 3 to 5 minutes. Add the liver and cook just until it loses its pinkness.

2. Transfer the liver mixture with all the pan drippings to a food processor and add the nutmeg, brandy, and remaining butter; process until smooth. Season with salt and pepper and more brandy if desired.

3. Press the processed liver mixture into a serving bowl, cover with plastic wrap, and chill for at least 3 hours. Serve within a day, cold or at room temperature.

Grilled Beef "Jerky" SOUTHEAST ASIA ■ ▪

MAKES **8 SERVINGS**

TIME **ABOUT 1 DAY, LARGELY UNATTENDED, PLUS TIME TO PREHEAT THE GRILL**

Although the ingredients of this great snack, which also makes a good starter, are the same as for a common marinated beef dish, this is all about process. The beef is first dried and then fried or grilled. If you live in a warm climate, you can dry the beef in the sun for a day, turning it once. To get the same effect in more temperate zones, you need an oven, which, needless to say, is easier and more reliable.

To crush the coriander seeds, put them in a plastic bag and press on them with the bottom of a pot, leaning on the pot if necessary. For information on

Southeast Asian fish sauces like nam pla and nuoc mam, see page 500; for information on trimming lemongrass, see page 143.

1½ pounds boneless beef sirloin or flank steak
2 tablespoons minced lemongrass
1 tablespoon crushed coriander seeds
2 tablespoons nam pla or nuoc mam
1 tablespoon honey or sugar
1 tablespoon minced garlic

1. Freeze the meat for 30 to 60 minutes, until it is semisolid. Slice as thinly as possible (if you have a slicing machine, this is the time to use it).

2. Combine the meat with all the remaining ingredients. Marinate for 2 to 24 hours. Drain the meat, then place it on a rack—the slices should not be touching one another—and put it in an oven set at its lowest temperature (or place in the sun, or use a dehydrator). "Cook" the meat, turning it occasionally, until dry but still pliable, at least 4 hours and probably more (if it takes less time than that, your oven is too hot; you can proceed, but next time look for a tamer heat source). Wrap and refrigerate the meat for up to a couple of days if you like.

3. Start a charcoal or gas grill; the fire should be quite hot and the rack no more than 4 inches from the heat source. Grill the slices quickly, until lightly browned on both sides. Serve hot or at room temperature.

COOKED APPETIZERS, PREPARED IN ADVANCE AND SERVED HOT OR WARM

These are cooked appetizers, usually served hot or warm, but that can be prepared in advance, reheated, or served at room temperature in a pinch. Just enough to give the entertaining cook the flexibility needed to make a meal work.

Crostini ITALY ■ ▨ ▨

MAKES **8 SERVINGS**

TIME **15 MINUTES**

Crostini is toast—no big deal. Yet it serves as a perfect base for dips and spreads, from Tapenade (page 604) to Fresh Tomato Salad (page 172). Good, too, with ricotta or goat cheese blended with chopped parsley or basil; tomato, country ham (like prosciutto), and olive oil; Brandade de Morue (page 56); or Canapés with Piquillo Peppers and Anchovies (page 48). Parsley or basil is always welcome as a garnish.

If you're making just a few crostini, you can use a toaster oven, but for large quantities a grill or oven works best. The toasted bread itself will keep for an hour or so; don't top it until you're ready or nearly ready to eat.

Extra virgin olive oil as needed

1 loaf Italian bread or French baguette, cut into ¹/₂-inch slices

1. Prepare a grill or preheat the oven to 400°F.
2. Lightly brush the oil onto both sides of each slice of bread. Grill or bake until grill lines appear or until golden and slightly crisp, about 10 minutes. Turning is unnecessary but doesn't hurt.

Garlic Crostini. Cut a clove of garlic in half and rub the bread with the cut side after grilling. For a more subtle version, mince a couple of cloves of garlic and mix with the olive oil before brushing it on the bread.

Crostini with Beans and Greens

ITALY ■ ▨ ▨

MAKES **6 TO 8 SERVINGS**

TIME **30 MINUTES**

A typical topping for crostini (and not a bad dish on its own), this hearty combination makes a great starter for a vegetarian meal. Cannellini beans are traditional here, but any white bean will work.

The spread and bread may be made well in advance, but don't combine them until just before serving.

Crostini (see preceding recipe)

3 tablespoons extra virgin olive oil

2 garlic cloves, minced

1 onion, diced

2 cups White Beans with Garlic (page 441), or any canned white beans, drained and liquid reserved

1 pound spinach, trimmed and roughly chopped

10 fresh sage leaves or about 1 teaspoon dried, crumbled

Salt and black pepper to taste

1. If you need to make the crostini, start with these. Place the oil in a skillet over medium heat. Add the garlic and onion and cook, stirring occasionally, until fragrant and softened, about 5 minutes. Add the beans and spinach and stir. Cook, stirring occasionally, until the spinach wilts, about 5 minutes.
2. Add the sage and 2 tablespoons of the reserved bean liquid. Cover and cook for another 5 minutes. (You can prepare all of this before assembling the crostini and even refrigerate; bring back to room temperature before proceeding.)
3. Remove from the heat and season with salt and pepper. Spoon on top of crostini and serve immediately.

Farinata Genovese

Ligurian Chickpea Pancake ITALY ■

MAKES **4 TO 6 SERVINGS AS A STARTER OR SIDE DISH**
TIME **1 HOUR, PLUS TIME FOR THE BATTER TO REST**

Farinata, which is nearly identical to the socca of Provence, is a cross between firm polenta and a primitive pizza. To me it's the perfect no-work Mediterranean appetizer, a great thing to have in your repertoire if you want to make sure there's something warm for guests to eat when they arrive—or if you just want to round out a pasta dinner for the family on a weeknight.

Keep the pepper mill nearby when you serve the farinata; it's best with an almost perverse amount of freshly ground black pepper.

You can buy chickpea flour at health food stores, Italian markets, Middle Eastern stores, and specialty food shops.

1 cup chickpea flour

1 teaspoon salt

1 teaspoon freshly ground black pepper, plus more to taste

5 tablespoons extra virgin olive oil, plus more to taste

1/2 small yellow onion, thinly sliced (1/4 to 1/2 cup, loosely packed, to taste), optional

1 tablespoon fresh rosemary leaves, optional

1. Combine the chickpea flour with $1^3/4$ cups water in a bowl; whisk together to eliminate lumps. Whisk in the salt and two tablespoons of the olive oil and let the batter sit on the kitchen counter for at least 1 hour and as long as 12. The batter will become slightly thicker as it sits.

2. Preheat the oven to 400°F. Put a well-seasoned or nonstick 12-inch pizza pan or skillet over medium-high heat and add 3 tablespoons of the olive oil. When the oil is hot, after 1 or 2 minutes, add the onion and rosemary if you're using them;

let them sizzle for a minute, then add the batter. Drizzle with a little olive oil and bake for 20 to 40 minutes, until the farinata is no longer custardy in the center. If you have a separate broiler, preheat it during the last 10 minutes or so of cooking.

3. Turn the broiler on. Set the farinata a few inches away from the broiler heat for a minute or two, just long enough to brown it spottily, but not long enough so that it colors evenly or burns.

4. Remove the farinata from the pan with two spatulas—this is where a nonstick pan comes in very handy—and transfer it, carefully, to a cutting board. Let cool briefly, then cut it into wedges and grind a generous amount of black pepper over all. Eat while still warm out of the oven, with additional black pepper or olive oil as desired.

Falafel MIDDLE EAST ■ ▥

MAKES **6 SERVINGS AS A STARTER OR IN SANDWICHES**
TIME **1 HOUR, PLUS SOAKING TIME**

Falafel is the best known of bean fritters, and—because it's usually made from chickpeas and/or fava beans—the best tasting. Canned chickpeas are too soft for falafel, but the recipe is pretty easy anyway; the dried beans are soaked, not cooked, and the frying is straightforward.

The addition of an egg prevents the batter from falling apart, which is a common problem. It may not be strictly traditional, but it works.

The little fritters are best in a huge pita, with a pile of raw vegetables, but they're also nice served as a starter, with some greens and a little Tahini Sauce.

$1^3/4$ cups dried chickpeas or 1 cup dried chickpeas plus 3/4 cup dried split fava beans

2 garlic cloves, peeled and lightly crushed

1 small onion, peeled and quartered

1 teaspoon ground coriander

1 tablespoon ground cumin

1 scant teaspoon cayenne, or to taste

1 cup chopped fresh parsley or cilantro leaves

2½ teaspoons salt

½ teaspoon black pepper, or to taste

½ teaspoon baking soda

1 tablespoon fresh lemon juice

1 egg

Corn, grapeseed, or other neutral oil for deep-frying

1. Put the beans in a large bowl and cover with water by 3 or 4 inches. Soak for 24 hours, checking once or twice to see if you need to add more water to keep the beans submerged—they will triple in volume as they soak.

2. Drain the beans well and transfer them to a food processor with all the remaining ingredients except the oil; pulse until finely minced but not pureed, scraping the sides of the bowl down as necessary; add water a tablespoon at a time if necessary to allow the machine to do its work. Taste and make sure the mixture is seasoned adequately; add more of any seasoning you like.

3. Put at least 2 inches (more is better) of oil in a large, deep saucepan. (The narrower the saucepan, the less oil you need, but the more oil you use, the

more patties you can cook at the same time.) Turn the heat to medium-high and heat the oil to about 350°F (a pinch of the batter will sizzle immediately—or you can test it with a deep-frying thermometer).

4. Scoop out heaping tablespoons of the mixture and shape them into balls or small patties. Fry in batches, without crowding, until nicely browned, turning as necessary; total cooking time will be less than 5 minutes. Serve hot or at room temperature, with Tahini Sauce (page 597).

Supplì Fried Rice Balls ITALY ■ ■ ▨

MAKES **6 TO 8 SERVINGS AS A STARTER OR SNACK**

TIME **30 MINUTES (WITH PREPARED RICE)**

A Roman treat and a fine use for leftover rice (especially risotto). Formally called supplì al telefono because the stringy mozzarella center stretches when you bite through the center and is reminiscent of telephone wires, this is a snack, or a very informal starter. If you use packaged bread crumbs, make sure they're unseasoned.

3 eggs

2 cups cold cooked rice, preferably Risotto alla Milanese (page 521)

3 ounces fresh mozzarella, chopped

2 ounces prosciutto, minced, optional

2 cups fine bread crumbs, preferably homemade (page 580)

Corn, grapeseed, or other neutral oil for deep-frying

1. Break one of the eggs into the rice and mix well. Form the rice into 2-inch balls. With your thumb, make a small indentation in the center of each ball, fill with a little mozzarella, plus prosciutto if you're using it; reseal the ball with the risotto around it.

FALAFEL

2. Lightly beat the remaining two eggs and dip each ball into the egg mixture and then the bread crumbs. Set the finished balls on wax paper; they can be refrigerated for up to a couple of hours or cooked right away.

3. Put about 3 inches of oil in a deep saucepan and turn the heat to medium-high; bring to 350°F (heat until a bread crumb sizzles in the oil, but not violently). Gently slide the balls into the oil and fry until golden brown, turning once if necessary, about 4 minutes.

4. Drain on paper towels and serve hot or at room temperature.

Flan de Courgettes Zucchini Custard
FRANCE ■ ▨
MAKES **6 TO 8 SERVINGS AS A STARTER OR 4 AS A LIGHT
 MAIN COURSE**
TIME **ABOUT 1 HOUR**

The slices of this Provençal custard are gorgeous, a yellow-and-green mosaic enhanced by the tomato coulis (a fancy word for "sauce"). Best warm or at room temperature, but not as good if it sees the inside of a refrigerator, so serve—as an appetizer or a main course for a light meal—within three or four hours. With thanks to Marie Martin.

½ cup extra virgin olive oil

2 to 3 pounds zucchini, thinly sliced

Salt and black pepper to taste

1 tablespoon plus 1 teaspoon minced garlic

5 eggs

¼ cup heavy cream or milk

4 medium tomatoes, preferably very ripe, cored and
 roughly chopped

¼ cup chopped fresh basil leaves

1 tablespoon sugar

1. Put half the oil in a large skillet over medium heat. Add the zucchini, along with a large pinch of salt and some pepper, and cook, stirring occasionally, until it wilts and gives up its liquid, about 10 minutes. Add the tablespoon of garlic and continue cooking until the zucchini browns slightly, another 5 to 10 minutes.

2. Meanwhile, preheat the oven to 350°F and set a kettle of water to boil. Beat together the eggs, cream, and some more salt and pepper. When the zucchini is done, cool slightly, then scoop it into the egg mixture, using a slotted spoon. Stir. Lightly grease an 8 x 4-inch loaf pan (lined with wax paper if not nonstick or well seasoned) and pour the zucchini mixture into it. Place in a baking dish and put in the oven; add water to the baking dish to come as far up the sides of the pan as is practical, then bake until the flan is set but still slightly jiggly in the middle, about 30 minutes.

3. While the flan is cooking, make the tomato coulis. Put the remaining oil in a small saucepan over medium heat. Add the tomatoes, along with the remaining garlic, some salt and pepper, the basil, and the sugar. Bring to a boil, cover, and simmer for about 15 minutes.

4. When the flan is done, cool it on a rack for a few minutes. Invert over a plate and unmold. Cool until warm or room temperature, then slice and serve, with the tomato coulis.

Tarte Flambé Alsatian "Pizza" FRANCE ■
MAKES **4 OR MORE SERVINGS AS A STARTER OR LIGHT
 MAIN COURSE**
TIME **45 TO 60 MINUTES (WITH PREMADE DOUGH)**

This is a pizza in all but name, and it disproves the notion that "creative" pizzas began in California. Creamy, smoky, and crunchy, it's a real winner.

½ recipe Pizza Dough (page 572)

Flour as needed

Olive oil as needed

1 cup fromage blanc or crème fraîche or ¾ cup sour
  cream thinned with ⅓ cup milk

½ cup minced onion

½ cup minced bacon

Salt and black pepper to taste

1. Preheat the oven to at least 500°F (600 is better if your oven goes that high), with a pizza stone in place if you have one. Knead the dough lightly and place it on a lightly floured surface; sprinkle it with a little more flour and cover it with plastic wrap or a towel. Let it rest while the oven heats.

2. Pat or roll out the dough as thinly as possible, to a diameter of about 12 inches, using more flour or oil as necessary. The process will be easier if you let the dough rest occasionally between rollings. If you have a pizza stone in your oven, place the dough on a floured peel or long-handled board; if not, lay the dough on a baking sheet brushed lightly with olive oil. Let the dough rest for 15 to 30 minutes, or until it begins to puff ever so slightly.

3. Spread the fromage blanc on the dough. Sprinkle with onion, bacon, a little salt, and plenty of pepper. Bake until nicely crisp, about 10 minutes; if the tart is browning unevenly, rotate it back to front about halfway through the cooking time. Serve hot or, in a pinch, at room temperature.

Pissaladière Onion Pizza FRANCE ■ ▨

MAKES **4 OR MORE SERVINGS**

TIME **ABOUT 1 HOUR (WITH PREMADE DOUGH)**

The most exciting pissaladière I ever had was served at the open-air market in the heart of old Nice. It was baked in a wood-burning oven a few blocks away, sent to the market by bicycle, and eaten standing up or at picnic tables shaded by huge awnings. The wedges were gently sweet and intensely salty; the crust, just a half inch thick, was perfumed with the local olive oil and was perfectly browned and crisp. It was so simple—mostly just sweet onions on a wonderful crust.

You can make a wonderful pissaladière at home: just be sure to cook the onions very, very slowly.

½ recipe Pizza Dough (page 572)

Flour as needed

3 tablespoons extra virgin olive oil, plus more as needed

1½ pounds onions, about 3 large or 4 or 5 medium, thinly
  sliced

Salt and black pepper to taste

1 teaspoon fresh thyme leaves or ½ teaspoon dried

6 to 10 anchovies, optional

About 12 Niçoise or other good-quality black olives, pitted
  and cut in half, optional

6 to 8 thin slices tomato, optional

1. Preheat the oven to 450°F, with a pizza stone in place if you have one. Knead the dough lightly and place it on a lightly floured surface; sprinkle it with a little more flour and cover it with plastic wrap or a towel. Let it rest while the oven heats and you cook the onions.

2. Put the olive oil in a large skillet over medium-high heat and add the onions and some salt and pepper. Cook, stirring frequently, until the onions give up their liquid and become quite soft, at least 15 minutes; do not allow them to brown. When they are cooked, turn off the heat and stir in the thyme.

3. Pat or roll out the dough as thinly as possible, to a diameter of about 12 inches, using more flour or oil as necessary. The process will be easier if you let the dough rest between rollings. If you have a pizza stone in your oven, place the dough on a

floured peel or long-handled board; if not, lay the dough on a baking sheet brushed lightly with olive oil. Let the dough rest for 15 to 30 minutes, or until it begins to puff ever so slightly.

4. Spread the dough with onions and then decorate, if you like, with anchovies, olives, and tomato. Bake until nicely crisp, 15 minutes or more; if the tart is browning unevenly, rotate it back to front about halfway through the cooking time. Serve hot or at room temperature.

Sicilian Onion Pizza. Omit the tomatoes and olives. In step 2, stir the anchovies into the cooked onions and cook for 5 minutes. Stir a 6-ounce can of tomato paste into the onions and cook for a few more minutes over low heat. Season to taste. Drizzle the rolled-out dough with 2 tablespoons olive oil and bake for 10 to 12 minutes, or until the bottom begins to turn pale golden. Spread the partially baked dough with 1 cup plain bread crumbs, preferably fresh, then spread with the onion mixture. Return to the oven and bake for 15 to 20 minutes more, until the bottom is dark golden but not burned and the top is a richly colored caramel. Remove and allow to cool for a few minutes before cutting; best served hot or warm.

Piquillo Peppers Stuffed with Fish
SPAIN ■ ▨

MAKES **4 TO 6 SERVINGS**

TIME **20 MINUTES (WITH PRECOOKED FISH)**

Piquillos have so much going for them. Not only is their color stunning, their skin thin, and their flavor a near-perfect blend of sweet and hot, but one couldn't bioengineer a better shape for stuffing.

To precook the fish, simply put it in salted water to cover, bring the water to a boil, and turn off the heat. By the time the water cools, the fish will be done.

3 tablespoons extra virgin olive oil

2 garlic cloves, minced

2 shallots, minced

2 tablespoons flour

1/2 pound flaky white fish, like cod or haddock, cooked, skinned, and boned

1/4 cup dry white wine

1/4 cup heavy cream

1 tablespoon brandy, optional

Salt and black pepper to taste

8 to 12 piquillo peppers

3 tablespoons chopped fresh parsley leaves

1. Heat the oil in a deep skillet over medium-high heat. Add the garlic and shallots and cook, stirring occasionally, until softened and fragrant, about 2 minutes. Add the flour and cook, stirring constantly, until the mixture is well combined. Add the fish and stir, breaking it up into small pieces.

2. Add the white wine and cream and cook, stirring occasionally, until the mixture comes to a boil. Remove the fish with a slotted spoon and continue to cook the sauce until it has thickened and reduced

STUFFING A PIQUILLO PEPPER

Pimientos del Piquillo Piquillo Peppers

Pimientos del piquillo are delicious—sweet, slightly hot, and crimson. They're cone shaped (piquillo means "little beak") and from the Navarre region of Spain, most famously from the town of Lodosa, where the best are (supposedly) grown. Prime piquillos are harvested by hand, roasted over wood fires, then hand-peeled and packed (you may find flecks of charred skin remaining on them).

Until recently, piquillos were rarely seen outside Spain, but they are now shipped everywhere. Even with-

out preservatives (most are packed naturally), piquillos keep well and are a wonderful pantry item. Most specialty markets and some fine foods Web sites carry them.

Piquillos are perfect for stuffing (page 46), though they are also delicious sautéed (page 471) or even simply sprinkled with olive oil and salt.

---

by half. Stir in the brandy and season with salt and pepper.

3. Meanwhile, stuff the piquillos with the fish and arrange on a platter. Pour the sauce over the stuffed piquillos, garnish with parsley, and serve hot or warm.

Piquillos Stuffed with Crab. Substitute ½ pound cooked lump crabmeat for the fish.

Stuffed Piquillos with Brandade. Stuff the peppers with about ½ recipe prepared Brandade de Morue (page 56).

Pork, Piquillo, and Cheese Canapés
SPAIN ■ ■ ■

MAKES **6 TO 8 SERVINGS**

TIME **30 MINUTES (WITH PRECOOKED MEAT)**

You can use leftover pork (or any meat, really), for these canapés, because its flavor is not the most important thing here. What is important are the piquillos and the manchego. Without these the dish has no authenticity.

That said, this is a great basic recipe combining meat, cheese, and pepper, and you can substitute for any of them—I especially like this with a bit of chorizo and a strong blue cheese.

If you start with raw pork tenderloin, cut it into 4 slices and brown it in a little olive oil in a nonstick skillet over medium-high heat for about 3 minutes per side.

12 to 16 slices baguette or other narrow, crusty loaf

¼ pound cooked pork tenderloin, cut into 12 to 16 thin slices

Salt and black pepper to taste

Extra virgin olive oil

12 to 16 small slices manchego or other firm sheep's milk cheese

6 to 8 piquillo peppers, cut in half lengthwise

1. Toast the bread lightly. Put a piece of pork on each piece of bread. Sprinkle the pork with salt and pepper and drizzle it with a few drops of olive oil.
2. Top with a piece of cheese and a piquillo half. Skewer with a toothpick and serve within 30 minutes.

Canapés with Piquillo Peppers and Anchovies SPAIN ■ □ □

MAKES **5 TO 10 SERVINGS**

TIME **15 MINUTES**

Peppers and anchovies are a delicious standby appetizer, and when you use piquillos (page 47) and good anchovies (page 25)—packed in olive oil—they become even better.

If you think using the garlic this way may be too strong for your tastes, simply cut a clove in half and rub the bread with it, then discard—or omit the garlic altogether.

> **10 slices French or Italian bread, roughly ³/₄ inch thick, cut in half**
>
> **1 teaspoon minced garlic**
>
> **10 piquillo peppers, cut in half lengthwise, or 4 or 5 roasted peppers (page 470), cut into pieces**
>
> **20 anchovies**
>
> **Extra virgin olive oil, optional**

Lightly toast or grill the bread. Spread each piece with a tiny bit of garlic, then layer on a piece of piquillo and an anchovy. Drizzle with a little anchovy oil and/or olive oil. Serve within 1 hour.

Piquillo Peppers with Shiitakes and Spinach SPAIN ■ □ □

MAKES **6 SERVINGS**

TIME **ABOUT 30 MINUTES**

A tapa based on piquillo peppers (see page 47), which are sold in jars and cans at specialty food stores and many supermarkets and are naturals for stuffing.

> **¹/₄ cup extra virgin olive oil**
>
> **2 garlic cloves, sliced**
>
> **1 small dried hot red chile**
>
> **2 cups shiitake mushrooms, stems removed (reserved for stock, if desired), caps thinly sliced or chopped**
>
> **1 cup cooked spinach, squeezed dry and chopped**
>
> **Salt and black pepper to taste**
>
> **12 piquillo peppers**

1. Place the olive oil in a large skillet over medium heat. Add the garlic and chile and cook, stirring occasionally, until the garlic browns lightly, about 5 minutes. Remove the chile and add the shiitakes. Cook, stirring occasionally, until the shiitakes release their liquid and become tender, about 10 minutes. Stir in the spinach and season with salt and pepper.

2. Stuff each of the peppers with some of the shiitake-spinach mixture. Serve at room temperature or warm gently in a 250°F oven for about 15 minutes.

Empanadas MEXICO, CARIBBEAN ■ ■ □

MAKES **12, ENOUGH FOR 12 SNACKS OR 4 MAIN COURSES**

TIME **ABOUT 1 HOUR (WITH PRECOOKED MEAT)**

A street snack of Central America and the Caribbean, empanadas can really be filled with anything you have on hand. This recipe and its variations offer several of the traditional fillings. Masa harina can be found at most supermarkets and Latin grocery stores. It adds a nice crunch to the dough, but regular flour works well, too.

> **1¹/₂ cups all-purpose flour, plus a little flour for rolling the dough**
>
> **¹/₂ cup masa harina, fine cornmeal, or more all-purpose flour**
>
> **1¹/₂ teaspoons baking powder**
>
> **1 teaspoon salt**

$\frac{1}{2}$ cup lard (traditional), shortening, or vegetable oil

$2\frac{1}{2}$ cups Shredded Pork (page 396)

$\frac{1}{2}$ cup milk

1. Mix the all-purpose flour, masa harina, baking powder, and salt together in a food processor; process for about 5 seconds. With the machine running, add the lard and process for 10 seconds. Then, with the machine still running, gradually add about $\frac{1}{2}$ cup cold water, stopping when the dough forms a ball; the dough should be fairly dry. Knead by hand until smooth, just a minute or so.

2. Divide the dough into 12 pieces, roll each piece into a ball, wrap in plastic or cover with a damp towel, and let rest for at least 20 minutes. (You can refrigerate the dough overnight; be sure to let it come to room temperature before proceeding.) On a well-floured surface, roll each piece into a 6-inch circle, adding flour as necessary.

3. Preheat the oven to 450°F. Place a couple of table-spoons of the pork on each of the circles, then fold each circle over; seal the seam with a few drops of water and press with the tines of a fork to close. Place on an ungreased baking sheet and brush lightly with milk. Bake until the dough is golden brown and hot, about 20 minutes. Serve immediately or at room temperature.

Chicken Empanadas. Substitute $2\frac{1}{2}$ cups of the chicken mixture from Chicken Tacos (page 323) for the filling.

Chorizo Empanadas. A very easy one: substitute $2\frac{1}{2}$ cups chopped or crumbled cooked, fresh Mexican chorizo (remove it from its skin first) for the filling.

Seafood Empanadas. Substitute $2\frac{1}{2}$ cups cooked shrimp, crabmeat, fish, or a mixture for the filling. Or use canned tuna.

Bean and Cheese Empanadas. Substitute $2\frac{1}{2}$ cups cooked beans (page 431) for the filling. Sprinkle crumbled queso fresco, blanco, añejo, or cojita (page 85) or grated Monterey Jack cheese on the beans and proceed as directed.

Vegetable Empanadas. Omit the pork. Cook 1 medium onion, diced, in 2 tablespoons corn, grape-seed, canola, or other neutral oil until softened. Mix with Roasted Red Peppers (page 470), diced, and use as the filling for the empanadas.

Grilled Octopus GREECE ■ ▩

MAKES **4 TO 6 SERVINGS**

TIME **2 HOURS OR MORE, PLUS TIME TO PREHEAT THE GRILL**

Wherever you find octopus, you find grilled octopus, though it is most closely associated with Greece, where it is prepared wonderfully. Most octopus in the U.S. is sold frozen, so make sure you think ahead (the benefit is that frozen octopus is also cleaned octopus). If you buy fresh, be sure to ask to have it cleaned or be prepared to do it yourself.

One more thing: Allow plenty of time for simmering until the octopus becomes tender—it's a simple but usually time-consuming process. (Sometimes octopus becomes tender quickly—but it's an unpredictable occurrence, not something you can count on.)

3 pounds cleaned octopus

1 bay leaf

4 fresh thyme branches

20 peppercorns

Salt and black pepper to taste

1 head of garlic, cut in half through its equator

3 lemons

3 tablespoons extra virgin olive oil
Minced fresh parsley leaves for garnish

1. Combine the octopus, bay leaf, thyme, peppercorns, 1 teaspoon salt, the garlic, and one of the lemons, cut in half, in a saucepan along with water to cover. Turn the heat to medium, cover, and bring to a boil. Adjust the heat so that the liquid simmers slowly and cook until the octopus is tender, 30 to 90 minutes (check with the point of a sharp knife). Drain, discarding all the solids (except the octopus). You can prepare this 24 hours in advance up to this point; cover and refrigerate the octopus.

2. Start a charcoal or wood fire or preheat a gas grill; the fire should be quite hot and the grill rack about 4 inches from the heat source. Cut the octopus into large serving pieces, brush it with half of the olive oil, and sprinkle it with salt and pepper.

OCTOPUS

Grill it quickly, so that the outside browns before the inside dries out. Cut the remaining lemons into wedges.

3. Brush the octopus with the remaining olive oil. Serve with lemon wedges, hot or at room temperature, garnished with the parsley.

Grilled Squid with Vinaigrette GREECE, ITALY, SPAIN, ETC. Much simpler: Cut cleaned squid into big rings (or use baby squid, cleaned but left whole) and skewer it. Grill or pan-grill it over quite high heat until browned, less than 5 minutes. Serve as directed or drizzled with Vinaigrette (page 600).

Warm Octopus and Potatoes SPAIN ■
MAKES **6 TO 8 SERVINGS**
TIME **UP TO 2 HOURS, LARGELY UNATTENDED**

A nice little appetizer from Galicia—northwestern Spain—great served warm or at room temperature. Your olive oil should be of the highest quality possible. For more about cooking octopus, see Grilled Octopus (page 49).

3 pounds cleaned octopus
2 bay leaves
Several fresh thyme sprigs
1 head of garlic, cut in half through its equator
2 pounds waxy potatoes, peeled and sliced 1/4 inch thick
1 teaspoon good-quality paprika, or to taste
1/3 cup extra virgin olive oil, or to taste
Coarse salt to taste

1. Put the octopus in a pot with water to cover; add the bay leaves, thyme, and garlic. Turn the heat to medium, cover, and bring to a boil. Adjust the heat so that the liquid simmers slowly and cook until

the octopus is nearly tender, 30 to 90 minutes (check with the point of a sharp knife). Add the potatoes to the water and cook for another 10 to 20 minutes, or until the potatoes are tender. Drain and discard everything but the octopus and potatoes.

2. Transfer the potatoes to a platter (wood is traditional) and the octopus to a cutting board. Let cool for a couple of minutes, then cut it into bite-sized pieces. Add to the potatoes, sprinkle with paprika, drizzle with plenty of olive oil, and toss gently. Sprinkle with salt and serve.

Octopus "Confit" JAPAN ■ ▩

MAKES **6 OR MORE SERVINGS**

TIME **1½ TO 2 HOURS**

An inspiration from Tadashi Ono, a talented Japanese chef now living in the United States. Succulent beyond belief and a most refreshing and appetizing starter. Most octopus sold in this country is frozen, which is not necessarily a bad thing. But if you can find fresh, sweet-smelling specimens, by all means use them. In either case, have the fishmonger clean the octopus. (Or do it yourself, by inverting the head and discarding its contents.)

About 2 pounds cleaned octopus

About 3 cups extra virgin olive oil

12 garlic cloves, peeled

2 small dried chiles

5 fresh thyme branches

Large pinch of salt

2 tablespoons soy sauce

2 tablespoons fresh lime juice

1. Wash the octopus well. Put it in a saucepan and add olive oil to cover, the garlic, chiles, thyme, and

salt. Bring to a very slow simmer over medium-high heat (if you have a thermometer, the ideal temperature is about 190°F). Adjust the heat to maintain this slow simmer and cook until the octopus is tender, an hour or more (check with the point of a sharp knife).

2. Transfer the garlic and octopus to a platter and discard the chiles, thyme, and oil or reserve the oil for another use, like sautéing fish or other seafood. Serve warm or cool, drizzled with soy sauce and lime juice.

Gogi-Jun Meat and Tofu Pancakes KOREA ■ ▩

MAKES **8 OR MORE SERVINGS AS A STARTER**
OR SIDE DISH

TIME **45 MINUTES**

Serve these spicy little pancakes as an appetizer—they'd even work at a cocktail party—or as part of a meal. They're not especially delicate (in fact they're pretty filling), and they're frequently served at room temperature, so feel free to make them in advance.

1 pound firm tofu

1 pound ground beef

10 scallions, trimmed and minced

2 long hot red chiles or about 1 teaspoon hot red pepper
    flakes

1 teaspoon black pepper

6 garlic cloves, minced

1 tablespoon dark sesame oil

1 tablespoon soy sauce

Large pinch of salt

2 tablespoons minced fresh chives

2 eggs

Corn, grapeseed, or other neutral oil for frying

1 cup instant (Wondra) or cake flour

1. Put the tofu in a towel and wring as much water as possible from it. Combine in a bowl with the next 9 ingredients. Squeeze the mixture through your hands for a minute or two, until it is very fine and well combined. Taste (you can cook a bit of the mixture if you're worried about eating raw beef) and adjust the seasoning as necessary; the pancakes should be well seasoned but not very hot.
2. Beat the eggs in a bowl. Put a couple of tablespoons of oil in a large skillet, preferably nonstick, and turn the heat to medium-high. Put the flour on a plate. Make the mixture into small pancakes, about 2 inches across and $\frac{3}{8}$ inch thick.
3. Dip each pancake into the flour and then the egg, then transfer to the skillet. Cook as many at a time as will fit without crowding, adjusting the heat so they brown but do not burn; turn each after 2 or 3 minutes. As they finish, stack on a plate. Serve hot or at room temperature.

Crisp Dried Anchovies THAILAND ■ ▣ ▣
MAKES **6 SERVINGS AS A SNACK OR SIDE DISH**
TIME **5 MINUTES**

Like the nut and bean preparations on pages 27–28, these savory crisp snacks from Southeast Asia (closely related to the similar recipe from Korea that follows) can be eaten out of hand. Also like them, they're great with beer. Though unfamiliar to some people, they're instantly liked by most. (You can buy dried baby anchovies—described on page 25—at most Asian, and some Latin, markets.) In Thailand, they're sometimes tossed with Fried Peanuts (page 27), a lovely little combo.

½ cup dried baby anchovies
About 3 tablespoons corn, grapeseed, or other neutral oil
3 shallots, minced

3 garlic cloves, minced
1 tablespoon peeled and minced or grated fresh ginger
**1 small fresh chile, stemmed, seeded, and minced,
    or ½ teaspoon hot red pepper flakes, or to taste**
1 teaspoon sugar
½ teaspoon salt, or to taste

1. Rinse the anchovies, then soak them in water to cover while you prepare the other ingredients.
2. Coat the bottom of a medium skillet with the oil and heat over medium-high heat until a wisp of smoke appears. Add the shallots, garlic, ginger, and chile and cook, stirring occasionally, until fragrant, just 15 to 30 seconds.
3. Add the anchovies and continue to cook and stir until light brown and crisp, less than 5 minutes. Add the sugar and salt and stir once or twice. Remove the anchovies, drain on paper towels, and serve immediately or within an hour.

Sweet Dried Anchovies KOREA ■ ▣ ▣
MAKES **4 SERVINGS**
TIME **20 MINUTES**

It's quite possible that nothing has ever sounded worse to you, but believe me, nearly everyone who tries these crisp, salty, sweet tidbits falls in love with them (some prefer the less assaultive Thai version in the preceding recipe). Best served as a little nibble, but hard to stop eating once you start, these rank as one of my favorite snacks to accompany an ice-cold beer or cold sake (or some soju, the deceptively mild Korean vodka). Buy the smallest dried anchovies (page 25) you can find for this dish, preferably no more than an inch or so long.

1 cup dried baby anchovies
3 tablespoons corn, grapeseed, or other neutral oil

1 teaspoon minced garlic

1 tablespoon sugar, or more to taste

2 tablespoons dark sesame oil, or more to taste

1 teaspoon go chu jang (Korean chili paste) or
   Chinese chile-bean paste, or more to taste

1 tablespoon soy sauce, or more to taste

1 teaspoon toasted sesame seeds (page 596), optional

1. Rinse the anchovies, then soak them in water to cover while you prepare the other ingredients.
2. Put the oil in a 10-inch skillet, preferably nonstick, over medium heat. A minute later, add the anchovies and cook, stirring occasionally and adjusting the heat so they brown and become crisp without burning, 8 to 10 minutes. Add the garlic, sugar, and sesame oil and cook, stirring, for about 30 seconds.
3. Add the go chu jang and soy sauce and cook for a minute more, stirring constantly. Taste and add more sesame oil, soy sauce, or go chu jang as you like. Remove the anchovies, drain on paper towels, and garnish with the sesame seeds. Serve immediately or within several hours.

Chawan-Mushi Savory Egg Custard
JAPAN ■ ■

MAKES 4 SERVINGS

TIME 40 MINUTES

Chawan-mushi is an egg custard flavored with stock and soy and laced with a number of tasty tidbits. In Tokyo, I had a bowl that contained tiny amounts of myoga (a potent member of the ginger family), shrimp, chicken, ginkgo nut, and yuzu, an Asian citrus fruit. None of these is essential, and you can substitute for any or all of them, as I do here. The fillings, called gu, are supposed to be whatever you have on hand.

If you have covered ramekins, they are ideal for this preparation. But covering the pot works just as well.

12 watercress leaves

4 sea scallops, each cut into 4 pieces, $\frac{1}{4}$ pound ground
   pork, or a little of each

1 tablespoon minced shallot

Salt and black pepper to taste

5 eggs

1$\frac{1}{2}$ cups chicken stock (page 160), beef stock
   (page 160), or Dashi (page 162)

1 tablespoon soy sauce

1 teaspoon sesame oil, optional

1. Put a quarter each of the watercress, scallops, and shallot in each of four 6-ounce ramekins and sprinkle with salt and pepper. Beat the eggs lightly and combine with the stock, soy, and sesame oil, if using.
2. Put the ramekins in a baking pan or skillet and fill them with the egg mixture. Add boiling water to reach about halfway up the sides of the ramekins and turn the heat to high. When the water returns to the boil, turn the heat to low and cover tightly.
3. Simmer for 15 minutes, then check. The custards are done when they have set and are no longer watery but are still quite jiggly. Immediately remove them from the water and serve hot or at room temperature.

Polpette Meatballs ITALY ■ ■ ■
MAKES 8 SERVINGS AS A STARTER, 4 SERVINGS WITH
   PASTA AS A MAIN COURSE

TIME 30 MINUTES

Needless to say, you can put these in almost any tomato sauce (pages 606–607) and use them for spaghetti and meatballs. But they're often served in Italy as a small first course, sometimes over cabbage.

I like the combination of veal and pork best, but you can use any combination you like or even all beef.

½ pound each ground veal and pork or any combination
    of ground meats

1 egg

¼ cup freshly grated Parmesan cheese

¼ cup chopped fresh parsley leaves

¼ cup minced onion

Salt and black pepper to taste

2 tablespoons extra virgin olive oil

Flour for dredging

1. Combine the meat in a bowl with the egg, cheese, parsley, onion, and salt and pepper. Mix well but do not knead. Form into balls of any size you like; tiny (½-inch diameter) ones are kind of nice but take longer to form.

2. Put the oil in a large skillet and turn the heat to medium. One by one, dredge the meatballs in the flour and add them to the oil. Cook, turning as necessary, until nicely browned all over, 10 to 15 minutes. Serve hot or at room temperature.

Almond Meatballs SPAIN ■ ▨ ▨

MAKES **8 OR MORE SERVINGS**

TIME **30 MINUTES**

Unlike the preceding Italian meatballs, these are strongly flavored with garlic, contain no cheese, and are spiked with almonds. They are unusual and great served on a toothpick with a glass of sherry.

½ pound each ground veal and pork or any combination
    of ground meats

1 egg

½ cup bread crumbs, preferably homemade (page 580)

1 tablespoon minced garlic

¼ cup blanched almonds, roughly chopped

Salt and black pepper to taste

2 tablespoons extra virgin olive oil

Flour for dredging

1. Combine the meat in a bowl with the egg, bread crumbs, garlic, almonds, and salt and pepper. Mix well but do not knead. Form into balls of any size you like; tiny (½-inch diameter) ones are kind of nice but take longer to form.

2. Put the oil in a large skillet and turn the heat to medium. One by one, dredge the meatballs in the flour and add them to the oil. Cook, turning as necessary, until nicely browned all over, 10 to 15 minutes. Serve hot or at room temperature.

HOT APPETIZERS WITH FLEXIBILITY

Following are appetizers that *must* be served hot or warm but still allow the cook some leeway. Some recipes allow for much or even all of the cooking to be done in advance and the cooking to be finished at the last minute. Others take well to reheating.

Mushrooms with Sherry SPAIN ■ ▨

MAKES **4 SERVINGS**

TIME **20 MINUTES**

A deluxe version of sautéed mushrooms, often served on small plates in tapas bars. This is a wonderful starter for a sitdown dinner, but be sure to serve it with plenty of bread; you will want it to sop up the sauce.

2 tablespoons butter

2 garlic cloves, minced

1 pound button or other mushrooms, trimmed and
quartered

1 tablespoon fresh lemon juice

2 tablespoons Fino, Amontillado, or Manzanilla sherry

3/4 cup Beef Stock (page 160)

1 small dried hot red chile, crumbled, or 1 teaspoon hot
red pepper flakes, or to taste

Salt and black pepper to taste

3 tablespoons chopped fresh parsley leaves

1. Put the butter in a deep skillet and turn the heat to medium-high. Add the garlic and mushrooms and cook until the mushrooms have given up their liquid and are beginning to brown, 5 to 10 minutes. Add the lemon juice, sherry, stock, and chile to the pan and bring to a boil. Lower the heat and let the mixture simmer, uncovered, for about 10 minutes, or until the liquid is quite syrupy and nearly evaporated.

2. Season with salt and pepper, garnish with parsley, and serve with crusty bread. Or let sit for a while and then reheat.

Mushrooms with Herbs and Butter
FRANCE ■ ▦

MAKES **4 SERVINGS**

TIME **30 MINUTES**

Most cultures enjoy mushrooms, but none treats them more regally than the French. This prime example is best made with lots of butter (not bad with the smaller amount, either, of course) and wild mushrooms. But if you have access only to cultivated mushrooms, combine a couple of varieties—button with shiitake and portobello, for example, and, if possible, a small handful of dried porcini, reconstituted

as on page 112. This can also be served as a side dish, especially with poultry.

3 to 6 tablespoons butter

2 tablespoons minced shallot

1 pound mushrooms, preferably an assortment, trimmed
and sliced

1/4 cup chopped fresh parsley leaves

1 teaspoon fresh thyme or tarragon leaves

2 tablespoons chopped fresh chervil or basil leaves

2 tablespoons snipped fresh chives

1 teaspoon minced garlic, optional

Salt and black pepper to taste

1. Put the butter in a skillet over medium-high heat. When the butter foam subsides, add the shallot and cook for a minute. Reduce the heat to medium and add the mushrooms. Cook, stirring occasionally, for about 5 minutes.

2. Add the remaining ingredients and cook, stirring, for another minute or two. Turn off the heat and serve hot or warm; these can also sit for a little while and then be reheated.

Mushrooms with Cream. Quite the luxury: Step 1 remains the same. In step 2, before adding the herbs and garlic, stir in 1/2 cup heavy cream or crème fraîche. Bring to a boil, stirring, then reduce the heat, add the remaining ingredients, and finish as directed.

Mushrooms with Herbs and Oil. In step 1, substitute extra virgin olive oil for the butter; omit the shallots. In step 2, use parsley only (though it won't hurt to add the other herbs), along with 1 tablespoon minced garlic and about 1/4 cup fresh bread crumbs (page 580). Finish with a few drops of fresh lemon juice.

Bagna Cauda Warm Olive Oil Bath

FRANCE ■ ▨

MAKES **4 SERVINGS**

TIME **30 MINUTES**

A classic Niçoise appetizer that is like fondue—a "warm bath"—of anchovies, garlic, and olive oil (you can use butter in place of some of the olive oil if you're feeling indulgent), served with fresh raw vegetables. It's an unusual dish by today's standards but remains a wonderful combination.

A fondue pot is the ideal serving vessel, because it's important to keep the sauce hot at the table; an earthenware dish that retains heat well will work if you preheat it and serve the Bagna Cauda immediately.

¼ **pound anchovy fillets packed in olive oil**

1 **tablespoon minced garlic**

1 **cup extra virgin olive oil**

1 **tablespoon chopped fresh savory or rosemary leaves or 2 teaspoons dried**

Salt and black pepper to taste

Crudités: a large and varied assortment like carrots, celery, endives, zucchini, and radishes

1. Place the anchovies, garlic, and oil in a fondue pot or saucepan. Place on the stove, turn the heat as low as possible, and cook, stirring constantly, until the anchovies break up, about 10 minutes. Do not let the garlic brown at all. Season with savory and pepper and place over the fondue burner or in a preheated earthenware dish. Taste and add a bit of salt if necessary. (You can prepare the oil an hour or two ahead to this point; reheat before serving.)

2. Serve warm, dipping the cold crudités into the olive oil mixture.

Brandade de Morue FRANCE ■

MAKES **6 TO 8 SERVINGS**

TIME **45 MINUTES (WITH PRESOAKED SALT COD)**

Salt cod is an ancient food, the result of a need to preserve a plentiful catch while still at sea. It has been used in many different ways, but one of the greatest is brandade de morue, a Provençal classic that is rich, filling, and truly special.

Though salt cod isn't available everywhere, it can be found in many supermarkets, without much trouble, and making brandade is easier than ever thanks to the food processor (use a mortar and pestle if you insist on tradition). Brandade can be served with crusty bread, spread on Crostini (page 41), or stuffed into roasted tomatoes or peppers, especially piquillo peppers (page 492 or 47).

1 **pound boneless salt cod (bacalao), soaked overnight in several changes of cold water (page 245)**

2 **garlic cloves, peeled, or to taste**

⅔ **cup extra virgin olive oil**

⅔ **cup heavy cream or milk**

Salt and black pepper to taste

Juice of 1 lemon, or to taste

⅛ **teaspoon freshly grated nutmeg**

1. Place the salt cod in one layer in a skillet or saucepan with water to cover; bring the water to a boil, turn off the heat, and let cool for 15 to 20 minutes. Drain and pick out any stray bones or pieces of skin.

2. Place the cod in a food processor with the garlic and a couple tablespoons of the olive oil. Start processing and, through the feed tube, add small amounts of olive oil alternating with small amounts of cream. Continue until the mixture becomes smooth, creamy, and light. (You may not need all of the oil and cream.) Add pepper, some

of the lemon juice, and the nutmeg. Blend and taste; the mixture may need a bit of salt and more lemon juice. (You can prepare the dish several hours or even a day ahead to this point; cover and refrigerate until you're ready to eat.)

3. Reheat the brandade if necessary, in a double boiler or in a 300°F oven, covered. Serve with bread, toast, or crackers.

Panfried Fish "Sandwiches"

SWEDEN ■ ▨

MAKES **8 SERVINGS, 4 AS A MAIN COURSE**

TIME **40 MINUTES**

In Sweden these little fish "sandwiches" are made with Baltic herring, but you can make them with any small fish from which you can remove the backbone, such as smelts, anchovies, and sardines (the names of all of these fish are confused anyway—many true herring and anchovies are called sardines and vice versa).

To bone these fish, grasp the head and pull straight down; most of the innards will come out along with it; use your thumb to open the fish up from the front, then grasp the backbone and remove. You'll be left

with two tiny fillets joined by the skin. Plan to make eight of these—four sandwiches—for each serving if you make them as a main course.

6 tablespoons (³⁄₄ stick) butter

¹⁄₂ cup snipped fresh dill leaves

1 teaspoon Dijon mustard

Salt and black pepper to taste

32 sardines, anchovies, small herrings, or smelts, boned (see headnote)

2 tablespoons extra virgin olive oil

2 eggs

Bread crumbs, preferably homemade (page 580), for dredging

Lemon wedges

1. Cream together 4 tablespoons of the butter with the dill, mustard, and some salt and pepper. (You can do this in a small food processor; make sure the butter is nearly ice cold.) Rinse and dry the cleaned fish well. Spread a small amount of the dill butter on the inside of half of the fillets, then top with another fillet to create a sandwich; sprinkle these with salt and pepper.

2. Put the remaining butter, along with the olive oil, in a large skillet, preferably nonstick, over medium-high heat. Dip each sandwich in the egg,

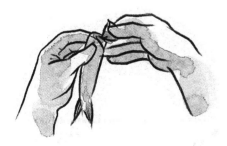

BONING FRESH ANCHOVIES OR SARDINES

then dredge in the bread crumbs; when the butter melts, add the sandwiches to the skillet. Cook until lightly browned on both sides, a total of less than 5 minutes. Adjust the heat so that the fat is bubbling but not burning. Serve hot or at room temperature, with the lemon wedges.

Wrappers for Vareniki, Pelmeni, or Pierogi Filled Dumplings EURASIA ■

MAKES **50 OR MORE WRAPPERS**

TIME **ABOUT 1 HOUR, PARTLY UNATTENDED**

Whether the noodle and wrappers made from its dough moved west from China or east from Italy is anyone's guess, but it wound up everywhere. There is barely a square mile of turf between Mongolia and Hungary that doesn't boast some kind of dumpling, and the variety is staggering. (And, if you consider the ravioli and empanada dumplings, they are universal.)

But though shape and filling vary wildly, the doughs are pretty much the same throughout the world: they're made either with egg or without. These are mostly made with, making the dough essentially the same as that used for fresh pasta.

2 cups flour, plus more as needed

1 teaspoon salt

2 egg yolks

1. Combine the flour and salt in a food processor and pulse to mix. Add the egg yolks and, with the machine running, 1/4 cup water; after that, add water about 1 tablespoon at a time, until a dough ball forms; transfer to a lightly floured surface and knead by hand for a couple of minutes.

2. Cut the dough into 2 pieces, form into balls, dust with flour, and cover with plastic wrap, a damp towel, or an upside-down bowl. Let rest for 20 to 60 minutes. (At this point you can wrap the dough tightly in plastic and freeze for up to a couple of weeks; defrost at room temperature before proceeding.) Meanwhile, make your filling from one of the following recipes.

3. Knead one of the balls for a minute on a lightly floured surface. Roll each ball into a thin sheet, about 1/16 inch thick, and cut into 2- to 3-inch squares or use a cookie cutter or glass to form 2- to 3-inch circles. You can lightly flour the dumplings, stack, and refrigerate (up to a day) or freeze them (up to 2 weeks), or form them immediately.

FILLING DUMPLINGS

Dumplings

The term *dumpling* can be used to describe almost any form of dough boiled in liquid, but we tend to define it as filled dough—think of a wonton—cooked in liquid or, sometimes, butter or oil. Filled dumplings are found almost everywhere: Asia is well known for its dumplings, which probably originated (like so much else) in China, around three thousand years ago.

And they're even more varied than you might think: dumplings may be thick or thin skinned, filled with meat or vegetables or cheese or grains, and cooked in any way you like. In short, definitive statements about them are difficult to make. In northern China alone, there are the familiar dumplings known as jiao zi, with a thick, flour-based skin and meat and vegetable fillings; these are usually boiled and served with a dipping sauce. But siew loong bao—"little dragon buns"—have a thin, delicate skin and especially juicy filling and are steamed on a bed of Chinese cabbage and served with Chinese red vinegar and fine slivers of ginger.

On the other end of the spectrum, saan jeen bao have a thicker, breadlike skin and are panfried on the bottom. Shanghai specializes in panfried dumplings, which are called wor teep and are shaped in half-moons; the Japanese gyoza are similar to these, as are some of the Korean mandoo (which themselves take many forms). Farther south in the Guandong province, wontons are the dumpling of choice. These have a thin flour- and egg-based skin and a shrimp and pork filling. Many dim sum dumplings are unusual, featuring rice paper skins, seafood fillings, or open-faced wrappings.

Russia is also well known for its dumplings, called pelmeni, whose origins are thought to be in Siberia (just a half-continent away from China); these are generally filled with meat and boiled in broth. Eastern European dumplings in general probably stem from these, but, again, there are too many varieties to count.

Then there are ravioli and the other stuffed pastas of Italy, none of which are called dumplings, even though . . . well, they are. And when you think of it, there are various stuffed and baked or fried doughs from all over the world—empanadas, for example, or samosas—that are forms of dumplings as well.

Potato-Filled Vareniki or Pierogi
EURASIA

MAKES **ABOUT 50, ENOUGH FOR 10**

TIME **ABOUT 1 HOUR (WITH PREMADE WRAPPERS)**

My favorite dumplings, these are creamy, savory, and salty and, when served with the cooked onion garnish and some sour cream, irresistible. Like the cheese-filled version on page 60, they may be boiled and served with melted butter, but I think they're best when fried in butter and served with sour cream.

In addition to the variation, you can stuff these with cooked cabbage, cooked mushrooms, sauerkraut, or almost anything else you can think of.

6 tablespoons ($^3/_4$ stick) butter, more or less

2 large onions, diced

Salt and black pepper to taste

1 teaspoon minced garlic, optional

2 cups well-seasoned mashed potatoes

1 recipe Wrappers for Vareniki, Pelmeni, or Pierogi (page 58)

2 egg whites, lightly beaten

Sour cream for garnish

1. Put 2 tablespoons of the butter in a skillet over medium heat and add the onions, along with a liberal sprinkling of salt and pepper. Cook, stirring occasionally, until the onion wilts, then turns

brown, as long as 30 minutes. It's okay if the onion gets a bit crisp on the edges, but don't cook it too fast; basically you want a kind of onion compote. Combine half the onions and the garlic, if you're using it, with the mashed potatoes, then taste and adjust the seasoning.

2. Lay a wrapper on a work surface, then place 1 to 2 teaspoons of the filling in the center of it; brush the edges of the wrapper with egg white, then pinch tightly to close. If you have cut circles, form half-moons; if you have cut squares, form triangles. Press the seam tightly to seal; it's best if no air is trapped between the filling and wrapper. Set on a lightly floured plate or wax paper. (At this point, you may cover tightly and refrigerate for up to a day or freeze for a couple of weeks.)

3. To boil the dumplings, melt the remaining butter, set a large pot of water to boil, and preheat the oven to 200°F. Salt the water and boil the dumplings a few at a time until they rise to the surface. A minute or two later, taste a bit of the dough to see whether it is tender. As they finish, remove the dumplings with a slotted spoon and put them in an ovenproof bowl; drizzle them with some of the butter and put the bowl in the oven. When the dumplings are done, make sure they are coated evenly with butter. Reheat the reserved onions and toss them with the pierogi. Serve hot with sour cream.

Panfried Dumplings. Put about 2 tablespoons butter in a large skillet, preferably nonstick, over medium heat. When the butter melts, add as many dumplings as will fit without crowding and brown them quickly, turning once or twice. Keep warm on a plate in the oven, cooking the remaining dumplings and adding butter to the skillet as needed. Serve hot.

Kasha-Filled Vareniki or Pierogi. Use Kasha with Bacon and Onions (page 529) or Kasha with Mushrooms (page 529) as a filling.

Cheese-Filled Vareniki or Pierogi
MAKES **ABOUT 50, ENOUGH FOR 10**

TIME **ABOUT 1 HOUR (WITH PREMADE WRAPPERS)**

These are usually quite sweet but served as a main course nevertheless, because they're incredibly filling. Most frequently boiled and served with melted butter, like the meat-filled dumplings in the preceding recipe, but I grew up eating them fried in butter, and they are superior that way. (Ideally, they're served with sour cream as well.) These, served with some of the other vareniki or pierogi on these pages, are just great.

2 cups small-curd cottage cheese, well drained in a
    strainer, or 2 cups farmer or pot cheese

Pinch of salt

2 tablespoons sugar, or to taste

1 egg

1/2 cup sour cream, plus more for serving

1 recipe Wrappers for Vareniki, Pelmeni, or Pierogi
    (page 58)

2 egg whites, lightly beaten

4 tablespoons (1/2 stick) butter, more or less

1. Combine the cottage cheese with the salt, sugar, egg, and 1/2 cup sour cream in a bowl; taste and adjust the seasoning.

2. Lay a wrapper on a work surface, then place 1 to 2 teaspoons of the filling in the center of it; brush the edges of the wrapper with egg white, then pinch tightly to close. If you have cut circles, form half-moons; if you have cut squares, form triangles. Press the seam tightly to seal; it's best if no air is trapped between the filling and wrapper. Set on a lightly floured plate or wax paper. (At this point you may cover tightly and refrigerate for up to a day or freeze for a couple of weeks.)

3. To boil the dumplings, melt the butter, set a large pot of water to boil, and preheat the oven to 200°F.

Salt the water and boil the dumplings a few at a time until they rise to the surface. A minute or two later, taste a bit of the dough to see whether it is tender. As they finish, remove the dumplings with a slotted spoon and put them in an ovenproof bowl; drizzle them with some of the butter and put the bowl in the oven. When the dumplings are done, make sure they are coated evenly with butter and serve hot with sour cream.

Panfried Dumplings. Put about 2 tablespoons butter in a large skillet, preferably nonstick, over medium heat. When the butter melts, add as many dumplings as will fit without crowding and brown them quickly, turning once or twice. Keep warm on a plate in the oven, cooking the remaining dumplings and adding butter to the skillet as needed. Serve hot, with sour cream.

Meat-Filled Pelmeni, Vareniki, or Pierogi

MAKES **ABOUT 50, ENOUGH FOR 10**

TIME **ABOUT 1 HOUR (WITH PREMADE WRAPPERS)**

Pelmeni were traditionally frozen before cooking (they're from Siberia; one would just make a few hundred, throw them in a bag, and put the bag in a barn or outdoors), and some people insist that they're best when frozen first, though I cannot imagine why that would be. But all dumplings can be frozen successfully after filling and can even be cooked directly from the freezer. Just make sure they're floured enough to prevent sticking during freezing, or the dough might tear.

You may not use all of this filling, but it's best not to run short. As with pot stickers (Wor Teep, page 63), be sure not to overfill the dumplings or the seams will burst. Any combination of meats will do well as a fill-ing here. If you grind your own, it will be even better; the meat should be ground quite finely. Though the butter suffices as a sauce, you can serve these with sour cream as well if you like.

$^3/_4$ **pound meat, preferably a mixture of pork and beef, preground or cut into chunks**

Salt and black pepper to taste

1 large onion, finely diced, or 1 cup diced scallion

1 recipe Wrappers for Vareniki, Pelmeni, or Pierogi (page 58)

2 egg whites, lightly beaten

4 tablespoons ($^1/_2$ stick) melted butter

Minced fresh dill leaves for garnish, optional

1. Put the meat in a food processor along with a large pinch of salt and some pepper. Process, along with a couple of tablespoons of cold water, until the mixture is finely ground and almost fluffy. Mix in the onion by hand.

2. Lay a wrapper on a work surface, then place 1 to 2 teaspoons of the filling in the center of it; brush the edges of the wrapper with egg white, then pinch tightly to close. If you have cut circles, form half-moons; if you have cut squares, form triangles. Press the seam tightly to seal; it's best if no air is trapped between the filling and wrapper. Set on a lightly floured plate or wax paper. (It is at this point that the pelmeni are traditionally frozen, and you can do so if you like, or refrigerate them for a day or so.)

3. To boil the dumplings, melt the butter, set a large pot of water to boil, and preheat the oven to 200°F. Salt the water and boil the dumplings a few at a time until they rise to the surface. A minute or two later, taste a bit of the dough to see whether it is tender. As they finish, remove the dumplings with a slotted spoon and put them in an ovenproof bowl; drizzle them with some of the butter and put the bowl in the oven. When the pelmeni are

done, grind some fresh pepper over them, make sure they are coated evenly with butter, garnish with dill if you like, and serve hot.

Pelmeni in Broth. Drain the cooked pelmeni and put them in a bowl filled with hot, rich broth, like chicken stock (page 160). Omit the butter. Garnish with fresh dill or parsley leaves and serve.

Dumpling Wrappers CHINA ■

MAKES **ABOUT 50 WRAPPERS**

TIME **40 MINUTES**

An all-purpose wrapper, useful for many of the recipes on the following pages: dumplings, pot stickers, wontons, and so on. Of course you can buy these, ready made, at any supermarket, but they are fun and pretty easy to make—a good afternoon project and one kids will like.

Note that the wrappers are made in stages, with a resting period in between; this period can be extended up to a day if you wrap the dough ball in plastic and refrigerate—just be sure to let it come to room temperature once again before proceeding.

2 cups flour, plus more as needed

1 teaspoon salt

1. Combine the flour and salt in a large mixing bowl and gradually stir in about $1/2$ cup cold water, until the dough comes together in a ball. The dough should be quite dry. Turn onto a floured surface and knead until smooth and elastic, about 5 minutes, flouring as necessary to prevent sticking.

    You can also do this in a food processor: add the water gradually to the flour and salt in a food processor while the machine is running, adding as much water as necessary to form a dough ball— again, the dough should be dry—then let the machine run for about 15 seconds. Finish the kneading by hand, using as much flour as necessary to keep it from sticking.

2. Shape the dough into a ball, dust with flour, and cover with plastic wrap or a damp towel. Let it rest for 20 minutes to 2 hours (or longer; see headnote).

3. Knead the ball for a minute, then cut into 4 pieces. On a lightly floured surface, roll each piece into a 1-inch log, then cut into 1-inch pieces and roll each one out from the center to form a 4-inch round or square, adding a bit of additional flour if necessary. Use immediately or dust with flour, stack, and refrigerate for up to a couple of days or freeze for up to 2 weeks.

Egg Roll Wrappers. These may be used as slightly richer dumpling wrappers or for egg rolls: Add 1 egg to the flour-salt mixture, then reduce the water to a little less than $1/2$ cup. In step 3, cut the dough ball into 4 pieces and roll out each one. Cut 3-inch squares for dumpling wrappers, 6-inch squares for egg roll wrappers.

Noodles. In step 3, after cutting the dough into 4 pieces, roll out each piece into a rectangle. Try to roll the dough as thinly as possible without ripping it, preferably to $1/8$ inch thick. Lightly dust the rectangles, fold into quarters lengthwise, then use a sharp knife to cut each folded rectangle into thin strips. Alternatively, use a pasta machine: put the dough rectangles through the smallest setting, then roll them through the spaghetti setting. Dust lightly with flour to prevent sticking. Cook in boiling water just until tender, about 3 minutes, then drain, rinse, drain again, and serve immediately.

Egg Noodles. Use the dough recipe for the egg roll wrappers, then follow the instructions for noodles.

Fried Wontons CHINA ◼

MAKES **ABOUT 60, ENOUGH FOR 12**

TIME **30 MINUTES (WITH PREMADE WRAPPERS)**

Though not traditional, fried wontons are extremely popular. They are an easy finger food for parties and a snack that your kids will love. If you're making the wrappers, try to get 60 out of the dough, or you may have a little filling left over.

> 1 pound ground pork or peeled shrimp, minced, or a
> combination
>
> 2 cups chopped fresh chives (if you can find Chinese,
> or garlic, chives, so much the better)
>
> 1 tablespoon peeled and minced or grated fresh ginger
>
> 1 egg, lightly beaten
>
> 1 tablespoon soy sauce
>
> 2 teaspoons Shaoxing wine or dry sherry
>
> 2 teaspoons dark sesame oil
>
> 2 teaspoons black pepper
>
> Large pinch of salt
>
> 1 recipe Dumpling Wrappers (page 62) or about
> 60 store-bought wrappers
>
> Peanut or neutral oil like corn or grapeseed, as needed

1. In a bowl, mix together the pork or shrimp, chives, ginger, egg, soy sauce, wine, sesame oil, pepper, and salt.
2. Place 1 scant tablespoon of the filling in the center of each wrapper. Moisten the edges of the wrapper with a few drops of water (use a brush or your finger) and fold into a triangle or semicircle. Press the edges together tightly to seal, making sure no air is

trapped between the filling and wrapper. Set aside on a floured plate or wax paper and repeat until all the filling is used.

3. Put about 2 inches of oil in a deep saucepan and turn the heat to medium-high; heat to about 250°F on a deep-frying thermometer. Working in batches and adjusting the heat as necessary, gently put as many of the wontons as will fit without crowding into the oil and cook, turning once, until golden brown, less than 10 minutes.
4. Drain on paper towels and serve with Soy Dipping Sauce (page 583).

Vegetable Wontons. For the pork and shrimp, substitute one 10-ounce package of spinach, thawed, drained, and chopped, 2 minced scallions, and 4 or 5 fresh (or reconstituted dried) shiitake (black) mushrooms.

Wonton Soup. In step 1, bring a large pot of water to a boil. Fill and seal the wontons as directed. Depending on the size of your pot, boil the wontons in one or two batches for about 10 minutes per batch. Gently stir intermittently to prevent sticking. Immediately transfer to bowls of good chicken stock (page 160) and garnish with chopped scallions.

Wor Teep Pot Stickers, or Panfried Dumplings
CHINA

MAKES **24 DUMPLINGS**

TIME **40 MINUTES (WITH PREMADE WRAPPERS)**

These are the pot stickers popular in Shanghai and many other southern Chinese cities. Panfried until crisp on the bottom and then cooked through by steaming, they have a delicious combination of crunch and chew in the dough and a springy, flavorful center. They are best served hot out of the pan (but beware of their tongue-burning juices!).

Gyoza is the Japanese version of this type of dumpling and mandoo the Korean version. They may be filled with pork or have a vegetarian stuffing; usually, their skin is somewhat thinner. You can buy gyoza or mandoo skins at the market or just roll the Chinese skins a little thinner yourself.

Dumplings may be filled and dusted with flour and refrigerated, covered, for a couple of hours or frozen for a few days. But they're really best when cooked right after being filled.

Leeks are usually full of sand. The easiest way to clean them in this recipe is to chop them, rinse in a strainer, and shake dry.

½ pound ground pork, chicken, or other meat

¼ cup minced scallion

1 cup chopped leek, cleaned, Napa cabbage, or bok choy

1 teaspoon peeled and minced fresh ginger

1 teaspoon rice wine or dry sherry

1 teaspoon sugar

1 tablespoon soy sauce

1 tablespoon dark sesame oil

1 egg, lightly beaten

1 teaspoon black pepper

Large pinch of salt

½ recipe Dumpling Wrappers (page 62), or about 24 store-bought wrappers

Peanut or neutral oil like corn or grapeseed, as needed

Soy Dipping Sauce (page 583)

1. Combine the first 11 ingredients and mix gently but thoroughly. Place about 2 teaspoons of the filling in the center of a wrapper, then moisten the edge of the wrapper with water and fold over to form a half-moon. Press the seam tightly to seal; it's best if no air is trapped between the filling and wrapper. Set on a lightly floured plate or wax pa-

per. (At this point you may cover tightly and refrigerate for up to a day or freeze for a couple of weeks.)

2. Coat a large, deep skillet with a thin layer of oil and turn the heat to medium-high. Place the dumplings, one at a time, into the skillet, seam side up, leaving space between them (you will probably have to cook them in two batches). Turn the heat to medium, then cover and cook for about 5 minutes. Add ½ cup water to the skillet, then cover and cook for another 2 minutes. Remove the lid, turn the heat to high, and cook until the water has evaporated, about 3 minutes. Remove the dumplings and serve with the dipping sauce. (Repeat to cook all the pot stickers if necessary.)

Vegetarian Gyoza JAPAN. Substitute ½ pound drained and mashed soft tofu for the meat. Cut the amount of leeks in half and add ¼ cup shredded Napa cabbage, ¼ cup chopped fresh mushrooms, ¼ cup shredded carrot, and ¼ cup chopped walnuts to the filling.

Mandoo KOREA. Use pork or beef for the meat. Omit the leeks. Add ¼ cup minced scallion, ¼ cup minced mushrooms, ¼ cup minced carrot, and ¼ cup chopped soaked bean thread vermicelli to the filling. Double the amount of black pepper.

Steamed Dumplings. Set up a steamer or place a heatproof plate on a rack above 1 to 2 inches of boiling water in a covered pot. Lightly oil the steamer or plate to prevent sticking. Steam the dumplings in one or two batches for about 10 minutes per batch. Serve immediately with Soy Dipping Sauce (page 583).

Manti Lamb-Filled Dumplings

TURKEY, AFGHANISTAN

MAKES **25 OR MORE DUMPLINGS**

TIME **ABOUT 1 HOUR (WITH PREMADE WRAPPERS)**

Like Wor Teep, Chinese pot stickers, these meat-filled dumplings are filling and delicious (with store-bought dumpling wrappers, they're also quite easy). But the serving style is completely different: these are usually cooked and served in broth, with yogurt. Alternatively, you can boil them in water and serve them with yogurt or melted butter.

> 1½ cups yogurt
>
> 1 pound lean boneless lamb, preferably from the leg
>
> Salt and black pepper to taste
>
> 1 medium onion, roughly chopped
>
> 6 cups good stock of any kind (pages 160–163)
>
> ½ recipe Wrappers for Vareniki, Pelmeni, or Pierogi (page 58) or Dumpling Wrappers (page 62), or about 25 store-bought wrappers
>
> 2 eggs, lightly beaten
>
> Minced fresh scallion or chives for garnish

1. Drain the yogurt in a cheesecloth-lined strainer while you prepare the dumplings. Combine the lamb, salt, pepper, and onion in a food processor and pulse to chop coarsely; be careful not to over-process. Set a large pot of water to boil and add salt (if you have a large steamer, you can use this as well). In a separate pot, warm the stock.

2. Place 1 to 2 teaspoons of the filling in the center of a wrapper, then brush the edges of the wrapper with the egg. If you have circles, form half-moons; if you have squares, form triangles. Press the seam tightly to seal; it's best if no air is trapped between the filling and wrapper. Set on a lightly floured plate or wax paper. Proceed, cover and refrigerate for up to a day, or freeze for up to a week.

3. Boil the dumplings without crowding—you may have to do this in batches—stirring occasionally, until heated through, about 10 minutes. As they finish cooking, transfer them to the hot broth. Just before serving, taste and adjust the broth's seasoning. Serve the manti in a bowl, with broth, garnished with some yogurt and scallion.

Meat Samosas INDIA ▥

MAKES **24 SAMOSAS, ENOUGH FOR 8**

TIME **AT LEAST 45 MINUTES**

One of the world's great dumplings, the samosa has migrated to Southeast Asia and elsewhere. As with most dumplings, the filling is easily varied. And, as with most dumplings, you can use store-bought dumpling wrappers or the simple homemade ones on page 62. But the superrich wrappers here are really the best.

Traditionally, you would deep-fry samosas, but more and more often they are baked. They're terrific either way.

> 2 cups flour, plus more as needed
>
> Salt and black pepper to taste
>
> 2 tablespoons cold butter
>
> 2 tablespoons yogurt
>
> 1 large baking potato, like Idaho or russet, peeled and roughly chopped
>
> 1 large carrot, roughly chopped
>
> 2 tablespoons corn, grapeseed, or other neutral oil, or more butter
>
> 1 tablespoon minced garlic
>
> 1 tablespoon peeled and minced fresh ginger
>
> 1 medium onion, diced
>
> ½ pound ground meat: pork, beef, lamb, chicken, or turkey
>
> 1 teaspoon ground turmeric

1 teaspoon ground cumin

1 teaspoon ground coriander

1/2 teaspoon ground cinnamon

1/2 cup thawed frozen or fresh green peas

Corn, grapeseed, or other neutral oil for deep-frying,
    optional

1. Combine the flour with a large pinch of salt, the butter, and the yogurt in a food processor; turn on the machine and, a few seconds later, add about 1/2 cup water. Let the machine run, adding a little more water if necessary, until a dough ball forms. Knead the dough for a moment by hand, adding a little more flour if necessary, and wrap it in plastic.

2. Put the potato and carrot in a pot and add salted water to cover. Bring to a boil and cook until quite soft, 10 to 20 minutes; drain and mash.

3. Put the 2 tablespoons oil in a large skillet, preferably nonstick, over medium-high heat. A minute later, add the garlic, ginger, and onion and cook, stirring occasionally, until the onion softens, about 5 minutes. Add the meat and stir-fry, separating the clumps, until it loses its pinkness, about 5 minutes. Stir in the spices, some pepper, and a large pinch of salt. Add the mashed potatoes and carrots and the peas and cook for another minute, stirring to combine. Remove from the heat, taste and adjust the seasoning, and cool. (You can prepare both the dough and the filling to this point a day or so ahead and refrigerate until ready to proceed.)

4. Sprinkle a work surface with flour, then divide the dough into quarters. Cover three of the pieces and divide the fourth into 6 pieces; roll each piece into a round ball. Roll each ball out to a 3-inch diameter. When you have rolled out the first 6, put about 1 tablespoon of the filling in the center of each. Brush the rim (you can use your fingertip) with a little water, then fold over and seal. Keep covered with plastic wrap while you repeat with the remaining dough.

5. Preheat the oven to 350°F or put at least 3 inches of oil in a saucepan or other deep vessel, turn the heat to medium-high, and heat the oil to about 350°F. If you're baking, put the samosas on a nonstick or lightly greased baking sheet and bake until golden brown, about 30 minutes. If you're deep-frying, cook as many as will fit without crowding in the hot oil until lightly browned, about 3 minutes, turning once or twice. Drain on paper towels and serve hot. (Or keep them warm in a low oven or serve at room temperature, but in any case within an hour.)

Vegetarian Samosas. Simply substitute 1/2 cup chopped cabbage and 1/2 cup mashed cooked beans for the meat. Or try the following.

Potato-and-Pea Samosas. Step 1 remains the same. In step 2, omit the carrot and use 3 large potatoes. Omit the ginger, onion, and meat and mash the potatoes with the spices along with 2 tablespoons yogurt and 1 stemmed, seeded, and minced jalapeño (or 2 smaller chiles or hot red pepper flakes to taste). Cook the peas briefly in boiling salted water to cover; drain and add to the potato mixture, then taste and adjust the seasoning. Skip step 3 and proceed with steps 4 and 5.

Chicken or Shrimp Egg Rolls CHINA
MAKES 20, ENOUGH FOR 10 OR 20
TIME 40 MINUTES (WITH PREMADE WRAPPERS)

This finger food is popular in the south of China, Southeast Asia, and, of course, many American Chinese restaurants. It's perfect for parties and supereasy to make, especially with store-bought egg roll wrappers. They can be filled an hour or two ahead of time and fried immediately before serving or—though it isn't ideal—fried an hour or two ahead of time and crisped in a warm oven later.

> 1 teaspoon sugar
>
> 2 teaspoons soy sauce
>
> 2 teaspoons rice wine or dry sherry
>
> ½ pound boneless, skinless chicken, either white or dark meat, cut into thin shreds, or roughly chopped peeled shrimp
>
> Peanut or neutral oil like corn or grapeseed, as needed
>
> 5 fresh (or reconstituted and drained; see page 112) shiitake (black) mushrooms, stems discarded and caps sliced
>
> 3 scallions, trimmed and roughly chopped
>
> 2 cups bean sprouts or shredded Napa cabbage
>
> 1 tablespoon peeled and minced fresh ginger
>
> 20 egg roll wrappers, homemade (page 62) or store-bought
>
> Hot mustard like Colman's, Soy Dipping Sauce (page 583), hoisin sauce, and/or Worcestershire sauce for serving

1. Whisk together the sugar, soy sauce, and rice wine and then toss with the chicken or shrimp. While it sits, put 2 tablespoons of oil in a large skillet and turn the heat to medium-high. A minute later, add the mushrooms, scallions, and bean sprouts; cook, stirring occasionally, for about 3 minutes. Remove from the pan with a slotted spoon.

2. Add another tablespoon of oil to the skillet and cook the ginger, stirring, until fragrant, about 30 seconds. Add the chicken or shrimp and its marinade and cook until it loses its pinkness, stirring occasionally to separate the pieces, about 3 minutes. Return the vegetables to the pan, mix well with the chicken or shrimp, and cook for another minute. Remove the mixture with a slotted spoon. (You can prepare this filling, covered and refrigerated, up to a day in advance.)

3. Add at least 3 inches of oil to a heavy saucepan or deep-fryer (a narrow vessel will save you oil; a broad one will allow you to cook more egg rolls at once); heat over medium-high heat until it reaches about 350°F. Meanwhile, moisten the edges of an egg roll wrapper with water and put 2 tablespoons of the filling down a line in the center; fold in the sides and roll tightly. Seal the seam with a few drops of water.

4. Working in batches, place the egg rolls in the oil and turn occasionally to brown evenly; the cooking will be easy and quick, about 5 minutes per batch (you just have to heat them through and brown the outside; everything inside is already cooked). Adjust the heat as necessary so that the egg rolls brown evenly. As they finish, drain on paper towels. Serve hot, with any of the sauces.

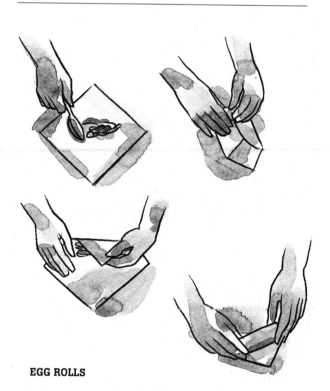

EGG ROLLS

Vegetarian Egg Rolls. Omit the chicken or shrimp and use both bean sprouts and Napa cabbage, along with 2 cups shredded or grated carrots.

Chicken or Shrimp Rice Paper Rolls SOUTHEAST ASIA. These are egg rolls Southeast Asian style, often wrapped in a leaf of red or green lettuce before serving, making a nice contrast between hot and cold. Substitute twenty 8- to 10-inch rice paper sheets for the egg roll wrappers. Soften the rice paper in hot water (110–120°F) for about 10 seconds (see page 38 for details). Fill and roll them on a damp kitchen or paper towel; you won't need water to seal. Fry and serve immediately with Sweet Nam Pla Dipping Sauce (page 586) or plain soy sauce.

Lumpia Wrappers PHILIPPINES 🔳

MAKES **8 OR MORE WRAPPERS**

TIME **20 MINUTES**

These are very similar to crêpes—the staple of Brittany (page 86)—but thinner and more delicate (and the filling, which follows, is like nothing you'll find in the French tradition). Though they're often called "Philippine Egg Rolls," lumpia—again, like most crêpes—require no cooking once they're filled.

1 cup flour

1 egg

Corn, grapeseed, or other neutral oil as needed

1. Whisk together the flour, egg, and 1 cup water until very smooth.
2. Heat an 8- or 10-inch nonstick skillet over medium heat. When a drop of water skitters across the surface before evaporating, add a little oil—just a teaspoon or so. Ladle about 2 tablespoons of the batter into the skillet and swirl it around so that it forms a thin layer on the bottom of the pan. Pour the excess batter back into the bowl.
3. When the wrapper is just cooked through and the edges lift away from the pan, remove it carefully (you need not turn it over). Repeat with the remaining batter. If you like, keep the wrappers warm, covered, in a 200°F oven, for up to an hour before filling and serving.

Lumpia Rolls PHILIPPINES 🔳

MAKES **8 ROLLS, ENOUGH FOR 4**

TIME **20 MINUTES**

This well-known Philippine starter combines attributes of many of the wrapped foods of other countries. It's filled like an egg roll, has an egg wrapper like a crêpe, and is served warm but not fried. All the components, which can be varied according to what you have in your kitchen, are cooked before assembly.

3 tablespoons corn, grapeseed, or other neutral oil

2 garlic cloves, minced

2 shallots, minced

1 pound pork, chicken, shrimp, or a combination, minced

½ cup grated or shredded carrot

½ cup shredded Napa or other cabbage

½ cup sliced fresh or canned bamboo shoots, drained if canned

2 teaspoons salt

2 teaspoons black pepper

2 teaspoons Shaoxing wine or dry sherry

8 Lumpia Wrappers (page 68)

8 green- or red-leaf lettuce leaves

Sweet Garlic Soy Sauce (page 590) or Hoisin Chili Sauce (page 584)

1. Put the oil in a large skillet and turn the heat to medium. A minute later, add the garlic and shal-

lots and cook, stirring occasionally, until fragrant, 15 to 30 seconds. Add the pork and cook, breaking up any lumps and stirring occasionally, until the meat loses its pinkness, about 3 minutes. Add the vegetables and cook, stirring occasionally, until softened, about 5 minutes. Add the salt, pepper, and wine and remove from the heat.

2. Lay a lumpia wrapper flat on a work surface and place a piece of the lettuce on top. Line 2 heaping tablespoons of the stir-fry mixture on top of the lettuce. Fold in the sides and roll tightly, sealing the seam, if necessary, with a few drops of water spread with a brush or your fingertip. Serve with either or both of the sauces.

TAQUITOS

Taquitos Fried Pork-Filled Tortillas MEXICO ■

MAKES **20 TAQUITOS, ENOUGH FOR 4 OR MORE**

TIME **45 MINUTES**

This is an amazing finger food, best set up using a simple assembly line of two or even three people. (You can also roll all the taquitos ahead of time and fry them immediately before serving; if you do this, and have cooperative friends, it's almost as easy to make forty or even eighty taquitos as it is to make twenty.) Best served immediately from the skillet, they can also be made ahead and reheated in the oven. Serve with sour cream, any salsa (pages 610–612), Guacamole (page 22), or a combination.

Twenty 5-inch corn tortillas

½ to 1 pound Shredded Pork (page 396)

2 or 3 fresh jalapeños, stemmed, seeded, and cut into thin strips, optional

Corn, grapeseed, or other neutral oil for deep-frying

1. Heat a small skillet over medium heat and toast a tortilla on both sides until pliable. Put a heaping tablespoon of the pork in a line near the edge of the tortilla and top with a jalapeño strip if desired. Tightly roll the tortilla and secure with a toothpick. Repeat with the remaining tortillas and pork.

2. Heat at least 2 inches of oil in a deep, heavy saucepan to about 350°F. Gently slide in the taquitos and fry until crisp, 2 to 3 minutes per side, turning once. Work in batches; do not overcrowd. Drain on paper towels and serve.

Gougères FRANCE ■ ▨ ▨

MAKES **30 TO 40 GOUGÈRES, ENOUGH FOR 8 TO 12 SERVINGS**

TIME **ABOUT 30 MINUTES**

Gougères are perfect dinner party fare; they're elegant, delicious, and filling, all of which buys you a few extra minutes when you're getting the main course ready.

Gougères are fried as commonly as they're baked, but baked gougères hold numerous advantages for the home cook: they're less messy, they can be baked in advance (even a day ahead: let them cool to room temperature, store in an airtight container overnight, then reheat in a 200°F oven), and they can be served at room temperature. I like them best made with well-aged Gruyère, but any of the cheeses suggested below will work well.

> 4 tablespoons (1/2 stick) butter
>
> 1/2 teaspoon salt
>
> 1 1/2 cups flour
>
> 3 eggs
>
> 1 cup freshly grated aged Gruyère, Emmental, Cantal, or Cheddar cheese
>
> 1 cup freshly grated Parmesan or other hard cheese

1. Lightly grease 2 baking sheets and preheat the oven to 425°F.
2. Combine 1 cup water, the butter, and the salt in a medium saucepan; turn the heat to medium-high and bring to a boil. Cook, stirring, until the butter melts, just a minute or two longer. Add the flour all at once and cook, stirring constantly, until the dough holds together in a ball, 5 minutes or less. The dough will get stiffer as you stir it; keep at it until the dough is smooth. Transfer the batter to a large mixing bowl or the workbowl of a stand mixer.
3. Add the eggs one at a time, beating hard after each addition (this is a little bit of work; use a stand mixer if you have one; a hand mixer will likely not be powerful enough). Stop beating when the mixture is glossy. Stir in the cheeses.
4. Drop teaspoonfuls onto the baking sheets and bake until puffed and lightly browned, 10 to 15 minutes. Serve warm or at room temperature.

Chorizo in Red Wine SPAIN ■ ▨

MAKES **6 TO 8 SERVINGS**

TIME **20 MINUTES**

A classic tapa that's challenging only to the extent that it's hard to find good chorizo; it should not be too well dried but rather fresh and soft. Plenty is being made in the States now, especially in Florida, California, and New York—the major centers of Latin cuisine. Since chorizo is so intensely flavored already, it takes few ingredients to make this dish, but it's still pretty powerful.

In northwestern Spain they make this with the local sidra Asturiana, or hard cider; to try it that way, omit the garlic and parsley and substitute hard cider (English, French, or American hard cider is fine) for the red wine.

> 1 pound dried chorizo, thinly sliced
>
> 1 cup dry red wine
>
> 2 tablespoons minced garlic
>
> Salt and black pepper to taste
>
> Chopped fresh parsley leaves for garnish

1. Preheat the oven to 450°F. Put the chorizo in an ovenproof skillet and turn the heat to high. Cook, stirring occasionally, until it is nicely browned, about 10 minutes, adjusting the heat as necessary to avoid burning the meat.
2. Stir in the wine and garlic and transfer the skillet to the oven. Cook, more or less undisturbed, until about half the liquid has evaporated and what's left is dark and thick, 10 to 15 minutes. Taste and add salt and pepper if necessary. Garnish with parsley and serve very hot, with toothpicks or pieces of bread. Or prepare the dish an hour or two ahead and reheat it.

HOT APPETIZERS

Last minute only: these are hot appetizers, those that must be cooked and served right away. Some—especially those that are deep-fried—are best served while your guests are standing in the kitchen; others are true first courses, elegant and satisfying.

(it's unlikely you'll need to do this in batches, but if your pan is small, you might), turning as necessary, until golden brown, 5 to 10 minutes.

3. Drain on paper towels, sprinkle with salt, and serve immediately—on a plate lined with a cloth napkin, if you want to be fancy—with the lemon wedges.

Carciofi Fritti Fried Artichoke Hearts ITALY ▪

MAKES **4 SERVINGS**

TIME **30 MINUTES**

Best made with the hearts of fresh artichokes, but that is an expensive, time-consuming, and labor-intensive route. I won't say frozen artichoke hearts are just as good, but they are worth using, and that's what most people do—increasingly, even in Italy. The tenderness and subtle flavor of the vegetable still comes through. I like to fry these in olive oil, but it's not essential.

> **Extra virgin olive oil or neutral oil like corn or grapeseed as needed**
>
> **Salt and black pepper to taste**
>
> **2 eggs, lightly beaten**
>
> **½ cup freshly grated Parmesan cheese, optional**
>
> **1 cup fairly fine bread crumbs, preferably homemade (page 580)**
>
> **8 artichoke hearts, fresh (see page 72) or thawed frozen**
>
> **Lemon wedges for serving**

1. Heat at least 1 inch of oil in a wide saucepan or deep skillet over medium to medium-high heat.
2. Season the eggs and, if you like, combine the Parmesan cheese and bread crumbs; season this mixture, too. When the oil is ready—a pinch of the bread crumbs will sizzle—dip each heart in the eggs, then roll in the bread crumbs. Add them to the oil, one at a time, and fry without crowding

Nadroo Korma Lotus Root Fries INDIA ▪

MAKES **6 TO 8 SERVINGS**

TIME **30 MINUTES**

The first time I ate these—I was in Delhi—I was convinced they were pork rind; that's how crisp and delicious they are. Frying them is foolproof, and they rank with the great finger foods of the world. Lotus roots are sold at many Asian markets and top-notch supermarkets as well.

> **Corn, grapeseed, or other neutral oil as needed**
>
> **2 lotus roots, 1 to 2 pounds, peeled and cut into matchsticks 2 to 3 inches long**
>
> **1 teaspoon pure chile powder, like ancho or New Mexico, or to taste, optional**
>
> **1 teaspoon Fragrant Curry Powder (page 593), or other mild curry powder, or to taste, optional**
>
> **Salt to taste**

1. Put at least 2 inches of oil in a saucepan or other deep vessel and heat over medium-high heat to about 350°F on a deep-frying thermometer.
2. Add a handful of lotus root pieces and cook, stirring occasionally, until crisp, about 3 minutes. Drain and repeat with the remaining lotus root.
3. Sprinkle with the seasoning(s) of your choice and serve immediately.

Artichoke Hearts

1. With small to medium artichokes, cut off the top third or so of the leaves (serrated knives work well with artichokes). 2. Snap off most of the remaining outside leaves—until you get to the pale green tender inner leaves—then trim the bottom. 3. Use a spoon to scoop out every bit of the choke.

1. With large artichokes, cut them into halves or quarters from top to bottom. 2. Remove all tough leaves and choke from around the heart. (With especially large artichokes, parboil the heart for about 1 minute in salted water before proceeding). In either case, what remains is the heart, and it's all edible.

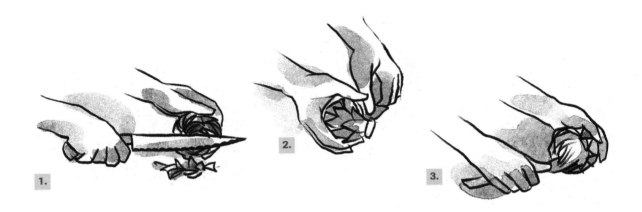

SMALL AND MEDIUM ARTICHOKES

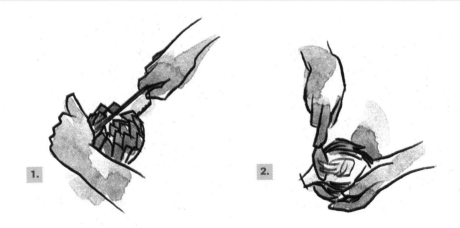

LARGE ARTICHOKES

Hou Bao Daan Pocket Eggs CHINA ■

MAKES **4 SERVINGS**

TIME **10 MINUTES**

I am such a soy sauce fanatic I essentially "invented" this dish before ever having been served it; imagine my surprise to find it is legitimate, basically an egg over easy with an instantly made soy-based sauce. The Chinese name for this popular late-night snack describes the runny center encased by the crisp-fried edges.

> **1 tablespoon soy sauce**
>
> **1 tablespoon sweet black vinegar or balsamic vinegar**
>
> **3 tablespoons corn, grapeseed, or other neutral oil**
>
> **4 eggs**
>
> **Salt to taste**

1. Mix together the soy sauce and vinegar. Set aside.
2. Heat a quarter of the oil in a small nonstick skillet over high heat. Swirl the oil to coat the bottom of the pan and crack one of the eggs into the pan. Season with salt. When the edges of the egg begin to brown and the white begins to set, fold the egg in half. Splash on a quarter of the soy-vinegar mixture and immediately remove from the skillet. Repeat with the remaining eggs and serve hot.

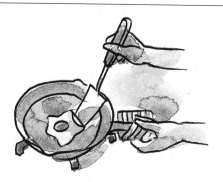

FOLDING A POCKET EGG

Grilled Chicken Wings JAPAN

MAKES **6 SERVINGS**

TIME **40 MINUTES, PLUS MARINATING TIME AND TIME TO PREHEAT THE GRILL**

I had the best Japanese-style chicken wings at the Gonpachi Restaurant in Tokyo. They arrived at the table crackling on a little hibachi grill. Salty, sweet, and aromatic, they were great with chilled sake. To me, this is perfect contemporary Japanese cooking.

> **3 tablespoons soy sauce**
>
> **2 tablespoons sake**
>
> **2 tablespoons mirin or honey**
>
> **3 scallions, trimmed and roughly chopped**
>
> **2 garlic cloves, chopped**
>
> **One 1-inch piece fresh ginger, peeled and chopped**
>
> **3 pounds chicken wings, wing tips removed, drumettes and wings separated**

1. Mix together everything but the chicken wings in a large baking dish. Add the chicken wings and turn to coat, then cover with plastic wrap and refrigerate for at least 2 hours or as long as overnight. Turn the wings occasionally in the marinade.
2. Start a charcoal or wood fire or preheat a gas grill or broiler; the fire should be only moderately hot and the rack about 6 inches from the heat source. If you are going to broil the wings, line your pan with foil.
3. Remove the wings from the marinade and put on the grill or in the broiler. Cook for about 10 minutes on each side, remove from the heat, and serve immediately.

Grilled Chicken Wings, Chinese Style. Substitute Shaoxing wine for the sake and oyster sauce for the mirin. Add 2 star anise to the marinade.

Brik Egg in Pastry TUNISIA ■

MAKES **4 SERVINGS**

TIME **15 MINUTES (WITH PREMADE WRAPPERS)**

Like Moroccan briouat, Tunisian briks use warka, a phyllolike wrapper, to contain a filling. This one is most commonly filled with a whole egg—a spicy sort of poached egg in a thin, crisp shell—rather great.

Tuna is a nice complement to the egg filling, but you can do without it. These are best eaten hot, but beware of egg running onto your shirt—which is exactly what happened to me. If you use warka or phyllo, keep it covered with a damp cloth while you work. Egg roll wrappers need no special treatment, but they're not as thin or crisp.

FOLDING A RAW EGG INSIDE A BRIK

One 6-ounce can tuna, preferably packed in olive oil, drained, optional

3 tablespoons chopped fresh parsley leaves

3 tablespoons fresh lemon juice

1/2 teaspoon salt

1/2 teaspoon black pepper

4 warka, phyllo, or egg roll sheets, thawed if frozen

Corn, grapeseed, or other neutral oil for frying

4 small eggs

1 lemon, cut into quarters

1. Mix the tuna, if you're using it, parsley, lemon juice, salt, and pepper. Use a pair of scissors or a jar to cut the wrappers into 4- to 5-inch circles (squares will work too) and moisten the edges very lightly with drops of water.
2. Put about 1/2 inch of oil in a medium skillet or wide saucepan and turn the heat to medium-high. Divide the tuna mixture among the wrappers. Working quickly, crack an egg on top of each, fold into a semicircle, and seal the edge tightly.
3. When the oil shimmers, fry the briks, two at a time, until golden brown, turning once; total cooking time will be less than 2 minutes per brik. Serve hot with lemon wedges.

Mushrooms and Eggs SPAIN ■

MAKES **4 TO 6 SERVINGS AS A STARTER OR 2 AS A MAIN COURSE**

TIME **15 MINUTES**

In *pais Vasco*—Basque country—many tapas are substantial and filling. This meets that requirement, but it is also quick and simple. I once had it made with chanterelles, which of course produced a sublime version. If you can get them, or other wild mushrooms, the dish will be really special, but it's quite wonderful with shiitakes.

As for an omelet, you can put most anything you want in here; especially good is about a cup of chopped shrimp added just before the eggs. You can serve this on toast or bread, as is often done in tapas bars, or just by itself. It also makes a fine main course for two.

3 tablespoons extra virgin olive oil

2 garlic cloves, minced

2 shallots, sliced

$1/4$ pound shiitake or other mushrooms, tough stems removed and caps chopped

$1/4$ cup chopped fresh parsley leaves

5 eggs

1 tablespoon milk

Salt and black pepper to taste

Crostini (page 41), optional

1. Put the oil in a large skillet, preferably nonstick, and turn the heat to medium. Add the garlic and shallots and cook, stirring, until softened and fragrant, about 2 minutes. Stir in the mushrooms and half the parsley; cover and cook until the mushrooms are soft, about 10 minutes.
2. Meanwhile, beat the eggs with the milk. When the mushrooms are done, turn the heat to low and stir in the egg and milk mixture. Cook, stirring occasionally, just until the eggs have set. Season with salt and pepper, spoon on top of crostini if you like, garnish with the remaining parsley, and serve.

Grilled Mushrooms and Bacon
SPAIN ▨

MAKES **4 SERVINGS**

TIME **20 MINUTES, PLUS TIME TO PREHEAT THE GRILL**

A staple of many tapas bars, and among the most elementary of appetizers, this is a surefire crowd pleaser—as long as your crowd isn't vegetarian. Even if some members are, you can skewer plain mushrooms or mushrooms and other vegetables—like red peppers and zucchini, for example.

12 medium button mushrooms, trimmed

About $1/4$ pound slab bacon, cut into 12 pieces, or 6 thick slices bacon, cut in half

Vinaigrette (page 600) or Aïoli (page 603)

1. Start a charcoal or gas grill or preheat the broiler: the fire should be medium-hot and the grill rack at least 4 inches from the heat source. Make 4 small skewers, alternating mushrooms and bacon. (If you are using sliced bacon, cut the 6 pieces in half, then fold each over onto itself as you skewer it.)
2. Grill, turning frequently, until the bacon is crisp on the outside and the mushrooms tender, 10 to 15 minutes. Serve, offering vinaigrette or aïoli as a dipping sauce.

Pan-Cooked Mushrooms and Bacon. Half of an English breakfast: Put 1 tablespoon extra virgin olive oil in a skillet and turn the heat to medium-high. A

SKEWERING BACON AND MUSHROOMS

minute later, add the mushrooms and bacon and cook, stirring occasionally, until the bacon is crisp and the mushrooms browned and tender, about 10 minutes. Skewer if you like (it's a nicer presentation) and serve.

Mushroom Caviar RUSSIA

MAKES **4 TO 6 SERVINGS**

TIME **15 MINUTES**

This "caviar," most commonly spread on toast, is little more than sautéed mushrooms, but with an unusual texture and a decidedly Russian character. Do not mince the mushrooms too finely or they will become pasty.

2 tablespoons butter or extra virgin olive oil

1 medium onion, diced

2 garlic cloves, minced

1 pound button mushrooms, trimmed and cut into
¼-inch dice

2 tablespoons fresh lemon juice

3 tablespoons sour cream

Salt and black pepper to taste

2 tablespoons chopped fresh dill for garnish

1. Put the butter in a skillet and turn the heat to medium. A minute later, add the onion and garlic and cook until softened, stirring occasionally, about 5 minutes. Add the mushrooms, raise the heat to medium-high, and cook until lightly browned, 10 minutes or so.
2. Remove from the heat and stir in the lemon juice and sour cream. Season with salt and pepper, then garnish with dill and serve.

Marie Martin's Tarte aux Tomates

Tomato Tart FRANCE

MAKES **4 TO 8 SERVINGS AS A STARTER OR SNACK**

TIME **ABOUT AN HOUR**

The taste of strong mustard distinguishes this Provençal specialty, which can be served as a snack or a first course. Although you can make this simple, rich crust in the food processor (follow the procedure for Sweet Tart Pastry, page 654), it's so simple and straightforward it's almost as easily done by hand.

2 cups flour, plus more for rolling the dough

1 egg

Salt and black pepper to taste

8 tablespoons (1 stick) butter at room temperature

Extra virgin olive oil as needed

4 to 5 tablespoons Dijon mustard as needed

4 large tomatoes

1 tablespoon fresh thyme leaves

1. Combine the flour and egg in a bowl with a pinch of salt; quickly mix in the butter with your hands, then add cold water by the tablespoon until you can gather the dough into a ball. If time allows, refrigerate for 30 minutes or longer (you can leave it in the refrigerator, well wrapped, for up to a day or freeze for up to a month).
2. Preheat the oven to 450°F. Use some butter or olive oil to lightly grease a 10- to 12-inch round pizza pan. Roll out the dough on a lightly floured surface or simply press it into the pan, right up to the edges. Bake for about 10 minutes or until it is just beginning to color. Remove and set on a rack. (You can proceed immediately or wait an hour or two before finishing the tart.)
3. Set the oven at 400°F. Spread the crust with mustard. Core the tomatoes; if they are very juicy, cut in half through the equator and squeeze out some

of the juice, shaking out most of the seeds as well. Cut into about ¼-inch-thick slices and place in one layer on the crust. Sprinkle with salt, pepper, and thyme, then drizzle with olive oil. Bake the tart for about 30 minutes, until the tomatoes are shriveled and hot and the crust is browned. Serve hot or warm; this does not keep very well.

Zucchini Tart with Bacon FRANCE

MAKES **4 TO 8 SERVINGS AS A STARTER OR SNACK**
TIME **ABOUT AN HOUR**

This tart calls for the same procedures as the Tomato Tart (preceding recipe), with a different but equally summery—and, with its bit of curry powder, more unusual—topping.

> 2 cups flour, plus more for rolling the dough
>
> 1 egg
>
> Salt and black pepper to taste
>
> 8 tablespoons (1 stick) butter at room temperature
>
> Extra virgin olive oil as needed
>
> ½ cup diced bacon
>
> 4 to 6 medium zucchini, thinly sliced or shredded
>
> 1 teaspoon curry powder, or to taste

1. Follow steps 1 and 2 in the preceding recipe to make the crust.
2. Meanwhile, put 2 tablespoons olive oil in a large skillet over medium heat; a minute later, add the bacon and cook, stirring occasionally, until it is lightly but not completely browned; remove from the skillet with a slotted spoon and add the zucchini. Cook, stirring occasionally and sprinkling with salt and pepper, until it shrivels and its liquid evaporates. Stir in the curry powder, then taste and adjust the seasoning.

3. Set the oven at 400°F. Spread the crust with the zucchini and scatter the bacon over it. Bake the tart for about 30 minutes or until the zucchini has browned somewhat and the crust is golden, adjusting the heat as necessary. Serve hot or warm; this does not keep very well.

Fried Green Chiles SPAIN ■

MAKES **4 OR MORE SERVINGS**
TIME **10 MINUTES**

This simple starter is served all over the world—at least wherever chiles are grown—but I first had it in Basque country.

Here they're fried, but you can grill fresh chiles as well; in either case they taste fresh, smoky, salty, and spicy all at the same time. The chiles you use can be mild or hot. If you use mild long chiles, like Anaheim, most people will be happy.

> Extra virgin olive oil as needed
>
> 1 pound fresh small green frying chiles, rinsed and dried
>
> Coarse salt

1. Put about ½ inch of oil in a deep skillet and turn the heat to medium-high. When the oil is hot but not smoking, add the chiles (do not overcrowd). Cook them, turning occasionally, until the peppers are browned lightly on all sides, about 10 minutes. Repeat with the remaining chiles.
2. Remove from the heat with a slotted spoon, drain on paper towels, and sprinkle with coarse salt. Serve immediately.

Sautéed Peppers with Miso JAPAN ▦

MAKES **4 TO 6 SERVINGS**

TIME **20 MINUTES**

Every culture that grows peppers grills them, and the people who eat them always swear "they're not that hot." Well, in Japan, not only are they not that hot, they are often sautéed; and only in Japan are they sauced with miso. Use mild long green chiles like Anaheims or—if you can find them—mild long red chiles, and you'll come pretty close to duplicating the original.

> 3 tablespoons dark sesame oil
>
> 12 to 24 long mild fresh chiles (depending on size; use your judgment), rinsed and dried
>
> Salt and black pepper to taste
>
> 2 tablespoons mirin or 1 tablespoon honey mixed with 1 tablespoon water
>
> ½ cup white or red miso

1. Put the sesame oil in a large skillet and turn the heat to medium-high. When the oil is hot, after a minute or two, add the peppers. Cook, shaking the pan every once in a while, until they are nicely browned and shriveled, about 10 minutes. As they cook, sprinkle them with salt and pepper.

2. Meanwhile, whisk together the mirin and miso. When the peppers are done, turn off the heat and pour this mixture over the peppers; stir to combine and serve immediately.

Scallion Pancakes CHINA

MAKES **8 OR MORE SERVINGS**

TIME **1½ HOURS, LARGELY UNATTENDED**

This tough, chewy little pancake is a staple in China. Though the dough requires at least an hour of resting time, it's easy to make. Cut it into small pieces and serve as finger food for a crowd or into larger wedges and serve at the table, as part of a general Chinese feast. Lard is the traditional (and best) fat for cooking these; substitute oil if you prefer.

> 2 cups flour, plus a little more for rolling the dough
>
> 1 teaspoon salt
>
> ¾ cup boiling water, or as needed
>
> 1 tablespoon dark sesame oil, or as needed
>
> 1 cup finely chopped scallion
>
> Lard (traditional) or neutral oil, such as corn or grapeseed, as needed
>
> Coarse salt to taste

1. Place the flour and salt in a food processor; turn on the machine and add the water through the feed tube until the dough forms a ball. Alternatively, you can slowly pour the water into the flour-salt mixture and stir rapidly with a fork until the dough forms a ball around the fork.

2. Knead by hand for about 1 minute, until the dough is smooth. Place it in a bowl, cover with plastic wrap, and let rest for about 1 hour (or up to a day, refrigerated).

3. On a lightly floured surface, pinch and roll the dough into 2-inch balls, then flatten the balls into disks. Lightly brush one of the disks with sesame oil and sprinkle a few scallions on top. Place another disk on top of that one and use a rolling pin to roll the dough into a 5-inch-long oval. Lightly brush one side of the oval with sesame oil, sprinkle a few scallions on top, and fold the oval in half. Roll into a circle about ¼ inch thick, adding flour as necessary. Repeat with the remaining dough; you'll probably make about 6 pancakes with this amount of dough.

4. Generously coat a large, deep skillet with the lard or oil and turn the heat to medium-low. When the lard has melted or the oil is hot, place one of the

pancakes in the skillet. Cook until browned lightly, 3 to 5 minutes, then turn and brown the other side. Repeat with the remaining dough, then sprinkle with coarse salt, cut, and serve warm.

Char Siu Bao Steamed Barbecued Pork Buns
CHINA ■

MAKES **18 BUNS**

TIME **2¹/₂ HOURS, LARGELY UNATTENDED**

To make these classic steamed rolls at home, you might pick up char siu—barbecued pork—in one of the myriad of Chinatown restaurants that have roast meats hanging in the window. Or you can make the Barbecued Pork (page 373) and the buns a day or two later.

Fortunately, the buns themselves are easy to make, and they can be made as much as a month in advance: let them cool to room temperature after they've steamed (which should only take 15 minutes or so), then line them up on a baking sheet, cover tightly with plastic wrap, and freeze. Once they are frozen you can transfer them to a freezer bag or other airtight container. To serve, reheat the dumplings in a steamer over an inch of boiling water for 5 minutes.

Serve these as a starter or a snack.

3 tablespoons sugar

1¹/₂ teaspoons active dry yeast

1¹/₂ teaspoons baking powder

1¹/₂ cups cake or pastry flour

1¹/₂ cups all-purpose flour, plus more for rolling out the dough

1 tablespoon lard, butter, or oil

1 teaspoon corn, grapeseed, or other neutral oil

1 tablespoon cornstarch

1 tablespoon soy sauce

1 tablespoon oyster sauce

1 tablespoon honey

¹/₂ teaspoon sesame oil

White pepper to taste

¹/₂ pound char siu (¹/₄ recipe Barbecued Pork, page 373), cut into ¹/₄-inch dice

1. Stir together 2 tablespoons of the sugar, yeast, baking powder and 1 cup of warm water in a measuring cup and let the mixture sit until frothy, about 10 minutes.

2. Meanwhile, combine the flour and lard in a food processor and pulse until the mixture resembles cornmeal. With the machine running, slowly add the yeast mixture through the feed tube. Process for about 30 seconds, adding more water, a little at a time if necessary, until the mixture forms a ball and is slightly sticky to the touch. If it is dry, add another tablespoon or two of water and process for another 10 seconds. (In the unlikely event that the mixture is too sticky, add flour a tablespoon at a time.) Turn the dough out onto a lightly floured work surface and knead by hand for about 5 minutes. You don't want the dough to tear easily when you tug on it, but it need not be perfectly smooth.

3. Use the oil to grease a large bowl. Shape the dough into a ball, place it in the bowl, and cover with plastic wrap or a damp towel. Let rise until doubled in bulk, about 2 hours.

4. Meanwhile, make the filling. Stir together the cornstarch and 1 tablespoon of water in a small bowl; set aside. Combine the remaining tablespoon of sugar with the soy sauce, oyster sauce, honey, and ³/₄ cup of water in a small saucepan and set over high heat. Cook, stirring constantly, just until the sugar dissolves. Immediately transfer the sauce to a bowl and cool for a few minutes.

5. When the sauce has cooled, stir in the remaining ingredients and the cornstarch slurry. Let the pork marinate in the sauce at room temperature until you're ready to make the dumplings.

6. Cut eighteen 2-inch squares of parchment paper and set aside. Deflate the dough, transfer to a lightly floured work surface, knead for a minute, and roll it into a long snake. Cut the snake crosswise into 18 equal pieces. Lightly flour your work surface and your rolling pin and cover the dough you're not using with a piece of plastic wrap or a kitchen towel. Flatten one of the 18 pieces into a 2-inch disk with the palm of your hand, then use the rolling pin to shape it into a thin round, about 4 inches in diameter, dusting with flour as necessary.

7. Mound about 1 scant tablespoon of the filling (use a slotted spoon—you don't want any of the excess marinade) into the center of the disc. Bring the edges of the round up over the top of the filling and press them together to make a pouch. Twist the "neck" of the pouch together, then pinch the dough together in a few places to seal the top shut. Put one of the squares of parchment on the bottom of the bun, then set it aside on a plate, covered with a sheet of plastic wrap. Repeat with remaining ingredients. Let the finished buns sit for 10 minutes before you steam them.

8. Put at least an inch of water in a large steamer, cover, and bring to a steady simmer. Put the buns in the steamer, at least ½ inch apart, and steam until cooked through, about 12 minutes. Do not overcrowd; work in batches if necessary. Let them cool briefly and serve warm.

Mantou. Steamed buns, with no filling, wonderful warm with—believe it or not—a pat of butter; serve in place of rice at a Chinese meal. Omit the cornstarch, soy sauce, oyster sauce, sesame oil, white pepper, char siu, 1 tablespoon sugar, and steps 4–8. When the dough has risen, deflate it, transfer it to a lightly floured work surface, and knead for 1 minute. Pull off a small handful of dough and roll into a ball. Cover with a piece of plastic wrap or a kitchen towel and repeat with remaining dough. Prepare a large steamer and lightly oil the steamer rack. Put the dough balls directly on the steamer rack and steam for about 15 minutes. Remove and serve immediately.

Pajon Crisp Vegetable Pancake KOREA
MAKES **6 TO 8 SERVINGS AS A STARTER OR SIDE DISH**
TIME **45 MINUTES**

In Korea, this popular starter and snack is served at home, in restaurants, and on street corners. (It's also one of the most popular dishes in Korean restaurants in the States.) At its most basic, it's a large egg batter scallion pancake, but other vegetables, meat, and seafood are often added to make it a fancier and more substantial dish. Glutinous rice flour creates a wonderfully chewy texture, but if you can't find it, all-purpose flour is perfectly fine. Serve these immediately after making them.

> 2 cups flour, preferably half all-purpose, half glutinous rice
>
> 2 eggs, lightly beaten
>
> 1 tablespoon corn, grapeseed, or other neutral oil, plus more for frying
>
> 5 scallions, green parts only, trimmed, cut into 3-inch lengths, and sliced lengthwise
>
> 20 chives, preferably Chinese ("garlic") chives, roughly chopped
>
> 2 medium carrots, grated
>
> 1 small yellow or green summer squash, grated
>
> Soy Dipping Sauce (page 583)

1. Mix the flour, eggs, and oil with 1½ cups water to form a smooth batter. Let it rest while you prepare the vegetables. When you're ready to cook, stir the scallions, chives, carrots, and squash into the batter.

2. Heat a large nonstick skillet over medium-high heat and coat the bottom with oil. Ladle in a quar-

ter of the batter and spread it out evenly into a circle. Turn the heat to medium and cook until the bottom is browned, about 5 minutes, then flip and cook for another 5 minutes. Repeat with the remaining batter.

3. As the pancakes finish, remove them and, if necessary, drain on paper towels. Cut into small triangles and serve with Soy Dipping Sauce.

Steak Pajon. Add $1/4$ pound finely chopped steak, preferably sirloin, to the batter.

Seafood Pajon (called Hoy Tod in Thailand). Add $1/2$ pound chopped peeled shrimp, clams, mussels, or a combination to the batter along with 1 cup bean sprouts and $1/2$ cup chopped fresh cilantro leaves.

Kimchi Pajon. Add about 1 cup chopped Kimchi (page 444) to the batter.

Okonomiyaki Savory Pancakes JAPAN

MAKES **4 PANCAKES, ENOUGH FOR 4 STARTER OR SIDE DISHES**

TIME **40 MINUTES**

Okonomiyaki, a savory pancake, is a Japanese bar snack, something that you eat (or make) while you're drinking. There are restaurants in Japan that make nothing but okonomiyaki, where you sit at a bar or table with a griddle set into it and pick what you want in your "pancake." Everything is fair game, from sliced roasted pork to enoki mushrooms—even to the loose bits of fried batter that are a by-product of tempura called tenkasu.

This batter, which includes shredded cabbage, is made in the style linked with Osaka; in Hiroshima, the other part of Japan where the pancake is popular,

they add soba noodles to the batter. Obviously it's a very flexible recipe. Here I use bean sprouts and peas, but vary it as you like. For example, omit the sprouts and peas and use $1/2$ cup sliced squid and $1/2$ cup asparagus tips; in the summer, substitute 1 cup fresh corn kernels scraped off the cob.

You might look for Japanese Kewpie brand mayonnaise to finish the okonomiyaki; the container makes it easy to do the very 1980s squeeze bottle garnish of mayo and okonomiyaki sauce (which is like ketchup and also comes in a squeeze bottle, available at Japanese markets) that is part of the dish's charm. Personally, what I like is the eerie way the bonito shimmy when they're scattered across the pancake.

2 eggs

1 cup flour

Salt

1 cup Dashi (page 162) or water, or as needed

1 cup white or green cabbage, finely shredded

2 or 3 scallions, trimmed and roughly chopped

1 tablespoon corn, grapeseed, or other neutral oil

1 cup bean sprouts

$1/2$ cup frozen peas, thawed under running water

Mayonnaise for garnish

Okonomiyaki sauce for garnish

Bonito flakes for garnish

1. Preheat a griddle or medium nonstick skillet over medium-low heat while you make the batter.

2. Mix together the eggs, flour, and a pinch of salt. Stir in the dashi, mixing in only enough to moisten the flour; don't worry about a few lumps. Stir in the cabbage and scallions and, if the batter seems thick at this point, add a little more water or dashi to thin it out.

3. Grease your griddle or pan with a teaspoon of the oil and, when the oil shimmers, ladle the batter onto the griddle or skillet, using about a quarter of the batter for each 6- to 8-inch pancake.

4. After 2 or 3 minutes, when the first side is beginning to color, scatter the top of the pancake with a handful of bean sprouts and 2 tablespoons of the peas, patting them down a little to anchor them in the batter. Flip the pancake and cook the second side for 2 or 3 minutes, then flip and continue cooking, flipping as necessary to ensure even coloration, for another 5 minutes; the okonomiyaki needs to spend about 10 minutes in total over the heat.

5. Transfer the okonomiyaki to a warmed plate, spread a little mayonnaise across the top of it (or drizzle it across the top if you're using Japanese mayonnaise in one of those squirt bottles), drizzle liberally with okonomiyaki sauce, and top with a generous handful of bonito flakes. Serve at once, cutting it into wedges at the table. Repeat for the remaining batter. (You can also hold the pancakes on an ovenproof plate in a 200°F oven for up to 15 minutes while you cook the second batch, but they're best hot out of the pan. If you're going to hold them in the oven, garnish just before serving.)

Spinach Pancakes FINLAND

MAKES **6 TO 8 SERVINGS**

TIME **30 MINUTES**

Another good pancake starter or side dish. At their best hot, but still good warm. You can use frozen spinach for this if that's all you have.

  10 ounces fresh spinach, large stems removed, or one 10-ounce package frozen chopped spinach, thawed and drained

  2 cups flour

  $\frac{1}{2}$ teaspoon baking soda

  $\frac{1}{2}$ teaspoon salt

  $\frac{1}{8}$ teaspoon freshly grated nutmeg

  1 tablespoon sugar

  2 eggs

  $1\frac{1}{2}$ to 2 cups buttermilk, as needed

  2 tablespoons melted and cooled butter

  Butter or neutral oil, like corn or grapeseed, for frying

  1 cup sour cream, optional

  1 tablespoon minced lemon zest, optional

1. Put the fresh spinach in a covered saucepan over medium heat with just the water clinging to its leaves after washing or plunge it into a pot of salted boiling water. Either way, cook it until it wilts, just a couple of minutes. Drain, cool, squeeze dry, and chop.

2. Preheat a large skillet, preferably nonstick, over medium-low heat while you make the batter. Preheat the oven to 200°F. Mix together the dry ingredients. Beat the eggs into $1\frac{1}{2}$ cups of the buttermilk, then stir in the melted butter. Stir this into the dry ingredients, adding a little more buttermilk if the batter seems thick; stir in the spinach.

3. Use a teaspoon or two of butter or oil each time you add batter (you can use less with a nonstick skillet if you like). When the butter foam subsides or the oil shimmers, ladle batter onto the griddle or skillet, making any size pancakes you like. Adjust the heat as necessary; usually the first batch will require higher heat than subsequent batches. The idea is to brown the bottom in 2 to 4 minutes, without burning it. Flip only when the pancakes are fully cooked on the bottom; they won't hold together well until they're ready.

4. Cook until the second side is lightly browned; as the pancakes are done, put them on an ovenproof plate in the oven for up to 15 minutes. Mix the sour cream and lemon zest together and place a small dollop on each pancake.

Mixed-Herb Pancakes. Substitute 1/4 cup chopped mixed fresh herbs, like parsley, mint, and chives, for the spinach.

Clam Cakes KOREA ▦

MAKES **4 TO 6 SERVINGS**

TIME **25 MINUTES**

The Korean coast is known for its variety of delicious clams, which inspired this local specialty. More like superflavorful pancakes than the highly breaded clam cakes sometimes served in the States, they are a good use for our sea clams, which are sold fresh, chopped, in their own liquid (canned clams, which are acceptable, will not be as flavorful). These are best eaten with your fingers, by the way.

> 1 pound chopped clams, with liquid if possible
>
> 1 egg, lightly beaten
>
> 1/4 cup chopped fresh cilantro leaves
>
> 1/2 cup chopped scallion
>
> 1 small fresh chile, stemmed, seeded, and minced, or about 1 teaspoon cayenne or hot red pepper flakes
>
> 1 teaspoon baking soda
>
> Salt and black pepper to taste
>
> 2 tablespoons flour, or more as needed
>
> Corn, grapeseed, or other neutral oil for frying
>
> Soy Dipping Sauce (page 583)

1. Mix together the clams, their liquid or 1/4 cup water, the egg, cilantro, scallion, chile, baking soda, salt, and pepper. Add just enough flour to bind the mixture and form a stiff batter; start with 2 tablespoons and use more if you need it.
2. Preheat a large skillet, preferably nonstick, over medium-high heat for 2 or 3 minutes, coat the bottom with oil, and heat for another minute. Drop the batter by spoonfuls into the skillet and smooth out the batter to make flat cakes. Do not overcrowd. Cook until browned, about 5 minutes, flip, and cook for another 5 minutes. Repeat with the remaining batter.
3. Drain on paper towels and serve with Soy Dipping Sauce.

Tod Mun Fish or Shrimp Cakes THAILAND ▦

MAKES **6 OR MORE SERVINGS**

TIME **30 MINUTES (WITH PEELED SHRIMP)**

Tod mun—Thai fish cakes—are usually made with mackerel or other dark-fleshed fish, but shrimp are just as good, and most of my friends seem to prefer them made this way. Both mackerel and shrimp have enough natural gelatin to hold together without egg or bread crumbs or mashed potatoes or any of the other binders necessary in so many fish cakes. In fact, they have so much natural gelatin that if you over-process the fish it becomes rubbery, which in fact is characteristic of tod mun. My little trick—of pureeing some of the fish and simply chopping the rest—keeps it a little softer; you can do it either way. If you make these with shrimp, they can also be grilled. See page 500 for information on Thai fish sauce (nam pla).

> 1/4 cup fresh cilantro leaves, plus more for garnish
>
> 1 teaspoon hot red pepper flakes, or to taste
>
> 1 large shallot, roughly chopped
>
> 1 garlic clove, peeled
>
> 2 tablespoons nam pla or soy sauce
>
> One 1/2-inch piece fresh ginger, peeled and roughly chopped
>
> 2 limes
>
> 1 1/2 pounds shrimp, peeled, or 1 1/2 pounds skinned mackerel fillet
>
> Corn, grapeseed, or other neutral oil for frying

1. Put the cilantro, hot pepper, shallot, garlic clove, nam pla, ginger, and juice and zest of 1 lime in a food processor. Process until the mixture is pureed, stopping to scrape down the sides if necessary. Add a third to half of the shrimp or mackerel and puree; add the remaining fish and pulse just until chopped and combined.

2. Put ¼ inch of oil in a large skillet (you can use less if you use a nonstick skillet) and turn the heat to medium-high. Shape the mixture into small balls or 4 or 8 burgerlike patties. When the oil shimmers, cook the patties until browned on both sides, a total of about 10 minutes. Meanwhile, quarter the remaining lime.

3. Serve the fish cakes with the lime wedges, garnished with the remaining cilantro.

Shrimp Cakes, Indian Style. Follow the same procedure, omitting the lime juice and zest but using the cilantro, hot red pepper flakes, and shallot as above, along with 3 garlic cloves, peeled, 1 teaspoon ground cumin, and 1 tablespoon any curry powder or garam masala (see pages 592–594).

SHALLOTS

Queso Fundido Melted Cheese MEXICO ▣
MAKES **4 TO 6 SERVINGS**
TIME **30 MINUTES**

The original and superior version of nachos with cheese has the smoky spiciness of roasted chile and chorizo. While it can be served with tortilla chips, it is best scooped and wrapped into warm corn or flour tortillas. This makes a great simple lunch served with salad or soup.

1 small fresh chile, preferably serrano
Butter for greasing the baking dish
1 tablespoon corn, grapeseed, or other neutral oil
1 small onion, diced
½ pound Mexican chorizo, casing removed and diced or crumbled
1 pound melting cheese, like queso asadero, Chihuahua, or Menonita (see page 85), Monterey Jack, or mozzarella, cut into ½-inch cubes
Warm corn or flour tortillas

1. Preheat the oven to 375°F. Roast the chile in a dry skillet over medium heat (or over an open flame), turning to brown on all sides. Cool it, then peel, seed, stem, and chop.

2. Liberally butter a 9-inch gratin or similar baking dish and put it in the oven. Meanwhile, put the oil in a large skillet and turn the heat to medium-high. Add the onion and cook, stirring occasionally, until translucent, 3 to 5 minutes. Add the chile and chorizo and cook, stirring occasionally, until the chorizo is cooked through, about 5 minutes more. Drain the oil from the pan.

3. Layer the cheese across the bottom of the heated gratin dish and sprinkle the chorizo mixture on top. Bake until the cheese melts, about 10 minutes. Scoop the hot melted cheese and chorizo into warm tortillas and serve.

Queso Frito Fried Cheese SPAIN ■

MAKES **4 SERVINGS**

TIME **20 MINUTES**

Variations of this exist around the world, but I like the Spanish version for its paprika and because I like Spanish cheese. A fresh cheese made of sheep's milk is ideal here, but you can use any soft cheese you like, even mozzarella. This is best when it's really hot, when the cheese is soft and the outside crisp; serve immediately after making it.

3 tablespoons flour

1 teaspoon paprika

½ pound mild soft sheep's milk cheese, like manchego or Tuscan pecorino, or other cheese, cut into ½-inch slices

2 eggs, beaten

½ cup fine bread crumbs, preferably homemade (page 580)

Extra virgin olive oil for frying

1. Mix the flour and paprika together. Dredge the cheese slices in the flour, then the beaten egg, and finally the bread crumbs. If time allows, put on wax paper and refrigerate for an hour or longer.
2. Put at least ½ inch of oil in a heavy skillet and turn the heat to medium-high. When the oil shim-

Mexican Cheeses Too much of the Mexican food served in the States is smothered with a gooey layer of Cheddar or Monterey Jack, itself usually no more than mild Cheddar. But real Mexican cooking rarely uses melting cheese, and stateside Mexican markets—and, increasingly, good supermarkets—stock the more popular queso fresco, or fresh cheese, and a variety of other types. Here, then, is a mini–field guide to this wide variety of Mexican cheeses.

Name	Taste and Texture	Use	Substitutes
Queso Fresco, Queso Ranchero, Queso Blanco	Milky, fresh, slightly salty, a little acidic, wet, crumbly; ranges from smooth to coarse; sometimes spongy; doesn't melt	Crumble on top of or into any Mexican dish; use to fill empanadas or chiles	Dry, fresh farmer cheese (add salt), dry cottage cheese (drain), mild fresh goat cheese
Queso Añejo, Queso Cotija, Queso Oreado, Queso Seco	Salty, fairly sharp, but still a little milky, dry, crumbly	Good for grating and sprinkling onto dishes, especially Choclo (page 454)	Feta (rinse and drain), young mild Parmesan, mild Romano
Queso Asadero, Quesilla	Mild, creamy, relatively dry	Good for melting or heating until soft, especially in Quesadillas (page 103)	Whole-milk mozzarella; mild Monterey Jack
Queso Chihuahua, Queso Menonita	Mild, slightly salty, gooey when melted	Good for shredding and melting, specifically for Queso Fundido (page 84) or Enchiladas (page 324)	Mild Cheddar, mild Monterey Jack
Quesilla, Queso Panela	Sweet, soft, silky, delicate; fresh, not aged or ripened	Best served alone as a side dish or an appetizer; also a nice addition to salads	Ricotta, cottage cheese

mers, fry the cheese slices until golden brown, about 30 seconds, then turn and brown the other side. Drain on paper towels and serve as soon as possible.

Ham and Cheese Puffs SCANDINAVIA ■

MAKES **4 SERVINGS**

TIME **10 MINUTES (WITH PREPARED CHEESE MANTECAOS)**

This is my cross-cultural take on a frequently served Swedish snack. If you're making the North African mantecaos specifically for this dish, you might omit the cumin, but I think they're more interesting with it.

You can also make these with standard biscuits, in which case they're pretty simple.

2 tablespoons butter or neutral oil, like corn or grapeseed

5 shallots, sliced

2 cups diced cooked ham, pork, or slab bacon

½ cup sour cream

1 egg

¼ cup chopped fresh parsley or dill leaves

Black pepper to taste

Cheese Mantecaos (page 35), cooled and sliced in half horizontally

1. Melt the butter in a skillet over medium heat. Add the shallots and cook until soft and golden, about 3 minutes. Lower the heat and add the meat; cook, stirring occasionally, until hot, about 5 minutes.

2. Meanwhile, whisk together the sour cream, egg, and herbs. Add to the meat mixture and cook until just heated through. Season with pepper and spoon into the Cheese Mantecaos, making little sandwiches. Serve immediately.

Buckwheat Crêpes FRANCE

MAKES **4 SERVINGS**

TIME **ABOUT 1½ HOURS, LARGELY UNATTENDED**

Everyone knows about sweet crêpes (page 645), but visitors to France quickly become addicted to these—the classic snack food of Brittany—especially the ham-and-cheese variation.

Traditionally, the batter sits for an hour before starting to cook. As long as you plan ahead a bit, that shouldn't be a problem. But in a pinch you can skip the resting period—it doesn't make too much difference—and overall these are easy to make and great as savory starters or a light lunch or supper.

¼ cup all-purpose flour

1 cup buckwheat flour

2 eggs

½ cup milk

Butter or neutral oil, like corn or grapeseed, for frying

1. Combine the first 4 ingredients in a bowl with 1 cup water; whisk until smooth and let sit for at least an hour if time allows.

2. Heat an 8- or 10-inch nonstick skillet over high heat for about 2 minutes. Add a teaspoon or two of butter or a thin layer of oil, then pour most of it out (you can use it for the next crêpe), leaving just a trace behind.

3. Pour in ¼ cup of the batter and swirl it around so that it coats the bottom of the pan completely; pour the excess back into the remaining batter. Adjust the heat so that the batter dries on top before it burns on the bottom; it will be ready to turn in 1 to 2 minutes. Turn and cook the second side for about 30 seconds. Repeat with the remaining batter, adding more oil to the pan if necessary (it will not always be). Stack the crêpes as they finish, then fill as desired and serve.

Ham and Cheese Crêpes. Make a layer of thinly sliced ham and cheese—Gruyère or Emmental is best—in the center of each crêpe; fold the bottom edge a third of the way toward the center. Fold the sides in and then the bottom over, to make kind of an envelope. You can serve as is, but it's better to lightly brown the folded crêpes in melted butter just before serving.

Fried Egg Crêpes. You will add the egg as you make the crêpes. Cook the first side as in step 3, then turn and break an egg into the center of the crêpe. Quickly fold in the sides and bottom to make kind of an envelope, cover, and cook just until the yolk is set, about 2 minutes. Season to taste with salt and pepper and serve immediately.

Smoked Fish and Crème Fraîche Crêpes. Spread a thin layer of crème fraîche on each crêpe and line the smoked fish in the center of the crêpe. Fold in the sides and bottom, garnish with chopped fresh chives, and serve.

Black-Eyed Pea Fritters CARIBBEAN
MAKES 6 TO 8 SERVINGS
TIME 30 MINUTES, PLUS SOAKING TIME

These fritters, which you'll also find in Texas and Florida, have their origins in the Caribbean—and, if you want to trace them further back, India; see the variation.

2 cups (about 1 pound) dried black-eyed peas, soaked overnight and drained

4 garlic cloves, peeled

1 teaspoon salt

½ teaspoon black pepper

2 small fresh chiles, preferably habanero, or small dried chiles, stemmed and seeded, or ½ teaspoon Tabasco sauce, optional

Corn, grapeseed, or other neutral oil for deep-frying

1 lime, cut into wedges, for serving

1. Rinse and dry the peas and then place them in a food processor with the garlic, salt, pepper, and chiles. Process until the mixture is well combined and then pulse until the mixture becomes fluffy.
2. Put about 3 inches of oil in a deep saucepan and heat over medium-high heat until it reaches 350°F on a deep-frying thermometer or a pinch of the batter sizzles, but not violently. Using a tablespoon, gently drop spoonfuls of the pea mixture into the oil and fry, turning once, until golden brown, about 5 minutes or a little more. Work in batches, taking care not to crowd the fritters.
3. Drain on paper towels and serve with lime wedges.

Phulouri Split Pea or Chickpea Fritters INDIA. Substitute dry green or yellow split peas or chickpeas for the black-eyed peas and add 1 small chopped onion, ½ teaspoon hot red pepper flakes, or to taste, 1 tablespoon peeled and minced fresh ginger, 1 teaspoon minced garlic, ½ cup chopped fresh cilantro leaves (some stems are okay), 1 teaspoon each ground coriander and cumin, and ½ teaspoon ground fenugreek.

Buñuelos Yucca Fritters CARIBBEAN
MAKES 10 SERVINGS
TIME 1½ HOURS

These sweet fritters are a cross between doughnuts and potato pancakes. That may sound strange, but, like doughnuts or churros, they make a great breakfast or snack food. Bunuelos are most often made from a combination of three roots. One is yucca (also known as cassava and, confusingly enough, tapioca and manioc); it has a tough brown skin, bright white flesh, and a tough core that should be cut out before cooking. The second is malanga (also called taro), which resembles a hairy yam but has a lovely, creamy interior, sometimes streaked with purple.

Finally, there's boniato, also known as batata or Cuban sweet potato. It's in the same family as sweet potatoes and yams (and either can be substituted here). The reddish skin encases white flesh, which is dry and has a subtle sweetness.

All three of these can be found at major good supermarkets and Latin groceries, right next to one another.

1½ pounds yucca, peeled, cored, and cut into 2-inch cubes

½ pound malanga, peeled and cut into 1-inch cubes, or more boniato

½ pound boniato, yam, or sweet potato, peeled and cut into 1-inch cubes, or more malanga

1½ cups sugar

2 cinnamon sticks

2 star anise

½ teaspoon ground aniseed

1 teaspoon salt

2 eggs, lightly beaten

1 cup flour, plus more as needed

Corn, grapeseed, or other neutral oil for deep-frying

1. Put the yucca, malanga, and boniato into a large saucepan and cover with cold water. Bring to a boil, then lower the heat and simmer until tender, about 30 minutes.

2. Meanwhile, put the sugar, cinnamon, and star anise into a medium saucepan and stir in 3 cups water until the sugar dissolves. Set over medium-low heat and simmer until syrupy and golden, about 40 minutes. Remove from the heat and cool.

3. Transfer the yucca, malanga, and boniato and ½ cup of their cooking liquid to a large mixing bowl. Mash with a potato masher or fork until smooth. When the mixture has cooled, stir in the aniseed, salt, and eggs. Using a wooden spoon, stir in the flour, adding more as necessary, until a moldable dough is formed.

4. Divide the dough in half, then roll each piece into a long snake, 1 inch in diameter. Cut each snake into 7-inch lengths and form each piece into a figure eight, pinching the ends and center shut.

5. Put about 3 inches of oil in a deep saucepan and heat over medium-high heat until it reaches 350°F (a pinch of the dough sizzles, but not violently). Gently drop the figure eights into the oil and fry, turning once, until golden brown, 5 to 10 minutes. Work in batches, taking care not to crowd the fritters. Drain on paper towels, drizzle with the syrup, and serve immediately.

Simpler Bunuelos. Omit the spicy sugar syrup; sprinkle confectioners' sugar or a mixture of 3 tablespoons sugar mixed with 1 tablespoon ground cinnamon over the bunuelos.

Eggplant Fritters ITALY ■

MAKES **ABOUT 6 SERVINGS**
TIME **30 MINUTES**

You can make eggplant into fritters, seasoned with almost anything you like, but my taste here runs to Parmesan; the combination is magical. Fritters are usually deep-fried, but it isn't necessary in this case. Here they are made into flat, pancakelike forms and cooked in far less oil. Like most fried foods, these are best hot; but, as with most fritters, they're acceptable up to a half hour after they've been made (and, though I wouldn't serve them to company this way, they're pretty good cold).

About 1½ pounds eggplant

Salt

1 egg

½ cup fresh parsley leaves

½ cup freshly grated or roughly chopped Parmesan cheese

1 garlic clove, peeled

Pinch of cayenne

½ cup bread crumbs, preferably homemade (page 580), or flour

Corn, grapeseed, or other neutral oil for frying

Lemon wedges for serving

1. Trim and peel the eggplant and cut it into 1-inch cubes. If the eggplants are large, sprinkle them with salt, put them in a colander, and let them sit for at least 30 minutes, preferably 1 hour. Rinse.

2. Set a large pot of water to boil. Blanch the eggplant in the boiling water for about 5 minutes or until soft. Drain in a colander, pressing to get rid of as much moisture as possible. Combine in a food processor with the egg, parsley, Parmesan, garlic, and cayenne and process until smooth. Pulse in enough bread crumbs or flour to make a batter that will hold together.

3. Put enough oil in a large nonstick skillet to coat the bottom to a depth of about ¼ inch. Turn the heat to medium-high and wait until the oil is hot; when it's ready, a pinch of flour will sizzle. Drop the batter from a spoon, as you would pancake batter, and cook until nicely browned on both sides. Do not crowd the fritters, and adjust the heat as necessary so they brown without burning. Total cooking time per pancake will be about 6 minutes. Serve hot or warm, with lemon wedges.

Zucchini Fritters. Somewhat easier, if anything. In step 1, grate or shred an equal amount of zucchini; wring in a towel to squeeze out as much moisture as possible (if the zucchini are salted, the resulting pancakes will have slightly better texture, but it isn't imperative). Blanching is not necessary. Combine by hand with the remaining ingredients and cook as directed.

Fresh Corn Fritters SOUTHEAST ASIA

MAKES **ABOUT 6 SERVINGS**

TIME **30 MINUTES**

If you're accustomed to sweet corn fritters—even served with maple syrup—these are going to come as either a joyous revelation or a rude awakening. They're just as crunchy, but spicy and mildly hot.

2 Anaheim or poblano chiles

1 jalapeño or habanero chile, stemmed, seeded, and minced, or 1 teaspoon hot red pepper flakes, or to taste

3 cups fresh corn kernels, from 5 or 6 ears

1 egg

½ cup flour, or a little more as needed

½ teaspoon ground coriander

1 teaspoon ground cumin

½ cup fresh cilantro leaves

Salt and black pepper to taste

Corn, grapeseed, or other neutral oil for deep-frying

1. Roast the whole chiles in a dry skillet, the broiler, or over a grill (page 470), until lightly charred all over. Cool, then peel, stem, and seed. Combine the mild chiles in a food processor with the hot chile and 2 cups of the corn; process until quite smooth, about 1 minute, stopping the machine to scrape down the sides if necessary.

2. Combine the puree with the whole corn kernels, egg, flour, spices, cilantro, and some salt and pepper. The mixture should hold together when you clump it; if it does not, add a little more flour.

3. Put at least 2 inches of oil in a deep saucepan or skillet and heat over medium-high heat to 350°F or until a pinch of flour sizzles. Use a spoon or your hands to form the batter into golf ball–sized or smaller fritters; gently slide them into the oil and fry until golden brown, turning once, about 4 minutes. Serve immediately.

Bacalaitos Salt Cod Fritters CARIBBEAN
MAKES **6 TO 8 SERVINGS**

TIME **30 MINUTES, PLUS SOAKING TIME**

These traditional bite-sized treats are served as a starter or a snack throughout the Caribbean (and, for that matter, in parts of Europe). They must be served hot: I recommend that you serve them to your guests while they're standing around the stove and let them eat them with their fingers (or on toothpicks).

If you want to serve them at the table, consider Aïoli (page 603) as a dipping sauce. Or you can follow Moorish traditions and serve them with honey or molasses.

> 1 pound salt cod (bacalao), soaked overnight in several changes of cold water, drained, cooked, and shredded (page 56)
>
> 1 onion, minced
>
> 2 garlic cloves, minced
>
> 1/2 teaspoon black pepper, or more to taste, or cayenne to taste
>
> 1 cup flour
>
> 2 eggs
>
> 1/2 cup chopped fresh parsley leaves

Corn, grapeseed, or other neutral oil for deep-frying
Lime wedges

1. Combine the salt cod, onion, garlic, and pepper in a bowl and mix well with a wooden spoon. Add the flour and stir a few times, then beat in the eggs one at a time. Add about 1/2 cup water and stir until a batter forms—it should be a bit thicker than pancake batter, but not much—then stir in the parsley.

2. Let the mixture rest while you put about 3 inches of oil in a deep saucepan and heat it over medium-high to 350°F (a drop of the batter will sizzle energetically but not violently). Using a tablespoon, gently drop spoonfuls of the cod mixture into the oil and fry, turning once, until golden brown, 3 to 5 minutes. Work in batches, taking care not to crowd the fritters.

3. Drain on paper towels and serve with lime wedges or keep in a warm oven until ready to serve.

Spanish Shrimp Fritters. Substitute 1 pound shrimp, peeled, and ground, for the salt cod.

Indian Shrimp Fritters. Substitute 1 pound shrimp, peeled and ground, for the salt cod. Add 1 teaspoon ground cumin and 1 teaspoon ground turmeric to the shrimp, onion, garlic, and pepper mixture. Substitute 2 hot green chiles, stemmed, seeded, and minced, for the parsley.

Pakoras Batter-Fried Vegetables INDIA
MAKES **6 TO 8 SERVINGS**

TIME **ABOUT 40 MINUTES**

Similar to Tempura (recipe follows), these are usually made only with vegetables—but a very wide assortment—and the batter is best when prepared with chickpea flour (also called besan or gram flour and available at Indian and many Asian markets and most health food stores). Traditionally, the batter also often contains anardana, a powder made from ground pomegranate seeds—if you can find some (try the same stores that have besan), add a teaspoon to the batter, along with the garam masala.

Pakora batter can also be fried on its own, as a fritter; mix a medium onion, chopped, into it, and drop it by the tablespoon into the hot oil.

> Corn, grapeseed, or other neutral oil for deep-frying
> 2 cups chickpea flour
> 1 teaspoon baking powder
> 1 teaspoon salt
> Pinch of cayenne
> 1 tablespoon garam masala or fairly mild curry powder (pages 593–594)
> 1 tablespoon clarified butter (page 241) or more oil
> 1 1/2 to 2 pounds assorted vegetables, cut into chunks, slices, or rings: potato, onion, eggplant, winter squash or sweet potato, bell pepper, cauliflower, even leaves of spinach or chard

1. Put at least 3 inches of oil in a large, deep saucepan; a larger pan with more oil will allow you to cook more at once. Turn the heat to high and keep it there until the temperature reaches 350°F (a pinch of flour will sizzle). Then adjust the heat as necessary to maintain this temperature. While the oil is heating, prepare the batter and the vegetables.

2. To make the batter, combine the flour, baking powder, salt, spices, and butter in a bowl. Add about 1/2 cup cold water and whisk, adding more water as necessary until the mixture is smooth and about the consistency of thick cream.

3. When the oil is ready, dip the vegetables in the batter, then slide them into the oil; do not crowd. Fry each piece until golden, turning once if necessary, less than 5 minutes total. Drain on paper towels and serve immediately.

Tempura Batter-Fried Fish and Vegetables JAPAN
MAKES **6 TO 8 SERVINGS**
TIME **ABOUT 40 MINUTES**

Tempura is not the only batter-fried appetizer in the world; in fact, many cuisines have a similar dish, and some of these recipes follow. But tempura is very light, easy to make, and pretty much foolproof; chances are you'll get it right even on your first try.

Shrimp is the most common seafood, and probably the best, for use in tempura, but there's no reason you couldn't use other shellfish or even finfish. As for vegetables, it's a matter of whatever is on hand. Harder vegetables, like winter squash and carrots, should be cut into thin slices so they become tender at about the same time they are browned. More tender vegetables—zucchini, eggplant, mushrooms, and the like—can be made larger or even, in the case of mushrooms or green beans, kept whole.

Tempura, like most fried foods, must be served immediately. It will hold in a low oven for a few minutes, but as we all know it's at its best the second it's done. As long as you're comfortable with your guests, serve each piece as you make it, in your kitchen.

For frying, use a light, clean oil; grapeseed is probably best, but the more common (and cheaper) corn and safflower are good too. A frying or instant-read thermometer is a good idea, and temperatures of 330–350°F will work well for both vegetables and fish. If you don't have a thermometer, put a drop of batter into the oil when you think it's ready; it should neither sink to the bottom (too cold) nor immediately dance on the surface (too hot), but sink slightly beneath the surface and then rise to the top and skitter a bit.

> Corn, grapeseed, or other neutral oil for deep-frying
> 1½ to 2 pounds assorted vegetables: zucchini, eggplant, winter squash or sweet potato, mushrooms, bell pepper, green beans, broccoli or cauliflower, leeks, onions, etc.
> 4 to 8 large shrimp, peeled and sliced in half lengthwise
> Soy Dipping Sauce (page 583) or lemon wedges
> 2½ cups flour
> 3 egg yolks

1. Put at least 3 inches of oil in a large, deep saucepan. Turn the heat to high and keep it there until the temperature reaches 350°F (a pinch of flour will sizzle; also see headnote). Then adjust the heat as necessary to maintain this temperature. While the oil is heating, prepare the vegetables, shrimp, and sauce.

2. When you are ready to cook, combine 2 cups water and 2 cups ice; let sit for a minute, then measure 2 cups ice water. Beat lightly with 1½ cups of the flour and the egg yolks; the batter should be lumpy and quite thin.

3. One piece at a time, dredge the vegetables and shrimp in the remaining flour, then dip into the batter. Fry each piece until golden, turning once if necessary, less than 5 minutes total. Drain on paper towels and serve immediately, with the dipping sauce or lemon wedges.

Rebozados Crisp-Fried Shrimp SPAIN

MAKES **4 TO 6 SERVINGS**

TIME **30 MINUTES**

The Spanish version of Tempura (page 91), this produces a much thicker crust. It is most often made with shrimp, but you can use any seafood or vegetable or even bits of meat. It's a simple but superflavorful frying technique.

In much of Spain, olive oil is used for deep-frying, and it's good; furthermore, it has become so inexpensive that it's no longer impractical. But you can use a neutral oil, like corn or vegetable oil, if you prefer.

> 2 eggs
> 1 teaspoon extra virgin olive oil
> 1 tablespoon minced fresh parsley leaves
> ¼ teaspoon crumbled saffron, or more if you have it
> ½ teaspoon baking soda
> ¼ teaspoon salt
> ¼ teaspoon cayenne
> ¾ cup flour
> Oil for deep-frying (see headnote)
> 1 pound small shrimp, peeled
> Lime or lemon wedges for serving

1. Beat the eggs with ¼ cup water and the extra virgin olive oil. Stir in the parsley, saffron, baking soda, salt, cayenne, and flour until you have a smooth batter. Let the mixture rest while you put about 3 inches of oil in a deep saucepan and heat it over medium-high to 350°F (a drop of the batter will sizzle energetically but not violently).

2. Fold the shrimp into the batter, then transfer them to the oil one at a time with tongs or a spoon, working in batches. Cook until golden brown and puffed, about 4 minutes. Repeat with the remaining shrimp.

3. Drain on paper towels and serve immediately with lime wedges.

Vegetable Rebozados. Substitute 1 pound vegetables, like broccoli, cauliflower, or chard, cut into bite-sized pieces, for the shrimp.

About Cooking Oil

Oil is almost as much a part of cooking as heat. Few cuisines do not use a refined oil of some kind (some people get their essential fatty acids directly from animal fat, but these are increasingly rare), and therefore few do not employ and enjoy deep-frying. Cooking oils, then, are a staple in nearly every pantry.

Not all oils are the same, of course, and choosing the right one makes a difference. Cooking oils are made from fruits, like the olive, which is amazingly easy to produce; nuts, like almond and walnut, which are very flavorful; seeds, like sesame and rapeseed—better known as canola; vegetables, like corn; and legumes, like soy and peanut.

Three primary factors should be considered in choosing the proper oil: smoke point, flavor, and healthfulness. Freshness is also an issue.

Smoke point. The smoke point is the temperature at which an oil begins to smoke and break down. All cooking oils have smoke points high enough to deep-fry food (in case you're curious, avocado oil has the highest smoke point but is not readily available), which should never be done at temperatures higher than 375°F. If oil is kept at or below this temperature and not reused (each reuse lowers the smoke point, for a variety of reasons), you can pretty much ignore smoke points.

Pan-searing and sautéing require higher temperatures but usually for a briefer time, so again, any oil—any cooking fat, for that matter, including lard, butter, and rendered duck fat—will do the job. Corn and canola oils have high smoke points and work well in these cases.

Flavor. Flavor is the most important factor in cooking oils. For many cooked dishes and almost all deep-fried dishes, you want a neutral oil, which has little or no flavor. Grapeseed is ideal and becoming more and more widely available; corn is also good. To me, canola and soy, as popular as they are, have off flavors that I could do without.

The process of producing oils also affects flavor; cold-pressed oils are always preferable to oils that are extracted chemically. Extra virgin olive oil is *always* cold pressed; it's not ideal for deep-frying, but for sautéing, and certainly for vinaigrettes and many other sauces, it's often the best choice and the closest thing to an all-purpose oil there is. (It's now used in all parts of the world, including Japan.) "Virgin," "pure," "light," and "pomace" olive oils are less expensive, but generally the savings are not worth the sacrifice in quality.

Aside from olive oil, the most strongly flavored oils are from nuts or roasted seeds, like dark sesame oil; these are usually used in dressings (alone or in combination with olive oil), or—like good olive oil—for adding to a dish when it has been cooked (sesame oil is frequently used this way in Asian cooking).

Healthfulness. A third factor in choosing oil is its healthfulness. No cooking oil contains cholesterol, but those with low amounts of saturated fat—like grapeseed, canola, and olive—are better for you. Also, cooking oils with proportionally less polyunsaturated fat (and thus, more monounsaturated fat) are better for you. Extra virgin olive oil is among the "best" for you in this regard.

Storage and freshness. Oil, like all fat, can go bad. Stored in a cool, dark place (or in an opaque container), most oil will keep well for about a year. If you plan to keep it longer than that, or you live in a warm climate, it's best to use the refrigerator. (I keep all oil except that which I intend to use within a week or two in the fridge.) And always use the refrigerator for nut oils, which become rancid more quickly than other oils.

Fritto Misto Lightly Fried Fish and Vegetables

ITALY

MAKES **6 OR MORE SERVINGS**

TIME **45 MINUTES**

Like Tempura (page 91), the Fritto Misto batter and technique can be used with almost any morsel of food. An old-fashioned Fritto Misto might have bits of veal or other meat, frog's legs, cock's combs, artichoke hearts, chanterelles or other mushrooms, zucchini or other vegetables, pieces of cheese, and, of course, fish.

These days, it seems most people—including me—like a fish-based Fritto Misto, with perhaps a few pieces of vegetable thrown in. I have some suggestions here, but please use whatever you like.

Because you'll have to fry in batches, and because it's good only when very hot, it's best to serve Fritto Misto as an appetizer and usually only to those guests who are willing to stand around in the kitchen.

I don't think Fritto Misto needs more than fresh lemon as a "sauce," but you can use aïoli or even a light tomato sauce if you like.

Corn, grapeseed, or other neutral oil for deep-frying

1 medium zucchini, cut into chunks

1 large onion, peeled, sliced, and separated into rings

1 red bell pepper, cored, stemmed, and sliced

2 cups flour

1 teaspoon baking powder

1 teaspoon salt

Black pepper to taste

1 egg

¾ cup white wine or beer

1 pound or more assorted fish: peeled shrimp, cleaned
and sliced squid, crabmeat, shucked clams, pieces of
skate or finfish, etc.

Coarse salt

Lemon wedges or Aïoli (page 603) for serving

1. Put at least 3 inches of oil in a large, deep saucepan; a larger pan with more oil will allow you to cook more at once. Turn the heat to high and keep it there until the temperature reaches 350°F (a pinch of flour will sizzle). Then adjust the heat as necessary to maintain this temperature. While the oil is heating, prepare the vegetables.

2. Make the batter: Combine 1 cup of the flour, the baking powder, salt, and pepper in a bowl; mix lightly with a fork. Mix together the egg and wine, then stir the mixture into the batter until smooth; the mixture should be just about the consistency of pancake batter.

3. Dredge each piece of food lightly in the remaining flour, then dip into the batter and add to the oil. Do not crowd the food; you will have to cook in batches. Cooking time will be just as long as it takes for the pieces to become an appealing shade of gold, just 5 minutes or so.

4. Drain on paper towels, sprinkle with coarse salt, and serve immediately, with lemon wedges or aïoli.

Amritsari Spicy Fried Fish INDIA

MAKES **4 SERVINGS**

TIME **40 MINUTES**

Crisp-fried ladyfish are a specialty in India, and even though ladyfish themselves are part of the reason they're so great and we don't see them here, we can come pretty close to duplicating the dish; both batter and marinade are spicy, distinctive, and exciting. Plan on serving immediately.

One 1-inch piece fresh ginger, peeled

2 garlic cloves, peeled

1 small hot fresh chile, stemmed and seeded, or about
1 teaspoon hot red pepper flakes

Salt and pepper

3 tablespoons fresh lemon or lime juice

About 1 1/2 pounds white fish fillets, like red snapper or
black sea bass, skinned, boned, and cut into 2-inch
cubes or 4-inch strips about 1 inch wide (almost like
fish fingers)

3/4 cup flour

1 teaspoon pure chile powder, like Ancho or New Mexico,
or 1/2 teaspoon cayenne

1 egg, beaten

Corn, grapeseed, or other neutral oil for deep frying

1 lemon, cut into wedges, for serving

1. Mince together the ginger, garlic and chile (you can do this in a small food processor if you prefer). Combine the mixture in a bowl with a healthy pinch of salt and pepper, the lemon or lime juice, and the fish. Refrigerate for at least 20 minutes and up to an hour.

2. Meanwhile, heat at least 2 inches of oil in a 6-quart saucepan to about 350°F. (A drop of the batter will sizzle energetically but not violently when the oil reaches this temperature.) Combine the flour, chile powder, and egg in a large bowl. Add enough water to make a thick batter, about 1/2 cup.

3. Dip each piece of fish in the batter and gently slide into the oil; do not overcrowd—you'll probably manage 3 or 4 pieces at once. Fry, turning occasionally, until the fish is crisp and golden brown on all sides, about 7 minutes. Drain on paper towels and serve immediately with lemon wedges.

Fish Quenelles with Herbs FRANCE

MAKES **6 TO 8 SERVINGS**

TIME **ABOUT 1 HOUR**

Quenelles, like gefilte fish (page 36), are fish balls, but they are elegant fish balls, containing cream, herbs,

and butter. As a result, they're more expensive and more caloric than gefilte fish, but faster and easier to make. Also like gefilte fish, they traditionally were made from freshwater fish (especially pike), but you can use any delicate white-fleshed fish you like. This is a big, fancy first course, best followed with something light and simple, unless you're planning an elegant dinner.

Chervil is the best possible herb to use here, but it is almost always difficult to find; dill is the standard second choice.

2 to 3 pounds fish heads, bones, and skin

1 onion, peeled and quartered

2 carrots, roughly chopped

2 celery stalks, roughly chopped

1 bay leaf

10 peppercorns

Salt and black pepper to taste

Stalks from a bunch of dill or chervil

1 1/2 pounds assorted white fish fillets, carefully picked
over for bones, rinsed, and patted dry

1 cup snipped fresh dill leaves or minced chervil

2 egg whites

1 teaspoon fresh lemon juice

1 1/2 cups heavy cream

4 tablespoons (1/2 stick) butter, cut into bits

FORMING FISH QUENELLES

1. Combine the first 8 ingredients with water to cover in a pot and bring to a boil. Turn the heat to low and simmer for 30 minutes while you prepare the fish.

2. Combine the fish fillets and $1/2$ cup of the dill in a food processor and pulse until the fish is chopped and blended. Add the egg whites and process until just blended, no longer. Add the lemon juice, 1 cup of the cream, and a bit of salt and pepper and, again, process briefly, until the mixture is combined and smooth, but no longer.

3. When the stock is done, strain it into a clean pot and bring it to a simmer. Use 2 tablespoons or your hands to form 8 to 16 ovals of the fish mixture, depending on size. Place them in the pot and simmer for 5 minutes. Turn them and simmer for 5 minutes more. Remove the quenelles with a slotted spoon and drain on paper towels. Place on warmed plates and cover with foil.

4. Boil the stock until it is reduced to about 1 cup. Reduce the heat to low and stir in the butter a bit at a time. When the sauce thickens, add the remaining cream and $1/4$ cup of the remaining dill. Stir and heat through, but do not boil.

5. Serve the quenelles hot, with the sauce, garnished with the remaining dill.

Jansson's Temptation SWEDEN
MAKES **6 TO 8 SERVINGS AS A SNACK OR SIDE DISH**
TIME **1 HOUR**

This combination of crusty potatoes and salty anchovies will either appeal to you enormously or make no sense. One of the best-known dishes in Sweden, it's served at almost every holiday party—logically, if you ask me, because it's great snack food. It makes a good side dish for a hearty roast as well.

6 to 8 potatoes, about 2 pounds

3 tablespoons butter, more or less

2 medium onions, roughly chopped

At least a dozen anchovy fillets (about one 2-ounce tin), chopped

Black pepper to taste

2 tablespoons bread crumbs, preferably homemade (page 580)

2 cups milk, cream, or half-and-half

1. Preheat the oven to 375°F. Peel the potatoes and slice them $1/8$ to $1/4$ inch thick (I use a food processor or mandoline). Place them in cold water to keep them from discoloring.

2. Put 2 tablespoons of the butter in a skillet and turn the heat to medium. When the butter melts, turn the heat up to medium-high and add the onions. Cook, stirring occasionally, until the onions are soft, about 5 minutes, then turn off the heat.

3. Butter a baking pan. Drain the potatoes and alternate layers of potatoes, anchovies, and onions, with potatoes as the top and bottom layers. Sprinkle black pepper liberally over each layer; you don't need any salt. Top with the bread crumbs and a few dots of butter, then pour the milk or cream over the top. Bake for about 40 minutes or until the top is browned, the liquid is absorbed, and the potatoes are tender.

Broiled ("Grilled") Sardines or Smelts ENGLAND ▪
MAKES **2 SERVINGS**
TIME **15 MINUTES**

Sardines are not sold fresh as often as they might—or should—be. But when they are, and they're in good shape (make sure they don't look tired and old), they're worth grabbing. Fresh anchovies or smelts make a good substitute, again as long as they're gleaming. All of these little fish may be sold gutted, but if yours are whole, simply make a slit along the belly of each and, under running water, run your finger along the inside cavity to remove the innards. (You can eat them with their guts too, as many Europeans do; they're delicious that way.)

Though I usually "grill" these in the broiler, they can also be cooked over a fire, using a fish basket, just until browned on each side. You can also fry sardines; treat them as you would Fritto Misto (page 94), and serve them with any light tomato sauce, like Fast, Fresh Tomato Sauce (page 606).

12 to 16 large sardines, at least 1 pound, cleaned, rinsed,
    and dried
Melted butter or olive oil for brushing the fish
Salt and black pepper to taste
¼ cup extra virgin olive oil or melted butter for drizzling
    on the cooked fish, optional
1 teaspoon minced garlic, optional
½ cup chopped fresh parsley leaves for garnish

GUTTING FISH

1. Preheat the broiler; the rack should be about 4 inches from the heat source. Brush the fish inside and out with a little butter or oil, then sprinkle with salt and pepper. Lay them in a baking dish that can hold them, side by side, without crowding. Broil, turning once, until browned on both sides, about 5 minutes total.

2. Drizzle with more oil or butter and sprinkle with the garlic if you like; garnish with the parsley and serve hot.

Grilled Baby Squid SPAIN ■
MAKES **4 TO 6 SERVINGS**
TIME **20 MINUTES OR LESS, PLUS TIME TO PREHEAT
    THE GRILL**

These are not "grilled" at all but cooked on a plancha, a hot flat-top griddle similar to those used by short-order chefs. But you can grill them, too. Both ways work fine, but in either case the heat should be very intense and the cooking time very short.

The squid should be the smallest you can find, preferably about the size of an average adult's thumb.

1 pound cleaned baby squid or 1½ pounds whole baby
    squid
Coarse salt to taste
About 3 tablespoons extra virgin olive oil
1 tablespoon fresh lemon juice or sherry vinegar, or to
    taste

1. Start a charcoal or wood fire or preheat a gas grill; the fire should be quite hot (on a gas grill, as hot as you can get it) and the rack no more than 4 inches from the heat source and preferably less. Or preheat a heavy pan over high heat (and turn on an exhaust fan if you have one) for about 5 minutes.

2. If you need to clean the squid, pull off the head and tentacles and separate them by cutting just behind the head; save the tentacles and discard the head. Rinse out the inside of the bodies and dry well.

3. Sprinkle the squid with coarse salt and toss them lightly with a tablespoon or two of olive oil. If you are grilling, skewer the squid. Grill or pan-grill the squid quickly, about 1 minute per side; they should brown nicely but remain moist inside.

4. Put the squid on a plate. Drizzle with a little more olive oil and sprinkle with lemon juice or vinegar and a bit more salt. Serve immediately.

Grilled Baby Squid, Japanese Style. Here the grill is requisite, because the soy sauce coating would burn on a griddle: After cleaning the squid, marinate them briefly in a mixture of ¼ cup soy sauce and 2 tablespoons mirin (or 1 tablespoon honey mixed with 1 tablespoon white wine). Grill and garnish with toasted sesame seeds (page 596). (Black sesame seeds are more commonly used here, and they look nice against the white squid, so if you can find them, by all

CLEANING SQUID

means use them. Look in Japanese, Chinese, or Indian stores.)

Shrimp with Garlic SPAIN ■
MAKES **4 SERVINGS**
TIME **10 MINUTES**

A classic Spanish tapa, cooked quickly in small ramekins and served sizzling. In Spain, the ramekins are put over direct heat, which, frankly, makes me nervous; I use a heavy skillet and take that right to the table.

The Spanish are practically obsessed with the type of shrimp they use and prefer them to be fresh rather than frozen; but most of us don't have much choice. That's okay: as long as the shrimp are of high quality, the dish will be delicious.

Double the amounts here if you want to serve this as a main course, and, no matter when you serve it, be sure to offer bread as well; the sauce is incredible.

½ cup extra virgin olive oil

6 garlic cloves, peeled and sliced

1 small dried chile, coarsely chopped, or 1 teaspoon hot
    red pepper flakes, or to taste

1 pound peeled shrimp, preferably small (more than
    40 per pound), or larger shrimp, cut up

½ teaspoon coarse salt, or to taste

Chopped fresh parsley leaves for garnish

1. Combine the oil, garlic, and chile in an 8- to 10-inch skillet, preferably cast iron, and turn the heat to medium. When the garlic begins to sizzle and turn golden, add the shrimp. Cook, stirring, until the shrimp just turn pink and opaque, 2 to 4 minutes.

2. Stir in the salt, garnish with the parsley, and serve immediately, directly from the pan.

Shrimp with Garlic, Tomatoes, and Chiles. Use 2 or 3 chiles, or to taste. When the garlic sizzles, add 1 cup cut-up seeded tomatoes (canned are fine; drain them first) and cook, stirring occasionally, until the mixture becomes saucy, about 10 minutes. Add the shrimp and proceed as directed. If you like, you can also increase the amount of tomatoes and use this as a pasta sauce.

Hardshell Clams with Garlic ITALY ▪

MAKES **4 SERVINGS**

TIME **30 MINUTES**

The classic recipe for steaming clams and a good topping for pasta. In Italy, the smallest clams possible are used—with shells often not much bigger than your thumbnail—and here the best to use for that purpose are tiny littlenecks, mahogany clams, or cockles.

When buying hardshell clams, make sure the shells are undamaged and tightly shut; this means the clams are alive. The only remaining challenge is to make sure the clamshells are entirely free of sand (you need not worry about the interior; that's the advantage of these clams over steamers). Wash the shells well and even scrub them if necessary. If any clams remain closed after cooking, simply pry them open with a knife or your fingers.

> ¼ cup extra virgin olive oil
>
> 3 pounds tiny hardshell clams or cockles
>
> 1 tablespoon minced garlic
>
> 1 teaspoon hot red pepper flakes, or to taste, optional
>
> Salt and black pepper to taste
>
> Chopped fresh parsley leaves for garnish
>
> Lemon wedges for serving

1. Put half the olive oil in a large, deep skillet and turn the heat to high. Add the clams and cook, shaking the skillet or stirring the clams occasionally, until the first few of them open, about 5 minutes.

2. Add the garlic and, if you're using them, the hot pepper flakes, and cover for a minute. Uncover, then continue to cook, stirring occasionally, until almost all of the clams are open, another 5 to 10 minutes. (Any that are not open at this point may be opened at the table with an ordinary butter knife or your fingers.) Sprinkle with salt and pepper, drizzle with the remaining olive oil, garnish with the parsley, and serve with the lemon wedges.

Pasta with White Clam Sauce. In step 1, set a large pot of water to boil and add salt. While the clams are cooking, cook 1 pound pasta, preferably linguine, until it still has quite a bit of crunch (you must taste frequently once it begins to soften). When the clams are almost done, turn off the heat and cover the skillet. Drain the pasta, reserving about 1 cup of the cooking liquid. Add the pasta to the clams and cook, stirring, until the pasta is tender, adding the reserved cooking liquid if the mixture seems dry. Stir in the parsley, taste and adjust the seasoning, and serve, omitting the lemon.

Pasta with Red Clam Sauce. Follow the preceding variation, but just before adding the pasta to the clams, add about 1½ cups chopped fresh or canned tomatoes (you can peel and seed them first if you have the time and energy).

Migas Chorizo and Bread SPAIN ▪

MAKES **4 TO 8 SERVINGS**

TIME **30 MINUTES, PLUS SOME ADVANCE PLANNING**

An ingenious way of turning leftover bread into a substantial dish, migas is best served as an appetizer, because a little goes a long way. Eat it straight from the pan if you like, but in any case, hot, hot, hot.

If your bread is stale, you can start this right away. If not, slice it and let it sit out overnight to harden.

> 1 stale baguette or French or Italian loaf, 8 to 12 ounces, sliced
>
> ¼ cup extra virgin olive oil, or more as needed
>
> ½ pound dried chorizo, more or less, cut into quarter-sized pieces about ¼ inch thick
>
> ¼ cup roughly chopped garlic
>
> Salt and black pepper to taste

1. Soak the bread in water to cover until soft, just a few minutes, then squeeze out the water and wring the bread as dry as possible in a towel. The drier you get it, the quicker the cooking time.

2. You can start cooking while the bread is soaking: Put the oil in a large skillet, preferably nonstick, over medium-high heat. Add the chorizo slices and cook, stirring occasionally, until browned, about 5 minutes. Add the garlic and cook, stirring occasionally, until it begins to soften, another 5 minutes or so.

3. Add the squeezed-out bread and continue to cook, stirring infrequently, until the bread begins to brown, 10 to 15 minutes. If the mixture becomes dry before the bread browns, add a bit more olive oil. Season with a bit of salt and a lot of pepper and serve.

Fried Satay THAILAND ▪

MAKES **4 SERVINGS**

TIME **30 MINUTES**

This is similar to Grilled Satay, which follows, only in that it is meat on a stick. But this deep-fried version is crunchier, and the skewer itself is best when made from lemongrass or sugarcane, either of which imparts a subtle aroma to the meat (and gives you something to gnaw on, if your tastes go in that direction). Since the meat is pressed around the skewer like a meatball—the result is kind of a meat lollipop—it needs to be finely minced to hold together well; a food processor does the job perfectly.

> Four 5-inch lemongrass stalks, peeled and sliced sugarcane stalks, or wood skewers
>
> Corn, grapeseed, or other neutral oil for deep-frying
>
> 1 pound boneless pork, boneless, skinless chicken, or peeled shrimp, roughly chopped
>
> 2 garlic cloves, peeled and lightly smashed
>
> 2 shallots, peeled and quartered
>
> 1 teaspoon ground coriander
>
> 1 teaspoon salt
>
> 1 teaspoon black pepper
>
> 1 lime or lemon, cut into quarters, for serving

1. If you're using wood skewers, soak them in water to cover. Put at least 4 inches of oil in a deep, heavy saucepan and turn the heat to medium-high. Combine all the ingredients except the skewers and citrus in a food processor and process until very smooth, scraping down the sides of the bowl a couple of times if necessary.

2. Mold the mixture into four 3-inch balls and stick one of the lemongrass or sugarcane stalks halfway into each ball. Tightly press the meat mixture against the stalk.

3. The oil is ready to fry when it reaches 350°F or a little more. Gently place the balls into the oil and fry, turning occasionally, until evenly golden brown and cooked through, about 10 minutes total. Drain on paper towels and serve within 10 minutes, with the lime or lemon.

Grilled Satay MALAYSIA

MAKES **4 SERVINGS**

TIME **1 HOUR, PLUS TIME TO PREHEAT THE GRILL**

Most satays are thin slices of meat threaded through a bamboo skewer and grilled; they are almost inevitably dry. But this Malaysian version is made like kebabs, with bigger chunks of meat, which remain juicy and tender. Since they can be assembled ahead of time, they make a convenient starter, especially if you're going to be grilling anyway. More on tamarind on page 587 and on nam pla on page 500.

> 3 garlic cloves, peeled
>
> 3 shallots, peeled
>
> One 1-inch piece fresh ginger, peeled and roughly
> chopped
>
> 1 teaspoon ground coriander
>
> 1 teaspoon ground turmeric
>
> 1/2 teaspoon salt, or to taste
>
> 1 tablespoon palm or brown sugar
>
> 1 teaspoon tamarind pulp, dissolved in 2 tablespoons hot
> water, 2 tablespoons Tamarind Paste (page 585),
> dissolved in 1/4 cup hot water and strained, or
> 1 tablespoon Worcestershire sauce mixed with
> 1 tablespoon fresh lime juice
>
> 2 tablespoons nam pla
>
> 1 pound boneless, skinless chicken breast, boneless beef
> sirloin, or boneless pork shoulder or loin, cut into
> 1-inch cubes
>
> Fresh cilantro leaves for garnish
>
> Peanut Sauce (page 586) or lime wedges

1. If you're using wood (versus metal) skewers, soak them in water to cover. Place the first 9 ingredients in a food processor and process until completely smooth (you can add a tablespoon or two of water if the mixture is too thick to process), stopping the machine and stirring the mixture down occasionally if necessary. Combine with the meat in a large bowl and let it sit while you start a charcoal or wood fire or preheat a gas grill or broiler. (You can also cover the meat and refrigerate it for up to a day.)

2. Thread the meat onto the skewers, leaving 3 inches at the end and slight gaps between the chunks. Grill or broil for 3 to 4 minutes on each side, or until lightly browned all over. Garnish with cilantro and serve immediately with Thai Peanut Sauce or lime wedges.

Swedish Kottbullar or Danish Frikadeller Meatballs

SWEDEN, DENMARK

MAKES **12 OR MORE SERVINGS**

TIME **45 MINUTES**

In general, these are milder than Italian-style meatballs (Polpette, page 53), with cooked onion and no garlic or cheese. Often served with a cream sauce (and lingonberries), they can be made without one, skewered on toothpicks, and passed at parties.

A combination of pork, veal, and beef is best here, but if I had to choose only one meat it would unquestionably be pork.

> 1/2 cup bread or cracker crumbs
>
> 1 cup cream or half-and-half, 2/3 cup optional
>
> 4 tablespoons (1/2 stick) butter, 1 tablespoon optional
>
> 1 medium onion, minced
>
> Salt and black pepper to taste
>
> 1/2 pound each ground pork, veal, and beef, or 1 1/2 pounds
> ground pork
>
> Pinch of ground cloves or allspice or 1/2 teaspoon ground
> ginger
>
> 2 tablespoons flour, optional
>
> 3/4 cup beef or chicken stock, preferably homemade
> (page 160), or water, optional

1. Soak the bread or cracker crumbs in $1/3$ cup of the cream. Put 1 tablespoon of the butter in a large skillet over medium-high heat. Add the onion and a bit of salt and pepper and cook, stirring occasionally, until the onion softens, about 5 minutes. Turn off the heat.

2. Combine the bread crumbs, onion, meat, and spice, along with some more salt and pepper; do not overmix or overhandle. With wet hands or wet spoons, shape the meat into small meatballs (I would say as small as you have the patience for, but no more than an inch in diameter).

3. Put 2 tablespoons of the remaining butter in the skillet and turn the heat to medium-high. When the butter melts, begin adding the meatballs, a few at a time; you may have to cook in batches. Brown nicely on all sides and turn off the heat. Serve immediately or proceed to the next step.

4. To make a sauce, remove all but a trace of fat from the pan. Return the pan to the stove over medium heat and add the remaining butter and, after it melts, the flour. Stirring constantly, add the stock and cook until slightly thickened. Add the remaining cream and continue to cook for a few more minutes or until thickened. Taste and adjust the seasoning, then pour the meatballs into the sauce to reheat before serving.

Negima Beef-Scallion Rolls JAPAN
MAKES **4 TO 8 SERVINGS**

TIME **30 MINUTES, PLUS TIME TO PREHEAT THE GRILL**

The most difficult part of making negima, the popular Japanese appetizer in which meat is wrapped around scallions or chives, is slicing the meat thin enough. You can ask your butcher for ultra-thin-cut sirloin, and you might get it, but it's probably easier to use pork, chicken, or veal, all of which are regularly sold as thin cutlets. With a little gentle pounding, they're thin enough, and the process becomes easy.

$1/4$ cup soy sauce, plus more for brushing the meat

1 tablespoon rice vinegar or white wine vinegar

1 tablespoon mirin or 2 teaspoons honey mixed with
2 teaspoons water

Green parts from about 2 dozen scallions or a big fistful
of chives

8 thin slices of beef, chicken, veal, or pork, each
about 3 inches wide and 5 to 6 inches long,
about $1 1/4$ pounds

1. Start a charcoal or wood fire or preheat a gas grill or broiler; the fire should be quite hot. Mix together the first 3 ingredients, then soak the scallions or chives in this mixture while you prepare the meat.

2. Place the meat between 2 layers of wax paper or plastic wrap and pound it gently with a mallet, the bottom of a cast-iron pan, or a rolling pin until it is about $1/8$ inch thick. Brush one side of each piece of meat with a little soy sauce.

3. Remove the scallions or chives from their soaking liquid and cut them into lengths about the same width as the meat. Place a small bundle of them at one of the narrow ends of each slice, on the soy-brushed side. Roll the long way, securing the roll with a toothpick or two. (You can prepare the rolls in advance up to this point; cover and refrigerate for up to 2 hours before proceeding.) Brush the exterior of the roll with a little of the soaking liquid.

4. Grill or broil until brown on all sides, a total of about 6 minutes for chicken, 4 to 5 minutes for pork or veal, 4 minutes or less for beef.

Tabak Maaz Fried Lamb Ribs INDIA

MAKES **8 SERVINGS**

TIME **1 HOUR, SOMEWHAT UNATTENDED**

An unusual appetizer, in both its meat (lamb ribs, while delicious, are not seen that frequently) and its spicing. Ask the butcher for a lamb breast, cut into ribs; give him a couple of days' notice to make sure he can get one.

> **4 pounds lamb ribs (breast), or 2 to 3 pounds shoulder lamb chops**
>
> **Salt**
>
> **1/4 teaspoon cayenne pepper**
>
> **1 tablespoon fennel seeds, ground**
>
> **1 tablespoon peeled and minced fresh ginger**
>
> **1 teaspoon ground turmeric**
>
> **2 bay leaves**
>
> **4 cloves**
>
> **4 cardamom pods**
>
> **1 cinnamon stick**
>
> **1/2 cup milk**
>
> **2 tablespoons butter or neutral oil, like corn or grapeseed**
>
> **1 tablespoon minced garlic**
>
> **Chopped fresh cilantro leaves for garnish**

1. Combine the ribs in a large skillet with a pinch of salt and the cayenne, fennel, ginger, turmeric, bay leaves, cloves, cardamom, cinnamon, milk, and about 1/2 cup water. Bring to a boil, then adjust the heat so the mixture simmers; cook, turning the meat occasionally, until tender, adding more water if the mixture dries out, 30 to 45 minutes.

2. When the ribs are tender, remove them. If any liquid remains in the pan, cook over medium-high heat, stirring with a wooden spoon to loosen any bits that have stuck to the bottom, until the mixture is just about dry. Remove the cardamom pods, cloves, cinnamon stick, and bay leaves.

3. Add the butter to the pan over medium heat and when it's hot, brown the ribs. Remove the ribs to a warm platter and add about 1/2 cup water to the pan. Once again, cook over medium-high heat, stirring with a wooden spoon to loosen any bits that have stuck to the bottom, until the liquid is reduced by about half. Pour over the ribs, garnish with cilantro, and serve.

Cheese and Chile Quesadillas

MEXICO ■

MAKES **6 TO 12 SERVINGS AS AN APPETIZER OR A MIDDAY SNACK OR LIGHT LUNCH**

TIME **15 MINUTES**

In their simplest form, quesadillas are warm corn tortillas encasing spicy melted cheese, but the basic construction simply begs to be built upon. See the variations and keep in mind that the possibilities are endless—take advantage of what you have in the refrigerator or garden.

Fresh corn tortillas are best, but flour ones are acceptable. You may dry-sauté the quesadillas, with no oil, in a nonstick or well-seasoned cast-iron skillet.

> **2 tablespoons extra virgin olive oil, plus more for the pan, optional**
>
> **2 garlic cloves, minced**
>
> **1 pound pasilla or poblano chiles, stemmed, seeded, and chopped**
>
> **1/4 cup chopped fresh cilantro leaves**
>
> **Twelve 6-inch corn tortillas or eight 8-inch flour tortillas**
>
> **1 cup grated Mexican melting cheese, like quesilla, queso asadero, Chihuahua, or Menonita (see page 85), mild Cheddar, or a combination**
>
> **1/4 cup salsa (pages 610–612), Guacamole (page 22), or sour cream, optional**

1. Heat the oil in a skillet over medium heat. Add the garlic and chiles and cook, stirring occasionally, until softened, about 2 minutes. If the mixture begins to brown, add a little water to the skillet. Remove from the heat, stir in the cilantro, and set aside.

2. Set a large skillet, preferably nonstick or well-seasoned cast iron, over medium-low heat. Add just enough oil to lightly coat the bottom of the skillet, if desired, and build your quesadilla: put a tortilla on the skillet, spread on an even layer of cheese and the chile mixture, then top with another tortilla. When the cheese begins to melt, about 2 minutes, use a spatula to flip the quesadilla over. Cook just until the bottom tortilla is warm and lightly toasted, about 2 minutes. Repeat with the remaining ingredients.

3. Cut the quesadillas into wedges and serve immediately with salsa, guacamole, or sour cream, if desired. (You can keep these warm in a 200°F oven for a few minutes if you like.)

Grilled Cheese and Chile Quesadillas. Start a charcoal or wood fire or preheat a gas grill; the fire should be moderately hot and the rack about 4 inches from the heat source. In step 2, brush one side of a tortilla with oil and set on the grill. Build your quesadilla, brush oil on the top tortilla, and proceed as directed.

Additional Fillings. All of the following are delicious.
- Chopped cooked chicken (the Chicken Taco filling, page 323, would be perfect)
- Chopped cooked pork (try the Shredded Pork, page 396)
- Chopped cooked beef
- Chopped cooked shrimp
- Sautéed sliced mushrooms
- Refried beans or thin slices of ripe avocado and tomato spread on the melted cheese
- Caramelized onions

Soups Soup is the least rule-bound of all categories of food. Soup can be cooked quickly or left on a back burner; its ingredients can taste fresh and distinct, or they can be allowed to marry and become mellow; it may be rich or lean. You can start with great stock, or you can start with water. And so on.

As varied as the well over one hundred soup recipes in this chapter are, they all follow just a few simple patterns. Of course there are differences, but you'll find that the techniques change little; what you're doing is changing ingredients and seasonings.

Yet soup is not only for beginners; most veteran cooks still thrill at the thought of extracting the maximum flavor from ingredients and presenting a dish that, in a single spoonful, contains either a riot of flavors or just the concentrated essence of a single one.

Note: in this chapter, ■ indicates soups that can double as main courses. While this is somewhat arbitrary—any soup can be a "main course," given enough side dishes—the ones I've chosen are by their nature quite hearty and filling.

Note, too, that almost any soup can be prepared in advance; the ones that are not distinguished by the ■ simply require a bit more last-minute preparation than the others.

VEGETARIAN SOUPS

This huge category includes soups that either are vegetarian by their nature or do not suffer when made with water instead of stock. Many of them contain meat as optional ingredients, some contain dairy, but most can be made not only "vegetarian" but vegan with little trouble.

Having said that, I'll also say that I believe that almost every soup is best when it begins with stock. This can be anything from vegetable stock or a stock made with mushroom broth, to full-fledged chicken stock. The body and extra flavor provided by this base will improve any soup. And, in fact, vegetarian soups made with water can be insipid if you're not careful (soups containing meat, poultry, or fish rely less on stock because of their richer ingredients).

Cabbage and Potato Soup POLAND ■
MAKES **4 SERVINGS**
TIME **35 MINUTES**

Caraway seeds bring their interesting, bitter character to this simple soup, which is produced throughout Eastern Europe. It's light but flavorful when made vegetarian, richer and more robust with bacon and beef stock. The Scandinavian variation is even simpler (and sweeter).

To crush the caraway seeds, put them in a small plastic bag or wrap them in plastic or wax paper and press on them with the bottom of a pot (or other heavy object) or go over them with a rolling pin.

2 thick slices bacon, diced, optional

1 medium onion, diced

1 small head of cabbage, preferably Savoy, cored and
    shredded

1 tablespoon caraway seeds, lightly crushed

2 medium to large potatoes, peeled and cut into ½-inch
    dice

6 cups beef, chicken, or vegetable stock, preferably
    homemade (page 160 or 162)

Salt and black pepper to taste

1 cup croutons (page 580)

1. Cook the bacon in a large saucepan over medium heat, stirring occasionally, until some of the fat is rendered, 3 to 5 minutes. Add the onion and cook—or cook the onion in 2 tablespoons butter or oil if you're not using the bacon—stirring, until it's translucent, about 4 minutes. Add the cabbage and cook, stirring occasionally, until it wilts, about 5 minutes.

2. Add the caraway seeds and potatoes and lightly brown the potatoes, about 5 minutes. Add the stock and bring to a boil. Reduce heat and simmer for 20 minutes or until the potatoes are very tender. Taste and adjust the seasoning as necessary. Thin with a bit of water or stock if the soup seems too rich. Garnish with the croutons and serve immediately.

Brown Cabbage Soup Scandinavia. This version has a sweetness that many people will like. (You can add a tablespoon of vinegar to it as well.) Omit the caraway seeds and potatoes. After the cabbage wilts, add 2 tablespoons brown sugar and stir well. When the sugar is completely dissolved, add the stock and proceed.

Cabbage Soup with Thyme and Apples EASTERN EUROPE
MAKES **4 SERVINGS**
TIME **40 MINUTES**

The thyme really shines in this soup, which is unusual for its use of sautéed apples as a slightly crisp, sweet garnish. In the old days, during times of bounty, a piece of meat would be added with the cabbage; you can do that too, but the cooking process will get much longer. I find this light, first-course soup much more useful without it.

> 1 tablespoon extra virgin olive oil
>
> 3 tablespoons butter
>
> 1 large onion, sliced
>
> 1 small head of cabbage, just over a pound, preferably Savoy, cored and shredded
>
> 10 fresh thyme sprigs
>
> Salt and black pepper to taste
>
> 6 cups beef, chicken, or vegetable stock, preferably homemade (page 160 or 162)
>
> 3 Golden Delicious or other good apples, peeled, cored, and cubed

1. In a medium saucepan, combine the oil and 1 tablespoon of the butter and turn the heat to medium-high. When the butter melts, add the onion and cabbage and cook, stirring occasionally, until they wilt and begin to brown, 10 to 15 minutes. Add 8 of the thyme sprigs and cook for a few minutes more. Sprinkle with salt and pepper.

2. Add the stock and turn the heat to medium; stir occasionally as it heats. Put the remaining butter in a skillet and turn the heat to medium-high. When the butter foam subsides, add the apple pieces; cook, stirring occasionally, until they brown and become tender, about 10 minutes. Strip the leaves from the remaining 2 thyme sprigs and sprinkle them over the apples, along with a bit of salt.

3. Taste the soup and adjust the seasoning; remove the thyme sprigs. Serve the soup hot, garnished with the apple chunks.

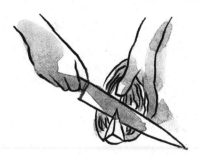

CORING AND SHREDDING CABBAGE

Carrot, Spinach, and Rice Stew
TURKEY ■

MAKES **4 SERVINGS**

TIME **45 MINUTES**

I first ate this soupy stew (or stewy soup) at a lunch counter in Istanbul and was taken by its depth of flavor. It seemed that either the whole was greater than the sum of its parts or there were some hidden ingredients. It turned out to be the former, or nearly so; through an interpreter, I learned that the dish did not begin with stock but with water and that the only ingredient I was not seeing was a bit of garlic. The cook offered that one might add a bit of butter for richness but that he hadn't done so with this batch.

If you want to turn this into a more filling main course, use stock instead of water, add some cubed boneless chicken or lamb, season it with a little cumin or dill, and finish it with lemon. You'll wind up with a bigger, more substantial Turkish-style stew, though not necessarily a better one.

1/2 pound carrots, about 3 medium, peeled and cut into
    1/4-inch dice
3/4 cup long-grain rice, like basmati
Salt and black pepper to taste
1 pound fresh spinach, thick stems removed, roughly
    chopped
1 teaspoon minced garlic, optional
2 tablespoons butter, optional

1. Combine the carrots with 6 cups of water in a saucepan and turn the heat to high. Bring to a boil, then stir in the rice and a large pinch of salt. When the mixture returns to the boil, add the spinach, then adjust the heat so that it simmers gently.

2. Cook, stirring occasionally, until the rice and carrots are very tender and the mixture takes on the consistency of a thick stew, about 30 minutes. Stir in the garlic or butter (if you're using either or both) and cook for another 5 minutes. Taste and adjust the seasoning and serve or cover and refrigerate for up to a day before reheating, adding a little more water if necessary.

Potage de Lentilles à l'Oseille
Lentil Soup with Sorrel FRANCE ■

MAKES **4 SERVINGS**
  TIME **ABOUT 1 HOUR**

Here sorrel brings both acidity and lightness to an often heavy mixture. You can substitute watercress or spinach for the sorrel to similar effect, especially if you add a squeeze of lemon at the end. Though it has only two primary ingredients, this soup is quite complex, particularly when you begin with good stock.

The best lentils to use here are lentilles du Puy or other small dark green ones. Use the greenish brown variety only if you cannot find these.

1/3 pound dried lentils, preferably small dark green lentils,
    rinsed and picked over
6 cups beef, chicken, or vegetable stock, preferably
    homemade (page 160 or 162), or water
1 to 3 tablespoons butter
1/4 pound sorrel or spinach, or a little more, chopped
Salt and black pepper to taste
1 teaspoon sugar
Fresh lemon juice to taste (if using spinach)

1. Place the lentils in a large saucepan and add the stock. Simmer over low heat until softened, 30 minutes or so.

2. Meanwhile, melt 1 tablespoon of the butter in a deep skillet over medium heat and cook the sorrel until softened, about 5 minutes. Stir the sorrel into the simmering lentils along with the salt, pepper, and sugar; bring the mixture to a boil, then lower the heat and simmer, stirring occasionally, for about 10 minutes.

3. At this point you can adjust the seasoning—now is the time to add lemon if you think the soup needs some—and serve, or you can puree the soup, which is somewhat more elegant. To do so, use a food mill, an immersion blender, or an upright blender and puree the mixture until smooth, working in batches if necessary. (In this as in every instance, take care when pureeing hot liquid; it's best, if you have the time, to let the mixture cool to room temperature before pureeing.) Reheat the soup in the pan and stir in the remaining butter, or cover and refrigerate the soup for up to a couple of days, adding the butter (and a little water if necessary) when you reheat it.

On Pureeing Soups

Until quite recently, pureed soups were made in a food mill, a tool that you may have never used or even seen. Though hand-operated, it's still as good a tool as any.

But now there are other options, and chances are good you already own at least one of these tools: the blender. Here's a summary of the possibilities, but there are a couple of general rules to follow no matter which you choose.

If at all possible, wait until your mixture cools before using an electric gadget to puree soup. Burns are far more common—and far more dangerous—than cuts, and if the idea of boiling hot puree flying through your kitchen doesn't give you pause, well, you're tougher than I am. Or it's never happened to you. If you must puree a soup mixture while it's still very hot, be very careful.

It helps to work in batches to avoid overloading your machine. Not only will this make it operate more efficiently; it will also reduce the chance of an accident.

The standard blender. Though limited in size, this is the best, cheapest, and most common tool for pureeing. You'll almost certainly have to puree in batches; spoon or ladle equal amounts of solids and liquids into the container. Cover tightly (I hold the cover on with a towel) and pulse the blender on and off once or twice to get the mixture moving, then let 'er rip. Blend until smooth.

The immersion blender. Not nearly as efficient, at least the home models (the industrial-strength immersion blenders used in restaurants are another story); you'll never get a perfectly smooth puree. Still, easy and convenient. Immerse the blade part of the blender into the solid and liquid mixture and turn on. Slowly move the blender around the pot until the soup is smooth, turn off the blender, and remove from the pot. Be sure to keep the blade under the soup to prevent the liquid from spraying.

The food processor. Not ideal, because food processors, unlike blenders, are not leak-proof. Best, then, for thicker soups and in small quantities. Spoon the solids and a little bit of liquid into the bowl of the food processor, cover, and process until smooth, stopping the machine to scrape down the sides if necessary. You may have to incorporate some of the liquid by hand after pureeing.

The food mill. Easy and straightforward. Use the finest hole setting if you have the option. Spoon the solids into the food mill placed over a large bowl, scraping the bottom of the mill at the end. Slowly stir in the liquid until well combined.

Onion Soup FRANCE ■
MAKES **4 SERVINGS**
TIME **ABOUT 1 HOUR**

There's some sort of misunderstanding in many American "French" restaurants, which seem to believe that onion soup should look like pizza, overloaded with gooey cheese. The real thing—and this is it—is something else entirely; robust, flavorful, and elegant.

This is as compelling a reason as there is to make your own beef stock.

4 tablespoons ($\frac{1}{2}$ stick) butter

4 large onions, thinly sliced (about 6 cups)

5 cups beef or chicken stock, preferably homemade (page 160), warmed

2 or 3 fresh thyme sprigs or a pinch of dried

2 or 3 fresh parsley sprigs

1 bay leaf

Salt and black pepper to taste

2 tablespoons cognac or other brandy, optional

4 croutons (page 580), made with bread slices and butter
   instead of oil

1 cup freshly grated Parmesan cheese

1. Melt the butter in a large, deep saucepan or casserole over medium heat. Add the onions and cook, stirring occasionally, until very soft and just beginning to brown, 30 to 45 minutes. Adjust the heat so they do not brown too fast but rather slowly turn into a melting mass.

2. Preheat the oven to 400°F. Add the stock, turn the heat to medium-high, and bring just about to a boil. Turn down the heat so that the mixture sends up a few bubbles at a time. Add the herbs, bay leaf, salt, pepper, and cognac and cook for 15 minutes. Fish out the bay leaf and herb sprigs, if any. (You may prepare the soup in advance up to this point; cover and refrigerate for up to 2 days, then reheat before proceeding.)

3. Place a crouton in each of 4 ovenproof bowls. Add soup and top with cheese. Place the bowls in a roasting pan or on a sturdy cookie sheet and bake for 5 to 10 minutes, just long enough to melt the cheese. Serve immediately.

Potage Crème de Tomates et de Pommes de Terre

Creamy Tomato-Potato Soup FRANCE ■

MAKES **4 SERVINGS**

TIME **1 HOUR**

In the States, cream soup usually conjures up images of thick, starchy soup with canned vegetables. But real cream soup, as made in France, is relatively thin, supersmooth, and fragrant with fresh vegetables and herbs. For convenience, you might prepare the vegetable puree ahead of time and refrigerate it; you can then finish the soup right before serving. Note that Vichyssoise, cold leek and potato soup, the variation that follows, is a direct descendant.

3 tablespoons butter

3 leeks, white parts only, sliced and well rinsed, or 1 large
   onion, sliced

3 medium tomatoes, preferably peeled (drained canned
   are fine)

About 1 pound baking potatoes, like Idaho or russet,
   peeled and diced

Salt and black pepper to taste

5 cups chicken or vegetable stock, preferably homemade
   (page 162)

$\frac{1}{2}$ cup cream or half-and-half, plus more as needed

Chopped fresh chervil or parsley leaves for garnish

1. Melt the butter in a large saucepan over medium-low heat. As soon as it melts, add the leeks and cook, stirring occasionally, until softened, about 5 minutes. Keep the heat moderate—you want the butter and leeks to remain pale in color. Meanwhile, cut the tomatoes in half through their equators, squeeze and shake out the seeds, then chop the pulp.

2. Stir in the tomatoes and cook, stirring occasionally, for 5 minutes; add the potatoes. Season with salt and pepper and add the stock. Bring the soup to a boil, then reduce the heat and simmer for 30 minutes.

3. Using a food mill, an immersion blender, or an upright blender, puree the mixture until smooth, working in batches if necessary. (In this as in every instance, take care when pureeing hot liquid; it's best, if you have the time, to let the mixture cool to room temperature before pureeing.) Reheat the soup (or refrigerate for up to a day before reheating); stir in the cream and additional salt and pep-

per as needed. If the soup seems too thick, thin it with cream or water. Garnish with chervil and serve immediately.

Vichyssoise Chilled Leek and Potato Soup. Omit the tomatoes. Cook through the pureeing of the soup. Rather than reheat, cool the soup and then refrigerate for at least 2 hours or until completely chilled. Stir the cream into the chilled soup immediately before serving and garnish with snipped chives. (You can also serve this soup hot if you like.)

Potage Crécy Creamy Carrot Soup
FRANCE ■ ▤
MAKES **4 SERVINGS**
TIME **45 MINUTES**

Few things are more uplifting in the dead of winter than a bowl of this bright orange soup, which is equally good served cold in the summer. Don't overcook the carrots or you'll lose the beautiful color.

This soup can be made ahead of time and refrigerated, then reheated if necessary.

3 tablespoons butter

2 shallots, sliced

1 pound carrots, roughly chopped or grated

1 large baking potato, like Idaho or russet, peeled and roughly chopped or grated

Salt and black pepper to taste

2 teaspoons sugar

5 cups chicken or vegetable stock, preferably homemade (page 160 or 162)

1/2 cup crème fraîche or sour cream, optional

1/4 cup chopped fresh chervil or parsley leaves for garnish

1. Melt the butter in a large saucepan over medium heat. Add the shallots, carrots, potato, salt, pepper,

and sugar and cook, stirring occasionally, for about 15 minutes, until the carrots begin to break down. Add the stock, raise the heat to high, and bring the mixture to a boil. Turn the heat to low and simmer for about 15 minutes.

2. Using a food mill, an immersion blender, or an upright blender, puree the mixture until smooth, working in batches if necessary. (In this as in every instance, take care when pureeing hot liquid; it's best, if you have the time, to let the mixture cool to room temperature before pureeing; or cover and refrigerate for up to a couple of days before pureeing.)

3. To serve hot, reheat the soup in the saucepan. To serve it cold, refrigerate, covered, for at least 2 hours. Stir in the crème fraîche or sour cream if you're using it, then garnish with chervil and serve.

Soupe au Pistou Vegetable Soup with Basil
FRANCE ■
MAKES **4 SERVINGS**
TIME **1 HOUR, PLUS SOAKING TIME IF YOU USE DRIED BEANS**

Pistou is a garlic-basil paste almost identical to pesto—the names in fact are the same, just in different dialects. In France it's used less to dress pasta than to thicken soups while heightening their flavor. Pistou is usually passed at the table so your guests can add as much as they like.

1 1/2 cups fresh shell beans, preferably a combination of white, red, and black, or 1/2 cup dried beans, soaked overnight and drained

2 leeks, white and light green parts only, sliced and well rinsed, or 1 large onion, sliced

2 carrots, chopped

Dried Mushrooms

While good fresh wild mushrooms are hard to come by, dried wild mushrooms—which arguably have a more intense flavor—can be bought relatively inexpensively and keep forever; they are an ideal pantry item. I buy dried porcini—the best-flavored dried mushroom—either online or in a specialty shop (or, if the time is right, in Italy), and a pound, which usually costs about fifty bucks, lasts me a couple of years. Dried shiitakes, purchased at Asian markets, cost about a quarter of that price; they are not as flavorful, but they're pretty good.

Reconstituting dried mushrooms is easy. You just soak them in hot water until they are softened. This can take from five to thirty minutes (you might even have to change the water a couple of times), depending on the thickness and toughness of the mushrooms. This soaking liquid can be good to use as a substitute for stock.

---

2 celery stalks, chopped

2 potatoes, peeled and chopped

2 zucchini, chopped

4 medium tomatoes, cored, seeded, and chopped

4 garlic cloves, peeled

2 cups fresh basil leaves

¼ cup extra virgin olive oil, plus more as needed

Salt and black pepper to taste

1 cup small pasta, like ditalini or capellini, broken into pieces

Freshly grated Parmesan to taste

1. Place the beans, leeks, carrots, celery, and potatoes in a large saucepan and cover with 7 cups water. Bring to a boil and then simmer, stirring occasionally, for 30 minutes. Add the zucchini and 3 of the tomatoes and simmer for another 20 minutes.

2. Meanwhile, pound the garlic and basil in a mortar and pestle or process in a food processor until pasty. Add the remaining tomato and combine until smooth. Slowly add the oil until very well combined and smooth. Season with salt and pepper.

3. Just before serving, add the pasta to the soup and cook until al dente, about 7 minutes. Stir 1 tablespoon of the pistou into the soup and then season with salt and pepper. Serve immediately with the Parmesan and remaining pistou.

Mushroom-Barley Soup

EASTERN EUROPE ■ ■

MAKES **4 SERVINGS**

TIME **45 MINUTES**

When my grandmother was a girl, this was a staple winter dish, and it still is in Poland and much of the rest of Eastern Europe. You might think of porcini as Italian or French, but good dried mushrooms, including porcini, come out of Poland to this day.

1 ounce dried porcini or other mushrooms (about 1 cup)

2 tablespoons extra virgin olive oil

DRIED PORCINI

¼ pound or more fresh shiitake or button mushrooms,
stemmed and roughly chopped

2 medium carrots, sliced

¾ cup pearl barley

Salt and black pepper to taste

1 bay leaf

1. Soak the porcini in 3 cups very hot water (see page 112). Put the olive oil in a medium saucepan and turn the heat to medium-high. Add the shiitakes and carrots and cook, stirring occasionally, until they begin to brown, about 10 minutes. Add the barley and continue to cook, stirring frequently, until it begins to brown; sprinkle with a little salt and pepper. Remove the porcini from their soaking liquid (do *not* discard the liquid); sort through and discard any hard bits.

2. Add the porcini to the pot and cook, stirring, for about a minute. Add the bay leaf, the mushroom soaking water, and 3 cups additional water (or stock if you prefer). Bring to a boil, then lower the heat to a simmer; cook until the barley is very tender, 20 to 30 minutes. Taste and add more salt if necessary, plus plenty of pepper. Serve hot or cover and refrigerate for up to a day before reheating, adding a little more water to thin the soup if necessary.

Mushroom-Potato Soup RUSSIA. Add 1 onion, diced, when cooking the shiitakes and carrots. Substitute 3 potatoes, peeled and diced, for the barley.

Avgolemono Egg-Lemon Soup GREECE
MAKES **4 SERVINGS**

TIME **ABOUT 30 MINUTES**

Truly one of the great delights of Eastern Mediterranean cooking, always refreshing and comforting.

For an easier version, try Simplest Egg-Lemon Soup (or the Lithuanian recipe that follows) as a variation. I am tempted to say you *must* use good homemade stock for this, but I'll leave it as a recommendation.

I had the soup made with tomatoes once—a regional variation—and enjoyed it very much. But the color may not be what you're expecting.

5 cups chicken or vegetable stock, preferably homemade
(page 160 or 162)

½ cup long-grain rice or orzo

1 carrot, thinly sliced

1 celery stalk, minced

Salt and black pepper to taste

1 cup chopped tomato, optional

2 eggs

1 teaspoon grated lemon zest

3 tablespoons fresh lemon juice, or more to taste

Minced fresh dill or parsley leaves for garnish

1. Put the stock in a large, deep saucepan or casserole and turn the heat to medium-high. When it is just about boiling, turn the heat down to medium so that it bubbles but not too vigorously. Stir in the rice, carrot, and celery and cook, stirring occasionally, until the vegetables are all tender, about 20 minutes. Season with salt and pepper and add the tomato if you're using it; turn the heat under the soup to low.

2. Use a whisk to beat the eggs in a bowl with the lemon zest and juice; still beating, add about ½ cup of the hot stock. Gradually add about another cup of the stock, beating all the while. Pour this mixture back into the soup and reheat, *but under no circumstances allow the mixture to boil or the eggs will scramble.*

3. Taste and add salt, pepper, or lemon juice as necessary. Garnish with the dill and serve.

Simplest Egg-Lemon Soup. Here good stock really *is* a must, because you are not adding much to it at all. Omit the carrot, celery, tomatoes, and zest. Heat the stock, cook the rice, and proceed to step 2.

Lemon Soup LITHUANIA ▧

MAKES **4 SERVINGS**

TIME **20 MINUTES**

This northern European sour soup makes a rich, wonderful, and full-bodied starter. The acidity of lemon complements the richness and near-sweetness of the stock, and the combination is simply amazing. For Greek egg-lemon soup, see the preceding recipe.

> 6 cups homemade jus rôti or chicken stock (page 163 or 160) or the best stock you can find
>
> 1 large lemon, or more to taste
>
> 2 egg yolks
>
> 2 tablespoons flour
>
> 1 cup sour cream
>
> 1 cup croutons (page 580)

1. Put the jus rôti in a medium saucepan and bring it to a boil over medium-high heat; turn off the heat as soon as it boils. Meanwhile, grate the zest of the lemon. Juice the lemon.

2. Use a whisk, an electric mixer, or a blender to combine the egg yolks, flour, and sour cream until smooth. Continue to mix while slowly adding the jus rôti.

3. Stir in the grated lemon zest and lemon juice. Transfer everything back to the saucepan and reheat the soup gently; taste and adjust the seasoning (you might like to add more lemon juice), then garnish with the croutons and serve.

Kapusniak Sauerkraut Vegetable Stew

POLAND ■

MAKES **4 SERVINGS**

TIME **40 MINUTES**

If you think sauerkraut is only for hot dogs or choucroute garni (page 404), think again. Here's a vegetable stew from Poland that demonstrates quite nicely that sauerkraut has roles beyond garnishing meat.

Buy sauerkraut from packages or barrels, not cans, and make sure it contains just cabbage and salt. That's all it takes.

> 5 cups beef, chicken, or vegetable stock, preferably homemade (page 160 or 162)
>
> 2 large celery stalks, chopped
>
> 2 large carrots, chopped
>
> 2 tart apples, peeled, cored, and chopped
>
> 1 ounce dried porcini or other mushrooms, reconstituted (page 112) and chopped
>
> 3 tablespoons butter or extra virgin olive oil
>
> 1 large onion, diced
>
> 1 pound sauerkraut, drained and chopped, juices reserved
>
> 1 tablespoon caraway seeds
>
> Salt and black pepper to taste

1. Bring the stock to a boil in a large saucepan; add the celery, carrots, apples, and mushrooms (taste the water in which you soaked the mushrooms; if it tastes good, add that too). Simmer over low heat until everything is soft, about 20 minutes.

2. Meanwhile, melt the butter in a large skillet over medium heat and cook the onion and sauerkraut, stirring occasionally, until browned and softened, about 10 minutes. Lower the heat and stir in the caraway seeds. Stir the sauerkraut mixture into the simmering stock and cook until the soup thickens slightly, 5 to 10 minutes. Season with salt if necessary, pepper, and the reserved sauerkraut juice.

Egg Flower Soup CHINA ▓

MAKES **4 SERVINGS**

TIME **10 MINUTES**

This improvement on the American Chinese restaurant classic has one thing in common with egg-drop soup: when properly made, the egg looks like delicate flowers. While many versions of this soup are thickened with cornstarch, I think the egg thickens the broth sufficiently.

Like the Chicken and Watercress Soup on page 140, this has an Italian relative; see the variation.

Any of these soups can be made more substantial by adding some shredded leftover chicken—or diced raw chicken, added while the stock is heating; don't add the egg until the chicken is just about cooked.

6 cups beef or chicken stock, preferably homemade
(page 160)

1 tablespoon dark sesame oil

Salt to taste

6 eggs, beaten

¹/₂ cup thinly sliced scallion

¹/₄ cup fresh cilantro leaves, roughly chopped

1. Put the stock in a saucepan, turn the heat to medium-high, and bring to a boil. Reduce the heat to low and add the oil and salt to taste. Carefully pour in the eggs in a slow stream, whisking constantly, until thin, nearly translucent egg "flowers" form, about 1 minute.

2. Remove from the heat and garnish with the scallions and cilantro. Serve hot.

Stracciatella ITALY. Use olive oil in place of sesame oil. Omit the scallions and cilantro. After adding the eggs, stir in 1 cup freshly grated Parmesan cheese. Garnish with ¹/₄ cup roughly chopped parsley leaves and pass additional Parmesan at the table.

Consommé, Jerez Style SPAIN. Use olive oil in place of sesame oil; omit the cilantro. Before adding the eggs, stir about 2 tablespoons dry (Fino) sherry into the broth. Swirl in the eggs, garnish with scallions, and serve.

Mulligatawny Spicy Vegetable Soup

INDIA ■ ■

MAKES **4 SERVINGS**

TIME **40 MINUTES**

Originally an Indian vegetable soup, this became popular among British colonialists, who added chicken to the mix. I like it better in something approaching its original form, but see the variations for more substantial versions.

2 tablespoons corn, grapeseed, or other neutral oil

2 garlic cloves, minced

1 teaspoon ground cumin

1 teaspoon ground turmeric

2 medium onions, chopped

3 medium carrots, sliced

4 celery stalks, chopped

1 white turnip, peeled and sliced, optional

6 cups chicken or vegetable stock, preferably homemade
(page 160 or 162), or water

3 tablespoons curry powder, preferably homemade
(pages 592–593)

Salt and black pepper to taste

¹/₄ cup chopped fresh cilantro leaves

1. Heat the oil in a deep, heavy saucepan over medium-high heat. Add the garlic, cumin, and turmeric and cook until fragrant, about 30 seconds. Add the onions, carrots, celery, and turnip if you're using it and cook, stirring occasionally, until the vegetables begin to soften, about 10 min-

---

■ make ahead   ▓ serve at room temp./cold   ▓ 30 minutes or less   ■ main course   SOUPS **115**

utes. Add the stock, bring to a boil, then lower the heat and simmer for 15 minutes.

2. Stir in the curry powder and cool the mixture slightly if time allows (it's never a good idea to puree boiling hot mixtures if you can avoid it). Use a food mill, an immersion blender, or an upright blender to puree the stew.

3. Reheat the stew in the saucepan, season with salt and pepper, garnish with cilantro, and serve.

Mulligatawny with Coconut Milk. Stir $1/2$ cup coconut milk, homemade (page 584) or canned, into the soup after seasoning with salt and pepper; heat through and serve.

Chunky Mulligatawny with Chicken. Add 1 pound chicken breasts or thighs, skinned, boned, and cut into $1/2$-inch cubes, to the saucepan with the vegetables. Do not puree the soup.

Simple Vegetarian Borscht
EASTERN EUROPE ■ ■ ■
MAKES **4 SERVINGS**
TIME **ABOUT 1 HOUR, PLUS CHILLING TIME**

Borscht, like gazpacho, is difficult to define; there are more versions than you can count. But at least we know they all (or almost all, anyway) contain beets (it's likely that the word *borscht* comes from the same root as the word for beet). And usually borscht is served cold. But it can be a vegetarian affair or a big meaty stew. The vegetarian version is usually served cold, while the beefy version is usually a hot winter dish.

Here's a fairly simple cold borscht with hot potatoes, a style I have made for thirty years (and first ate, at my grandmother's table, before that). For a meaty borscht, see page 148.

2 pounds beets, peeled

1 large white onion, peeled

1 bunch of fresh dill

Salt and black pepper to taste

4 hard-cooked eggs (page 338), peeled and quartered, for garnish, optional

1 medium cucumber, peeled, cut in half, seeded, and diced

4 medium red or white waxy potatoes, boiled until tender and kept hot, for garnish, optional

Fresh lemon juice to taste

Sour cream or yogurt for serving

1. Grate the beets and the onion together; you can do this on a box grater or, faster and easier, in a food processor; use either the basic metal blade and pulse carefully (do not puree) or the grating disk. Put them in a large saucepan with the stems of the dill (tie them in a bundle) and water to cover, about 6 cups.

2. Bring to a boil, then adjust the heat so the liquid simmers steadily but not violently, until the beets are tender, 15 to 20 minutes. Add salt and pepper, remove the dill stems, and chill. Meanwhile, prepare the eggs, cucumber, and/or potato.

3. When the soup is cold, taste and add lemon juice, salt, and pepper as necessary. Snip or chop the remaining dill. Serve the borscht in bowls, with any of the garnishes you like as well as the dill; pass sour cream at the table.

Borscht Consommé. An elegant and unusual starter: Cook the beets and onion in about 6 cups beef or chicken stock (page 160), along with a bay leaf. When tender, strain; discard the beets and, to the liquid, add the lemon juice, salt, and pepper to taste. Reheat and serve hot, garnished with chives, with or without sour cream.

Basic Red Gazpacho SPAIN ■ ■ ■

MAKES **4 SERVINGS**

TIME **20 MINUTES, PLUS RESTING TIME**

Having eaten countless dishes called gazpacho—both in and out of Spain—I feel less an authority than anyone to define it. Some people would have you believe that all gazpachos contain soaked bread, and indeed many do. Some say it must have vinegar; but I've been served plenty of good cold soups called gazpacho that were barely acidic. Others call any cold, drinkable soup that meets the need for both food and drink gazpacho. (A chilled can of crushed tomatoes would meet this definition and, with parsley and garlic, wouldn't be too bad on a hot day.)

I do have a few rules of my own for gazpacho: First, try to avoid green bell pepper. Even if it looks nice, this underripe fruit adds crunch at the price of bitterness; use red or yellow peppers instead. Second, the raw flavors of uncooked gazpacho really do seem to mellow when you allow them to meld for a few hours or even overnight; while not essential, this is a nice touch. And finally, sherry vinegar (or high-quality wine vinegar) is preferable to balsamic vinegar in gazpacho; not only is it more authentic, but its cleaner flavor provides better balance.

See the next recipe for a more complex version of this classic. Or add some cumin or paprika to this one, use tomato or V-8 juice in place of the water, and add fresh herbs—especially basil—as you find them.

About 2 pounds ripe tomatoes, roughly chopped

1 red or yellow bell pepper, seeded, stemmed, and roughly chopped

2 pickling (Kirby) cucumbers, 1 small firm cucumber, or about $\frac{1}{3}$ seedless ("English") cucumber, peeled if necessary and roughly chopped

4 slices stale good-quality white bread (about $\frac{1}{4}$ pound), crusts removed

1 garlic clove, peeled

1 tablespoon or more sherry vinegar or good-quality wine vinegar, or to taste

$\frac{1}{4}$ cup extra virgin olive oil

Salt and black pepper to taste

1. Mince a bit of the tomato, pepper, and cucumber for garnish and set aside. Soak the bread in a cup of water for 5 minutes, then squeeze out the excess water.

2. Place the bread in a blender or food processor with the unminced tomato, pepper, and cucumber, 6 cups water, the garlic, and the vinegar. Process until smooth, then add the olive oil slowly, with the machine running.

3. Season with salt and pepper and refrigerate until ready to serve; the flavor will improve over a few hours. Before serving, check the seasoning again and garnish with the reserved tomato, pepper, and cucumber.

Ignacio Blanco's Roasted Vegetable Gazpacho SPAIN ■ ■

MAKES **4 SERVINGS**

TIME **ABOUT 1 HOUR, PLUS RESTING TIME**

Ignacio Blanco is a friend from Galicia, the northwestern corner of Spain. He taught me this delicious (and, yes, traditional, though it is cooked) gazpacho. Best made in August, when all these vegetables are at their peak.

4 ripe tomatoes

2 small or 1 medium eggplant, peeled and cut into large chunks

4 small or 2 medium zucchini, cut into large chunks

2 medium onions, peeled and cut into large chunks

About 10 garlic cloves, peeled

$\frac{1}{2}$ cup extra virgin olive oil

¼ cup sherry vinegar

Salt and black pepper to taste

4 slices stale good-quality bread, crusts removed, torn up

Garlic croutons (page 580) or roasted tomatoes
    (page 493) for garnish

1. Preheat the oven to 400°F. In a roasting pan, combine the tomatoes, eggplant, zucchini, onions, garlic, and olive oil; roast until the eggplant is tender, stirring occasionally, about 30 minutes.

2. Turn the mixture into a bowl and add the vinegar, salt, pepper, 1 quart water, and bread. Refrigerate and let sit several hours or overnight.

3. Use a food processor or blender to blend the mixture until smooth. Put it through a food mill or strainer and discard the solids. Check the seasoning, garnish with garlic croutons or roasted tomatoes, and serve.

Almond Soup SPAIN ■ ■

MAKES **4 SERVINGS**

TIME **40 MINUTES**

This is an unusual soup, with flavors that may mystify but undoubtedly will please your guests. It's often served cold—and called a gazpacho—but I like it equally well hot.

5 cups chicken or vegetable stock, preferably homemade
    (page 160 or 162), or water

1 cup dry white wine or water

1 bay leaf

2 fresh parsley sprigs, plus more for garnish

3 tablespoons extra virgin olive oil

1 cup blanched almonds

1 onion, sliced

4 thick slices French or Italian bread, cut into ½-inch
    cubes

¼ teaspoon saffron threads

½ teaspoon ground cumin

Salt and black pepper to taste

1. Place the stock and wine in a large saucepan with the bay leaf and parsley sprigs and turn the heat to medium-high; when the first bubbles appear, turn the heat to low and maintain a gentle simmer.

2. Meanwhile, put the oil in a skillet and turn the heat to medium-high. Add the almonds, onion, and bread and cook, stirring occasionally, until the onions are softened, about 5 minutes. Cool slightly; remove about a quarter of the bread cubes and set aside.

3. Place the remaining almond mixture in a food processor with the saffron and cumin. Process until the mixture is a smooth paste. With the machine running, slowly pour 1 cup of the broth into the almond paste to blend.

4. Remove the bay leaf and parsley sprigs from the broth and stir in the almond paste. Bring the soup to a boil, then lower the heat and simmer for 10 minutes. Taste and add salt and pepper as necessary, then garnish with a few parsley sprigs and the reserved bread cubes and serve.

Sopa de Aguacate Avocado Soup

MEXICO ■ ■

MAKES **4 SERVINGS**

TIME **20 MINUTES, PLUS CHILLING TIME**

This creamy soup is wonderful on hot days; pair it with tortilla chips and you have a great lunch. Unlike most avocado soups, which are cream based, this one features the sweetness of tomatoes and the bite of chiles. You can make this into a dip by adding another avocado or two and reducing the amount of stock to just enough to allow the mixture to be pureed.

A nice touch is to use a third avocado, diced, as a garnish.

2 tablespoons corn, grapeseed, or other neutral oil

3 garlic cloves, minced

1 small onion, diced

2 fresh chiles, preferably serrano, stemmed, seeded, and minced

1 large ripe tomato, cored and chopped

1 quart chicken or vegetable stock, preferably homemade (page 160 or 162)

2 ripe medium avocados, peeled and pitted

Salt and black pepper to taste

1/2 cup chopped fresh cilantro leaves

1/2 cup tortilla chips, optional

1. Heat the oil in a large saucepan over medium heat. Add the garlic, onion, and chiles and cook, stirring occasionally, until fragrant, about 1 minute. Stir in the tomato and cook for 4 minutes, stirring now and then.

2. Add the stock and bring to a boil. Simmer for 10 minutes, uncovered, stirring occasionally. Cool slightly, then strain and cool.

3. Put the mixture in a blender along with the avocados and puree until smooth. Season with salt and pepper. Refrigerate until cold, about 2 hours.

4. Stir again, garnish with cilantro and tortilla strips chips if you like, and serve.

Sopa Fria de Mango
Savory Cold Mango Soup CARIBBEAN ■ ■

MAKES **4 SERVINGS**

TIME **20 MINUTES, PLUS CHILLING TIME**

Mangoes abound not only in the Caribbean but also, these days, in the United States. When they're cheap (in Latin markets they're often four for a dollar) there is no better use for them than this sweet soup, which can be served as an appetizer, especially in hot weather (or for dessert; see the variation). It's also lovely at Sunday brunch.

4 large or 8 small ripe mangoes, peeled, pitted, and chopped, or 4 cups frozen mango, thawed

1 cup milk

3/4 cup yogurt

1 1/2 cups coconut milk, homemade (page 584) or canned

1 tablespoon pure chile powder, like ancho or New Mexico, or to taste

1/4 teaspoon cayenne, or to taste

1/4 cup chopped fresh mint leaves for garnish, plus a few sprigs if you like, optional

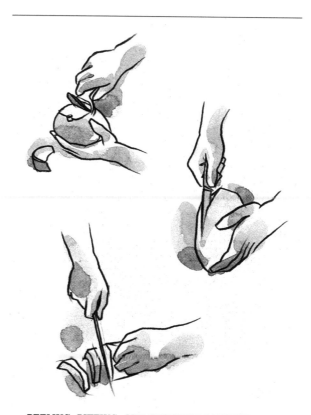

PEELING, PITTING, AND CHOPPING A MANGO

1. Put the mango in a food processor or blender and puree, adding enough milk to allow the machine to do its work easily. (Work in batches if necessary.) Add the remaining milk along with the yogurt, coconut milk, chile powder, and cayenne and process until smooth. Taste and adjust the seasoning.
2. Transfer the soup to a bowl and refrigerate until cold, about 1 hour. Ladle into bowls, garnish with the mint if you like, and serve.

Sweet Cold Mango Soup. This is a dessert: Omit the chile powder and cayenne (though a suspicion of chile powder remains a nice touch). Add 3 tablespoons sugar, or to taste, and 3 tablespoons dark rum, or to taste.

Green Bean Soup with Mint SPAIN ■ ■
MAKES **4 SERVINGS**
TIME **35 MINUTES**

If you want a little crunch, process the soup without the green beans, then stir them back into the puree before serving. This is best served at room temperature, since heat will dull the mint's bright flavor.

¼ pound bacon, diced, or 2 tablespoons oil or butter

2 garlic cloves, chopped

1 onion, diced

1 potato, peeled and diced

1 quart beef, chicken, or vegetable stock, preferably homemade (page 160 or 162)

½ pound fresh green beans, trimmed and cut into ½-inch pieces

Salt and black pepper to taste

¼ cup chopped fresh mint leaves, plus more for garnish

1. If you're using bacon, cook it in a heavy saucepan over medium-high heat until browned and crisp, then remove from the pan and reserve. Cook the garlic and onion in the same saucepan, adding 2 tablespoons oil or butter if you did not use bacon, until softened, about 3 minutes. Add the potato and stock and bring to a boil, then lower the heat, cover, and simmer until the potato is tender, about 20 minutes.
2. Meanwhile, cook the green beans in 2 cups salted boiling water. When tender, remove them from the pot, reserving the cooking liquid.
3. Cool the potato mixture and green bean water slightly if time allows (it's never a good idea to puree boiling hot mixtures if you can avoid it). Place the potato mixture, green beans, green bean liquid, and mint in a blender or food processor. Puree the mixture until smooth. Season with salt and pepper, garnish with the mint and bacon pieces, if desired, and serve.

Cucumber Seaweed Soup
JAPAN, KOREA ■ ■ ■
MAKES **4 SERVINGS**
TIME **20 MINUTES**

The only thing this has in common with the familiar European-style cucumber soups is the cucumber. Otherwise the ingredients—from the dashi to the soy sauce—are strictly Asian. This sublimely refreshing soup can be served hot or cold. When chilled, it's especially good with a few pieces of shrimp added to each bowl.

5 cups Dashi (page 162) or vegetable or chicken stock (page 162)

One 1½-pound block firm tofu, cut into ½-inch cubes

1 tablespoon soy sauce

1 tablespoon mirin or 1 1/2 teaspoons honey

Salt and black pepper to taste

One 8-inch sheet nori

1 medium cucumber, peeled if necessary and cut into
   paper-thin slices

1. Put the dashi in a medium saucepan and bring almost to a boil, then lower the heat so the mixture is steaming but not bubbling. Add the tofu and heat through, about 5 minutes. Stir in the soy sauce, mirin, salt, and pepper; taste and adjust the seasoning.

2. Toast the nori by either holding it over a flame for a few seconds per side or drying it in a 300°F oven for about 10 minutes. Crumble the nori and divide it and the cucumber slices among 4 soup bowls. Ladle the hot soup over them and serve immediately. Alternatively, refrigerate the soup and serve it cold, garnished with the cucumber and nori.

Coconut Milk Soup INDIA ■

MAKES **4 SERVINGS**

 TIME **35 MINUTES**

The creamy, rich, and mildly spicy flavor of this soup makes it a great starter before Indian entrees like Crunchy Curried Shrimp or Fish (page 217) or Patra ni Machhi (page 231).

3 tablespoons corn, grapeseed, or other neutral oil

1 small onion, chopped

One 1-inch piece fresh ginger, peeled and minced

1/4 cup chopped fresh cilantro leaves, plus more for
   garnish

1/2 teaspoon ground cinnamon

2 cups coconut milk, homemade (page 584) or canned

2 cups heavy cream or whole milk

Salt and black pepper to taste

1. Heat the oil in a saucepan over medium-high heat. Add the onion and ginger and cook, stirring occasionally, until the onion softens, 5 to 10 minutes. Stir in the cilantro and cinnamon and cook until fragrant, about 20 seconds.

2. Pour in the coconut milk and cream and bring to a boil; immediately turn the heat to low and simmer gently for 15 minutes, or until the mixture thickens slightly.

3. Season with salt and pepper, garnish with the remaining cilantro, and serve hot.

Coconut Soup with Clams and Shrimp. As done on the Kerala coast of India: In step 1, add 1/2 teaspoon cayenne, 1 tablespoon paprika, and 1 teaspoon ground coriander along with the cilantro and cinnamon. In step 2, after the soup has simmered for 15 minutes, add 2 dozen well-scrubbed small clams (or 4 dozen cockles) and 12 to 24 (depending on their size) peeled shrimp. Cook until the clams open, about 10 minutes.

Cilantro and Garlic Soup PORTUGAL ▨

MAKES **4 SERVINGS**

 TIME **30 MINUTES**

This is different from most garlic soups, not only for the addition of plenty of cilantro (parsley is more common, yet this is traditional, too) but also because the garlic-cilantro mixture is uncooked except by the heat of the broth poured over it, so it remains quite strong. If you have good beef or chicken stock, use it both to poach the eggs and as the base of the soup. And if you have an extra 5 minutes, don't toast the bread in a toaster but brown it lightly in a skillet on both sides in olive oil—there's nothing more delicious.

3 garlic cloves, peeled and crushed

2 cups chopped fresh cilantro leaves, plus more for garnish

Salt and black pepper to taste

1/4 cup extra virgin olive oil

4 thick slices French or Italian bread, toasted

4 eggs, preferably poached in beef or chicken stock (page 160), cooking liquid reserved

1. Place the garlic, 2 cups cilantro, and 1 teaspoon salt in a food processor and process until well incorporated. With the machine running, slowly pour in the oil and process until a paste is formed; stop the machine to scrape down the sides of the bowl if necessary.

2. Place the toast in 4 soup bowls and top with the poached eggs. Bring 5 cups of the egg poaching liquid to a gentle simmer, whisk in the cilantro paste, and season with salt and pepper.

3. Ladle the soup into bowls, garnish with cilantro, and serve.

Miso Soup with Tofu JAPAN ▦

MAKES **4 SERVINGS**

TIME **ABOUT 15 MINUTES**

"Real" miso soup begins with dashi, but you can make a pretty good version starting with water or other stock; see the variations. Start with traditional unpasteurized miso, which is inexpensive and lasts for several months in the refrigerator. Dark brown hatcho miso is traditionally used for soup, but the lighter varieties, which are more often used to make dressings and sauces, are fine as well. You'll find a good selection at Japanese markets and a decent selection at many health food stores.

Whenever you cook miso, it's best to keep the heat fairly tame to preserve its flavor and aroma.

1 quart Dashi (page 162)

1/3 cup dark or other miso

1/4 pound any tofu, cut into small cubes

1/4 cup minced carrot

4 scallions, trimmed and cut into 1-inch lengths

1. Heat the dashi in a medium saucepan just until bubbles begin to form along its edges. Turn the heat to low, then mix about 1/2 cup of the dashi with the miso in a bowl or blender; whisk or blend until smooth. (If you have an immersion blender, the fastest and easiest tool here, do this in a tall measuring cup.)

2. Pour the miso mixture back into the hot dashi and add the tofu and carrot; stir once or twice and let sit for a minute, just long enough to heat the tofu through. Add the scallions and serve.

Water- or Stock-Based Miso Soup. Use water or light chicken, beef, or vegetable stock (page 160 or 162) instead of dashi. Proceed as directed, adding a bit more miso if necessary.

Miso Soup with Shrimp or Chicken. Substitute 1/2-inch cubes of peeled shrimp or boneless, skinless chicken for the tofu. Cook for 2 minutes or until nearly done. Add the carrot and, when the soup is done, the scallions.

Miso Soup with Pork or Beef. Start with water and add about 1/2 pound not-too-lean thinly sliced pork (preferably from the shoulder) or beef (sirloin is good), along with a piece of kombu (dried kelp, page

Miso

Miso, a traditional Japanese food, is a fermented, aged paste made of soybeans (or other beans), grain (usually rice or barley), salt, and the *Aspergillus orzyae* bacteria. High-quality naturally made miso may go through a cycle of fermentation and aging that lasts as long as three years; it's as delicious, complex, and valuable as Parmesan. Commercial, or "quick," miso may undergo this process for a few weeks or even less (it's the equivalent of the "Parmesan" sold in green cardboard cylinders).

In Japan, where miso is eaten daily by many people, it is thought to have healing properties, and certainly as a low-fat, high-soy-protein, low-carbohydrate food it's probably pretty good for you.

Miso is sold in plastic tubs, tubes, jars, or plastic bags and keeps, refrigerated, for a long, long time—months at least. The best is organic, unpasteurized, traditionally made miso, which contains live cultures (pasteurized miso is no longer a living food). There are many kinds of miso, but generally speaking most fall into three categories:

Sweet miso is usually white or light beige in color, smooth in texture, and has a hint of sweetness. It may be called mellow miso, white miso, or sweet white miso. This miso is best used in dressings; some people use it as a dairy substitute.

Medium or mild miso, which can be used as an all-purpose miso, is usually smooth textured and golden colored. It is sometimes called yellow miso.

Red miso, barley miso, and hatcho miso are darker in color, saltier, and more earthy flavored; they are best when used in soups and stews. Their textures range from smooth to chunky.

In fact, I use the three misos more or less interchangeably, because I keep only one in the refrigerator at a time. If you cook with it more often, you might like to change among them.

---

484), 1 tablespoon soy sauce, and 1 tablespoon mirin. Bring to a boil, then turn the heat to low. Remove the kombu and simmer until the meat is tender. Mix about ½ cup of this broth with the miso as above, return to the simmering broth, and proceed as directed.

Miso Soup with Clams. In a covered pot over high heat, steam open 24 tiny clams (cockles are best) in about ½ cup water; they will be done when open, in about 10 minutes. Cool a bit, then remove the clams from the shells (pry open any that don't "pop") and rinse them in the broth. Strain and reserve the broth. Proceed as directed, starting with either dashi or water and adding the clams and broth instead of the tofu in step 2.

Jook Congee, or Rice Porridge CHINA ■
MAKES **6 SERVINGS**
TIME **ABOUT 2½ HOURS**

At its most basic, jook is soupy rice, perhaps with some salt or soy sauce. Conceptually, this would not appeal to most Americans, and the notion of congee did not appeal to me for many years. Yet when it was first served to me I thought it miraculous—of course it had a few more ingredients—and it turns out to be even better when made at home, where you can cook the rice in stock rather than water. A great part of a Chinese feast, as well as a wonderful breakfast or lunch.

½ cup short-grain rice
½ cup glutinous rice or more short-grain rice

---

2 cups chicken stock, preferably homemade (page 160), or water

One 3-inch piece fresh ginger, peeled and roughly chopped

¼ pound slab bacon, optional

¼ cup minced scallion

¼ cup minced crisp cooked bacon, optional

½ cup roasted peanuts, optional

Dark sesame oil for drizzling, optional

1. Wash the rices and put them in a stockpot with the stock or water. Place over high heat until the stock boils, then add about 1 quart water; bring to a boil and turn the heat to low.
2. Partially cover the pot and simmer for about 1½ hours, stirring occasionally to make sure the rice is not sticking to the bottom of the pot. Add the ginger and the slab bacon if you're using it and simmer for another hour. The jook should have a porridgelike consistency, so if it becomes very thick too quickly, turn down the heat and stir in more water. When it is done, the jook will be soupy and creamy.
3. Remove the slab bacon and serve the jook in individual bowls; garnish with scallion and, if you like, minced bacon and peanuts. Drizzle with sesame oil if desired.

Jook with Vegetables. Soak 4 or 5 dried black (shiitake) mushrooms in hot water until softened, then remove their stems and chop them. Omit the bacon from step 2 and add the mushrooms along with the ginger and 2 finely diced carrots. When the jook is almost done, stir in 1 cup fresh or frozen peas and cook for another 10 minutes or so. Garnish and serve.

Jook with Pork and Tea Eggs. In step 2, during the last half hour of simmering, add ½ pound lean ground pork and 2 or 3 sliced tea eggs (page 34) or regular hard-cooked eggs (page 338).

Jook with Meat. Cut the ginger into thin slivers instead of chopping it. Add it in step 2 along with ½ pound sirloin, sliced, or ½ pound boneless, skinless chicken breast, sliced, during the last 15 minutes of simmering.

Jook with Seafood. In step 2, during the last half hour of simmering, add ¼ pound cleaned squid, sliced; during the last 5 minutes of simmering, add ¼ pound peeled shrimp and ¼ pound firm white fish, skinned and sliced.

Jook with Dried Scallops. In step 2, substitute 2 ounces Chinese dried scallops for the slab bacon. (You can buy dried scallops, or conpoy, at most Chinese markets and spend almost as much as you want for them; they're a delicacy.) The scallops will soften and shred as the jook simmers. Omit the minced bacon.

Domburi Rice Soup with Chicken or Tofu and Egg
JAPAN ▨ ■
MAKES **4 SERVINGS**
TIME **30 MINUTES**

I had this as a late-night snack in Japan, but it's great at breakfast, too, a soothing, homey soup that is also good made with tofu or leftover chicken. Even if you don't have dashi, you can execute this dish in a half hour or so. You can make fresh rice for this, of course, but if you use leftover rice—which is fine—heat it first; the microwave does a fine job of this. Some Japanese make small individual omelets for each bowl, but others use the easier, if somewhat odd, technique of cooking the egg in the soup, as here.

3 cups Dashi (page 162)

¼ cup good-quality soy sauce

¼ cup mirin or 2 tablespoons honey

2 tablespoons sake

¼ to ½ pound chopped boneless, skinless chicken
    or firm tofu

4 eggs

4 scallions, chopped

4 cups cooked short-grain rice (page 507), hot

½ sheet nori, lightly toasted (page 121), optional

1. Combine the dashi in a medium saucepan with the soy sauce, mirin, and sake and bring to a boil. Lower the heat a bit, then add the chicken or tofu; adjust the heat so the mixture simmers and cook, stirring occasionally, for 2 or 3 minutes.

2. Beat the eggs in a bowl with the scallions and add, slowly, to the bubbling mixture; let cook, undisturbed, until the eggs' edges are set, then stir once or twice. (The egg should not be fully set; it will finish cooking before you eat it.) Put the hot rice in 4 deep soup bowls and pour the soup over it. Crumble the nori and sprinkle it over the top if you're using it and serve.

Rice Soup with Tofu and Vegetables. In step 1, you may use water instead of dashi (though dashi is still preferable). Add the seasonings, then 1 thinly sliced carrot, 1 thinly sliced onion, 4 thinly sliced fresh shiitake mushroom caps, and, if you like, a few leaves of spinach. Simmer for about 10 minutes, until the vegetables soften. Add the tofu and proceed.

Curry Soup Noodles MALAYSIA ■

MAKES **4 SERVINGS**

TIME **45 MINUTES**

A dish that combines the style of Chinese soup noodles with the flavors of Indian curries. This version, made entirely with fresh ingredients, is probably superior to any you've had at a restaurant.

3 garlic cloves, peeled

3 shallots, peeled

One 1½-inch piece fresh ginger, peeled

2 fresh chiles, preferably Thai, stemmed and seeded,
    or hot red pepper flakes, to taste

1 tablespoon Tamarind Paste (page 585), optional

2 teaspoons ground turmeric

2 teaspoons ground coriander

2 tablespoons corn, grapeseed, or other neutral oil

1 lemongrass stalk, trimmed and smashed (page 143)

1 quart beef, chicken, or vegetable stock, preferably
    homemade (page 160 or 162), or water

Salt to taste

1 pound fresh Chinese egg noodles

1½ cups bean sprouts, trimmed

1 cup coconut milk, homemade (page 584) or canned

4 hard-cooked eggs (page 338), sliced

½ pound tofu, pressed (page 491) and sliced

1 cucumber, peeled, cut in half, seeds removed
    (page 169), and sliced

1. Put the first 7 ingredients in a food processor or blender and process until pasty. Put the oil in a large saucepan over medium-high heat. Add the curry paste and cook until fragrant, about 1 minute. Add the lemongrass and stock and bring to a boil. Lower the heat and simmer, uncovered, for 15 minutes.

2. Meanwhile, bring a large pot of water to a boil and add salt. Add the noodles and bean sprouts and cook, stirring occasionally, just until the noodles are tender, about 3 minutes. Drain and transfer the noodles and bean sprouts to large serving bowls.

3. Add the coconut milk to the curry soup and cook, stirring occasionally, for another 5 minutes. Remove from the heat and divide the soup among the bowls of noodles. Top the noodles with the eggs, tofu, and cucumber and serve.

Passatelli ITALY ■

MAKES **4 SERVINGS**

TIME **30 MINUTES**

This is one of those soups that contain so few ingredients that it's really best to use good stock as opposed to canned broth. (On the other hand, the broth should not be too strong, or it will overwhelm the delicate, fresh pasta.)

If you already have fresh pasta dough prepared for another dish, you can substitute it for the passatelli, but this stuff is worth making for its own sake—and easy.

> 1 quart beef, chicken, or vegetable stock, preferably homemade (page 160 or 162)
>
> 1/3 cup fresh bread crumbs, preferably homemade (page 580)
>
> 3/4 cup freshly grated Parmesan cheese, plus more to taste
>
> 1/8 teaspoon freshly grated nutmeg
>
> 1/4 cup minced fresh parsley leaves
>
> 2 eggs

1. Bring the stock to a steady simmer in a large saucepan. Meanwhile, combine the bread crumbs, Parmesan, nutmeg, and parsley on a work surface and make a well in the center. Break the eggs into the well and knead the mixture until it forms a soft, granular dough.

2. Place the dough into a ricer or food mill with large holes. (If you do not have a ricer or food mill, place the dough in a colander and press the dough through with a wooden spoon.) Press the dough into the simmering stock and cook until tender but firm, just about 2 minutes.

3. Serve immediately, passing more Parmesan at the table.

Pasta Grattata. Known as tarhana in the Middle East: Instead of making passatelli, use about 1/4 pound of fresh egg pasta (page 541), formed into a ball.

Using the big holes on a box grater, grate the pasta directly into the simmering broth (or onto wax paper, where you can store it for a few hours; just make sure the shreds remain separate). Cook in the stock until the pasta is tender but firm, 3 or 4 minutes. Season the stock with the nutmeg and serve, passing Parmesan at the table.

Matzo Ball Soup EASTERN EUROPE. To make matzo balls, which are not all that different in spirit, beat 3 eggs with 1/2 cup stock. Add 1/4 cup minced onion, 1/4 cup rendered chicken fat or oil, salt and black pepper to taste, and enough matzo meal to make a moist, barely stiff dough—about a cup. Shape into balls and cover; refrigerate, preferably overnight,

PASSATELLI

but for at least an hour. Cook the matzo balls in abundant boiling salted water until expanded and set, about 30 minutes, then add them to the soup.

Sopa de Ajo al Tomate Garlic-Tomato Soup
CARIBBEAN

MAKES **4 SERVINGS**

TIME **40 MINUTES**

A staple of homes in Cuba and much of the rest of the Caribbean, where tomatoes are available year-round, this soup clearly derives from the classic Mediterranean "boiled water" (see the variation), a soup based on garlic, bread, and whatever else can be found. Despite its humble origins, this is a wonderful dish for entertaining (be sure to warn your guests that the bowls are hot!).

2 tablespoons extra virgin olive oil

6 garlic cloves, peeled

8 ripe plum tomatoes, peeled and chopped (canned are fine)

1 bay leaf

6 cups chicken or vegetable stock, preferably homemade (page 160 or 162), or water

Four 1-inch-thick slices French or Italian bread, at least a day old

4 eggs

Salt and black pepper to taste

2 tablespoons chopped fresh parsley leaves

1. Preheat the oven to 450°F. Place a large saucepan over medium-high heat. Add the olive oil and garlic cloves and cook, stirring occasionally, until the garlic is softened and lightly browned, about 5 minutes. Stir in the tomatoes and bay leaf and continue stirring until the tomatoes begin to break down, about 5 minutes. Pour in the chicken stock

and bring to a boil; lower the heat and simmer for 20 minutes. (You can prepare the dish up to this point and let sit for a few hours or cover and refrigerate for up to a day; reheat before proceeding.)

2. Meanwhile, prepare the soup bowls. Place the bread slices in the bottom of 4 individual heatproof dishes and then break an egg over each slice.

3. When the soup is ready, season with salt and pepper, then strain the soup into the individual bowls. Sprinkle the parsley on top of the soup and bake for 5 minutes. Serve piping hot.

"Boiled Water" PROVENCE. The meager, ultrasimplified version, which is still quite good. Omit the tomatoes and use water in place of stock. Omit the eggs; instead, toast the bread (better still, fry it on both sides in extra virgin olive oil). Finish with freshly grated Parmesan cheese.

Lime and Garlic Soup MEXICO. Omit the bread and eggs. Finish the simple soup with about $1/4$ cup chopped fresh cilantro leaves and loads of fresh lime juice.

Spinach and Chickpea Soup
PORTUGAL ■ ■

MAKES **4 SERVINGS**

TIME **AT LEAST 2 HOURS (FAR SHORTER WITH PRECOOKED OR CANNED CHICKPEAS)**

Most people seem to adore chickpeas, and one of their strongest attributes is that, unlike other dried legumes, they produce delicious cooking liquid. So if you lack stock for this dish, don't worry about it. But—and this is true for the several chickpea recipes that follow as well as this one—the cooking time for chickpeas is unpredictable. Cook the beans the day before you plan to make the soup if at all possible, or at least soak them for several hours to reduce the cooking time (or, in a pinch, use canned chickpeas). Once they're done, the cooking time is just a few minutes.

If you are so inclined, this soup remains equally authentic and becomes more substantial if you add $\frac{1}{2}$ to 1 pound browned sausage chunks. You can brown the sausage right before the onions, in the same skillet.

½ pound dried chickpeas or about 2 cups cooked

¼ cup extra virgin olive oil

1 large onion, chopped

3 garlic cloves, finely chopped

Salt and black pepper to taste

1 quart beef, chicken, or vegetable stock, preferably
   homemade (page 160 or 162), or water

1 pound fresh spinach, trimmed and coarsely chopped

Chopped fresh parsley leaves for garnish

1. If time allows, soak the chickpeas for several hours or overnight in water to cover. (If it does not, boil them for 2 minutes, then soak for 2 hours; or just start cooking them, unsoaked.) Place in a pot with fresh water to cover by at least 2 inches. Bring to a boil, turn down the heat, and simmer, covered, for at least 1 hour or until tender.

2. Put half of the oil in a deep skillet or casserole and turn the heat to medium-high. A minute later, add the onion, garlic, a large pinch of salt, and some pepper. Cook, stirring occasionally, until the onion softens and begins to brown, about 10 minutes. Reduce the heat to medium-low.

3. Add the stock, stir, and adjust the heat so the mixture simmers. Add the spinach, stir, and continue to cook while you proceed.

4. When the chickpeas are tender, remove them from the heat and drain them, reserving their cooking water. Puree half of the chickpeas, using a food

mill, an immersion blender, or an upright blender, adding enough of the reserved cooking water to keep the mixture moving smoothly. (Take care when pureeing hot liquid; it's best, if you have the time, to let the mixture cool to room temperature before pureeing. You may need to work in batches.)

5. Transfer the puree to the casserole containing the spinach, along with the remaining chickpeas. Cook for a few minutes longer, taste and adjust the seasonings, then garnish with parsley and serve.

Chickpeas in Their Own Broth, with Fried Bread Crumbs SPAIN ■
MAKES **4 SERVINGS**
TIME **30 MINUTES (WITH PRECOOKED CHICKPEAS)**

A soupy appetizer (you can make it a little drier if you like) and a good one, a terrific example of making something delicious out of a few scraps. You *must* cook dried chickpeas yourself for this one; canned chickpeas will not cut it. Likewise, you must make homemade bread crumbs. Do these two things and you will love this dish.

One hunk French or Italian bread a day or two old, about
   6 inches long

½ cup extra virgin olive oil

Salt and black pepper to taste

½ cup chopped dried chorizo, optional

3 cups cooked chickpeas (preceding recipe), with about
   2 cups of their cooking liquid (5 cups total)

1 tablespoon minced garlic

Chopped fresh parsley leaves for garnish

1. Roughly chop the bread and put it in a food processor; pulse until it is shredded, with no chunks larger than a pea, but most not much

smaller either. Put all but 2 tablespoons of the olive oil in a skillet over medium heat. Add the bread and a sprinkling of salt and cook, shaking the pan occasionally, until the crumbs are nicely browned, 5 to 10 minutes. Use a slotted spoon to remove the bread crumbs from the skillet (drain them on paper towels if you wish; I do not) and, if you're adding the chorizo, brown it lightly in the skillet.

2. Warm the chickpeas in their broth with the garlic and salt and pepper. Divide the soup among 4 bowls, then top with the bread crumbs and, if you're using it, the chorizo. Garnish with parsley, drizzle with the remaining olive oil, and serve.

Chickpea and Pasta Soup ITALY ■ ▓ ■

MAKES **4 SERVINGS**

TIME **30 MINUTES (WITH PRECOOKED CHICKPEAS)**

A substantial soup (if you use chicken stock instead of water, it will be even more so) and a perfect winter lunch or a solid dinner when teamed with a light grilled dish, like Grilled Swordfish Rémoulade (page 256) or "Grilled" Mackerel with Garlic and Rosemary (page 266). Remember, though, that chickpeas can take a long time to cook, so if you have any inkling you're going to make this soup, cook the chickpeas in advance. (Canned chickpeas are also good, or you can use lentils for speed; see the variation.) This soup can be refrigerated for a few days and reheated before serving, but it's best to add the pasta at the last minute.

3 tablespoons extra virgin olive oil, plus more to taste

2 garlic cloves, peeled and crushed

1 carrot, chopped

1 celery stalk, chopped

1 onion, chopped

1 teaspoon dried rosemary

2 cups cooked (page 431) or canned chickpeas, drained

¼ cup small pasta, like elbow macaroni or broken spaghetti

Salt and black pepper to taste

Fresh parsley sprigs, optional

1. Put the 3 tablespoons oil in a large saucepan or stockpot over medium-high heat. Add the garlic, carrot, celery, and onion and cook, stirring occasionally, until the vegetables are fragrant and softened, about 5 minutes. Add the rosemary and chickpeas and stir well. Pour in enough water to cover the chickpeas, cover, lower the heat, and simmer for 10 minutes.

2. Cool the mixture slightly if time allows (it's never a good idea to puree boiling hot mixtures if you can avoid it). Use a food mill, an immersion blender, or an upright blender to puree the mixture. If you are going to refrigerate the soup, do so now. If not, return it to the saucepan and reheat over low heat. Meanwhile, cook the pasta in boiling salted water until nearly tender; drain.

3. Just before serving, stir the pasta into the soup and reheat. Season with salt and pepper, garnish with parsley, and serve, drizzled with a little more olive oil.

Lentil and Pasta Soup. Add ½ cup canned plum tomatoes, chopped, with their juices, after the vegetables have softened. Cook for 5 minutes and then substitute 1 cup dried lentils (no need to soak) for the chickpeas. Stir well, add enough water to cover, cover the pot, and simmer for 30 minutes. Cook the pasta as in step 2 and proceed directly to step 3.

Chunky Chickpea and Pasta Soup. Do not puree the soup mixture. Instead, just add the cooked pasta before serving.

Pasta with Chickpeas. Add $^1/_2$ cup canned plum tomatoes, chopped, with their juices after the vegetables have softened. Cook for 5 minutes and add the cooked chickpeas. Do not add water to cover. Instead, continue stirring and cook over low heat for 10 minutes. Meanwhile, cook 1 cup short Italian pasta, like penne, rigatoni, or fusilli. Toss the cooked pasta with the chickpea mixture, season with salt and pepper, garnish with parsley, and serve.

Mediterranean Squash and Chickpea Soup MOROCCO ■ ■

MAKES **4 SERVINGS**

TIME **1$^1/_2$ HOURS, LARGELY UNATTENDED**

Brilliant orange pumpkinlike squash fill the vegetable stands of Morocco and most other Mediterranean countries every fall, and they show up in stews, couscous, pasta, and soups like this. You may find the same squash in the States, but butternut, acorn, or sugar pumpkin—pumpkin grown for flavor, not size—are perfect substitutes and easy enough to find. (Canned pumpkin is an acceptable if not ideal alternative; drain it well.) Make this up to a day in advance, reserving the cream and cilantro to add just before serving.

1 butternut or acorn squash or sugar pumpkin, about
    2 pounds

2 tablespoons butter

1 large onion, diced

1 large tomato, cored and chopped

2 cups cooked chickpeas (page 431) plus their liquid
    or one 14-ounce can, drained and liquid reserved

1 quart beef, chicken, or vegetable stock, preferably
    homemade (page 160 or 162), or water

Salt and black pepper to taste

$^1/_2$ teaspoon cayenne, or to taste

2 tablespoons heavy cream, sour cream, or yogurt,
    optional

$^1/_4$ cup chopped fresh cilantro leaves for garnish

1. Preheat the oven to 350°F. Cut the squash in half and put it in a casserole dish. Cover tightly with aluminum foil and bake until soft, about 1 hour. Remove from the oven, cool, and remove the seeds and strings. Scoop the pulp from the shell to a bowl.

2. While the squash is baking, melt the butter in a large saucepan over medium heat; add the onion and cook, stirring occasionally, until transparent, about 5 minutes. Stir in the tomato and cook until softened, about 5 minutes. Add the squash, half the chickpeas along with their liquid, and the stock. Bring to a boil, then remove from the heat.

3. Using an immersion or an upright blender or a food mill, puree the mixture until smooth. Add the remaining chickpeas, then season with salt and the peppers. Heat through just before serving, then garnish with the heavy cream if desired and cilantro.

Laotian-Style Squash Soup. Use coconut milk, homemade (page 584) or canned, in place of half of the stock. Omit the cream and stir 2 tablespoons fish sauce (see page 500) into the final pureed mixture. Garnish with cilantro and $^1/_4$ cup minced scallion.

Sopa de Habas Fava Bean Soup MEXICO

MAKES **4 SERVINGS**

TIME **1$^1/_2$ HOURS, LARGELY UNATTENDED**

When families in Mexico give up meat—either for Lent or for other reasons—they turn to soups like this one. You might have trouble finding fresh favas, though Latin markets frequently stock them, especially in spring, and I've even seen them at supermarkets in recent years. Their wonderful flavor has no exact match, but fresh peas are a good substitute. The best chile for this dish is the mildly hot dried chile negro; it's best when toasted, which is an easy enough process: put the chiles in a dry, ungreased skillet over medium heat and cook, turning as each side browns, until browned and fragrant, 5 to 10 minutes.

1 pound fresh fava beans or peas or ¹/₂ pound split dried
   fava beans, soaked overnight

6 cups beef, chicken, or vegetable stock, preferably
   homemade (page 160 or 162), or water

6 garlic cloves, sliced

1 large onion, chopped

2 tablespoons corn, grapeseed, or other neutral oil

3 tomatoes, cored and sliced

2 tablespoons cider vinegar

¹/₂ teaspoon dried oregano, preferably Mexican

Salt and black pepper to taste

¹/₂ cup fresh cilantro leaves, chopped

2 tablespoons fresh mint leaves, chopped

3 dried chiles, preferably chile negro, toasted, stemmed,
   seeded, and chopped

¹/₂ cup crumbled queso fresco or feta cheese, optional

1. Place the beans or peas, stock, and half the garlic and onion in a stockpot and bring to a boil. Turn the heat to low and simmer for 40 minutes, or until the beans are soft. If you are using dried beans, cook for at least an hour and add water if the liquid level begins to run low.

2. Meanwhile, in a large skillet, heat the oil over medium heat. Cook the remaining garlic and onion, stirring occasionally, until soft, about 5 minutes. Add the tomatoes and cook until softened, about 5 minutes. Add the vinegar and oregano and cook for 2 minutes, or until the sauce in the pan is slightly thickened.

3. Add the tomato mixture to the beans and stir well to combine. Simmer for another 10 minutes, stirring occasionally and mashing some of the beans to create a somewhat smooth consistency. Season with salt and pepper.

4. Stir in the cilantro, mint, chiles, and cheese if you like and serve immediately.

Pancotta ITALY

MAKES **4 SERVINGS**
TIME **40 MINUTES**

There are as many versions of pancotta—cooked bread—as there are towns in Italy (and, it seems sometimes, Italian Americans); so feel free to improvise. Some versions are quite dry, some incorporate cooked white beans, and some are run under the broiler just before serving, just to give you a few ideas. This is the perfect way to use leftover bread, though you can also make it with fresh bread.

3 tablespoons extra virgin olive oil

3 garlic cloves, minced

¹/₄ cup chopped fresh parsley leaves

1 dried hot chile, stemmed and crumbled, optional

4 thick slices Italian bread, cut into 1-inch cubes

5 cups beef, chicken, or vegetable stock, preferably
   homemade (page 160 or 162), or water

Salt and black pepper to taste

Freshly grated pecorino Romano or Parmesan cheese, to
   taste

1. Place the oil in a large saucepan over medium heat. Add the garlic, parsley, and chile if using and cook, stirring constantly, until fragrant, about 1

minute. Add the bread and cook, stirring occasionally, until it turns golden, about 5 minutes.

2. Pour the stock into the saucepan and simmer, uncovered, for 30 minutes; the mixture should be quite thick. Season with salt and pepper, then serve warm or at room temperature with the freshly grated cheese.

Chestnut Soup ITALY

MAKES **4 SERVINGS**

TIME **45 MINUTES (WITH PRECOOKED CHESTNUTS)**

Throughout the northern Mediterranean littoral, chestnuts not only grow on trees; they fall to the ground each autumn and are, for many people, a free crop. (They once did the same on this continent, but a blight wiped them out.) The first fall I visited northern Italy, I saw them drop and realized there were more than anyone could possibly eat. As a result, they are used in a much wider array of dishes there than they are here.

This is a rich soup, one that can be made in a matter of minutes with cooked, frozen, or even canned chestnuts, and the results are inevitably good. Add a little splash of port just before serving to give this a bit of a kick.

2 tablespoons butter

1 onion, chopped

1½ pounds fresh chestnuts, boiled and peeled (page 453), or 2 cups thawed frozen or canned chestnuts, drained and rinsed

1 quart beef, chicken, or vegetable stock, preferably homemade (page 160 or 162), or water

Salt and black pepper to taste

½ cup heavy cream, or more to taste

1. Melt the butter in a large saucepan over medium heat, add the onion, and cook until softened and translucent, about 5 minutes. Add the chestnuts and stock and simmer until the chestnuts are very soft, about 30 minutes. (You can prepare the soup up to this point and let sit for a few hours or cover and refrigerate for up to a couple of days.)

2. Cool the mixture slightly if time allows (it's never a good idea to puree boiling hot mixtures if you can avoid it). Use a food mill, an immersion blender, or an upright blender to puree the mixture. Return the soup to the saucepan and reheat it over low heat. Season with salt and pepper. Stir in the cream and serve immediately.

Peanut Soup CARIBBEAN ▧

MAKES **4 SERVINGS**

TIME **20 MINUTES**

This unusual soup is popular in the Dutch Caribbean and the island of St. Kitts, where peanuts are called—as they are in much of the world—groundnuts. Though many groundnuts have a stronger flavor than American varieties, you can use any unsalted roasted peanuts—or even peanut butter—in this rich soup.

2 cups unsalted roasted peanuts or 1 cup peanut butter

1 medium onion, peeled and quartered

1 quart chicken or vegetable stock, preferably homemade (page 162)

1 cup milk or heavy cream

Salt to taste

Cayenne, hot red pepper flakes, or Tabasco sauce to taste

1. Place the peanuts in a food processor and process until the mixture is smooth and buttery, stopping the machine to scrape down the sides as necessary.

If you are using peanut butter, just place it in the processor. Add the onion and process until well combined. With the machine running, pour in the stock.

2. Transfer the peanut mixture to a saucepan and place over medium-low heat. Simmer until the mixture thickens, about 7 minutes. Slowly stir in the milk, then season with salt and cayenne. Serve with simple crackers.

Plantain Soup CARIBBEAN ■

MAKES **4 SERVINGS**

TIME **45 MINUTES**

An unusual and quite useful plantain recipe, usually associated with Cuba. Like many soups, this one can be made in advance and reheated, though you'll probably want to add a little more lime juice just before serving for freshness. See page 623 for information on plantains.

> 2 green plantains, peeled (page 623) and cut into chunks
>
> 1 tablespoon fresh lime juice, or to taste
>
> 6 cups beef, chicken, or vegetable stock, preferably homemade (page 160 or 162)
>
> 1 garlic clove, peeled and crushed
>
> Cayenne or hot red pepper flakes to taste, optional
>
> Salt and black pepper to taste

1. Place the plantains, lime juice, stock, and garlic in a large saucepan over medium-high heat and bring to a boil. Turn the heat to low and simmer until the plantains are very soft, about 30 minutes.

2. Use a slotted spoon to transfer the plantains and garlic to a food processor or blender and process, gradually adding just enough broth, about 1 cup, to make a smooth paste. Pour the paste back into the saucepan and whisk over low heat until the soup is thickened and heated through. Season with cayenne if desired and salt and pepper and serve hot.

Thin Plantain Soup. This is more of a broth than a creamy puree: Instead of slicing the plantains, grate them. Place all the ingredients in a large saucepan, bring to a boil, and then simmer for 30 minutes. Strain and serve with lime wedges (garnish with cilantro if you have it).

Chunky Plantain Soup. No straining or pureeing here: Instead of slicing the plantains, grate them; mince the garlic. Place all the ingredients in a large saucepan, bring to a boil, and then simmer for 30 minutes. Stir well and serve.

PEELING PLANTAINS

FISH SOUPS

Fish stock (page 161) is delicious and far quicker and easier to make than chicken or meat stock. It improves most fish soups, but it's rarely essential. What is essential, as with all dishes containing fish, is freshness; see page 206 for a discussion of this.

Unlike most soups, fish soups are usually best prepared at the last minute, because many fish—especially finfish—overcook in the heat of a soup. You can often make the base one day and add the fish the next, but as a group these are so quick and easy that there isn't much point.

West Lake Fish Soup CHINA ■

MAKES **4 SERVINGS**

TIME **30 MINUTES**

Quite similar to the beef soup recipe on page 145, except at the outset, when shallots are browned to give the soup a little extra color and complexity.

> 2 tablespoons peanut or neutral oil like corn or grapeseed
>
> $\frac{1}{2}$ cup chopped shallot or onion
>
> 6 cups chicken or other stock, preferably homemade (pages 160–163)
>
> 3 tablespoons soy sauce, or to taste
>
> 1 teaspoon black pepper, or more to taste
>
> 1 cup fresh or thawed frozen peas
>
> $\frac{3}{4}$ to 1 pound skinless white fish fillets, like flounder, roughly chopped
>
> 2 tablespoons cornstarch
>
> 2 egg whites, lightly beaten
>
> 1 cup chopped fresh cilantro leaves
>
> Salt to taste

1. Put the oil in a saucepan large enough to contain all the ingredients and turn the heat to medium. A minute later, add the shallot and cook, stirring occasionally, adjusting the heat to prevent burning, until golden brown, about 10 minutes.
2. Add all but $\frac{1}{4}$ cup of the stock and turn the heat to medium-high. When it begins to steam, add the soy sauce, pepper, peas, and fish and cook at a gentle simmer (adjust the heat as necessary), stirring occasionally, until the peas are tender and the fish falling apart, 5 to 10 minutes. Mix the remaining $\frac{1}{4}$ cup stock with the cornstarch in a small bowl.
3. Drizzle in the egg whites, stirring constantly with a whisk or chopsticks. Stir in the cornstarch mixture. When the soup thickens, stir in the cilantro. Taste and add more pepper or soy sauce if you like and salt if necessary. Serve immediately.

Mussel Soup FRANCE ■

MAKES **4 SERVINGS**

TIME **30 MINUTES (WITH CLEANED MUSSELS)**

This delicate soup is classy yet simple, and leaving the mussels in their shells makes for a beautiful presentation; a touch of cream is a nice addition but an optional one. Serve this with a loaf of good, crusty bread; soaking the bread in the broth is one of this dish's great pleasures.

You can transform this into an entree, using pasta; see the variation.

> 4 pounds mussels, picked through and cleaned (page 208)
>
> 2 shallots, sliced
>
> 2 cups dry white wine
>
> 3 tablespoons butter or extra virgin olive oil
>
> 2 leeks, white and light green parts only, sliced and well rinsed
>
> 2 garlic cloves, minced
>
> Large pinch of saffron

¼ teaspoon cayenne, or to taste, optional

½ cup heavy cream, optional

1 tablespoon fresh lemon juice, plus more to taste

Salt and black pepper to taste

Chopped fresh basil or chervil leaves for garnish, optional

1. Put the mussels, shallots, and wine in a saucepan and turn the heat to high. Cover and cook, shaking the pan occasionally, just until the mussels open, about 5 minutes. Remove them from the broth with a slotted spoon, then strain the broth through cheesecloth or a fine strainer and set aside.

2. Melt the butter in a saucepan over medium heat. Add the leeks and cook until fragrant and softened, about 5 minutes. Stir in the garlic and crumble the saffron into the saucepan. Pour in the reserved mussel broth, the cayenne if you're using it, and enough water to make about 5 cups of soup; add the cream if you're using it. Bring just to a boil, then turn off the heat and season with lemon juice, salt, and pepper.

3. Arrange the mussels in soup bowls and pour the hot broth over them. Garnish with the basil or chervil if desired and serve.

Pasta in Mussel Broth. Cook ½ pound cut pasta, like penne, in salted boiling water until tender but not mushy, about 8 minutes. Add the pasta to the mussel soup, garnish, and serve.

Crab Soup, Korean Style KOREA ■

MAKES **4 SERVINGS**

TIME **30 MINUTES**

This is just about the best crab soup I have ever tasted, and it's also the easiest. (One of the messiest, too; you must eat the crab with your hands.)

At its base is miso, combined with go chu jang, a red pepper paste mixed with beans, kind of a spicy version of hoisin sauce. If you live anywhere near a Korean market, you'll find it; if not, use hoisin mixed with Tabasco.

Buy the crabs live and have them cleaned and chopped up by the fishmonger. Or follow the directions for cleaning them in step 1.

6 blue or rock crabs

2 tablespoons dark miso

2 tablespoons light miso

2 tablespoons minced garlic

1 tablespoon go chu jang or 1 tablespoon hoisin sauce
mixed with 1 teaspoon Tabasco or other hot sauce

About 4 cups cooked short-grain white rice (page 507)

1. If you must clean the crabs yourself, bring a large pot of water to a boil. Plunge the crabs in and cook for just a minute. Drain in a colander and rinse under cold water. Working over a bowl (and saving any liquids or soft parts of the crab that come out during cleaning), break off the "apron," the triangle of shell on the crab's bottom, then remove the upper shell entirely (save any innards attached to it). On each side of the crab you will find the gills—spongy and off-white—remove and discard. Now cut the crab into quarters. To make eating easier, use the back of your knife to crack the claws.

2. In a saucepan, whisk the next 4 ingredients with 1 quart water; bring to a boil, stirring. Add the crabs, cover, and cook at a steady boil for about 20 minutes; during the last 5 minutes of cooking, add any parts of the crab you reserved during cleaning.

3. Serve the broth with a few pieces of crab in it; when people have eaten the crabs, clean up the shells and add the rice to the broth. Eat the rice.

Clam Soup JAPAN, KOREA ▪

MAKES **4 SERVINGS**

TIME **20 MINUTES**

This soup is incredibly simple and quick and as different from American clam chowder as it could possibly be. Rather than overwhelming the flavor of the clams with cream or tomatoes, here the seaside flavors of the clams are accented subtly with a seaweed-based broth. More on seaweed on page 483.

Use the smallest hardshell clams you can find (do not use steamers) and, before cooking, discard clams with broken shells or shells that are not tightly closed. Be sure to wash the clams thoroughly—no trace of sand should remain on their shells. Any clams that do not open during the cooking process can be pried open with a dull knife at the table.

1/4 **pound dried kombu (kelp), rinsed**

24 **small clams, like littlenecks or mahogany clams, or**
   cockles, scrubbed and washed well

4 **scallions, trimmed and cut into 2-inch lengths**

1 **tablespoon sake or mirin or 1 teaspoon honey**

2 **tablespoons soy sauce**

1 **teaspoon dark sesame oil**

Salt to taste

1. Combine 5 cups water and the kombu in a large saucepan; turn the heat to medium and cook the kombu until tender, about 10 minutes, never letting the water come to a full boil. Remove and discard the kombu and add the clams, then cook just until the clams open, about 5 minutes.

2. Stir in the scallions, sake, soy sauce, sesame oil, and salt; taste and adjust the seasoning. Serve immediately.

Hot and Sour Fish Soup SOUTHEAST ASIA

MAKES **4 SERVINGS**

TIME **40 MINUTES**

Unlike the viscous and peppery Chinese version of this soup on page 145, this one is brothlike and derives its heat from chiles and its intriguing sour flavor from lime and lemongrass. It's the Southeast Asian equivalent of chicken soup, often eaten to treat a cold. See page 500 for information on nam pla.

1 **tablespoon corn, grapeseed, or other neutral oil**

2 **garlic cloves, sliced**

2 **shallots, sliced**

1 **pound shrimp, peeled, shells reserved**

6 **cups fish or chicken stock, preferably homemade**
   (page 161 or 160), or water

3 **lemongrass stalks, trimmed, smashed, and cut into**
   2-inch lengths (page 143)

One 3-inch piece fresh galangal or ginger, sliced and
   smashed

4 **fresh chiles, or to taste, preferably Thai, stemmed,**
   seeded, and chopped, or hot red pepper flakes to taste

4 **lime leaves, preferably fresh, minced**

1 **tablespoon grated lime zest**

1 **cup trimmed and sliced button mushrooms**

1 **cup fresh or canned sliced bamboo shoots, drained if**
   canned,

2 **tablespoons nam pla**

1 **tablespoons fresh lime juice**

2 **teaspoons sugar**

1/4 **cup chopped fresh cilantro leaves or scallion for**
   garnish

Lime wedges

1. Put the oil in a large saucepan and turn the heat to medium. A minute later, add the garlic and shallots and cook until softened, stirring occasionally, 3 to 5 minutes. Add the reserved shrimp shells and

cook, stirring occasionally, until they turn pink, about 2 minutes.

2. Add the stock, lemongrass, galangal, chiles, lime leaves, and lime zest; turn the heat to high and bring to a boil. Lower the heat and simmer, uncovered, for about 20 minutes.

3. Carefully strain the stock; return it to the saucepan and bring to a boil. Add the shrimp and turn the heat to low; cook until the shrimp turn pink, 3 to 5 minutes. Add the mushrooms and bamboo shoots and simmer for another minute.

4. Remove from the heat and stir in the nam pla, lime juice, and sugar. Stir, taste and adjust the seasoning, then garnish with cilantro or scallion and serve with the lime wedges.

Bourride Fish Stew with Aïoli
PROVENCE/LIGURIA ■
MAKES **4 SERVINGS**
TIME **1 HOUR**

A simple version of Bouillabaisse (page 138) that uses only one type of fish and is thickened by aïoli, the wonderful garlicky mayonnaise of Provence and Liguria (also called "the Italian Riviera"). Ask your fishmonger to gut and fillet the fish and to give you the head and bones for the stock, which of course can be made in advance. (Within limits you can use as many heads and bones as you like. See Fish Stock, page 161.) Serve this stew with crusty bread and a salad.

2 tablespoons butter or extra virgin olive oil

1 onion, chopped

3 pounds firm-fleshed fish, like red snapper or sea bass, gutted, filleted, and skinned, bones and heads reserved

3 tablespoons extra virgin olive oil

2 leeks, white and light green parts only, chopped and well rinsed

1 pound Swiss chard leaves or spinach, well rinsed and chopped

1 cup Aïoli (page 603) or to taste

Salt and black pepper to taste

Chopped fresh parsley or chervil leaves for garnish

1. Melt the butter in a large saucepan or stockpot over medium-high heat. Add the onion and cook, stirring occasionally, until softened and translucent, about 5 minutes. Raise the heat to high and add the fish bones and heads; cook, stirring occasionally, for another 5 minutes or so. Add 6 cups water, bring to a boil, then reduce the heat so the mixture bubbles a bit and simmer for about 30 minutes, skimming any foam from the surface. Strain the mixture.

2. Meanwhile, heat the 3 tablespoons olive oil in a large saucepan over medium-high heat and add the leeks; cook, stirring occasionally, until softened and browned lightly, about 5 minutes. Stir in the chard; add 1 cup of the fish stock, then cover and cook for another 5 minutes.

3. Add about half of the remaining stock and bring to a boil; reduce the heat so that the mixture barely simmers, then add the fish. Poach until just cooked through, 10 minutes (the fish is done when easily pierced with a thin-bladed knife; try not to overcook).

4. Whisk 1/2 cup aïoli into the remaining stock, then gently stir the mixture into the soup. Season with salt and pepper, garnish with the herb, and serve, passing more aïoli at the table.

Bouillabaisse PROVENCE ∎

MAKES **8 SERVINGS**

TIME **1 HOUR**

Every seaside culture has its own fish stew, but in the West, bouillabaisse is the best known. Older recipes are quite specific about the kind of fish and the technique, but in my experience bouillabaisse, no matter how wonderful, is neither more nor less than a highly seasoned soup made with the day's catch. So vary this recipe according to what you find at the store (or what you bring home from a day's fishing).

> 1 tablespoon extra virgin olive oil
>
> 2 medium onions, roughly chopped
>
> 1 navel or other orange
>
> 1 tablespoon fennel seeds
>
> Large pinch of saffron, optional
>
> 1 small dried chile or a pinch of cayenne, or to taste
>
> 2 cups chopped tomatoes (drained canned are fine)
>
> 1 to 1½ pounds monkfish, catfish, or blackfish, cut into 1-inch cubes
>
> 3 pounds small hardshell (littleneck or mahogany) clams, cockles, or mussels, well washed
>
> 1 to 1½ pounds peeled shrimp or scallops, cut into bite-sized pieces if necessary
>
> 1 to 1½ pounds cod or other delicate white fish, cut into 6 large chunks
>
> 1 tablespoon minced garlic
>
> ½ cup roughly chopped parsley leaves

1. Put the olive oil in a flameproof casserole or large saucepan over medium heat. Add the onions and cook, stirring occasionally, until softened, about 5 minutes. Meanwhile, use a vegetable peeler to strip the zest from the orange (save the orange itself for another use). Add the zest, fennel, saffron, and chile or cayenne and cook for about a minute. Add the tomatoes and turn the heat to medium-high. When the mixture boils, reduce the heat to medium and cook, stirring occasionally, until the mixture becomes saucelike, 10 to 15 minutes. (You can prepare the dish several hours ahead up to this point; cover and set aside until you're ready to proceed.)

2. Add the monkfish and raise heat to medium-high. When the mixture begins to boil, reduce heat to medium-low and cook, stirring occasionally, until fish is just about tender, 10 minutes or so.

3. Add the clams, raise the heat to high, and stir; when the mixture boils, reduce heat to low, cover, and cook until clams begin to open, 5 to 10 minutes. Add the shrimp or scallops and white fish, stir, and cover; cook, stirring gently once or twice, until the fish is just about done (a thin-bladed knife will pierce it with little resistance), about 5 minutes. (If the mixture is very thick—there should be some broth—add a cup or so of hot water.) Stir in the garlic and cook for 1 minute more. Stir in the parsley and serve, with crusty bread.

MEAT SOUPS

These soups can be big meals in themselves or surprisingly light and quick. Of all the categories of soup, these are the ones where you are safest using water in place of stock, because the long simmering times and the presence of meat virtually guarantee that you'll wind up with a flavorful broth.

Caldo Cantina Chicken-Rice Soup MEXICO ∎

MAKES **4 SERVINGS**

TIME **40 MINUTES**

A great place to use leftovers and to improvise. Plenty of lime, raw onion, and cilantro are key; if you include them in abundance, the soup will be delicious and authentic.

Though I have never seen it in Mexico, you could use vegetable stock here if you prefer.

6 cups chicken stock, preferably homemade (page 160)

1/4 cup long-grain rice

Salt and black pepper to taste

1 cup diced fresh tomato

1/2 cup minced onion, preferably white

1 cup diced cooked chicken, optional

1/4 cup fresh lime juice, or to taste

1/2 cup roughly chopped fresh cilantro leaves, or more to taste

Minced fresh jalapeños or other chiles to taste, optional

1. Put the stock in a medium saucepan and bring it to a boil over medium-high heat. Add the rice along with some salt and pepper and lower the heat so the mixture just bubbles. Cook, stirring occasionally, until the rice is quite tender, about 20 minutes.

2. Meanwhile, combine the vegetables with the chicken if you're using it, lime juice, cilantro, and chiles if you're using them, in the bottom of 1 large or 4 small bowls. When the soup is ready, ladle it over the vegetables and spices, taste and adjust the seasoning if necessary, and serve.

Chicken Soup with Chipotle Paste

MEXICO ■ ▨

MAKES **4 SERVINGS**

TIME **30 MINUTES**

A staple in Mexico, often garnished with diced raw onion, avocado, tomato, and a squeeze of lime. You can make the chipotle paste by buying canned chipotles in adobo (sold at almost all Latin markets and many supermarkets) and simply whizzing them in a blender. The results, however, are searingly, blindingly hot and not at all like what you get in restaurants in Mexico, where the paste is made from scratch.

Fortunately, making the paste from scratch takes all of 20 minutes, 10 of which are spent soaking dried chipotles (available at most places that sell dried chiles or online at www.penzeys.com and other mail-order sources). The lovely brick-red paste, used in small quantities, converts the blandest chicken soup into something hot, smoky, and delicious. Leftover paste is also great on broiled or grilled chicken or pork or stirred—again, in small quantities—into poached or steamed vegetables.

7 cups chicken stock, preferably homemade (page 159)

2 medium carrots, cut into 1/4-inch dice

2 celery stalks, cut into 1/4-inch dice

1 medium to large onion, cut into 1/4-inch dice

4 to 6 dried chipotles, to taste

1/3 cup long-grain rice

Salt and black pepper to taste

2 garlic cloves, peeled

2 tablespoons tomato paste

1 teaspoon dried oregano

1. Put the stock in a saucepan with the carrots, celery, and onion; bring to a boil. Soak the chipotles in just-boiled water to cover for 10 minutes. Reduce the heat so the stock simmers steadily and, when the carrots are just about tender, add the rice, salt, and pepper and stir. Bring back to a boil and continue to simmer.

2. When the chipotles are soft, remove them from the liquid; open them up on a cutting board and, using the back of a knife, scrape out all the seeds and stems. Combine the chiles in a blender with the garlic, tomato paste, oregano, and a large pinch of salt. Add either sufficient chicken stock (you can use some from the simmering soup) or, if

you're extremely heat-tolerant, the soaking liquid, to allow the blender to puree the chiles and other ingredients well.

3. When the rice is tender—this will take about 20 minutes—taste the soup and adjust the seasoning. Divide among 4 soup bowls, passing the chipotle paste at the table and warning your fellow diners about its intense heat.

Ajiaco Creamy Chicken Soup with Vegetables
COLOMBIA ■

MAKES **4 SERVINGS**

TIME **1½ HOURS, LARGELY UNATTENDED**

This popular soup—a fun dish for a casual meal since the corn is left on the cob—is traditionally seasoned with the fragrant local herb guascas. Unfortunately, I've only rarely seen guascas in the States, so I use a combination of cumin and thyme, which approximates the real thing.

Fortunately, you can often find yucca, also known as cassava, at most major supermarkets. This root vegetable, native to South America and largely grown in Africa and the Caribbean, has a subtle sweetness, not unlike yams. If you can find it, try the variation. Serve with arepas (page 575) or crusty bread.

3 tablespoons butter

1 tablespoon neutral oil, like corn or grapeseed

2 pounds boneless, skinless chicken thighs, cut into
   2-inch pieces

1 medium onion, chopped

1 teaspoon ground cumin

2 teaspoons fresh thyme leaves or 1 teaspoon dried

4 medium potatoes, peeled and cut into ½-inch cubes

Salt and black pepper to taste

5 cups chicken stock, preferably homemade (page 160)

2 ears yellow corn, shucked and cut crosswise into 2-inch
   pieces

1 cup heavy cream

2 tablespoons drained capers

1 ripe avocado, peeled, pitted, and sliced

1. Combine the butter and oil in a large flameproof casserole or saucepan over medium-high heat. When the butter foam subsides, add the chicken and brown it, turning the pieces as they brown, 5 to 10 minutes. Stir in the onion and cook until softened, about 5 minutes.

2. Stir in the cumin and thyme, followed by the potatoes and a liberal sprinkling of salt and pepper; stir until the vegetables are coated with oil and spices. Add the chicken stock, bring the mixture to a boil, then turn the heat to low, cover partially, and let the stew cook for about 30 minutes.

3. Add the corn and cook just until tender, about 10 minutes. Use a wooden spoon to crush some of the potato pieces against the side of the casserole to thicken the soup.

4. Divide the cream and capers among 4 serving bowls. Ladle the soup over the cream and capers, top with avocado slices, and serve immediately.

Ajiaco with Yucca. Substitute 1 large yucca, peeled and cut into ½-inch cubes, for 2 of the potatoes.

Chicken and Watercress Soup
CHINA ▩

MAKES **4 SERVINGS**

TIME **15 MINUTES**

One of the many recipes that bridge the short distance between Chinese and Italian cooking. The main recipe makes a light soup that complements stir-fry dishes well; the Italian variation is substantial enough to serve as a light main course.

½ pound boneless, skinless chicken breasts, cut into thin shreds

2 teaspoons Shaoxing wine or dry sherry

6 cups chicken stock, preferably homemade (page 160)

½ pound watercress, trimmed

Salt to taste

2 teaspoons dark sesame oil

2 scallions, trimmed and finely chopped

1. Put the chicken in a bowl with the wine to marinate while you bring the chicken stock to a boil in a large saucepan. Add the chicken with its marinade, reduce the heat to low, and simmer until the chicken loses its pinkness, about 3 minutes.
2. Add the watercress and simmer until softened, about 5 minutes. Remove the soup from the heat and season with salt and sesame oil. Serve hot, garnished with the scallions.

Chicken and Watercress Soup with Parmesan ITALY. Marinate the chicken in the wine, but omit the sesame oil and scallions. When the chicken is done, stir about ⅛ teaspoon freshly grated nutmeg and 1 cup freshly grated Parmesan into the soup. Serve, passing more Parmesan at the table.

Cream-Style Corn Soup CHINA ■

MAKES **4 SERVINGS**

TIME **15 MINUTES**

This soup has become popular in the kitchens of Chinese Americans in the past few decades. It's best, of course, when you start by making creamed corn (see

the second variation), but canned creamed corn—a concoction that Americans of various ethnicities and generations have long enjoyed (sometimes in secret)—allows you to make this tasty soup quickly at any time of year. See page 500 for information on Thai fish sauce (nam pla).

2 tablespoons corn, grapeseed, or other neutral oil

2 garlic cloves, sliced

3 shallots, sliced

3 cups chicken stock, preferably homemade (page 159)

½ pound shredded crabmeat, diced peeled shrimp, or diced boneless, skinless chicken breast

1 tablespoon nam pla or soy sauce

1 tablespoon Shaoxing wine or dry sherry

One 15-ounce can creamed corn

2 eggs, lightly beaten

½ cup chopped fresh cilantro leaves or scallion, optional

1. Heat the oil in a large saucepan over medium heat. Add the garlic and shallots and cook, stirring occasionally, until softened, 3 to 5 minutes. Add the chicken stock and bring to a boil; then add the crabmeat. Lower the heat to medium and cook for about 2 minutes, until nearly done.
2. Stir in the nam pla, wine, and corn. While stirring, pour in the eggs in a slow stream so they cook in thin strands. Garnish if you like and serve immediately.

Vegetarian Cream-Style Corn Soup. Substitute vegetable stock (page 162) for the chicken stock. Omit the meat.

Fresh Corn Cream-Style Corn Soup. This will take a little longer. Shuck 8 ears of corn and use a knife to slice off the kernels; reserve. Place the ears in a stockpot and cover with 6 cups water. Bring to a boil, then lower the heat and simmer, covered, for about 30 minutes; strain, reserving the liquid. Place half the kernels and half the corn stock in a blender or food processor and puree until not quite smooth. Use the remaining corn stock in place of the chicken stock in the recipe, adding the remaining kernels along with the meat; use the puree in place of the cream-style corn. Good with a cup of heavy or sour cream stirred in during the last minute or two of cooking.

Chicken and Egg Soup KOREA ▨ ■

MAKES **4 SERVINGS**

TIME **20 MINUTES**

Much like the Egg Flower Soup (and Stracciatella variation) on page 115, but far more substantial and suitable as a main course. This is a perfect soup for a cold winter night; many Koreans would add considerably more garlic and a bit of ground hot pepper as well.

> 5 cups chicken stock, preferably homemade (page 160)
>
> 2 tablespoons corn, grapeseed, or other neutral oil
>
> 4 eggs, beaten
>
> 1 pound chicken breasts or thighs, skinned, boned, and cut into 1-inch chunks
>
> 1 garlic clove, peeled and crushed, or more to taste
>
> 3 scallions, trimmed and cut into 2-inch lengths
>
> 1 tablespoon soy sauce
>
> 1 teaspoon dark sesame oil
>
> Salt and black pepper to taste
>
> Tabasco sauce or cayenne to taste, optional
>
> 2 tablespoons toasted sesame seeds (page 596)

1. Bring the chicken stock to a boil in a medium saucepan. Meanwhile, heat the oil in an 8- or 10-inch skillet, preferably nonstick, over medium-high heat. Add the eggs and spread out thinly into a circle. When the eggs are cooked through and set, carefully flip them over and cook just until the other side is lightly browned. Remove from the heat, cool, cut into thin strips, and set aside.

2. When the stock is boiling, add the chicken and garlic and simmer until the chicken is cooked through and tender, about 10 minutes. Stir in the scallions, soy sauce, sesame oil, salt and pepper, and, if you like, hot sauce or cayenne. Ladle into soup bowls; top with the egg strips and sesame seeds and serve.

Dom Yam Gai Chicken and Coconut Soup

THAILAND ■

MAKES **4 SERVINGS**

TIME **40 MINUTES**

The subtle blend of sweet, creamy, and sharp flavors in this Thai classic makes it one of the first Thai dishes most people learn to love. Although the best version I ever had began with cracking real coconuts—a chore I wouldn't wish on an enemy—if you make coconut milk from dried coconut or use canned coconut milk, the dish is easy to re-create at home and really great. For information on Thai fish sauce (nam pla), see page 500.

Lemongrass

Lemongrass, which looks like a long, tough scallion, is usually used in one of two ways: It is bruised all over (use the back of a chef's knife), then tossed into stews or other dishes, whole or chopped into easier-to-handle lengths. It flavors dishes this way, and you can gnaw on it after it's cooked, but you can't chew it.

Alternatively, trim the ends and peel off as many of the outer layers as necessary (use a small knife to make a lengthwise slit to make this easier) until the relatively tender inner core is exposed. Mince this, or, if a small food processor is handy, chop it and then mince it in the food processor. Expect each stalk to yield a tablespoon, at most, of minced lemongrass.

---

1 quart coconut milk, homemade (page 584) or canned

1 cup chicken stock, preferably homemade (page 160)

1 pound boneless, skinless chicken breast or thigh, cut into 1-inch strips

3 lemongrass stalks, trimmed, smashed, and cut into 2-inch lengths (page 143)

10 nickel-sized slices of fresh ginger

2 fresh chiles, preferably Thai, stemmed, seeded, and minced, or hot red pepper flakes to taste

4 lime leaves, preferably fresh, roughly chopped

1 cup sliced button mushrooms or drained canned straw mushrooms

3 tablespoons nam pla

3 tablespoons fresh lime juice

1 teaspoon sugar

Salt and black pepper to taste

1/4 cup chopped fresh cilantro leaves, optional

1. Combine the coconut milk and stock in a large saucepan, turn the heat to medium-high, and bring to a boil. Lower the heat a bit, add the chicken pieces, and simmer until cooked through, about 10 minutes. Remove the chicken with a slotted spoon and set aside.

2. Add the lemongrass, ginger, chiles, and lime leaves; simmer for 15 minutes. Remove the larger pieces of spices with a slotted spoon. Return the chicken to the saucepan along with the mushrooms and heat through, about 3 minutes. (You can prepare the dish up to this point and let sit for a few hours or cover and refrigerate for up to a day before reheating and proceeding.) Turn off the heat and stir in the nam pla, lime juice, and sugar. Season with salt and pepper, garnish with the cilantro if desired, and serve.

Sopa de Tortilla Tortilla Soup MEXICO

MAKES **4 SERVINGS**

TIME **1 HOUR**

This classic Mexican soup is the perfect solution for leftovers—stale tortillas, cold chicken, and overly ripe tomatoes. It can be garnished with a variety of toppings, from the classic avocado and cheese to steamed greens.

1/2 cup corn, grapeseed, or other neutral oil

6 corn tortillas (stale are fine), cut into 1/4-inch strips

3 garlic cloves, sliced

1 large onion, diced

2 dried chiles, preferably pasilla, stemmed, seeded, and sliced

---

■ make ahead　　■ serve at room temp./cold　　■ 30 minutes or less　　■ main course　　SOUPS　　**143**

3 fresh tomatoes, roasted (page 493) or blanched and
   peeled, or canned tomatoes
6 cups chicken or vegetable stock, preferably homemade
   (page 160 or 162)
1 cup shredded cooked chicken
2 tablespoons fresh lime juice, or to taste
Salt and black pepper to taste
1 cup chopped fresh cilantro leaves
1 cup cubed Mexican fresh cheese, such as queso fresco,
   blanco, or ranchero (see page 85), or Monterey Jack
   cheese
1 ripe avocado, peeled, pitted, and sliced

1. Put the oil in a saucepan over medium-high heat; a couple of minutes later, when the oil is hot, begin to fry the tortilla strips in batches until golden brown and crisp, turning after a minute or two, for a total of 2 to 4 minutes. Drain on paper towels and set aside.

2. Discard all but 2 tablespoons of the oil. Turn the heat to medium, add the garlic and onion, and cook, stirring occasionally, until softened, about 5 minutes. Add the chiles, tomatoes, and half the tortilla strips and cook for another 5 minutes. Pour in the chicken stock and bring the mixture to a boil, then simmer for 20 minutes. (You can prepare the soup up to this point and let sit for a few hours or cover and refrigerate for up to a day before proceeding.)

3. Cool slightly. Using an immersion blender or an upright blender (be careful to prevent spattering), puree the mixture until smooth. Return to the stove over medium heat, stir in the chicken, and heat through. Season with the lime juice, salt, and pepper. Garnish with the cilantro, cheese, avocado, and remaining tortilla strips and serve.

Caldo Gallego SPAIN ■ ■
MAKES **4 SERVINGS AS A MAIN COURSE, 6 AS A STARTER**
TIME **1 1/2 HOURS, LARGELY UNATTENDED**

Galicia's hearty bean and meat stew makes a terrific one-pot meal but is often served in cups as a starter. The rich flavors of the meat and beans are complemented by the sharp turnip and greens.

In Galicia, the meat base is made from unto, a cured pork belly that I would tell you how to find if I knew. It's not unlike pancetta but most like the fatty part of prosciutto, which would make a great substitute; salt pork or bacon is also fine—here I use a combination.

There are as many ways to vary Caldo Gallego as there are to vary beef stew. For example, substitute chickpeas for the white beans; add chunks of pork shoulder, ribs, beef brisket, shin, chuck, or oxtail with the beans (increase the cooking time somewhat); replace the chorizo with other sausage; add peeled chunks of winter squash, pumpkin, apple, or pear; or substitute green beans or kale, collards, or chard for the cabbage.

2 tablespoons extra virgin olive oil
1/4 pound salt pork or bacon, diced
1/4 pound ham, preferably Serrano or prosciutto, with
   some of its fat, diced
1 cup dried white beans, soaked overnight (if you have the
   time) and drained
1/2 pound waxy ("new") potatoes, peeled and cut into
   small chunks
1 onion, sliced
1/4 pound turnips, trimmed, peeled, and diced
1 dried chorizo sausage, about 1/2 pound, peeled and
   sliced
1 small head of cabbage, preferably Savoy
Salt and black pepper to taste

1. Heat the oil in a large, heavy saucepan or flameproof casserole over medium-high heat. Add the pork and ham and brown, then stir in the beans. Pour in enough water to cover the beans by 3 inches and bring to a boil, then lower the heat, cover, and simmer for 40 minutes or until the beans are nearly tender.

2. Add the potatoes, onion, and turnips and simmer until the potatoes are tender, about 20 minutes. Then add the chorizo and cabbage and cook just until the chorizo is heated through and the greens are soft, 10 to 20 minutes more. Season with salt and pepper and serve. (You can prepare the soup entirely in advance, but do not let sit for more than a few hours or the potatoes will begin to disintegrate.)

West Lake Beef Soup CHINA ■

MAKES **4 SERVINGS**

TIME **30 MINUTES**

Too few soups are both hearty and quick to make, but West Lake soups—named after their area of origin (West Lake is in the northern Chinese city of Hangzhou)—are stunning exceptions.

I've eaten West Lake soup only in restaurants and homes in this country, but the preparations have always offered wonderfully clear and intense flavors and a marked richness. This comes not only from dropped egg whites but from loads of meat or fish, cilantro, peas, and, as I found out in the cooking, a bit of cornstarch, which is not altogether necessary but is harmless enough.

If you're interested in West Lake Fish Soup, which uses a slightly different procedure, see page 134. See page 274 for more on Shaoxing wine.

½ pound beef, preferably sirloin, trimmed and chopped

1 tablespoon Shaoxing wine or dry sherry

3 tablespoons soy sauce

6 cups beef or chicken stock, preferably homemade (page 160)

1 teaspoon white pepper, or more to taste

2 tablespoons cornstarch

1 cup fresh or thawed frozen peas

2 egg whites, lightly beaten

1 cup chopped fresh cilantro leaves

1. Mix the beef with the wine and 1 tablespoon of the soy sauce; set aside. Bring the stock to a boil in a large saucepan. Season with the remaining soy sauce and the white pepper. In a small bowl, combine 2 tablespoons of the stock with the cornstarch.

2. Add the peas and beef to the stock and cook, stirring occasionally, just until the peas are bright green and the beef loses its pinkness, about 2 minutes. Using a whisk or chopsticks, drizzle in the egg whites, stirring constantly.

3. Stir in the cornstarch mixture. When the soup thickens, remove it from the heat and stir in the cilantro. Serve immediately.

West Lake Crab Soup. Substitute ½ pound shredded crabmeat or lobster meat for the beef and fish stock (page 161) for the beef or chicken stock. In step 2, add the crabmeat after the egg whites (it will cook almost instantly).

Hot and Sour Soup CHINA

MAKES **4 SERVINGS**

TIME **30 MINUTES**

Much northern Chinese food is spicy, and this well-known soup follows that pattern, deriving its heat from freshly ground pepper (use a lot of it) and its sourness from rice vinegar. Don't be put off by the long ingredient list: this doesn't take much time to prepare and is guaranteed to be better than the version served at most Chinese restaurants. Normally, I think thickening with cornstarch is unnecessary, but here it feels appropriate to give the soup its signature thickness; you can eliminate it if you like.

Any of the dried ingredients that you can't get at your supermarket can be found at almost any Chinese market.

1 teaspoon Shaoxing wine or dry sherry

3 tablespoons soy sauce

1 tablespoon dark sesame oil

3 tablespoons cornstarch

1/2 pound lean boneless pork loin, chicken breast, or flank steak, cut into thin shreds against the grain

6 cups chicken stock, preferably homemade (page 160)

1 garlic clove, minced

One 1-inch piece fresh ginger, peeled and minced

5 dried black mushrooms, soaked in hot water for at least 10 minutes

5 dried Chinese wood ear mushrooms, soaked in hot water for at least 10 minutes

10 dried lily buds, soaked in hot water for at least 10 minutes

1/2 pound extra-firm tofu, cut into small cubes

1/4 cup rice vinegar, or more to taste

1 tablespoon freshly ground black pepper, or more to taste

2 eggs, lightly beaten

1/4 cup chopped fresh cilantro leaves

1/2 cup chopped scallion

1. Whisk together the wine and 1 teaspoon each of the soy sauce, sesame oil, and cornstarch. Combine the meat shreds with this mixture to marinate while you combine the stock with the garlic and ginger in a large saucepan and bring to a boil over medium-high heat. Drain the mushrooms and lily buds, trim off all the hard ends, cut into thin slices, and add to the stock. Reduce the heat to low and simmer for 5 minutes.

2. Bring the stock back to a boil over medium heat and add the meat. Stir to make sure the pieces do not stick together and cook until the meat loses its pinkness, about 3 minutes. Then add the tofu, vinegar, pepper, and remaining soy sauce. Reduce the heat to low again and simmer for 5 minutes.

3. Mix the remaining cornstarch with 1/4 cup cold water and stir that mixture into the soup until it thickens, about 1 minute. Continue to stir and pour in the eggs in a slow stream. The eggs should form thin, almost transparent ribbons. Remove from the heat and season with the remaining sesame oil and more vinegar or pepper to taste. Garnish with the cilantro and scallion and serve hot.

Vegetarian Hot and Sour Soup. Omit the meat and add 1/2 pound more tofu and 1/4 pound slivered bamboo shoots. Substitute vegetable stock (page 162) for the chicken stock.

Jota Pork, Bean, and Sauerkraut Soup
SLOVENIA ■

MAKES **6 TO 8 SERVINGS**

TIME **2 HOURS, LARGELY UNATTENDED, PLUS SOAKING TIME**

Jota, often referred to as Slovenia's national dish, is also found throughout Friuli, in extreme northeastern Italy, and especially in the area around Trieste. It's a good one-dish meal, not unlike a soupy version of cassoulet. The addition of sauerkraut, however, cuts through the rich pork and the beans, and while it might not exactly "lighten" the dish, it makes it somewhat less dense. Buy "pure" sauerkraut—just cabbage and salt—packed in plastic bags or a barrel. Serve with good crusty bread.

2 cups dried kidney beans, soaked overnight or boiled for 2 minutes and soaked for 2 hours

One ¼-pound piece salt pork

3 medium thin-skinned waxy potatoes, peeled and cut into 1-inch cubes

1 pound sauerkraut, rinsed and drained

2 tablespoons extra virgin olive oil

½ pound slab bacon, diced

3 garlic cloves, chopped

1 medium onion, chopped

3 tablespoons flour

3 bay leaves

Salt and black pepper to taste

1. Drain the beans and put in a large saucepan with the salt pork. Add enough water to cover the beans by 2 inches. Set over high heat, bring to a boil, then lower the heat and simmer, uncovered, until tender, about 45 minutes. Remove the pork from the saucepan; dice the meat, discarding the fat, and return it to the saucepan.

2. Meanwhile, put the potatoes in a medium saucepan and barely cover with water. Set over medium-high heat, bring to a boil, then lower the heat and cook, partially covered, until tender, about 20 minutes. Stir in the sauerkraut.

3. Put the oil in a large casserole or Dutch oven and turn the heat to medium. Add the bacon and cook, stirring occasionally, until the fat is rendered. Add the garlic and onion and cook, stirring occasionally, until the onion is golden and softened, 3 to 5 minutes.

4. Whisk in the flour and cook, stirring frequently, until golden brown, 3 to 5 minutes. Add the bean mixture with its cooking liquid and the potatoes and sauerkraut with their cooking liquid. Stir in the bay leaves, bring the mixture to a boil, then lower the heat and simmer, uncovered, for 20 more minutes.

5. Mash some of the potatoes and beans to thicken the soup, season with salt and pepper, and serve.

Shchi Sauerkraut Soup RUSSIA ■ ■
MAKES **6 TO 8 SERVINGS**
TIME **2 HOURS, LARGELY UNATTENDED**

This classic Russian soup is rich and full of complex flavors. While there are probably as many versions as there are families, the key ingredient is always sauerkraut. (It's best served with a whole head of soured cabbage, but you're going to have trouble finding that; just stick with good sauerkraut, sold in bulk or in plastic packages, which contains nothing but cabbage and salt.)

This is one of those soups that pretty much requires good stock, and it's nice to make it especially for this dish, because the beef is a good addition. If you don't have time (or you're a vegetarian), use premade stock or make a quick vegetable stock with the bay leaf, parsley, carrots, onions, and celery.

2 pounds boneless beef chuck, cut into 1-inch cubes

1 bay leaf

½ bunch of fresh parsley

3 carrots, roughly chopped

2 onions, roughly chopped

2 celery stalks, roughly chopped

1 pound good-quality sauerkraut

3 tablespoons butter

2 garlic cloves, minced

½ pound button mushrooms, trimmed and sliced

1 small head of cabbage, about $\frac{1}{2}$ pound, cored and
shredded

1 potato, peeled and diced

Salt and black pepper to taste

3 tablespoons chopped fresh dill leaves for garnish

1 cup sour cream

1. Put the beef, bay leaf, parsley, and half the carrots, onions, and celery in a large saucepan with 7 cups cold water. Bring the mixture to a boil, then lower the heat and simmer for at least an hour, longer if you have time. Remove the beef from the stock and set aside; when it's cool, chop it roughly. Strain the stock, discarding the vegetables.

2. Lightly rinse the sauerkraut and drain well. Melt the butter in a large, heavy saucepan or flameproof casserole over medium heat. Add the remaining carrots, onion, and celery and cook, stirring occasionally, until softened, about 5 minutes. Add the garlic, mushrooms, sauerkraut, and cabbage and cook, stirring occasionally, for about 10 minutes. Add the potato, beef cubes, and reserved stock and simmer for another 30 minutes, or until the vegetables are tender. (You can prepare the soup up to this point in advance; let sit for a few hours or cover and refrigerate for up to 2 days before reheating and proceeding.) Add some salt and pepper, then ladle into bowls. Garnish with the dill and serve, passing the sour cream at the table.

Borscht with Meat RUSSIA ■ ■

MAKES **4 SERVINGS**

TIME **1$\frac{1}{2}$ HOURS, LARGELY UNATTENDED**

An unusual and unexpected variation on the traditional beef-and-vegetable stew, differing largely in its inclusion of beets, which deliver their distinctive sweetness and color. In fact it's close to the vegetarian version of borscht (page 116), especially if you add the optional sour cream.

If you use chuck or brisket here, the cooking time will be longer but the stew will taste better; if you're in a hurry, use tenderloin—you'll save time but lose flavor.

2 thick slices bacon, chopped

1 pound boneless beef, preferably from the chuck or
brisket, cut into 1-inch cubes

2 onions, chopped

1 head of cabbage, preferably Savoy, cored and shredded

3 beets, peeled and roughly chopped

3 carrots, chopped

3 tomatoes, chopped

6 cups beef, chicken, or vegetable stock, preferably
homemade (page 160 or 162), or water

2 cups cooked or canned white beans, like navy or Great
Northern, drained

1 cup sour cream, optional

Salt and black pepper to taste

1. Put the bacon in a large saucepan or flameproof casserole and turn the heat to medium. When it begins to render its fat, turn the heat up a bit and add the beef. Brown quickly, just 1 or 2 minutes per side. Add the onions and cook, stirring occasionally, until they begin to soften, 3 to 5 minutes.

2. Stir in the cabbage and cook, stirring occasionally, until wilted, about 5 minutes. Add the beets, carrots, tomatoes, and stock. Bring the mixture to a boil, then reduce the heat and simmer, stirring occasionally, for at least 40 minutes, or until the meat and carrots are tender. (You can prepare the borscht up to this point and let sit for a few hours or cover and refrigerate for up to a day before reheating and proceeding.)

3. Stir in the beans and sour cream if you're using it and heat through, stirring. Taste and add salt and pepper as necessary, then serve with crusty bread.

Grand Borscht EASTERN EUROPE ■

MAKES **6 SERVINGS**

TIME **ABOUT 3 HOURS, LARGELY UNATTENDED**

As noted in the previous recipe, borscht can become quite elaborate. Here it becomes a full meal.

> 2 quarts beef, chicken, or vegetable stock, preferably
> homemade (page 160 or 162)
> 1 carrot
> 1 celery stalk
> 1 whole medium onion, plus 2 large onions, chopped
> 4 pounds beef short ribs or beef shank or 2 pounds brisket
> 1 ham hock, optional
> 1 bay leaf
> ¹/₂ cup dried small white beans, like navy or pea, soaked
> overnight or boiled for 2 minutes and soaked for
> 2 hours, if time allows, and drained
> 1¹/₂ pounds beets, peeled and diced
> 4 medium or 8 small baking potatoes, like Idaho or russet,
> peeled and diced
> 4 tablespoons (¹/₂ stick) butter
> 6 garlic cloves, roughly chopped, optional
> 2 cups shredded cabbage
> Salt and black pepper to taste
> 2 Granny Smith or other tart apples, peeled, cored, and
> roughly chopped
> ¹/₄ cup cider vinegar or red wine vinegar, or to taste
> Minced fresh dill leaves or chives for garnish
> Sour cream for serving

1. Combine the stock, carrot, celery, whole onion, beef, ham hock if you're using it, bay leaf, and beans in a stockpot; bring to a boil, then cover partially and adjust the heat so the mixture simmers steadily. Cook until the meat and beans are very tender, at least 2 hours. Remove the bay leaf and vegetables and discard. Remove the beef and cool, then cut it into chunks. If you used the ham hock, remove the meat from the bone; reserve the meat and discard the bone. (This can all be done days in advance; cover and refrigerate until you're ready to proceed.)

2. Meanwhile, add the beets and potatoes to the stock along with the beef and ham and simmer while you proceed with the recipe.

3. Put the butter in a large skillet and turn the heat to high. When it melts, add the chopped onions, garlic, and cabbage, along with a large pinch of salt and a sprinkling of pepper, and cook, stirring occasionally, until the onions and cabbage are tender, 10 to 15 minutes. Add the apples and cook, stirring occasionally, about 5 minutes more. Turn off the heat and stir in the vinegar.

4. Add the onion-cabbage mixture to the bubbling stock, then taste and adjust the seasoning. Garnish and serve hot, passing the sour cream at the table.

Naengmyon Cold Buckwheat Noodle Soup

KOREA ▨ ■

MAKES **6 TO 8 SERVINGS**

TIME **SEVERAL HOURS (PREFERABLY OVERNIGHT),
LARGELY UNATTENDED**

Here's an unusual dish: a grand cold soup that is essentially a whole meal. (You might, if you have the inclination and want to be wholly authentic, serve with Kong Namul, page 182; Black Beans with Soy, page 432; or other panchan.) Pickle the cucumber and daikon in advance if you can or substitute kimchi. Though this dish contains some chiles, it is not meant to be blazing hot, so use mild long red chiles if you can find them or the more common long green (Italian frying, or Anaheim) peppers.

> 2 pounds beef brisket
> 2 pounds beef bones
> 1 carrot, peeled

1 onion, peeled

10 thin slices peeled fresh ginger

2 garlic cloves, peeled and lightly crushed

1 tablespoon sugar

1 tablespoon white wine or rice wine vinegar

¼ cup soy sauce, plus more for serving

Salt and black pepper to taste

1 pound Korean buckwheat and potato starch noodles
    or Japanese buckwheat (soba) noodles

1 cup Lightly Pickled Cucumber (page 455)

1 cup daikon kimchi, diced, or sliced daikon, pickled as for
    Lightly Pickled Cucumber (page 455)

1 Asian pear or Granny Smith apple, peeled, cored, and
    grated

2 fresh long red chiles or long green Italian peppers,
    stemmed, seeded, and minced

3 or 4 hard-cooked eggs (page 338), peeled and cut
    in half

About 1 teaspoon hot red pepper flakes, preferably Korean

Hot mustard, like Colman's, for serving

1. Combine the first 6 ingredients in a pot with water to cover; bring to a boil, then adjust the heat so the mixture simmers. Cook, partially covered, for about 2 hours, or until the meat is quite tender; add water if necessary to keep the meat covered. Transfer the meat to a plate; cover and refrigerate. Strain the broth and chill for several hours or overnight; skim off excess fat. You should have about 2 quarts of stock. Add water to make 2 quarts if you have less; if you have more, that's fine. Add the sugar, vinegar, soy sauce, and salt and pepper if necessary; taste and adjust the seasoning—the broth should be delicious on its own.

2. Set a large pot of water to boil and add salt. Cook the noodles until tender, just a few minutes. Drain, then run under cold water until cool; drain again and set aside.

3. Put a portion of noodles in each of 6 to 8 large bowls; spoon a portion of broth over them. Thinly slice the beef and put a few slices in each bowl. Garnish with a bit of cucumber, daikon, pear, chile, and ½ egg sprinkled with salt and hot red pepper flakes. Serve with mustard and soy sauce.

Beef and Tofu Soup KOREA ■
MAKES **4 SERVINGS**

TIME **45 MINUTES, PLUS MARINATING TIME**

Korean soups like this one are often served in heavy stone pots that keep the soup sizzling hot at the table—in fact, they're often still boiling when you (attempt to) start to eat them. (In some restaurants they're served over flames so they continue to boil as you eat them; this is tricky for Westerners.) The pots may be hard to come by unless you can get to a Koreatown in a city like New York or Los Angeles, but this soup is just as good served in an ordinary soup bowl; just preheat the bowl so you can serve it very hot.

You can serve this as an entree. In Korea, it would be teamed with Sticky Rice (page 508); spoon some of it right into the hot soup.

3 tablespoons soy sauce

1½ tablespoons dark sesame oil

3 scallions, trimmed and chopped

3 garlic cloves, chopped

One 1-inch piece fresh ginger, chopped

1 teaspoon sesame seeds

1 pound lean steak, preferably sirloin, sliced as thinly as
    possible across the grain

3 tablespoons corn, grapeseed, or other neutral oil

1 pound firm tofu, cut into ½-inch cubes

Salt and black pepper to taste

1. Mix together the soy sauce, sesame oil, scallions, garlic, ginger, and sesame seeds in a large bowl. Add the meat, toss well to coat, cover, refrigerate,

and marinate for about 1 hour—longer if time allows, shorter if you're in a hurry.

2. Heat the oil in a heavy saucepan over medium-high heat. Drain the meat, reserving the marinade, and brown it, turning once or twice. Add 6 cups water and bring to a boil; lower the heat and simmer for 20 minutes.

3. Add the tofu and reserved marinade and heat through, about 5 minutes. Season with salt and pepper and serve hot.

Hearty Beef and Tofu Soup. This is more flavorful and substantial, because you are really making stock with the beef; but it takes far longer, too. Substitute 1½ pounds beef short ribs, cut into 2-inch pieces, for the steak. Proceed as in step 2, adding time to brown the bigger pieces and at least an hour more of simmering to tenderize them. Remove the ribs and strip the meat from the bones; cut into bite-sized pieces, return to the broth, and proceed to step 3.

Gori Gom Tang Oxtail Soup KOREA ■
MAKES **4 SERVINGS**

TIME **2½ HOURS, LARGELY UNATTENDED**

Although oxtail is no longer a common meat in American households, it's still sold in many supermarkets (it's really "steertail," of course) and makes a great soup base, contributing wonderful flavor and body. Though you might think otherwise, this is actually a fairly light soup, extremely tasty and, when made traditionally, quite spicy.

Traditionally, you use the seasoning mixture as a dipping sauce at the table for the oxtail pieces, eating them with the soup on the side. While that can be fun for a dinner party, the soup is easier to make and just as tasty when all the ingredients are combined at the end.

If you can't find oxtail, use short ribs, shank, or brisket; or try the variation, which is a bit mellower.

2 pounds oxtail, cut into 2-inch lengths

1 tablespoon salt, plus more to taste

4 nickel-sized slices fresh ginger

2 garlic cloves, minced

1 small fresh hot red chile, stemmed, seeded, and minced, or 1 teaspoon hot red pepper flakes, or to taste

2 teaspoons black pepper, plus more to taste

2 tablespoons soy sauce

2 teaspoons dark sesame oil

3 scallions, trimmed and chopped

1 tablespoon toasted sesame seeds (page 596)

1. Place the oxtail, salt, ginger, and 7 cups water in a stockpot or large saucepan. Simmer, partially covered, skimming the foam from the surface if necessary, until the meat is quite tender but not yet falling off the bone, about 2 hours.

2. Remove the oxtail from the stock, cool slightly, and cut the meat off the bone into bite-sized pieces. Return the meat to the stock with the garlic, chile, pepper, soy sauce, and sesame oil. Bring to a light boil and simmer, uncovered, for 20 minutes or longer, until the meat is fork-tender. (You can prepare the dish several hours, or even a day, in advance up to this point; cover and refrigerate, skim the congealed fat off if you like, then reheat when you're ready.)

3. Taste and adjust the seasoning, garnish with the scallions and sesame seeds, and serve hot.

Sul Long Tang Korean Beef Soup. Omit the chile. Substitute beef shank or brisket for the oxtail. Add 1 medium daikon radish, trimmed and peeled, in step 1. In step 2, cut the meat into thin slices across the grain and cut the radish into 1-inch chunks.

Pho Bo Meat and Noodle Soup with Herbs
VIETNAM ■

MAKES **6 TO 8 SERVINGS**

TIME **SEVERAL HOURS, LARGELY UNATTENDED**

While pho originated in the north of Vietnam, it has become a national dish. Carts and small shops sell it everywhere, usually for breakfast (since I'm a big fan of savory breakfasts, this was ideal for me).

The clear, fragrant beef broth is the flavorful base of this dish, and the sliced sirloin, noodles, and condiments provide the texture. (The sirloin must be sliced as thinly as possible, because it cooks in the serving bowl; freeze it for 30 minutes or so to facilitate thin slicing.) Information on Thai fish sauce—nam pla—is on page 500. Rice vermicelli (mai fun) is available at most supermarkets and all Chinese markets, and is sometimes called "rice stick."

10 star anise

5 peppercorns

5 cloves

1 cinnamon stick

4 garlic cloves, peeled and lightly smashed

1 small onion, roughly chopped

One 3-inch piece fresh ginger, peeled and sliced

4 pounds oxtail or beef bones

2 pounds boneless chuck, cut into a few pieces

¼ cup nam pla, or more to taste

1 tablespoon sugar, or more to taste

Salt and black pepper to taste

1 pound dried rice vermicelli

1 pound lean sirloin, thinly sliced across the grain

1 cup fresh bean sprouts, rinsed

10 fresh cilantro sprigs

10 fresh basil (preferably Thai) or mint sprigs

2 fresh chiles, preferably Thai, stemmed, seeded, and minced

2 scallions, trimmed and chopped

2 limes, cut into wedges

1. Set a large flameproof casserole or stockpot over medium heat. Add the star anise, peppercorns, cloves, and cinnamon stick and toast until fragrant, about 1 minute; scoop out and set aside for the moment. Add the garlic, onion, and ginger and char, about 5 minutes.

2. Add the oxtail or beef bones, chuck, and reserved spices. Add water to cover and bring to a boil, then lower the heat and simmer, uncovered, until the chuck is tender, at least an hour. Remove, shred, and set it aside. Simmer the broth for a total of about 3 hours, then add the nam pla, sugar, salt, and pepper, adding more of each to taste. At some point during this period, cook the rice noodles in boiling salted water until tender, just a few minutes. Strain, rinse in cold water, and set aside.

3. When the broth is done, strain and reheat until it's just about boiling. Divide the noodles, sirloin, and reserved shredded meat among the serving bowls and then pour in the broth. Garnish with the bean sprouts, cilantro, basil, chiles, and scallions and serve, squeezing lime juice over all.

Quicker Pho with Meatballs VIETNAM ■
MAKES **6 TO 8 SERVINGS**

TIME **LESS THAN 1 HOUR**

Start with stock, use just about the same seasoning as in regular pho (preceding recipe), and substitute quick-cooking meatballs for chuck. The result is a relatively fast pho with all the flavor of its slow-cooked big brother. See page 500 for information on nam pla, Thai fish sauce.

2 tablespoons corn, grapeseed, or other neutral oil

1 tablespoon minced garlic

1 small onion, roughly chopped, plus 1 medium onion, minced

1 pound ground pork

Salt to taste

10 cups chicken or beef stock, preferably homemade
   (page 160)

1 teaspoon ground anise

1/4 teaspoon black pepper

Pinch of ground cloves

1/2 teaspoon ground cinnamon

One 3-inch piece fresh ginger, peeled and sliced

1/4 cup nam pla

1 tablespoon sugar

1 pound dried rice vermicelli

1 cup bean sprouts, rinsed

10 fresh cilantro stems

10 fresh basil (preferably Thai) or mint stems

2 fresh chiles, preferably Thai, stemmed, seeded, and
   minced

2 scallions, trimmed and chopped

2 limes, cut into wedges

1. Set a large flameproof casserole or stockpot over medium heat and add the oil. A minute later, add the garlic and chopped onion and cook, stirring occasionally, until softened, about 5 minutes. Meanwhile, combine the pork and minced onion with a large pinch of salt and form into about 20 small meatballs.

2. When the onion is cooked, remove with a slotted spoon. Add the meatballs to the pan and turn heat to high; brown quickly, about 5 minutes. Return onion to the pan along with the stock, anise, pepper, cloves, cinnamon, ginger, nam pla, and sugar.

3. Bring to a boil, then lower the heat and simmer, uncovered, for about 20 minutes, until the meatballs are cooked through and the seasonings have married. Meanwhile, cook the rice noodles in boiling salted water until tender, just a few minutes. Strain, rinse in cold water, and set aside.

4. When the meatballs are cooked, add the noodles to the broth and reheat them. Divide the noodles

and meatballs among 6 to 8 serving bowls and pour in the broth. Garnish with the bean sprouts, cilantro, basil, chiles, and scallions and serve, squeezing lime juice over all.

Harira Ramadan Soup NORTH AFRICA ■ ■
MAKES **4 TO 6 SERVINGS**
TIME **2 HOURS, LARGELY UNATTENDED (WITH PRECOOKED CHICKPEAS)**

In the holy month of Ramadan, Muslims fast from sunrise to sunset and partake of a hearty meal after sunset. This often includes harira, a filling, flavorful, and easily varied soup. If your cilantro comes with roots, wash them well, tie them in a bundle, and add them to the stew for extra flavor; remove before serving.

1 tablespoon butter or olive oil

1 pound boneless lamb shoulder or boneless, skinless
   chicken thighs, cut into 1-inch cubes

1 medium onion, chopped

1 bunch of fresh parsley, large stems removed, chopped

1 bunch of cilantro, large stems removed, chopped

1 teaspoon ground cinnamon

1 teaspoon ground turmeric

Salt and black pepper

1/2 cup dried chickpeas, soaked overnight, or 1 cup
   canned or precooked chickpeas, drained

1/2 cup dried lentils, picked over

2 large tomatoes, peeled, seeded, and chopped, or about
   2 cups drained canned

1/4 cup vermicelli or other thin noodles broken into small
   pieces

2 lemons

1. Put the butter in a large saucepan or flameproof casserole and turn the heat to medium-high.

When it melts, add the lamb or chicken and brown evenly, about 2 minutes per side. Add the onion and cook, stirring occasionally, for about 3 minutes, until it softens a bit. Stir in the parsley, cilantro, cinnamon, turmeric, a large pinch of salt, and about 1 teaspoon pepper.

2. Add the chickpeas and 6 cups water. Bring the mixture to a boil, turn the heat to medium-low, and simmer, partially covered, until the chickpeas begin to soften, at least 30 minutes. (If you're using canned or precooked chickpeas, add them and the lentils at the same time.) Add the lentils and simmer for another 30 minutes, stirring now and then. Add the tomatoes and simmer for a final 30 minutes, stirring occasionally. (You can prepare the soup up to this point a day or two ahead; refrigerate if it will be more than an hour or two, then reheat before adding the noodles and finishing.)

3. Add the noodles to the simmering stew about 10 minutes before serving. Add the juice of one of the lemons, along with more salt and pepper if necessary. Serve, with the remaining lemon cut into wedges.

Vegetarian Harira. Omit the lamb or chicken and use a good vegetable stock (page 162) instead of water. As the noodles become tender, stir in 2 lightly beaten eggs.

Mandoo Kuk Dumpling Soup KOREA ▪

MAKES **4 SERVINGS**

TIME **20 MINUTES (WITH PREMADE DUMPLINGS)**

Mandoo are Korean dumplings almost identical to gyoza, though they are more often steamed than pan-fried. If you don't feel like making dumplings, you can use this broth to make soup with duk, Korean rice cakes; these are sold fresh or frozen at most Korean markets. Sometimes noodles are added to this soup as well, a nice but unnecessary touch.

> 2 ounces Korean potato starch noodles or mung bean
>   noodles, optional
> 3 tablespoons dark sesame oil
> 1 medium onion, chopped
> 2 tablespoons minced garlic
> 6 cups beef or chicken stock, preferably homemade
>   (page 160)
> Salt and black pepper to taste
> 12 to 24 gyoza or similar dumplings (pages 63–64)
> 3 tablespoons soy sauce
> 1/2 cup minced scallion for garnish

1. If you're using the noodles, soak them in hot water to cover while you proceed with the recipe.

2. Put 2 tablespoons of the sesame oil in a saucepan or casserole and turn the heat to medium. Add the onion and cook, stirring occasionally, until it softens, about 5 minutes. Add the garlic and cook, stirring once or twice, for another minute. Add the stock and bring almost to a boil, then lower the heat so the mixture simmers. Taste and add salt if necessary, along with plenty of black pepper.

3. Add the dumplings and continue to simmer. If the soaked noodles are very long, cut them into manageable lengths with scissors and add them to the stock. Cook until the dumplings are hot, 5 to 10 minutes longer. Add the soy sauce and remaining sesame oil to the soup, divide it among 4 bowls, garnish with scallion, and serve.

Duk Kuk Rice Cake Soup. Omit step 1. Step 2 remains the same, though if you like you can add 1/4 to 1/2 pound beef sirloin, cut into small cubes. In step 3, add about 1/2 pound duk (Korean rice cake), cut into 1/2-inch-thick slices. Simmer until the rice cake is hot, about 5 minutes. Garnish and serve.

Seaweed Soup KOREA

MAKES **4 SERVINGS**

TIME **1 ½ HOURS, LARGELY UNATTENDED**

If you like seaweed salad, try this. Traditionally offered to nursing mothers, it's soothing in the winter and cooling in the summer (see variation).

To slice the beef thinly, freeze it until it is just beginning to harden, 30 to 60 minutes.

Miyuk is the Korean word known to the Japanese as wakame and elsewhere as alaria (see page 484); you should be able to find it at Asian markets.

½ pound lean beef, preferably sirloin, sliced as thinly as
    possible

2 garlic cloves, minced

3 tablespoons soy sauce

1 tablespoon dark sesame oil

3 ounces miyuk (wakame) seaweed, broken into bits

2 tablespoons corn, grapeseed, or other neutral oil

2 scallions, cut into 2-inch lengths, plus chopped scallion
    for garnish

Salt and black pepper to taste

1. Mix the beef with the garlic, soy sauce, and sesame oil and marinate for a few minutes. Meanwhile, thoroughly wash the seaweed under cold running water.

2. Heat the oil in a large saucepan over medium-high heat. Add the beef with its marinade and brown, about 2 minutes, then add the seaweed and cook, stirring, for another 2 minutes. Add the scallions and 5 cups water to the saucepan and bring to a boil. Lower the heat and simmer, partially covered, until the seaweed is soft, about 1 hour.

3. Season with salt and pepper, garnish with chopped scallion, and serve.

Summer Seaweed Soup. Cook through step 2, then cool. Meanwhile, seed and thinly slice 1 cucumber and peel and thinly slice one 2-inch piece of daikon radish. Add to the cooled soup, along with 6 ice cubes, and serve.

Pork and Posole with Chipotles
MEXICO ■

MAKES **4 SERVINGS**

TIME **AT LEAST 1 HOUR, LARGELY UNATTENDED**

Posole is dried corn treated with limestone, a traditional American food that predates the arrival of Europeans by some thousands of years. In its ground form it is the main ingredient in tortillas, but for some reason the whole kernels are largely ignored in this country outside of the Southwest. (Hominy, which is essentially the same thing, has a bit of a following in the South, but again mostly in its ground form: grits.)

Posole is also the name of a soupy stew containing, well, posole. It can be varied in many ways, but it is always delicious and distinctive. If you have time, soak and cook the dried kernels yourself: Rinse the posole, then soak it in water to cover if time allows, for up to 12 hours; cook in boiling water to cover, stirring occasionally, for 1 hour and probably longer. Season with salt and drain.

Canned posole (or hominy) is almost as good, and reduces the time it takes to make this soup to about an hour.

4 cups precooked posole or canned hominy

1 pound boneless pork shoulder, trimmed of excess fat
    and cut into chunks

Salt and black pepper to taste

1 tablespoon fresh oregano or marjoram leaves or
    1 teaspoon dried

1 dried chipotle or 1 chipotle chile in adobo, or to taste

1 tablespoon ground cumin, or to taste

1 large onion, chopped

1 tablespoon minced garlic

Chopped fresh cilantro leaves for garnish

Lime wedges for serving

1. Combine the posole, pork, salt, pepper, oregano, chile, cumin, and onion in a saucepan that will hold them comfortably. Add water or some of the hominy cooking liquid to cover by about an inch and turn the heat to medium-high. Bring to a boil, then adjust the heat so the mixture simmers steadily but not violently. Cook, stirring occasionally, until the pork is tender, about an hour; add liquid if necessary.

2. Stir in the garlic and cook for a few more minutes. Taste and adjust the seasoning, then serve in bowls—the mixture should be soupy—garnished with the cilantro and lime wedges.

Posole with Pumpkin Seeds. A traditional variation: Toast 1 cup hulled pumpkin seeds (pepitas, page 612) in a small dry skillet over medium heat, shaking the pan frequently until the seeds pop and color slightly, about 5 minutes. Combine them with a bit of the broth in a blender and process until smooth. Stir them into the stew and heat through.

Polpette and Orzo in Broth ITALY ■

MAKES **4 SERVINGS**

TIME **ABOUT 40 MINUTES**

Here, meatballs—usually called polpette, at least in Rome—are made with a load of fresh Parmesan, lightened with parsley, and served in a delicious broth, with just a bit of pasta. It's filling soup but not overwhelming.

Although you can assemble many of its compo-

nents in advance—the meatballs, pasta, carrots—it's best to do the actual cooking at the last minute. This soup will lose its light texture if allowed to sit with the meatballs and pasta in it for too long.

1 thick slice white bread

$1/2$ cup milk

6 cups beef, chicken, or vegetable stock, preferably homemade (page 160 or 162)

1 cup orzo, ditalini, or other small pasta

1 pound ground sirloin or other good-quality beef

$1/2$ cup minced onion

1 cup freshly grated Parmesan

$1/2$ cup minced fresh parsley leaves

Salt and black pepper to taste

3 medium carrots, julienned or shredded

1. Soak the bread in the milk until soggy, about 5 minutes. Meanwhile, heat the stock and bring a pot of water to a boil. When the water is ready, cook the pasta until it is nearly done; drain, rinse, drain again, and set aside.

2. Squeeze the milk from the bread and combine the bread gently with the meat, onion, half of the cheese, half of the parsley, and some salt and pepper. Shape into 1-inch meatballs, pressing no more than is necessary. Season the stock and add the carrots, then gently lower the meatballs into the

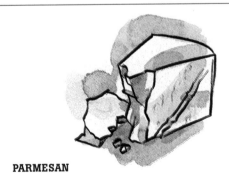

PARMESAN

stock. Adjust the heat so that the liquid bubbles gently.

3. Simmer for about 10 minutes, until the carrots are tender; add the orzo and cook for another 2 minutes. Taste and adjust seasoning, then serve, sprinkling with remaining Parmesan and parsley.

Kofte in Broth Meatball Soup with Lemon
MIDDLE EAST ■

MAKES **4 SERVINGS**

TIME **45 MINUTES**

A filling, bright-tasting soup that would certainly qualify as a main course. To make it even more substantial, cut up a couple of potatoes and simmer them with the kofte.

1 pound boneless lamb, preferably from the shoulder,

    excess fat removed

1 medium onion, peeled and quartered

Salt and black pepper to taste

1/3 cup fresh parsley leaves, plus more for garnish

1/3 cup fresh dill leaves

Pinch of ground allspice

1/2 teaspoon ground cinnamon

5 cups beef, chicken, or vegetable stock, preferably

    homemade (page 160 or 162)

2 tablespoons extra virgin olive oil

1/2 cup dry white wine, water, or more stock

Fresh lemon juice to taste

1. Cut the lamb into large chunks and put in a food processor with the onion, a large pinch of salt, some pepper, and the parsley, dill, allspice, and cinnamon; process until quite smooth, stopping the machine and scraping down the sides if neces-

sary. With wet hands, form into meatballs about 1 inch in diameter.

2. Heat the stock and hold it at a gentle simmer. Put the oil in a large skillet and turn the heat to medium-high. A minute later, add the meatballs and cook, turning occasionally, until browned, about 10 minutes. As they finish, add them to the stock. Pour off any excess fat from the skillet and add the wine. Raise the heat to high and cook, stirring and scraping with a wooden spoon, until the liquid and any solids in the skillet are incorporated. Add this liquid to the stock.

3. Taste and adjust seasoning, then add the lemon juice. Garnish with parsley and serve.

Lion's Head Meatballs in Broth CHINA

MAKES **4 SERVINGS**

TIME **3 HOURS, LARGELY UNATTENDED**

These Chinese meatballs are so named because of their large size. When served in the center of cabbage leaves, the dish resembles a lion's head and mane; or at least that's what they say. In any case it is an unusual, delicious dish that's easy to make.

2 pounds boneless pork shoulder (butt or picnic), coarsely

    ground in a food processor or meat grinder

1 scallion, trimmed and minced

One 1-inch piece fresh ginger, peeled and minced

2 tablespoons soy sauce

1 tablespoon Shaoxing wine or dry sherry

2 teaspoons sugar

1 teaspoon white pepper

2 egg whites

2 tablespoons corn, grapeseed, or other neutral oil

1/2 pound Napa cabbage, cut into 2-inch pieces

Salt to taste

1 quart beef or chicken stock, preferably homemade (page 160)

1 tablespoon dark sesame oil, or to taste

1. Mix the first 8 ingredients together, just until combined, using your hands or a wooden spoon. Set aside.
2. Heat the oil in a large casserole over medium-high heat. Add the cabbage and stir-fry until softened, about 5 minutes, seasoning with salt. Add the stock and bring to a steady simmer.
3. With wet hands, form 4 meatballs with the pork mixture; handle gently. Slide the meatballs into the stock, cover, and simmer, undisturbed, until cooked through, about 2 hours.
4. Place the cabbage in a soup tureen and put the meatballs on top. Spoon the stock over the dish, season with sesame oil, and serve immediately.

Deluxe Lion's Head. Add $1/2$ cup chopped reconstituted wood ear mushrooms (see page 112) and $1/4$ cup chopped peeled, fresh water chestnuts (or peeled jicama) to the pork mixture.

SAVOY CABBAGE

Lion's Head Pie. A kind of delicious meat loaf: Omit the cabbage and stock. Press the pork mixture into a large shallow dish. Steam over hot water until cooked through, about 1 hour.

Pearl Balls. You may have eaten these in a dim sum house: Omit the cabbage, stock, and sesame oil. Soak 1 cup glutinous or sticky rice in water for 1 hour, then drain. Form the meat mixture into 1-inch balls, then roll them in the sticky rice to cover. Place the balls in a steamer and cook until the meat cooks through and the rice puffs and becomes sticky, about 30 minutes. Remove and serve.

Cabbage and Sausage Soup
EASTERN EUROPE   ■
MAKES **4 SERVINGS**
TIME **40 MINUTES**

Interestingly, though this is usually and correctly associated with Eastern Europe, I had it first in northeastern Italy. That's not entirely surprising, because the Alto Adige region of Italy, also known as the Tyrol, was part of Austria until after World War I.

Often thickened with rice, this soup can also be used as a sauce for pasta; see the variation.

2 tablespoons extra virgin olive oil

$1/2$ pound mild fresh sausage, removed from its casing

1 large onion, minced

1 small head of Savoy cabbage, about 1 pound, cored and shredded

Salt and black pepper to taste

1 tablespoon minced garlic

6 cups chicken stock, preferably homemade (page 160)

$1/2$ cup short-grain rice, like Arborio

Freshly grated Parmesan cheese

1. Put the olive oil in a broad, deep skillet or flame-proof casserole over medium heat. A couple of minutes later, add the sausage and cook, stirring to break up any lumps, until it loses its pinkness. Remove with a slotted spoon and set aside.

2. Add the onion to the skillet and cook, stirring occasionally, until it begins to soften, about 3 minutes; add the cabbage, a large pinch of salt, and some pepper. Cook, stirring occasionally, until the cabbage is tender, 10 minutes or so. Stir in the garlic and cook for another minute, then add the stock. Bring to a boil and adjust the heat so the mixture simmers steadily; stir in the rice, sausage, and (probably) some more salt.

3. Cook, stirring occasionally, until both the rice and cabbage are very tender, about 15 minutes more. Taste and adjust the seasoning and serve, passing Parmesan at the table.

Pasta with Cabbage and Sausage. Step 1 remains the same. In step 2, set a large pot of water to boil and salt it. Reduce the stock to 1 cup and omit the rice; cook until the cabbage is soft and the mixture "saucy." Cook 1 pound cut pasta until tender but not mushy; drain, reserving a little of the cooking water. Toss the pasta with the cabbage and sausage mixture, adding a little of the reserved water if the mixture seems dry. Toss with Parmesan and serve.

STOCKS

Stock—the essence of meat, poultry, fish, vegetables, or a combination made liquid—is considered the fond, or base, of classic French cuisine, and simple chicken stock is an essential part of home cooking. Not only soups but sauces, risotto, and many low-fat preparations all rely on good, rich broth for much of their flavor.

But no one has stock on hand all the time. In fact, few people have the time or energy to make stock from scratch. And even those who do find so many uses for it—there are few ingredients that have more applications—that it quickly runs out. Eventually, all cooks turn to canned stock or the dreaded bouillon cubes.

Barring homemade stock, the best solution is undoubtedly to use the best canned stock you can find. I've come to expect nothing more than a little bit of flavor from canned stock; it's a step above water (and water isn't a bad alternative). You've just got to add the ingredients that will transform it.

The flavor of real chicken stock, for example, is derived from meat, bones, and aromatics, the last of which can mean just about anything but usually includes carrot, onion, and perhaps celery. Canned stock can be improved markedly by simmering it with some chicken trimmings—wing tips, back, neck, and so on—and some of those magical aromatic vegetables.

At the minimum, canned stock simmered for 20 or even 10 minutes with an onion (you need not bother to peel it), a carrot, and a clove of garlic will be improved measurably. Some herbs, a bay leaf, and a few peppercorns will make it even better. Parsley and celery are also good choices; ginger, scallions, and a dash of soy are great in stocks destined for Asian dishes; a bit of thyme or rosemary might be useful; and a few dried mushrooms (or trimmings from fresh ones) can add a huge flavor boost. All of these techniques will work if you start with water in place of canned stock, too.

All stocks can be refrigerated for a couple of days before using (or longer if you bring the stock to a boil every second or third day) or frozen more or less indefinitely.

Chicken Stock FRANCE ■

MAKES **ABOUT 6 CUPS**

TIME **1¼ HOURS, LARGELY UNATTENDED**

Easy to make—you can use a slow cooker and cook for about 6 hours—but, ironically, so easy to consume. When you make it, you'll find uses for it, and it will be time to make it again. You can always use canned stock or water, but there is nothing like real stock.

- 1 medium onion
- 2 pounds chicken, preferably wings, thighs, and legs
- 1 medium carrot
- 1 celery stalk
- 4 garlic cloves
- 1 bay leaf

1. Combine all the ingredients in a large saucepan with 6 cups water and turn the heat to high. Bring to a boil, then lower the heat so that the mixture bubbles steadily but not rapidly. Cook, skimming any foam that accumulates, for at least 1 hour (more than 2 hours is counterproductive).
2. Cool slightly, then strain. Refrigerate (you can skim off fat after the stock cools completely) and use within 3 days or freeze.

Chicken Stock, Chinese Style. Omit the bay leaf; add 10 nickel-sized slices fresh ginger and, if you like, 1 star anise.

Beef Stock FRANCE ■

MAKES **ABOUT 1 GALLON**

TIME **AT LEAST 3 HOURS, LARGELY UNATTENDED**

Beef stock is made everywhere there's beef—it's a fine use for scraps and not-too-meaty bones—but it's associated most closely with France, where, along with other stocks, it is considered the fond, the foundation or basis for many important sauces and dishes. While canned chicken stock is an often-acceptable substitute for fresh, canned beef stock is nearly useless, and bouillon cubes completely so. Though I don't make beef stock even a tenth as often as I do chicken stock, I'm never sorry when I do; it's incomparably flavorful.

- 3 to 4 pounds meaty beef bones, like shank, shin, tail, or short ribs
- 2 medium onions, chopped
- 2 medium carrots, chopped
- 2 celery stalks, chopped
- 3 fresh thyme sprigs or ½ teaspoon dried
- 10 fresh parsley sprigs, or more to taste
- 1 teaspoon salt, plus more to taste
- 3 cloves
- 10 peppercorns

1. Rinse the beef bones well under cold running water, then transfer to a large stockpot and add the remaining ingredients. Add about 1 gallon water or enough to cover by a couple of inches.
2. Bring just about to a boil, then partially cover and adjust the heat so the mixture sends up a few bubbles at a time. Cook, skimming off any foam that accumulates at the top, until the meat falls from the bones and the bones separate from one another, 2 to 3 hours.
3. Strain, pressing on the vegetables and meat to extract as much juice as possible. Taste and add salt if necessary. Refrigerate, then skim any hardened fat from the surface. Refrigerate for 4 to 5 days (longer if you boil it every third day, which will keep it from spoiling) or freeze.

Beef Stock, Asian Style. Omit the thyme, parsley, and cloves. Add 4 garlic cloves, peeled and crushed, 3 scallions, trimmed and chopped, and 7 nickel-sized pieces of fresh ginger to the stock.

Consommé FRANCE ■ ▤

MAKES **ABOUT 6 CUPS**

TIME **ABOUT 30 MINUTES (WITH PREMADE STOCK)**

If you thought consommé was for sick people, you'll think differently after you try it. It's deceptively addictive, a rich, clear soup with wonderful, deep flavor. There's a reason this is a traditional starter at elegant meals; it whets your appetite without filling you up at all.

You can use a food processor to chop the chicken and vegetables together; pieces about $1/4$ inch in diameter are about right, so don't overprocess.

6 cups chicken stock (page 160), refrigerated and
　skimmed of excess fat
10 to 12 ounces boneless, skinless chicken, white or dark
　meat, chopped
1 medium onion, chopped
1 medium carrot, chopped
1 celery stalk, chopped
$1/2$ leek, trimmed, chopped, and well rinsed
1 tomato, cored and cut into quarters
4 egg whites
Salt and black pepper to taste

1. Place the stock in a large saucepan and turn the heat to medium-high; bring to a boil. Adjust the heat so that the mixture bubbles steadily but not too rapidly. Combine the chicken, onion, carrot, celery, leek, and tomato in a bowl; stir in the egg whites and add 1 cup ice cubes.
2. Add this mixture all at once to the simmering stock, along with some salt and pepper. Whisk once or twice and bring back to a boil. Adjust the heat so that the liquid bubbles steadily but not too rapidly; the solids will form a "raft" on top of the liquid. Create a "chimney," a hole on one edge of the raft, simply by spooning some of the solids out of the way. Let it cook that way for about 10 min-

utes, gradually enlarging the chimney by scooping solids from the edge of the raft onto the middle.
3. Ladle the liquid (it's okay if you take some of the raft with it, but try to minimize this) through a strainer lined with cheesecloth. Serve (hot, in small bowls), refrigerate (you can skim off fat after the stock cools completely) and use within 3 days, or freeze for up to 2 weeks.

Fish Stock FRANCE ■

MAKES **ABOUT 1 QUART**

TIME **1 HOUR, LARGELY UNATTENDED**

Though the fish industry is more factory oriented than ever, you can still grab a few heads and racks (skeletons) from fishmongers for free, even at supermarkets. All you have to know is that usually you want white-fleshed fish, without their guts (which are strong tasting) or gills (which are bitter). Once you have those, you can make good fish stock in less than an hour.

1 tablespoon butter or olive oil
1 medium to large onion, quartered
1 carrot, roughly chopped
1 celery stalk, roughly chopped
$1/2$ cup sweet or dry white wine
1 pound bones and/or cleaned heads from white fish
1 bay leaf

1. Combine all the ingredients in a saucepan and add 1 quart water. Bring to a boil, lower the heat, and simmer for about 30 minutes.
2. Turn off the heat, then cool the broth for about 15 minutes. Strain and use immediately, refrigerate for up to 3 days, or freeze for up to a few weeks.

Shrimp Shell Stock ■

MAKES **ABOUT 1 QUART**

TIME **30 MINUTES, LARGELY UNATTENDED**

The easiest and most economical stock there is. And not only can it substitute for fish stock, but it's useful in its own right. You can add vegetables, as you do for Fish Stock (preceding recipe), but it isn't essential.

Shells from 2 pounds shrimp
Salt and black pepper to taste

1. Put the shells in a medium saucepan and add about 1 quart water or enough to cover. Bring it to a boil, then take the pan off the heat and let the shells steep until the water cools. (Or, if you're in a hurry, use it right away.)
2. Strain the stock, discard the shells, and add salt and pepper. Use immediately, refrigerate for up to 2 days, or freeze for up to a month.

Vegetable Stock ■

MAKES **1 GALLON**

TIME **1½ HOURS**

This vegetable stock is not unlike Jus Rôti (page 163) but without the meat—the roasting step adds a layer of flavor that is a welcome addition to otherwise one-dimensional vegetable stocks.

Although this is hardly a bare-bones stock, the addition of mushrooms or more root vegetables (especially parsnips) will give it even more oomph.

5 tablespoons extra virgin olive oil
3 leeks, both white and green parts, cut in half lengthwise
    and well rinsed, or 3 large onions, quartered
5 carrots, cut in half
3 celery stalks, cut in half
3 potatoes, peeled or well washed and quartered
7 garlic cloves or 4 shallots
12 fresh parsley sprigs
4 fresh thyme sprigs
10 peppercorns
½ cup dry white wine
Salt to taste

1. Preheat the oven to 400°F. Put the olive oil in a large roasting pan and add the leeks, carrots, celery, potatoes, and garlic; toss well to coat the vegetables with the oil and put the pan in the oven.
2. Roast, shaking the pan occasionally and turning the vegetables over once or twice, until everything is nicely browned, about 45 minutes.
3. Use a slotted spoon to scoop all the vegetables into a stockpot; add the remaining ingredients except salt and 3 quarts water. Set over high heat.
4. Put the roasting pan over a burner set to high and add about 1 quart water, depending on the depth of the pan. Bring it to a boil and cook, scraping off all the bits of food that have stuck to the bottom. Pour this mixture into the stockpot, then bring to a boil. Partially cover and adjust the heat so the mixture sends up a few bubbles at a time. Cook until the vegetables are very soft, 30 to 45 minutes.
5. Strain, pressing on the vegetables to extract as much juice as possible. Taste and add salt if necessary. Use, refrigerate for 4 to 5 days (longer if you boil it every third day, which will prevent spoiling), or freeze.

Dashi JAPAN ■ ■

MAKES **ABOUT 2 QUARTS**

TIME **15 MINUTES**

The smell of dashi—the basic stock common to hundreds of Japanese dishes—is everywhere in Japan.

And that makes sense: it's a quickly made stock that gives all kinds of foods a good, distinctive flavor.

The two main ingredients—kelp (a kind of seaweed also called kombu; see page 484) and dried bonito flakes (bonito is a type of tuna)—are esoteric, but they're sold at every Japanese market and now at many more general Asian markets and health food stores. The process is simple, the results reliable; try it.

But whatever you do, steer clear of instant dashi, which is just about as good as chicken bouillon cubes, which is to say not good at all.

1 piece dried kelp (kombu), 4 to 6 inches long

¹/₂ to 1 cup dried bonito flakes

1. Combine the kelp and 2 quarts water in a medium saucepan and turn the heat to medium. Do not allow the mixture to come to a boil; as soon as it is about to, turn off the heat and remove the kelp (you can use it as a vegetable in stir-fries or salads if you like).
2. Immediately add the bonito flakes and stir; let sit for a couple of minutes, then strain. Use the dashi immediately or refrigerate for up to 2 days.

Jus Rôti Dark Stock FRANCE ■
MAKES **ABOUT 6 CUPS**

TIME **ABOUT 1¹/₂ HOURS, LARGELY UNATTENDED**

This takes a little time and a little care; the chicken must be browned fully before you add the vegetables, since the liquid they exude will stop the browning process. If you like, you can strain this stock and reduce it over high heat to a cup or two of shiny glaze, enough to make a flavorful sauce for meat, chicken, fish, or vegetables (store the sauce as you would the stock itself).

To make this even richer and darker, substitute

beef or veal (using the same cuts you'd use for beef stock, page 160) for some or all of the chicken.

2 pounds chicken wings, cut into 3 pieces each

2 tablespoons extra virgin olive oil

¹/₂ onion

1 carrot

4 garlic cloves

¹/₂ celery stalk

3 fresh thyme sprigs

1. Preheat the oven to about 500°F and place a rack in the lowest possible position (if you can roast on the floor of the oven, so much the better).
2. Combine the chicken and olive oil in a roasting pan just large enough to hold the chicken in one layer. Roast for about 45 minutes, stirring and scraping occasionally, until the meat is nicely browned. Add the remaining ingredients and stir once or twice, scraping, then return to the oven for about 20 minutes more, stirring once or twice.
3. Place the pan on top of the stove (careful—it will be very hot) and add 6 cups water. Bring to a boil over medium heat and cook for 30 minutes, stirring and scraping occasionally. Cool slightly, then strain. Use, refrigerate for 4 to 5 days (longer if you boil it every third day, which will prevent spoiling), or freeze.

BONITO FLAKES

Salads Salads are universal and universally enjoyed. From the light green salad, which can be more of a refreshing interlude, start, or finish to a meal—a few leaves, barely dressed—to the what-can-we-throw-in-here thing that comprises a meal, the salad is so broadly defined that attempts are almost futile. About the only generalization you can make about salads is that they're cold.

Key to any salad—beyond the obvious, like fresh ingredients—is the dressing. Learning how to make a good dressing, which can be as simple as oil and vinegar, or nam pla and lime juice, or even just a bit of lemon, is essential. But in this instance (and it's unusual), "learning" is following not so much recipes as your taste: Everyone likes different levels of acidity, and moods change too. Sometimes you'll want a salad with just olive oil, and sometimes just lemon; sometimes you'll want to make mayonnaise that's sharp and even fiery, and sometimes you'll want it mild. In no aspect of cooking is the phrase *to taste* more appropriate than in making salads.

Of course the same is true of how you construct a salad. There are barely rules or rights and wrongs. If a hunk of iceberg lettuce with "Russian dressing" (ketchup and mayonnaise) is a salad (and it is), and a gorgeous minimalist creation like Cold Spinach with Sesame (page 184) is a salad, and a showstopper like a classic Niçoise (page 196) is a salad, then anything goes. This is an arena in which you don't need to "know" how to cook to produce something you like.

SIMPLE, LIGHT, RAW SALADS

These are what might be called side salads; they need no cooking or advance preparation (though some can be prepared in advance) and are, for the most part, basic combinations of greens or other raw vegetables and dressings. Most are lightning-quick to make.

Green Salad with Oil and Vinegar

FRANCE ■ ■

MAKES **4 SERVINGS**

TIME **15 MINUTES**

Simple, basic, and essential. You can always make a true Vinaigrette (page 600), but as is, this is the simplest green salad, as good for entertaining as it is for weeknights.

Almost any greens are good with this dressing, from romaine, Boston, or iceberg lettuce to frisée or radicchio, but a mixture is best. The prepacked mesclun mixtures now sold in almost all supermarkets make it even easier.

2 tablespoons minced shallot or red onion, optional
1/4 cup sherry, balsamic, or wine vinegar
4 to 6 tablespoons extra virgin olive oil, to taste
Salt and black pepper to taste
About 1/2 pound lettuce and/or other greens, preferably a mixture

1. Whisk together the first four ingredients, beginning with 4 tablespoons oil and adding more as necessary.
2. Dress and toss the lettuce, adjust the seasoning if necessary, and serve.

Green Salad with Nut Oil FRANCE. Substitute 2 tablespoons hazelnut or walnut oil for half the olive oil.

Green Salad with Lemon ITALY. Substitute fresh lemon juice for the vinegar.

Green Salad with Vinaigrette, Roquefort, and Walnuts FRANCE ■ ■

MAKES **4 SERVINGS**

TIME **15 MINUTES**

One of the most delicious salads, offered at many Paris bistros and throughout the countryside. Good with a ripe pear on the side or cut into cubes and added to the mix.

10 or 15 walnuts or about 1/4 cup sliced almonds (blanched or not)
About 1/2 pound lettuce and/or other greens, preferably a mixture
About 1/2 cup Vinaigrette (page 600)
1/4 pound ripe Roquefort or other soft blue cheese, like Stilton or Gorgonzola
Minced fresh chervil or parsley leaves or chives for garnish, optional

1. Toast the walnuts in a dry skillet over medium heat, shaking the pan occasionally, until fragrant, about 3 minutes. Set aside.
2. Toss the lettuce with the vinaigrette, then toss in the walnuts and cheese. Garnish if you like and serve.

■ make ahead   ■ serve at room temp./cold   ■ 30 minutes or less

Handling Salad Greens

Obviously, greens should look fresh—no brown spots, no bashed-in parts, no chewed-up leaves, nothing dried out, nothing moldy, nothing slimy, and so on. That's the starting place.

Once out of the ground, greens begin to wilt unless they're kept cool and moist. Supermarkets have elaborate spraying systems and packaging; most greens keep best slightly moist, wrapped in plastic in the fridge, but the sooner you use them the better.

These days many greens are prewashed, at least theoretically. Some, especially those that are not mass-produced and packaged three thousand miles away, are still quite sandy. I recommend washing everything: Fill a large pot or the bottom portion of a salad spinner with cold water; put the greens in a colander or the colander-like bottom of the salad spinner; plunge into the water and swish; remove, drain the water, and repeat until the water is clean. This may take anywhere from one rinse to four.

Dry the greens using a salad spinner or (more complicated) paper towels.

LETTUCE *top row: radicchio, escarole, bib; bottom row: romaine, endive, Boston, arugula*

The Mandoline

If you've ever used a mandoline, you probably understand its charm: it makes quick work of repetitive, volume slicing tasks, it makes precise cuts precisely, and it cleans up in seconds. In short, it makes up for the unprofessional knife skills of the home cook. I use mine almost daily.

For a long time the only mandolines available here were the handsome and expensive steel French variety, but now plastic Japanese and Korean models are available for a fraction of the price. And the plastic models handle the same tasks with comparable aplomb, so only economy and aesthetics will dictate which one ends up in your kitchen. Regardless of how cavalier you're feeling when you start using your new mandoline, always use the guard whenever your fingers are getting close to the blade—everyone I know has learned this lesson the hard way once.

Caesar Salad MEXICO ■ ▪

MAKES **4 SERVINGS**
TIME **20 MINUTES**

You might think Caesar Salad is American, but legend has it that it was invented in Tijuana in the 1920s by an Italian named Caesar Cardini, who originally called it "aviator's salad" because so many of the U.S. Air Force pilots based in San Diego loved it.

In any case, the secret to a great Caesar salad is making sure everything is as fresh as you can get it—this includes the eggs and lettuce—and the best quality possible: freshly grated (and real) Parmesan and good anchovies, packed in either salt or olive oil.

2 heads romaine lettuce

1 garlic clove, cut in half

6 tablespoons extra virgin olive oil

1 tablespoon sherry or red wine vinegar

1 to 2 tablespoons minced anchovies, or to taste

2 eggs or $\frac{1}{2}$ cup pasteurized egg product

Salt and black pepper to taste

$\frac{1}{2}$ to 1 cup freshly grated Parmesan cheese

2 tablespoons fresh lemon juice, or to taste

Croutons (page 580), rubbed with garlic

1. Peel away all of the dark green (and even medium-dark green) outer leaves of the romaine heads; you want only hearts and tender inner leaves.
2. Rub the inside of your salad bowl with the garlic clove; discard it. Add the oil, vinegar, and anchovies to the bowl and whisk to combine. Whisk in the eggs, salt and pepper, and $\frac{1}{2}$ cup of the Parmesan. Taste the dressing on a leaf of romaine at this point and assess how much more acidity it needs and whether or not it will need any additional salt (remembering that you're going to add more salty Parmesan in a minute) or pepper. Add lemon juice to taste and salt and pepper as necessary.
3. Toss the lettuce in the dressing; top with the croutons and remaining Parmesan, then bring to the table and toss again. Serve immediately.

Salad of Artichoke Hearts and Parmesan ITALY ■ ▪

MAKES **4 SERVINGS**
TIME **20 MINUTES**

This is why people want to move to Italy: you can buy raw fresh artichoke hearts already trimmed (occasionally you can find these in this country's best markets too, especially in California), and layer them with the best Parmesan and olive oil. The cheese and artichoke have some kind of symbiotic magic going on, making the whole far greater than the sum of its parts. Fantastic.

4 to 8 raw fresh artichoke hearts (12 if very small)

2 lemons, more or less

Several thin slices Parmesan cheese

Extra virgin olive oil as needed

Salt and black pepper to taste

1. Slice the artichoke hearts as thinly as you can (a mandoline is ideal for this), rubbing each with lemon juice as you do so. Layer them on a plate with slices of Parmesan and drizzle all with olive oil, salt, and pepper.

2. Taste and adjust the seasoning, adding more lemon juice if necessary, and serve immediately.

Cabbage and Beet Salad

SCANDINAVIA ■ ▨ ▨

MAKES **4 SERVINGS**

TIME **10 MINUTES**

Beet salads in general are wonderful, but this one is a refreshing change. For one thing, the beets are raw. For another, their sweetness is offset by the sharp taste of raw cabbage; it's a fine if odd marriage. Think of it as Swedish coleslaw (like coleslaw, it can be made a few hours in advance).

Whenever you peel beets—and especially when you're grating them—be sure to wear an apron or clothing you don't care about.

About 3 cups shredded cabbage (¹/₂ pound, more or less)

¹/₂ pound carrots, grated

1 pound beets, peeled and grated

¹/₂ cup Mustard Dill Sauce (page 608), or to taste

Salt and black pepper to taste

1. Toss the cabbage, carrots, and beets with just enough dressing to coat the vegetables evenly. Season to taste with more dressing and salt and pepper.

2. Chill well and serve.

Sauerkraut Salad

POLAND ■ ▨ ▨

MAKES **4 SERVINGS**

TIME **10 MINUTES**

This is best when you have freshly made sauerkraut—especially a whole head, which you can sometimes find at Eastern European specialty markets. There will, of course, be times when that's impossible, and then you must turn to packaged sauerkraut. This is not a problem as long as you steer clear of the canned stuff and look for that packed in plastic bags, containing nothing but cabbage and salt.

Serve this strong, tart salad with a hearty meat dish, like "Deviled" Pork Chops (page 362), Baeckoffe of Pork and Lamb (page 399), or Carbonnade (page 385).

One 2-pound head or 2 pounds packaged sauerkraut

1 heaping tablespoon sweet paprika

¹/₃ cup walnut, hazelnut, dark sesame, or extra virgin olive oil

¹/₂ cup pitted and chopped black olives, preferably not canned

1. If using a whole head of sauerkraut, quarter, core, and shred it as finely as possible. If using packaged sauerkraut, rinse lightly and drain well.

2. Stir in the paprika and oil and garnish with the olives.

Sauerkraut Salad, Russian Style. Prepare the sauerkraut as in step 1. Substitute sugar for the paprika and use extra virgin olive oil; substitute an apple (Granny Smith is good here), peeled, cored, and shredded on a grater (or in a small food processor), for the olives. Add 2 scallions, trimmed and chopped, and 1 cup chopped jarred or canned plums (or dried prunes, soaked in a little water or port). Toss all the ingredients together and serve.

Cucumber Salad, European Style
POLAND ■ ▦ ▧

MAKES **4 SERVINGS**

TIME **15 MINUTES**

Not unlike the better-known Middle Eastern and Indian combinations of yogurt and cucumbers, this Polish version is more tart than its Eastern cousins, making it especially refreshing as a part of a meal with heavy dishes.

> 4 cucumbers (about 1 1/2 pounds), peeled if necessary
> Salt and black pepper to taste
> 1 cup sour cream
> 2 tablespoons white or white wine vinegar
> 1/4 cup chopped fresh dill leaves, or more to taste

1. Cut the cucumbers in half lengthwise, then scoop out the seeds with a spoon. Slice, salt, and put in a colander; let drain over a bowl or in the sink for 10 to 20 minutes. Rinse, drain, and spin or pat dry. (If you want supercrunchy cucumbers, wring dry in a towel.)
2. While the cucumbers are draining, combine the sour cream and vinegar. When the cucumbers are ready, toss them with the dressing. Season with salt and pepper, garnish with the dill, and serve, or refrigerate for up to an hour.

Leek Salad NORTH AFRICA ■ ▦ ▧

MAKES **4 SERVINGS**

TIME **10 MINUTES**

This North African salad will give you a wonderful new perspective on leeks. Uncooked, they are deliciously refreshing, especially when paired with tomatoes and cucumbers.

> Juice of 1 lemon, or to taste
> 3 tablespoons extra virgin olive oil
> Salt and black pepper to taste
> 4 leeks, white parts only, sliced, well rinsed, and dried
> 2 ripe tomatoes
> 1 firm medium cucumber
> At least 1/2 cup chopped fresh parsley or cilantro leaves

1. Whisk together the lemon and oil along with a healthy pinch of salt and several grindings of pepper. Toss with the leeks.
2. Core the tomatoes, then cut them in half horizontally and shake out the seeds, squeezing gently; chop. Peel the cucumber if necessary, then cut in half lengthwise and scoop out the seeds with a spoon; chop.
3. Combine all the ingredients, then taste and adjust the seasoning; refrigerate, if you like, for up to a couple of hours. Garnish with additional parsley or cilantro if you like.

Leek and Olive Salad. In step 2, substitute 1/2 cup pitted black olives, preferably oil-cured, for the cucumber.

Vinegar Like wine or spirits, vinegar can be made from just about any fruit, vegetable, or grain. It's a two-step process: first an alcoholic fermentation to convert sugars in the base material to alcohol; then an acetic fermentation to convert the resulting brew to (acetic) acid. Some vinegars have other steps at either end of the process—barley is malted to convert starches to fermentable sugars, and some wine vinegars (most famously, real balsamic vinegar) are finished in wood barrels to add extra dimensions of flavor. But all traditionally made vinegars have more in common than you might think.

SHERRY VINEGAR

Still, choosing vinegar can be difficult because there are so many varieties. It pays to know that almost all inexpensive vinegars are nothing but "white" vinegar—distilled vinegar, essentially diluted acetic acid—combined with artificial flavorings. This is great for cleaning your windows, but not for salad dressing.

I recommend that you stock sherry vinegar (which is similar to real balsamic vinegar, but less expensive), or a real wine vinegar, along with rice vinegar, which is lower in acidity and great for Asian foods. You don't really need more than that, though having a range of great vinegars on hand is a luxury that, unlike many gastronomic money pits, pays real flavor dividends.

Since all vinegars are different, not only in acid levels but also in flavor, unless you stick to the same vinegar all the time, most vinaigrettes are best made "to taste."

Type	Acidity	Info
Lemon/Lime Juice	Roughly 3%	Not vinegar at all, of course, but frequently used in its place, and supremely useful.
White (or Distilled) Vinegar	5%	White vinegar can be made from just about anything and is most commonly either distilled malt vinegar or, more likely, a mix of pure acetic acid and water. Used primarily for pickling, it can be used in cooked dishes when you want just straight acidity, with no added flavor.
Cider Vinegar	5%	Cider vinegar is made—unsurprisingly—from cider, apple juice, or by-products from the cider-making process. The best I've had came from Normandy, a cider-making region in northern France, though there are probably some small American producers doing a good job with it as well. Used primarily for pickling, a good-quality cider vinegar can be salad-worthy. Most cider vinegar, however, is white vinegar with flavoring.
White Wine Vinegar	5–7%	White wine vinegar—like white wine—can be insipid or wonderful. Some versions sold as "champagne vinegar"—though only infrequently actually from Champagne—are of better quality. My advice in buying white wine vinegar is not to buy the cheapest or the most expensive. White vinegar works well in vinaigrettes and makes a more subtly flavored pickle than straight white vinegar.

Type	Acidity	Info
Sherry Vinegar	8%	My personal favorite. For the money, the best and most flavorful vinegar out there. Make sure the bottle says "Vinagre de Jerez." This is my go-to vinegar for salads, cooked dishes—just about anything other than pickles. Use anywhere you would use balsamic. But look out—it's very acidic. Use less than you're used to, or cut it with a little water.
Red Wine Vinegar	6–7%	If you're not going to invest in a good bottle of red wine vinegar—one that will probably run you between $8 and $30 (!)—use sherry vinegar. If you do decide to spring for a bottle, find one that tells you what grape it's made from. Look to Spain for the best value and California for the opportunity to spend the most money. Use on salads or in cooked dishes.
Balsamic Vinegar	6%	Mention of Modena or not, most balsamic vinegar sold in this country is distilled vinegar flavored with caramel syrup, which doesn't mean it's bad. At $4 a bottle, it has some flavor, which makes it uncommon and useful. Real balsamic vinegar is a luxury—see below.
Aceto Balsamico Tradizionale di Modena	6% or less	Aceto Balsamico Tradizionale di Modena—real balsamic vinegar—is hard to make, hard to find, and hard to afford. Somewhat surprisingly, dark, sweet, syrupy aceto balsamico starts out as Trebbiano grapes, which make a rather innocuous white wine (called Ugni Blanc in France, they're the base for cognac, too). Through an archaic process wherein the unfermented must of the grapes is aged in a series of wooden barrels (each of a different wood type and size), it's converted to a prized condiment that works not only on greens but on ice cream, strawberries, and cheese. Plan to spend at least $30 for 100 milliliters, about a cup.
Malt Vinegar	4–5%	Malt vinegar has a malty (think of amber-colored beer) aroma and flavor. Like beer, it's made from malted grain and, mirroring the common range for alcoholic content in beer (alcohol turns into acetic acid during the vinegar-making process), is usually around 4 or 5% acid, though I've seen it as high as 8%. Malt vinegar adds a distinctive note to pickles and is a requisite for British-style fish 'n' chips. Though it's never expensive, it's worth spending an extra couple dollars to get real malt vinegar instead of something labeled non-brewed condiment, which is—just like industrial balsamic—water, acetic acid, and coloring.
Rice Wine Vinegar	4.5%	A pantry staple. Essential for Japanese and other East Asian cuisines and good light vinaigrettes across the board. Also sold as "rice vinegar." Even the cheap varieties are decent.
Chinese Black Vinegar	4.5%	Sweet and smoky, Chinese black vinegar (teem ding tenh cho) is made from glutinous rice and is unusual and delicious. Used in cooked dishes and as a dipping sauce or condiment. Look for a black vinegar with a short list of ingredients and the word *Chinkiang* on it.

Radish Salad TURKEY ■ ■ ▨

MAKES **4 SERVINGS**

TIME **20 MINUTES, LARGELY UNATTENDED**

The peppery bite of radishes is the featured player in this crunchy salad, which is served all over the Arab world in one form or another. Salting the radishes first improves both flavor and texture, but if you're pressed for time, just salt the salad as you normally would.

About 16 radishes, sliced

1 celery stalk, diced

1 tablespoon salt

$1/4$ teaspoon black pepper

3 tablespoons fresh lemon juice or 2 tablespoons sherry
  or white wine vinegar, or to taste

2 tablespoons extra virgin olive oil

1 orange, peeled and segmented, optional

2 tablespoons chopped fresh parsley or cilantro leaves,
  optional

1. Toss the radishes and celery with the salt in a strainer and let sit for 15 minutes; rinse and drain. Meanwhile, stir together the pepper, lemon juice, and olive oil.
2. Toss the radishes and celery with the dressing; taste and add more salt, pepper, or lemon juice as needed. Refrigerate for up to an hour or serve right away, after garnishing with orange segments and parsley if you like.

Mexican Radish Salad. Omit the celery, orange, and oil; substitute fresh lime juice for the lemon juice. Toss the radishes with $1/2$ cup finely chopped fresh mint or cilantro leaves, the salt and pepper, the lime juice, and the juice of $1/2$ orange. Garnish as directed if you wish.

Fresh Tomato Salad ITALY ■ ▨

MAKES **4 SERVINGS**

TIME **20 MINUTES**

The first time I ate this great summer salad, I could not figure out how the raw garlic flavor could be strong without being overpowering, but the reason is simple: the garlic is mixed with the dressing, then strained out. Peeling the tomatoes is far from necessary, but it's a nice refinement. More important is to use delicious ripe tomatoes.

4 to 6 garlic cloves, peeled and smashed

Salt and black pepper to taste

1 tablespoon red wine vinegar

3 tablespoons extra virgin olive oil

2 pounds tomatoes, preferably plum, cored, peeled if you
  like, and sliced

20 fresh basil leaves, torn into small pieces

1. Whisk together the garlic, salt, vinegar, and olive oil. Place the tomatoes on a platter and strain the dressing over them.
2. Top with the basil leaves, a little more salt, and some pepper. Serve immediately.

Fresh Tomato and Green Bean Salad FRANCE. Trim the ends from 1 pound of green beans. Cook them in a large pot of boiling salted water for 2 minutes or until bright green, then immediately drain and rinse under cold running water to stop the cooking. Instead of dressing the tomatoes, toss the green beans with the strained dressing and place on top of the tomatoes. Top with the basil, salt, and pepper and serve.

Spicy Fresh Tomato Salad MEXICO. Use the same dressing, along with $1/2$ red onion, chopped, and 1 stemmed, seeded, and chopped fresh chile (jalapeño or Thai, for instance) or hot red pepper flakes to taste.

Basil is still good here, but so is cilantro, mint, or a combination.

Tomato Salad with Ginger INDIA ■ ■

MAKES **4 SERVINGS**

TIME **20 MINUTES**

An unusual tomato salad, exceptionally fresh tasting—it contains no oil—and terrific with any grilled food. You certainly don't need to be making an Indian meal to serve it.

3 large or 4 medium tomatoes

Salt and black pepper to taste

1 tablespoon peeled and minced fresh ginger

1 small fresh chile, like Thai or jalapeño, stemmed, seeded, and minced, or to taste

3 tablespoons fresh lime juice, or to taste

Chopped fresh cilantro leaves for garnish

1. Core the tomatoes, then slice them. Arrange them on a plate and sprinkle with salt and pepper; let sit for about 10 minutes.
2. Meanwhile, combine the ginger with some more salt and pepper, the chile, and about 3 tablespoons lime juice.

SLICING FENNEL ON A MANDOLINE

3. Drain any liquid that has accumulated around the tomatoes, then dress with the ginger-lime mixture. Taste and add more lime juice if necessary, then garnish and serve.

Fennel and Orange Salad ITALY ■ ■

MAKES **4 SERVINGS**

TIME **10 MINUTES**

A superrefreshing salad, great on hot summer days. If you have a mandoline, use it here, since the fennel is best when cut into thin slices.

This salad can be made more substantial with cooked scallops, shrimp, or crabmeat and is also delicious with grapefruit. Peel the fruit over a bowl to catch the juices, then cut the segments between the membranes.

4 juicy oranges, ideally blood oranges

1 fennel bulb, trimmed and very thinly sliced

3 scallions, trimmed and sliced

1 teaspoon ground cumin

Salt to taste

3 tablespoons extra virgin olive oil

Chopped fresh parsley or basil leaves for garnish

1. Peel the oranges over a bowl with a knife, removing the peel and white membrane, then roughly chop the whole orange on a cutting board; strain and reserve the juice. Put the orange pieces in a bowl with the fennel and scallions.
2. Whisk the reserved juice with the cumin, salt, and oil. Toss with the salad; taste and adjust the seasoning and garnish with parsley or basil.

Orange, Fennel, and Olive Salad. In step 2, add the juice of a lemon. Omit the scallions and cumin and add $1/4$ cup or more good-quality black olives, pitted and chopped, and $\frac{1}{2}$ teaspoon fresh thyme leaves (or a pinch of dried thyme). Garnish with parsley leaves.

Orange, Artichoke, and Olive Salad. Starting with the preceding variation, substitute 4 large artichokes or 2 cups canned artichoke hearts, drained and quartered, for the fennel (or use in addition to the fennel). If using fresh artichokes, prepare as directed on page 71 for Carciofi Fritti: Fried Artichoke Hearts (Italy)—cooking them just short of complete tenderness—and proceed as above.

Orange, Red Onion, and Rosemary Salad. Starting with the first variation, substitute 1 red onion for the fennel and 1 teaspoon minced fresh rosemary leaves for the olives. Trim, peel, and thinly slice the onion and immerse it in salted water to cover for at least 10 minutes (30 is better) before draining, drying, and adding to the salad. Toss the rosemary with the oranges, onion, and dressing.

Orange and Walnut Salad

NORTH AFRICA ■ ■

MAKES **4 SERVINGS**

TIME **10 MINUTES**

Morocco's oranges are renowned for their distinctive sweetness, but they're not common here. Use good California or Florida navels or clementines (you'll need six or eight) instead. Removing the thin membranes from the individual segments is an optional refinement.

> **3 navel oranges**
>
> **Juice of 1 orange**
>
> **Juice of 1 lemon**
>
> **1 tablespoon sugar**

PEELING AN ORANGE

> **1 teaspoon ground cinnamon**
>
> **1 teaspoon salt**
>
> **1 tablespoon extra virgin olive oil**
>
> **1 small head of romaine lettuce, chopped**
>
> **1 cup chopped walnuts, lightly toasted (page 165)**
>
> **Chopped fresh cilantro leaves for garnish**

1. Peel the oranges with a knife, removing the peel and, if you like, the white membrane, then separate into segments.
2. Whisk together the orange juice, lemon juice, sugar, cinnamon, salt, and oil. Toss with the lettuce; taste and adjust the seasoning. Serve topped with the orange pieces, walnuts, and cilantro.

Som Tum Green Papaya Salad THAILAND ■ ■

MAKES **4 SERVINGS**

TIME **20 MINUTES**

This fiery, strong northern Thai specialty (if it's made correctly, you will really reek after eating it, but it's worth it) has become one of the most popular dishes in Thailand and at Thai restaurants in the States. When I was in Bangkok, I could not walk down the streets or through the markets without at least a dozen offers of Som Tum from the vendors, and it was hard not to stop for a little dish with some grilled meat and sticky rice. You can usually find green, or unripe, papayas and yard-long beans (and the Thai fish sauce called nam pla) at Asian or Latin groceries, but you can also substitute Granny Smith apples for the papaya and Napa cabbage for the beans.

> 2 garlic cloves, peeled and lightly smashed
>
> 1 shallot, minced
>
> 2 small fresh chiles, preferably Thai, stemmed, seeded, and minced
>
> 2 tablespoons nam pla
>
> 3 tablespoons fresh lime juice, or more to taste
>
> 2 teaspoons sugar, or more to taste
>
> 1 green (unripe) papaya, peeled, seeded, and shredded
>
> 2 or 3 yard-long beans or about a dozen green beans, trimmed and cut into 1-inch lengths
>
> 1 small tomato, cored and cut into eighths
>
> 2 tablespoons finely chopped dry-roasted peanuts
>
> Chopped fresh cilantro leaves for garnish

1. Combine the garlic, shallot, and chiles on a cutting board and mince and press with the side of a knife until pasty (or, as is traditional, use a mortar and pestle). Combine in a bowl with the nam pla, lime juice, sugar, papaya, beans, and tomato and mash with the back of a wooden spoon (or a potato masher) until the vegetables are softened and everything is well combined.

2. Taste and adjust the seasoning; the mixture will be hot but may need more nam pla, lime juice, and/or sugar. Garnish with peanuts and cilantro and serve.

Raita INDIA ■ ■ ■

MAKES **4 SERVINGS**
TIME **20 MINUTES**

Raita is salad, relish, dip, and side dish in one. Yogurt-based, it usually includes something sharp to balance the sour blandness: onion, spices, mustard, even chiles. (It's most closely associated with India, but similar mixtures are made in the Middle East.)

The recipe here is the basic foundation of many raitas and is usually not eaten as is but added to according to preference. There are infinite variations, of which the ones that follow are among the most popular. All balance spicy curries well but are also good eaten on their own or as a dip for flatbreads, like those on pages 559–565.

> 2 cups plain yogurt
>
> 1 teaspoon sugar
>
> $\frac{1}{4}$ teaspoon ground cumin
>
> $\frac{1}{4}$ teaspoon dry mustard
>
> Pinch of salt

1. Whisk the yogurt until smooth and creamy. If it remains thick and stiff, thin it with a little water and continue whisking.

2. Stir in the sugar, cumin, mustard, and salt, along with any of the combined ingredients that follow.

Cucumber-Mint Raita. Stir 1 large cucumber, peeled, seeded, and diced, and $\frac{1}{4}$ cup chopped fresh mint leaves into the yogurt. Season to taste with black pepper and salt if necessary.

Tomato Raita. Stir 1 large tomato, cored, seeded, and diced, 1 onion, peeled and diced, and 1 small hot green chile, stemmed, seeded, and minced, into the yogurt. Garnish with 2 tablespoons chopped fresh cilantro leaves and season to taste with cayenne or pure chile powder, like ancho or New Mexico.

Mixed-Vegetable Raita. Stir 1 cup diced fresh vegetables, like bell pepper, celery, radish, or fennel, into the yogurt. Season to taste with black pepper and garnish with 2 tablespoons chopped fresh cilantro leaves.

Beet Raita. Stir $^1/_2$ cup cooked, peeled, and diced beets and 1 small hot green chile, stemmed, seeded, and minced, into the yogurt. Season to taste with black pepper and garnish with 2 tablespoons chopped fresh cilantro leaves.

Potato Raita. Stir 2 potatoes, cooked, peeled, and diced, and 1 small hot green chile, stemmed, seeded, and minced, into the yogurt. Season to taste with hot paprika and garnish with 2 tablespoons chopped fresh cilantro leaves.

Chickpea Raita. Stir 1 cup cooked or drained canned chickpeas and 1 teaspoon hot red pepper flakes into the yogurt. Season to taste with black pepper.

Banana-Coconut Raita. A sweet raita, good with very spicy dishes: Omit the sugar and substitute about 1 teaspoon garam masala (page 594) or curry powder for the cumin and mustard. Add $^1/_4$ cup dried shredded unsweetened coconut and 2 ripe bananas, peeled and not-too-thinly sliced. Add chopped fresh mint leaves and a little bit of cayenne, or to taste.

COOKED, SALTED, OR MARINATED SALADS

This is another group of simple salads. These require some cooking or advance preparation, but of course at times this can make them more convenient than the salads in the preceding group, because a great many of them can be made at leisure and allowed to marinate or simply sit for hours or even a day or two. By and large they are still quite easy to prepare.

Bitter Greens with Sour Cream Dressing POLAND ■ ▩

MAKES **4 SERVINGS**
TIME **15 MINUTES**

This creamy dressing, popular throughout central and eastern Europe, is a deliciously indulgent protein shake with its eggs and sour cream. You can use any firm greens here, but stay away from tender greens, like Boston lettuce and delicate mesclun mixes; they will not stand up well to the dressing.

3 hard-cooked eggs (page 338)
2 teaspoons sugar
Juice of 1 lemon, or to taste
1 cup sour cream
Salt and black pepper to taste
6 cups roughly chopped greens, preferably romaine,
     endive, escarole, or chicory

1. Cut the peeled eggs in half and transfer the yolks to a bowl. Mash them with the sugar and lemon juice, then beat in the sour cream with a wooden spoon until smooth. Season with salt and pepper. (You can do this in a food processor or mixer, but it's easy enough by hand.)
2. Slice the egg whites into thin strips and toss with the greens and dressing. Serve immediately.

Marinated Mushrooms FRANCE ■ ▩

MAKES **4 SERVINGS**
TIME **AT LEAST 2 HOURS, PREFERABLY OVERNIGHT**

An unusually versatile preparation, good as an appetizer, a side dish, or a salad, and as appropriate over lettuce as it is solo. Can be made days and days in advance.

Endive and the Bitter Greens

Endives, chicories, and escaroles are all related—they may be white, green, or red; they're all bitter and mostly crunchy. Belgian endive (also called witloof and simply endive) is one of these plants, grown in darkness to keep it mild and white.

Chicory—which the Italians call *radicchio*—can be grown in heads but is also curly, sometimes with an almost sharp texture, like frisée. Escarole is similar. All of these are great in salads and also braised or grilled (page 462).

---

1 pound button mushrooms, trimmed and sliced

⅓ cup extra virgin olive oil

¼ cup fresh lemon juice

Salt and black pepper to taste

Chopped fresh parsley leaves for garnish

1. Combine the first 3 ingredients in a bowl with a small pinch of salt and some pepper. Cover and refrigerate for at least 2 hours and up to several days, tossing occasionally.
2. Taste and adjust the seasoning, then garnish and serve.

Ginger Cucumber Salad

SOUTHEAST ASIA ■ ▥

MAKES **4 SERVINGS**

TIME **1½ HOURS, LARGELY UNATTENDED**

This salad is found throughout Southeast Asia. It's a great dish for entertaining since it must marinate for at least an hour before being served and can sit for a couple of hours after that.

½ cup rice or white vinegar

One 1-inch piece fresh ginger, peeled and minced or grated

3 tablespoons sugar

1 teaspoon salt

2 large cucumbers, peeled, halved, seeded (page 169), and sliced

3 tablespoons corn, grapeseed, or other neutral oil

1 onion, sliced

½ teaspoon ground turmeric

2 tablespoons toasted sesame seeds (page 596)

1. Mix together the vinegar, ginger, sugar, and salt and toss with the cucumbers. Let stand for at least 1 hour (if it's a warm day, and you're going to marinate for more than an hour, refrigerate). Drain off the excess liquid.
2. Just before serving, put the oil in a skillet and turn the heat to medium; a minute later, add the onion and turmeric. Cook until softened, about 5 minutes. Stir this mixture into the cucumbers, garnish with the sesame seeds, and serve.

Spicy Cucumber Salad. In step 2, add 2 stemmed and minced small green chiles, preferably Thai, and 10 whole peppercorns to the skillet with the onion. The peppercorns will become fragrant and brown slightly. You do not need to remove them from the pan—they are delicious—but your guests should be forewarned.

Cucumber Tofu Salad. In step 2, press the water from an 8-ounce block of firm tofu (see page 491).

■ make ahead   ▥ serve at room temp./cold   ▦ 30 minutes or less

SALADS   **177**

Brown it on both sides in the oil in a nonstick skillet, then remove and cook the onion. Cut the tofu into $1/2$-inch strips and add to the salad.

Cucumber, Jicama, and Fruit Salad

MEXICO ■ ▧

MAKES **4 SERVINGS**

TIME **AT LEAST 35 MINUTES**

The spicy sweetness of this Mexican salad is super-refreshing and delicious as long as you have ripe fruit; vary the ingredients depending on what you find. Really, any fruit is suitable, from oranges and apples to pineapples and papayas; peaches and melons are wonderful summer options.

1 medium jicama (less than a pound), peeled and cut into
   $1/2$-inch cubes
1 cucumber, peeled, seeded (page 170), and diced
$1/2$ cup fresh lime juice
Salt to taste
2 cups fresh fruit in bite-sized pieces, peeled and seeded
   if necessary
Cayenne or pure chile powder, like ancho or New Mexico,
   to taste (the dish should be at least slightly hot)
Chopped fresh cilantro leaves for garnish

1. Toss the jicama and cucumber with the lime juice and salt in a nonreactive bowl and let it sit for at least 30 minutes. Meanwhile, prepare the fruit.

2. When ready to serve, toss in the fruit and cayenne. Taste and adjust the seasoning, then garnish and serve.

Fruit Salad "Salsa." To use this salad as a sauce for grilled or broiled fish, chicken, or pork, similar to Xec (page 615), omit the jicama and add 1 tablespoon extra virgin olive oil.

Beet Salad with Horseradish

SCANDINAVIA ■ ▧

MAKES **4 SERVINGS**

TIME **1 HOUR, LARGELY UNATTENDED, PLUS
   MARINATING TIME**

Beets are earthy and sweet; horseradish is earthy and seismic; the combination is fortuitous. Fresh horseradish is best, but you can substitute prepared horseradish if necessary (make sure the jar hasn't been opened for too long, or the horseradish will have lost its intensity). This salad is best after marinating in the refrigerator for a day or two, so prepare it ahead of time if you think of it.

1 pound beets, or a little more, well washed
One 2-inch piece fresh horseradish, peeled and grated,
   or 1 tablespoon prepared horseradish, or to taste
Salt and black pepper to taste
3 tablespoons corn, grapeseed, or other neutral oil
1 tablespoon white or red wine vinegar
2 tablespoons minced fresh chives

1. Preheat the oven to 375°F. Put the beets, still wet, in a roasting pan and cover with foil. Bake until soft, about 45 minutes (use a thin-bladed knife to pierce through the foil and into the beets to test for doneness). Remove the beets, then allow them to cool before peeling and slicing into rounds $1/2$ inch thick. (You can cook the beets a day or two in advance if you like; cut them up at the last minute.)

2. In a blender or bowl, whisk together all the remaining ingredients except the chives until creamy. Toss the mixture with the beets, then taste and adjust the seasoning. Cover and refrigerate or serve, garnished with the chives.

Pickled Beets SCANADINAVIA ■ ■

MAKES **6 TO 8 SERVINGS**

TIME **1 HOUR, PLUS MARINATING TIME**

This dish is served everywhere in Scandinavia and for a long time was a staple of restaurants throughout North America—though it seems to be disappearing along with the relish trays and the family restaurants that featured them.

About 2 pounds medium beets

2 cups white vinegar

1 cup sugar

2 tablespoons kosher, canning, or other noniodized salt

2 bay leaves

¹/₄ teaspoon ground cloves

1 onion, sliced

Grated fresh or prepared horseradish to taste, optional

1. Remove all but an inch of the beet greens, reserving the rest of the greens for another use. Wash and scrub the beets, then simmer in boiling water to cover until tender, 30 to 60 minutes. Cool enough to peel off the skins. Cut the beets into ¹/₂-inch slices. (You can cook the beets a day or two in advance if you like; cut them up at the last minute.)

2. Bring the vinegar, sugar, salt, bay leaves, and cloves to a boil. Add the beets and the onion and cook for about a minute. Cool, then add the horseradish and refrigerate. Eat within 2 weeks, as a side dish or as a garnish.

Beet Salad with Cumin NORTH AFRICA ■ ■

MAKES **4 SERVINGS**

TIME **1 HOUR, LARGELY UNATTENDED**

This salad is a popular item on the Sabbath table of Moroccan Jews. It's at its best after sitting in the dress-

ing for a couple of hours; in fact, you can store it for up to a week in the refrigerator.

1 pound beets, or a little more

Juice of 1 lemon

1 garlic clove, minced

1 teaspoon ground cumin

Salt and black pepper to taste

¹/₄ cup extra virgin olive oil

¹/₂ cup chopped fresh parsley leaves

1. Preheat the oven to 375°F. Wash the beets, then put them, still wet, in a roasting pan and cover with foil. Bake until soft, about 45 minutes (use a thin-bladed knife to pierce through the foil and into the beets to test for doneness). Remove the beets, then allow them to cool before peeling and slicing into rounds ¹/₂ inch thick. (You can cook the beets a day or two in advance if you like; cut them up at the last minute.)

2. In a blender or bowl, whisk together all the remaining ingredients except the parsley until creamy. Taste and adjust the seasoning as necessary. Toss the beets with the dressing and refrigerate or serve, garnished with the parsley.

Chickpea Salad FRANCE ■ ■

MAKES **4 SERVINGS**

TIME **AT LEAST 2¹/₂ HOURS, LARGELY UNATTENDED**

The countryside chef who showed me this dish told me that soaking and cooking chickpeas in rainwater makes them taste better. (Unless you live in a pristine environment, it's probably not a good idea; or maybe that's exactly the point.) Anyway, this classic salad is great warm, at room temperature, or cold. Of course the chickpeas can be cooked a day or more in advance, allowing you to make this at the last minute.

The chickpeas will cook somewhat faster if you soak them overnight or boil them for a minute and then let soak for a couple of hours; but it isn't necessary.

2 cups dried chickpeas, washed and picked over

1 garlic clove

1 bay leaf

1 carrot, chopped

3 shallots, minced

Fresh lemon juice or good-quality vinegar of your choice, to taste

Salt and black pepper to taste

3 tablespoons extra virgin olive oil

1/2 cup chopped fresh parsley leaves

1. Drain the chickpeas if necessary and place them in a large pot with the garlic, bay leaf, and carrot; cover with cold water. Bring the water to a boil over medium-high heat; reduce the heat and simmer until done, about 2 hours.

2. Drain and remove the garlic and bay leaf; stir in the shallots. Season to taste with lemon juice, salt, and pepper. Then let the chickpeas sit for a few hours or cover and refrigerate for a day or so; bring back to room temperature before serving.

3. Immediately before serving, stir in the oil and parsley, then taste and adjust the seasoning.

Chickpea Salad with Ginger

INDIA ■ ▨ ▨

MAKES **4 SERVINGS**

TIME **10 MINUTES (WITH PRECOOKED CHICKPEAS)**

This isn't unlike French Chickpea Salad (preceding recipe), but it has an entirely different feel; for best flavor, use young, fresh ginger if possible.

Canned chickpeas work well for this dish, but, as always, freshly cooked ones are preferable. Make this salad up to two hours in advance, but no more.

3 cups cooked (page 431) or canned chickpeas

2 bell peppers, red, yellow, or orange, stemmed, seeded, and diced

1 red onion, diced

One 1-inch piece fresh ginger, peeled and minced

1 tablespoon ground cumin, lightly toasted in a dry pan until fragrant

1 tablespoon sugar

3 tablespoons fresh lemon juice

Salt and black pepper to taste

Chopped fresh cilantro leaves for garnish

1. Toss the chickpeas, peppers, onion, and ginger together in a large bowl. Sprinkle on the cumin, sugar, and lemon juice and mix well. (You can prepare the dish up to this point in advance; let sit for up to 2 hours.)

2. Season with salt and pepper, garnish with cilantro, and serve.

Yogurt Chickpea Salad. Substitute 1 cup lightly toasted cashews for the peppers. Add 1/4 cup yogurt along with the cumin, sugar, and lemon juice.

Cold Lemony Greens GREECE ■ ▨ ▨

MAKES **4 SERVINGS**

TIME **20 MINUTES**

Throughout the eastern Mediterranean, you'll find cool cooked greens sprinkled with olive oil and doused with lemon. Every green you can cook is used in this way, from spinach to wild greens I'd never heard of. It's great with collards, dandelions, mustard, broccoli raab . . . you get the idea. If you know you're cooking greens one night, make a double batch and prepare these the next day. Juicy, tart, and refreshing, this is the ideal summer vegetable dish.

Salt and black pepper

1 pound or more greens, any type, like spinach or collards, trimmed of thick stems (or at least 2 cups cooked greens)

Extra virgin olive oil to taste

Fresh lemon juice to taste

Lemon wedges

1. Bring a large pot of water to a boil and salt it (or you can steam the greens over an inch or so of boiling water). Cook the greens until tender, from about 3 minutes for spinach to up to 15 for the stems of tougher greens like collards. Drain well, then wrap in plastic or place in a covered bowl and refrigerate (you can leave them in the fridge for up to 2 days). Or cool by plunging them into ice water or running under cold water.

2. Squeeze excess moisture from the greens, then chop them coarsely. Toss with olive oil, lemon juice, salt, and pepper, then taste and add more of anything necessary. Serve immediately, with lemon wedges.

Garlic Bread Salad with Tomatoes
ITALY ■ ▨

MAKES **4 SERVINGS**

TIME **20 TO 30 MINUTES**

Stale bread is not only okay for this dish but preferable. You can make a similar dish (called fattoush and Middle Eastern in origin) using pita bread; make sure it's nice and crunchy before tossing with the tomatoes and olive oil. Use ripe, flavorful tomatoes here. And add some chopped shallots or red onion to the mix if you like.

About $1/2$ pound crusty bread (slightly stale is fine)

1 garlic clove, cut in half

$1/4$ cup extra virgin olive oil

2 tablespoons fresh lemon juice or good-quality vinegar

2 tomatoes, roughly chopped

Salt and black pepper

$1/4$ cup or more roughly chopped fresh basil or parsley leaves

1. Rub the bread all over with the garlic and toast or grill until crunchy and lightly browned.

2. Cut or tear the bread into $1/2$- to 1-inch cubes (no larger) and toss it with the remaining ingredients. Taste, adjust the seasoning, and serve within 15 minutes.

Garlic Bread Salad with Tomatoes and Green Beans. Trim about $1/2$ pound green beans and cut them into $1/2$-inch lengths. Drop into boiling salted water and cook until bright green and just tender, about 5 minutes. Drain and run under cold water to stop the cooking. Drain again, then toss into the salad.

Fennel and Cucumber Salad ITALY ▨ ▨
MAKES **4 SERVINGS**

TIME **25 MINUTES**

A crunchy mixed vegetable salad given a twist by the addition of bread. Feel free to improvise with whatever is in your garden or kitchen. The key to this salad is not the choice of vegetables but slicing them as thinly as possible. Use a mandoline if you have one.

About $1/4$ pound crusty bread (stale is fine), torn into pieces

1 tablespoon balsamic vinegar

$1/4$ cup extra virgin olive oil

Salt and black pepper to taste

2 cucumbers, peeled and sliced

1 fennel bulb, trimmed and sliced

2 tomatoes, preferably plum, cored and sliced

2 celery stalks, sliced

1 red bell pepper, stemmed, seeded, and sliced

6 radishes, trimmed and sliced

1/2 cup pitted small black olives

8 cornichons, chopped

1 cup chopped fresh basil leaves, optional

1. Broil or grill the bread until lightly browned and crunchy, then place in a salad bowl.
2. Whisk together the vinegar, oil, salt, and pepper. Toss the remaining ingredients with the bread and dressing and serve immediately.

Chicken and Cucumber Salad

JAPAN ■ ■ ■

MAKES **4 SERVINGS**

TIME **30 MINUTES**

Crunchy, mildly sweet, and lightly spicy, this is a lovely little salad I learned in Kyoto. If you can find myoga—a lily root that looks something like garlic and is sold at some Asian markets—use it instead of the onion. Like onion, it's spicy and peppery; unlike onion, if you eat too much of it, you forget everything—or so I was told.

Salt

1 large red onion, thinly sliced and separated into rings

1 thin-skinned (English) cucumber

1 whole boneless, skinless chicken breast, 1/2 to 3/4 pound

1/2 cup sake

2 tablespoons rice or other mild vinegar

1 tablespoon sugar

1 tablespoon soy sauce

1. Put 1 tablespoon salt in a bowl of cold water and stir; add the onion. Rub the cucumber with salt, but do not peel it. Slice it thinly (a mandoline is ideal for this), put it in a colander, and sprinkle it lightly with salt. Combine the chicken and sake in a shallow bowl or deep plate and steam over hot water until cooked, about 10 minutes.
2. Drain and rinse the onion. Rinse the cucumber and wring the slices dry in a towel. Reserve the chicken-cooking liquid; shred the chicken.
3. Combine the onion, chicken, and cucumber in a bowl. Combine the vinegar, sugar, soy sauce, and 2 tablespoons of the chicken-cooking liquid and dress the salad with this. Serve within an hour, at room temperature.

Kong Namul Bean Sprout Salad KOREA ■ ■ ■

MAKES **6 OR MORE SERVINGS**

TIME **15 MINUTES**

Usually served as a panchan (side dish or small appetizer), this makes a fine little salad, too. Like many panchan, it contains sesame oil. To trim bean sprouts—a process I consider unnecessary but many people worldwide believe essential—simply pull off the thin little tail.

Salt

1 pound mung or soybean sprouts, trimmed if you like

1 tablespoon soy sauce

1 tablespoon dark sesame oil

1 teaspoon minced garlic

1 teaspoon sugar

1 teaspoon toasted sesame seeds (page 596)

2 scallions, trimmed and minced

1. Bring a medium pot of water to a boil and add salt. Poach the sprouts in this water for about 1

Making Bean Sprouts

Rinse about ½ cup mung beans well, then soak in water to cover for about 12 hours. Drain, then put in a jar topped with cheesecloth or other coarse cloth or a clean screen. Rinse and drain the beans; put the jar on a plate, propping it so its mouth is tilted down. Cover the jar with a towel to protect it from the light. Rinse and drain at least twice a day (more if the weather is dry or your air conditioner is on). After a few days, the seeds will have sprouted. Continue until they reach the length you want, then drain and refrigerate; they'll keep for a few more days. You can sprout other beans, seeds, or even whole grains the same way.

minute; drain and immediately toss with the soy sauce, sesame oil, garlic, and sugar.

2. Taste and adjust the seasoning, adding salt or more soy sauce or sesame oil if you like. Serve or refrigerate and serve cold, garnished with the sesame seeds and scallions.

Tomato and Onion Salad

MIDDLE EAST ■ ■ ■

MAKES **4 SERVINGS**

TIME **30 MINUTES**

Don't be deceived by this salad's simplicity: the lemon dressing and fresh herbs bring out the complex flavors of the tomatoes and onions, and if the ingredients are good, the results are practically miraculous. Note the extremely useful technique of "killing" the onions—as they say in Turkey—which you might try whenever you use raw onions, to tame their harshness.

You can make this salad an hour ahead of time, refrigerate, and toss again before serving.

1 large red onion, diced

Salt and black pepper to taste

1 garlic clove, minced

2 tablespoons fresh lemon juice

⅓ cup extra virgin olive oil

1 teaspoon ground cumin

4 medium tomatoes, cored, seeded, and chopped

½ cup chopped fresh parsley leaves

1. Soak the onion in salted ice water for about 30 minutes, then drain and dry. Meanwhile, whisk together the garlic, lemon juice, olive oil, and cumin; season with salt and pepper.

2. Toss the onion, tomatoes, and parsley with the dressing; taste and adjust the seasoning.

Tomato and Onion Salad with Tahini. Add another tablespoon of lemon juice to the dressing and substitute tahini for the olive oil. Whisk well before proceeding.

Tomato and Tapenade Salad ITALY ■ ■

MAKES **4 SERVINGS**

TIME **5 MINUTES (WITH PREMADE TAPENADE)**

A simple summer salad that is best with tomatoes that have just started to ripen. You can also toss this salad into hot or leftover pasta for a quick hot dish or pasta salad.

> **3 large or 4 medium tomatoes, cored, seeded, and chopped**
> **1 teaspoon minced garlic**
> **About ¹/₂ cup Tapenade (page 604)**
> **Salt and black pepper to taste**
> **¹/₂ cup fresh basil leaves, torn**

1. Toss the tomatoes with the garlic, tapenade, salt, and pepper.
2. Stir in the basil leaves; taste, adjust the seasoning, then serve.

Cold Spinach with Sesame JAPAN ■ ■ ■

MAKES **4 SERVINGS**

TIME **20 MINUTES**

A delicious way to prepare spinach ahead and present it beautifully. This is a place where perfectly fresh spinach will really strut its stuff. (You could use frozen spinach for this preparation, but it will not taste as good.)

For a really stunning look, roll the cold cooked spinach in a bamboo sushi-rolling mat, then slice the log on the diagonal before dipping it in the sesame seeds.

> **Salt to taste**
> **10 to 16 ounces fresh spinach, tough stems removed**
> **1 teaspoon soy sauce, or to taste**

> **¹/₂ cup toasted sesame seeds (page 596)**
> **1 teaspoon dark sesame oil, or to taste**

1. Bring a large pot of water to a boil and add salt. Add the spinach and cook until it wilts and the stems become tender, 30 seconds to 2 minutes. Remove it with a strainer or slotted spoon and immediately plunge it into a bowl of ice water. When it has cooled off, squeeze the excess water from it and finely chop it.
2. Sprinkle the spinach with a little salt and the soy sauce and shape it into a 1-inch-thick log (or press the spinach into small balls or mounds). Cut the log into 1-inch slices. Dip each end of each slice into the sesame seeds and arrange on a plate. Drizzle with the sesame oil. Serve immediately or refrigerate for up to 2 hours before serving.

COLD SPINACH WITH SESAME

Spinach and Dried Shrimp Salad

CHINA ■ ■ ■

MAKES **4 SERVINGS**

TIME **15 MINUTES**

A Chinese salad that contains one unusual but powerful ingredient: dried shrimp. These tiny bay shrimp are used throughout East Asia (especially Indonesia) and can be found at any Asian market. They're intensely flavored with the sea and salt and are so powerful they may be an acquired taste. This, however, is a great way to try them.

Salt

10 dried shrimp

10 ounces fresh spinach, tough stems removed

2 tablespoons soy sauce

2 tablespoons dark sesame oil

1. Bring a large pot of water to a boil and add salt. Meanwhile, barely cover the shrimp with boiling water (it should be less than ½ cup) and soak while you prepare the rest of the salad.
2. Plunge the spinach into the boiling water, then drain it immediately. Run it under cold water and drain again. Remove the shrimp from the soaking liquid and chop coarsely. Strain the soaking liquid into a large bowl; whisk with the soy sauce and sesame oil. Toss with the shrimp and spinach and serve within an hour.

DRIED SHRIMP

Pressed Tofu Salad CHINA ■ ■

MAKES **4 TO 6 SERVINGS AS A SALAD OR STARTER**

TIME **20 MINUTES, PLUS 2 HOURS TO MARINATE**

There are two keys to this salad. The first is buying dry, pressed tofu (bean curd), which is sold at most Asian food markets and some natural food stores. It's much firmer than regular tofu and has a dense, chewy texture and a brown skin. (If you can't find it, use extra-firm tofu and press it yourself; see page 491.)

The second key is allowing the salad to marinate long enough for the tofu to absorb the dressing. That part's easy, but it does require advance planning.

1 pound dry pressed tofu

2 medium to large carrots

2 large celery stalks

2 tablespoons soy sauce

1 teaspoon Tabasco sauce

¼ cup dark sesame oil

1. Cut the bean curd into 2-inch matchsticks; grate the carrots and celery. Whisk together the remaining ingredients.
2. Toss everything together and let it marinate for at least 2 hours in the refrigerator. Toss again immediately before serving.

Eggplant Salad with Mustard-Miso Dressing JAPAN ■ ■ ■

MAKES **4 SERVINGS**

TIME **ABOUT 30 TO 60 MINUTES**

One of the few recipes in which eggplant is boiled. It's an unusual preparation, and a good one, but you can also sauté it, as in Sautéed Eggplant (page 456).

Small eggplants are almost always preferable to large ones, and the Japanese know this better than anyone; you don't even see large eggplants there. (If you must use a larger eggplant, try to get a very firm one, which will have fewer seeds.)

Typically, this is made with wasabi powder; but I had it prepared with Dijon mustard in Japan, so I consider this version perfectly legitimate.

About 1 pound eggplant

Salt and cayenne to taste

1/3 cup white or other miso, or to taste

1 tablespoon soy sauce

1/4 cup Dijon mustard

Lemon wedges for serving

1. Trim the eggplant and cut it into 1-inch cubes. (If the eggplant is large, sprinkle with salt, put in a colander, and let it sit for at least 30 minutes, preferably 60. Rinse, drain, and pat dry.)
2. Bring a large pot of water to a boil and add salt. Immerse the eggplant in the boiling water and cook until tender, about 5 minutes. Drain well and set in a colander to cool. (You can refrigerate the eggplant, covered, for up to a day at this point. Bring it back to room temperature before proceeding.)
3. Dry the eggplant with paper towels. Whisk together the miso, soy sauce, and mustard in a serving bowl. Add the eggplant along with salt and cayenne, then toss. Taste and adjust the seasoning if necessary. Serve with the lemon wedges.

Cold Eggplant Salad with Sesame Dressing JAPAN ■ ▪

MAKES **4 SERVINGS**

TIME **20 TO 60 MINUTES**

Not unlike the preceding recipe, this one, too, is best with fresh, firm small eggplants. Serve as a starter or side dish, especially in summer.

About 1 1/2 pounds eggplant, preferably 4 to 6 small to medium

Salt

2 tablespoons toasted sesame seeds (page 596)

2 tablespoons soy sauce

1 tablespoon fresh lemon juice

1/2 teaspoon sugar

1. Trim the eggplant and cut it into 1/4-inch cubes or thin strips. (If the eggplant is large, sprinkle with salt, put in a colander, and let it sit for at least 30 minutes, preferably 60. Rinse, drain, and pat dry.)
2. Bring a large pot of water to a boil and add salt. Blanch the eggplant in the boiling water for 2 minutes, no more; it will just become tender. Drain in a colander as you would pasta.
3. Dry the eggplant with paper towels. Combine the remaining ingredients and toss with the eggplant in a small bowl. Serve at room temperature or refrigerate until ready to serve; covered well, this will remain flavorful for up to a day.

Batrik Bulgur and Tomato Salad with Nuts
TURKEY ■ ▪

MAKES **4 SERVINGS**

TIME **ABOUT 1 HOUR, LARGELY UNATTENDED**

Bulgur, which is precooked cracked wheat (see page 525), needs only to be reconstituted to be ready to eat. Usually this is done with water or stock, but here freshly made tomato juice is the liquid. (I had no idea what I was tasting when I first had this, but fortunately it was explained to me so I could experiment.) The nuts add a welcome crunchiness to this wonderful salad.

4 medium tomatoes, cored (canned are fine)

1/2 cup fine (#1) or medium (#2) bulgur

Sesame Seeds

In the American culinary pantheon, we most often see sesame seeds on top of burger buns, a site that belies their importance to many of the world's cuisines. Sesame, specifically as tahini, a thick nut butter made from roasted ground sesame, has been part of the Middle Eastern diet since antiquity and is an essential component of popular spreads like hummus and baba ghanoush.

Whole sesame seeds are commonly used in the garnish and flavoring of sweets and confections from Sicily to Saigon. Sesame seeds are also pressed for oil, of course (it is the hulls from this process that form the basis of the kind of halvah most commonly seen in the States). In the Middle East and India, this is generally a light, all-purpose oil. In China, Korea, and elsewhere in East Asia, it is made with roasted sesame seeds and used primarily as a seasoning, to finish dishes (though many Koreans cook with dark sesame oil—see, for example, Sautéed Spinach with Sesame, page 33—with good and unusual results).

Japan's Buddhist vegetarian tradition places a good deal of importance on the flavor of sesame; the oil tempura is traditionally fried in is flavored with a percentage of (roasted) sesame oil.

The various colors sesame seeds are available in—black, brown, and beige—taste almost identical, so you can pick which you'll use with visual effect in mind. Purchase sesame seeds in small quantities, keep them in the fridge or freezer, and toast them (see page 596) as you need them—pretoasted sesame seeds, sold at many Asian markets, lack the nutty aroma of freshly toasted seeds.

I should note that in my kitchen, the only sesame oil I use is the dark East Asian variety. If you can find light sesame oil and want to substitute it for the neutral oils called for throughout the book—corn or grapeseed (the latter being my favorite when I can find it at a decent price)—go right ahead; it's a fine choice.

---

2 tablespoons fresh lemon juice

3 tablespoons extra virgin olive oil

1 teaspoon pure chile powder, like ancho or New Mexico, or hot red pepper flakes, plus more to taste

1 small red or white onion, diced

1/3 cup shelled pistachios or chopped walnuts

Salt and black pepper to taste

Chopped fresh parsley leaves for garnish, optional

1. Puree the tomatoes in a blender or food processor; strain. Mix the bulgur with the tomato juice and lemon juice and set aside for about an hour or until the grains are tender.

2. Toss the bulgur mixture with the remaining ingredients except the parsley. Taste and adjust the seasoning, then serve, garnished with parsley if you like, or let stand for up to a couple of hours before garnishing and serving.

Tabbouleh MIDDLE EAST ■ ▨

MAKES **4 SERVINGS**

TIME **40 MINUTES**

Tabbouleh, the well-known salad that uses bulgur as its base (usually; there's also a rice version, which I've included as a variation), should be dominated by its herbs, mostly parsley but also mint. You can prepare the bulgur ahead of time and toss in the herbs right before serving.

2⁄3 cup fine (#1) or medium (#2) bulgur

1⁄2 cup extra virgin olive oil

1⁄4 cup fresh lemon juice, or to taste

Salt and black pepper to taste

2 cups roughly chopped fresh parsley, leaves and small stems only

1 cup roughly chopped fresh mint leaves

1⁄2 cup chopped scallion

4 medium tomatoes, cored, seeded, and chopped

1. Soak the bulgur in hot water to cover until tender, 15 to 30 minutes. (Meanwhile, prepare the other ingredients.) Drain the bulgur well, squeezing out as much of the water as possible. Toss the bulgur with the oil and lemon juice and season to taste.
2. Just before you're ready to eat, add all the remaining ingredients and toss gently. Taste, adjust the seasoning if necessary, and serve.

Tabbouleh with Rice. You can make this in 10 minutes if you have leftover rice; basmati (page 505) is best. Simply substitute 2 cups cooked rice for the bulgur; since rice is more starchy than bulgur, it may require a little more olive oil and lemon juice.

Mixed Vegetable Salad with Horseradish LITHUANIA ■ ■

MAKES **4 SERVINGS**

TIME **30 MINUTES**

A northern European salad that is a great accompaniment to grilled sausages or cooked ham. It combines fall fruits and vegetables with a creamy dressing spiked with horseradish. If you cannot find a rutabaga—the thick-skinned yellow turnip also called a swede—substitute a couple of white turnips or a daikon radish.

2 medium waxy potatoes, peeled and cut into 1⁄2-inch cubes

Salt and black pepper to taste

2 celery stalks, diced

2 carrots, grated

2 apples, preferably Granny Smith, peeled, cored, and grated

1 small rutabaga (about 1⁄2 pound), peeled and grated

1 tablespoon caraway seeds

One 3-inch piece fresh horseradish, peeled and grated, or 2 tablespoons prepared horseradish, or to taste

1⁄3 cup sour cream

1 tablespoon vinegar (if using fresh horseradish)

1. Put the potatoes in a saucepan with salted water to cover. Bring to a boil and simmer until tender, about 10 minutes; drain. (Meanwhile, prepare the other ingredients.)
2. Place all the vegetables and fruits in a large bowl; stir in the caraway seeds and a large pinch of salt and pepper.
3. Mix together the horseradish, sour cream, and, if necessary, vinegar. Pour over the salad and toss. Taste, adjust the seasoning, and serve.

Arborio Rice Salad ITALY ■ ■

MAKES **4 TO 6 SERVINGS**

TIME **30 MINUTES**

When you want a rice dish that screams "northern Italy," but you don't want something as rich (or as much work) as risotto, try throwing together this Italian rice salad, which was first made for me outside of Milan, served alongside a simply roasted chicken. You could add leftover chicken, shredded cheese, or other more substantial foods to make this into a meal, but it's a wonderful side dish.

Salt and black pepper to taste

2 cups Arborio, Vialone Nano, or other short-grain Italian
   or Spanish rice

¼ cup extra virgin olive oil

1 tablespoon sherry or red wine vinegar

¼ cup chopped fresh parsley leaves

¼ cup chopped fresh basil leaves

½ small red onion, thinly sliced

1 pint cherry tomatoes, halved

2 or 3 anchovy fillets, coarsely chopped, optional

2 tablespoons drained capers, optional

1. Bring a large pot of water to a boil and add salt. Drop the rice in, stir occasionally, and cook for about 15 minutes, until just tender. Drain, rinse briefly under running water—you want to stop the cooking, but it's nice if the rice stays a little warm, so it absorbs some of the vinegar—and shake well to drain off any excess moisture.

2. Transfer the rice to a serving bowl or platter and toss it with the remaining ingredients, including salt and pepper. Taste and add more olive oil, vinegar, salt, or pepper as needed. Serve at room temperature.

Bean and Tuna Salad ITALY ■ ■ ■

MAKES **4 SERVINGS**

TIME **15 MINUTES (WITH PRECOOKED BEANS)**

This classic combination of beans and tuna is great when made with white beans that have been cooked with garlic and other spices, like White Beans with Garlic (page 441). If you use bland or canned or frozen beans, jack up the seasonings here; add, for example, a bit of garlic, some fresh thyme, and/or a little cayenne.

A great picnic recipe, this can be made well in advance; note the green bean and salami variations,

which are also good. Any of these salads would be great toppings for Crostini (page 41) as well.

2 cups cooked, frozen, or canned white beans, like
   cannellini

One 7-ounce can tuna, preferably packed in olive oil

2 tablespoons extra virgin olive oil, plus more to taste

1 tablespoon fresh lemon juice, plus more to taste

1 red onion, finely chopped

Salt and black pepper to taste

¼ cup finely chopped celery leaves for garnish, optional

1. Drain the beans if necessary. Put the tuna in the bowl and flake with a fork, then stir in the beans.

2. Drizzle the olive oil and lemon juice over the salad, add the onion, and toss well. Season with salt and pepper, then taste and add more olive oil, lemon juice, salt, or pepper as needed. Garnish if you like and serve at room temperature; this will keep well, unrefrigerated, for an hour or two.

Green Bean and Tuna Salad. Substitute 1 pound green beans, trimmed, for the white beans. Cook them in salted boiling water just until tender and bright green; immediately plunge them into ice water to stop the cooking. Drain, then cut into 1-inch pieces and proceed as directed.

Bean and Salami Salad. Substitute 3 ounces salami, cut into narrow strips, for the tuna and red wine vinegar for the lemon juice.

MORE COMPLICATED SALADS

The salads that follow are "bigger" in a couple of senses. They might require real cooking and perhaps significant advance preparation as well. They're also hearty combinations approaching main-dish salads—

without meat or fish (these come later) but substantial nonetheless.

Asparagus Salad with Soy-Mustard Dressing JAPAN ■ ■ ■
MAKES **4 SERVINGS**

TIME **15 MINUTES**

Think of asparagus with mayonnaise but with a very sharp (and relatively low-fat) twist. As in most recipes for poached asparagus, thick spears are best; they retain some of their crispness while becoming tender. Those that weigh an ounce or more each—that is, eight to sixteen per pound—are the best. Their only disadvantage is that they must be peeled before cooking to remove the relatively tough skin. Fortunately, it's an easy job, with either a vegetable peeler or a paring knife.

Salt to taste

1 pound asparagus, trimmed and peeled if necessary

1 tablespoon dry mustard, dissolved in 1 tablespoon water

2 egg yolks

1 tablespoon soy sauce

1 tablespoon fresh lemon juice

1. Bring a large pot of water to a boil and add salt. Cook the asparagus just until tender, about 2 minutes for thin spears, up to 4 or 5 for thicker ones. Drain and immediately rinse with cold water (or, better still, plunge into ice water) to stop the cooking. Drain again and set aside. (You can wrap the asparagus and refrigerate for up to a day at this point. Bring to room temperature before serving.)
2. Whisk together the mustard, egg yolks, soy sauce, and lemon juice until well combined and smooth. Toss with the asparagus and serve.

Green Beans with Sesame-Miso Dressing JAPAN ■ ■ ■
MAKES **4 SERVINGS**

TIME **15 MINUTES**

Green beans (or almost any other vegetable for that matter) gain an exciting twist from this miso-based dressing. You can find miso (see page 123) at well-stocked supermarkets and Asian markets; red miso (which is actually brown) is most often used in this dressing, but you can also use white. If you cannot find miso, see the variation, which is worth trying in any case.

Salt to taste

1 1/2 pounds green beans, trimmed and cut into 2-inch lengths

1 tablespoon sugar or honey

1 tablespoon mirin, sweet sake, or other sweet wine

2 tablespoons toasted sesame seeds (page 596)

3 tablespoons miso, preferably red

1. Bring a large pot of water to a boil and add salt. Cook the green beans just until tender, about 3 minutes, drain, and rinse under cold water (better still, plunge them into a bowl of ice water) to stop the cooking. Drain again and set aside.
2. Whisk the sugar into the mirin until it is dissolved; stir in the sesame seeds and miso until well combined. Toss with the green beans until well coated, then serve or let stand for up to an hour before serving.

Green Beans with Sweet Sesame Dressing. Substitute 1 tablespoon soy sauce and 1 teaspoon honey for the miso.

Houria Spicy Carrot Salad NORTH AFRICA ■ ■ ■

MAKES **4 SERVINGS**

TIME **30 MINUTES**

Houria is a great starter, but you can also serve it alongside North African meat dishes, like Lamb Tagine with Prunes (page 407) or Chicken and Lentil Tagine (page 284). It comes in many forms but always combines the sweetness of carrots with the typically earthy spices of North Africa. It's best with cooked carrots, but if you're in a hurry you can make it with raw carrots; see the variation.

Julienning carrots for houria is easiest with a mandoline (see page 167); if you don't have one, slice or chop them roughly.

1½ pounds carrots, julienned, sliced, or diced

2 garlic cloves, peeled

2 teaspoons sugar

Salt and black pepper to taste

2 teaspoons caraway seeds

1 teaspoon cumin seeds

1 teaspoon sweet paprika

2 tablespoons extra virgin olive oil

1 teaspoon Harissa (page 598) or cayenne to taste

12 good-quality black olives, pitted, optional

¼ pound feta cheese, crumbled, optional

¼ cup chopped fresh cilantro leaves for garnish, optional

1. Put the carrots, garlic, sugar, salt, caraway, cumin, paprika, and oil in a wide skillet or saucepan; add just enough water to cover the carrots and turn the heat to medium-high. Bring to a boil and turn the heat to medium. Cook the carrots, stirring occasionally, until softened and most of the water has evaporated, about 15 minutes. Drain and transfer to a large bowl.
2. Remove and mince the garlic cloves. Return to the carrot mixture and toss with the harissa, along

with more salt plus pepper to taste. Mix with the optional olives, feta, and/or cilantro and serve warm or at room temperature. (You can prepare the dish in advance and let sit for a few hours at room temperature or cover and refrigerate for up to a day; bring back to room temperature before serving.)

Quick Carrot Salad. Omit the garlic, sugar, and caraway seeds. Squeeze the juice of 1 lemon over the raw carrots and then toss with the cumin, paprika, oil, harissa, and salt to taste. Garnish with olives, feta, orange slices, or cilantro leaves—or not at all—and serve.

Grilled Eggplant Salad NORTH AFRICA ■ ■

MAKES **4 SERVINGS**

TIME **45 MINUTES, PLUS TIME TO PREHEAT THE GRILL AND CHILLING TIME**

This cooked salad can be prepared in many different ways, including a twice-fried method that by most standards is overwhelmingly oily. These options are all suitable, though the first one, in which the eggplant is grilled, is my favorite. The salad is best served cold, so plan to prepare it ahead of time and refrigerate. It's quite good warm or at room temperature too.

1 pound eggplant, preferably small ones

3 garlic cloves, minced

1 small onion, minced

2 medium tomatoes

2 teaspoons sweet paprika

2 teaspoons ground cumin

1 tablespoon fresh lemon juice

3 tablespoons extra virgin olive oil

1 tablespoon Harissa (page 598), or to taste

Salt and black pepper to taste

Chopped fresh parsley leaves for garnish, optional

¼ cup drained capers, optional

1 cup good-quality black olives, pitted, optional

1. Start a charcoal or wood fire or preheat a gas grill (or the broiler); the rack should be 4 to 6 inches from the heat source. Cut the eggplants in half lengthwise up to the stem, but do not cut through. Spread the garlic and onion in between the eggplant halves and press the halves back together.

2. Grill the tomatoes and eggplants, turning once or twice, until they are blackened and soft, 5 to 10 minutes for the tomatoes, 10 to 15 for the eggplants.

3. Let cool a bit, then peel off the skins and let cool further. Roughly chop the vegetables, reserving any juices, then mix with the paprika, cumin, lemon juice, oil, harissa, and salt and pepper.

4. Chill if time allows or serve warm or at room temperature; in any case, garnish if you like with the parsley, capers, and olives just before serving.

Sautéed Eggplant Salad. Cut the eggplants and tomatoes into 1-inch cubes. Sprinkle the eggplant pieces with salt, put them in a colander, and let them sit for at least 30 minutes, preferably 60. Rinse, drain, and pat dry. Heat the oil in a large skillet and cook the eggplant until almost soft, about 7 minutes, then add the garlic, onion, and tomatoes and cook for another 5 minutes. Remove from the heat and stir in the remaining seasonings. Serve warm or chill and garnish if you like.

Roasted Eggplant Salad. Preheat the oven to 375°F. Cut the eggplants and tomatoes into 1-inch cubes. Sprinkle the eggplant pieces with salt, put them in a colander, and let them sit for at least 30 minutes, preferably 60. Rinse, drain, and pat dry.

Place the eggplant, tomatoes, garlic, onion, paprika, cumin, and oil into an ovenproof baking dish. Stir well and cover with foil. Bake for 50 to 60 minutes, stirring once or twice and adding some water if the mixture looks too dry (unlikely but not impossible). Remove from the oven and let cool. Stir in the lemon juice, harissa, salt, and pepper. Garnish if you like and serve.

Eggplant and Yogurt Salad
MIDDLE EAST ■ ▦

MAKES **4 SERVINGS**

TIME **40 MINUTES, PLUS TIME TO PREHEAT THE GRILL AND CHILLING TIME**

Eggplant is everywhere in the Middle East; you see it as often as you do tomatoes. Here are three takes on a creamy, mild dish of eggplant and yogurt. The first relies on the charred flavor you get when you grill or broil eggplant; especially when seasoned this way, it's really the best. The variations are easier and still very good.

As always, small eggplants are best; regardless of size, they should be as firm as you can find.

1 pound eggplant, preferably small ones

1 medium onion, minced

3 garlic cloves, minced

1½ cups yogurt, preferably whole-milk

Salt and black pepper to taste

Pinch of cayenne

¼ cup chopped fresh parsley or mint leaves

1. Start a charcoal or wood fire or preheat a gas grill (or the broiler); the rack should be no more than 4 inches from the heat source. Cut the eggplants in half lengthwise up to the stem, but do not cut

through. Spread about two thirds of the onion and garlic between the eggplant halves and press the halves back together.

2. Grill the eggplants, turning once or twice, until they are blackened and collapsed, 10 to 15 minutes. Don't worry if the skin burns a bit. Meanwhile, mix the remaining garlic and onion with the yogurt; season to taste with salt, pepper, and a little cayenne.

3. When cooked, let the eggplants cool a bit, then peel off the skins and let cool further. Roughly chop the eggplants, reserving any juices, then mix with the yogurt dressing. Chill if time allows or serve at room temperature; in either case, garnish with the parsley or mint.

Sautéed Eggplant and Yogurt Salad. Use half as much onion and garlic. Cut the eggplants into 1-inch cubes, then sprinkle them with salt and put them in a colander; let them drain for at least 20 minutes and up to an hour. Rinse, drain, and pat dry. Put the oil in a large skillet over medium-high heat and cook the eggplants, stirring occasionally, until almost soft, 10 to 15 minutes. Remove from the heat, cool, and mix with the onion, garlic, yogurt, and seasoning. Serve warm, at room temperature, or cold.

Roasted Eggplant and Yogurt Salad. Cut the eggplants into 1-inch cubes, then sprinkle them with salt and put them in a colander; let them drain for at least 20 minutes and up to an hour. Rinse, drain, and pat dry. Meanwhile, preheat the oven to 375°F. Lightly oil a baking dish and put the eggplant into it. Stir well, cover with foil, and bake for about an hour, stirring once or twice and adding some water if the mixture looks too dry (unlikely but not impossible). Remove from the oven and let cool. Use half as much onion and garlic and mix the eggplant with these, the yogurt, and the seasoning. Garnish and serve.

Roast Pepper Salad with Tomatoes and Preserved Lemon

NORTH AFRICA ■ ■

MAKES **4 SERVINGS**

TIME **ABOUT 1 HOUR (WITH PREROASTED PEPPERS), LARGELY UNATTENDED**

North African spices enhance the smoky flavor of the peppers here, and the preserved lemon—which you can buy at a specialty shop or make yourself (page 598)—makes it exotic. You can prepare this salad ahead of time since it is best after marinating for an hour or so. For extra color, use bell peppers of a couple of different colors.

> 1 pound bell peppers, roasted, stemmed, seeded, and peeled (page 470)
> ¾ pound tomatoes (2 large or 3 or 4 medium), cored (and seeded and peeled too if you like)
> 1 garlic clove, minced
> 2 teaspoons sweet paprika
> 1 teaspoon ground cumin
> ½ teaspoon cayenne, or to taste
> Salt to taste
> Juice of 1 lemon
> ¼ cup extra virgin olive oil
> ¼ cup chopped fresh parsley leaves
> 1 preserved lemon, cut into thin strips

1. Cut the peppers into 1-inch strips; coarsely chop the tomatoes. Toss in a large bowl with the garlic, paprika, cumin, cayenne, salt, lemon juice, and oil. Let rest for about an hour.

2. Garnish with parsley and preserved lemon strips before serving.

Roasted Pepper, Anchovy, and Caper Salad ITALY ■ ▦

MAKES **4 SERVINGS**

TIME **20 MINUTES (WITH PREROASTED PEPPERS), PLUS MARINATING TIME**

A well-known standard, this marinated salad combines the sweetness of peppers with the saltiness of anchovies and capers, using a good olive oil to tie all the flavors together.

You can use jarred roasted peppers ("pimientos") for this if you like. Canned or jarred piquillo peppers (page 47) are better, but still not as good as peppers you roast yourself. The best anchovies commonly available are sold in jars, packed in olive oil.

It's best to make this salad ahead of time so the flavors marry. Eat this at lunch, as a starter, or as a side dish with something flavorful, like Beef Stew with Dried Mushrooms (page 380).

> 1 pound red, yellow, and/or orange bell peppers, roasted, stemmed, seeded, and peeled (page 470)
> $1/4$ pound anchovy fillets
> 3 garlic cloves, peeled and crushed
> 3 tablespoons drained capers
> 1 tablespoon dried oregano
> Salt and black pepper to taste
> $1/4$ cup extra virgin olive oil, plus more as needed
> Chopped fresh parsley leaves for garnish, optional

1. Cut the roasted peppers into 1-inch strips and lay a quarter of them on the bottom of a casserole dish. Spread a third of the anchovies, 1 garlic clove, 1 tablespoon of the capers, and 1 teaspoon of the oregano evenly on top. Sprinkle on salt and pepper. Repeat two more times and then top with the remaining peppers.
2. Pour enough olive oil over the salad to cover the top layer of peppers. Marinate for at least 2 hours at room temperature. If marinating overnight,

cover and refrigerate, but bring back to room temperature before serving. Use the parsley at the last minute if you choose to do so.

Potato Salad with Mustard Vinaigrette FRANCE ■ ▦

MAKES **4 SERVINGS**

TIME **30 MINUTES, PLUS COOLING TIME**

Potato salad is an American classic, but this is a lot more flavorful than the mayonnaise-based version. It's great served warm, but the important thing to remember is that it's far better at room temperature than cold.

If you like, add about $1/4$ pound diced slab bacon, cooked until crisp, along with $1/2$ cup minced shallot or mild onion for a Germanic twist.

> Salt and black pepper to taste
> $1^1/2$ to 2 pounds waxy or Yukon Gold potatoes
> $1/3$ cup Dijon mustard
> $1/4$ cup extra virgin olive oil
> 1 tablespoon balsamic, sherry, or other flavorful vinegar, or to taste
> 3 tablespoons chopped fresh parsley leaves

1. Bring a pot of water to a boil and add salt. Peel the potatoes, then cut them into bite-sized pieces. Cook them in the water until tender but still firm and not at all mushy, 15 minutes or so. Drain.
2. Combine the mustard, oil, and vinegar in a bowl or blender and whisk or blend until well combined. Toss with the potatoes while they're still warm; season with salt and pepper and garnish with the parsley. Serve warm or at room temperature or refrigerate for up to a day, but bring back to room temperature before serving.

Roasted Corn and Black Bean Salad

MEXICO ■ ■ ■

MAKES **4 SERVINGS**

TIME **20 MINUTES (WITH PRECOOKED BEANS)**

You can use canned black beans for this (you can even use frozen corn), but the salad is best with beans that have been cooked, with good spices, until tender but not mushy.

> 2 tablespoons extra virgin olive oil
>
> 4 ears corn, husked and stripped of their kernels
>
> Salt and black pepper to taste
>
> 1 garlic clove, minced
>
> 1 ½ cups cooked black beans (page 431), at room temperature
>
> 1 ripe tomato, cored and diced, optional
>
> 1 teaspoon minced jalapeño or other small chile
>
> 2 tablespoons fresh lime juice
>
> Chopped fresh cilantro leaves for garnish

1. Put the oil in a large nonstick skillet and turn the heat to high. Add the corn, along with a large pinch of salt and some pepper, and cook, shaking the pan or stirring occasionally, until the corn is lightly charred, 5 to 10 minutes. Add the garlic and cook for 1 minute more, stirring.

2. Combine the corn with all the remaining ingredients. Taste and adjust the seasoning and serve or cover and refrigerate for up to a couple of hours, then bring back to room temperature before serving.

MAIN-COURSE SALADS

There are times when everyone wants nothing more than a simple salad for dinner, or at least lunch; these will fit the bill, and some are even more substantial than that, salads that can serve as light main courses or even not-so-light ones. Not surprisingly, many contain fish, chicken, or meat.

Tofu Salad with Peanut Sauce

SOUTHEAST ASIA ■

MAKES **4 SERVINGS**

TIME **30 MINUTES**

This is a warm salad, combining a wide range of textures and flavors, great as a light lunch or a starter for any Asian meal. Although you can buy packaged fried tofu at many Asian markets—and that is undeniably convenient—it is much better homemade. Just be sure to remove as much of the water as you can, by firmly pressing the tofu between paper towels as detailed on page 491. For information on shrimp paste, see page 9; for information on nam pla, see page 500.

> Neutral oil, such as corn or grapeseed, for deep-frying
>
> ½ pound firm tofu, drained, dried, and cut into 2-inch cubes
>
> 3 small fresh chiles, preferably Thai, stemmed and seeded
>
> 2 garlic cloves, peeled
>
> 1 teaspoon shrimp paste or 1 tablespoon nam pla
>
> 1 tablespoon sugar
>
> 1 tablespoon soy sauce
>
> ½ cup peanuts, chopped
>
> Salt to taste
>
> ¼ cup bean sprouts
>
> ¼ cup Chinese yard-long beans or haricots verts, trimmed
>
> 1 small cucumber, peeled and sliced

1. Heat 2 inches of oil in a deep, heavy pot over medium heat to 400°F. When the oil is hot, carefully slide in the tofu cubes and fry, turning occa-

CHINESE LONG BEANS

sionally, until golden brown and puffy, 5 to 10 minutes. Work in batches to avoid overcrowding. Remove with a slotted spoon and drain on paper towels.

2. Put the chiles, garlic, and shrimp paste in a food processor. Process into a paste. Heat 1 tablespoon oil in a small skillet over medium heat and fry the chile paste until fragrant, about 30 seconds. Stir in the sugar, soy sauce, and ¼ cup water. When the sugar has dissolved, remove from the heat. Stir in the peanuts and season with salt.

3. Toss the peanut sauce with the bean sprouts, long beans, and cucumber. Transfer to a serving plate and top with the fried tofu.

Salade Niçoise FRANCE ■ ■ ■
MAKES **4 SERVINGS**

TIME **15 MINUTES**

The definition of a classic Niçoise salad is often contested, especially now that it is so popular at cafés and restaurants. It is, however, essentially a country salad, so the ingredients depend on what is in season. The basics of this rough country salad are lettuce, hard-cooked eggs, anchovy fillets, black olives, tomatoes, and garlic in the dressing. Most people add tuna, too, but you can consider it optional. Among the myriad other possible additions are cooked green beans, potatoes, and artichoke hearts, raw or roasted bell pepper, capers, and basil.

6 cups torn assorted lettuces and other salad greens

2 hard-cooked eggs (page 338), sliced

1 cup good-quality black olives, preferably oil-cured

3 ripe tomatoes, cored, seeded, and cut into quarters or
    eighths

6 anchovy fillets

One or two 6-ounce cans tuna, preferably packed in olive
    oil, or grilled fresh tuna, cut into chunks, optional

2 tablespoons red wine vinegar, plus a little more if
    needed

About ½ cup extra virgin olive oil

Salt and black pepper to taste

1 garlic clove, minced

1 small shallot, minced

1 teaspoon Dijon mustard

ANCHOVIES *packed in olive oil*

1. Arrange all the salad ingredients nicely on a platter—greens on the bottom, topped with egg slices, olives, tomatoes, anchovies, and tuna, if using. Or—less attractive but easier to serve—toss all the ingredients together.
2. Make the vinaigrette by adding the vinegar to the oil, along with the salt and pepper, garlic, shallot, and mustard. Stir and taste. Add more vinegar if necessary and adjust the seasoning. Stir or shake vigorously, pour over the salad, and serve.

Mediterranean-Style Seafood Salad

ITALY ■ ▦

MAKES **4 SERVINGS**

TIME **30 MINUTES PLUS CHILLING TIME**

In most parts of the world, and certainly throughout the Mediterranean, seafood salad is as simple as this: you dress some poached fish with olive oil and loads of lemon. (Actually some people prefer vinegar, and it's certainly traditional in many places, but I always go with lemon if I have it.) If you want to make it more elaborate, you add poached vegetables or serve it on a bed of greens.

So view this simple recipe as a guideline, not as dogma; use whatever fish you have, a variety or something as simple and common as shrimp. Add vegetables and vary the seasonings if you like. It will be fine any way you do it.

Salt and black pepper to taste

1/2 pound swordfish, skinned and cut into
   1/2-inch chunks

1/2 pound shrimp, peeled (halved if large)

1/2 pound sea scallops, cut in half through their
   equators (or quartered if very large)

1/2 cup minced fresh parsley leaves

1 tablespoon capers with a little of their liquid, or to taste

1 shallot, minced

1/4 cup extra virgin olive oil

Fresh lemon juice to taste

1. Bring a saucepan of water to a boil and add salt. (If you have Fish Stock, page 161, use it; when you're done, strain it and save it for reuse.) Turn the heat to medium-low and add the swordfish; 30 seconds later, add the shrimp and scallops. Cover and turn off the heat; let the fish sit in the liquid for about 10 minutes. Drain and cool, then chill. (You can prepare the fish to this point up to 24 hours in advance; cover and refrigerate until you're ready to eat.)
2. Toss the fish with the parsley, capers, shallot, olive oil, salt, and pepper. Add lemon juice, then taste and adjust the seasoning as necessary.

Fish Salad with Horseradish Dressing RUSSIA ■ ▦ ▦

MAKES **4 SERVINGS**

TIME **15 MINUTES**

A great cool salad, especially wonderful if you use fresh horseradish. (If you never have, buy just a small piece of the root, which looks like a tree root; peel and grate it, being careful not to get any of its juices in your eyes.) You can prepare the fish and dressing ahead of time and toss together immediately before serving.

Salt and black pepper to taste

1 1/2 pounds white fish fillets, like red snapper, cod, or
   halibut, skinned, boned, and cut into 2-inch chunks

3 tablespoons fresh lemon juice

One 2-ounce piece fresh horseradish, peeled and grated,
   or 1 tablespoon prepared horseradish or wasabi paste,
   or to taste

¼ cup mayonnaise, preferably homemade (page 602)

2 teaspoons sugar

1 cucumber, peeled and diced

¼ cup chopped fresh parsley leaves

2 tablespoons chopped fresh dill leaves

1. Bring a large saucepan of salted water to a boil, then adjust the heat so the water bubbles gently. Add the fish pieces and cook for about 5 minutes, or until a skewer or thin-bladed knife pierces them easily. Do not overcook. Drain and sprinkle with half the lemon juice.

2. Whisk the remaining lemon juice with the horseradish, mayonnaise, sugar, salt, and pepper. When you're ready to serve—the salad is good warm, cold, or at room temperature—gently toss the dressing with the fish and cucumber, top with parsley and dill, and serve.

Salt Cod Salad SPAIN ■

MAKES **4 SERVINGS**

TIME **20 MINUTES (WITH PREPARED SALT COD)**

This is an odd-sounding salad, but everyone who tastes it loves it. The saltiness of the bacalao, salt cod, which is not overwhelming as long as you've handled it properly, is balanced by the other flavors, and the crunch of vegetables is a welcome addition.

2 tablespoons fresh lemon juice

2 tablespoons cider or red wine vinegar

⅓ cup extra virgin olive oil

Salt and black pepper to taste

4 to 6 cups salad greens, preferably a mixture, roughly chopped

1 pound dried salt cod, soaked, cooked, and shredded (page 245)

1 orange, peeled and segmented

1 tomato, cored and chopped, or a handful of cherry tomatoes, cut in half

⅓ cup pitted black olives, preferably oil-cured, roughly chopped

⅓ cup chopped fresh parsley leaves

1. Mix the lemon juice and vinegar in a large bowl; whisk in the oil in a slow, steady stream until well combined. Season with salt and pepper and toss in the salad greens. Transfer the salad to a serving bowl or plate.

2. Toss the salt cod, orange, tomato, olives, and parsley together and arrange on top of the salad greens. Serve immediately.

Green Papaya Salad with Shrimp

VIETNAM ■ ■

MAKES **4 SERVINGS**

TIME **30 MINUTES, PLUS TIME TO PREHEAT THE GRILL IF YOU'RE USING IT TO COOK THE SHRIMP**

Not surprisingly—Vietnamese food is only occasionally hot—this isn't as blistering as the vegetarian Thai version on page 174. You can buy Vietnamese chili-garlic paste at any store selling Asian ingredients; it keeps nearly forever in the refrigerator. Fish sauces like nam pla and nuoc mam are discussed on page 500. Palm sugar is available at many Asian markets, but brown sugar is indistinguishable in flavor.

Salt and black pepper

12 large shrimp, peeled

4 cups peeled, seeded, and shredded green papaya, Granny Smith apple, jicama, or a combination

2 cups mung bean sprouts

1 cup roughly chopped fresh cilantro leaves

½ cup roughly chopped fresh mint leaves

½ cup chopped scallion

1 teaspoon Vietnamese chili-garlic paste, or to taste

Juice of 2 limes

¼ cup nam pla or nuoc mam

1 tablespoon brown or palm sugar

½ cup finely chopped dry-roasted peanuts

1. Salt the shrimp, then grill or broil it until just cooked, or put it in a saucepan with salted water to cover, bring the water to a boil, then turn off the heat and let the shrimp sit in the water until cool. When cool, slice the shrimp in half lengthwise, as if you were butterflying it.

2. Meanwhile, toss the papaya, sprouts, herbs, and scallion together in a large bowl. Whisk together the chili-garlic paste, lime juice, nam pla, and sugar, along with a little salt and a lot of pepper; taste and adjust the seasoning. Toss the dressing with the papaya-herb mixture, then top with the shrimp and peanuts. Toss again at the table and serve.

Salade Olivier RUSSIA ■ ■
MAKES **4 SERVINGS**

TIME **20 MINUTES (WITH PREPARED INGREDIENTS)**

The story about this so-called Russian classic is that it was created by a nineteenth-century French chef, M. Olivier, who ran The Hermitage, a famous restaurant in Moscow. It is essentially a potato salad–chicken salad combo and, as such, eminently useful. This recipe outlines the basic salad; you can improvise as you would for Salade Niçoise (page 196).

2 teaspoons mustard, preferably Dijon

1 cup mayonnaise, preferably homemade (page 602)

2 tablespoons fresh lemon juice

1 pound cooked chicken or turkey meat, cut into ½-inch cubes

3 waxy potatoes, boiled until tender, peeled, and cut into 1-inch cubes

1 medium onion, diced

Salt and black pepper to taste

2 hard-cooked eggs (page 338), shelled and sliced crosswise

¼ cup chopped fresh parsley or dill leaves

1. Whisk the mustard, mayonnaise, and lemon juice together. Toss with the chicken, potatoes, and onion. Season with salt and pepper, then gently stir in the eggs.

2. Chill if you like (the salad will keep well for a few hours), garnish with parsley or dill, and serve.

Laarb Minced Chicken "Salad"
THAILAND ■ ■

MAKES **4 SERVINGS**

TIME **25 MINUTES**

You could call this chicken salad Thai-style, but whatever you call it—you'll see larb, larp, laarb, and other variations on menus—this is a quick, delicious, appetite-rousing starter. Teaming it with any of the more substantial Thai dishes in this book and some rice makes for an impressive meal. (If you need information on nam pla, see page 500.)

Most laarb served in this country is made from chicken, and certainly that's good and easy. But laarb is even more delicious made with pork shoulder or beef tenderloin. In any case, this is one place where you should mince the meat together with the garlic by hand; food-processed meat is just a little too mushy here. The process shouldn't take more than five minutes, though, so don't be put off.

1 pound boneless, skinless chicken thighs, pork shoulder, or beef tenderloin

1 garlic clove, peeled

2 tablespoons corn, grapeseed, or other neutral oil

Salt and black pepper to taste

1 teaspoon sugar, or to taste

1 tablespoon nam pla, or to taste (see page 500)

Pinch of cayenne, or to taste

Juice of $1/2$ lime, or to taste

1 cup loosely packed mixed herbs, like cilantro, basil,
    mint, or Thai basil

1 shallot, sliced

1 small fresh chile, such as Thai or serrano, stemmed,
    seeded, and sliced, optional (use it only if you like your
    food very spicy)

About 12 outer leaves of cabbage or iceberg lettuce

2 tablespoons Khao Koor: Ground and Toasted Rice (page
    587), optional

Lime wedges for garnish

1. Mince the chicken and garlic together with a sharp
   knife or cleaver.

2. Coat the bottom of a medium skillet or wok with
   the oil and turn the heat to medium-high. When a
   wisp of smoke appears, add the minced chicken
   and garlic. Season immediately with pinches of
   salt, pepper, and sugar and cook, stirring infrequently, until the meat browns a bit, 3 or 4 minutes.

3. Transfer the meat to a medium salad bowl and toss
   it with the nam pla, cayenne, and lime juice. Let
   the mixture sit for 30 seconds, then taste and adjust the seasonings. Stir in the herbs, shallot, and
   chile if you're using it.

4. Tear or cut the cabbage or lettuce leaves into
   roughly two-bite-sized pieces (2 inches by 1 inch
   or slightly larger) and arrange them on a large plate
   or platter like little serving bowls. Spoon a little of
   the chicken-herb mixture into each of them, sprinkle the ground and toasted rice over all if you like,
   and garnish with the lime wedges. Serve within a
   couple hours, before the herbs start to wilt.

Seaweed Salad with Cucumber and Chicken or Shrimp JAPAN ■ ■

MAKES **8 SERVINGS**

TIME **20 MINUTES**

This is simply a kind of sea-based mesclun with a distinctively sesame-flavored dressing. Wakame, a dark
green, leafy seaweed, is sold dried almost everywhere
and is the most common seaweed used in salad. Other
seaweeds, ranging in color from light green to bright
red to black and in texture from leafy to ferny, are all
fine (see page 483).

At most Japanese markets and some health food
stores, you can find a prepackaged assortment of seaweed salad greens; these are a little more expensive
than buying individual seaweeds but will give you a
good variety without a big investment. You don't need
much: an ounce of dried seaweed, or even less, is
enough to make a salad for four.

2 ounces wakame or assorted seaweeds

2 medium to large cucumbers, preferably thin skinned,
    like English or Japanese

1 pound shredded cooked chicken or roughly chopped
    cooked shrimp, optional

$1/2$ cup minced shallot, scallion, or red onion

3 tablespoons soy sauce

2 tablespoons rice or other light vinegar

2 tablespoons mirin

2 tablespoons dark sesame oil

$1/2$ teaspoon cayenne, or to taste

Salt to taste

2 tablespoons toasted sesame seeds (page 596), optional

1. Rinse the seaweed once and soak it in at least 10
   times its volume of water for 5 minutes, until tender. Meanwhile, wash and dice the cucumbers; do
   not peel unless necessary.

2. Drain and gently squeeze the seaweed to remove
   excess water. Pick through the seaweed to sort out

any hard bits (there may be none) and chop or cut up (it may be easier to use scissors than a knife) if the pieces are large. Combine the cucumbers and seaweed in a bowl. Add the chicken or shrimp if using.

3. Toss with the remaining ingredients except the sesame seeds; taste and add salt or other seasonings as necessary and serve, garnished with the sesame seeds if you like.

Chicken Salad with Tarator TURKEY ■ ■ ■
MAKES **4 SERVINGS**

TIME **30 MINUTES (WITH PREPARED CHICKEN)**

Tarator, or skordalia (page 600), is one of the most useful dressings I know, a mayonnaiselike sauce that contains neither egg nor oil. Here it transforms ordinary chicken salad.

2 ounces good-quality bread

1 cup milk or stock

$1/4$ pound walnuts (about 1 cup)

1 small garlic clove, peeled

Salt and black pepper to taste

$1/4$ cup extra virgin olive oil

Pure chile powder, like ancho or New Mexico, or paprika to taste

2 to 3 cups shredded cooked chicken

1 cup chopped fresh cilantro leaves

1. Soak the bread in the milk or stock while you put the walnuts, garlic, and some salt in a food processor and pulse the machine to grind coarsely. Gently squeeze some of the liquid from the bread and add to the processor along with the oil. Process until combined but not pureed. Add as much of the remaining milk or stock as you need to give the mixture a mayonnaiselike consistency.

2. By hand, add the chile powder or paprika; bind the chicken with as much of the sauce as is necessary to give it the texture you like. Taste and adjust the seasoning, then stir in about two thirds of the cilantro. Serve or refrigerate for up to a day; garnish with the remaining cilantro before serving.

Chicken Salad with Vietnamese Seasonings ■ ■
MAKES **4 SERVINGS**

TIME **15 MINUTES (WITH PRECOOKED CHICKEN)**

The ideal herb for seasoning this salad is rau ram, which is not impossible to find if a well-stocked Asian store or supermarket is in your area; you can pick up your Thai fish sauce (page 500) while you're there. The best alternative is a combination of cilantro and mint, which comes pretty close.

If you don't have precooked chicken, just simmer chicken breasts (bone-in are best) in water to cover for 10 to 15 minutes. When the meat is done, pull it from the bone (continue cooking the bones, perhaps with a few vegetables like carrots and onions, to make stock) and chop or shred.

1 tablespoon nam pla

1 teaspoon cracked or coarsely ground black pepper

1 teaspoon sugar

1 small fresh chile, preferably Thai, minced, or
$1/2$ teaspoon hot red pepper flakes, or to taste

2 tablespoons fresh lime juice

1 teaspoon minced garlic

2 medium to large shallots, chopped

2 cups chopped or shredded cooked chicken

$1/2$ cup chopped rau ram or $1/4$ cup each mint and cilantro leaves

Salt to taste

12 or 16 leaves Boston, red leaf, or green leaf lettuce

1. Combine the first 7 ingredients in a bowl and toss with the chicken; set a bit of the herb aside for garnish, then stir the rest into the mixture. Taste and adjust the seasoning, adding salt if necessary.

2. Arrange the lettuce on 4 plates and top each leaf with a portion of the chicken salad. Garnish with the remaining herb and serve.

Salade Lyonnaise FRANCE ■ ▨

MAKES **4 SERVINGS**

TIME **ABOUT 30 MINUTES**

In Lyon, fat remains king, which makes it a pleasure to eat there—assuming you can put your guilt aside. This salad is best made with a mixture of greens, some of which should be bitter, like dandelion. The poached egg (which ideally will be hot) softens everything, the bacon provides salt, crunch, and fat, the vinegar spices it all up—the combination is really a treat. One of my favorite lunches and a knockout first course, which should be followed by something light.

2 tablespoons extra virgin olive oil

$\frac{1}{4}$ to $\frac{1}{2}$ pound slab bacon, cut into $\frac{1}{2}$-inch cubes

1 tablespoon chopped shallot

6 cups mixed salad greens

About $\frac{1}{4}$ cup top-quality red wine vinegar

1 teaspoon Dijon mustard

Salt and black pepper to taste

4 Poached Eggs (page 337)

1 cup small Croutons (page 580), optional

1. Place the olive oil in a skillet and turn the heat to medium. Add the bacon and cook slowly until it is crisp all over, 10 minutes or more. Add the shallot and cook for a minute or two longer, until the shallot softens. Keep the bacon warm in the skillet.

2. Heat a salad bowl by filling it with hot water and letting it sit for a minute. Dry it and toss in the greens. Add the vinegar and mustard to the skillet and bring just to a boil, stirring. Pour the liquid and the bacon over the greens and season to taste; they shouldn't need much salt.

3. Divide the salad among 4 plates. Top each portion with a poached egg, sprinkle with croutons if you're using them, and serve immediately.

Neua Nam Tok Grilled Beef Salad

VIETNAM ■ ▨

MAKES **4 SERVINGS**

TIME **30 MINUTES, PLUS TIME TO PREHEAT THE GRILL OR BROILER**

The first time I had this salad—it was in Saigon—I ate so much of it I could barely eat anything else. So, obviously, you can make it as a main course (serve it with rice). Technically, it's a starter and a great use for leftover steak. For a traditional, unusual, and wonderful Thai version, toss the beef with $\frac{1}{4}$ cup Khao Koor powder (page 587) before dressing. For information on nam pla, see page 500.

1 to $1\frac{1}{2}$ pounds strip steak, about 1 inch thick

Salt to taste

1 teaspoon black pepper, or more to taste

$\frac{1}{4}$ cup nam pla

3 tablespoons fresh lime juice

1 garlic clove, minced

2 shallots, sliced

2 small fresh chiles, preferably Thai, stemmed, seeded, and minced, or 2 teaspoons hot red pepper flakes, or to taste

2 teaspoons sugar

Roughly 4 cups red or green leaf lettuce, chopped

1 cucumber, peeled if necessary, cut in half lengthwise,
   seeded (see page 171), and sliced
1 cup fresh mint leaves
1 cup fresh cilantro leaves

1. Preheat a grill or broiler. Sprinkle the steak with salt and pepper, then grill for about 4 minutes per side or until medium-rare. Remove from the heat and let rest for about 10 minutes.
2. Meanwhile, whisk together the nam pla, lime juice, garlic, shallots, chiles, and sugar. Cut the steak into ¼-inch slices and immediately toss the steak with the dressing.
3. Place the lettuce, cucumber, mint, and cilantro on a plate and top with the steak and dressing. Serve immediately.

NAM PLA

1. Start a charcoal or wood fire or preheat a gas grill or broiler; the rack should be about 4 inches from the heat source. Grill or broil the beef until medium-rare, 5 to 10 minutes; set it aside to cool.
2. Toss the lettuce with the mint, onion, and cucumber. Combine the remaining ingredients with 1 tablespoon water—the mixture will be thin—and toss the greens with this dressing. Transfer the greens to a platter, reserving the dressing.
3. Thinly slice the beef, reserving its juice; combine the juice with the remaining dressing. Lay the slices of beef over the salad, drizzle the dressing over all, and serve.

Beef Salad with Mint THAILAND ■ ■

MAKES **4 SERVINGS**

TIME **25 MINUTES, PLUS TIME TO PREHEAT THE GRILL OR BROILER**

A simple, bright, and light salad with tons of flavor. One of the best possible lunch dishes. See page 500 for information on fish sauces like nam pla.

½ pound beef tenderloin or boneless sirloin
4 cups torn Boston or romaine lettuce, mesclun, or any
   mixture of salad greens
1 cup torn fresh mint leaves
¼ cup minced red onion
1 medium cucumber, peeled if necessary, cut in half
   lengthwise, seeded (see page 169), and diced
Juice of 2 limes
1 tablespoon nam pla or soy sauce
⅛ teaspoon cayenne, or to taste
½ teaspoon sugar

Green Mango Salad with Meat
VIETNAM ■ ■

MAKES **4 SERVINGS**

TIME **20 MINUTES**

Here's a salad that combines the fresh tartness of green—unripe—mangoes with a little stir-fried meat.

Unripe mangoes are more common than the ripe variety at most supermarkets, but if you can't find them, substitute Granny Smith apples. Nam pla—Thai fish sauce—is described on page 500. Palm sugar is authentic but pretty indistinguishable from brown sugar.

2 green mangoes, peeled, pitted, and julienned or diced (see illustration on page 119)

Salt to taste

¼ cup fresh lime juice

3 tablespoons corn, grapeseed, or other neutral oil

3 garlic cloves, sliced

3 shallots, sliced

2 small fresh chiles, preferably Thai, stemmed and minced, or 2 teaspoons hot red pepper flakes, or to taste

¼ pound ground beef or pork

1 teaspoon black pepper

¼ cup nam pla

1 tablespoon brown or palm sugar

3 tablespoons dry-roasted peanuts, chopped

3 tablespoons chopped fresh cilantro leaves

1. Toss the mango pieces with the salt and lime juice and set aside. Put the oil in a large skillet and turn the heat to medium. A minute later, add the garlic, shallots, and chiles and cook, stirring, until fragrant, about 1 minute.

2. Add the meat and pepper to the pan and cook, stirring occasionally, until it loses its pinkness. Stir in the nam pla and sugar and cook for 1 minute more. Drain any excess oil from the pan, then add the beef mixture to the mangoes. Mix well, garnish with the peanuts and cilantro, and serve.

Green Mango Salad with Smoked Fish. Substitute 1 small smoked trout, skinned, boned, and broken into ½-inch pieces (it will fall apart as you handle it), for the meat. Proceed as directed, cooking the trout only long enough to heat it through.

Fish No aspect of food buying has changed in the last twenty years more than that of fish. Once fresh fish was strictly local, and frozen fish was of generally poor quality. Now markets are as likely to offer fish from around the world as from local waters, living inland is not nearly as great a handicap as it was, and frozen-at-sea fish may be "fresher" than fish that has merely been refrigerated.

One thing hasn't changed, though: you cannot count on finding any particular species at the market. That's why the recipes in this chapter offer suggestions for substitutions. The good news is that once you get into the right category—mollusks, shellfish, fish steaks, and so on—the techniques are pretty much consistent from one variety to the next. And that's why the chapter is divided by fish and shellfish category.

BUYING FRESH FISH

Fish buying has changed a great deal in the last twenty years, and, in a way, it's become easier. The first thing to know is that most supermarkets specialize in only the most popular fish. As of this writing, these are salmon (mostly farm raised and almost always fresh), shrimp (mostly frozen before sale; more on this in a moment), cod, and, lately, tuna.

Unless you have a great supermarket fish counter, you have to thoroughly check out any fish other than these (you might as well check out these, too, but the supermarkets stock them because they sell, and because they sell they're usually in good shape). It's easy enough:

1. Does the fish look good, that is, moist and whatever color it should be?

2. Does it smell good? (If the clerk won't let you smell it, take your package and open it on the spot—hand it back if it smells bad.)

Shrimp should be bought frozen; in 90 percent of the cases, it will have been frozen anyway. This way you can defrost it (in the refrigerator or in cold water) at your convenience, and you know it's "fresh." Many other fish—swordfish, for example—are often better frozen than "fresh."

Whole lobster, crab, oysters, mussels, and clams should be alive when you buy them. They should smell like seawater.

At a real fish market, sadly decreasing in number each year, trust is key. You should—really—be able to buy any fish and assume it's good. Once burned, twice shy, as the saying goes, and if you're given bad fish at a local fish store, march right back there and complain. Again, however, if you smell it before leaving, that isn't going to happen.

MOLLUSKS

Whole clams, oysters, and mussels should be alive when you buy them. Their shells should be closed tightly or—as is often the case with steamers and mussels—if gaping, still hard to pry apart. They should smell really good. In this condition, iced or refrigerated and allowed to breathe (never store them in closed plastic bags), they will remain alive and healthy for days. Wash them well before cooking; there may be times you need to scrub clams to remove all the grit.

Shucked mollusks—as scallops almost always are—can be treated in the same way as other fish. Ice or refrigerate them and use them as soon as possible.

Stir-Fried Clams with Black Bean Sauce CHINA ■
MAKES **4 SERVINGS**
TIME **20 MINUTES**

Simple and incredibly delicious. If you prefer a thick sauce, like that served at many Chinese restaurants, add cornstarch (as directed) at the end of cooking; it's by no means necessary, however.

Use the smallest clams you can find, preferably just an inch or so in diameter. Cockles, which are even smaller, are often the best choice; manila clams (which are brown) are also good. Serve this dish with Basic Long-Grain Rice (page 506).

4 pounds littleneck, cherrystone, or manila clams or cockles

2 tablespoons fermented black beans (page 207)

2 tablespoons Shaoxing wine or dry sherry

3 tablespoons corn, grapeseed, or other neutral oil

2 tablespoons minced garlic

Fermented Black Beans

Fermented black beans—the kind called for in many Chinese-style stir-fries—are not like the black beans you're going to find in a Goya can. First of all, they begin life as soybeans, turned brown-black through a curing process first devised about two thousand years ago.

They have a distinctively salty and pungent taste (I love it) and a shriveled, soft but chewy texture—a little like what you'd expect a "fermented" bean to feel like.

They're usually packed in salt (hence their other common moniker, salted black beans), in plastic bags or cardboard boxes at Asian stores.

Sometimes black beans are soaked to remove excess salt, but this isn't necessary. Just keep an eye on the soy sauce or other salty ingredients in the dish so it doesn't end up too salty.

---

2 tablespoons peeled and minced fresh ginger

1 tablespoon soy sauce

1 teaspoon sugar

2 scallions, trimmed and roughly chopped

2 teaspoons cornstarch, dissolved in 1 tablespoon plus
   1 teaspoon water, optional

2 teaspoons dark sesame oil

1. Use a stiff brush to scrub the clam shells under running water to remove all traces of sand. Rinse the black beans in a strainer and soak them in the wine.
2. Place a wok or heavy skillet over high heat. A minute later, add the oil and reduce the heat to medium-high. When the oil shimmers, add the garlic and ginger. Cook, stirring, for about 15 seconds, then raise the heat to high and add the clams. Stir for a minute, then stir in the black bean/sherry mixture, soy sauce, sugar, and scallions. Cover, then cook over medium-high heat for 5 minutes, or until most of the clams are open. (Any clams that do not open during cooking can be opened with a dull knife at the table.)
3. Reduce the heat to low. If you choose to use the cornstarch mixture, stir and add it to the clams; cook, stirring occasionally, until the sauce is thick-

ened and smooth, about 15 seconds. Drizzle with the sesame oil and serve, with the sauce, over white rice.

Spicy Stir-Fried Clams with Black Bean Sauce. Add 2 to 4 dried red chiles (with their seeds if you want the dish extra-hot) to the stir-fry as you are adding the garlic and ginger.

Stir-Fried Crabs in Black Bean Sauce. Start with 4 blue or softshell crabs, cleaned and cut up as directed on page 225; they will cook a little more quickly than the clams.

Clams in Sherry Sauce SPAIN ■
MAKES **4 SERVINGS**
TIME **30 MINUTES**

Every winemaking culture in the world cooks with its local product, but only Spain has sherry. And while sherry is not quite all-purpose, as simple white wine is, it is manifestly more powerful and incomparably more complex; in fact it rivals stock in the character it adds to many dishes. (When Spanish food comes with a good-tasting but anonymous "brown sauce," you can bet it contains a hefty dose of sherry.) Sherry combined with seafood, olive oil, and garlic, as in this recipe, produces a magically Spanish dish, one that is not only classic but awesome and one you can consider a template for many others.

You can spend a fortune on sherry, but since each bottle is the product of several different vintages it is consistent from year to year, and the fact that it is stabilized by alcohol enhances its shelf life (refrigerated, an opened bottle retains flavor good enough to drink for several days, and sometimes even longer if used for cooking). In short, all real sherry is good, and bottles costing ten bucks are more than acceptable. Fino is probably best for drinking, but the slightly sweeter, nuttier Amontillado and Oloroso are perhaps a little better for cooking.

As is almost always the case in cooking, the clams you use here should be as small as you can find. Tiny ones the size of a quarter are fun, but the slightly larger cockles or West Coast "butter" clams are equally tender and easier to eat. Mahogany clams or good littlenecks are also fine; do not use "steamers," whose sand will spoil the dish. In any case, buy only live clams; their shells should be undamaged and nearly impossible to pry open. Rinse them, scrubbing their shells if necessary, to rid them of all sand. Those that do not open during the cooking are fine; just pry them open at the table with a dull knife.

Serve this as an appetizer or a main course, with good bread for sopping up the sauce.

¼ cup extra virgin olive oil

2 garlic cloves, peeled and slivered

2 shallots or 1 small onion, diced

3 to 4 pounds clams, the smallest you can find, scrubbed of all sand

½ cup Fino, Amontillado, or Oloroso sherry

Black pepper to taste

2 tablespoons butter, more or less, or more olive oil

1 teaspoon fresh lemon juice, or to taste

Chopped fresh parsley leaves for garnish

1. Put the oil in a deep skillet or flameproof casserole over medium heat. Add the garlic and shallots and cook, stirring occasionally, until softened, about 5 minutes.

2. Add the clams and raise the heat to high; cook, stirring occasionally, until the clams begin to open and release their juices, 5 to 10 minutes. Transfer them to a bowl with a slotted spoon and add the sherry to the pan. Cook until reduced and slightly thickened, about 5 minutes more, then stir in the pepper and butter.

3. Return the clams to the pan and cook, stirring frequently, for another 2 or 3 minutes. Put the clams on your serving dish; add the lemon juice to the sauce, then taste and adjust the seasoning. Pour the sauce over the clams, garnish with parsley, and serve.

MUSSELS

When you buy mussels, you may have a choice: wild or farm raised. Wild are harder to clean and less predictable, but they can be incredibly delicious. Farm raised are easy to clean, uniform in size, and—this is the downside—milder in flavor. I usually gamble on wild. Allow about a pound of mussels per person.

When cleaning mussels, discard any with broken shells. If the mussels have beards—the hairy vegetative growth attached to the shell—trim them off. Wild mussels may require scrubbing—they might even have barnacles attached here and there. Those mussels that remain closed after the majority have been steamed open can be pried open with a knife (a butter knife works fine) at the table.

Steamed Mussels ITALY ▓

MAKES **4 SERVINGS**

TIME **30 MINUTES**

I'd had mussels in New York, even as a child, but never did they look so appealing as they did my first night in Rome, laced with onion, garlic, tomato, parsley, and lemon. Since then I've learned to love and prepare mussels in a variety of ways, but I always come back to these.

Serve with lots of bread for sopping up the broth.

2 tablespoons extra virgin olive oil

1 medium onion, chopped

6 garlic cloves, peeled and lightly smashed

1 cup cored and chopped tomato, optional

4 pounds mussels, cleaned (page 208)

Fresh parsley leaves or sprigs for garnish

1 lemon, quartered

1. Put the oil in a saucepan large enough to hold all the mussels and turn the heat to medium. A minute later, add the onion and garlic and cook, stirring occasionally, until the onion begins to soften, 5 minutes. Add the tomato, if using, and raise the heat a bit; cook for 5 minutes more, until the tomato begins to break up.

2. Add the mussels, turn the heat to high, and cover the pot. Cook, shaking the pot occasionally, until they all (or nearly all) open, about 10 minutes. Turn off the heat.

3. Scoop the mussels into a serving bowl. Strain the accumulated liquid through a fine strainer—preferably one lined with cheesecloth—and pour it over the mussels. Garnish with parsley and serve with the lemon wedges.

Steamed Mussels, French Style. Substitute butter for the oil and use 2 or 3 chopped shallots in place of the onion. The garlic is optional; omit the tomato and lemon. Proceed as directed, adding $1/2$ cup white wine to the pot just before adding the mussels. If you like, you can finish the sauce with $1/2$ cup heavy cream.

Steamed Mussels, East Asian Style. Substitute peanut or canola oil for the olive oil and $1/4$ cup chopped scallion for the onion; add 1 tablespoon peeled and minced fresh ginger along with the garlic and proceed as directed, omitting the tomato and lemon. Add 1 tablespoon soy sauce to the liquid after cooking and serve with lime wedges.

Steamed Mussels, Thai Style. Omit the oil, onion, tomato, lemon, and parsley. Combine the mussels in a pot with the garlic; 2 lemongrass stalks, bruised with the back of a knife and roughly chopped; $1/2$ cup roughly chopped fresh Thai basil leaves; 1 small fresh or dried chile; the juice of 1 lime; and 1 tablespoon nam pla. Steam as in step 2, then strain as in step 3. Garnish the mussels with more Thai basil and a squeeze of fresh lime.

Steamed Mussels with Pasta. Steps 1 and 2 remain the same (it's nice to add a dried chile to the mix). When the mussels are done, shell them, reserving all the liquid that comes out of them, as well as their (strained) cooking liquid. Let them rest in the liquid. Cook a pound of linguine or spaghetti in boiling salted water. While the pasta is cooking, reheat the mussels gently in their cooking liquid. Drain the pasta and dress it with the mussels and as much of the liquid as needed to make a sauce. Garnish with parsley and serve.

Mussels with Linguiça PORTUGAL ■

MAKES **4 SERVINGS**

TIME **30 MINUTES**

More than anywhere else, cooks in Portugal combine seafood and meat with abandon, and it usually works. This dish cries out for crusty bread.

If you want a milder garlic flavor, add it along with the tomatoes so it cooks a little longer.

> ½ to 1 pound linguiça or kielbasa
>
> 1 tablespoon extra virgin olive oil
>
> 2 plum tomatoes, cored and roughly chopped (canned are fine)
>
> About 3 pounds mussels, cleaned (page 208)
>
> 1 tablespoon minced garlic
>
> Chopped fresh parsley leaves for garnish

1. Cut the sausage into slices about ⅛ inch thick. Put the olive oil in a wide, deep skillet or flameproof casserole, turn the heat to medium-high, and add the sausage. Cook, stirring occasionally, until the sausage begins to brown, about 10 minutes. Add the tomatoes. Cook about 5 minutes, stirring occasionally, until the tomatoes begin to break up.

2. Add the mussels and cook, shaking the pan occasionally, until they open, about 10 minutes. (This will happen more quickly if you cover the pan, but it isn't really necessary.)

3. When almost all the mussels are open, add the garlic and cook, stirring once or twice, for another minute or so. Garnish and serve immediately.

SCALLOPS

There are three important kinds of scallops:

Sea scallops, primarily from the North Atlantic, can be quite large and are best cooked so that their interior remains underdone and creamy. They are sometimes sold as "diver" scallops, which means they were hand-harvested by a scuba diver—at least in theory. Diver scallops are generally regarded as being of a higher quality than other sea scallops, which are gathered by a ship dragging a heavy net across the ocean floor, and are clearly more ecologically friendly.

Bay scallops may be wild or farm raised and are about the size and shape of a small cork. The wild variety, caught off the coast of southern New England in the winter months, are rare and therefore quite expensive (about $20 a pound); they're also unbelievably good (and great raw). Farm-raised bay scallops, most often from China, are much cheaper. They're decent but cannot compare to Nantucket bays.

Calico scallops, sometimes mislabeled "bays," are quite small and have a tendency to be overcooked. Even when treated well, they are the least flavorful of the scallops.

Regardless of the type of scallop you buy, look for specimens that are sold as "dry" or "dry-packed," which means they haven't been soaked in phosphates, which cause them to absorb water and lose flavor.

Miso-Broiled Scallops JAPAN ■

MAKES **4 SERVINGS**

TIME **15 TO 30 MINUTES**

The usefulness of miso is nearly unlimited, and it can convert the simplest of ingredients into an exotic dish, a secret of much of Japanese cooking. Here the fermented soybean paste is combined with scallops and a little seasoning, then allowed to sit for a while before being grilled or broiled. It's a traditional dish, in some parts of Japan the home-cooking equivalent of slathering something with barbecue sauce before cooking.

For ease of use and strict authenticity, the miso should be thinned—it's too thick to use straight—with mirin, the sweet, golden-colored wine made from rice (and Japan's most important sweetener before the introduction of white sugar). Mirin, too, comes in a naturally brewed form called hon-mirin; it's preferable to aji-mirin, which may be boosted with corn syrup; check the label. But the amount of mirin is so small, and its flavor in this dish so subtle, that you can use a fruity, sweet white wine in its place or even honey.

If you can, try this with Asparagus Salad with Soy-Mustard Dressing (page 190) or a plain salad. And a bit of short-grain rice, of course.

¹/₂ cup miso

2 tablespoons mirin

¹/₂ cup minced onion

Salt and cayenne to taste

1¹/₂ pounds scallops, preferably bay

Juice of 1 lime

1. Preheat a broiler (or grill), setting the rack as close as possible to the heat source. Put the miso in a bowl, add the mirin, and whisk until smooth. Stir in the onion, a little bit of salt, and a pinch of cayenne. Add the scallops and marinate while the

MIRIN

broiler or grill preheats, or refrigerate for up to a day.

2. Broil until lightly browned, without turning, for 2 to 3 minutes, or grill, turning once after a minute or 2. Sprinkle with the lime juice and serve.

Miso-Broiled Fish. You can also marinate sturdy white fillets this way—catfish, blackfish, monkfish, red snapper, and grouper are all good examples—or the old standby, salmon. Like the scallops, they should not be turned if you're using the broiler. They should, however, be placed about 4 inches from the heat source so that the coating does not burn before the fish cooks through.

Sautéed Scallops with Garlic FRANCE ■

MAKES **4 SERVINGS**

TIME **15 MINUTES**

You can make this with sea scallops or true bay scallops (which are rare and quite expensive); don't bother to try it with the tiny calicos, which are guaranteed to overcook and become rubbery.

If you look at a sea scallop, you'll see a little stark-white hinge on one side; remove that if you have the time; it's much chewier than the rest of the meat. And if you're lucky enough to find scallops with their roe (it's red or beige; you'll know it when you see it), by all means use them here.

2 tablespoons extra virgin olive oil

2 tablespoons butter or more oil

2 pounds sea scallops, cut in half horizontally if very large

Flour for dredging

Salt and black pepper to taste

1 tablespoon minced garlic

Chopped fresh chervil or parsley leaves or chives for garnish

1. Put the oil and butter in a large nonstick skillet and turn the heat to medium-high; begin to dredge the scallops lightly in the flour. When the butter foam subsides, add the scallops swiftly but not all at once. Turn them individually, as they brown, allowing about 2 minutes per side. Season with salt and pepper as they cook.

2. Once you have turned all the scallops, add the garlic and lower the heat a bit. Stir or, even better, shake the pan gently so the garlic cooks a bit and is distributed among the scallops. Garnish and serve.

Sautéed Scallops with Bacon and Shallots. A venerable tradition: In step 1, use only 1 tablespoon butter or oil; in it, sauté about $\frac{1}{4}$ cup bacon or pancetta over medium heat until crisp, 5 to 10 minutes; halfway through the cooking time, add $\frac{1}{4}$ cup minced shallots. Quarter the scallops; do not dredge them in flour. Stir them into the bacon/shallot mixture and cook, stirring occasionally, for a couple of minutes, until stark white. Season to taste (omit the garlic), garnish, and serve.

Sautéed Scallops with White Wine. You can finish either the main recipe or the variation this way: Transfer the cooked scallops to a warm platter and turn the heat to high. Add 1 cup dry white wine (a really good one will not be wasted here) and cook, stirring and scraping the pan with a wooden spoon, until the wine is reduced by more than half and is syrupy and thick. Pour this over the cooked scallops, garnish, and serve.

SHRIMP, SQUID, AND CRAB

SHRIMP

Shrimp may be wild or farm raised—the former are always more flavorful than the latter—but almost all

are frozen before sale, and this has been true for about seventy years. But shrimp freeze well and keep well; in some ways, it makes sense to buy frozen shrimp and defrost them yourself, which gives you more control than buying thawed shrimp. "IQF" (individually quick frozen) shrimp are often a good buy.

When you're buying any shrimp, look for a firm, full shell and firm meat. The meat should not be white (that's freezer burn) or pink, which means it has been defrosted at too high a temperature.

Shrimp are graded by size (U-60, for example, means there are under sixty shrimp to a pound); tiny ones run two hundred and more to a pound, giants may run close to a half pound each. Generally, I stick to those in the U-20 to U-30 range, which provide a good combination of handling ease (you have to peel them, after all) and economy. I don't devein shrimp, but certainly you can if you prefer to do so.

Drunken Shrimp CHINA ■
MAKES 4 SERVINGS
TIME 30 MINUTES, LARGELY UNATTENDED

Because this dish has only two ingredients, finding the best shrimp is of utmost importance. In Hong Kong, where only live fish is considered fresh, live shrimp are common. Here you may find them at some fishmongers (especially in Chinese neighborhoods) and even in some Western supermarkets. The wine traditionally used for this dish in the south of China is Mei Kuei Lu Chiew and is quite strong and a little sweet; you can find it at many Chinese markets. Shopping hassles aside, this dish is worth trying. Serve it with an assortment of other Chinese dishes or as a starter.

1 pound medium shrimp, preferably live
1¼ cups Mei Kuei Lu Chiew, dry Gewürztraminer, or gin

1. If you are using live shrimp, run them under cold water to clean them thoroughly. In any case, leave the shells on. Place the shrimp in a bowl with 1 cup of the wine, cover, and refrigerate for 20 minutes.

2. Heat a wok or deep skillet over high heat, then add the remaining $1/4$ cup wine. When the wine is almost boiling, carefully ignite it, then immediately add the shrimp with its marinade. (If you are not comfortable igniting the wine, bring it to a rolling boil.) Cook the shrimp, stirring, until they turn pink, about 5 minutes. Remove from the heat and serve.

Stir-Fried Shrimp with Cabbage and Black Beans CHINA ■

MAKES **4 SERVINGS**

TIME **30 MINUTES**

Though Chinese cabbages, like bok choy and Napa, have become more widely available here, I still prefer this dish with ordinary green cabbage; its crunch is unsurpassed. Serve this with Basic Long-Grain Rice or Fried Rice (page 506).

2 tablespoons fermented black beans (page 207)

2 tablespoons Shaoxing wine, dry sherry, or white wine

3 tablespoons peanut or vegetable oil

1 pound green or other cabbage, cored and roughly chopped (not finely shredded)

1 tablespoon chopped garlic

1 tablespoon peeled and minced fresh ginger

4 or 5 small dried chiles

$1^1/2$ pounds shrimp, roughly 30 to 40, peeled

2 tablespoons soy sauce

Salt to taste

1 teaspoon dark sesame oil

$1/4$ cup minced scallion, green part only, for garnish

1. Soak the black beans in the wine. Put 2 tablespoons of the oil in a wide skillet, preferably nonstick, and turn the heat to high. A minute later, add the cabbage and cook, stirring occasionally, until glossy and beginning to brown, 3 to 5 minutes. Remove with a slotted spoon.

2. Still over high heat, add the remaining oil, along with the garlic, ginger, and chiles; cook, stirring once or twice, for 15 to 30 seconds. Add the shrimp and cook, stirring occasionally, for about 2 minutes. Turn the heat to medium.

3. Return the cabbage to the skillet, along with the black beans and their liquid and the soy sauce. Cook, stirring, for about a minute. Taste and salt. Drizzle with the sesame oil, garnish with the scallion, and serve.

Minced Shrimp in Lettuce Wrappers

CHINA ■

MAKES **4 SERVINGS**

TIME **15 MINUTES**

This wrapped dish, best assembled at the table, is great fun, either as a starter or as part of your main meal, and as fitting for a weeknight as tacos. It has a wonderful combination of contrasting flavors and textures: the spicy filling is offset by the sweetness of hoisin sauce and the cool crunch of lettuce.

2 tablespoons corn, grapeseed, or other neutral oil

2 garlic cloves, minced

One $1^1/2$-inch piece fresh ginger, peeled and minced

1 scallion, trimmed and chopped

1 small fresh hot red chile, stemmed, seeded, and minced, or a few pinches of hot red pepper flakes

1 red bell pepper, stemmed, seeded, and chopped

$1/4$ pound water chestnuts, preferably fresh, trimmed, peeled, and chopped

3/4 pound small shrimp, peeled and minced

2 teaspoons Shaoxing wine or dry sherry

2 teaspoons soy sauce

2 teaspoons oyster sauce

1 teaspoon dark sesame oil

1 head of iceberg lettuce, leaves separated

Hoisin sauce for serving

1. Heat the oil in a wok or skillet over medium-high heat. Add the garlic, ginger, scallion, and chile and cook until fragrant, about 15 seconds. Add the red pepper and water chestnuts and cook until bright and crisp, about 2 minutes.

2. Stir in the shrimp, wine, soy sauce, and oyster sauce and cook, stirring occasionally, until the shrimp is pink and the sauce bubbling, about 4 minutes. Remove from the heat, transfer to a serving dish, and sprinkle with sesame oil.

3. Assemble the dish while eating: take a piece of lettuce, spread some hoisin sauce in it, and top with a spoon or two of the shrimp mixture.

Shrimp with Peas and Ham CHINA

MAKES **4 SERVINGS**

TIME **15 MINUTES**

A quick little stir-fry, great for a weekday dinner, and especially good if you can get a chunk of country ham, like prosciutto, Serrano, or Smithfield. Great, too, with sautéed Chinese sausages (sold at every Chinese supermarket) in place of ham. With white rice, this makes a nice little meal.

1 pound small shrimp, peeled

1 tablespoon Shaoxing wine or dry sherry

1 cup fresh or frozen peas

2 tablespoons corn, grapeseed, or other neutral oil

One 1 1/2-inch piece fresh ginger, peeled and minced

3 scallions, trimmed and chopped

1/4 pound ham (see headnote), cut into 1/4-inch cubes

Salt and black pepper to taste

1. Place the shrimp in a bowl with the wine. Toss to coat and marinate for 5 minutes. Cook the peas in boiling salted water to cover until tender, just a few minutes. Drain and set aside.

2. Put the oil in a wok or skillet and turn the heat to high. A minute later, add the ginger and scallions and cook until fragrant, about 15 seconds. Add the ham and brown lightly.

3. Stir in the shrimp, its marinade, and the peas. Cook, stirring occasionally, until the shrimp is cooked through, about 5 minutes. Season with salt and pepper and serve.

Shrimp in Tamarind Sauce

SOUTHEAST ASIA

MAKES **4 SERVINGS**

TIME **20 MINUTES**

Tamarind is a large seed pod grown and used in the cuisine of almost every equatorial country. Its pulp is processed into a dark brown paste, which is used as you might tomato paste, concentrated stock, or, for that matter, ketchup—as a simple flavor enhancer that completely changes the nature of the sauce into which it is stirred. You can make your own paste (page 585) or buy the paste now sold in bottles at many Asian stores. (There is also a kind of instant tamarind powder, which is not very good.) The bottled paste is concentrated to increase its strength, so if you use homemade tamarind paste, double the quantity (or add to taste).

As for this recipe, you can use the same process to make almost anything in a tamarind sauce, but shrimp, because it requires minimal cooking time, is by far the easiest. I like to brown the shrimp first for a little more flavor, but you could actually start this recipe with the second step and add the shrimp after the onion. The dish is best when quite sour and not—as happens at too many restaurants—a sticky combination of sweet and sour.

2 pounds shrimp, peeled

4 tablespoons ($^1/_2$ stick) butter

1 medium onion, chopped

2 tablespoons peeled and minced fresh ginger

1 small fresh chile, stemmed, seeded, and diced, or

    1 teaspoon hot red pepper flakes, or to taste

$^1/_4$ cup tamarind paste, or to taste

$^1/_4$ cup fresh lime juice, or to taste

Salt and black pepper to taste

Chopped fresh cilantro leaves for garnish

Lime wedges for serving

1. Place a large nonstick skillet over high heat. After a minute, add as many shrimp as will fit comfortably in one layer—do not try to brown all the shrimp at once. As soon as they begin to brown, about a minute later, turn them, cook them for about 30 seconds on the other side, and remove them from the pan. Repeat until all the shrimp are done, then turn off the heat for a minute.

2. Turn the heat to medium and add the butter; when it melts, add the onion, turn the heat to medium-high, and cook, stirring occasionally, until the onion softens, about 5 minutes. Add the ginger and chile and cook for 30 seconds, then add the tamarind paste and $^1/_4$ cup water. Stir to blend, then taste and add more tamarind paste if necessary. Return the shrimp to the pan, bring to a boil, then stir in the lime juice. Cook, stirring occasionally, until the mixture thickens, a minute or so.

3. Taste and adjust the seasoning, then garnish and serve over rice with the lime wedges.

Shrimp on Lemongrass Skewers

THAILAND ■

MAKES **4 SERVINGS**

TIME **15 TO 30 MINUTES**

Lemongrass stalks are used as skewers throughout Southeast Asia, where lemongrass grows like . . . well, grass. (It will grow that way for you, too, if you stick a couple of stalks in the ground, especially if you live in a warm climate and keep it well watered.) Simply trim the stalks, skewer the shrimp on them, and grill; you can gnaw on the stalks when you've finished the shrimp.

Serve these with Nam Prik (page 586) or Soy Dipping Sauce (page 583). For information on Thai fish sauce (nam pla), see page 500.

4 lemongrass stalks

32 to 40 shrimp, about 1$^1/_2$ pounds, peeled

Salt and black pepper to taste

$^1/_4$ teaspoon cayenne

1 teaspoon minced garlic

1 tablespoon peanut or neutral oil, like corn or grapeseed

1 tablespoon nam pla

Chopped fresh cilantro leaves for garnish

Lime wedges for serving

SHRIMP ON LEMONGRASS SKEWERS

1. Trim the tough ends and exterior sheaths from the lemongrass; roughly chop the trimmings and toss them with the shrimp, salt, pepper, cayenne, garlic, oil, and nam pla. Let rest while you preheat the grill or broiler; the fire should be quite hot and the heat source roughly 4 inches from the rack. Bruise the lemongrass stalks with the back of a heavy knife.

2. Remove the shrimp from the marinade and skewer them on the stalks. Grill the shrimp until firm and pink, 2 or 3 minutes per side. Garnish with cilantro, then serve hot with a sauce and the lime wedges.

Steamed Shrimp with Lemongrass-Coconut Sauce THAILAND ■ ▪

MAKES **4 SERVINGS**

TIME **30 MINUTES, PLUS CHILLING TIME**

You have an aesthetic choice to make in preparing this dish, which is great as part of a cool meal in summer. Add a couple of Asian-style salads, like Tomato Salad with Ginger (page 173) or Green Papaya Salad (page 174), and you're in business. The coconut sauce, with its sugar, lemongrass, and chile—all typical Thai flavors—is wonderfully flavorful but stark white. Adding a large pinch of saffron turns it a glorious yellow and adds the distinctive complexity of that spice, a nice touch. If you prefer, you can use some ground turmeric—whose flavor is bitter but not at all unpleasant—or curry powder. Or just leave the sauce as is. See page 500 for information on Thai fish sauce (nam pla).

  4 lemongrass stalks

  2 tablespoons nam pla

  3 limes

  2 pounds shrimp, peeled

1 small dried chile

1 cup coconut milk, homemade (page 584) or canned

1 tablespoon sugar

1 large pinch of saffron threads or 1 teaspoon ground
   turmeric or curry powder

Salt to taste

1. Trim the ends from the lemongrass, then bruise 3 of the stalks all over with the back of a knife. Cut them in half and put them in the bottom of a saucepan with the nam pla. Squeeze the juice of two of the limes into the pot, then throw the limes themselves in there. Top with the shrimp, cover tightly, and turn the heat to medium-high. Cook for 5 to 10 minutes, or until the shrimp are pink and firm. Remove the shrimp and chill.

2. Remove the hard outer layers from the remaining lemongrass stalk and mince the tender core; you won't get much more than a teaspoon or two. Combine this with the chile, coconut milk, sugar, and saffron in a small saucepan over low heat. Cook, stirring occasionally, until the mixture is a uniform yellow. Remove and discard the chile and chill. Cut the remaining lime into wedges.

3. Taste the sauce and add a little salt if necessary. Serve the cold shrimp topped with the cold sauce and accompanied by lime wedges.

Blazing Hot Shrimp Curry in Coconut Milk INDIA ■

MAKES **4 SERVINGS**

TIME **30 MINUTES**

The sweetness of coconut milk tames the heat of this quick stew somewhat, but it remains a dish for fans of fiery food. If you cut the number of chiles to one, however, that will change. In any case, you will want a fair amount of plain white rice with this one.

2 large onions

10 garlic cloves

25 to 30 dried red chiles

2 tablespoons neutral oil, like corn or grapeseed

3 tablespoons curry powder, preferably homemade
(pages 592–593)

3 cups coconut milk, homemade (page 584) or canned
(about two 13-ounce cans)

1 1/2 to 2 pounds shrimp, peeled

Salt and black pepper to taste

1/4 cup fresh lime juice

Chopped fresh cilantro leaves for garnish

1. Combine the onions, garlic, and two or more of the chiles in a food processor (the more chiles you grind, the hotter the dish; the remaining chiles are primarily for appearance). Process until ground.

2. Put the oil in a large skillet over medium-high heat. Add the onion mixture and the curry powder and cook, stirring, until it begins to brown, 5 to 10 minutes. Add the coconut milk and remaining chiles, bring to a boil, and add the shrimp. Adjust the heat so the mixture simmers and cook until the shrimp are all pink, 5 to 10 minutes. Taste and add salt and pepper as necessary, then stir in the lime juice. Garnish and serve.

Crunchy Curried Shrimp or Fish

INDIA ■

MAKES **4 SERVINGS**

TIME **30 MINUTES**

I have been making this dish for more than thirty years—it's one of the first South Asian recipes I learned—and I've never stopped loving it. After having a similar preparation in Delhi, I loved it even more. Basically, you coat shrimp with a spicy mix, then with a simple batter. Originally it was deep-fried,

but shallow-frying, which uses less oil and makes less of a mess, works just as well.

Don't limit yourself to shrimp here; any seafood—scallops, oysters, clams, or fish fillet—will work wonderfully. Cooking time will remain about the same in almost every case.

1 1/2 to 2 pounds shrimp, the bigger the better, peeled,
or any fish fillet

1 tablespoon vinegar, any kind

Salt to taste

1/2 teaspoon black pepper

1 teaspoon ground turmeric

2 teaspoons curry powder, preferably homemade
(pages 592–593), or garam masala (page 594)

1/4 teaspoon cayenne, optional

Peanut or vegetable oil for frying

2 cups flour

Lime wedges

Chopped fresh cilantro leaves for garnish

1. Preheat the oven to 200°F. Toss the shrimp or fish with the vinegar. Combine the salt, pepper, turmeric, curry powder, and cayenne, if using, and rub this mixture into the fish.

2. Put at least 1/8 inch of oil in a large nonstick skillet and turn the heat to medium-high. Combine the flour with enough warm water to make a paste about as thick as yogurt.

3. When the oil is hot (a pinch of flour will sizzle), dip each piece of shrimp into the batter and cook, raising the heat to high and rotating the pieces as necessary to promote even browning, until golden and crisp on each side, 5 to 8 minutes total. Do not crowd; you will have to cook in batches. As each piece is done, keep it warm in the oven while you continue to cook. Serve with the lime, garnished with the cilantro.

■ make ahead　■ serve at room temp./cold　■ 30 minutes or less

Crunchy Curried Shrimp or Fish with Onions and Chiles. A more fiery version, though you can keep the chiles to a minimum; the onions alone make it interesting: Steps 1 and 2 remain the same. In step 3, transfer the shrimp or fish to a plate after browning quickly, about 2 minutes per side. Pour out all but 2 tablespoons of the oil, then add 3 large onions, sliced and separated into rings, another tablespoon curry powder or garam masala, and 3 stemmed, seeded, and minced fresh or dried chiles (or to taste). Cook over medium-high heat, stirring occasionally and adjusting the heat so the onions cook as quickly as possible without burning, until the onion has wilted and browned, at least 10 minutes. Add a cup of water, bring to a boil, and return the fish to the skillet. Cook at a gentle simmer until the fish is done, another 5 minutes or so. Serve over white rice.

Chile-Fried Shrimp MEXICO ■
MAKES **4 SERVINGS**
TIME **20 MINUTES**

Just because I identify a dish with a country doesn't mean it's made exclusively there, and chile-fried shrimp is practically universal. So calling this a Mexican dish is a little like calling grilled steak an American dish.

But I like to make this with the relatively mild chiles used in Mexico, and I like to serve it with rice and beans, so there it is. This is best made with homemade Chili Powder (page 609), but if you prefer, use a chile powder dominated by ancho or New Mexican chiles, which have warmth but not high levels of heat.

Arroz a la Mexicana (page 517) is a great side dish for this, along with a green salad.

2 tablespoons pure chile powder, like ancho or New Mexico, or to taste

Cayenne to taste, optional

2 tablespoons cornmeal

Salt and black pepper to taste

$1/2$ cup neutral oil, like corn or grapeseed

$11/2$ to 2 pounds shrimp, preferably large, peeled

Chopped fresh cilantro leaves for garnish

Lime or lemon wedges

1. Combine the chile powder, cayenne if using, cornmeal, salt, and pepper in a bowl. Put the oil in a large skillet and turn the heat to medium-high. Toss the shrimp in the spice mixture to coat.
2. When the oil is hot (a pinch of cornmeal will sizzle), toss in about half the shrimp or whatever number will fit in one layer. Turn the heat to high and cook until brown on one side, then turn and brown the other side, adjusting the heat so the shrimp brown without burning—4 to 5 minutes total. Repeat with the remaining shrimp. Garnish and serve with the lime or lemon.

Garlic-Fried Shrimp, Indian Style. Substitute curry powder for the chile powder.

Shrimp in Annatto Sauce MEXICO ■
MAKES **4 SERVINGS**
TIME **40 MINUTES (WITH PREMADE RECADO ROJO)**

Along with Cochinita Pibil (page 351), this is among the best uses for the annatto-based Recado Rojo, one of the most beautiful and flavorful sauces in the world. Serve with loads of plain white rice.

$1/4$ cup extra virgin olive or other oil

2 large onions, sliced

Salt to taste

2 cups chopped tomatoes (drained canned are fine)

$1/4$ teaspoon cayenne or black pepper to taste

2 tablespoons Recado Rojo (page 609), or to taste

2 pounds shrimp, peeled

Chopped fresh cilantro leaves for garnish

1. Put the oil in a large skillet and turn the heat to medium-high. Add the onions and a pinch of salt and cook, stirring occasionally, until they are soft, about 10 minutes. Add the tomatoes and cayenne or black pepper and cook, stirring once or twice, until the tomatoes break down, 10 minutes or so. Stir in the Recado Rojo and simmer until the mixture is thick, about 10 minutes. (You can prepare the dish to this point and let sit for an hour or two before reheating and adding the shrimp.)

2. Add the shrimp and cook, stirring occasionally, until pink and firm, 5 minutes or so. Taste and adjust the seasoning, adding more salt, pepper or cayenne, or Recado Rojo as you like. Garnish with the cilantro and serve immediately.

Ribs in Annatto Sauce. Incredibly, not much different, but more time-consuming: Before beginning, parboil about 4 pounds of spareribs in water to cover until tender, at least 30 minutes (you can do this in advance, then drain the ribs, wrap them well in foil, and refrigerate). Step 1 remains the same. In step 2, add the drained ribs to the sauce and cook, stirring occasionally, until very tender and nearly falling from the bone, perhaps another half hour or so. Serve as directed.

Garlic Shrimp, Yucatecan Style
MEXICO ■

MAKES **4 SERVINGS**

TIME **30 MINUTES**

I ate this by the Gulf of Mexico, in a place with pink and avocado-green walls, a mariachi, and an outside

shower. It tasted just as good last winter in Connecticut. Serve this, if you like, with Cebollas Curtidas (page 615) or any other relish or salad. Rice is also good, as are French fries.

¼ cup extra virgin olive or other oil

10 garlic cloves, thinly sliced

Salt and black pepper to taste

24 large shrimp or about 1 pound smaller shrimp, peeled

4 plum tomatoes, cored and sliced

Chopped fresh cilantro leaves for garnish

1. Put the oil in a skillet large enough to hold the shrimp and turn the heat to medium. Add the garlic and cook, stirring occasionally, until it turns brown and crisp, about 10 minutes; do not burn. Sprinkle with salt and remove.

2. Raise the heat to high and add the shrimp, along with a sprinkling of salt and pepper. Cook, turning once or twice, until pink and firm, about 5 minutes. Put the shrimp and oil on a platter and garnish with the garlic, tomatoes, and cilantro. Serve hot.

Chipotle Shrimp MEXICO ■
MAKES **4 SERVINGS**

TIME **30 MINUTES**

Chipotles are smoked jalapeños, and they're available dried (soak them in warm water until soft before use) or in cans. When canned, they're called chiles in adobo; adobo is a red sauce from Veracruz that's perfect for this dish.

Serve this spicy dish with plain white rice and lots of it.

1½ to 2 pounds medium to large shrimp (20 to 30 per pound), peeled

¼ cup fresh lime juice

Salt and black pepper

4 garlic cloves, peeled

½ pound tomatoes (about 2 small), cored and quartered

1 small can chiles in adobo, or less to taste (even
   1 chipotle will make this dish quite hot)

2 tablespoons extra virgin olive oil

1 small onion, chopped

1 teaspoon dried oregano, preferably Mexican

¼ cup chopped fresh cilantro leaves for garnish

1. Toss the shrimp with the lime juice, salt, and pepper. Set aside.
2. Place the garlic, tomatoes, and chipotles in a food processor or blender. Process until smooth.
3. Heat the oil in a large skillet over medium-high heat. Add the onion and cook, stirring occasionally, until softened, about 5 minutes. Stir in the chipotle sauce and cook, stirring constantly, until thickened and dark, about 5 minutes or so. Add the shrimp with its marinade and cook, stirring occasionally, for 4 minutes. Add the oregano, salt, and pepper, taste and adjust the seasoning, then garnish and serve.

Chipotle Scallops. Substitute fresh scallops, sea or bay, for the shrimp.

Chipotle Crabs. Omit the lime juice marinade. Substitute 3 pounds live blue or rock crabs for the shrimp. Wash well and chop in half lengthwise. Before cooking the onion, cook the crabs in the skillet for 3 minutes on each side. Remove, then proceed as directed, reheating the crabs with the sauce for about 2 minutes.

Shrimp in Green Sauce PORTUGAL ■
MAKES **4 SERVINGS AS A MAIN COURSE, 8 AS A STARTER**
TIME **30 MINUTES**

This should be hot, garlicky, and spicy, a dish you want to serve over rice or with crusty bread; once the shrimp juices have mingled with it, the sauce is irresistible.

Although it's a perfect weeknight dish, this also makes a great appetizer at a dinner party.

6 garlic cloves, peeled

⅓ cup extra virgin olive oil

6 scallions, trimmed and roughly chopped

1 cup parsley without any thick stems

2 pounds medium to large shrimp (20 to 30 per pound), peeled

Salt and black pepper to taste

4 small dried chiles or a few pinches of hot red pepper flakes, or to taste

⅓ cup shrimp shell, fish, or chicken stock, preferably homemade (page 162, or 160), white wine, or water

1. Preheat the oven to 500°F. Combine the garlic and oil in a small food processor and blend until smooth, scraping down the sides as necessary. Add the scallions and parsley and pulse until the mixture is minced. Toss with the shrimp, salt, pepper, and chiles.
2. Put the shrimp in a roasting pan that will hold them comfortably. Add the liquid and place the pan in the oven. Roast, stirring once, until the mixture is bubbly and hot and the shrimp are all pink, 10 to 15 minutes. Serve immediately.

Shrimp in Green Sauce, Indian Style. In step 1, substitute cilantro for the parsley and add 1 tablespoon good curry powder (pages 592–593 or store-bought).

SQUID

SQUID

Almost all squid is now sold so clean it needs just a quick rinse to be ready for cooking; some of it is even sold cut into rings. (If you need to clean it yourself, see the instructions and illustration on page 98.) To make it even more convenient, squid, like shrimp, is one of those rare seafoods whose quality barely suffers when frozen, so you can safely tuck a two-pound bag in the freezer and let it sit for a month or two, defrosting it the day you're ready to cook. (Like shrimp, it will defrost quickly and safely when covered with cold water.)

Thai basil is so unlike Italian basil that they might as well be different herbs; not only does the Thai variety look different, but it is infinitely mintier. If you're using Italian basil, therefore, you might consider adding a small handful of mint leaves. See page 500 for information on Thai fish sauce (nam pla). If your squid hasn't already been cleaned, see page 98.

1½ pounds cleaned squid, rinsed well

2 tablespoons peanut oil

1 tablespoon minced garlic

2 small fresh chiles, preferably Thai, stemmed, seeded, and chopped, or to taste, or crumbled dried chiles or hot red pepper flakes to taste

¼ teaspoon ground coriander

1 tablespoon sugar

2 tablespoons nam pla

1 lime leaf, minced, if available

½ cup basil leaves, preferably Thai, roughly chopped if large

Salt to taste

1. Dry the squid well with cloth or paper towels. Cut vertically through the group of tentacles if it is large; otherwise, leave whole. Cut the squid bodies into rectangles, diamonds, or squares, with no dimension greater than 1 inch. The pieces should be

Stir-Fried Squid with Basil and Garlic
THAILAND ■

MAKES **4 SERVINGS**

TIME **15 MINUTES**

A very, very fast dish, because the squid must be cooked only briefly to prevent toughness. So make your side dishes first; rice is the natural choice, and it will keep perfectly well over low heat while you stir-fry.

THAI BASIL

■ make ahead　　■ serve at room temp./cold　　■ 30 minutes or less　　FISH　**221**

fairly uniform in size. Have everything else ready and at hand before you begin to cook.

2. Put a large nonstick skillet over high heat; add the oil and, when it shimmers, add the garlic, chiles, and coriander. Cook, stirring almost constantly, for 15 seconds. Raise the heat to high, add the squid, and cook, stirring occasionally, for about 3 minutes, just until it loses its raw look.

3. Lower the heat to medium and stir in the sugar, nam pla, lime leaf if you have it, and basil. Cook, stirring, for another few seconds, just until the basil wilts. Taste, add salt or more chile or nam pla if necessary, and serve.

Stir-Fried Squid, Korean Style. Same technique, different ingredients: In step 3, stir in ¼ cup water, 1 tablespoon go chu jang (page 591) or 1 tablespoon miso mixed with a pinch of cayenne, 2 tablespoons soy sauce, 1 tablespoon toasted sesame seeds (page 596), and 1 teaspoon dark sesame oil. Instead of basil, garnish with minced scallion.

Squid in Red Wine Sauce FRANCE ■
MAKES **4 SERVINGS**
TIME **1 HOUR**

Among my favorite squid dishes. Although sautéing, stir-frying, and deep-frying are good, fast techniques for squid, they tend to be messy because of squid's marked tendency to spatter when cooked in oil. A gentle braise in flavorful liquid and seasonings is the perfect alternative, and this one, with its Provençal spirit, is delicious and warming. See page 98 if you buy squid that hasn't been cleaned. Crusty bread is a must; keep the vegetable simple.

3 tablespoons extra virgin olive oil
5 garlic cloves, peeled and crushed

2 pounds cleaned squid, the bodies cut up if large
1 cup fruity red wine
Several fresh thyme sprigs or 1 teaspoon dried
Salt and black pepper to taste
Chopped fresh parsley leaves for garnish, optional

1. Put 2 tablespoons of the oil in a large skillet that can later be covered and turn the heat to medium-high. Add the garlic and cook, stirring, until lightly browned. Add the squid and stir, then lower the heat and add the wine. Stir, add the thyme, and cover.

2. Cook at a slow simmer until the squid is tender, about 45 minutes. (You can prepare the dish to this point and let sit for an hour or two, covered, before proceeding.) Uncover, season with salt and pepper, raise the heat, and cook until most but not all of the liquid has evaporated. Stir in the remaining olive oil, garnish, and serve.

Pasta with Squid in Red Wine. Add 2 cups chopped tomato (canned are fine), with their juice, to the sauce along with the wine. Cook as directed, reducing the sauce over high heat at the last moment if it is too watery and adding a teaspoon of minced garlic during the last 5 minutes of cooking. This will sauce about a pound of pasta.

Squid (or Cuttlefish) with Artichokes and Garlic ITALY
MAKES **4 SERVINGS**
TIME **ABOUT 1 HOUR**

The presence of artichokes in Liguria (the "Italian Riviera") is enough to make you envious; they're everywhere, they're good, and everyone seems to know what to do with them. Here's a simple dish, assuming you can get your hands on some good artichoke hearts. This is wonderful with either crusty bread or a simple rice dish, like Rice with Onions, Garlic, and Herbs (page 518). See page 98 for squid-cleaning instructions if you need them.

¼ cup extra virgin olive oil

1 tablespoon minced garlic

1½ pounds cleaned squid or cuttlefish, cut into pieces

Salt and black pepper to taste

½ cup chopped fresh parsley leaves

2 anchovy fillets

½ pound artichoke hearts, sliced ¼ inch thick

1 cup dry white wine

1. Put the oil in a large skillet that can later be covered and place it over medium heat. Add the garlic and, when it sizzles, the squid, along with a large pinch of salt and pepper, a couple of tablespoons of the parsley, and the anchovies. Cook, stirring occasionally, until whatever liquid appears has evaporated.

2. Add the artichokes and some more salt and pepper and stir; add the wine and let it bubble away for a minute. Cover and adjust the heat so the mixture simmers steadily but not violently. Cook until the squid is tender, at least 30 minutes and probably a little longer.

3. Taste and adjust the seasoning, stir in the remaining parsley, and serve.

Braised Stuffed Squid SPAIN
MAKES **4 SERVINGS**

TIME **1 HOUR**

I have seen stuffed squid recipes with forty ingredients, and some are quite good; often, they contain squid ink, which—though hard to find (or to collect from the squid's sacs)—is undeniably delicious. But those recipes are too time consuming for me.

Still, squid—like piquillo peppers—seem to have been created for stuffing. So, over the years, I have devised this simple, sensible procedure, which produces a stuffed squid much like the one I was served a couple of years ago in northern Spain.

Beware that squid shrinks significantly during cooking, so be careful to stuff it very loosely; overstuffing may result in burst squid.

Great with Peasant-Style Potatoes (page 477) or Potatoes with Bay Leaves (page 481).

¼ cup extra virgin olive oil, or more as needed

½ cup fresh bread crumbs, preferably homemade (page 580)

¼ cup pine nuts or chopped walnuts

8 large squid (bodies at least 6 inches long, about 1½ pounds), cleaned (page 98)

4 or 5 medium shiitake mushrooms, stems discarded, or 2 ounces dry-cured ham, like prosciutto

1 small onion, peeled and quartered

4 garlic cloves, peeled

6 anchovy fillets or 1 teaspoon drained capers, optional

Salt and black pepper to taste

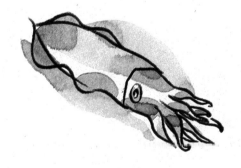

CUTTLEFISH

1 or 2 small dried chiles, or to taste

1 cup dry white wine

Chopped fresh parsley leaves for garnish

1. Put 2 tablespoons of the oil in a medium skillet and turn the heat to medium. Add the bread crumbs and nuts and cook, stirring occasionally, until lightly browned, about 5 minutes. Put the squid tentacles in a food processor along with the shiitakes, onion, 2 garlic cloves, and half the anchovies or capers if you're using them. Process until fairly fine but not pureed. Combine with the bread crumb mixture and a bit of salt and pepper. If the mixture seems dry, add a little olive oil.

2. Use a small spoon to stuff the squid bodies about half full with this mixture. Close the openings with 1 or 2 toothpicks (round ones are less likely to break than flat ones).

3. Chop the remaining garlic and anchovies or capers. Put the remaining 2 tablespoons olive oil in a large nonstick skillet and place over medium heat; add the garlic, anchovies, and chiles and cook until the garlic begins to gain color. Carefully add the squid (it will spatter) and partially cover the pan. Brown the squid on both sides, adjusting the heat as necessary; this will take only a couple of minutes.

4. Add the wine, bring to a boil, reduce the heat so the mixture simmers, and cover. Cook for about 30 minutes, or until the squid is tender (a toothpick will penetrate it fairly easily, but it will be tender like shrimp, not tender like cod). Remove the cover and, if the sauce is very thin, raise the heat and let it reduce a bit.

5. Serve the squid whole or sliced, garnished with parsley and a spoonful or two of the pan juices, avoiding the chiles.

Stuffed Squid with Tomato Sauce ITALY. This is good over pasta: Set the squid aside after browning, and, in the same pan, make Fast, Fresh Tomato Sauce (page 606), adding a sprig of fresh rosemary or $1/2$ teaspoon dried. After the sauce has simmered for about 5 minutes, add the squid and cook, covered, until the squid is tender.

Squid Stuffed with Pine Nuts and Currants SPAIN. A simpler stuffing: Omit the shiitakes, garlic, and anchovies and add $1/4$ cup currants or raisins.

CRAB

Steamed Dungeness Crab with Ginger CHINA ■

MAKES **4 SERVINGS**

TIME **30 MINUTES**

Unless you live in Alaska or know a good fishmonger in the Pacific Northwest, it's almost impossible to buy Dungeness crab that has not already been cooked. That's not a problem; they can still be steamed, as they are here. This is a subtle preparation, but Dungeness is so wonderful that's all it takes. (You can use lobster if you prefer.)

2 to 4 Dungeness crabs, depending on size

$1/2$ cup Shaoxing wine, sake, or white wine

10 slices fresh ginger, plus 1 teaspoon peeled and minced

$1/4$ cup plus 2 tablespoons soy sauce

2 tablespoons rice, black, or white vinegar

1 teaspoon dark sesame oil

2 teaspoons sugar

Put water in the bottom of a steamer. Put the crabs on a plate and spread the wine, sliced ginger, and $1/4$ cup soy sauce over them. Place in the steamer and cover; cook until the crabs are hot and cooked through, about 10 minutes. Meanwhile, combine the remaining ingredients to make a dipping sauce. Serve hot with the dipping sauce.

Steamed Crabs with Soy Dipping Sauce CHINA

MAKES **4 SERVINGS**

TIME **1 HOUR, LARGELY UNATTENDED**

This is one of those odd dishes that are easier to cook than to eat. Blue crabs take a lot of work; but they're so delicious they're worth the effort. If you live on the West Coast, you'll probably use Dungeness crab, which will be easier.

Salt to taste

20 live blue crabs

2 tablespoons Shaoxing wine or dry sherry

3 scallions, trimmed and roughly chopped

3 slices fresh ginger, smashed

1 teaspoon peeled and minced fresh ginger

2 tablespoons soy sauce

2 tablespoons rice, black, or white vinegar

1 teaspoon dark sesame oil

2 teaspoons sugar

Minced scallion for garnish, optional

Fresh cilantro leaves for garnish, optional

1. Bring a large pot of water to a boil and add salt. Boil the crabs for about a minute (you may have to do this in batches), then rinse them in cold water. Combine the wine, scallions, and ginger slices in a large bowl and add the crabs. For the dipping sauce, combine the minced ginger with the soy sauce, vinegar, sesame oil, and sugar and stir to blend. Let sit for about 30 minutes.
2. Put about an inch of water in a steamer, wok, or roasting pan. Place the crabs on a plate and put the plate in the steamer or on a rack in a wok or other pan. Cover and bring to a boil, then steam for 5 to 10 minutes, until hot. Garnish the crabs if you like and serve with the dipping sauce.

Chile Crab SINGAPORE ■

MAKES **4 SERVINGS**

TIME **20 MINUTES**

One of the most popular snacks sold at the famous open-air food bazaars of Singapore is a huge platter of fresh crabs stir-fried in a sweet, spicy sauce. You eat this crab dish, like many others, with your fingers; it's worth the mess. (If that doesn't appeal to you, try this dish with precooked crabmeat.)

Remember, crabs must be alive and kicking (or cooked) when you buy them. Information on Thai fish sauce (nam pla) is on page 500.

8 or more live blue or rock crabs or 2 Dungeness crabs

One 2-inch piece fresh ginger, peeled

3 garlic cloves, peeled and lightly crushed

2 shallots, roughly chopped

4 fresh or dried small red or green chiles, stemmed and seeded

3 tablespoons corn, grapeseed, or other neutral oil

2 tablespoons tomato paste

2 tablespoons fresh lime juice

2 tablespoons nam pla

2 teaspoons soy sauce

1 tablespoon sugar

1. Bring a large pot of water to a boil. Plunge the crabs in and cook for less than a minute, just until they stop kicking (Dungeness crabs will take a little longer). Drain in a colander and rinse under cold water. Working over a bowl (to save any liquid or soft parts that come out), break off the "apron," the triangle of shell on the crab's bottom, then remove the upper shell entirely (save any innards attached to it). On each side of the crab, you will find the gills—they're spongy and off-white— remove and discard them. Now cut the crab into quarters. To make eating easier, use the back of your knife to crack the claws.

■ make ahead ■ serve at room temp./cold ▩ 30 minutes or less

2. Put the ginger, garlic, shallots, and chiles in a food processor and process until minced. Put the oil in a wok or large skillet and place over medium-high heat; a minute later, add the minced seasonings and cook, stirring constantly, for about 30 seconds.

3. Stir in the tomato paste, lime juice, nam pla, soy sauce, sugar, and 2 tablespoons water. Add the crab and coat with the sauce. Cook just until the sauce is bubbling and the crab is heated through, about 5 minutes, then stir in any reserved crab parts or liquid and cook for another minute.

4. Serve the crabs on a platter, with the sauce spooned over and around them. To eat, pick out the meat with your fingers and dip in the surrounding sauce.

Crab with Ginger, Chinese Style. Simpler, milder, and very good: In step 2, for seasoning, use 6 scallions, trimmed and roughly chopped, and 2 tablespoons peeled and minced or shredded fresh ginger. Use peanut oil if possible; heat, add the ginger and scallions, and cook for about 15 seconds, then add the crab. Add a large pinch of coarse salt and 3 tablespoons Shaoxing wine, dry sherry, or sake. Cook, stirring frequently, until the crabs are done, about 5 minutes. Stir in 1 tablespoon soy sauce and 1 teaspoon dark sesame oil and serve.

Chile Shrimp. Far, far easier, not as exotic, but delicious: Omit the crabs and step 1. Proceed as directed, using about 1 pound small peeled shrimp in step 2. Cooking time will be about the same.

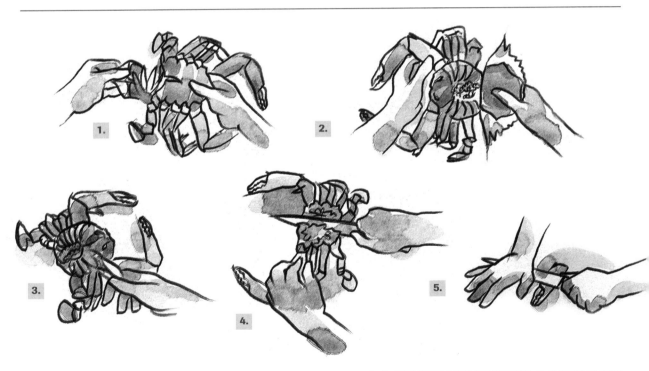

1. BREAK OFF APRON. 2. REMOVE UPPER SHELL. 3. REMOVE GILLS. 4. CUT CRAB INTO QUARTERS. 5. CRACK CLAWS WITH FLAT SIDE OF A KNIFE.

Grilled Crab with Cilantro Salsa

SOUTH AMERICA ■

MAKES **4 SERVINGS**

TIME **20 MINUTES, PLUS TIME TO PREHEAT THE GRILL**

We typically associate king crab legs with Alaska (and butter), but they are indigenous to the waters of the South Pacific as well. Down there, the accompaniment is a little more interesting. You can grill softshell crabs this way as well and serve them with the same salsa.

8 to 12 king crab legs, thawed, or 8 to 12 softshell crabs, cleaned

Cilantro Salsa (page 616)

1. Start a charcoal or gas fire; don't make it too hot. Position the grill rack at least 4 inches from the heat source.
2. Grill the crab legs, turning once, just until the shells are too hot to touch, 5 to 8 minutes (if the legs have been split, grill them flesh side up so the juices do not spill out). Serve immediately with the salsa.

FILLETS

By far the most popular cut of finfish. Though fillets vary wildly in quality, many can be substituted for one another. Thin fillets, mostly cut from flatfish like flounder and sole, are almost all interchangeable; they're tender, mild, and cook quickly. Thicker fillets have more variety of flavors and texture: red snapper and grouper, for example, are meaty, whereas cod has a fine, tender texture. Dark fillets, like mackerel, are oilier and more heavily flavored. (Then there's salmon . . .) But in general, it's safe to say this: if two fillets look the same, they may be treated the same; if you go to the market looking for nice white sole and you find nice white flounder, go for it.

Quick-Braised Fish Fillets in Black Bean Sauce CHINA ■

MAKES **4 SERVINGS**

TIME **30 MINUTES**

When you don't have the time, energy, or inclination to braise a whole fish, try this simpler, faster version; the flavors are much the same. Serve this over rice.

Peanut or neutral oil, like corn or grapeseed, for frying

$1/4$ cup fermented black beans (page 207)

$1/4$ cup Shaoxing wine, dry sherry, or water

2 cups flour

$1^1/2$ pounds fillets of grouper, sea bass, or red snapper

Salt and black pepper to taste

1 tablespoon peeled and minced fresh ginger

1 tablespoon minced garlic

4 scallions, trimmed and roughly chopped

1 large onion, sliced

2 cups chopped tomatoes (drained canned are fine)

Soy sauce to taste

1. Pour about $1/8$ inch of oil into a wide, deep skillet, preferably nonstick. Place over medium-high heat. Soak the beans in the wine. Mix the flour with enough water to make a paste the consistency of sour cream. Season the fish with salt and pepper.
2. When the oil is hot—it will shimmer, and a pinch of flour tossed into it will sizzle—coat the fillets with the batter and brown them quickly, about 2 minutes per side. You may have to work in batches; do not crowd the fish. As you finish browning, transfer it to a plate. Turn off the heat and let the pan cool down a bit, then discard the oil and wipe out the pan.

3. Put 2 tablespoons oil in the pan and turn the heat to high. A minute later, add the ginger, garlic, and scallions and cook, stirring, for about 30 seconds. Add the onion and cook, stirring occasionally, for about 2 minutes, just until it begins to soften. Turn the heat to medium and add the tomatoes and the black beans and their liquid. Cook, stirring occasionally, for about 5 minutes, just until the tomatoes begin to break up.

4. Return the fish to the pan (now it's okay to crowd) and continue to cook until it is done, about 5 minutes more (a thin-bladed knife inserted into the center will meet little resistance). Taste and add soy sauce if the dish is not salty enough; serve the fillets with the sauce over rice.

Sea Bass or Other Fillets Wrapped in Bean Curd CHINA ▪

MAKES **4 SERVINGS**

TIME **25 MINUTES**

Bean curd sheets, which have a wonderful chewy texture and the mild flavor of tofu, are sold at Asian groceries, fresh (refrigerated) or dried. They are not difficult to handle; in fact they're a lot of fun and create a wonderful crisp exterior that offsets the flaky, soy-marinated fish inside.

If you cannot find them, substitute the rice paper sheets traditionally used for spring rolls (see the variation).

> 1 1/2 pounds fillets of sea bass, grouper, halibut, or red snapper
>
> 2 teaspoons soy sauce
>
> 2 teaspoons Shaoxing wine or dry sherry
>
> 2 teaspoons rice or white wine vinegar
>
> 1 teaspoon dark sesame oil
>
> 2 teaspoons peeled and grated fresh ginger

> 2 teaspoons sugar
>
> 1 sheet fresh or dried bean curd
>
> Corn, grapeseed, or other neutral oil for deep-frying

1. Cut the fillets into 4 equal rectangular pieces. Whisk together the next 6 ingredients until the sugar dissolves, then add the fish to this marinade and set aside for 10 minutes.

2. If using a dried bean curd sheet, soak it in hot water until softened, about 5 minutes. Cut the sheet into four 5-inch squares.

3. Heat at least 2 inches of oil in a large, deep saucepan to 375°F. Meanwhile, remove the fish from the marinade and put each fillet along the edge of one of the bean curd sheets. Roll the fish in the bean curd sheet, like a jelly roll, leaving the ends open. The bean curd will stick to itself and seal shut.

4. Gently slide the fish rolls into the hot oil and fry, turning once, until golden brown and crisp on the outside, about 2 minutes on each side. Remove, drain on paper towels, and serve.

Fish Wrapped in Rice Paper SOUTHEAST ASIA. Substitute 5-inch-square rice paper sheets for the bean curd, but do not soak until the fish and oil are ready. Immediately before you are ready to roll, soak the sheets in warm water until softened, about 15 seconds. Drain them briefly on a towel and proceed as directed.

Grouper or Other Fillets with Chiles and Tomatoes SOUTHEAST ASIA ▪

MAKES **4 SERVINGS**

TIME **30 MINUTES**

A glance at the ingredients might convince you this is an Italian dish. But this sweet-and-spicy concoction, laced with nam pla (see page 500 for information on this Thai fish sauce), could not be less Mediterranean in character. It's great with fillets, but you can also make it with whole fish; see the variation.

2 small fresh or dried chiles

3 tablespoons corn, grapeseed, or other neutral oil

2 pounds fillets of grouper, red snapper, black sea bass, or catfish

Salt and black pepper to taste

2 garlic cloves, minced

1 medium onion, diced

3 medium tomatoes, cored and chopped

1 tablespoon nam pla

2 teaspoons sugar

$1/4$ cup fish or chicken stock, preferably homemade (page 161 or 160), or water

1 scallion, trimmed and chopped

$1/4$ cup chopped fresh cilantro leaves for garnish

1. If you have fresh chiles, stem and seed them; if dried, soak in warm water for a few minutes until softened, then remove the stems and seeds. Meanwhile, heat the oil in a large skillet, preferably nonstick, over medium-high heat. Season the fish fillets with salt and pepper, then slide them into the hot oil. Cook, turning once, until golden brown, about 2 minutes per side. Remove the fish with a slotted spatula and drain on paper towels.

2. Add the garlic, onion, and chiles to the skillet and cook, stirring occasionally, until the onion is softened, about 5 minutes. Add the tomatoes and cook until they release their juices, about 5 minutes. Stir in the nam pla, sugar, and stock.

3. After the sauce reduces and thickens slightly, about 5 minutes, add the scallion and return the fish to the pan. Cook just until the fish is heated through, about 5 minutes. Garnish with cilantro and serve.

MAKING SHALLOW CUTS IN A GROUPER

Whole Fish in Spicy Tomato Sauce. Prepare the chiles as directed. Use about a 3-pound grouper, sea bass, or red snapper, gutted and scaled. Make 3 shallow cuts, from top to bottom, on each side of the fish. Put $1/2$ cup oil in a nonstick skillet that will accommodate the fish and turn the heat to high. A few minutes later, when the oil is hot—a pinch of flour will sizzle—dredge the fish heavily on both sides in flour, then gently lower it into the oil. Cook until golden brown on both sides, turning just once and adjusting the heat if necessary to prevent scorching. Transfer the fish to a platter and pour off the oil; wipe it out with a towel. Return the skillet to the stove over medium-high heat and add the 3 tablespoons of oil. Proceed to step 2. In step 3, when you return the fish to the skillet, partially cover the skillet with a lid or a piece of foil, and cook the fish without turning for 10 to 15 minutes, until the meat near the bone is pearly white. Serve, scooping the meat from the bone and serving it with the sauce.

■ make ahead   ▨ serve at room temp./cold   ▨ 30 minutes or less

Red Snapper or Other Fillets in Red Sauce SOUTHEAST ASIA ■

MAKES **4 SERVINGS**

TIME **15 MINUTES**

The heat from the sauce—red because of the chiles—and the tartness of the tamarind give these otherwise mild fillets a wonderful kick. For sweet and spicy flavors, try the variation. The spice mixture can be made well ahead of time and this dish finished in just a few minutes. See page 500 for information on Thai fish sauce (nam pla).

Serve with any simple rice dish.

> 4 small fresh red chiles, stemmed, seeded, and roughly
> chopped
>
> 2 garlic cloves, peeled
>
> 2 shallots, roughly chopped
>
> One 1-inch piece fresh ginger, peeled and roughly
> chopped
>
> 1 teaspoon ground turmeric
>
> 1^1/$_2$ to 2 pounds fillets of red snapper, sea bass, grouper,
> or halibut, skinned and cut into 2-inch chunks
>
> 2 tablespoons corn, grapeseed, or other neutral oil
>
> 2 tablespoons Tamarind Paste (page 585)
>
> 1 teaspoon nam pla, plus more to taste
>
> 2 scallions, trimmed and chopped, for garnish

1. Place the chiles, garlic, shallots, ginger, and turmeric in a food processor and process until pasty. Spread the mixture on the fish fillets (you can prepare the fish to this point, then cover and refrigerate for a few hours).
2. Heat the oil in a large skillet, preferably nonstick, over medium-high heat. About 2 minutes later, when the oil is hot, add the fish fillets and cook until the fish is fragrant, about 30 seconds.
3. Combine the tamarind paste with 1 cup water and add to the pan; bring to a boil. Lower the heat to

medium and simmer, stirring gently once or twice, until the fish is cooked through, 5 to 10 minutes. Season to taste with nam pla, garnish with scallions, and serve.

Shrimp in Red Sauce. Substitute 2 pounds medium shrimp, peeled, for the fish.

Fish in Sweet and Spicy Red Sauce. Substitute palm or brown sugar for the tamarind.

Halibut or Other Fish Steamed in Banana Leaves SOUTHEAST ASIA

MAKES **4 SERVINGS AS A MAIN COURSE,**
8 AS A STARTER

TIME **45 MINUTES**

This dish is dead easy to make and will wow everyone you serve it to. Dried banana leaves are sold at many Asian food markets, and though they're not likely to be the kind of thing you use every week, they are cheap and keep forever. For steaming Sticky Rice (page 508) or a dish like this, they are enormous fun and add a wonderful woody, smoky flavor. Furthermore, they seal in so much moisture that it's difficult to overcook the fish this way. See page 500 for information on Thai fish sauce (nam pla).

> 8 dried banana leaves, each about 8 inches square
>
> 1^1/$_2$ to 2 pounds fillets of halibut, red snapper, grouper,
> or sea bass, cut into 8 pieces
>
> 1 teaspoon minced garlic
>
> 1 tablespoon peeled and minced fresh ginger
>
> 1 tablespoon nam pla
>
> 1 tablespoon sugar
>
> ^{1}/$_2$ teaspoon cayenne, or to taste
>
> ^{1}/$_4$ cup chopped shallot

½ cup roughly chopped fresh cilantro leaves

Salt to taste

1. Put at least 2 inches of water in the bottom of a steamer. Soak the banana leaves in hot water until soft, just a few seconds.
2. Toss together the fish, garlic, ginger, nam pla, sugar, and cayenne. Put a piece of the seasoned fish in the center of each of the banana leaves and top with shallot, cilantro, and a light sprinkling of salt. Fold in the sides of the leaves and seal shut with toothpicks or skewers.
3. Steam for about 15 minutes, or until the fish is done (peek into one of the packages to check). Be careful of the steaming liquid when removing the packages. Remove each of the fish pieces from its package before serving and spoon some of the juices over it.

Lemongrass Halibut (or Other Fish) Steamed in Banana Leaves. In step 2, toss the fish with 1 teaspoon hot red pepper flakes, 2 tablespoons minced lemongrass, 1 teaspoon ground coriander, 1 tablespoon fresh lime juice, and the nam pla and sugar. Put it in the packages as directed and top with the shallots, ½ cup chopped fresh chives or scallion, and ½ cup fresh basil leaves, preferably Thai basil. Seal and steam as directed.

Patra ni Machhi Fish and Coconut Chutney
Steamed in Banana Leaves INDIA ■ ▨

MAKES **4 SERVINGS**

TIME **25 MINUTES**

One of the most popular dishes in Parsi (Zoroastrian) cuisine and wonderful with basmati (or brown) rice, this is traditionally made with pomfret, a fish that is not always readily available here. Use pompano, if you can find it, or any fillets, from mackerel to sole. You can prepare the banana leaf packages up to 3 hours in advance—just cover and refrigerate until ready to cook.

8 dried banana leaves (page 230), each about 8 inches square

5 garlic cloves, chopped

One 1½-inch piece fresh ginger, peeled and chopped

3 small hot fresh green chiles, stemmed, seeded, and minced, or to taste

1 cup roughly chopped fresh cilantro leaves

2 tablespoons roughly chopped fresh mint leaves

1 cup unsweetened shredded coconut, rinsed and drained

2 teaspoons ground cumin

3 tablespoons fresh lime juice

3 tablespoons corn, grapeseed, or other neutral oil

Salt to taste

1½ to 2 pounds fillets of pomfret, pompano, mackerel, sole, flounder, or sea bass, cut into 8 pieces

1. Put at least 2 inches of water in the bottom of a steamer. Soak the banana leaves in hot water until soft, just a few seconds.
2. Put the next 7 ingredients into a food processor and pulse until finely ground. Add the lime juice, oil, and a pinch of salt and process until nearly smooth; taste and adjust the seasoning as necessary.
3. Put a piece of the fish in the center of each of the banana leaves and season with salt, then top with the coconut chutney. Fold in the sides of the leaves and seal shut with toothpicks or skewers.
4. Steam for about 15 minutes, or until the fish is done (peek into one of the packages to check, but be careful—it's hot). Serve each guest 2 packages.

Fish Fillets Poached in Caramel Sauce VIETNAM ■

MAKES **4 SERVINGS**

TIME **30 MINUTES**

There were two things I couldn't get enough of in Vietnam: crunchy lemongrass dishes and caramel sauce dishes. Here's one of the latter, in which the caramel sauce—essentially melted sugar, which becomes oddly bitter while retaining its sticky sweetness as it browns—is used to poach the fish. Make sure you use lots of black pepper, which is one of the characteristic seasonings of Vietnam, and serve this unusual, delicious dish with Basic Long-Grain Rice (page 506). Information on Thai fish sauce (nam pla) is on page 500.

1 cup sugar

$1/2$ cup nam pla, or to taste

$1/2$ cup sliced shallot

1 teaspoon black pepper, or more to taste

Fresh lime juice to taste (at least 2 limes)

$1^1/2$ pounds fillets of red snapper, grouper, black sea bass, or catfish

Chopped fresh cilantro leaves for garnish

1. Put a 10-inch nonstick skillet over medium heat and add the sugar and a tablespoon or two of water. Cook, occasionally shaking the pan gently, until the sugar liquefies and begins to bubble, about 10 minutes. When the sugar is all liquid, cook for another minute or so, until it darkens; turn off the heat. Mix the nam pla with $1/2$ cup water; carefully, and at arm's length in case the hot caramel spatters, add the liquid and turn the heat to medium-high. Cook, stirring constantly, until the caramel melts into the liquid. Add the shallot and cook, stirring occasionally, until it softens, about 5 minutes.

2. Add the black pepper and some lime juice, then lay the fish in the sauce. If the sauce does not reach at least halfway up the fish, add water as necessary. Simmer until the fish is done, probably less than 10 minutes (a thin-bladed knife inserted into its center will meet little resistance). Taste and add more lime juice or pepper if necessary, then garnish and serve.

Soy-Glazed Flounder or Other Fillets

JAPAN ■

MAKES **4 SERVINGS**

TIME **20 MINUTES**

This is an ultraquick recipe, lightly sweet, and one that will work for any white fillet—even thick ones if you extend the cooking time slightly. I prefer very thin ones, though, because the sauce almost permeates them and the cooking time is so short. The soy glaze makes this a natural over white rice.

1 tablespoon peanut or neutral oil, like corn or grapeseed

1 tablespoon minced garlic

1 tablespoon peeled and minced fresh ginger

1 cup fish or chicken stock, preferably homemade (page 161 or 160), or water

2 tablespoons soy sauce

1 tablespoon sugar

4 to 8 fillets of flounder or sole, a total of about $1^1/2$ pounds

1 teaspoon dark sesame oil

$1/4$ cup minced scallion

1. Put the oil in a large skillet, preferably nonstick, and place over medium-high heat. A minute later, add the garlic and ginger and cook, stirring occasionally, until they soften, about 2 minutes. Add

the stock, soy sauce, and sugar and bring to a boil; cook until reduced by about half, 5 to 10 minutes.

2. Add the fillets, in one layer if possible, turn the heat to low, and cover. Cook for about 2 minutes, uncover, and turn the fillets.

3. Cook for another 2 minutes, then drizzle with the sesame oil, sprinkle with the scallion, and serve.

Mackerel Fillets Simmered in Soy Sauce JAPAN ■

MAKES **2 TO 4 SERVINGS**

TIME **20 MINUTES**

Many Japanese cooks treasure dark, oily, full-flavored fish and treat it with a simple dose of powerful seasonings and a simple cooking technique that might be called "pan-steaming." If you think you don't like mackerel, try it this way; it may change your mind. Serve this with short-grain white rice (page 507).

$1/2$ cup soy sauce

$1/3$ cup sake or dry sherry

1 tablespoon sugar

2 tablespoons rice or white wine vinegar

5 or 6 thin slices peeled fresh ginger

3 or 4 garlic cloves, crushed

4 mackerel fillets, about 1 pound total, skin on

Finely grated peeled fresh ginger or lemon zest for garnish

1. In a 12-inch skillet with a lid, mix together all the ingredients except the fish and garnish. Add $1/2$ cup water, bring to a boil, and simmer over medium heat for about 5 minutes, uncovered.

2. Add the fish, skin side down, cover, and simmer until the fish is cooked through (the smallest fillet should just flake when prodded with a fork or knife, and the fish should all be opaque), 7 to 10

minutes. Spoon a fillet and some sauce onto a mound of white rice; garnish and serve.

Black Cod or Mackerel Fillets in Miso Sauce JAPAN

MAKES **4 SERVINGS**

TIME **2 TO 3 HOURS, LARGELY UNATTENDED**

Black cod, a Pacific fish also known as sable, is treasured in Japan (and at elite Japanese restaurants here) for its richness and slightly smoky flavor. With miso it is astonishingly delicious. (Mackerel is not the same but still very good.) Use white (it's actually beige) miso if you can find it.

As is common before cooking many types of fish in Japan, this is salted to firm up the flesh; you can skip this step if you prefer.

This is not a super-saucy dish, but well-made short-grain rice (page 507) is still a good accompaniment, as would be any salad.

1 tablespoon salt

$1 1/2$ to 2 pounds fillets of black cod (sable) or mackerel

1 cup miso

$1/4$ cup sake or mirin

1 tablespoon peeled and finely shredded fresh ginger

1. Sprinkle the salt all over the fish and let sit refrigerated for at least 45 and up to 90 minutes. Rinse and dry the fish.

2. Combine $3/4$ cup of the miso with 3 tablespoons of the sake. Smear this mixture all over the fillets and let sit refrigerated again for 45 to 90 minutes. Rinse and dry again.

3. Preheat the broiler; the rack should be about 4 inches from the heat source. Soak the ginger in cold water to cover. Combine the remaining miso

and sake and smear over the flesh side of the fillets. Put on a nonstick or greased baking sheet and broil carefully, until the mixture bubbles but does not burn and the fish is done (the point of a thin-bladed knife inserted into its thickest part will meet little resistance). If the top threatens to burn before the fish is cooked through, move the rack down a notch or move the fish into a hot oven. Drain the ginger and use it to garnish the fish; serve immediately.

Grilled Black Cod or Mackerel. In step 2, do not rinse off the miso mixture; simply use your fingers to remove most but not all of it. Grill over moderate heat, turning once, until the outside is crisp and the inside cooked through.

Sweet-and-Spicy Broiled Mackerel or Other Fillets KOREA ■

MAKES **4 SERVINGS**

TIME **30 MINUTES**

Like Japan, Korea makes good use of fermented beans, in the form of soy sauce and the terrific chili-bean paste known as go chu jang (page 591). If you cannot find that, use the Sesame-Chile Paste on page 591 or hoisin, spiked with a couple of pinches of cayenne or dried red chile flakes, but don't make the dish too hot—it should be predominantly sweet, sticky, and spicy. Serve with white rice, preferably short grain (page 507), and a salad or vegetable.

>   1 tablespoon go chu jang (see headnote) or 1 tablespoon
>   hoisin sauce mixed with about $1/2$ teaspoon cayenne
>   or hot red pepper flakes
>   2 tablespoons soy sauce

1 tablespoon mirin or sugar

1 tablespoon minced garlic

1 tablespoon dark sesame oil

4 fillets of mackerel or bluefish, preferably with skin on,
   or 2 swordfish steaks, a total of $1 1/2$ to 2 pounds

Toasted sesame seeds (page 596) for garnish

Minced scallion, green part only, for garnish

1. Preheat the broiler; adjust the rack so that it is about 4 inches from the heat source. (These can also be grilled, but you'll need a basket, because they'll stick if grilled directly on the grate.) Combine the go chu jang, soy sauce, mirin, garlic, and sesame oil and rub this mixture all over the fish, but primarily on the flesh side. Place skin side down in a broiling pan, preferably nonstick or lined with lightly oiled foil (you can use more sesame oil for this).

2. Broil until the top is brown and bubbly, less than 10 minutes. If the fish is not cooked through (a thin-bladed knife will pierce its thickest part easily), move it to the oven for a couple of minutes or lower the broiling rack a couple of inches. Serve immediately, garnished with the sesame seeds and scallion.

Crisp-Fried Fillets or Shrimp in Spicy Tomato Sauce INDIA

MAKES **4 SERVINGS**

TIME **1 HOUR**

Fish or shrimp in a powerful sauce is a common dish in India; this is a good example. If you're comfortable in the kitchen, you can produce this dish far more quickly by beginning with the onion-tomato mixture and sautéing the fish in a separate skillet.

Serve this with Coconut Rice (page 516) or Home-

Fried Potatoes with Onion and Amchoor (page 477) or any Indian vegetable dish.

2 tablespoons fresh lime juice

Salt and black pepper to taste

1 teaspoon ground turmeric

3 teaspoons curry powder, preferably homemade
(pages 592–593), or garam masala (page 594)

¼ teaspoon cayenne

1½ to 2 pounds fillets of red snapper, sea bass, or other
firm, white-fleshed fish or shrimp, peeled

Peanut or neutral oil, like corn or grapeseed, for frying

1 large onion, thinly sliced

1 jalapeño or other fresh chile, stemmed, seeded, and
minced, or 1 teaspoon hot red pepper flakes, or to
taste

1 tablespoon minced garlic

1 tablespoon peeled and minced fresh ginger

3 cups peeled and chopped tomato (canned are fine;
strain them first)

Chopped fresh cilantro leaves for garnish

1. Mix together the lime juice, salt, pepper, turmeric, 1 teaspoon of the curry powder, and the cayenne and rub this mixture all over the fish or shrimp. (You can allow the fish to sit in this mixture, refrigerated, for a couple of hours.)

2. Put at least ⅛ inch of oil in a large nonstick skillet and turn the heat to medium-high. When the oil is hot, add the fish or shrimp and quickly brown on each side, about 5 minutes total; don't worry about whether the fish is cooked through. Transfer to a plate.

3. Wipe out the skillet, turn the heat to high, and add 2 more tablespoons of oil. Cook the onion, stirring occasionally, until wilted and browned along the edges. Add the chile, garlic, and ginger and cook, stirring, for about a minute. Add the remaining curry powder, the tomatoes, and some salt and

pepper and reduce the heat to medium. Cook, stirring occasionally, until the tomatoes break up and become saucy. Taste and adjust the seasoning.

4. Return the fish to the pan and heat through, about 5 minutes. Garnish and serve.

Escabeche with Mackerel
SOUTH AMERICA ■ ■
MAKES **4 SERVINGS**
TIME **45 MINUTES, PLUS COOLING TIME**

Generally speaking, escabeche is a method used for flavoring (and preserving—but we don't use it for this purpose) fish after it has been cooked. It's great with dark-fleshed fish like mackerel, tuna, and bluefish, but it also works nicely with cod and even flatfish like flounder. All that changes is the cooking time, and, of course, the flavor.

Serve this as part of a buffet with other South American or almost any Western European dishes.

¾ cup extra virgin olive oil

1½ to 2 pounds mackerel fillets, with or without skin

Flour for dredging

Salt and black pepper to taste

10 garlic cloves, peeled and lightly crushed

2 bay leaves

5 fresh thyme sprigs or 1 teaspoon dried

½ teaspoon cayenne, or to taste

1 cup red wine vinegar or other vinegar

1 cup red wine

1 cup chicken stock, preferably homemade (page 160),
or water

1. Put about ½ cup of the oil in a large nonstick skillet and turn the heat to medium-high. About 3 minutes later, when the oil is hot, dredge the fillets

lightly in the flour and add them, one at a time, to the skillet. Do not crowd: it's likely you'll have to cook in batches. Sprinkle the fillets with salt and pepper as they cook. As the fillets brown, turn them and brown the other side. Total cooking time for each fillet will be about 6 minutes. When the fish are done, transfer them to a platter or gratin dish; they may overlap slightly.

2. Cool the pan and wipe it out. Add the remaining oil and turn the heat to medium. A minute later, add the garlic and cook, stirring occasionally, until it begins to turn color. Add the bay leaves, thyme, and cayenne and stir; add the vinegar, bring to a boil, and simmer for a minute. Add the wine, bring back to a boil, and simmer for about 5 minutes. Add the stock, bring back to a boil, and cook quickly to reduce the mixture to about half its volume.

3. Pour the liquid over the fish. Let cool to room temperature and serve or cover and refrigerate for up to a couple of days, bringing it back to room temperature before serving.

SALMON

These days it's not a question so much of whether salmon is sold in steaks or fillets—both are widely available, all the time, at reasonable prices (this was not the case even twenty years ago)—but whether it is wild or farm raised.

Farm-raised salmon is almost all Atlantic salmon (which is endangered in the wild). It's fatty (theoretically, these are "good" fats), easy to cook, and pretty tasty. But the usual questions about farm-raised animals apply: its impact on the environment, its feed, what's accumulated in its fatty tissues (in this instance PCBs), and the breeding and raising practices. In short, it's inexpensive, popular, widely available . . . and beleaguered.

Wild salmon is Pacific salmon, mostly from Alaska,

and in season from spring through fall (sometimes you can find frozen wild salmon, and I wish there were more of that). There are five types: king (or chinook), the most prized and usually the most expensive; sockeye (or red), the leanest and my personal favorite; coho (or silver), which is hardest to find and quite good; chum, often very inexpensive when in season and not bad; and pink, most of which is canned.

Crisp-Skin Salmon Fillets with Chimichurri Sauce

SOUTH AMERICA ■

MAKES **4 SERVINGS**

TIME **30 MINUTES**

Strictly speaking, chimichurri is Argentinean, but there is far more salmon in Chile than elsewhere in Latin America, and chimichurri has become pan-continental. Keep the skin on the salmon (make sure it's scaled), and making it perfectly crisp is nearly effortless as long as you use a nonstick skillet. I love this with Peasant-Style Potatoes (page 477) or Potatoes with Bay Leaves (page 481).

> 1 cup finely chopped (but not minced) fresh parsley leaves, preferably flat-leaf
> $^1/_3$ cup plus 2 tablespoons extra virgin olive oil
> 3 tablespoons fresh lemon juice
> 1 tablespoon finely chopped garlic
> 1 teaspoon hot red pepper flakes, or to taste
> Salt to taste
> Four 6-ounce salmon fillets, preferably cut from the center of a thick fillet, skin on and scaled

1. Combine the parsley, $^1/_3$ cup of the olive oil, the lemon juice, garlic, and red pepper flakes in a bowl and stir to combine. Season to taste with salt and add more red pepper if you like (it should be quite

hot). Let sit while you prepare the fish or up to a couple of hours.

2. Preheat the oven to 500°F. Put the remaining 2 tablespoons olive oil in a large ovenproof skillet, preferably nonstick, and turn the heat to high. When the oil smokes, add the salmon, skin side down. Cook for about 30 seconds, shaking the pan once or twice to make sure the fillets don't stick. Transfer to the oven and roast for 5 minutes or until the fish is medium-rare to medium.

3. Sprinkle the top of the fish with salt and serve it with the sauce.

Lime-Cooked Fish with Crisp Garlic

MEXICO ■

MAKES **4 SERVINGS**

TIME **30 MINUTES**

Limes and hot weather go together; I first had this at a three-walled restaurant in a Yucatán port on the Gulf of Mexico. I loved it immediately, and I love it still. It works just as well with shrimp as it does with flatfish.

As for the chiles, the amount is your call. I like just a touch of heat—a pinch of cayenne does the trick for me—but this dish is often prepared scorchingly hot.

Serve with rice (Mexican Rice, page 517, is good), or tortillas.

¼ cup neutral oil, like corn or grapeseed

5 garlic cloves, thinly sliced

Salt to taste

4 large or 8 small fillets of flounder or other flatfish, 1½ pounds or more

3 small hot dried red chiles, or to taste

½ cup fresh lime juice

1 cup cherry or grape tomatoes, optional

½ cup chopped fresh cilantro leaves

1. Combine 2 tablespoons of the oil with the garlic in a small heavy saucepan over medium-low heat. Cook, shaking the pan occasionally, until the garlic browns, 5 to 10 minutes; season with a little salt and turn off the heat.

2. Meanwhile, put the remaining 2 tablespoons oil in a large nonstick skillet over medium-high heat. A minute later, add the fish and chiles and cook, undisturbed, for about 2 minutes. Reduce the heat to medium and add all but a tablespoon or two of the lime juice, along with the tomatoes if you're using them. Cook for another 2 minutes or so, until the fish is cooked through. (There is no need to turn the fish; if you are using shrimp instead of flatfish, stir occasionally.)

3. Transfer the fish to a platter. Stir the cilantro into the pan juices and pour the contents of the pan over the fish, along with the garlic and its oil and the remaining lime juice. Serve immediately.

Pan-Cooked Grouper or Other Fillets with "Killed" Onions MEXICO ■

MAKES **4 SERVINGS**

TIME **ABOUT 30 MINUTES**

Like the preceding dish, this one is wickedly strong tasting, not fiery-hot but potent with garlic, onions (which are salted to "kill" their harshness), and lime. Not for the faint of heart, but many people (including me) love it. You can use any firm-fleshed white fish: halibut, swordfish, striped bass, red snapper, and so on.

Ideally, you'd serve this with Mexican Radish Salad (page 172), along with some beautiful tomatoes. Rice and beans would also be good.

1 large white onion, sliced

Salt and black pepper

½ cup plus 2 tablespoons fresh lime juice

¼ cup extra virgin olive or other oil

1½ to 2 pounds fillets of grouper or other firm-fleshed
fish, in 2 or 4 pieces

6 garlic cloves, thinly sliced

Chopped fresh cilantro leaves for garnish

1. Peel and slice the onion; sprinkle liberally with salt and toss. Let sit for 30 minutes or so, then rinse and toss with 2 tablespoons of the lime juice.

2. Put 3 tablespoons of the oil in a large nonstick skillet and turn the heat to medium-high. Add the fish and cook, rotating if necessary but not turning, and sprinkling with salt and pepper as it cooks, until nicely browned on one side, 4 to 5 minutes. Turn and lower the heat to medium; continue to cook until the fish is tender (a thin-bladed knife will pass through its thickest part with little resistance), another 2 to 5 minutes, depending on its thickness. Transfer to a warm platter.

3. Add the remaining oil to the skillet along with the garlic and cook, stirring constantly, just until the garlic begins to color—less than a minute. Turn off the heat, add the remaining ½ cup lime juice, and stir, scraping the bottom of the pan if necessary to incorporate the garlic, lime juice, oil, and whatever solids remain. Taste and add more salt and pepper if necessary. Pour over the fish, garnish with cilantro, and serve with the onion.

Fish Tacos MEXICO ■

MAKES **4 SERVINGS**

TIME **20 MINUTES**

Fish tacos, long a staple of coastal Mexico (and coastal California), have become popular throughout the U.S. I prefer the fish fried, but you can grill or even steam it if you like.

Eight 5-inch corn tortillas

1 to 1½ pounds fillets of firm white fish, like red snapper,
sea bass, grouper, or halibut, skinned and boned

3 garlic cloves, minced

Salt and black pepper to taste

2 tablespoons fresh lime juice

½ cup cornmeal

2 tablespoons pure chile powder, like ancho
or New Mexico

Corn, grapeseed, or other neutral oil for frying

½ cup shredded cabbage

Lime wedges for serving

Salsa Fresca (page 610) or other salsa for serving

1. Put at least 1 inch of water in the bottom of a steamer. When the water simmers, wrap the tortillas in a kitchen towel and set in the steamer. Steam for 3 minutes, then turn off the heat and keep the cover on the steamer while you prepare the fish.

2. Cut the fish into 8 equal pieces. Mix the garlic, salt, pepper, and lime juice together and rub into the fish.

3. Mix the cornmeal and chile powder together. Remove the fish from the marinade and dredge lightly in the cornmeal mixture. Pour ⅛ inch of oil into a large skillet and place over medium-high heat. After a couple of minutes—when a pinch of cornmeal sizzles in the oil—gently lay the fish pieces in the skillet. Fry, turning once, until golden brown and tender (a thin-bladed knife will meet little resistance). Do not overcrowd; work in batches if necessary. Drain on paper towels.

4. Remove the tortillas from the steamer and place a piece of fish in the center of each. Top with shredded cabbage and serve with lime wedges and salsa.

Grilled Fish Tacos. Omit the cornmeal. Marinate the fish as directed. Start a charcoal fire or preheat a gas grill or broiler; the fire should be quite hot, the rack 3 or 4 inches from the heat source. Remove the fish from the marinade, drizzle with the oil, and sprinkle with the chile powder. Grill the fish for about 4 minutes, inserting a metal spatula between the fish and the grill every 2 minutes or so to minimize sticking. Turn the fish and grill for another 4 minutes, again making sure the fish doesn't stick. Check for doneness; the fish will still be firm and juicy but will have lost its translucence, and a thin-bladed knife will pass through it fairly easily. Proceed as directed.

Run Down Jamaican Codfish Curry

MAKES **4 SERVINGS**

TIME **1 ½ HOURS**

This dish is usually made with pickled or salted fish, but it's simpler (and, in my opinion, better) when made with lightly salted fresh fish. To be truly authentic, the chile should be a Scotch bonnet (habanero), which has a distinctive though fiery flavor, but any chile will do in a pinch.

Serve this with Coconut Rice (page 516) or, even better, Coconut Rice and Beans (page 516).

Salt to taste

1 ½ to 2 pounds fillets of cod, red snapper, sea bass, or other white-fleshed fish, in 1 or 2 pieces

2 tablespoons corn, grapeseed, or other neutral oil

3 garlic cloves, minced

1 large onion, chopped

1 Scotch bonnet or other chile, stemmed, seeded, and minced, or to taste

1 teaspoon black pepper

1 ½ to 2 cups coconut milk, homemade (page 584) or canned

1 cup chopped tomato with its juice

Juice of 1 lime

Chopped fresh cilantro leaves for garnish

1. Salt the cod lightly on both sides and let rest refrigerated for about an hour, but at least 30 minutes and up to 24 hours.
2. Put the oil in a deep skillet or wide saucepan and place over medium-high heat. A minute later, add the garlic, onion, chile, and pepper. Cook, stirring occasionally, until the onion softens, 5 to 10 minutes. Stir in the coconut milk and tomato, bring to a boil, and cook, stirring occasionally, until the mixture reduces by about half.
3. Rinse the fish and add it to the pot. Adjust the heat so that the mixture bubbles steadily but not violently. When the fish is done, after about 10 minutes—a thin-bladed knife will meet little resistance—add the lime juice, garnish, and serve.

Fish Tagine MOROCCO

MAKES **4 SERVINGS**

TIME **45 MINUTES**

An easy fish stew with exotic flavors. You can make the same style dish using chicken thighs in place of the fish; just boost the oven temperature to 400°F and increase the cooking time by 15 minutes or so. This is great served with couscous (page 526), bread, or rice.

⅓ cup chopped fresh parsley or cilantro leaves, plus more for garnish

One ½-inch piece fresh ginger, peeled and minced

3 teaspoons sweet paprika

¼ cup fresh lemon juice

½ cup extra virgin olive oil, plus more as needed

1 ½ to 2 pounds fillets of red snapper, halibut, grouper, sea bass, or other firm fish, cut into 4 equal portions

3 garlic cloves, peeled

¼ teaspoon cayenne, or to taste

5 small tomatoes, cored

3 teaspoons ground cumin

Salt and black pepper to taste

1 large onion, sliced

1 lemon, thinly sliced crosswise

¼ cup olives, preferably green, pitted

1. Preheat the oven to 350°F. Whisk together the first 5 ingredients in a shallow baking dish. Place the fish in the marinade and turn to coat. (Refrigerate if your kitchen is very warm.)

2. Place the garlic, cayenne, tomatoes, cumin, a large pinch of salt, and a sprinkling of pepper in a food processor and pulse until the mixture is coarsely chopped. Oil the bottom of a casserole or baking dish. Lay the onion slices across the bottom, then top with the tomato mixture. Cover the pan with foil and bake for about 15 minutes, or until the mixture becomes juicy.

3. Remove the foil and lay the fish on top of the tomato mixture; sprinkle with salt and pepper. Lay the lemon slices on top of the fish, then pour on the fish marinade; top with the olives. Cover and bake for another 15 minutes, or until a thin-bladed knife passes through the fish with little re-sistance. Garnish with additional parsley or cilantro and serve immediately.

Red Snapper or Other White Fillets Meunière FRANCE ■

MAKES **4 SERVINGS**

TIME **15 MINUTES**

Classically, meunière refers to fillets of sole that are floured and quickly sautéed in clarified butter, then finished with parsley, lemon juice, and a little melted butter. Over the years the definition has expanded to encompass a series of flexible techniques that can be applied to just about any thin cut of meat, poultry, or fish. You can serve this with a salad and bread, or with any good potato and vegetable combination.

True sole is a uniquely firm fish, best replaced not by local "soles" (like gray sole or Pacific sole) but by sturdy fillets like red snapper, grouper, catfish, black-fish, or sea bass.

4 red snapper fillets, about 1½ pounds

Salt and black pepper to taste

Flour or cornmeal for dredging

Extra virgin olive oil, other oil, butter, clarified butter
    (page 241), or a combination for sautéing

1 to 2 tablespoons butter, optional

1 tablespoon fresh lemon juice

2 tablespoons minced fresh parsley leaves

1. Heat a 12-inch skillet, preferably nonstick, over medium-high heat for about 2 minutes. While it is heating, sprinkle the fish with salt and pepper and place the flour or cornmeal on a plate.

2. Place enough oil or butter in the skillet to coat the bottom well and place over high heat. When the oil is hot, dredge a fillet in the coating, turning it over a few times and pressing it down so that it is well covered. Add the fillet to the pan, then repeat.

3. Cook until the fillets are nicely browned on the first side, about 3 minutes, then turn and cook on the second side for 2 to 4 minutes, lowering the heat a bit if the coating begins to scorch, until the fish is firm to the touch. As the fish is cooking, melt the butter, if you're using it, over medium heat until it is nut brown.

4. When the fish is done, drain it briefly on paper towels, then transfer to a warm platter. Drizzle with lemon juice and top with half the parsley. At the last minute, pour the browned butter over all, add the remaining parsley, and serve.

Clarified Butter

Removing the white milk solids from melted butter "clarifies" it, leaving only the golden butterfat behind. It's a useful trick, because the solids burn at high temperatures. Once clarified, butter can be used to sauté over very high heat.

In India, a variation on clarified butter called ghee is still commonly used in cooking and flavoring. It differs only slightly from European-style clarified butter in that it's heated for longer to boil off the tiny amount of water suspended in butter, thereby rendering it almost impervious to spoilage, and to impart a characteristically nutty, toasted taste. Ghee is sold bottled in Indian markets, though clarified butter as made here and left on the stove a minute or two longer—just until it smells slightly nutty—is a perfectly good and probably preferable substitute.

Smen is a sometimes-clarified butter (sometimes it's just made with whole butter) used in North African cooking. It is flavored with spices or herbs and traditionally aged for a period of weeks or even months before being used, and its principal role is that of a flavoring agent, not to preserve the butter or make it a more versatile cooking medium.

To make clarified butter, melt a stick (or more) of butter over low heat and cook it over very low heat for 3 to 5 minutes, skimming the clusters of white milk solids off the top of the butter as you do. When the butter is clear, let the pan stand off the heat for a minute or two (unless you're making ghee, in which case you should heat it a little longer). Decant the clear golden oil off the milk solids (which will have settled to the bottom of the pan) and use immediately or store in an airtight container in the refrigerator for up to a month.

Sea Bass or Other Fillets in Saffron Sauce SPAIN ▤

MAKES **4 SERVINGS**

TIME **30 MINUTES**

A lovely, flavorful, and colorful sauce with an elusive perfume that is the result of the saffron-vinegar combination. This is suitable for any firm-fleshed fish fillet.

If you make the variation with the potato salad, you'd pretty much have a one-dish meal here; bread and salad would be nice additions.

5 tablespoons extra virgin olive oil

1$\frac{1}{2}$ to 2 pounds fillets of sea bass, red snapper, catfish, monkfish, wolffish, or other firm fillets

Flour for dredging

6 garlic cloves, peeled and lightly crushed

1 medium onion, chopped

1 red bell pepper, stemmed, seeded, and cut into strips

About $\frac{1}{2}$ teaspoon saffron threads

$\frac{1}{2}$ cup dry white wine or water

1 cup fish or chicken stock preferably homemade (page 161 or 160) or water

Salt and black pepper to taste

1. Put 3 tablespoons of the oil in a nonstick skillet over medium-high heat. A couple of minutes later, when the oil is hot (a pinch of flour will sizzle), dredge each fillet in the flour and add to the skillet. Cook until brown, turning, once, about 3 minutes per side. Remove the fillets and set aside. Let the pan cool a bit, then wipe it out.

2. Heat the remaining 2 tablespoons oil and add the garlic. Stir until fragrant, about 1 minute, then add the onion and bell pepper. Cook, stirring occasionally, until the onion becomes translucent, about 5 minutes.

---

3. Add the saffron, wine, stock, and salt and pepper. Return the fish to the pan, cover, and adjust the heat so the mixture simmers. Cook until the fish is done, about 5 minutes more.

Sea Bass with Saffron and Potatoes. A more substantial dish: In step 2, add 1 pound potatoes, peeled and cut into 1-inch chunks, along with the onions. After adding the wine and stock, bring to a boil, then simmer until the potatoes are tender, about 20 minutes. Add the browned fish and finish as directed.

Cod with Chickpeas and Sherry
SPAIN ■

MAKES **4 SERVINGS**

TIME **30 MINUTES (WITH PRECOOKED CHICKPEAS)**

Sherry, garlic, and chickpeas, a decidedly Andalusian combination of flavors, is served by itself or as a side dish with almost any cut of meat, fish, or poultry. But I like it best with cod: the subtlety and tenderness of the fish are offset wonderfully by the big, almost meaty flavors of the scented chickpeas yet are not overwhelmed by them.

If you have any advance inkling at all that you're going to be tackling this recipe, try to cook dried chickpeas for it in advance (page 431).

The best sherry to use here is Amontillado, which is slightly but not overpoweringly sweet; a ten-dollar bottle of Amontillado will suffice, and since you're only going to use about a quarter of the bottle, there will be plenty left to chill and drink. Second choices would be slightly sweeter Oloroso or drier Fino.

¼ cup plus 2 tablespoons olive oil

2 fillets of cod, each about 1 inch thick,
   1½ to 2 pounds total

Flour for dredging

Salt and black pepper

2 medium Spanish onions, cut into ¼-inch slices

4 cups cooked or drained canned chickpeas

¾ cup sherry, preferably Amontillado

2 tablespoons minced garlic

¼ cup chopped fresh parsley leaves

1. Preheat the oven to 300°F. Put 2 tablespoons of the oil in a nonstick skillet large enough to hold the cod in one layer; place over medium-high heat. Dredge the fillets lightly in the flour and, when the oil is hot, add them to the skillet one at a time, skin (it won't have skin, so shiny) side up. Cook, undisturbed, for about 5 minutes or until the cooked side is browned evenly. Turn the fish onto an ovenproof plate, browned side up, sprinkle with salt and pepper, and put it in the oven.

2. Immediately add 2 more tablespoons of the oil and the sliced onions to the pan and cook, stirring, for about a minute or two, just until they start to color.

3. Add the chickpeas (with about ½ cup of their liquid if they were not canned) to the skillet and cook, stirring, for about a minute. Add all but a tablespoon of the sherry and raise the heat to high. Cook, shaking the pan now and then, until the liquid is all but evaporated and the chickpeas are beginning to brown. Stir in the garlic along with some salt and pepper and cook for 1 minute, stirring occasionally; stir in the remaining 2 tablespoons olive oil and remaining tablespoon of sherry.

4. By this time, the fish will be done. (If it is not, hold the chickpeas over low heat until it is.) Serve it on top of the chickpeas, scattered with parsley.

Monkfish or Other Fillets in Almond Sauce SPAIN

MAKES **4 SERVINGS**

TIME **45 MINUTES**

Almonds grow abundantly in Spain—you see the trees throughout the South and easily find fresh almonds, which are a rarity here—and play an integral role in many dishes, offering a rich flavor and body to sauces. This dish is a perfect weeknight offering, but it's also a fine main course at a dinner party.

I like monkfish here, but striped bass, grouper, red snapper, and black sea bass are all suitable; each will cook at slightly varying rates (the monkfish will take the most time, red snapper the least).

This is wonderful over either white rice or a pilaf (page 513) or with crusty bread.

3 tablespoons extra virgin olive oil

1 thick slice bread, roughly chopped

$\frac{1}{2}$ cup blanched almonds

1 tablespoon minced garlic

1 medium onion, chopped

$\frac{1}{4}$ cup chopped fresh parsley leaves, plus more for
   garnish

1 teaspoon fresh paprika

$\frac{1}{2}$ cup dry white wine

1 cup fish stock, preferably homemade (page 161),
   or water

1$\frac{1}{2}$ to 2 pounds fillets of monkfish or other firm white fish

Salt and black pepper to taste

1. Preheat the oven to 350°F. Heat half the oil in a skillet over medium heat. Add the bread pieces and almonds and toast, stirring occasionally, until golden brown. Transfer to a food processor. Add the remaining oil to the skillet and heat. Add the garlic and onion and cook, stirring occasionally, until softened, about 5 minutes. Stir in the parsley and paprika, then transfer the mixture to the food processor.

2. Process the mixture until coarsely ground, then, with the machine running, add the wine. Continue processing until a smooth paste is formed. Return the mixture to the skillet and stir in the stock.

3. Bring the mixture to a steady simmer over medium heat and cook for 15 minutes, stirring occasionally. Meanwhile, season the fish with salt and pepper and place in a casserole. When the sauce is cooked, season it with salt and pepper and pour over the fish.

4. Put the fish in the oven and bake, uncovered, until the point of a thin-bladed knife inserted into the thickest part of the fish meets little resistance (monkfish will remain firm, but there will be a noticeable difference between underdone and done). Garnish and serve hot.

Bacalao a la Vizcaina
Salt Cod, Basque Style SPAIN ■

MAKES **4 SERVINGS**

TIME **1$\frac{1}{2}$ HOURS (WITH PREPARED SALT COD)**

Like so many other cultures that have traditionally relied on salt cod, that of the Basque region of Spain and France still cherishes the flavor. This stew is one of the region's best-known dishes, and it's a good one. Like most stews, it's terrific when made a day ahead of time and reheated.

Serve with rice or crusty bread or boiled potato.

1 pound boneless salt cod, soaked and cooked
   (page 245)

Extra virgin olive oil for frying

Flour for dredging

3 garlic cloves, minced

1 large onion, diced

2 large tomatoes, cored and chopped

1 cup dry white wine or water, more or less

1 tablespoon drained capers

1 bay leaf

Pinch of cayenne

Salt and black pepper to taste

Chopped fresh parsley leaves for garnish

1. Drain the salt cod and pick out any stray bones or pieces of skin, then cut into bite-sized pieces. Heat enough oil to liberally coat the bottom of a large skillet over medium-high heat; dredge the cod in the flour, then add to the skillet. Cook, turning once, until lightly browned and crisp, about 5 minutes. Remove with a slotted spoon and set aside.

2. Wipe or rinse out the pan; return it to the stove over medium heat and add 2 tablespoons olive oil. A minute later, add the garlic and onion and cook, stirring occasionally, until the garlic softens, about 5 minutes; leave the onion fairly crisp. Stir in the tomatoes, wine, capers, bay leaf, and cayenne.

3. Adjust the heat so the mixture simmers steadily; add the cod and cook, uncovered, for about 45 minutes or until the fish is quite tender. Add more water if necessary; the mixture should not dry out but have the texture of a tomato sauce. When the fish is ready, taste and adjust the seasoning, garnish, and serve hot or warm. (You can prepare the dish and let it sit for a couple of hours or cover and refrigerate for up to a day before reheating and serving.)

Bacalao with Eggplant. In step 2, add 1 pound small eggplants, trimmed and cubed, to the skillet with the tomatoes.

Salt Cod in Tomato Sauce SPAIN

MAKES **4 SERVINGS**

TIME **45 MINUTES (WITH PREPARED SALT COD)**

You find this dish, or one like it, everywhere there is salt cod—which is to say, almost everywhere in the North Atlantic and parts of the Mediterranean. I like the Spanish version, which is reminiscent of a strong pasta sauce. In fact, thinned just a bit, this would make an excellent sauce for pasta, though I still prefer it with crusty bread.

You can poach almost any fish in this sauce—any white-fleshed fish will work, though cod is the most obvious and logical choice—but it will never have the character brought to the table by salt cod, especially if you take the time to fry it first, as in the variation.

1 pound boneless salt cod, soaked
   and cooked (page 245)

2 tablespoons extra virgin olive oil

3 garlic cloves, peeled and lightly smashed

3 anchovy fillets, or to taste

One 28-ounce can whole plum tomatoes, drained
   and chopped

Salt and black pepper to taste

2 tablespoons drained capers

1/2 cup pitted green olives

Hot red pepper flakes to taste

Chopped fresh parsley leaves for garnish

1. Drain the salt cod and pick out any stray bones or pieces of skin, then cut it into chunks. Combine the oil and garlic in a large skillet over medium heat. Add the anchovies and cook, stirring occasionally, until the garlic is lightly golden and the anchovies broken up. Raise the heat to medium-high and add the tomatoes along with a little salt and some pepper. Cook for a few minutes, stirring occasionally, until the mixture gets saucy, about 15 minutes.

Salt Cod

Bacalao—cod that has been salted and dried—is originally from northern Europe, though perhaps most closely associated with Spain and Portugal. The Grand Banks off Newfoundland, also known as terra de Bacalhau, were the great source of cod. Since there was no refrigeration when these waters were first fished heavily in the late fifteenth century, the gutting and packing of the fish in salt or brine on board before exporting became a standard practice. (There is evidence that Basque, Irish, English, and northern European fishermen began fishing the Newfoundland waters before this time but on a smaller scale.)

Now, of course, cod and other fish can be refrigerated or frozen on board, but the taste for salt cod remains. Portugal considers it one of its national foods (the annual per-capita consumption is something around 20 pounds), and there is still plenty of it in Spain, Italy, Brazil, and Scandinavia.

Most supermarkets sell salt cod (often in cute little wooden boxes). It will keep well for weeks or even months in your refrigerator (and eternally in your freezer). And using it is pretty straightforward, if time consuming: Soak it for at least a few hours (overnight is better), changing the water when you think of it, until the water is not intolerably salty when you taste it. Then poach for a few minutes in water or milk until tender. Proceed with any of the recipes here (or elsewhere).

---

2. Add the capers, olives, pepper flakes, and cod. Cook for about 10 minutes, stirring occasionally and gently, until the cod is hot. Taste and adjust the seasoning, then garnish and serve.

Fried Salt Cod in Tomato Sauce. More work, but better: After poaching the salt cod, cut it into chunks. Drain well on paper towels, then dredge in flour and fry on both sides in at least $1/4$ inch of hot olive oil. Add to the tomato sauce as directed.

Monkfish or Other Fillets with Artichokes ITALY
MAKES **4 SERVINGS**

TIME **40 MINUTES**

I had this dish in Genoa, which is near Albenga, a part of Liguria best known for its artichokes. All the work is in preparing the artichokes, and the results are fantastic. In true Ligurian fashion, you might begin this meal with Pasta with White Clam Sauce (page 99) or Pansotti (page 550).

4 large artichokes

1 tablespoon vinegar, any kind

2 tablespoons extra virgin olive oil

1$1/2$ to 2 pounds fillets of monkfish, red snapper, striped bass, or other firm white fish (2 or 4 fillets)

2 tablespoons flour, plus more as needed

Salt and black pepper to taste

2 garlic cloves, sliced

3 tablespoons fresh lemon juice

$1/2$ cup dry white wine

3 fresh rosemary sprigs or 2 teaspoons dried

1. Trim the artichokes: Cut off their pointy tops to within 1 or 1$1/2$ inches of the base; remove all but about $1/2$ inch of the stem. Cut all around the artichoke, removing all of the hard parts. Open up the center and dig out the choke with a blunt-edged

spoon. Trim any remaining hard parts. What's left is the artichoke bottom; cut it into $1/4$-inch slices and put in water to cover; add the vinegar (this keeps the slices from becoming discolored).

2. Heat the oil in a large nonstick skillet over medium heat. Lightly dredge the fish fillets in the flour, then put them in the skillet. Brown quickly—no more than 2 minutes on each side—seasoning with salt and pepper. Transfer to a plate and keep warm.

3. Add the garlic and the drained artichokes and cook, stirring occasionally, until softened, about 5 minutes. Add the lemon juice, wine, and rosemary and cook for another 5 minutes. Return the fish to the skillet and cook without turning until it is cooked through, about 5 minutes more, perhaps a little longer with monkfish (most fillets are done when the point of a thin-bladed knife inserted into the thickest part meets little resistance; monkfish will still be resilient, but far less so than when it was raw). Taste and adjust the seasoning, then serve with the pan juices.

Baked Fish with Artichokes. Omit the flour. Preheat the oven to 350°F. Spread half the oil in a ceramic casserole or baking dish and place the fish in it. Toss the garlic and artichokes with the lemon juice and remaining oil and spoon around the fish. Top with the rosemary and wine and bake, uncovered, until the fish is cooked through and the vegetables soft, 20 to 30 minutes.

Cod Baked in Foil ITALY

MAKES **4 SERVINGS**
TIME **40 MINUTES**

People cook food in packages all over the world—the tamale counts as one, too—but leave it to the Italians to do it simply. In Rome, you would have this with bass or turbot, but really it can be made with any fillet you like.

Cooking in packages requires a small leap of faith to determine that the food is done, because once you open the packages you want to serve them. This method has always worked well for me.

1$1/2$ to 2 pounds thick cod fillet, cut into 4 equal pieces
$1/4$ cup extra virgin olive oil
Salt and black pepper to taste
1 teaspoon minced garlic
$1/4$ cup chopped fresh parsley or basil leaves
Lemon wedges for serving

1. Put a baking pan in the oven and preheat it to 400°F. Take 8 sheets of aluminum foil, each about 18 inches long, and place one piece on top of the other (you will make 4 packages). Rub the fish with some of the olive oil; it should be nice and moist. Season it with salt and pepper and put it on a piece of the foil. Sprinkle with garlic and parsley and fold the foil onto itself, crimping the edges as tightly as possible. Repeat the process. (You can refrigerate the packages until you're ready to cook, no more than 6 hours later.)

2. Put the packages in the baking dish and bake for about 15 minutes (or about 8 minutes from the time it starts sizzling). Let sit for a couple of minutes before carefully slitting open the packages. Then spoon out the fish and serve with the lemon.

Cod Baked in Foil with Vegetables. Add any or all of the following to each of the packages: 1 seeded and diced plum tomato, a few black olives, some capers, some very thinly sliced potato or onion.

Cod Baked with Vegetables. You don't need to make packages to produce the same flavor: Use either the original recipe or the variation and place the fish and other ingredients in a covered baking dish (Corning Ware is ideal for this). Bake at 350°F to 400°F until the fish is cooked through (the fish is done when the point of a thin-bladed knife inserted into the thickest part meets little resistance), 10 to 15 minutes.

Cod Poached in Cider FRANCE ■

MAKES **4 SERVINGS**

TIME **30 MINUTES**

The ideal fish for this Norman preparation is Dover sole—the real thing, a fish with great flavor and unmatched texture. But this isn't an ideal world—you're unlikely to find Dover sole and equally unlikely to want to pay the asking price if you do. Fortunately, cod is a good substitute. In fact, as long as you don't overcook it, it's fantastic here. Any firm but not tough white fillet will also work: red snapper and black sea bass are excellent choices.

If you can pick up mussels at the same time, by all means go for the variation; the broth and overall results will be improved markedly.

In Normandy, this would inevitably be accompanied by a potato gratin like the one on page 482 and, if you were lucky, a salad.

2 tablespoons butter

1 large onion, sliced

Salt and black pepper to taste

1½ to 2 pounds fillets of cod or red snapper, about 1 inch thick, in 1 or 2 pieces

2 cups dry sparkling cider

Chopped fresh parsley leaves for garnish

1. Preheat the oven to 400°F. Put the butter in a small skillet and turn the heat to medium. Add the onion and a sprinkling of salt and pepper and cook, stirring occasionally, until the onion is soft

but not yet beginning to brown. Turn off the heat. Transfer the onion to a flameproof ceramic or nonstick baking dish just large enough to contain the fish. Sprinkle the fish with salt and pepper and put it over the onion. Pour the cider around all and bring to a boil on top of the stove.

2. Cover with foil and bake for 12 to 15 minutes, or until the fish is done (a thin-bladed knife inserted into its center will meet little resistance). Garnish with parsley and serve the fish with the onion and juices spooned over it.

Cod Poached in Cider with Mussels. Clean 2 pounds mussels (page 208) and combine them with the cider in a covered pot. Turn the heat to high and cook, shaking the pan occasionally, until the mussels open, about 10 minutes. When they are cool enough to handle, remove them from their shells; pass the cider through a cheesecloth-lined strainer. Proceed as directed, using the mussel-scented cider for the liquid and adding the shelled mussels to the fish about halfway through its cooking time.

Cod Poached in Cider with Mushrooms. In step 1, when the onion begins to soften, add 1 cup trimmed and chopped white, cremini, or portobello mushrooms and continue to cook, stirring occasionally, until the mushrooms have given up their liquid, about 10 minutes more. Proceed as directed.

Roast Catfish or Other Fillets with Sauerkraut and Bacon

EASTERN EUROPE ■

MAKES **4 SERVINGS**

TIME **30 MINUTES**

This dish sparks a vision of an ice fisher on a frozen Eastern European lake, bringing home a fresh carp, combining it with two of that region's winter staples—bacon and sauerkraut—and roasting it over a hot fire. What a treat that must have been and what a relief from what might have been months without any fresh meat or fish at all.

It's a great dish in a warm winter kitchen in the twenty-first century, too. Use sauerkraut that is fresh or packed in plastic (never canned), which contains no more than cabbage and salt; real sauerkraut needs no preservatives.

Serve the dish with mashed or boiled potatoes.

1/2 pound slab bacon, cut into 1/2-inch cubes

2 pounds sauerkraut, rinsed and drained

1 tablespoon sweet paprika

2 pounds fillets of catfish, red snapper, grouper, carp,
**   or mackerel**

Salt and black pepper to taste

1. Preheat the oven to 500°F. Put the bacon in a skillet and over medium heat cook, stirring occasionally, until the bacon renders its fat and becomes crisp, 10 to 15 minutes.

2. Toss the sauerkraut with half the paprika and half the bacon, with some of its fat, then spread this along the bottom of a roasting pan or casserole.

3. Brush the fish with a little bacon fat, then season it on all sides with salt, pepper, and the remaining paprika. Place on top of the sauerkraut and roast, uncovered, for about 5 minutes. Sprinkle with the remaining bacon and cook until the fish is white throughout, about 5 minutes more. Serve immediately.

Red Snapper or Other Fish Fillets in Paprika Sour Cream EASTERN EUROPE
MAKES **4 SERVINGS**
TIME **30 MINUTES**

Sour cream sauce is standard throughout Eastern Europe, and it's not as bland as you might think or as you might have experienced. The dish should be quite sour, for one thing, and a bit hot—if your paprika has little flavor, either buy a new supply or spike it with cayenne—and it should be finished with fresh herbs.

Serve this over rice or buttered noodles or with crusty bread.

1 1/2 to 2 pounds fillets of red snapper, halibut, or grouper,
**   skinned and cut into 1-inch cubes**

1/4 cup fresh lemon juice

Salt and black pepper

3 tablespoons extra virgin olive oil

1 small onion, chopped

1/2 cup sour cream

1/2 cup fish stock, preferably homemade (page 161),
**   or water**

2 teaspoons hot paprika, plus more to taste

1/4 cup chopped fresh dill leaves

1/4 cup chopped fresh parsley leaves

1. Toss the fish in a bowl with the lemon juice and some salt and pepper.
2. Put the oil in a large skillet with a lid, preferably nonstick, and place over medium-high heat. Add the onion and cook, stirring occasionally, until softened, about 5 minutes. Stir in the sour cream and stock and lower the heat to medium-low to maintain a gentle simmer. Add the fish with its marinade, cover, and cook until a thin-bladed knife passes through the fish with just a little resistance, about 5 minutes.
3. Stir in the paprika and dill and simmer until the sauce thickens slightly. Taste and adjust the seasoning, garnish with the parsley, and serve hot.

Baked Fish in Paprika Sour Cream. Preheat the oven to 450°F. Use the oil (or, better still, softened butter) to grease a baking dish or casserole. Toss the fish with the salt, pepper, lemon juice, onion, paprika, and dill. Stir in the sour cream and just $1/4$ cup fish stock. Place in the baking dish and bake, uncovered, until the fish flakes when probed with a fork, about 10 minutes. Garnish with parsley and serve.

Poached Fillets in Caraway Sauce
EASTERN EUROPE ▦
MAKES **4 SERVINGS**
TIME **30 MINUTES**

Caraway seeds have too long been relegated to the tops of rye bread; their bitter, nutty flavor is distinctive and easy to like. Here they dominate a simple Romanian sauce used for fish. To crush the seeds, put them in a plastic bag and press on it with the bottom of a pot—really lean into it, rock back and forth a bit, and you'll get it.

If you can lay your hands on crusty rye or pumpernickel bread, this is the place for it. Salad or any simple vegetable dish, along with rice if you don't have or want bread, would also be good.

2 tablespoons corn, grapeseed, or other neutral oil
1 medium onion, diced
2 tablespoons caraway seeds, crushed
2 tablespoons snipped fresh chives, plus more for garnish
$1/2$ cup fish stock, preferably homemade (page 161), or water
$1/4$ cup fresh lemon juice
$1/4$ cup dry white wine or more stock or water
Salt and black pepper to taste
$1^{1}/2$ to 2 pounds fillets of sea bass, red snapper, grouper, or other firm fish, skinned

1. Heat the oil in a large deep skillet with a lid over medium heat, then add the onion, half the caraway seeds, and the chives. Cook until the onion softens, about 5 minutes, then add the stock and the other liquids; raise the heat to high and reduce by about half; this will take just a few minutes. Season with salt and pepper.
2. Sprinkle the fillets with salt and pepper and the remaining caraway seeds. Lay the fillets in the liquid, cover, turn the heat to medium, and poach until the fillets are white and opaque throughout, about 5 minutes (the fish is done when it offers little resistance to a thin-bladed knife). Garnish with chives and serve immediately.

Catfish or Other Fillets with Rice
EASTERN EUROPE ▦
MAKES **4 SERVINGS**
TIME **30 MINUTES**

Think of this as a simpler take on paella. It's Eastern European in origin, so it was often made with freshwater fish, but you can use any fillets you want. With a salad, this is a wonderful—and very fast—one-pot meal.

If you're using water instead of stock, you might augment its flavor slightly by simmering it for 15 minutes with a carrot, an onion, and a celery stalk, along with a few peppercorns, a garlic clove, a bay leaf, and a teaspoon of vinegar; strain before proceeding. If you don't have time for this, that's fine too—the dish will still be good, even if you just use water.

2½ cups fish or chicken stock, preferably homemade
    (page 161 or 160), or water (see headnote)
1½ cups long-grain rice, rinsed and drained
1 large or 2 medium tomatoes, cored, chopped, and
    mashed (with their juices), or 1 cup canned chopped
    tomatoes with their juices
3 tablespoons butter, melted
¼ cup Madeira, sweet sherry, or white wine
1 to 1½ pounds fillets of catfish, perch, bass, or other
    freshwater fish or fillets of red snapper, sea bass,
    halibut, or other firm white saltwater fish, cut into
    bite-sized pieces

1. Bring the fish stock to a gentle boil in a medium saucepan or wide skillet with a lid, preferably nonstick. Add the rice and bring to a boil; turn the heat to medium-low and cover. Cook for 15 minutes, or until the water is nearly absorbed and the rice nearly tender.
2. Turn the heat to low and stir in the tomatoes with their juices, the butter, and the Madeira. Gently fold in the fish pieces, cover, and simmer for another 15 minutes, or until the fish is cooked and heated through. Serve hot.

Steamed Red Snapper or Other Fillets with Hard-Cooked Egg Sauce
EASTERN EUROPE
MAKES **4 SERVINGS**
TIME **30 MINUTES**

An unexpected but delicious use for hard-cooked eggs that, of course, can be made in advance. If you have fish stock, poach the fish in it, but if you don't, don't worry about it. Serve this with plain boiled potatoes.

2 extra-large eggs
1 cup good-quality stock, any kind
1½ to 2 pounds fillets of red snapper, grouper, sea bass,
    or any other firm fish
Salt and black pepper to taste
2 tablespoons butter
2 tablespoons fresh or sour cream, optional
Chopped fresh parsley leaves for garnish

1. Put the eggs in a small saucepan, add water to cover, and turn the heat to high. When the water boils, cover the pan, turn off the heat, and set a timer for 10 minutes. (Meanwhile, set up the steamer; don't start steaming the fish, though, until the eggs are done.) When the eggs are done, cool them under cold running water, then peel and chop.
2. Put the stock in the bottom of a tight-lidded steamer and the fish above it. Season the fish with salt and pepper. Bring the stock to a boil and adjust the heat so that it continues to bubble, but not violently. The fish will cook through in 5 to 10 minutes.
3. While the fish is steaming, put the butter in a small saucepan and turn the heat to medium. When its foam subsides and it begins to turn brown, add the chopped eggs and some salt and pepper. When the fish is done, lay it on a plate and

thin the egg sauce with about $\frac{1}{4}$ cup of the stock. Stir in the cream if you're using it, taste and adjust the seasoning, and spoon the sauce over the fish. Garnish and serve.

Baked Cod or Other Fillets with Dried Mushroom Sauce

EASTERN EUROPE ▨

MAKES **4 SERVINGS**

TIME **30 MINUTES**

Remember fish dishes baked with canned cream of mushroom soup? This is the original, and you may not believe how good it is.

Never buy dried porcini in the tiny packages sold at stores. A package should contain at least an ounce, and the mushrooms should look like mushrooms, not powder. Given that you can buy a pound of dried porcini for as little as $25 (look on the Internet), you should expect to pay no more than $5 for an ounce.

Serve this with buttered rice or noodles.

$\frac{1}{2}$ ounce dried porcini mushrooms

1 cup hot fish stock, preferably homemade (page 161), or water

2 tablespoons butter

$\frac{1}{4}$ cup chopped shallot or red onion

$1\frac{1}{2}$ to 2 pounds cod, red snapper, striped bass, halibut, or any other thick fillet, in 1 or 2 pieces

Salt and black pepper to taste

1 cup sour cream

1. Preheat the oven to 400°F. Soak the mushrooms in the stock until softened, about 10 minutes. Trim any hard parts and chop roughly. Pour the soaking liquid through a cheesecloth-lined strainer.
2. Use about half the butter to grease a baking dish just large enough to hold the fish. Add the shallot,

then the fish; sprinkle the fish with salt and pepper. Cover lightly with foil and bake for about 5 minutes.
3. Meanwhile, combine the mushrooms, sour cream, and enough of the soaking liquid to make a thin sauce. Pour this over and around the fish, re-cover the pan, and continue to bake until the fish is done (a thin-bladed knife inserted into its center will meet little resistance), 5 to 10 minutes more. Serve hot.

Poached Fish with Russian Sauce

RUSSIA ▨

MAKES **4 SERVINGS**

TIME **30 MINUTES**

"Russian Sauce" is probably the origin of Russian dressing, though the two no longer have much in common; still, the pickles and capers mark the relationship. This is most traditionally made with sturgeon (which is a wonderfully sturdy and flavorful fish) but can be made with any firm white fillet, from carp, catfish, or sturgeon to red snapper, sea bass, or grouper. Serve with boiled potatoes or plain white rice.

2 tablespoons extra virgin olive oil

$\frac{1}{2}$ pound fresh button mushrooms, cleaned and sliced

1 small onion, chopped

1 pound tomatoes, cored and chopped (canned are fine), with their juices

$\frac{1}{4}$ cup good-quality black olives, pitted

$\frac{1}{2}$ cup diced sour pickles (cornichons are good; do not use sweet pickles)

1 tablespoon drained capers

1 cup fish stock, preferably homemade (page 161), or water

Salt and black pepper to taste

1½ to 2 pounds fillets of carp, sturgeon, sea bass, red snapper, or other firm fish, skin removed

2 tablespoons cornstarch

¼ cup chopped fresh parsley leaves for garnish

1. Put the oil in a deep skillet and turn the heat to medium-high. A minute later, add the mushrooms and onion and cook, stirring occasionally, until softened, about 5 minutes. Add the tomatoes and cook until they break down and release their juices, about 10 minutes. Stir in the olives, pickles, capers, stock, and salt and pepper and bring to a steady simmer.

2. Sprinkle the fish with salt and pepper, then gently slide the fillets into the stock and cook just until a thin-bladed knife passes through with little resistance, less than 10 minutes. Transfer the fish to a warmed serving dish.

3. Bring the sauce to a boil and reduce slightly. If you want a thickened sauce, as is traditional, mix the cornstarch with 2 tablespoons cold water and stir into the sauce. Lower the heat, then simmer until the sauce thickens; taste and adjust the seasoning. Spoon the sauce over the fish, garnish with parsley, and serve.

STEAKS: HALIBUT, TUNA, SALMON, SWORDFISH

Fish steaks—cross-cuts of larger fish or thick "fillets" taken from long boneless sections of fish like tuna and swordfish—are great for grilling, though of course they can be cooked by other methods too. Many (especially those from salmon, tuna, and swordfish) are best left a little (or a lot) underdone in the center.

Sweet Black Pepper Halibut or Other Fish Steaks, Vietnamese Style
SOUTHEAST ASIA ▓

MAKES **4 SERVINGS**

TIME **30 MINUTES**

A fine recipe for fish steaks, from halibut to Spanish mackerel, even swordfish (it's also good with shrimp or scallops). The lemongrass is essential if you want authentic flavor, though the dish will be good without it, because the real keys are the quickly made caramel and an abundance of black pepper, which is used more in Vietnam than any place I've ever been. See page 500 for information on Thai fish sauce (nam pla). Serve with plain white rice.

¼ cup sugar

¼ cup nam pla

¼ cup minced lemongrass (page 143)

1 tablespoon minced garlic

1 teaspoon black pepper, or to taste

4 scallions, trimmed and roughly chopped

1½ to 2 pounds halibut or other fish steaks or sturdy fillets

Salt to taste

Chopped fresh cilantro leaves for garnish

1. Combine the sugar, nam pla, and ¼ cup water in a skillet just large enough to hold the fish. Place over medium heat and cook, stirring infrequently, until the sugar melts and the mixture bubbles, 5 to 10 minutes. Add the lemongrass, garlic, and black pepper and cook, stirring occasionally, for about 3 minutes more.

2. Add the scallions, fish, and another ¼ cup water. Cook over medium-high heat, turning the fish occasionally (if you're using fillets, turn it less often so that it doesn't break up), until the sauce is very thick and the fish cooked through, about 10 min-

utes. Taste, add salt if necessary, then garnish and serve.

Halibut Simmered in Soy and Sake
JAPAN ▨

MAKES **4 SERVINGS**

TIME **30 MINUTES**

A quick and simple dish, one that produces a beautiful sauce to use on white rice. Halibut is ideal here, but swordfish steaks are great too, and you can even make this preparation with thick white fillets of grouper, red snapper, or sea bass.

Use dashi (which can be prepared in just a few minutes) if at all possible, chicken stock if not.

$\frac{1}{2}$ **cup sake**

2 tablespoons mirin, honey, or sugar

1 cup Dashi (page 162) or chicken stock, preferably
   homemade (page 160)

$\frac{1}{4}$ **cup good-quality soy sauce**

5 or 6 thin slices peeled fresh ginger

1 tablespoon peeled and finely shredded fresh ginger
   or $\frac{1}{2}$ cup minced scallion, green part only, or both,
   for garnish

$1\frac{1}{2}$ **to 2 pounds halibut fillets or steaks (see headnote)**

1. Combine the sake, mirin, dashi, soy sauce, and sliced ginger in a skillet or saucepan with a lid; it should be just wide enough to hold the fish. Bring to a boil over medium-high heat. Meanwhile, if you are using shredded ginger, soak it in cold water to cover.

2. After the liquids have boiled for 1 minute, reduce the heat to medium and gently add the fish, skin side down. Cover and adjust the heat so the mixture simmers steadily. Cook for about 5 minutes, or until the point of a thin-bladed knife meets little resistance when inserted into the thickest part of the fillet.

3. Carefully remove the fish from the poaching liquid. Drain the ginger if you're using it and garnish the fish. Pass the sauce separately to spoon over the fish and white rice.

Seared Swordfish with Lemongrass, Tamarind, and Fried Garlic
SOUTHEAST ASIA ▨

MAKES **4 SERVINGS**

TIME **30 MINUTES**

A wonderful technique and combination of flavors that works so well with swordfish that I would be reluctant to substitute (Spanish mackerel, usually quite difficult to find, would be a good alternative). If you're unfamiliar with lemongrass, trim its ends, then slit and peel its tough outer layer to expose the tender core; you usually get about 1 tablespoon from each stalk. See page 500 for information on Thai fish sauce (nam pla).

Sticky Rice (page 508) is the thing here, along with a lightly dressed salad or very simple vegetable dish.

6 tablespoons peanut or neutral oil, like corn or grapeseed

2 swordfish steaks, each $\frac{3}{4}$ to 1 pound

Salt and black pepper to taste

2 tablespoons minced lemongrass

1 tablespoons minced garlic

1 tablespoon peeled and minced fresh ginger

1 small fresh chile, stemmed, seeded, and minced,
   or to taste

3 tablespoons tamarind paste (page 585) mixed with
   1 cup water

■ make ahead   ▨ serve at room temp./cold   ▨ 30 minutes or less   FISH   **253**

3 tablespoons nam pla

5 large garlic cloves, thinly sliced

Chopped fresh cilantro leaves for garnish

1. Put 2 tablespoons of the oil in a large skillet, preferably nonstick, over medium-high heat. A minute later, add the fish (in batches if necessary) and brown quickly on both sides, sprinkling with salt and pepper as it cooks, for a total of about 4 minutes. Turn the heat to low and transfer the fish to a plate.

2. Add the lemongrass, minced garlic, ginger, and chile to the skillet and cook, stirring frequently, until the garlic begins to brown, 3 to 5 minutes. Add the tamarind mixture and nam pla and bring to a boil; adjust the heat so the mixture simmers steadily. Return the swordfish to the pan and cover.

3. Meanwhile, put the remaining $1/2$ cup oil in a small saucepan over medium heat. Add the sliced garlic and cook, stirring once in a while, until it is brown and crisp, about 5 minutes; do not let it burn. Remove with a slotted spoon and drain on a paper towel (you can reuse the oil if you like).

4. The fish is done when a thin-bladed knife inserted into its thickest part meets little resistance. Transfer it to a plate. The sauce should be syrupy; if it is not, reduce it over high heat, stirring constantly, for a couple of minutes. (If it is too dry, add a little water and stir to incorporate.) Pour the sauce over the fish and garnish with the fried garlic and the cilantro.

Tuna with Miso-Chile Sauce JAPAN ▪

MAKES **4 SERVINGS**

TIME **30 MINUTES**

This is a more complicated use of miso, useful not only for fish but for meat (just substitute tenderloin for the tuna). I learned it from Japanese-born chef Tadashi Ono, who now lives in New York. His dual lives encouraged Ono to take a few liberties of the type that few would take in Japan, with a classic sauce like this one; but if this is fusion cooking, it's the good kind.

The Japanese chili paste called tohbanjan is strictly traditional here, but you can use Vietnamese or Korean chili paste or simply cayenne. I love this with Basmati Rice with Shiso (page 510).

1 teaspoon butter

1 teaspoon minced shallot

$1/2$ teaspoon peeled and minced fresh ginger

$1/2$ teaspoon minced garlic

$1/8$ teaspoon Japanese or other chili paste (see headnote)

$1/2$ cup red wine

1 tablespoon mirin or honey

2 tablespoons dark miso

1 tablespoon corn, grapeseed, or other neutral oil

Four 1-inch-thick tuna steaks, each 6 to 8 ounces

Salt and black pepper to taste

1. Preheat the broiler; the rack should be fairly close to the heat source. Put the butter in a small saucepan over medium heat. Add the shallot, ginger, garlic, and chili paste and stir. Cook, stirring occasionally, until the vegetables begin to soften, about 5 minutes. Add the red wine and mirin and continue cooking until most of the liquid has evaporated, about 10 minutes. Add the miso and incorporate well, then set aside.

2. Place an ovenproof skillet large enough to hold all 4 steaks and preferably nonstick over medium-high heat. When warm, add the oil. Season the tuna on both sides with salt and pepper, then add it to the hot oil. Cook for about 3 minutes per side for medium-rare, then remove the pan from the heat. Brush some of the miso glaze on the top side of each steak.

3. Place the tuna under the broiler to caramelize; it should take no more than 1 minute. Remove and serve.

be cooked adequately (it should still be slightly uncooked in its center). Serve hot or at room temperature.

Salmon Teriyaki JAPAN ■ ▦ ▨

MAKES **4 SERVINGS**

TIME **ABOUT 20 MINUTES**

Spring through fall, you may be able to find wild Alaska king or sockeye salmon (if you live in the Northwest or even on the West Coast, this won't be a problem), and that is ideal for this dish. Farm-raised salmon, available year-round everywhere, is certainly an acceptable substitute, but it is fattier and has less flavor, so it'll make a bit more of a mess when you brown it, and it will not stand up quite as well to the sauce. Serve this with short-grain rice (page 507).

4 salmon steaks, each 6 to 8 ounces

$^{1}/_{3}$ cup sake or slightly sweet white wine, like a German Kabinett or Spätlese

$^{1}/_{3}$ cup mirin or 2 tablespoons honey mixed with 2 tablespoons water

2 tablespoons sugar

$^{1}/_{3}$ cup soy sauce

1. Preheat a large nonstick skillet over medium-high heat for about 2 minutes, then add the salmon. Brown quickly on both sides, not more than 2 minutes per side. Transfer the fish to a plate and turn the heat to medium. Add 2 tablespoons water, followed by the wine, mirin, sugar, and soy sauce. Stir to blend and, when the mixture is producing lively bubbles and beginning to thicken, return the salmon to the pan.

2. Cook, turning the salmon in the sauce, until it becomes more of a glaze than a liquid, not more than a couple of minutes. By that time the salmon will

Halibut with Vegetables EASTERN EUROPE

MAKES **4 SERVINGS**

TIME **1 HOUR**

The fish equivalent of classic beef stew, and definitely a winter dish, with its base of root vegetables. You can, of course, vary the vegetables according to what you have in your pantry—cauliflower, zucchini, eggplant, and even okra will work well.

The stew should be very thick, not really soupy at all; so though you may add water as necessary while cooking, be sure not to add too much. Since the fish is added when the vegetables are just about done, you can substitute almost any white-fleshed fish or even shellfish. Just adjust the cooking time as necessary.

Serve this on top of rice or with crusty bread.

3 tablespoons corn, grapeseed, or other neutral oil

3 garlic cloves, minced

1 large onion, roughly chopped

2 carrots, roughly chopped

2 potatoes, peeled and roughly chopped

2 parsnips, peeled and roughly chopped

1 turnip, peeled and roughly chopped

2 celery stalks, roughly chopped

2 large tomatoes (canned are fine), cored and chopped, with their juice

2 pounds halibut or other fish, cut into chunks

1 tablespoon paprika

Salt and black pepper to taste

Chopped fresh parsley leaves for garnish

1. Heat the oil in a large saucepan or casserole with a lid over medium-high heat. Add the garlic and

onion and cook, stirring occasionally, until softened, about 5 minutes. Add all the vegetables and stir once or twice. Turn the heat to medium, cover, and cook for 20 minutes, stirring occasionally. If the mixture dries out, add a little water.

2. When the carrots are nearly tender, lay the fish pieces on top of the vegetables and sprinkle with paprika, salt, and pepper. Re-cover and cook until the fish is done (a thin-bladed knife inserted into its center will meet little resistance).

3. Taste and adjust the seasoning (this will take plenty of black pepper), then garnish and serve.

Halibut with Vegetables with Mustard-Cream Sauce. Combine $1/2$ cup heavy or sour cream with at least 2 tablespoons Dijon mustard. Pour this over the stew and stir gently just before the fish finishes cooking.

Halibut or Other Fish Braised in Red Wine FRANCE

MAKES **4 SERVINGS**

TIME **1 TO 1$1/2$ HOURS**

A delicate and subtle preparation that can also be made with monkfish, striped bass, sea bass, or other firm-fleshed fish. Serve with Braised Leeks (page 465).

> 5 tablespoons butter
>
> $1/4$ cup chopped shallot
>
> 1$1/2$ cups red wine
>
> 2 bay leaves
>
> 1 cup fish or chicken stock, preferably homemade (page 161 or 160)
>
> 1$1/2$ pounds halibut steak, 1 inch or more thick
>
> Salt and black pepper to taste
>
> Chopped fresh parsley leaves for garnish

1. Put 3 tablespoons of the butter in a 10- or 12-inch skillet over medium heat. When the butter melts, add the shallot and cook, stirring occasionally, until tender, 2 or 3 minutes. Add the wine and bay leaves, raise the heat to high, and cook until the mixture is reduced to about $1/2$ cup, about 20 minutes.

2. Add the stock and reduce to about 1 cup, about 10 minutes. Add the halibut along with some salt and pepper, turn the heat to low, and cover. Cook for about 10 minutes or until the halibut is tender (a thin-bladed knife will pass through it with little resistance). Transfer the halibut to a warm plate and stir in the remaining butter, cooking and stirring until the sauce is smooth. Taste and adjust the seasoning, pour the sauce over and around the fish, garnish, and serve.

Grilled Swordfish Rémoulade

FRANCE ■ ■ ■

MAKES **4 SERVINGS**

TIME **30 MINUTES, PLUS TIME TO PREHEAT THE GRILL**

Rémoulade is an all-purpose fish sauce, a superspicy, chunky variation on mayonnaise and perhaps the Platonic ideal of tartar sauce. You can use it with poached, baked, fried, even leftover fish, but I think it's best with grilled fish. Swordfish is the most obvious candidate, but you can grill steaks of cod, mahimahi, mako, salmon, or tuna and serve them with rémoulade; monkfish is also good.

This combination is pretty rich; I'd be satisfied with a decent bread and a salad or steamed vegetable dressed with no more than lemon juice.

> 1 cup mayonnaise, preferably homemade (page 602)
>
> Salt and black pepper to taste
>
> 1 small garlic clove, minced

2 tablespoons chopped drained capers

2 tablespoons chopped fresh parsley leaves

1 teaspoon chopped fresh tarragon leaves or a pinch
   of dried

1 tablespoon Dijon mustard

2 anchovy fillets, minced

$1/4$ teaspoon cayenne, or to taste

$1^1/_2$ to 2 pounds swordfish, in 1 or 2 steaks

1. Start a wood or charcoal fire or preheat a gas grill (or broiler); the fire should be quite hot and the rack about 4 inches from the heat source. While it's heating, make the mayonnaise and combine it with all the remaining ingredients except the fish. (If you're making the mayonnaise in a food processor or blender, you can save yourself some mincing by adding the garlic at the beginning and pulsing in the other solid ingredients while the sauce is still in the machine.)
2. Grill the fish, turning when nicely browned, about 4 or 5 minutes, then cook for 4 or 5 minutes more. The fish is done when just a bit of translucence remains in its center; use a thin-bladed knife to check. Serve hot or cold, with the rémoulade sauce.

Pan-Seared Swordfish with Tomatoes, Olives, and Capers SICILY ▥

MAKES **4 SERVINGS**

TIME **30 MINUTES**

Call this fish with puttanesca sauce—strong flavored, and swordfish can really take it. Serve with plenty of crusty bread or scoop out the fish after it cooks, put the sauce over pasta, and serve the fish on the side

3 tablespoons extra virgin olive oil

$1^1/_2$ to 2 pounds swordfish, in 1 piece

Salt and black pepper to taste

1 tablespoon minced garlic

2 tablespoons drained capers

2 small dried chiles or a large pinch of hot red pepper
   flakes, or to taste

$1/4$ cup black or green olives, preferably not canned

4 cups (about one 28-ounce can) chopped tomatoes with
   their juice

Chopped fresh parsley leaves for garnish

1. Put the oil in a deep skillet, preferably nonstick, over medium-high heat. When the oil is hot, add the fish and brown it well, rotating and turning it as necessary and sprinkling it with salt and pepper; the process should take less than 10 minutes. Turn off the heat and remove the fish.
2. Turn the heat to medium and add the garlic, capers, chiles, and olives. Cook, stirring occasionally, for about a minute; add the tomatoes and bring to a boil. Gently slide the fish into the sauce and cook, turning once, until it is tender, about 5 minutes more. Taste and adjust the seasoning as necessary, then garnish and serve.

Grilled or Broiled Skewered Swordfish Chunks with Salmoriglio
ITALY

MAKES **4 SERVINGS**

TIME **20 TO 45 MINUTES, PLUS TIME TO PREHEAT
   THE GRILL**

Simple skewers brushed, after grilling, with an easy, traditional Sicilian sauce. Grill some vegetables at the same time if you like. For an indoor version, see the variation.

$1^1/_2$ to 2 pounds swordfish, cut into large chunks

$1/3$ cup extra virgin olive oil, plus a little more for brushing
   on the fish

Salt and black pepper to taste

2 garlic cloves, peeled

1 tablespoon fresh oregano leaves
or 1 teaspoon dried

Juice of 1 lemon

Chopped fresh parsley leaves for garnish

1. Start a charcoal or gas grill, or preheat a broiler; the fire should be quite hot and the rack about 3 inches from the heat source. Thread the fish onto 4 skewers (it will be easier to turn the fish if you use 2 skewers per kebab, for a total of 8 skewers, 4 kebabs). Brush the fish with a little olive oil and sprinkle it with salt and pepper.

2. Combine the remaining oil, salt, pepper, garlic, and oregano in a small food processor and puree; the mixture should be smooth (scrape down the sides of the container if necessary). Stir in the lemon juice and set aside.

3. Grill or broil the fish, turning as each side browns, a bit more than 2 minutes per side. Swordfish is best cooked until tender but not dry; when a thin-bladed knife inserted into the center meets only a little resistance, it's done. Drizzle with the salmoriglio, garnish with the parsley, and serve.

Pan-Grilled Swordfish Steaks with Salmoriglio.
It's nice to enhance the sauce with a tablespoon or 2 of capers when you do it this way: Use 2 steaks, each about a pound. Put a large heavy skillet over medium-high heat and wait a couple of minutes. Add 2 or 3 tablespoons olive oil to the pan and cook the fish until nicely browned, 4 to 5 minutes; turn and cook until the fish is done. Serve with the sauce.

Roast Tuna with Onions and Lemon
ITALY ■ ▨ ▨
MAKES **4 SERVINGS**
TIME **30 MINUTES**

A useful technique for any dark-fleshed fish, including whole mackerel or bluefish (which may be stuffed with the onion mixture), steaks of Spanish mackerel, or fillets of pompano; adjust the cooking time accordingly.

I really like pasta before this—something quite simple, like Pasta with Pepper and Cheese (page 547) or Pasta with Broccoli Raab (page 552).

¼ cup extra virgin olive oil, plus a little more to taste

1 large onion, roughly chopped

1 tablespoon minced garlic

1 small fresh chile, a piece of jalapeño, or cayenne to taste, optional

½ cup chopped fresh parsley leaves

Several fresh tarragon leaves or ½ teaspoon dried or 1 teaspoon fresh thyme leaves or ½ teaspoon dried

½ cup fresh bread crumbs (page 580)

Salt and black pepper to taste

2 lemons, thinly sliced

4 small or 2 large tuna steaks, 1½ to 2 pounds total

Juice of 1 lemon

1. Preheat the oven to 450°F. Put half the olive oil in a medium skillet or saucepan and turn the heat to medium; a minute later, add the onion and cook, stirring occasionally, until softened, about 5 minutes; add the garlic and chile if you're using it and cook, stirring occasionally, for about 1 minute more. Turn off the heat and stir in the parsley, tarragon, and bread crumbs, along with some salt and pepper.

2. Layer half the lemon slices in the bottom of a small roasting pan. Rub the fish with the remaining olive

oil, sprinkle it with salt and pepper, and place it in the pan. Put the onion mixture and remaining lemon slices on top of the fish.

3. Roast the fish until done, about 10 minutes for medium-rare (cut into it and take a look). Drizzle with the lemon juice and a little more olive oil and serve hot or at room temperature.

WHOLE FISH

The least frequently used and most challenging of all forms of fish, though often the most rewarding. When you buy whole fish, it should have bright eyes and a clean smell. When you cook it, you often need a lot of room and a fair amount of patience. Until you're used to dealing with whole fish, stick with specimens under 3 pounds, which are easiest to handle.

Salt-Grilled (Broiled) Fish JAPAN ▓

MAKES **4 SERVINGS**
TIME **20 MINUTES**

Best done with small fish—four 1-pound red snappers or black bass are ideal—this technique, among the world's easiest and most reliable, can also be used with larger fish. But I wouldn't go above a couple of pounds each, or cooking them through under the broiler will be tricky.

Bear in mind that some broilers (especially electric ones) may cycle on and off, which is undesirable here; if you prop open the door, the heating element is more likely to remain on.

You could, of course, serve this as you would any plain broiled fish, with a salad and vegetable or starch, for example. Typical Japanese choices might be rice

(of course), along with Chicken and Cucumber Salad (without the chicken, page 182) or Eggplant Salad with Mustard-Miso Dressing (page 185).

4 small fish, like red snapper, $^{3}/_{4}$ to 1 pound each, gilled, gutted, and scaled, heads may be on or off
Coarse salt
Lemon wedges for serving

1. Preheat the broiler; the rack should be about 4 inches from the heat source. Rinse the fish well and dry it thoroughly. Cut 3 or 4 diagonal gashes on both sides of each fish, right down to the bone. Sprinkle liberally with the salt, rubbing a bit so the salt penetrates the gashes.

2. Put the fish on a broiling pan, preferably nonstick, and place under the broiler. Cook for about 5 minutes or until well browned, rotating the pan if necessary to give all the fish even heat. Turn and repeat on the other side. Serve immediately, with lemon wedges.

Shallow-Fried Small Fish with Ginger Sauce CHINA ▓

MAKES **4 SERVINGS**
TIME **30 MINUTES**

Not far from the cooking traditions of American freshwater fishermen, this is simple panfried fish with a separately made sauce. If you're shopping, look for small specimens of black sea bass or red snapper; if you're fishing, largemouth bass, croaker, spot, and porgies are all good. In any case, you need the fish to fit in your pan. In fact, two small fish are better than one large one in this instance.

Use the best soy sauce you can find for this dish.

There's not much sauce here, so unless you're from

a rice-eating culture, you might find rice a bit dry. Cold Noodles with Sesame Sauce (page 532) would make a great starter, or you could serve this with Egg Noodles with Spring Onions (page 536). For vegetables, try Quick-Braised Root Vegetables with Hoisin (page 499) or Snow Peas with Ginger (page 470).

Peanut or vegetable oil for frying

One 2- to 3-pound or two 1- to 1½-pound black sea bass or other fish (see headnote), gilled, gutted, scaled and thoroughly dried, heads may be on or off

Cornstarch or flour for dredging

1 tablespoon peeled and minced fresh ginger

1 teaspoon minced garlic

2 tablespoons soy sauce

Chopped fresh cilantro leaves for garnish

1. Put about ¼ inch of oil in a large skillet, preferably nonstick, over medium-high heat. After 3 or 4 minutes, when the oil is hot—a pinch of cornstarch or flour will sizzle—dredge both sides of the fish in the cornstarch. Add 1 fish; wait a couple of minutes before adding the other if you are using 2. Cook, adjusting the heat as necessary—at some point you will have to lower it—so the underside browns without burning, about 10 minutes. Turn and brown the other side.

2. Meanwhile, put 2 tablespoons oil in a small saucepan and turn the heat to medium. Add the ginger and garlic and swirl the pan, then cook, stirring, until the garlic begins to color, 2 or 3 minutes. Turn the heat to very low.

3. When the fish is done (a thin-bladed knife will pass right down to the bone with little resistance), drain briefly on paper towels, then transfer to a platter. Pour the ginger-garlic mixture over it, then splash it with soy sauce. Garnish and serve immediately.

Braised Whole Fish in Hot-and-Sour Sauce CHINA

MAKES **4 SERVINGS**

TIME **45 MINUTES**

It doesn't take long, but this dish requires a fairly large pan. A long, narrow roasting pan will do in a pinch, especially if it's nonstick. If you have trouble getting the fish to fit into your pan, by all means cut off its head and tail. Or try making this with smaller fish, in the 2- to 3-pound range. Then, when you feel you've gotten the hang of browning a whole fish, move on to larger specimens.

This is a blast to eat—and should have enough sauce to make plain white rice a terrific accompaniment. A simple Chinese-style vegetable like Snow Peas with Ginger (page 470) would make the meal even better.

One 3- to 5-pound grouper, red snapper, carp, or sea bass, gilled, gutted, and scaled, head may be on or off

1 cup fish or chicken stock, preferably homemade (page 161 or 160), or water

4 fresh or dried shiitake (black) mushrooms

½ cup plus 2 tablespoons peanut or neutral oil, like corn or grapeseed

Flour for dredging

Salt to taste

1 large onion, sliced

2 teaspoons minced garlic

1 tablespoon peeled and minced or grated fresh ginger

2 or 3 dried red chiles, stemmed, seeded, and minced, or 1 teaspoon hot red pepper flakes, or to taste

1 tablespoon fermented black beans (page 207)

2 tablespoons Shaoxing wine or dry sherry

2 tablespoons soy sauce

¼ cup rice or white wine vinegar

2 teaspoons dark sesame oil

Minced scallion and chopped fresh cilantro leaves for garnish

1. Make 3 shallow cuts, from top to bottom, on each side of the fish. If you're using dried mushrooms, heat the stock or water and soak the mushrooms in it.

2. Put the $1/2$ cup oil in a nonstick skillet that will accommodate the fish and place over high heat. A few minutes later, when the oil is hot—a pinch of flour will sizzle—dredge the fish heavily on both sides in the flour, then gently lower it into the oil. Cook, sprinkling with salt, until golden brown on both sides, turning just once and adjusting the heat if necessary to prevent scorching. Transfer the fish to a platter and pour off the oil from the skillet. Return it to the stove over medium heat and add the remaining 2 tablespoons oil.

3. Drain the mushrooms if dried (reserving the stock) and slice them thinly, discarding their stems. Add them to the skillet along with the onion and turn the heat to high. Cook, stirring occasionally, until the onion softens, about 5 minutes. Add the garlic, ginger, chiles, and black beans and cook, stirring, for another minute. Add the wine, soy sauce, vinegar, and stock. Bring to a boil, then turn the heat to low and return the fish to the pan.

4. Cover and cook gently until the fish is cooked through (peek into one of the slashes; the meat should be opaque clear to the bone), about 15 minutes. Use a pair of spatulas to gently move the fish to a platter. If the mixture is very soupy, turn the heat to high and reduce it until thick, stirring occasionally (if it's not, proceed). Spoon the sauce over and around the fish, then drizzle with the sesame oil and garnish with the scallion and cilantro.

Braised Whole Fish in Sweet-and-Sour Sauce.
Omit the chiles or not, as you like. After adding the liquids in step 3, stir in $1/2$ cup honey or sugar and cook until it dissolves. Proceed as directed.

Braised Whole Fish in Mushroom–Bamboo Shoot Sauce. Omit the onion, chiles, black beans, and vinegar. Add $1/4$ cup bamboo shoots, sliced, with the mushrooms to the skillet in step 3. Proceed as directed.

Whole Steamed Sea Bass or Other Fish CHINA ■

MAKES **4 TO 8 SERVINGS**
TIME **ABOUT 30 MINUTES**

The highlight of many meals in Chinese restaurants, yet few dishes are easier to prepare at home. Start with a medium-sized firm-fleshed fish—black bass and red snapper are ideal, but grouper or, if you can find it, small striped bass, are also good—preferably with its head on (if the head won't fit in your steamer, cut it off, along with the tail). Scales must be removed and the fish must be thoroughly cleaned; any fishmonger can do this for you. Serve the fish with white rice and, preferably, a few other Chinese dishes.

2 tablespoons soy sauce

1 tablespoon rice or white wine vinegar

2 teaspoons dark sesame oil

One 3- to 5-pound sea bass or red snapper, gilled, gutted, and scaled, head may be on or off

2 tablespoons peeled and shredded or minced fresh ginger

4 scallions, trimmed and shredded, for garnish

Chopped fresh cilantro leaves for garnish

1. Combine the soy sauce, vinegar, and sesame oil in a bowl. Score each side of the fish 3 or 4 times, diagonally from top to bottom, right down to the bone. Rub the soy mixture into the fish, then put the fish on a plate and refrigerate while you prepare the steamer.

2. Put about an inch of water in a steamer, wok, or roasting pan. Place the fish, still on the plate, in the steamer or on a rack in the wok or pan; scatter the ginger over it. Cover and bring to a boil, then steam the fish for about 15 minutes, or until done (the meat near the bone will be opaque or nearly so).

3. Garnish the fish with the scallions and cilantro and serve immediately.

Whole Steamed Fish with Black Beans. This is considerably less subtle, and many people like it more: to the seasoning mixture, add 1 tablespoon minced garlic and 2 tablespoons fermented black beans (page 207).

Whole Steamed Fish, Italian Style. The technique is identical, the ingredients completely different: In step 1, mix together $1/4$ cup extra virgin olive oil (the best you have), the juice of a lemon, $1/4$ cup chopped fresh parsley leaves, and 1 tablespoon minced garlic. Steam as directed and garnish with more chopped fresh parsley. Serve with lemon wedges.

Lemongrass Fish SOUTHEAST ASIA

MAKES **4 TO 6 SERVINGS**

TIME **30 MINUTES**

Lemongrass, the seasoning most closely associated with Southeast Asia, plays a major role here, despite the presence of many other ingredients. Nothing else "cleans" the taste of the fish quite like it. Serve with any rice dish.

2 lemongrass stalks, trimmed (page 143) and smashed

1 small fresh chile, stemmed and seeded

2 garlic cloves, peeled

2 tablespoons corn, grapeseed, or other neutral oil

1 tablespoon chopped fresh cilantro leaves

1 tablespoon chopped fresh mint leaves

1 tablespoon chopped fresh Thai basil leaves

One 3- to 5-pound sea bass or red snapper, gilled, gutted, and scaled, head may be on or off

Salt and black pepper to taste

Lime wedges for serving

1. Preheat the oven to 350°F. Place the lemongrass, chile, and garlic in a food processor. Process until finely minced. Add the oil and process until pasty; stir in the herbs.

2. Place the fish on a baking sheet and sprinkle with salt and pepper. Make 2-inch-long cuts, about 1 inch apart, on each side of the fish. Stuff the cavity and the cuts with the herb mixture and spread the remaining mixture on top of the fish.

3. Bake for about 15 minutes or until the fish is done (the meat near the bone will appear opaque, and the flesh will flake). Serve immediately, with lime wedges.

Grilled or Broiled Fish with Lime

SOUTHEAST ASIA

MAKES **4 SERVINGS**

TIME **35 MINUTES**

This dish is popular throughout Southeast Asia (I had it in Vietnam), where firm-fleshed river fish are plentiful. Carp is an excellent choice for freshwater fish, as is wild catfish (I'm not a fan of farmed catfish), but red snapper or sea bass is also good. Lime leaves are not always available; substitute grated lime zest if necessary. See page 500 for information on Thai fish sauce (nam pla). This would be great with Green Papaya Salad (without the shrimp, page 198).

One 2- to 3-pound carp, catfish, red snapper, or sea bass, gilled, gutted, and scaled, head may be on or off

⅓ cup fresh lime juice

2 tablespoons nam pla

2 tablespoons corn, grapeseed, or other neutral oil

Salt and black pepper to taste

4 lime leaves, chopped, or the grated zest of 1 lime

3 garlic cloves, minced

2 lemongrass stalks, trimmed (page 143) and cut into
**   5-inch lengths**

1. Make 3 or 4 parallel diagonal slashes on each side of the fish, just about down to the bone. Mix together the lime juice, nam pla, oil, salt, and pepper and marinate the fish in this while you start a charcoal or gas grill or broiler; the fire should be medium-hot, and the grill rack should be about 4 inches from the heat source.

2. Remove the fish from the marinade and stuff the cavity with the lime leaves and garlic. Lay the lemongrass stalks directly on the grill or broiler pan and place the fish on top.

3. Grill the fish or broil for at least 5 minutes per side, basting three or four times with the marinade, then check for doneness (peek down to the bottom of the gashes, where the meat should be white). Serve hot.

LIME LEAVES

Grouper or Other Fish Steamed in Its Own Juice, with Cilantro Sauce

SOUTH AMERICA

MAKES **4 SERVINGS**

TIME **40 MINUTES**

This is an interesting technique: the fish is oven-steamed, with just a tiny bit of liquid, thus retaining all of its own juices. Traditionally the packages would be made with banana or other large leaves, and they would be buried in hot ashes. Foil is much more convenient, if not quite as interesting or flavorful.

If you make this with fillets, the cooking time will be under 10 minutes. Serve this with Peasant-Style Potatoes (page 477) and a lightly dressed vegetable.

One 3-pound or larger grouper, red snapper, black sea
**   bass, or other firm white fish, gilled, gutted, and**
**   scaled, head may be on or off**

Salt and black pepper to taste

½ cup fresh lime juice

½ cup chopped fresh cilantro leaves, stems reserved

¼ cup extra virgin olive oil

2 garlic cloves, minced

1 small onion, chopped

1 small tomato, cored and chopped

1. Preheat the oven to 500°F. Tear off 2 pieces of aluminum foil, each large enough to wrap the fish, then put one on top of the other. Put the fish on the foil, then in a large baking dish. Sprinkle salt, pepper, and half the lime juice in the cavity, then stuff the cavity with the cilantro stems. Sprinkle all the remaining ingredients over the fish and fold the foil over to seal in the fish.

2. Bake until the fish flakes when probed with a fork, 15 minutes or more; don't overcook. (Unfortunately, there is no way to check the fish without unwrapping, so don't check for at least 15 minutes; rewrap if necessary.)

3. Carefully unseal the foil (watch out for hot steam) and transfer the fish toppings and any accumulated juices to a food processor or blender. Process until the mixture forms a creamy sauce, adding some lime juice or olive oil if needed. Transfer the fish to your serving dish and top with the cilantro sauce. Serve immediately.

Quick Baked Fish in Cilantro Sauce. In step 3, omit the blending of the sauce; serve the fish with the toppings and accumulated juices spooned over and around the fish.

Quick Baked Fish with Butter FRANCE. This procedure will work with any seasonings: Try wrapping fish with salt, pepper, fresh lemon juice, and butter (about 4 tablespoons, cut into bits). Use about half as much herb, about ¼ cup; fresh parsley, dill, or chervil are best in this.

Quick Baked Fish with Fennel, Olive Oil, and Lemon ITALY. Wrap the fish with salt, pepper, fresh lemon juice, 3 tablespoons extra virgin olive oil, 1 trimmed and sliced fennel bulb, and about ¼ cup chopped fresh parsley, treated as the cilantro in the original recipe or the first variation.

Baked Whole Fish with Dates

NORTH AFRICA

MAKES **4 TO 6 SERVINGS**

TIME **1 HOUR**

Dates, of course, are a staple food of the Sahara and many other deserts; they grow on palm trees, keep forever, and, to nomads, are far more important than any bread product. But only in coastal North Africa and parts of the Middle East does date country meet the sea and a dish like this come about.

Substitute prunes for dates if you prefer.

A simple pilaf, chosen from among those on pages 513 to 514, would be great here, as would Houria (page 191).

One 3- to 4-pound grouper, red snapper, carp, or sea bass, gilled, gutted, and scaled, head may be on or off

Salt and black pepper to taste

1½ cups pitted dates

4 tablespoons (½ stick) butter

1 large onion, sliced

½ cup dry white wine

1 teaspoon ground cinnamon

½ teaspoon ground ginger

1. Preheat the oven to 325°F. Season the fish with salt and pepper inside and out. Roughly chop the dates and put them in the fish's cavity along with half the butter. Use some of the remaining butter to grease the bottom of a roasting pan and dot the top of the fish with the rest of it. Toss the onion with the wine, cinnamon, ginger, and a little more salt and pepper and place in the bottom of the roasting pan; put the fish on top of this mixture. Seal the top with aluminum foil.

2. Bake the fish for about 30 minutes, undisturbed. Uncover, raise the oven heat to 450°F, and continue to roast, basting once or twice with the pan juices, until the fish begins to brown on top, about 15 minutes more. Serve the fish immediately with the dates, onions, and pan juices.

Baked Fish with Almonds. Make a paste by combining 1 cup blanched almonds, 1 tablespoon sugar, and 1 teaspoon ground cinnamon in a food processor with 2 tablespoons chilled butter; process, scraping down the sides of the processor as necessary, until smooth. You can mix this paste with the chopped dates or use it alone.

Fish Couscous NORTH AFRICA

MAKES **6 TO 8 SERVINGS**

TIME **45 MINUTES**

Couscous is a small pasta—not a grain as most people believe—as well as the name of almost every North African dish that contains it. So there are innumerable fish, vegetable, meat, and chicken couscous dishes (see pages 526 and 527 for a couple of others). You can cook the couscous separately (see page 526) or steam it on top of the simmering stew, a nice touch for which you will need either a special utensil called a couscoussière or a steamer rigged inside of a covered pot in which you cook the sauce.

If you are not comfortable cooking pieces of whole fish, substitute a firm fillet like red snapper or grouper and reduce the fish cooking time to about 10 minutes; do not overcook.

2 tablespoons extra virgin olive oil

2 garlic cloves

2 dried hot red chiles

1 large onion, peeled and quartered

2 carrots, chopped

2 celery stalks, chopped

2 medium potatoes, preferably waxy, peeled and cut into chunks

2 bay leaves

1 tablespoon ground cumin

2 tomatoes, cored and chopped

1 teaspoon saffron threads, optional

Salt and black pepper to taste

1 tablespoon mild paprika

Cayenne to taste

One 3-pound red snapper, grouper, black sea bass, or other firm fish, gilled, gutted, scaled, and cut crosswise through the bone into big chunks

2 medium zucchini, cut into chunks

4 cups cooked couscous (page 526)

Chopped fresh parsley leaves for garnish

1. Combine the oil, garlic, and chiles in a large saucepan or casserole and place over medium heat. Cook, stirring occasionally, until fragrant, about 15 seconds. Add the onion and cook, stirring occasionally, until translucent, about 5 minutes. Then stir in the carrots, celery, potatoes, bay leaves, and cumin; stir once or twice. Add 1 quart water (or fish stock if you have it) and bring to a boil, then lower the heat to maintain a steady simmer.

2. Stir in the tomatoes and saffron if you're using it and raise the heat again; cook, uncovered, until the tomatoes break down, about 10 minutes. Add some salt and pepper along with the paprika; taste and add more of any of these, along with cayenne if necessary (the dish should be slightly hot). Cover and cook until the vegetables are just about tender.

3. Add the fish and the zucchini. (If you are steaming the couscous over the stew, set that up also and cover.) Simmer the fish for about 20 minutes, or until it is cooked through (a thin-bladed knife inserted into its center will meet little resistance).

4. Toss the couscous with some of the cooking broth to soften it. Place it on your serving dish and top with the stew. Garnish and serve.

Broiled Sea Bass or Other Fish with Olives FRANCE ▧

MAKES **4 SERVINGS**

TIME **30 MINUTES**

We tend to think of grilling as the ideal way to cook many foods, but the broiler is more valuable when you want to save a marinade and the fish's pan juices. A recipe like this one was originally cooked in a pan over an open fire, and you can certainly follow that tradition, but the broiler makes quick work of it.

Though the dish is French, it's very southern, and I might serve a simple pasta beforehand; Tomatoes Provençal (page 494) would also be in the right spirit, as would a simple salad.

One 3-pound sea bass, red snapper, grouper, or sturdy
   white-fleshed fish, gilled, gutted, and scaled, head may
   be on or off
3 tablespoons extra virgin olive oil
1/4 cup dry white wine
Salt and black pepper to taste
2 teaspoons fresh thyme leaves or 1 teaspoon fresh
   rosemary leaves
1 teaspoon fennel seeds
1/2 cup or more pitted black olives
Chopped fresh parsley leaves for garnish
Lemon wedges for serving

1. Preheat the broiler; adjust the rack so that it is about 4 inches from the heat source. Cut 3 or 4 gashes on each side of the fish, from top to bottom. Mix together the oil, wine, salt, pepper, thyme, and fennel in a baking pan large enough to accommodate the fish. Put the fish in the pan and rub it with the oil mixture.

2. Broil the fish, adjusting the distance between it and the heat source so that it browns evenly but not too quickly. Try to turn the fish only once; total cooking time will be approximately 15 minutes.

3. When the fish is done, transfer it to a platter. Working quickly, add the olives to the pan and cook on the stove over high heat, stirring, for just a minute, to heat them up and combine them with the pan juices. Spoon or pour the olive sauce over the fish, garnish, and serve with the lemon wedges.

"Grilled" Mackerel with Garlic and Rosemary FRANCE ▪

MAKES **4 SERVINGS**
TIME **30 MINUTES**

I had a dish similar to this one in Provence at least twenty years ago and have never stopped making it. Few preparations do as much justice to dark-fleshed fish. Like many "grilled" dishes, this one is better made in the broiler, where you have far more control.

A potato gratin, like the one on page 482, would be suitable here, as would Peasant-Style Potatoes (page 477). Of course, a simple vegetable dish or two would also be wonderful, as mackerel is pretty rich in its own right.

Four 1-pound mackerel, gilled, gutted, and cleaned (they
   have no scales), heads may be on or off
2 tablespoons extra virgin olive oil
Salt and black pepper to taste
1 tablespoon minced garlic
Several fresh rosemary sprigs
4 lemons
Chopped fresh parsley leaves for garnish

1. Preheat the broiler; adjust the rack so a roasting pan will sit about 6 inches from the heat source. Use a sharp knife to make a few diagonal gashes on each side of the fish, right down to the bone. Combine the olive oil with some salt and pepper and the garlic. Rub the fish all over, inside and out, with this mixture, making sure to get some in the gashes. Tuck some sprigs and leaves of rosemary into and on the fish. Thinly slice 2 of the lemons and put these slices in the cavities of the fish.

2. Broil on a rack in a roasting pan, until the top is nicely browned, about 5 minutes. Turn carefully and cook for another 5 minutes or so, until browned on the other side. If the fish are done

now—they may well be—remove from the oven. If not, turn off the broiler and turn on the oven, finishing the cooking by indirect rather than direct heat (the fish is done when its flesh is opaque down to the bone).

3. Cut the remaining lemons into wedges. Garnish the fish with the parsley and serve with the lemon.

Skate with Brown Butter FRANCE ■
MAKES **4 SERVINGS**
TIME **20 MINUTES**

I once thought that poached skate with brown butter was the highest and best use of this relative of shark, but then I began to sauté the fish, which is even better. Which you prefer depends, to some extent, on your tolerance for butter. I offer the sautéed version first and the more classic poached fish as a variation.

For either, it's easiest if you buy skate that has been "filleted," that is, removed from its central cartilage (if it isn't, just cook it a little longer; it will practically come off the "bone" by itself). But never, ever buy skate that has not been skinned; you simply will not get it off unless you resort to a pair of pliers—and even then it won't be easy.

This is a rich dish; serve it with salad and a light vegetable, no more, and you'll be satisfied.

Flour for dredging

Salt and black pepper to taste

Extra virgin olive or other oil (or clarified butter, page 241) for frying

1¹⁄₂ to 2 pounds skate, skinned

4 tablespoons (¹⁄₂ stick) butter

2 tablespoons drained capers, lightly crushed

¹⁄₄ cup wine vinegar, preferably white

Chopped fresh parsley leaves for garnish

1. Put a large skillet over medium-high heat. While it is heating, season the flour with salt and pepper and put it on a plate. Add the oil or clarified butter to the skillet—it should coat the bottom well—and turn the heat to high. When the oil is hot, dredge the skate lightly in the flour and add it to the pan. Cook until the skate is nicely browned on the first side, 3 to 5 minutes, then turn. Cook on the second side for 2 to 4 minutes—lower the heat a bit if the coating begins to scorch—until it is firm to the touch.

2. Just before serving, put the butter in a small saucepan over medium-high heat. Cook, stirring occasionally, until the butter foam subsides and the butter turns nut-brown, then cook for another 15 seconds or so. Add the capers and swirl them around, then pour the butter over the fish. Immediately add the vinegar to the pan that the butter was in, swirl it around, and pour it over the fish. Garnish with parsley and serve immediately.

Poached Skate with Brown Butter. Put the skate in a deep, wide saucepan or skillet and add enough Fish Stock (page 161)—or water with about 10 percent vinegar added—to cover. Bring to a boil over high heat, skim off any foam, and turn the heat to medium-low. Cook the skate until tender, about 10 minutes. Remove the skate, drain it, and place it on a hot platter. Proceed to step 2 and finish as directed.

Coastal-Style Roasted Sea Bass or Other Large Whole Fish GREECE
MAKES **4 SERVINGS**
TIME **1 HOUR**

Try to use branches of fresh oregano, marjoram, or fennel here; they really make a tremendous difference.

The first two are grown by many gardeners, and a good gardener can probably spare some. Bronze—herb—fennel grows wild all over southern California and is easy to find (it's also grown by some gardeners). Occasionally you can find one of these in a big bunch at a market, too; you'll need a big bunch to try the grilling option.

In any case, choose a fish with a simple bone structure so it can be served and eaten easily. The best for this purpose are sea bass, red snapper, grouper, striped bass, and mackerel. One advantage in using the oven over the grill is that in roasting you can add some peeled, chunked potatoes to the bottom of the roasting pan as well; they'll finish cooking along with the onions.

One 3-pound sea bass, gilled, gutted, and scaled, with
    head left on or removed

1 teaspoon salt

2 garlic cloves, cut into very thin slivers

1/4 cup extra virgin olive oil

1 lemon, thinly sliced

20 fresh oregano or marjoram sprigs or 1 teaspoon dried

8 small onions, peeled and cut in half

1 cup dry white wine or fish, chicken, or vegetable stock,
    preferably homemade (page 161, 160, or 162), or
    water, plus a little more if needed

Black pepper to taste

1. Cut 3 or 4 gashes on each side of the fish, from top to bottom. Salt the gashes and salt the fish's cavity as well. Let it sit while you prepare the other ingredients. Preheat the oven to 450°F.
2. Push half of the garlic slivers into the gashes. Rub the fish with a little of the olive oil and pour the rest into the bottom of a large baking pan. Spread the lemon slices over the bottom of the pan and top it with most of the oregano. Lay the fish over all, then spread the onions and remaining garlic around the fish. Pour the wine over all and sprin-

kle with salt and pepper. Top with the remaining oregano.
3. Cover with aluminum foil and bake, undisturbed, until the onions are nearly tender, 20 to 30 minutes. Uncover and continue to bake, shaking the pan occasionally, until the fish is cooked through, another 5 to 10 minutes (look at one of the gashes in the thickest part of the fish; the meat will appear opaque clear down to the central bone). If the pan is drying out, add a little more liquid.
4. To serve, scoop the flesh from the fish with a spoon and top with some sauce.

Coastal-Style Grilled Fish Fillets. If the weather's good, and you have access to fennel branches, this is easier: Start by preheating a charcoal or gas grill; the fire should be quite hot and the grill rack about 4 inches from the heat source. Make a bed of fennel stalks directly on the grill bed. Sprinkle 1 1/2 to 2 pounds of sturdy fish fillets, like halibut (these may be steaks), striped bass, monkfish, or cod, with salt and cayenne. Grill right on the branches. While the fish is cooking, grind a teaspoon or more of fennel or dill seeds; juice 1 lemon and thinly slice another. When the fish is done, remove it from the grill, leaving as much of the stalks behind as possible (some of the burned fronds will adhere to the fish; this is fine). Sprinkle the fish with the fennel or dill seeds, then decorate it with the lemon slices. Drizzle with the lemon juice and a bit of olive oil and serve.

Fish with Raisin Almond Sauce
EASTERN EUROPE ■
MAKES **4 SERVINGS**
TIME **30 MINUTES**

This is a typical Eastern European dish, rich with flavor, its sweetness tempered by the lemon juice. It makes a nice presentation, especially if you use a meaty fish like carp. The same technique can be applied to any fish fillet: reduce the cooking time to 10 minutes (or less; the fish is done when the point of a thin-bladed knife inserted into the thickest part meets little resistance).

You might want some mashed potatoes or rice here, along with a simple salad.

> 5 cups fish stock, preferably homemade (page 161), or
>   water
> One 3-pound carp, gilled, gutted, and scaled
> Salt and black pepper to taste
> 2 tablespoons butter
> $^1/_2$ cup blanched almonds, sliced
> $^1/_2$ cup raisins
> $^1/_3$ cup fresh lemon juice
> $^1/_4$ cup sweet white wine

1. Bring the fish stock to a steady, gentle boil in a large saucepan or skillet with a lid. Season the fish, inside and out, with the salt and pepper and gently slide it into the stock. Cover and simmer over low heat until the fish is cooked through, at least 20 minutes.
2. Meanwhile, melt the butter in a small saucepan over medium-high heat. Add the almonds and cook, stirring occasionally, until golden brown, about 5 minutes. Stir in the raisins and cook until plump, about 3 minutes. Add $^1/_4$ cup of the lemon juice and the wine; bring to a boil, then lower the heat and simmer until reduced by about half, about 5 minutes. Season to taste with salt and pepper, then refresh with the remaining lemon juice.
3. Remove the fish from the broth and place on your serving dish. Pour the sauce over the fish and serve.

MIXED FISH DISHES

Red Fish Stew, Fast and Spicy INDIA ■
MAKES **4 SERVINGS**
TIME **30 MINUTES**

This is a fast stew you can make with a variety of fish—a few scraps if that's all you have—or with one or more types of prime fish. For example, it's great with shellfish only: shrimp or a combination of shrimp, scallops, and a mollusk, like mussels (make sure they're well washed). But you can make it with a single piece of sturdy fish, like monkfish or halibut. In any case, be sure to serve it with plenty of white rice, preferably basmati.

> 5 small dried red chiles, or to taste
> 1 large onion, peeled and cut into chunks
> 5 garlic cloves, peeled
> One 1-inch piece fresh ginger, peeled and cut into chunks
> 1 teaspoon ground turmeric
> $^1/_4$ cup Tamarind Paste (page 585), optional
> 2 cups fish or chicken stock, preferably homemade
>   (page 161 or 160), or water
> $^1/_2$ cup coconut milk, homemade (page 584) or canned,
>   optional
> Salt and black pepper to taste
> $1^1/_2$ to 2 pounds firm white fish, shrimp, or any
>   combination of seafood (see headnote)
> Lime wedges (especially if you don't use tamarind)
>   for serving

1. Combine the chiles, onion, garlic, ginger, turmeric, and tamarind if you're using it in a small food processor and blend until smooth, scraping down the sides if necessary. Combine with all the remaining ingredients except the fish and lime in a pot and turn the heat to medium; bring to a boil and add the fish. Cover and cook, more or less

undisturbed, until the fish is tender, about 10 minutes.

2. Taste and adjust the seasoning as necessary. Serve with the lime wedges.

Choucroute de Poissons FRANCE

MAKES **4 SERVINGS**

TIME **1 HOUR**

A choucroute need not be meat, as is the more familiar one on page 404. Alsace, where the dish originated, has a long tradition of combining sauerkraut with fish. As is always the case, buy sauerkraut that is either sold in bulk or packed in plastic and contains no more than cabbage and salt.

Serve with boiled potatoes.

1 pound sauerkraut, rinsed

1 teaspoon juniper berries, lightly crushed with the side of a knife

1 teaspoon fresh thyme leaves or $1/2$ teaspoon dried

1 bay leaf

1 cup dry white wine

Salt and black pepper to taste

$1/2$ pound fillet of cod, snapper, or other white fish

$1/2$ pound smoked haddock, trout, or other smoked white fish

$1/2$ pound salmon fillet, skinned

1 shallot, minced

$1/4$ cup cream

8 tablespoons (1 stick) butter, slightly softened

Juice of 1 lemon

Chopped fresh parsley leaves for garnish

1. Combine the sauerkraut in a deep skillet or flame-proof casserole with the juniper, thyme, bay, and all but 2 tablespoons of the white wine. Place over medium-high heat. When the mixture begins to bubble, lower the heat and cover, adjusting the heat so the mixture simmers. Cook for about 40 minutes, stirring occasionally and seasoning with salt and pepper as necessary. Lay the fish fillets on top of the sauerkraut and cover the pan once again.

2. In a small saucepan over medium-high heat, cook the remaining 2 tablespoons white wine with the shallot until the liquid has almost evaporated, just a few minutes. Turn the heat to low, add the cream, and stir. Add the butter a little bit at a time, stirring all the while. When the mixture is creamy, stir in the lemon juice, along with some salt and pepper. Keep warm.

3. When the fish is tender, about 10 minutes after adding it, spoon the sauerkraut and fish onto a platter; drizzle the sauce over all. Garnish with parsley and serve.

Zarzuela SPAIN

MAKES **4 SERVINGS**

TIME **45 MINUTES**

Zarzuela—the word means "medley" in Spanish—unites a variety of fish and is, like bouillabaisse, a dish whose ingredients can be varied according to what you can find. The traditional sauce accompaniment for Zarzuela is Romesco (page 606), but the variation makes that superfluous. I love this with crusty bread.

3 tablespoons extra virgin olive oil

1 tablespoon minced garlic

1 large onion, chopped

3 tablespoons Spanish brandy or cognac

1 small dried chile or $1/2$ teaspoon hot red pepper flakes

Pinch of saffron threads, optional

2 large tomatoes (drained canned are fine), cored and
   diced
Salt and black pepper to taste
$1/2$ cup dry white wine
$1 1/2$ pounds mussels, cleaned (page 208)
$1 1/2$ pounds littleneck or mahogany clams or cockles,
   well scrubbed
$1/2$ pound shrimp (15 to 30 per pound), peeled
$1/2$ pound squid, cleaned (page 98), cut into rings,
   tentacles left intact
1 pound fillets of halibut, monkfish, grouper, or other firm
   white fish, skinned and cut into 1-inch chunks
Chopped fresh parsley leaves for garnish

1. Put the oil in a deep skillet or flameproof casserole
   with a lid and place over medium-high heat. Add
   the garlic and onion and cook until the onion is
   soft, about 5 minutes. Add the brandy and bring
   the mixture to a boil. Crumble the chile and saffron if you're using it into the skillet, then stir in
   the tomatoes along with a little salt and pepper.
   When the tomatoes break up, add the wine and
   bring to a boil.

2. Add the mussels and clams and cover. Cook until
   the first of these begin to open, about 5 minutes.
   Add the shrimp, squid, and fish and cook until the
   shrimp is pink, the fish cooked through, and most
   of the mollusks open, another 5 to 10 minutes.
   Taste and adjust the seasoning, then garnish and
   serve.

Nutty Zarzuela. In a food processor or blender,
process 1 cup toasted almonds or hazelnuts with the
garlic, onion, and $1/2$ cup water until a paste is
formed. Add this paste to the skillet in step 1 where
you would have added the garlic and onion. Double
the amount of white wine and proceed as directed.

Poultry Chicken, once an occasional treat—before the advent of mass production, it was something of a luxury—is now a staple, not only in the United States but in much of the world. Though quality varies widely, even bland supermarket chicken can be cooked in ways that make it delicious, especially when you apply the techniques and flavors of the rest of the world. And it's almost always dependably good served with rice or bread—if you automatically think of these when you're planning a meal with chicken, you're more than halfway there.

For the simplest chicken dishes—those with only a few, sometimes subtle, ingredients—it still pays to look a little harder and spend a little more for higher-quality birds. These may be free-range, kosher, or (sometimes—the word is often meaningless) "natural" chickens. At least one of these options is now offered at most supermarkets.

WHOLE CHICKEN

Whole chicken is easy to cook and universally loved. And unlike most other chicken preparations, its appearance creates an elegant, even festive atmosphere. Generally speaking, when you buy a whole chicken, you may have to pull out its neck, liver, and perhaps heart (stored, wrapped in plastic or paper, in the cavity); you can cook or discard these. Though it's not essential, many people like to rinse chicken before cooking; if you do so, dry it well before proceeding.

White Cut Chicken CHINA ■ ▨

MAKES **4 SERVINGS**

TIME **40 MINUTES, LARGELY UNATTENDED**

Served throughout China to celebrate the New Year, birthdays, and anniversaries, this simple poached chicken is often accompanied by no more than soy sauce for dipping, though the equally appropriate Ginger-Scallion Dipping Sauce (page 583) is my favorite. Since this is served at room temperature or cold, you can easily make it ahead of time.

> One 1-inch piece fresh ginger, peeled and cut into
> ¼-inch slices
> 5 scallions, trimmed and cut into 2-inch lengths
> 2 whole star anise
> 2 tablespoons salt
> 2 tablespoons sugar
> One 3- to 4-pound chicken, trimmed of excess fat

1. Place all the ingredients except the chicken in a large pot with 2 quarts water. Bring to a boil over high heat.
2. Carefully place the chicken in the pot, breast side up, and bring the water back to a boil. Then turn the heat to low, cover, and simmer for 20 minutes.

Remove from the heat and then let the chicken sit in the water for another 10 minutes.
3. Remove the chicken from the pot, cool to room temperature, and cut into serving pieces. Serve with soy sauce and Ginger-Scallion Dipping Sauce or cover and refrigerate until ready to serve.

Drunken Chicken CHINA ■ ▨

MAKES **4 TO 6 SERVINGS**

TIME **1 HOUR, PLUS MARINATING TIME**

This simple steamed chicken is usually served cold, and it's refreshing on warm summer days, like a good chicken salad. Shaoxing wine, with its full, distinctive flavor, is best for this dish, but Fino (dry) sherry is a good substitute. Start this as long as a day in advance; the more marinating time, the better.

If you don't have a large steamer, you can use a big pot with a rack set inside. Or simply poach the chicken, as in the variation.

> 1 tablespoon salt, plus more to taste
> 1 tablespoon sugar, plus more to taste
> One 3- to 4-pound chicken, trimmed of excess fat
> 4 scallions, trimmed and cut into 3-inch lengths
> Five ¼-inch-thick slices peeled fresh ginger
> ⅓ cup Shaoxing wine or dry sherry

1. Put at least an inch of water in a large steamer, cover, and bring to a rolling boil. Meanwhile, sprinkle the salt and sugar in the cavity and all over the outside of the chicken. Place half the scallions and 2 slices of ginger in the cavity of the chicken. Place the chicken in the steamer and top with the remaining scallions and ginger. Set a kettle of water to boil.
2. Cover and steam for about 50 minutes, adding water from the kettle if necessary. Carefully transfer

Shaoxing Wine

Shaoxing, the Chinese cooking wine made from rice, originated in the Shaoxing region but is now produced throughout China. The highest-quality wines are aged for over a hundred years (it's said), but most brands and varieties are aged for just a few years (or, in the case of the least expensive types, not at all).

Most Shaoxing wines are intended for cooking only

(I have yet to meet someone who enjoys drinking them). They have a distinctive, somewhat sherrylike flavor (dry sherry is the common and best substitute) that varies depending on the kind of rice used, the process, the aging, and so on—just like wines made from grapes. You can find Shaoxing cooking wines at Asian groceries and some major supermarkets.

---

the chicken to a large bowl. When the chicken has cooled, cut it into small serving pieces.

3. Meanwhile, combine the wine with 1/4 cup of the steaming liquid and add a pinch of salt and sugar to taste. Pour this mixture over the cut chicken and cover. Refrigerate for at least 5 hours and preferably overnight.

Poached Drunken Chicken. Bring a large pot of water to a rolling boil and add the chicken, salt, sugar, scallions, and ginger. Cover, turn the heat as low as possible, and cook for 35 minutes. Carefully transfer the chicken to a large bowl and proceed as directed, substituting the boiling liquid for the steaming liquid.

Soy-Poached Chicken CHINA ■ ▪
MAKES **4 SERVINGS**

TIME **40 MINUTES**

Traditionally this bird is taken from the liquid and served without further cooking, hot or at room temperature. But I like to finish it by placing it in a hot oven where, in just five minutes, it develops a dark brown, crispy crust; this browning can also be done a few hours later.

Perhaps the best thing about this sauce is that it can be used time and again, as long as you freeze it between uses (or refrigerate it and bring it to a rolling boil every few days) and top up the liquids now and then.

Mei Kuei Lu Chiew wine is available at most Chinese markets for about $2 a bottle, and yellow rock sugar can be found at Chinese markets too.

3 cups soy sauce

3 cups (1 bottle) Mei Kuei Lu Chiew wine or any floral, off-dry white wine, like Gewürztraminer or Muscat

2 whole star anise

One 14-ounce box yellow rock sugar or 1 cup granulated sugar

3 ounces (about a 5-inch knob) fresh ginger, peeled, cut into thick slices, and bruised with the side of a knife

10 medium scallions, untrimmed

One 2 1/2 - to 3-pound chicken, trimmed of excess fat

1. In a narrow pot with about a 6-quart capacity, combine the soy sauce, wine, 2 cups water, and the star anise over high heat. While the sugar is still in its box (or wrapped in a towel), smack it several times with a hammer or rolling pin to break it up; it need not be too fine. Add the sugar and ginger to the liquid and bring it to a rolling boil.

Soy Sauce

Shoyu—soy sauce—is irresistible, the heart and soul of Japanese food and a staple throughout Asia and now the United States.

Like many Japanese foods, shoyu probably originated in China. There are references to it from the first millennium A.D., but it was only in the seventeenth century that the process used today was developed fully. The best soy sauce takes eighteen months to produce, and even decent commercial soy sauce, like the kind commonly sold at supermarkets, requires six months. The ingredients remain the same: soy, wheat, a yeastlike culture, salt, and water. Good soy sauce lists those ingredients and no others.

Contrast this to the cheap black soy sauce made throughout Asia, which sells for around a dollar a bottle. It can be called "soy sauce" only because its base of hydrolyzed vegetable protein is made from soy, which is treated with hydrochloric acid, then combined with salt and caramel. The process takes three days, and the result is—not to put too fine a point on it—worthless.

---

2. Add 6 of the scallions, then gently and slowly lower the chicken into the liquid, breast side down. (In a narrow pot, the liquid will easily cover the chicken; if it is close, just dunk the chicken under the liquid as it cooks. If it is not close, add a mixture of soy sauce and water to raise the level.) Bring the liquid back to a boil and boil steadily for 10 minutes. Turn off the heat and turn the chicken over so the breast side is up. Let it sit in the hot liquid for 15 minutes. Meanwhile, trim and mince the remaining 4 scallions and preheat the oven to 500°F.

3. Carefully remove the chicken from the liquid and serve it hot or at room temperature. Or place it in a skillet or roasting pan. Roast for 5 minutes, or until nicely browned; keep an eye on it, because it can burn easily. In either case, reheat the sauce and, when the chicken is ready, carve it. Serve the chicken with a few spoonfuls of sauce on it. Put another cup or so of the sauce in a bowl and add the remaining scallions; pass this at the table.

Hainanese Chicken Rice CHINA
MAKES 4 SERVINGS
TIME 1½ HOURS, PLUS RESTING TIME

A Chinese dish that is also seen in parts of Southeast Asia. Serve with Ginger-Chile Sauce. Even more than usual, be sure to use a good-quality chicken here; its flavor is what makes the rice special.

One 3- to 4-pound chicken, trimmed of excess fat

1 teaspoon salt

3 tablespoons roughly chopped garlic

5 slices fresh ginger, peeled and smashed

¼ cup peanut or neutral oil, like corn or grapeseed

3 shallots, roughly chopped

2 cups long-grain rice

Salt and black pepper to taste

2 tablespoons dark sesame oil

Ginger-Chile Sauce (page 584)

2 tomatoes, sliced

2 cucumbers, peeled and sliced

¼ cup minced scallion

Chopped fresh cilantro leaves for garnish

■ make ahead   ■ serve at room temp./cold   ▨ 30 minutes or less   POULTRY **275**

1. Bring a large pot of water to a boil. Rub the inside and outside of the chicken with salt and put 2 tablespoons of the garlic and the ginger in its cavity. Add the chicken to the water; it should be completely submerged, but just barely. Cover, reduce the heat to medium, and cook for 10 minutes. Turn off the heat and let the bird remain in the water for 2 hours, covered.

2. Remove the chicken from the pot (reserve the stock) and place it in a large bowl of ice water until cool. (Or refrigerate it and proceed with the recipe when you're ready.) Place the peanut oil in a skillet over medium heat. When the oil is hot, add the remaining garlic and the shallots; cook, stirring occasionally, until lightly browned, about 5 minutes. Add 1 quart of the reserved chicken stock and bring to a boil. Add the rice, bring to a boil again, then reduce the heat to low and cover; cook for about 20 minutes, until the rice has absorbed all the liquid. Stir in salt and pepper to taste.

3. Drain the chicken and rub it with the sesame oil. Cut it into bite-sized pieces (you can decide whether you want to include the bones or not) and arrange it over the rice. Drizzle some of the Ginger-Chile Sauce over the chicken and decorate with the tomatoes and cucumbers. Sprinkle the scallion and cilantro over all or, if you like, heat the remaining chicken stock and serve in small bowls, sprinkled with the scallion; stir in some sauce to taste.

Pollo al Mattone Chicken Under a Brick
ITALY ■ ▨
MAKES **4 SERVINGS**
TIME **45 MINUTES**

You will need two ovenproof skillets or a skillet and a couple of bricks or rocks to use this simple, wonderful method, which yields crisp, delicious skin and succulent meat. As a bonus, much of the chicken's own moisture remains at the bottom of the pan and produces a perfect natural sauce. You can buy split chickens at most supermarkets, or any butcher will split it for you. You can also do it yourself: use a knife or poultry shears to cut out the backbone, then press down on the breast to flatten it.

One 3- to 4-pound chicken, trimmed of excess fat, and
    split, backbone removed
1 tablespoon minced fresh rosemary leaves or 1 teaspoon
    dried
Salt and black pepper to taste
1 tablespoon coarsely chopped garlic
2 tablespoons extra virgin olive oil
2 fresh rosemary sprigs, if available
1 lemon, cut into quarters

CHICKEN UNDER A BRICK

1. Place the chicken on a cutting board, skin side down, and press down as hard as you can with your hands to make it as flat as possible. Mix together the minced rosemary, salt, pepper, garlic, and 1 tablespoon of the olive oil and rub this all over the chicken. Tuck some of the mixture under the skin as well. If time permits, cover and marinate in the refrigerator for up to a day (even 20 minutes of marinating is helpful).

2. When you are ready to cook, preheat the oven to 500°F. Preheat an ovenproof 12-inch skillet (preferably nonstick) over medium-high heat for about 3 minutes. Press the rosemary sprigs into the skin side of the chicken. Put the remaining olive oil in the pan and wait about 30 seconds for it to heat up.

3. Place the chicken in the skillet, skin side down, along with any remaining pieces of rosemary and garlic; weight it with another skillet or one or two bricks or rocks wrapped in aluminum foil. The basic idea is to flatten the chicken by applying a fair amount of weight evenly over its surface.

4. Cook over medium-high to high heat for 5 minutes, then transfer to the oven. Roast for 15 minutes. Remove from the oven and remove the weights; turn the chicken over (it will now be skin side up) and roast for 10 minutes more or until done (large chickens may take an additional 5 minutes or so). Serve hot or at room temperature, with lemon wedges.

Classic Roast Chicken FRANCE

MAKES **4 SERVINGS**

TIME **45 TO 60 MINUTES**

Since it is made everywhere, it may be a stretch to call roast chicken "French"—but not to call it one of the simplest of the world's great recipes. There are three keys to success: One, pay attention to the technique; it works. Two, start with a good chicken (find a free-range or kosher chicken you like and stick with it); without it, the technique is wasted. And three, use butter if at all possible; the difference is profound.

You can use this technique or any of the variations with baby chicken (poussin) or Cornish hens.

One 3- to 4-pound chicken, trimmed of excess fat
2 tablespoons soft butter or extra virgin olive oil
Salt and black pepper to taste

1. Preheat the oven to 450°F. Rub the chicken with the butter and season it with salt and pepper. Five minutes after turning on the oven, place a cast-iron or other heavy ovenproof skillet on a rack set low in the oven.

2. When the oven is hot, about 10 minutes later, carefully place the chicken, breast side up, in the hot skillet. Roast, undisturbed, for 30 to 40 minutes, or until an instant-read thermometer inserted in the meaty part of the thigh registers 155°F. Remove from the oven, let rest 3 to 5 minutes, then carve and serve.

Roast Chicken with Tarragon FRANCE. In step 1, make a compound butter of 4 tablespoons (½ stick) butter and 1 tablespoon chopped fresh tarragon leaves—simply mash them together. Rub this over the chicken—put some under the skin of the breast too—and put whatever remains in the bird's cavity. In step 2, baste the bird with the pan juices about every 10 minutes. Because you will be opening the oven door periodically, the cooking time will increase somewhat.

Roast Chicken with Paprika CENTRAL EUROPE. A very-good-looking bird: Follow the same method as for Roast Chicken with Tarragon, using paprika to taste in place of the tarragon—about 1 teaspoon hot paprika or 1 tablespoon sweet or, better still, a combination. Rub the outside of the top of the bird with more paprika too.

Roast Chicken with Ponzu JAPAN. Before roasting, season the chicken with salt and pepper and rub it with about 2 tablespoons of Ponzu (page 591). When the chicken is done, let it rest for a couple of minutes. Put about a cup of ponzu in a bowl or gravy boat. Carve the chicken, splash it with 2 or 3 tablespoons of the ponzu, and serve, passing the remaining ponzu at the table.

Chicken with Walnut Sauce

EASTERN EUROPE, RUSSIA ■ ■

MAKES **4 SERVINGS**

TIME **45 MINUTES**

Boiled chicken may seem a thing of the past, but if the chicken is good to begin with, you don't overcook it, and you serve it with this classic walnut sauce—sometimes called tarator or skordalia—it can be quite fabulous. Make the chicken and the sauce in advance if you like; both are good at room temperature. And, if you prefer, sauté the chicken and serve it with this sauce; see, for example, Chicken Escabeche (page 294) for the cooking technique.

If you want to make the sauce without stock, see page 600.

Walnut sauce, or tarator, is good not only with chicken but also with plain steamed vegetables—that's what I'd serve with this, perhaps along with a rice or potato dish.

Chicken stock, preferably homemade (page 160), or water
   as needed

One 3- to 4-pound chicken, trimmed of excess fat

2 medium onions, peeled and quartered

2 carrots, chopped

2 celery stalks, chopped

$1/4$ cup fresh parsley leaves, stems reserved and tied
   together

Salt and black pepper to taste

1 thick slice day-old bread

1 cup walnuts, blanched

3 garlic cloves, peeled

1 fresh hot red chile, stemmed and seeded, or 1 teaspoon
   pure chile powder, like ancho or New Mexico

1. Bring a pot of chicken stock or water to a boil (starting with stock will mean even more flavorful chicken and even better stock when you're done). Add the chicken, onions, carrots, celery, parsley stems, salt, and pepper; the liquid should just cover the chicken. Simmer, uncovered, over low heat, until the chicken is cooked through, about 30 minutes. Remove the chicken and cool to room temperature. Strain the stock and set aside.

2. Put the bread in a bowl and saturate it with some of the stock. Squeeze any excess liquid out of the bread, then place it in a food processor with the parsley leaves, walnuts, garlic, and chile. Process until the walnuts are ground, then, with the machine running, pour in enough of the reserved stock to form a creamy sauce, about 2 cups. Reserve the remaining stock for another use.

3. Season the sauce with salt and pepper. Carve the chicken and serve it with the sauce.

Walnut Chicken Salad. When the chicken is cooked, remove the meat from the bones and chop into small pieces; combine with enough of the sauce to create a chicken salad. Serve at room temperature.

CUT-UP CHICKEN OR BONE-IN PARTS

A few years ago a milestone was reached in the sale of chicken: chicken parts outsold whole chickens. Though cutting up a whole chicken is about the easiest of all butchering chores to master—and is also economical and provides you with parts for making stock—most people no longer bother with it because chicken parts are readily available.

In most dishes calling for bone-in chicken parts, you have a choice between breasts and legs, just breasts, and just legs. You can use the whole leg (with thighs) or the drumstick or thigh alone. At home I choose to cook thighs alone more often than not—they are simply the tastiest part of the bird (and, as a bonus, they're the least expensive). But you can use any combination you like in most of these recipes.

BRAISED OR POACHED CHICKEN PARTS

This is a quick, easy, and reliable way to deal with bone-in chicken parts, because most chicken becomes so tender so quickly. In fact, the danger often lies in overcooking.

Braised Chestnut Chicken CHINA ■

MAKES **4 SERVINGS**

TIME **1¼ HOURS, LARGELY UNATTENDED, PLUS TIME TO SOAK MUSHROOMS (AND POSSIBLY CHESTNUTS)**

This popular winter stew is often served on special occasions, but I think its very nature makes an occasion special. Chestnuts, so rarely used in cooking here, add a rich and subtle sweetness to the dish. Fresh chestnuts are best, but frozen chestnuts are almost as good, and Asian markets carry dried chest-

nuts that are suitable as well. Forget canned chestnuts, though—they're too soft to hold up to the long cooking.

Like most braises, this is even better the second day, so feel free to make it in advance.

¼ cup dried black Chinese mushrooms

2 tablespoons corn, grapeseed, or other neutral oil

2 scallions, trimmed and chopped

One 2-inch piece fresh ginger, peeled and minced

1 chicken, 3 to 4 pounds, cut into serving pieces, or 2½ to 3 pounds chicken parts, trimmed of excess fat

¼ cup soy sauce

2 tablespoons Shaoxing wine or dry sherry

2 tablespoons sugar

1 cup fresh chestnuts, boiled or roasted and peeled (page 453), or 1 cup frozen chestnuts, thawed, or ½ cup dried Chinese chestnuts, soaked in hot water for 3 hours

1. Put the mushrooms in a bowl or measuring cup and cover with boiling water. Let sit until soft, 20 to 30 minutes. Put the oil in a large, deep skillet or flameproof casserole, preferably nonstick, over medium-high heat. A minute later, add the scallions and ginger and cook, stirring once or twice, for about 30 seconds. Add the drained mushrooms and cook, stirring occasionally, until lightly browned, about 2 minutes. Transfer the mushrooms and spices with a slotted spoon to a plate and set aside.

2. Put the chicken pieces in the skillet, skin side down, and brown well, rotating and turning the pieces as necessary, 10 to 15 minutes. Return the mushrooms and spices to the pan along with the soy sauce, wine, and sugar.

3. Add enough water just to cover the chicken, about 2 cups, and then the chestnuts. Stir well, cover, and turn the heat to low. Simmer for 20 to 30 minutes, or until the chicken and chestnuts are tender.

4. If the sauce has not thickened to a stewlike consistency, raise the heat and cook off some of the liquid as necessary. Serve hot with rice or cover and refrigerate overnight before reheating (it may be necessary to add a little water to thin the sauce).

Lemongrass-Steamed Chicken
SOUTHEAST ASIA
MAKES **4 SERVINGS**
TIME **45 MINUTES**

The simplest and easiest way to infuse the flavor of lemongrass into chicken. For the ultraswell version, see Lemongrass Chicken (page 287). Like that dish, this one is great with steamed Sticky Rice (page 508).

8 chicken thighs, trimmed of excess fat

Salt and black pepper to taste

3 tablespoons corn, grapeseed, or other neutral oil

6 lemongrass stalks, trimmed (page 143), halved
    lengthwise, and smashed

3 tablespoons soy sauce

Lime wedges for serving

Chopped fresh cilantro leaves for garnish

1. Sprinkle the chicken with salt and pepper. Put the oil in a deep skillet or casserole with a lid over medium-high heat. Spread the lemongrass evenly over the skillet.
2. When the lemongrass begins to fry and is fragrant, place the chicken, skin side down, on top, turn the heat to medium, and cover the skillet. Cook, turning and basting with the soy sauce every 10 minutes or so, until the chicken is cooked through, about 30 minutes. Discard the lemongrass and serve the chicken with the lime wedges, garnished with cilantro.

Red-Cooked Chicken MALAYSIA
MAKES **4 SERVINGS**
TIME **45 MINUTES**

This fragrant, sweet-smelling Malaysian version of braised chicken is complex and delicious. The vaguely red color (it's actually brown) comes from the chiles and tamarind. But if you don't have tamarind, or you want a truly red sauce, substitute tomato paste for the tamarind paste; it's a nice change of pace and actually makes the dish more attractive.

Serve this with Nasi Lemak (page 515) or another rice dish.

2 small fresh or dried red chiles, preferably Thai

3 tablespoons corn, grapeseed, or other neutral oil

1 chicken, 3 to 4 pounds, cut into serving pieces,
    or 2½ to 3 pounds chicken parts, trimmed of
    excess fat

2 garlic cloves, minced

One 1-inch piece fresh ginger, peeled and minced

1 small onion, diced

1 cinnamon stick

2 whole star anise

1 teaspoon whole cloves

1 tablespoon tamarind paste (page 585)

1 cup coconut milk, homemade (page 584) or canned

1. If you have fresh chiles, stem, seed, and mince them; if dried, soak in warm water for a few minutes until softened, then remove the stems and seeds and mince them. Put the oil in a deep skillet or flameproof casserole, preferably nonstick, with a lid. Place it over medium-high heat and wait a minute or so, until the oil is hot. Add the chicken, skin side down, and brown it well, rotating and turning the pieces as necessary, 10 to 15 minutes. Remove the chicken and drain all but 2 tablespoons of the fat from the skillet.

2. Turn the heat to medium and add the chiles, garlic, ginger, and onion to the skillet. Cook, stirring occasionally, until the onion softens, about 3 minutes. Add the cinnamon stick, star anise, and cloves and cook until fragrant, about 1 minute.

3. Stir in the tamarind paste and coconut milk until the paste dissolves, then return the chicken to the skillet. Add 1 cup water, bring the mixture to a boil, turn the heat to low, cover, and simmer for 20 minutes or until the chicken is done. Serve immediately, with white rice.

Kari Ayam Chicken Curry MALAYSIA

MAKES **4 SERVINGS**
TIME **1 HOUR**

This recipe doesn't demand anything particularly exotic to produce an authentically Malaysian flavor. But instead of relying on canned curry paste as so many similar dishes do, this one offers a good deal more fragrance and sweetness by starting with fresh spices. If you've got access to a good market and would like to try a more unusual chicken curry from Southeast Asia, try the Red-Cooked Chicken (preceding recipe) or the Braised Duck or Chicken with Fresh Curry Paste on page 328, which incorporates Thai ingredients like dried shrimp or fish sauce.

This curry is great with white rice but even better with the Malaysian coconut rice, Nasi Lemak, on page 515. You can make this curry a day in advance—keep it covered in the refrigerator overnight and warm it gently over low heat before serving.

One 1-inch piece fresh ginger, peeled and coarsely
    chopped
5 shallots, coarsely chopped
3 garlic cloves, coarsely chopped

1 tablespoon corn, grapeseed, or other neutral oil
1 chicken, 3 to 4 pounds, cut into serving pieces,
    or 2$\frac{1}{2}$ to 3 pounds chicken thighs, trimmed of
    excess fat
Salt to taste
$\frac{1}{2}$ cinnamon stick
1 whole star anise
2 whole cloves
3 tablespoons curry powder, preferably homemade
    (pages 592–593)
1$\frac{1}{2}$ cups coconut milk, homemade (page 584) or canned

1. Combine the ginger, shallots, and garlic in a food processor or blender and puree to a coarse paste. Set aside.

2. Heat the oil in a large skillet over medium-high heat. When it shimmers, season the chicken with salt, add it, skin side down, and brown well, rotating and turning the pieces as necessary, 10 to 15 minutes.

3. When the chicken has browned, transfer it to a plate and add the shallot-ginger-garlic paste to the pan. Cook, stirring, until lightly colored and fragrant, about 4 minutes. Add the cinnamon stick, star anise, cloves, and curry powder and cook for a minute more, then return the chicken to the skillet and season well with salt.

4. Add the coconut milk to the pan, scraping with a wooden spoon to incorporate any solids into the sauce. Lower the heat so the coconut milk is simmering gently and cook, partially covered, for 30 minutes, or until the chicken is cooked through (you may want to remove the breast meat from the sauce after 20 minutes and warm it through just before serving—this will keep it from overcooking). Remove the whole spices from the pan and serve warm with Nasi Lemak or plain jasmine rice.

Red-Braised Chicken INDIA

MAKES **4 SERVINGS**

TIME **ABOUT 1 HOUR**

A basic spicy braised dish (non-Indians might call it a curry) that can be varied as you like (a couple of ideas follow the main recipe) and can also be made with lamb, pork, or seafood. Though it is traditionally made quite hot in its northern India home (as much food there is), you can reduce the number of chiles to one for a much milder version or increase them if your tastes run that way.

Because the chicken is not browned, the dish is relatively easy to make; you can remove its skin if you like, because without the browning it adds nothing.

I love this with a Paratha (page 559) but that might be too much work; it's delicious with any rice dish also.

2 tablespoons butter or neutral oil, like corn or grapeseed

2 large onions, sliced

Salt and black pepper to taste

1 tablespoon minced garlic

1 tablespoon peeled and minced fresh ginger

3 small hot fresh chiles, like jalapeños, stemmed, seeded,
   and minced, or 3 small hot dried chiles, crumbled, or
   2 teaspoons hot red pepper flakes, or to taste

1 teaspoon ground cinnamon

1 teaspoon ground cardamom

Pinch of ground cloves

2 cups chopped tomatoes (canned are fine; don't bother
   to drain)

1 chicken, 3 to 4 pounds, cut into serving pieces, or 2$\frac{1}{2}$ to
   3 pounds chicken parts, trimmed of excess fat,
   skinned if you like

Chopped fresh cilantro leaves for garnish

1. Put the butter in a 12-inch skillet or flameproof casserole over medium-high heat. Add the onions along with some salt and pepper and cook, stirring occasionally, until quite soft, 10 to 15 minutes. Stir in the garlic, ginger, and chiles and cook, stirring, for about a minute. Add the remaining spices and the tomatoes and cook, stirring occasionally, until the mixture is saucy, about 10 minutes.

2. Add the chicken, along with some more salt and pepper, and adjust the heat so the mixture simmers energetically but not violently. Cook, uncovered, until the chicken is tender, 30 to 40 minutes. Taste and adjust the seasoning, then serve (on white rice is best), garnished with the cilantro.

Red-Braised Chicken with Potatoes. Potatoes are just a "for instance"; this dish is made with okra, peas, green beans, nuts, dried fruits, even green bananas: In step 2, when the chicken is about half cooked, stir in 4 large or 6 to 8 small to medium potatoes, peeled and cut into chunks. You will need more salt and pepper.

Red-Braised Chicken with Coconut Milk. In step 2, just before adding the chicken, stir in 1$\frac{1}{2}$ cups coconut milk, homemade (page 584) or canned, or yogurt, preferably whole milk.

Chicken Adobo PHILIPPINES ■

MAKES **4 SERVINGS**

TIME **45 MINUTES, PLUS TIME TO PREHEAT THE GRILL**

The Philippines is not renowned for its cuisine, but chicken adobo is the well-known exception. The basic idea is this: You poach chicken in a mixture of diluted soy sauce, vinegar, and spices until it's just about done, and then you grill or broil it. Before serving, the poaching liquid is boiled until reduced (thus eliminating any fears of bacterial contamination) and used as a sauce; it's delicious over rice.

If you know you are going to make the dish a day or two before eating it, you can poach the chicken in advance and refrigerate it, in or out of its liquid, until you're ready, then proceed with the recipe. But because the grilling or broiling time will be a little longer than if you proceed without stopping—the cold chicken must heat through—you should use slightly lower heat to avoid burning.

Serve this with plain white rice.

1 cup soy sauce

$^1/_2$ cup white or rice vinegar

1 tablespoon chopped garlic

2 bay leaves

$^1/_2$ teaspoon black pepper

1 dried chipotle chile

1 chicken, 3 to 4 pounds, cut into serving pieces, or 2$^1/_2$ to 3 pounds chicken parts, trimmed of excess fat

Chopped fresh cilantro leaves for garnish

1. Combine all the ingredients except the garnish with 1 cup water in a covered pot large enough to hold the chicken in one layer. Bring to a boil over high heat; reduce the heat to medium-low or low (you want a slow simmer, nothing more) and cook, covered, for about 30 minutes, turning once or twice, until the chicken is cooked through. (You may prepare the recipe to this point and refrigerate the chicken in the liquid for up to a day before proceeding.)

2. Meanwhile, start a charcoal or wood fire or preheat a gas grill or broiler. The fire need not be too hot, but place the rack just 3 or 4 inches from the heat source.

3. Remove the chicken and dry it gently with paper or cloth towels. Boil the sauce over high heat until it is reduced to about 1 cup; discard the bay leaves and keep the sauce warm. Meanwhile, grill or broil the chicken until brown and crisp, about 5 minutes per side. Garnish, then serve the chicken with the sauce.

Chicken Adobo with Coconut Milk. In step 1, add about $^3/_4$ cup coconut milk, homemade (page 584) or canned, to the cooking liquid. In step 3, after the liquid has been reduced, add another $^3/_4$ cup coconut milk and reduce again until about 1 cup remains.

Asopao de Pollo PUERTO RICO
MAKES **4 SERVINGS**

TIME **1$^1/_2$ HOURS, LARGELY UNATTENDED**

This soupy rice and chicken stew is a cousin to Arroz con Pollo and Paella (pages 293 and 520), but it's much looser, and you must eat it right away; otherwise, the rice will absorb too much of the liquid and the stew will lose its soupy texture.

For the ham, it's best to buy a thick slice and cut it into chunks; you don't want shreds of thinly sliced ham. Very lean bacon or a piece of smoked pork will work nicely too. Some ideas for varying this dish: Don't add the chopped tomatoes, but put them in the bottom of each bowl before adding the soup; garnish with chopped fresh avocado; add fresh lime juice, onion, or chopped fresh cilantro leaves to taste, just before serving; or serve with chopped chiles in adobo (from a can) or Tomato-Chipotle Salsa (page 611).

3 garlic cloves, minced

2 teaspoons dried oregano

1 teaspoon salt, plus more to taste

1 teaspoon black pepper, plus more to taste

1 chicken, 3 to 4 pounds, cut into serving pieces, or 2$^1/_2$ to 3 pounds chicken parts, trimmed of excess fat

3 tablespoons corn, grapeseed, or other neutral oil

¼ pound ham, diced

1 onion, chopped

1 green bell pepper, stemmed, seeded, and chopped

3 tomatoes, cored and chopped

2 tablespoons drained capers

¼ cup green olives, pitted

1 cup long-grain rice

5 cups chicken stock, preferably homemade (page 160), or water

¼ cup fresh or frozen green peas, cooked, for garnish

¼ cup Roasted Red Peppers (page 470) or canned pimientos, for garnish, optional

1. Thoroughly combine the garlic, oregano, salt, and pepper in a small bowl and sprinkle on the chicken pieces.
2. Put the oil in a deep skillet or flameproof casserole, preferably nonstick, with a lid. Place over medium-high heat and wait a minute or so, until the oil is hot. Add the chicken, skin side down, and brown it well, rotating and turning the pieces as necessary, 10 to 15 minutes. Remove from the skillet and set aside. Add the ham, onion, bell pepper, and tomatoes to the skillet and cook, stirring occasionally, until the ham is browned and the onion softened, about 5 minutes. Return the chicken to the skillet, cover, and cook over medium-low heat for 30 minutes.
3. Raise the heat to medium and stir in the capers, olives, and rice. Add the chicken stock, then cover and simmer over low heat until the rice is softened but the mixture is still quite moist, about 15 minutes.
4. Season with salt and pepper, garnish with peas and red peppers if you like, and serve immediately.

Chicken and Lentil Tagine MOROCCO ■

MAKES **4 SERVINGS**

TIME **1 HOUR, LARGELY UNATTENDED**

A tagine is the name of both a stew and the pot it's served in. A North African specialty, it differs from other stews primarily in its sweet spicing. This one, featuring chicken, is bright yellow and alluring. Serve it with rice, warmed pitas, or crusty bread.

2 tablespoons extra virgin olive oil

1 chicken, 3 to 4 pounds, cut into serving pieces, or 2½ to 3 pounds chicken parts, trimmed of excess fat

2 garlic cloves, sliced

2 onions, sliced

2 tomatoes, cored and chopped

2 teaspoons ground turmeric

Salt and black pepper to taste

1 large bunch fresh cilantro or parsley sprigs, tied together with kitchen string

2 cinnamon sticks

1 cup dried lentils, picked over

1. Put the oil in a deep skillet or flameproof casserole, preferably nonstick, with a lid. Place over medium-high heat and wait a minute or so, until the oil is hot. Add the chicken, skin side down, and brown it well, rotating and turning the pieces as necessary, 10 to 15 minutes.
2. Stir in the garlic, onions, tomatoes, turmeric, and some salt and pepper. Pour in 1 quart water, along with the cilantro bundle and cinnamon sticks. Cover, turn the heat to low, and simmer for about 20 minutes.
3. Add the lentils, cover, and simmer until they're soft, about 25 minutes more. Discard the cilantro bundle and cinnamon sticks, season to taste with salt and pepper, and serve. (You can prepare the dish up to this point and let sit for a few hours or

cover and refrigerate for up to a day before reheating and serving; you may have to add a little water to thin the sauce a bit.)

Chicken and Chickpea Tagine. In step 3, substitute 1 cup cooked (page 431) or nearly cooked chickpeas for the lentils.

Chicken and Chickpea Tagine with Vanilla MOROCCO

MAKES **4 SERVINGS**

TIME **1 TO 1½ HOURS (WITH PRECOOKED CHICKPEAS), LARGELY UNATTENDED**

This tagine is similar to the preceding Chicken and Lentil Tagine but, with the addition of dates and vanilla, far more exotic. My version of this tagine may not compare with those that begin with toasting and grinding spices and peeling grapes, but it's easily executed (especially since the chicken is not browned first, which spares the cook a fair amount of time and energy) and, I think, quite divine.

Some things to look out for: First, work with dark-meat chicken only. In Morocco, the breast might be propped up out of the way so it almost steams and remains moist, but this is impractical without a special pot (also called a tagine). Be aware that tagines are on the dry side, so don't add liquid to the sauce unless it's threatening to burn. Home-cooked chickpeas and fresh tomatoes are, of course, preferable to the canned varieties, but in this dish the differences are not marked. Do, however, use a vanilla bean. If all you have is vanilla extract, omit the vanilla entirely.

2 tablespoons neutral oil, like corn or grapeseed

2 tablespoons butter

1 large onion, thinly sliced

2 garlic cloves, minced

Salt to taste

Pinch of freshly grated nutmeg

½ teaspoon ground cinnamon

1 teaspoon ground ginger

1 teaspoon ground cumin

1 teaspoon ground coriander

½ teaspoon black pepper

Pinch of cayenne

1½ to 2 cups chopped tomatoes (drained canned are fine)

4 cups cooked (page 431) chickpeas (canned are fine; drain and rinse first)

½ cup raisins or chopped pitted dates

½ vanilla bean

8 chicken thighs or 4 leg-thigh pieces, cut in 2

Chopped fresh cilantro or parsley leaves for garnish

1. Put the oil and butter in a large skillet or flameproof casserole with a lid and place over medium-high heat. When the butter melts, add the onion and cook, stirring occasionally, until it softens, 5 to 10 minutes (do not let it brown). Add the garlic, a large pinch of salt, and the spices and cook, stirring, for about 30 seconds. Add the tomatoes, chickpeas, raisins, and vanilla and bring to a boil, stirring (if the mixture is very dry, add about ½ cup water). Taste and add salt as necessary.

2. Sprinkle the chicken pieces with salt and nestle them into the sauce. Cover and, 5 minutes later, adjust the heat so the mixture simmers steadily but not violently. Cook until the chicken is very tender, 45 to 60 minutes. Taste and adjust the seasoning, then garnish and serve.

Chicken with Clams PORTUGAL

MAKES **4 SERVINGS**

TIME **ABOUT 1 HOUR**

I have never seen this wonderful stew appear in any other cuisine, but it is a great one, the brininess of the clams vastly improving the taste of the chicken. This dish is often served with Peasant-Style Potatoes (page 477).

2 tablespoons olive oil

1 chicken, 3 to 4 pounds, cut into serving pieces, or 2$^1/_2$ to 3 pounds chicken parts, trimmed of excess fat

Salt and black pepper to taste

2 large onions, sliced

1 tablespoon minced garlic

1 cup beef or chicken stock, preferably homemade (page 160)

2 dozen littleneck clams, well washed and scrubbed

Chopped fresh parsley leaves for garnish

1. Put the oil in a deep skillet or flameproof casserole, preferably nonstick, with a lid. Place over medium-high heat and wait a minute or so, until the oil is hot. Add the chicken, skin side down, and brown it well, rotating and turning the pieces as necessary and sprinkling them with salt and pepper as they cook, 10 to 15 minutes. As the pieces brown, transfer them to a platter.

2. Still over medium-high heat, add the onions to the pan and cook, stirring occasionally, until they brown nicely, about 15 minutes. Add the garlic and cook, stirring occasionally, for another minute or so. Add the stock and the chicken.

3. Cover and adjust the heat so the mixture simmers; cook for about 10 minutes. Add the clams and raise the heat to high; cook just until the clams open (if one or two are stubborn, don't worry about it; you can open them with a knife at the table), 5 to 10 minutes. Taste and adjust the seasoning, then garnish with the parsley and serve.

Braised Chicken with Vinegar ITALY

MAKES **4 SERVINGS**

TIME **45 MINUTES**

Slightly more complicated than the French version on page 303, resulting in more tender meat but less crisp skin. I'd make this with leg and thigh pieces rather than including breasts—which almost invariably dry out during braising—but the choice is yours. The sauce will keep things relatively moist in any case.

This is great with risotto (page 521) and a vegetable dressed with good olive oil.

3 tablespoons extra virgin olive oil

$^1/_4$ cup chopped pancetta or bacon

1 teaspoon chopped fresh rosemary leaves or $^1/_2$ teaspoon dried

2 fresh thyme sprigs or $^1/_2$ teaspoon dried

3 garlic cloves, peeled and lightly smashed

1 chicken, 3 to 4 pounds, cut into serving pieces, or 2$^1/_2$ to 3 pounds chicken parts, trimmed of excess fat

Salt and black pepper to taste

$^1/_2$ cup good-quality red wine or balsamic vinegar

Chopped fresh parsley leaves for garnish

1. Set a large skillet with a lid over medium-high heat. Add the oil, pancetta, herbs, and garlic and cook, stirring occasionally, until the pancetta browns, about 5 minutes. Remove the garlic and place the chicken in the skillet; brown it well, rotating and turning the pieces as necessary and sprinkling them with salt and pepper, 10 to 15 minutes.

2. Add the vinegar and $^1/_2$ cup water; raise the heat to high and cook for a minute or two, until the mix-

ture has reduced slightly and thickened somewhat. Reduce the heat to low and cover the skillet; cook until the chicken is tender and there is only the barest trace of pink near the bone, about 20 minutes more. Transfer the chicken to a warm platter and, if the sauce is thin, raise the heat to high, stirring and reducing the sauce as necessary until it is thick and glossy, just a few minutes. Taste the sauce and add salt and pepper to taste.

3. Spoon the sauce over the chicken, garnish, and serve.

Fast Braised Chicken with Vinegar. Made with boneless breasts, this is a fine, fast weeknight dish (30 minutes, tops): In step 1, the bacon is optional; quickly brown 4 pieces boneless, skinless chicken breasts in the oil on both sides. Add salt, pepper, vinegar, and $1/4$ cup water. Turn the heat to low and cover; cook until the breasts are done, less than 10 minutes. Uncover, taste and adjust the seasoning, garnish, and serve.

ROASTED, BROILED, OR GRILLED

Along with frying, these are the best cooking methods for adding flavor to chicken. Both (I consider grilling and broiling two sides of the same coin, as a broiler is little more than an upside-down grill) brown chicken beautifully, and both are easily mastered and usually convenient (whenever you don't have a grill handy or when the weather turns foul, use the broiler).

The key to roasting chicken is high heat—usually 450°F or higher. The key to grilling is variable heat; you want part of the grill hot enough to sear the chicken and part of it cool enough to cook the chicken through without setting it on fire. To achieve the same effect while broiling, you will have to adjust the height of the broiling rack.

Lemongrass Chicken SOUTHEAST ASIA
MAKES **4 SERVINGS**
TIME **1 HOUR (MORE IF YOU HAVE TIME)**

From Southeast Asia via New York, a recipe based on one developed by my sometime coauthor and longtime Asian hand, Jean-Georges Vongerichten. Included here not because it is "authentic" in the true sense but because the flavor is truly Thai and it's among the best Thai-inspired chicken recipes I know. Serve it with Sticky Rice (page 508). For information on Asian fish sauces like nam pla, see page 500.

2 lemongrass stalks, trimmed (page 143) and thinly sliced

2 large shallots, roughly chopped

2 garlic cloves, roughly chopped

1 small fresh red chile, stemmed and roughly chopped, or 1 teaspoon hot red pepper flakes

1 tablespoon nam pla or nuoc mam

1 chicken, 3 to 4 pounds, cut into serving pieces, or $2^1/2$ to 3 pounds chicken parts, trimmed of excess fat

Salt and black pepper to taste

1 tablespoon corn, grapeseed, or other neutral oil

1. Combine the first 5 ingredients in a food processor and puree roughly, stopping the machine to scrape down the sides once or twice. If possible, do this the day before you want to eat.

2. Loosen the chicken's skin wherever you can and spread the marinade between the meat and the skin, pressing it into the flesh. Sprinkle with salt and pepper. If time allows, wrap the chicken in plastic and let rest for several hours, refrigerated.

3. When you're ready to cook, preheat the oven to 500°F. Place the oil in a large nonstick skillet over high heat. When the oil is hot, place the chicken in the skillet. When the chicken begins to brown, 3 or 4 minutes later, put the skillet in the oven. Cook for about 8 minutes or until the bottom is crisp, then turn and return to the oven for another 5

minutes or so, again until crisp. Turn once more and cook until the chicken is done, about 5 minutes, then serve.

Spicy Grilled Chicken SOUTHEAST ASIA ■ ▨

MAKES **4 SERVINGS**

TIME **45 MINUTES, PLUS TIME TO PREHEAT THE GRILL**

No one does grilled chicken better than in Southeast Asia, where it seems to come straight from heaven. The key ingredients were all exotic and hard to find here just ten years ago, but now you can make this routinely. Once you try it, you probably will.

This is wonderful teamed with Sticky Rice (page 508) and Green Papaya Salad (page 174). But it's fine with any rice dish and vegetable, too, because it is really a star.

2 small fresh or dried chiles, preferably Thai

2 garlic cloves, peeled

One 1-inch piece fresh ginger, peeled and roughly chopped

1 tablespoon tamarind paste (page 585)

1 tablespoon sugar

1 cup coconut milk, homemade (page 584) or canned

1 chicken, 3 to 4 pounds, cut into serving pieces, or 2^1/2 to 3 pounds chicken parts, trimmed of excess fat

Salt and black pepper to taste

Lemon or lime wedges for serving

1. If you have fresh chiles, stem and seed them; if dried, soak in warm water for a few minutes until softened, then remove the stems and seeds. Place them, along with the garlic, ginger, tamarind paste, sugar, and coconut milk, in a food processor or blender. Process until the ingredients have broken down and the mixture is well combined.

Transfer the mixture to a saucepan and simmer over medium-low heat, stirring occasionally, until the sauce thickens, about 15 minutes. Remove from the heat. Cool a bit, then make a series of angular slashes in the chicken parts—two or three per part—and spread about half of the sauce on the chicken and into the slashes. (You can let the chicken rest, refrigerated, for an hour or two at this point.)

2. Meanwhile, start a charcoal or wood fire or preheat a gas grill or broiler. The fire should be only moderately hot, and the rack should be at least 6 inches from the heat source. You want to grill the chicken fairly slowly.

3. If you're broiling, spread a tablespoon or so of the sauce on a nonstick broiling or baking pan; place the chicken pieces on top and sprinkle them with salt and pepper. Broil or grill the chicken, turning and basting frequently with the sauce, until nicely browned all over and cooked through, 30 to 40 minutes. Brush once more with the sauce and serve hot or at room temperature with the lemon or lime wedges.

Soy Barbecued Chicken. Substitute ^{1}/2 cup Sweet Garlic Soy Sauce (page 590) for the tamarind paste and coconut milk.

Thai Barbecued Chicken. Omit the chiles and tamarind and use only half the amount of coconut milk. Add 2 lemongrass stalks, trimmed (page 143) and roughly chopped, 6 fresh cilantro sprigs, 2 teaspoons ground turmeric, and 2 tablespoons nam pla to the sauce. Process the sauce well—the lemongrass will never become completely smooth, but don't worry about it—and proceed as directed.

Grilled Chicken in Chipotle Sauce

MEXICO ■ ▨

MAKES **4 SERVINGS**

TIME **40 MINUTES, PLUS TIME TO PREHEAT THE GRILL**

A near no-brainer, as long as you have Tomato-Chipotle Salsa on hand. Even if you don't, not a lot of trouble, and one of the best grilled chicken recipes I know. See the variations for an even faster way to make this and one that works as an appetizer.

Don't serve this, however, to people who do not like hot food. There is no taming chipotles, though most people find them delicious.

You need rice here; Arroz a la Mexicana (page 517) would be ideal. Some slices of (cooling) avocado would be welcome as well.

8 chicken thighs or an equivalent amount of other parts

2 garlic cloves, peeled and cut in half

Corn, grapeseed, or other neutral oil as needed

Salt and black pepper to taste

1 cup Tomato-Chipotle Salsa (page 611) or more to taste

Chopped fresh cilantro leaves for garnish

Lime wedges for serving

1. Start a charcoal or wood fire or preheat a gas grill or broiler; the fire should be only moderately hot and the rack about 6 inches from the heat source.
2. Rub the chicken with the cut side of the garlic cloves, brush on the oil, and season with salt and pepper. Grill carefully so the chicken doesn't burn, making sure the skin crisps and browns and the interior cooks through; it will take about 20 minutes.
3. Brush the chicken heavily with the chipotle sauce on both sides and cook for just another minute or two. Serve, hot or at room temperature, garnished with cilantro and with the lime wedges on the side.

Chicken or Turkey Breasts in Chipotle Sauce (an appetizer). Substitute about 1 pound boneless, skinless chicken or turkey breast, which will take less than 10 minutes to grill. When done, cut into chunks and toss with the chipotle sauce. Serve on toothpicks.

Pork Chops in Chipotle Sauce. Bone-in pork chops, preferably from the shoulder end, can be done exactly like the chicken in the main recipe; cooking time will be a little shorter (do not allow them to dry out). Boneless pork (like tenderloin) can be used as in the chicken breast variation.

Two-Way Chicken SOUTHEAST ASIA ■ ▨

MAKES **4 SERVINGS**

TIME **30 MINUTES, PLUS MARINATING TIME**

Dark, glazed, and bittersweet, this is another marvel of simple cooking from Southeast Asia. It takes no longer than a classic European chicken sauté, yet when you make it you will impress not only your guests but yourself. You can stop after step 2 and have a Thai-style dish, which is good, or proceed to step 3 and have one of the best Vietnamese-style chicken dishes you've ever tasted. Either way, serve with rice. For information on Thai fish sauce (nam pla), see page 500.

1 chicken, 3 to 4 pounds, cut into serving pieces,
    or 2¹/₂ to 3 pounds chicken parts, trimmed of
    excess fat

3 tablespoons soy sauce

1 tablespoon minced garlic

1 tablespoon peeled and minced fresh ginger

1 teaspoon hot red pepper flakes

1 tablespoon corn, grapeseed, or other neutral oil

Lime wedges for serving, optional

Chopped fresh cilantro leaves for garnish

¹⁄₄ cup sugar, optional

2 tablespoons nam pla, optional

1. Place the chicken in a large bowl with the soy sauce and half the garlic, ginger, and hot pepper flakes. Toss well to coat and proceed or cover and refrigerate for up to a day.

2. Put the oil in a large deep nonstick skillet over medium-high heat. After a minute or so, when the oil is hot, remove the chicken from its marinade and add it, skin side down, to the skillet. Brown it well on both sides, rotating and turning the pieces as necessary, about 10 minutes (the soy will help it brown faster than usual). Then lower the heat and continue to cook, turning as necessary, until the chicken is cooked through, about 15 minutes longer, removing the pieces as they finish cooking.

3. At this point you can serve the chicken with the lime wedges if you like, hot, warm, or at room temperature, garnished with cilantro. Or proceed to the next step.

4. Turn the heat to low and add the sugar and remaining garlic, ginger, and hot pepper flakes to the skillet, along with 2 tablespoons water. Raise the heat to high and cook, stirring occasionally, until the sugar melts and the sauce thickens and becomes foamy (you'll know it when you see it), about 5 minutes. Add the nam pla and any juices that have accumulated around the chicken and cook for another minute, then return the chicken to the pan and cook, turning the pieces in the sauce a few times until they are nicely glazed and the chicken is hot. Remove it from the skillet, spoon the sauce over it, garnish with cilantro, and serve.

Grilled Chicken with Sesame KOREA ■ ■

MAKES **4 SERVINGS**

TIME **40 MINUTES, PLUS TIME TO PREHEAT THE GRILL AND MARINATING TIME**

Koreans are big on sesame seeds, and they're big on marinating. They're also big on big flavors, as this wonderful grilled chicken demonstrates.

You can buy pretoasted sesame seeds and even sesame seed powder at Korean markets, something you might consider if you become addicted to this cuisine; but toasting them takes no time at all.

If you're really feeling energetic, serve this with Potato Pancakes with Scallions and Kimchi (page 474). But plain white rice and a salad would also be fine, especially if the salad were made with seaweed, like the one on page 200 (omit the chicken or shrimp).

¹⁄₄ cup toasted sesame seeds (page 596)

2 tablespoons minced garlic

1 tablespoon peeled and minced fresh ginger

¹⁄₄ cup soy sauce

2 tablespoons dark sesame oil

2 tablespoons sugar or mirin

Salt and black pepper to taste

1 chicken, 3 to 4 pounds, cut into serving pieces, or 2¹⁄₂ to 3 pounds chicken parts, trimmed of excess fat

Chopped fresh scallion for garnish

1. Grind half of the toasted sesame seeds to a powder and set the other half aside for garnish. Combine this powder in a large bowl with the garlic, ginger, soy sauce, sesame oil, sugar, salt, pepper, and about ¹⁄₄ cup water. Make a couple of deep slashes on the skin side of each piece of chicken and add the chicken to the marinade. Let rest while you prepare the grill or refrigerate for up to 24 hours, turning occasionally.

2. Start a charcoal or gas grill; the fire should be only moderately hot and the rack about 4 inches from the heat source. (You can broil or roast the chicken if you prefer. To broil, follow the grilling directions; to roast, cook at 450°F for about 30 minutes.) Grill the chicken carefully—this mixture will burn easily—starting at the cooler part of the fire and, as the chicken's fat drips less, moving to a hotter part, turning the pieces as necessary to brown them.

3. Serve the chicken hot or at room temperature, garnished with the scallion and reserved sesame seeds.

Grilled Chicken with Chiles. Not much different in ingredients, but quite different in flavor: Omit the sesame seeds and oil. Add 2 or more small fresh chiles (preferably Thai), stemmed, seeded, and minced, or 2 teaspoons chili paste, or to taste. When the chicken is nearly done, baste it with a couple of tablespoons of fresh lime or lemon juice.

Tandoori Chicken INDIA

MAKES **4 SERVINGS**

TIME **45 MINUTES, PLUS TIME TO PREHEAT THE GRILL AND MARINATING TIME**

You cannot make "authentic" tandoori chicken without a tandoor, the clay oven closely associated with Indian cooking and used to make many of that country's wonderful breads. But you can replicate the seasonings and grill or broil it so that it becomes very similar to the original. It isn't difficult, and it's really rewarding.

Most tandoori chicken gets its bright red color from food coloring, but some cooks use a mild chile powder or a healthy dose of paprika, and that's what I do here.

Nice with Tomato Salad with Ginger (page 173) or Panfried Spicy Potatoes with Eggplant (page 476). Equally good with Paratha (page 559) or even plain rice.

1 chicken, 3 to 4 pounds, cut into serving pieces, or 2^{1}/2 to 3 pounds chicken parts, trimmed of excess fat

1 cup yogurt

1 tablespoon garam masala (page 594) or curry powder, preferably homemade (pages 592–593)

1 tablespoon paprika

1 teaspoon peeled and minced fresh ginger

1 teaspoon minced garlic

1 teaspoon ground coriander

1 teaspoon ground cumin

^{1}/2 teaspoon cayenne, or to taste (less if your curry powder is strong)

Salt to taste

1. Remove the skin from the chicken and make diagonal slashes in the flesh, right down to the bone. Combine all the remaining ingredients in a large bowl or roasting pan and marinate the chicken in this mixture in the refrigerator for at least a couple of hours or as long as overnight.

2. When you're ready to cook, start a charcoal or gas grill or preheat the broiler. The heat should be only moderate (the fire should be past its peak if you're using charcoal) and the rack 4 to 6 inches from the heat source. Grill or broil the chicken, turning each piece as it browns—you'll probably turn it several times during cooking—until done (there will be no traces of blood, which will be easy to see thanks to the gashes in the flesh), 20 to 30 minutes. Serve hot.

SAUTÉED CHICKEN

This is a huge category, worldwide probably the most popular way to cook chicken after grilling. Though panfrying can be messy—there is almost no way to avoid spattering during the initial browning—it smells great, and it's a wonderful way to add flavor and often crunch without much effort.

Chicken Biryani INDIA ■ ▪

MAKES **4 SERVINGS**

TIME **1 HOUR**

When you open the lid of a pot containing good biryani—the Indian equivalent of arroz con pollo or paella—the smell should drive you wild: chicken (or lamb), butter, and spices should dominate, followed by the subtle aroma of basmati rice. When it's prepared correctly, it seems to me, you can even smell the salt.

This is one of India's—indeed the world's—great dishes, and yet too often in restaurants it is underwhelming, underspiced, and made without care. The spice mixture makes the dish exotic, but though it must be made carefully it isn't difficult. (The chicken isn't browned, which actually makes it easier than many similar preparations.) One key is to use real butter (in sufficient quantity; I'm sure the ultimate biryani has more butter than this version) and good spices: cardamom in the pod, whole cloves, cinnamon stick, and real saffron. Good coarse salt doesn't hurt either and, needless to say, the better the chicken, the happier you'll be when you bite into it.

It's also important to leave the lid on as much as possible. I'm not one of these people who believes that rice must be cooked undisturbed (on the contrary, I think it stands up to all kinds of abuse), but in this instance you want to make sure the chicken cooks fairly quickly and that as much of the aroma as possible remains in the pot. The goal, remember, is to smell everything.

Serve with Dal (page 433) or any Indian-style vegetable.

4 tablespoons (½ stick) butter

1 large onion, chopped

Salt and black pepper to taste

Large pinch of saffron threads

10 whole cardamom pods, preferably 5 white or green and 5 black

5 whole cloves

1 cinnamon stick

1 tablespoon peeled and minced or grated fresh ginger

1½ cups basmati rice

3 cups chicken stock, preferably homemade (page 160)

1 chicken, 3 to 4 pounds, cut into serving pieces, or 2½ to 3 pounds chicken parts, trimmed of excess fat

¼ cup slivered blanched almonds, optional

1. Put 2 tablespoons of the butter in a deep skillet, flameproof casserole, or wide saucepan with a lid. Turn the heat to medium-high and wait a minute or so. Add the onion, along with some salt and pepper, and cook, stirring occasionally, until the onion softens without browning, 5 to 10 minutes. Add the spices and cook, stirring, for another minute.

2. Add the rice and cook, stirring occasionally, until it is glossy and all ingredients are well combined, 2 or 3 minutes. Add the stock, chicken, and some more salt and pepper and bring to a boil; cover and adjust the heat so the mixture simmers.

3. Cook, undisturbed, for about 25 minutes, then check. When the chicken and rice are both tender and the liquid has been absorbed, turn the heat off and re-cover. (If either chicken or rice is not quite done, add a little—no more than ½ cup—boiling water and re-cover with the heat still on.)

4. Meanwhile, melt the remaining 2 tablespoons butter in a small skillet over medium heat. Add the almonds if you're using them (if you're not, simply melt the butter) and brown them very lightly, just for 3 minutes or so. Pour this mixture over the biryani, sprinkle with a bit more salt, and re-cover; let rest for another 2 or 3 minutes. (You can keep the dish hot at this point in a 200°F oven for up to 30 minutes without sacrificing its quality.) Take the pot to the table, uncover, and serve.

Chicken Korma Pulao
Chicken with Yogurt and Rice   INDIA

MAKES **4 TO 6 SERVINGS**
TIME **ABOUT 1 HOUR**

This variation of Biryani (preceding recipe) is spicier, creamier, and somewhat more complicated. Go easy on the cayenne: this is meant to be a fragrant dish, not a fiery one.

Serve with Dal (page 433) or any Indian-style vegetable.

3 tablespoons butter or oil
1 chicken, 3 to 4 pounds, cut into serving pieces, or 2^1/$_2$ to 3 pounds chicken parts, trimmed of excess fat
Salt and black pepper to taste
2 large onions, sliced
1 tablespoon minced garlic
1 tablespoon peeled and minced fresh ginger
1 cinnamon stick
3 whole cloves
6 cardamom pods
1 tablespoon ground coriander
1 teaspoon ground cumin
^{1}/$_4$ teaspoon cayenne, or to taste
Pinch of saffron threads or 1 teaspoon ground turmeric
1^1/$_2$ cups basmati rice

1^1/$_2$ cups yogurt
Chopped fresh cilantro leaves for garnish

1. Put the butter in a large deep skillet, preferably nonstick, with a lid. Turn the heat to medium-high. When the butter melts, add the chicken, skin side down. Brown it well, rotating and turning the pieces as necessary and sprinkling with salt and pepper, 10 to 15 minutes. Transfer the chicken to a plate and add the onions to the pan. Cook, stirring occasionally, until they soften, 5 to 10 minutes.

2. Reduce the heat to medium and add the garlic, ginger, cinnamon, cloves, cardamom, coriander, cumin, cayenne, saffron, and some salt and pepper. Cook, stirring occasionally, for about 3 minutes. Add the rice and cook, stirring, until the mixture is well combined and the rice is glossy. Carefully add the yogurt and 1^1/$_2$ cups hot water and stir. Nestle the chicken in the rice mixture and cover tightly. Adjust the heat so the mixture simmers gently.

3. Cook for 20 to 30 minutes, until the liquid is nearly absorbed, the rice is tender, and the chicken is cooked through. If the mixture is soupy, boil out the excess water by turning up the heat a bit. If it is dry or the rice is undercooked (unlikely), add a little more water and continue to cook. Garnish with the cilantro and serve.

Arroz con Pollo   Chicken with Rice
CARIBBEAN ■

MAKES **4 SERVINGS**
TIME **ABOUT 1 HOUR**

You can make arroz con pollo, the Caribbean specialty, fast or slow. For weeknights, go with the stripped-down variation. But when you have a little time—and you don't need much—make the full-fledged version, with bacon for smokiness, real chicken stock for extra flavor, and saffron for best color and complexity.

If you don't have stock, don't worry too much. Since the chicken and vegetables are cooking in the liquid, the dish will taste good even if you make it with water.

A few slices of tomatoes would go well here, or any salad you like. You don't need much to round out this meal.

¼ pound good slab bacon, cut into ¼-inch dice

3 cups chicken stock, preferably homemade (page 160), or water

2 medium onions (about ½ pound), sliced

1 chicken, 3 to 4 pounds, cut into serving pieces, or 2½ to 3 pounds chicken parts, trimmed of excess fat

1 tablespoon minced garlic

1 red bell pepper, stemmed, seeded, and chopped

Salt and black pepper to taste

1½ cups white rice

1 ripe tomato, cored, seeded, and chopped

⅛ teaspoon ground allspice

2 bay leaves

Large pinch of saffron threads, optional

1 cup fresh or frozen peas, optional

Freshly minced parsley or cilantro leaves for garnish

Lemon or lime wedges for serving

1. Put the bacon in a deep skillet that has a lid and is large enough to hold the chicken; turn the heat to medium-high. Cook, stirring occasionally, until the fat is rendered and the bacon is browned and crisp, about 10 minutes. Meanwhile, warm the stock in a small saucepan.
2. Add the onions and the chicken, skin side down, to the bacon and brown the chicken well, rotating and turning the pieces as necessary, about 10 minutes. About halfway through the browning, add

the garlic and bell pepper and sprinkle everything with salt and pepper.

3. Transfer the chicken and everything else in the pan with a slotted spoon to a bowl. Add the rice and cook, stirring occasionally, until the rice is glossy, about 5 minutes. Add the tomato, allspice, bay leaves, saffron and peas if you're using them, and stock; stir, then return the chicken mixture to the pan. Adjust the heat so the liquid boils steadily but not violently and cover.
4. Cook for 20 minutes, until all the water is absorbed and the chicken is cooked through. (You can keep the dish warm over very low heat for another 15 minutes, and it will retain its heat for 15 minutes beyond that and still be good warm rather than hot.) Garnish with parsley and serve with lemon or lime wedges.

The Minimalist's Arroz con Pollo. Fast, easy, and still really good. Omit the bacon, stock, red pepper, tomato, allspice, bay leaves, and peas. Bring 3 cups water to a boil. Put 2 tablespoons olive oil in a skillet and turn the heat to medium-high. Add the onions and a sprinkling of salt and pepper. Cook, stirring occasionally, until the onions soften and become translucent, 5 to 10 minutes; meanwhile, remove the skin from the chicken. Add the rice to the onions and cook, stirring occasionally, until glossy. Add the saffron if you're using it, then the chicken, some salt and pepper, and the boiling water. Adjust the heat and finish cooking as directed.

Chicken Escabeche CARIBBEAN ■ ■
MAKES 4 SERVINGS
TIME AT LEAST 1 HOUR

Escabeche (see also pages 235 and 350) is a great way to flavor food, by marinating it after it's cooked rather than before. The cooked chicken (in this case) is bathed in an aromatic marinade. The soaking need not be long, but since the dish is best served at room temperature (it makes a good picnic option), you should plan to wait a while between cooking and eating. Use this as part of a picnic or buffet.

2 tablespoons extra virgin olive oil

1 chicken, 3 to 4 pounds, cut into serving pieces, or 2½ to 3 pounds chicken parts, trimmed of excess fat

Salt and black pepper to taste

1 large white or red onion, cut in half and sliced into half-moons

2 medium carrots, roughly chopped

2 celery stalks, roughly chopped

1 red bell pepper, stemmed, seeded, and roughly chopped

1 green bell pepper, stemmed, seeded, and roughly chopped

2 bay leaves

5 fresh thyme sprigs or 1 teaspoon dried

5 fresh marjoram or oregano sprigs or 1 teaspoon dried marjoram or ½ teaspoon dried oregano

1 small dried or fresh chile, optional

3 garlic cloves, peeled and lightly crushed

1 cup red wine or other vinegar

1 cup red wine

1 tablespoon sugar

1. Put the oil in a deep skillet or flameproof casserole, preferably nonstick, with a lid. Turn the heat to medium-high and wait a minute or so, until the oil is hot. Add the chicken, skin side down, and brown it well, rotating and turning the pieces as necessary and sprinkling them with salt and pepper as they cook, 10 to 15 minutes. Adjust the heat to prevent burning and continue to cook the chicken until it is done, another 15 minutes or so. Transfer the chicken to a deep platter. (Breasts will be done before legs and thighs; remove them first.)

2. Turn the heat to medium and add the onion, carrots, celery, peppers, bay leaves, herbs, chile if using, garlic, a pinch of salt, and about ½ teaspoon pepper. Cook, stirring occasionally, until the onion softens, about 10 minutes. Add the vinegar, wine, sugar, and 1 cup water and bring to a boil; lower the heat and simmer for about 10 minutes.

3. Pour the hot mixture over the chicken and let rest until the dish reaches room temperature before serving. Or cover well and refrigerate; the escabeche will keep for at least a couple of days (bring back to room temperature before serving).

Onion and Saffron Chicken NORTH AFRICA
MAKES **4 SERVINGS**

TIME **1 HOUR**

Little more than chicken braised with onions but with a couple of "secret" ingredients. The first is a lot of saffron. Saffron takes a bit of an initial investment (it's $30 or more an ounce), but it lasts a very long time; I use it regularly, and an ounce lasts me years. (Of course, I usually add it in pinches; this is a more extravagant dish.)

The second is preserved lemon. If you can buy this at a Middle Eastern store, you're in luck. If you can't, you'll have to make your own, but it takes weeks, so this recipe requires what you might call advance planning. However, the results are great even without the lemon.

Couscous (page 526) is a natural here, as is the Spicy Carrot Salad on page 191.

4 large or 8 small chicken thighs, excess fat removed

Salt and black pepper to taste

2 tablespoons extra virgin olive oil, plus more to taste

2 large onions, sliced

1 teaspoon saffron threads

¼ cup chopped fresh parsley leaves, plus more for
    garnish
Three ½-inch slices Preserved Lemon (page 598),
    optional

1. Season the chicken thighs with salt and pepper. Put the oil in a skillet with a lid over medium-high heat. Add the chicken, skin side down, and cook, rotating the pieces as necessary, until nicely browned, about 10 minutes; turn and brown the other side. Stir in the onions and saffron, cover, turn the heat to low, and cook for about 15 minutes.
2. Add the parsley and 1 cup water (or chicken stock, if you have it), then cover and cook for another 10 minutes. If you're using preserved lemon, add it now. Turn the heat to high and cook, uncovered, until the sauce reduces by half, about 10 minutes.
3. Taste and adjust the seasoning, then drizzle with a little olive oil, garnish with parsley, and serve.

Nketia Fla
Groundnut (Peanut) Stew with Chicken   GHANA
MAKES **4 SERVINGS**
  TIME **ABOUT 1½ HOURS, LARGELY UNATTENDED**

Groundnut (peanut) stew is savory, sweet, and rich. Its origins are in West Africa, where it remains a staple, but you see it in the Caribbean and even occasionally in the American South too. Traditionally made with raw African groundnuts, which are smaller than American peanuts, it is commonly made with peanut butter now.

For a true West African experience, serve this with Foo Foo (page 473).

2 tablespoons corn, grapeseed, or other neutral oil
8 chicken thighs, trimmed of excess fat

Salt and black pepper to taste
1 medium onion, chopped
One 1-inch piece fresh ginger, peeled and minced
½ teaspoon cayenne, or more to taste
1½ cups chopped tomatoes (canned are fine)
1 quart chicken stock, preferably homemade (page 160)
¾ cup natural peanut butter, preferably chunky

1. Put the oil in a deep skillet over medium-high heat. When it shimmers, put the chicken in the skillet, skin side down. Season with salt and pepper and brown well, rotating and turning them as necessary, 10 to 15 minutes. Transfer the meat to a plate and drain all but 2 tablespoons of the fat.
2. Add the onion and ginger and cook, stirring occasionally, until softened and fragrant, about 3 minutes. Stir in the cayenne and tomatoes and cook until the tomatoes have softened, about 5 minutes.
3. Return the chicken pieces to the casserole and add 3½ cups chicken stock. Bring to a boil, then lower the heat and simmer until the chicken is cooked through and tender, 20 to 30 minutes.
4. Whisk or blend together the remaining chicken stock and the peanut butter; stir the mixture into the stew. Cook for another 20 minutes or so, then taste, adjust the seasoning, and serve.

Chicken with Nuts and Raisins
MIDDLE EAST
MAKES **4 SERVINGS**
  TIME **ABOUT 45 MINUTES**

An ancient dish that is made almost everywhere nuts and grapes are grown. Serve with rice or bread.

2 tablespoons extra virgin olive oil
1 chicken, 3 to 4 pounds, cut into serving pieces, or 2½ to
    3 pounds chicken parts, trimmed of excess fat

Salt and black pepper to taste

4 garlic cloves, peeled and lightly smashed

1 large onion, sliced

1 cup dry white wine

1 cup walnuts or hazelnuts, roughly chopped

1 cup raisins or currants

Fresh lemon juice to taste

1. Put the oil in a deep skillet or flameproof casserole, preferably nonstick, with a lid. Turn the heat to medium-high and wait a minute or so, until the oil is hot. Add the chicken, skin side down, and brown it well, rotating and turning the pieces as necessary, 10 to 15 minutes. About halfway through the browning, add some salt and pepper along with the garlic, allowing the garlic to brown with the chicken. Transfer the chicken to a plate as it browns.

2. Reduce the heat to medium and add the onion; cook, stirring occasionally, until it softens and begins to color, 5 to 10 minutes. Add the wine and let it bubble away for a minute or so. Add the nuts and raisins and return the chicken to the pan, skin side up. Cover and turn the heat to low; cook until the chicken is done, 10 to 15 minutes more.

3. Add about a tablespoon of lemon juice, then taste and adjust the seasoning, adding more salt, pepper, or lemon juice as necessary. Serve immediately.

Chicken with Almond Garlic Sauce
SPAIN

MAKES **4 SERVINGS**

TIME **45 MINUTES**

This dish incorporates many of the distinctive elements of Spanish cuisine: almonds, garlic, saffron, and sherry. The addition of hard-cooked eggs to poultry dishes, traditional and still popular, is called pepitoria.

Serve with Yellow Rice (page 518) or any other rice or potato dish and whatever vegetable you like.

2 tablespoons extra virgin olive oil

1 cup blanched almonds

4 garlic cloves, peeled and lightly smashed

1 chicken, 3 to 4 pounds, cut into serving pieces, or 2½ to 3 pounds chicken parts, trimmed of excess fat

Salt and black pepper to taste

1 large onion, chopped

Large pinch of saffron threads

¼ cup chicken stock, preferably homemade (page 160), or water

2 hard-cooked eggs (page 338), optional

1 cup dry sherry

1. Put the oil in a deep skillet or flameproof casserole, preferably nonstick, over medium-high heat. After a minute or so, when the oil is hot, add the almonds and half the garlic and toast until golden. Remove with a slotted spoon and transfer to a food processor or blender. Let cool.

2. Add the chicken to the skillet, skin side down, and brown it well, rotating and turning the pieces as necessary, 10 to 15 minutes. About halfway through the browning, add some salt and pepper along with the onion, allowing the onion to brown with the chicken.

3. Meanwhile, add the saffron, stock, remaining garlic cloves, and one of the eggs to the food processor or blender. Process the mixture until a smooth paste is formed. Add this mixture to the skillet with the sherry and stir well.

4. Turn the heat to medium-low and simmer, uncovered, for 20 minutes, turning the chicken pieces occasionally; taste and adjust the seasoning. Meanwhile, slice the remaining egg. Transfer the

chicken with the sauce to your serving dish, garnish with the sliced egg, and serve.

Chicken with Green Olives MOROCCO

MAKES **4 SERVINGS**

TIME **45 MINUTES**

You see this dish made with a lot of liquid, the chicken simmered until tender, and you see it with the chicken sautéed and crisp, the liquid minimal. I opt for the second version, which I like very much.

> 2 tablespoons extra virgin olive oil
>
> 3 to 4 pounds chicken leg-thigh pieces, each cut into
>
>   2 pieces, trimmed of excess fat
>
> Salt and black pepper to taste
>
> 1 large onion, chopped
>
> 2 teaspoons peeled and minced fresh ginger
>
> About 1 inch cinnamon stick or $^1/_4$ teaspoon ground
>
> A few saffron threads or $^1/_2$ teaspoon ground turmeric
>
> 1 tablespoon minced garlic
>
> 1 bay leaf
>
> 1 teaspoon ground cumin
>
> 1 teaspoon paprika
>
> Pinch of cayenne, or to taste
>
> 2 cups chicken stock, preferably homemade (page 160)
>
> 2 cups good-quality green olives, pitted
>
> Fresh lemon juice to taste, at least 2 tablespoons
>
> Chopped fresh cilantro leaves for garnish

1. Put the oil in a deep skillet or flameproof casserole, preferably nonstick, over medium-high heat. After a minute or so, when the oil is hot, add the chicken, skin side down, and brown it well, rotating and turning the pieces as necessary and sprinkling them with salt and pepper as they cook, 10 to 15 minutes. Transfer the chicken to a plate and pour off all but 2 tablespoons of the fat.

2. Reduce the heat to medium, and add the onion, ginger, $^1/_2$ teaspoon or more pepper, the cinnamon, saffron, garlic, bay leaf, cumin, paprika, cayenne, and some salt and cook, stirring occasionally, for about 5 minutes, until the onion softens. Add the stock and raise the heat to medium-high. Return the chicken to the pan, skin side up, and cook at a lively simmer while you prepare the olives.

3. Put the olives in a small saucepan and cover with water; bring to a boil, drain, and repeat. Add the drained olives to the chicken. Cook until the chicken is done, about 15 minutes from the time you returned it to the pan. Add lemon juice, then taste and adjust the seasoning—it's unlikely, but not impossible, that the mixture will need some salt. Garnish and serve.

Chicken Thighs with Chickpeas

MOROCCO

MAKES **4 SERVINGS**

  TIME **40 MINUTES (WITH PRECOOKED CHICKPEAS)**

A deceptively easy weeknight chicken dish (as long as you have cooked or canned chickpeas around) with much of the exotic spicing that makes North African cuisine so enjoyable. With the added chickpeas and vegetables, it's also very nearly a one-pot meal; just serve it with rice or—more in keeping—couscous (page 526) and you're all set.

> 8 chicken thighs, about 2 pounds
>
> Salt and black pepper to taste
>
> 1 tablespoon ground cumin
>
> 1 teaspoon ground cardamom or 5 or 6 whole white
>
>   cardamom pods
>
> $^1/_2$ teaspoon ground cinnamon
>
> $^1/_4$ teaspoon cayenne, or to taste

2 tablespoons extra virgin olive oil

2 medium zucchini (about ½ pound), trimmed and cut into chunks

1 cup drained cooked (page 431) or canned chickpeas

1 cup peeled and seeded tomatoes (drained canned are fine)

½ cup chicken stock, preferably homemade (page 160), or water

1 tablespoon fresh lemon juice, or to taste

Chopped fresh cilantro leaves for garnish

1. Remove the skin from the chicken. Combine the salt, pepper, cumin, cardamom, cinnamon, and cayenne and rub this mixture all over the meat.

2. Put the oil in a deep skillet or flameproof casserole, preferably nonstick, with a lid. Turn the heat to medium-high and wait a minute or so, until the oil is hot. Add the chicken, smooth side down, and brown it lightly, rotating and turning the pieces as necessary, about 10 minutes.

3. Add the zucchini. Raise the heat to high and cook, stirring occasionally, until the zucchini begins to brown, about 10 minutes. Add the chickpeas and tomatoes and cook, stirring occasionally, for 5 minutes; do not let the mixture dry out completely.

4. Add the stock and bring to a boil; turn down the heat, cover, and cook for about 20 minutes, or until the thighs are tender and cooked through. Season with lemon juice, salt, and pepper; taste and adjust the seasoning, then garnish and serve.

Mushroom Sherry Chicken SPAIN

MAKES **4 SERVINGS**

TIME 1½ **HOURS, LARGELY UNATTENDED**

Dry sherry—ask for Fino—is among the world's most distinctive wines and also among the best for cooking. Here it's used as the basis for a rich but low-fat sauce that is an absolute classic. With bread or rice, this is an incredible dish.

2 tablespoons extra virgin olive oil

1 chicken, 3 to 4 pounds, cut into serving pieces, or 2½ to 3 pounds chicken parts, trimmed of excess fat

Salt and black pepper to taste

2 garlic cloves, chopped

1 large onion, chopped

½ pound fresh mushrooms, trimmed and sliced

1 cup dry sherry

¼ cup chopped fresh parsley leaves

1. Heat the oil in a large deep skillet with a lid over medium-high heat. Add the chicken to the skillet, skin side down, and brown it well, rotating and turning the pieces as necessary, 10 to 15 minutes. About halfway through the browning, add some salt and pepper.

2. Remove the chicken with a slotted spoon and drain all but 1 tablespoon of the fat. Add the garlic, onion, and mushrooms and cook until softened and lightly browned, about 5 minutes.

3. Return the chicken to the skillet and add the sherry. Bring the mixture to a boil, then lower the heat, cover partially, and simmer until the chicken is tender, about 45 minutes. If the mixture becomes dry, add some water.

4. Season to taste with salt and pepper, garnish with parsley, and serve.

Roast Mushroom Sherry Chicken. Preheat the oven to 400°F. Coat the bottom of a roasting pan with the oil and arrange the chicken pieces, skin side up, in the pan. Put the garlic, onion, and mushrooms around the chicken and sprinkle everything with salt and pepper. Pour the sherry into the pan and bake, uncovered, for 45 minutes, basting every 10 minutes. If the mixture becomes dry, add some water to the

■ make ahead   ■ serve at room temp./cold   ▨ 30 minutes or less

pan. Season to taste with salt and pepper, garnish with parsley, and serve.

Chicken with Mole Sauce MEXICO

MAKES **4 SERVINGS**

TIME **ABOUT 1 HOUR**

Real mole takes many forms, often using dozens of ingredients and taking days to make. This is an extremely simplified version of a dark, rich one that, not atypically, includes a bit of chocolate, for both flavor and color, a practice that does not, as some people believe, make the mixture sweet or even chocolaty. In fact, the presence of the chocolate should go undetected.

You can substitute dark-meat turkey for the chicken; cut the legs into pieces and increase the cooking time by about 50 percent or until the turkey is quite tender.

For a simpler, more straightforward flavor, try the chile sauce variation.

Serve with plain rice here, or Yellow Rice (page 518) or Arroz a la Mexicana (page 517), and a simple salad.

2 tablespoons lard or extra virgin olive oil

1 chicken, 3 to 4 pounds, cut into serving pieces,
    or 2$^{1}/_{2}$ to 3 pounds chicken or turkey parts, trimmed
    of excess fat

Salt and black pepper to taste

1 medium onion, chopped

2 garlic cloves, minced

$^{1}/_{2}$ cup fresh cilantro leaves, roughly chopped

1 cup chopped tomatoes with their juice

1 bay leaf

1 teaspoon fresh thyme leaves or $^{1}/_{2}$ teaspoon dried

1 cinnamon stick or 1 teaspoon ground

1 cup chicken stock, preferably homemade (page 160),
    or water

1 dried chipotle chile, or to taste

1 dried pasilla or ancho chile

$^{1}/_{2}$ cup pepitas (hulled green pumpkin seeds)

$^{1}/_{2}$ ounce unsweetened chocolate

1. Put the lard in a deep skillet or flameproof casserole, preferably nonstick, with a lid. Turn the heat to medium-high and wait a minute or so, until the lard melts. Add the chicken, skin side down, and brown it well, rotating and turning the pieces as necessary and sprinkling them with salt and pepper as they cook, 10 to 15 minutes. Use a slotted spoon to transfer the chicken to a plate.

2. Add the onion, garlic, and half the cilantro and cook, stirring occasionally, until the onion softens, about 5 minutes. Add the tomatoes, bay leaf, thyme, cinnamon, and stock, along with the chicken. Bring to a boil, lower the heat, and cover; the mixture should bubble steadily but not violently. Meanwhile, toast the chiles and the pepitas in a dry skillet over medium heat until browned and fragrant, about 5 minutes; when they're done (they'll probably start to pop), add them to the sauce.

3. When the chicken is tender, 20 to 30 minutes later, remove it from the sauce and keep it warm in a low oven. If the sauce seems very watery, reduce it over high heat. Add the chocolate to the sauce, taste the sauce, and add more salt and pepper if needed. Cool the sauce slightly, then transfer it to a blender and blend until smooth.

4. Return the sauce to the skillet, turn the heat to medium, and reheat. Taste and adjust the seasoning and serve the chicken topped with the sauce and the remaining cilantro.

Baked Chicken Mole. Do not cook the chicken on the stove, but prepare the sauce as directed. Marinate the chicken in the blended sauce for at least 30 minutes. Preheat the oven to 400°F. Place the chicken and marinade in a casserole or baking dish and bake, covered with foil, for 1 hour.

Pollo Enchilado Chicken with Chile Sauce. In step 2 omit the cilantro, tomatoes, bay leaf, thyme, pepitas, and chocolate. Cook the chicken as directed. Meanwhile, toast the chiles, then soak in hot water until softened, about 20 minutes. Place the chiles, onion, garlic, and cinnamon in a blender and blend until smooth. Season to taste with salt and pepper, place in the skillet with the chicken to reheat, and then serve the chicken with the sauce and the cilantro.

Almendrado de Pollo
Chicken in Almond Mole MEXICO

MAKES **8 SERVINGS**

TIME **ABOUT 1 HOUR**

One of the classic moles of Oaxaca, now popular throughout Mexico. Though no mole is simple, this is among the easiest and most straightforward, something you can actually consider making on a weeknight (especially if you're an experienced cook and can brown the chicken and make the sauce at the same time).

To be entirely authentic—or, at least, more authentic, since true authenticity is never really possible north of the border—you should roast most of the sauce ingredients before combining them in the skillet. Toast the almonds in a dry skillet, shaking occasionally, until fragrant; heat the peeled garlic in a dry skillet until lightly browned; roast the onions and tomatoes in a hot oven until blistered; and so on,

right down to toasting and grinding fresh whole spices. (In fact, old-style cooks brown unblanched almonds and then peel them.) All of this does make a difference, and if you have the time, please try it. Believe me, though, the mole will be sensational without these steps.

If you've never cooked with lard, have no fear: It has less saturated fat than butter and is still sold in virtually every supermarket. It remains a wonderful cooking fat. Serve with rice or Arroz a la Mexicana (page 517).

---

2 dried ancho or other fairly mild chiles (the dish should
    not be too fiery)

¹/₄ cup lard (preferred) or neutral oil, like corn or
    grapeseed

1 large white onion, chopped

1 cup blanched almonds

Salt and black pepper to taste

10 garlic cloves, peeled

3 or 4 tomatoes, cored and chopped (about 3 cups)

1 teaspoon ground cinnamon

Pinch of ground cloves

1 tablespoon red wine or other vinegar

1 chicken, 3 to 4 pounds, cut into serving pieces,
    or 2¹/₂ to 3 pounds chicken parts, trimmed of
    excess fat

Chicken stock, preferably homemade (page 160),
    as needed

Slivered almonds for garnish, optional

---

1. Soak the chiles in hot water to cover. When they're softened, after about 30 minutes, remove their stems and seeds.
2. Put half the lard in a deep skillet or flameproof casserole and turn the heat to medium-high. Add the onion and cook, stirring occasionally, until it begins to soften, 3 to 5 minutes. Add the almonds, salt, pepper, garlic, tomatoes, cinnamon, cloves,

chiles, and vinegar and cook, stirring occasionally, until the tomatoes begin to break up. Cool slightly (in this as in every instance, take care when pureeing hot liquid; it's best, if you have the time, to let the mixture cool to room temperature before pureeing), then puree in a blender. (You can prepare the dish to this point, cover, and set aside for several hours, until you're ready to eat.)

3. Meanwhile, or when you are ready to continue, put the remaining lard in a skillet, preferably nonstick. Turn the heat to medium-high and wait a minute or so, until the lard melts. Add the chicken, skin side down. Season it with salt and at least $1/2$ teaspoon pepper and brown it well, rotating and turning the pieces as necessary, 10 to 15 minutes.

4. Return the tomato mixture to the skillet or casserole and turn the heat to medium; bring to a gentle boil and cook, stirring frequently, until slightly thickened (if the mixture is too thick, add a bit of chicken stock). Taste and adjust the seasoning, then add the browned chicken and cook, uncovered, turning the chicken once or twice, until tender and cooked through, about 20 minutes. Garnish, if you like, and serve.

Pollo con Salsa Verde
Chicken in Green Sauce MEXICO

MAKES **4 SERVINGS**
TIME **40 MINUTES**

There are as many green sauces in the world as there are red ones, and this is one of my favorites. Fresh tomatillos are best for this dish, and those, like pepitas (pumpkin seeds) are increasingly easy to find.

Though it's probably at its best with Arroz a la Mexicana (page 517), you can serve this with almost any rice dish.

$1/3$ cup hulled pumpkin or squash seeds

1 cup chopped fresh cilantro leaves

1 cup roughly chopped scallion

1 cup husked, cored, and sliced fresh tomatillos or sliced drained canned

1 jalapeño or other fresh hot green chile, stemmed and seeded, or to taste

Chicken stock, preferably homemade (page 160), or water as needed

3 tablespoons lard or neutral oil, like corn or grapeseed

1 chicken, 3 to 4 pounds, cut into serving pieces, or $2 1/2$ to 3 pounds chicken parts, trimmed of excess fat

Salt and black pepper to taste

1. Put the pumpkin seeds in a dry skillet and toast over medium heat, shaking the pan occasionally, until they brown lightly, less than 5 minutes (they'll probably begin to pop). Combine in a blender with the cilantro, scallion, tomatillos, chile, and enough stock or water to make a smooth, thin paste. Set aside.

2. Put the lard in a large deep skillet or flameproof casserole, preferably nonstick, with a lid. Turn the heat to medium-high and wait a minute or so, until the lard melts. Add the chicken, skin side down, season it with salt and pepper, and brown it well, rotating and turning the pieces as necessary, 10 to 15 minutes. Pour out any excess fat.

3. Add the salsa verde to the pan with about $1/2$ cup more stock or water; the mixture should be loose, almost soupy. Turn the heat to high and bring to a boil, then adjust the heat so the mixture simmers gently. Cook, uncovered, until the chicken is tender and the sauce somewhat reduced, 20 to 30 minutes. Serve hot or warm.

Chicken alla Cacciatora

Chicken with Vegetables and Herbs   ITALY

MAKES **4 SERVINGS**

TIME **50 MINUTES**

The name refers to "hunter's style," whatever that is supposed to mean. I doubt that hunters in Italy, or anywhere else, ever carried all these ingredients, but this is a traditional southern Italian dish. This is a far better version than those popularized in the sixties, which were essentially chicken with canned tomato sauce.

This is great with bread, even better with a simple risotto (page 521).

3 tablespoons extra virgin olive oil

1 chicken, 3 to 4 pounds, cut into 8 pieces, or 2$\frac{1}{2}$ to
    3 pounds chicken legs and thighs

Salt and black pepper to taste

1 medium onion, sliced

1 tablespoon minced garlic

2 medium carrots, thinly sliced

$\frac{1}{4}$ pound shiitake or button mushrooms, stems removed
    and discarded (or reserved for stock), sliced

1 tablespoon juniper berries, lightly crushed

2 bay leaves

1 cup dry white wine

1 cup canned tomatoes, coarsely chopped,
    with their juice

Chopped fresh parsley leaves for garnish

1. Put the oil in a deep skillet or flameproof casserole, preferably nonstick, with a lid. Turn the heat to medium-high and wait a minute or so, until the oil is hot. Add the chicken, skin side down. Season it with salt and pepper and brown it well, rotating and turning the pieces as necessary, 10 to 15 minutes. Transfer the chicken to a plate and pour off the excess fat.

2. Reduce the heat to medium, add the onion, garlic, carrots, mushrooms, juniper berries, and bay leaves, and cook, stirring occasionally, until the onion softens, about 10 minutes. Add the wine and let it bubble away for a minute or two, then add the tomatoes and the chicken. Stir, then partially cover the pan; reduce the heat to low and cook for about 20 minutes, or until the chicken is cooked through. Garnish and serve.

Pasta alla Cacciatora. It's perhaps odd that this variation begins "omit the chicken," but aside from that the recipe is markedly similar: Omit the chicken. Brown about $\frac{1}{2}$ cup minced pancetta or bacon in 1 tablespoon olive oil and leave it in the skillet. Proceed with step 2. After adding the tomatoes, cook a pound of broad, long pasta, like fettuccine, and toss it with the sauce. Good with or without freshly grated Parmesan cheese.

Chicken with Vinegar   FRANCE

MAKES **4 SERVINGS**

TIME **40 MINUTES**

A French peasant classic, popularized internationally by the great Paul Bocuse. My version is leaner; for something approaching the glorious original, see the variation. Bread is a must, with salad to follow.

2 tablespoons butter or extra virgin olive oil

1 chicken, 3 to 4 pounds, cut into serving pieces, or 2$\frac{1}{2}$ to
    3 pounds chicken parts, trimmed of excess fat

Salt and black pepper to taste

$\frac{1}{4}$ cup minced shallot or scallion

1 cup good-quality red wine vinegar

1 tablespoon butter, optional

1. Preheat the oven to 450°F. Set a large skillet—preferably with steep sides to minimize spattering—over medium-high heat. Add 2 tablespoons butter and wait a minute. When it is good and hot, place the chicken in the skillet, skin side down. Cook undisturbed for about 5 minutes, or until the chicken is nicely browned. Turn and cook for 3 minutes on the other side. Season with salt and pepper.

2. Place the chicken in the oven. Cook for 15 to 20 minutes, or until it is just about done (the juices will run clear, and there will be the barest trace of pink near the bone). Transfer the chicken to an ovenproof platter and place the platter in the oven; turn off the oven and leave the door slightly ajar.

3. Pour most but not all of the cooking juices out of the skillet. Place the skillet over medium-high heat and add the shallot; sprinkle with a little salt and pepper and cook, stirring, until tender, about 2 minutes. Add the vinegar and raise the heat to high. Cook for a minute or two, or until the powerful smell has subsided somewhat. Add ½ cup water and cook for another 2 minutes, stirring, until the mixture is slightly reduced and somewhat thickened. Stir in the butter if desired.

4. Return the chicken and any accumulated juices to the skillet and turn the chicken in the sauce. Serve immediately.

Paul Bocuse's Poulet au Vinaigre. This is closer to the original and much richer: In step 1, brown the chicken in 8 tablespoons (1 stick) butter. In step 3, add 3 tablespoons butter to the reduced vinegar sauce, stirring until it thickens.

Mushroom and Cranberry Chicken
EASTERN EUROPE
MAKES **4 SERVINGS**
TIME **1 HOUR**

A standard braised chicken, with a not-so-standard tart fruit sauce whose acidity cuts through the richness of the meat to make a dish that is always a surprising hit.

The sauce can also be used with roast chicken or, for that matter, pork or turkey. Any of these can be served with Kasha (page 528) or any other simple grain dish, and a salad or vegetable.

1½ cups fresh cranberries, rinsed and picked over
⅓ cup sugar
2 tablespoons corn, grapeseed, or other neutral oil
1 chicken, 3 to 4 pounds, cut into serving pieces, or 2½ to 3 pounds chicken parts, trimmed of excess fat
Salt and black pepper to taste
3 garlic cloves, chopped
1 medium onion, chopped
½ pound button, cremini, or shiitake mushrooms, trimmed and sliced, shiitake stems discarded (or saved for stock)
1 fresh rosemary sprig, chopped, or 1 teaspoon dried
½ cup dry white wine

1. Combine the cranberries, sugar, and ¾ cup water in a small saucepan and turn the heat to medium-low. Cover and cook, stirring occasionally, until the berries are broken and the mixture is saucy, 10 to 15 minutes. Remove from the heat and set aside.

2. Meanwhile, put the oil in a deep skillet or flameproof casserole, preferably nonstick, with a lid. Turn the heat to medium-high and wait a minute or so, until the oil is hot. Add the chicken, skin side down, and brown it well, rotating and turning the

pieces as necessary, and sprinkling with salt and pepper as it cooks, 10 to 15 minutes. Finish the browning with the skin side up.

3. Stir in the garlic, onion, mushrooms, rosemary, and wine. Turn the heat to low, cover, and simmer until the chicken is tender, 20 to 30 minutes. Serve the chicken with the mushrooms and pan juices and top with the cranberry sauce.

Chicken with Apricots EASTERN EUROPE

MAKES **4 SERVINGS**

TIME **45 MINUTES**

The pairing of sweet dried-fruit sauce with poultry or pork is common not only throughout Eastern Europe but in North Africa, the Middle East, and parts of Western Europe as well. To prevent the dish from being too sweet, it's important to add a little vinegar or lemon juice.

The easiest way to "chop" dried apricots—which can be quite sticky—is with scissors.

Serve with a simple pilaf (page 513).

½ pound dried apricots, roughly chopped

3 tablespoons corn, grapeseed, or other neutral oil

1 chicken, 3 to 4 pounds, cut into serving pieces, or 2½ to 3 pounds chicken parts, trimmed of excess fat

1 onion, chopped

2 teaspoons sugar

½ teaspoon ground cinnamon

¼ cup dry white wine, stock, or water

2 teaspoons balsamic or sherry vinegar or lemon juice, or to taste

Salt and black pepper to taste

1. Bring 2 cups water to a boil in a small saucepan. Add the apricots, turn the heat to low, and simmer,

uncovered, for 20 minutes. Remove the apricots with a slotted spoon and reserve the liquid.

2. Meanwhile, put the oil in a deep skillet or flame-proof casserole, preferably nonstick. Turn the heat to medium-high and wait a minute or so, until the oil is hot. Add the chicken, skin side down, and brown it well, rotating and turning the pieces as necessary, 10 to 15 minutes. Remove the chicken and set aside; drain all but 2 tablespoons of fat from the skillet.

3. Turn the heat to medium-low and add the onion. Cook, stirring occasionally, until softened, about 5 minutes. Stir in the apricots, sugar, and cinnamon; add the wine, the reserved apricot liquid, and the vinegar. Raise the heat to high and cook, stirring occasionally and sprinkling with some salt and pepper, until the mixture has thickened and reduced by half.

4. Return the chicken to the skillet and stir to coat with the sauce. When the chicken is reheated, about 5 minutes, taste, adjust the seasoning, and serve.

Chicken with Apricots, Moroccan Style. Before browning the chicken, rub it with a mixture of 1 teaspoon ground cinnamon, 1 teaspoon ground cumin, ½ teaspoon ground coriander, ½ teaspoon ground ginger, and ½ teaspoon cayenne. Proceed as directed, browning the chicken over slightly lower heat to avoid burning the spices. Garnish with chopped fresh cilantro leaves before serving.

Chicken in Garlic Sour Cream ROMANIA

MAKES **4 SERVINGS**

TIME **40 MINUTES**

Boiled potatoes and sour cream are a classic Eastern European combination, but this recipe takes the idea a step further to produce a rich, full-flavored main course that is especially great in winter. Serve with a light salad and rice or crisp bread.

Salt and black pepper to taste

2 large potatoes, peeled and cut into ½-inch cubes

3 tablespoons butter or extra virgin olive oil

1 chicken, 3 to 4 pounds, cut into serving pieces, or 2½ to 3 pounds chicken parts, trimmed of excess fat

4 garlic cloves, minced

½ cup chopped fresh scallion, plus more for garnish

½ cup chopped fresh dill leaves, plus more for garnish

¼ cup sour cream

1. Bring a large pot of water to a boil and add salt. Add the potatoes and cook until tender, about 15 minutes. Drain and set aside.

2. Meanwhile, put the butter in a deep skillet or flameproof casserole, preferably nonstick. Turn the heat to medium-high and wait a minute or so, until the butter melts. Add the chicken, skin side down, and brown it well, rotating and turning the pieces as necessary, 10 to 15 minutes. Remove the chicken from the skillet and set aside. Drain all but 3 tablespoons of the fat.

3. Reduce the heat to medium-low and add the garlic, scallion, and dill. Cook, stirring occasionally, until the garlic is softened and the mixture fragrant, about 1 minute. Add the potatoes to the skillet and stir to coat with the herb mixture; add the chicken pieces and stir again. Turn the heat to low and stir in the sour cream.

4. Season to taste with salt and pepper and simmer very gently for another 10 minutes. Garnish with scallion and dill and serve.

Provence-Style Chicken FRANCE

MAKES **4 SERVINGS**

TIME **40 TO 50 MINUTES**

There are more versions of this dish than you can count. You can add cayenne if you like or a little wine or stock. Some olive oil at the end contributes freshness, and ½ cup or more of rice cooked with the chicken (add twice as much boiling water or stock as rice, at about the same time) makes the dish more substantial. And so on. In short, it's one of those universal recipes, but in all forms associated with southern France. Bread is the most common accompaniment, but this saucy chicken is good over rice or other grains as well.

2 tablespoons extra virgin olive oil

4 chicken leg-thigh pieces, each cut into 2 pieces

Salt and black pepper to taste

1 tablespoon minced garlic

2 anchovy fillets, minced, optional

1 large or 2 medium onions, chopped

1 red bell pepper, stemmed, seeded, and chopped

Large pinch of saffron threads, optional

1 teaspoon fresh marjoram (preferred), oregano, or thyme or ¼ teaspoon dried

2 tablespoons drained capers

2 cups cored and chopped tomatoes (canned are fine), with their liquid

1 cup good-quality black or green olives (or a mixture), pitted

Chopped fresh parsley leaves for garnish

1. Put the oil in a large deep skillet, preferably nonstick, and turn the heat to medium. A minute later, add the chicken pieces, skin side down, and brown well, seasoning with salt and pepper and adjusting the heat and rotating the pieces so they brown evenly, about 10 minutes. When they are done, transfer them to a plate.

2. Add the garlic and anchovies if you're using them and cook, stirring occasionally, until the garlic begins to take on some color, about 5 minutes. Add the onions and the bell pepper and cook, stirring occasionally, until they soften, about 10 minutes. Add the saffron, herb, and capers and stir, then add the tomatoes and olives. Stir, bring to a boil, and return the chicken, skin side up, to the skillet.

3. Cover and cook over medium-low heat—the mixture should bubble, but gently—until the chicken is done, 20 to 30 minutes. Garnish and serve.

Coq au Vin FRANCE

MAKES **4 SERVINGS**

TIME **ABOUT 1 HOUR**

My version of an old-fashioned French recipe, with a little corner cutting. If you ever come across an old, tough chicken, this is the place to use it; increase the cooking time as necessary until the bird becomes tender. If you use one of our typical chickens, it's actually a pretty quick recipe to prepare. Use a decent but not too expensive red wine.

Pearl onions are quite nice here, even frozen ones. If you start with fresh ones, however, which are best, drop them into boiling water for 30 to 60 seconds to make peeling (much) easier.

The French would serve crusty bread with this, and you couldn't do any better.

¼ pound good slab bacon, cut into ¼-inch dice

20 pearl onions, peeled, or 1 large onion, sliced

1 chicken, 3 to 4 pounds, cut into serving pieces, or 2½ to 3 pounds chicken parts, trimmed of excess fat

6 garlic cloves, peeled

Salt and black pepper to taste

2 cups chicken stock, preferably homemade (page 160)

2 cups Burgundy (Pinot Noir) or other fruity red wine

2 bay leaves

Several fresh thyme sprigs

Several fresh parsley sprigs

½ pound button mushrooms, trimmed and roughly chopped

2 tablespoons butter

Chopped fresh parsley leaves for garnish

1. Put the bacon in a large deep skillet that will hold the chicken and has a lid. Turn the heat to medium-high and cook, stirring occasionally, until the fat is rendered and the bacon is browned and crisp, about 10 minutes. Add the onions and chicken, skin side down, and brown the chicken well, rotating and turning the pieces as necessary, about 10 minutes. About halfway through the browning, add the garlic and sprinkle the chicken with salt and pepper.

2. Pour or spoon off any excess fat and add the stock and wine, along with the herbs. Adjust the heat so that the mixture bubbles gently but steadily. Cover and cook for about 20 minutes, or until the chicken is tender and cooked through. (If you like, you can remove the breast pieces, which will finish cooking first, and keep them warm while the leg pieces remain.) Transfer the chicken to a platter and keep warm. Remove the garlic, bay leaves, and herb sprigs and discard.

3. Add the mushrooms to the remaining liquid and turn the heat to high. Boil as quickly as you can until the mixture is reduced by about three fourths and becomes fairly thick and saucy. Lower the heat, stir in the butter, and return the chicken to the pan, just to reheat a bit and coat with the sauce. Taste and adjust the seasoning, then garnish with parsley and serve.

Chicken Breasts with Sage ITALY ■

MAKES **4 SERVINGS**

TIME **30 MINUTES**

It's still rare to see boneless chicken breasts in Italy, probably because people understand how difficult it is to keep them from drying out. The simplest solution is to leave them on the bone, which helps retain moisture (and, arguably, makes for a nicer presentation). This is a nice, simple, fast stovetop braise, especially pleasant in spring and fall. (The first variation, which uses boneless breasts, is even faster.) Fresh herbs are a must.

Serve with plain white rice or—even better, of course—any risotto (pages 521–522).

> 3 tablespoons extra virgin olive oil, butter, or a
>   combination
> 2 garlic cloves, peeled and lightly crushed
> 20 or 30 fresh sage leaves or 3 or 4 fresh rosemary or
>   thyme sprigs
> 4 chicken breast halves, preferably with wings attached
> Salt and black pepper to taste
> 1/4 cup plus 1 tablespoon balsamic vinegar or fresh lemon
>   juice
> 1/2 cup chicken stock, preferably homemade (page 160),
>   or water
> Chopped fresh parsley leaves for garnish

1. Put the oil in a deep skillet or flameproof casserole, preferably nonstick, with a lid. Turn the heat to medium-high and wait a minute or so, until the oil is hot. Add the garlic and half the sage, then the chicken, skin side down, and brown it well, rotating the pieces as necessary (you don't really have to brown the bone side); the process will take 5 to 10 minutes. Turn the meat browned side up and sprinkle it with salt and pepper.
2. Add the remaining sage, along with the 1/4 cup vinegar and the stock. Turn the heat down to low

and cover; cook until the chicken is tender and no trace of blood remains near the bone, 15 minutes or so.

3. Transfer the chicken to a warm platter and, if the sauce is thin, raise the heat to high, stirring and reducing the sauce as necessary until it is thick and glossy, just a few minutes. Stir in the remaining tablespoon of vinegar or lemon juice. Taste the sauce and add salt and pepper. Spoon the sauce over the chicken, garnish, and serve.

Boneless Chicken Breasts with Sage. Start with 4 pieces of boneless breast, about 1 1/2 pounds. Add the garlic and sage (all at once) and brown the breasts well on both sides, adjusting the heat and rotating and turning the pieces as necessary until done, about 10 minutes. Transfer to a platter and add the 1/4 cup vinegar or lemon juice along with 1/4 cup water. Cook, stirring and scraping with a wooden spoon to incorporate any solids into the sauce. If you like, stir in 1 tablespoon butter at this point to enrich the sauce. Add the remaining vinegar or lemon juice, taste and adjust the seasoning, and serve.

Chicken Breasts with Mint. You can use this variation with either bone-in or boneless breasts. Substitute 1 cup chopped fresh mint leaves for the sage. Add half of them, along with a teaspoon of sugar, when you first turn the chicken breasts (after one side has been browned). Add the other half to the sauce after removing the chicken.

FRIED CHICKEN

Frying chicken—or anything else—takes good-quality oil (page 93), lots of space, and a deep vessel. Given that, and a little bit of practice, it can become routine and almost effortless.

I like fried chicken from the American South, but I don't think it can touch any of the following recipes, which have a ton more flavor.

Fried Chicken, Caribbean Style

CARIBBEAN ■ ■

MAKES **4 SERVINGS**

TIME **2 HOURS, LARGELY UNATTENDED**

Whenever you're deep-frying, remember this: A vessel with deep sides will reduce spattering. A broader vessel will allow you to fry more pieces at once but will require considerably more oil; a narrower vessel will conserve oil but will mean you must cook in batches. The choice is yours.

Coconut Rice (page 516) or Plantains in Coconut Milk (page 472) would be sensational here, but as you know, fried chicken goes well with anything.

8 chicken thighs or an assortment of chicken pieces,
    trimmed of excess fat

Salt and black pepper to taste

1 tablespoon curry powder, preferably homemade
    (pages 592–593)

$1/2$ teaspoon ground allspice

2 tablespoons minced garlic

1 Scotch bonnet (habanero) or other fresh chile, stemmed,
    seeded, and minced, or cayenne to taste, optional

1 egg

1 cup flour

Corn, grapeseed, or other neutral oil for deep-frying

Lemon or lime wedges for serving

1. Toss the chicken in a bowl with the salt, pepper, curry, allspice, garlic, chile, 2 tablespoons water, and the egg. When thoroughly combined, blend in the flour, using your hands. The mixture will be a mess; keep mixing until most of the flour is blended with the other ingredients and coat the chicken—it will never be perfect, so don't spend too much time on it. Refrigerate for at least an hour and up to a day.

2. When you're ready to cook, put about 2 inches of oil in a skillet or large deep saucepan and turn the heat to medium-high. When the oil reaches about 325°F—a pinch of flour will sizzle—you can begin to fry the chicken. Dredge each piece in any flour that remains in the bottom of the bowl and gently place in the oil. Do not crowd; cook in batches if necessary (this chicken will stay hot for a good 15 to 20 minutes after it's done anyway). Fry, turning 3 or 4 times, until nicely browned all over, about 20 minutes. At that point the pieces will be done, but if you want to make sure, make a small slit in each piece and check for blood.

3. Serve hot, warm, at room temperature, or cold, with lemon or lime wedges.

Fried Chicken, Thai Style SOUTHEAST ASIA. Not starkly different, but noticeably so: Omit the allspice; use a Thai chile if you have it. Add 1 tablespoon peeled and minced fresh ginger to the mix and use 2 tablespoons soy sauce or nam pla (Thai fish sauce) instead of water. Everything else remains the same.

Creole Fried Chicken CARIBBEAN ■

MAKES **4 SERVINGS**

TIME **40 MINUTES, PLUS MARINATING TIME**

American fried chicken is almost always covered in batter or another dry coating. Elsewhere, however, chicken is often fried after a brief marinade in a sauce; the results are not as crunchy but really different and quite delicious. (Plus, fried chicken without batter keeps better.) If you want a supercrunchy fried chicken, see the previous recipe. The marinade for this Cuban version traditionally contains sour orange juice, but a mixture of orange and lime juice is a good substitute. Serve this with Arroz a la Mexicana (page 517).

4 garlic cloves, minced

1 small onion, sliced

1 teaspoon dried oregano

1 teaspoon ground cumin

$\frac{1}{4}$ cup fresh orange juice

$\frac{1}{4}$ cup fresh lime juice

1 chicken, 3 to 4 pounds, cut into serving pieces,
    or 2$\frac{1}{2}$ to 3 pounds chicken parts,
    trimmed of excess fat

Corn, grapeseed, or other neutral oil for deep-frying

1. Combine the first 6 ingredients in a large dish, then add the chicken and turn to coat with the marinade. Cover and refrigerate for at least 30 minutes. When ready to cook, remove the chicken from the marinade.

2. Heat 2 inches of oil over medium-high heat in a large deep skillet or wide saucepan with a lid. When the oil reaches 350°—use an instant-read thermometer or a pinch of flour or cornmeal, which will sizzle at the right temperature—raise the heat to high and begin to add the chicken pieces slowly but steadily, skin side down (if you add them all at once, the temperature will plummet). When they have all been added, cover the skillet, reduce the heat to medium-high, and set a timer for 7 minutes. After 7 minutes, uncover the skillet, turn the chicken, and continue to cook, uncovered, for another 7 minutes. Turn the chicken skin side down again and cook for about 5 minutes more, turning as necessary to ensure that both sides are golden brown.

3. As the chicken pieces finish cooking (the juices near the bone will run clear), remove them from the skillet and drain them on paper towels. Serve hot, warm, or at room temperature.

Fried Chicken, Parsi Style INDIA ■ ■
MAKES **4 SERVINGS**
TIME **2 HOURS, LARGELY UNATTENDED**

Yet another take on spicy fried chicken, this one bordering on fiery, but with a pleasant, feathery crust from the eggs. Marinate for up to a day if you like.

You could serve this with almost anything, ranging from plain old cole slaw to Stewed Apples and Eggplant (page 458) to any of the Indian breads (pages 559–565).

8 chicken thighs or an assortment of chicken pieces,
    trimmed of excess fat

Salt and black pepper to taste

1 tablespoon minced garlic

1 tablespoon peeled and minced fresh ginger

2 jalapeños or 4 small fresh chiles, stemmed, seeded, and
    minced

1 tablespoon cumin seeds

1 teaspoon ground coriander

Corn, grapeseed, or other neutral oil for deep-frying

1 cup flour

4 eggs, beaten

Lime wedges for serving

1. Use a sharp knife to make deep gashes, right down to the bone, on the skin side of the chicken pieces. Combine the salt, pepper, garlic, ginger, chiles, cumin, and coriander. Rub the chicken all over with this mixture. Wrap tightly in plastic and refrigerate for at least an hour and up to a day.

2. When you're ready to cook, put about 2 inches of oil in a skillet or large deep saucepan and turn the heat to medium-high. When the oil reaches about

325°F—a pinch of flour will sizzle—you can begin to fry the chicken. Dredge each piece in the flour, then dip in the egg; gently place in the oil. Do not crowd; cook in batches if necessary (this chicken will stay hot for a good 15 to 20 minutes after it's done anyway). Fry, turning 3 or 4 times, until nicely browned all over, about 20 minutes. At that point the pieces will be done, but if you want to make sure, make a small slit in each piece and check for blood.

3. Serve hot, warm, at room temperature, or cold, with the lime wedges.

BONELESS, SKINLESS CHICKEN BREASTS AND THIGHS

Boneless, skinless breasts are undeniably popular, but this is due in large part to their low fat content, which rivals that of even lean white fish. If it's ease of cooking and low fat you're after, you cannot go wrong with boneless, skinless breasts. Boneless thighs, which are now widely available, can be substituted in any of these recipes; the cooking time will be marginally longer.

STIR-FRYING BONELESS CHICKEN

Not unlike other methods of panfrying, stir-frying—usually—has one important difference: you cut the food into bite-sized pieces before cooking it instead of afterward. This makes for lightning-fast cooking.

Generally speaking, with home equipment it's best to stir-fry most or even all of the ingredients separately, combining them only at the last minute. That's the only way to brown each of them and to cook them by direct heat instead of simmering the pieces in their own juices, which is what will happen if you crowd them, no matter how high the heat. Most of these recipes reflect that reality.

Stir-Fried Chicken with Walnuts

CHINA ▓
MAKES **4 SERVINGS**
TIME **20 MINUTES**

A basic stir-fry and—like every other—one that you can vary however you like. Cashew nuts or peanuts are also great here. Start with Spicy Cold Celery (page 17) and serve this with rice.

2 tablespoons peanut or neutral oil, like corn or grapeseed

1 pound boneless, skinless chicken breasts or thighs, cut into roughly 1-inch chunks

1 cup walnuts

1 tablespoon minced garlic

1 tablespoon peeled and minced fresh ginger

4 scallions, trimmed and roughly chopped

1/2 cup chicken stock, preferably homemade (page 160), or water

1 tablespoon Shaoxing wine, dry sherry, or white wine

2 tablespoons soy sauce

1 teaspoon dark sesame oil

1. Put the oil in a deep skillet or wok, preferably nonstick, over medium-high heat. When it smokes, add the chicken and cook, stirring occasionally, until the chicken browns a bit, 3 or 4 minutes. Remove the chicken with a slotted spoon. Add the walnuts, garlic, and ginger and cook, stirring, for about 30 seconds.

2. Add the scallions, then almost immediately the stock, wine, and soy sauce. Cook for a moment, then return the chicken to the pan. Cook, stirring, for 1 minute more, then stir in the sesame oil and serve immediately.

Kung Pao Chicken CHINA

MAKES **4 SERVINGS**

TIME **20 MINUTES**

You can find this dish at almost any Chinese restaurant, but it is easy to make at home—and usually better, too. Some people deep-fry the chicken first, but stir-frying is much quicker and less complicated, and the results are still great. Serve with plain rice.

> **¹/₂ teaspoon cornstarch**
>
> **1 tablespoon Shaoxing wine or dry sherry**
>
> **1¹/₂ to 2 pounds boneless, skinless chicken breasts, cut into ¹/₂-inch chunks**
>
> **3 tablespoons corn, grapeseed, or other neutral oil**
>
> **5 small dried chiles**
>
> **2 garlic cloves, minced**
>
> **One ¹/₂-inch piece fresh ginger, peeled and minced**
>
> **1 teaspoon sugar**
>
> **3 tablespoons soy sauce**
>
> **1 teaspoon dark sesame oil**
>
> **1 scallion, trimmed and chopped**
>
> **¹/₂ cup roasted peanuts, chopped, for garnish**

1. Whisk the cornstarch into the wine until it dissolves, then coat the chicken pieces with the mixture. Marinate while you prepare the remaining ingredients.
2. Heat the oil in a wok or large nonstick skillet over medium-high heat. Add the chiles and cook, stirring occasionally, until slightly blackened, about 5 minutes. Add the garlic and ginger and cook until fragrant, about 10 seconds, then stir in the chicken. Cook the chicken, stirring constantly, until it loses its pinkness, about 5 minutes.
3. Turn the heat to low, then sprinkle the sugar over the chicken; stir in the soy sauce and cook for another 5 minutes, stirring occasionally. Remove from the heat, then stir in the sesame oil and scallion. Garnish with peanuts and serve.

Kung Pao Shrimp. Substitute 2 pounds peeled shrimp for the chicken. Cooking time will be about the same.

Thai Spicy Chicken. Omit the wine and cornstarch. Substitute nam pla (Thai fish sauce) for the soy sauce and chopped fresh cilantro leaves for the peanuts.

Stir-Fried Chicken with Creamed Corn HONG KONG

MAKES **4 SERVINGS**

TIME **20 MINUTES**

Hong Kong, where East and West have met and exchanged ideas for a long time, has devised some dishes that to most American palates may seem more bizarre than stewed pigs' ears. Among them is this recipe, stir-fried chicken with creamed corn. Yes: canned cream corn, as in Jolly Green Giant or Clarence Birdseye.

It's not fancy, but it's a good home-cooked dish, quick, easy, and convenient.

> **1 pound boneless, skinless chicken breasts or thighs, cut into roughly 1-inch chunks**
>
> **2 tablespoons soy sauce**
>
> **1 teaspoon dark sesame oil**
>
> **1 tablespoon Shaoxing wine, dry sherry, or white wine**
>
> **2 tablespoons peanut or neutral oil, like corn or grapeseed**
>
> **1 tablespoon minced garlic**
>
> **1 tablespoon peeled and minced fresh ginger**
>
> **1 small fresh chile, stemmed, seeded, and minced, or hot red pepper flakes to taste**
>
> **One 15-ounce can creamed corn**
>
> **1 cup fresh, frozen, or canned corn kernels**
>
> **Chopped fresh cilantro leaves for garnish**

1. In a small bowl, mix the chicken with the soy sauce, sesame oil, and wine. Marinate while you prepare the other ingredients.
2. Put the oil in a deep skillet or large wok, preferably nonstick, and turn the heat to high. Drain the chicken. When the oil is hot, add the chicken to the skillet and cook, undisturbed, until the bottom browns, about 2 minutes. Stir once or twice and cook for another 2 minutes. Turn the heat to medium-low.
3. Add the garlic, ginger, and chile and stir; 15 seconds later, add both types of corn. Cook, stirring occasionally, until heated through, 3 or 4 minutes. Garnish and serve over white rice.

Stir-Fried Beef with Creamed Corn. Substitute 1 pound ground beef for the chicken. Proceed as directed, breaking it into small pieces while browning.

Ginger Chicken THAILAND ■

MAKES **4 SERVINGS**

TIME **30 MINUTES**

A simple stir-fry, one made with a great deal of ginger and typical Thai seasonings. It makes a great weeknight meal; serve it with jasmine or sticky rice. Information on Thai fish sauce (nam pla) is on page 500.

2 small fresh or dried chiles, preferably Thai

2 tablespoons corn, grapeseed, or other neutral oil

3 shallots or 1 medium onion, sliced

2 tablespoons minced garlic

One 3-inch piece fresh ginger, peeled and cut into thin matchsticks or minced

1 pound boneless, skinless chicken breast, cut into 1/2- to 3/4-inch chunks

3 fresh or reconstituted (page 112) dried shiitake mushrooms, stems discarded, sliced

2 scallions, trimmed and chopped

2 tablespoons soy sauce

2 tablespoons nam pla

2 teaspoons sugar

Fresh lime juice to taste

Salt and black pepper to taste

1. If you have fresh chiles, stem, seed, and chop them; if dried, soak in warm water for a few minutes until softened, then remove the stems and seeds and chop them. Heat a wok or large deep skillet over medium-high heat for 2 to 3 minutes. Add the oil, swirl it around, and add the shallots. Cook, stirring occasionally, until softened, about 2 minutes. Add the garlic, about two thirds of the ginger, and the chiles and cook, stirring, for 15 seconds.
2. Add the chicken and raise the heat to high. Stir the chicken once, then let it sit for a minute before stirring again. Cook, stirring occasionally, until the chicken has lost its pinkness, 3 to 5 minutes. Reduce the heat to medium.
3. Add the mushrooms and scallions and cook, stirring occasionally, about 2 minutes. Stir in the soy sauce, nam pla, and sugar and cook until the sauce thickens slightly, about 2 minutes more. Add a couple of tablespoons of lime juice, a bit of salt if necessary, and a lot of black pepper. Taste and adjust the seasoning, then garnish with the reserved ginger and serve.

Peanut Chicken THAILAND ■

MAKES **4 SERVINGS**

TIME **25 MINUTES**

Like Ginger Chicken (preceding recipe), a Thai-style stir-fry that is superfast and very flavorful. If you use a mild, fragrant curry powder, like the one on page 593, this will appeal to many kids; it's more sweet than spicy. Serve with jasmine or other white rice. Thai fish sauce (nam pla) is discussed on page 500.

1½ to 2 pounds boneless, skinless chicken breasts, cut
    into 1-inch chunks

2 garlic cloves, minced

One 1-inch piece fresh ginger, peeled and minced

1 tablespoon curry powder, preferably homemade
    (pages 592–593)

2 tablespoons corn, grapeseed, or other neutral oil

1 small onion, sliced

⅓ cup roasted peanuts, chopped

1 tablespoon sugar

1 tablespoon nam pla

½ cup coconut milk, homemade (page 584) or canned

1. Put the chicken, garlic, ginger, and curry powder in a large bowl and toss well to coat. Marinate while you prepare the rest of the ingredients.
2. Put the oil in a large nonstick skillet or wok and turn the heat to medium. Add the onion and cook, stirring occasionally, until softened and translucent, about 5 minutes. Raise the heat to medium-high and add the chicken. Cook, stirring occasionally, until the chicken loses its raw look and begins to brown, about 5 minutes.
3. Stir in the peanuts, sugar, nam pla, and coconut milk. Cook, stirring occasionally, until the sauce is thickened and the chicken tender, 5 to 10 minutes. Serve immediately.

Peanut Chicken with Vegetables. Bring a medium pot of water to a boil and add salt. Parboil about ½ head broccoli, cut into chunks, and 6 trimmed scallions, cut into 2-inch lengths, for about 3 minutes each or until barely tender. Drain well and add to the pan along with the chicken. Increase the coconut milk to ¾ cup.

PANFRYING BONELESS CHICKEN

Sautéing boneless chicken gives you the best of many worlds: a crisp crust with little mess and fast cooking with loads of flavor. Again, it often pays to use boneless thighs unless keeping the fat to a minimum is your primary goal.

Lemon Chicken CHINA
MAKES **4 SERVINGS**
    TIME **40 MINUTES, PLUS MARINATING TIME**

There are many versions of this popular Cantonese pairing, and they are almost always too sweet—sometimes abominably so. I've reduced the sugar in this one, so it's more sour and savory.

I do love the chicken fried, but you can also steam or stir-fry it; both variations are faster and easier than the main recipe. In any case, serve the chicken over white rice.

1½ to 2 pounds boneless, skinless chicken breasts or
    thighs, cut crosswise into ½-inch strips

1 scallion, trimmed and chopped

One ½-inch piece fresh ginger, peeled and minced

3 tablespoons soy sauce

1 tablespoon oyster sauce, optional

1 teaspoon Shaoxing wine or dry sherry

¼ teaspoon black pepper

Corn, grapeseed, or other neutral oil for deep-frying

1 egg, lightly beaten

½ cup flour

¼ cup fresh lemon juice

½ cup chicken stock, preferably homemade (page 160)

2 tablespoons sugar

2 teaspoons cornstarch

Salt to taste

1. Place the first 7 ingredients in a bowl and combine thoroughly. Cover, refrigerate, and marinate for at least 30 minutes and up to 2 hours. When ready to cook, pour 2 inches of oil in a deep heavy skillet or saucepan and heat to about 375°F (use an instant-read thermometer to check, or add a pinch of flour to the oil; it will sizzle at the right temperature). Remove the chicken from the marinade and coat with the egg and then the flour; carefully slide the chicken into the oil. Do not overcrowd; cook in batches if necessary. Cook, turning once, until golden brown and cooked through, about 7 minutes. Remove and drain on paper towels.

2. Meanwhile, in a medium saucepan, combine the lemon juice, chicken stock, sugar, and cornstarch and cook over medium-low heat, stirring occasionally, until the sugar is dissolved and the mixture thickens. Taste and season with salt, then turn the chicken pieces in the sauce and serve.

Stir-Fried Lemon Chicken. Omit the egg and flour. Heat 3 tablespoons corn, grapeseed, or other neutral oil in a wok or large nonstick skillet over medium-high heat. Add the chicken and cook until it loses its pinkness. Stir in the ginger and cook until fragrant, about 10 seconds. Add the soy sauce, oyster sauce if you're using it, wine, pepper, lemon juice, stock, sugar, and cornstarch. Mix everything together thoroughly and cook until the sauce thickens. Season to taste with salt, garnish with scallion, and serve.

Steamed Lemon Chicken. Omit the egg, flour, stock, and cornstarch. Place the chicken in a bowl with the ginger, soy sauce, oyster sauce if you're using it, wine, pepper, lemon juice, and sugar. Combine everything thoroughly, cover, refrigerate, and marinate for at least 30 minutes and up to 2 hours. When ready to cook, set up a steaming rack over at least 2 inches of water. Transfer the chicken to a heatproof plate and pour the marinade over it. Steam until the chicken is cooked through, about 20 minutes. Season to taste with salt, garnish with scallion, and serve.

Chicken Potato Patties NORTH AFRICA
MAKES **4 SERVINGS**
TIME **1 HOUR**

These are chicken croquettes with North African flavors. Leftover mashed potatoes and chicken are absolutely acceptable and you can use cooked cod (or other white-fleshed fish) in place of chicken. Any vegetable or salad will round this out nicely.

Salt
1½ pounds potatoes, peeled and cut into 1-inch chunks
  or at least 2 cups leftover mashed potatoes
1 pound boneless, skinless chicken breasts, cut into
  roughly 1-inch pieces
2 garlic cloves, minced
1 small onion, finely chopped
1 egg, lightly beaten
3 tablespoons chopped fresh parsley or cilantro leaves,
  plus more for garnish
½ teaspoon ground cinnamon
1 teaspoon ground turmeric
Pinch of cayenne, or to taste
Black pepper
Flour, as needed
Neutral oil, like corn or grapeseed, for shallow frying

1. Bring a large pot of water to a boil and add salt. Cook the potatoes until easily pierced with a knife, 10 to 15 minutes. Remove with a slotted spoon, then add the chicken; cook until it is done, 5 to 10 minutes. Remove the chicken (reserve some of the cooking water), cool it, then dice it finely.

2. Use a fork to mash the potatoes—they should remain a little chunky—in a bowl with the garlic, onion, and egg, then the chicken, parsley, cinnamon, turmeric, cayenne and salt and black pepper to taste. If the mixture seems dry, add a little of the cooking liquid; then add enough flour to enable you to shape the mixture into patties. (If you chill it first this will be easier, but it isn't necessary.)

3. Wet or flour your hands and shape the mixture into patties of any size, or simply scoop large spoonfuls of the batter into the pan, flattening them with the back of a spatula.

4. In a heavy skillet, heat about ½ inch of oil to 350°F. When the oil is ready—a pinch of flour will sizzle, and the oil will thin and start to shimmer (don't let it smoke)—slide in the chicken-potato patties and cook until golden brown, 3 to 5 minutes per side. Do not crowd the pan; work in batches if necessary. Drain on paper towels and serve immediately, garnished with the parsley or cilantro.

Chicken with Citrus Sauce CARIBBEAN ▨

MAKES **4 SERVINGS**

TIME **20 MINUTES**

Here are two versions of this delicious sweet-and-sour dish, which is prepared at roadside stands and restaurants on many Caribbean islands: Pan-cook it in the winter, grill it in the summer. Serve it with Coconut Rice and Beans (page 516).

3 tablespoons extra virgin olive oil

2 pounds boneless, skinless chicken breasts, cut into
½-inch cubes

Salt and black pepper to taste

2 garlic cloves, sliced

1 red onion, sliced

½ cup fresh orange juice

2 tablespoons fresh lemon juice

2 tablespoons fresh lime juice

2 tablespoons honey

2 tablespoons drained capers for garnish

1. Heat the oil in a skillet over medium-high heat. Add the chicken pieces and cook, stirring occasionally, until lightly browned and cooked through, seasoning to taste with salt and pepper, about 10 minutes. Remove and place in your serving dish.

2. Add the garlic and onion to the skillet and cook, stirring occasionally, until the onion is slightly softened, about 3 minutes. Stir in the orange juice, lemon juice, lime juice, and honey. Cook only until the honey has completely dissolved, about 30 seconds.

3. Pour the onion-citrus mixture over the chicken, garnish with capers, and serve.

Grilled Chicken with Citrus Sauce. Grill about 3 pounds bone-in chicken—this can be thighs, wings, or a variety of parts—over a fairly low fire until crisp, browned, and cooked through (see page 289 for detailed grilling directions). Make the sauce separately, as in step 2, using 2 tablespoons olive oil. Serve the grilled chicken hot, warm, or at room temperature, with the sauce spooned over it.

Chicken and Sausage in Vinegar

ITALY ▨

MAKES **4 SERVINGS**

TIME **30 MINUTES**

Best made with boneless thighs, this is not bad with breasts either, as long as you don't overcook them. Serve with crusty bread.

1 tablespoon extra virgin olive oil

$^1/_2$ pound sweet or hot Italian sausage, cut into 1-inch
chunks

1 pound boneless, skinless chicken thighs or breasts,
cut into 1 $^1/_2$-inch chunks

Salt and black pepper to taste

1 tablespoon minced garlic

1 medium onion, chopped

2 red bell peppers, stemmed, seeded, and roughly
chopped

2 tablespoons butter, optional

$^1/_2$ cup red wine vinegar or balsamic vinegar

$^1/_2$ cup chicken stock, preferably homemade (page 160),
or water

Chopped fresh parsley leaves for garnish

1. Put the oil in a large skillet, preferably nonstick, over medium-high heat. Add the sausage pieces and brown well, turning as necessary, for a total of about 10 minutes. Add the chicken and sprinkle it with salt and pepper. Brown it quickly, about 5 minutes. Reduce the heat to medium and add the garlic, onion, and peppers.
2. Cook, stirring occasionally, until the vegetables soften a bit, about 2 minutes. Add the butter if you're using it and stir until melted.
3. Add the vinegar and raise the heat to high; boil, uncovered, until the vinegar is almost evaporated, 2 to 3 minutes. Add the stock and let it boil until the sauce thickens, just a minute or so. Garnish and serve.

Chicken Teriyaki JAPAN ■ ▦ ■
MAKES **4 SERVINGS**

TIME **20 MINUTES**

You can make this ever-popular Japanese dish with boneless chicken breasts, and it's great that way, but the breasts have a tendency to overcook. Better to use boneless or even bone-in thighs. The technique remains the same no matter what cut you use (and even if you use salmon or beef; see pages 255 and 360); only the cooking time differs.

Teriyaki does not really produce a sauce, but a glaze, so something like Basmati Rice with Shiso (page 510) is preferable to plain rice (though plain rice is perfectly fine). A good salad with soy vinaigrette (page 601) is another fine pairing.

1 $^1/_2$ to 2 pounds boneless chicken thighs or breasts

$^1/_3$ cup sake or slightly sweet white wine, like a German
Kabinett or Spätlese

$^1/_3$ cup mirin or 2 tablespoons honey mixed with
2 tablespoons water

2 tablespoons sugar

$^1/_3$ cup soy sauce

1. Preheat a large nonstick skillet over medium-high heat for about 2 minutes, then add the chicken. Brown quickly on both sides, not more than 2 minutes per side. Transfer the chicken to a plate and reduce the heat to medium. Add 2 tablespoons water, followed by the wine, mirin, sugar, and soy sauce. Stir to blend and, when the mixture is producing lively bubbles, return the chicken to the pan.
2. Cook, turning the chicken in the sauce, until it becomes thick and sticky, more of a glaze than a liquid, just a few minutes. By that time the chicken should be cooked through but not overcooked; if the chicken needs another couple of minutes, add a little more water to the pan and continue to cook. Serve hot or at room temperature.

Chicken Teriyaki with Bone-In Thighs or Drumsticks. Slower to cook, but still popular and traditional: In step 1, preheat the pan and add 8 pieces bone-in chicken thighs or drumsticks, or a combination, skin side down. Brown the pieces well, rotating and turning the pieces as necessary and adjusting the heat so that they brown without burning, until they are nicely browned and almost cooked through, 15 to 20 minutes. Remove and proceed as directed.

Chicken Kiev RUSSIA

MAKES **4 SERVINGS**

TIME **ABOUT 3 HOURS, LARGELY UNATTENDED**

This classic Ukrainian dish is one of pure indulgence, and was common in French restaurants in the middle of the last century. Warn your guests: When made properly, butter spurts out of the chicken when it is cut; it's quite spectacular. You can prepare the chicken rolls ahead of time and fry just before serving, but it cannot be said that this is a dish that takes no work— it's about as complicated as I care to get.

Traditionally, Chicken Kiev is served alongside crispy potatoes and fresh green peas, but rice and salad are good too.

> 8 tablespoons (1 stick) butter, softened
>
> 2 garlic cloves, minced
>
> 2 tablespoons chopped fresh parsley leaves, dill leaves, chives, or a combination, plus more for garnish
>
> 4 boneless, skinless chicken breasts
>
> Salt and black pepper to taste
>
> $1/4$ cup flour
>
> 2 eggs, beaten
>
> $1/4$ cup fresh bread crumbs, preferably homemade (page 580)
>
> Corn, grapeseed, or other neutral oil for deep-frying
>
> Lemon wedges for serving

1. Mix the butter with the garlic and herbs. Form the mixture into eight 1-inch by $1/2$-inch logs. Place on wax paper, cover, and freeze for at least 1 hour.

Meanwhile, put each breast piece between 2 pieces of wax paper or plastic wrap and pound gently with the bottom of a pot, a rolling pin, or the palm of your hand until about $1/2$ inch thick. Cut each in half so you have 8 pieces. Sprinkle each with salt and pepper.

2. When the butter mixture is frozen, place a piece of the frozen butter in the center of each chicken breast. Fold in the sides and roll the chicken tightly around the butter. Make sure the butter is completely enclosed and the chicken sealed shut.

3. Coat the chicken rolls in the flour, eggs, then bread crumbs. Place on wax paper, cover, and refrigerate for at least 1 hour.

4. About 30 minutes before you're ready to eat, put at least 2 inches of oil in a deep heavy skillet or saucepan and turn the heat to medium-high. When it reaches 350°F—a pinch of flour will sizzle, and the oil will thin and start to shimmer (don't let it smoke)—gently slide in the chicken rolls and cook, turning once or twice, until golden brown, about 4 minutes. Do not overcrowd; work in batches if necessary. Drain on paper towels, garnish, and serve hot, with the lemon wedges.

CHICKEN KIEV

GRILLED BONELESS CHICKEN

Once you take the skin off chicken, it becomes almost as easy to grill as hot dogs. The danger of incineration just about vanishes, and cooking time—especially for breasts—is reduced to less than 10 minutes.

Remember, too, that you can always use the broiler instead of the grill, with far more control and convenience.

Chicken Tikka Grilled Boneless Chicken INDIA

MAKES **4 SERVINGS**

TIME **30 MINUTES, PLUS TIME TO PREHEAT THE GRILL AND MARINATING TIME**

As is so often the case in Indian cooking, butter is the "secret" ingredient here, one that gives the chicken extra moisture and richness. The combination of that, mild spices, and grilling is what has made this dish so popular in the West.

Serve with plain Paratha (page 559) and mint chutney, if you can.

> **1 1/2 pounds boneless, skinless chicken breasts or thighs**
> **1/4 cup yogurt**
> **1/4 cup ground cashews**
> **Pinch of ground mace**
> **1 teaspoon ground cardamom**
> **1 teaspoon ground coriander**
> **1 teaspoon peeled and minced fresh ginger**
> **1 teaspoon minced garlic**
> **Salt and black pepper to taste**
> **2 tablespoons butter, melted**
> **1/2 teaspoon ground fennel**
> **Chopped fresh cilantro leaves for garnish**

1. Cut the chicken into 1-inch chunks (no smaller). Combine the chicken in a bowl with all the ingredients except the butter, fennel, and cilantro. Marinate while you heat the grill or refrigerate for several hours or overnight.

2. Start a charcoal or gas grill; the fire need be only moderately hot, and the rack should be 4 to 6 inches from the heat source. If you're using wooden skewers, soak them for a few minutes. Thread the meat onto the skewers, leaving a little bit of space between pieces.

3. Grill, basting with the melted butter, until the chicken is nicely browned and cooked through, 10 to 15 minutes. Sprinkle with the ground fennel and cilantro and serve.

Yakitori Grilled Chicken on Skewers JAPAN

MAKES **4 SERVINGS**

TIME **20 TO 40 MINUTES, INCLUDING TIME TO PREHEAT THE GRILL**

Yakitori shops—small places, mostly joints, where you sit at the counter—specialize in chicken, though you can use this sauce and technique for almost anything that can be cut into bite-sized pieces: chicken wings, chicken skin, chicken livers or gizzards, bits of pork, shiitake mushrooms, scallions, even garlic cloves. Sometimes different things are combined on skewers, too, so feel free to go that route. A good hot fire, preferably made with real charcoal (not gas and certainly not briquettes) is requisite. Chicken thighs are often boned before sale; if you can find only bone-in thighs, you will quickly figure out how to remove the meat from them—it's simple (and the bones make great stock). Do not use breasts in this recipe unless you are a fan of dry meat.

As long as you have the grill going, you might make some Roasted Red Peppers (page 470). Or, if you feel like it, Sautéed Peppers with Miso (page 78). Either is a great accompaniment. Shichimi pepper is a spice mixture sold in Japanese markets.

¹/₂ cup sake

¹/₄ cup mirin or 2 tablespoons honey

¹/₂ cup soy sauce

2 tablespoons sugar

2 pounds boneless, skinless chicken thighs, cut into
1-inch chunks

Shichimi pepper, optional

Lemon wedges for serving

1. Start a charcoal fire or preheat the broiler; it should be very hot, with the rack set not more than 4 inches from the heat source and preferably somewhat less. Combine the first 4 ingredients in a small saucepan and bring to a boil; simmer for about a minute, stirring. Remove from the heat.

2. Traditionally, yakitori is skewered on wood, but you can use metal if you prefer (because the cooking time is so short, there's really no need to soak the skewers first). Skewer the chicken pieces, leaving a little bit of space between pieces. Brush once, lightly, with the sauce.

3. Grill or broil, basting frequently but lightly (since the sauce is sweet, it will burn, so it's best if it does not drip directly onto the coals) and turning the skewers as the chicken browns. Total cooking time will be less than 10 minutes. Sprinkle with shichimi if you like and serve immediately, with the lemon wedges.

Chicken Kebab MIDDLE EAST

MAKES **4 SERVINGS**

TIME **45 MINUTES, PLUS TIME TO PREHEAT THE GRILL**

I don't know how strongly to stress that the boneless chicken meat to be used for kebabs should be from the thighs rather than the breasts. Thigh meat will remain juicy and tender, whereas breast meat—almost no matter how careful you are—will become dry,

pasty, and tough. Buy boneless thighs (or, as I've seen recently, boneless legs) or bone them yourself (and save the bones for stock)—the process is intuitive and easy.

As with Shish Kebab (page 354), if you want to grill other vegetables—tomatoes, peppers, mushrooms, more onions, whatever—skewer them separately, then brush them with a little olive oil and sprinkle them with salt and pepper before grilling.

Sumac is a sour spice found at Middle Eastern food stores.

2 large onions, peeled

2 tablespoons extra virgin olive oil

Juice of 1 lemon

1 tablespoon minced garlic

Salt and black pepper to taste

3 bay leaves, crumbled into bits

1 tablespoon fresh marjoram or oregano leaves or
1 teaspoon dried oregano

2 pounds boneless, skinless chicken thighs or legs,
cut into 1¹/₂-inch chunks

Lemon wedges or ground sumac

1. When you're ready to cook—if you choose not to marinate the meat—start a charcoal or wood fire or preheat a gas grill; the fire should be moderately hot and the rack about 4 inches from the heat source. Mince one of the onions and combine it in a large bowl with the oil, lemon juice, garlic, salt, pepper, bay leaves, and marjoram; taste and adjust the seasoning. Marinate the chicken in this mixture for at least a few minutes or for up to 12 hours in the refrigerator.

2. If you're using wooden skewers, soak them in water to cover for a few minutes. Cut the remaining onion into quarters, then separate it into large pieces. Thread the chicken and onion alternately onto the skewers, leaving a little space between pieces. Grill, turning as each side browns and

brushing with the remaining marinade, for 12 to 15 minutes, or until the chicken is cooked through. Serve with the lemon wedges or sprinkle with a bit of sumac.

Skewered Chicken Thighs with Peanut Sauce THAILAND ▨

MAKES **4 SERVINGS**

TIME **30 MINUTES, INCLUDING TIME TO PREHEAT THE GRILL AND MARINATING TIME**

These are best grilled slowly so that the sweet sauce caramelizes slowly as the chicken cooks through. You can use boneless breasts for these, but they will almost invariably dry out. Do not marinate these for more than an hour or so; the meat will begin to get mushy. In fact I don't bother to marinate them at all unless it fits into my schedule. Thai fish sauce (nam pla) is described on page 500.

$^1/_2$ cup natural peanut butter, preferably chunky

1 tablespoon curry paste (page 9) or curry powder, preferably homemade (pages 592–593), or to taste

About $^1/_2$ cup coconut milk, homemade (page 584) or canned

2 tablespoons nam pla or soy sauce

1 tablespoon fresh lime juice

1$^1/_2$ pounds boneless chicken thighs, cut into large chunks

Lime wedges for serving

Chopped fresh cilantro leaves for garnish

1. Start a charcoal or gas grill or preheat the broiler; the fire should be only moderately hot, and the rack should be at least 4 inches from the heat source. Put the peanut butter in a small saucepan over medium heat; add the curry paste and enough coconut milk to achieve a creamy, stirrable

consistency. Cook over low heat, whisking, for about 5 minutes; do not boil. Stir in the nam pla and lime juice.

2. Marinate the chicken in this mixture for 5 minutes or up to an hour. Grill or broil slowly, until nicely browned and cooked through, 10 minutes or longer.

3. Serve hot, sprinkled with fresh lime juice and garnished with cilantro.

MISCELLANEOUS CHICKEN RECIPES

Steamed Chicken Cups THAILAND

MAKES **4 SERVINGS**

TIME **35 MINUTES**

Steamed dishes are not common even in Thailand (most Thai dishes are stewed or stir-fried). But this is a lovely, mild, sweet dish I had at an upscale restaurant in Bangkok; I thought it was an innovation, but it turns out to be quite traditional. You can prepare the mixture ahead of time, cover, and refrigerate the ramekins until you are ready to steam them. Serve it with rice and a salad or vegetable dish.

To make ground chicken yourself, cut boneless, skinless breasts or thighs into chunks and put them in a food processor; pulse until ground, being careful not to overprocess. You can use turkey or pork in place of the chicken if you like. Information on Thai fish sauce (nam pla) is on page 500.

3 garlic cloves, peeled

6 fresh cilantro sprigs, leaves and stems separated

1 teaspoon black pepper

1 pound ground chicken

$^1/_2$ pound ground pork

■ make ahead   ▨ serve at room temp./cold   ▨ 30 minutes or less   POULTRY **321**

1 tablespoon palm sugar (page 9) or brown sugar

2 tablespoons coconut milk, homemade (page 584) or
    canned, plus a drizzle for garnish

2 tablespoons nam pla

2 eggs, beaten

1. Put at least 2 inches of water in the bottom of a steamer. Put the garlic, cilantro stems, and pepper into a food processor and process until the garlic is pasty and the cilantro finely minced. By hand, mix with the chicken, pork, sugar, coconut milk, nam pla, and 1 egg.

2. Spoon and press down the mixture into ½-cup ceramic ramekins or small heatproof paper cups, like the aluminum-lined ones you might use for cupcakes. Brush the remaining egg on top and place the ramekins in the steamer. Cover and cook until the mixture is firm, 15 to 20 minutes.

3. Remove from the heat and cool slightly. Invert the ramekins onto plates and tap gently to release the steamed chicken. Drizzle with a little coconut milk, garnish with the reserved cilantro leaves, and serve.

Chicken B'stilla MOROCCO
MAKES **4 SERVINGS**
TIME **1½ HOURS**

This is something like a chicken pot pie, but far more exotic and quite wonderful. Like a chicken pot pie, it is serious work; it will keep you busy for a good solid hour. (You can, however, prepare the chicken filling and almond topping in advance and assemble it just before baking.) The sweet almond topping may deceive your guests into thinking it's a dessert, but the savory chicken filling counters it perfectly.

As always, when working with phyllo dough, make sure you keep the pieces that you are not working with covered with a damp towel; see Baklava (page 628) for more details.

2 tablespoons corn, grapeseed, or other neutral oil

2 garlic cloves, minced

1 onion, chopped

2 pounds boneless, skinless chicken thighs

½ cup chopped fresh parsley or cilantro leaves

1 teaspoon ground turmeric

½ teaspoon saffron threads, crumbled, optional

One 1½-inch piece fresh ginger, peeled and minced

3 cups chicken stock, preferably homemade (page 160),
    or water

Salt and black pepper to taste

4 eggs, lightly beaten

½ cup blanched almonds

2 teaspoons ground cinnamon

¼ cup confectioners' sugar

½ pound (about 12 sheets) phyllo

8 tablespoons (1 stick) butter, melted, plus more as
    needed

1. Heat the oil in a large saucepan over medium heat. Cook the garlic and onion until softened and fragrant, about 3 minutes. Add the chicken, parsley, turmeric, saffron if desired, ginger, and stock. Season with salt and pepper, bring to a boil, then cover and simmer until the chicken is cooked through, about 20 minutes. Remove the chicken from the pot and set aside to cool.

2. Slowly pour the eggs into the simmering stock, stirring constantly. Continue to simmer the stock, uncovered, until reduced by half, about 10 minutes. Cut the chicken into bite-sized pieces and return to the reduced stock. Continue simmering until almost all the liquid has evaporated, another 10 minutes or so. Remove from the heat and set aside.

3. Preheat the oven to 425°F. Lightly toast the almonds in a dry skillet over medium heat, shaking

frequently, until fragrant, just a couple of minutes. Grind them in a coffee or spice grinder and mix them with the cinnamon and sugar.

4. Lay 4 or 5 of the phyllo sheets in a greased 9-inch pie pan, brushing a little melted butter between sheets. The edges of the phyllo sheets should hang over the rim of the pie pan. Spread the chicken mixture evenly in the pan over the phyllo sheets. Top the chicken mixture with the remaining phyllo sheets, again brushing with a little melted butter. Fold in the edges to enclose the pie, sealing with melted butter.

5. Cut a few small slits in the top of the pie to allow hot air to escape while baking. Place in the oven and cook until golden brown and crisp, about 30 minutes. Remove and immediately sprinkle the almond mixture on top. Serve hot.

Chicken Tacos MEXICO
MAKES **4 SERVINGS**
TIME **35 MINUTES**

If you have had only the fast-food variety of tacos or made them using a mix, these will come as a revelation, yet they're quite easy to make. Top them with sour cream, any salsa (pages 610–612), Guacamole

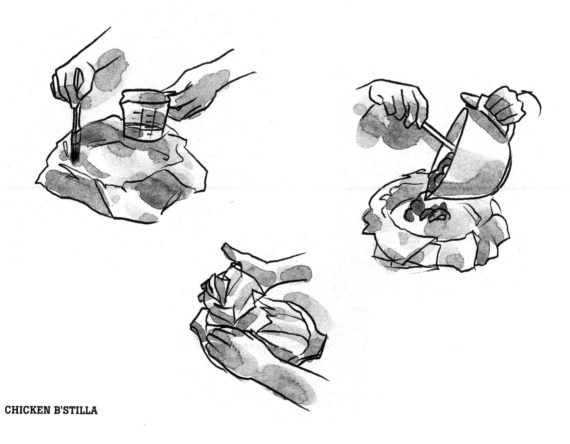

CHICKEN B'STILLA

■ make ahead   ■ serve at room temp./cold   ■ 30 minutes or less

(page 22), or a combination; they are also delicious on their own. There is a wealth of variations here; if you're not interested in frying, see the soft taco version.

The chicken can be cooked by any method you like; poaching with aromatic vegetables and spices will work, along with producing a decent stock.

3 tablespoons lard (traditional) or corn, grapeseed, or
    other neutral oil, plus more for deep-frying
2 garlic cloves, minced
2 jalapeños, stemmed, seeded, and diced, or to taste
1 small onion, diced
1 pound ripe tomatoes, cored and diced
About 3 cups skinned and shredded cooked chicken
Salt and black pepper to taste
Twelve 5-inch corn tortillas
$\frac{1}{2}$ cup shredded lettuce or cabbage
$\frac{1}{2}$ cup queso fresco, crumbled, or grated Cheddar cheese

1. Heat 3 tablespoons lard or oil in a skillet over medium-high heat. Add the garlic and jalapeños and cook until fragrant, about 10 seconds. Add the onion and cook until softened, about 5 minutes. Stir in the tomatoes and cook for 10 minutes or so, until their juices are released, then add the chicken. Cook until all the liquid is absorbed, 5 to 10 minutes, then season with salt and pepper and remove from the heat.

2. Add at least 2 inches of lard or oil to a heavy skillet or saucepan. Heat to 350°F (the fat will be shimmering, and a piece of taco will sizzle when added to it; or use an instant-read thermometer). Spread the chicken over one half of each tortilla. Fold the tortilla in half and secure with a toothpick. When the oil reaches 350°F, gently slide the tacos into the oil and cook, turning occasionally, until crisp and golden, about 5 minutes. Do not overcrowd; work in batches if necessary.

3. Drain on paper towels, remove the toothpicks, add lettuce and cheese, and serve.

Smoky Chicken Tacos. Roast or broil the tomatoes and onion, preferably over a charcoal or wood fire, before cooking in the skillet.

More Authentic Chicken Tacos. Substitute tomatillos for the tomatoes.

Chicken Flautas. In step 3, roll the tacos into cylinders and secure with a toothpick. Proceed as directed and serve on a bed of the lettuce, topped with the cheese.

Steamed Soft Tacos. Do not fry. Instead, set up a steamer and steam the unfilled tortillas until softened, about 15 minutes. They can also be toasted lightly in a dry skillet, just until warm (do not brown). Fill them with the chicken, lettuce, and cheese and serve.

Chicken Salbutes. Little guys, great for snacks or hors d'oeuvres: Substitute tortilla chips for the tortillas. Place a spoonful of the chicken mixture on each tortilla chip and top with cheese and lettuce.

Shredded Pork Tacos. Omit the first seven ingredients. Use Shredded Pork (page 396) to fill the tacos.

Enchiladas MEXICO
MAKES **8 SERVINGS**
TIME **1 HOUR**

This is a classic taqueria dish that is even better when made at home. Although the preparation takes some time, enchiladas are delicious and fun for parties or potlucks. You can fill and roll the tortillas ahead of time and then top with the sauce and cheese and bake immediately before serving. To make cheese enchiladas, omit the chicken and fill the tortillas with cheese; pour the sauce over all and proceed.

1 cup corn, grapeseed, or other neutral oil

5 garlic cloves, peeled

1 onion, peeled and quartered

4 tomatoes, cored and quartered

6 dried mild chiles, like guajillo or California, stemmed and seeded

2 teaspoons ground cumin, plus more to taste

Salt and black pepper to taste

1 quart chicken stock, preferably homemade (page 160)

About 2 cups cooked, shredded chicken

Forty 5-inch corn tortillas

1 cup queso Chihuahua (page 85), or shredded Cheddar or Monterey Jack cheese

1. Heat 3 tablespoons of the oil in a large skillet over medium heat. Add the garlic and onion and cook until softened, about 5 minutes. Add the tomatoes and chiles and cook until the tomato juices are released and the chiles are soft, about 5 minutes. Season with cumin, salt, and pepper.

2. Transfer this mixture to a blender and blend until smooth, adding sufficient chicken stock to make a loose but still creamy mixture. Taste and adjust seasoning. Moisten the chicken with about half of the sauce, or enough to make it pasty.

3. Preheat the oven to 350°F. Meanwhile, heat the remaining oil in a deep skillet over medium-low heat. Cook the tortillas, one at a time, until softened and pliable, about 10 seconds. Drain on paper towels.

4. Line a heaping tablespoon of the chicken mixture in the center of each tortilla, roll tightly, and put in a large baking dish. The rolls should be placed snugly against one another. Pour the remaining sauce over, top with the cheese, and bake for about 25 minutes, or until heated through. Serve hot.

Simpler Enchiladas. Omit the tomatoes, chiles, and cumin. The chicken is optional. Add 2 tablespoons mild chile powder to the softened garlic and onion and cook, stirring occasionally, until fragrant. Add the chicken stock and cook until the sauce thickens. Proceed as directed.

DUCK, GOOSE, OTHER BIRDS, AND RABBIT

DUCK

Our much-maligned duck ("It's so fatty!") is actually pretty easy to cook. And if you keep a thin layer of liquid in the bottom of the roasting pan, the fat drips into it and stays there, reducing spattering. (You'll need a rack to elevate the duck.)

It's also worth noting that the popularity of duck breast in many restaurants has led to the appearance of duck legs in many supermarkets. These are a wonderful ingredient, for which I've included some recipes. (I'm not a fan of boneless duck breasts, so I use them only rarely.)

Roast Duck CHINA ■ ■

MAKES **4 SERVINGS**
TIME **ABOUT 1 HOUR**

While Peking Duck—which is a big deal—is reserved for special occasions, the simpler Cantonese version of roast duck is made far more routinely. It's the duck you see hanging in rows in restaurant windows in every Chinatown in the country.

Because this is often served at room temperature—or as an ingredient in stir-fries—you can make it ahead of time. If you want to serve it hot, accompany it with rice, noodles, or a panfried noodle cake like the one that forms the base for Shrimp with Crisp-Fried Noodles (page 534), and use hoisin as a dipping sauce.

3 tablespoons soy sauce

2 tablespoons Shaoxing wine or dry sherry

3 tablespoons brown sugar

2 teaspoons five-spice powder

4 scallions, trimmed, cut into 2-inch lengths, and smashed

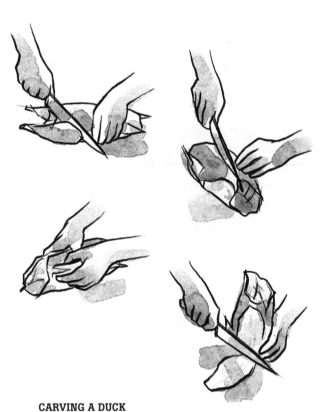

CARVING A DUCK

Six 1/4-inch slices peeled fresh ginger, smashed

1 tablespoon salt, plus more as needed

4 whole star anise

One 4- to 5-pound duck, trimmed of excess fat

1/2 cup hoisin sauce

1. Preheat the oven to 400°F. Combine the soy sauce, wine, brown sugar, five-spice powder, scallions, and ginger in a bowl; stir until the sugar dissolves. Sprinkle the salt all over the duck and inside the cavity. Rub half the marinade into the cavity.

2. Prick the duck skin all over with a sharp fork, skewer, or thin-bladed knife; try not to hit the meat (the fat layer is usually about 1/4 inch thick). Place the duck, breast side down, on a rack in a roasting pan.

3. Roast the duck for 15 minutes, prick the exposed skin again, then roast for another 15 minutes. Brush with half the remaining marinade and then turn it breast side up. Prick again, brush with the remaining marinade, then roast until the meat is done, about another 20 minutes; all juices, including those from the interior, should run clear, and the leg bone should wiggle a little in its socket. When the bird is done, an instant-read thermometer inserted into the thigh will read about 180°F.

4. Carve the duck and serve, passing the hoisin at the table.

Vietnamese Roast Duck. Sharper and less complex, but interesting. Omit the wine, five-spice powder, and scallions. Add 6 garlic cloves, peeled and minced, double the soy sauce, and mince the ginger. Whisk the soy sauce, sugar, ginger, and garlic together to make the marinade. Proceed as directed.

Tea-Smoked Duck or Chicken

CHINA ■ ▨

MAKES **4 SERVINGS**

TIME **ABOUT 1 ½ HOURS**

This is a simple smoking technique that doesn't take long, though if your aluminum foil seal is not tight, you run the risk of really smoking up your kitchen. So the first time you try it, pick a day that's warm enough to open the windows and have a fan handy. (I don't say this to dissuade you, but from very real experience. I do love this recipe, and it works well; but sometimes unfortunate events occur!)

The duck is best cut up and served as part of a larger meal of Chinese food or as part of a multinational buffet or used in stir-fries.

Chicken is even easier; you can skip the initial steaming if you like.

One 4- to 5-pound duck, trimmed of excess fat

½ cup soy sauce

1 tablespoon five-spice powder

½ cup white rice

1 cup black tea leaves

½ cup sugar

10 pieces dried orange peel (available at Chinese markets) or fresh orange peel

2 cinnamon sticks, broken up

1 tablespoon dark sesame oil

1. Prick the duck skin all over with a sharp fork, skewer, or thin-bladed knife; try not to hit the meat (the fat layer is usually about ¼ inch thick). Rub the duck all over with all but 2 tablespoons of the soy sauce, then the five-spice powder. Place the duck on a steaming rack over (not in) abundant boiling water, cover the pot, and turn the heat to high. Steam for about 45 minutes, adding more (boiling) water if necessary. Remove the duck. (At this point you can cool and wrap it well, then refrigerate for a day or two before proceeding.)

2. Line a heavy pot with a tight-fitting lid with 2 layers of heavy aluminum foil (a wok is okay, but it won't have a lid). Mix the rice, tea, sugar, orange peel, and cinnamon in the bottom. Use a rack of some kind to create a platform for the duck, at least an inch over the smoking mixture (but remember that the duck must not protrude over the top of the pan). Place the duck, breast side up, on the platform, then cover the pot very tightly with a double thickness of heavy aluminum foil or its cover or, preferably, both. The seal should be as tight as you can make it (without resorting to epoxy; duct tape isn't bad, though).

3. Turn the heat to high and, after 10 minutes (or when smoke appears; despite your best efforts, there will probably be at least a small leak), turn the heat to medium. Smoke for another 15 to 20 minutes. Turn off the heat, but do not remove the cover for another 15 minutes (as soon as you do, remove and discard the smoking mixture).

4. Serve the duck hot or at room temperature; do not refrigerate at this point unless you're going to add it to a stir-fry (in which case wrap it well and refrigerate for up to 2 days). If you're serving the duck solo, cut it into small pieces and drizzle with the remaining soy sauce and the sesame oil.

Garlic Duck and Rice LAOS

MAKES **4 TO 6 SERVINGS**

TIME **1 HOUR**

This Laotian version of arroz con pollo is a rich, flavorful, and gorgeous one-pot dish, unusual and quite easy. See page 500 for information on Thai fish sauce (nam pla).

2 cups jasmine or other long-grain rice

2 whole heads garlic, cloves separated and peeled

2 teaspoons pepper

1 teaspoon salt, or to taste

1 tablespoon ground turmeric

3 tablespoons nam pla

One 4- to 5-pound duck, cut into serving pieces and
   trimmed of excess fat

Chopped fresh cilantro leaves for garnish

Lime wedges for serving

1. Put the rice in a strainer and rinse it well, then
    soak in cold water to cover.

2. Meanwhile, put the garlic, pepper, salt, turmeric,
    and nam pla into a food processor or blender.
    Process until the garlic is pasty and the ingredients
    are well incorporated, stopping the machine and
    scraping the sides if necessary.

3. Place a deep skillet or flameproof casserole with a
    lid over medium-high heat. A minute later, add
    the duck, skin side down, and brown well, adjust-
    ing the heat and rotating the pieces so they brown
    evenly, 10 to 15 minutes. As they brown, turn them
    and briefly brown the other side. When they are
    done, transfer them to a plate and pour off all but
    a couple tablespoons of the fat.

4. Add the garlic paste to the skillet and cook, stirring
    constantly, until fragrant, about 15 seconds. Re-
    turn the duck to the pan and stir to coat with the
    sauce.

5. Add 3½ cups water to the pan with the duck and
    bring to a boil. Drain the rice and slowly stir it into
    the pan. Bring the water to a boil again, cover, turn
    the heat to medium-low, and simmer until the rice
    is cooked through, about 20 minutes. Turn off the
    heat and let the duck and rice sit for 10 minutes.
    Garnish with the cilantro and serve with lime
    wedges.

Braised Duck or Chicken with Fresh Curry Paste THAILAND

MAKES **4 SERVINGS**

TIME **1 HOUR**

A basic Thai-style curry, most often made with a convenient canned product from Thailand called "curry
paste." Here I make my own version, for a fresher
taste. The technique is simple: First you brown the
main ingredient; I use poultry here, but it can be
meat, seafood, vegetables, or tofu, and the process
would barely change. Then you cook the curry paste,
loosening it with some liquid (typically coconut
milk), and finish the dish by simmering. Straightforward and authentic. Serve with Basic Short-Grain
Rice (page 507) or steamed Sticky Rice (page 508).
See page 9 for information on dried shrimp and page
500 for details on Thai fish sauce (nam pla).

One 3-pound duck or chicken, cut into serving pieces, or
   3 pounds duck legs or chicken thighs

Salt and black pepper to taste

1 tablespoon dried shrimp, nam pla, or soy sauce

2 small fresh or dried red chiles or cayenne to taste

1 medium onion, peeled and cut into chunks

4 large garlic cloves, peeled

One 1-inch piece fresh ginger, peeled and roughly
   chopped

1 tablespoon ground cumin

1 teaspoon ground coriander

1½ cups coconut milk, homemade (page 584) or canned

2 limes

½ cup chopped fresh cilantro or basil leaves

1. Put the pieces of duck or chicken in a 12-inch skil-
    let or flameproof casserole, preferably nonstick,
    and turn the heat to medium-high. Brown care-
    fully on both sides, rotating and turning as neces-
    sary and sprinkling with salt and pepper as they
    cook. Take your time to do this thoroughly, allow-

ing up to 15 or 20 minutes total; remove the pieces as they are browned.

2. Meanwhile, soak the dried shrimp in water to cover and soak the dried chiles, if you're using them, in warm water to cover. Combine the onion, garlic, ginger, and spices in a food processor. When the shrimp are tender, add them to the processor, reserving the liquid. When the chiles are soft, remove and discard the stems; add the flesh (and seeds, if you want extra heat) to the processor. If you're using nam pla or soy sauce, add it to the processor. Pulse the machine on and off, using enough of the reserved liquids or some of the coconut milk to loosen the mixture so the machine can do its work, until a thick paste is formed.

3. Remove all but a couple tablespoons of the fat from the skillet (you will have to remove more if you use duck than if you use chicken), add the curry paste, and cook over medium heat, stirring occasionally, until the mixture becomes fragrant, a minute or two. Add the remaining coconut milk and bring to a boil; nestle the pieces of the bird in there, adding any juices that have accumulated around them. Adjust the heat so that the mixture simmers energetically but not violently and cook, uncovered, until the duck or chicken is tender, 20 to 40 minutes. Meanwhile, juice 1 lime and quarter the other. Stir the lime juice into the curry.

4. Serve (on white rice is best), garnished with the cilantro and accompanied by the quartered lime.

Roast Duck with Bay Leaves and Marsala ITALY

MAKES **2 TO 4 SERVINGS**
TIME **1¼ HOURS**

Italians use leaner ducks than we do, so this is a compromise recipe: Italian flavors with American duck.

The best Marsala is called vergine. It is really delicious and makes a subtle but real difference here. But standard Marsala will work fine.

If you have time, make a quick stock using the duck neck and giblets—just simmer them in water to cover while you are roasting the duck. Then you'll have it for the final sauce. This would be great with polenta, if you feel like making it (page 529), but also with crusty bread or even plain rice.

One 4- to 5-pound duck
1 cup Marsala or Oloroso sherry
Salt and black pepper to taste
10 bay leaves
½ cup duck, chicken, beef, or vegetable stock, preferably homemade (pages 160 or 162), or water

1. Preheat the oven to 450°F. Discard the duck neck and giblets or use them to make stock; remove excess fat from the duck's cavity. Rub the duck all over with a bit of Marsala, then sprinkle it with salt and pepper. Place it, breast side down (wings up), on a rack in a roasting pan; add water to come to just below the rack and put half the bay leaves in the water.

2. Roast undisturbed for 30 minutes. Prick the back all over with the point of a sharp knife, then flip the bird onto its back. Brush with Marsala again. (If the bottom of the pan dries out, add a little water, but carefully.)

3. Roast for 10 minutes, prick the breast all over with the point of a knife, and brush with Marsala. Roast for 10 minutes and brush again. Roast for another 5 or 10 minutes if necessary, or until the duck is a glorious brown all over and an instant-read thermometer inserted into the thigh reads at least 155°F. Transfer the duck to a warm platter.

4. Pour or spoon off as much fat (but not the dark juices) as possible from the roasting pan. Put it over a burner and turn the heat to high. Add the

remaining Marsala, bay leaves, and the stock and cook, stirring and scraping with a wooden spoon to incorporate any solids, until the sauce is glossy and thick, 5 to 10 minutes. Taste and add salt and pepper if necessary. Carve the bird and serve with the sauce.

Duck Confit FRANCE ■
MAKES **4 SERVINGS**
TIME **A FEW DAYS, LARGELY UNATTENDED**

Duck confit is one of those foods that began as a method of preserving and continues because it tastes so damn good. It's a simple enough process, and the results are dependable.

It's best when you use duck fat as a cooking medium. While not exactly a pantry staple, duck fat isn't terribly expensive if you buy it from a specialty retailer that makes most of its money from other parts of the duck (like Hudson Valley Foie Gras: www.hudsonvalleyfoiegras.com).

Fortunately, confit is not bad with olive oil either, though when you do the math on the two and figure in how delicious potatoes sautéed in leftover confit fat are, duck fat becomes increasingly appealing.

My favorite way to serve duck confit is with a simple and strongly flavored salad of bitter greens—like the Green Salad with Vinaigrette, Roquefort, and Walnuts on page 165 minus the blue cheese and made, if possible, with a fifty-fifty walnut oil/olive oil dressing.

1 cup salt

2 tablespoons dried thyme

2 bay leaves

1 tablespoon black pepper

8 duck legs

20 garlic cloves, peeled, optional

About 2 quarts rendered duck fat or grapeseed or extra virgin olive oil

1. Mix or grind together the salt, thyme, bay leaves, and pepper. Put the duck in a roasting pan or broad, shallow bowl and rub this mixture all over it. Nestle the garlic if you're using it in among the legs and refrigerate for 24 to 48 hours.

2. Remove the duck from the salt mixture and rub off any excess salt. Preheat the oven to 300°F. Warm the duck fat so that it is pourable. Place the duck and garlic in a baking dish in one layer. Cover the legs with the duck fat. (You may not need all the fat, depending on the size of your pan; and if you do not have enough, add olive or other oil as necessary.) Put in the oven and cook, undisturbed—the mixture should send up a few bubbles a minute, but no more than that; adjust the heat accordingly—for 3 to 4 hours or until a fork pierces the leg with little resistance. Cool in the fat for about an hour.

3. The legs can be stored in or out of the fat. To store them in the fat, simply refrigerate the whole roasting pan or combine the duck and the fat in a bowl and refrigerate. To store out of the fat, remove from the fat while still warm, then cool to room temperature. Wrap each leg individually and refrigerate. The legs (and garlic) will keep for up to 2 weeks; the fat will keep, refrigerated, indefinitely.

4. To serve, heat a couple of tablespoons of the fat in a skillet over medium-low heat. Add 1 or more legs (and a clove or 2 of garlic) and brown slowly, turning as necessary, until crisp, 10 to 15 minutes. Serve with a salad (see the headnote) or with warm crusty bread.

Crisp-Braised Duck Legs with Aromatic Vegetables FRANCE ■

MAKES **4 SERVINGS**

TIME **ABOUT 2 HOURS, LARGELY UNATTENDED**

"Crisp-braised" might seem like a contradiction in terms, since braising is geared to develop full tenderness, usually at the cost of crispness. But browned duck skin has such an astonishing capacity for holding its crispness that duck legs can be browned, then carefully braised, with the result being a crackling skin covering sublimely soft meat.

This is a grand winter dish, the kind you would eat ecstatically at a neighborhood bistro, were you lucky enough to live near such a place. Serve with bread and a salad.

4 duck legs, trimmed of excess fat

Salt and black pepper to taste

2 leeks, trimmed, cleaned (page 465), and diced,
    or 1 large onion, diced

1/2 pound carrots, diced

3 celery stalks, diced

5 garlic cloves, peeled and lightly crushed

6 fresh thyme sprigs

2 cups chicken stock, preferably homemade (page 160)

Chopped fresh parsley leaves for garnish

1. Put the duck legs, skin side down, in a skillet large enough to accommodate all the ingredients comfortably; turn the heat to medium. Brown the duck legs slowly, carefully, and evenly—it will take about 20 minutes total—sprinkling them with salt and pepper as they cook. Meanwhile, chop the vegetables.

2. When the legs are nicely browned, turn and sear the meat side for just a minute or two. Transfer to a plate; remove all but enough of the fat to moisten the vegetables (there's plenty more fat where that came from). Preheat the oven to 400°F. Add the vegetables and garlic, thyme, and some salt and pepper and cook, stirring occasionally, over medium-high heat, until they begin to brown, 10 to 15 minutes. Return the duck legs, skin side up, to the pan and add the stock; it should come about halfway up the duck legs but in no case should it cover them. Turn the heat to high, bring to a boil, and transfer to the oven.

3. Cook for 30 minutes, then turn the heat to 350°F. Continue to cook, undisturbed, until the duck is tender and the liquid reduced, at least another half hour and probably a bit longer. (When done, the duck will hold nicely in a warm oven for up to another hour.) Garnish and serve.

Crisp-Braised Duck Legs with Apricots or Prunes. In step 2, substitute shallots for the leeks; omit the celery and garlic and add 1 1/2 cups dried apricots or prunes (or a mixture). Proceed as directed.

Crisp-Braised Duck Legs with Parsley. In step 2, cook 1/4 cup peeled and chopped shallot until softened (omit the other vegetables). Add 2 cups chopped fresh parsley leaves; use 2 cups dry white wine (or 1 cup wine and 1 cup stock) in place of the stock. Finish as directed, garnishing with more fresh parsley.

Pan-Roasted Duck with Olives

FRANCE ■

MAKES **4 SERVINGS**

TIME **ABOUT 2 HOURS, LARGELY UNATTENDED**

You can make this Provençal dish with whole duck, but it's also great with legs. The covered pan-roasting does a good job of keeping the duck's breast from drying out, while the legs become tender. It makes a lovely presentation, and the sauce is delicious.

If you have only black olives, that's fine, but add a tablespoon or two of capers to the mix.

As with many (if not most) French dishes, this is best with bread and a salad.

1 whole duck, the larger the better

10 or more garlic cloves, peeled and lightly smashed

Several fresh thyme sprigs

2 bay leaves

Salt and black pepper to taste

1 cup fruity red wine

1 cup chopped tomatoes (canned are fine), with their juice

2 cups good-quality olives, preferably a combination of green and black

Chopped fresh parsley leaves for garnish

1. Discard the duck neck and giblets or keep them for another use; remove excess fat from the duck's cavity. In the bottom of a casserole or broad saucepan large enough to hold the duck comfortably, put the garlic, thyme, and bay leaves. Salt the duck well, then place the duck, breast side down (wings up), on top of this bed. Add the wine and tomatoes and sprinkle with pepper. Bring to a boil over high heat, then cover the pan and adjust the heat so the mixture simmers steadily but not violently.

2. Cook undisturbed for 30 minutes; the duck should be starting to brown. Baste it with the pan juices and re-cover; continue to cook, basting occasionally, until the duck is nicely browned and the legs tender when pierced with the tip of a thin-bladed knife, at least another half hour. Add the olives and cook for another 30 minutes or so. (This will keep nicely over very low heat for at least another 30 minutes.) Garnish with parsley and serve.

Duck Legs with Olives. This can serve 8 people, as long as you include a couple of side dishes. Substitute 8 duck legs for the whole duck; trim them of all visible fat. Set up a flameproof casserole or broad skillet as described. If you like, add 1 large onion, roughly chopped, 2 carrots, roughly chopped, and 2 celery stalks, roughly chopped, to the bottom of the skillet. Turn the heat to medium and add all the remaining ingredients except the parsley. When the mixture reaches a lively simmer, turn the heat to low and cover; adjust the heat as directed. The duck will be tender in about 1½ hours. Transfer the duck to a warm plate and cover (or place in a very low oven), then turn the heat to medium-high under the remaining sauce. Cook, stirring occasionally, until the mixture is reduced to a thick, saucelike consistency, about 10 minutes. Spoon over the duck legs, garnish with the parsley, and serve.

GOOSE

Roast Goose with Sauerkraut
EASTERN EUROPE
MAKES **4 TO 6 SERVINGS**
TIME **ABOUT 3 HOURS**

Sauerkraut complements roast goose perfectly. The acidity cuts through the grease and adds a wonderful flavor.

Don't overestimate the number of people a goose will serve; it's a large bird, but not a very meaty one.

One 8- to 10-pound goose, trimmed of excess fat

Salt and black pepper to taste

1 pound sauerkraut, preferably fresh, shredded, rinsed, and drained

2 tablespoons sugar

½ cup dry white wine

1. Preheat the oven to 350°F. Prick the goose skin all over with a sharp fork, skewer, or thin-bladed knife; try not to hit the meat (the fat layer is usually about ¼ inch thick). Season the goose with salt and pepper and place it, breast side down, on a rack in a roasting pan.

2. Roast the goose for 20 minutes, prick the exposed skin again, then roast for another 20 minutes, or until it begins to brown. Then turn the goose breast side up, prick again, and baste with some of the accumulated pan juices (there will be plenty). Roast for another hour, pricking the skin and basting 2 or 3 times during that period.

3. Take the roasting pan out of the oven and remove the goose. Lay the sauerkraut on the bottom of the roasting pan and return the goose to the pan. Raise the heat to 400°F and continue to roast until the meat is done, about another 30 minutes. At that point, all juices, including those from the interior, should run clear, and the leg bone should wiggle a little in its socket. When the bird is done, an instant-read thermometer inserted into the thigh will read about 180°F.

4. Remove the goose from the pan and set the pan over low heat on the stovetop. Stir in the sugar and wine, scraping the browned bits from the pan, and simmer until the sauce has reduced slightly and the sauerkraut is moist but not swimming in liquid.

5. Carve the goose and serve with the sauerkraut.

Braised Goose with White Wine and Coffee ALSACE ■

MAKES **4 TO 6 SERVINGS**

TIME **AT LEAST 2½ HOURS, LARGELY UNATTENDED**

Bizarre, huh? But this is how I learned this dish, which originated with the mother of my sometime coauthor Jean-Georges Vongerichten. And it's great: the wine adds fruitiness and the coffee bitterness and, of course, great color. No one will guess what's in here. Unlike most goose preparations, this one can be stretched—with bread, side dishes, and salad—to serve six or even, in a pinch, eight.

One 8- to 10-pound goose, trimmed of excess fat

2 tablespoons butter

2 tablespoons neutral oil, like corn or grapeseed

Salt and black pepper

2 cups chopped celery

2 cups chopped onion

2 cups chopped carrot

10 fresh thyme sprigs

2 cups not-too-dry white wine, like Gewürztraminer

1 cup strong brewed coffee

1 tablespoon cornstarch

Chopped fresh parsley leaves for garnish

1. Preheat the oven to 300°F. Cut the goose into about 8 pieces, discarding the neck. (If you can get your butcher to do this for you, so much the better; the bones are tough and the joints not readily apparent. But you can hack right through with a heavy knife or cleaver.) Put the butter and oil in a large flameproof casserole that can later be covered and turn the heat to medium-high; wait a minute or so, until the butter melts into the oil. Add the goose, skin side down, season it with salt and pepper, and brown it well, rotating and turning the pieces as necessary, 10 to 15 minutes. Transfer the goose to a plate.

2. Add the celery, onion, carrot, and thyme to the pan. Sprinkle with salt and pepper and cook, stirring occasionally, until the vegetables are softened, about 10 minutes. Add the wine and cook, stirring and scraping the bottom of the pan, until the wine bubbles and is slightly reduced. Return the goose to the pot, cover, and put in the oven. Cook, check-

ing every now and then just to make sure the mixture is not drying out (it will not), for at least 2 hours, or until the meat is very tender and almost falling from the bone. (The dish may be prepared to this point and set aside for a few hours or refrigerated for up to a day, then reheated before proceeding.)

3. Mix together the coffee and the cornstarch and stir into the sauce, cooking until it thickens slightly. Taste and adjust the seasoning, garnish, and serve.

OTHER BIRDS

Marinated and Grilled Squab, Quail, or Cornish Game Hen VIETNAM

MAKES **4 SERVINGS**

TIME **2 HOURS OR MORE, PLUS TIME TO PREHEAT THE GRILL, LARGELY UNATTENDED**

Squab is the best bird for this—in fact it's one of the best eating birds there is—but it's expensive and not easy to come by. If you use quail instead, you'll need eight birds (one is not enough for even a light eater). If you use Cornish game hens, you'll need only two. Note the simple finishing "sauce" of salt and pepper mixed together. In Vietnam, this is more common than salt alone. See page 500 for information on fish sauces like nam pla and nuoc mam.

3 garlic cloves, minced

1/3 cup minced shallot

1 tablespoon peeled and minced fresh ginger

1/4 cup honey

1/2 cup nuoc mam, nam pla, or light soy sauce

4 squabs, about 1 pound each

2 tablespoons black pepper

1 tablespoon salt

1 teaspoon dark sesame oil

1. In a small saucepan, combine the garlic, shallot, ginger, honey, nuoc mam, and 1/2 cup water. Bring to a boil, stir once or twice, and cool.

2. Split the birds in half—through the breastbone and backbones—and marinate them in this mixture for at least 1 hour and preferably overnight (in the refrigerator for longer marinating times).

3. Start a charcoal or gas grill; the fire should be only moderately hot and the rack about 4 inches from the heat source. Drain the birds and grill them for about 6 minutes per side or until done to your taste; squab is at its best when still fairly pink. (Quail will take about the same amount of time; game hens will take about 20 minutes total). Meanwhile, mix the pepper and salt together.

4. When the birds are done, drizzle them with the sesame oil and serve, passing the pepper-and-salt mixture at the table.

Marinated and Sautéed Squab. In step 3, drain the birds well and dry with paper towels. Place 2 tablespoons oil in one or more large skillets and turn the heat to high. Cook the birds until nicely browned, about 4 minutes. Turn and brown the other side for 2 to 4 minutes, or until the squab are done. (Quail will take about the same amount of time; I would not recommend doing Cornish hens this way.) Finish and serve as directed.

Deep-Fried Squab. This is quite a different procedure, more work, but very good. Double the amount of marinade. Bring the marinade to a boil in a large saucepan and cook the birds in it, sequentially if necessary, for about 10 minutes each. Remove and let dry on a rack (you can do this a day ahead of time; let dry in the refrigerator). When you're ready to cook, bring a large pot of corn, grapeseed, or other neutral oil to about 350°F (a pinch of flour will sizzle, and the oil will thin and start to shimmer). Fry the birds, sequentially if necessary, until browned and crisp, about 10 minutes. (Quail are excellent this way; reduce the initial cooking time to 5 minutes each; I would not recommend doing Cornish hens this way.) Serve with salt and pepper.

RABBIT

Civet of Rabbit, or Hasenpfeffer

FRANCE, GERMANY

MAKES **4 TO 6 SERVINGS**

TIME **12 HOURS OR MORE, LARGELY UNATTENDED**

An unusual dish with the traditional addition of chocolate for richness. This is best with hare but very nice with the much milder domestic rabbit (and quite good with chicken, too). This is one of those rare occasions when I find a long marinade really helps. You can begin the dish in the morning and finish it that day or start it twenty-four hours (or even more) in advance.

> **2 cups good-quality red wine**
> **¹⁄₂ cup red wine vinegar**
> **1 carrot, roughly chopped**
> **1 onion, roughly chopped**
> **Several fresh parsley or thyme sprigs**
> **1 rabbit or hare, cut into serving pieces**
> **Salt and black pepper to taste**
> **4 thick slices good-quality bacon**
> **2 cups chopped onion**
> **1 cup diced carrot**
> **1 cup diced celery**
> **¹⁄₂ pound wild or button mushrooms, or 1 ounce dried**
>   **porcini, reconstituted (page 112), the soaking liquid**
>   **reserved, and mixed with ¹⁄₂ pound button mushrooms**
> **Flour for dredging**
> **1 ounce unsweetened chocolate, grated or chopped**

1. Mix together the wine, vinegar, chopped carrot, and roughly chopped onion in a bowl large enough to hold the rabbit. Add the herb and the rabbit, along with some salt and pepper. Marinate in the refrigerator, turning the rabbit pieces occasionally, for at least 8 hours. Strain the marinade, reserving it, and dry the rabbit pieces.

2. Cut the bacon into bits and render it over medium-low heat in a Dutch oven or steep-sided skillet. After 5 or 10 minutes, when it has given up much of its fat and is becoming crisp, remove it and add the chopped onion, diced carrot, and celery. Cook, stirring, over medium-low heat; chop the mushrooms and add them, too. If you have soaked dried mushrooms, strain and reserve the soaking liquid. When the vegetables are soft, after about 10 minutes, remove them with a slotted spoon and set aside with the bacon.

3. Turn the heat to medium. Dredge the rabbit pieces in the flour and brown them in the fat that remains in the pan, turning as needed to brown evenly and seasoning with salt and pepper as they brown. When they are browned, lower the heat and return the vegetables and bacon to the skillet; stir, then add the reserved marinade and mushroom soaking liquid, if any. Raise the heat a bit, bring to a boil, stir, then add the chocolate, some salt, and plenty of pepper.

4. Lower the heat even further, cover, and cook until the rabbit is tender and the sauce thick, about an hour. If the sauce is too thin, transfer the meat to a warm oven and reduce the sauce over high heat, stirring almost constantly, until it is thickened. Taste and adjust the seasoning and serve immediately, with buttered noodles, rice, or crusty bread.

Sweet and Sour Rabbit or Chicken

ITALY

MAKES **4 SERVINGS**

TIME **45 TO 50 MINUTES**

A classic Sicilian preparation, with exotic, contrasting flavors. Domesticated rabbit is sold in many supermarkets these days, but since it really does taste like chicken, you can use that if you prefer. Either way, start the meal with a simple pasta dish or serve this with bread and a cooked vegetable.

¼ cup extra virgin olive oil

1 rabbit, cut into 8 pieces, or 1 chicken, 3 to 4 pounds, cut into serving pieces, or 2½ to 3 pounds chicken parts, trimmed of excess fat

Flour for dredging

Salt and black pepper to taste

1 onion, sliced

4 celery stalks, chopped

3 tablespoons drained capers

¼ cup pine nuts

¼ cup currants or raisins

¼ cup sugar

½ cup red wine vinegar

½ cup chicken stock, preferably homemade (page 160)

1 cup red wine

Chopped fresh basil leaves for garnish

1. Put half the oil in a deep skillet or flameproof casserole, preferably nonstick, with a lid. Turn the heat to medium-high and wait a minute or so, until the oil is hot. Dredge the rabbit or chicken pieces in the flour, shaking to remove the excess, then put them, skin side down, in the skillet. Season the meat with salt and pepper and brown it well, rotating and turning the pieces as necessary, 10 to 15 minutes. Transfer the meat to a plate and wipe out the pan.

2. Put the remaining 2 tablespoons oil in the skillet, turn the heat to medium-high, and add the onion and celery; cook, stirring occasionally, until the onion softens, about 5 minutes. Add the capers, pine nuts, and currants and cook, stirring occasionally, for about 5 minutes more. Add the sugar, vinegar, stock, and wine and bring to a boil.

3. Simmer for a minute, then return the rabbit, skin side up, to the pan. Cover and adjust the heat so the mixture simmers steadily. Cook for about 20 minutes, or until the rabbit is tender. Garnish with the basil and serve.

Stifado Rabbit or Chicken Stew GREECE ■

MAKES **4 SERVINGS**

TIME **ABOUT 90 MINUTES**

A dark, fairly intensely flavored stew that is best made with rabbit (or, traditionally, hare), but is quite good with chicken. You can make the entire dish in advance and let it rest at room temperature for a few hours before reheating (or cover and refrigerate overnight).

This is lovely just with crusty bread, or with any potato dish.

¼ cup extra virgin olive oil

1 rabbit or 1 chicken, 3 to 4 pounds, cut into 8 pieces

Salt and black pepper to taste

2 large onions, roughly chopped

4 garlic cloves, sliced

2 cups dry red wine

1 tablespoon red wine vinegar

2 cups chopped tomatoes (canned are fine), with their juice

1 cinnamon stick

3 whole cloves

1 bay leaf

2 allspice berries

1 teaspoon sugar

1. Put half the oil in a deep skillet or flameproof casserole, preferably nonstick, with a lid. Turn the heat to medium-high and wait a minute or so, until the oil is hot. Put the rabbit pieces in the skillet; season with salt and pepper and brown the pieces well, rotating and turning them as necessary, 10 to 15 minutes. Transfer the meat to a plate and wipe out the pan.

2. Put the remaining 2 tablespoons oil in the skillet, turn the heat to medium-high, and add the onions and garlic; cook, stirring occasionally, until the onions soften, about 5 minutes. Add the wine and cook, stirring occasionally, and allowing it to bubble away for a minute or two. Stir in the vinegar and tomatoes and cook, stirring occasionally, until the tomatoes break up, about 10 minutes. Tie the cinnamon stick, cloves, bay leaf, and allspice in a small cheesecloth bag and add to the sauce, along with the sugar and some salt and pepper.

3. Return the meat to the pan, cover, and adjust the heat so the mixture simmers steadily. Cook until the meat is tender but not dry, 20 to 40 minutes (chicken is likely to require less cooking time than rabbit). If the sauce is thin, transfer the meat to a plate and keep it warm, then reduce the sauce over high heat until thickened. Spoon over the meat and serve.

EGG DISHES

What can one say about the egg, one of the most useful, inexpensive, long-keeping, and underrated of all of our animal ingredients? Only, perhaps, that we should be thankful that increasing amounts of cage-free, chemical-free eggs are appearing at many supermarkets; these are not only presumably more humane and healthier but are noticeably more flavorful.

Poached Eggs ■ ▪

MAKES **2**

TIME **10 MINUTES**

The perfect poached egg isn't easy to achieve, and it's unlikely you'll produce one on your first try. Patience. If you want to get good at it, sacrifice a dozen or two and practice. Or don't worry so much; a ragged-looking poached egg tastes just as good as a lovely one. Just don't overcook.

1 teaspoon salt

1 teaspoon white or cider vinegar

2 eggs

1. Bring about an inch of water to a boil in a deep, small skillet, add the salt and vinegar, and lower the heat to the point where it barely bubbles. One at a time, break the eggs into a shallow bowl and slip them into the water. At this point, cover the skillet or begin to spoon the water over the tops of the eggs.

2. Cook for 3 to 5 minutes, just until the white is set and the yolk has filmed over. Remove with a slotted spoon. (Poached eggs can be handled as long as you are careful; to reheat them, dip into a saucepan of simmering water for 30 seconds.)

Hard-Cooked Eggs ■ ■ ■

MAKES **4 SERVINGS**

TIME **15 MINUTES, LARGELY UNATTENDED**

Few people hard-cook eggs correctly (and I myself have changed my technique about five times in the last thirty years, though I do think this is it). For one thing, they should not be boiled. For another, they should not be overcooked. Here's how:

4 large or extra-large eggs

1. Put the eggs in a small saucepan with water to cover and turn the heat to medium-high. Bring to a boil, then turn off the heat and cover.
2. Let sit for 9 minutes. Run under cold water to cool, then refrigerate or peel.

Akoori Spicy Scrambled Eggs INDIA ■

MAKES **4 SERVINGS**

TIME **20 MINUTES**

Eggs are a significant source of protein in India, and when you eat a lot of eggs you look for ways to vary them. This is a standard preparation and a great one for lunch, a late supper, or for those who like really savory breakfasts. They're also made as street food, which is how I first had them—prepared at a cart and eaten from a paper plate standing up (and, in a hurry, in the back of a car).

In India, these eggs might have cooked lentils (Dal, page 433), black-eyed peas (page 434), or cooked shredded potatoes stirred into them.

3 tablespoons butter or neutral oil, like corn or grapeseed

1 tablespoon minced garlic

1 tablespoon peeled and minced fresh ginger

½ cup roughly chopped scallion

1 jalapeño or other small fresh chile, stemmed, seeded, and minced, or to taste

Salt and black pepper to taste

8 eggs

⅓ cup chopped fresh cilantro leaves

1. Put the butter in a skillet, preferably nonstick, and turn the heat to medium-high. Add the garlic, ginger, scallion, chile, and a sprinkling of salt and pepper and cook, stirring occasionally, until the garlic begins to color, about 3 minutes.
2. Meanwhile, beat the eggs lightly with a little more salt and pepper. With the heat still at medium-high, add them to the pan and stir. Immediately remove the pan from the heat and stir until the curds stop forming, a minute or so. Return to the heat and cook, stirring constantly, until the eggs are creamy and thick but not dry (they will continue to cook under their own heat after you remove them, so stop a moment short of your desired consistency). Stir in the cilantro and serve immediately.

Hard-Cooked Eggs in Spicy Tomato Sauce INDIA

MAKES **4 SERVINGS**

TIME **40 MINUTES**

In a largely vegetarian country, eggs take on more importance than they have traditionally in the States. Indians eat eggs in a variety of interesting ways and at all meals. Here they're hard-cooked, simmered in a spicy tomato sauce, and served as a main course. It's a great, easy, and inexpensive weeknight dish. Serve with Pilaf (page 513) or another rice preparation.

3 tablespoons neutral oil, like corn or grapeseed

2 large onions, chopped

1 jalapeño or other small fresh chile, stemmed, seeded, and minced, or 1 or 2 dried red chiles, crumbled, or to taste

1 tablespoon minced garlic

1 tablespoon peeled and minced fresh ginger

8 eggs

1 teaspoon ground cumin

1 teaspoon ground coriander

1 teaspoon ground turmeric

$\frac{1}{2}$ teaspoon ground fenugreek

$\frac{1}{4}$ teaspoon ground cinnamon

3 cups chopped tomatoes (canned are fine, drain them lightly before chopping)

Salt and black pepper to taste

Chopped fresh cilantro leaves for garnish

1. Put the oil in a 10- or 12-inch skillet and turn the heat to medium. A minute or two later, add the onions, chile, garlic, and ginger. Cook, stirring, for a minute or two, then cover the pan and reduce the heat to medium-low. Cook until the onions are dry and beginning to brown, about 10 minutes.

2. Meanwhile, put the eggs in cold water to cover. Turn the heat to medium-high, bring to a boil, then turn off the heat and cover; set a timer for 9 minutes.

3. When the onions are done, uncover and raise the heat to medium-high. Add the spices and cook, stirring occasionally, for about a minute. Add the tomatoes, a pinch of salt, and some pepper and cook, stirring occasionally, until the mixture bubbles. Cook for about 5 more minutes.

4. When the eggs are done, plunge them into a bowl of cold water and place under running water until they feel cool, then peel. When the tomato sauce is ready, add them; cook 5 minutes or so more. Taste and adjust the seasoning, garnish, and serve hot.

Spicy Tomato Sauce with Vegetables. This will take a little longer; you can include the eggs or not, as you prefer. In step 3, add 3 or 4 cups chopped mixed vegetables, such as carrots, green beans, potatoes, zucchini, cauliflower, and/or eggplant, along with $\frac{1}{2}$ cup water; simmer until the vegetables are done, then—if you are using them—add the eggs.

Huevos Rancheros MEXICO
MAKES **4 SERVINGS**

TIME **35 MINUTES**

As long as you are not a person who eats only sweets for breakfast, there is nothing more satisfying than huevos rancheros, the original "breakfast burrito." Since you finish the dish in the oven, you can prepare all but the eggs ahead of time, which makes it a great brunch dish when you have guests; the recipe is easily doubled or even tripled.

$\frac{1}{4}$ cup corn or grapeseed oil for frying, or more as needed

Four 5-inch corn tortillas

$\frac{1}{4}$ cup Refried Beans (page 438) or any soft, well-seasoned beans

4 eggs

Salt and black pepper to taste

$\frac{1}{2}$ cup Salsa Roja (page 610) or any tomato-based salsa, preferably homemade

$\frac{1}{4}$ cup crumbled fresh Mexican cheese, like queso fresco, blanco, or ranchero (page 85)

1. Preheat the oven to 350°F. Heat the oil in a small skillet over medium heat. When the oil is hot but not smoking, fry the tortillas one at a time until softened and heated through, about 3 seconds per side. Make sure they do not crisp. Drain on paper towels.

2. Spread 1 tablespoon of the beans in the center of each tortilla and set aside. Meanwhile, use a little more oil to fry the eggs sunny side up (a nonstick skillet will make your life easier), sprinkling with salt and pepper as they cook. Place an egg in the center of each tortilla, then top with 2 tablespoons salsa and 1 tablespoon cheese.

3. Carefully transfer the tortillas to a baking dish that fits them snugly. Bake until the cheese is melted, about 5 minutes, then serve immediately.

Simplest Huevos Rancheros. Omit the tortillas and Refried Beans. Scramble the eggs in oil; as they are beginning to set in the pan, stir in the salsa and cheese. Season to taste with salt and pepper and serve.

Baked Eggs, West Indian Style
CARIBBEAN

MAKES **4 SERVINGS**

TIME **35 MINUTES**

Shirred eggs with a spicy sauce make a great brunch dish. Serve with toast or Arroz a la Mexicana (page 517).

> 2 tablespoons extra virgin olive oil
>
> 1 or 2 small dried hot red chiles or about 1 teaspoon hot red pepper flakes, or to taste
>
> 3 garlic cloves, chopped
>
> 1 medium onion, chopped
>
> 1 small bell pepper, preferably red, stemmed, seeded, and chopped
>
> 2 cups chopped plum tomatoes (drained canned are fine)
>
> Salt and black pepper to taste
>
> 8 eggs
>
> 2 tablespoons butter, melted

1. Preheat the oven to 350°F. Put the olive oil in a large skillet over medium-high heat; a minute later, add the chiles and garlic and cook for about 30 seconds, stirring. Add the onion and bell pepper and cook, stirring occasionally, until the onion softens, 5 to 10 minutes. Add the tomatoes and cook, stirring occasionally, until the mixture becomes saucy, 10 to 15 minutes. Season with salt and pepper.

2. Put a portion of the sauce in each of 4 ramekins or put all of it in the bottom of a gratin dish. If you're using a gratin dish, make 8 nests in the sauce using the back of a spoon; crack 1 egg into each nest or 2 eggs into each ramekin. Top with salt, pepper, and the melted butter.

3. Bake for 8 to 12 minutes, or until the eggs are barely set. The yolks should still be soft and runny—take care not to overcook.

Baked Eggs "Flamenco" SPAIN

MAKES **4 SERVINGS**

TIME **35 MINUTES**

I love baked eggs, so I was delighted to come across this elaborate version, served as an appetizer before a Spanish dinner (I like it at brunch). When it was made for me, it contained small amounts of asparagus and peas, but you could use bits of any vegetable you like; leftovers are the best option. Use both meats, either, or neither; this is essentially a dish that was created to combine eggs with whatever else is on hand.

> 2 tablespoons extra virgin olive oil
>
> 1/4 pound ham, preferably prosciutto, cubed or chopped
>
> 1/4 pound chorizo, thinly sliced
>
> 1 cup tomatoes, chopped (drained canned are fine)

8 eggs

Salt and black pepper to taste

1/2 cup chopped cooked green vegetables, like peas,
    green beans, and/or asparagus

8 strips Roasted Red Peppers (page 470), or canned
    piquillo peppers or pimientos

Chopped fresh parsley leaves for garnish

1. Preheat the oven to 425°F. Put the oil in a large
skillet and turn the heat to medium-high; add the
ham and chorizo and cook, stirring occasionally,
until the chorizo begins to brown, about 5 minutes. Turn off the heat.

2. Distribute the tomatoes among four ³/₄-cup
ramekins, making a layer at the bottom of each.
Layer a portion of the meat mixture on top of the
tomatoes.

3. Break 2 eggs into each ramekin, taking care to keep
the yolks whole; sprinkle with salt and pepper.
Add the vegetables and top with the pepper strips.
Bake for 8 to 12 minutes, or until the eggs are
barely set. The yolks should still be soft and
runny—take care not to overcook. Garnish and
serve immediately.

Cuban-Style Baked Eggs. These are vegetarian:
Omit the ham and chorizo. In step 1, cook 1 onion,
chopped; 1 small red bell pepper, stemmed, seeded,
and chopped; and 1 tablespoon minced garlic in the
oil, stirring occasionally, until the onion softens. In
step 2, add the tomatoes to the mix and cook over
medium heat, stirring occasionally, until the mixture
becomes saucy; taste and add salt and pepper if necessary. Put the sauce in the bottom of 4 ramekins or 1
larger dish and break the eggs onto it. Dot with a little butter if you like and sprinkle with salt and pepper.
Omit the chopped vegetables and additional peppers
and bake as directed. Garnish and serve.

Tortilla SPAIN ■

MAKES **3 TO 6 SERVINGS**

TIME **ABOUT 40 MINUTES**

Perhaps the most commonly seen tapa of all, this is a
dish I have loved eating (and making) since I first visited Spain more than twenty years ago. Don't be put
off by the large quantity of olive oil; much of it will be
poured off (and will have a lovely taste, so you can use
it for sautéing; refrigerate in the meantime).

1 cup extra virgin olive oil

1¼ pounds (3 to 4 medium) waxy potatoes, peeled and
    thinly sliced

1 medium onion, thinly sliced

Salt and black pepper to taste

6 extra-large or jumbo eggs

1. Put the oil in a large, nonstick, ovenproof skillet
over medium heat. About 3 minutes later, add a
slice of potato; if bubbles appear, the oil is ready.
Add all of the potatoes and onion, along with
some salt and pepper. Turn the potato mixture in
the oil with a wooden spoon and adjust the heat so
that the oil bubbles lazily.

2. Cook, turning the potato mixture gently every few
minutes and adjusting the heat so the potatoes do
not brown, until they are tender when pierced
with the point of a small knife, 15 to 20 minutes.
Meanwhile, beat the eggs with some salt and pepper in a large bowl.

3. Drain the potato mixture in a colander, reserving
the oil. Wipe out the skillet and return it to medium
heat, along with 2 tablespoons of the oil. Combine
the potato mixture with the eggs and add to the
skillet. As soon as the edges firm up—this will take
only a minute or so—reduce the heat to medium-
low and cook, undisturbed, for 5 minutes.

4. Insert a rubber spatula all around the edges of the
cake to make sure it will slide from the pan. Care-

fully slide it out—the top will still be quite runny—onto a plate. Cover with another plate and, holding the plates tightly, invert them. Add another tablespoon of oil to the skillet and use a rubber spatula to coax the cake back in. Cook for another 5 minutes, then slide the cake from the skillet to a plate. (Alternatively, finish the cooking by putting the tortilla in a 350°F oven for about 10 minutes.) Serve warm (not hot) or at room temperature. Do not refrigerate.

Chilaquiles MEXICO
MAKES **6 SERVINGS**
TIME **1 HOUR**

A wonderful brunch dish, often served for breakfast in Mexico as a way to use up the previous day's leftovers. But the combination of crunchy tortillas, spicy tomato sauce, and melted cheese is so irresistible you'll want to make it just for its own sake. If you do not want to fry the tortillas, you can either bake them until quite crisp—this will take 15 minutes or so—or simply substitute unsalted (or lightly salted) corn tortilla chips.

> Fifteen 5-inch corn tortillas, cut into 1-inch strips
>
> Corn, grapeseed, or other neutral oil as needed
>
> 3 garlic cloves, minced
>
> 1 medium onion, diced
>
> 4 chipotle, serrano, or jalapeño chiles, stemmed, seeded, and minced, or to taste
>
> 4 cups diced tomatoes (canned are fine; don't bother to drain)
>
> 2 cups chicken stock, preferably homemade (page 160)
>
> Salt and black pepper to taste
>
> 4 eggs, lightly beaten
>
> 2½ cups grated Mexican melting cheese, like queso asadero, Chihuahua, or Menonita (page 85)

> ¼ cup Mexican crema or sour cream
>
> ¼ cup chopped fresh cilantro leaves

1. Preheat the oven to warm. Put the tortilla strips on a baking sheet and let them dry out in the oven for about 5 minutes. Meanwhile, put 1 inch of oil in a large deep heavy skillet over medium heat. Remove the tortilla strips from the oven and raise the oven temperature to 350°F.

2. When the oil is hot, add some tortilla strips and cook until almost crisp. Remove and drain on paper towels. Repeat with the remaining tortilla strips.

3. Carefully drain all but 2 tablespoons oil from the skillet. Set the skillet over medium-high heat and add the garlic, onion, and chiles and cook, stirring, until softened, about 3 minutes. Add the tomatoes, cook until softened, then stir in the chicken stock. Bring to a boil, then lower the heat and simmer until thickened, about 20 minutes. Season with salt and pepper, then stir in the eggs.

4. Coat the bottom of a glass or ceramic baking dish with some of the sauce. Put an even layer of tortilla strips on top of the sauce and sprinkle the cheese on top of the tortilla strips. Repeat this layering, ending with sauce and cheese.

5. Cover with foil and bake until the cheese bubbles, about 20 minutes. Cool slightly, garnish with crema and cilantro, then cut into squares and serve.

Chilaquiles with Meat. Add 1½ cups shredded cooked chicken, turkey, beef, or pork to the simmering tomato sauce. Proceed as in the original recipe.

Fried Egg Chilaquiles. Do not stir the eggs into the sauce, but make the chilaquiles without them. Instead, top each serving of chilaquiles with a fried egg.

One-Pot Chilaquiles. Omit steps 4 and 5, but make sure your skillet is ovenproof. After the sauce has thickened, remove it from the heat and stir in the tortilla strips and cheese. Bake, uncovered, for 20 minutes, cool slightly, then scoop onto serving plates and garnish as directed.

Quick Chilaquiles. Omit steps 4 and 5. Divide the tortilla strips among serving plates and top with the tomato sauce, cheese, crema, and cilantro. Serve immediately.

Omelette aux Fines Herbes FRANCE ▦

MAKES **2 SERVINGS**

TIME **15 MINUTES**

The omelet remains the standby dinner for many accomplished French cooks, and it remains on the menu of many restaurants. Delicious and gorgeous, it's a bit trickier than a frittata (page 558), but considerably faster, and nonstick pans have made it a lot more reliable.

Fresh herbs are a must here; I would say butter is a must also, but I'd rather you made the omelet with olive oil than not at all.

Once you learn how to do this, it will become a staple for you, and variations will be second nature. I offer a few to get you started.

5 eggs

2 tablespoons plus 1 teaspoon finely chopped fresh herbs, preferably a combination of chervil, tarragon (less than a teaspoon of fresh leaves), chives, and parsley

Salt and black pepper to taste

2 tablespoons cream, optional

2 tablespoons plus 1 teaspoon butter (preferred) or extra virgin olive oil

1. Beat together the eggs, 2 tablespoons herbs, and some salt and pepper in a bowl; add the cream if you're using it.

2. Put a 10-inch nonstick skillet over medium-high heat and wait a minute. Add the 2 tablespoons butter; when it melts, swirl it around the pan until its foam subsides, then pour in the egg mixture. Cook, undisturbed, for about 30 seconds, then use a rubber spatula to push the edges of the eggs toward the center. As you do this, tip the pan to allow the uncooked eggs in the center to reach the perimeter.

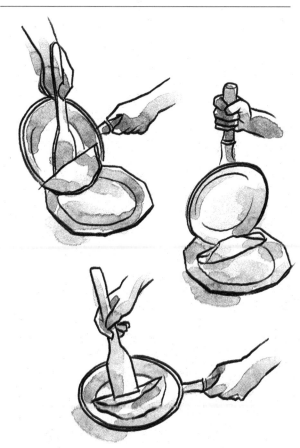

THREE WAYS OF FINISHING AN OMELET

3. Continue this process until the omelet is mostly cooked but still quite runny in the center, a total of about 3 minutes (you can cook until the center firms up if you prefer).

4. There are several ways to proceed. You can try rolling the omelet out of the pan to form a cylinder; this is the most traditional, elegant (and, of course, difficult) method; to do this, hold the pan's handle at about a 45-degree angle above the plate and begin to roll from the handle end. Or you can fold the omelet in thirds, which is almost as nice, using a large spatula. The easiest thing to do, and it's not only acceptable but lovely, is to fold the omelet in half and slide it from the pan.

5. Rub the top of the omelet with the remaining teaspoon of butter, garnish with the remaining teaspoon of herbs, and serve.

Tomato Omelet. Cut a tomato (or 2 if you prefer) in half through its equator and, over a sink, squeeze and shake to discard seeds. Chop finely and add to the eggs—in a line along the axis on which you will fold or roll—about a minute before finishing the omelet.

Ham or Bacon Omelet. Add $1/4$ cup finely chopped ham or cooked bacon to the eggs—in a line along the axis on which you will fold or roll—about a minute before finishing the omelet. Reduce the salt in the eggs.

Sorrel Omelet. A lovely old delicacy: Omit the other herbs. Before cooking the eggs, melt a tablespoon of butter in a small pan over medium heat and add $1/4$ cup chopped sorrel leaves; cook for about 5 minutes, until the sorrel begins to melt. Remove from the heat. Cook the eggs as directed; add the sorrel—in a line along the axis on which you will fold or roll—about a minute before finishing the omelet.

Meat I don't remember who said to me, "You must have meat at a big meal; it brings closure." It could be an ancient statement or a recent one. But the fact is that the heaviness and richness of most meat dishes give a kind of satiety that it is difficult to obtain with other foods. I believe this is why we continue to eat it, regardless of ethics or health. Also: we like the flavor.

This chapter is organized not by types of meat but by cooking technique, perhaps a bit unusual. But meats can often be substituted so freely for one another that I believe this makes sense.

Best Beef Cuts for Grilling

Sirloin. All cuts of sirloin can be grilled successfully. Strip sirloin (also called *New York strip*) is the best by far.

Ribeye. Super steak, probably more flavor than any other cut.

Filet. Also called *tenderloin*. Not extremely flavorful, but very tender. Usually best with some kind of sauce.

Skirt. As long as it isn't overcooked, a terrific steak.

T-bone. A combination of filet and sirloin—tender and tasty. Porterhouse is almost the same but with more of the filet.

GRILLING

The simplest, most straightforward, and oldest of meat-cooking techniques is grilling. Many, many cuts of meat can be grilled with nothing more than a little salt, and that method can hardly be improved on. These recipes build on that idea; they preserve the intrinsic flavor of good meat and complement it with simple sauces and dressings.

Bistecca alla Fiorentina

Tuscan Grilled Steak ITALY ■

MAKES **4 SERVINGS**

TIME **30 MINUTES, PLUS TIME TO PREHEAT THE GRILL**

It's not much different from an American steak, but the combination of cut (almost always a T-bone, though occasionally you'll see ribeye), olive oil, and lemon juice marks this preparation as distinctly Tuscan. If you can find a piece of dry-aged prime meat, go for it.

I love the combination of steak and bread, and of course tomato or other salad, but you can use any typical steak side dishes you like—even in Italy they might serve this with French fries.

One 2-pound porterhouse or T-bone steak, about 1³/₄ inches thick

Coarse salt and freshly ground black pepper to taste

Extra virgin olive oil

1 lemon, cut into wedges

1. Start a charcoal or gas grill or preheat the broiler; the fire should be quite hot and the rack 4 to 6 inches from the heat source. Grill the steak for about 5 minutes per side for medium-rare, turning only once (an instant-read thermometer should read about 125°F when inserted into the thickest part); cooking time, of course, will depend on the thickness of the steak and the heat of the fire.

2. Sprinkle both sides liberally with salt and pepper. Put on a platter and drizzle with a little olive oil. Serve with the lemon wedges.

Fleica Grilled Steak with Garlic ROMANIA

MAKES **4 TO 6 SERVINGS**

TIME **1¹/₂ HOURS, LARGELY UNATTENDED, PLUS TIME TO PREHEAT THE GRILL**

If you think Eastern European cuisine is boring, this will change your mind. It's probably the most famous dish from Romania and something that may become a part of your summer grilling repertoire.

Flank steak is classic for this, but I like it best with sirloin or ribeye. Omit the butter if you're feeling health-conscious, but it adds a wonderful richness. Garnish with the parsley and serve.

3 or 4 garlic cloves, peeled

Juice of 2 lemons

¹⁄₂ teaspoon salt

Freshly ground black pepper to taste

One 2- to 3-pound flank steak or 4 sirloin (New York) strip
or ribeye steaks or an equivalent amount of skirt steak

3 tablespoons butter, melted

¹⁄₄ cup chopped fresh parsley leaves

1. If you have a mortar and pestle, pound the garlic with the lemon juice and salt until a paste is formed. Otherwise, mince the garlic finely and stir it with the salt into the lemon juice. Use the back of a wooden spoon to smash the garlic as much as you can. Press the pepper into the steak and then spread the garlic mixture evenly on both sides. Let the steak marinate for an hour at room temperature.

2. Meanwhile, start a charcoal or gas grill or preheat the broiler; the fire should be moderately hot and the rack about 4 inches from the heat source. When ready to cook, brush the melted butter onto the steak and then place on the grill. Continue to baste with any remaining butter while the steak is cooking, about 4 minutes per side for medium-rare. Garnish with the parsley and serve.

Grilled Steak with Roquefort Sauce

FRANCE ■

MAKES **4 SERVINGS**

TIME **20 MINUTES, PLUS TIME TO PREHEAT THE GRILL**

A dish that often appears on bistro menus in France and increasingly here in the States. It's best, I think, with Roquefort, which is made from sheep's milk. But Stilton, Gorgonzola, Maytag blue, or any high-quality fairly soft blue cheese will work well. Don't bother, however, trying to make this sauce with commercially produced domestic blue cheese, such as that sold pre-crumbled for salads. Not only will its taste be inferior, but it will not give the sauce the same creaminess.

You need a salad here, to provide some offsetting lightness. Some bread wouldn't be bad either; whatever your side dishes, they should be relatively uncomplicated.

1 tablespoon butter or neutral oil, like corn or grapeseed

¹⁄₄ cup minced shallot

2 tablespoons white wine vinegar or cider vinegar

6 ounces crumbled Roquefort or other blue cheese

Salt and black pepper to taste

A good pinch of cayenne

1¹⁄₂ to 2 pounds sirloin (New York) strip, filet mignon,
or ribeye steaks

Minced fresh parsley leaves or chives for garnish,
optional

1. Start a charcoal fire or preheat a gas grill or broiler; the fire should be quite hot and the rack no more than 4 inches from the heat source.

2. Put the butter in a small saucepan and turn the heat to medium; when the butter melts and its foam begins to subside, add the shallot and cook until soft, stirring occasionally, about 5 minutes. Add the vinegar, stir, and cook until it is just about evaporated, 1 or 2 minutes. Turn the heat to low and stir in the cheese, a few grindings of black pepper, and the cayenne. Stir occasionally until the cheese melts, then taste and adjust the seasoning as necessary (it's unlikely that the sauce will need any salt). Keep warm while you grill the steaks.

3. Season the steaks well with salt and pepper, then grill or broil for 3 to 4 minutes per side for medium-rare, longer or shorter according to your taste. Serve the steaks with a spoonful or two of

sauce over each, garnished with the parsley or chives if you like.

Grilled Skirt Steak with Sauce au Chien CARIBBEAN ■ ▨

MAKES **4 SERVINGS**

TIME **30 MINUTES, PLUS TIME TO PREHEAT THE GRILL**

I was in a restaurant in Martinique where this sauce—which translates as "dog sauce," for reasons I don't want to know—was served on everything, from kidneys to chicken to vegetables. I liked it best on steak. As with so many Caribbean dishes, this would be served with Coconut Rice and Beans (page 516).

Other cuts of meat you can use here: almost anything, from liver to bone-in dark-meat chicken, to pork chops or ribs.

1 tablespoon peeled and slivered or minced garlic

6 scallions, trimmed and minced

1 jalapeño or habanero (Scotch bonnet) chile, stemmed, seeded, and minced, or chili paste or hot red pepper flakes to taste (start with about $1/2$ teaspoon)

Salt and black pepper to taste

$1/2$ teaspoon ground allspice, or to taste

1 tablespoon peanut or neutral oil, like corn or grapeseed

$11/2$ to 2 pounds skirt, sirloin (New York) strip, or ribeye steak

Juice of 1 lime

1. Start a charcoal or gas grill or preheat the broiler; the fire should be moderately hot and the rack about 4 inches from the heat source. Meanwhile, prepare the sauce: Combine the garlic, scallions, chile, $1/2$ teaspoon each of salt and pepper, the allspice, and the oil in a small bowl. Add $1/2$ cup boiling water; stir and let sit.

2. Sprinkle the meat with salt and pepper and grill or broil it, 3 or 4 minutes per side for skirt steak, somewhat longer for sirloin or ribeye, turning 2 or 3 times, until cooked through, about 15 minutes. Taste the sauce and add more chile, salt, pepper, or allspice if needed. Stir in the lime juice. Serve the meat hot or at room temperature, passing the sauce at the table.

Tenderloin with Miso JAPAN ▨

MAKES **4 SERVINGS**

TIME **30 MINUTES, PLUS UP TO 1 DAY FOR MARINATING, AND TIME TO PREHEAT THE GRILL**

Tenderloin—most commonly sold as filet mignon—has just about the least flavor of any cut of beef, but it is wonderfully tender and juicy, and it sure takes well to this sauce, which everyone seems to love.

I'm not usually a big fan of long marinating periods, but here it seems to make a big difference; the miso completely changes the flavor of the meat in a spectacular way. I grill these, but you can broil the meat or roast it at 500°F for just a few minutes. (In any case, cook until the interior of the meat is about 125°F.)

Other cuts of meat you can use here: ribeye; pork tenderloin, cut into medallions as you would the filet.

1 cup dark (red) miso

1 tablespoon peeled and minced fresh ginger

1 teaspoon minced garlic

$1/2$ teaspoon cayenne, or to taste

Mirin or sake as needed

$11/2$ to 2 pounds beef tenderloin, cut into medallions, or ribeye, or sirloin (New York) strip

1. Combine the first 4 ingredients in a large bowl, then thin with a little mirin or sake, just until the mixture is pasty. Spread the meat with this paste, then proceed or cover and refrigerate for up to 24 hours.
2. Start a charcoal fire or gas grill or preheat the broiler or oven; the rack should be 4 inches or less from the heat source. Grill, broil, or roast the meat, 2 to 4 minutes per side, until the outside is crisp and the inside medium-rare. Serve immediately.

Grilled Lemongrass Beef VIETNAM

MAKES **4 SERVINGS AS A MAIN COURSE, 8 AS A STARTER**

TIME **1 HOUR, LARGELY UNATTENDED, LONGER FOR MARINATING IF YOU HAVE TIME, PLUS TIME TO PREHEAT THE GRILL**

Lemongrass has a distinctive flavor that is instantly likable and very closely associated with the cuisine of Vietnam (it's grown and used elsewhere, especially in Southeast Asia, but nowhere quite as widely). This dish is often served on a flat bed of plain rice noodles, but I like it best over a salad, dressed with a little nuoc

THREADING BEEF ONTO SKEWERS

cham. For information on Asian fish sauces like nam pla, see page 500.

Other cuts of meat you can use here: pork, cut from either the loin or the shoulder.

1½ to 2 pounds beef tenderloin or boneless sirloin
1 tablespoon toasted sesame seeds, (page 596)
2 lemongrass stalks, trimmed (page 143) and finely chopped
2 large or 4 medium shallots, roughly chopped
2 large garlic cloves, roughly chopped
1 small dried chile, or to taste
1 tablespoon fresh lime juice
1 tablespoon sugar
2 tablespoons nam pla, plus a little more if needed
Salt if necessary
½ teaspoon black pepper, or to taste
Nuoc Cham (page 590) for dipping

1. Freeze the beef for 30 to 60 minutes to facilitate slicing. If you're using wood skewers, soak them in water to cover. Meanwhile, combine all the remaining ingredients except the Nuoc Cham in a small food processor and blend to a paste, stopping the machine to stir down the sides if necessary.
2. When the beef is semifrozen, slice it as thinly as you can. Marinate it for as little as 20 minutes and as long as overnight in the spice paste (if the paste is too thick, thin it with a bit more nam pla).
3. Start a charcoal or gas grill; the fire should be quite hot and the rack about 4 inches from the heat source. Skewer the beef slices, using the skewer as you would a needle to weave once or twice through the meat. Grill quickly, about 1 minute per side, until nicely browned. Serve hot with the Nuoc Cham.

Lemongrass "Hamburgers" VIETNAM ▨

MAKES **4 SERVINGS**

TIME **30 MINUTES, PLUS TIME TO PREHEAT THE GRILL**

Of all the powerful ingredients in these burgers—lemongrass, shallots, garlic, chile, and nam pla (called nuoc mam in Vietnamese; see page 500 for information on these Asian fish sauces)—none survives the cooking as well as the lemongrass, whose distinctive scent and flavor override all the others, reducing them to bit players.

Lemongrass is changed less by cooking than most seasonings, and this goes for its woody texture too, which is why you remove the tough outer layers. You can grind the tender cores with the meat instead of chopping them if you like. Serve the burgers on rolls, rice noodles, or salad.

Other cuts of meat you can use here: ground beef sirloin or chuck, which may be combined with pork if you like.

1½ to 2 pounds boneless pork, preferably from the shoulder

3 or 4 large shallots or 1 medium red onion, peeled

4 garlic cloves, peeled

2 lemongrass stalks, trimmed (page 143) and finely chopped

1 teaspoon stemmed, seeded, and minced fresh chile or hot red pepper flakes, or to taste

Salt and black pepper to taste

1 tablespoon nam pla

1 teaspoon sugar

Lime wedges or Dijon mustard for serving

1. Start a charcoal fire or preheat a gas grill; the fire should not be too hot, and the rack should be 4 inches or more from the heat source. (You can also cook the patties in a nonstick skillet or a broiler.) If the meat is preground, mince the shallots, garlic, and lemongrass and combine them and the chile with the pork, salt, pepper, nam pla, and sugar. If the meat is in chunks, combine it in a food processor with those ingredients and process until everything is minced together; do not overprocess—it's best if the meat is minced, not pureed.

2. Shape the meat mixture into 8 small patties (or 4 larger ones if you're serving them on buns) and grill until nicely browned on both sides and cooked as you like the meat (pork should be cooked to at least 150°F), about 10 minutes. Serve with the lime wedges or mustard.

Grilled Escabeche with Pork SPAIN ■ ▨

MAKES **4 SERVINGS**

TIME **45 MINUTES, LONGER FOR MARINATING IF YOU HAVE TIME, PLUS TIME TO PREHEAT THE GRILL**

Often the most effective marinating happens not before but after cooking. This technique, usually called escabeche, was once used to preserve food. It's really a form of pickling: hot food was put into hot liquid containing a good deal of vinegar. Treated thus, it would keep for some time (if canned, for a long time).

Since we don't need escabeche for preserving, the postgrilling marinating time can be as little as a few minutes, but it can also be as long as overnight—it doesn't make much difference; in either case, it produces a highly flavored, prepared-in-advance, room-temperature dish that is good as part of a buffet with a variety of other dishes (none of which should be noticeably acidic).

Other cuts of meat you can use here: any cut of chicken, bone in or out (be careful not to overcook), or mackerel or other fish (typically floured and sautéed or fried before marinating).

½ cup red wine or other vinegar

1 cup red wine

2 bay leaves

5 fresh thyme sprigs or 1 teaspoon dried

5 fresh marjoram or oregano sprigs or 1 teaspoon dried
marjoram or $\frac{1}{2}$ teaspoon dried oregano

1 small dried or fresh chile, optional

1 large onion, white or red, cut in half and sliced into half-
moons

3 garlic cloves, peeled and lightly crushed

1 tablespoon sugar

Salt and black pepper to taste

2 pork tenderloins, 1$\frac{1}{2}$ to 2 pounds total

1. Start a charcoal or gas grill or preheat the broiler; the fire should be moderately hot and the rack 4 to 6 inches from the heat source. As it is heating, combine all the ingredients except the pork (including a pinch of salt and a liberal grinding of pepper, at least $\frac{1}{2}$ teaspoon) in a medium saucepan with 1 cup water. Bring to a boil, reduce the heat to medium-low, and simmer for about 5 minutes, or until the onion has softened just a bit. Pour into a deep platter large enough to accommodate the pork.

2. Sprinkle the pork liberally with salt and pepper and brown it on all sides until it is nearly cooked through (an instant-read thermometer inserted into the meat should read 150°F), 10 to 15 minutes. Remove the pork, let it rest for a few minutes to cool, then put it on the platter with the marinade.

3. If you are eager to eat, wait 10 minutes or so, then slice the pork about 1 inch thick and put it back in the marinade; wait another 15 minutes or so before eating. If you have time, let the pork sit in the marinade, whole, for a couple of hours (or overnight, refrigerated) before slicing and serving at room temperature, spooning a bit of the marinade (including some onion) over each slice.

Cochinita Pibil Yucatecan Pit-Roasted Pork
MEXICO ■ ▨

MAKES **ABOUT 10 SERVINGS**

TIME **24 HOURS, LARGELY UNATTENDED**

Here's how you really make cochinita pibil: Dig a pit and build a large wood fire in it. Cover the wood with rocks. When the rocks crack, they're ready. Rub the pork as directed here, then wrap it in banana leaves. Put in the pit, then cover with leaves and douse the whole thing with water. Cover the pit. Let sit for a day or so. Eat.

Or try my method, which is not bad at all.

1 boneless pork shoulder (picnic or Boston butt),
about 6 pounds

6 garlic cloves, slivered

1 recipe Recado Rojo (page 609)

$\frac{1}{4}$ cup fresh orange juice

$\frac{1}{4}$ cup fresh lemon juice

1 recipe Habanero-Garlic Salsa (page 611)

1. Use a thin-bladed knife to poke holes all over the pork; as you do so, shove slivers of garlic in there. Combine the Recado Rojo with the orange and lemon juices and rub all over the pork. Wrap loosely in foil and refrigerate overnight.

2. Five or 6 hours before you're ready to eat, turn the oven to 300°F or prepare a charcoal or gas grill to cook over low indirect heat (ideally with some wood or wood chips as a flavoring source; see the headnote on page 352). Open the top of the foil and put the pork in a roasting pan in the oven or directly on the grill rack; if you're grilling, cover the grill. Cook, checking occasionally and basting with the pan juices (add water or orange juice to the bottom of the foil package if the mixture dries out), until the pork is brown and very, very tender—4 hours or more.

3. Serve hot or at room temperature, with the pan juices and Habanero-Garlic Salsa.

Jerked Pork JAMAICA ■

MAKES **ABOUT 10 SERVINGS**

TIME **24 HOURS, LARGELY UNATTENDED**

Among the most mistreated and overused terms in cooking is jerked, which, at least when I had it in the central Jamaican highlands—Cockpit Country, as it's called—is essentially a beautifully seasoned pork (or, originally, boar) shoulder slow-cooked over coals. (You cannot make a "jerked" pork tenderloin; it will simply dry out.) The distinctive flavors are nutmeg, allspice (which is called pimento in the islands), and habanero peppers. If possible, crack a nutmeg into pieces and toast about half of it in a skillet until fragrant, with about a tablespoon of allspice berries, then grind them together. If not, use dried spices as directed here.

If you have a gas grill, this will be easy; but if at all possible, set up an aluminum tray of soaked wood chips over the side with the heat and replenish as necessary. If you use charcoal, use real charcoal instead of briquettes if you can.

Serve this with Coconut Rice and Beans (page 516) and, if you dare, Habanero-Garlic Salsa (page 611).

Other cuts of meat you can use here: bone-in chicken legs (cooking time will be considerably shorter, about 1 hour); spareribs, though not traditional, are also good.

10 scallions, trimmed and finely chopped

2 tablespoons minced garlic

1 or 2 habanero (Scotch bonnet) chiles, stemmed, seeded, and minced

1 teaspoon freshly grated nutmeg

1 teaspoon ground allspice

1 tablespoon fresh thyme leaves or 1 teaspoon dried

Salt and black pepper to taste

1/2 cup fresh lime juice, more or less

1 boneless pork shoulder (picnic or Boston butt), about 6 pounds

1. Combine the first 6 ingredients with some salt and pepper, then moisten with enough lime juice to make a paste. Use a thin-bladed knife to poke holes all over the pork and stick some of the paste in there; rub the pork with that which remains. Wrap loosely in foil and refrigerate overnight or, if you're in a hurry, proceed.

2. Five or 6 hours before you're ready to eat, turn the oven to 300°F or prepare a charcoal or gas grill to cook over low indirect heat (ideally with some wood chips as a flavoring source; see the headnote). Open the top of the foil and put the pork in a roasting pan in the oven or directly on the grill rack; if you're grilling, cover the grill. Cook, checking occasionally and basting with the lime juice, until the pork is brown and very, very tender—4 hours or more. To serve, chop into pieces (the meat will be very tender).

Grilled Lamb Chops with Mint Chutney INDIA ■

MAKES **4 SERVINGS**

TIME **30 MINUTES, PLUS TIME TO PREHEAT THE GRILL**

You can make this easy mint chutney quite hot, and it still seems balanced, especially when served with a rich, flavorful meat like lamb. Heat, as aficionados know, comes in a wide variety of flavors, and what works best here is a bit of roasted fresh habanero (also called Scotch bonnet), the hottest chile you can find. But minced raw jalapeño or hot red pepper flakes are also good. No matter what you use, add a little at a time (I'd start with a quarter teaspoon if you're using habanero) and taste repeatedly, bearing in mind that the heat of chiles can "bloom" after a few minutes.

Serve this with a neutral dish like plain rice, and perhaps a cooling salad.

Juice of 2 limes

1 garlic clove, peeled

One 1-inch piece fresh ginger, peeled and roughly chopped

Fresh or dried chile to taste

1 cup yogurt

1 tablespoon sugar

2 cups fresh mint leaves

Salt and black pepper to taste

8 lamb chops, preferably from the shoulder

1. Start a charcoal or gas grill or preheat the broiler; the fire should be moderately hot and the rack 4 to 6 inches from the heat source. To make the chutney, combine the lime juice, garlic, ginger, chile, yogurt, and sugar in a food processor or blender and puree. Stir in the mint by hand, then add salt and pepper.
2. Grill the chops for 3 to 4 minutes per side, by which time they will be medium-rare, or until they reach the desired degree of doneness.
3. Serve the lamb chops hot with the cool chutney.

Marinated Lamb "Popsicles" with Fenugreek Cream INDIA

MAKES **4 SERVINGS AS A MAIN COURSE, 8 AS A STARTER**

TIME **2 HOURS, LARGELY UNATTENDED, PLUS TIME TO PREHEAT THE GRILL**

This is the recipe of my friend Vikram Vij, whose Vancouver restaurant, Vij's, is among the best Indian restaurants in North America.

Other cuts of meat you can use here: beef tenderloin (filet mignon), cut into medallions.

Pilaf (page 513), Dal (page 433), and other standard Indian accompaniments would do nicely here.

2 racks of lamb, 8 ribs each, or 16 rib chops

$\frac{1}{4}$ cup dry white wine

$\frac{1}{4}$ cup grainy yellow mustard

Salt to taste

2 tablespoons corn, grapeseed, or other neutral oil

1 tablespoon minced garlic

1 teaspoon ground turmeric

2 cups heavy cream

2 teaspoons dried green fenugreek flakes (kasuri methi) or ground fenugreek

$\frac{1}{4}$ teaspoon cayenne

2 tablespoons fresh lemon juice

$\frac{1}{4}$ teaspoon paprika

1. Cut the racks into individual ribs; combine in a bowl with the wine, mustard, and a large pinch of salt. Cover and refrigerate for a couple of hours.
2. When you're ready to cook, start a charcoal or gas grill or preheat the broiler; the fire should be quite hot and the rack 2 to 4 inches from the heat source (a little farther away if you're using the fattier shoulder chops). Put the oil in a small pot over medium heat and add the garlic. As the garlic turns golden, add the turmeric and cook, stirring constantly, for about a minute. Add the cream, fenugreek, cayenne, lemon juice, and paprika and turn the heat to low. Keep warm while you grill the ribs.
3. Grill the ribs quickly, just a couple of minutes per side (3 or 4 minutes for shoulder chops). Serve, either doused with the cream sauce or with the sauce on the side for dipping.

Tandoori Raan

Grilled or Roast Lamb with Spices INDIA

MAKES **6 OR MORE SERVINGS**

TIME **1 HOUR, PLUS UP TO 1 DAY FOR MARINATING,
AND TIME TO PREHEAT THE GRILL**

In India, it should be noted, much "mutton" is actually goat, and—except in the most expensive restaurants or wealthiest homes—this spice mixture would be used on meat that would later be braised in a yogurt sauce, much like the one for the meatballs on page 424. But with our relatively young, tender lamb, you can just rub the meat with the spices and grill. (If you refrigerate for an hour or a day, the taste will be somewhat improved, but it's not imperative.) I find this dish just as elegant as the French version, page 358, especially when it is on the spicy but mild side, with the chiles omitted.

Serve with simple Pilaf (page 513) and, if you like, Curried Carrots (page 451).

Other cuts of meat you can use here: beef steaks like skirt, sirloin (New York) strip, or ribeye are all good treated this way.

1 large onion, peeled

4 garlic cloves, peeled

**One 1-inch piece fresh ginger, peeled and roughly
   chopped**

1 teaspoon fennel seeds

**1 teaspoon cardamom seeds (if you have pods, crush
   them to extract seeds), preferably black**

6 cloves

1 tablespoon cumin seeds

1 cinnamon stick

6 black peppercorns

**2 small dried chiles or 2 teaspoons hot red pepper flakes,
   or to taste, optional**

One 3- to 4-pound butterflied leg of lamb

Salt to taste

1. Combine the onion, garlic, and ginger in a food processor and grind until pasty. Put in a fine strainer and drain as much water as possible from the mixture. Meanwhile, toast the spices in a small dry skillet over medium heat, shaking the pan frequently until they become aromatic, about 3 minutes. Grind together until very fine.

2. Trim the lamb of any excess fat and, if any parts seem overly thick, make a horizontal cut in the meat so they lie fairly flat; sprinkle with salt. Combine the spice mixture and the onion mixture and rub this all over the meat. Use a thin-bladed knife to poke some holes in the lamb and stick a little bit of the mixture into each of them, too. If time allows, fold the meat in half, wrap tightly in plastic, and marinate, refrigerated, for up to a day.

3. When you're ready to cook, start a charcoal or gas grill or preheat the broiler; the fire should be quite hot and the rack at least 4 inches from the heat source. Grill or broil the meat until it is nicely browned, even a little charred, on both sides, 20 to 30 minutes, and the internal temperature at the thickest part is about 125°F; this will give you some lamb that is quite rare as well as some that is nearly well done. Let rest for 5 minutes before slicing thinly, as you would a thick steak.

Shish Kebab Skewered Lamb MIDDLE EAST

MAKES **4 SERVINGS**

TIME **1 HOUR, PLUS UP TO 1 DAY FOR MARINATING,
AND TIME TO PREHEAT THE GRILL**

Meat to be grilled for shish kebab, usually lamb, is ideally marinated in a paste of yogurt, minced onion, and spices, even if it's only for a few minutes. If you prefer to eliminate the yogurt, use a couple of tablespoons of olive oil instead. And if you have dried ground sumac—a sour spice found at all Middle

Grinding Your Own Meat

There are a few reasons to grind your own meat. One, there have been some (legitimate) safety concerns about preground hamburger. Two, grinding your own gives you control over the cut you use, the amount of fat you include, and the texture with which you end up. Finally, preground lamb and pork are not always available.

Fortunately, if you have a food processor, grinding your own meat is easy. Start with not-too-lean cuts: for pork or lamb, use shoulder (butt); for beef, use chuck (or, if you like, sirloin). Cut the meat into chunks, discarding hard pieces of fat (and gristle and bone, of course). Then process, pulsing the machine on and off until you achieve the consistency you need.

Eastern stores—sprinkle a little of it on the meat just before serving (you won't need the lemon).

If you choose to grill other vegetables—tomatoes, peppers, mushrooms, more onions, whatever—skewer them separately. Simply brush them with a little olive oil and sprinkle them with salt and pepper. These skewers, of course, are ideal with Pilaf (page 513).

Other cuts of meat you can use here: beef tenderloin (filet mignon) or boneless chicken thighs (which will require a little longer cooking time).

> 2 large onions, peeled
>
> 1 cup yogurt
>
> 2 tablespoons extra virgin olive oil
>
> Juice of 1 lemon
>
> 1 tablespoon minced garlic
>
> 1 tablespoon ground cumin
>
> Salt and black pepper to taste
>
> 1/4 teaspoon cayenne
>
> 2 pounds boneless lamb shoulder or leg, cut into
>   1 1/2- to 2-inch chunks
>
> Lemon wedges for serving
>
> Tarator (page 600) or Thin Yogurt Sauce (page 597) for
>   serving

1. When you're ready to cook—if you choose not to marinate the meat—start a charcoal or gas grill; the fire should be moderately hot and the rack about 4 inches from the heat source. Mince one of the onions and combine it in a large bowl with the yogurt, oil, lemon juice, garlic, cumin, salt, pepper, and cayenne; taste and adjust the seasoning. Marinate the lamb in this mixture for at least a few minutes, for several hours at room temperature, or overnight in the refrigerator.

2. If you're using wooden skewers, soak them in water to cover for a few minutes. Cut the remaining onion into quarters, then separate it into large pieces. Thread the meat and onion alternately onto the skewers, leaving a little space between pieces. Grill, turning as each side browns and brushing with the remaining marinade, for 6 to 10 minutes for rare meat, longer if you like it more well done. Serve, with the lemon wedges and Tarator or Thin Yogurt Sauce.

Grilled Meat Kofte

Lamb "Burgers" MIDDLE EAST ▨

MAKES **4 SERVINGS**

TIME **30 MINUTES, PLUS TIME TO PREHEAT THE GRILL**

Kofte are at home in a dozen or more countries, under a variety of names. The most basic combine ground lamb and onion in a fairly smooth paste—not chopped, like the best hamburgers are, but quite dense—and are grilled on skewers (you can, if you prefer, shape them into burgers or meatballs and grill that way). Beyond the basic, there are infinite varieties; I get into some of them, but this is a subject on which one could write a book . . . Serve, if you like, with Parsley-Onion Condiment (page 596).

> 1 1/2 pounds boneless lamb, preferably from the shoulder, excess fat removed
>
> 1 medium onion, peeled and quartered
>
> Salt and black pepper to taste
>
> Lemon wedges for serving

1. Start a charcoal or gas grill or preheat the broiler; the fire should be moderately hot and the rack 4 to 6 inches from the heat source. Cut the lamb into large chunks and put in a food processor with the onion, a pinch of salt, and some pepper; process until smooth, stopping the machine and scraping down the sides if necessary. With wet hands, form into elongated meatballs on metal skewers or shape into 4 elongated "burgers."
2. Grill or broil the kofte, undisturbed, until nicely browned on one side, about 5 minutes. Turn and brown the other side; these can be medium to well done and will still be moist (though I think they're best rare). Serve hot, with the lemon wedges.

Kofte with Cumin and Pine Nuts. Add 1 teaspoon ground cumin (or to taste) to the mix. After the meat is processed, blend in 1/4 cup pine nuts by hand.

Kofte with Tomato Sauce and Yogurt. Grill or broil the kofte as directed. Prepare Fast, Fresh Tomato Sauce (page 606). Mix 1 cup yogurt with some salt and a tablespoon of extra virgin olive oil. Top the meatballs with the tomato sauce and yogurt, sprinkle with parsley, and serve.

Kofte with Stewed Onions. Peel and thinly slice 4 large onions. Put them in a large skillet, cover it, and turn the heat to medium-low. Cook, undisturbed, until the onions are dry and almost sticking to the pan, at least 30 minutes. Then uncover and add 4 table-spoons (1/2 stick) butter or extra virgin olive oil, along with some salt and pepper. Turn the heat to medium and cook, stirring occasionally, until browned and almost falling apart. Use this mass as a bed for kofte.

Lamb Kebabs with Peppers and Yogurt MIDDLE EAST

MAKES **4 SERVINGS**

TIME **40 MINUTES**

You might think of this as a kind of indoor shish kebab, one that contains its own built-in sauce, a combination of yogurt and the juices exuded by the lamb and roasted vegetables. Serve with rice or pita bread.

Other cuts of meat you can use here: beef tenderloin (filet mignon) or boneless chicken thighs (which will require a little longer cooking time).

> 2 pounds boneless lamb shoulder or leg, cut into 2-inch chunks
>
> 3 red or yellow bell peppers
>
> 2 or 3 fresh Anaheim or other mild chiles (use red bell peppers if you must substitute)
>
> 1 onion, peeled and cut in half
>
> 2 tomatoes
>
> Salt and black pepper to taste
>
> 1 teaspoon fresh thyme leaves or a pinch of dried
>
> 2 cups yogurt
>
> Lemon wedges for serving

1. Turn the heat to high under a cast-iron or other large heavy skillet; a couple of minutes later, add

the lamb and quickly sear on all sides. Don't worry about cooking it through, but brown the exterior well.

2. Remove the lamb and put the peppers and chiles in the same skillet, still over high heat. Add the onion, cut sides down. Cook until the peppers blacken on all sides, turning as necessary (the onion will blacken quickly; remove it and set aside). When the peppers are beginning to collapse, after a total of 10 to 15 minutes, remove the skillet from the heat and cover with foil or a lid. Preheat the broiler and adjust the rack so it is 2 to 4 inches from the heat source.

3. When the peppers cool slightly, remove them from the pan and peel and seed them, then cut or tear them into strips; seperate the onions into rings. Cut the tomatoes in half through their equator and, over a sink, squeeze and shake them to extract the seeds. Put the tomatoes, cut side down, in the skillet and char them, 3 to 5 minutes; roughly chop the tomatoes.

4. Combine the vegetables with the lamb, salt, pepper, thyme, and yogurt in a roasting pan just large enough to hold the lamb in one layer. Broil until charred on top, just a few minutes, then serve over pita or rice, with the lemon wedges.

Grilled Lamb Skewers with Bay Leaves TURKEY ▥

MAKES **4 SERVINGS**

TIME **30 MINUTES, PLUS TIME TO PREHEAT THE GRILL**

When I was served this dish, of alternating bay leaves and chunks of lamb, the bay leaves were fresh (I was told that the world's best bay leaves are grown around Smyrna, in Turkey). I couldn't imagine that dried bay leaves would be much less delicious, and indeed

they're not. Either a rice dish or ordinary crusty bread is fine here, along with a salad like Spicy Carrot Salad (page 191), any of the eggplant salads on pages 191–193, or simply some plain roasted peppers or grilled vegetables.

Other cuts of meat you can use here: chunks of boneless pork shoulder (which will need somewhat longer cooking) or beef tenderloin (filet mignon).

1¹⁄₂ to 2 pounds boneless lamb shoulder, cut into 1¹⁄₂-inch chunks

3 tablespoons extra virgin olive oil

Salt and black pepper to taste

1 tablespoon minced garlic

Bay leaves, preferably fresh

1. Start a charcoal or gas grill; the fire should be only moderately hot and the rack about 4 inches from the heat source. If you're using wooden skewers, soak them in water while you prepare the meat.

2. Toss the meat with the olive oil, along with the salt, pepper, and garlic. When you're ready to cook, skewer pieces of meat alternately with bay leaves; don't worry if some of the leaves break; just jam them between pieces of meat.

3. Grill the meat for 2 to 5 minutes per side, depending on the heat of the fire and the desired degree of doneness. Remove and serve.

Grilled or Roast Leg of Lamb with Thyme and Orange GREECE

MAKES **6 OR MORE SERVINGS**

TIME **1 HOUR, PLUS TIME TO PREHEAT THE GRILL**

How wonderful is the marriage between thyme and lamb? So wonderful that this dish conjures up visions of Greeks spit-roasting lamb or goat on rocky hills above the sea, basting it with branches of thyme dipped in olive oil. (Which is not a bad recipe itself, especially if you have the rocky hills and sea.) This lamb is lovely with a rice dish or simply with bread.

Note, interestingly, that this recipe is virtually the same as the one that follows—except the flavors are distinctly different. Under many circumstances, I would have made one a variation of the other, but it would have seemed, in this case, to give one or the other short shrift. They're both great.

Other cuts of meat you can use here: thick cuts of "London broil" or flank steak.

One 3- to 4-pound butterflied leg of lamb

10 to 12 fresh thyme sprigs

2 garlic cloves

Zest of 1 orange

1 teaspoon black pepper

Coarse salt to taste

1. Start a charcoal fire or preheat a gas grill or broiler; the fire should be quite hot and the rack at least 4 inches from the heat source. Trim the lamb of any excess fat and, if any parts seem overly thick, make a horizontal cut in the meat so they lie fairly flat. Strip the thyme leaves from the stems and mince them with the garlic and orange zest (a small food processor will handle this well); combine with the pepper and a healthy pinch of salt. Use a thin-bladed knife to poke some holes in the lamb and stick a little bit of the mixture into each of them; rub the meat with that which remains.

2. Grill or broil the meat until it is nicely browned, even a little charred, on both sides, 20 to 30 minutes, and the internal temperature at the thickest part is about 125°F; this will give you some lamb that is quite rare as well as some that is nearly well done. Let rest for 5 minutes before slicing thinly, as you would a thick steak.

Grilled or Roast Lamb with Herbs
FRANCE

MAKES **6 OR MORE SERVINGS**

TIME **1 HOUR, PLUS TIME TO PREHEAT THE GRILL**

You can use a whole leg for this or a butterflied boneless leg—usually, you can buy boneless leg of lamb in the supermarket. You can grill or broil it (or, for that matter, roast in a hot oven); there are differences in timing and in flavor, but all the results are excellent, and it's a dish you can use at any time of year.

You can also make it more simply: rub a leg of lamb with olive oil, salt, pepper, and fresh thyme or rosemary. But I like it best as it is done in Provence, with a variety of herbs, along with some garlic.

If you're cooking this inside, serve it with Potatoes with Bay Leaves (page 481) or another roasted potato dish and a simple steamed vegetable. Outside, I'd grill some vegetables and perhaps some Crostini (page 41).

One more comment: this is also great with boneless lamb shoulder, but because that is higher in fat, you must grill over lower heat, and carefully, to prevent burning.

One 3- to 4-pound butterflied leg of lamb

¼ cup extra virgin olive oil

1 teaspoon minced garlic

1 teaspoon fennel seeds

1 tablespoon fresh lavender leaves
    or 1 teaspoon dried

1 tablespoon fresh rosemary leaves
    or 1 teaspoon dried

2 teaspoons fresh thyme leaves

Salt and black pepper to taste

Lavender flowers or rosemary sprigs for garnish,
    if available

Lemon wedges for serving

1. Start a charcoal or gas grill or preheat the broiler; the fire should be quite hot and the rack at least 4 inches from the heat source. Trim the lamb of any excess fat and, if any parts seem overly thick, make a horizontal cut in the meat so they lie fairly flat.

2. Combine the oil, garlic, fennel seeds, and herbs with some salt and pepper. Use a thin-bladed knife to poke some holes in the lamb and stick a little bit of the mixture into each of them; rub the meat with that which remains.

3. Grill or broil the meat until it is nicely browned, even a little charred, on both sides, 20 to 30 minutes, and the internal temperature at the thickest part is about 125°F; this will give you some lamb that is quite rare as well as some that is nearly well done. Let rest for 5 minutes before slicing thinly, as you would a thick steak. Garnish the lamb with lavender or rosemary and serve with lemon wedges.

Grilled or Roast Lamb with Cilantro Salsa ARGENTINA. Make Cilantro Salsa (page 616). In step 2, use Cilantro Salsa in place of the herb mixture; don't bother to put any in the meat, just on it.

PAN-COOKED MEAT

Meat isn't sautéed as often as poultry or fish, because adding fat to it is superfluous (think of chicken-fried steak, which is the classic example of overkill). There are exceptions, of course, especially with pork and veal, both of which are quite lean. Generally you want fairly tender cuts of meat for sautéing, and that's reflected in the recipes here.

Beef Tenderloin in Caramelized Sugar VIETNAM ■
MAKES **4 SERVINGS**
TIME **30 MINUTES**

Though you occasionally see this technique in other cuisines, I know of nowhere but Vietnam where caramelized sugar is used as the basis for a savory sauce in such a wide variety of dishes. You see it with pork, beef, shrimp, finfish, chicken, and even frog. You see it in fancy urban restaurants and in rural three-sided structures. Completed by plenty of onions and black pepper, the result is wickedly forceful, decidedly delicious, and, in the sauce's dark brown glossiness, downright gorgeous, an astonishing creation given the number of ingredients and the time it requires. See page 500 for information on Asian fish sauces like nam pla.

Other cuts of meat you can use here: boneless chicken thighs, pork steaks cut from the loin—both of which will require longer cooking times—or any fish or shrimp (see Fish Fillets Poached in Caramel Sauce, page 232).

Sticky Rice (page 508) is not entirely traditional here, but it's great, as is any other plain rice dish. A strong-flavored salad (like Green Papaya Salad, page 198, but without the shrimp) would round things out perfectly.

4 filets mignons, each at least 1 inch thick

1 cup sugar

1/2 cup nam pla, or to taste

1 large onion, sliced into half-moons

1 teaspoon black pepper, or more to taste

1. Heat a 10-inch skillet over high heat, then brown the meat well on both sides; it won't take more than a minute or two per side. Turn off the heat and transfer the steaks to a plate.

2. A minute later, add the sugar to the pan and turn the heat to medium. Cook, occasionally shaking the pan gently, until the sugar liquefies and begins to bubble. When the sugar is all liquid, cook for another minute or so, until it darkens; turn off the heat. Mix the nam pla with $1/2$ cup water; carefully, and at arm's length, add the liquid and turn the heat to medium-high. Cook, stirring constantly, until the caramel melts into the liquid. Add the onion and cook, stirring occasionally, until it softens, about 5 minutes. Stir in any liquid that has accumulated around the meat.

3. Stir in the black pepper and return the meat to the pan. Cook over medium heat, turning the meat once in a while, until it is done to your liking (5 to 8 minutes for medium-rare). Taste and adjust the seasoning, then serve, spooning a bit of the onion and sauce over each steak.

Steak Teriyaki JAPAN ▥
MAKES **4 SERVINGS**
TIME **20 TO 30 MINUTES**

Teriyaki is an old preparation, but using steak is relatively new, as beef was not widely eaten in Japan until the second half of the twentieth century. So this might be considered a new classic. I love it with a simple salad (you might use Sesame-Miso Dressing, page 190) and perhaps Basmati Rice with Shiso (page 510).

Other cuts of meat you can use here: the teriyaki treatment is widely used for chicken, bone in or out (see page 317), pork, and shrimp.

> 4 sirloin (New York) strip or ribeye steaks, 6 to 8 ounces each, or 2 larger steaks
> $1/2$ cup sake or slightly sweet white wine, like a German Kabinett or Spätlese

> $1/3$ cup mirin or 2 tablespoons honey mixed with 2 tablespoons water
> 2 tablespoons sugar
> $1/3$ cup soy sauce

1. Heat a large heavy skillet over high heat for about 3 minutes, then add the steaks. Brown quickly on both sides, not more than 2 minutes per side. Transfer the meat to a plate and turn off the heat for a minute or two.

2. Turn the heat to medium, add the sake, and cook, stirring, to loosen any bits of meat adhering to the bottom of the pan. Add the mirin, sugar, and soy sauce. Stir to blend and, when the mixture is producing lively bubbles, return the meat to the pan.

3. Cook, turning the meat in the sauce, until it becomes thick and sticky, more of a glaze than a liquid; this will take only 5 minutes or so. By that time the steaks should be rare to medium-rare (if you're not sure, cut into a piece). Continue to cook if necessary, adding a spoonful or two of water if the sauce threatens to burn. Serve immediately.

Steak au Poivre FRANCE ▥
MAKES **4 SERVINGS**
TIME **20 MINUTES**

This remains a luxurious dish, though it is quite simple. Traditionally, so many cracked (not ground) black peppercorns are pressed into the meat that they form a crispy crust. For some this is overwhelming. But if you slice the steak before serving, the surface area per bite is not as great. Or you could, of course, use much less pepper.

> 2 tablespoons freshly cracked black pepper, more or less
> 4 filets mignons or sirloin (New York) strip steaks, each 6 to 8 ounces

1 tablespoon extra virgin olive oil

3 tablespoons butter

Salt to taste

2 tablespoons minced shallot

1 tablespoon Dijon mustard

¼ cup heavy cream (preferred) or water

Chopped fresh parsley leaves for garnish

1. Press the pepper into the steaks to form an even coating. Preheat the oven to 200°F. Put the oil and 1 tablespoon of the butter in a large skillet and turn the heat to medium-high. When the butter melts, add the steaks and turn the heat to high. Sear on the first side for about 3 minutes, then turn and sprinkle with salt. Sear on the second side for 2 or 3 minutes; lower the heat and cook until just short of desired level of doneness, about 7 minutes total for medium-rare. Keep warm in the oven while you make the sauce.

2. Pour out any fat from the skillet, but leave brown bits in there. Over medium-high heat, add the remaining butter and shallot and cook until soft, stirring occasionally, about 3 minutes. Add the mustard and cream and cook, stirring, for 30 seconds. Spoon the sauce over the steaks, garnish, and serve.

Tonkatsu Breaded Pork Cutlets JAPAN ▪

MAKES **4 SERVINGS**

TIME **30 MINUTES**

Said to have been brought to the islands by the Dutch, these are now as deeply ingrained in Japanese cooking as fried chicken is in ours. They are typically served on a simple bed of shredded cabbage, with a commercially prepared tonkatsu sauce. I have re-created the sauce from scratch here, and believe me, it's far better than the bottled stuff.

These can be deep-fried if you prefer (use about 2 inches of oil), but at home most Japanese shallow-fry them, as I do.

Other cuts of meat you can use here: veal, chicken, or turkey cutlets.

1 tablespoon Dijon mustard

1 tablespoon soy sauce

1 tablespoon mirin or honey

2 teaspoons rice or other mild vinegar

4 boneless pork steaks, preferably from the shoulder, about 6 ounces each

Salt and black pepper to taste

¼ cup neutral oil, such as corn or grapeseed

Flour for dredging

2 eggs, lightly beaten in a wide, shallow bowl

2 cups panko (Japanese bread crumbs, page 8) or other bread crumbs, preferably homemade (page 580)

2 cups shredded cabbage

Lemon wedges for serving

1. Combine the first 4 ingredients and set aside. Sprinkle the meat with salt and pepper. Put a large

nonstick skillet over medium-high heat and add the oil. When the oil is hot—a pinch of flour will sizzle—begin to prepare the pork: dip a piece in the flour, then the egg, and finally the bread crumbs—the more of this coating that adheres, the better. Put the piece of pork in the pan and repeat until done; you may have to cook in batches (keep any cooked pieces in a low oven until you're finished cooking).

2. Adjust the heat so the meat cooks rapidly but the coating does not burn. Rotate the pieces so they brown evenly and turn each as the first side becomes deep golden brown, 3 to 4 minutes. Cook about the same amount of time on the second side.

3. Make a mound of cabbage on each of 4 plates. Drizzle the cabbage with a bit of the sauce, then top with a cutlet. Serve with lemon wedges and any remaining sauce.

"Deviled" Pork Chops FRANCE ■
MAKES **4 SERVINGS**
TIME **20 MINUTES**

A laughably simple weeknight dish that packs a lot of flavor. Try to buy shoulder (rib) end pork chops, which will dry out less in the pan than others. Serve with a salad and a cooked vegetable or starch, like any of the mashed potato dishes on page 480.

Other cuts of meat you can use here: bone-in chicken thighs (which will require more cooking) or pork medallions cut from the tenderloin (which will cook more quickly).

    4 pork chops, each 6 to 8 ounces
    Salt and black pepper to taste
    2 tablespoons or more Dijon mustard

    3 tablespoons extra virgin olive oil
    Chopped fresh parsley leaves for garnish

1. Put a large skillet, preferably nonstick, over medium-high heat. Sprinkle the chops with salt and pepper and smear them all over with mustard. Add the oil to the pan and, when it is hot, the chops.

2. Cook for about 3 minutes per side, or until nicely browned, then lower the heat and continue to cook, turning occasionally, until cooked through, another 10 minutes or so.

3. Transfer the chops to a plate and add $1/2$ cup water (or stock) to the skillet. Cook, stirring, until the water has incorporated any solids in the pan. When there are only a couple of tablespoons of liquid left, spoon it over the chops, garnish, and serve.

Pork Chops with Prunes and Cream
FRANCE
MAKES **4 SERVINGS**
TIME **45 MINUTES**

A Norman recipe, easily identified with the region because of the combination of dairy and meat. It may sound overly rich, but pork is so lean these days that the added fat is welcome, and the taste is incredible. A wonderful dish for midwinter; serve it with simple boiled potatoes or rice and a steamed vegetable.

Other cuts of meat you can use here: veal chops or bone-in chicken breasts.

    2 tablespoons butter (preferred) or extra virgin olive oil
    4 thick pork chops, cut from the rib (shoulder) end
        of the pork
    Salt and black pepper to taste

2 fresh thyme sprigs

2 garlic cloves, peeled and lightly smashed

1 cup not-too-dry white wine or cider

1 cup pitted prunes

1/2 to 1 cup heavy cream

Chopped fresh chervil leaves for garnish, optional

1. Put the butter in a large skillet with a lid over medium-high heat. When the butter melts, add the pork chops and brown them well on both sides, rotating them in the pan so they brown evenly, turning as needed, and sprinkling with salt and pepper. When they are just about browned, after about 10 minutes, add the thyme and garlic.

2. Pour in the wine and scatter the prunes around the pork. Cover and adjust the heat so the mixture simmers steadily but not violently. Cook just until the pork chops are tender, 20 minutes or so, or until their internal temperature is 145°F on an instant-read thermometer.

3. Transfer the meat to a platter and, if there is a lot of liquid, reduce it over high heat until only about 1/2 cup remains. Over medium heat, slowly add half the cream and cook, stirring constantly, until the mixture is thick. Add a little bit more, up to the remaining 1/2 cup, until the sauce has a consistency you like. Spoon the prunes and sauce over the chops, garnish with chervil if you like, and serve.

Sandwich Cubano
Grilled Ham and Cheese Sandwich   CUBA   ■

MAKES **1 SERVING**

TIME **20 MINUTES**

If you have leftover roast pork, especially from Lechon Asado, this is how to use it. Combined with ham, Swiss cheese, and pickles, it makes the classic grilled sandwich of the Latin Caribbean. Though purists insist on Cuban bread (essentially a fairly soft French loaf), the best I ever had was in San Juan, made on a sweet roll. A definite bastardization but one that demonstrated that almost any kind of bread will do and that this sandwich is great in many guises.

Ordinary yellow mustard is the norm for this, but consider Dijon or brown mustard instead. Similarly, bad dill pickles are standard, but if you can lay your hands on some half-sour pickles (or use Lightly Pickled Cucumbers, page 455), the results will be better—if less "authentic."

One 6- to 8-inch loaf Cuban, French, or Italian bread

Butter for the bread

Several thin slices Lechon Asado (page 375) or other roast pork

Several thin slices ham

Several slices Swiss cheese

Sliced dill pickles

Mustard

1 tablespoon butter if needed

1. Cut the bread in half the long way and butter it. Layer with pork, ham, cheese, and pickles. Spread with mustard. Top with the other half of the bread and squash the sandwich with your hand.

2. Use a sandwich press or put 1 tablespoon butter in a cast-iron or nonstick skillet over medium heat. When it melts, add the sandwich and weight it with a plate and something heavy—a filled teakettle, a big rock, some cans, whatever. You really want to squash the sandwich. Cook for about 3 minutes, or until lightly browned, then turn and brown the other side. Lower the heat if necessary so the cheese melts before the bread becomes too browned.

3. Cut in half on the diagonal and serve.

Breaded Lamb Cutlets ROMANIA

MAKES **4 SERVINGS**

TIME **35 MINUTES**

This central European dish brings the breading technique to lamb, a meat with enough flavor and tenderness to taste great underneath a crunchy exterior. While cuts of meat from the loin or leg can be used, the medallions of meat from the rack are far superior in texture. It's not unusual to finish the dish with a sprinkle of white wine sauce, but you can skip that and simply squeeze some lemon juice over the lamb; that's what I usually do.

Twelve 1-inch-thick medallions of lamb, cut from
    2 boneless racks (about 1$\frac{1}{2}$ pounds) or the
    equivalent amount from the loin or leg

3 tablespoons extra virgin olive oil

1 teaspoon ground cumin, plus more to taste

1 tablespoon chopped fresh thyme

2 garlic cloves, peeled and crushed

2 eggs, lightly beaten

Bread crumbs for dredging, preferably fresh (page 580), or
    panko (Japanese bread crumbs, page 8)

Salt and black pepper to taste

$\frac{1}{2}$ cup dry white wine

Chopped fresh parsley leaves for garnish, optional

2 lemons, cut into wedges, for serving

1. Preheat the oven to 200°F. If using medallions from racks, press to a $\frac{1}{2}$-inch thickness with the palm of your hand. If using cuts from the loin or leg, place the meat between sheets of wax paper and pound to a $\frac{1}{2}$-inch thickness with a mallet or rolling pin. Place a nonstick skillet over medium-high heat and add the oil, cumin, thyme, and garlic.
2. When the oil shimmers, remove the garlic and discard. Dip the lamb pieces into the egg, press into the bread crumbs on both sides, and add to the skillet. Do not crowd—you will have to cook in batches. When the meat is in the skillet, season it with salt and pepper and sprinkle it with a pinch of cumin.
3. Brown one side, then flip and brown the other; adjust the heat so that each side takes about 2 minutes. The meat should remain rare. Remove the pieces, drain, and then transfer to a warm platter in the oven. When all the pieces are done, drain the oil from the pan, leaving the browned bits, and then add the wine to the pan. Allow the mixture to simmer until it reduces by half, 3 to 5 minutes.
4. Garnish the lamb with the parsley if you like and serve it alongside the wine sauce and lemon wedges.

Wiener Schnitzel Crisp Veal Cutlets AUSTRIA

MAKES **4 SERVINGS**

TIME **1 HOUR**

Wiener schnitzel, one of Austria's most famous culinary exports, is traditionally made with a pounded out boneless veal chop, though at $15 to $16 per chop (also per serving) it's a lot more feasibly reproduced with cutlets.

If the cutlets you buy are thicker than those called for here, pound them gently between two sheets of wax paper using the bottom of a small saucepan. And if you opt for the more opulent—but not necessarily better—veal chops, you may want to have two skillets going at the same time, as a properly flattened boneless veal chop will be 8 to 9 inches in diameter and you'll have to cook them one at a time.

You can, of course, follow this recipe using chicken, turkey, or pork cutlets.

1 cup flour

3 cups bread crumbs, preferably fresh (page 580)

3 eggs, beaten

Salt and black pepper to taste

1 pound thinly sliced veal from the leg (scaloppine), about ⅛ inch thick

2 tablespoons butter plus 2 tablespoons olive oil or all oil or all clarified butter (page 241)

Chopped fresh parsley leaves for garnish

1 lemon, cut into quarters, for serving

1. Preheat the oven to 200°F. Set out the flour, bread crumbs, and beaten eggs on plates or in shallow bowls next to each other on your counter and have a stack of parchment or wax paper ready. Season the eggs liberally with salt and pepper.

2. Dredge the cutlets, one at a time, in the egg, then the flour, then dip in the egg again, then dredge in the bread crumbs. Stack the breaded cutlets between layers of wax paper and, when all the veal is breaded, transfer the stack to chill in the refrigerator for at least 10 minutes and up to 3 hours.

3. Heat the butter and oil in a large skillet over medium heat until a pinch of flour dropped into the pan sizzles. Cook in batches as necessary, making sure not to crowd the pan, adding fat to the pan as needed. Turn the cutlets as soon as they're browned, then cook the other side. The total cooking time should be 5 minutes or less. As each piece of veal is done, transfer it to an ovenproof platter; place the platter in the oven.

4. Serve as soon as all the cutlets are cooked, garnished with the parsley and with the lemon wedges on the side.

Cotolette alla Milanese Veal Cutlets Milan Style ITALY. Simply omit the parsley and you have the Italian classic on which veal Parmigiana—really quite an American dish—with its topping of cheese and tomato sauce, is based.

Involtini di Vitello
Veal Rolled with Mushrooms ITALY

MAKES **4 SERVINGS**

TIME **1 HOUR**

These rolls take some time and require a bit of assembly—not that there's anything especially challenging—so I always feel like if I'm going to bother with them, I might as well make a big batch and double the amounts here. In any case, you can prepare the rolls in advance and cook them just before serving.

I cook the rolls in a mixture of stock and wine (you could use either instead of both), but many cooks use a light tomato sauce for simmering, like Fast, Fresh Tomato Sauce (page 606). The filling can be varied, too: substitute ground pork or pork sausage for the

INVOLTINI DI VITELLO

ushrooms or use a bit of mozzarella instead of or along with the Parmesan.

Other cuts of meat you can use here: cutlets of chicken, turkey, pork, or even beef (see Negima, page 102).

1/4 cup extra virgin olive oil

1 medium onion, finely chopped

2 tablespoons bread crumbs, preferably fresh (page 580)

1 tablespoon chopped garlic

1/2 pound chanterelle or shiitake mushrooms, trimmed (discard shiitake stems or reserve for stock) and roughly chopped

Salt and black pepper to taste

2 tablespoons pine nuts

1 tablespoon fresh marjoram leaves or 1/2 teaspoon dried

1/4 cup chopped fresh parsley leaves, plus more for garnish

1/4 cup freshly grated Parmesan cheese

8 thin slices veal from the leg (scaloppine), pounded if necessary to less than 1/4 inch thick

3 tablespoons butter

1/2 cup dry white wine plus 1/2 cup beef or chicken stock, preferably homemade (page 160), or 1 cup of either

1. Put half the oil in a large skillet or casserole, preferably nonstick, over medium-high heat. A minute later, add the onion and cook, stirring occasionally, until it wilts, about 5 minutes. Add the bread crumbs, garlic, mushrooms, and salt and pepper and cook, stirring occasionally, until the mushrooms have given up their liquid and become soft, 10 to 15 minutes. Turn off the heat and stir in the pine nuts, marjoram, parsley, and Parmesan. Cool slightly.

2. Put a portion of the filling into the center of each of the pieces of veal and roll up; seal with a toothpick and season the outside of the rolls with some salt and pepper. Put the remaining oil in the skillet and add 2 tablespoons of the butter. Turn the heat to medium-high. Brown the veal rolls quickly, just a couple of minutes per side (it may be easier to do this in batches), adjusting the heat so the meat browns without burning.

3. With all the veal in the pan, add the wine and/or stock and let it bubble away for a moment. Turn the heat to low, then cover the pan and adjust the heat so the mixture simmers gently. Cook until the veal is tender, about 20 minutes.

4. Transfer the veal to a warm platter; if the pan juices are thin, raise the heat to high and reduce, stirring, until less than 1/2 cup of liquid remains. Taste and adjust the seasoning, then stir in the remaining butter. Pour this over the veal rolls, garnish with parsley, and serve.

Veal Paprikás HUNGARY ▪

MAKES **4 SERVINGS**

TIME **25 MINUTES**

This classic Hungarian dish employs paprika liberally, but it does not overpower the dish, because the spiciness is tempered by the sour cream. This is good over buttered noodles or rice or with bread.

Other cuts of meat you can use here: cutlets or chunks of pork, chicken, or turkey.

Salt and black pepper to taste

1/4 cup fresh lemon juice

12 thin slices veal from the leg (scaloppine)

1 cup sour cream

1/2 cup chicken stock, preferably homemade (page 160)

3 tablespoons corn, grapeseed, or other neutral oil

1/2 cup flour

1 onion, sliced

1 tablespoon hot paprika, plus a sprinkling for garnish

Chopped fresh parsley leaves for garnish, optional

1. Lightly sprinkle salt, pepper, and the lemon juice over the veal; let sit while you prepare the other ingredients. Whisk together the sour cream and stock.

2. Heat the oil in a large skillet over medium-high heat. Dip a piece of the veal into the flour and slide into the skillet; repeat until the skillet is full but not crowded. Fry until nicely browned on both sides, just a minute or two on each, adjusting the heat so that the meat browns quickly and nicely but does not burn; remove each piece from the skillet as it finishes cooking.

3. When all the meat is cooked, sauté the onion in the same skillet until softened, about 5 minutes. Sprinkle the paprika over the onion and return the meat to the pan. When the meat is warm again, pour in the sour cream–stock mixture and heat through, being careful not to let the sauce boil. Sprinkle with a little paprika, garnish with parsley if you like, and serve.

Veal with Garlic. In step 3, add 1 tablespoon minced garlic along with the onion.

Veal with Capers. In step 3, add 2 tablespoons drained capers along with the sour cream–stock mixture.

3 tablespoons extra virgin olive oil
3 tablespoons butter or more oil
1 pound calf or lamb liver, cut into chunks
Flour for dredging
Salt and black pepper to taste
4 eggs
Parsley-Onion Condiment (page 596)

1. Put 2 tablespoons each of the butter and oil in a large nonstick skillet and place over medium-high heat. When the butter has melted, dredge each of the pieces of liver in the flour, shaking to remove the excess, and add them to the skillet. Sprinkle with salt and pepper and brown well on all sides, until the meat is done to your liking (I recommend medium for this dish). Turn off the heat and transfer the liver to a warm plate.

2. Wipe out the pan with paper towels and return it to the stove over medium-high heat. Add the remaining oil and butter to the skillet and, when the butter melts, fry the eggs, sprinkling them with salt and pepper as they cook. Serve a portion of the liver with an egg and the condiment.

Fried Liver with Egg and Cheese. In step 2, leave the eggs quite underdone; top them with a couple of 1/8- to 1/4-inch-thick slices of cheese and run under the broiler until the cheese melts. Serve as directed.

Fried Liver with Egg TURKEY ■

MAKES **4 SERVINGS**

TIME **20 MINUTES**

If you are a steak-and-eggs kind of person, and a liver kind of person, this is a great dish. (I love it, especially at breakfast.) Serve with warm pita bread.

Other cuts of meat you can use here: chicken livers (clean them well and do not overcook them); strip, skirt, or other steak.

Liver with Garlic, Sage, and White Wine ITALY ■

MAKES **4 SERVINGS**

TIME **20 MINUTES**

Good, tender calf liver is one of our most underrated meats, in part, I suspect, because nearly everyone overcooks it. It is best rare, and this recipe takes advantage of that.

2 tablespoons extra virgin olive oil

2 tablespoons butter or more oil

4 slices calf liver, each at least $\frac{1}{2}$ inch thick, about
   $1\frac{1}{2}$ pounds total

Flour for dredging

Salt and black pepper to taste

2 teaspoons minced garlic

$\frac{1}{2}$ cup dry white wine

10 or 15 sage leaves, preferably fresh

Juice of 1 lemon

Chopped fresh parsley leaves for garnish

1. Put half the oil and butter in a large skillet, preferably nonstick, over medium-high heat. When the butter has melted, dredge each of the pieces of liver in the flour, shaking to remove the excess, and add them to the skillet. Sprinkle with salt and pepper and brown quickly on both sides, for a total of 4 or 5 minutes; the meat should be rare when you're done. Transfer to a warm plate and turn the heat to medium.

2. Add the remaining oil and butter to the skillet along with the garlic. Cook, stirring occasionally, until the garlic begins to color, a minute or two. Add the wine and the sage and cook, stirring, until all the elements are incorporated and the wine has been reduced by half. Add the lemon juice, then taste and adjust the seasoning. Pour the sauce over the meat, garnish, and serve.

STIR-FRIES

To a very real extent, the technique for all stir-fried dishes is the same. It's almost equally true that you can freely substitute for the protein in any stir-fry recipe; since you're cutting pieces into small bits in any case, cooking time for everything is minimal.

Stir-Fried Spicy Shredded Beef

CHINA ■

MAKES **4 SERVINGS**

TIME **20 MINUTES**

This Szechwan specialty gets its heat from fresh chiles and its flowery, smoky aroma from Szechwan peppercorns. Since the beef is cut into such thin shreds, it takes little time to cook. Serve this with rice or noodles, along with stir-fried greens (page 463).

Other cuts of meat you can use here: pork, preferably from the shoulder or leg (fresh ham); lamb, preferably from the shoulder or leg; boneless chicken.

1 to 1$\frac{1}{2}$ pounds sirloin (New York) strip, cut into thin
   shreds (this will be easier if you freeze the beef for
   30 to 60 minutes)

2 teaspoons soy sauce

1 egg white, lightly beaten

3 tablespoons corn, grapeseed, or other neutral oil

1 garlic clove, minced

1 tablespoon fresh ginger, peeled and grated or minced

1 tablespoon whole Szechwan peppercorns

2 fresh hot chiles, preferably Thai chiles, stemmed,
   seeded, and chopped, or crumbled dried chiles or hot
   red pepper flakes to taste

2 celery stalks, thinly sliced, or about 1 cup shredded
   cabbage

1 tablespoon Shaoxing wine or dry sherry

Salt to taste

1 scallion, trimmed and chopped, for garnish

1. Combine the beef shreds with the soy sauce and egg white. Heat the oil in a wok or deep skillet over high heat. When the oil is almost smoking, stir in the garlic, ginger, peppercorns, and chiles. Cook until fragrant, about 15 seconds. Add the celery and cook until almost translucent, about 2 minutes.

Szechwan Peppercorns

Until quite recently, Szechwan peppercorns were banned from import into the United States because they carried a bacterial disease that causes citrus plants to drop leaves and fruit. Though there was no evidence that the dried peppercorns (really the dried berry of the prickly ash tree) could actually transmit the disease, the ban stood until July 2005, when the situation was resolved by a number of manufacturers agreeing to heat-treat their peppercorns. Now, they're widely available again.

This is fortunate, since Szechwan peppercorns are an essential ingredient in Szechwan cookery; their flowery, smoky aroma, somewhat lemony-medicinal flavor, and tongue-numbing "spiciness" (it's less like heat and more like local anesthesia) are part of the spectrum of flavors that makes Szechwan cooking so unusual.

You should be able to buy Szechwan peppercorns in almost any Asian market now—check out your local Chinatown—but if not, try mail-order sources such as Kalustyan's (www.kalustyans.com) or Penzeys (www.penzeys.com).

---

2. Stir in the beef and cook until lightly browned. Add the wine and cook until the liquid evaporates, a minute or less. Season, garnish, and serve immediately.

Stir-Fried Curry Beef CHINA ■

MAKES **4 SERVINGS**

TIME **20 MINUTES**

This stir-fry has only curry powder in common with the stews that are usually labeled curries. Unlike those, this is quick and easy. Serve it over steamed rice.

Other cuts of meat you can use here: pork, preferably from the shoulder or leg (fresh ham); lamb, preferably from the shoulder or leg; boneless chicken; shrimp (which will cook much faster).

1 pound boneless beef, preferably sirloin, cut into ½-inch slices across the grain

1 tablespoon soy sauce

1 tablespoon Shaoxing wine, dry sherry, stock, or water

1 teaspoon sugar

2 tablespoons corn, grapeseed, or other neutral oil

2 garlic cloves, minced

One 1½-inch piece fresh ginger, peeled and minced

1 small onion, sliced

3 tablespoons curry powder, preferably homemade (pages 592–593)

Chopped fresh cilantro leaves for garnish

1. Mix the beef with the soy sauce, wine, and sugar. Set aside.

2. Heat the oil in a skillet with a lid over medium-high heat. Add the garlic, ginger, and onion and cook until the onion is softened, about 5 minutes. Stir in the curry powder and cook until fragrant, about 30 seconds.

3. Add the beef and cook, stirring occasionally, until browned. Add ¼ cup water to the skillet and continue to cook, stirring occasionally, for another 2 minutes or so. Garnish and serve immediately.

Stir-Fried Pork in Garlic Sauce CHINA ■

MAKES **4 SERVINGS**

TIME **20 MINUTES**

The most challenging part of this recipe is cutting the pork into thin shreds; freeze the meat for 30 or even 60 minutes first, which will make it easier, but plan on spending the bulk of the time allotted for this recipe on this single task. The cooking itself takes only 5 minutes (in fact, if you want to serve rice with this, which you should, cook it beforehand and keep it warm).

Don't mince the garlic; you want its flavor to be strong in this dish. Serve this with white rice.

Other cuts of meat you can use here: beef, preferably sirloin; lamb, preferably from the shoulder or leg; boneless chicken.

    2 tablespoons peanut or vegetable oil

    2 tablespoons chopped garlic

    2 small dried chiles

    1½ pounds boneless pork, preferably from the shoulder
        (Boston butt or picnic), cut into thin shreds and
        thoroughly dried

    1 bunch of scallions, trimmed and cut into 2-inch lengths,
        white and green parts separated

    3 tablespoons soy sauce

1. Put the oil in a large nonstick skillet (12-inch is best) and turn the heat to high; a minute later, add the garlic and chiles and cook, stirring occasionally, until the garlic begins to color, just a minute or so.

2. Add the pork and stir once or twice. Cook until it begins to brown, about a minute. Add the white parts of the scallions and stir; cook for another minute, stirring occasionally.

3. Add the green parts of the scallions and stir; cook for 30 seconds, then turn off the heat and add the soy sauce. Serve immediately.

Stir-Fried Pork in Garlic Sauce, Thai Style. In step 3, add 1 tablespoon sugar with the green parts of the scallions and substitute nam pla for the soy sauce.

Stir-Fried Pork with Asparagus

CHINA ■

MAKES **4 SERVINGS**

TIME **20 MINUTES**

If you like a really strong garlic flavor, reserve half of the garlic and stir it in at the end of the cooking, along with the optional sesame oil. Serve with rice.

Other cuts of meat you can use here: beef, preferably sirloin; lamb, preferably from the shoulder or leg; boneless chicken; shrimp (which will cook more quickly).

    2 tablespoons peanut or vegetable oil

    3 or 4 small dried red chiles, optional

    1 pound boneless pork, preferably shoulder or tenderloin,
        thinly sliced or cut into ½-inch chunks

    2 cups trimmed pencil-thin asparagus, cut into
        1-inch-long pieces

    1 tablespoon minced garlic

    1 tablespoon peeled and minced fresh ginger

    ½ cup sliced scallion

    ½ cup chicken stock, preferably homemade (page 160),
        or water

    1 tablespoon soy sauce

    2 teaspoons dark sesame oil, optional

1. Have all the ingredients ready, including cooked white rice if you're planning to serve it. Preheat a large skillet over high heat for about 2 minutes. Immediately add half the peanut oil, the chiles if you're using them, and the pork, spreading it in one even layer. Cook, stirring only occasionally, until the pork browns, about 3 minutes. Transfer

the pork to a bowl (discard the chiles) and lower the heat slightly.

2. Add the remaining oil and the asparagus to the skillet. Again, cook, stirring occasionally, until the asparagus turns bright green and begins to become tender, 3 or 4 minutes. Add the garlic, ginger, and scallion and cook, stirring once or twice, for 30 seconds.

3. Add the stock and soy sauce, stir, and cook for 15 seconds. Add the sesame oil if you like and serve.

Stir-Fried Pork in Coconut Milk

SOUTHEAST ASIA ▦

MAKES **4 SERVINGS**

TIME **30 MINUTES**

Akin to the preceding recipe, this one and its Japanese variation use additional liquid. This, plus the braising time, makes for a saucier dish that can be stretched, with white rice, to serve more people if you like. But in any case, it's delicious. See page 500 for information on Asian fish sauces like nam pla.

Other cuts of meat you can use here: boneless chicken.

3 tablespoons peanut or neutral oil, like corn or grapeseed

1 large white onion, sliced

2 tablespoons chopped garlic

2 small dried chiles

1½ pounds boneless pork, preferably from the shoulder (Boston butt or picnic), cut into thin shreds and thoroughly dried

About 1½ cups coconut milk, homemade (page 584) or canned

3 lime leaves, preferably fresh, or the zest of 1 lime

3 tablespoons nam pla

Lime wedges for serving

1. Put 2 tablespoons of the oil in a large nonstick skillet (12-inch is best) and turn the heat to high; a minute later, add the onion and cook, stirring only occasionally, until the onion begins to char a little, a couple of minutes. Add the garlic and chiles and cook, stirring occasionally, for another minute. Remove this mixture with a slotted spoon and add the remaining oil.

2. Add the pork and stir once or twice. Cook without stirring until it begins to brown, about a minute; stir once and let sit for another minute. Return the onion mixture to the pan, stir, and turn the heat to medium. Add the coconut milk, lime leaves, and nam pla and adjust the heat so that the mixture simmers steadily but not too violently.

3. Cook for 10 minutes or so, until the mixture thickens slightly. Taste, adjust the seasoning, and serve with the lime wedges.

Pork in Sweet Soy Sauce JAPAN. The technique is similar, but the ingredients and results quite different: Omit the chiles in step 1. In step 2, add ½ cup good-quality soy sauce mixed with ½ cup water and 2 tablespoons mirin or 1 tablespoon honey; omit the lime leaves and nam pla. Simmer as directed and serve with lemon wedges.

Stir-Fried Lamb with Bitter Melon or Green Peppers and Black Beans

CHINA ▦

MAKES **4 SERVINGS**

TIME **30 MINUTES**

Bitter melon is a cucurbit; so is cucumber, and they resemble one another. (But so is a cantaloupe, so the melon reference isn't far off.) Its flavor, though, is akin to that of green peppers, which are much easier to find. Serve this over white rice.

If you have access to bitter melons, by all means use them; cut them in half the long way, then scoop out the seeds and fluffy insides, which are like those found in overripe zucchini, before chopping and proceeding as directed.

Fermented black beans are available at most Asian markets and many supermarkets (see page 207).

The lamb will be easier to slice if you freeze it for 30 minutes or so.

1/4 cup fermented black beans

1/4 cup Shaoxing wine, dry sherry, sake, or white wine

3 tablespoons neutral oil, like corn or grapeseed

3 or 4 green bell peppers, stemmed, seeded, and sliced, or 2 or 3 bitter melons, prepared as described in the headnote

1 pound boneless lamb, from the leg or shoulder, cut into thin slices

1 tablespoon minced garlic

1 tablespoon peeled and minced fresh ginger

1/3 cup chicken stock, preferably homemade (page 160), or water

2 tablespoons soy sauce

1/2 cup roughly chopped scallion

1. Soak the black beans in the wine. Put 1 tablespoon of the oil in a large skillet or wok over high heat. When the oil shimmers, add the peppers and cook, stirring only occasionally, until they brown and soften, 5 to 10 minutes. Transfer to a bowl.

2. Add another tablespoon of the oil to the skillet and heat; add the lamb, a couple of pieces at a time. Do not crowd; you may need to cook the lamb in 2 batches. Brown well on each side, then transfer to the bowl with the peppers.

3. Add the remaining tablespoon of oil, along with the garlic and ginger; cook, stirring, for 30 seconds, then add the pepper-lamb mixture, along with the soaked beans and their liquid, the stock, and the soy sauce. Cook, stirring occasionally, until the liquid is somewhat reduced (if it dries

out immediately, add a little more stock or water), just a couple of minutes. Stir in the scallion and serve.

ROASTING MEAT

Although large cuts of meat roast beautifully, this method is not prevalent worldwide, probably because not only the meat but the necessary cooking fuel are prohibitively expensive in so many places. (It takes a lot less fuel to stir-fry than it does to roast.) Still, the roasting of meat is second, perhaps, only to grilling and broiling as a method that can bring out the best flavors with the least work.

Matambre Stuffed Flank Steak ARGENTINA ■
MAKES **6 TO 8 SERVINGS**

TIME **2 1/2 HOURS, PLUS OVERNIGHT CHILLING IF DESIRED**

Matambre, which means "hunger killer" or "hunger fighter" in Spanish, is one of Argentina's best and best-known culinary exports, a rolled flank steak stuffed with spices, vegetables, and hard-cooked eggs that makes a fabulous presentation.

Matambre is prepared and served in a variety of ways. I like it best roasted, then chilled, pressed, and sliced. Prepare it on a Saturday night during the summer, unveil it Sunday afternoon, and spend the remainder of the day picking at it and drinking well-chilled Argentinean red wine. Serve with Chimichurri (page 617) or any salsa.

Freeze the meat for 30 minutes or so before slicing; the firmer meat will make the job easier.

1 flank steak, 1 1/4 to 1 1/2 pounds

Salt and black pepper to taste

1 teaspoon dried or fresh oregano leaves

1 teaspoon ground cumin

2 to 3 garlic cloves, to taste, minced

1 bunch of fresh parsley or ¹/₂ bunch of parsley plus
    ¹/₂ bunch of fresh cilantro

3 small carrots, peeled and cut lengthwise into quarters

2 hard-cooked eggs (page 338), sliced

2 small red onions, peeled and cut into wedges

1 bunch of spinach or watercress

2 tablespoons extra virgin olive oil

1. Preheat the oven to 375°F. Butterfly the flank steak: using a long, sharp knife, cut the steak almost in half with the grain, then flip it open, like a book.

2. Season the meat liberally on both sides with salt and pepper, then flip it cut side up, wide side facing you. Season with the oregano, cumin, and garlic and cover it with a fairly even layer of the parsley. Arrange the carrots, eggs, and onions in neat vertical rows, making two rows of each—you won't have enough to make rows across the entire steak because you need a couple inches free to make it into a neat roll. Scatter a relatively even layer of spinach over all.

3. Roll the whole thing up like a jelly roll; the grain of the steak should run the length of the roll; tie in 3 or 4 places with butcher's twine.

4. Heat the olive oil in a Dutch oven or roasting pan large enough to accommodate the rolled steak. Deeply brown it on all sides, about 15 minutes, and then transfer the pan to the oven and roast for 1¹/₄ to 1¹/₂ hours, until the meat is tender to the touch. Transfer the matambre to a cutting board if you want to eat it at this point or a clean baking dish if you're going to chill it overnight. Let it rest for 30 minutes regardless of when you're eating it—it will be tough hot out of the oven.

5. Weight it with a plate with something relatively heavy on it (this book?) and chill overnight. Take the matambre from the fridge and slice it into ¹/₂- to 1-inch pieces about an hour before you want to start in on it. Serve at room temperature.

Barbecued Pork CHINA ■

MAKES **4 SERVINGS**

TIME **50 MINUTES, PLUS MARINATING TIME**

This traditional Cantonese dish can be eaten with rice or noodles, tossed into a fried rice or noodle dish, or used to stuff into a sweet bun. It's beloved by all meat eaters and a great dish for parties.

1¹/₂ pounds boneless pork loin, cut from the shoulder end,
    or 2 pounds boneless pork shoulder, trimmed

3 tablespoons honey

2 tablespoons hoisin sauce

2 tablespoons soy sauce

2 tablespoons Shaoxing wine or dry sherry

2 tablespoons oyster sauce

¹/₂ teaspoon five-spice powder

1. Cut the pork lengthwise into 1-inch by 2-inch strips. Pierce the meat all over with the point of a knife. Combine the remaining ingredients and pour over the meat in a shallow baking dish. Cover and refrigerate for at least 4 hours and up to a day.

2. When you're ready to cook, preheat the oven to 400°F. Transfer the meat to a rack in a roasting pan and bake for 45 minutes, turning and basting occasionally. Cool, slice, and serve warm or cover and refrigerate for up to a day (reheat gently before serving).

Barbecued Pork, Southeast Asian Style. Add 1 tablespoon nam pla (Thai fish sauce) and 3 garlic cloves, minced, to the marinade.

Roast Pork with Prunes and Apricots

SCANDINAVIA

MAKES **4 TO 6 SERVINGS**

TIME **1$\frac{1}{2}$ HOURS OR MORE**

Ginger may not be a spice you associate with Sweden, but it's there (as is cardamom), and it makes its mark in this winter dish. When I was first served this, it was done in traditional, fancy style: a large roast of pork with a hole poked right through its center, stuffed with the dried fruit. It's a glorious presentation and my first choice. But I have since been served it, and made it, in the simpler, stewed fashion of the variation, which is equally legit.

I like this with Potato and Horseradish Gratin (page 482), but it's good with most any potato dish.

12 prunes

12 dried apricots

1 cup port, dry red wine, or water

One 2- to 3-pound piece boneless pork loin, cut from the
    rib (shoulder) end

Salt and black pepper

1 tablespoon peeled and minced fresh ginger

1 tablespoon sugar

$\frac{1}{2}$ teaspoon cayenne

1 cup dry white wine

$\frac{1}{2}$ cup heavy cream, optional

1. Preheat the oven to 450°F. Combine the prunes, apricots, and liquid in a small saucepan and turn the heat to medium. Simmer gently until tender, about 10 minutes (longer if the fruit was very dry to begin with).

2. Cut the roast open lengthwise, leaving a bit of a hinge along one side, and sprinkle it with salt and pepper. Drain the fruit and layer it on the meat with the ginger. Close the meat and tie or skewer it to something approaching its original shape. Mix together a large pinch of salt, some pepper, the sugar, and the cayenne and rub the roast all over with this mixture. Place in a roasting pan and put in the oven.

3. Roast, undisturbed, for about 15 minutes. Pour about $\frac{1}{2}$ cup of the white wine or stock over the roast and lower the heat to 350°F. Continue to roast, adding about $\frac{1}{4}$ cup wine every 15 minutes or so to keep the bottom of the pan moist, for about 45 minutes. Check the roast; an instant-read thermometer will register 145°F when it's done (and it may take up to 1$\frac{1}{2}$ hours).

4. Transfer the meat to a warm platter and put the pan on the stove over medium-high heat. If necessary, reduce the liquid to about $\frac{3}{4}$ cup, scraping the bottom of the pan with a wooden spoon to release any brown bits. (If the pan is dry, add more white wine.) When the sauce is reduced, stir in the cream, if you're using it, and cook for another minute or two. Taste and adjust the seasoning, then carve the meat and serve it with the sauce.

Stewed Pork with Prunes and Apricots. Much faster and easier. Cut the meat into cubes and brown them over medium-high heat in 2 tablespoons butter or extra virgin olive oil. Add 1 cup white wine or stock, the fruits (don't bother to soak first), salt, pepper, ginger, sugar, and cayenne. Cover and adjust the heat so the mixture simmers steadily. Cook until the pork is tender, about 30 minutes; reduce the liquid a bit, then add the cream if you like.

Sausage and Orange with Bay Leaves MEDITERRANEAN ▪

MAKES **4 SERVINGS**

TIME **30 MINUTES**

This is a Mediterranean dish that can be done more authentically if you can get your hands on branches of fresh edible bay (laurel), but that's not always easy (you could use rosemary or fennel branches quite successfully, and they're equally traditional, though obviously different in flavor). In the original version, you throw a few branches of bay (laurel) onto a grill and top with sausage. My oven method uses somewhat less bay and is virtually foolproof.

Other cuts of meat you can use here: chunks of pork or lamb, cut from the shoulder, or boneless chicken thighs.

1 or 2 branches fresh bay leaves or 50 or 60 dried bay leaves
1¹/₂ to 2 pounds fresh garlic sausage
3 navel oranges

1. Preheat the oven to 450°F. Lay the bay leaves on the bottom of a roasting pan and top them with the sausage; prick the sausage in a few places with a thin-bladed knife. Put in the oven for about 15 minutes, turning once or twice, until browned.
2. Meanwhile, peel the oranges and cut them into ¹/₄-inch-thick slices. Top the sausage with the orange slices and bake until the sausage is cooked through, about 10 more minutes. Serve the sausage and the orange slices (do not eat the bay leaves).

Lechon Asado Roast Pork CUBA ■ ▧

MAKES **6 SERVINGS**

TIME **AT LEAST 2 HOURS, LARGELY UNATTENDED**

An international dish if ever there was one (the Philippine version is quite similar and you can find others around the globe) and one that can be spiced with as little as a rub of garlic, salt, and pepper or a little more elaborately, as is this one. Use a bone-in loin cut, from the rib (shoulder) end, or simply a boneless shoulder (picnic or butt) roast.

This is the pork that is best used for Sandwich Cubano (page 363).

2 tablespoons minced fresh oregano leaves or
**   2 teaspoons dried**
1 tablespoon minced garlic
2 teaspoons ground cumin
1 tablespoon salt
1 tablespoon black pepper
One 3-pound bone-in pork roast, from the shoulder end,
**   excess fat removed**
¹/₄ cup fresh lemon juice
1 large onion, thinly sliced
Lemon wedges for serving

1. Combine the first 6 ingredients. Use a sharp knife to poke some holes all over the meat and insert small amounts of the garlic rub into them. Combine the remaining rub with the lemon juice and onion and rub all over the exterior of the roast; if time allows, wrap in plastic or place in a resealable plastic bag and refrigerate for 24 hours. If not, proceed.
2. When you're ready to cook, preheat the oven to 450°F. Put the pork on a rack in a roasting pan and put in the oven. Roast for 20 minutes, or until the pork begins to brown, then lower the heat to 350°F and add 1 cup water to the bottom of the pan. Continue to roast, basting the pork with the pan juices and adding water to the bottom of the pan if it threatens to dry out, for about 2 hours, or until the interior temperature of the pork reaches 150°F on an instant-read thermometer.
3. Remove the pork and let it rest. (You can prepare the dish up to this point in advance; let sit for a few hours or cover and refrigerate for up to a day. Make the sauce and refrigerate it separately; reheat before serving.) Add more water to the bottom of the pan if necessary and cook over high heat, stirring and scraping to incorporate any browned bits

of meat that may be stuck to the bottom. Carve the pork, spoon a little of this pan juice over it, and serve with the lemon wedges.

BRAISING

All of the recipes in this section rely on braising—cooking in liquid, either a little or a lot, over low heat. Braising will tenderize even the toughest cuts, and these are the cuts that are most likely to be not only the least expensive but the most flavorful. The flavors of added seasonings and vegetables have plenty of time to mellow and marry with those of the meat. Furthermore, though it usually takes a long time, braising meats can almost always be more or less ignored for long stretches. All of this goes a long way to explain why this part of the chapter is huge and incredibly useful.

Beef Stew with Bean Paste KOREA ■
MAKES **4 SERVINGS**
TIME **45 MINUTES**

This is a very fast and almost equally flavorful relative of Kalbi Jim (page 388). If you cannot find go chu jang, the chili-bean paste sold in Korean markets, substitute a couple of tablespoons of good miso and add more hot red pepper flakes to taste. All you need to complete this meal is white rice.

Other cuts of meat you can use here: boneless pork, preferably from the shoulder or leg (fresh ham); boneless chicken thighs.

1½ pounds boneless beef sirloin, cut into 1-inch cubes
2 tablespoons minced garlic
¼ cup soy sauce

3 tablespoons dark sesame oil
1 large potato, peeled and diced
1 large onion, chopped
2 medium carrots, chopped
2 long fresh red chiles, 2 small fresh chiles, or hot red pepper flakes to taste
2 tablespoons go chu jang or dark miso, or to taste
2 tablespoons toasted sesame seeds (page 596) for garnish
2 tablespoons chopped scallion for garnish

1. Marinate the meat in a mixture of the garlic, soy sauce, and 1 tablespoon of the sesame oil while you prepare the other ingredients.
2. Put the remaining sesame oil in a broad skillet or flameproof casserole with a lid over medium-high heat. Add the potato, onion, and carrots and cook, stirring occasionally, until the onion is softened and the potato and carrots begin to brown, about 10 minutes. Stir in the chiles and cook for another minute. Remove with a slotted spoon.
3. Add the meat and its marinade to the skillet and cook for about 2 minutes, stirring. Return the vegetable mixture to the pan and stir once or twice, then add the go chu jang and about 1 cup water (or use stock). Bring almost to a boil, then lower the heat and cover; cook the mixture gently until the meat is fairly tender, about 20 minutes. (You can prepare the dish to this point several hours in advance, cover, and set aside until you're ready to eat, then reheat; or cover and refrigerate overnight before reheating.) Garnish and serve.

Korean Beef Stew with Tofu and Kimchi. Lighter and spicier: Reduce the meat to ½ pound. In step 3, add 1 cup chopped kimchi (page 444; also available at most Asian markets) along with the vegetables. When the meat is done, add ½ to ¾ pound firm tofu, cut into ½- to 1-inch cubes. Heat through gently and serve as directed.

Best Beef Cuts for Braising

Chuck and brisket. Meat from the front of the animal has tons of flavor but must be cooked for long periods of time to become tender.

Short ribs. Like spareribs and lamb shank, a superb choice for braising.

Round. Not ideal—it is usually too lean—but can be made into a good pot roast or stew.

Odd cuts. Cheeks, shanks, tail, and so on can all be braised nicely.

Beef Stew with Winter Squash JAPAN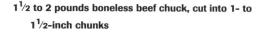

MAKES **4 SERVINGS**

TIME **AT LEAST 1 HOUR, LARGELY UNATTENDED**

Although this stew has much in common with the humble American beef stew, it is legitimately Japanese and wonderfully flavored with soy, ginger, mirin (the Japanese sweet cooking wine, for which sugar or honey is an adequate substitute), winter squash, and,

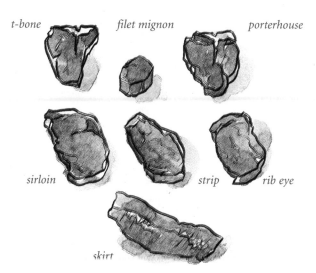

t-bone   filet mignon   porterhouse

sirloin   strip   rib eye

skirt

SOME BEEF CUTS

perhaps best of all, the peel and juice of a lemon. The combination is one of simple and delicious counterpoints that make this a great stew. Ambitious cooks may want to include dashi, the quickly made stock that is one of the most fundamental flavors of Japanese cooking, but the stew is great when made with chicken stock or, for that matter, water.

Other cuts of meat you can use here: short ribs (which will require longer cooking time), bone-in chicken thighs (which will cook more quickly), veal shoulder or round.

1½ to 2 pounds boneless beef chuck, cut into 1- to
   1½-inch chunks

2 cups Dashi (page 162), chicken stock, preferably
   homemade (page 160), or water

¼ cup soy sauce

¼ cup mirin, honey, or sugar

10 nickel-sized slices peeled fresh ginger

Salt and black pepper to taste

1 lemon

1½ pounds peeled and seeded butternut, pumpkin,
   or other winter squash, or sweet potatoes, cut into
   1-inch chunks

1. In a large skillet, preferably nonstick, sear the meat over medium-high heat in two batches until nicely browned, only about 5 minutes per batch, since it's sufficient to brown the meat well on one side. As you finish, transfer the chunks to a medium-sized flameproof casserole with a lid.

2. When the meat is all browned, add the stock to the skillet and cook over high heat, stirring and scraping occasionally, until all the solids are integrated into the liquid. Pour into the casserole with the soy sauce, mirin, ginger, and a couple of grindings of pepper. Peel the lemon and add the peel to the mixture; juice the lemon and reserve the juice.

3. Cover and cook on top of the stove (or in a 350°F oven), maintaining a steady simmer. Stir after 30 minutes and begin to check the meat at 15-minute intervals.

4. When the meat is tender, or nearly so, stir in the squash and continue to cook as before, checking every 15 minutes, until the squash is tender but not mushy. (If you choose to prepare the dish in advance, undercook the squash slightly and stop cooking here. Let sit at room temperature for up to a couple of hours or cover and refrigerate for up to a day. If you like, skim excess fat before reheating and proceeding, adding a little water if necessary.) Taste and add salt if needed, then stir in the reserved lemon juice and serve.

Faster Japanese Beef Stew. Use beef tenderloin (filet mignon). Brown the meat as directed and reduce the liquid in the pan. Combine the meat, liquid, and all the other ingredients except the lemon juice. Cook until the squash is tender, 20 to 30 minutes; stir in the lemon juice and serve.

Beef Stew with Prunes MIDDLE EAST ■
MAKES **4 SERVINGS**

TIME **2 HOURS, LARGELY UNATTENDED**

A wonderful spin on beef stew containing both dried fruits and vegetables. You see this combination throughout Central Asia (and occasionally in the Middle East and Europe), and it's an easy one to exploit.

Dried fruits keep forever and take no preparation to add their wonderful body, sweetness, and acidity to what otherwise might be a dull dish. Other fruits often used here are quinces, chestnuts, or dried apricots.

You can make this up to a day ahead of time and reheat before serving—it only gets better with time. Serve with couscous (page 526) or any other simple grain dish.

Other cuts of meat you can use here: lamb or pork shoulder, lamb shanks or short ribs (both of which will take considerably longer to become tender).

3 tablespoons extra virgin olive oil

2 pounds lean boneless beef, preferably chuck, cut into 2-inch or smaller cubes

Salt and black pepper to taste

1 onion, chopped

3 plum tomatoes, stemmed and chopped (canned are fine)

1 teaspoon sweet paprika, or more to taste

1 cinnamon stick

1 bay leaf

1 cup chicken stock, preferably homemade (page 160)

1 cup dry red wine

2 tablespoons sugar

1 cup pitted prunes

1 tablespoon sherry or other vinegar, or to taste

Chopped fresh parsley leaves for garnish

1. Place a deep skillet or flameproof casserole with a lid over medium-high heat and add the oil. Brown the meat well on all sides, seasoning it and adjusting the heat as necessary, about 10 minutes; remove with a slotted spoon.

2. In the same pot over medium-high heat, sauté the onion and tomatoes with a large pinch of salt and some pepper. When they soften, after about 5 minutes, stir in the paprika, cinnamon, and bay leaf. Return the meat to the pan and add the stock and wine; bring to a boil, then lower the heat, cover,

and simmer for 30 minutes, adjusting the heat so the mixture simmers steadily. (It's unlikely but not impossible that you'll need to add a little water or stock during the simmering; check every 20 minutes or so.)

3. Remove the cinnamon stick and bay leaf and stir in the sugar and prunes. Simmer until the prunes and meat are soft, another 30 to 45 minutes or so. (You can prepare the dish to this point and let sit for a few hours or cover and refrigerate for up to a day before reheating and proceeding.) When the meat is very tender, uncover the pot and, if necessary, raise the heat a bit so the sauce thickens and becomes glossy. Stir in the vinegar, then taste and adjust the seasoning as necessary. Serve hot, garnished with the parsley.

Sour Beef Stew with Horseradish

EASTERN EUROPE ■

MAKES **4 SERVINGS**

TIME **1¹/₂ HOURS OR MORE, LARGELY UNATTENDED**

A simple beef stew with some guts. If you can get your hands on fresh horseradish, substitute peeled ¹/₄-inch-thick slices of it for about half the potatoes; it develops a mild flavor and pleasant texture as it cooks. (Horseradish loses most of its harshness with heat; that's why you do not add the prepared horseradish until the last few minutes of cooking.)

Other cuts of meat you can use here: lamb or veal shoulder.

> 2 tablespoons corn, grapeseed, or other neutral oil
>
> 1¹/₂ to 2 pounds boneless beef chuck, cut into 1-inch chunks
>
> Salt and black pepper to taste
>
> 2 tablespoons butter or more oil
>
> 1 large onion, chopped

> 1 celery stalk, chopped
>
> 2 carrots, chopped
>
> 2 or 3 medium waxy potatoes, peeled and cut into chunks
>
> 1 cup beef or chicken stock, preferably homemade (page 160)
>
> ¹/₄ cup white or wine vinegar
>
> 1 bunch of fresh dill
>
> Sharp Horseradish Sauce (page 607) or prepared horseradish to taste

1. Put the oil in a large deep skillet or flameproof casserole with a lid and place over medium-high heat. Add the beef and brown it well, 10 minutes or more (you may have to brown it in batches), sprinkling it with salt and pepper as it cooks. As the pieces brown, transfer them to a plate. Turn off the heat and allow the pan to cool a bit.

2. Return the heat to medium and put the butter in the pan; when it melts, add the onion, celery, carrots, and potatoes and cook, stirring occasionally and sprinkling with salt and pepper, until the onion is soft, 5 to 10 minutes. Add the stock and vinegar and let the mixture bubble for about a minute; return the meat to the pan. Remove about ¹/₂ cup of dill leaves and reserve; tie the dill stems with the remaining attached leaves into a bundle and add to the bubbling liquid.

3. Cover the pan and adjust the heat so the mixture simmers steadily but not violently. Cook until the meat is tender, at least an hour. Taste and adjust the seasoning. (The dish may be prepared in advance to this point, cooled, then covered and refrigerated for up to a couple of days. If you like, skim the fat before reheating.) Stir in a tablespoon or two of horseradish sauce; taste again and add more if you like. Serve hot, garnished with the reserved dill.

Sour Beef Stew, Scandinavian Style. In step 1, use half butter, half oil. In step 2, add 6 anchovy fillets and 2 bay leaves along with the onion and other vegetables; add 1 tablespoon sugar along with the stock. Proceed as directed; the horseradish sauce is optional (though it is commonly used).

Beef Stew with Dried Mushrooms

EASTERN EUROPE ■

MAKES **4 SERVINGS**

TIME **AT LEAST 1 1/2 HOURS, LARGELY UNATTENDED**

We tend to associate dried mushrooms with France and Italy, but of course they're used wherever mushrooms grow wild, and that includes almost all of central Europe. In fact, some of the best (and least expensive) dried porcini (cèpes) sold in this country come from Poland.

Make this a day in advance if you like and refrigerate, covered; reheat when you're ready.

Serve this with boiled potatoes, buttered noodles, or a rice dish, along with a vegetable or salad. This is also good served with grated fresh horseradish or Creamy Horseradish Sauce (page 608).

Other cuts of meat you can use here: lamb, veal, or pork shoulder, all of which will cook more quickly than the beef.

2 cups beef or chicken stock, preferably homemade (page 160), or water

1 ounce dried porcini

3 tablespoons butter, lard, or neutral oil, like corn or grapeseed

2 large or 3 medium onions, sliced

2 pounds boneless beef chuck, brisket, or round, cut into 1 1/2-inch chunks

Salt and black pepper to taste

2 tablespoons tomato paste, optional

2 bay leaves

Chopped fresh parsley leaves for garnish

1. Heat the stock in a small saucepan or in the microwave; the liquid need not boil, just become hot to the touch. Soak the mushrooms in it. Put 2 tablespoons of the fat or oil in a large skillet or flameproof casserole with a lid and place over medium-high heat. When the fat or oil is hot, add the onions and cook just until they soften, about 5 minutes. Remove with a slotted spoon.

2. Add the remaining fat or oil to the pan and wait a minute or so. Add the beef and brown it well on both sides, about 10 minutes, adjusting the heat so the meat browns but does not burn. Sprinkle the meat with salt and pepper as it browns. Meanwhile, trim the softened mushrooms of any tough parts.

3. When the meat is browned, return the onions to the pan along with the tomato paste if you're using it, the mushrooms and their soaking liquid, and the bay leaves; stir once, then cover. Adjust the heat so the mixture simmers steadily but not violently and cook until the meat is tender (this may be as short as 45 minutes or as long as 1 1/2 hours); check occasionally to make sure the mixture is not drying out (unlikely, but if it is, add a little more stock or water). When the meat is tender, taste and adjust the seasoning, garnish, and serve.

Beef Stew with Sour Cream. When the meat is almost tender, stir in 1 cup sour cream into which you have whisked 1 tablespoon flour. Finish as directed.

Cholent EASTERN EUROPE ■

MAKES **8 SERVINGS**

TIME **AT LEAST 3 HOURS, PREFERABLY LONGER, LARGELY UNATTENDED**

Like tsimmes (page 502), this recipe was originally designed to sit in an oven after a fire had been built, cooking slowly overnight and even into the next day to provide a hot Sabbath meal for Jews who were not allowed to (actively) cook after sunset on Friday. Provided you have no such restrictions, it's a little easier to make cholent, a wonderful stew of any meat, beans, barley, and potatoes; I believe it's especially good with limas, which in any case are traditional in at least parts of Europe.

Other cuts of meat you can use here: lamb shoulder is also good and, if you're not too worried about tradition, so is pork shoulder.

1 pound dried lima or other white beans

2 tablespoons extra virgin olive oil

3 pounds beef brisket or boneless beef chuck, cut into
     large chunks

Salt and black pepper to taste

2 large onions, roughly chopped

5 garlic cloves, roughly chopped

1 tablespoon peeled and minced fresh ginger or
     1 teaspoon ground

$\frac{1}{2}$ teaspoon ground cinnamon

1 teaspoon ground cardamom

1 bay leaf

8 small or 4 medium waxy potatoes, peeled, halved if
     medium-sized

$\frac{1}{2}$ cup pearl barley or kasha

1. Soak the beans overnight or for several hours if time allows; drain.
2. Put the oil in a large deep skillet or flameproof casserole with a lid over medium-high heat. A couple of minutes later, add the meat and cook, turning as necessary, to brown the meat on all sides. This will take at least 10 minutes and probably longer; sprinkle the meat with salt and pepper as it browns. Remove the meat and turn the heat to medium. Add the onions and cook, stirring occasionally, until they wilt and begin to brown, about 10 minutes. Add the garlic, ginger, cinnamon, cardamom, bay leaf, and some more salt and

pepper and cook, stirring, for about a minute. Add the beans, potatoes, barley if you are using it, and water to cover.

3. Bring to a boil, then cover and adjust the heat so the mixture simmers as slowly as possible, with just a few bubbles rising to the surface each second. Cook for 3 hours or preferably longer, until all the ingredients are very tender. (You can also cook in a 250°F oven overnight.) If you are using kasha, add it during the last hour of cooking. Taste and adjust the seasoning and serve in bowls or cover and refrigerate for up to a day before reheating, adding a little more water to thin the stew if necessary.

Real Beef Stroganoff RUSSIA ▨

MAKES **4 SERVINGS**

TIME **30 MINUTES OR LESS**

Few Americans have ever had the real thing, probably because the frozen and cafeteria concoctions have given this old and rather rich dish a bad name. But it's a simple preparation and a nice one; serve over buttered noodles or plain white rice or with bread.

This is a good place to use beef tenderloin, because the cooking is quick and the meat should be tender. Both the mushrooms and the tomatoes are optional; the dish is perfectly fine without either or with both.

Other cuts of meat you can use here: boneless veal shoulder or round.

3 tablespoons butter

2 large onions, sliced

Salt and black pepper to taste

$\frac{1}{2}$ pound mushrooms, trimmed and sliced, optional

$1\frac{1}{2}$ to 2 pounds beef tenderloin or boneless sirloin,
     cut into $1\frac{1}{2}$- to 2-inch chunks

1 tablespoon Dijon mustard

2 plum tomatoes (canned are fine), chopped, or ½ cup
good tomato sauce, optional

1 cup beef or chicken stock, preferably homemade
(page 160)

½ cup sour cream

Chopped fresh dill or parsley leaves for garnish

1. Put the butter in a large deep skillet or flameproof casserole with a lid and place over medium-high heat. When it melts, add the onions, along with a sprinkling of salt and pepper and the mushrooms if you're using them, and cook, stirring occasionally, until the onion is very soft but not brown, about 10 minutes. Add the beef and cook, stirring, for just a minute.

2. Stir in the mustard, tomatoes if you're using them, and stock. Adjust the heat so the mixture simmers steadily but not violently and cook for about 5 minutes, or until the meat is tender. Stir in the sour cream, taste and adjust the seasoning, garnish, and serve.

Beef Stew with Cinnamon GREECE ■

MAKES **4 SERVINGS**

TIME **ABOUT 2 HOURS**

A recipe that beautifully demonstrates the affinity that beef and cinnamon have for each other. If you use fresh pearl onions, parboil them for about 30 seconds to loosen the skins, which will make peeling far easier (or use frozen pearl onions; they're quite good). Serve this over rice or broad buttered noodles.

Other cuts of meat you can use here: lamb, pork, or veal shoulder, all of which will cook a little more quickly; boneless chicken thighs, which will cook much more quickly; lamb shanks or short ribs, which will require much longer cooking time.

2 tablespoons extra virgin olive oil

1½ to 2 pounds boneless beef chuck or brisket, cut into
1- to 2-inch cubes

Salt and black pepper to taste

1 large onion, chopped

20 pearl onions, fresh or frozen, peeled

1 tablespoon minced garlic

½ cup dry red wine

½ cup chicken or beef stock, preferably homemade
(page 160), or water

2 bay leaves

2 cloves

½ teaspoon ground cinnamon

One 6-ounce can tomato paste

¼ cup red wine vinegar

1. Put the oil in a skillet or flameproof casserole with a lid and place over medium-high heat. Brown the meat on all sides, seasoning it with salt and pepper as it cooks and turning it only when each side is browned. (The meat can also be browned in the oven; see page 412.) As the meat browns, remove each piece with a slotted spoon and set aside.

2. Pour or spoon off most of the fat and brown the chopped onion lightly over medium heat. Remove and add to the meat. Add the pearl onions and brown them quickly; remove them and set aside separately.

3. Add the garlic to the pan and cook, stirring occasionally, for about 30 seconds. Return the meat and chopped onion along with the red wine, stock, bay leaves, cloves, cinnamon, tomato paste, and additional salt and pepper. Cover tightly and adjust the heat so the mixture simmers gently. Cook for about an hour, or until the meat is fairly tender.

4. Add the vinegar and pearl onions and continue to simmer until the meat is very tender, roughly 30 minutes more. (You can prepare the dish to this

point in advance and let sit for a few hours or cover and refrigerate for up to a day before reheating, adding a little water if necessary.)

Boeuf Bourguignon Beef Stew with Bacon, Red Wine, and Mushrooms FRANCE ■
MAKES **4 SERVINGS**

TIME **AT LEAST 2 HOURS, SOMEWHAT UNATTENDED**

Like coq au vin, this is a slow recipe that takes careful attention to a couple of ingredients: the bacon must be good slab bacon, nice and smoky and not too lean, and the wine should be fruity and worthy of drinking (there are Burgundies and American Pinot Noirs that meet this requirement and cost around ten bucks a bottle).

By all means make this a day or two in advance if you like, then refrigerate and skim the fat if that's your preference. Reheating will take only about 15 minutes.

New potatoes, roasted in olive oil or butter, are terrific alongside this stew, but so is crusty bread. Round things out with a steamed vegetable or salad.

1 tablespoon extra virgin olive oil

$^1/_4$ pound good-quality slab bacon, cut into $^1/_2$-inch cubes

2 pounds boneless beef chuck or brisket, cut into
$1^1/_2$- to 2-inch cubes

Salt and black pepper to taste

1 large onion, chopped

3 or 4 fresh thyme sprigs

3 bay leaves

2 garlic cloves, peeled and lightly crushed

$^1/_2$ cup chopped fresh parsley leaves, plus more for garnish

12 small button mushrooms, trimmed and halved or quartered

12 pearl onions, peeled (frozen are okay)

1 cup good-quality red wine, preferably Burgundy (Pinot Noir)

Stock or water if necessary

1. Put the olive oil in a Dutch oven or flameproof casserole with a lid and place over medium heat. Add the bacon and cook, stirring occasionally, until it is crisp and has given up most of its fat, about 10 minutes. Remove with a slotted spoon, add the meat, and raise the heat to medium-high. Cook, turning the cubes as they brown and sprinkling them with salt and pepper, until the meat is brown and crisp all over, at least 10 minutes. Remove with a slotted spoon.

2. Reduce the heat to medium and add the chopped onion, thyme, bay leaves, garlic, and parsley, along with some more salt and pepper, and cook, stirring occasionally, until the onion softens, about 5 minutes. Remove with a slotted spoon, then add the mushrooms and pearl onions and cook, stirring occasionally, until lightly browned, 5 to 10 minutes; transfer with a slotted spoon to a separate bowl. Add the wine and let it bubble for a minute, then return the meat to the pan, along with the chopped onion mixture.

3. Cover and adjust the heat so the mixture simmers gently for about an hour, then return the mushroom–pearl onion mixture, along with the bacon. Re-cover and continue to cook until the meat is tender, adding a little more liquid if the mixture threatens to dry out. Depending on the meat, the dish could be done in as little as 30 minutes more or in three times as long. Taste and adjust the seasoning, then garnish and serve or cover and refrigerate for up to 2 days before reheating.

Beef Daube FRANCE ■

MAKES **4 SERVINGS**

TIME **AT LEAST 2 HOURS, SOMEWHAT UNATTENDED**

The Provençal version of boeuf bourguignonne, with different vegetables and seasonings. I think the variation, Beef Daube with Olives, is the superior recipe, but you may prefer this simpler version. Serve this with crisp-roasted potatoes or crusty bread.

Other cuts of meat you can use here: boneless lamb shoulder, cut into chunks.

1 tablespoon extra virgin olive oil

1/4 pound good-quality slab bacon, cut into
    1/2-inch cubes

2 pounds boneless beef chuck or brisket, cut into
    1 1/2- to 2-inch cubes

Salt and black pepper to taste

2 large onions, chopped

2 celery stalks, chopped

3 carrots, chopped

5 garlic cloves, peeled and lightly smashed

3 or 4 fresh thyme sprigs

1 fresh rosemary sprig or 1 teaspoon dried

2 or 3 strips orange peel

1 cup rough red wine, preferably from the south of
    France—something like Cahors or Côtes-du-Rhône

1 tablespoon red wine vinegar

Stock or water if necessary

1. Put the olive oil in a Dutch oven or flameproof casserole with a lid and turn the heat to medium. Add the bacon and cook, stirring occasionally, until it is crisp and has given up most of its fat, about 10 minutes. Remove with a slotted spoon, add the meat, and raise the heat to medium-high. Cook, turning the cubes as they brown and sprinkling them with salt and pepper, until the meat is brown and crisp all over, at least 10 minutes. Remove with a slotted spoon.

2. Reduce the heat to medium and add the onions, celery, carrots, garlic, thyme, rosemary, and orange peel, along with some more salt and pepper, and cook, stirring occasionally, until the onions soften, about 5 minutes. Add the wine and vinegar and let them bubble for a minute, then return the meat to the pan.

3. Cover and adjust the heat so the mixture simmers gently for about an hour, then add the bacon. Recover and continue to cook until the meat is tender, adding a little more liquid if the mixture threatens to dry out. Depending on the meat, the dish could be done in as little as 30 minutes more or in three times as long.

4. Taste and adjust the seasoning, then garnish and serve or cover and refrigerate for up to 2 days before reheating.

Beef Daube with Olives or Dried Fruit. In step 2, replace the rosemary with 1 teaspoon fennel seeds. When you return the bacon to the pan in step 3, add 1 cup good-quality green or black olives, preferably pitted, or 1 cup dried prunes or apricots.

Beef Braised with Sweet White Wine
FRANCE ■

MAKES **4 TO 6 SERVINGS**

TIME **AT LEAST 2 HOURS, LARGELY UNATTENDED**

A specialty of southwestern France, where some of the world's best sweet wines are made. Since you need only about a cup (you could get away with less, if you like), it won't do that much harm to use a good Sauternes or Barzac, the best of the lot. But I have made this very successfully with Montbazillac, which costs about $10 a bottle and is certainly good enough to drink. The resulting sauce is nicely but not cloyingly sweet and wonderful over buttered noodles.

You can make this a day in advance (it might even be better that way) and easily double it to serve a crowd.

Other cuts of meat you can use here: pork or lamb chops or chunks of boneless pork, lamb, or veal shoulder, all of which will cook much more quickly.

3 tablespoons extra virgin olive oil

2 to 3 pounds beef brisket or boneless beef chuck in one piece

Salt and black pepper to taste

3 large or 4 medium onions, sliced

1 tablespoon minced garlic

2 or 3 medium carrots, cut into chunks, optional

1 cup sweet white wine

1. Put 2 tablespoons of the oil in a large skillet or flameproof casserole with a lid and place over medium-high heat. Wait a minute or so and when the oil is hot, add the beef and brown it well on both sides, about 10 minutes, adjusting the heat so the meat browns but does not burn. Sprinkle the meat with salt and pepper as it browns.

2. Transfer the meat to a plate and reduce the heat to medium. Add the remaining oil and the vegetables to the pan; stir once, then cover. Cook for 10 to 15 minutes, stirring once or twice, until the onions are browned, dry, and almost sticking to the pan. Uncover, then add the wine and stir. Add the meat and cover again. Adjust the heat so the mixture simmers steadily but not violently and cook until the meat is tender (this may be as short as 90 minutes or as long as 3 hours).

3. Transfer the meat to a cutting board and let it rest for a couple of minutes. Taste and adjust the sauce seasoning; you should be able to taste the pepper. If the mixture is very thin (unlikely), boil it down for a few minutes, as necessary. Carve the meat and serve it with the sauce spooned over it or cool and refrigerate the meat (uncarved) and sauce for up to a day before reheating gently.

Carbonnade Beef and Onions Stewed in Beer
BELGIUM ■

MAKES **4 TO 6 SERVINGS**

TIME **ABOUT 2 HOURS, LARGELY UNATTENDED**

A simple beef stew that is good over buttered noodles or with plain boiled potatoes. For the beer, use Guinness stout or another dark, bitter beer. Like many stews, this is equally good (or better) when refrigerated and reheated the next day.

Other cuts of meat you can use here: though not traditional, this works well with chunks of lamb shoulder or veal shoulder.

3 cups thinly sliced onion

3 tablespoons lard or neutral oil, like corn or grapeseed

2 to 2^1/$_2$ pounds boneless beef chuck, brisket, or round, cut into 1^1/$_2$-inch cubes

Salt and black pepper to taste

1 tablespoon minced garlic

1 bay leaf

1 teaspoon fresh thyme leaves or ^{1}/$_2$ teaspoon dried

1 teaspoon fresh oregano leaves or ^{1}/$_2$ teaspoon dried

1 bottle (about 1^1/$_2$ cups) good dark, bitter beer

1 tablespoon Dijon mustard, or to taste

Chopped fresh parsley leaves for garnish

1. Put the onion in a large flameproof casserole or deep skillet with a lid and cover it; place over medium heat and cook, checking and stirring every few minutes, until the onion is dry and almost sticking to the pan, about 15 minutes. At that point, add 2 tablespoons of the lard and cook, stirring occasionally, until the onion becomes a brown, soft mass, another 15 minutes or so. Remove with a slotted spoon and add the remaining lard to the skillet.

2. Raise the heat to medium-high and brown the meat on all sides, sprinkling it with salt and pepper as it browns. When the meat is brown, add the

garlic and cook, stirring, for about 30 seconds. Return the onion to the pan, along with the herbs and beer. Bring to a boil, then adjust the heat so the mixture simmers; cover.

3. Cook, checking occasionally to make sure the mixture does not dry out (unlikely, but if it does, add more beer), for about an hour, or until the meat is quite tender. Uncover the pan; the mixture should be stewy but not soupy; if it is, raise the heat and boil out some of the liquid. Stir in the mustard, then taste and adjust the seasoning. Garnish and serve or cool, cover, and refrigerate.

Ropa Vieja Shredded Stewed Beef CUBA
MAKES **6 TO 8 SERVINGS**

TIME **3½ HOURS, HALF UNATTENDED**

"Old clothes" may not sound that appetizing, but it's one of those overcooked, funky, juicy, tender dishes you can't stop eating (at least I can't). And the only thing even remotely difficult about it is shredding the steaks into the ropy strands that give Ropa Vieja its fanciful name. Still, it's not you-can-do-it-wrong difficult; it's just a bit of an upper-body workout.

You could cut the recipe in half and cook one steak, but with a dish that takes this long and keeps as well as it does (you can refrigerate it for a few days or even freeze it), I think this is a sensible amount.

As a bonus, when you braise this much meat you end up with at least a quart of rich, dark beef stock, redolent of bay and cloves—perfect for cooking Arroz a la Mexicana (page 517)—which, not coincidentally, is a perfect side dish for Ropa Vieja.

A couple of preparation notes: green bell peppers are a bit more traditional here, but I prefer to make Ropa Vieja with the sweeter red bell peppers. You choose.

Cutting the steaks in half to make two thin steaks (hold the knife parallel to the cutting board) is a bit of a challenge, but if you freeze the steaks for about 30 minutes first, the firmer flesh will make it easier. Take your time, but don't worry about doing too good a job—you're going to shred the meat anyway.

2 tablespoons corn, grapeseed, or other neutral oil

2 to 3 pounds flank steaks, split in half lengthwise (with the knife held parallel to the cutting board)

Salt and black pepper to taste

2 bay leaves

1 yellow onion, halved (unpeeled), each half stuck with a clove

5 garlic cloves

¼ cup extra virgin olive oil

1 tablespoon cumin seeds

1 cinnamon stick or 1 teaspoon ground cinnamon

2 large yellow or white onions, thinly sliced

1 or 2 red bell peppers, stemmed, seeded, and cut into ½-inch strips

4 plum tomatoes, coarsely chopped, or one 8-ounce can whole tomatoes, drained and chopped

3 tablespoons capers, soaked if salted, drained if in vinegar

Lime wedges for serving

Tabasco or other hot sauce for serving

1. Put the neutral oil in a wide deep skillet or Dutch oven with a lid over medium-high heat. Season the steaks well with salt and pepper. Brown the beef in the pan in two or more batches, making sure the meat colors deeply on all sides, about 20 minutes in all.

2. Drain the fat from the pan and cover the meat with 2 quarts water. Turn the heat to high and add the bay leaves, onion halves, and 2 unpeeled garlic cloves. When the water comes to a boil, partially cover the pan and adjust the heat so the mixture simmers gently; braise for about 2 hours, or until the meat is tender.

3. Remove the meat from the pan and transfer to a wide baking dish or a deep skillet (you want to collect the juices it will release). Strain the broth, discarding the aromatics. Reserve 1 cup for this recipe and the rest for another use.

4. Peel the remaining 3 garlic cloves and mash to a paste with the flat side of a knife. Return the pan to the stove, turn the heat to medium, and add the olive oil. When it shimmers, add the garlic paste, cumin seeds, and cinnamon stick (if you're using ground cinnamon, add it with the sliced onions). Cook for a minute, stirring, until fragrant and lightly colored, then add the sliced onions. Turn the heat up a bit and cook, stirring occasionally, until the onions are deeply golden; add the bell pepper strips and cook until they soften slightly, 3 or 4 minutes more. Season everything well with salt and pepper and add the tomatoes, reserved broth, and reserved juices. Reduce the heat to low and simmer until half of the liquid in the pan is gone, about 15 minutes; remove the cinnamon stick and, if you choose to, the bay leaves.

5. Meanwhile, shred the beef: anchor one end of the flank steak with a fork (or, better yet, a carving fork) and run another fork the length of the steak, with the grain, shredding it into thin sinewy strips. When you've shredded all the beef, add it to the pan with the onion and pepper sauce and warm through. Garnish with the capers and serve with plenty of rice, lime wedges, and hot sauce.

Poached Beef Tenderloin FRANCE ■

MAKES **6 SERVINGS**
TIME **30 MINUTES**

Poaching a tenderloin of beef is the surest way to obtain perfectly and uniformly rare meat. Whether you choose a 2-pound piece, which will easily serve four,

or a larger one, the procedure and results are consistently the same, making the dish ideal for dinner parties. As long as the meat is of fairly consistent thickness, every slice you cut—with the exception of the very ends—will look like the others. Buying the beef is simple but usually can be made even simpler with an advance call to the butcher; ask for the thick (châteaubriand) end of the tenderloin, 2 to 3 pounds (he will be willing to cut it to any size you like), in one piece, tied. If you allow the meat to reach room temperature before poaching, cooking time will be reduced by a few minutes; but it will be no longer than 20 and probably shorter anyway.

It's key to serve the meat with a variety of garnishes from which you and your guests can choose: minced shallots, good mustard, chopped cornichons, coarse salt, soy sauce, even ketchup. These can be combined—I favor mustard combined with shallots and cornichons. I'd like a potato gratin with this recipe (page 482), but any potato dish (including good old mashed potatoes) would be fine, as would almost any nicely prepared vegetable. Bread, too.

One 3-pound piece beef tenderloin from the thick end, preferably at room temperature
6 cups beef or chicken stock, preferably homemade (page 160), or water
Salt to taste
Garnishes, such as minced shallots, Dijon mustard, chopped cornichons, coarse salt, and salsa

1. Put the meat in a deep pan just large enough to hold it—a Dutch oven is usually ideal, but you can curve the meat into a wide saucepan too—and cover it with boiling water or stock. Add a large pinch of salt if you're using water or if the stock is unsalted. Adjust the heat so that the mixture bubbles gently—on my stove that's medium.

2. Cook until the meat's internal temperature reaches 120°F (use an instant-read thermometer);

125°F if you prefer medium-rare. Remove the meat and let it sit for about 5 minutes, then cut into ½- to 1-inch-thick slices. Serve immediately with the garnishes.

Kalbi Jim Braised Short Ribs KOREA ■
MAKES **6 SERVINGS**

TIME **2 HOURS, PLUS MARINATING TIME, LARGELY UNATTENDED**

Koreans prepare and enjoy dozens of different stews and usually eat them so hot (in temperature—they're often served over a flame so they are actually boiling while they're being eaten) that Westerners are astonished. Some are so mild that they seem almost French; others are dark and richly flavorful, like this classic. Serve with white rice.

Other cuts of meat you can use here: lamb shanks.

6 pounds beef short ribs

10 garlic cloves, chopped

1 cup soy sauce

5 tablespoons dark sesame oil

2 tablespoons peeled and minced fresh ginger

12 scallions, trimmed and roughly chopped

¼ cup toasted sesame seeds (page 596), ground

½ cup sake

¼ cup mirin or 2 tablespoons honey or sugar

2 tablespoons sugar

1 Asian pear or 2 crisp apples, peeled, cored, and chopped

1 or 2 fresh chiles, preferably long and red, minced, or to taste

2 large shallots, chopped

1 teaspoon black pepper, plus more to taste

¼ cup olive or neutral oil, like corn or grapeseed

1 large potato, peeled and chopped

2 medium onions, chopped

2 medium carrots, chopped

2 eggs for garnish, optional

Salt to taste

1. Combine the first 14 ingredients and marinate overnight, covered and refrigerated. About 2 hours before you're ready to eat, put half the oil in a wide deep saucepan or flameproof casserole with a lid and turn the heat to high. Remove the short ribs from the marinade, reserving the marinade, and brown them on all sides, 10 to 15 minutes.

2. Add the marinade to the meat, along with 2 cups water. Bring to a boil, then lower the heat and simmer, covered, for an hour or longer, until tender. (These are not cooked until falling-off-the-bone tender, but tender as if they were a good steak.)

3. Turn the heat back to high, uncover, and add the potato, onions, and carrots. Cook at a lively simmer until the stew is thick and the vegetables are done, about 20 minutes more. (You can prepare the dish to this point and let sit for a few hours or cover and refrigerate for up to a day before reheating and proceeding.)

4. Meanwhile, if you want to make a traditional egg garnish, put the remaining oil in a 12-inch nonstick skillet and turn the heat to medium-high. Beat the eggs with a little pepper and a pinch of salt, then add them to the skillet. Turn the heat to medium and let sit, undisturbed, until the bottom is lightly browned, 3 to 5 minutes. Flip and cook until the omelet is firm, just another minute or two. Turn out onto a cutting board and cool slightly, then roll up and cut into thin slices. Taste the stew and add a little salt if necessary. Garnish the meat if you like and serve.

Rabo de Toro Braised Oxtail SPAIN ■

MAKES **4 SERVINGS**

TIME **AT LEAST 2 HOURS, LARGELY UNATTENDED**

You can find oxtails at many supermarkets, but you can also braise any tough cut of beef this way. In Spain, traditionally, it's bull's tails (hence the Spanish name), and, surprisingly, it's almost always made with white wine. It's a simple enough recipe and one you can pretty much ignore while it cooks, especially if you put it in the oven. It'll take a while.

If you make this in advance, not only can you refrigerate it and skim the fat if you like, but you can remove the meat from the bone and use it in any stuffed dumpling, pasta, or vegetable. Having said that, it's great served from the pot, with mashed potatoes.

Other cuts of meat you can use here: short ribs, lamb shanks, chunks of boneless lamb or pork shoulder (which will be much faster) or beef chuck or brisket (which will be somewhat faster), bone-in chicken thighs (much quicker).

 1 tablespoon extra virgin olive oil

 ¼ pound good-quality slab bacon, cut into small cubes

 3 to 4 pounds oxtails, cut into 2-inch lengths

 Salt and black pepper to taste

 1 large onion, chopped

 2 carrots, roughly chopped

 2 celery stalks, peeled and roughly chopped

 1 head of garlic, excess papery skin removed, cut in half
   through its equator

 1 cup dry white wine

 2 bay leaves

 Several fresh thyme sprigs

 1 medium to large tomato, cored and roughly chopped

 Stock or water as needed

 Chopped fresh parsley leaves for garnish

1. Preheat the oven to 300°F. Put the olive oil in a Dutch oven or flameproof casserole with a lid and place over medium heat. Add the bacon and cook, stirring occasionally, until it is crisp and has given up most of its fat, about 10 minutes. Remove with a slotted spoon, add the meat, and turn the heat to medium-high. Cook, turning the chunks as they brown and sprinkling them with salt and pepper, until the meat is brown and crisp all over, at least 10 minutes. Remove with a slotted spoon.

2. Turn the heat to medium and add the onion, carrots, and celery, along with some more salt and pepper, and cook, stirring occasionally, until the onion softens, about 5 minutes. Add the garlic and cook for another minute. Add the wine and let it bubble for a minute, then return the meat and the bacon to the pan along with the bay leaves, thyme, and tomato. Stir.

3. Cover and put in the oven; cook, checking after about an hour and adding more liquid if needed, for at least 2 hours, or until the meat is very, very tender—falling off the bone. Taste and adjust the seasoning. If the mixture is soupy, reduce the liquid over high heat until it is more like a sauce. Garnish and serve or cover and refrigerate for up to 2 days before reheating.

Oxtail with Capers CARIBBEAN ■

MAKES **4 SERVINGS**

TIME **AT LEAST 2 HOURS**

The New World version of the preceding recipe, this includes Spain's capers (which, ironically, the Spanish version usually does not) and a bit more seasoning. Once again, you can use other meat in place of oxtails and can make this in advance, then refrigerate and skim the fat.

This would be great with Coconut Rice (page 516) or any rice and bean dish, and Platanos Maduros (page 472).

Other cuts of meat you can use here: short ribs, lamb shanks, chunks of boneless lamb or pork shoulder (which will be much faster) or beef chuck or brisket (which will be somewhat faster), bone-in chicken thighs (much quicker).

1 tablespoon extra virgin olive oil

3 to 4 pounds oxtails, cut into 2-inch lengths

Salt and black pepper to taste

2 large onions, roughly chopped

1 tablespoon minced garlic

2 cups chopped tomatoes (canned are fine)

1 cup red wine

1 teaspoon ground cumin

1 teaspoon dried oregano

1/4 teaspoon ground allspice

1 cup capers, with a bit of their juice

3 or 4 Roasted Red Peppers (page 470), cut into strips

Chopped fresh parsley leaves for garnish

1. Preheat the oven to 300°F. Put the olive oil in a Dutch oven or flameproof casserole with a lid and place over medium-high heat. Add the meat and cook, turning the chunks as they brown and sprinkling them with salt and pepper, until the meat is brown and crisp all over, at least 10 minutes. Remove with a slotted spoon.

2. Reduce the heat to medium and add the onions; cook until softened, stirring occasionally, about 5 minutes. Add the garlic and stir; add the tomatoes, wine, and spices, along with at least 1/2 teaspoon black pepper, and bring to a boil. Cook, stirring occasionally, until the mixture is saucy, about 15 minutes. Add the capers and return the meat to the pan.

3. Cover and put in the oven; cook, checking after about an hour and adding more liquid if needed, for at least 2 hours, or until the meat is very, very tender—falling off the bone. Taste and adjust the seasoning. If the mixture is soupy, remove the meat and reduce the liquid over high heat until it is more like a sauce. Stir in the peppers, garnish, and serve, or cover and refrigerate for up to 2 days.

Rendang Dry-Braised Beef with Spices MALAYSIA
MAKES **4 SERVINGS**

TIME **1 1/2 HOURS, LARGELY UNATTENDED**

Unlike most braised meat dishes, this one ends up dry. The sauce is reduced slowly with the meat, and the result is something like fresh beef jerky. Be sure to vary the amount of chile according to your taste; I tend to be quite conservative when using chiles, but this dish is traditionally quite hot. Serve with white rice and a moist vegetable dish, like Spinach with Coconut Milk (page 487).

2 hot dried red chiles

3 garlic cloves, peeled

3 shallots, peeled

One 1-inch piece fresh ginger or galangal, peeled and roughly chopped

1 teaspoon ground turmeric

1 teaspoon cumin seeds

1 teaspoon coriander seeds

2 tablespoons tamarind paste (page 585), or the juice and zest of 2 limes

2 tablespoons corn, grapeseed, or other neutral oil

GALANGAL

1 pound boneless beef, preferably chuck, cut into 1-inch
    cubes

1 cup coconut milk, homemade (page 584) or canned

Salt to taste

1. Put the chiles, garlic, shallots, ginger, turmeric, cumin, and coriander in a food processor. Process until everything is minced (or mince everything by hand and combine). Add the tamarind paste and process until smooth.

2. Heat the oil in a skillet with a lid and place over medium-high heat. Add the spice paste and cook, stirring occasionally, until fragrant, about 2 minutes. Add the beef and cook, stirring occasionally, until browned and covered with the sauce.

3. Pour in the coconut milk and bring the mixture to a boil. Lower the heat, cover, and simmer until the sauce dries out, about 1 hour. Season with salt and serve.

12345 Spareribs CHINA ■

MAKES **4 SERVINGS**

TIME **50 MINUTES, LARGELY UNATTENDED**

The name of this dish may be cute, but it also reflects its simplicity; it is an honest sweet-and-sour pork dish. While the ribs need to braise for at least 40 minutes, the preparation time is just 10 minutes or so. Ask your butcher to cut across the ribs to form 1-inch strips (a supermarket butcher can do this), then have him separate the ribs, or you can do that part yourself.

This dish reheats perfectly. Serve the ribs with white rice.

2 pounds spareribs, cut into 1-inch chunks

1 tablespoon Shaoxing wine or dry sherry

2 tablespoons white or rice vinegar

3 tablespoons soy sauce

4 tablespoons sugar

5 tablespoons water

1. Place a deep skillet with a lid over medium-high heat and brown the spareribs on each side, turning after 2 or 3 minutes.

2. Whisk together the remaining ingredients and pour into the skillet. Cover the skillet, turn the heat to low, and simmer for about 40 minutes, stirring the ribs occasionally to make sure they don't burn. When the ribs are fork-tender, serve hot or cover and refrigerate for up to a day before reheating.

Black Bean and Garlic Spareribs

CHINA

MAKES **4 SERVINGS**

TIME **45 MINUTES, LARGELY UNATTENDED**

Chinese fermented black beans (see page 207) keep forever and add a distinctive flavor to every dish they're used in; best yet, most people like them immediately. This classic highlights them perfectly. Ask the butcher to cut the ribs into small pieces for you (a supermarket butcher can do this).

Serve as a starter or an entree with steamed white rice.

3 tablespoons corn, grapeseed, or other neutral oil

2 pounds pork spareribs, cut into individual ribs and
    crosswise into 1-inch strips

4 garlic cloves, minced

1 tablespoon fermented black beans, rinsed, drained,
    and coarsely chopped

1 scallion, trimmed and chopped

One 1½-inch piece fresh ginger, peeled and minced

2 tablespoons soy sauce

1 tablespoon Shaoxing wine, dry sherry, stock, or water

$^{1}/_{2}$ cup chicken stock, preferably homemade (page 160),
   or water

1. Put the oil in a skillet with a lid and place over medium-high heat. A minute later, add the spareribs. Brown them lightly on both sides, then drain all but 2 tablespoons of oil from the pan.

2. Add the garlic, black beans, scallion, and ginger. Stir-fry until fragrant, about 1 minute. Stir in the soy sauce, wine, and stock and bring to a boil. Cover, turn the heat to low, and simmer, stirring occasionally, until the ribs are tender, 30 minutes or more. Remove from the heat and serve with the pan juices over white rice.

Sesame Spareribs KOREA
MAKES **4 SERVINGS**
   TIME **45 TO 60 MINUTES**

No rib-cooking technique makes more sense than the one used in Korea, which begins with a tenderizing poaching and continues with a kind of dry-roasting in the fat and juices exuded by the ribs themselves, along with a dose of strong seasonings. It results in ribs that are dark, glossy, and so tender that just a tug of the teeth will pull them off the bone. If possible, ask your butcher to cut the ribs into 2-inch lengths, which will make them easier to cook (and to eat).

I love these preceded by Pajon (page 80) and, of course, with some Kimchi (page 444) on the side, but you may serve them with white rice and a simple steamed vegetable.

Other cuts of meat you can use here: short ribs (which will take considerably longer to cook in step 2).

3 pounds spareribs, cut into 2-inch pieces
2 tablespoons chopped garlic

$^{1}/_{4}$ cup toasted sesame seeds (page 596)

$^{1}/_{3}$ cup sugar

5 nickel-sized pieces peeled fresh ginger

$^{1}/_{2}$ cup soy sauce

2 tablespoons dark sesame oil

Salt and black pepper to taste

$^{1}/_{2}$ cup chopped scallion

1. Put a large skillet that can hold the ribs in one layer over high heat and add the ribs and 1 cup water. Boil, turning the ribs occasionally, until the liquid has evaporated, then reduce the heat to medium and brown the ribs in their own fat, turning occasionally, for about 5 minutes.

2. Add the garlic and half the sesame seeds and stir; cook for 30 seconds. Add the sugar, ginger, soy, half the sesame oil, and another $^{1}/_{2}$ cup water; turn the heat to medium-high and cook, turning occasionally, until the liquid is thick and dark, about 10 minutes. If the ribs are tender at this point, they're ready. If not, add another $^{1}/_{2}$ cup water and repeat the process.

3. Add salt and pepper and the remaining sesame seeds and sesame oil. Stir once, sprinkle with the scallion, and serve.

Braised Spareribs with Cabbage, Root Vegetables, and Caraway
EASTERN EUROPE ■
MAKES **4 TO 6 SERVINGS**
   TIME **1$^{1}/_{2}$ TO 2 HOURS**

A big rustic one-pot meal. Easily expanded with the addition of more vegetables.

Serve with a salad for contrast, and some bread or rice if you like.

Other cuts of meat you can use here: short ribs, oxtail, or veal shanks.

Best Pork Cuts for Braising

Ribs. Most are far better cooked with liquid than grilled over direct heat (a combination of the first followed by the second is great, too), as is grilling over indirect heat.

Shoulder or butt. When cut up, this becomes tender more quickly than any meat except veal.

Odd cuts. Shank, feet, belly (fresh bacon), tail—all of these can be braised successfully.

---

3 to 4 pounds spareribs, cut into individual ribs, excess fat removed

2 tablespoons butter or extra virgin olive oil

1 large onion, sliced

2 medium carrots, roughly chopped

2 celery stalks, roughly chopped

1 small head of green or Savoy cabbage, about 1 1/2 pounds, cored and shredded

1/2 pound parsnips, peeled and roughly chopped

1/2 pound waxy potatoes, peeled and halved or quartered (the chunks should be large)

1 teaspoon fresh thyme leaves or 1/2 teaspoon dried

1 tablespoon caraway seeds

Salt and black pepper to taste

Chopped fresh parsley or celery leaves for garnish

1. Put the spareribs in a pot with water to cover and bring to a boil. Simmer while you prepare the other ingredients.
2. Put the butter in a large flameproof casserole with a lid and place it over medium heat. Add the onion and cook, stirring occasionally, until it begins to soften, about 5 minutes. Add the carrots, celery, cabbage, parsnips, potatoes, thyme, caraway, salt, and pepper and cook, stirring occasionally, until the cabbage begins to wilt, about 5 minutes.
3. Remove the ribs and nestle them in the cabbage as well as you can. Add about 2 cups of the rib-cooking liquid and bring to a boil. Cover and adjust the heat so the mixture simmers steadily. Cook for about an hour, then check; stir carefully

and see if the rib meat is tender. If it is, you're done. If not, cover and cook for another 15 minutes, then check again.

4. When the mixture is done, if it seems too soupy, turn the heat to high and cook, stirring occasionally and carefully, until it is more of a moist stew. Garnish and serve immediately or cover and refrigerate for up to a day before reheating.

Braised Spareribs with Cabbage, Roman Style ITALY ■

MAKES **4 SERVINGS**

TIME **ABOUT 1 1/2 HOURS, LARGELY UNATTENDED**

A Roman classic and, like so many of those dishes, smacking of garlic, chile, and bay.

You can serve this with just bread, of course, or precede it with a pasta dish or soup.

2 tablespoons extra virgin olive oil

4 garlic cloves, peeled and crushed

2 or more dried red chiles, like serrano

3 to 4 pounds spareribs, cut into individual ribs, excess fat removed

Salt and black pepper to taste

3 bay leaves

1 head of Savoy or green cabbage, 1 1/2 to 2 pounds, cored and shredded

1 cup dry white wine

Chopped fresh parsley leaves for garnish

1. Put the olive oil in a large deep skillet or flameproof casserole with a lid and place over high heat. A minute later, add the garlic and chiles. When they sizzle, add the ribs, meatiest side down; sprinkle with salt and pepper and add the bay leaves. Cook, more or less undisturbed, adjusting the heat so the meat browns nicely, for 5 to 10 minutes. Turn the ribs and brown again. Transfer the ribs to a plate.

2. Pour off any excess fat and add the cabbage and some more salt and pepper. Cook, stirring occasionally, until it browns a bit, then add the wine and stir to release any brown bits stuck to the bottom of the pan. Return the ribs to the pot; adjust the heat so the mixture simmers steadily but not violently, then cover.

3. Cook, checking occasionally to make sure the mixture does not dry out (if it does, add a little more white wine or water). When the ribs are tender and the cabbage is very soft—this will take at least 45 minutes and possibly up to an hour—uncover the skillet. If the mixture is soupy, turn the heat to high and cook, stirring occasionally and carefully, until it is more of a moist stew. Garnish and serve immediately or cover and refrigerate for up to a day before reheating.

Braised Ribs with Spicy Adobo
CARIBBEAN ■

MAKES **4 SERVINGS**

TIME **AT LEAST 1 1/2 HOURS**

Oven-baked ribs, which were once the standard, are now uncommon, because everyone thinks grilled ribs are the thing. But these are delicious, great with rice or polenta, and far easier than grilling.

But if you like, you can use this sauce for grilling, too: parboil the ribs in water until nearly tender, then grill them, basting with the sauce, until they are nicely browned.

Other cuts of meat you can use here: chunks of pork shoulder, short ribs (which will need much more time), bone-in chicken thighs (which will cook much more quickly).

3 to 4 pounds spareribs, more or less, separated into individual ribs

Salt and black pepper to taste

1 tablespoon minced garlic

1 medium onion, peeled and quartered

2 teaspoons fresh oregano or marjoram leaves

1 tablespoon pimentón (page 14) or 1 dried chipotle chile, soaked in hot water to soften, then minced

2 cups chopped tomatoes with their liquid (canned are fine)

1 tablespoon wine vinegar

1. Place a large deep skillet with a lid over medium-high heat and add the ribs. Cook, turning as necessary and sprinkling with salt and pepper, until they are well browned, at least 10 minutes. Transfer to a plate.

2. Preheat the oven to 350° F. Turn the heat under the pan to medium and add the garlic, onion, oregano, more salt and pepper, and pimentón. Cook, stirring occasionally, until the onion is well softened, about 10 minutes. Add the tomatoes and vinegar and cook, stirring occasionally, until the tomatoes begin to soften, 5 to 10 minutes. Add the ribs, cover, and put the pan in the oven.

3. Cook until the ribs are tender and just about falling from the bone, an hour or more. Serve immediately or cover and refrigerate for up to 2 days; reheat gently before serving.

Pork with Red Wine and Coriander

SPAIN ■

MAKES **4 SERVINGS**

TIME **ABOUT 1 HOUR**

This dish nicely combines the Mediterranean trio of garlic, red wine, and coriander. I first had it in southern Spain, where the culinary influence of North Africa remains strong. Like most braises, it takes time but, once the initial browning is done, very little work.

There are a couple of ways to deal with the coriander: You can leave the seeds whole and wrap them in cheesecloth or just leave them in the sauce and eat them. Or you can crack them first, either with a mortar and pestle or by putting them in a plastic bag and crushing them with a rolling pin or the bottom of a pot.

I like crusty bread here, plus a salad or steamed vegetable; the dish is complex and attention-grabbing enough not to bother with much more.

Other cuts of meat you can use here: lamb shoulder is a great substitute; chunks of beef chuck or brisket are also good.

1 tablespoon extra virgin olive oil

2 pounds boneless pork shoulder, cut into 1-inch cubes

1 head of garlic, excess papery skin removed, cut in half through its equator

2 cups red wine

3 tablespoons coriander seeds, cracked and wrapped in cheesecloth

1 tablespoon butter

Fresh lemon juice to taste

1/2 cup chopped fresh cilantro leaves

1. Put the oil in a large deep skillet with a lid and place over medium-high heat. A minute later, add the pork and cook, undisturbed, until brown on one side, about 10 minutes. Stir once and add the garlic; cook, stirring occasionally, for about a minute. Add 1 1/2 cups of the wine, then the cheesecloth with the coriander.

2. Turn the heat to low and cover. Adjust the heat so the mixture simmers gently. Cook for about an hour, until the pork is just about tender (You can prepare in advance up to this point; then cover and refrigerate for up to 2 days before proceeding.)

3. Stir in the remaining red wine; cook for 2 or 3 minutes. Stir in the butter, then taste and add lemon juice as necessary. Stir in half the cilantro, then serve, garnished with the remaining cilantro.

Pork Chops with Orange SPAIN

MAKES **4 SERVINGS**

TIME **ABOUT 1 HOUR**

In Spain, where the world's best oranges grow, they are used to season just about everything. One of my favorite encounters with the citrus fruit was an oven-braised dish of pork and oranges that I had in Seville. It could not have been simpler and can be reproduced easily.

Use either country-style ribs, ribs cut from the rib (shoulder) end, or even spareribs if you like; avoid center-cut or loin pork chops here because they will become dry and tasteless.

3 navel or other oranges

2 tablespoons extra virgin olive oil

About 2 pounds shoulder or rib end pork chops or country-style ribs

Salt and black pepper to taste

Chopped fresh parsley leaves for garnish

1. Grate or mince the orange zest. Peel the pith from the oranges and cut them into $\frac{1}{4}$-inch slices; reserve as much of their juice as you can.

2. Put the oil in a large skillet with a lid and place over medium heat. After a minute, add the ribs and brown them well on all sides, about 10 minutes, sprinkling the meat with salt and pepper as they cook. Reduce the heat to low and add the orange zest and any juice to the pan. Top the ribs with the orange slices, cover the skillet, and turn the heat to low.

3. Cook, undisturbed, until the meat is tender, at least 15 minutes and probably more like 30. Garnish the meat and serve with the pan juices.

Shredded Pork MEXICO ■

MAKES **4 OR MORE SERVINGS**

TIME **ABOUT 1 HOUR, LARGELY UNATTENDED**

Not exactly a dish, but the ideal filling for tacos and a preparation that plays many other roles, too. Use it to augment bean and rice dishes or to stuff cabbage, grape leaves, empanadas, or almost anything else. Do not use any cut of pork other than shoulder here; all others are more likely to become tough than tender.

2 pounds boneless pork shoulder, cut into 1-inch chunks

1 large white onion, peeled and quartered

5 garlic cloves, peeled and lightly crushed

2 bay leaves

1 tablespoon ground cumin

1 ancho or other large mild dried chile, optional

Salt and black pepper to taste

1. Combine all the ingredients in a saucepan with a lid and add water to cover. Turn the heat to high, bring to a boil, and skim any foam that comes to the surface. Partially cover and adjust the heat so the mixture simmers steadily. Cook until the meat is quite tender, about an hour, then cool.

2. Shred the meat with your fingers. Taste and adjust the seasoning; use within a couple of days.

Tamale Pie MEXICO

MAKES **12 OR MORE SERVINGS AS A STARTER, 6 TO 8 AS A MAIN COURSE**

TIME **1$\frac{1}{2}$ HOURS**

Despite its name, this is not a tamale (it's closer to polenta). It has neither the taste nor the texture of a real tamale, and, strictly speaking, it isn't even Mexican, unless you remember that Texas is as Mexican as it is American.

That being said, tamales are complicated, and this, at the very least, combines the earthy flavors of corn and pork. It's a true Tex-Mex dish, dating back at least a century. Serve with rice and beans.

3 pounds boneless pork shoulder, cut into 1-inch chunks

1 large white onion, chopped

5 garlic cloves, chopped

2 bay leaves

1 tablespoon ground cumin

1 poblano or other large mild chile, stemmed, seeded, and minced

Salt and black pepper to taste

3 cups crushed tomatoes (canned are fine)

1 cup coarse cornmeal

1 tablespoon butter, plus butter for the dish

1. Combine the first 6 ingredients in a saucepan and add water to cover. Turn the heat to high, bring to a boil, and skim any foam that comes to the surface. Partially cover and adjust the heat so the mixture simmers steadily. Cook until the meat is quite tender, about an hour, then cool. Discard the bay

leaves, shred the meat with your fingers, then taste and add salt and pepper. Stir in the tomatoes and set aside.

2. Preheat the oven to 400°F and grease a 9 × 12-inch baking dish, preferably glass. Bring 1 quart water to a boil in a large saucepan and add a large pinch of salt. Adjust the heat so the water simmers and begin to add the cornmeal in a steady stream, stirring or whisking all the while to prevent the formation of lumps. When it has all been added, turn the heat to low. Continue to cook, stirring frequently and whisking if necessary to break up lumps, until the mixture begins to pull away from the sides of the pot, about 15 minutes. Turn off the heat; taste and add more salt if necessary, along with some pepper. Stir in the butter until melted.

3. Spread a third of the cornmeal mixture onto the bottom of the baking dish, then spread all of the shredded pork mixture over it. Spoon the remaining cornmeal mixture on top of the pork and spread evenly to cover the pork. Transfer to the oven and cook until nicely browned and warmed through, about 40 minutes. Remove from the oven, cool slightly, then cut into squares and serve.

Braised Pork with Coconut Milk
SOUTHEAST ASIA ■
MAKES **4 TO 6 SERVINGS**
TIME **2 HOURS OR LESS**

A surprising cousin of the Italian Roast Pork with Milk (page 400), similar in its preparation and results, completely different (but equally superb) in the eating. Because the pork is cut up and braised, it cooks more quickly. Use meat from the shoulder end. See page 500 for information on Asian fish sauces like nam pla.

Serve this with Sticky Rice (page 508).

Other cuts of meat you can use here: boneless chicken thighs.

2 tablespoons corn, grapeseed, or other neutral oil
2 to 3 pounds boneless pork shoulder, cut into 2-inch chunks
Pinch of salt
1 teaspoon black pepper
1 tablespoon minced garlic
2 Thai or other small fresh chiles, stemmed, seeded, and minced
About 1 quart coconut milk, homemade (page 584) or canned
2 tablespoons nam pla
Chopped fresh cilantro leaves for garnish

1. Put the oil in a deep skillet or casserole with a lid and place it over medium-high heat. When the oil shimmers, add the meat. Brown it well on all sides, turning as necessary, about 10 minutes, perhaps longer. While the meat is browning, sprinkle it with salt and pepper.

2. Turn the heat to low and pour off all but a couple tablespoons of the fat. Add the garlic and chiles and cook, stirring, for about 30 seconds. Add the coconut milk and nam pla and raise the heat; bring to a boil, then turn the heat to low once again. Partially cover the pan and adjust the heat so the mixture simmers steadily. Cook for at least an hour, stirring every 15 minutes or so; do not let the bottom burn. If the mixture becomes too thick, add water, $1/2$ cup or so at a time.

3. Cook until the meat is quite tender. If the sauce is a good consistency at this point, simply plate and serve. If it is too thick, add a little water and cook, stirring occasionally, until the mixture is creamy. Garnish with the cilantro and serve or cover and refrigerate for up to a day before reheating, adding a little more water to thin the stew if necessary.

Sweet-and-Sour Braised Pork

SOUTHEAST ASIA

MAKES **8 OR MORE SERVINGS**

TIME **2 HOURS OR MORE, LARGELY UNATTENDED**

Perfect for a buffet or a large dinner or for when you want to cook for one night and eat for a few following, this is my take on the various pork stews served throughout Southeast Asia. It should be quite sweet and quite strong. (One of the traditional ingredients is salted bean curd, a cheeselike concoction that is—like nam pla, page 500—a bit of an acquired taste. I'd include it here, but it's quite difficult to find. Dried shrimp, page 185, equally legitimate, are a good alternative, as are fermented black beans, page 207).

Serve this over white rice with a simple stir-fried or steamed vegetable.

If you are in a hurry, use boneless pork, cut into 2-inch chunks; the dish will be ready in less than an hour. But I like the big presentation.

One bone-in pork shoulder (picnic or butt), about
    6 pounds
$1/2$ cup nam pla or soy sauce
1 cup palm or brown sugar
2 large onions, roughly chopped
$1/4$ cup peeled and minced fresh ginger
2 tablespoons dried shrimp or fermented black beans
$1/4$ cup minced garlic
$1/4$ cup rice or cider vinegar or fresh lime juice
Chopped fresh cilantro leaves for garnish

1. Put the pork in a pot that is large enough to hold it and has a lid. Add the nam pla, sugar, onions, ginger, dried shrimp, and about 1 quart water. Bring to a boil, then cover and adjust the heat so the mixture simmers steadily but not violently. Cook, checking every half hour or so to make sure the mixture is not drying out—add water if it is—until the pork is tender, 2 hours or more.

2. Transfer the pork to a large platter. Turn the heat to high and reduce the liquid to about 2 cups; it should be quite syrupy. Stir in the garlic and vinegar and cook for another 2 or 3 minutes; you don't want the garlic to mellow entirely. Carve the pork and serve with the sauce, garnished with cilantro.

Spicy Pork and Tofu Stew KOREA ■

MAKES **4 TO 6 SERVINGS**

TIME **1 HOUR**

Korean meat stews tend to be dark and flavorful; in this one, the last-minute addition of silky bean curd gives the stew an almost creamy dimension. If you can find a jar of go chu jang, the chili paste sold in Korean markets, the dish will gain authenticity. But I have had good results with a couple of tablespoons of good miso, which is far easier to find, and a large pinch (or more) of hot red pepper flakes. Rice completes this meal, but adding a vegetable makes it even nicer.

$1 1/2$ pounds boneless pork, preferably from the shoulder,
    cut into $1 1/2$-inch chunks
1 tablespoon minced garlic
1 tablespoon peeled and minced fresh ginger
2 tablespoons soy sauce
2 tablespoons sugar or mirin
2 tablespoons go chu jang or 2 tablespoons dark miso
    plus hot red pepper flakes to taste
$3/4$ to 1 pound silken tofu, cut into 1-inch cubes
1 tablespoon dark sesame oil
1 tablespoon toasted sesame seeds (page 596) for
    garnish
2 tablespoons chopped scallion for garnish

1. Turn the heat to high under a large skillet with a lid; add the pork cubes a few at a time and brown

well, adjusting the heat so the meat browns but does not burn and turning to brown all sides, about 10 minutes. Transfer the meat to a plate and turn the heat to low.

2. Add the garlic and ginger to the pan and cook, stirring occasionally, until the garlic colors, a couple of minutes. Add $1/4$ cup water, then the soy sauce, sugar, and go chu jang. Raise the heat slightly and bring to a boil, then return the meat to the pan and cover. Adjust the heat so the mixture simmers steadily but not violently and cook, stirring once in a while, until the pork is tender, 30 to 45 minutes. (You can prepare the dish to this point several hours in advance, cover, and set aside until you're ready to eat, then reheat; or cover and refrigerate overnight before reheating.)

3. Uncover, then add the tofu and stir gently; cook for just a few minutes to heat the tofu through. Taste and adjust the seasoning, then stir in the sesame oil, sprinkle with the sesame seeds and scallion, and serve immediately.

Pork Vindaloo INDIA ■

MAKES **4 TO 6 SERVINGS**

TIME **ABOUT 1 1/2 HOURS**

Like any "curry," this one contains several spices. But in this one, although it can be made quite hot, the flavor of cinnamon is dominant—and wonderfully offset by the addition of vinegar. If you can find mustard oil at an Indian or Pakistani market, use it here; not only is it the oil of choice for many Indian dishes, but it's great for simply sautéing vegetables. Serve this with white rice or a simple pilaf.

Other cuts of meat you can use here: beef chuck or brisket (cooking time will be longer); chicken thighs, bone in or out; or lamb shoulder.

2 tablespoons mustard oil (preferred) or other oil

1 tablespoon minced garlic

1 tablespoon peeled and minced fresh ginger

1 teaspoon ground coriander

$1/2$ teaspoon black pepper

Salt to taste

$1/2$ teaspoon cayenne or hot red pepper flakes, or to taste

Pinch of ground cloves

1 teaspoon mustard seeds (if not using mustard oil)

1 teaspoon ground cardamom

5 cinnamon sticks or 1 tablespoon ground cinnamon

2 pounds boneless pork shoulder (Boston butt or picnic), cut into chunks

$1/2$ cup rice wine vinegar or other good-quality mild vinegar

Chopped fresh cilantro leaves for garnish

1. Put the oil in a large skillet or flameproof casserole with a lid and turn the heat to medium. A couple of minutes later, add all the ingredients except the pork, vinegar, and cilantro and cook, stirring, for a minute or two, until the fragrances are released.

2. Add the pork and vinegar, stir, and bring to a boil. Adjust the heat so the mixture simmers gently, then cover and cook until the pork is tender, at least an hour. Stir from time to time; if the mixture dries out, add a little water. (You can prepare the dish to this point several hours in advance, cover, and set aside until you're ready to eat, then reheat; or cover and refrigerate overnight before reheating.)

3. Taste, adjust the seasoning, garnish, and serve.

Baeckoffe of Pork and Lamb FRANCE ■

MAKES **4 TO 6 SERVINGS**

TIME **ABOUT 3 HOURS, LARGELY UNATTENDED**

I first learned about baeckoffe—"baker's oven"—from the great chef (also my friend and sometime coauthor) Jean-Georges Vongerichten, who is from Alsace. It's one of those ancient unattended dishes given, in a pot, to the communal oven and picked up several hours later. Jean-Georges (like his mother) made it with pork, but when I was in Alsace I had it prepared with pork and lamb, which I liked a bit more. "My" version is below.

Baeckoffe is great made in advance; that, combined with its flexible cooking time, makes it a very easy dish to prepare. With a salad and some bread, it makes a pretty relaxed meal for a small crowd.

Other cuts of meat you can use here: traditionally, baeckoffe is a combination of slow-cooked meats, so with—or instead of—these two, you can use boneless beef (chuck or brisket is best) or veal.

1 pound boneless pork, preferably from the shoulder

1 pound boneless lamb, preferably from the shoulder

2 pounds waxy potatoes, peeled and sliced about $1/4$ inch thick

Salt and black pepper

2 large onions, sliced

4 bay leaves

$1/2$ cup roughly chopped fresh parsley

Several fresh thyme sprigs

1 cup dry white wine, preferably Riesling or Pinot Blanc

1 cup any stock, preferably homemade (pages 160–163), or water

1. Remove the excess fat from the meat and cut it into 1- to $1^{1}/2$-inch chunks. Preheat the oven to 325°F. In a casserole or terrine with a lid, put half the potatoes, along with some salt and pepper, then half the onions, half the herbs, the meat, the remaining potatoes, onions, and herbs, some more salt and pepper, and finally the liquids.

2. Cover and bake for at least 2 and probably 3 hours or until the meat is very tender.

Roast Pork with Milk ITALY

MAKES **4 TO 6 SERVINGS**

TIME **AT LEAST 2 HOURS**

An easy, luxurious, and always surprising dish in which the milk becomes curds and the pork wonderfully tender. As long as you use the right cut, that is: be sure to get a roast from the shoulder end, either a rib (shoulder) roast or a piece of shoulder (Boston butt).

The garlic variation is really majestic, but I begin with the milder version for those non-garlic-lovers out there. This is a very rich, very filling dish. You might serve it with nothing more than bread (or rice) and salad.

Other cuts of meat you can use here: to my surprise, a friend suggested I try this with bone-in chicken thighs, and it worked beautifully. Much quicker, too.

$1/4$ cup extra virgin olive oil

One 2- to 3-pound boneless pork rib roast or Boston butt

Salt and black pepper to taste

At least 1 quart whole milk

1. Put a heavy lidded pot or flameproof casserole that will hold the roast snugly over medium-high heat and add the oil, swirling to coat. When the oil shimmers, add the roast. Brown well on all sides, turning the meat as necessary, about 10 minutes, perhaps longer. While the meat is browning, sprinkle it with salt and pepper.

2. Add enough milk to the pan to come most of the way up the sides of the roast. Bring to a boil, then turn the heat to low. Simmer (adjust the heat as necessary), partly covered, for at least an hour, turning the roast once or twice.

3. Cook until the roast is quite tender and the milk is reduced to small nut-brown clumps. If the milk

begins to dry out before the roast is cooked, add $\frac{1}{2}$ cup milk, repeating if necessary. When the pork is done, transfer it to a warm serving platter.

4. Spoon off most of the fat from the sauce and add $\frac{1}{4}$ cup water. Turn the heat to high and reduce, scraping the bottom of the pan with a wooden spoon to dislodge bits of pork. Carve the meat into slices, then pour half of the sauce over the roast and pass the rest at the table. Serve immediately.

Roast Pork and Garlic with Milk. In step 1, separate 2 heads of garlic into cloves and peel them; brown the cloves in the oil, stirring occasionally, before adding the roast; this will take about 5 minutes. Remove the garlic as you brown the roast, then add it back to the pan with the milk and a fresh rosemary sprig. You can serve the sauce as is or use a food mill, an immersion blender, or an upright blender to puree the mixture, working in batches if necessary. (In this as in every instance, use care when pureeing hot liquid; it's best, if you have the time, to let the mixture cool to room temperature before pureeing. The meat may be covered with foil and held in a warm oven while you're working on the sauce.)

Sausage and Beans SPAIN, ITALY ■ ▨

MAKES **4 SERVINGS**

TIME **30 MINUTES (WITH PRECOOKED BEANS)**

If you like franks and beans, this is for you. There are, of course, more complicated versions, ending with cassoulet, but this is the starting point.

Other cuts of meat you can use here: longer, because they need some simmering time, but very good, are browned chunks of pork or lamb shoulder (or both), cooked in the beans in place of (or in addition to) the sausage.

4 cups White Beans with Garlic (page 441) or any well-
seasoned white beans
Salt and black pepper if necessary
Additional extra virgin olive oil if necessary
1$\frac{1}{2}$ pounds good-quality pork sausage

1. Gently warm the beans in a medium saucepan, partially covered. If you have not already added salt, pepper, and olive oil, do so, to taste.
2. Meanwhile, slowly grill or panfry the sausage until nicely browned all over, 15 to 20 minutes. Cut into chunks and bury in the beans. Cook, stirring occasionally, until heated through, another 5 minutes or so. Serve or cover and refrigerate for up to a day before gently reheating.

Chorizo and Beans. Even easier: Bury about $\frac{1}{2}$ pound dried (Spanish) chorizo (or other good garlicky sausage), cut into chunks, in 4 cups beans, along with a dried chile or hot red pepper flakes to taste. Heat through, about 10 minutes, then taste, adjust the seasoning, and serve.

Sausage with Aromatic Beans and Tomatoes. Substitute Aromatic White Beans with Chicken Stock and Tomatoes (page 442) for the White Beans with Garlic.

Fabada Pork and Beans Asturian Style SPAIN ■

MAKES **6 SERVINGS**

TIME **A DAY OR TWO, LARGELY UNATTENDED**

Some Spaniards, like my friend Jose Andres, a chef based in Washington, D.C., who taught me this recipe, can talk until they're blue in the face about fabada, the famous pork and bean stew they say is "the grandfather of the French cassoulet." They will remind you to use *only* real fabes (dried beans you can find only at gourmet stores or specialty Web sites and that cost up to $20 a pound), tell you that you must have fresh morcilla (blood sausage), and on and on until you're convinced that there's no way you could ever make fabada at home.

But dedication to the dish's origins, along with a couple of simple substitutions, allows you to retain its spirit without going nuts.

    1 pound fabes (large white beans from Asturias) or other
        dried large white beans, soaked overnight in water to
        cover (or boiled for 2 minutes and soaked for 2 hours)
        and drained
    3 tablespoons extra virgin olive oil
    Pinch of saffron threads
    1 head of garlic, cut in half through its equator
    $\frac{1}{2}$ pound salt pork, pancetta, or slab bacon, in one piece
    1 smoked ham hock, in one piece, about 1 pound
    $\frac{1}{2}$ pound dried (Spanish) chorizo
    2 morcilla (Spanish blood sausages) or another $\frac{1}{2}$ pound
        chorizo
    1 onion, peeled

1. Rinse the beans and place them in a large pot with a lid; add water to cover by an inch. Bring to a boil over high heat, skimming off any foam that rises to the top.
2. Add the olive oil, saffron, garlic, salt pork, and ham hock and stir. Partially cover, bring back to a boil, then reduce the heat and simmer for about an hour, adding water if the mixture threatens to dry out.
3. Add the chorizo, morcilla, and onion to the pot and let it simmer for another 60 to 90 minutes, until the beans are quite soft (some may have split at this point, which is fine and will help thicken the stew). Again, add water, a little at a time, if necessary.
4. Remove the pot from the heat, discard the onion and garlic, and transfer the meat to a cutting board. Pull the meat from the ham hock off the bone and slice the sausages and salt pork. You can serve the stew at this point or let it rest for hours or even a couple of days. Serve the beans warm in deep soup bowls with a few slices of each of the meats nestled into them.

Garbure Meaty Bean Stew from the Pyrenees
FRANCE, SPAIN
MAKES **4 SERVINGS**
TIME **ABOUT 3 HOURS, LARGELY UNATTENDED, PLUS TIME TO SOAK THE BEANS**

This is the cassouletlike dish of the mountains between Spain and France, claimed by several cultures. When I was there, I was told that each of twenty different versions was the "only" authentic one; in this way, too, it's like cassoulet. What they all had in common were the large white beans called Tarbais (after Tarbes, one of the larger towns of the region)—which you probably will not be able to find—and a stultifying heartiness.

Great stuff: you must serve it with crusty country bread and a good red wine.

    $\frac{1}{4}$ pound salt pork, diced
    4 small potatoes, peeled and halved
    2 garlic cloves, chopped
    2 leeks, trimmed, washed (page 465), and sliced
    2 carrots, cut into 2-inch lengths
    1 turnip, peeled and quartered
    1 small head of cabbage, cored and chopped
    1 cup dried large white beans, like Tarbais, cannellini, or
        limas, soaked overnight (or boiled for 2 minutes and
        soaked for 2 hours) and drained
    2 fresh thyme sprigs
    2 bay leaves

5 fresh parsley sprigs

5 whole peppercorns

$\frac{1}{2}$ to 1 pound Duck Confit (page 330), goose confit, fresh garlic or sweet sausage, or a combination

Salt to taste

1. Bring a large kettle of water to a boil. Put the salt pork in a large saucepan over medium heat. Cook, stirring occasionally, until the cubes brown nicely, adjusting the heat as necessary. Add all the vegetables except the beans and continue to cook, stirring occasionally, until they brown a bit. Add the beans, cover with water by about 2 inches, and bring back to a boil over high heat, then adjust the heat so the mixture simmers. Add the thyme, bay leaves, parsley, and peppercorns (if you like you can tie them into a little cheesecloth bag first). Simmer, uncovered, for about 2 hours, or until the beans and vegetables are tender.

2. Add the confit and/or sausage to the simmering soup and cook until the confit is warmed through and/or until the sausage is cooked through, 15 to 30 minutes more. Remove the confit and/or sausage, slice, and divide among serving bowls. Ladle the soup and its vegetables and beans into the bowls and serve hot.

Bigos POLAND ■

MAKES **4 SERVINGS**

TIME **1$\frac{1}{2}$ HOURS, LARGELY UNATTENDED**

"Hunter's stew" is probably one of the oldest and most popular dishes in Eastern Europe. Like cassoulet and bouillabaisse, it is one of those preparations that can be made with whatever is on hand—you most often see it with venison—and may be a casual dish that can be stored and reheated many times (and can ac-

commodate leftovers) or something served to beloved guests on holy days.

Traditionally, bigos took three days to make, but there's no need to stick to that tradition; it's just as good when made all at once.

Inexpensive dried black or shiitake mushrooms (sold at most Asian markets) are good here; pricier porcini are better. Or use a combination of dried and fresh mushrooms.

Serve with rye bread.

Other cuts of meat you can use here: anything—pork, veal, lamb, venison, duck, goose, or a combination; it's a mishmash.

$\frac{1}{4}$ pound bacon or salt pork, roughly chopped

$\frac{1}{4}$ pound sausage, optional

1$\frac{1}{2}$ pounds not-too-lean beef chuck or brisket, cut into small cubes

1 onion, chopped

2 pounds sauerkraut, fresh or packaged in plastic

1 ounce dried black mushrooms, soaked and sliced, liquid reserved

$\frac{1}{2}$ teaspoon caraway seeds

$\frac{1}{2}$ teaspoon black pepper

1 tablespoon sugar

$\frac{1}{2}$ cup Madeira or other sweet wine

1. Heat a Dutch oven or heavy flameproof casserole with a lid over medium-high heat and add the bacon. Cook, stirring occasionally, until most of the fat is rendered, then add the sausage if you're using it and the meat and brown. Remove the bacon, sausage, and meat with a slotted spoon and set aside.

2. Lower the heat to medium and cook the onion in the fat, stirring occasionally, until translucent, about 5 minutes. Add the sauerkraut, mushrooms, mushroom liquid, caraway seeds, pepper, and sugar. Stir to combine and add just enough water

to barely cover. Cover, turn the heat to low, and simmer for 15 minutes.

3. Return the meat to the pan and add the wine. Cover and simmer for an hour, or until the meat is tender (lamb, pork, and veal will probably take longer than beef). Serve or cool to room temperature and refrigerate, then reheat before serving.

Bigos with Fresh Cabbage. Omit the sauerkraut from step 2 and substitute one 2-pound head of fresh cabbage, cored and thinly sliced, 3 tablespoons white vinegar, and 2 tart apples, peeled and sliced.

Bigos with Prunes. For a sweeter stew, substitute $1/2$ pound diced pitted prunes for the dried mushrooms. You do not need to soak the prunes. Add them to the bigos when you would have added the mushrooms.

A Grand Choucroute
Sauerkraut with Smoked Meats FRANCE ■

MAKES **6 TO 8 SERVINGS**
TIME **ABOUT 2 HOURS**

Choucroute, the Alsatian specialty, is a near-perfect party dish: you can easily make it in advance and in quantity. This version, with boiled potatoes cooked right in, is also a one-pot dish. Serve it with bread—preferably good rye or pumpernickel—and you're all set. (Well, you'll also need some hot mustard and beer or Alsatian wine.)

Feel free to vary the meats however you like. But, as is always the case, buy sauerkraut that is either sold in bulk or packed in plastic and contains no more than cabbage and salt.

$1/4$ cup lard, butter, or extra virgin olive oil
1 large onion, sliced

2 pounds sauerkraut, rinsed
1 ham hock, salted or smoked
2 cups dry white wine, preferably Riesling
1 pound slab bacon, in one piece
Salt and black pepper
1 tablespoon minced garlic
1 teaspoon juniper berries, lightly crushed with the side of a knife
1 teaspoon caraway seeds
1 pound boneless smoked pork loin
2 pounds smoked sausages: bratwursts, frankfurters, kielbasa, or similar
16 small potatoes, peeled, or 4 or 5 larger potatoes, peeled and quartered

1. Put the lard in a large deep skillet or flameproof casserole with a lid and place over medium heat. A minute later, add the onion and cook, stirring occasionally, until it is quite soft, about 10 minutes. Add the sauerkraut, ham hock, wine, 1 cup water, and bacon. Cover and cook, adjusting the heat so the mixture simmers, until the ham hock begins to become tender, about 1 hour.

2. Taste the mixture and add some salt if necessary; add at least $1/2$ teaspoon pepper, along with the garlic, juniper berries, caraway seeds, and pork loin. Cover and cook for about 15 minutes.

3. Add the sausages and potatoes and re-cover. Adjust the heat so the mixture simmers. Taste and add more salt if necessary. At this point you can keep the mixture warm over very low heat for an hour or two, or turn it off and reheat after several hours.

4. To serve, slice the bacon and pork loin. Cut the sausages and ham hock into pieces. Put the sauerkraut in the middle of a large platter and surround and top it with the meats and potatoes.

Best Lamb Cuts for Braising

Shoulder. Truly wonderful, whether braised whole or in chunks.

Shanks. Along with pork ribs and beef short ribs, possibly the ideal cut.

Leg. A third choice, after the preceding two, because it is lean; but quite acceptable in many instances and always good flavored.

Hunkar Begendi

Braised Lamb in Eggplant Puree   TURKEY

MAKES **4 SERVINGS**

TIME **AT LEAST 2 HOURS**

I'd heard of hunkar begendi and even tried it in Turkish restaurants elsewhere before I went to Istanbul, but I was not prepared for the reverence it inspires. Not only is this dish delicious—its name means "Sultan's Delight"—but its appearance causes a hush to fall over a table. This is great stuff, a creamy, eggplant-laced béchamel topped with tender braised lamb. It's a fair amount of work, but worth it.

4 tablespoons (^{1}/$_2$ stick) butter

1 tablespoon extra virgin olive oil

1^1/$_2$ to 2 pounds boneless lamb, preferably from the shoulder, cut into 1^1/$_2$- to 2-inch chunks

Salt and black pepper to taste

1 large onion, thinly sliced

1 tablespoon minced garlic

2 cups chopped tomatoes with their liquid (canned are fine)

2 pounds eggplant (2 to 3 medium or several small)

Juice of ^{1}/$_2$ lemon

3 tablespoons flour

2 cups milk

^{1}/$_2$ cup grated kasseri cheese or pecorino Romano

Lemon wedges for serving

1. Combine 1 tablespoon of the butter with the olive oil in a large deep skillet or flameproof casserole with a lid and place over medium-high heat. When the butter foam subsides, add the chunks of meat, sprinkling them with salt and pepper as they brown. When the pieces are deeply browned, at least 10 minutes, transfer to a plate; pour or spoon off any excess fat.

2. Add the onion and garlic, along with some more salt and pepper, and cook, stirring occasionally, until the onion softens, 5 to 10 minutes. Add the tomatoes and about 1 cup water and bring to a boil; cover, then adjust the heat so the mixture simmers steadily. Cook, adding a little more water if necessary, until the lamb is perfectly tender, at least an hour. When done, the mixture should be moist but not soupy; cook out some of the liquid if necessary. (This portion of the recipe can be done in advance; cover and refrigerate for up to a day before proceeding if you like.)

3. Meanwhile, start a charcoal or gas grill or preheat the oven to 500°F. Prick the eggplant all over with a thin-bladed knife (they might explode otherwise) and grill or roast, giving quarter turns as they blacken, until completely collapsed, 15 to 30 minutes. When the eggplant is done, use a towel to hold it by its stem and a sharp knife to peel off the skin. Put the pulp, less as many seeds as you can do away with easily, into a bowl with the lemon juice.

4. Put the remaining butter in a 1-quart (approximately) saucepan over medium heat. Stir in the flour a bit at a time until the mixture is well blended. Then continue to cook, stirring constantly, until the mixture browns a bit. Add the milk a bit at a time, stirring (or, better still, whisking) after each addition to keep the mixture smooth. Season with salt and pepper and cook, stirring almost constantly, until the sauce is thick, 5 to 10 minutes.

5. When the eggplant is cooled, put it in a colander or strainer and squeeze it with your hands to remove as much excess water as possible and to break it up. Put it in another bowl and mash it with a fork until very smooth, then combine it with the sauce, beating with a wooden spoon until quite smooth. Put in a saucepan and reheat, then turn the heat to a minimum and stir in the cheese. Taste and adjust the seasoning. Put a puddle of the eggplant sauce on each plate, then top with a portion of the lamb. Serve immediately, with the lemon wedges.

Braised Lamb with Honey and Almonds NORTH AFRICA, MIDDLE EAST ■
MAKES **4 SERVINGS**

TIME **ABOUT 2 HOURS, LARGELY UNATTENDED**

This may sound like dessert—indeed it's sweet and crunchy—but the spice will shatter that image. A dreamy dish, easy to make and with an exotic aroma. If you would rather not mess with the spices, use about a tablespoon of Tabil (page 597), Garam Masala (page 594), or any curry powder. Brown the lamb in the oven if you prefer (see page 412).

If you have the energy, buy bone-in lamb, then cut the meat from the bones. Make stock from the bones and scrap meat; you need only a cup. (Simmer the bones with a carrot and a piece of onion in water to cover for about an hour, then drain. That's it.)

Serve with any bread you like or with Couscous (page 526) or rice.

Other cuts of meat you can use here: beef chuck or brisket, which will take somewhat longer to become tender; boneless chicken thighs, which will cook far more quickly.

> 2 tablespoons extra virgin olive oil
>
> 1 large onion, roughly chopped
>
> 2 pounds boneless lamb, from the shoulder or leg, cut into 1- to 2-inch chunks
>
> Salt and black pepper to taste
>
> 1/2 cup honey
>
> 1 garlic clove, minced
>
> 1 teaspoon ground coriander
>
> 1/4 teaspoon cayenne, or to taste
>
> 1 teaspoon ground caraway (use a spice or coffee grinder)
>
> 1/2 teaspoon ground cumin, optional
>
> 1/2 teaspoon ground fennel, optional
>
> 1 cup chicken or beef stock, preferably homemade (page 160), or water or lamb stock
>
> 1 cup whole blanched almonds
>
> 1 tablespoon butter, optional
>
> 1 teaspoon fresh lemon juice, or to taste
>
> Chopped fresh parsley or cilantro leaves for garnish

1. Put the oil in a large deep skillet with a lid over medium heat. A minute later, add the onion and cook, stirring occasionally, until quite soft, about 10 minutes. Remove with a slotted spoon and raise the heat to medium-high. Add as many chunks of lamb as will fit without crowding (you will inevitably have to brown in batches). It will take 3 or 4 minutes for the pieces to brown; when they do, turn them and sprinkle them with salt and pepper. Adjust the heat so the pieces brown as rapidly as possible without burning; the process will take 10 to 15 minutes.

2. Turn off the heat and wait a minute for the pan to cool a bit; pour off any excess fat. Turn the heat back to medium and add the honey; cook, stirring occasionally, until the honey has thinned and coated the lamb. Stir in the garlic and cook for a moment; then add the spices and finally the reserved onion and stock. Cover; adjust the heat so the mixture simmers steadily. Meanwhile, put the almonds in a skillet that will accommodate them in one layer over medium heat; cook, shaking the skillet, until lightly browned and fragrant, 5 minutes or so.

3. Cook, undisturbed (you can stir occasionally if you want to, but it's unnecessary), until the meat is very tender, an hour or more. Stir in the almonds and the butter if you're using it, followed by the lemon juice. Taste and adjust the seasoning, then serve (or cover and refrigerate for up to a day, stirring in the almonds only when you reheat the stew), garnished with the parsley.

Lamb Tagine with Prunes

NORTH AFRICA ■

MAKES **4 SERVINGS**

TIME **1 TO 1 ½ HOURS, LARGELY UNATTENDED**

A sweet, smooth stew. When prunes cook for a long time, as do half of these, they break down and create a rich if chunky sauce. Reserving some is a nice way to add a different texture back to the dish. You can substitute apricots for the prunes, if you like. You can also add more dried fruit and some chunks of carrots to the mix as well.

Other cuts of meat you can use here: boneless chicken thighs (which will cook more quickly), beef chuck or brisket (which will take a bit longer)

Best served with plain Couscous (page 526).

2 tablespoons butter or extra virgin olive oil

2 pounds boneless lamb shoulder, cut into roughly
    1 ½-inch chunks

Salt and black pepper to taste

1 cup pitted prunes

½ cup red wine, stock, or water

1 large onion, chopped

1 tablespoon minced garlic

1 teaspoon peeled and minced fresh ginger

1 tablespoon honey

Pinch of ground allspice

Pinch of cayenne, or to taste

½ teaspoon ground cinnamon

1 tablespoon fresh lemon juice, or to taste

2 tablespoons lightly toasted sesame seeds (page 596) for
    garnish

Chopped fresh parsley or cilantro leaves for garnish

1. Put the butter in a wide skillet with a lid and place over high heat. When the butter foam subsides, add the lamb, a little at a time. Let sear, undisturbed, for about 2 minutes, then turn and continue to cook until the meat is nicely browned all over, about 10 minutes; sprinkle the meat with salt and pepper as it browns. While the meat is browning, soak the prunes in the liquid. When the meat is browned, transfer it to a plate and turn the heat to medium.

2. Add the onion, garlic, ginger, honey, allspice, cayenne, and cinnamon, along with a little more salt and pepper, and cook, stirring occasionally, until the onion softens, about 10 minutes. Return the lamb to the skillet along with half the prunes and their soaking liquid. Bring to a boil, then reduce the heat so the mixture simmers. Cover and let the mixture simmer for about 45 minutes, stirring once or twice during that period; if at any point the mixture threatens to dry out, add a little water, wine, or stock. (You can prepare the dish to this point and let sit for a few hours or cover and

refrigerate for up to a day before reheating and proceeding.)

3. When the lamb is just about tender, add the remaining prunes, re-cover, and continue to cook until they and the lamb are soft, about 15 minutes more. Add the lemon juice, taste and adjust the seasoning, garnish, and serve.

Lamb Tagine with Fresh Fruit. Best with quince, if you can get a hold of any: In place of the prunes, use 4 quinces, apples, or not-too-ripe pears, trimmed and cored. Add the fruit all at once; quinces will need up to 45 minutes of cooking time, apples and pears just 30 minutes or so.

Choua Steamed Lamb Shoulder MOROCCO
MAKES **4 SERVINGS**
 TIME **ABOUT 2 HOURS**

Strange but true: If you steam a lamb shoulder with just a few spices (and some vegetables if you like), it becomes completely tender and succulent even if you ignore it completely. In that way, it is much like braising, so I've included it here. Although there *is* such a thing as overcooking this preparation, you would have to make an effort.

Sealing the pot with a paste of flour and water is traditional but unnecessary, as long as your steamer has a tight seal. If it does not, simply keep a kettle of water boiling and add to the pot as needed.

  1½ to 2 pounds boneless lamb shoulder, cut into
   1½-inch chunks
  Salt and black pepper to taste
  Large pinch of saffron threads
  1 tablespoon ground cumin
  4 medium carrots, cut into chunks, optional

  4 medium potatoes, waxy potatoes preferred, peeled and
   cut into chunks, optional
  8 shallots, peeled
  4 garlic cloves, peeled

1. Toss the lamb chunks with some salt and pepper. Crumble the saffron and add it to the mix, along with the cumin. Place in the top of a steamer over boiling water and cook, more or less undisturbed, for about 1 hour (if necessary, replenish the water).

2. Add whatever vegetables you're using and continue to cook until both lamb and vegetables are very tender, at least another half hour and probably longer. Serve immediately.

Braised Lamb with Garlic and Lemon GREECE
MAKES **4 SERVINGS**
 TIME **ABOUT 2 HOURS, LARGELY UNATTENDED**

Like most braised dishes, this stew takes time but, once the initial browning is done, very little work. There are times I consider browning optional, but this isn't one of them, because the dish is so simple that you need the complexity browning brings. Serve with Pilaf (page 513) or another rice dish.

Other cuts of meat you can use here: beef chuck, brisket, or round (all of which will take somewhat longer than the lamb); pork shoulder; lamb shanks (again, longer cooking); or veal shoulder or round.

  1 tablespoon extra virgin olive oil
  2 pounds boneless lamb, from the shoulder or leg, cut into
   1- to 2-inch chunks
  Salt and black pepper to taste
  5 or 6 garlic cloves, slivered

2 lemons

1 cup dry white wine, stock, or water

1. Put the oil in a large deep skillet with a lid and turn the heat to medium-high. A minute later, add as many chunks of lamb as will fit without crowding (you will inevitably have to brown in batches). It will take 3 or 4 minutes for the pieces to brown; when they do, turn them and sprinkle them with salt and pepper. Adjust the heat so the pieces brown as rapidly as possible without burning. After each has browned on 2 sides, remove it from the pan and add another piece or two. The entire browning process will take 10 to 15 minutes.

2. When all the meat has been removed from the pan, turn off the heat and wait a minute for the pan to cool a bit. Turn the heat back to medium and add the garlic; wash and slice one of the lemons and add it also. Cook for about 30 seconds, then add the liquid. Raise the heat to high and let the liquid bubble away for a minute. Return the meat to the pan and cover; adjust the heat so the mixture bubbles very gently. (If it cooks too quickly, you may have to add a little water once or twice.)

3. Cook, undisturbed (you can stir occasionally if you want to, but it's unnecessary), until the meat is very tender, about 1 1/2 hours. Taste and adjust the seasoning, then serve over the rice with the other lemon cut into wedges.

Braised Lamb with Egg-Lemon Sauce GREECE ■

MAKES **4 SERVINGS**

TIME **AT LEAST 1 HOUR, LARGELY UNATTENDED**

A more complicated lamb stew than the preceding recipe, but a very flexible one, finished with the classic rich and delicious avgolemono, egg-lemon sauce. This can be made with a large variety of vegetables, in which case it's a meal in a pot, always best served with pita bread or pilaf.

Other cuts of meat you can use here: lamb shanks (which will take longer to cook) or shoulder chops, beef chuck or brisket (which also will require longer cooking time), or veal shoulder.

2 tablespoons extra virgin olive oil

4 lamb shanks or about 2 pounds boneless lamb shoulder, cut into 1-inch cubes

Salt and black pepper to taste

2 large onions, cut into chunks

4 medium potatoes, peeled and cut into chunks

4 medium carrots, roughly chopped

10 garlic cloves, slivered

1 teaspoon dried oregano

1 cup dry white wine

1 bunch of fresh dill

1 cup beef or chicken stock, preferably homemade (page 160), or make lamb stock and use it

Avgolemono (page 596), preferably made with the broth from this stew

1. Put the oil in a large deep skillet or flameproof casserole with a lid and turn the heat to medium-high. Add the lamb, sprinkling the meat with salt and pepper as it browns. When the pieces are deeply browned, after at least 10 minutes, transfer to a plate; pour or spoon off any excess fat.

2. Add the vegetables and the oregano, along with some more salt and pepper, and cook, stirring occasionally, until the onions soften, 5 to 10 minutes. If you are using shanks, remove the vegetables with a slotted spoon and set aside.

3. Add the wine and let the mixture bubble for about a minute. Remove about 1/2 cup of dill leaves and reserve; tie the dill stems with the remaining at-

tached leaves into a bundle and add to the pot along with the stock. Return the lamb to the pot and cover. Adjust the heat so the mixture simmers steadily but not violently.

4. If you're using lamb shanks, return the vegetables to the pot when they are nearly tender, an hour or more later. In any case, cook until the lamb is tender. (You can prepare the dish to this point and let sit for a few hours or cover and refrigerate for up to a day before reheating and proceeding.)

5. When the lamb is nearly done, make the Avgolemono. Turn the heat to low, then stir the sauce into the lamb and heat through; do not boil. Taste and adjust the seasoning and serve in bowls, garnished with the reserved dill.

Braised Lamb with Lemon Sauce. If you do not wish to make Avgolemono, simply prepare the stew as directed and finish it with the juice of a lemon, or more to taste.

Lamb Stew with Mushrooms ITALY ■
MAKES **4 TO 6 SERVINGS**
TIME **1 1/2 TO 2 HOURS, LARGELY UNATTENDED**

What I suggest here—since most of us don't have access to truly wild mushrooms—is a combination of dried porcini with fresh shiitakes and white (button) mushrooms.

Serve this with buttered noodles, a risotto (even Bare-Bones Risotto, page 522, would be great), or crisp bread.

Other cuts of meat you can use here: boneless pork shoulder, veal shoulder, or beef chuck or brisket (which will require somewhat longer cooking time).

1/2 ounce dried porcini
2 tablespoons extra virgin olive oil

2 pounds boneless lamb shoulder, trimmed of excess fat
and cut into 2-inch cubes, or 3 to 4 pounds bone-in
shoulder or neck, cut into roughly 2-inch chunks
Salt and black pepper to taste
1/2 pound fresh shiitake mushrooms, stems discarded or
reserved for stock, caps sliced
1/2 pound button mushrooms, trimmed and sliced
3 or 4 fresh thyme sprigs
1 tablespoon minced garlic
1 cup red wine or stock, preferably homemade
(pages 160–163)
Minced fresh parsley leaves for garnish

1. Soak the porcini in hot water to cover. Put the olive oil in a large deep skillet or flameproof casserole with a lid and place over medium-high heat. Add the lamb chunks a few at a time, removing them as they brown and seasoning with salt and pepper as they cook. When they are all nicely browned—this will take 15 minutes or so—pour or spoon off the excess fat, then add the shiitakes, button mushrooms, drained porcini (reserve the soaking liquid), and thyme. Cook, stirring occasionally, until the mushrooms begin to brown, 5 to 10 minutes, then add the garlic.

2. Two or three minutes later, add the wine, about 1/2 cup of the porcini liquid, and some salt and pepper. Bring to a boil, return the lamb to the pan, turn the heat to low, and cover. Cook at a steady simmer, checking and stirring occasionally, until the lamb is tender, about an hour (or 90 minutes at most). (You can prepare the dish to this point and let sit for a few hours or cover and refrigerate for up to a day before reheating and proceeding.)

3. Remove the cover; if the mixture is soupy, raise the heat a bit and cook until the sauce thickens. Taste and adjust the seasoning, then garnish and serve.

Lamb Stew with Vinegar. Use a whole head of garlic, separated into cloves, in place of the tablespoon of minced garlic. For the liquid, use $\frac{1}{2}$ cup good red wine vinegar mixed with $\frac{1}{2}$ cup stock. All else remains the same.

Lamb Stew with Mushrooms and Olives. Steps 1 and 2 remain the same. As the lamb draws close to tenderness, add $\frac{1}{2}$ pound good-quality black or green olives, or a mixture (pitted or not, your choice), and finish the cooking with them in the pot.

Navarin FRANCE
MAKES **4 SERVINGS**

TIME **ABOUT 2 HOURS, LARGELY UNATTENDED**

A classic French lamb stew, this happy marriage of fruit and meat is updated here by the addition of a bit of orange, which enlivens the flavor. The peas and potatoes are an optional accompaniment; you could serve this with mashed potatoes or a potato gratin like the one on page 482.

2 pounds boneless lamb shoulder, cut into 1$\frac{1}{2}$- to 2-inch
   cubes

Salt and black pepper to taste

Flour for dredging

2 tablespoons olive oil

1 tablespoon butter

1 large onion (unpeeled), quartered

2 carrots, roughly chopped

3 celery stalks, roughly chopped

1 head of garlic, cut in half along its equator

1 orange, halved

$\frac{1}{4}$ bunch of fresh thyme

1 clove

2 quarts Jus Rôti (page 163) or veal stock, or as needed

4 waxy potatoes, boiled and quartered

$\frac{1}{2}$ cup frozen peas

1. Preheat the oven to 375°F. Season the lamb liberally with salt and pepper, then dredge it lightly in the flour. Heat the olive oil in a lidded large deep skillet or flameproof casserole over medium-high heat. When the oil is shimmering, add the lamb (working in batches, if necessary) and brown evenly on all sides, 10 to 15 minutes. Remove the meat from the pan and discard the fat. (You can also do the initial browning in the oven; see the headnote for Lamb Pilaf with Cinnamon, page 412.)

2. Return the pan to the stove and add the butter, onion, carrots, and celery (you can add the garlic at this stage if you want a stronger garlic flavor in the dish). Cook over medium heat, stirring, until the vegetables soften and just begin to color, about 10 minutes.

3. Squeeze the orange juice into the pan, scraping to get all the browned bits off the bottom of the pan, then add the meat, garlic, and thyme. Stick the clove through one of the halves of the juiced orange, reserving the other; add it and enough stock to barely cover the contents of the pan. Bring to a boil, then lower the heat and reduce to a simmer. Cover and transfer to the oven.

4. Check the pan after 10 minutes to make sure it isn't boiling; if it is, lower the heat to 300°F. Cook for an hour or more, as necessary, until the meat is tender and the liquid in the pan has reduced slightly.

5. Remove the pan from the oven and transfer the braised meat to a platter or cutting board to rest. Strain the sauce, pressing on the vegetables to extract as much liquid as possible, then put the sauce in a pan on the stove and reduce it over high heat until thickened considerably. Discard the vegetables and the orange half. Warm the peas and potatoes in the sauce briefly, then divide them and the lamb among 4 serving plates. Pour the sauce through a strainer over each of the 4 portions. Zest

the remaining half of the juiced orange and garnish each plate with a pinch of the zest. Serve immediately.

Lamb Stew with Dill SCANDINAVIA

MAKES **4 SERVINGS**

TIME **1 TO 1 1/2 HOURS, LARGELY UNATTENDED**

Lamb stew is a quintessential spring dish that can be a real celebration—or unbearably heavy. The difference has little to do with the lamb and much to do with the vegetables: If the stew sports color and lots of different flavors, it is lovely, almost light. If, on the other hand, it contains little besides lamb and potatoes, it becomes the cafeteria-style "Irish stew" that gave the dish a bad name in the first place. This is how it's done in Scandinavia—bright, colorful, and fresh tasting. In other parts of northern Europe, parsley might be substituted for the dill; it's just as good.

Other cuts of meat you can use here: beef chuck or brisket (which will require somewhat longer cooking time), veal shoulder.

> 2 tablespoons butter or extra virgin olive oil
>
> 2 pounds boneless lamb shoulder, cut into roughly 1 1/2-inch chunks
>
> 8 shallots, peeled
>
> 8 to 12 very small waxy potatoes, washed
>
> Salt and black pepper
>
> 2 carrots, diced into roughly pea-size bits, optional
>
> 1 cup green peas (frozen are okay)
>
> 8 scallions, trimmed and sliced, optional
>
> 1/2 cup snipped dill leaves, or more to taste
>
> Lemon wedges for serving

1. Put the butter in a wide skillet with a lid and place over high heat. When the butter foam subsides, add the lamb, a little at a time. Let sear, undisturbed, for about 2 minutes, or until the underside is nicely browned. Stir, then add the shallots and potatoes. Let cook for another couple of minutes, then add the salt, pepper, and a cup of water. Stir, scraping the bottom if necessary to loosen any bits of meat that may have stuck. Turn the heat to low, cover, and let the mixture simmer for about 45 minutes, stirring once or twice during that period.

2. Uncover and add the carrots if you're using them; stir once and simmer for about 15 minutes more, or until the lamb and potatoes are tender.

3. Uncover and add the peas and scallions. Raise the heat if necessary to boil away excess liquid. Taste and adjust the seasoning, then serve, garnished with the dill and accompanied by a lemon wedge.

Lamb Pilaf with Cinnamon GREECE

MAKES **4 TO 6 SERVINGS**

TIME **1 HOUR**

Great for a small crowd, this one-pot meal is intensely flavorful and sweet and will fill your kitchen—indeed, your home—with the wonderful aromas of cinnamon and simmering meat.

If you have the time and the energy, this is even better if you brown the lamb chunks first: Put about 2 tablespoons of olive oil in a separate skillet, turn the heat to medium-high, and brown the chunks on all sides, turning as needed; this will take about 15 minutes. (The lamb chunks can also be browned in the oven; just put them in a skillet or roasting pan and place in a 450°F oven. Roast, stirring occasionally, until they are browned all over, 20 to 30 minutes.)

Other cuts of meat you can use here: boneless beef chuck, boneless pork shoulder or leg (fresh ham).

4 medium or 2 large onions, sliced

1½ to 2 pounds boneless lamb shoulder, cut into 1- to
    2-inch chunks

4 garlic cloves, roughly chopped

2 cups undrained canned or fresh tomatoes, chopped

½ cup raisins

1 cup red wine

2 tablespoons extra virgin olive oil

Salt and black pepper to taste

2 cinnamon sticks or 1 teaspoon ground cinnamon

1 bay leaf

½ cup pine nuts

1½ cups long-grain or basmati rice

Chopped fresh parsley leaves for garnish

1. Place the onions in a deep 12-inch skillet or flame-proof casserole with a lid over medium heat; cover the pan. Let them stew, undisturbed, while you cut up the lamb, chop the garlic, and chop the tomatoes. Soak the raisins in the wine. After 5 or 10 minutes, uncover the pan and stir the onions; re-cover. When the onions are dry, slightly brown, and almost sticking to the pan, another 10 minutes or so, add the olive oil and raise the heat to medium-high.

2. Cook, stirring occasionally, until the onions are nicely browned. Add the garlic and stir. Add the tomatoes, raisins and wine, salt and pepper, cinnamon, bay leaf, pine nuts, and rice; stir. Bring to a simmer and add the lamb and 2 cups hot water. Cover and cook very slowly for about 30 minutes, checking after about 20 minutes to make sure the mixture has not dried out; if it has, add a bit more water and re-cover.

3. Check that the rice is done; if it is not, add a bit more water. Raise the heat to medium-high and cook until the mixture is moist but not swimming in liquid and the rice is fully cooked. Check the seasoning, garnish with parsley, and serve.

Lamb Chops with Sherry SPAIN ■

MAKES **4 SERVINGS**

TIME **30 MINUTES**

An Andalusian dish, featuring the wonderfully distinctive flavor of sherry. Dry (Fino) sherry is most commonly used here, but I have had it with the slightly nuttier Amontillado and even sweeter Oloroso, and I liked it just as well, though it is different. Don't use cream sherry in any case.

Serve this with crusty bread, by all means; the sauce is delicious.

Other cuts of meat you can use here: pork or veal chops, bone-in chicken.

1 tablespoon extra virgin olive oil

4 lamb shoulder chops, each 6 to 8 ounces

Salt and black pepper to taste

1 medium onion, roughly chopped

1 carrot, roughly chopped

1 tablespoon minced garlic

1 cup dry or other sherry

1. Put the oil in a large skillet with a lid and turn the heat to medium-high. A minute later, add the chops and quickly brown them on both sides, about 5 minutes, sprinkling the meat with salt and pepper as it browns. Transfer to a plate and reduce the heat to medium.

2. Put the onion, carrot, and garlic in the pan and cook, stirring occasionally, until the onion softens, about 5 minutes. Add the sherry, raise the heat to high, and cook until the liquid is somewhat reduced, 5 minutes or so. Return the lamb chops to the pan, cover, and cook, adjusting the heat so the mixture simmers steadily but not violently.

3. The lamb is done when cooked through and tender, 10 to 15 minutes. Transfer to a platter. If the mixture is soupy, reduce it over high heat until it

has a nice saucy consistency. Pour over the meat and serve.

Lamb Shanks Cooked in Yogurt
MIDDLE EAST ■

MAKES **4 SERVINGS**

TIME **2 HOURS OR MORE, LARGELY UNATTENDED**

This lamb braises in its own juices and those produced by the onions. A large quantity of whole garlic cloves brown and become sublimely tender during the long cooking process, nicely offsetting the creamy, almost bland sauce. Do not skimp on the herb garnish, which is essential in this case.

Serve with crusty bread, warm pita, or a good pilaf (page 513).

Other cuts of meat you can use here: chunks of boneless lamb shoulder, which will cook considerably faster.

1 tablespoon extra virgin olive oil

4 lamb shanks, each about 1 pound, trimmed of excess fat

Salt and black pepper to taste

10 to 20 garlic cloves, peeled

2 large onions, roughly chopped

2 tablespoons cornstarch

1 quart yogurt

1 teaspoon minced garlic

Chopped fresh dill or mint leaves for garnish

1. Put the olive oil in a large deep skillet or flameproof casserole with a lid and place over high heat. A minute later, add the lamb shanks and brown well, turning as necessary, at least 10 minutes. Sprinkle the meat with salt and pepper as it browns.
2. When the meat is nicely browned, add the whole garlic cloves and cook for another couple of min-

utes; then add the onions, stir to distribute them evenly, turn the heat down to low, and cover. Cook gently, checking to see that the mixture does not dry out and adding water or stock about $1/2$ cup at a time if it does. Cook until the lamb is quite tender, about $1^1/2$ hours (it may take a little longer). (The dish may be cooked to this point, cooled, then covered and refrigerated. If you like, skim excess fat before reheating and proceeding.)
3. Thin the cornstarch with 2 tablespoons water and whisk it into the yogurt, along with the minced garlic. Stir this mixture into the lamb and simmer, uncovered, for a few minutes. Taste and adjust the seasoning, then garnish and serve.

Stewed Lamb Shanks with Mushrooms and Pasilla Chile Sauce
MEXICO ■

MAKES **4 SERVINGS**

TIME **AT LEAST 2 HOURS, LARGELY UNATTENDED**

This dish is all about patience; the chile sauce takes just a few minutes to prepare and can be done while the lamb shanks are browning. But after combining the two with the mushrooms you must wait, sometimes for a few hours, for the shanks to become completely tender. Once that's done, you can eat the meat with a rice dish (try Arroz a la Mexicana, for example, on page 517), or use it as a filling for tacos.

Ideally, you'd use wild mushrooms here—I once made it with chanterelles, and the combination was magical—but fresh shiitakes are also great.

Other cuts of meat you can use here: short ribs (which will also take a long time); chunks of lamb or pork shoulder (which will be faster) or beef chuck or brisket; bone-in chicken parts (which will be much quicker), preferably thighs.

2 tablespoons lard (preferred) or neutral oil, such as corn
   or grapeseed
4 lamb shanks, each about 1 pound
Salt and black pepper to taste
1 large white onion, chopped
1/2 pound fresh shiitake mushrooms, stems discarded or
   reserved for stock, caps sliced
1 tablespoon fresh marjoram or oregano leaves or
   1 teaspoon dried oregano, preferably Mexican
1 teaspoon ground cumin
1 recipe Pasilla Salsa (page 612)

1. Put the lard in a large deep skillet or flameproof
   casserole with a lid and place over high heat. A
   minute later, add the lamb shanks and brown well,
   turning as necessary, at least 10 minutes. About
   halfway through the browning, sprinkle the lamb
   with salt and pepper. If you have not made the
   Pasilla Salsa, now is the time.

2. Turn the heat to medium, transfer the lamb to a
   plate, and add the onion and mushrooms to the
   skillet; cook, stirring occasionally and sprinkling
   the vegetables with salt and pepper, until the
   onion is soft, about 5 minutes. Add the marjoram,
   cumin, salsa, and about 1/2 cup water. Nestle the
   lamb in the sauce and adjust the heat so the mixture simmers slowly; cover.

3. Cook, turning and checking the meat every 30
   minutes or so and adding a little water if necessary
   to keep the mixture from drying out. When the
   meat is very, very tender, at least an hour (and
   probably more like 2), turn off the heat and serve
   or keep warm over low heat until you're ready to
   serve. Or cover and refrigerate for up to 2 days before reheating.

Lamb Shanks with Potatoes GREECE ■
MAKES **4 SERVINGS**
TIME **ABOUT 2 1/2 HOURS, LARGELY UNATTENDED**

The combination of lamb, thyme, garlic, and lemon is
so perfect that this dish—simple as it is—is among
my favorites. Needless to say, the slow-cooked potatoes, stewed in the pan juices, become rather fabulous.

Other cuts of meat you can use here: boneless
lamb or pork shoulder or shoulder lamb chops, all of
which will cook more quickly than the shanks; short
ribs; beef chuck or brisket; veal shank (osso buco).

1 tablespoon extra virgin olive oil
4 lamb shanks, each about 1 pound
Salt and black pepper to taste
4 garlic cloves, crushed and peeled
4 fresh thyme sprigs or 1 teaspoon dried thyme, plus a few
   fresh leaves for garnish
2 cups stock, preferably homemade (pages 160–163),
   white wine, or water
2 pounds waxy potatoes, scrubbed, or all-purpose
   potatoes (such as russet or Yukon Gold), peeled and
   cut into 1- to 2-inch chunks
Juice of 1 lemon

1. Put the olive oil in a large deep skillet or flameproof casserole with a lid and turn the heat to
   high. A minute later, add the lamb shanks and
   brown well, turning as necessary; this will take at
   least 10 minutes. About halfway through the
   browning, sprinkle the lamb with salt and pepper
   and add the garlic and thyme.

2. When the meat is nicely browned, add the liquid,
   turn the heat down to low, and cover. Cook at a
   slow simmer until the lamb is quite tender, about
   1 1/2 hours or a little longer. (The dish may be prepared to this point, then covered and refrigerated
   for up to a day.) Add the potatoes and re-cover.

3. Raise the heat if necessary (the mixture should continue to boil, but not too rapidly) and cook until the potatoes are just about tender, 30 to 45 minutes more. If the stew is very thin, raise the heat to high and uncover to boil out some of the liquid. When the potatoes are tender, taste and adjust the seasoning, stir in the lemon juice, garnish with a few fresh thyme leaves if you have them, and serve.

Lamb Shanks with Lentils FRANCE ■
MAKES **4 SERVINGS**

TIME **AT LEAST 2 HOURS, LARGELY UNATTENDED**

A typical dish from the southern French countryside. Lentils are combined with lamb shanks, red wine, and not much else, and they cook for a couple of hours. While becoming beyond tender, the lentils also absorb the flavors of the lamb, the wine, and the aromatics sprinkled among them. The result is a one-pot meal—a salad or a little bread, or both, would round things out nicely—that takes some time but little work or attention.

Other cuts of meat you can use here: short ribs.

³/₄ pound dried lentils, rinsed and picked over

2 medium carrots, chopped

1 onion, chopped

4 fresh thyme sprigs or 1 teaspoon dried

1 tablespoon minced garlic

2 bay leaves

1 bottle dry red wine

4 lamb shanks

Salt and black pepper to taste

1. Preheat the oven to 400°F. Combine the first 7 ingredients in a roasting pan or flameproof casserole and stir; bring to a boil on top of the stove, then nestle the lamb shanks among the lentils, cover the pan (aluminum foil will do), and put in the oven. Lower the heat to 350°F and cook, undisturbed, for about an hour.

2. Uncover and stir the lentils gently; season with salt and pepper. Re-cover and cook for about 1 hour more, until the lentils are very tender and the lamb begins to pull away from the bone; if at any point the mixture threatens to dry out, add more wine or water. And don't worry about overcooking the lentils; just make sure the lamb is done. When the lamb is tender, uncover the pan, raise the heat to 400°F, and cook for another 15 minutes or so, just to brown the top a bit. Taste, adjust the seasoning, and serve or cool, cover, and refrigerate for up to a day before reheating.

Veal Stew with Dill and Sour Cream
EASTERN EUROPE ■

MAKES **4 SERVINGS**

TIME **1 HOUR**

A fairly quick stew—some would call it fricassee, but that term is so widely used as to be meaningless—that gives you loads of uncommon flavor for very little work. Great with polenta (page 529), which you must call mamaliga in this instance.

Other cuts of meat you can use here: pork shoulder.

2 tablespoons butter or extra virgin olive oil

1¹/₂ to 2 pounds boneless veal, from the shoulder or round, cut into roughly 1¹/₂-inch chunks

Salt and black pepper to taste

2 large onions, roughly chopped

1 tablespoon sweet paprika, or to taste

Best Veal Cuts for Braising

Shank. Takes a while, and a little short on meat, but the marrow makes it worth it.

Shoulder. Cut into chunks, about the fastest-braising meat there is (pork and lamb shoulder are also quick).

Breast. Unwieldy, sometimes a little fatty, but often wonderful. Figure about one veal rib per serving.

---

¹/₂ cup white wine, stock, or water

1 bunch of fresh dill

¹/₂ cup sour cream

1. Put a large skillet with a lid over high heat and, a minute later, add the butter. Add the meat in one layer to be sure it browns (if you use the larger amount of meat, you may have to cook in batches; it's worth the effort). Cook, undisturbed, adjusting the heat so the meat browns but does not burn and sprinkling the meat with salt and pepper as it cooks, until the meat is nicely browned on the bottom, about 5 minutes. Stir, then brown a little more, another 3 to 5 minutes. Remove with a slotted spoon and reduce the heat to medium.

2. Add the onions and paprika, along with some more salt and pepper. Cook, stirring occasionally, until the onions soften and any bits of meat stuck to the bottom of the pan are released, about 5 minutes. Return the meat to the pan and stir. Add the liquid, stir, and reduce the heat to low. Cut the dill leaves from the stems, chop, and set aside. Tie the stems in a bundle, and add to the pot. Cover, adjusting the heat so the mixture simmers steadily but not violently, and cook for 30 to 40 minutes, or until the meat is tender. (You can prepare the dish to this point and let sit for a few hours or cover and refrigerate for up to a day before reheating and proceeding.) Meanwhile, chop the dill leaves.

3. Uncover, remove the bundle of dill stems, and discard; stir in the sour cream. Cook for about 5 min-

utes more, until heated through. Taste and adjust the seasoning, garnish with the chopped dill, and serve.

Veal Stew with Pickles. I ordinarily cannot stand dill pickles in cooked dishes, but I find this one irresistible. Along with the sour cream, stir in about ¹/₂ cup chopped dill pickles or cornichons and 1 tablespoon strong mustard, such as Dijon.

Blanquette de Veau White Veal Stew
FRANCE
MAKES **4 TO 6 SERVINGS**
TIME **2 HOURS, LARGELY UNATTENDED**

A longtime symbol of cuisine bourgeois—the simple, hearty home cooking of France (which is more valuable to most of us than haute cuisine, the four-star stuff)—this is an immensely satisfying dish and quite straightforward. Serve it over white rice or with crusty bread.

6 tablespoons (³/₄ stick) butter

2 pounds boneless veal shoulder, cut into 2-inch cubes

1 onion, peeled and quartered

2 carrots, cut into chunks

2 turnips or parsnips, trimmed, peeled, and cut into chunks

Salt and black pepper to taste

6 cups chicken stock, preferably homemade (page 160)

2 bay leaves

7 fresh thyme sprigs

$\frac{1}{4}$ cup flour

2 egg yolks

$\frac{1}{2}$ cup heavy cream

1 tablespoon fresh lemon juice

Chopped fresh parsley leaves for garnish, optional

1. Put a large flameproof casserole or Dutch oven with a lid over medium-high heat for 2 or 3 minutes. Add 2 tablespoons of the butter. A minute later, when the foam subsides, brown the veal chunks, adding a few at a time, turning them to brown all over, and removing the pieces as they brown. Take your time and brown the veal in batches if necessary so they darken nicely; depending on your heat level and the size of your pan, this will take from 10 to 20 minutes.

2. If necessary, drain all but 2 tablespoons of the fat from the pan and add the onion, carrots, and turnips. Cook, stirring occasionally, for 5 minutes, then add the salt, pepper, stock, bay leaves, and thyme. Bring to a boil and return the veal to the casserole. Adjust the heat so the stew simmers steadily and cook, partially covered, stirring occasionally, until the veal is tender, 45 to 60 minutes.

3. Transfer the veal and vegetables to a large bowl. Strain and reserve the stock. Melt the remaining butter in a medium saucepan over low heat. Add the flour and whisk constantly for 3 minutes; do not let the mixture brown. Whisk in 2 cups of the reserved stock and cook, whisking occasionally, until the mixture thickens, about 5 minutes. Add the egg yolks and cream and cook, whisking constantly, for another 2 minutes. Whisk in the lemon juice and remove from the heat.

4. Pour the sauce over the veal and vegetables, garnish, and serve.

Veal Shanks with Cherries RUSSIA ■

MAKES **4 SERVINGS**

TIME **AT LEAST 2 HOURS, LARGELY UNATTENDED**

Think of this as osso buco, Russian style; the technique is almost identical to that in the following, better-known classic, but the result is sweeter and more fragrant. Serve with pilaf or buttered noodles.

If you are lucky enough to find fresh sour cherries, by all means use them; pit about a pound and add them to the pan as you would bottled sour cherries, along with about $\frac{1}{4}$ cup sugar and a bit more stock.

Other cuts of meat you can use here: as in classic osso buco, you will lose something by substituting chunks of boneless veal for the shank, but you will gain time, and the results will still be quite good.

1 tablespoon extra virgin olive oil

4 tablespoons ($\frac{1}{2}$ stick) butter or more oil

4 center-cut slices veal shank, at least 2 pounds

Salt and black pepper to taste

1 large onion, roughly chopped

$\frac{1}{2}$ cup chopped carrot

10 white cardamom pods

One 16- or 17-ounce jar sour cherries, with their juice

1 cup chicken or beef stock, preferably homemade (page 160), or red wine

1 teaspoon grated lemon zest

1. Combine the oil and 2 tablespoons of the butter in a wide deep skillet or flameproof casserole, preferably nonstick, with a lid and place over medium-high heat. Wait a couple of minutes and, when the butter foam subsides, add the veal shanks and brown them well, rotating and turning the pieces as necessary, 15 minutes or more. Sprinkle the meat with salt and pepper as it cooks; when the meat is brown, transfer it to a plate.

2. Reduce the heat to medium, add the onion and carrot, and cook, stirring occasionally, until they

soften, about 10 minutes. Stir in the cardamom, then the cherries and their juice, along with the stock. Bring to a boil and turn the heat to low.

3. Return the veal shanks to the pan and cover the skillet; adjust the heat so the mixture simmers steadily. Cook until the meat is very tender and pulling away from the bone, at least 90 minutes and probably more; turn the veal every half hour or so. (When the meat is tender, you may turn off the heat and refrigerate the dish for up to 24 hours; reheat gently before proceeding.)

4. If the sauce is thin, transfer the meat to a warm platter and turn the heat to high; boil the sauce until it becomes thick and glossy, about 5 minutes. Stir in the remaining butter, a bit at a time, then add the lemon zest and turn off the heat. Serve the meat with the sauce spooned over it.

Osso Buco ITALY ■

MAKES **4 SERVINGS**

TIME **AT LEAST 2 HOURS, LARGELY UNATTENDED**

One of the greatest Italian dishes and, when done properly (it takes time; do not rush), one of the best meat dishes you can make. The marrow-filled veal shanks (the name means "bone with hole") practically cook themselves after the initial browning and seasoning. (And the dish holds well enough overnight so you can cook almost the whole thing in advance.)

Buy center-cut shank, about 1½ inches thick. (The slices from the narrow end have very little meat; those from the thick end contain little or no marrow.)

The mixture of garlic, lemon zest, and parsley stirred in at the last minute, known as gremolata, is a lovely little fillip, but consider it optional.

Serve, classically, with Risotto alla Milanese (page 521) or a simpler, leaner rice dish.

Other cuts of meat you can use here: it will not be osso buco, but a veal stew made with chunks of veal shoulder in the same style, with the same ingredients, is quite good and considerably faster.

2 tablespoons extra virgin olive oil

4 center-cut slices veal shank, at least 2 pounds

Salt and black pepper to taste

4 anchovy fillets, optional

1 cup chopped onion

½ cup chopped carrot

½ cup chopped celery

1 tablespoon plus 1 teaspoon minced garlic

2 bay leaves

3 or 4 fresh thyme sprigs or ½ teaspoon dried

1 cup dry white wine, chicken or beef stock, preferably homemade (page 160), or water

1 teaspoon grated lemon zest

2 tablespoons chopped fresh parsley leaves

1. Put the oil in a wide deep skillet or flameproof casserole, preferably nonstick, with a lid and place over medium-high heat. Wait a couple of minutes and, when the oil is hot, add the veal shanks and brown them well, rotating and turning the pieces as necessary, 15 minutes or more. Sprinkle the meat with salt and pepper as it cooks. Transfer the veal shanks to a plate.

2. Turn off the heat for a minute, then turn it to medium. Add the anchovies if you're using them and cook, stirring occasionally, until they break up, a minute or two. Add the onion, carrot, celery, 1 tablespoon of the garlic, the bay leaves, and thyme and cook, stirring occasionally, until the vegetables soften, about 10 minutes. Add the wine, bring to a boil, and turn the heat to low.

3. Return the veal shanks to the pan and cover the skillet. Five minutes later, check to see that the mixture is simmering—just a few bubbles appearing at once—and adjust the heat accordingly. Cook until the meat is very tender and pulling

away from the bone, at least 90 minutes and probably more; turn the veal every half hour or so. (When the meat is tender, you may turn off the heat and refrigerate the dish for up to 24 hours; reheat gently before proceeding.)

4. If the sauce is thin, transfer the meat to a warm platter and turn the heat to high; boil the sauce until it becomes thick and glossy, about 5 minutes. Mix together the remaining teaspoon of garlic, the lemon zest, and the parsley to make the gremolata. Stir the gremolata into the sauce and turn off the heat. Serve the meat with the sauce spooned over it.

Osso Buco, French Style. Brown the meat as in step 1, then simmer it in Fast, Fresh Tomato Sauce (page 606), made with a tablespoon of garlic and a teaspoon of fresh marjoram. Once the meat is tender, finish, if you like, by covering with about $1/2$ cup fresh bread crumbs (page 580) and baking in a 375°F oven for about 15 minutes.

GROUND MEAT DISHES

You'll find a few hamburgerlike recipes in the grilling section at the beginning of this chapter, but the following recipes are either simmered or panfried. What they have in common is that they are all based on ground meat. The meats themselves are essentially interchangeable—not only can beef, pork, lamb, and veal almost always fill in for one another, but chicken and turkey do nicely in most instances, too. The difference is not so much in the type of meat but in the fat content: higher-fat "burgers," sausages, koftes, and the like will always be juicier and have more flavor than those that are lean.

Plantain and Meat Casserole
CARIBBEAN ■ ▨

MAKES **4 TO 6 SERVINGS**
TIME **ABOUT 1 HOUR**

A fairly complicated, lasagnelike dish and, like lasagne, perfectly homey. With advance preparation (you can make the sauce a day ahead and sauté the plantains several hours ahead), you can throw this together quickly, but even if you do it all at once you can make quick work of it. Great with a salad, this needs nothing else.

Other meat you can use here: ground turkey, chicken, veal, or pork.

2 tablespoons extra virgin olive oil or neutral oil, like corn or grapeseed

1 pound ground beef

Salt and black pepper to taste

1 large onion, roughly chopped

1 red or green bell pepper, stemmed, seeded, and roughly chopped

1 tablespoon minced garlic

1 tablespoon paprika

1 tablespoon ground cumin

2 teaspoons dried oregano, preferably Mexican

2 cups chopped tomatoes (canned are fine)

1 recipe Platanos Maduros (page 472)

2 eggs, lightly beaten, optional

1. Preheat the oven to 350°F. Put the oil in a large skillet and turn the heat to medium-high. A minute later, add the meat and some salt and pepper and cook, stirring to break up lumps, until it loses its color, just a couple of minutes. Remove with a slotted spoon and add the onion and bell pepper. Cook, stirring occasionally, until quite soft, about 10 minutes. Add the garlic, paprika, cumin, oregano, and tomatoes and some more salt and pepper and cook, stirring occasionally, until

the mixture is saucy, 15 to 20 minutes. (This is a good time to sauté the plantains if you have not already done so.)

2. Return the beef to the sauce and cook for another 5 minutes; taste and adjust the seasoning as necessary. Use about a third of the sauce to make a thin layer at the bottom of an 8- or 9-inch square casserole or similar-size dish. Top with a layer of plantains, then more sauce, then the remaining plantains, then finally the remaining sauce. Pour the eggs over all if you like. Bake for 20 to 30 minutes, until heated through, then serve hot or at room temperature or cover and refrigerate overnight before covering with foil and reheating in a 250°F oven.

Pytt i Panna Meat Hash SWEDEN ■

MAKES **4 SERVINGS**

TIME **ABOUT 30 MINUTES**

The ideal dish for when you have leftover meat and potatoes, this can also be made from scratch, by cutting raw potatoes into small cubes and browning them, then cutting meat into small cubes and browning it with the onions. This preparation is undeniably more elegant, but the recipe here, I feel, is more in tune with the spirit of the dish.

If you don't like the idea of raw egg (which, I assure you, is entirely in keeping with tradition), fry or poach the eggs, then top the hash with them.

Other cuts of meat you can use here: boneless pork.

4 tablespoons (¹/₂ stick) butter or extra virgin olive oil

2 cups cooked or raw beef, cut into ¹/₂-inch cubes

Salt and black pepper to taste

2 cups boiled potatoes (2 or 3 potatoes) in ¹/₂-inch cubes

1 cup diced onion

4 eggs

1. Put 1 tablespoon of the butter in a large skillet, preferably nonstick, over medium-high heat. When its foam begins to subside, add the beef and cook, shaking the pan occasionally, until brown and crisp all over, about 10 minutes, sprinkling the meat with salt and pepper as it cooks. Transfer to a bowl.

2. Put another 2 tablespoons of butter in the pan and cook the potatoes as you did the meat, until brown and crisp, also about 10 minutes. Remove and add to the meat.

3. Repeat with 1 more tablespoon of butter and the onion, cooking until it is browned on the edges. Return the meat and potatoes to the pan and cook, stirring occasionally, until all ingredients are hot, brown, and crisp. Taste and adjust the seasoning.

4. Put portions of the hash on 4 plates; make a small well in the top of each portion and break a raw egg into it; diners will stir the egg into the hash before eating.

Fresh Sausage Patties FRANCE, ETC. ■ ■

MAKES **6 TO 12 SERVINGS (DEPENDING ON TIME OF DAY AND ACCOMPANIMENTS)**

TIME **30 MINUTES**

These are made wherever there are pigs, which is most of the world. And everywhere (except in American supermarkets), they contain a great deal of fat. In fact, you cannot make real sausage without fat, ideally in a ratio of about two parts lean to one part fat. ("Lean" sausage is not sausage; it's hamburger.) So if you're entirely antifat, pass this recipe by.

For the rest of you, there is nothing like homemade sausage, not on your first try, but on about your third or fourth, when you know exactly what seasonings turn you on. This is my favorite; it makes a lot, but the mixture freezes very well.

These are great served with Creamy Horseradish Sauce (page 608). Or serve them on a bed of White Beans with Garlic (page 441). Or make a quick pan gravy—just add some white wine or water to the fat left in the pan and cook, stirring frequently, until the mixture is saucy—and serve over mashed potatoes. If you like highly flavored food in the morning, try them at breakfast.

> 2 pounds boneless pork, preferably from the shoulder
> 1/2 to 3/4 pound fresh pork fatback, more if the pork itself is very lean
> 1 tablespoon salt
> 1/2 teaspoon cracked black pepper
> 1 tablespoon minced garlic
> 1 tablespoon fennel or coriander seeds
> 1/4 teaspoon hot red pepper flakes
> Tiny pinch each of ground cloves, ground allspice, and freshly grated nutmeg

1. Cut the pork and fat into small cubes and combine with all the other ingredients. Grind with a meat grinder or food processor (probably in batches, unless your machine is very large) until finely chopped—that is, ground, not pulverized. (Some small chunks are okay.) Add a little water or red wine if the mixture is so dry that it won't hold together. Panfry a tiny piece of the meat to check the seasoning; add more of anything you like.

2. Shape the meat into thin patties; you will have at least 10 or 12 (freeze any you are not going to cook within a day). Heat a large skillet, preferably nonstick, over medium heat for 2 or 3 minutes, then add the patties. Cook, rotating as necessary so they brown evenly, then turn and cook on the other side until done; they'll be firm but not tough when cooked through. Serve.

Poached Sausage with Garlic. This will work nicely with the fresh sausage patties or store-bought patties or links: In step 2, brown the meat on one side, with about 10 garlic cloves, peeled, moving the garlic so it browns but does not burn. Add 1/2 cup dry white wine, cover, and cook until the sausage is done, another 5 minutes or so. Serve over mashed potatoes.

Mititei Fresh Sausages ROMANIA
MAKES **4 SERVINGS**
TIME **30 MINUTES, PLUS RESTING TIME AND TIME TO PREHEAT THE GRILL**

Almost every country has a sausage or two. These skinless Romanian ones are among the easiest, essentially well-seasoned hamburgers that were undoubtedly created in a pinch and are known as "the little sausages without skin" and remain popular today. Note that these contain caraway seeds, one of the distinctive flavorings of Eastern Europe—the Italian variation uses fennel instead.

Other cuts of meat you can use here: ground beef, veal, or a combination.

> 1 1/2 pounds well-ground pork
> 1 tablespoon extra virgin olive oil
> 1 tablespoon water
> 3 garlic cloves, minced
> 1 egg, lightly beaten
> 1 teaspoon hot red pepper flakes or hot paprika
> 1 teaspoon caraway seeds
> Salt and black pepper to taste

1. Place all the ingredients in a large bowl. Wet your hands and knead the mixture for about 5 minutes, rewetting your hands if the mixture begins to stick. Cover the bowl and refrigerate for at least 2 and up to 24 hours.

2. When you're ready to cook, start a charcoal or gas grill or preheat the broiler; the fire should be medium-hot and the rack no more than 4 inches from the heat source. Meanwhile, shape the meat mixture into little sausages, about 3 inches long and 1 inch in diameter. Grill or broil the sausages, turning occasionally with a spatula or tongs, until nicely browned and cooked through, about 10 minutes.

Ma Po Tofu Simmered Tofu with Ground Pork

CHINA ▓

MAKES **8 SERVINGS**

TIME **20 MINUTES**

This is not a stir-fry but a simmered dish, easy and fast. The cooking time totals about 10 minutes, and the preparation time is about the same, so make sure to start a pot of rice before anything else.

Other meat you can use here: ground turkey, chicken, veal, or beef.

   2 tablespoons peanut or other oil

   2 tablespoons minced garlic

   2 tablespoons peeled and minced fresh ginger

   1/4 teaspoon hot red pepper flakes, or to taste

   1/2 pound ground pork

   1 cup chopped scallion, green part only

   1 cup stock, preferably homemade (pages 160–163), or water

   2 pounds soft or silken tofu, cut into 1/2-inch cubes

   1/4 cup soy sauce

   Salt to taste

   Minced fresh cilantro leaves for garnish, optional

1. Put the oil in a deep 12-inch skillet or wok, preferably nonstick, and turn the heat to medium-high. A minute later, add the garlic, ginger, and red pepper flakes and cook just until they begin to sizzle, less than a minute. Add the pork and stir to break it up; cook, stirring occasionally, until it loses most of its pink color.

2. Add the scallion and stir; add the stock. Cook for a minute or so, scraping the bottom of the pan with a wooden spoon if necessary to loosen any stuck bits of meat, then add the tofu. Cook, stirring once or twice, until the tofu is heated through, about 2 minutes.

3. Stir in the soy sauce, taste, and add salt and hot pepper flakes as necessary. Garnish with the cilantro if you like and serve.

Minced Pork and Shrimp in Coconut Milk SOUTHEAST ASIA ▓

MAKES **4 SERVINGS**

TIME **20 MINUTES**

Incredibly quick and perfect on a weeknight with steamed Sticky Rice (page 508), which of course takes twice as long as the dish itself! See page 500 for information on nam pla.

Other meat you can use here: ground turkey, chicken, veal, or beef.

   1 cup coconut milk, homemade (page 584) or canned

   2 fresh red chiles, preferably Thai, stemmed, seeded, and minced

   1 tablespoon peeled and minced fresh ginger

   1 tablespoon minced garlic

   1/2 pound ground pork

   1/2 pound shrimp, peeled and finely chopped

   1 tablespoon nam pla

   Salt and black pepper to taste

   2 scallions, trimmed and chopped

   2 tablespoons chopped fresh cilantro leaves

   2 tablespoons chopped fresh mint leaves

1. Put the coconut milk, chiles, ginger, and garlic in a medium saucepan. Bring the mixture to a boil.

2. Stir in the pork and adjust the heat so the mixture simmers steadily. A minute later, add the shrimp. Cook, stirring, until both pork and shrimp are cooked through, about 3 minutes more.

3. Stir in the nam pla, then salt and pepper if necessary. Remove from the heat and transfer to a serving bowl; garnish with the scallions, cilantro, and mint, and serve.

Goshtaba Lamb Meatballs Simmered in Milk
INDIA

MAKES **4 SERVINGS, MORE AS PART OF A LARGER MEAL**

TIME **45 MINUTES**

There is a whole class of Kashmiri, Pakistani, and northern Indian meatballs that have the reputation of being extremely difficult to make, because the meat must be minced and pounded repeatedly until very, very smooth. But guess what? The food processor is so efficient at this that the meatballs are now practically fast food. Typically quite large, meaning one or two per person is plenty. Serve with any rice dish, or Paratha (page 559). Haaq (page 487) is another typical dish from Kashmir that would go well here.

$1\frac{1}{2}$ pounds boneless lamb shoulder

Salt and black pepper to taste

2 teaspoons ground ginger

1 tablespoon ground cardamom

1 teaspoon ground fennel or anise

Pinch of cayenne

$1\frac{1}{2}$ cups yogurt

2 tablespoons butter

1 tablespoon Fragrant Curry Powder (page 593), Garam Masala (page 594), or any mild good-quality curry powder

2 cups whole milk

Chopped fresh mint leaves for garnish

1. Combine the lamb, salt, pepper (about $\frac{1}{2}$ teaspoon), ginger, cardamom, fennel, and cayenne in a food processor. Process, stopping the machine and scraping down the sides if necessary, until the meat is very smooth. Add about $\frac{1}{4}$ cup of the yogurt and process until even smoother. Bring a large pot of water to a boil and add salt.

2. Shape the meat into large balls, $1\frac{1}{2}$ inches or so in diameter, and add to the boiling water; adjust the heat so the mixture simmers and cook until the meatballs swell, about 15 minutes.

3. Put the butter in a large skillet or flameproof casserole with a lid over medium heat. A minute later, add the curry powder and stir for 30 seconds. Add the milk and remaining $1\frac{1}{4}$ cups yogurt, stir until smooth, and bring to a gentle simmer. Add the meatballs, then cover and adjust the heat so the mixture simmers steadily. Cook for another 15 minutes, then serve, garnished with the mint.

Alubukhara Kofta
Prune-Stuffed Meatballs in Yogurt Sauce   INDIA

MAKES **4 SERVINGS**

TIME **ABOUT 1 HOUR**

Like much of the food from the northern reaches of India (these are actually Kashmiri in origin), these fruit-stuffed meatballs have an exotic air about them. Serve with pilaf or one of the Indian breads on pages 559–565.

Other meat you can use here: ground veal, pork, or beef.

Salt and black pepper to taste

$1\frac{1}{2}$ pounds ground lamb

$^1/_2$ teaspoon ground fennel

$^1/_2$ teaspoon ground ginger

$^1/_4$ teaspoon cayenne

16 small pitted prunes or apricots or 8 large,
cut in half

2 tablespoons corn, grapeseed, or other neutral oil

1 tablespoon Fragrant Curry Powder (page 593),
Garam Masala (page 594), or any mild, good-quality
curry powder, or to taste

2 cups yogurt

Chopped fresh mint leaves for garnish

1. Bring a large pot of water to a boil and add salt. Mix the lamb with salt, pepper, fennel, ginger, and cayenne. Shape into 16 meatballs and stuff each with a prune or an apricot. Add the meatballs to the boiling water and adjust the heat so the mixture simmers steadily. Cook for about 10 minutes, until the meatballs are firm, then remove with a slotted spoon.

2. Put the oil in a deep skillet or flameproof casserole over medium heat. A minute later, stir in the curry powder and cook, stirring constantly, for about 30 seconds. Reduce the heat to low and stir in the yogurt and about $^1/_2$ cup water—enough to thin the yogurt. Add the meatballs, cover, and adjust the heat so the mixture simmers. Cook for about 15 minutes more, or until the meatballs are cooked through.

3. Taste and adjust the seasoning, garnish, and serve.

Panfried Kofte with Potatoes
MIDDLE EAST ■ ▨

MAKES **4 SERVINGS**

TIME **40 MINUTES**

Sweeter than grilled kofte like the one on page 355—and too delicate for the grill—these may be broiled but are at their best when panfried. Serve with any Raita (page 175) and a cooked vegetable.

1 baking potato, about $^1/_2$ pound, or about 1 cup mashed
potatoes

Salt and black pepper to taste

1 pound boneless lamb, preferably from the shoulder,
excess fat removed

1 egg

Pinch of ground allspice

$^1/_4$ cup pine nuts

$^1/_4$ cup currants or raisins

4 tablespoons ($^1/_2$ stick) butter or oil for panfrying,
optional

Flour for dredging, optional

1. Peel the potato and cut it into chunks; simmer in salted water to cover until tender, 15 minutes or so. Meanwhile, cut the lamb into large chunks and put into a food processor with the egg, a large pinch of salt, some pepper, and the allspice. When the potato is done, run it under cold water, then drain and add it to the food processor; process until quite smooth, stopping the machine and scraping down the sides if necessary. By hand, mix in the pine nuts and currants.

2. To panfry, shape the kofte into 8 small patties. Put the butter if you're using it in a large skillet, preferably nonstick, over medium heat. When the butter melts, dredge each of the patties lightly in the flour if you wish—shaking lightly to shed the excess—and fry, rotating as necessary and turning once or twice, until crisp and golden on each side, about 10 minutes.

   To broil, preheat the broiler—the rack should be about 4 inches from the heat source—and shape the kofte into 4 or 6 elongated (small football-shaped) meatballs. Broil, turning once, until nice and brown, about 10 minutes total. Serve hot or at room temperature.

Kofte with Bulgur MIDDLE EAST ■

MAKES **4 SERVINGS**

TIME **1 HOUR, SOMEWHAT UNATTENDED**

While most kofte are quite smooth in texture, this one has the nutty graininess of bulgur, the staple grain of the Middle East. It's best to season these even more than you would Grilled Meat Kofte (page 355)—the bulgur cuts the lamb's flavor—and broil or panfry them; they are too delicate to grill.

1/2 cup fine bulgur

1 pound boneless lamb, preferably from the shoulder, excess fat removed

1 medium onion, peeled and quartered

Salt and black pepper to taste

2 garlic cloves

Pinch of cayenne

1 teaspoon cumin

1 egg

1/2 cup chopped fresh parsley leaves

4 tablespoons (1/2 stick) butter or oil for panfrying, optional

Flour for dredging, optional

1. Rinse the bulgur, then put it in a bowl. Cover with boiling water (about 2 cups) and let sit until tender (taste it), 15 to 30 minutes. Drain thoroughly.

2. Cut the lamb into large chunks and put in a food processor with the bulgur, onion, a large pinch of salt, some pepper, the garlic, cayenne, cumin, and egg. Process until quite smooth, stopping the machine and scraping down the sides if necessary. Mix in the parsley by hand.

3. To broil, preheat the broiler—the rack should be about 4 inches from the heat source—and shape the kofte into 4 or 6 elongated (small football-shaped) meatballs. Broil, turning once, until nice and brown, about 10 minutes total.

   To panfry, shape the kofte into 8 small patties. Put the butter if you're using it in a large skillet, preferably nonstick, over medium heat. When the butter melts, dredge each of the patties lightly in the flour if you wish—shaking lightly to shed the excess—and fry, rotating as necessary and turning once or twice, until crisp and golden on each side, about 10 minutes. Serve hot or at room temperature.

Kofte with Chickpeas or Nuts. Substitute 1 cup cooked chickpeas or toasted walnuts (see Toasted Sesame Seeds, page 596) for the bulgur. Do not cook, but grind thoroughly before adding the meat. Proceed as in step 2.

Vegetables Our taste for vegetables has grown with their increased availability and increased variety. Still, it's arguable that locally grown vegetables, in season, beat the pants off anything else and that simple vegetable preparations are best of all. Nothing, for example, tastes better than freshly picked steamed peas or asparagus.

That's not always what you'll have, of course, so we look for ways to add flavor to store-bought vegetables (which are usually less than ideal; there are times you can do better with frozen).

Although many traditional recipes relied on gardens and markets that provided local vegetables in season, many recipes went far beyond the basics, because "seasonality" often means a surplus, so variety was key. What I've tried to include here are some of the best of the world's simple and traditional vegetable recipes.

This chapter is simply organized alphabetically by vegetable, but since so many vegetables can be substituted for one another, I've included those possibilities whenever appropriate.

ARTICHOKES

In this country, artichokes are usually quite large, which means they're most often steamed (or poached) and served as an appetizer, with melted butter, mayonnaise, vinaigrette, or another sauce. But if you can find small artichokes, trim and slice them, then sauté or even eat them raw (as on page 167). Larger artichokes can also be eaten this way, but you must first either scoop out the choke from the top (use a spoon) or, more efficiently, cut them in quarters the long way, trim, and cut out the choke.

Stewed Baby Artichokes with Fava Beans and Peas ITALY ■ ▪

MAKES **4 SERVINGS**

TIME **1 HOUR**

This is a classic combination of Italian spring vegetables, but it's also a template for stewing any fresh veggies you like in olive oil. If you cannot get small artichokes—those so small they have no choke, so you can simply trim and quarter them—use frozen artichoke hearts. If you cannot get favas, use limas; here, too, frozen are okay, and the same with peas. This stew makes a good sauce for cut pasta, like penne.

Other vegetables you can prepare this way: This is nearly a universal recipe; almost anything you can think of will work here, from spinach to potatoes to asparagus, as long as you adjust the cooking time accordingly. Mix and match as you like.

$1/3$ cup extra virgin olive oil

4 spring onions, trimmed and quartered, or 12 scallions, trimmed and cut into 2- or 3-inch lengths

4 to 8 baby artichokes, trimmed of any hard parts and cut into quarters or eighths

1 cup fresh small fava or lima beans

1 cup shelled fresh peas

Salt and black pepper to taste

$1/2$ cup chicken stock, preferably homemade (page 160), or as needed

1 fresh tarragon sprig, optional

1. Put the oil in a large skillet or flameproof casserole with a lid over medium heat. Add the onions and cook, stirring occasionally, until wilted, 5 to 10 minutes; do not let the onions brown. One at a time, add the remaining vegetables; in each instance, cook, stirring, for about a minute. Add some salt and pepper, the stock, and, if you're using it, the tarragon. Turn the heat to low, cover, and adjust the heat so the mixture simmers gently.

2. Cook, uncovering and stirring every 10 minutes or so and adding a little more liquid if needed, until the vegetables are completely tender, at least 30 minutes more but quite likely 45. Taste and adjust the seasoning, then serve hot or at room temperature.

Artichokes with White Wine and Lemon ITALY ■ ▪

MAKES **4 SERVINGS**

TIME **1 HOUR**

A simple and basic artichoke recipe that may well become your default method. The acidity of the white wine keeps the artichokes nice and green and also contrasts nicely but not too jarringly with their mild flavor.

Other vegetables you can prepare this way: Not all vegetables take to white wine, but many do, especially those with a little sweetness. Think carrots, beets, sweet potatoes, and winter squash.

4 medium to large artichokes

¼ cup extra virgin olive oil

1 cup dry white wine

3 garlic cloves, peeled and lightly smashed

Juice of 1 lemon

Salt and black pepper to taste

Melted butter, lemon juice, or mayonnaise, preferably
  homemade (page 602), for serving

1. To trim the artichokes, cut off their pointy tops, then remove a row or two of the hardest outer leaves. Peel the bottom stem with a paring knife, trimming the hard bottom but leaving the rest, unless it appears extremely stringy.

2. Choose a deep saucepan or flameproof casserole with a lid that will hold the artichokes in one layer. Add the oil, wine, garlic, lemon juice, a large pinch of salt, at least ½ teaspoon pepper, and 1 cup water. Turn the heat to medium-high and bring to a boil. Add the artichokes, stems down, cover, and adjust the heat so the mixture simmers.

3. Cook the artichokes until tender but not mushy, 30 to 60 minutes. Serve hot or at room temperature, with melted butter, lemon juice, or mayonnaise. Or reduce the cooking liquid over high heat, then strain and pour it over the artichokes.

ASPARAGUS

Always break off the bottom, woody part of asparagus stalks. They usually snap off at about the right place, or you can use a knife. As for peeling, pencil-thin asparagus don't need it, but with all others, use an ordinary vegetable peeler to remove the outer skin from the base of the flower to the bottom of the stalk.

Steamed Asparagus with Sauce Gribiche FRANCE ■ ▩
MAKES **4 OR MORE SERVINGS**

TIME **30 MINUTES**

Plain vinaigrette is lovely over steamed vegetables (or poached or grilled fish for that matter), but gribiche surpasses it. Just the thought of this bistro classic makes my mouth water.

Other vegetables you can prepare this way: any vegetable you can steam and sauce—potatoes, broccoli, and carrots, for example.

1½ to 2 pounds asparagus, trimmed and peeled

Salt and black pepper to taste

1 cup Vinaigrette (page 600)

2 tablespoons chopped cornichons or gherkins

1 teaspoon minced lemon zest

1 hard-cooked egg (page 338), finely chopped

2 tablespoons minced fresh chives or chopped fresh
  parsley leaves

1. You can steam or simmer the asparagus; each method takes 5 to 10 minutes (steaming is a little faster because you don't have to bring a large pot of water to a boil).

   To **steam, stand** them up in a pot with about an inch of salted water on the bottom, then cover and turn the heat to high; or just lay them in a steamer over boiling water. Cook just until the thick part of the stalks can be pierced with a knife.

   To simmer, plunge into boiling salted water and cook until the thick part of the stalks can be pierced with a knife.

2. While the asparagus is cooking, combine the remaining ingredients except the herb and blend with a fork.

3. Drain the asparagus and serve hot or at room temperature, with some of the sauce spooned over it. Garnish with the herb.

White Asparagus with Aïoli. White asparagus is produced by "blanching" the spears as they grow: dirt is mounded up around each stalk so it doesn't develop chlorophyll—which is what turns it green. Steam or simmer as directed, giving it plenty of time to become tender. Serve warm, with Aïoli (page 603).

Asparagus with Eggs and Parmesan
ITALY ▪

MAKES **4 SERVINGS**

TIME **20 MINUTES**

I've had variations of this spring creation in a number of places. In Holland, they use ham; in Italy, they use Parmesan; in Germany, they use both. The key ingredients, however, are good asparagus and fried eggs, and the results are as delicious as they are easy. The combination of melted butter and runny egg yolk mimics Hollandaise sauce, though I think browning the butter yields a more flavorful result.

The most difficult decision may be when to serve this. I like it as a light supper, but it's also great at brunch.

Other vegetables you can prepare this way: cauliflower would be equally nice.

> 1 to 1^1/$_2$ pounds asparagus, trimmed and peeled
>
> Salt and black pepper to taste
>
> 6 tablespoons (^{3}/$_4$ stick) butter, or more
>
> 4 eggs
>
> 8 thin slices ham, optional
>
> 12 or 16 paper-thin slices Parmesan cheese

1. Poach or steam the asparagus in or over boiling salted water until it is bright green and just tender, 3 to 7 minutes, depending on its thickness. Meanwhile, put 4 tablespoons of the butter in a small saucepan and turn the heat to low.

2. Add at least 2 tablespoons butter to a large skillet, preferably nonstick, and turn the heat to medium. When the butter melts, crack the eggs into the skillet and cook, sprinkling with salt and pepper and adjusting the heat as necessary, until the whites are no longer runny, about 5 minutes.

3. Drain the asparagus when it is done and divide among 4 plates. Turn off the heat under the butter the moment it begins to turn brown; if the eggs are not quite ready, keep it warm over the lowest possible heat.

4. Top the asparagus with a portion of ham if you're using it, then a fried egg, then a drizzle of the browned butter, and finally a few slices of Parmesan. Serve immediately.

BEANS (LEGUMES)

If cereals and grasses—think wheat and rice—provide the human race with the bulk of its caloric intake, legumes are the next most important plant family. They are also, arguably, our chief source of protein. Legumes are the edible fruits or seeds of a range of shrubs, trees, and plants that are members of the Fabaceae family, including peas, beans, and lentils, as well as other not immediately apparent relatives, like tamarind, fenugreek, licorice, and carob.

Most parts of the world have their own star legume (often matched with a particular starch). East Asia obviously favors soybeans (which can be the familiar beige or black), not only as soy sauce but in soy milk, tofu, miso, and edamame. From the southern coast of Europe to the Middle East, lentils, peas, and chickpeas are most popular. France is associated with pale-green flageolets and much of the rest of Europe with favas. Red beans, kidney beans, and white beans are all indigenous to the New World. Africa grows cowpeas (and peanuts, a legume). And India draws from everywhere—there is hardly a legume that is not eaten in this largely vegetarian country and hardly a meal that does not contain some form of dal (page 433).

There is more than just culinary synergy between legumes and cereals. The relatively high protein content of legumes, when matched with carbohydrate-rich cereals and grasses, makes for a nutritionally balanced and healthy meal (providing "complete" protein, meaning all the essential amino acids).

If you think legumes are one-dimensional, consider how different cultures treat the same bean. In the south of France, chickpeas are ground into flour to make socca. In Italy, the flour is used to make a kind of polenta, which may be fried (page 530), and the whole beans are included in stews, braises, and pastas. In the Middle East, they're ground with garlic, lemon, and sesame to create hummus (page 19) or loosely bound and fried for falafel (page 42). In India, they're stewed as dal, or ground into flour and turned into little fried dumplings that are served in yogurt (page 435).

Cooking beans is easy. The timing, however, is difficult, largely because the age of the beans strongly in-

fluences how much they cook. (The older they are, the drier and the longer they take to soften.) In general, fresh beans and peas cook quickly, and many, like green beans and sugar snap peas, don't necessarily have to be cooked at all. Lentils cook more quickly than most beans and may be done in as little as twenty minutes.

Dried beans and peas are usually cooked in water to cover for a long enough period to tenderize them without making them mushy—canned peas and beans are about as mushy as you'd ever want your legumes to be. Many people advocate presoaking beans for several hours—or longer—and, while this does shorten cooking time, if I fail to plan that far in advance, I just allow extra cooking time.

Many, many dried legumes can be substituted for one another, if imperfectly (I make what I consider appropriate suggestions in most recipes). Though the best lentils (lentilles du Puy and their ilk) are arguably unique, all lentils (and other pulses, like split peas) can be used interchangeably in most recipes. Similarly, all the dried North American legumes, whether white, red, pink, or spotted, will work in most recipes. The results will be different, but usually good (size and age will affect cooking time more than color).

TAMARIND POD

Cooked Chickpeas or Other Legumes ■ ▨

MAKES **6 TO 8 SERVINGS**

TIME **AT LEAST 2 HOURS, LARGELY UNATTENDED, PLUS SOAKING TIME**

Like all dried beans, chickpeas are far better when you cook them yourself than when you simply open a can. But unlike lentils, split peas, and even to some extent white and red beans, you must plan ahead to use chickpeas in other dishes. Overnight soaking reduces the cooking time somewhat, as does a quick boil and a shorter soak; but mostly the cooking takes time, unless you use a pressure cooker.

Once done, chickpeas can be stored in their cooking liquid (this is another unusual aspect of chickpeas; their cooking liquid is delicious), covered and refrigerated, for a few days or frozen indefinitely.

Other legumes you can prepare this way: this procedure can be followed for any legume, but most will cook faster than the chickpeas.

1 pound dried chickpeas, rinsed and picked over
Salt to taste

1. Soak the chickpeas overnight or for as long as possible or boil for a couple of minutes and soak for a couple of hours. Or simply cover with water and start cooking.
2. Put in a medium-to-large pot (they will triple in size) with water to cover and bring to a boil over medium-high heat. Skim any foam that forms on the surface and adjust the heat so the mixture simmers; cover partially to reduce evaporation. Stir every 15 minutes or so, adding water as necessary. Cook until the chickpeas are tender, about 2 hours, then salt the water and cook for a few minutes more.
3. Drain excess liquid. The best way to store is in enough liquid to keep them moist, refrigerated for up to a couple days, frozen for up to a couple of weeks.

Chickpeas or Other Legumes with Aromatic Vegetables. Once the chickpeas begin to get tender, add 1 onion, peeled and quartered; 1 carrot, broken in half; 1 celery stalk; a couple of garlic cloves, peeled; and a few fresh thyme sprigs (or pinches of dried). Remove these vegetables when the chickpeas are done.

Black Beans with Soy JAPAN, KOREA ■ ▨
MAKES **4 OR MORE SERVINGS**
TIME **ABOUT 2 HOURS, PLUS SOAKING TIME**

Soy-glazed black beans are a common panchan—little side dish—in Korea, but they're also served in Japan; in both countries they're usually served at room temperature. They are about as far from the cumin- and garlic-laced black beans of Mexico (see page 438) as they could be. In Asia, they're made with black soybeans, which are larger and rounder than the more common black ("turtle") beans you see everywhere. But you can use either. Serve this as if it were a little salad, with any Korean or Japanese cooked dish.

$^1/_2$ pound dried black beans, rinsed and picked over
$^1/_4$ cup sugar, or more to taste
2 tablespoons mirin or a little more sugar
$^1/_4$ cup soy sauce
2 tablespoons dark sesame oil
1 tablespoon sesame seeds

1. If time allows, soak the beans for several hours or overnight, then drain. (If not, proceed, but expect cooking time to be somewhat longer.) Place in a pot, add water to cover, and bring to a boil over medium-high heat. Partially cover, adjust the heat so the mixture simmers steadily, and cook, stirring occasionally, until the beans are nearly tender and most of the water has evaporated, at least an hour and probably more. (Add water as necessary to keep the beans covered, but bear in mind that eventually you will want no water at all, so don't drown them.)
2. Add the sugar, mirin, and soy sauce and raise the heat a bit. Continue to cook, stirring frequently now, until the beans are glazed and still firm, not quite as tender as you're used to; leave them quite

moist (the soy sauce will burn if the mixture dries out). Stir in the sesame oil.

3. You can serve the beans immediately, at room temperature, or chilled. Just before serving, toast the sesame seeds in a small dry skillet over medium heat, shaking the pan frequently until the seeds color slightly. Sprinkle the beans with the seeds and serve.

Edamame JAPAN ▨

MAKES **4 SERVINGS**

TIME **10 MINUTES**

Edamame—fresh soybeans—are rarely seen "fresh" in this country, but they're now sold frozen at most supermarkets. You buy them still in their pods and pop the little beans out to eat them (the pods are inedible). Eaten as a little snack at the table or as a side dish, with no more than salt, they're rather great.

Coarse salt

1 pound edamame

1. Bring a pot of water to a boil and add salt. Add the edamame (still frozen is fine) and cook until bright green and tender, 5 to 10 minutes.
2. Drain, sprinkle with coarse salt, and serve.

Dal Slow-Cooked Lentils or Other Legumes

INDIA ■

MAKES **8 OR MORE SERVINGS**

TIME **1 TO 1½ HOURS, PLUS SOAKING TIME IF DESIRED**

One of the staples of the subcontinent, dal is not only daily fare but something to be relished with many meals. Serve this with Basic Long-Grain Rice (page 506) or any pilaf (pages 513–514).

If you have the time (and forethought) to soak the lentils, they'll cook more quickly, but it is far from necessary.

Other legumes you can prepare this way: chickpeas (far longer cooking time), red beans.

1 pound dried lentils or small beans, rinsed and
picked over

1 onion, roughly chopped

One 2-inch piece fresh ginger, peeled and minced

3 garlic cloves, minced

1 tablespoon curry powder, preferably homemade
(pages 592–593)

2 teaspoons ground cumin

2 dried red chiles or hot red pepper flakes or cayenne
to taste

3 or 4 tomatoes, cored and roughly chopped,
optional

Salt and black pepper to taste

1. Combine all the ingredients except salt and pepper in a large pot, along with water to cover. Bring to a boil over high heat and adjust the heat so the mixture simmers steadily but not violently. Cook, stirring occasionally, until the lentils are soft, about an hour.
2. Season to taste and serve or cover and refrigerate for up to several days before reheating.

Dal with Butter and Cream. The ne plus ultra of dal and proof that the French have no monopoly on adding butter to legumes: About 10 minutes before serving, stir in 1½ sticks of butter (you can use less if you want, but it won't be the same) and 1 cup heavy cream. Cook to heat through and melt the butter, then adjust the seasoning and serve.

Dal with Shrimp. As the dal is finishing, cook $\frac{1}{2}$ pound shrimp, peeled and cut into bite-sized pieces, in 3 tablespoons butter or neutral oil, like grapeseed or corn, until cooked through (and even lightly browned). Pour the shrimp and their cooking liquid into the dal and serve.

Dal with Coconut INDIA ■
MAKES **8 OR MORE SERVINGS**
TIME **1 TO 1½ HOURS**

A very simple but flavorful dal, one as successful with chickpeas or beans as with lentils. Serve this with Basic Long-Grain Rice (page 506) or any pilaf (pages 513–514).

If you have the time (and forethought) to soak the lentils, they'll cook more quickly, but it is far from necessary.

Other legumes you can prepare this way: red beans.

> 1 pound dried lentils or small beans, rinsed and picked over
>
> 1 cup unsweetened shredded coconut or 1 can coconut milk, or 1½ cups homemade coconut milk (page 584)
>
> ½ cup palm or brown sugar, or to taste
>
> Salt and black pepper to taste

1. Combine all the ingredients except salt and pepper in a large pot, along with water to cover. Bring to a boil over high heat and adjust the heat so the mixture simmers steadily but not violently. Cook, stirring occasionally, until the lentils are soft, about an hour.
2. Season to taste and serve or cover and refrigerate for up to several days before reheating.

Black-Eyed Peas with Coconut Milk
INDIA ■
MAKES **4 SERVINGS**
TIME **AT LEAST 1 HOUR, PLUS SOAKING TIME**

More complicated than the preceding recipe, this sweet, spicy, unusual preparation is one I adore. You can make it with other legumes, of course, but black-eyed peas are traditional, and they cook more quickly than most others. (If you can find them frozen—or, better still, fresh—they'll cook very quickly.)

Other legumes you can prepare this way: lentils, chickpeas, black beans, red beans.

> 2 cups dried black-eyed peas, rinsed and picked over
>
> 2 tablespoons corn, grapeseed, or other neutral oil
>
> 1 tablespoon minced garlic
>
> 1 tablespoon peeled and minced fresh ginger
>
> ¼ teaspoon cayenne, or to taste (this dish is not normally made fiery hot)
>
> 1 tablespoon tamarind paste, homemade (page 585) or store-bought, or fresh lime juice
>
> 2 cups coconut milk, homemade (page 584) or canned
>
> Salt and black pepper to taste

1. Soak the beans for several hours or overnight, then drain. If you have no time to soak at all, that's okay too—just allow for more cooking time. Drain the beans and cook in water to cover until tender, usually 30 to 60 minutes. Drain.
2. Put the oil in a large skillet or saucepan over medium-high heat. A minute later, add the garlic and ginger and cook, stirring, until the garlic colors, about a minute. Add the beans, then the cayenne, tamarind (if you're using lime juice, hold it out until the last minute), and coconut milk. Bring to a boil, then adjust the heat so the mixture simmers.
3. Cook until most of the coconut milk is absorbed and the beans are very soft, another 20 minutes or

so. Taste and adjust the seasoning, then serve or cover and refrigerate for up to a couple of days before reheating gently.

Chickpea Dumplings in Yogurt Sauce INDIA ■

MAKES **4 SERVINGS**

TIME **1 HOUR OR MORE**

One of the best vegetarian dishes of India, the chickpea dumpling is the equal of those made of meat without mimicking them, and the yogurt sauce is creamy and delicious. Some people soak the chickpea dumplings in water after frying them, which gives them a lovely and delicate texture; others leave them crisp, adding them to the sauce at the last minute. The choice is yours; I enjoy the crisp version more but happily eat and make both.

You can buy chickpea flour and hing (asafetida, page 10) at any store selling Indian ingredients and at many Middle Eastern stores as well.

One word about the preparation: Skilled cooks can make the sauce first, then the dumplings, or mix the dumpling batter, then turn to the sauce, then fry the dumplings while the sauce is simmering. The level of activity required to do this is somewhat frenetic, but if you are comfortable with kitchen multitasking, it will work out.

2 cups chickpea flour

Salt and black pepper to taste

¼ teaspoon cayenne

Pinch of asafetida (hing)

1½ teaspoons ground turmeric

1 teaspoon ground coriander

½ teaspoon baking soda

2½ cups yogurt

Oil for deep-frying

1 small dried chile

1 teaspoon cumin seeds

1 teaspoon fennel seeds

1 cinnamon stick

1 teaspoon coriander seeds or more ground coriander

1 large onion, sliced

Chopped fresh cilantro leaves for garnish

1. Put 1 cup of the chickpea flour, some salt and pepper, the cayenne, asafetida, 1 teaspoon of the turmeric, the coriander, baking soda, and ½ cup of the yogurt in a food processor and pulse a few times to combine; scrape the sides of the container if necessary. With the machine running, gradually add warm water, a tablespoon or so at a time, until the mixture forms a smooth paste. Process, stopping to scrape the sides of the container if necessary, until the mixture is smooth and light.

2. Add at least 2 inches of oil to a pot (a narrow pot will allow you to use less oil, but a broader one will allow you to cook more dumplings at once). Turn the heat to medium-high and bring the oil to about 350°F (a pinch of the chickpea batter will sink about halfway to the bottom before bouncing back up to the top when the oil is ready). Drop in

ASAFETIDA (HING)

the batter by teaspoons (it's easiest to pick up a bit of the batter with one teaspoon and scrape it off with another). Do not crowd; turn the dumplings once or twice and cook them until nicely browned, just 2 or 3 minutes. As the dumplings finish, transfer them to a bed of paper towels to drain.

3. Now make the sauce: Combine the remaining chickpea flour and yogurt in a blender with 1 cup warm water; turn on the blender and process until smooth. Combine this mixture in the blender if it is large or in a bowl with another quart of water.

4. Put 2 tablespoons oil into a saucepan or deep skillet and turn the heat to medium. A minute later, add the chile, cumin, fennel, cinnamon, coriander, and remaining $1/2$ teaspoon turmeric and cook, stirring, for about 30 seconds. Add the onion and cook, stirring occasionally, until it is soft, about 5 minutes. Turn the heat to low and add the yogurt–chickpea flour mixture, along with a large pinch of salt. Cover and simmer for about 20 minutes. (You can prepare the dish several hours in advance to this point; cover and set aside until you're ready to eat.)

5. Taste and adjust the sauce's seasoning; it should be mild with a touch of heat and quite fragrant. Fish out the cinnamon stick and the chile (you can eat the other spices). Add the dumplings and re-cover; cook just until they are heated through, 5 to 10 minutes. Garnish with the cilantro and serve.

Feijoada Spicy Beans, Goan Style INDIA ■

MAKES **4 SERVINGS**

TIME **ABOUT 2 HOURS, PLUS SOAKING TIME**

In Brazil, feijoada is a meat dish with beans. In Goa, another former colony of Portugal, it is a bean dish in which meat is optional. I have been served and pre-pared it with both kidney beans and black-eyed peas and prefer it with the latter.

To serve more people, simply double the beans and increase the remaining ingredients slightly or add meat; it won't be much more effort.

Serve over rice and make this entirely in advance if you like; it will keep, refrigerated, for a couple of days.

Other legumes you can prepare this way: kidney or other red beans, black beans.

$1/2$ pound dried black-eyed peas or kidney beans, rinsed and picked over

2 large onions, peeled

6 garlic cloves, peeled

1 small dried chile or 1 teaspoon hot red pepper flakes, or to taste

One 1-inch piece fresh ginger, peeled and roughly chopped

2 tablespoons corn, grapeseed, or other neutral oil

Salt and black pepper to taste

1 tablespoon Fragrant Curry Powder (page 593) or any mild, good-quality curry powder

2 large tomatoes, cored, seeded, and roughly chopped (canned are fine; use about $1^1/2$ cups)

1 cup coconut milk, homemade (page 584) or canned

4 Italian or other large sausages, optional

1 tablespoon tamarind paste, homemade (page 585) or store-bought, or fresh lime juice to taste

1. If time allows, soak dried beans for several hours overnight or boil them in water to cover for a minute, then soak for a couple of hours. If you have not soaked the beans, rinse them and put them in a pot with water to cover; bring to a boil and simmer while you prepare the remaining ingredients. Otherwise, drain and add them in step 3.

2. Combine the onions, garlic, chile, and ginger in a food processor and grind until pasty. Put the oil in a large deep saucepan or flameproof casserole with

a lid over medium heat and add the onion mixture, along with some salt and pepper and the curry powder. Cook, stirring occasionally, until the onion begins to brown, 5 to 10 minutes.

3. Add the tomatoes and coconut milk and bring to a boil. Whether you've soaked or parboiled the beans, drain them and add them to the simmering mixture, along with enough water to barely submerge the beans. Partially cover and adjust the heat so the mixture simmers steadily but not violently. Cook until the beans are tender, 30 to 90 minutes.

4. If you are using the sausages, cut them into 1-inch chunks and brown them at any time while the beans are cooking. Stir into the bean mixture. Just before serving, add the tamarind. Taste and adjust the seasoning and serve.

Rajma Spicy Red Beans INDIA ■

MAKES **6 TO 8 SERVINGS**

TIME **ABOUT 2 HOURS, PLUS SOAKING TIME**

Chickpeas and lentils are the staple legumes of India, but red beans are cooked from time to time and, typically, done in an extremely flavorful manner. You can add meat to this preparation, which is already quite a bit like chili.

Like Dal with Butter and Cream (page 433), this is excellent with some butter (and cream, if you like) stirred in toward the end of cooking.

Make it entirely in advance if you like; it will keep, refrigerated, for a couple of days. Serve with rice.

Other legumes you can prepare this way: chickpeas, black beans.

1 pound dried red beans, any kind, rinsed and picked over

¹/₂ teaspoon cayenne, or to taste

2 tablespoons corn, grapeseed, or other neutral oil

1 tablespoon peeled and minced fresh ginger

1 tablespoon minced garlic

1 teaspoon fennel seeds

1 teaspoon ground cinnamon

Pinch of ground cloves

1 tablespoon ground cardamom

1 bay leaf

1 teaspoon ground turmeric

2 cups chopped tomatoes (canned are fine)

Salt to taste

1 tablespoon garam masala (page 594) or curry powder, preferably homemade (pages 592–593), or to taste

1. If time allows, soak dried beans for several hours or overnight, then drain. (If not, proceed, but expect cooking times to be somewhat longer.) Place the drained beans in a large pot with water to cover and the cayenne and cook until they are just about tender; this will take 1 to 2 hours, depending on their freshness and whether you soaked them. Continue to cook while you proceed to step 2.

2. Put the oil in a wide skillet or flameproof casserole over medium heat. Add the ginger, garlic, fennel, cinnamon, cloves, cardamom, bay leaf, and turmeric and cook, stirring, for about a minute. Add the tomatoes and cook, stirring occasionally, until they break up a bit, 5 minutes or so.

3. Drain the beans, reserving a little of their cooking liquid, and add them to the tomato sauce, along with a large pinch of salt. Continue to cook until the beans are fully tender, probably less than 15 minutes longer, adding a little of the bean-cooking liquid if necessary. When the beans are done, add the garam masala, taste and adjust the seasoning, and serve.

Black Beans with Garlic and Cumin

MEXICO ■

MAKES **8 OR MORE SERVINGS**

TIME **ABOUT 2 HOURS, PLUS SOAKING TIME**

The familiar version, served in Latin American restaurants everywhere. Leave the beans soupy if you plan to serve them over rice. Allow plenty of time, because black beans can take a while, and they're best served quite soft. But by all means prepare them in advance if you can and reheat before serving.

Epazote is a typical addition to black beans in Mexico, and it contributes a distinctive flavor, but the beans are just fine without it.

Other legumes you can prepare this way: red beans, white beans.

> **1 pound dried black beans, rinsed and picked over**
>
> **Several fresh epazote sprigs or 1 teaspoon dried, optional**
>
> **2 garlic cloves, peeled and crushed**
>
> **1 tablespoon ground cumin, or to taste**
>
> **Salt and black pepper to taste**
>
> **1 teaspoon minced garlic**
>
> **¹/₂ cup minced onion**

1. If time allows, soak the beans overnight or for several hours in water to cover, then drain. (If not, proceed but expect cooking time to be somewhat longer.) Combine with water to cover in a pot over medium-high heat. When the mixture boils, add the epazote if you're using it, crushed garlic, and cumin, partially cover, and adjust the heat so the mixture simmers steadily. Cook, stirring infrequently, until the beans are tender and most of the water is evaporated, at least an hour and probably more; add water as necessary to keep the beans covered.

2. When the beans are tender, add salt, pepper, more cumin if you like, and the minced garlic. Cook for another 5 minutes, then stir in the onion. Taste, adjust the seasoning, and serve.

Refried Beans MEXICO

MAKES **4 SERVINGS**

TIME **ABOUT 1¹/₂ HOURS, PLUS SOAKING TIME**

You can use precooked (or canned) beans here, and the total time will be a mere twenty minutes, but if you cook dried beans with the proper spicing to begin with, the ultimate dish will be somewhat better. The traditional medium for frying beans is lard and with good reason; it's delicious. But you can also make wonderful refried beans with a combination of cumin and well-browned onion.

Other legumes you can prepare this way: red beans are standard; neither black nor white beans are as common, but they work well.

> **¹/₂ pound dried red beans, rinsed and picked over**
>
> **Several fresh epazote sprigs, or 1 teaspoon dried, optional**
>
> **2 garlic cloves, peeled and crushed**
>
> **2 tablespoons ground cumin, or to taste**
>
> **Salt and black pepper to taste**
>
> **1 teaspoon minced garlic**
>
> **¹/₄ cup corn, grapeseed, or other neutral oil**
>
> **1 cup chopped onion**
>
> **Salt and black pepper to taste**
>
> **¹/₄ teaspoon cayenne, plus more if desired**

1. If time allows, soak the beans overnight or for several hours in water to cover, then drain. (If not, proceed, but expect cooking time to be somewhat longer.) Combine with water to cover in a pot over medium-high heat. When the mixture boils, add the epazote if you're using it, crushed garlic, and 1 tablespoon of the cumin, partially cover, and ad-

just the heat so the mixture simmers steadily. Cook, stirring occasionally, until the beans are tender and most of the water has evaporated, at least an hour and probably more; add water as necessary to keep the beans covered.

2. When the beans are tender, add salt, pepper, and the minced garlic. Put the oil in a large skillet, preferably nonstick, and turn the heat to medium. When the oil is hot, add the onion and cook, stirring, until it is golden brown, about 10 minutes.

3. Add the remaining cumin and cook, stirring, for 1 minute more. Add the beans and mash with a large fork or potato masher. Continue to cook and mash, stirring, until the beans are more or less broken up (some remaining chunks are fine).

4. Season with salt and pepper, add the cayenne and more cumin if you like, and serve.

Traditional Refried Beans. Substitute ½ cup lard for the oil and reserve the onion and second tablespoon of cumin. Add the beans to the hot lard. When they are nicely mashed, stir in the onion and cumin and cook for 5 minutes more, stirring frequently. Season as directed and serve.

Lentils and Rice with Caramelized Onions MIDDLE EAST

MAKES **4 TO 6 SERVINGS**

TIME **1 HOUR**

A slightly labor-intensive but wonderful vegetarian dish that, with its contrasting textures and slight sweetness, makes a terrific main course or a first-rate side dish.

Other legumes you can prepare this way: split yellow or green peas.

3 large onions, thinly sliced

¼ cup extra virgin olive oil

Salt and black pepper to taste

2 cups dried brown or green lentils, rinsed and picked over

1 cup long-grain rice

1. Put the onions in a large skillet with a lid and turn the heat to medium. Cover and cook, stirring occasionally, until the onions are dry and almost sticking to the pan, about 20 minutes. Add the oil and a large pinch of salt and cook, stirring occasionally, until the onions brown, another 10 to 15 minutes.

2. Meanwhile, put the lentils in a 4-quart or other medium saucepan and add 1 quart water; turn the heat to medium-high, then cover and cook, stirring occasionally, for about 20 minutes. Turn off the heat if the lentils become tender before the onions are done.

3. Coarsely chop half the onions, making just a few passes with a knife. Add these and the rice to the lentils and stir. Continue cooking until both the rice and lentils are tender and all the water is absorbed, another 15 minutes or so. If the mixture begins to dry out before it is completely cooked, add another ½ cup water, repeating as necessary. When the mixture is done, taste and adjust the seasoning; keep warm over low heat.

4. Meanwhile, continue to cook the onions left in the skillet over medium-high heat, stirring frequently, until they are a dark brown and threatening to burn, about 15 minutes. Remove with a slotted spoon and drain on paper towels.

5. Garnish the rice and lentils with the caramelized onions and serve.

Lentils with Bulgur MIDDLE EAST ■ ■

MAKES **4 TO 6 SERVINGS**

TIME **1 1/2 HOURS, MOSTLY UNATTENDED, PLUS SOAKING TIME**

A relative of tabbouleh, but (usually) served hot and made with lentils. This is a good vegetarian main course, but also a fine side dish at a Middle Eastern or other meal. The onion-mint garnish is terrific stuff.

1/2 cup dried brown or green lentils, rinsed and picked over

5 tablespoons extra virgin olive oil

1 teaspoon minced garlic

2 jalapeños or other fresh chiles, stemmed, seeded, and minced, or to taste

1 ripe medium tomato, chopped

1 teaspoon ground cumin or 1/4 teaspoon ground allspice

1 cup medium bulgur

About 3 cups chicken, beef, or vegetable stock, preferably homemade (page 160 or 162), or water

1 large onion, cut in half and thinly sliced

1/2 cup chopped fresh mint leaves

1. If time allows, soak the lentils in cold water to cover for an hour or more (overnight is fine). Drain.
2. Put 2 tablespoons of the oil in a large deep saucepan over medium heat. A minute later, add the garlic and cook until fragrant, another minute or so. Add the jalapeños, tomato, and cumin and cook until the tomato is soft, 2 or 3 minutes.
3. Add the bulgur and cook, stirring, for 3 to 4 minutes, then add the stock and lentils. Bring to a boil, then cover and adjust the heat so the mixture simmers steadily; cook for 20 to 30 minutes, or until the lentils and bulgur are tender and all the liquid is absorbed. If the mixture threatens to dry out, add another 1/2 cup liquid and continue cooking;

if the mixture is too wet, raise the heat a bit and cook, uncovered and stirring, until it dries out.
4. While the lentil mixture is cooking, add the remaining 3 tablespoons oil to a skillet and cook the onion over medium heat, stirring occasionally, until deep brown, caramelized, and on the verge of blackening, at least 20 minutes. Stir in most of the mint and remove from the heat.
5. When the lentil-bulgur mixture is done, garnish it with the onion and remaining mint and serve.

Mashed White Beans GREECE ■ ■

MAKES **4 SERVINGS**

TIME **ABOUT 1 1/2 HOURS, PLUS SOAKING TIME**

An unexpected and even elegant side dish (I love that it can also be served cold, as a dip). You can make this with leftover cooked beans, canned beans, or frozen beans—in which case it will take 10 minutes—but if you cook dried beans this way, with these seasonings, they'll be sensational.

Other legumes you can prepare this way: chick peas (allow for longer cooking time), flageolets.

1/2 pound dried navy or other white beans, rinsed and picked over

1 medium onion, chopped

1 medium carrot, chopped

2 garlic cloves, peeled

1 teaspoon fresh thyme leaves or a pinch of dried

1/3 cup extra virgin olive oil

1 teaspoon minced garlic

Salt and black pepper to taste

Fresh lemon juice to taste

Chopped fresh parsley leaves for garnish

1. If time allows, soak the beans overnight or for several hours, then drain. (If not, proceed, but expect cooking time to be somewhat longer.) Combine the beans with the onion, carrot, garlic cloves, and thyme with water to cover in a pot over medium-high heat. Bring to a boil, then partially cover and adjust the heat so the mixture simmers steadily. Cook until the beans are very tender, at least 45 minutes and possibly twice that long; add water as necessary.

2. Drain the beans, reserving their cooking liquid. Cool slightly, then puree in a food mill or food processor, using only as much of the reserved liquid as necessary to make a smooth puree.

3. Put about half the oil in a nonstick skillet over medium heat. Add the beans and stir, adding the minced garlic along with salt and pepper to taste. When the mixture is smooth and hot and the rawness of the garlic is gone, turn off the heat. Stir in the remaining olive oil and at least a tablespoon of lemon juice. Taste and adjust the seasoning, garnish, and serve.

Mashed White Beans in the Style of Northern France. Also great with roasted meats: In step 3, substitute 4 tablespoons ($^{1}/_{2}$ stick) butter for the olive oil and 1 tablespoon minced shallot for the garlic. Stir in $^{1}/_{4}$ cup heavy cream in place of the lemon juice.

White Beans with Garlic ITALY ■ ■
MAKES **4 SERVINGS**

TIME **1 TO 2 HOURS, LARGELY UNATTENDED, PLUS SOAKING TIME**

One of the most basic, simple, and delicious bean dishes. When my kids learned how to make this, they would open a can of beans, heat it with olive oil and garlic, and add some salt. Period. My way is a tiny bit more sophisticated, but not much. These are great on their own but also fantastic as a side dish with grilled meats of any kind.

As with all legumes, if you have a chance to soak the beans ahead of time, they will cook a little more quickly, but it isn't essential.

About $^{1}/_{2}$ pound dried white beans, rinsed and picked over, or 2 to 3 cups canned

1 teaspoon fresh thyme leaves or a pinch of dried or

1 tablespoon chopped fresh sage or dried to taste

Salt and black pepper to taste

2 teaspoons minced garlic

2 tablespoons extra virgin olive oil, or to taste

1. If time allows, soak dried beans for several hours or overnight, then drain. (If not, proceed, but expect cooking time to be somewhat longer.) Place the drained beans in a large pot with water to cover. Turn the heat to high and bring to a boil. Add the herb and partially cover; adjust the heat so the mixture simmers steadily.

2. Cook, stirring occasionally, until the beans are tender, about an hour. Add about $^{1}/_{2}$ teaspoon salt and some pepper. Continue to cook, adding water if necessary, until the beans are quite soft, another 15 to 30 minutes or so.

3. If the mixture is very soupy, raise the heat a bit and cook off any remaining liquid. When the beans are moist but not soupy, add the garlic and cook, stirring occasionally, for another 5 minutes or so. Add the olive oil, taste and adjust the seasoning, and serve or refrigerate for up to 3 days before reheating. (Or add water to cover and freeze for up to a month.)

Aromatic White Beans with Chicken Stock and Tomatoes FRANCE ■

MAKES **4 SERVINGS**

TIME **1 TO 2 HOURS, LARGELY UNATTENDED, PLUS SOAKING TIME**

The addition of stock boosts this simple bean preparation (not much different from the preceding one in technique) to another level, and it's a good one. This is a more elegant bean dish, at home with any good dish of roast meat, like Lechon Asado (page 375) or Grilled or Roast Lamb with Herbs (page 358). As with all legumes, if you have a chance to soak the beans ahead of time, they will cook a little more quickly, but it isn't essential.

Other legumes you can prepare this way: chickpeas (allow for longer cooking time), flageolets (the traditional French accompaniment to leg of lamb).

About $1/2$ pound dried white beans, rinsed and picked over

About 6 cups chicken stock, preferably homemade (page 160)

1 teaspoon fresh thyme leaves or a pinch of dried

1 tablespoon minced garlic

1 medium carrot, finely chopped

1 celery stalk, finely chopped

1 medium onion, finely chopped

Salt and black pepper to taste

2 medium tomatoes, cored

2 tablespoons butter, optional

1. If time allows, soak dried beans for several hours or overnight. (If not, proceed, but expect cooking time to be somewhat longer.) Place the drained beans in a large pot with all but a cup of the stock and the thyme, garlic, carrot, celery, and onion; add water if necessary (or more stock, if you have it) to cover. Turn the heat to high and bring to a boil; partially cover and adjust the heat so the mixture simmers steadily.

2. Cook, stirring occasionally, until the beans are tender, about an hour. Add about $1/2$ teaspoon salt and some pepper. Continue to cook, adding water if necessary, until the beans are quite soft, another 15 to 30 minutes or so.

3. Add the remaining cup of stock and raise the heat so the mixture bubbles energetically. Cut the tomatoes in half through their equators, then, over the sink, shake and squeeze them to rid them of their seeds and some of their juices. Chop finely and add to the beans. Cook, stirring occasionally, until the beans are moist but not soupy, 10 to 15 minutes. Taste and adjust the seasoning, then stir in the butter if you're using it and serve or refrigerate for up to 3 days before reheating and adding the butter. (Or add water to cover and freeze for up to a month.)

BEETS

We now see golden beets, white beets, and candy-striped beets, but there's little difference in flavor. In fact, fresh beets are among the most reliable vegetables, sweet at any size and—unlike turnips and parsnips—rarely becoming woody as they grow larger.

Roasted Beets ITALY ■ ■

MAKES **4 SERVINGS**

TIME **AT LEAST 1 HOUR**

Most vegetables can be prepared with little more than olive oil and salt, but few are as rewarding as beets, which can be stunningly delicious when done this way. One key is to bake them—which dries out their flesh a little bit and concentrates their flavor—rather than boil them. (Think of the difference between a baked and a boiled potato.) It takes some time, but it is easy and reduces staining.

Other vegetables you can prepare this way: carrots or parsnips (peel before roasting), turnips or rutabagas; cooking time will vary.

4 medium beets, a little over a pound

Extra virgin olive oil

Salt and black pepper to taste

Chopped fresh parsley leaves for garnish

1. Preheat the oven to 375°F. Wash the beets well and put them in a roasting pan, still wet; cover the pan with foil. Bake until soft, about 45 minutes (use a thin-bladed knife to pierce through the foil and into the beets to test for doneness). Remove the beets, then allow them to cool a bit.

2. When the beets are cool enough to handle, peel them (the peels will slip off easily), then slice or dice them, as you prefer. Toss with olive oil, salt, and pepper, garnish with the parsley, and serve warm or at room temperature.

Pkhali Beets with Walnut-Garlic Sauce
RUSSIA ■ ▩ ▩

MAKES **6 OR MORE SERVINGS**

TIME **10 MINUTES (WITH PRECOOKED VEGETABLES)**

Made throughout the Balkans, into Russia and Turkey, this is essentially a chopped vegetable—it can be almost anything—combined with a strong version of Tarator (page 600). It can be eaten alone or used as a spread or as a dip for pita. Most people let it sit for a few hours before serving, which allows the garlic to mellow and the flavors to marry. This isn't a bad idea, but if you're in a hurry, plunge right in.

Other vegetables you can prepare this way: eggplant (roasted or quickly boiled, as in Eggplant Salad with Mustard-Miso Dressing, page 185); red beans, cooked until tender; green beans; spinach or other greens.

1 cup walnuts, toasted

2 garlic cloves, peeled

1 onion, peeled and quartered

1 teaspoon cayenne

¹/₂ teaspoon ground coriander

2 tablespoons red wine vinegar

Salt to taste

1¹/₂ pounds cooked beets, finely chopped

1. Place the walnuts, garlic, onion, cayenne, coriander, and vinegar in a food processor. Process until the mixture is smooth, adding a little water if necessary to achieve the consistency of a thick sauce. Taste and season with salt.

2. Thoroughly stir the beets and walnut sauce together and serve with pita or other bread or cover and refrigerate for up to a day.

CABBAGE

Cabbage belongs to a huge family of vegetables that includes broccoli, cauliflower, mustard, and kale, all of which have fairly strong flavors. When it comes to cabbage itself, the head cabbages and the leafy kind, like bok choy and Napa, are pretty much interchangeable. Red cabbage is often the odd man out, not so much because of its flavor (it's hard to tell the difference between the taste of red and that of ordinary green) but because its color tends to overwhelm that of any other ingredient.

Oshinko Pickled Cabbage JAPAN ■ ■

MAKES **ABOUT 10 SERVINGS**

TIME **2 TO 3 DAYS, LARGELY UNATTENDED**

Essentially a simplified sauerkraut and a very light pickle. Use good-quality soy sauce and serve this as a side dish with Japanese or other Asian food. Do not try to make this in very hot weather; fifty or sixty degrees is ideal.

Other vegetables you can prepare this way: any mixture of vegetables, as in the variation.

One 2-pound head of Napa cabbage

¹⁄₄ cup coarse salt

1 small dried chile, seeded and minced

Good-quality soy sauce, optional

1. Trim the cabbage of hard parts and discard any discolored leaves; chop the rest into pieces no bigger than 2 inches along any dimension. Toss in a nonmetal bowl with the salt and chile.
2. Cover with plastic wrap and a plate that will fit inside the bowl; weight the plate as well as you can with cans, a rock, or a resealable plastic bag filled with water. Let sit, unrefrigerated, for a day or longer, tossing the cabbage occasionally and draining liquid as it accumulates. With each passing day, the cabbage will become softer and more translucent; you can eat it at any stage. When it reaches the stage you like, refrigerate. Serve as a small side dish, with or without soy sauce.

Mixed Pickled Vegetables. You can treat an assortment of vegetables the same way. Combine, for example, thinly sliced cucumbers, thinly sliced carrots, and peeled and thinly sliced turnips. Eggplant, onion, and radish (especially daikon), all peeled and thinly sliced, are also good. You can also add trimmed and chopped scallions, peeled and thinly sliced garlic, and/or a few slices of peeled fresh ginger to the mix.

Kimchi KOREA ■ ■

MAKES **12 SERVINGS**

TIME **3 HOURS, LARGELY UNATTENDED**

Kimchi, the world's best-known Korean ingredient, generally describes pickled vegetables, though cabbage is the most common choice. Originally a basic salt pickle, chiles were introduced in the sixteenth century, followed soon thereafter by fish or shrimp paste. Regional influences determine the level of pungency, with warmer regions producing kimchi heavily seasoned with chile powder and anchovy paste. Some take to kimchi immediately; for others it is an acquired taste. For information on nam pla (Thai fish sauce), see page 500.

If you love kimchi, you'll enjoy making this version. Even though it's quick, the results will be as good as that found at most restaurants and better than almost any version you've bought in jars. Kept refrigerated, it will last for about a week.

Dried salted shrimp are inexpensive and keep forever; you'll find them at most Asian markets.

1 head of green, Savoy, or Napa cabbage, about 2 pounds, separated into leaves

¹⁄₂ cup coarse salt, more or less

20 scallions, including most of the greens, trimmed and roughly chopped

1 tablespoon hot red pepper flakes (or use Korean co chu cara, chile powder), or to taste

¹⁄₄ cup nam pla

¹⁄₄ cup minced garlic

2 tablespoons peeled and minced or grated fresh ginger

¹⁄₄ cup sugar

3 tablespoons dried salted shrimp, optional

1. Layer the cabbage leaves in a colander, sprinkling a little salt between layers. Let sit over a bowl for at least 2 hours. When the cabbage is wilted, rinse it. Spin it dry in a salad spinner.

2. Use a wooden spoon to mix together the scallions, red pepper, nam pla, garlic, ginger, sugar, and salted shrimp. Roughly chop the cabbage and toss with the spice mixture. Serve immediately or refrigerate for up to a week; it will become stronger every day.

Chongak Kimchi. Substitute 3 pounds Korean white radish (or daikon) for the cabbage. Trim and peel the radish, then cut into 1-inch cubes. Proceed as directed.

Pa Kimchi. Omit the cabbage. Use about 30 scallions. Trim the scallions if you like (I've seen them made with and without their roots), but do not chop them. Treat them as you would the cabbage in step 1. In step 2, use kitchen string to tie the scallions together in bunches of 5. Put the bundles in a container that will hold them snugly and pour the spice mixture over them. Proceed as directed.

Braised Red Cabbage with Apples
SCANDINAVIA
MAKES **4 TO 6 SERVINGS**
TIME **ABOUT 1 HOUR**

Traditionally served throughout Scandinavia as part of the smorgasbord or Christmas dinner. The apples dissolve, leaving a sweetness that is balanced by the tartness of the vinegar. To emphasize one element or the other, add either the (sweet) jelly or the (astringent) red wine. Lovely in midwinter.

Other vegetables you can prepare this way: any cabbage, including white, Savoy, or Napa.

    4 tablespoons (1/2 stick) butter
    2 tablespoons sugar
    3 tablespoons red or white wine vinegar

    Salt and black pepper to taste
    1 medium head of red cabbage, about 2 pounds, cored
        and shredded
    2 apples, preferably Cortland or Golden Delicious, peeled,
        cored, and cut into chunks
    1/4 cup black or red currant jelly or red wine, optional

1. Combine the butter, sugar, and vinegar with a large pinch of salt and a sprinkling of pepper in a large deep skillet with a lid over medium heat. Bring to a boil.
2. Add the cabbage, stirring to coat. When the cabbage begins to glisten and soften a bit, add the apple pieces and stir. Reduce the heat to medium-low and simmer, covered, until the cabbage is soft, about 45 minutes.
3. Stir in the currant jelly or wine if you're using it. Taste and adjust the seasoning, then serve.

Braised Cabbage with Chestnuts. Omit the sugar from step 1. In step 2, substitute green cabbage for red and 1 cup peeled and roughly chopped chestnuts (page 453) for the apples. Cook until both chestnuts and cabbage are tender, as directed, then serve.

Stuffed Cabbage MIDDLE EAST ■
MAKES **8 OR MORE ROLLS, ABOUT 4 SERVINGS**
TIME **ABOUT 1 HOUR (WITH PREMADE STUFFING)**

The major difference between stuffed cabbage and most other stuffed vegetables is that cabbage is inevitably cooked in a sauce; you can use the sweet-and-sour sauce here or simply simmer the leaves in Fast, Fresh Tomato Sauce (page 606). Serve either with crusty bread or, if your filling does not have much rice, over rice.

Cabbage leaves also may be filled and stuffed exactly as you would grape leaves (page 446) and served hot or cold, again as you would grape leaves.

You will have plenty of cabbage left over after you remove the leaves for stuffing; use it in any stir-fry or in rice or soup.

Other vegetables you can prepare this way: any large leaves can be stuffed—grape leaves, collards, and turnip greens, for example.

Salt and black pepper to taste

1 medium head of green or Savoy cabbage

$1/4$ cup extra virgin olive oil

1 large onion, chopped

4 cups chopped tomatoes with their liquid (canned are fine; use the juice, too)

$1/2$ cup raisins, optional

$1/4$ cup sugar, or to taste

$1/2$ cup red wine or other good vinegar, or to taste

$1/4$ teaspoon cayenne, or to taste

1 recipe stuffing (pages 448–449)

Stock, water, or tomato juice, if needed

Chopped fresh parsley leaves for garnish

1. Bring a large pot of water to a boil and salt it. Meanwhile, use a thin-bladed sharp knife to cut a cone-shaped wedge out of the bottom of the cabbage, removing its core. Put the cabbage into the boiling water and leave it there until the outer leaves soften, at least 5 minutes or more. Remove and plunge into cold water; gently remove as many leaves as you can. Put the cabbage back in the boiling water and repeat the process until you have 12 to 15 leaves (you'll probably mess some up, so it's worth having extra). Make a V-cut in each leaf to remove the tough central stem.

2. Make the sauce so it can simmer while you stuff the cabbage leaves (or stuff them in advance): Put the olive oil in a deep skillet or flameproof casserole with a lid and turn the heat to medium. Add the onion and cook, sprinkling with salt and pepper and stirring occasionally, until softened, about 5 minutes. Add the tomatoes, raisins, sugar, vinegar, and cayenne and stir. Adjust the heat so the mixture simmers steadily and cook for about 20 minutes.

3. To stuff the cabbage leaves, put a leaf, curved side up, on a counter or cutting board. Put $1/4$ cup or so of filling in the center of the leaf, near where you cut off the stem. Fold over the sides, then roll up from the stem end, making a little package; you'll quickly get the hang of it. Don't roll too tightly—the mixture will expand as it cooks. Skewer the rolls with a toothpick or two to hold them together.

4. Taste the sauce and adjust its seasoning as necessary; it should be quite sweet and sour. If it seems very thick, add a little stock, water, or tomato juice. Carefully add the cabbage rolls, turn the heat to low, cover, and cook, undisturbed, until the leaves are tender and the rolls are hot throughout, about 30 minutes. Garnish and serve.

Stuffed Grape Leaves MIDDLE EAST ■ ■

MAKES **ABOUT 30 GRAPE LEAVES, 6 OR MORE SERVINGS**
TIME **ABOUT 1 HOUR, PLUS RESTING TIME**

I'll never forget the first time I made these; I went out with a friend to his small "vineyard"—he had a few wild grapevines growing in his backyard—and we picked the leaves and painstakingly cut the heavy veins from all of them, then blanched them and began. I've never eaten better, though canned or bottled grape leaves make the process much easier.

Unlike most stuffed vegetables, grape leaves are usually served cold. However, they can be served hot, just after cooking, topped with Avgolemono (page

596) or simply some yogurt thinned with a little water and warmed with a tablespoon or two of minced garlic and some salt and pepper.

Other vegetables you can prepare this way: cabbage leaves (see page 445).

> Salt and black pepper to taste
>
> 35 or so fresh or bottled grape leaves (about 1 jar, usually)
>
> 1 recipe stuffing (pages 448–449)
>
> 1 cup chicken stock, preferably homemade (page 160), or water
>
> Juice of 1 lemon
>
> $3/4$ cup extra virgin olive oil
>
> Chopped fresh mint or parsley leaves for garnish
>
> Lemon wedges for serving

1. Bring a large pot of water to a boil; salt it only if you're using fresh leaves. Blanch the leaves, a few at a time, for about a minute—or until they're tender—if they're fresh, just 15 seconds or so if they're bottled. Rinse under cool water. Remove any thick stems.

2. To stuff, put a leaf, vein (bottom, or dull) side up, on a counter or cutting board. Put a tablespoon or so of filling in the center of the leaf, near the stem. Fold over the sides, then roll up from the stem end, making a little package; you'll quickly get the hang of it. Don't roll too tightly—the mixture will expand as it cooks. Put each finished package on a plate, seam side down.

3. If you have any unused leaves, put them in the bottom of a wide deep skillet or flameproof casserole with a lid. Add the stock to the pot, along with a large pinch of salt and the lemon juice. Arrange the stuffed leaves in the pot, seam sides down, packing them as tightly together as is necessary; if you have to layer them, that's fine too. Drizzle about half the olive oil over all, then cover with a plate (this helps the rolls maintain their shape).

STUFFED GRAPE LEAVES

Bring to a boil, then lower the heat and cover. Cook for about 30 minutes, checking once or twice just to make sure there is still liquid in the pan (if it is running low, add a little boiling water).

4. Turn off the heat. (If you wish to serve the grape leaves hot, see the headnote.) Let cool to room temperature, then remove the rolls, put them on a plate, cover, and chill. (They may remain in the refrigerator for up to 2 days.) Drizzle with the remaining olive oil, sprinkle with a bit of pepper and mint, and serve with lemon wedges.

Meat Filling for Grape Leaves, Cabbage Leaves, Peppers, and Tomatoes MIDDLE EAST ■ ▨

MAKES **ENOUGH TO FILL 4 TO 6 LARGE TOMATOES OR**
PEPPERS, 8 OR MORE CABBAGE LEAVES, OR UP TO
30 OR SO GRAPE LEAVES

TIME **30 MINUTES**

The more-or-less standard meat filling for stuffed vegetables, made with a lot of herbs and spices. It's so delicious that you can bake the vegetables with no sauce around them, as in the recipe on page 492, or use one of the preparations on pages 445–447. You can add pine nuts and currants to this mixture if you like or make the vegetarian version that follows.

> 2 tablespoons butter or extra virgin olive oil
>
> 1 large onion, chopped
>
> Salt and black pepper to taste
>
> 1/4 cup long-grain rice
>
> 1/4 teaspoon ground allspice
>
> 1/2 teaspoon ground cumin
>
> 1/4 teaspoon ground cinnamon
>
> 3/4 pound ground lamb, preferably from the shoulder
>
> 1/2 cup chopped fresh parsley leaves
>
> 1/2 cup chopped fresh dill leaves
>
> Zest of 1 lemon, minced

1. Put the butter in a small saucepan or skillet with a lid and place over medium-high heat. When the butter melts, add the onion and a sprinkling of salt and pepper and cook, stirring occasionally, until the onion is soft but not at all browned, about 5 minutes. Add the rice and spices and cook, stirring, until the rice is glossy, about a minute. Add 1/2 cup water, cover, and turn the heat to low; cook until all the liquid is absorbed, about 15 minutes; don't worry if the rice isn't quite tender.

2. Combine the rice in a bowl with the lamb, some more salt and pepper, the herbs, and lemon zest.

(If you are stuffing tomatoes with this mixture, include the tomato pulp here too.) Use immediately or cover and refrigerate for up to a day before stuffing tomatoes, peppers, or grape or cabbage leaves.

Rice, Pine Nut, and Currant Filling for Grape Leaves, Cabbage Leaves, Peppers, and Tomatoes MIDDLE EAST ■ ▨

MAKES **ENOUGH TO FILL 4 TO 6 LARGE TOMATOES OR**
PEPPERS, 8 OR MORE CABBAGE LEAVES, OR UP TO
30 OR SO GRAPE LEAVES

TIME **30 MINUTES**

A flavorful vegetarian filling for stuffed vegetables (pages 445–447 and 492) that is simple, quick, and easy to make in advance. If you have a mild chile powder (like one made from Aleppo or New Mexican chiles), use 1/2 teaspoon or more of it in place of the cayenne.

Some cooks add about 1/2 cup grated hard sheep's cheese, of a type like pecorino Romano, to this mix.

> 1/4 cup extra virgin olive oil
>
> 2 large onions, chopped
>
> Salt and black pepper to taste
>
> 1/3 cup pine nuts
>
> 1/3 cup currants or raisins
>
> 1/4 teaspoon ground allspice
>
> 1/4 teaspoon ground cinnamon
>
> Pinch of cayenne
>
> 1 cup long-grain rice
>
> 2 cups chicken, beef, or vegetable stock, preferably homemade (page 160 or 162), or water
>
> 1/4 cup chopped fresh parsley leaves
>
> 1/4 cup chopped fresh dill leaves
>
> 1/4 cup chopped fresh mint leaves
>
> Zest of 1 lemon, minced

1. Put the olive oil in a wide saucepan or deep skillet with a lid and place over medium heat. A minute later, add the onions and cook, stirring occasionally and sprinkling with salt and pepper, until they are well softened but not at all browned, at least 5 minutes. Add the pine nuts, currants, allspice, cinnamon, cayenne, and rice. Cook, stirring occasionally, until the rice is glossy, a minute or two. (If you are stuffing tomatoes or other vegetables with pulp, add the pulp at this point and cook for another 5 minutes or so.)

2. Add the stock, bring to a boil, reduce the heat so the mixture barely simmers, and cover. Cook until the liquid is absorbed, 15 to 20 minutes. Let cool a bit, then stir in the herbs and the minced lemon zest. Taste and adjust the seasoning. Use immediately or cover and refrigerate for up to a day before stuffing tomatoes, peppers, or grape or cabbage leaves.

Bean and Nut Filling for Grape Leaves, Cabbage Leaves, Peppers, and Tomatoes MIDDLE EAST ■ ▨

MAKES **ENOUGH TO FILL 4 TO 6 LARGE TOMATOES OR PEPPERS, 8 OR MORE CABBAGE LEAVES, OR UP TO 30 OR SO GRAPE LEAVES**

TIME **30 MINUTES (WITH PRECOOKED BEANS)**

You can definitely use leftover beans for this recipe, but especially White Beans with Garlic (page 441) or Aromatic White Beans with Chicken Stock and Tomatoes (page 442). If you must cook beans from scratch, it would be best to combine them with some garlic and other aromatic vegetables and a few sprigs of thyme while they cook.

¼ cup extra virgin olive oil
1 large onion, chopped

Salt and black pepper to taste
1 cup pine nuts or chopped walnuts
1 cup well-seasoned cooked chickpeas, white beans, or red beans (page 431)
½ cup cooked rice
1 teaspoon fennel seeds
Pinch of cayenne
About ½ cup mixed fresh herbs: parsley, dill, mint, and/or basil leaves
Zest of 1 lemon, minced

1. Put the olive oil in a skillet over medium heat. A minute later, add the onion and cook, stirring occasionally and sprinkling with salt and pepper, until well softened but not at all browned, at least 5 minutes. Add the pine nuts and cook, stirring occasionally, until lightly browned, about 5 minutes.

2. Add the beans, rice, fennel seeds, cayenne, and some more salt and pepper and cook, mashing and stirring, until the mixture is pasty and well combined, about 5 minutes. (If you are stuffing tomatoes or other vegetables with pulp, add the pulp at this point and cook for another 5 minutes or so.)

3. Stir in the herbs and minced lemon zest. Taste and adjust the seasoning. Use immediately or cover and refrigerate for up to a day before stuffing tomatoes, peppers, or grape or cabbage leaves.

Cabbage Pie RUSSIA ■ ▨

MAKES **4 TO 6 SERVINGS AS A MAIN COURSE, MANY MORE AS A STARTER OR SNACK**

TIME **1¼ HOURS**

Savory pies are favorites in Russia, and cabbage pie is the most common. I have not been there, but my friend Jacqueline Mitchell has, and she returned with this, certainly the easiest cabbage pie ever. I think it is best suited as an appetizer or a snack, but it's an odd dish, good hot or at room temperature, mysteriously simple, and quite glorious when it's done.

Other vegetables you can prepare this way: any cabbage (red will not look too great, though it will taste fine), including Savoy and Napa.

2 tablespoons butter, plus more as needed

1 medium or ¹/₂ large head of green cabbage, about
    2 pounds, cored and shredded

1 medium onion, sliced

Salt and black pepper to taste

²/₃ cup chopped fresh dill leaves

6 eggs

1 cup whole-milk yogurt or sour cream

3 tablespoons mayonnaise

¹/₂ teaspoon baking powder

1¹/₄ cups flour

1. Preheat the oven to 375°F. Put the butter in a large skillet, preferably nonstick, over medium heat. A minute later, add the cabbage and onion. Sprinkle with salt and pepper and cook, stirring occasionally, until the cabbage is quite tender, about 10 minutes; do not brown. Remove from the heat, add the dill, then taste and adjust the seasoning.

2. Meanwhile, hard-cook 3 of the eggs (page 338). When they are done, peel and coarsely chop. Add to the cooked cabbage mixture and let cool while you make the batter.

3. Combine the yogurt, mayonnaise, and remaining 3 eggs. Add the baking powder and flour and mix until smooth. Lightly butter a 9 × 12-inch ceramic or glass baking dish. Spread half the batter over the bottom, then top with the cabbage filling; smear the remaining batter over the cabbage, using your fingers or a rubber spatula to make sure there are no gaps in what will form the pie's top crust.

4. Bake for 45 minutes; it will be shiny and golden brown. Let the pie cool for at least 15 minutes be-

fore slicing it into as many squares or rectangles as you like. Eat warm or at room temperature.

CARROTS

We take carrots for granted—they're almost always there, and they are rarely treated as a cooked vegetable. But carrots are so ubiquitous, and so inexpensive, that it's worth rethinking that policy. These two recipes will help you do just that.

Glazed Carrots FRANCE ▪
MAKES **4 SERVINGS**
TIME **ABOUT 30 MINUTES**

This easy, fast cooking process turns carrots into a luxury vegetable. For even better flavor, add the grated zest of an orange or a lemon when about five minutes of cooking time remain.

Other vegetables you can prepare this way: turnips, radishes, onions, beets, parsnips, or other root vegetables.

1 pound carrots, cut into chunks

Salt to taste

2 tablespoons butter

Chopped fresh parsley, chervil, or mint leaves for garnish,
    optional

1. Put the carrots in a saucepan with a pinch of salt and water to cover them about halfway. Add the butter, cover the pan, and turn the heat to medium-high.

2. Simmer until the carrots are nearly tender, about 20 minutes. Uncover; much of the water will have evaporated. Continue to cook until the carrots are

shiny; if they threaten to burn, add a tablespoon or two of water. When they're done, taste and adjust seasoning if necessary; garnish if you like, and serve.

Curried Carrots INDIA ■

MAKES **4 SERVINGS**

TIME **30 MINUTES**

Tender, sweet carrots with delicious garlic cloves and a hint of exotic spice, this is another Indian dish that goes well as a side dish with food from almost anywhere. Add a few dried chiles, left whole, if you like, or hot red pepper flakes to taste.

Other vegetables you can prepare this way: parsnips.

> 1 pound carrots, cut into nickel-thick coins
>
> 16 garlic cloves, peeled
>
> 2 tablespoons butter or neutral oil, like corn or
>
>   grapeseed
>
> Salt to taste
>
> 1 tablespoon curry powder, preferably homemade
>
>   (pages 592–593), or garam masala (page 594)
>
> 2 tablespoons unsweetened shredded coconut, optional

1. Combine all the ingredients except the coconut in a medium saucepan with about $1/2$ cup water. Cover and bring to a boil, then adjust the heat so the mixture simmers steadily. Cook, checking occasionally and adding water $1/4$ cup at a time if the mixture dries out, until the carrots are tender, about 20 minutes.

2. Uncover and continue to cook until the water has evaporated and the carrots are nicely glazed, another 5 minutes or so. If you like, toast the coconut in a small dry skillet over medium heat, shaking the pan frequently until it colors slightly. Garnish the carrots with the coconut and serve hot.

CAULIFLOWER AND BROCCOLI

Cauliflower and broccoli are essentially interchangeable, though you might not think so until you saw a broccoflower or Romanesco broccoli; the appearance of each makes the link clear. Broccoli cooks a little faster, and the trimming and cleaning techniques are a little different (I think it's worth it to peel the stems of broccoli; cauliflower has no stems to speak of), but almost every recipe for one can be used for the other. Cauliflower's white color and slightly richer but milder flavor make it, I believe, a little more versatile.

Curried Cauliflower INDIA ■ ■ ■

MAKES **4 SERVINGS**

TIME **20 MINUTES**

A staple dish of India, often made with potatoes added (cook large chunks of the potato in the same water, at the same time, as the cauliflower and simply increase the amount of oil and spice). Best with homemade curry powder or garam masala. The cumin seeds add a nice bit of crunch but are not essential.

Other vegetables you can prepare this way: broccoli, potatoes, carrots, turnips, radishes.

> Salt and black pepper to taste
>
> 1 medium head of cauliflower, about $1^1/2$ pounds
>
> 3 tablespoons peanut or vegetable oil
>
> 1 tablespoon curry powder, preferably homemade
>
>   (pages 592–593), or garam masala (page 594), or to
>
>   taste
>
> 1 teaspoon cumin seeds, optional
>
> Juice of $1/2$ lemon

1. Bring a large pot of water to a boil and add salt. Meanwhile, trim the cauliflower but leave it whole.

Add it to the boiling water and cook until a thin-bladed knife pierces the cauliflower with little resistance, 10 to 20 minutes. Immediately transfer the cauliflower to a bowl of ice water and run water over it until it is cool enough to handle.

2. Cut or break the cauliflower into florets. Put a 12-inch skillet, preferably nonstick, over medium-high heat. Add the oil and curry powder and cook, stirring, until the powder turns brown and becomes aromatic, just a minute or so. Toss in the cauliflower and some salt and pepper and cook, stirring, until it is nicely coated with the oil and reheated, 3 to 4 minutes. Add the cumin seeds and lemon juice and stir, then taste and adjust the seasoning; serve hot or at room temperature.

Gobi Taktakin Curried Sautéed Cauliflower

INDIA ■ ▨ ▨

MAKES **4 SERVINGS**

TIME **20 MINUTES**

Marginally different from the preceding dish, but enough so that I thought its inclusion worthwhile, Gobi Taktakin is a dish made on the streets of India, where they use knives to mince the cauliflower as it sautés on huge flat griddles. (The dish's onomatopoeic name alludes to the *tak-tak-tak* sound of two knives simultaneously mincing and tossing the cauliflower as it sautés. To spare your pans the extra wear, it's better to chop the cauliflower in advance.)

Best with homemade curry powder or garam masala. Cumin seeds add a nice crunch, and cilantro adds a fresh note at the end, but neither is essential.

Other vegetables you can prepare this way: broccoli, potatoes, carrots, turnips, radishes.

3 tablespoons corn, grapeseed, or other neutral oil

1 tablespoon cumin seeds, optional

1 small red onion, finely chopped

1 medium head of cauliflower, about 1 1/2 pounds, broken into florets and very finely chopped

1 tablespoon curry powder, preferably homemade (pages 592–593), or garam masala (page 594), or to taste

Salt and black pepper to taste

Pinch of cayenne

1/4 cup chopped fresh cilantro leaves

Lime wedges for serving

1. Put the oil in a nonstick skillet wide enough for the cauliflower to fit into in one layer and place over medium-high heat. A minute later, add the cumin seeds if you're using them, let them fry for 30 seconds, then add half the onion and all the cauliflower. Add the curry powder and season with salt, pepper, and cayenne. Cook, stirring or tossing, until the onion has caramelized and the florets are lightly browned, 3 to 5 minutes.

2. Add the cilantro to the pan, toss once, and transfer to a serving platter. Garnish with the raw onion and serve hot or at room temperature, accompanied by lime wedges.

Broccoli or Cauliflower with Garlic and Lemon, Two Ways ITALY ■ ■ ▨

MAKES **4 SERVINGS**

TIME **30 MINUTES**

This is broccoli as it's done in Rome: garlic, olive oil, and lemon (almost everything—from mussels to beans to veal—can be cooked with these flavorings and called Roman-style). The first method is more familiar and perhaps a tad more reliable for beginning cooks; the second requires a bit more judgment, but it's better.

If you like, add a few anchovy fillets along with the garlic.

Other vegetables you can prepare this way: almost anything—dark leafy greens like collards and kale, cauliflower, green beans, carrots, and beets, for example.

Salt and black pepper to taste

1 head of broccoli or cauliflower, 1 pound or so, trimmed
and cut into bite-sized pieces

3 tablespoons extra virgin olive oil

1 tablespoon minced garlic, optional

Zest and juice of 1 lemon

1. Bring a large pot of water to a boil and add salt. Plunge the vegetable into the boiling water and cook until fairly tender, 3 to 6 minutes, depending on the size of your pieces. Drain and plunge into a bowl of ice water or run under cold water. Drain again.

2. Put 2 tablespoons of the olive oil in a large skillet over medium heat. Add the garlic, if using, and cook, stirring occasionally, until it is golden, about 3 minutes. Add the drained vegetable and turn the heat to high. Cook, stirring only when necessary— you don't want the broccoli to fall apart—until the vegetable begins to brown; add the lemon zest and cook for another minute or two.

3. Add the remaining olive oil and the lemon juice, taste and adjust the seasoning, and serve hot or at room temperature.

Alternative method. Skip step 1. In step 2, start with ¼ cup olive oil (and, if you like, add a dried chile). Thirty seconds after adding the garlic, add the broccoli or cauliflower and ¼ cup water. Cover the pan. Cook, uncovering and stirring occasionally, until the vegetable is tender, 10 to 15 minutes. Taste and adjust the seasoning and serve.

CHESTNUTS

We rarely cook chestnuts as a vegetable, I suspect because there has been no native chestnut crop in nearly a century, thanks to a blight that wiped out the American chestnut. But they are delicious this way (and can form the basis for a couple of classic turkey stuffings).

Chestnuts are best when they feel heavy; lighter ones have started to dry out, will take longer to cook, and may never become fully tender. Chestnuts are in season in the fall; I would not bother with them past Christmas.

Glazed Chestnuts EASTERN EUROPE
MAKES **4 SERVINGS**
TIME **1 HOUR**

Boiling is the easiest way to shell chestnuts, though it's still a pain. Frozen, pre-peeled chestnuts are a good alternative.

Other vegetables you can prepare this way: see Glazed Turnips (page 496).

1 pound chestnuts

Salt and black pepper to taste

4 tablespoons (½ stick) butter or extra virgin
olive oil

1. Cut a ring around each chestnut, then place them in boiling salted water to cover and cook for 3 minutes. Remove them from the water, a few at a time, and peel (both outer shell and inner skin) while still hot.

2. Put the butter in a saucepan and turn the heat to medium. A minute later, add the chestnuts, a sprinkling of salt and pepper, and ¼ cup water. Cover and cook, stirring occasionally, until the chestnuts are quite tender, about 30 minutes,

adding a little more water if necessary. When the chestnuts are ready, uncover and boil away any excess water, leaving the chestnuts glazed with the butter. Serve hot.

CORN

Corn has become more reliable, with new super hybrids that retain their sweetness in the market for days. Some people, in fact, would say corn has become too sweet; but these super-savory recipes will take care of that.

STRIPPING CORN KERNELS

Pan-Grilled Corn with Chiles MEXICO ■
MAKES **4 SERVINGS**
TIME **20 MINUTES**

You'll need a nonstick skillet for this or at least a very well-seasoned cast-iron or steel pan (or cheat and start with a tablespoon or two of corn oil). Although this recipe will work with frozen corn kernels, it is far, far superior when you strip the kernels from fresh cobs. Corn cooked this way is terrific in salads—either green or bean—where you are looking for extra crunch and flavor.

> 6 ears corn, shucked
> 1 jalapeño or ¹/₂ habanero (Scotch bonnet) chile,
>   stemmed, seeded, and minced, or ¹/₂ teaspoon hot red
>   pepper flakes, or to taste
> Salt to taste
> ¹/₂ cup chopped fresh cilantro leaves
> Lime wedges for serving

1. Use a knife to strip the kernels from the corn. It's easiest if you stand the corn up on a cutting board or in a shallow bowl and just cut down the length of each ear as many times as is necessary; you'll quickly get the hang of it.
2. Put a large nonstick skillet over high heat; when it begins to smoke, add the corn and chile and let sit for a moment. As the corn browns, shake the pan to distribute it so each kernel is blackened on at least one surface.
3. Remove from the heat, then add salt and stir in the cilantro. Serve immediately, with lime wedges.

Choclo or Elote Asado Grilled Corn
MEXICO, CHILE, PERU
MAKES **4 TO 8 SERVINGS**
TIME **30 MINUTES, PLUS TIME TO PREHEAT THE GRILL**

If you think nothing beats grilled fresh corn in the summer, think again: street vendors in Mexico, Chile, Peru, and other Central and South American countries figured out how to make a great thing even better, adding a little lime juice and chile powder to what is already a near-perfect food. The tart lime juice is incredibly refreshing, and a little smoky heat from the chiles brings out the crisp sweetness of the corn. For a more indulgent version, see the variation.

8 ears fresh sweet corn

3 tablespoons butter

1 lime, cut into wedges

1 tablespoon pure chile powder, like ancho or New Mexico, plus more to taste

1. Start a charcoal fire or preheat a gas grill; the fire should be moderately hot, and the rack no more than 4 inches from the heat source. Peel back the husks of the corn without removing them and remove the silks. Smooth the husks back into place, but don't worry if they don't completely cover the kernels.

2. When the grill is ready, grill the corn, turning occasionally, for 10 to 15 minutes. As the ears start to brown, carefully peel back the husks. Coat the corn with the butter and return to the grill with the husks peeled back. Grill, turning occasionally, until nicely browned—some of the kernels will blacken, and that's fine—another 5 to 10 minutes.

3. Squeeze lime juice on the corn, sprinkle with chile powder, and serve immediately.

Grilled Corn with Cream and Cheese. Omit the lime juice. After sprinkling with chile powder, coat with Mexican crema, or thinned sour cream, about 1 tablespoon per person, and sprinkle with grated cotija cheese, about 2 tablespoons per person.

CUCUMBERS

A couple of words about cucumbers, which also appear in the salad (and even soup) chapter: In almost every case, smaller and thinner is better. Look for Japanese hybrids, firm Kirbys, and any other variety that contains a minimum of seeds. If you are forced to use a heavily seeded cucumber, it's almost always worth splitting it in half and scooping the seeds out with a spoon.

Lightly Pickled Cucumber or Other Vegetables ■ ■ ■
MAKES **4 SERVINGS**
TIME **15 MINUTES**

You can use this technique for radish (especially daikon), eggplant, zucchini, even cabbage; salting time will vary, but in every case you will wind up with an ultra-crisp vegetable that is great as a snack, a garnish, or an addition to salads and soups.

4 cucumbers, about 1$\frac{1}{2}$ pounds, peeled if necessary

1 tablespoon coarse salt

1. Cut the cucumbers in half lengthwise, then scoop out the seeds with a spoon. Slice thinly (a mandoline is best for this), then toss with the salt and put in a colander; let drain (over a bowl or in the sink) for 10 to 20 minutes.

2. Rinse, drain, and wring dry in a towel. Use immediately or wrap in plastic and refrigerate for up to a day.

Quick Salted Vegetables with Mirin and Soy. In step 2, after drying, toss the cucumbers or other vegetables with 2 teaspoons rice vinegar, $\frac{1}{2}$ teaspoon dark sesame oil, 1 tablespoon soy sauce, and 1 teaspoon mirin.

EGGPLANT

Eggplant come in a dizzying array of shapes and sizes. There is an oval off-white variety that it probably seemed sensible to name *eggplant,* there are tiny green eggplant prized for their bitterness, and there are the more widely available varieties we concern ourselves with here: the long, slender, usually lavender "Japanese" or "Asian" type and the more common dark purple Mediterranean breed.

Though you might follow geographic clues for which to use—pick the Asian type for Middle Eastern and Asian recipes and the globe eggplant for Western European recipes—I think the lavender variety is generally so superior (unless you have a garden or gardenlike source, in which case they're all great) that I select it whenever I have a choice. In general, the smaller the eggplant, the better (I love the golf-ball-sized ones, which do not require any trimming or cleaning), but—also in general—firmness is the most important characteristic when buying an eggplant (after, of course, obvious lack of damage).

If the skin is very thick and tough, it is best peeled; if not, it is better to leave it on. Salting eggplants (see following recipe) does remove some of their bitterness, but it's an undeniable hassle. If this process keeps you from cooking with them, try skipping it. Many strains are now bred to minimize potential bitterness, and salting is unnecessary. If the eggplant is fresh and firm, chances are it will taste pretty good without salting, regardless of the variety.

Sautéed Eggplant ITALY ■ ■
MAKES **4 SERVINGS**
TIME **30 TO 90 MINUTES**

There is nothing like a simply cooked dish of eggplant, one of the world's most beloved vegetables and one that several cuisines—Italian, Turkish, and Indian, most notably—treat with near reverence.

> 6 or 8 small, 2 or 3 medium, or 1 or 2 large eggplant, about 2 pounds
> Salt and black pepper to taste
> 1/3 cup extra virgin olive oil
> 1 tablespoon minced garlic, or more if you like
> Chopped fresh parsley or basil leaves for garnish

1. Peel the eggplant if you like. If you have any doubt about its quality, cut it into 1-inch cubes and place them in a colander. Sprinkle liberally with salt, at least a tablespoon; toss the eggplant to distribute the salt. Let sit in a sink or over a bowl, undisturbed, for at least 30 and preferably 60 minutes. It will shed a good deal of liquid. Squeeze out as much liquid as you can, rinse with fresh water, and pat dry.

2. Put the oil and all but 1/2 teaspoon of the garlic in a large nonstick skillet over medium heat. Two minutes later, add the eggplant; cook, stirring occasionally, until the eggplant is tender and lightly browned, 15 minutes or longer, adjusting the heat as necessary so the eggplant browns as quickly as possible without burning.

3. Add the remaining garlic and cook, stirring, for 1 minute more; taste and adjust the seasoning, then stir in a handful of parsley and cook for a few more seconds. Garnish with some more parsley and serve hot, warm, or at room temperature.

Stewed Eggplant with Tomatoes FRANCE. This is good with a few capers, too: In step 3, before adding the garlic, stir in about 2 cups chopped tomatoes (ripe, fresh ones are best, but canned are acceptable). Cook for about 10 more minutes, stirring occasionally, until the tomatoes break up, then add the garlic and proceed.

Crunchy Eggplant. In step 3, before adding the garlic, stir in about ½ cup bread crumbs, preferably fresh (page 580). Cook for about a minute, until they begin to brown, then add the garlic.

Basic Sautéed Eggplant, Indian Style. In step 2, use butter if you prefer; add 2 cups sliced onion and 1 or more stemmed, seeded, and minced fresh green chiles, like jalapeños. Cook until the onion softens, then add the eggplant and proceed. In step 3, add 1 teaspoon peeled and minced fresh ginger along with the garlic and use cilantro and mint in place of the parsley or basil.

Eggplant with Peppers and Yogurt MIDDLE EAST. In step 2, cook 2 bell peppers—red, yellow, green, or a combination (or you can use mild poblano chiles), cored, seeded, and cut into strips—with the eggplant, until tender. In step 3, mix the remaining garlic with 1 cup yogurt, beaten until smooth, a tablespoon of extra virgin olive oil, and some salt and pepper. Remove the eggplant and peppers from the pan and pour this sauce over them; serve hot.

Eggplant with Pine Nuts ITALY. Just before serving, lightly brown ¼ cup pine nuts in 2 tablespoons extra virgin olive oil; stir this into the cooked eggplant.

Eggplant with Sweet Miso JAPAN ■ ▥
MAKES **4 SERVINGS**
TIME **50 MINUTES**

The Japanese not only love eggplant; they also produce some of the best—the slender, long, lavender-colored varieties are sweeter and firmer than the fat, almost black ones. Here the skinny ones are essential.

Make this up to an hour in advance; like many eggplant dishes, it's good at room temperature. Or make in advance and run under the broiler to reheat, until the miso topping bubbles (reserve the sesame seeds until after you do this).

4 small or 2 large thin, long eggplant
¼ cup peanut oil or neutral oil, like corn or grapeseed
¼ cup dark ("red") miso
1 teaspoon sugar
1 tablespoon mirin or 1½ teaspoons honey thinned with water
1 tablespoon rice or other mild vinegar, or to taste
Lightly toasted sesame seeds (page 596)

1. Remove the caps from the eggplant and cut them in half lengthwise.
2. Put the peanut oil in a large skillet, preferably non-stick, over medium heat. About 2 minutes later, add the eggplant, skin side down. Cook until nicely browned, adjusting the heat and rotating the pieces so they brown evenly, about 10 minutes. Turn and cook on the flesh side until brown, then continue to cook, turning as necessary, until tender, another 10 minutes or so.
3. When the eggplant is almost done, combine the miso, sugar, mirin, and vinegar in a small saucepan over medium heat. Cook for about 1 minute, stirring. Remove the eggplant and spread a thin coating of the miso mixture over each half; top with the sesame seeds. Serve hot or at room temperature.

Grilled or Broiled Eggplant with Sweet Miso. Start a charcoal or gas grill or preheat the broiler; the rack should be about 6 inches from the heat source. Brush the eggplant slices well with oil. Place, flesh side down, on a baking sheet or directly on the grill. Broil or grill, turning as necessary, until browned on both sides, brushing with more oil if the eggplant looks dry. Proceed with step 3.

Choonth Wangan Stewed Apples and Eggplant INDIA

MAKES **4 SERVINGS**

TIME **30 TO 40 MINUTES**

It took me a long time to figure out what was in this mysteriously flavored concoction, and even then I had to ask my host (who was from Kashmir, where this is common) what was going on here. The apples and eggplant complement each other perfectly, to the point where each loses a bit of its identity and gains something unusual. Serve this as a side dish any time you like, not just with Indian food.

> ¼ cup corn, grapeseed, or other neutral oil
>
> 1 pound eggplant, preferably the small lavender kind, cut into 1-inch cubes
>
> 1 pound Granny Smith or other tart, crisp apples, peeled, cored, and cut into eighths
>
> ½ cup tamarind paste, homemade (page 585) or store-bought
>
> 1 teaspoon fennel seeds
>
> 1 tablespoon peeled and minced fresh ginger
>
> 1 teaspoon ground cardamom
>
> 1 teaspoon ground cinnamon
>
> Pinch of ground cloves
>
> ¼ teaspoon cayenne
>
> ¼ teaspoon asafetida (hing; see page 10), optional
>
> Salt and black pepper to taste
>
> Chopped fresh cilantro leaves for garnish

1. Put the oil in a large skillet, preferably nonstick, over medium heat. A minute later, add the eggplant and apples and cook, stirring occasionally, until the eggplant and apples are both quite tender, 15 to 20 minutes.
2. Gently stir in all the remaining ingredients except the cilantro, along with ½ cup water; adjust the heat so the mixture simmers. Cook, stirring gently, until the mixture is thick. Taste and adjust the seasoning, then garnish and serve.

Pastry for Savory Tarts ■ ■

MAKES **ENOUGH FOR AN 8- TO 10-INCH TART**

TIME **20 MINUTES, PLUS RESTING TIME**

A pastry suitable for any pie, though for desserts I would go with the Sweet Tart Pastry on page 654. Here you can use olive oil in place of butter, with quite good results. The keys to easy success: use a food processor and chill the dough before rolling it out.

> 1½ cups unbleached flour, plus more for rolling
>
> ½ teaspoon salt
>
> 8 tablespoons (1 stick) cold unsalted butter, cut into about 8 pieces, or ½ cup extra virgin olive oil, or a combination

1. Combine the flour and salt in a food processor and pulse once or twice. Add the butter or oil all at once; process until the mixture is uniform, about 10 seconds (do not overprocess).
2. Put the mixture in a bowl and add 3 tablespoons ice water; mix with your hands until you can form the dough into a ball, adding another tablespoon or two of ice water if necessary (if you overdo it and the mixture becomes sodden, add a little more flour). Form into a ball, wrap in plastic, and freeze for 10 minutes or refrigerate for at least 30 minutes. (You can refrigerate for up to a couple of days or freeze for up to a couple of weeks.)
3. Sprinkle a countertop with flour and put the dough on it; sprinkle with flour. Alternatively, roll the dough between 2 sheets of lightly floured plastic wrap (this is untraditional, but it works well). Use a rolling pin to roll with light pressure, from

Savory Tarts

Few dishes are more impressive than a gorgeous savory tart served at the beginning or middle of a meal, and few are easier. The crust (which can actually be omitted!) is thrown together in a food processor, then refrigerated and rolled out. The filling is essentially whatever vegetables you want to include, bound by eggs and, if you like, cheese; though the proportions remain pretty much the same, the vegetables themselves can be varied at will. The result is a rich, filling, and good-looking creation that will please anyone lucky enough to eat it.

the center out. If the dough is sticky, add a little flour (if it continues to become sticky, and it's taking you more than a few minutes to roll it out, refrigerate or freeze again). Roll, adding flour and rotating and turning the dough as needed; use ragged edges of dough to repair any tears, adding a drop of water while you press the patch into place.

4. When the diameter of the dough is about 2 inches greater than that of your tart pan, move the dough to the tart pan by draping it over the rolling pin and then place it in the pan. Press the dough firmly into the pan all over. Refrigerate for about an hour before filling or baking (if you're in a hurry, freeze for a half hour or so).

Torta di Melanzane Eggplant Pie ITALY ■ ▨
MAKES **4 OR MORE SERVINGS**
TIME 1½ **HOURS, SOMEWHAT UNATTENDED**

This may be called a torte, sformata, crostata, teglia, or quiche, not to mention a dozen other names in different countries, mostly Mediterranean. They all begin with a simple pie shell and a pile of cooked vegetables (and sometimes meat). (The recipe will take less time if you have a premade crust.) Cheese, eggs, or other enriching ingredients may be added.

The result may be a first course, a light lunch, or the centerpiece of a larger meal.

You can also use any of these mixtures to make a crustless "torte"—see the variation.

Other vegetables you can prepare this way: zucchini or summer squash may be substituted for the eggplant.

1 Pastry for Savory Tarts (preceding recipe)

6 or 8 small, 2 or 3 medium, or 1 or 2 large eggplant, about 2 pounds

Salt and black pepper to taste

⅓ cup extra virgin olive oil, plus a little more for the tart

1 large onion, chopped

2 red or yellow bell peppers, stemmed, seeded, and sliced

½ cup chopped pitted olives, optional

½ cup chopped fresh basil leaves

5 eggs

½ cup grated Gruyère, Cantal, Cheddar, or other firm but not dry cheese

¼ cup freshly grated Parmesan cheese

1. Roll out the crust and chill it, either in the freezer for 15 minutes or in the fridge for at least 30 minutes. Peel and/or salt the eggplant if you like (see page 456). Rinse with fresh water and squeeze out excess moisture.

2. Preheat the oven to 400°F and set the rack in the middle. Tear off a piece of foil twice as large as the

crust. Fold it in half and smear it with butter or oil; lay the greased side onto the crust. Weight the foil with a pile of dried beans or rice (these can be reused for this same purpose), pie weights, or a tight-fitting skillet or saucepan—anything that will sit flat on the surface. Bake 12 minutes, then remove the foil and continue to bake at 350°F, until the crust is a beautiful shade of brown. Remove and let cool on a rack while you prepare the filling.

3. Put the oil in a large nonstick skillet over medium heat. Two minutes later, add the onion and bell peppers; cook, stirring occasionally, until softened, about 5 minutes. Add the eggplant and cook until all the vegetables are softened, 10 minutes or longer. Stir in the olives if you're using them, then taste and adjust the seasoning, cool slightly, and combine with the remaining ingredients.

4. Spoon this mixture into the partially baked shell and bake for 30 to 40 minutes, or until almost firm and lightly browned on top; reduce the oven heat if the shell's edges are darkening too quickly. Cool for at least 10 minutes before slicing and serving.

Crustless Vegetable Pie. Essentially a gratin: Butter a casserole dish large enough to hold the filling comfortably. Pour the mixture in, sprinkle with ½ cup bread crumbs if you like, and bake for 30 to 40 minutes, until almost firm; the center should still jiggle a little, but a thin-bladed knife inserted near the edge will come out clean.

GREEN BEANS

For the most part, green beans are available year-round, because they grow easily and store and ship well. This makes them something of a staple, taken for granted by most of us. But when featured in dishes like these they really come into their own.

Green Beans, Pears, and Ham
GERMANY ■
MAKES **4 SERVINGS**
TIME **30 MINUTES**

I never did find out what this was called in Germany, but I do know it's surprisingly good even though it's the kind of concoction you'd come up with to make use of the last three ingredients in the house. The pears' sweetness offsets the saltiness of the ham (this is a good place to use ordinary ham, as long as it's not too sweet; prosciutto or the like would be overkill), the green beans add freshness (and welcome color), and the three distinct textures make the eating fun. Serve with simply cooked meat or fish.

> 2 tablespoons butter or extra virgin olive oil
> 1 large onion, thinly sliced
> 1 pound ham or very lean bacon in one piece
> 2 or 3 large pears, preferably Bosc, not overly ripe
> ¾ pound green beans
> Salt and black pepper to taste
> 1 cup chicken stock, preferably homemade (page 160)

1. Put the butter in a large deep skillet over medium-high heat. When hot, add the onion and cook, stirring occasionally, for about 5 minutes. Meanwhile, cut the ham into ½-inch chunks. Add it and raise the heat to high.

2. While the ham cooks—stir it occasionally, but let it brown a bit on the bottom—peel and core the pears and cut them into 1-inch chunks. Lower the heat to medium and add them to the pan; stir occasionally. Trim the beans, cut them into roughly 2-inch lengths, rinse them quickly, and add them to the skillet along with a sprinkling of salt and at least ½ teaspoon pepper. Cook for a minute, then raise the heat to medium-high, add the chicken stock, and stir.

3. Cook, stirring occasionally, until the beans are bright green and semitender, the pears are quite tender, and the liquid so reduced that it is essentially a sauce, 10 to 15 minutes. Taste, adjust the seasoning, and serve.

GREENS

Bitter greens are not only the backbone of many salads (see page 177) but wonderful cooked, too. Most are interchangeable.

Green Beans with Yogurt and Dill
GREECE ■ ■
MAKES **4 SERVINGS**
TIME **40 MINUTES**

Like many Mediterranean vegetables, these are cooked until quite soft—none of this crisp-tender business—and commonly served at room temperature, making it a fine dish to prepare in advance.

> 1/4 cup extra virgin olive oil
>
> 1 large onion, roughly chopped
>
> Salt and black pepper to taste
>
> 1 1/2 pounds green beans, trimmed
>
> 1/2 cup snipped fresh dill
>
> Juice of 1/2 lemon
>
> 1 cup yogurt

1. Put the oil in a large skillet or flameproof casserole with a lid over medium heat. A minute later, add the onion, along with some salt and pepper, and cook, stirring occasionally, until it wilts, about 5 minutes. Add the beans, about half the dill, and 1 cup water. Lower the heat, cover, and adjust the heat so the mixture simmers steadily. Cook until the beans are quite tender, 20 to 30 minutes.
2. Uncover and raise the heat so any excess liquid boils away. Add the lemon juice, then stir; taste and adjust the seasoning. Turn off the heat, stir in the yogurt, garnish with the remaining dill, and serve.

Radicchio with Bacon ITALY ■ ■ ■
MAKES **4 SERVINGS**
TIME **20 MINUTES**

Closely related in flavor and spirit to the classic French pissenlit (dandelion greens with bacon), this differs in that the greens are cooked from the start. Also, though it may be finished with lemon, vinegar is almost never used.

Other vegetables you can prepare this way: any relatively tender, bitter green—curly endive, escarole, dandelion, even Belgian endive, cut crosswise.

> 2 tablespoons extra virgin olive oil
>
> 1/4 pound slab bacon, cut into 1/4- to 1/2-inch chunks
>
> 1 pound radicchio, roughly chopped
>
> Salt and black pepper to taste
>
> Lemon wedges for serving, optional

1. Put the olive oil in a large skillet, preferably nonstick, over medium-high heat. Add the bacon and cook, stirring occasionally, until crisp, 5 to 10 minutes. Remove with a slotted spoon and set aside for the moment.
2. Reduce the heat to medium, add the radicchio, and cook, stirring occasionally, until it wilts and becomes tender, about 10 minutes. Add some pepper and salt if necessary, then return the bacon to the pan and cook, stirring occasionally, until the bacon reheats. Serve hot or at room temperature, with the lemon wedges if you like.

Grilled Radicchio ITALY ■ ■ ■

MAKES **4 SERVINGS**

TIME **30 MINUTES, PLUS TIME TO PREHEAT THE GRILL**

This is an excellent side dish, drizzled with olive oil and sprinkled with salt, the base of an elegant salad—combine it with Gorgonzola and walnuts, for example—or a fine topping for Grilled Polenta (page 530) or Crostini (page 41).

Other vegetables to prepare this way: split Belgian endives (use four), or even small heads of romaine lettuce.

2 heads of radicchio

1/4 cup extra virgin olive oil, or more to taste

Salt and black pepper to taste

1 teaspoon minced garlic, optional

Lemon wedges for serving

1. Start a charcoal or gas grill; the fire should be only moderately hot and the rack about 4 inches from the heat source. Cut the radicchio in half and drizzle the cut sides with olive oil, then sprinkle with salt and pepper. If you like, rub with the garlic.
2. Grill, cut side down, until nicely browned, about 2 minutes, then turn and brown the other side. Continue to cook, turning occasionally, for a total of 5 to 10 minutes, or until the exterior is browned and crisp (the interior will barely cook; that's fine).
3. Serve hot or at room temperature with lemon wedges and drizzled with a little more olive oil.

Braised Endives FRANCE ■

MAKES **4 SERVINGS**

TIME **1 HOUR**

Endives have a couple of things going for them: they're grown inside (mostly in the dark, so they stay white), so they're fresh all year round; they have great form and nice crunchy texture; they are unusually bitter, but in a pleasant way. Cooked—especially with good stock—they are elegant and delicious.

Other vegetables you can prepare this way: leeks (split and washed), romaine lettuce (quartered, the long way), or any root vegetable—especially carrots.

2 tablespoons butter or extra virgin olive oil

4 Belgian endives, trimmed

Salt and black pepper to taste

3/4 cup chicken or vegetable stock, preferably homemade (page 160 or 162), white or red wine, or water

Fresh lemon juice to taste

1. Preheat the oven to 350°F. Put the butter in a flameproof casserole or an ovenproof skillet with a lid over medium heat. When the butter melts, add the endives, along with a sprinkling of salt and pepper. Add the stock, cover, and bring to a boil.
2. Put the dish in the oven and cook for 30 to 40 minutes, until the endives are very tender and almost—but not quite—falling apart. (You can prepare the dish to this point, let sit for up to an hour, then reheat in the oven.) Sprinkle with a little lemon juice and serve.

Braised Endives with Bacon or Ham. Add 1/4 cup minced bacon or prosciutto along with the stock.

Escarole with Olive Oil, Anchovies, and Pepper ITALY ■ ■ ■

MAKES **4 SERVINGS**

TIME **30 MINUTES**

Do not skimp on the olive oil here; its flavor is integral. Really, this is escarole braised in olive oil, an extremely useful and wide-ranging technique.

You can omit the anchovies if you like or add pine nuts (about ¼ cup), raisins (¼ cup), pitted black or green olives (about ½ cup), or about ½ cup chopped tomato. You can also use wine or stock in place of the water, for a richer taste.

Other vegetables you can prepare this way: this is a classic and basic recipe that can be used for almost any green or in fact for "harder" vegetables like cauliflower or broccoli, following exactly the same procedure. Cooking time will vary.

½ cup extra virgin olive oil

1 tablespoon minced garlic

6 anchovy fillets

2 to 4 small dried chiles or 1 teaspoon hot red pepper flakes, or to taste

1 pound escarole, radicchio, endive, or other bitter green or vegetable, trimmed

Salt and black pepper to taste

1. Put all but a tablespoon of the oil in a large deep skillet or flameproof casserole with a lid and place over medium heat. Set aside a teaspoon of the garlic and put the rest in the oil, along with the anchovies and chiles. Cook, stirring occasionally, until the garlic begins to color, a minute or two. Add the escarole and ½ cup water and adjust the heat so the mixture simmers steadily. Cover.
2. Cook for about 20 minutes, checking and stirring occasionally and adding water if the mixture threatens to dry out. When the escarole is tender, remove the lid and raise the heat if necessary to cook off excess liquid; stir in the reserved garlic and cook for another minute. Taste and adjust the seasoning, then serve hot or at room temperature, drizzling with the reserved olive oil just before serving.

Gai Lan (Chinese Mustard Greens) with Oyster Sauce CHINA ■

MAKES **4 SERVINGS**

TIME **15 MINUTES**

The bright green stir-fry of Chinese restaurants.

Other vegetables you can prepare this way: if you can't find gai lan, use broccoli raab or even collards or kale; broccoli or cauliflower will work too.

1½ pounds gai lan

2 tablespoons peanut oil

1 tablespoon minced garlic, optional

¼ cup oyster sauce

1. Separate the leaves and stems of the gai lan; cut the stems into 2-inch lengths.
2. Put the peanut oil in a large skillet or wok and turn the heat to high. Add the leaves of the greens and toss until they wilt, about 3 minutes; put on a platter. Add the stems, the garlic if you're using it, and about ¼ cup water. Toss until the stems are crisp-tender, 3 to 5 minutes. Remove them and put on top of the greens. Top with oyster sauce and serve.

Collards, Kale, or Other Dark Greens Cooked in Yogurt MIDDLE EAST ■ ■ ■

MAKES **4 SERVINGS**

TIME **30 MINUTES**

Think of this as the Middle Eastern version of creamed spinach, served at room temperature. The yogurt is uncooked, which keeps it fresh and tangy.

Other vegetables to prepare this way: spinach.

Salt and black pepper to taste

About 1 pound dark leafy greens, like collards or kale, stems and leaves separated

2 cups whole-milk yogurt

2 tablespoons extra virgin olive oil

1 tablespoon fresh marjoram or oregano leaves

1 small or ½ large garlic clove, minced

Pinch of cayenne, optional

1. Bring a large pot of water to a boil and add salt. Meanwhile, roughly chop the collard stems; you can leave the leaves whole. Add the stems to the boiling water and, about 3 minutes later, the leaves. Cook until both are tender, 5 to 10 minutes more. Drain and rinse under running water until cool enough to handle. Squeeze dry and chop.

2. Whisk the yogurt and olive oil together in a large bowl until smooth. Stir in the marjoram, some pepper, garlic, cayenne if you're using it, and a large pinch of salt. Stir the greens into this and serve immediately or cover and refrigerate for up to an hour.

Flash-Cooked Kale or Collards with Lemon Juice BRAZIL ■ ■ ■

MAKES **4 SERVINGS**

TIME **15 MINUTES**

Kale and collards are interchangeable here; just make sure to discard any stems more than ⅛ inch thick—they will not cook in time.

Other vegetables you can prepare this way: any dark greens, like turnip, mustard, dandelion; shredded cabbage of any type.

1 to 1½ pounds kale or collard greens

3 tablespoons peanut oil or extra virgin olive oil

Salt and black pepper to taste

⅓ to ½ cup fresh lemon juice, wine vinegar, or sherry vinegar

1. Separate the stems and leaves of the greens. Chop the stems into 1-inch sections and shred the greens: stack them, then roll them up like a cigar and cut into thin strips.

2. Put the oil in a large skillet or wok, well seasoned or nonstick, over high heat. When the oil smokes, toss in the stems. Cook, stirring almost constantly, until they begin to brown, 3 to 5 minutes.

3. Add the greens and continue to cook, stirring, until the greens wilt and begin to brown, less than 5 minutes. Turn off the heat, season with salt and pepper, and add about ⅓ cup lemon juice. Taste, adjust the seasoning, and serve immediately or at room temperature.

LEEKS

The most expensive member of the onion family (they take the longest to grow), leeks are also the best as a stand-alone vegetable. Cleaning them, if you want to serve them intact, is tricky (see page 465). If you chop them, you can simply wash them as you would a green. Nothing else about them presents any challenge.

Leeks Vinaigrette FRANCE ■ ■ ■

MAKES **4 SERVINGS**

TIME **15 MINUTES**

Leeks have an alluring, herbaceous flavor unlike any other allium, and this simple salad is a great way to show it off. With slight adjustments in cooking time and quantity of vinaigrette you could substitute scallions, ramps, or, for that matter, shallots or pearl onions.

1 pound leeks, preferably small and evenly sized, trimmed and cleaned (see the following recipe)

3 to 4 tablespoons extra virgin olive oil, to taste

1½ tablespoons sherry or other wine vinegar, or more to taste

1 teaspoon Dijon-style mustard

1 teaspoon minced shallot

Salt and black pepper to taste

1 hard-cooked egg (page 338), minced or put through a coarse-mesh strainer

1. Put the leeks in a steamer over about 1 inch of boiling water; steam until tender, 10 minutes or more. Transfer the leeks to a platter.

2. While the leeks are steaming, make a vinaigrette: Whisk together the oil, vinegar, mustard, and shallot. Add a pinch of salt and a few turns of the pepper mill, then taste and add more vinegar, salt, or oil as necessary.

3. Dress the leeks with the vinaigrette, scatter with the egg, and serve, lukewarm or at room temperature.

Braised Leeks with Olive Oil and Rice MIDDLE EAST ■ ▨

MAKES **4 SERVINGS**

TIME **1 HOUR**

A simple little thing (the hardest part is cleaning the leeks) but delicious. The sweetness of the carrots really comes through, and the reserved olive oil adds a nice touch. Good with sautéed or roast poultry or meats.

Other vegetables you can prepare this way: Belgian endive (cut in half the long way), bok choy, and chard are all good.

4 large or 8 medium leeks, about 2 pounds

⅓ cup extra virgin olive oil

2 small carrots, roughly chopped

Salt and black pepper to taste

¼ cup white long-grain rice

Juice of ½ lemon

1. Trim the hard green parts from the leeks; split in half from about an inch below the root end (leave this intact for now) to the leafy end. Carefully wash between all the layers, removing all traces of sand. Cut off the root end and cut the leeks into 4-inch sections.

2. Put all but a tablespoon of the oil in a skillet with a lid or a saucepan large enough to hold the leeks in one layer. Turn the heat to medium. When the oil is hot, add the leeks and carrots, along with a sprinkling of salt and pepper, and cook for about 25 minutes, turning occasionally, until the leeks are tender. Your goal is not to brown the leeks but to soften them; if they brown a little, however, that's fine.

3. Add the rice and 1½ cups of water, cover, and adjust the heat so the mixture simmers. Cook for about 30 minutes, or until the water is absorbed; the mixture should be moist but not soupy. Serve

CLEANING LEEKS

hot, at room temperature, or cold (this will keep well, covered and refrigerated, for a day, and can be reheated). Just before serving, drizzle with the remaining olive oil and the lemon juice.

Braised Leeks with Olives. In step 2, omit the carrots. In step 3, omit the rice and add ½ cup pitted black olives, like Kalamatas. Use only ½ cup liquid and cook for only 5 to 10 minutes, until hot. Add the lemon juice at the end.

Braised Leeks with Egg-Lemon Sauce. You can use this formula with almost any braised vegetable: When the leeks are done, beat 2 eggs in a bowl with the minced or grated zest and juice of a lemon; still beating, add about ½ cup of the leek-cooking liquid. Gradually add the remaining cooking liquid, beating all the while. Dress the leeks with this sauce and serve.

Leeks in Red Wine FRANCE ■ ▣
MAKES **4 SERVINGS**
TIME **35 MINUTES**

As with all braised vegetable dishes, the results here depend largely on the quality of two ingredients: the vegetable itself and the braising liquid. Since it's easy enough to find good leeks, you have to be certain that the red wine is, if not great, then at least drinkable; and if you have good homemade stock, this is the place to use it.

Other vegetables you can prepare this way: Belgian endive, split in half the long way; onions, halved or quartered (or spring onions, left whole).

  2 tablespoons butter, extra virgin olive oil, or a
    combination
  4 leeks, trimmed and cleaned (page 465)
  Salt and black pepper to taste

  2 cups good-quality red wine
  2 tablespoons beef or chicken stock, preferably
    homemade (page 160), or water

1. Put the butter in a skillet with a lid or a saucepan large enough to hold the leeks in one layer and place over medium heat. A minute later, add the leeks; sprinkle them with salt and pepper and cook, turning once or twice, for about 5 minutes, until they begin to brown.
2. Add the wine and stock and bring to a boil. Reduce the heat to low, cover, and adjust the heat so the mixture simmers steadily. Cook until the leeks are tender, 20 to 30 minutes.
3. Use a slotted spoon to transfer the leeks to a platter. Raise the heat under the liquid and cook, stirring occasionally, until it thickens and is reduced to about ½ cup. Pour it over the leeks and serve immediately or serve at room temperature or cold.

Leeks in White Wine GERMANY. A less rich, more tart preparation: In step 2, substitute white wine for the red; omit the stock. Finish with the juice of ½ lemon.

Torta di Porri Leek Pie ITALY ■ ▣
MAKES **4 OR MORE SERVINGS**
TIME **1½ HOURS, SOMEWHAT UNATTENDED**

Somewhat more elegant than its more famous French cousin, which is featured in the variation. Good hot, perhaps even better warm or at room temperature, this is an ideal buffet or picnic preparation. Like the eggplant pie on page 459, this may be prepared without a crust.

Other vegetables you can prepare this way: onions of any type.

1 Pastry for Savory Tarts (page 458)

4 tablespoons (¹/₂ stick) butter or extra virgin olive oil,
    plus a little more for the tart

3 pounds leeks, trimmed, sliced, and washed (page 465)

Salt and black pepper to taste

¹/₂ cup dry white wine or water

¹/₂ cup chopped fresh parsley leaves

4 eggs

¹/₂ cup heavy cream, half-and-half, or milk

1 cup grated Gruyère, Cantal, Cheddar, or other firm but
    not dry cheese

¹/₄ cup freshly grated Parmesan cheese

1. Preheat the oven to 400°F. Tear off a piece of foil twice as large as the crust. Fold it in half and smear it with butter or oil; lay the greased side onto the crust. Weight the foil with a pile of dried beans or rice (these can be reused for this same purpose), pie weights, or a tight-fitting skillet or saucepan—anything that will sit flat on the surface. Bake for 12 minutes, then remove the foil and continue to bake at 350°F until the crust is a beautiful shade of brown, just a few minutes more. Remove and let cool on a rack while you prepare the filling.

2. Meanwhile, put the 4 tablespoons butter in a large nonstick skillet with a lid over medium heat. Two minutes later, add the leeks, along with a large pinch of salt and some pepper. Cook, stirring occasionally, until they begin to soften, about 5 minutes. Add the liquid and bring to a boil; cover and adjust the heat so the mixture simmers. Cook, stirring occasionally, until the leeks are very soft, at least 20 minutes. If a great deal of liquid remains, remove the lid and cook over medium heat until you have a moist but not soupy mass. Taste and adjust the seasoning, then cool slightly.

3. Combine the leeks with the remaining ingredients and pile this mixture into the prebaked shell. Bake for 30 to 40 minutes, or until almost firm and

lightly browned on top; reduce the oven heat if the shell's edges are darkening too quickly. Cool for at least 10 minutes before slicing and serving.

Quiche Lorraine. In step 2, begin by cooking ¹/₄ pound slab bacon, cut into ¹/₄-inch cubes, until crisp. Remove with a slotted spoon. Substitute onions (about 4 very large) for the leeks and cook in the bacon fat as directed. Then proceed to step 3, stirring the bacon in along with the eggs.

MUSHROOMS

Mushrooms are one of our most underrated culinary treasures and I use them freely. Here's a wonderful side dish that highlights their pure, earthy flavor.

Mushrooms Poached in Sour Cream
EASTERN EUROPE ▨
MAKES **4 SERVINGS**
TIME **30 MINUTES**

This is a mild, rich side dish, one that can double as a sauce for buttered noodles or rice (it can be served on toast too). With chanterelles or other wild mushrooms, it's a dream, but even with button mushrooms it's super. If you have spring onions, this is the place to use them; otherwise, leeks are a great substitute.

4 tablespoons (¹/₂ stick) butter

¹/₂ pound spring onions or leeks, trimmed, cleaned
    (page 465), and chopped

1 pound mushrooms, trimmed and sliced

Salt and black pepper to taste

1 tablespoon flour

1 cup sour cream

Juice of $1/2$ lemon

$1/4$ cup chopped fresh dill or parsley leaves

1. Put the butter in a skillet over medium-high heat. When the butter foam subsides, add the onions and cook for a minute. Reduce the heat to medium and add the mushrooms, along with some salt and pepper. Cook, stirring occasionally, for about 10 minutes, or until the mushrooms have given up most of their liquid and begun to brown.
2. Stir in the flour and cook for a moment, then add the sour cream and reduce the heat to low. Simmer for 3 to 5 minutes, then stir in the lemon juice. Taste and adjust the seasoning, stir in the dill, and serve immediately.

Cabbage in Sour Cream. Oddly enough, this works equally well; a tablespoon of dill (or caraway) seeds added along with the sour cream is a nice addition: Use 1 to $1^1/2$ pounds cored and shredded cabbage in place of the mushrooms and add about $1/2$ cup water to the skillet along with the cabbage. Cooking time may be a little longer, and you may have to add a bit more water to the mix. Finish as directed.

OLIVES

Olives—detailed on page 18—are almost always served as a snack, as part of a salad, or in tapenade; you rarely see them cooked. But they're great that way; you can incorporate them into many sauces or braised dishes, and their essence lends an incomparable juiciness. Here's a terrific example.

Braised Olives with Tomatoes ITALY ■ ▨
MAKES **4 SERVINGS**

TIME **45 MINUTES**

An unusual preparation, though you might not think so if it included meat. I like it best with a combination of medium-sized black olives, like Kalamatas, and large green ones, particularly the type that come from Sicily, but any combination will do. A great side dish, especially with sautéed chicken, useful too as a topping for Crostini (page 41) or—thinned if necessary—as a pasta sauce.

If the olives are very, very salty—only an occasional problem—parboil them in water to cover for a few minutes before starting.

2 tablespoons extra virgin olive oil

2 large onions, thinly sliced

1 pound olives, preferably a combination of black and green, rinsed, and pitted if you have time

3 cups chopped tomatoes (canned are fine)

Salt and black pepper to taste

Several fresh thyme sprigs, or 1 tablespoon fresh oregano leaves or 1 teaspoon dried, or about $1/4$ cup coarsely chopped fresh basil leaves

1 tablespoon balsamic or sherry vinegar or fresh lemon juice

1. Put the oil in a skillet over medium heat; a minute later, add the onions. Cook, stirring, until quite soft, 10 to 15 minutes. Add the olives and cook, stirring occasionally, for a minute, then add the tomatoes and plenty of black pepper. If you're using thyme or oregano, add it now.
2. Cook, stirring occasionally, until the mixture is saucy and the olives quite tender, about 30 minutes; add the vinegar, then taste and adjust the seasoning (you might need a little salt, but it's unlikely). Stir in the basil and serve or cover and refrigerate for up to a couple of days.

ONIONS

Sweet and Sour Onions MIDDLE EAST ■ ▦

MAKES **4 TO 6 SERVINGS**

TIME **45 MINUTES**

I like this best with shallots, which are prettier and tastier than boiling onions. Some people add raisins (about ¼ cup, from the beginning), which does not turn me on. Others garnish with toasted pine nuts, a nice but unnecessary touch.

Other vegetables you can prepare this way: almost any member of the onion family, including leeks, scallions, and any kind of onion—if the onions are large, peel and quarter them, then insert a toothpick into each quarter to hold it together during the cooking.

> **3 tablespoons extra virgin olive oil or butter**
>
> **1 pound small white boiling onions or shallots, peeled**
>
> **½ cup white wine, preferably not too dry**
>
> **1 bay leaf**
>
> **3 tablespoons good-quality red or white wine vinegar**
>
> **2 teaspoons sugar**
>
> **Salt and black pepper to taste**
>
> **Pine nuts, toasted briefly in a dry skillet for garnish, optional**
>
> **Chopped fresh parsley leaves for garnish, optional**

1. Put the oil in a skillet that is large enough to hold the onions in one layer and has a lid and place over medium-high heat. A minute later, add the onions and cook, shaking the pan occasionally, until they brown lightly, about 5 minutes. Add the wine and let it bubble away for a minute. Add 1 cup water and the bay leaf and cook the onions until soft, about 15 minutes.
2. Add the vinegar, sugar, salt, and pepper and cover. Adjust the heat so the mixture simmers and cook for at least 20 minutes longer, adding a little more water if the mixture threatens to dry out. When the onions are browned all over and very soft, garnish if you like and serve hot or at room temperature, with the juices.

Onion Gratin FRANCE

MAKES **4 SERVINGS**

TIME **45 MINUTES**

A simple and delicious way to use onions as a vegetable, one that long ago became part of the Middle American repertoire but has sadly dropped out. Time for a revival?

This dish is unquestionably best with small onions—pearl onions—or with cipollini, the squat Italian variety, or the very fresh spring onions, usually sold only at that time of year and looking like scallions on steroids. It will work almost as well with leeks, which should be trimmed first, then parboiled for 2 or 3 minutes. If you must use larger onions, parboil for a good 10 minutes before peeling and baking.

Convert this to a gorgeous spring gratin by adding a handful each of fresh wild mushrooms, like morels, and fresh peas to the mix.

Other vegetables you can prepare this way: shallots, treated exactly as you would pearl onions.

> **Salt and black pepper to taste**
>
> **1½ pounds pearl or spring onions, trimmed**
>
> **Butter for the dish**
>
> **A small grating of nutmeg**
>
> **1 cup heavy cream**

1. Bring a pot of water to a boil and add salt. Preheat the oven to 400°F.
2. Drop the onions into the water and leave them there for a minute. Peel them, then put them in a buttered ovenproof dish large enough to hold

them in one layer. Sprinkle them with salt, pepper, and a little nutmeg, then pour the cream over all. Bake until the top is brown and the onions are soft, about 30 minutes.

PEAS

Peas in all their delicious forms—dried and fresh, with pods and without—can be found in recipes around the world and throughout this book. Shell peas are an undeniable hassle (though frozen peas are almost always an adequate if not perfect substitute), but edible-podded peas—snow peas and snap peas—are almost effortless. Here's a favorite using snow peas.

Snow Peas with Ginger CHINA ▓

MAKES **4 SERVINGS**

TIME **10 MINUTES**

A small and perfectly easy dish. The finishing touch of hot sesame oil is a common garnish in Hong Kong and a nice one.

   1 tablespoon peanut or neutral oil, like corn or grapeseed

   1 teaspoon peeled and minced fresh ginger, or more to taste

   2 cups snow peas, edible-podded peas, pea pods, or any combination

   1 tablespoon soy sauce

   1 tablespoon dark sesame oil

   Salt and black pepper to taste

1. Put the oil in a 10- or 12-inch skillet, preferably nonstick, over high heat. A minute later, add the ginger and peas and stir and toss occasionally, un-

til they are lightly browned and their green color is vivid, about 2 minutes.

2. Add the soy sauce and transfer to a platter. Add the sesame oil to the same pan and heat for about 10 seconds. Pour over the snow peas, season with salt and pepper, and serve immediately.

SWEET PEPPERS

Sweet peppers, though not as varied as chiles (page 588), still have their differences. Green peppers are unripe peppers; though they have their uses, they're never as sweet as red (or orange or yellow) ones. A mixture of more than one color is always great. Longer peppers have thinner flesh and generally are better for frying than grilling (it's too easy to burn them on a grill).

Roasted Red Peppers MEDITERRANEAN ▓ ▓

MAKES **4 TO 8 SERVINGS**

TIME **20 TO 60 MINUTES**

Everyone who grows red peppers roasts red peppers, because it is, to use a legal term, their highest and best use. Once they're roasted, you can include them in a variety of recipes found here and in other books, or you can sauté them with onion and tomato, include them in stews, or put them on sandwiches. Arguably, they are at their best when served at room temperature, drizzled with oil and perhaps with some capers and anchovies. (They also keep very, very well, up to a few days, refrigerated.)

You can roast these, grill them, or broil them; all methods work about equally well.

Obviously, if you grill over wood, you're going to get some added (and welcome) flavors.

8 red bell peppers, washed

Extra virgin olive oil for rubbing the peppers

Salt to taste

Sherry or balsamic vinegar, optional

1. Rub the peppers all over with a couple of table-spoons of olive oil.

   To roast or broil: Preheat the oven to 450°F or turn on the broiler and place the rack about 4 inches from the heat source. Put the peppers in a foil-lined roasting pan. Roast or broil, turning the peppers as each side browns, until the peppers have darkened and collapsed, 15 or 20 minutes in the broiler, up to an hour in the oven.

   To grill: Start a charcoal or wood fire or preheat a gas grill; the rack should be about 4 inches from the heat source. When the fire is hot, put the peppers directly over the heat. Grill, turning as each side blackens, until they collapse, about 15 minutes.

2. Wrap the cooked peppers in foil (if you roasted the peppers, you can use the same foil that lined the pan) and cool until you can handle them, then remove the skin, seeds, and stems. Don't worry if the peppers fall apart.

3. The peppers can be served immediately or stored in the refrigerator for up to a few days; bring back to room temperature before serving. When you're ready to serve, sprinkle with a bit of salt, drizzle with olive oil, and, if you like, add a few drops of vinegar.

Peperonata ITALY ■ ▩

MAKES **4 TO 6 SERVINGS**

TIME **45 MINUTES**

A sweet classic, peperonata, like many vegetable stews, is easily varied: add chunks of potato, chicken, or zuc-chini or some minced garlic; a small chile or a bit of cayenne is also appropriate. Serve it hot as a side dish, warm as a topping for Crostini (page 41), or cold as a relish.

2 tablespoons extra virgin olive oil

2 tablespoons butter (or use more oil)

2 large onions, thinly sliced

Salt and black pepper to taste

2 red bell peppers, stemmed, seeded, and sliced

2 yellow bell peppers, stemmed, seeded, and sliced

3 cups chopped tomatoes with juice (canned are fine)

¼ cup fresh basil leaves, roughly chopped

1. Put the oil and butter in a large skillet or flame-proof casserole over medium-high heat. When the butter melts, add the onions, a large pinch of salt, and some pepper and cook, stirring occasionally, until the onions are soft, about 10 minutes. Add the peppers and continue to cook until wilted, another 10 minutes or so.

2. Add the tomatoes, bring to a boil, and adjust the heat so the mixture simmers steadily but not violently. Cook, stirring occasionally, until the mixture is thick, at least 15 minutes more. Taste and adjust the seasoning, stir in the basil, and serve hot or at room temperature or cover and refrigerate for up to a couple of days. The peperonata can be reheated or served cold.

Sautéed Piquillo Peppers SPAIN ■ ▩ ▨

MAKES **4 SERVINGS**

TIME **10 MINUTES**

This is a side dish or an appetizer, but a very quick one, since piquillos (sold in cans or jars) are already cooked. You can use freshly roasted red peppers (page 470) as a substitute, but not canned pimientos, which will fall apart (and, in most cases, are tasteless anyway). Add a few anchovy fillets along with the garlic if you like.

2 tablespoons extra virgin olive oil, or a little more

2 teaspoons slivered garlic

8 to 12 piquillo peppers, cut into strips

Salt and black pepper to taste

Sherry vinegar to taste, optional

1. Place the olive oil in a large skillet over medium-low heat and add the garlic. Cook, shaking the pan occasionally, until the garlic begins to color, about 5 minutes.
2. Add the peppers and turn the heat to medium. Cook, shaking the pan, until the peppers just begin to change color on the bottom, less than 5 minutes; turn and repeat. Season and serve hot or at room temperature, drizzled, if you like, with a little more olive oil and some sherry vinegar.

PLANTAINS

The plantain is a type of banana that is always cooked and at different stages of ripeness. It may range from green to black, with every stage of greenish yellow to yellow spotted with black in between. The blacker, the sweeter and the softer.

Platanos Maduros Sautéed Ripe Plantains
CARIBBEAN ▧

MAKES **4 SERVINGS**

TIME **20 MINUTES**

The hardest part of making these beauties is waiting for the plantains to turn black, though if you live in a neighborhood with a Latin market, you can probably buy them that way. Otherwise, buy the ripest (yellowest, with spots of black) plantains you can find and let them sit on your counter until they have turned black with no traces of yellow. To peel, cut off the tips, then cut crosswise into thirds; make a slit in the skin of each piece, then remove the skin.

For Plantain and Meat Casserole (page 420), cut the plantains into thirds and then split each piece lengthwise—rather than cutting them crosswise—before sautéing.

3 or 4 very ripe plantains, peeled

Corn, grapeseed, or other neutral oil for frying

Salt and black pepper to taste

Lime wedges for serving

1. Cut the plantains into about 1-inch pieces. Put about $1/16$ inch of oil in a large skillet over medium heat and, a minute later, add the plantains.
2. Cook, turning as necessary and adjusting the heat so the plantains brown slowly without burning, 10 to 15 minutes. Serve hot, sprinkled with salt and pepper, with lime wedges on the side.

Ndizi wa Nazi Plantains in Coconut Milk
CONGO, ZANZIBAR ▧

MAKES **4 SERVINGS**

TIME **20 MINUTES**

Plantains, a staple throughout much of Africa, are spiced up here to be served as a slightly sweet side dish. Warm, deeply satisfying, and quick, this is unusual and good even on weeknights. Best with West African, Caribbean (especially Lechon Asado, page 375), Mexican, and South American dishes.

Other vegetables you can prepare this way: green bananas or potatoes, both of which will need longer cooking time.

4 ripe (yellow-black) plantains, peeled (page 473) and cut into 1-inch rounds

$\frac{1}{2}$ teaspoon salt

$\frac{1}{2}$ teaspoon curry powder, preferably homemade (pages 592–593)

Pinch of ground cloves

$\frac{1}{2}$ teaspoon ground cinnamon, plus more to taste

$\frac{1}{2}$ teaspoon ground allspice or cardamom

$1\frac{1}{2}$ cups coconut milk, homemade (page 584) or canned

1. Put all the ingredients into a large saucepan over medium-low heat. Stir, then bring the mixture to a steady simmer.

2. Cook, stirring occasionally, until the plantains are tender and have absorbed almost all of the coconut milk, about 15 minutes. Serve immediately, sprinkled with a little more cinnamon if you like.

Foo Foo Mashed Plantains GHANA
MAKES **4 SERVINGS**
TIME **1$\frac{1}{2}$ HOURS, LARGELY UNATTENDED**

Foo foo, a staple in West Africa, is unlike any other starchy dish I've ever eaten. Traditionally, boiled plantains (or yucca) are pounded in large wooden mortars until they break down into a springy mash with a sticky, stretchy texture. Pieces are then pulled off by hand (you can use a spoon) and then dipped into a sauce, soup, or stew. I like to pull off pieces before serving and drop into Groundnut Stew (page 296).

2 tablespoons coarse salt, plus more to taste

4 yellow plantains, cut into 2-inch lengths and peeled (page 472)

1. Stir 1 tablespoon salt into a large bowl of cold water to dissolve; add the plantains and let sit for 20 minutes.

2. Meanwhile, bring a large pot of water to a boil and add the remaining salt. Transfer the plantains to the boiling water and cook until very tender, about 30 minutes.

3. Remove from the water, cut crosswise into 1-inch pieces, and put in a food processor. Pulse until finely chopped, then transfer to a mixing bowl and beat with a wooden spoon until smooth, sticky, and springy. (Alternatively, use a mortar and pestle. Put in a mortar, season to taste with salt, then pound with the pestle until the plantains become a sticky, springy mass, about 30 minutes.)

4. Pull off walnut-sized pieces with your fingers and serve immediately.

POTATOES

One important thing about potatoes: the baking potato (commonly called Idaho or russet) is best for baking, essential for gnocchi, and good for French fries and mashing. But for most other uses, you're best off with "all-purpose" potatoes, like Yukon Gold (a relatively new variety that is very good) or the waxy white or red-skinned potatoes sometimes called "new" potatoes. (Any potato can be "new," but the red ones most frequently are dug small.)

Stir-Fried Potatoes with Chiles CHINA ▦
MAKES **4 SERVINGS**
TIME **30 MINUTES**

The first time I was served this I found it completely bizarre, as you may. But I loved it instantly. It's from Szechwan but is equally at home with Asian and European dishes, as long as they have some guts.

The quality of this dish is maintained for only a few minutes; as it gets cold, it becomes far less appealing. So—really—prepare it at the last minute and serve it immediately.

> **Salt and black pepper to taste**
>
> **4 medium potatoes, peeled**
>
> **3 tablespoons peanut or neutral oil, like corn or grapeseed**
>
> **2 fresh Thai chiles or 1 jalapeño, stemmed, seeded, and minced, or 5 or 10 small dried chiles, or about 1 teaspoon hot red pepper flakes, or to taste**

1. Bring a large pot of water to a boil and add salt. Shred the potatoes, using the julienne blade of a mandoline, the shredding disk of a food processor, or a box grater. Plunge into the boiling water and remove after 30 seconds; immediately rinse under cold running water. The potatoes should remain quite crunchy; do not cook them until they are tender. Drain.

2. Put the oil in a large skillet, preferably nonstick, over medium-high heat. Add the chiles and cook until they sizzle, about a minute, then add the potatoes. Cook, stirring constantly, just until they begin to brown, about 5 minutes. Add some salt and pepper, then taste and adjust the seasoning and serve immediately.

THAI CHILES

Potato Pancakes with Scallions and Kimchi KOREA

MAKES **4 SERVINGS**

TIME **40 MINUTES**

We're accustomed to seeing shredded potatoes in hash browns or in the Eastern European pancakes commonly known as latkes. These are deliciously different.

The easiest way to prepare the potatoes is with the shredding disk of a food processor, but you can also use the normal steel blade and pulse until they are chopped. Or, of course, you can grate them by hand. In any case, do not grate too finely. Serve with any stewed meat dish and not just Korean-flavored ones.

Other vegetables you can prepare this way: you can substitute carrots or sweet potatoes for half of the white potatoes here.

> **4 scallions, trimmed and chopped**
>
> **¹⁄₃ cup soy sauce**
>
> **1 tablespoon peeled and minced fresh ginger**
>
> **2 tablespoons toasted sesame seeds (page 596)**
>
> **1 tablespoon dark sesame oil**
>
> **1 tablespoon sugar**
>
> **3 or 4 potatoes, peeled and grated to make about 3 cups**
>
> **¹⁄₂ cup Kimchi (page 444), drained and chopped**
>
> **1 egg**
>
> **2 tablespoons flour**
>
> **Salt and black pepper to taste**
>
> **Cayenne to taste or about 1 small fresh chile, stemmed, seeded, and minced**
>
> **About ¹⁄₃ cup corn, grapeseed, or other neutral oil**

1. Mince 2 of the scallions and combine with the soy sauce, ginger, sesame seeds, sesame oil, and sugar; set aside.

2. Put the potatoes in a strainer and squeeze to extract excess liquid. Combine in a bowl with the kimchi, egg, flour, salt, pepper, and cayenne.

3. Preheat the oven to 200°F. Put a couple of table-spoons of oil in a large skillet, preferably nonstick, over medium-high heat. When the oil is hot, add the potato batter by the large spoonful, to make pancakes about 3 inches across. Fry until nicely browned on one side, then turn and brown the other side, less than 10 minutes total. Drain on paper towels and keep warm in the oven while you repeat the process to use up all the batter.

4. Spoon a little of the sauce over the pancakes and pass the rest at the table.

Potato Croquettes with Meat JAPAN ■

MAKES **4 SERVINGS**

TIME **45 MINUTES**

I had been making meatless potato croquettes for years when I found that my favorite condiment (for these and many other fried foods) was soy sauce mixed with lemon—so imagine my self-satisfaction when I was served these at a Tokyo lunch counter with exactly that dipping sauce.

I like to add curry powder, for both flavor and color, but it's not essential. Substitute canned salmon or tuna for the meat if you like, but don't cook it; simply toss it with the onion and seasonings after cooking the onion. The Japanese bread crumbs called panko are available at Japanese markets and many supermarkets.

In Japan, these are almost always deep-fried; I find panfrying suffices, though of course you can deep-fry if you prefer. They're usually served on a bed of plain shredded cabbage, sometimes as an appetizer, sometimes as a main course.

You can make both mashed potatoes and the meat mixture in advance; you can also make the patties in advance and cover and refrigerate them for up to a day before cooking.

3 cups mashed potatoes, made with a minimum of milk
  and no butter (leftovers are fine)
Salt and black pepper to taste
3 tablespoons extra virgin olive oil or neutral oil, like corn
  or grapeseed
1 medium onion, chopped
1/2 pound ground beef, pork, chicken, or turkey, or a
  combination of ground meats
5 tablespoons soy sauce
2 teaspoons curry powder, preferably homemade
  (pages 592–593), optional
2 tablespoons butter or more oil
Flour for dredging
2 eggs, lightly beaten in a bowl
Bread crumbs, preferably fresh (page 580), or panko
  (Japanese bread crumbs, page 8) for dredging
Juice of 1 lemon
2 cups shredded cabbage, optional

1. If you're making mashed potatoes expressly for this dish, cook the meat while the potatoes are boiling. Season the potatoes well, but do not over-salt. Put 1 tablespoon oil in a medium to large skillet over medium-high heat. Add the onion and cook, stirring frequently, just until it softens, 5 minutes or so. Crumble the meat and add it, stirring to break up clumps. Cook, stirring, just until it loses its color, another 5 minutes. Turn off the heat, then add 1 tablespoon of the soy sauce, the curry powder if you're using it, and salt and pepper.

2. When the meat is cool enough to handle, combine with the potatoes. Again, taste and adjust the seasoning. Form into 4 large or 8 small patties.

3. Put the butter and remaining 2 tablespoons oil in a large skillet, preferably nonstick, over medium-high heat. When the butter melts, dredge each patty in the flour, then run through the egg, then dredge in the bread crumbs, pressing to help the crumbs adhere. Cook the patties as you would

hamburgers, turning—carefully, so as not to dislodge the coating—as each side browns, about 5 minutes per side. Since all the ingredients are already cooked, the crust is your main concern; the interior will get hot as long as the exterior browns.

4. Combine the remaining ¼ cup soy sauce with the lemon juice. If you're using the cabbage, spread it on a platter and moisten with a bit of the soy-lemon sauce. Put the patties on the cabbage bed and serve, passing the remaining sauce at the table.

Meatless Potato Croquettes with Curry. A side dish, not a main course: Omit the meat and soy sauce; finely chop the onion, but don't bother to cook it. Combine the potatoes with the onion, 1 teaspoon minced garlic, 1 egg, the curry powder, and ¼ cup chopped fresh cilantro leaves. Finish as directed, omitting the cabbage and serving with lemon wedges.

Panfried Spicy Potatoes with Eggplant INDIA ■ ▣

MAKES **4 SERVINGS**

TIME **ABOUT 40 MINUTES**

An unusual combination of textures and flavors, but—like the eggplant and apple mixture on page 458—one that really works. Serve in combination with other Indian dishes or as an unusual side dish with Western food.

Other vegetables you can prepare this way: for the eggplant, substitute cauliflower or thick slices of red or yellow bell pepper or a combination.

About 1½ pounds waxy potatoes

About 1½ pounds firm eggplant, preferably a small variety

¼ cup peanut oil (preferred) or neutral oil, like corn or grapeseed, or butter

1 jalapeño or 2 smaller fresh chiles, stemmed, seeded, and minced, or 1 teaspoon hot red pepper flakes, or to taste

1 tablespoon minced garlic

1 teaspoon mustard seeds

1 teaspoon cumin seeds

Salt and black pepper to taste

½ cup chopped onion

Fresh lemon juice to taste

Chopped fresh cilantro leaves for garnish

1. Peel the potatoes and cut them the long way into wedges, 6 to 10 per potato. Peel the eggplant (salt it if necessary; see page 456) and cut it into similar-sized wedges.

2. Put the oil in a 12-inch nonstick skillet with a lid over medium heat. Wait a couple of minutes, then add the chiles, garlic, mustard, and cumin; cook, stirring, until the garlic colors and the mustard seeds pop, a couple of minutes. Add the potatoes and eggplant, along with ¼ cup water and a sprinkling of salt and pepper, and cover. Cook for about 10 minutes, checking once or twice and adding a little water if necessary, until the vegetables begin to soften. Remove the cover and raise the heat to medium-high. Cook, stirring occasionally, until both potatoes and eggplant brown nicely and become completely tender, another 10 to 15 minutes.

3. Add the onion and continue to cook, stirring occasionally, until it softens and begins to brown, another 5 minutes or so. Stir in the lemon juice, taste and adjust the seasoning, then garnish and serve hot or at room temperature.

Panfried Spicy Potatoes with Tomatoes. You can make these with or without the eggplant: In step 3, add 2 cups seeded and chopped tomatoes about 2 minutes after adding the onion. Cook, stirring occasionally, until the tomatoes begin to break up, about 5 minutes. Serve as directed.

Home-Fried Potatoes with Onion and Amchoor INDIA ■ ▦

MAKES **4 SERVINGS**

TIME **ABOUT 40 MINUTES**

A real twist on American home fries, so good they can be eaten cold. Amchoor is dried mango powder, a supersour element; substitute lemon juice if you prefer. Amchoor powder is available at Indian markets. Serve these as you would any home fries.

If you cook these in butter, they'll be more authentic and more delicious. But oil is fine, too.

> About 2 pounds waxy potatoes
>
> Salt and black pepper to taste
>
> 2 tablespoons butter, peanut oil, or neutral oil, like corn
>   or grapeseed
>
> 1 cup chopped onion
>
> $^1/_4$ teaspoon cayenne, or to taste
>
> 1 tablespoon curry powder, preferably homemade (pages
>   592–593), or garam masala (page 594), or to taste
>
> 1 teaspoon amchoor powder, or to taste

1. Peel the potatoes, cut them into 1-inch chunks, and boil in salted water to cover until tender, 10 to 15 minutes. Drain.
2. Put the butter in a 12-inch skillet, preferably nonstick, over medium heat. Wait a couple of minutes, then add the potatoes. Raise the heat to medium-high and cook, turning to brown each side but not stirring too often. Add the onion when the potatoes are nearly done, after 10 to 15 minutes of cooking; cook, stirring, until the onion softens and begins to brown, 5 to 10 minutes. Add the seasonings, then taste and add more salt, cayenne, or amchoor if you like and serve hot or at room temperature.

Spicy Indian Home Fries. In step 2, cook 1 tablespoon mustard seeds in the oil before adding the potatoes. Omit the onion and, along with the potatoes, add 1 tablespoon whole cumin seeds and 1 teaspoon ground turmeric. Add 1 jalapeño, stemmed, seeded, and minced, or to taste, and cook for another minute or two, then finish with some chopped fresh cilantro leaves and about $^1/_4$ cup chopped cashews (optional).

Spicy Indian Home Fries with Tomato and Egg. A popular vegetarian dish: Follow the preceding variation and add 3 or 4 hard-cooked eggs (page 338), each cut into about 8 pieces, and 2 cored, seeded, and chopped tomatoes along with the chiles. Cook for another 2 minutes or so, then garnish and serve.

Peasant-Style Potatoes SPAIN ▦

MAKES **4 SERVINGS**

TIME **30 MINUTES**

This is closely related to the Tortilla (page 341) so frequently served as a tapa in Spain, but it's simply potato and olive oil, kind of Spanish home fries. A little garlic is nice but not essential. Serve as you would any home fries.

You can use all-purpose potatoes for this (like Yukon Gold) or red or white waxy potatoes, but don't use baking potatoes, which will simply fall apart as they soften.

> 2 pounds (4 or 5 medium) potatoes, preferably
>   Yukon Gold
>
> $^1/_3$ cup extra virgin olive oil
>
> Salt and black pepper to taste
>
> 1 teaspoon minced garlic, optional
>
> Chopped fresh parsley leaves for garnish

1. Peel and thinly slice the potatoes; if you have a mandoline, use it, but on its thickest setting—you want slices about $^1/_8$ inch thick.

2. Put the oil in an 8- or 10-inch nonstick skillet and turn the heat to medium; 3 or 4 minutes later, drop in a slice of potato. When tiny bubbles appear around the edges of the potato, the oil is ready; add all of the potatoes along with a fair amount of salt and pepper.

3. Gently turn the potatoes occasionally, keeping the heat at medium until, 15 to 20 minutes later, they are tender. At that point, turn the heat up so the potatoes brown a bit. Add the garlic, if you're using it, during the last 5 minutes of cooking. Taste and adjust the seasoning, then garnish and serve hot.

Peasant-Style Potatoes with Onion and Tomato
ITALY. Slightly more complicated, but this can also be turned into a soup (add water or stock along with the tomato) or a pasta sauce: In step 3, add 1 medium onion, diced, and about 1 cup chopped tomato (canned is fine); cook for 5 minutes or so, then add 1 cup water. Cook gently, stirring occasionally, until the potatoes are very soft and the water is absorbed, 10 to 15 minutes. Add the garlic (and a pinch of cayenne) if you like.

Gnocchi ITALY
MAKES **4 SERVINGS**
TIME **1 1/2 HOURS**

Labor intensive but highly rewarding. Perhaps not on the first try, but by your second or third, you will be making the best gnocchi you have ever eaten. (On the first try, you should probably use too much flour to make them a little firmer, but as you get used to the odd dough you will eventually make them lighter.) These make a great first course or side dish, served with Fast, Fresh Tomato Sauce (page 606) or simply melted butter and freshly grated Parmesan. And be sure to take a look at Potato Dumplings (recipe follows).

1 pound baking potatoes
Salt and black pepper to taste
About 1 cup flour

1. Put the potatoes in a pot with water to cover and add salt; adjust the heat so the water simmers and cook until the potatoes are quite tender, about 45 minutes. Drain and peel (use a pot holder or towel to hold the potatoes and peel with a small knife; it will be easy). Rinse the pot and once again fill it with salted water and bring to a boil.

2. Use a fork, potato masher, or ricer to mash or rice the potatoes in a bowl, along with some salt and pepper. Add about 1/2 cup of the flour and stir; add more flour until the mixture forms a dough you can handle. Knead for a minute or so on a lightly floured surface. Pinch off a piece of the dough and boil it to make sure it will hold its shape; if it does not, knead in a bit more flour.

3. Roll a piece of the dough into a rope about 1/2 inch thick, then cut the rope into 1-inch lengths; traditionally, you would spin each of these pieces off

ROLLING GNOCCHI OFF A FORK

the tines of a fork to score it lightly. As each gnoccho is ready, place it on a sheet of wax paper; do not allow them to touch.

4. A few at a time, add the gnocchi to the boiling water and stir. A minute after they rise to the surface, the gnocchi are done; remove with a slotted spoon. Put in a bowl and add sauce or reheat in butter within a few minutes; these do not keep well at all.

Potato Dumplings EASTERN EUROPE ■ ▨

MAKES **4 SERVINGS**

TIME **30 MINUTES**

The now-familiar gnocchi (preceding recipe) have gotten all the attention, but these—if a bit less elegant—are quite wonderful, considerably easier to handle, and far swifter to prepare. They are ideal alongside dishes like Sour Beef Stew with Horseradish (page 379).

> **Salt and black pepper to taste**
>
> **1 pound potatoes, peeled**
>
> **1 cup flour, or less**
>
> **2 eggs**
>
> **About 1/4 cup extra virgin olive oil or butter or a combination**

1. Bring a large pot of water to a boil and add salt. Grate or shred the potatoes by hand or in a food processor. Squeeze in a strainer or towel to remove as much liquid as possible. Combine with 1/2 cup of the flour and some salt, pepper, and the eggs. Stir, adding enough additional flour to make a dough that will hold together when squeezed in your hands.

2. Adjust the heat so the water simmers steadily. Make dumplings with a spoon or your hand, each

about the size of a walnut or small egg, and add to the water. Cook for about 3 minutes after they float to the surface; taste one and make sure the potato is cooked. Drain. (You may wrap or cover tightly and refrigerate these for up to a day at this point.)

3. When you're ready to cook, put the oil in a skillet over medium-high heat. When the oil is hot, brown the dumplings lightly, for about 5 minutes, seasoning them with salt and pepper as they cook if necessary. Serve hot.

Helen Art's Potato "Nik"

EASTERN EUROPE ■ ▨

MAKES **8 OR MORE SERVINGS**

TIME **ABOUT 40 MINUTES**

A big potato pie, one of my grandmother's favorites. She made this in a big cast-iron skillet, usually without butter, but it *is* better this way and can usually be made a couple of hours before eating; it remains quite crisp. Serve to a crowd, along with a stew or roast.

> **3 to 4 pounds baking potatoes, peeled**
>
> **1 large onion**
>
> **3 eggs**
>
> **Salt and black pepper to taste**
>
> **1/2 cup plain bread crumbs, preferably homemade (page 580), matzo meal, or flour, or as needed**
>
> **2 tablespoons butter**
>
> **2 tablespoons corn, grapeseed, or other neutral oil**

1. Grate the potatoes and onion on a box grater or with the grating disk of a food processor; if the mixture is very moist, drain in a colander or strainer for a minute.

2. In a large bowl, beat the eggs with the salt, pepper, and bread crumbs. Stir in the potatoes and onion.

The mixture should just barely hold together if you pinch a bit; if it does not, add a few more bread crumbs.

3. Preheat the oven to 400°F. Put the butter and oil in a 12-inch nonstick, ovenproof skillet over medium heat. When the butter melts and bubbles, pour the batter into it. Cook for a minute or two, then transfer to the oven. Bake for 20 to 30 minutes, or until nicely browned on the bottom; slide the cake out onto a plate (it will hold together). Cover with another plate, then invert the plates. Slide the pie back into the pan, cooked side up, and return to the oven until the bottom is brown; this will take only 10 minutes or so. Remove from the skillet and serve hot, warm, or at room temperature.

Mashed Potatoes with Anchovies

ITALY ▨

MAKES **4 TO 6 SERVINGS**

TIME **30 MINUTES**

About as far from the classic "American" mashed potatoes as you can get, these are equally rich (especially with the butter), but far more flavorful. They're great with simple roasted meat or poultry but are not for the faint of heart.

> 1¹⁄₂ pounds waxy red or white potatoes, peeled and cut into chunks
>
> Salt and black pepper to taste
>
> 3 tablespoons extra virgin olive oil
>
> 2 ounces (1 small can) anchovy fillets, with their oil
>
> 1 teaspoon minced garlic
>
> 2 tablespoons butter, optional
>
> 2 tablespoons chopped fresh parsley leaves, plus more for garnish

1. Put the potatoes in a pot with salted water to cover and bring to a boil. Partially cover and adjust the heat so the mixture simmers steadily. Don't mess with the potatoes much, but check one of them with the point of a knife after 10 minutes or so and cook until soft. Drain and place in a bowl. Mash with a large fork or potato masher until mealy.

2. Add the olive oil to a skillet, preferably nonstick, large enough to hold the potatoes. Place over medium heat, add the anchovies and garlic, and cook, stirring frequently, until the garlic begins to soften and the anchovies break up, just a minute or so. Turn the heat to low, add the potatoes to the pan, and stir until all the ingredients are well combined; add the butter if you're using it and continue to stir. Taste and adjust the seasoning, stir in the parsley, garnish, and serve.

Mashed Potatoes with Mushrooms and Onions EASTERN EUROPE ■

MAKES **4 SERVINGS**

TIME **ABOUT 40 MINUTES**

Once not only a staple but a main course, this is one of those side dishes many people can't get enough of. Serve with something light and lean, like plain broiled fish.

> 2 pounds baking potatoes, peeled and cut into quarters
>
> Salt and black pepper to taste
>
> 5 tablespoons butter
>
> 1 large onion, chopped
>
> ¹⁄₂ pound button mushrooms, trimmed and chopped
>
> ¹⁄₂ cup sour cream, or more to taste

1. Boil the potatoes in a pot with salted water to cover until soft, at least 15 minutes. Meanwhile,

put 2 tablespoons of the butter in a skillet over medium-high heat. When its foam subsides, add the onion and mushrooms, along with a large pinch of salt and a sprinkling of pepper, and cook, stirring occasionally, until they soften and brown, 10 to 15 minutes. Both onion and mushrooms should become a little crispy on the edges.

2. When the potatoes are done, drain them, then mash them well or put them through a food mill. Return them to the pot over the lowest possible heat and stir in the remaining 3 tablespoons butter, along with the sour cream. Stir in the onion and mushrooms, along with any butter remaining in that pan. Taste and adjust the seasoning, adding more salt, pepper, or sour cream as necessary. Serve immediately, keep warm, or reheat in a microwave.

Potatoes with Bay Leaves FRANCE
MAKES **4 SERVINGS**
TIME **ABOUT 1 HOUR**

Amazing how minor touches in familiar dishes can make such a huge difference. Anyone who grew up eating baked potatoes with butter and sour cream will be pleased and surprised at how aromatic and delicate these are.

4 baking potatoes
Salt and black pepper to taste
8 bay leaves
¼ cup extra virgin olive oil or melted butter

1. Preheat the oven to 400°F. Make a deep slit lengthwise in each potato, almost to the point of cutting it in half. Sprinkle salt and pepper in there and tuck in the bay leaves, 2 per potato. Put the potatoes in a baking dish and drizzle with the olive oil, smearing some on the insides as well as making sure the outsides are well coated. Push the potato halves back together and sprinkle their outsides with salt and pepper.

2. Bake for about an hour; the potatoes are done when you can easily poke a thin-bladed knife right through them. Serve immediately.

Potato Puffs FRANCE
MAKES **4 TO 6 SERVINGS**
TIME **1 HOUR**

A sort of deep-fried gnocchi that I was first served—sans onion—dipped in sugar, as a dessert. I like these better, however, as a side dish, with a roast. Old-fashioned and killer. Other vegetables you can prepare this way: substitute carrots or sweet potatoes for all or some of the white potatoes.

1½ pounds baking potatoes, peeled and cut into quarters
Salt and black pepper to taste
½ cup flour
1 egg
½ cup minced onion
Corn, grapeseed, or other neutral oil for deep-frying

1. Boil the potatoes in salted water to cover until soft, at least 15 minutes. Drain, then mash them well or put them through a food mill or ricer. Combine with the remaining ingredients except the oil. (You can prepare this mixture several hours ahead if you like; cover and refrigerate.)

2. Put at least 1 inch, preferably 2 inches, of oil in a heavy skillet or saucepan over medium-high heat. Bring the oil to a temperature between 325 and 350°F. Roll the potato mixture out on a floured

surface and, using a cookie cutter or glass, cut into 2-inch circles; or simply roll into small balls with your hands.

3. Fry the circles or balls until golden brown on both sides, about 2 minutes. Drain on paper towels and serve hot.

Caramelized Potatoes SCANDINAVIA ▨

MAKES **6 TO 8 SERVINGS**

TIME **30 MINUTES**

Even more so than most other people in the world with access to refined sugar, the Swedes and their fellow Scandinavians incorporate it into the most unlikely dishes. In this one, the caramel is not cooked until it becomes strongly bitter, but just slightly so. The butter then mellows it out. Not exactly health food by today's standards, but a glorious side dish at any feast.

24 small waxy red or white potatoes or 6 larger ones,
    peeled and cut into chunks
Salt and black pepper to taste
$^1/_2$ cup sugar
8 tablespoons (1 stick) butter

1. Put the potatoes in a pot with salted water to cover and bring to a boil. Partially cover and adjust the heat so the mixture simmers steadily. Don't mess with the potatoes much, but check one of them with the point of a knife after 10 minutes or so and cook until soft. Drain. (You can cook the potatoes and then cover them with plastic and refrigerate them for up to a day.)

2. Put the sugar in a 12-inch skillet, preferably nonstick, over low heat, along with a tablespoon of water. Cook, shaking the pan gently (but not stirring), until the sugar liquefies, bubbles, and turns light brown, about 10 minutes. Add the butter a bit at a time, stirring after each addition, until the mixture is smooth.

3. Turn the potatoes in the caramel, working in batches if necessary and rolling them so they become coated. When the potatoes are evenly covered and golden brown, add some pepper (and more salt if necessary), transfer to a plate, and serve.

Potato and Horseradish Gratin

EASTERN EUROPE ■

MAKES **4 SERVINGS**

TIME **45 MINUTES**

Horseradish, as I've noted elsewhere, loses most of its potency when heated. It also retains its flavor, making it a great accompaniment to potatoes in this simple gratin. The trick is finding fresh horseradish—and then peeling and slicing it (some people wear goggles, not a terrible idea). If none of this appeals to you, just make the gratin with potatoes—it's a beaut either way. Serve with roast chicken or meat.

Other vegetables you can prepare this way: any root vegetable or tuber—carrots, parsnips, or turnips, for example—will work fine prepared in this style, alone or in combination.

1 pound fresh horseradish, peeled and thinly sliced (use
    a mandoline if you have one)
1 pound potatoes, preferably Yukon Gold
Salt and black pepper to taste
4 tablespoons ($^1/_2$ stick) butter
2 to 3 cups half-and-half or milk, or more

1. Put the horseradish in a saucepan with water to cover and bring to a boil; simmer for about 5 minutes, then drain and rinse with cold water. Mean-

while, peel the potatoes and rinse them; slice them thinly with a knife or mandoline.

2. Preheat the oven to 400°F. Layer the potatoes and horseradish in a large nonstick, ovenproof skillet or roasting pan, sprinkling the layers with salt and pepper. Dot with the butter, then add enough half-and-half to come about three-quarters of the way up to the top.

3. Turn the heat under the gratin to high and bring to a boil. Turn the heat to medium-high and cook for about 10 minutes, or until the level of both liquid and vegetables has dropped somewhat. Put in the oven and cook, undisturbed, until the top is nicely browned, about 10 minutes. Turn the oven down to 300°F and continue cooking until the potatoes and horseradish are tender (a thin-bladed knife will pierce them with little or no resistance), about 10 minutes more. Serve immediately or keep warm in the oven or over very low heat for up to 30 minutes.

Potato and Gruyère Gratin FRANCE. Substitute ¼ pound of good-quality Gruyère, grated, for the horseradish and add an additional pound of potatoes. Layer the two as described in step 2, but instead of bringing the whole mixture to a boil on top of the stove, put the pan directly into the preheated oven and bake for 1 to 1½ hours, until tender. Run the gratin under the broiler for 30 seconds or so to crisp, then serve hot or warm.

SAUERKRAUT

Good sauerkraut is sold either from a barrel or in plastic bags; the canned stuff is terrible. And no matter how it's sold, it should contain no more than salt and cabbage; no preservatives are necessary (that's what the salt is for).

Sauerkraut Braised in Wine GERMANY
MAKES **4 SERVINGS**
TIME **ABOUT 40 MINUTES**

The combination of sauerkraut, juniper, and fruity wine is a divine one. You might as well use a German wine to be completely consistent. Best with pork, like Baeckoffe (page 399).

2 tablespoons lard or neutral oil, like corn or grapeseed
1½ to 2 pounds sauerkraut, rinsed
1 onion, sliced
1 bay leaf
1 teaspoon juniper berries, crushed with the side of a knife
1 cup Gewürztraminer or Riesling, not too dry
Freshly ground black pepper to taste

1. Heat the lard in a large skillet over medium heat until hot. Add the sauerkraut and onion and toss until the onion begins to wilt, 5 to 10 minutes. Add the remaining ingredients except the pepper, stir, and cook until some of the wine bubbles away, a minute or two.

2. Cover, lower the heat, and cook until the sauerkraut is tender, about 30 minutes. Add a good grinding of black pepper and serve.

SEAWEED

These are marine algae, not plants and definitely not weeds. Though we could call them sea vegetables, we're not going to. They were undoubtedly among the first foods consumed by humans, are still harvested off the coasts of almost every continent, and are (obviously) natural and incredibly nutritious—high in protein, vitamins (even B$_{12}$, rarely found outside of meat), minerals, and trace elements (rapidly disappearing from land vegetables due to soil depletion).

Seaweed has been a staple of Japanese and Chinese cooking for thousands of years and has a history as a snack food in northern Europe, Canada, and even Maine. These days it's usually dried and packed in resealable plastic. Some can be eaten out of the bag as a snack; others, especially nori, are toasted and used as a wrap or crumbled as a condiment. Most are best thrown into a pot of soup or stew or reconstituted and made into a salad or added to one.

You can usually find seaweeds at natural food stores, but you can also buy directly from producers (try www.seaveg.com and www.seaweed.net).

A quick primer:

NORI (LAVER)
Best known as the sushi wrapper; deep purple black or green. Sold as sheets, toasted or not toasted. It can be crumbled and used to flavor soup, rice, a stir-fry, even popcorn. Dry-roasting (in the oven, in a hot pan, or run quickly and carefully over an open flame) brings out its nutty, salty flavor. Brush it with a little sesame oil or soy sauce afterward for even better results.

KELP (KOMBU OR KONBU)
A key ingredient of Dashi (page 162), kelp is most often used as a flavor enhancer (it is a natural source of monosodium glutamate) in soups or stews, but it can also be cooked as a vegetable.

ARAME AND HIJIKI
These are both mild-tasting sea vegetables. Dark, almost black, thin and wiry, they must be soaked in water before being used in salads, soups, or stews and can be sautéed or braised.

ALARIA AND WAKAME
These close relatives are olive brown in color and have distinct spatula-shaped leaflets. Before using they must be soaked in water. Best used in soups, chopped for salads, or cooked with grains. They can also be dried, crumbled, and used as a salty seasoning. Called miyuk in Korea.

DULSE
Soft and chewy, mild and sweet, a lovely shade of red, this makes a colorful addition to salad and can be eaten as a snack (even dried, it remains soft and pli-

able). It can also be pan-roasted and served like chips and is good in sandwiches and salads after a brief rinse (it softens so quickly that actual soaking is unnecessary). Added to soups or chowders, it cooks in five minutes or less.

Hijiki with Shiitakes and Beans JAPAN ■

MAKES **4 SERVINGS**

TIME **30 MINUTES**

A splendid seaweed-based dish that can be made completely from the pantry (to be sure, a well-stocked pantry, and one that will require a little forethought). Hijiki is the seaweed of choice, a common curly black variety that looks as beautiful as black pasta once it's been soaked; you can buy it at any health food store or, of course, a Japanese market. (Buy some mirin, the sweet Japanese cooking wine, while you're there; it keeps forever and adds a distinctive flavor to many Japanese dishes.)

About 1$\frac{1}{2}$ ounces hijiki (about 1 cup)

5 large or 10 small dried shiitake ("black") mushrooms

2 tablespoons extra virgin olive oil

1 cup diced chicken, shrimp, or shucked small clams (canned are fine if you can find good ones), optional

2 medium or 1 large carrot, shredded

1 cup cooked soybeans, flageolets, peas, or black-eyed peas

1 cup Dashi or chicken stock, preferably homemade (page 162 or 160)

2 tablespoons mirin or 1 tablespoon honey

$\frac{1}{4}$ cup soy sauce, or to taste

Salt if necessary

1. Soak the hijiki in cold water to cover for about 10 minutes; soak the shiitakes in very hot water to cover for about 10 minutes. Meanwhile, prepare the remaining ingredients. Slice the shiitakes, discarding the tough stems but reserving the soaking liquid.

2. Put the olive oil in a 12-inch skillet over medium-high heat. If you're using chicken or shrimp, brown the pieces quickly in the oil, 2 or 3 minutes, stirring only once or twice. Remove with a slotted spoon.

3. Drain the hijiki and put it in the skillet; stir once, then add the carrot and shiitakes. Stir again; add the chicken, shrimp, or clams, along with the beans, the shiitake-soaking liquid, dashi, mirin, and soy sauce. Stir, turn the heat to medium-low, and cook, stirring occasionally, until the carrot is tender, about 10 minutes. Reduce the liquid further if necessary—the mixture should be stewy but not soupy—then taste, add more soy sauce or salt if necessary, and serve.

Nori Snacks KOREA ■

MAKES **4 SERVINGS**

TIME **10 MINUTES (WITH PRECOOKED RICE)**

Nori, the familiar seaweed used for rolling sushi, is a popular snack in Korea, especially when treated this way. And if you use the pieces of nori to pick up clumps of rice—a common after-school snack—you may find yourself making this frequently.

4 or more sheets nori

Dark sesame oil for brushing the nori

Salt to taste

Cooked short-grain rice (page 507), optional

1. Preheat the oven to 400°F. Brush each sheet of nori with sesame oil and sprinkle with salt. Put on a baking sheet and roast until crisp, about 10 minutes. Remove and cut into strips or quarters.

2. Eat or, if desired, use to wrap rice for a simple Oni-giri (page 511).

SPINACH

One of the first real vegetables of spring, spinach is easy to grow and available, fresh, year-round. Ironically, it's also one of the vegetables that freezes most successfully.

Saag Paneer
Cheese (or Tofu) with Spinach Sauce INDIA
MAKES **4 SERVINGS**
TIME **40 MINUTES**

Back in the days when I tackled such challenging projects, I made my own paneer, the fresh cheese that is integral to this dish of spicy spinach. Although you can buy paneer at markets specializing in Indian ingredients (and you can find these in almost every city), there is a superb substitute, and it's sold everywhere: tofu. Like paneer, tofu is a fresh, quickly made cheese; it just happens to have a soy base rather than a cow's milk base. But both are supremely bland, tender, and delicate.

The curry powder used here should not be especially fiery or laden with black pepper, but on the sweet side, containing spices like nutmeg, cardamom, and cinnamon. (If you're making your own, you'll find a recipe on page 593; if you're buying, just try to avoid mixes labeled *hot*.)

1 1/2 pounds fresh spinach
3/4 pound paneer or firm or extra-firm tofu
2 tablespoons butter or oil
1 tablespoon peeled and minced fresh ginger

1 tablespoon minced garlic
3 small dried chiles
2 tablespoons curry powder, preferably homemade (pages 592–593)
Salt to taste
1/2 cup yogurt
1 1/2 cups light cream or half-and-half

1. Trim the spinach of its tough, thick stems (with bunched spinach, you can often simply cut off the bottom couple of inches) and wash it to remove all traces of sand; do not dry it. Chop it into pieces no more than an inch or so along any dimension. Cut the block of tofu in half horizontally and wrap it in several layers of paper towels. Put it under a couple of plates; you want some weight on it, but not a lot.

2. Put the butter in a large skillet, preferably non-stick, over medium-high heat. A minute later, add the ginger, garlic, and chiles and cook, stirring occasionally, just until the garlic begins to color, a minute or two. Stir in the curry powder and a large pinch of salt and cook, stirring, for about 30 seconds. Add the spinach all at once. Cook, stirring, until the spinach wilts, then add the yogurt and a cup of the cream. Fish out the chiles and discard.

3. Let the mixture boil fairly rapidly, over medium to medium-high heat; at first, the spinach will give up its water and the amount of liquid in the pan will increase. Then it will begin to evaporate, and the mixture will become drier and drier. When it is nearly dry but still creamy, cut the tofu into 1/2-inch pieces and incorporate. When the tofu is hot, add the remaining cream to make the mixture a bit saucier. Taste and adjust the seasoning, stir, and serve.

Spicy Spinach Sauce. The same dish, without the paneer or tofu, used in India on dishes from grilled chicken to steamed broccoli: In step 3, omit the tofu and puree the mixture with enough of the cream to allow the machine to do its work. Add a squeeze of lime juice and serve with grilled or pan-grilled meat, poultry, fish, or vegetables.

Haaq Spinach with Hing INDIA ▣

MAKES **4 SERVINGS**

TIME **20 MINUTES**

Haaq is actually the name of a bitter green from Kashmir, not unlike spinach but perhaps a little more strongly flavored. In any case, spinach is used as a substitute throughout India, and this simple preparation is widespread. Neither mustard oil nor the amount of chile (I use only one) is key; but asafetida—also known as hing—the odd yellow powder (it's made from a resin that is exuded by the roots of the plant) with the offputting aroma, most definitely is. In fact, this is the place to use it and learn to love it, as I believe you will.

You can serve this as a side dish (in which case halve the quantities) or as a main course, with rice. It's also often served with fried fish on top of it.

1/2 cup mustard oil or neutral oil, like corn or grapeseed

5 small dried red chiles, or to taste

1 teaspoon asafetida (hing)

2 pounds fresh spinach, large stems removed

Salt to taste

1. Put the oil in a large skillet or flameproof casserole over medium heat; a minute later, add the chiles and asafetida and cook until the chiles sizzle a bit, just a minute or so.
2. Add the spinach and about 1/2 cup water. Cook, stirring occasionally, until the spinach wilts and is tender, about 15 minutes. Season with salt if necessary and serve hot or warm.

Spinach with Coconut Milk

SOUTHEAST ASIA ▣

MAKES **4 SERVINGS**

TIME **25 MINUTES**

Like the recipe on page 486, here is yet another super version of "creamed" spinach (true creamed spinach is on page 490), this one popular in Thailand and elsewhere. You can add curry powder or garam masala to this mix or make it into more of a stew by adding some minced pork or shrimp.

1 cup coconut milk, homemade (page 584) or canned

1 teaspoon peeled and minced fresh ginger

1 small fresh chile, stemmed, seeded, and minced, or hot red pepper flakes to taste

1 pound fresh spinach, large stems removed, chopped

Salt to taste

1. Combine the coconut milk, ginger, and chile in a saucepan over medium heat; bring to a boil, then add the spinach.
2. Adjust the heat so the mixture simmers and cook, stirring, until the spinach is wilted and the mixture thick, 5 to 10 minutes. Taste and adjust the seasoning, then serve.

Spinach Croquettes TURKEY ■ ▩ ▨

MAKES **4 SERVINGS**

TIME **30 MINUTES**

The ingredients are similar to those of Spinach Gratin (page 489), but these are faster and crunchier, lightly thickened spinach patties that are cooked until crisp.

Other vegetables you can prepare this way: none will be as quick as spinach, but you can make these with other greens—chard is especially good, but also kale and collards and even arugula and watercress.

Salt and black pepper to taste

2 pounds fresh spinach, large stems removed

1 medium onion, roughly chopped

2 eggs, lightly beaten

$\frac{1}{2}$ cup Gruyère, Cantal, or other fairly strong-flavored cow's milk cheese, grated

$\frac{1}{2}$ cup bread crumbs, preferably fresh (page 580)

2 tablespoons extra virgin olive oil

2 tablespoons butter or more oil

1. Bring a large pot of water to a boil and add salt. Add the spinach and onion and cook for just about a minute, until the spinach wilts. Drain thoroughly and cool a bit. Chop the spinach and put it and the onion in a bowl along with the eggs, cheese, and bread crumbs. Mix well, then add salt and pepper. If the mixture is too loose to form into cakes, add some more bread crumbs; if it's too dry, add a little milk or another egg.

2. Put half the oil and butter into a large skillet, preferably nonstick, over medium heat. Form the spinach mixture into small cakes (this amount will make 8 to 12) and cook without crowding—you will have to cook in batches—until nicely browned, about 5 minutes, adjusting the heat so the cakes brown evenly without burning, about 5 minutes. Turn once, then brown the other side, again about 5 minutes. Continue until all the spinach mixture is used up. Serve hot or at room temperature.

Spanakopita Cheese and Spinach Pie

GREECE ■ ■

MAKES **6 OR MORE SERVINGS**

TIME **1$\frac{1}{2}$ HOURS**

Spanakopita is among the best-known Greek dishes in the States, though the leaden, soggy versions you often encounter here are wildly different from the cheese and spinach pies served in Greece. The key to making a light spanakopita is to use a relatively small amount of strongly flavored fillings, butter every layer of phyllo—which helps the pastry stay flaky, light, and crisp—and start with good feta.

As always, when working with phyllo dough (page 629), make sure you keep the pieces that you are not working with covered with a damp towel; see Baklava (page 628) for more details.

2 tablespoons extra virgin olive oil

1 bunch of scallions or spring onions, trimmed and roughly chopped

Two 10-ounce packages frozen chopped spinach, thawed and drained, or 1$\frac{1}{2}$ pounds fresh spinach, large stems removed

Salt and black pepper to taste

3 tablespoons pine nuts

2 tablespoons sultanas (golden raisins) or raisins, optional

2 cups feta cheese

2 eggs

$\frac{1}{4}$ teaspoon freshly grated nutmeg, or a bit more to taste

4 tablespoons ($\frac{1}{2}$ stick) butter, melted

10 to 12 phyllo sheets

1. Preheat the oven to 300°F. Heat the oil in a large skillet over medium heat; add the scallions a minute later. Cook until they begin to soften, 3 to 5 minutes, then add the spinach. Season with salt and pepper and cook, stirring occasionally, until the spinach is completely wilted, less than 5 minutes. Turn the mixture out into a bowl and let it cool, then stir in the pine nuts and sultanas if you're using them.

2. Beat together the feta and eggs in a separate bowl. Season the mixture with the nutmeg and some black pepper, then taste and adjust the seasoning.

3. Brush the bottom of a 9 × 13-inch baking dish with butter. Lay 6 or 7 phyllo sheets in the pan,

brushing each sheet with melted butter; the edges of the sheets should hang over the rim of the pan.

4. Spread half of the cheese mixture over the phyllo and top it with half of the sautéed spinach and scallions. Lay another 4 sheets of phyllo on top of the spinach, buttering each sheet, then top the phyllo with the remaining cheese and spinach. Fold in the edges to enclose the pie, sealing with melted butter and additional buttered phyllo if necessary.

5. Score the top of the pie into squares or triangles and bake for 35 to 45 minutes, until golden brown. Serve warm or at room temperature.

Spinach with Raisins and Pine Nuts
ITALY ■ ■ ▦

MAKES **4 SERVINGS**
TIME **20 MINUTES**

You can spin this wonderful side dish in so many ways: add more pine nuts or raisins; use a lot of garlic, adding some at the end, so that it stays strong; add a dried chile or two to the olive oil; finish it with fresh lemon juice; or drizzle it with more olive oil at the end. Or serve it over pasta, thinned with some of the pasta-cooking liquid.

Other vegetables you can prepare this way: Chard is great; collards, kale, and dandelions are also good. Just make sure the initial simmering time is long enough to make the green (and its stems) fully tender; nothing is as fast as spinach.

> ¼ cup raisins or currants
> 1 pound fresh spinach, large stems removed
> ¼ cup extra virgin olive oil
> 1 teaspoon minced garlic
> ¼ cup pine nuts
> Salt and black pepper to taste

1. Soak the raisins or currants in warm water for 10 minutes while you prepare the spinach. Steam or parboil the spinach until tender, less than 5 minutes.

2. When the spinach is cool enough to handle, squeeze all the excess moisture from it; chop it roughly. Put the olive oil in a large skillet over medium heat. Add the garlic and cook, stirring occasionally, until golden, about 3 minutes. Add the spinach and raise the heat to medium-high. Cook, stirring occasionally, for about 2 minutes. Drain the raisins and add them, along with the pine nuts, to the pan. Reduce the heat to medium.

3. Cook, stirring occasionally, for another 3 or 4 minutes, until everything glistens. Season with salt and pepper and serve hot or at room temperature.

Spinach Gratin FRANCE ■ ■

MAKES **6 TO 8 SERVINGS**
TIME **45 MINUTES**

There are many ways to make spinach gratin: you can use heavy cream as a medium (essentially making creamed spinach, then baking it with cheese) or stir spinach into a white sauce. This is the most substantial, essentially a custard, and my favorite.

> Salt and black pepper to taste
> 2 pounds fresh spinach, large stems removed
> 1 medium onion, roughly chopped
> 1 teaspoon minced garlic
> 3 eggs, lightly beaten
> ½ cup milk
> 1 cup freshly grated Parmesan cheese
> 2 tablespoons butter
> ½ cup bread crumbs, preferably fresh (page 580)

1. Preheat the oven to 450°F. Bring a large pot of water to a boil and add salt. Add the spinach and

onion and cook for just about a minute, until the spinach wilts. Drain thoroughly and cool a bit. Chop the spinach and put it and the onion in a bowl along with the garlic, eggs, milk, and about half the Parmesan. Mix well, then add salt and pepper.

2. Use a little of the butter to grease a gratin dish or similar baking dish that will hold the spinach mixture at a depth of about 1 inch. Pour the spinach mixture into the dish, then top with the remaining Parmesan, the bread crumbs, and, finally, dots of the remaining butter. Bake until the mixture is hot and set and the top brown, about 20 minutes (if the top threatens to scorch before the mixture is set, lower the heat a bit). Serve hot, warm, or at room temperature.

Creamed Spinach FRANCE ■

MAKES **4 SERVINGS**

TIME **30 MINUTES**

The real deal. It doesn't matter how you cook the spinach in step 1: you can steam, microwave, or boil it, and there's no difference in the final result. However, if you can get fresh cream, not ultrapasteurized, you'll see a real difference in both texture and taste in the final dish.

Salt and black pepper to taste

11/2 pounds fresh spinach, large stems removed

1 cup cream

2 tablespoons butter

Small grating of nutmeg, optional

1. Bring a large pot of water to a boil and add salt. Plunge the spinach into it and cook for about a minute; drain well, then cool a bit and chop thoroughly.

2. Put the cream and butter in a wide saucepan over medium heat. Add the spinach and bring to a boil; cook, stirring occasionally, until the spinach has absorbed much of the cream and is thick. Add a tiny bit of nutmeg if you like, taste and adjust the seasoning, and serve hot.

TOFU

In the thousand or so years since it was first developed, in China, tofu has established itself as an essential ingredient in many Asian cuisines. Some cultures (like the Japanese) adopted it along with Buddhism's vegetarian tenets, though today it is regularly combined with meat and fish in soups, stir-fries, and noodle dishes.

Tofu starts as rehydrated dried soybeans, which are ground to a slurry, traditionally in a stone mill. The slurry is separated into the "milk" that will become tofu (and is, of course, soy milk) and a mix of solids used as animal feed in rural areas or, frequently, as a "meat extender" (in hamburgers, etc.) for the processed-food industry.

The soy milk, mixed with a coagulant and heated carefully, yields curds and whey, exactly as it does in cheese making (tofu is neither more nor less than soy cheese), and it's the curds that, when pressed, become tofu (hence its other common name, bean curd). The pressing of the curds determines the style of tofu:

Silken: Very fragile. Great in soups or other dishes where it will not be handled much, like Ma Po Tofu (page 423).

Soft: Still quite tender, but more easily handled; can be pressed (see next paragraph).

Firm: All-purpose.

Extra-firm: Best for stir-fries.

For stir-fries, it's wise to drain tofu on a few layers of paper or cloth towels to remove excess moisture. It's even better to press it: Cut it in half horizontally, then put each half on a cutting board that is propped at an angle so excess liquid can drain off (ideally, it will drain into the sink). Top with another, somewhat heavy object—a cutting board or a skillet, for example—and let sit for a half hour or so. Pat dry and proceed with any recipe.

Stuffed Tofu SOUTHEAST ASIA, CHINA

MAKES **4 SERVINGS**

TIME **40 MINUTES**

Tofu is often, perhaps even usually, eaten as part of a vegetarian meal, but it's also delicious when paired with shrimp or pork. This dish has some of the flavors and textures of Tod Mun (page 83), but the tofu adds a smooth texture and subtle flavor. For information on fish sauces like nam pla, see page 500. Serve this as an appetizer or as one of the centerpieces of a larger Asian meal.

Use all shrimp if you like or substitute other meat for the pork.

Corn, grapeseed, or other neutral oil for deep-frying

1 pound (1 package) firm tofu, drained and patted dry

¼ pound shrimp, peeled

¼ pound lean pork, trimmed

1 garlic clove, peeled

1 tablespoon nam pla

Salt and black pepper to taste

1 scallion, trimmed and chopped

2 tablespoons soy sauce

2 teaspoons rice vinegar

2 teaspoons sugar

1 small fresh chile, preferably Thai, stemmed, seeded, and minced

1. Pour 2 inches of oil into a deep heavy pot. Bring to 400°F over medium heat. Meanwhile, cut the tofu into 3-inch blocks at least 1 inch thick. Press the cubes between paper towels to dry well. Carefully slide the tofu into the oil and cook, turning occasionally, until golden brown and puffy, about 10 minutes. Work in batches to avoid overcrowding. Drain on paper towels and cool.

2. Meanwhile, put the shrimp, pork, and garlic in a food processor and process until everything is minced well. Add the nam pla, salt, and pepper and process until pasty. Stir in the scallion. In a separate bowl, whisk together the soy sauce, vinegar, sugar, and chile until the sugar is dissolved. Set aside.

3. Cut the fried tofu cubes in half diagonally to create tofu triangles. Spread the shrimp mixture on the uncooked side of each tofu triangle, pressing firmly. Heat 2 tablespoons oil in a large skillet over

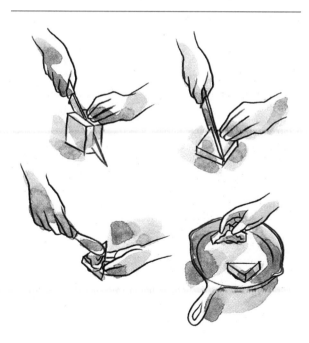

PREPARING STUFFED TOFU

medium heat. Put the tofu triangles in the skillet, shrimp side down, and cook until the shrimp mixture is browned and cooked through, about 4 minutes. Drain on paper towels, then serve, with the dipping sauce.

Tofu with Black Beans CHINA ▨
MAKES **4 SERVINGS**
TIME **20 MINUTES**

If you're a tofu fan, chances are you're always on the lookout for ways to spice it up. This is one of the best. For a meatier texture, use the technique in step 1 of the previous recipe. For a bigger stir-fry, add some vegetables—red bell peppers are nice.

Salted black beans are sold in supermarkets and in every Chinese store. They're almost always soaked before being used.

>   1 package (1 pound) firm or extra-firm tofu
>   2 tablespoons fermented black beans (page 207)
>   2 tablespoons Shaoxing wine, dry sherry, or water
>   3 tablespoons peanut oil or neutral oil, like corn or
>   grapeseed
>   1 tablespoon minced garlic
>   1 tablespoon peeled and minced fresh ginger
>   4 or 5 small hot dried chiles, or to taste
>   2 scallions, trimmed and roughly chopped
>   1 tablespoon soy sauce
>   1 tablespoon dark sesame oil
>   Chopped fresh cilantro leaves for garnish

1. Cut the tofu in half through its equator. Put the halves on 4 sheets of paper towels, and cover with another 4 sheets. Cover with a heavy cutting board, or a plate weighted with cans, or another similar weight. Change the towels if they become saturated. Weight the tofu for a total of 20 to 30 minutes, or as time allows. At the same time, soak the black beans in the wine or water.

2. Cut the pressed tofu into $1/2$-inch cubes. Put the oil in a large skillet or wok, preferably nonstick, over high heat. A minute later, add the garlic, ginger, and chiles and cook, stirring, for about 30 seconds. Drain the black beans and add them, along with the tofu and about 2 tablespoons water. Cook, stirring occasionally, until the tofu is hot, about 5 minutes. Add the scallions and stir for about 30 seconds.

3. Turn off the heat, then stir in the soy sauce and sesame oil; garnish and serve.

TOMATOES

Needless to say, the best tomatoes are grown locally and harvested ripe. And although it might appear that the supply of year-round tomatoes is better than it once was, it seems to me that the major difference is that the hard, tasteless tomatoes sold in February (and grown, for the most part, in hothouses in Holland) are simply redder than their orange counterparts of years ago; they are no more tasty. Often—more often than not—canned tomatoes are preferable to bad "fresh" tomatoes, especially if they are going to be cooked.

Stuffed Roasted Tomatoes or Peppers MIDDLE EAST ■ ▨
MAKES **4 SERVINGS**
TIME **ABOUT 1 HOUR (WITH PREMADE STUFFING)**

You can stuff any vegetable you like, from onions to zucchini, but peppers and tomatoes are the most popular because they have the best natural shapes, are attractive and flavorful, and, in the case of peppers, are already hollow. (Tomatoes are easily hollowed out, and their pulp can be used in the stuffing.)

> 4 to 6 firm ripe tomatoes, about 6 ounces each (see
>   variation for peppers)
> Salt and black pepper to taste
> 1 recipe stuffing (pages 448–449)
> ½ cup extra virgin olive oil
> Chopped fresh parsley or basil leaves for garnish

1. Preheat the oven to 450°F. Cut a ¼-inch slice from the smooth end of each tomato (reserve these slices) and use a spoon to scoop out all of the insides, leaving a wall about ¼ inch thick. Sprinkle the inside of the tomatoes with salt and pepper. Discard the woody core and seeds and chop the pulp; mix it with the stuffing.
2. Stuff each tomato with one-quarter of the mixture and replace the top slices. Spread half the olive oil in a shallow roasting pan that will allow for a little room between the tomatoes, then place them in the pan. Sprinkle all with salt and pepper and put the roasting pan in the oven.
3. Roast the tomatoes for 30 to 40 minutes, until the tomato is shriveled and the stuffing is hot (pierce the stuffing to its center with a skewer and touch the skewer to your wrist or lip). Serve hot, warm, or at room temperature, drizzled with the remaining olive oil and garnished with the herb.

Stuffed Roasted Peppers. Cut the top off 4 to 6 red bell peppers; scoop out and discard the insides; rinse, then sprinkle inside and out with salt and pepper. Stuff the peppers and replace their caps. Stand them up (it's okay if they support each other) in a roasting pan. Add ¼ cup olive oil and about a cup of stock or water. Roast as in step 3.

Faster Roasted Tomatoes GREECE ■ ▨

MAKES **4 SERVINGS**

TIME **40 MINUTES**

These are not elaborate, like the stuffed tomatoes in the preceding recipe, but are essentially seasoned baked tomatoes you can throw together in a hurry. The tomatoes themselves should be ripe and delicious, though ironically this treatment is a good one for green tomatoes as well.

> 1 teaspoon minced garlic, optional
> 1 cup bread crumbs, preferably fresh (page 580)
> ¼ cup fresh parsley leaves, plus chopped parsley for
>   garnish
> Salt and black pepper to taste
> ¼ cup extra virgin olive oil
> 2 pounds ripe tomatoes, cored and cut into ¼-inch-thick
>   slices

1. Preheat the oven to 400°F. If you're using the garlic, process it with the bread crumbs, the ¼ cup parsley leaves, and some salt and pepper; if not, just finely chop the parsley leaves and stir them into the bread crumbs along with some salt and pepper.
2. Use half the olive oil to grease the bottom of an ovenproof dish or pan that can just about hold the tomatoes in one layer (it's okay for them to overlap a bit). Layer the tomatoes in there and sprinkle with salt and pepper; top with the bread crumb mixture and drizzle with the remaining olive oil.
3. Bake for 20 to 30 minutes, or until the bread crumbs are lightly browned and the tomatoes softened; check once or twice and rotate the pan if necessary so the top browns evenly. Garnish with the remaining parsley and serve hot or at room temperature.

Torta di Patate e Pomodori

Potato and Tomato Pie ITALY ■ ▨

MAKES **AT LEAST 4 SERVINGS**

TIME **1 ¹/₂ HOURS, SOMEWHAT UNATTENDED**

A beauty—mild, soothing, and delicious. Be sure to use waxy ("new") potatoes, which will not fall apart. As with the other tarts in this chapter, this is best warm or at room temperature and may be prepared without any crust at all. If you're using a crust, the recipe will take less time if you have a premade crust.

> 1 Pastry for Savory Tarts (page 458)
>
> 4 tablespoons (¹/₂ stick) butter or extra virgin olive oil, plus a little more for the tart
>
> 1 large onion, sliced
>
> Salt and black pepper to taste
>
> 1 pound waxy potatoes, red or white, peeled and diced
>
> 2 cups chopped seeded tomatoes (canned are fine)
>
> ¹/₂ cup pitted black olives, like Kalamatas, roughly chopped
>
> Pinch of cayenne
>
> ¹/₂ cup chopped fresh parsley leaves
>
> 4 eggs
>
> ¹/₂ cup cream, half-and-half, or milk
>
> 1 cup grated Gruyère, Cantal, Cheddar, or other firm but not dry cheese
>
> ¹/₄ cup freshly grated Parmesan cheese

1. Preheat the oven to 400°F. Tear off a piece of foil twice as large as the crust. Fold it in half and smear it with butter or oil; lay the greased side on the crust. Weight the foil with a pile of dried beans or rice (these can be reused for this same purpose), pie weights, or a tight-fitting skillet or saucepan—anything that will sit flat on the surface. Bake for 12 minutes, then remove the foil and continue to bake at 350°F until the crust is a beautiful shade of brown, just a few minutes more. Remove and let cool on a rack while you prepare the filling.

2. Meanwhile, put the 4 tablespoons butter in a large nonstick skillet over medium heat. Two minutes later, add the onion, along with salt and pepper. Cook, stirring occasionally, until the onion begins to soften, about 5 minutes. Add the potatoes and continue to cook, stirring, until the potatoes look glossy, about 5 minutes. Add the tomatoes, olives, and cayenne, stir, and bring the mixture to a boil. Adjust the heat so the mixture simmers and cook, stirring occasionally, until the potatoes are soft and the mixture thick, about 15 minutes. If a great deal of liquid remains, raise the heat until most of it is gone. Taste and adjust the seasoning; cool slightly.

3. Combine the potato mixture with the remaining ingredients and pile into the prebaked shell. Bake for 30 to 40 minutes, or until almost firm and lightly browned on top; reduce the oven heat if the shell's edges are darkening too quickly. Cool for at least 10 minutes before slicing and serving.

Tomatoes Provençal FRANCE ■ ▨ ▨

MAKES **4 SERVINGS**

TIME **20 MINUTES**

A great way to handle good tomatoes that are not perfectly ripe and a great way to convert tomatoes to a cooked vegetable without much trouble.

> 4 medium to large tomatoes
>
> ¹/₄ cup extra virgin olive oil
>
> 1 tablespoon minced garlic
>
> ¹/₂ cup bread crumbs, preferably homemade (page 580)
>
> Salt and black pepper to taste
>
> ¹/₂ cup chopped fresh parsley leaves

1. Core the tomatoes, then cut them in half horizontally. Over the sink, squeeze and shake them to rid them of their seeds and some of their juice.

2. Put the oil in a large skillet, preferably nonstick, with a lid over medium heat. A minute later, add the tomatoes, cut sides down; cook until they brown but do not burn, about 5 minutes, then turn. Combine the remaining ingredients and sprinkle the interior of the tomatoes with this mixture; sprinkle the outsides of the tomatoes with a little more salt and pepper.

3. Partially cover and cook until the tomatoes are tender, about 10 more minutes. Serve hot or at room temperature.

TURNIPS AND RADISHES

Turnips and radishes share membership in the mustard family, the group of earthy-spicy greens and roots that includes horseradish, most "winter" greens, like kale, collards, and mustard, and kohlrabi. They're also two roots the English-speaking part of the world has never handled with any particular aptitude—though they are used to great effect pretty much everywhere else.

In France turnips are picked small and used quickly, most famously with duck, but the French are quick to include them in many of the preparations that make potatoes seem so transcendent—fries, gratins, and the like. The Chinese brown and braise them, playing up their natural sweetness. And they are pickled across Asia, much like their cousins, radishes, because both are excellent canvases for different pickling flavors.

Radishes come in a range of colors and sizes. Baseball-sized black radishes with bright white interiors are used in and around Eastern Europe; the daikon is a staple in Japan; and you may have seen a Chinese variety called watermelon radish, pale green on the outside and rosy-pink inside.

Many radishes are cooked to temper their considerable spiciness, the two most common exceptions being breakfast radishes (the kind you might have in France with a little butter and coarse salt) and the giant, rather mild daikon, which you may find grated raw next to your sushi.

Both turnips and radishes are easy to grow, easy to store, and available year-round.

Rutabaga Pudding SCANDINAVIA
MAKES **4 TO 6 SERVINGS**
TIME **1 1/2 HOURS**

As good warm as hot, this is a nice homey casserole to go with a roast or other dish in the spirit of Sunday dinner.

Other vegetables you can prepare this way: rutabagas are not only traditional but wonderful, but other turnips are great too, as are carrots, potatoes, parsnips, and celeriac (celery root).

> Salt and black pepper to taste
> 2 medium rutabagas (yellow turnips), about 2 pounds, peeled and cut into chunks
> 1/2 cup bread crumbs, preferably homemade (page 580)
> 1/2 cup cream, half-and-half, or milk
> 2 eggs
> Small grating of nutmeg
> 1 tablespoon butter, plus some for greasing the pan

1. Preheat the oven to 350°F. Bring a large pot of water to a boil and add salt. Add the rutabaga and cook until it is quite soft, 15 to 20 minutes. Drain thoroughly.

2. Put the rutabaga in a food processor with the bread crumbs, cream, and eggs; puree, stopping the machine to scrape down its sides if necessary. Stir in the nutmeg, then taste and add salt and pepper as needed.

3. Butter a baking dish that will hold the puree at a depth of about 1 inch (you can also bake the pudding in individual ramekins). Dot the top of the pudding with butter and bake until firm and lightly browned on top, about 1 hour.

Glazed Turnips FRANCE ■

MAKES **4 SERVINGS**

TIME **20 MINUTES**

There is no easier way to make a humble veg seem elegant than glazing it in this manner; turnips become royal enough to serve with any dish, but I like them best with roast chicken or beef.

Other vegetables you can prepare this way: carrots, radishes, onions, beets, parsnips, or other root vegetables.

> 2 tablespoons butter
>
> 1 pound turnips, carrots, radishes, onions, or other vegetable, trimmed, peeled, and cut into pieces about the size of radishes
>
> Salt and black pepper to taste
>
> 1 teaspoon sugar
>
> About 1 cup chicken, beef, or vegetable stock, preferably homemade (page 160 or 162)
>
> Minced fresh parsley leaves for garnish

1. Put the butter in a medium saucepan, one that will hold the vegetable in one layer, over medium heat. Add the vegetable and sprinkle with salt and pepper. Cook, stirring once in a while, until the vegetable begins to brown, about 10 minutes.
2. Add the sugar and enough stock to cover; bring to a boil and cook, more or less undisturbed, until the liquid has mostly evaporated and the vegetable is tender and brown, 20 to 30 minutes. When done, the shiny vegetable should be sitting in a small puddle of syrupy liquid.

3. Taste and add more salt and pepper if you like, then garnish and serve.

WATERCRESS

Nowadays, we mostly buy watercress, but I can remember every place I've ever found watercress growing wild—what a treat—and I can only imagine how treasured it once was, a wild, free-growing, distinctively delicious green. These days, it's mostly cultivated, but this doesn't detract from its flavor one bit.

Stir-Fried Watercress with Bean Sauce SOUTHEAST ASIA ■

MAKES **4 SERVINGS**

TIME **30 MINUTES**

Stir-fried vegetables are almost as common in Southeast Asia as they are in China, and even the spices are similar. But the addition of dried shrimp and the use of nam pla are dead giveaways that this dish is from Indochina. It's usually made on the fiery side, so feel free to increase the chiles if you like. Information on fish sauces like nam pla is on page 500.

Other vegetables you can prepare this way: green beans, parboiled broccoli or cauliflower, or a mixture of onions and peppers. All will take a little longer than fast-cooking watercress.

> 1 tablespoon dried shrimp (page 185), optional
>
> 2 small dried red chiles, or to taste
>
> 2 garlic cloves, peeled
>
> 2 shallots, roughly chopped

2 bunches of watercress, trimmed and roughly chopped

2 tablespoons corn, grapeseed, or other neutral oil, as needed

2 tablespoons yellow bean sauce (available at Chinese and Southeast Asian markets)

1 tablespoon sugar

2 tablespoons nam pla, or to taste

$\frac{1}{2}$ teaspoon black pepper, or to taste

Salt if necessary

About $\frac{1}{2}$ cup chopped fresh basil leaves, preferably Thai

1. If you're using them, soak the dried shrimp in hot water to cover until softened, just a few minutes. Combine them in a small food processor with the chiles, garlic, and shallots and process to a paste. Toss with the watercress.

2. Put the oil in a skillet or wok over high heat; a minute later, add the watercress and paste. Cook, stirring almost constantly, for about a minute, or until the watercress wilts. Stir in 2 tablespoons water, then the bean sauce, sugar, nam pla, and pepper; cook for 10 seconds, then turn off the heat.

3. Taste and add salt or other seasoning as necessary. Stir in the basil and serve.

WINTER SQUASH

Pumpkin, butternut, acorn, hubbard, and a dozen other winter squashes can all be readily substituted for one another (and most can be used in place of sweet potatoes and vice versa), but my preference is almost always butternut, because its smooth skin makes for easy peeling. And since peeling is the most challenging aspect of cooking winter squash, that's a strong advantage.

Masala Winter Squash INDIA
MAKES 4 SERVINGS
TIME 40 MINUTES

Most squash preparations are fairly bland, sweet, even insipid, but not this one, a lovely winter stew that can be a centerpiece for vegetarians (or for meat eaters with the addition of a few cubes of boneless chicken). A good rice pilaf (page 513) would suit this fine. It would also be at home alongside plain grilled steak.

Other vegetables you can prepare this way: semi-ripe plantains, potatoes, or sweet potatoes.

1 large onion, peeled

5 garlic cloves, peeled

1 small dried chile or 1 teaspoon hot red pepper flakes, or to taste

2 tablespoons corn, grapeseed, or other neutral oil

Salt and black pepper to taste

1 tablespoon curry powder, preferably homemade (pages 592–593) or to taste

1 cup chopped tomato (canned is fine), optional

About $1\frac{1}{2}$ pounds winter squash, like butternut or firm pumpkin, peeled and cut into 1-inch cubes

Lime wedges for serving

1. Combine the onion, garlic, and chile in a food processor and grind until pasty. Put the oil in a large skillet or flameproof casserole with a lid over medium heat and add the onion mixture along with some salt and pepper and the curry powder. Cook, stirring occasionally, until the onion begins to brown, 5 to 10 minutes.

2. Add the tomato or $\frac{1}{2}$ cup water along with the squash. Cover and adjust the heat so the mixture simmers steadily. Cook, stirring occasionally and adding more water if necessary, until the squash is tender, about 20 minutes. Serve with the lime wedges.

YAMS

The role of yams and sweet potatoes finally seems to be expanding, and rightly so. Their rich, sweet, tender flesh is closely related to that of winter squash, and they can be used in many of the same recipes.

Yam in Mirin JAPAN ▣

MAKES **4 SERVINGS**

TIME **30 MINUTES**

Wonderfully sweet, this side dish is the Japanese equivalent of butter-glazed carrots.

Other vegetables you can prepare this way: butternut or other winter squash or carrots.

> 1 pound yam or sweet potato, peeled and cut into 1-inch chunks
>
> 2 tablespoons plus 1 teaspoon good-quality soy sauce
>
> ¼ cup plus 1 teaspoon mirin or 2 tablespoons honey
>
> 1 tablespoon sugar

1. Combine the yam, 2 tablespoons soy sauce, ¼ cup mirin, and sugar in a small saucepan with about ½ cup water. Cover and cook over medium heat until the yam is tender, about 15 minutes, adding a little more water if necessary.
2. Uncover and cook, stirring occasionally, until the yam pieces are glazed and the mixture is almost dry. Add the remaining teaspoon of soy sauce and mirin, cook for another 5 seconds, and serve.

ZUCCHINI

Now, we see zucchini year-round—and it's not bad in winter, since it stores fairly well—but I still like it as a hot-weather vegetable, when it becomes ubiquitous and cheap. Prepared correctly, its subtle flavor shines.

Zucchini with Dill and Mint

MIDDLE EAST ■ ▣

MAKES **4 SERVINGS**

TIME **35 MINUTES**

The perfect midsummer dish, one that can be served hot or cold. Convert it to a pasta sauce by tossing it, hot, with cooked pasta, a couple of raw eggs, and some freshly grated Parmesan cheese.

Other vegetables you can prepare this way: any summer squash.

> ¼ cup extra virgin olive oil
>
> 2 pounds zucchini, cut into ½- to ¾-inch chunks
>
> 1 large onion, chopped
>
> Salt and black pepper to taste
>
> 1 tablespoon minced garlic
>
> ½ cup chicken or other stock, preferably homemade (pages 160–163), or water
>
> ¼ cup fresh dill leaves, roughly chopped
>
> ¼ cup fresh mint leaves, roughly chopped

1. Put half the oil in a large skillet with a lid over medium-high heat. A minute later, add the zucchini and onion along with a sprinkling of salt and pepper and cook, stirring occasionally, until the zucchini has softened slightly and begun to brown, about 10 minutes. Stir in the garlic and cook for another minute or so.
2. Turn the heat to low and add the stock; cover and adjust the heat so the mixture simmers. Cook for 5 to 10 minutes longer, or until the zucchini is very tender.
3. Stir in the herbs, taste and adjust the seasoning, and serve hot, at room temperature, or cold.

MIXED VEGETABLES

Quick-Braised Root Vegetables with Hoisin CHINA ▨

MAKES **4 TO 6 SERVINGS**

TIME **30 MINUTES**

A simple braised dish that brings a new look to root vegetables. Serve with stir-fries or with plain grilled or broiled fish.

Other vegetables you can prepare this way: turnips and radishes of any type will fill in nicely for the carrots or parsnips.

> 2 tablespoons peanut or neutral oil, like corn or grapeseed
>
> 1 tablespoon chopped garlic
>
> 1 tablespoon peeled and minced fresh ginger
>
> 4 medium carrots, roughly chopped
>
> 4 parsnips, peeled and roughly chopped
>
> 2 celery stalks, roughly chopped
>
> 2 tablespoons hoisin sauce
>
> 1 tablespoon soy sauce
>
> 3 scallions, trimmed and cut into 1-inch lengths

1. Heat a wok or large skillet with a lid over medium-high heat for about 3 minutes, or until it is quite hot. Add the oil, garlic, and ginger and stir for 10 seconds. Add the vegetables and cook, stirring, until they begin to brown, 2 or 3 minutes.

2. Lower the heat to medium and add ½ cup water (or stock), along with the hoisin sauce and soy sauce; stir. Cover and cook over medium-low heat until the vegetables are tender, about 10 minutes. Uncover, raise the heat to high, and add the scallions. Cook, stirring, until the liquid has all but evaporated, just a couple of minutes. Serve immediately.

Stir-Fried Vegetables with Nam Pla

VIETNAM ▨

MAKES **4 SERVINGS**

TIME **30 MINUTES**

The vegetables in Vietnam are as beautiful as any I've ever seen, and, because there was still little refrigeration when I visited the country, they were fresher than most. This might explain why I enjoyed the simple vegetable stir-fries so much. Then again, it may be the nam pla—or, to use the Vietnamese term, nuoc mam.

Other vegetables you can prepare this way: you can use whatever vegetables you like here—you want a total of three to four cups for four people—as long as you follow the basic principles of stir-frying (page 311).

> Corn, grapeseed, or other neutral oil for stir-frying
>
> 1 cup broccoli or cauliflower florets in about 1-inch pieces
>
> 2 medium carrots, thinly sliced
>
> ½ cup snow peas, trimmed
>
> 1 medium to large onion, thinly sliced
>
> 2 small dried chiles
>
> 1 tablespoon minced garlic
>
> 2 tablespoons nam pla, or to taste
>
> ½ teaspoon black pepper, or to taste
>
> Salt if necessary

1. Put 2 tablespoons oil in a skillet or wok over high heat; a minute later, add the broccoli. Cook, stirring occasionally, for about a minute, then add 1 tablespoon water. Continue to cook and stir until the vegetable is crisp-tender, about 5 minutes. Remove and repeat the process with the carrots and then the snow peas.

2. Put a little more oil in the pan and add the onion. Cook over high heat, stirring once in a while, until it softens and begins to char, 3 to 5 minutes. Add the chiles and garlic and cook, stirring, for another minute. Add ¼ cup water and the nam pla

Nam Pla

Nam pla translates as "fish water," and this salty, pungent-smelling sauce is a pillar of Thai cuisine, used in place of salt or as other cultures use soy sauce. Nam pla (which has different names in other languages, of course) is also prevalent in parts of Cambodia, Laos, Vietnam, Myanmar (Burma), Malaysia, the Philippines, Indonesia, and elsewhere.

Nam pla has been made for centuries if not millennia. The process starts with just-caught schooling fish, most often anchovies, which are rinsed and packed between layers of salt in open containers. The containers are left to ferment for up to a year, when the liquid generated by the process is decanted and bottled.

When buying nam pla, look for a bottle with an ingredient list on the side that's short and recognizable; brands with a preponderance of preservatives tend to be second flushes of the fermentation process—in other words, after the first batch of fish sauce is poured off, they "rinse" the fish again to obtain a lower-strength and lower-quality batch that is doctored with chemicals to make it palatable.

To the uninitiated (that includes most of us), nam pla smells musty and fishy, though sampled side by side with Worcestershire sauce (which is also made with fermented fish), it seems relatively tame. And for as much fuss as Westerners often make the first time they come across fish sauce, it's interesting to note that the Greeks and Romans made a similar condiment in a nearly identical fashion, called garum, that is called for throughout Apicius's fourth-century cookbook.

and pepper; return the cooked vegetables to the pan. Cook, stirring, until the mixture is combined, then taste and adjust the seasoning if necessary, and serve.

Subz Miloni Mixed Vegetable Curry INDIA

MAKES **4 SERVINGS**

TIME **1 HOUR**

Like many dishes from India, this one contains a lot of ingredients and requires a fair amount of precooking work but is easy to assemble. If you can find fresh paneer—the simple cheese that appears in many Indian dishes—by all means use it. But tofu makes a great substitute.

Serve over rice or as part of a larger Indian meal.

Salt to taste

1 pound fresh spinach, large stems removed

3 tablespoons peanut or neutral oil, like corn or grapeseed

1 medium carrot, cut into $^1/_4$-inch cubes

$^1/_4$ small cauliflower, trimmed and broken into small florets

$^1/_4$ pound shiitake or button mushrooms, trimmed and chopped, shiitake stems discarded or reserved for stock

1 or 2 fresh chiles, like jalapeño or serrano, stemmed, seeded, and minced, or 1 teaspoon hot red pepper flakes, or to taste

$^1/_4$ pound green beans, trimmed and roughly chopped

1 large onion, roughly chopped

3 green cardamom pods

3 black cardamom pods

6 cloves

4 peppercorns

1 cinnamon stick

1 tablespoon peeled and minced fresh ginger

1 teaspoon minced garlic

$^1\!/_2$ teaspoon ground fenugreek

1 teaspoon ground cumin

$^1\!/_2$ package firm tofu, 6 to 8 ounces, cubed

1 tablespoon curry powder, preferably homemade (pages
   592–593), or garam masala (page 594), or to taste

$^1\!/_2$ cup heavy cream

1. Bring a large pot of water to a boil and add salt. Add the spinach and cook for about 2 minutes, or until wilted. Drain, run under cold water, then squeeze out excess water and puree in a blender, adding back a tiny bit of water if necessary to allow the machine to do its work.

2. Put 2 tablespoons of the oil in a large deep skillet, preferably nonstick, over medium-high heat. Add the carrot and cauliflower and cook, stirring occasionally, until nearly tender, 10 to 15 minutes. Remove with a slotted spoon. Add the mushrooms, chiles, beans, and onion and cook, stirring occasionally, until softened, about 10 minutes. Remove and combine with the carrot mixture.

3. Add the remaining tablespoon of oil, then the whole spices, ginger, and garlic and stir for about a minute. Add the powdered spices and stir; add the cooked vegetables and tofu (or paneer) and cook, stirring gently and only occasionally, for about 5 minutes. Add the curry powder, cream, and salt as necessary. Serve hot or warm.

Ratatouille FRANCE ■ ■

MAKES **8 SERVINGS**

TIME **ABOUT 1 $^1\!/_2$ HOURS**

Ratatouille calls for a fairly specific list of vegetables: eggplant, tomatoes, zucchini, peppers, and usually onions. These are cooked slowly, together, with a lot of olive oil and some garlic. The dish is finished with fresh basil; how could it be bad?

Needless to say, ratatouille is best in midsummer, when the vegetables are at their peak. It can be served hot or at room temperature and is delicious both ways. It's especially good with grilled sausage.

2 large eggplant, about 2 pounds total, peeled if the skin
   is very thick and cut into $^1\!/_2$-inch chunks

2 medium zucchini, about 1 pound total, cut into $^1\!/_2$-inch
   chunks

Salt and black pepper to taste

$^1\!/_2$ cup extra virgin olive oil

2 large onions, thinly sliced

2 tablespoons minced garlic

2 red or yellow bell peppers, stemmed, seeded, and thinly
   sliced

4 ripe medium tomatoes, peeled, seeded, cored, and
   thickly sliced

$^1\!/_2$ cup chopped fresh basil or parsley leaves

1. Put the eggplant and zucchini in a colander and toss liberally with salt. Let stand for about an hour, if time allows, then rinse quickly and squeeze dry.

2. Put a wide flameproof casserole or deep skillet with a lid over medium heat. Add the olive oil and onions and cook, stirring occasionally, for about a minute; add the garlic, peppers, eggplant, and zucchini and cook, stirring to combine. Adjust the heat so the mixture simmers and cover. Cook, checking and stirring, for about 30 minutes, or until the vegetables are tender.

3. Add the tomatoes, stir, and re-cover. Cook for another 30 minutes, stirring occasionally, until the tomatoes have broken down and the vegetables are very soft. Taste and adjust the seasoning, stir in the basil, and serve hot or at room temperature.

Vegetarian Tsimmes EASTERN EUROPE ■ ▨

MAKES **4 TO 8 SERVINGS**

TIME **1 HOUR OR A LITTLE LONGER, SOMEWHAT UNATTENDED**

"Don't make a big tsimmes out of it" was a favorite expression of my mother's, as if making a tsimmes was a big deal and therefore making a big tsimmes— well, you get the idea. Making a tsimmes—a stew of fruits and vegetables, often on the sweet side, and sometimes grains—can be a big deal, especially if you begin with a piece of meat. But as a delicious mid-winter stew of dried fruits and root vegetables, served as a side dish or even a main course, it's hardly any work at all. To make one with meat, simply add these ingredients to the Cholent recipe on page 380.

Many tsimmes recipes call for cooking the fruit until it falls apart, which is all too easy to do. In this one, which has less water than most, the fruit is cooked until perfectly tender but still intact.

Other vegetables you can prepare this way: vary this as you like—not only is meat common, but so are turnips, beets, apples, barley, and the small egg noodles known as farfel. The key ingredients are the dried fruit, sweet potatoes, and carrots.

1 cup dried apricots

1 cup pitted prunes

1 cup dried pears

1 pound sweet potatoes, peeled and cut into 1-inch chunks

1 pound carrots, cut into 1-inch chunks

1 pound onions, thinly sliced

2 tablespoons butter or extra virgin olive oil

1/2 cup chopped dates

Salt and black pepper to taste

Pinch of ground cloves

1/2 teaspoon ground cinnamon

Pinch of cayenne

Juice of 1/2 lemon

1/4 cup honey

1. Bring a medium pot of water to a boil and preheat the oven to 375°F. Soak the apricots, prunes, and pears in warm water to cover. Parboil the sweet potatoes, carrots, and onions until just beginning to soften, 5 to 10 minutes. Drain, reserving 2 cups of the cooking liquid. Drain the dried fruit.

2. Use half the butter or oil to grease a large casserole or baking dish. Combine all the ingredients in a bowl and toss well; add to the casserole, along with about a cup of the reserved cooking liquid. Dot with the remaining butter and cover with foil; bake until everything is completely tender but not mushy, about 30 minutes, adding additional reserved cooking liquid if necessary to keep the mixture from drying out. Uncover and allow the top to brown a bit, then serve hot or at room temperature.

Vegetables with Dried Shrimp and Coconut Milk INDONESIA ▨

MAKES **4 SERVINGS**

TIME **30 MINUTES**

This dish contains a lot of flavors, but one distinguishes Indonesian cooking from almost every other: dried shrimp. These tiny crustaceans can be bought at most Asian markets and need only be soaked in hot water for a few minutes before use. (There's also a shrimp paste, which requires no soaking; you can use this instead.) But, like nam pla—Southeast Asian fish sauce—dried shrimp are an acquired taste for many people. I like them, but I've also made this successfully without them when I fear guests will balk.

Other vegetables you can prepare this way: I've

never seen this without green beans, but certainly you could substitute any root vegetable for the carrot and zucchini or any other summer squash for the eggplant.

2 tablespoons corn, grapeseed, or other neutral oil

2 tablespoons dried shrimp, optional

1 pound green beans, trimmed

½ pound carrots, cut into ½-inch slices

½ pound eggplant, cut into 1-inch chunks

1 small fresh chile, stemmed, seeded, and minced, or 1 small dried chile, or to taste

2 garlic cloves, roughly chopped

5 nickel-sized slices peeled fresh ginger

⅓ to ½ pound ground pork or turkey, optional

1 large tomato, roughly chopped, or about 1 cup canned tomatoes, drained and chopped

1½ cups coconut milk, homemade (page 584) or canned

½ cup unsweetened shredded coconut

Salt to taste

1 cup roughly chopped fresh basil leaves, preferably Thai

1. Heat the oil in a large skillet over high heat. If you're using them, soak the dried shrimp in hot water to cover. When the oil is hot, toss in the green beans and carrots. Cook, shaking the pan occasionally, for a minute, then add the eggplant, chile, garlic, and ginger. Again, cook and shake until the ingredients begin to brown. Crumble the meat if you're using it and add it, then cook, stirring occasionally, until the meat begins to lose its color. Stir in the soaked shrimp and their liquid and lower the heat to medium.

2. Add the tomato and about half the coconut milk. Cook, stirring occasionally, until the coconut milk is just about evaporated, then add a little more. Meanwhile, toast the coconut in a dry skillet over medium heat, tossing from time to time until lightly browned, about 5 minutes.

3. Whenever the mixture threatens to dry out, add a little more coconut milk, cook until the carrot is tender, the coconut milk is used up, and the mixture is moist but not soupy. Stir in the toasted coconut, taste and add salt if necessary (it will be if you did not use the dried shrimp), then stir in the basil and serve.

■ make ahead ■ serve at room temp./cold ■ 30 minutes or less

Grains This is the "carb" chapter, the one that includes not only some of the world's favorite foods but—according to the latest from the nutritional gurus—some of the healthiest. This is a marked change from even a couple of years ago, when almost anything containing carbohydrates was vilified.

Though highly processed grains like white flour may be something we should be limiting, our taste for good, crunchy bread will probably never diminish, though it's likely that the popularity of whole grain breads will surge. Pasta, most often made from semolina flour (or rice flour), remains among the most beloved foods on earth.

Most interesting, perhaps, is our newfound interest in ancient whole grains, like barley, oats, wheat, and spelt. They've been all but ignored for most of the last century (and thought of as "hippie food") but are finally coming back into their own.

This chapter is organized by grain (with rice first), then by pasta (with Italian pastas followed by rice noodles), and finally breads of all types.

RICE

Rice is easily one of the most popular and oldest foods worldwide. Archaeologists have traced its origins to about 10,000 B.C. in Asia, and since then, as the grain has spread west, the number of variations has consistently increased. Although there are only two primary types of rice—long grain (*Oryza sativa indica*) and short grain (*Oryza sativa japonica*)—there are something like forty thousand varieties of grain under those broad categories. The distinctions stem largely from the length of the grains, but also from fragrance, color, the degree to which the grains are milled, and the ability to absorb liquid. There are only a few basic ways of cooking rice, but an endless number of rice dishes from around the world.

Asian cuisine commonly features some form of rice at every meal. When served simply as a side dish with meat and vegetable dishes, it is steamed or boiled. Any leftover rice can be fried, stewed, or mixed with other ingredients to form a full meal. Korean and Japanese cuisines most commonly use short-grain (sometimes called medium-grain) white rice, which is slightly sticky and sweet. The stickiness is perfect for making sushi and rice balls. Brown rice, which is a more nutritious form of rice with its bran layer intact, is also popular in Korea. While the northern Chinese consume more bread than rice, southern Chinese have long-grain rice, which is dry and loose, at every meal.

Southeast Asian cuisine uses a variety of short- and long-grain rice. For example, jasmine rice, when left intact, boils like long-grain kernels, with a bit more moisture and a distinctive floral fragrance. When the jasmine kernels are broken into small shards and then steamed, the result is individual sticky kernels with a wonderful chewiness. Popular in Thailand, this sticky jasmine rice is scooped and eaten by hand, not with utensils. Southeast Asia also pro-duces black, green, and red varieties of rice, each of which has its own unique flavor and texture.

Glutinous rice is also popular throughout East and Southeast Asia and is often used in desserts. Glutinous rice is a starchy short-grain kernel that becomes sticky and gummy when cooked. It is often mixed with other short-grain kernels for dishes that require the rice to be formed into balls or molds. Glutinous rice can also be cooked and then pounded until a smooth elastic dough is formed to make chewy rice cakes or noodles, like Korean duk. This dough is used throughout East and Southeast Asia for sweets, most commonly filled with sweet red bean paste. Uncooked glutinous rice kernels are often ground into a rice flour to make similar filled chewy desserts or as a thickener for sweet soups.

On the other end of the spectrum is basmati rice, a thin, extra-long grain with a sublime aroma and flavor. Basmati rice is the grain of choice in South Asia, where it is first fried in oil, then boiled. Saffron or turmeric is often used to season the rice while cooking. Similar methods of preparation are found throughout the Middle East, Europe, and Central and South America, with different spices and vegetables mixed into the rice. Aside from basmati, most long-grain rice is quite basic—the husk and bran of each

DUK

grain are completely removed, and the kernel is fully milled, or polished. Long-grain rice is the rice of choice throughout most of Europe and the Americas, with the exception of Arborio and other short-grain rices, used for risotto in Italy and paella and similar dishes in Spain. The risotto method of sautéing the rice and then cooking it in stock while stirring constantly makes the dish creamy and rich in a unique way.

If you were to choose only one type of rice for your pantry, a basic long-grain white rice would be your best bet for versatility. However, keeping some short-grain rice on hand for Asian dishes or Arborio for risotto would easily expand your cooking repertoire. If you have a rice cooker, by all means, use it. Otherwise, follow the instructions for Basic Long-Grain Rice (recipe follows) or Basic Short-Grain Rice (page 507).

Basic Long-Grain Rice ◼

MAKES **4 SERVINGS**

TIME **20 MINUTES**

How quick-cooking rice came into existence I'll never know, given how easy this is. Basically, you can cook long-grain rice any way you want to, as long as you use sufficient water and stop the cooking (draining excess water if necessary) before it becomes mush. This is the most straightforward method.

1^{1}/2 cups long-grain rice, rinsed in a strainer
Large pinch of salt

1. Combine the rice with 2^{1}/4 cups water (or stock) and the salt in a medium saucepan with a lid and turn the heat to medium-high. Bring to a boil.
2. Turn the heat to medium-low and cover. Cook for 15 minutes, or until the water is absorbed and the

rice is tender. Serve or keep warm over absolutely minimal heat for up to 15 minutes.

Fried Rice CHINA, SOUTHEAST ASIA ◼

MAKES **4 SERVINGS**

TIME **30 MINUTES**

Leftover rice is not only acceptable here but practically mandatory: fresh or warm rice does not fry well, but clumps together and sticks to the wok. You need cold, stale rice, which separates during cooking.

If you have neither roast pork (even the Cuban Lechon Asado, page 375, will work) nor Chinese sausage, ham is a fine substitute. No meat at all is fine, too, of course; see the variations.

3 tablespoons corn, grapeseed, or other neutral oil
2 eggs, lightly beaten
^{1}/2 pound small shrimp, peeled, optional
^{1}/2 pound Barbecued Pork (page 373), Chinese sausage, or other meat, chopped into bits, optional
^{1}/2 cup chopped scallion
4 cups cooked long-grain rice (preceding recipe), chilled
1 tablespoon soy sauce
3 teaspoons dark sesame oil or toasted sesame seeds (page 596)
Salt and black pepper to taste

1. Heat 1 tablespoon of the oil in a wok or large skillet over medium heat, swirling the oil to coat the wok. Add the eggs and scramble, breaking the egg into small pieces, just until set. Remove and set aside.
2. Raise the heat to high and add the remaining oil. When hot, add the shrimp, if using, and cook until they turn pink, just a minute or so. Add the pork, if using, and brown lightly, then stir in the scallion. When fragrant, stir in the rice, eggs, and

soy sauce. Cook, stirring occasionally, until the rice is heated through, 3 to 5 minutes. Sprinkle the sesame oil over the rice, season with salt and pepper, and serve.

Yang Chow Fried Rice. In step 2, after the rice is heated through, add 2 cups thinly sliced iceberg lettuce.

Pineapple Fried Rice. In step 2, substitute nam pla (Thai fish sauce; see page 500) for the soy sauce. Add 1 cup chopped fresh pineapple along with the rice.

Vegetarian Fried Rice. Omit the shrimp and pork. In step 1, before adding the eggs, cook 1 medium carrot, chopped; 1 celery stalk, peeled and chopped; and 1 onion, chopped, until crisp-tender, about 5 minutes. Remove with a slotted spoon, then add the egg and proceed, stirring in the cooked vegetables after the rice is heated through.

Nasi Goreng Fried Rice, Malaysian Style. In step 2, substitute chopped cooked chicken for the pork. Substitute sliced shallot for the scallion and add 3 minced garlic cloves and 2 Thai chiles (or other small chiles, or to taste), stemmed, seeded, and minced, to the skillet. Substitute nam pla (Thai fish sauce) or shrimp paste (page 500 or 9) for the soy sauce. Omit the sesame oil and proceed as directed.

Basic Short-Grain Rice ■

MAKES **4 SERVINGS**

TIME **20 MINUTES, MORE IF TIME ALLOWS**

You can make short-grain rice in the same way as long-grain rice, but this traditional method, which takes a little more time, is slightly preferable.

1 1/2 cups short-grain rice
Large pinch of salt

1. Wash the rice thoroughly in several changes of water, then put it in the saucepan in which you intend to cook it with water to cover by about an inch, along with the salt. If time allows, let soak for 20 to 40 minutes.
2. Bring to a boil on top of the stove over medium heat. Cook, uncovered, until most of the water is absorbed, 8 to 12 minutes; small craters will appear on top of the rice. Turn the heat down to a minimum and cover. Cook for another 10 minutes or so, then turn off the heat. Serve immediately or let sit for up to 30 minutes more before serving.

Rice with Umeboshi JAPAN ■

MAKES **4 SERVINGS**

TIME **30 MINUTES**

Here the shopping is more challenging than the cooking, but it's worth the hunt: this tart rice preparation goes well with almost all Japanese food. It's pretty as well. Umeboshi (pickled plum) is available at all Japanese markets. Shiso is a seasonal herb that you may have trouble finding in winter; substitute a mixture of basil and mint or just one or the other. You can also use a rice cooker to cook the rice here.

1 1/2 cups short-grain rice
1/2 teaspoon salt
1/4 cup umeboshi, minced
1/4 cup minced fresh shiso
1 tablespoon toasted sesame seeds (page 596) for
    garnish

1. Wash the rice thoroughly in several changes of water, then put it in the saucepan in which you in-

tend to cook it with water to cover by about an inch, along with the salt. If time allows, let soak for 20 to 40 minutes.

2. Bring to a boil on top of the stove over medium heat. Cook, uncovered, until most of the water is absorbed, 8 to 12 minutes; small craters will appear on top of the rice. Turn the heat down to a minimum and cover. Cook for another 10 minutes or so, then turn off the heat.

3. Stir in the umeboshi and shiso, sprinkle with the sesame seeds, and serve immediately or let sit for up to 30 minutes.

Sticky Rice THAILAND

MAKES **4 SERVINGS**

TIME **ABOUT 2 HOURS, LARGELY UNATTENDED**

Served throughout China and Southeast Asia, sticky rice has become associated most closely with Thailand, where it is the equivalent of France's bread, eaten at almost every meal. It's addictive and easily made at home, as long as you plan ahead a bit.

Sticky rice is one of the few grains—indeed, foods—that can be prepared without salt and still taste great.

1 cup sticky (glutinous) rice

1. Rinse the rice, then soak it in water to cover for at least 1 hour and up to 24 hours.

2. Drain, then wrap in cheesecloth and put in a steamer above boiling water. Steam for about 30 minutes, until tender.

Sticky Rice with Nam Pla and Coconut Milk. Making a good thing better: Toss the cooked rice with 1 cup coconut milk, homemade (page 584) or canned, and 1 tablespoon nam pla (Thai fish sauce;

see page 500). Rewrap and steam (or microwave) for 5 more minutes to reheat.

Yau Mei Faan Flavorful Sticky Rice CHINA

MAKES **4 SERVINGS**

TIME **40 MINUTES**

Hearty and warming, this is a popular winter dish in China, and rightly so. If you have a rice cooker, this is a good place to use it; it will allow you both to make the rice and to keep it warm.

Even better is to wrap the rice in lotus leaves, as in the variation, which gives it a rich, smoky flavor and produces a dish often served at dim sum brunches. You can find lotus (or banana) leaves, as well as Chinese sausage and dried shrimp, at most Asian markets.

1½ cups sticky short-grain Chinese rice (sometimes
   called glutinous rice), rinsed well and drained
1 pound boneless, skinless chicken breast, cut into
   ½-inch chunks

SHAOXING WINE

2 tablespoons Shaoxing wine or dry sherry

⅓ cup soy sauce

1 tablespoon corn, grapeseed, or other neutral oil

2 Chinese sausage links, chopped

6 wood ear or shiitake mushrooms, reconstituted
(page 112), drained, and chopped

10 dried shrimp (page 185), soaked in hot water, drained,
and chopped

2 scallions, trimmed and minced

1. Cook the rice in a rice cooker or on the stovetop: Cover the rice with 3 cups cold water in a medium saucepan, bring to a boil, then turn the heat down and simmer, covered, until the rice absorbs the water and is cooked through, about 30 minutes.

2. Meanwhile, marinate the chicken in the wine and 2 tablespoons of the soy sauce. Heat the oil in a wok or large skillet over high heat. Add the sausage, mushrooms, and shrimp and brown, stirring occasionally, about 2 minutes. Add the chicken with its marinade and cook, stirring, until cooked through, about 4 minutes.

3. When the rice is done, stir in the chicken mixture and the remaining soy sauce until well combined. Garnish with the scallions and serve.

Sticky Rice Wrapped in Lotus Leaves. Soak 4 to 6 large lotus or banana leaves in hot water until soft, then rinse well and pat dry. Cut the lotus leaves so that you have eight 8 × 10-inch rectangles, with the grain of the leaves running the long way. Place one long end closest to your body and spoon a quarter of the rice mixture onto the middle of the leaf. Fold one long end over, then the other, and finally the 2 shorter ends. Seal with a toothpick or string. Repeat with the remaining leaves. (You may refrigerate these packages for up to 2 days.) When you're ready to serve, steam over boiling water until hot, about 10 minutes, or microwave for a couple of minutes to reheat.

STICKY RICE WRAPPED IN LOTUS LEAVES

Kayaku Gohan Rice with Vegetables JAPAN

MAKES **4 SERVINGS**

TIME **45 MINUTES**

This popular one-pot dish can be made with meat or vegetables and, like most casseroles, is easily varied. There are, of course, similar dishes throughout East Asia (and throughout this chapter), but this one is made distinctively Japanese by the addition of mirin and even more so if you use dashi for the cooking stock—a terrific touch.

Aburage—fried tofu—is available, precooked, at Japanese markets; it's slightly sweet.

1 1/2 cups short-grain rice

1/2 cup ground meat or diced chicken, optional

2 tablespoons corn, grapeseed, or other neutral oil,
    if you're using meat

Salt and black pepper to taste

1/4 pound shiitake mushrooms, stems discarded
    (or reserved for stock), caps sliced

1 small carrot, finely diced

1/4 cup chopped canned bamboo shoots, water chestnuts,
    or celery

1/4 pound fried tofu (aburage) or firm tofu, well pressed,
    (page 491), cut into chunks or strips

3 tablespoons soy sauce

3 tablespoons mirin or honey

2 1/2 cups Dashi or chicken stock, preferably homemade
    (page 162 or 160), or water

1. Wash the rice and soak it in water to cover while you prepare the other ingredients. If you are using the meat or chicken, put the oil in a medium skillet over medium heat. Add the meat or chicken and cook, stirring occasionally to break up lumps, until it browns; season with a bit of salt and pepper and turn off the heat.

2. In a medium saucepan or flameproof casserole with a lid, combine all the ingredients including the meat or chicken and the drained rice. Bring to a boil over medium heat, then stir once and cover. Reduce the heat to low and cook for about 20 minutes, or until the liquid is absorbed. Turn off the heat and let sit, covered, for 15 to 30 minutes. Taste and adjust the seasoning, then serve.

Basmati Rice with Shiso JAPAN ▪

MAKES **4 SERVINGS**

TIME **30 MINUTES**

A simple rice preparation that can serve as a great side dish for a variety of Japanese (and other) dishes. If you don't have shiso, use fresh mint, basil, cilantro, or a combination.

1 tablespoon butter

5 fresh shiso leaves

1 cup basmati rice

Salt and black pepper to taste

1. Preheat the oven to 350°F. Melt the butter over medium heat in an ovenproof saucepan with a lid. Chop two of the shiso leaves and cook them in the butter for 30 seconds.

2. Add the rice and cook, stirring, until the rice becomes transparent, just a couple of minutes. Add 1 1/2 cups water and some salt and pepper. Bring to a boil, cover, place in the oven, and set a timer for 10 minutes.

3. While the rice is cooking, mince the remaining shiso. When the 10 minutes are up, remove the rice but do not uncover; let it rest in a warm place for another 10 minutes. Stir in the remaining shiso, adjust the seasoning, and serve immediately.

Onigiri Rice Balls JAPAN ■ ■ ■

MAKES **4 SERVINGS**

TIME **30 MINUTES**

You might scoff at rice balls, and their close cousins, rice sandwiches, but I know plenty of people (self included) who lust after them. Even at their simplest—plain boiled rice, brushed with a little soy sauce and wrapped in a piece of nori—there is something enormously appealing about them. When you try a few of the variations, you'll find one you like as well.

Although there are several different shapes into which the Japanese form rice balls, there is really only one important rule to remember: press the rice just firmly enough to have it hold together; you do not want a tough, packed ball but a loose association of individual clumps.

Serve this as a side dish with Japanese food, or as an appetizer.

4 cups cooked short-grain rice (page 507), still hot

¼ cup soy sauce

4 sheets nori, lightly toasted (page 484)

1. Work with wet hands while the rice is still hot (or at least warm). Form 8 balls by cupping the rice gently between your hands. Brush each ball lightly with soy sauce, using about half the soy for this purpose.

2. Brush each of the nori sheets with a little of the remaining soy sauce, then cut each piece in half (done most easily with scissors). Wrap each ball with a piece of nori, shiny side out. Serve within a few hours.

Rice Balls with Sesame. Sprinkle the balls with toasted sesame seeds (page 596) before wrapping.

Rice "Sandwiches." Enclose any of the following in the rice balls: dried bonito flakes, lightly doused with soy sauce, about 1 tablespoon per ball; pitted pickled plums (umeboshi), 1 per ball; a small piece of cooked fish, preferably salmon grilled with soy sauce.

Rice Balls with Miso. Smear each of the rice balls with a bit of miso, thinned slightly with soy sauce, in place of the soy sauce alone.

Rice and Beans, Korean Style

MAKES **4 SERVINGS**

TIME **ABOUT 2 HOURS, MORE IF PRESOAKING BEANS**

Every culture that relies on rice mixes other common ingredients into it, to boost both flavor and nutrition. Most people are familiar with Fried Rice (page 506) and Coconut Rice (page 516), but this recipe is quite different from those.

If you make this dish with red beans only, use all the bean-cooking liquid for the rice; it will give it a lovely pink tinge.

¼ cup dried black beans

¼ cup dried adzuki or other red beans

¼ cup pearl barley

¼ cup sticky (glutinous) rice

1 cup short-grain rice

½ cup shelled and peeled chestnuts (page 453) or other nuts

¼ pound ground beef, pork, or other meat, optional

1 tablespoon dark sesame oil, optional

1. If time allows, soak the beans (together is fine) overnight or for several hours or boil together for 2 minutes, then soak for an hour or two. If time does not allow, simply proceed: cook the beans in water to cover until nearly tender, 1 to 2 hours. During their last half hour of cooking, soak the barley and rices in water to cover. Roast the chest-

nuts at 400°F or simmer in boiling salted water until tender, about 30 minutes.

2. When the beans are done, drain them, reserving about half the cooking water. Combine the beans, reserved cooking water, and grains in a saucepan with a lid with water to cover by about an inch. Bring to a boil and adjust the heat so the mixture simmers. When craters appear in the top of the rice mixture, after 10 to 15 minutes, the rice should be nearly tender. Add the chestnuts, turn the heat to low, cover, and cook for 15 minutes or so, until all the water is absorbed and all the ingredients are tender. If you're using the meat, cook it in the sesame oil over medium heat in a skillet until separate and brown, about 5 minutes.

3. Stir the meat into the rice, then taste and adjust the seasoning. Serve immediately or cover tightly and keep warm over the lowest heat for up to 30 minutes.

Rice with Mushrooms and Meat
KOREA

MAKES **4 TO 6 SERVINGS**

TIME **40 MINUTES**

Quicker and easier than the preceding recipe, this one usually relies on mushrooms and meat for flavor. Though it's a cross-cultural technique and not at all traditional, I think adding a small handful of soaked dried porcini to the fresh mushrooms as they cook is a big improvement.

You can buy toasted sesame seeds in Korean (and usually Japanese) markets, but toasting them yourself takes less than 5 minutes.

2 cups short-grain rice

2 tablespoons corn, grapeseed, or other neutral oil

1 large onion, chopped

1/2 pound button mushrooms, trimmed and sliced

1/2 pound ground beef or pork

Salt and black pepper to taste

2 tablespoons soy sauce

1 teaspoon dark sesame oil

2 teaspoons toasted sesame seeds (page 596)

2 or 3 scallions, trimmed and chopped, for garnish

1. Soak the rice in water to cover while you prepare the other ingredients. Put the oil in a large skillet with a lid over medium-high heat. A minute later, add the onion and cook, stirring occasionally, until softened, about 5 minutes. Add the mushrooms and meat and cook, stirring to break up any clumps of meat, until the mushrooms are softened and the meat browned, about 10 minutes.

2. Drain the rice and add it to the mixture, stirring to combine all the ingredients and adding some salt and pepper. Add water to cover by about 1/2 inch (more if you're using a narrow rather than broad pan) and cook, adjusting the heat so the mixture bubbles steadily. About 15 minutes later, the water should be mostly evaporated. Taste the rice; if it is not nearly done, add a bit more water and continue to cook.

3. When the rice is done, stir in the soy sauce, sesame oil, and sesame seeds, garnish with scallions, and serve or cover and hold over the lowest possible heat for up to 30 minutes.

Kimchi-Rice "Stew" KOREA ▪

MAKES **4 SERVINGS**

TIME **20 MINUTES (WITH PRECOOKED RICE)**

A great way to use leftover rice and a nice cooked treatment of kimchi, which you can buy at any Korean market if you don't want to make your own. Good as a side dish with Korean food, this also makes a fine snack or even a main course (add chicken, pork, beef, or shrimp if you like). The butter is a contemporary feature, but it's how I learned this (from a Korean-American friend), and I like it that way.

2 tablespoons dark sesame oil

1 cup roughly chopped Kimchi (page 444)

2 tablespoons butter or more sesame oil

4 cups cooked short-grain rice (page 507)

1 tablespoon soy sauce

1. Put the oil in a large skillet, preferably nonstick, over medium-high heat. Add the kimchi and cook until it softens a bit, just 5 minutes or so. Add the butter and rice and stir. Cook, stirring infrequently, until the rice is hot, 5 or 10 minutes.

2. Let the rice brown a bit on the bottom, then stir this browned part back into the mixture, season with soy sauce, and serve hot.

Red Lentils with Rice INDIA

MAKES **4 TO 6 SERVINGS**

TIME **40 MINUTES**

Rice and lentils are both daily fare in much of India, but rarely are they cooked together. An exception is made for the quite-quick-cooking red lentils, which are prepared in a manner not unlike that used in the Middle East.

2 tablespoons corn, grapeseed, or other neutral oil

1 large onion, chopped

1 tablespoon Fragrant Curry Powder (page 593)
   or any not-too-strong curry powder or garam masala (page 594)

3/4 cup dried red lentils

1 cup long-grain rice

Salt and black pepper to taste

2 tablespoons butter, optional

1. Put the oil in a large skillet or flameproof casserole with a lid over medium-high heat; a minute later, add the onion and cook, stirring occasionally, until it begins to brown on its edges, about 5 minutes. Stir in the curry powder, then 3 cups water. Bring to a boil and add the lentils and rice. Bring back to a boil, then cover and adjust the heat so the mixture simmers steadily.

2. Cook until the rice and lentils are tender, about 20 minutes. Uncover and, if necessary, boil off excess water. Season with salt and pepper, then stir in the butter if you're using it. When it has been incorporated, turn off the heat and serve.

Pilaf, Many Ways MIDDLE EAST

MAKES **4 SERVINGS**

TIME **ABOUT 1 HOUR, LARGELY UNATTENDED**

The procedure for basic pilaf—and here I'm focusing on the Middle Eastern rather than the Indian variety—is much simpler than that for risotto but truly no less rewarding. And like risotto's, its technique can lead you to many different dishes; note the variations, which are just a fraction of what you can do.

Long-grain rice (basmati is best) is the one to use here.

Leftover pilaf can be successfully reheated in a microwave; no kidding. Just add a tiny bit of water first.

4 tablespoons (1/2 stick) butter or extra virgin olive oil, or less if you must

1 medium onion, chopped

Salt and black pepper to taste

$1^{1}/_{4}$ cups long-grain rice

1 cup cored and chopped tomato (canned is fine; use the juice), optional

$1^{1}/_{4}$ to $1^{1}/_{2}$ cups chicken, beef, or vegetable stock, preferably homemade (page 160 or 162)

$^{1}/_{2}$ cup chopped fresh parsley leaves

2 tablespoons fresh lemon juice

1. Put the butter or oil in a large deep skillet with a lid and place over medium heat. Add the onion and a large pinch of salt and cook, stirring occasionally, until the onion turns translucent, 5 to 10 minutes. Add the rice and cook, stirring occasionally, until the rice is glossy and begins to brown, 3 to 5 minutes. Season with salt and pepper.

2. Add the tomato if you choose to and stir for a minute; add the stock (the smaller amount if you used tomato) and stir. Raise the heat and bring the mixture to a boil; cook for a minute or two, then reduce the heat to low and cover. Cook for about 15 minutes, or until most of the liquid has been absorbed. Turn the heat to the absolute minimum (if you have an electric stove, turn the heat off and let the pan sit on the burner) and let rest for another 15 to 30 minutes, until the rice is tender. Stir in the parsley and lemon juice and serve.

Pilaf with Currants and Pine Nuts. Along with the rice, add $^{1}/_{4}$ cup currants (or raisins), 2 tablespoons pine nuts, and $^{1}/_{2}$ teaspoon ground cinnamon.

Pilaf with Chickpeas or Peas. Just before adding the stock, stir in 1 cup cooked chickpeas or raw green peas (frozen are okay, and you need not defrost first).

Golden Pilaf. Before adding the stock, warm it with a large pinch ($^{1}/_{4}$ to $^{1}/_{2}$ teaspoon) of saffron threads.

Seafood Pilaf. Just before adding the stock, stir in 1 cup shrimp or scallops, cut into $^{1}/_{2}$-inch dice; they need not be cooked first. Or add 1 cup cooked, shelled, and rinsed mussels or 1 cup raw oysters or clams (chopped if large).

Vermicelli Pilaf. I love this: Sauté about $^{1}/_{2}$ cup vermicelli, broken into 1- or 2-inch lengths, along with the rice. Use the larger amount of stock.

Pilaf with Meat MIDDLE EAST
MAKES **4 SERVINGS**

TIME **1 HOUR, LARGELY UNATTENDED**

With a couple of good side dishes, this delicious standard makes a satisfying main course.

2 tablespoons butter or extra virgin olive oil

$^{1}/_{2}$ pound ground lamb, pork, turkey, chicken, beef, or a combination

Salt and black pepper to taste

1 medium onion, chopped

3 bay leaves

1 cup long-grain rice

$^{1}/_{2}$ teaspoon ground cinnamon

$1^{1}/_{2}$ cups chicken, beef, or vegetable stock, preferably homemade (page 160 or 162)

$^{1}/_{2}$ cup chopped fresh parsley leaves

2 tablespoons fresh lemon juice

1. Put 1 tablespoon of the butter in a large deep skillet with a lid and place over medium heat. Crumble the meat and add it to the pan along with a large pinch of salt; cook, stirring occasionally to break up the lumps, until the meat loses its color, less than 5 minutes. Remove with a slotted spoon.

2. Add the remaining butter to the skillet, followed by the onion and a little more salt; cook, stirring

occasionally, until the onion turns translucent, 5 to 10 minutes. Add the bay leaves and rice and cook, stirring occasionally, until the rice is glossy and begins to brown, 3 to 5 minutes. Return the meat to the pan, then stir the mixture and sprinkle with salt, pepper, and cinnamon.

3. Add the stock and stir. Raise the heat and bring the mixture to a boil; cook for a minute or two, then reduce the heat to low and cover. Cook for about 15 minutes, or until most of the liquid has been absorbed. Turn the heat to the absolute minimum (if you have an electric stove, turn the heat off and let the pan sit on the burner) and let rest for another 15 to 30 minutes, until the rice is tender. Stir in the parsley and lemon juice and serve.

Nasi Lemak Fragrant Coconut Milk Rice
MALAYSIA ■

MAKES **4 SERVINGS**

TIME **20 MINUTES**

Nasi Lemak is a favored breakfast dish in Malaysia, where you get it from streetside carts and busy little restaurants that are closed by lunchtime. You start with a pile of coconut rice (which is the nasi lemak, though the name always refers to the dish) and point to what you want to eat with it—salads of pickled pineapple, deep-fried shrimp; the possibilities vary from place to place.

The accompaniments suggested here are traditional and standard, and the recipes for the more unusual ones can be found in this book. Don't feel compelled to have all of them, though it wouldn't be hard to do so. The more things you have to eat the rice with, the more fun it is, especially at a dinner party. (I wouldn't suggest trying to get it all made by breakfast.)

1½ cups long-grain rice

1½ cups coconut milk, homemade (page 584) or canned (one 12- to 14-ounce can)

One ½-inch piece fresh ginger, peeled and finely sliced

½ teaspoon salt

½ cinnamon stick

Accompaniments (serve with some or all)

3 hard-cooked eggs (page 338), peeled and cut into wedges

1 cucumber, peeled if waxed or strips peeled to create a striped look, sliced

½ cup Fried Peanuts (page 27)

1 recipe Sambal Oelek (page 590) or Sambal Ikan Billis (following recipe)

1 recipe (or the leftovers from) Kari Ayam (page 281)

1. In a medium saucepan, combine the rice with the coconut milk, ginger, salt, and cinnamon and add enough water (probably only ¼ cup or so) to cover the rice with liquid. Bring to a boil over medium-high heat, then turn the heat to low and cover. Cook for 15 minutes, or until all the liquid is absorbed and the rice is tender. Serve or keep warm over absolutely minimal heat for up to 15 minutes.

2. Serve a pile of coconut rice in the center of each plate, flanked by wedges of hard-cooked eggs, sliced cucumber, and any or all of the other accompaniments.

Sambal Ikan Billis MALAYSIA ■ ■

MAKES **4 SERVINGS**

TIME **15 MINUTES**

This is the sambal traditionally served alongside Nasi Lemak, usually at breakfast; you might prefer these as a cocktail snack. For more about dried anchovies, see page 25.

Roughly ¼ cup dried anchovies

¼ cup corn, grapeseed, or other neutral oil

1 recipe Sambal Oelek (page 590)

1. Soak the dried anchovies in hot water for a few minutes while you heat the oil in a small saucepan over medium-high heat.

2. Drain the anchovies and add them to the oil. Fry them until golden brown, a minute or two, then transfer them to a paper-towel-lined plate. Add the sambal oelek to the oil and fry it, stirring, for a minute or two, until fragrant and darkened. Add the anchovies back to the pan, stir, and lower the heat to medium-low. Simmer for a minute and serve warm or at room temperature.

Coconut Rice CARIBBEAN ■

MAKES **4 SERVINGS**

TIME **30 MINUTES**

I call this Caribbean because that's where I first had it, but not surprisingly it's a staple in much of Southeast Asia as well. Great with jasmine rice, it's perfectly fine with any other short- or long-grain rice and can be varied in many ways. If you like, garnish with some chopped cashews or peanuts.

I love this with spicy stews.

3 cups coconut milk, homemade (page 584) or canned (about two 12- to 14-ounce cans)

1 bay leaf or 1 teaspoon peeled and minced fresh ginger, optional

1½ cups rice, preferably short-grain

Salt to taste

1. Combine the coconut milk, bay leaf if you're using it, and rice in a saucepan with a lid and bring to a boil over medium heat, stirring occasionally. Add

some salt, reduce the heat to low, and cover. Cook for 10 minutes, stirring occasionally to make sure the bottom doesn't stick or burn.

2. Uncover and continue to cook, stirring, over low heat until the rice is tender and the mixture is creamy, about 15 minutes. If the liquid evaporates before the rice is done, stir in water, about ½ cup at a time, and cook until done.

Coconut Rice and Beans. Stir ½ cup moist cooked kidney, pinto, pink, or black beans into the rice about 5 minutes before it finishes cooking.

Yellow Coconut Rice. In step 1, add ½ teaspoon ground turmeric to the mix.

Arroz con Coco Sweet Coconut Rice

SOUTH AMERICA

MAKES **4 SERVINGS**

TIME **40 MINUTES**

A different type of coconut rice, one that is made fairly sweet but served with savory (even spicy) foods, like Stewed Lamb Shanks with Mushrooms and Pasilla Chile Sauce (page 414). You can add about ⅓ cup raisins or corn or thinly sliced and lightly browned ripe plantains (page 472) or even a bit of cinnamon.

3 cups coconut milk, homemade (page 584) or canned (about two 12- to 14-ounce cans)

⅓ cup sugar

1½ cups long-grain rice

Pinch of salt

½ cup unsweetened shredded coconut, optional

1. Combine the coconut milk and sugar in a medium saucepan over medium heat. Bring to a boil, stir-

ring frequently, and cook until the mixture darkens in color, 5 to 10 minutes. Add the rice and salt, then cover; adjust the heat so the mixture simmers gently.

2. Cook until all the liquid is absorbed, 15 to 20 minutes; let stand for about 10 minutes before serving. During that time, if you like, toast the coconut in a dry skillet, shaking occasionally, until lightly browned. Stir into the rice just before serving.

Arroz a la Mexicana Mexican Rice MEXICO

MAKES **6 SERVINGS**

TIME **50 MINUTES**

Unlike the often inedible rice that comes on every combo platter of tacos or enchiladas in this country (and, increasingly and sadly, in Mexico as well), this is the real thing. It's the perfect side dish with any Mexican meal, especially when paired with Refried Beans (page 438). Whereas Spanish rice gets its color and flavor from saffron, the source here is fresh tomatoes.

 3 tablespoons lard or neutral oil, like corn or grapeseed

 2 cups long-grain rice, rinsed well and drained

 4 garlic cloves, peeled

 1 medium onion, peeled

 2 large tomatoes, cored, halved, and seeded

 1 quart chicken stock, preferably homemade (page 160),
    or water

 Salt and black pepper to taste

1. Heat the oil in a large saucepan with a lid over medium heat. Add the rice and cook, stirring occasionally, until golden brown, about 10 minutes.

2. Meanwhile, put the garlic, onion, and tomatoes in a food processor or blender and puree until smooth. Add this mixture to the rice and cook, stirring, for another 5 minutes.

3. Add the chicken stock and bring to a boil, then lower the heat, cover, and simmer until the water is absorbed and the rice tender, about 30 minutes. Fluff with a fork, season with salt and pepper, and serve.

Arroz Verde. In step 2, substitute 5 fresh poblano chiles, roasted (page 588) and stemmed, for the tomatoes. Add $1/4$ cup chopped fresh epazote or cilantro leaves with the chicken stock.

Rice with Vegetables MEXICO ▨

MAKES **4 SERVINGS**

TIME **30 MINUTES**

Sadly, throughout Mexico, you see rice cooked with mixed frozen vegetables—Birds Eye rice, essentially. Fortunately, the real thing is not that difficult to make and it's infinitely better.

 2 tablespoons lard or neutral oil, like corn
    or grapeseed

 $1/2$ cup chopped onion

 Salt and black pepper

 $1 1/2$ cups long-grain rice

 $1/3$ cup minced carrot

 $1/3$ cup peeled and minced celery

 $1/3$ cup minced red bell pepper

 $1/3$ cup minced green beans or $1/2$ cup peas

 3 cups chicken or beef stock, preferably homemade
    (page 160), or water

 Chopped fresh parsley or cilantro leaves
    for garnish

1. Put the lard in a saucepan or deep skillet with a lid and place over medium heat. A minute later, add the onion and some salt and pepper and cook, stirring occasionally, until the onion softens, about 5

minutes. Add the rice and cook, stirring, until it is glossy, about 2 minutes. Add the vegetables and a bit more salt and pepper and cook just until they begin to soften, 2 or 3 minutes.

2. Add the stock, bring to a boil, cover, and adjust the heat so the mixture simmers gently. Cook until all the liquid has been absorbed, 15 to 20 minutes. Serve immediately or let sit over the lowest possible heat (if you have an electric stove, turn the heat off and let the pan sit on the burner) for up to 30 minutes. Stir in the herb and serve.

Rice with Onions, Garlic, and Herbs
BRAZIL ■

MAKES **4 SERVINGS**

TIME **30 MINUTES**

This is a magnificent rice dish, one that could overwhelm other dishes with which you serve it. Therefore, it's best to give it its due and accompany it with a couple of grilled sausages or very simply cooked steak, chicken, or shrimp.

> 1 large onion, peeled and cut into chunks
>
> 6 to 10 garlic cloves, peeled
>
> $^{1}/_{2}$ cup fresh parsley leaves
>
> $^{1}/_{2}$ cup fresh basil or cilantro leaves
>
> 3 tablespoons corn, grapeseed, or other neutral oil
>
> 2 cups long-grain rice
>
> Salt and black pepper to taste
>
> 3 cups chicken stock, preferably homemade (page 160), or water

1. Combine the first 4 ingredients in a food processor and puree. Put the oil in a 6- or 8-cup saucepan with a lid over medium heat. A minute later, add the rice and cook, stirring occasionally, until it glistens, just a couple of minutes. Stir in all

but a tablespoon of the onion mixture and some salt and pepper and cook for a minute or two, stirring.

2. Add the stock, bring to a boil, and cover; turn the heat to medium-low and cook until the liquid is absorbed, 15 to 20 minutes. Stir in the reserved onion mixture and serve immediately.

Yellow Rice SPAIN AND ELSEWHERE ■
MAKES **4 SERVINGS**

TIME **30 MINUTES**

A kind of pilaf, really, but one that has become its own category, the mother of dishes ranging from Paella (page 519) to Coconut Rice and Beans (page 516). I cannot resist sautéing the rice in oil or butter first, but it's not entirely necessary; see the simpler variation. (You can also use any of the variations on Pilaf, Many Ways, page 513.)

Turmeric is a common and an inexpensive but one-dimensional substitute for saffron; it has none of the depth of flavor, though the color is terrific. You can put in a few roasted red peppers (page 470) or canned "pimientos" also, if you like; add them along with the rice. This is a side dish that has far-ranging applications but is especially fine with soupy beans.

> $2^{1}/_{2}$ cups chicken or beef stock, preferably homemade (page 160)
>
> Large pinch of saffron threads, about 1 teaspoon, or $^{1}/_{2}$ teaspoon ground turmeric
>
> 4 tablespoons ($^{1}/_{2}$ stick) butter or extra virgin olive oil
>
> 1 medium onion, chopped
>
> $1^{1}/_{2}$ cups Arborio or other short-grain rice
>
> Salt and black pepper to taste

1. Warm the stock gently in a saucepan with the saffron. Put half the butter in a deep skillet with a lid

over medium heat. A minute later, add the onion. Cook, stirring occasionally, until the onion softens, about 5 minutes. Add the rice and continue to cook, stirring, until the rice is glossy and begins to brown, about 5 minutes more.

2. Add the stock all at once, along with some salt and pepper. Cover and adjust the heat so the mixture simmers gently and cook until the rice is done, 15 to 20 minutes. Stir in the remaining butter, taste and adjust the seasoning, and serve.

Faster Yellow Rice. This is no work at all. Omit the onion. Combine the stock, saffron, rice, and a large pinch of salt in a saucepan with a lid and bring to a boil. Cover and simmer, stirring once after 5 minutes, until the rice is done, about 15 minutes. Stir in 2 tablespoons butter or extra virgin olive oil, taste and adjust the seasoning, and serve.

Yellow Rice with Chorizo SPAIN ▣

MAKES **4 SERVINGS**

TIME **30 MINUTES**

Somewhere in between a rice side dish and a one-pot meal—a form of paella, really—this can serve as either. A few bits of chicken browned along with the chorizo will go a long way. I love this with the warm taste of mild chile powder, but you can use hotter chiles or omit them entirely.

> 2¹/₂ cups chicken or beef stock, preferably homemade (page 160)
>
> Large pinch of saffron threads, about 1 teaspoon, or ¹/₂ teaspoon ground turmeric
>
> 2 tablespoons extra virgin olive oil
>
> ¹/₂ to 1 pound chorizo or other dry sausage (linguiça, kielbasa, or "Italian" sausage are all fine), sliced
>
> 1 tablespoon minced garlic

> 2 teaspoons pure mild chile powder, like ancho, or pimentón (Spanish smoked paprika), or to taste
>
> 1¹/₂ cups Arborio or other short-grain rice
>
> 1 tomato, preferably peeled, roughly chopped (or a couple of canned plum tomatoes, chopped)
>
> Salt and black pepper to taste
>
> Chopped fresh parsley leaves for garnish

1. Warm the stock gently in a saucepan with the saffron. Put the oil in a deep skillet with a lid over medium heat. A minute later, add the chorizo. Cook, stirring occasionally, until it begins to brown, about 5 minutes. Add the garlic, chile powder, and rice and continue to cook, stirring, until the rice is glossy, just a minute or two.

2. Add the tomato and the stock, along with some salt and pepper. Cover and adjust the heat so the mixture simmers gently. Cook until the rice is done, 15 to 20 minutes. Taste and adjust the seasoning, then garnish and serve.

The Original Paella SPAIN ▣

MAKES **4 SERVINGS**

TIME **30 MINUTES**

I didn't understand paella well until I had this dish in Spain. Rather than a major production, it's a simple combination of rice and shrimp, a terrific weeknight dish, as it has been in coastal Spain for centuries.

> 3¹/₂ cups chicken stock, preferably homemade (page 160)
>
> Pinch of saffron threads, optional
>
> 3 tablespoons extra virgin olive oil
>
> 1 medium onion, minced
>
> 2 cups short- or medium-grain rice, preferably Arborio
>
> Salt and black pepper to taste
>
> 2 cups peeled shrimp, cut into ¹/₂-inch chunks
>
> Minced fresh parsley leaves for garnish

1. Preheat the oven to 500°F or as near that temperature as you can get it. Warm the stock in a saucepan with the saffron if you're using it. Place an ovenproof 10- or 12-inch skillet over medium-high heat and add the oil. A minute later, add the onion and cook, stirring occasionally, until translucent, about 5 minutes.

2. Add the rice and cook, stirring occasionally, until glossy, just a minute or two. Season liberally with salt and pepper and add the warmed stock, taking care to avoid the rising steam. Stir in the shrimp and transfer the skillet to the oven.

3. Bake for about 25 minutes, until all the liquid is absorbed and the rice is dry on top (it's nice if it browns a little on the bottom, too). Garnish with parsley and serve immediately.

Paella de Setas y Pollo
Mushroom and Chicken Paella SPAIN

MAKES **6 SERVINGS**

TIME **1 HOUR**

Paella isn't always bright yellow rice studded with overcooked seafood—it's not even always made with seafood. Here's a great version made with chicken, chorizo, and mushrooms that I learned from Spanish chef Jose Andres, based in Washington, DC. It's a hearty one-dish meal impressive enough for any company.

Small handful of dried porcini

2 tablespoons extra virgin olive oil

6 bone-in, skin-on chicken thighs

1 yellow onion, chopped

3 garlic cloves, chopped

1 bay leaf

1/2 pound fresh mushrooms, preferably mixed

1/2 pound chorizo or other dry sausage

2 teaspoons pimentón (Spanish smoked paprika) or other paprika

1/2 cup dry white wine

1/2 cup tomato puree

2 cups Spanish or Arborio rice

3 cups chicken stock, preferably homemade (page 160), or as needed

Pinch of saffron threads

Salt to taste

1. Soak the dried mushrooms in hot water to cover. Put the oil in a 12-inch skillet over medium-high heat. When the oil shimmers, add the chicken thighs skin side down and cook them, flipping once or twice, until the skin is deeply browned, about 10 minutes.

2. Add the onion and cook, stirring occasionally, until it softens and starts to take on a little color, about 5 minutes. Add the garlic and bay leaf and cook for a minute more, until the garlic is golden.

3. Drain the dried mushrooms and add them, along with the fresh mushrooms, to the paella pan; cook, stirring, until the mushrooms have wilted slightly and begun to give up their liquid. Add the chorizo and pimentón and cook, stirring, for 30 seconds more, then add the wine and let it bubble away for a minute or so. Add the tomato puree and cook for 5 minutes, stirring occasionally.

4. Add the rice, scattering it across the pan in as even a layer as possible. Add the chicken stock and saffron and season well with salt. When the stock reaches a boil, set a timer for 20 minutes and adjust the heat so the paella cooks at a gentle simmer.

5. Check the rice—if it's still crunchy on the top, add a little more liquid and cook for a few minutes longer. When the rice is ready, turn the heat off, let the paella rest for 2 minutes, and serve.

Mixed Seafood and Rice JAPAN

MAKES **4 SERVINGS**

TIME **40 MINUTES**

Non-Japanese may think of this as Japanese paella. Like paella, it may be made with or without seafood. Like paella, it relies on good ingredients, including rice and stock, and, like paella, it's pretty straightforward to prepare and easy to vary. (You can make the recipe below not only with chicken but with almost any combination of seafood. You can also make it with vegetables; see page 510.)

There is, however, a critical difference. Whereas paella usually relies on chicken stock, wine, and tomatoes, Kayaku Gohan (along with, it seems, about a million other dishes in Japan) uses dashi. This isn't a problem, since dashi is easily made, as long as you stock kelp, a dried seaweed also known as kombu, and dried bonito flakes (bonito is related to tuna). Fortunately, each of these ingredients keeps forever, and each is readily available at Asian markets.

> 4 cups Dashi, preferably homemade (page 162)
> 5 fresh or dried shiitake mushrooms (caps only)
> 2 tablespoons neutral oil, like corn or grapeseed
> 1 medium onion, chopped
> 1/2 pound cleaned squid (page 98), tentacles halved and bodies sliced into rings, or shrimp, peeled
> 1 3/4 cups short-grain rice
> 1 cup fresh or thawed frozen peas
> 2 tablespoons soy sauce
> 1 tablespoon mirin or honey
> 1/2 pound shrimp, peeled and cut into small pieces
> Salt if necessary

1. Gently warm the dashi in a saucepan and if you're using dried shiitakes, add them to it. When the dried shiitakes are tender, 10 to 15 minutes later, remove and discard their stems and slice the caps.

2. Put the oil in a deep 10-inch skillet or fairly broad saucepan with a lid over medium-high heat. Add the onion, sliced mushroom caps, and squid and cook, stirring occasionally, until the edges of all three are brown, about 10 minutes. Reduce the heat to medium, add the rice, and cook, stirring, until combined. Add the peas, then strain the dashi and pour it in along with the soy sauce and mirin. Stir, reduce the heat to medium-low, and cover. A minute later, check that the mixture is simmering and adjust the heat if necessary; cook for 15 minutes.

3. When you remove the cover, the mixture should still be a little soupy (add a little dashi or water if it's dried out); add the shrimp and stir, then raise the heat a bit and cook until the rice is tender and the mixture is still moist but not soupy. Taste and adjust the seasoning, then serve.

Risotto alla Milanese ITALY

MAKES **4 TO 6 SERVINGS**

TIME **45 MINUTES**

In all but the best restaurants, risotto is abused—cooked in advance, baked, and who knows what else—so if you have never made risotto at home, you are in for a treat. It takes a little patience and a little practice, but it is not a difficult process at all.

True risotto alla Milanese contains—indeed, features—bone marrow, but don't be discouraged if you cannot (or will not) deal with that. Risotto is wonderful without it, and prosciutto makes an adequate substitute. What you do need are Arborio rice (now sold everywhere, but still best purchased in Italian markets), real saffron, and, ideally, good, homemade stock. (Having said that, see my "bare-bones" variation.)

I might add this: After years of trying every possible technique to make my risotto as creamy as the best I'd ever had, I realized that the "secret" was large quantities of butter. Don't hold back unless you must.

4 to 6 cups chicken, beef, or vegetable stock, preferably
    homemade (page 160 or 162)
Large pinch of saffron threads
4 to 6 tablespoons ($^{1}/_{2}$ to $^{3}/_{4}$ stick) butter
1 medium onion, minced
$^{1}/_{4}$ cup diced bone marrow or prosciutto, optional
$1^{1}/_{2}$ cups Arborio or other short- or medium-grain rice
Salt and black pepper to taste
$^{1}/_{2}$ cup dry white wine
$^{1}/_{2}$ cup freshly grated Parmesan cheese, or more to taste

1. Put the stock in a medium saucepan and turn the heat to low; add the saffron. Put 2 tablespoons of the butter in a large deep nonstick skillet and turn the heat to medium. (Allow the remaining butter to soften while you cook.) When it's hot, add the onion, along with the meat if you're using it, and cook, stirring occasionally, until it softens, 3 to 5 minutes.
2. Add the rice and cook, stirring occasionally, until it is glossy and coated with butter, 2 to 3 minutes. Add a little salt and pepper, then the white wine. Stir and let the liquid bubble away.
3. Use a ladle to begin to add the warmed stock, $^{1}/_{2}$ cup or so at a time, stirring after each addition and every minute or so. When the stock is just about evaporated, add more. The mixture should be neither soupy nor dry. Keep the heat medium to medium-high and stir frequently.
4. Begin tasting the rice 20 minutes after you add it; you want it to be tender but with still a tiny bit of crunch; it could take as long as 30 minutes to reach this stage. When it does, stir in the softened butter and Parmesan. Taste and adjust the seasoning and serve immediately.

Bare-Bones Risotto. A compromise, but still a very good dish in a pinch: Use water instead of stock and 2 tablespoons olive oil at the beginning of cooking (it's still worth stirring in a tablespoon of butter at the end). Omit the marrow and, if you must, the saffron.

Risotto al Limone. Lighter, more delicate, and perfectly fine when made with water instead of stock: Omit the saffron and marrow. In step 1, replace the onion with 2 or 3 chopped shallots, 1 celery stalk, chopped, and 1 fresh rosemary sprig (or $^{1}/_{2}$ teaspoon dried rosemary). In step 4, when the rice is almost done, stir in the grated zest of 1 lemon. Stir in the juice of the lemon, along with the butter, at the very end. For extra richness, add $^{1}/_{2}$ cup heavy cream if you like and cook for another minute, stirring. Add the Parmesan and serve.

Risotto with Red Wine. Omit the saffron, meat, and white wine. Substitute good red wine—something made with nebbiolo or sangiovese grapes will give you a taste most like that you'd have in Italy—for the stock. Both butter and Parmesan are needed to cut the wine's acidity.

Black Risotto with Seafood CROATIA
MAKES **4 TO 6 SERVINGS**
TIME **45 MINUTES**

Though there are similar rice-and-squid-ink dishes throughout the northern Mediterranean, I was introduced to this dish by a Croatian, so it is that country that gets the credit; Spaniards and Italians will no doubt be offended. The origins hardly matter, however; this is a wonderful and intensely flavorful dish.

It's unusual, too, for a few reasons: it's a no-stir (or, to be more precise, a low-stir) risotto; it's jet black;

and it combines cheese and seafood, which is not exactly common and, for many of us—usually including me—a no-no.

But it's also easy, delicious, and striking, a perfect dish for entertaining. Serve it with a simple salad, a white wine from northeastern Italy, Austria, or, if you can find one, Croatia, and fresh fruit for dessert.

You can find squid ink in small packages at fancy fish markets or European specialty shops (or, of course, on the Internet); it's shelf-stable though it must be refrigerated and relatively inexpensive. And though its taste is pure squid, it's the dramatic color that matters most.

4 to 6 tablespoons ($^1/_2$ to $^3/_4$ stick) butter

1 medium onion, diced

About $^1/_2$ pound squid, cleaned (page 98) and chopped

1$^1/_2$ cups Arborio or other short- or medium-grain rice

Salt and black pepper to taste

$^1/_2$ cup dry white wine

Four $^1/_2$- to 1-ounce packages squid ink

4 to 6 cups Shrimp Shell Stock (page 162) or water, warmed

$^1/_2$ pound medium to large shrimp, peeled (add their shells to the Shrimp Shell Stock)

$^1/_2$ cup freshly grated Parmesan cheese, or more to taste

Chopped fresh parsley leaves for garnish

1. Put 2 tablespoons of the butter in a large deep nonstick skillet and turn the heat to medium. (Allow the remaining butter to soften while you cook.) When it's hot, add the onion and squid and cook, stirring occasionally, until the onion softens, 3 to 5 minutes.
2. Add the rice and cook, stirring occasionally, until it is glossy and coated with butter, 2 to 3 minutes. Season with salt and a liberal amount of black pepper, then add the white wine. Stir and let the wine bubble away, then add the squid ink and

enough stock or water to cover the rice by about an inch.

3. Bring the pan to a simmer and cook for 15 to 18 minutes, stirring occasionally, until the rice is tender but still al dente. The mixture should be loose but not soupy at this point; if it isn't, add more water or stock by the tablespoonful.
4. Add the shrimp, stir once or twice to distribute them throughout the rice, and turn the heat to high. When they are just cooked through, after 3 or 4 minutes, remove the pan from the heat and stir in the softened butter and Parmesan. Taste and adjust the seasoning; garnish with parsley and serve immediately.

Variation. A nice refinement is to sear the shrimp (and some scallops if you have them) instead of stirring them into the rice: Substitute $^1/_4$ pound bay scallops for $^1/_4$ pound of the shrimp and, while the rice is cooking in step 3, put 2 more tablespoons of butter in a large nonstick skillet and turn the heat to medium-high. Dredge the scallops lightly in flour and, when the butter foam subsides, add them, along with the shrimp, a few at a time. Turn them individually as they brown, allowing about 2 minutes per side. Season with salt and pepper and nestle them into the risotto just before serving.

Ris in Cagnon   Rice with Cheese ITALY ■
MAKES **4 SERVINGS**

TIME **30 MINUTES**

From the land of risotto comes yet another rich, full-flavored (but far simpler) rice preparation; butter is nearly essential here. With thanks to the great food writer John Thorne (see his Simple Cooking Web site, www.outlawcook.com), who first made me aware of the existence of this Lombardian dish.

Salt and black pepper

1 cup Arborio or other short-grain rice

3 tablespoons butter

$\frac{1}{2}$ cup grated fontina or other good-quality semisoft
cheese

Freshly grated Parmesan cheese to taste

1. Bring a pot of water to a boil and salt it as you would to cook pasta. Add the rice in a steady stream and stir. When the water returns to a boil, lower the heat and simmer the rice until it is tender but not mushy, about 15 minutes. Drain.

2. Put the butter in a saucepan large enough to hold the rice and turn the heat to medium. When the butter melts and just begins to turn brown, add the rice and toss together. Stir in the fontina, then a handful of Parmesan, along with a bit of salt and some pepper. Serve, passing more Parmesan at the table.

Rice with Cheese and Garlic. In step 2, add 1 teaspoon minced garlic to the butter (or olive oil, which is fine in this variation) about 30 seconds before adding the rice.

Lemon Rice. In step 2, omit the cheeses; use the garlic as in the previous variation. Toss the rice with plenty of salt and pepper, then finish the dish with the juice of at least 1 lemon.

Rice with Spinach EASTERN EUROPE, GREECE
MAKES **4 SERVINGS**
TIME **40 MINUTES**

This is lovely, strong-tasting, and quite complex. It's a wonderful side dish but can also serve as the centerpiece of a vegetarian meal.

$\frac{1}{4}$ cup extra virgin olive oil

1 cup long-grain rice

Salt and black pepper to taste

1$\frac{1}{2}$ cups stock, preferably homemade (pages 160–163),
or water

1 pound fresh spinach, trimmed, washed, and drained
but still wet

Tiny grating of nutmeg

Juice of 1 lemon

2 tablespoons butter, cut into bits

$\frac{1}{2}$ cup grated pecorino Romano or crumbled
feta cheese

1. Put 2 tablespoons of the oil in a medium saucepan with a lid over medium heat. A minute later, add the rice along with some salt and pepper and cook, stirring, for about a minute. Add the stock, reduce the heat to low, and cover. Cook for about 15 minutes, or until the rice is done.

2. Meanwhile, put the remaining oil in a deep skillet over medium-high heat. A minute later, add the spinach and some salt and pepper and cook, stirring occasionally, until it wilts. Continue to cook until most of the liquid is gone; stir in the nutmeg and the lemon.

3. Toss the cooked rice with the butter and put on a platter; stir the cheese into the spinach, then immediately put on top of the rice and serve.

Barley with Dried Mushrooms
EASTERN EUROPE ■
MAKES **4 SERVINGS**
TIME **30 MINUTES**

Plain barley, cooked any way you would rice, is fine stuff (make sure you buy pearl barley; the whole-grain variety takes forever to cook). But barley with some butter and dried mushrooms is just a fantastic midwinter side dish.

Porcini mushrooms are best bought in large quantities; a pound might cost $40 or $50 but will last for years, whereas ½ ounce might cost $4 ($128 per pound) and last you a day.

> 1 ounce dried porcini
> 4 tablespoons (½ stick) butter or extra virgin olive oil
> 1½ cups pearl barley
> Salt and black pepper to taste
> 2½ cups stock, preferably homemade (pages 160–163),
>   or water
> Chopped fresh parsley leaves for garnish

1. Put the porcini in a bowl and cover with hot water. Put 2 tablespoons of the butter or oil in a medium saucepan over medium heat; a minute later, add the barley along with some salt and pepper and cook, stirring occasionally, until the barley is coated, just a minute or two. Add the stock (you can substitute ½ cup porcini soaking liquid for part of the stock if you like), cover, and adjust the heat so the mixture simmers. Cook for about 15 minutes, or until the barley is tender and the liquid absorbed.

2. When the mushrooms are tender, drain them. Trim them of any hard parts and, if necessary, slice them (usually they're already in quite small pieces so this won't be necessary). Put the remaining butter or oil in a small skillet over medium heat and toss the porcini in this briefly, sprinkling them with a little salt and pepper.

3. When the barley is done, top it with the sautéed porcini, being sure to get all the mushroom juices (and butter or oil) out of the skillet. Garnish and serve hot.

BULGUR

Bulgur (or bulghur, burghul, or bourghoul) is precooked whole wheat that is then dried, cracked, and finally sorted into different sizes. It has been a staple in Middle Eastern cuisine for thousands of years—the process has not changed much—and is easy to use and very quick cooking (often you can just soak the bulgur until it's rehydrated).

Bulgur is probably best known as one of the main ingredients of Tabbouleh (page 187), but it is also satisfying on its own—with a little butter, or olive oil and lemon—or cooked as a pilaf. Bulgur comes in four styles: fine, medium, coarse, and extra-coarse (these are sometimes numbered one through four). Medium is pretty much all-purpose.

Bulgur Pilaf with Meat
MIDDLE EAST
MAKES **4 SERVINGS**
TIME **1½ HOURS**

You can also make this pilaf with rice, but bulgur makes it unusual and special. Serve with a salad and you've got a meal.

> 6 tablespoons (¾ stick) butter or extra virgin olive oil
> 2 large onions, chopped
> Salt and black pepper to taste
> 1 pound boneless lamb shoulder or leg, cut into
>   1-inch cubes
> 2 bay leaves
> ½ teaspoon ground cinnamon
> Pinch of ground allspice
> 1 teaspoon ground cumin
> 3 cups cored and chopped tomatoes (canned are fine;
>   don't bother to drain)

About 2 cups chicken, beef, or vegetable stock, preferably
   homemade (page 160 or 162), or water,
   warmed
1½ cups medium or coarse bulgur
Chopped fresh parsley leaves for garnish
Lemon wedges for serving, optional

1. Put 4 tablespoons (½ stick) of the butter in a large
   skillet or flameproof casserole with a lid and turn
   the heat to medium. When the butter melts, add
   the onions, a large pinch of salt, and some pepper
   and cook, stirring occasionally, until the onions
   are quite soft, about 10 minutes.
2. Add the meat, bay leaves, and spices and cook, stirring, until everything is well combined. Add the
   tomatoes, stock, and (unless your stock is salty)
   some more salt and pepper. Cover, adjusting the
   heat so the mixture simmers. Cook for about 30
   minutes, until the meat is nearly tender.
3. Stir in the bulgur, cover again, and cook until the
   grain is nearly tender, about 15 minutes. At this
   point most of the liquid should be absorbed. If the
   mixture is dry and the grain not fully cooked, add
   some boiling water and cook for a few minutes
   more; if it is wet, uncover and raise the heat a bit
   to boil out the excess. Stir in the remaining butter.
   Turn off the heat and let sit for 15 minutes more.
   Taste and adjust the seasoning, garnish, and serve
   with the lemon if you like.

Fast Pilaf with Meat. In step 2, substitute ground
lamb (or beef). Add the bulgur along with the tomatoes and stock and finish as in step 3. (You may skip
the final resting period.)

Bulgur Pilaf with Chickpeas. In step 2, omit the
meat and add 1½ to 2 cups cooked chickpeas.

COUSCOUS NORTH AFRICA ■
MAKES **4 SERVINGS**
TIME **ABOUT 15 MINUTES**

Couscous, not actually a grain but a form of pasta,
cooks quickly. Ideally, it is steamed over a spicy stew,
from Stifado (page 336) to Chicken and Lentil Tagine
(page 284), and certainly you can do that. But you will
probably prepare it more frequently if you treat it
somewhat like rice, as I do here.

The couscous benefits from a short preliminary
toasting, which brings out more flavor (otherwise,
what you have is plain pasta); alternatively, turn it in
butter as I do in the variation.

1½ cups couscous
2¼ cups stock, preferably homemade (pages 160–163),
   warmed (or use warm water)
Salt and black pepper to taste

1. Put the couscous in a medium saucepan with a lid
   over medium heat. Cook, stirring occasionally,
   until it is aromatic and beginning to turn color, 3
   to 5 minutes. Add the stock all at once, along with
   some salt (unless your stock is very salty) and pepper. Cover and turn the heat to low.
2. Cook for 7 to 12 minutes, undisturbed, until the
   liquid is absorbed but the couscous is still quite
   moist. Fluff with a fork and serve immediately.

Couscous with Butter or Oil. This is good with
currants or raisins and pine nuts: In step 1, put 2 tablespoons butter or extra virgin olive oil in the
saucepan, and when it melts (or is hot), add the couscous. Cook, stirring occasionally, until it glistens, just
a minute or so. Proceed as directed. When the couscous is done, toss it with another tablespoon or two of
butter or oil.

Couscous with Apricots. For either the main recipe or the variation, stir in $1/2$ cup chopped or snipped dried apricots in step 1, along with the stock.

Couscous with Vegetables NORTH AFRICA

MAKES **4 SERVINGS**

TIME **1 HOUR (WITH PRECOOKED OR CANNED CHICKPEAS)**

A hearty, delicious vegetable stew, whose ingredients can be varied however you like. Chickpeas and squash—both summer (zucchini) and winter (pumpkin or butternut)—are the most commonly included vegetables.

4 tablespoons ($1/2$ stick) butter or extra virgin olive oil

2 large onions, roughly chopped

1 red bell pepper, stemmed, seeded, and roughly chopped

Salt and black pepper to taste

1 tablespoon peeled and minced fresh ginger

1 large pinch of saffron threads or $1/2$ teaspoon ground turmeric

$1/4$ teaspoon cayenne, or to taste

1 teaspoon ground coriander

3 cloves

$1/2$ teaspoon ground cinnamon

4 medium carrots, roughly chopped

1 pound winter squash, like butternut or pumpkin, trimmed and cut into chunks

2 medium zucchini, cut into chunks

1 cup or more chicken, beef, or vegetable stock, preferably homemade (page 160 or 162), or water

2 cups cooked (page 431) or canned chickpeas

$1/2$ cup raisins

1 recipe Couscous or Couscous with Butter or Oil (preceding recipe)

1. Put the butter in a large saucepan or flameproof casserole with a lid over medium heat. A minute or two later, add the onions and bell pepper, along with a couple of pinches of salt and at least $1/2$ teaspoon black pepper (you should really taste the pepper in this dish). Cook, stirring occasionally, until the onions are quite tender, about 10 minutes. Add the ginger, saffron, cayenne, coriander, cloves, and cinnamon and stir.

2. Add the carrots, winter squash, and zucchini, along with a cup of stock. Turn the heat to low, cover, and adjust the heat so the mixture simmers steadily. Cook until the carrots are tender, 20 to 30 minutes, checking and adding a bit more liquid if the mixture threatens to dry out. Add the chickpeas and raisins and cook for another 10 minutes, adding liquid if the mixture is dry, raising the heat and boiling some of it off if the mixture seems too soupy (it should be like a stew).

3. Taste and adjust the seasoning; the flavors of black pepper and cayenne should be pronounced. Serve immediately over the couscous.

Farro Salad ITALY ■ ■

MAKES **4 SERVINGS**

TIME **ABOUT 1 HOUR, LARGELY UNATTENDED**

Farro is a wheatlike grain grown in central Italy (known as spelt here). Barley makes a good substitute; cook it the same way. Here it is combined with a simple pesto; it's a lovely picnic or summer party side dish, with almost anything.

Salt and black pepper to taste

$1^1/2$ cups farro

$1/4$ cup walnuts or pine nuts

$1/2$ garlic clove

½ cup packed fresh basil leaves

¼ cup extra virgin olive oil, or more as needed

½ cup freshly grated Parmesan cheese

1. Bring a large pot of water to a boil and add salt. Cook the farro as you would pasta, tasting until it is tender, at least 15 minutes and probably about 30. Drain. (This can be done up to a day or two in advance; toss the farro with a little olive oil to keep it from clumping, then cover and refrigerate.)

2. Combine the walnuts, garlic, basil, oil, and a pinch of salt and some pepper in a blender or food processor and puree, adding a little more oil (or cold water) if necessary. Toss with the farro. Taste and adjust the seasoning, then add the Parmesan and serve hot or at room temperature, but not more than an hour or two later.

KASHA

In colder climates, where neither wheat nor rice will grow, buckwheat is an important grain (actually, it's a grass). Kasha, less attractively known as buckwheat groats (which simply means they have been hulled and cracked), has limited use, but it does make an unusual and delicious side dish; some people find it addictive, and it's certainly easy enough to prepare.

Most buckwheat is toasted before packaging, but it never hurts to toast it again in the skillet.

Kasha EASTERN EUROPE ▪
MAKES **4 SERVINGS**
TIME **ABOUT 20 MINUTES**

Here is kasha, simply prepared with butter. It's good with olive oil, too, but best with rendered chicken fat.

1½ cups kasha

2 to 4 tablespoons (¼ to ½ stick) butter or extra virgin olive oil

Salt and black pepper to taste

1. Bring about 1 quart of water (or, if you have it, stock) to a boil. Rinse the kasha in a strainer. Put half the butter in a skillet with a lid and turn the heat to medium. A minute later, add the kasha, along with some salt and pepper, and cook, stirring, until the mixture smells toasty, about 3 minutes.

2. Carefully add 3 cups of the boiling water, turn the heat to low, then cover and cook for about 15 minutes. If the liquid is absorbed and the kasha is tender but not mushy, it's done. If liquid remains, cook it a little more; if the mixture is dry and the kasha undercooked, add a little more water.

3. Stir in the remaining butter, taste and adjust the seasoning, and serve or keep warm over very low heat for up to 30 minutes.

Kasha with Cheese EASTERN EUROPE
MAKES **4 SERVINGS**
TIME **1 HOUR**

This can work as a main course, though it is better, perhaps, as a side dish with poultry or as a filling for Pierogi (page 59).

Given real-world options, fresh ricotta might be your best bet for cheese. If all you can find are packaged cheeses, small curd, full-fat cottage cheese is probably the best choice.

Salt and black pepper to taste

1 cup kasha

1 cup sour cream, plus more for garnish, if you like

1 cup farmer cheese, pot cheese, cottage cheese, or ricotta

2 tablespoons butter, plus a little for the pan

$\frac{1}{2}$ cup chicken stock, preferably homemade (page 160)

1. Preheat the oven to 350°F. Bring a medium pot of water to a boil and add salt. Rinse the kasha in a strainer. Cook the kasha in the water until barely tender, about 5 minutes; drain, but leave it quite moist.

2. Combine the kasha with the sour cream, cheese, butter, and stock; taste and add pepper and more salt if necessary. Use some more butter to liberally grease an 8- or 9-inch square pan. Spoon or pour in the kasha mixture and bake until heated through and lightly browned, about 30 minutes. Serve, with more sour cream if you like.

Kasha with Bacon and Onions

EASTERN EUROPE

MAKES **4 SERVINGS**

TIME **ABOUT 40 MINUTES**

A somewhat more elaborate procedure than the preceding recipe, to be sure, but super in flavor. See the excellent variation as well. This is practically a main course, good with a vegetable dish and a salad.

1$\frac{1}{2}$ cups kasha

1 tablespoon lard or extra virgin olive oil

$\frac{1}{2}$ pound good-quality slab bacon, minced

1 large onion, diced

Salt and black pepper to taste

1. Bring about 1 quart water (or, if you have it, stock) to a boil. Rinse the kasha in a strainer. Put the lard in a deep skillet with a lid over medium heat. A minute later, add the bacon and cook, stirring occasionally, until it is crisp, about 10 minutes. Remove it with a slotted spoon, add the onion, and raise the heat to medium-high. Cook, stirring occasionally, until the onion is brown and crisp, about 10 minutes. Remove with a slotted spoon; keep separate from the bacon so the bacon will remain crisp.

2. Add the kasha, along with some pepper, and cook, stirring, until the mixture smells toasty, about 3 minutes. Carefully add 3 cups of the boiling water, turn the heat to low, then cover and cook for about 15 minutes. If the liquid is absorbed and the kasha is tender but not mushy, it's done. If liquid remains, cook it a little more; if the mixture is dry and the kasha undercooked, add a little more water.

3. Taste and adjust the seasoning, adding salt and pepper if necessary. Stir in most of the bacon and onion, then garnish with the remaining bacon and onion and serve.

Kasha with Mushrooms. Soak a small handful of dried porcini in hot water. When they're tender, drain them, reserving their soaking liquid. Cook them with $\frac{1}{2}$ pound button mushrooms, trimmed and sliced, as you do the bacon in step 1, increasing the fat (use butter or olive oil) to 2 tablespoons; remove when they are lightly browned. Cook the kasha as above, using about a cup of the reserved mushroom soaking liquid in place of water. Stir in the mushrooms and serve.

Polenta alla Cibreo

Soft Polenta with Herbs ITALY

MAKES **6 TO 8 SERVINGS**

TIME **1$\frac{1}{4}$ HOURS, LARGELY UNATTENDED**

Given all the fuss that has been made about the difficulty of producing the real thing, I wouldn't blame you if you bought "instant" polenta. But polenta—and its identical Romanian cousin, mamaliga—is basically cornmeal mush, ethereal when made correctly and hardly neurosurgery.

First off, forget about stirring clockwise for 40 minutes with a long-handled wooden spoon or any of the other myths you've heard about how it has to be made. If you want great creamy polenta, cook the cornmeal very slowly and add as much butter as you can in good conscience. Second, this is a case where Parmigiano-Reggiano, the real Parmesan, will shine. Finally, note that the amount of water you use is variable: use 5 cups if you want to make very firm polenta that you can later grill or sauté; use more water if you want smooth, soft polenta, into which you will stir cheese and serve as a simple side dish or perhaps with a little tomato sauce.

The following recipe is based on one food writer Mitchell Davis learned from the chef at Cibreo in Florence, Italy. You could, of course, omit one or all of the herbs if you didn't have them on hand. With herbs or without, this polenta is great with any Italian roast or braised dish or with simply grilled Italian sausage.

1 cup milk, preferably whole

Salt and black pepper to taste

2 cups coarse cornmeal

2 teaspoons minced fresh sage leaves

2 teaspoons minced fresh rosemary leaves

1 garlic clove, minced

Pinch of freshly grated nutmeg

4 tablespoons (1/2 stick) unsalted butter

1/4 cup freshly grated Parmesan cheese, or more to taste

1. Bring the milk to a boil with 7 cups water in a medium saucepan; add a large pinch of salt. In a bowl, mix together the cornmeal, sage, rosemary, garlic, some pepper, and the nutmeg. Adjust the heat so the liquid simmers and begin to add the cornmeal mixture in a steady stream, stirring or whisking all the while to prevent the formation of lumps. When it has all been added, return the mixture to a boil, then turn the heat to low. The polenta should just barely be simmering; use a heat diffuser if necessary or, if you're cooking on an electric stove, move the pot to a second burner turned to low at this point.

2. Cook without stirring for 45 minutes. The polenta will have formed a crust on the bottom of the pan at this point; carefully stir it to incorporate the liquid in the pan without disturbing the crust. Cook for another 15 or so minutes, until the liquid is absorbed.

3. Taste and season the polenta with salt and pepper. Take the pan off the heat, stir in the butter and Parmesan, and serve immediately, passing more cheese at the table if you like.

Polenta "Gratin." Make the polenta with 5 cups water. Immediately spoon or pour the polenta into a buttered baking dish so that it is about an inch thick. Top with about a cup of freshly grated Parmesan cheese and broil until the cheese melts and browns slightly. Cut into squares and serve, with meat, poultry, or bean dishes.

Fried or Grilled Polenta. Make the polenta with 5 cups water. When it's done, turn the pot over and pour the polenta out onto a board. Let cool slightly, then cut with a string into 1/4- to 1/2-inch-thick slices. Now you can brush with olive oil and grill, with a little salt and pepper, or sauté in olive oil. Or dip in egg and grated Parmesan and sauté in melted butter.

Polenta with Fresh Corn. Stir 1 to 2 cups fresh corn kernels (or use canned or frozen, though obviously these are somewhat inferior) into the polenta during the last 5 minutes of cooking.

Tamales MEXICO ■

MAKES **24 TAMALES**

TIME **AT LEAST 2 HOURS**

Labor intensive, yes, but typically made as a group project and a fun one at that. The tamales in the frozen food aisle may be a quick fix, but they're barely worth eating. These, on the other hand, are worth the effort.

If you are using any of the chicken fillings, shred the chicken finely, then mix with the accompanying sauce.

You can buy dried corn husks at any market that carries a range of Latin products; same with masa harina, though finding fresh masa may be a bit more challenging, depending on where you live.

> **About 30 dried corn husks**
>
> **2 pounds fresh corn masa or 3$\frac{1}{2}$ cups masa harina**
>
> **2$\frac{1}{4}$ cups chicken stock, preferably homemade (page 160), plus more as needed**
>
> **2 cups lard or vegetable shortening, cubed**
>
> **1 teaspoon salt**
>
> **1 teaspoon baking powder**
>
> **1$\frac{1}{2}$ cups Shredded Pork (page 396), Grilled Chicken in Chipotle Sauce (page 289), Chicken with Mole Sauce (page 300), Chicken in Green Sauce (page 302), or Refried Beans (page 438)**

1. Soak the corn husks in warm water for at least 3 hours or overnight. Drain, then separate and clean the husks. Continue to soak until ready to use.
2. If you are using the dried masa harina, mix it and the stock together just until combined. The mixture will be crumbly. Set aside.
3. In a mixer, beat the lard with the salt and baking powder until fluffy. If you are using fresh masa, alternately add the masa and stock, beating continuously. If you are using the masa harina, add the masa harina mixture. Beat until the dough is light and fluffy, adding more stock if needed. The mixture is ready when a small ball of the dough floats in water.
4. Drain a husk and pat dry with paper towels. Spread 2 tablespoons of the masa dough in the center of the husk, then wet your fingers and pat into a 4 × 3-inch rectangle along the right edge of the husk, leaving at least 2 inches on each side. Spoon 1 tablespoon of your chosen filling lengthwise down the center of the dough rectangle. To wrap the tamales, fold the dough rectangle in half, bringing the right side of the dough over the filled center. Continue rolling tightly to the end of the husk, then secure the open ends with kitchen string. Repeat with the remaining ingredients. You may have some leftover husks, but often a few are split or too small to use.
5. Prepare a large steamer by setting a steamer rack about 2 inches above gently boiling water. Stack the tamales, seam down, on the rack. Cover and steam until done, about 45 minutes. To test for doneness, remove a tamale and open the husk—the filling should be firm and come away easily from the husk. Serve warm or at room temperature.

NOODLES AND PASTA

Books, of course, have been written about the simple combination of flour and water (and sometimes other ingredients) rolled into dough and boiled as noodles or other shapes. Call the result pasta, noodles, udon, or whatever you want, it's universal and beloved.

You can make your own pasta—there are some recipes in this section—and few things are as good. A Sunday afternoon with a pasta machine, followed by a Sunday dinner with fresh egg noodles and a nice dark sauce, is a wonderful experience, and store-bought "fresh" pasta is almost never the same, at least outside of Italy. But obviously dried pasta is a staple, one that is far easier to deal with than the fresh variety.

The basic rules for cooking pasta are simple and universal. One, use abundant water, about a gallon per pound. Two, don't forget to salt the cooking water; pasta that is salted after cooking is just not the same. And three, do not overcook. Once the pasta softens—this may be after as little as a minute, in the case of angel hair or the Japanese somen—start tasting. When it is mostly tender, with a still slightly firm interior, drain it, sauce it, and serve.

Cold Noodles with Sesame Sauce

CHINA ■ ■ ■
MAKES **4 SERVINGS**
TIME **30 MINUTES**

A perfect start to a Chinese meal, this can be prepared almost entirely in advance, varied in a number of ways, and even served as a main course if you like. Though it can be made with peanut butter (the natural kind, please, with no added sugar or fat), it's easy enough to buy sesame paste (tahini) at health food stores, stores specializing in Middle Eastern or Asian ingredients, and even supermarkets.

Sesame oil, which contributes mightily to the flavor of the finished dish, is a staple sold at Asian food stores (and, increasingly, supermarkets) and belongs in every refrigerator.

Chinese egg noodles are sold fresh at almost every Chinese market, most Asian supermarkets, and even many ordinary supermarkets. Regular dried pasta makes a good substitute here.

Salt to taste

1 pound cucumber

$^3/_4$ pound long pasta, such as linguine, or 1 pound fresh Chinese egg noodles

2 tablespoons dark sesame oil

$^1/_2$ cup tahini, peanut butter, or a combination

2 tablespoons sugar

3 tablespoons soy sauce, or to taste

1 teaspoon peeled and minced fresh ginger, optional

1 tablespoon rice or wine vinegar

Hot dark sesame oil or Tabasco sauce to taste

$^1/_2$ teaspoon black pepper, or more to taste

At least $^1/_2$ cup minced scallion for garnish

1. Bring a large pot of water to a boil and add salt. Peel the cucumber, cut in half, and, using a spoon, scoop out the seeds. Cut the cucumber into shreds (you can use a grater for this) and set aside.
2. When the water comes to a boil, cook the pasta until tender but not mushy. While the pasta is cooking, whisk together the sesame oil, tahini, sugar, soy sauce, ginger, vinegar, hot oil, and pepper in a large bowl. Thin the sauce with hot water so that it is about the consistency of heavy cream; you will need $^1/_4$ to $^1/_2$ cup. Stir in the cucumber. When the pasta is done, drain it and run it under cold water. Drain again.
3. Toss the noodles with the sauce and cucumber. Taste and adjust the seasoning as necessary (the dish may need salt), then garnish and serve.

Cold Noodles with Sesame Sauce and Chicken. This is a fine place to use leftovers of chicken, pork, beef, or seafood, or you can poach some chicken in the same water you use to cook the noodles or just add some fresh tofu. The amount is up to you.

Spicy Cold Noodles
CHINA ■ ■ ▨

MAKES **4 SERVINGS**

TIME **20 MINUTES**

Cold noodles, almost in salad form, with vegetables, spice, and meat. Perfectly fine with regular pasta, it is prettier and better with the fresh egg noodles now sold at many supermarkets and every Chinese market.

Salt to taste

1 pound fresh Chinese egg noodles

3 tablespoons soy sauce, or to taste

2 tablespoons rice vinegar

1 tablespoon dark sesame oil

2 teaspoons chile paste or oil, plus more to taste

1/2 pound Barbecued Pork (page 373) or ham, sliced

1 medium cucumber, peeled, seeded, and shredded

6 radishes, trimmed and sliced

1/2 cup bean sprouts, trimmed

1/2 cup chopped scallion for garnish

Chopped fresh cilantro leaves for garnish,
    optional

1. Bring a large pot of water to a boil and add salt. When the water comes to a boil, cook the pasta until tender but not mushy. Drain, run under cold water, and drain again.
2. Meanwhile, whisk together the soy sauce, vinegar, sesame oil, and chile paste in a large bowl. Add the noodles and all remaining ingredients except the scallion and cilantro to the bowl and toss well. Garnish and serve immediately or cover and refrigerate for up to a few hours before garnishing and serving.

Cold Soba Noodles with Dipping Sauce JAPAN ■ ■ ▨

MAKES **4 SMALL SERVINGS**

TIME **30 MINUTES**

Where the sesame sauce in the recipe on page 532 makes for a rich, hearty dish, this one is elegant and light. In Japan—where it gets plenty hot in the summer—cold soba noodles, served with a dipping sauce, are a common snack or light meal. Soba are brown noodles, made from wheat and buckwheat, and the sauce is based on dashi, the omnipresent Japanese stock. (You can also serve somen, thin wheat noodles, cold; cook them for a little less time, but also until tender.)

Dashi is close to essential here, though you can use chicken stock in a pinch. But dashi is so easy to make (and so good) that if you try it once you'll become devoted to it.

Salt to taste

1 cup Dashi or chicken stock, preferably homemade
    (page 162 or 160)

1/4 cup good-quality soy sauce

2 tablespoons mirin or 1 tablespoon honey mixed with
    1 tablespoon water

1/2 pound soba noodles

Peeled and finely grated or minced fresh ginger, minced
    scallion, and/or toasted sesame seeds (page 596) for
    garnish

1. Bring a large pot of water to a boil and add salt. Meanwhile, combine the dashi, soy sauce, and mirin; taste and add a little more soy sauce if it's not strong-flavored enough.
2. Cook the noodles until tender but not mushy, just as you would Italian pasta. Drain, quickly rinse under cold running water until cold, and drain well again. Serve the noodles with the garnishes,

with the sauce on the side for dipping (or spooning over).

Hiyashi Somen

Cold Noodles with Dipping Sauce JAPAN ■ ■

MAKES **6 SERVINGS**

TIME **20 MINUTES**

The first time I had hiyashi somen they were a revelation. It was a staggeringly hot day, and a Japanese friend was cooking dinner. When I found out we were having noodles, I was a little dismayed—I was more in the mood for a salad than for pasta. Then she brought out (what I now know as) hiyashi somen, in little bowls on top of ice with a cool dipping sauce to accompany them—perfect food for a blistering day.

You can top the somen with poached and chilled shrimp or room-temperature grilled shiitakes, but it's plenty good plain, as here. If you want to significantly speed up an already fast dish, skip the dried shrimp and sugar (or substitute homemade sugar syrup). For information on dried shrimp, see page 185.

2 cups Dashi, preferably homemade (page 162)

$^1/_2$ cup soy sauce

2 tablespoons mirin

2 tablespoons sugar

1 tablespoon dried shrimp, optional

Salt to taste

One 300-gram package (3 bundles) somen noodles

2 scallions, trimmed and minced

Wasabi, optional

1. Combine the dashi with the soy sauce, mirin, sugar, and dried shrimp if you're using them in a small saucepan over medium heat. Cook, stirring, just until the sugar is dissolved, then strain the dipping sauce into another container sitting on a bowl of ice to cool (you want it to be between ice cold and room temperature).

2. Bring a large pot of water to a boil and add salt. Drop in the somen and cook for 2 to 4 minutes, until tender, then rinse them in a colander under cold running water.

3. Serve each guest a small bowl of noodles twisted into a little nest on top of a couple of ice cubes and a small bowl with $^1/_2$ cup of the dipping sauce scattered with the minced scallions on the side. Pass a little dish of wasabi, if desired, to stir into the dipping sauce.

Shrimp with Crisp-Fried Noodles

CHINA

MAKES **4 SERVINGS**

TIME **45 MINUTES**

A different kind of noodle dish, one in which the noodles are fried crisp and then topped with a simply made stir-fry. Of course, you can use any stir-fry you like on top of a bed of noodles like this one; the noodles are essentially taking the place of rice.

Salt to taste

$^3/_4$ pound fresh Chinese egg noodles

$^1/_4$ cup peanut oil or neutral oil, like corn or grapeseed

1 tablespoon peeled and minced fresh ginger

1 tablespoon minced garlic

1 cup snow peas, trimmed

$^1/_4$ pound shiitake mushrooms, stems discarded (or reserved for stock), caps sliced

6 scallions, trimmed and cut into 2-inch lengths

1 pound shrimp, peeled and cut into pieces if large

3 tablespoons soy sauce, plus a little more to taste

2 teaspoons dark sesame oil

1. Bring a large pot of water to a boil and add salt. When it is ready, cook the noodles until tender, stirring occasionally—this will take only a few minutes. Drain, rinse with cold water, and drain again.

2. Meanwhile, put half the oil in a large skillet or wok, preferably nonstick, and turn the heat to medium-high. Add the ginger, garlic, snow peas, shiitakes, and scallions, along with about ¼ cup water (or use white wine or stock), and cook, stirring and shaking the pan, until the snow peas are bright green and the shiitakes softened slightly. Add the shrimp and soy sauce and, if the mixture is dry, add a little more water or stock. Cook, stirring occasionally, until the shrimp turn pink, 3 or 4 minutes. Transfer this mixture to a bowl and keep it warm.

3. Put the remaining oil in the skillet over medium-high heat and add the noodles. Cook, undisturbed, until brown and crisp on the bottom (adjust the heat so the noodles brown but do not burn). Use a large spatula to flip the noodles. Brown on the other side, then slide onto a platter. Quickly reheat the stir-fry mixture in the skillet, then put on top of the noodle cake; sprinkle with a little more soy sauce and sesame oil, cut into pieces, and serve.

Beef Lo Mein CHINA ■

MAKES **4 SERVINGS**

TIME **30 MINUTES**

A classic stir-fried noodle dish, just about the paradigm. You can make this with pork, chicken, shrimp, or any other bit of meat or fish you have or keep it entirely vegetarian; it's eminently flexible and an important part of every home cook's repertoire.

The variation that follows is a traditional dish for New Year's celebrations and wedding banquets. E-fu noodles, which are long, thin, flat egg noodles, symbolize long life. Most Asian groceries carry them, but if you cannot find them, regular egg noodles are fine too.

The meat will be easier to slice thinly if you freeze it for 30 to 60 minutes first. (This is always the case with any boneless meat or poultry.)

Salt to taste

½ pound fresh Chinese egg noodles

3 tablespoons peanut or neutral oil, like corn or grapeseed

½ pound sirloin (New York) strip steak, very thinly sliced and cut into 2-inch-long strips

2 tablespoons soy sauce

1 large onion, thinly sliced

1½ pounds broccoli, tops only, cut into bite-sized florets

1 red bell pepper, stemmed, seeded, and cut into thin strips

1 tablespoon minced garlic

2 teaspoons peeled and minced or grated fresh ginger

½ cup chicken stock, preferably homemade (page 160), or water

½ cup unsalted cashews, roughly chopped, or shelled peanuts, optional

1. Bring a large pot of water to a boil and add salt. Cook the noodles until tender but not mushy, then drain and rinse. Toss with 1 tablespoon of the oil to prevent sticking and set aside. Soak the meat in the soy sauce.

2. Put 1 tablespoon of the remaining oil in a deep skillet, preferably nonstick, and turn the heat to high. Add the onion and cook, stirring occasionally, until it begins to brown, about 5 minutes. Add the broccoli and red pepper and cook, stirring occasionally, until the broccoli is crisp-tender, 5 to 8 minutes. Add the garlic and ginger and cook for 1

minute, stirring almost constantly. Remove this mixture from the pan.

3. Add the remaining oil and turn the heat to high. Drain the meat (reserve the soy sauce) and cook, stirring occasionally, for about 1 minute. Add the reserved soy sauce, along with the chicken stock, and stir. Add the drained noodles, vegetables, and nuts if desired. Toss to mix and reheat, then serve.

Stir-Fried Noodles with Chives and Mushrooms. Substitute fresh or dried E-fu egg noodles for regular egg noodles. Omit the beef, onion, broccoli, red bell pepper, and cashews. Add 1 bunch of Chinese chives, cut into 2-inch lengths (about 2 cups), and 5 fresh shiitake mushrooms, trimmed and sliced. In step 2, add the chives and mushrooms and cook, stirring occasionally, until they brown and soften, about 5 minutes. Add the garlic, ginger, soy sauce, and stock and cook, stirring, for 1 minute. Add the noodles, toss to reheat, and serve.

Egg Noodles with Spring Onions
CHINA ▦

MAKES **3 TO 4 SERVINGS**

TIME **20 TO 30 MINUTES**

A prime example of the simplicity with which you can successfully treat fresh Chinese egg noodles, which are available at many supermarkets.

Salt to taste

1 pound fresh Chinese egg noodles

5 tablespoons peanut or neutral oil, like corn or grapeseed

1 pound spring onions or 4 or 5 bunches of scallions

$1/2$ cup minced chives, garlic chives, or a combination,
    plus 2 tablespoons for garnish

1 tablespoon soy sauce

1 teaspoon dark sesame oil

1. Bring a large pot of water to a boil and add salt. Cook the noodles as you would fresh pasta, stirring occasionally and tasting frequently; they cook very quickly, usually in about 3 minutes. When just tender, drain them thoroughly. Toss with a tablespoon of the oil (a little more if you are not proceeding with the recipe right away; you can wait an hour or two if you like) and set aside.

2. Heat a wok or large nonstick skillet over medium-high heat until it begins to smoke. Meanwhile, trim and chop the onions. Add 2 tablespoons of the remaining oil to the wok, wait about 15 seconds, and toss in the onions. Raise the heat to high and cook, stirring every 10 seconds or so, until they brown and begin to soften, about 5 minutes; do not cook them to the point of complete tenderness. Remove them from the pan with a slotted spoon. Keep the heat on high.

3. Add the remaining oil to the wok, heat briefly, then add the noodles and let them sit for about a minute, until they begin to brown on the bottom. Toss them once or twice and allow to sit again. If they begin to stick, add a bit of water and stir, scraping the wok to loosen any stuck particles. Add the chives and cooked onions and toss for a minute to blend and reheat the onions. Turn off the heat, add the soy sauce and sesame oil, toss again, and serve, garnished with the remaining chives.

Pad Thai THAILAND ▦
MAKES **4 SERVINGS**

TIME **30 MINUTES**

Though you don't see Pad Thai all that much in Thailand (I was told there that it was "a Chinese dish" and therefore inauthentic), it has become a standard at American Thai restaurants—and for good reason.

Asian Noodles

The variety of Asian noodles is vast, but the techniques used in cooking them are familiar. In China, most noodles are made with wheat, but in Southeast Asia rice noodles are more common. Japan produces buckwheat noodles (soba, page 533), and the bean thread, or cellophane noodle, made from ground mung beans, is seen almost everywhere. There are even noodles made from bean curd, usually called tofu shreds or strips.

Like Italian noodles, Asian noodles are sold dried or fresh; both are easy to find (even fresh rice noodles are now sold in most cities). All are sold in varying thicknesses, though thin threads and spaghettilike strands are most common. White wheat noodles are made from wheat and water; yellow ones have egg (and, frequently, food coloring) added. Depending on shape and texture, they might be called Shanghai noodle, Hong Kong noodle, soup noodle, lo mein, or panfried noodle. These all can be treated similarly, and the differences, though real, are subtle—just as the differences between linguine and bucatini are real but subtle.

Whether pale white wheat or yellow egg, fresh wheat noodles are almost always packed in plastic bags of twelve ounces to a pound. (They keep, refrigerated, for several days. Note, too, that they can easily be frozen in their own package. Defrost them in the refrigerator if you can or on the counter if you have less time. If you're really desperate, plunge them, still frozen, into boiling water; just be sure to separate them by stirring as they defrost.)

Rice noodles—the basis of the most popular Thai restaurant dish, Pad Thai (page 536)—have no equivalent in European cooking. Made from rice powder, even the dried ones are nearly as convenient as fresh wheat noodles, because they need only be soaked in hot water for a few minutes to become tender. (Optimally, they are soaked for a while, then dropped into boiling water for a few seconds, but you can skip this step in many recipes.)

Dried rice noodles are easily recognized by their grayish white, translucent appearance and by the fact that because of their somewhat irregular shapes they are never packed in as orderly a fashion as wheat noodles (they are quite long and are packaged folded up over themselves). Fresh ones are stark white.

The combination of sweet, salty, sour, and spicy in a variety of textures is irresistible.

There's nothing difficult about making Pad Thai at home. Just make sure you've portioned out all the ingredients before you start cooking and, especially if you're entertaining, take care of the first two steps before your guests arrive. Information on Asian fish sauces like nam pla is on page 500.

¾ pound dried flat rice noodles, ¼ inch wide

5 tablespoons corn, grapeseed, or other neutral oil

3 eggs, lightly beaten

4 garlic cloves, minced

¼ pound small shrimp, peeled

¼ pound pressed tofu (page 491) or extra-firm tofu, sliced

2 scallions, trimmed and cut into 1-inch lengths

1 cup bean sprouts, trimmed

2 tablespoons nam pla

2 teaspoons tamarind paste (page 585) or ketchup

2 teaspoons sugar

¼ cup chopped peanuts

¼ cup chopped fresh cilantro leaves

2 small fresh chiles, preferably Thai, stemmed, seeded, and sliced, optional

1 lime, cut into wedges

1. Put the noodles in a bowl and pour boiling water over them to cover. Allow to soak until softened, at

---

least 15 minutes, or until you're ready to use them (don't soak for longer than an hour or they may start to fall apart).

2. Put 2 tablespoons of the oil in a wok or large skillet, preferably nonstick, over medium heat. Add the eggs and scramble quickly for the first minute or so with a fork almost flat against the bottom of the pan; you're aiming for a thin egg crêpe of sorts, one with the smallest curd you can achieve. Cook just until set and transfer the crêpe to a cutting board. Cut into ¼-inch strips and set aside.

3. Raise the heat to high and add the remaining oil. When the oil is hot, add the garlic and shrimp and cook, stirring occasionally, until the shrimp lose their raw gray color. Remove from the pan with a slotted spoon and transfer to a plate next to the stove.

4. Add the tofu, scallions, and half the bean sprouts to the pan and cook, stirring occasionally, for 3 minutes. Transfer the tofu mixture to the plate with the shrimp.

5. Combine the drained noodles, egg crêpe, nam pla, tamarind, and sugar in the pan and cook, stirring occasionally, until the noodles are heated through, then add the stir-fried shrimp and tofu mixture. Toss once or twice and transfer the contents of the pan to a serving platter. Top with the peanuts, cilantro, chiles if desired, and remaining bean sprouts. Serve with the lime wedges on the side.

"Singapore" Noodles
Curried Rice Noodles with Pork or Chicken and Shrimp
SOUTHEAST ASIA 🔲

MAKES **4 SERVINGS**

TIME **30 MINUTES**

These curried noodles are a standby, and can be prepared much more simply: stir-fry the noodles with onions and curry powder, for example, or with a bit of egg. This is a relatively elaborate version, and can be made more so with the addition of bean sprouts (with the basil), sliced Chinese sausage (with the pork or chicken), egg (as in the Pad Thai on page 536), or vegetables like broccoli or asparagus (parboil it first), or tomato. Information on Asian fish sauces like nam pla is on page 500.

¾ pound thin rice noodles (often labeled "vermicelli" or "rice stick")

¼ cup peanut or neutral oil, like corn or grapeseed

¼ pound boneless pork or chicken, diced

¼ pound shrimp, peeled and diced

1 onion, diced

1 red or yellow bell pepper, stemmed, seeded, and chopped

1 tablespoon minced garlic

1 tablespoon peeled and minced fresh ginger

1 or 2 small dried chiles, chopped, or 1 teaspoon hot red pepper flakes, or to taste

1 tablespoon curry powder, preferably homemade (pages 592–593), or more to taste

1 tablespoon sugar

2 tablespoons soy sauce, or more to taste

2 tablespoons nam pla or more soy sauce, or more to taste

Stock or water as needed

½ cup torn fresh basil leaves, preferably Thai basil

Salt if necessary

½ cup minced scallion

¼ cup chopped peanuts

1. Put the noodles in a large bowl and cover them with boiling water. Prepare the other ingredients while the noodles sit.

2. Put half the oil in a large nonstick skillet or wok and turn the heat to high. Add the meat and cook, stirring constantly, until it loses its color, 3 or 4 minutes. Remove with a slotted spoon and set

aside. Add the shrimp and repeat the process; remove.

3. Add the remaining oil, wait a few seconds for it to become hot, and add the onion and bell pepper; cook, stirring occasionally, until the onion begins to brown, 3 to 5 minutes. Add the garlic, ginger, and chiles and cook, stirring, for 30 seconds. Add the curry powder and sugar and stir for a few seconds, then drain and add the noodles. Cook, stirring occasionally, for about a minute. Stir in the soy sauce and nam pla; return the meat and shrimp to the pan.

4. Add about $^1/_2$ cup stock or water to allow the noodles to separate and continue to cook, stirring occasionally, until the noodles begin to brown, 5 to 10 minutes. Turn off the heat and stir in the basil; taste and adjust the seasoning, adding salt and more curry, chile, soy sauce, or nam pla to taste. Garnish with the scallion and peanuts and serve.

Chop Chae
Glass Noodles with Vegetables and Meat KOREA ■ ▓

MAKES **8 SERVINGS**

TIME **1 HOUR**

A festive dish that takes a bit of preparation—a simple enough process, but quite a few steps. Nevertheless, it's a delicious and unusual noodle dish, and because it's best served at room temperature, you can make it a couple of hours in advance. Substitute shrimp or fish for the meat (or omit it entirely) if you like. Precooked fish cake is available at Korean or Japanese markets. Potato starch noodles are available at Korean markets.

2 tablespoons dark sesame oil, plus more as needed

$^1/_4$ pound boneless sirloin, cut into bits

2 medium carrots, julienned or minced

1 large onion, thinly sliced and separated into rings

About 6 ounces precooked fish cake, thinly sliced, optional

12 scallions, trimmed and roughly chopped

2 cups chopped cooked spinach

1 cup trimmed mushrooms, preferably a mixture of oyster, shiitake, and enoki

1 tablespoon minced garlic

$^1/_2$ pound potato starch noodles or glass (mung bean) noodles

2 tablespoons soy sauce, or more to taste

Salt and black pepper to taste

$^1/_4$ cup pine nuts, lightly toasted

$^1/_4$ cup lightly toasted sesame seeds (page 596)

1. Bring a large pot of water to a boil. Meanwhile, put 1 tablespoon of the sesame oil in a skillet over medium-high heat. Add the meat and cook, stirring occasionally, until browned, about 5 minutes. Remove with a slotted spoon and place in a large bowl. Cook the carrots in the same skillet, stirring occasionally, just until they lose their crunch, about 5 minutes. Add to the meat.

2. Put the remaining sesame oil in the skillet and add the onion; cook, stirring occasionally, until it begins to brown, about 5 minutes. Remove with a slotted spoon and add to the meat. If you're using the fish cake, add it to the pan now and cook, stirring occasionally, until it begins to brown, about 5 minutes. Remove and add to the meat mixture. Raise the heat to high, add the scallions, and cook, stirring, until they wilt, just 2 or 3 minutes. Add to the meat mixture.

3. Add a little more oil if necessary and stir-fry the spinach over medium heat until hot, 3 to 5 minutes. Add to the meat mixture. Add the mushrooms and garlic and cook, stirring occasionally, until softened, about 5 minutes. Add to the meat.

4. Add the noodles to the boiling water and turn off the heat. The noodles will be tender in about 5

minutes; drain. Add the noodles and soy sauce to the skillet and cook, stirring occasionally, for about 5 minutes. Add to the meat mixture.

5. Toss the noodles and meat mixture well, adding salt, pepper, and more sesame oil or soy sauce to taste. Garnish with the pine nuts and sesame seeds and serve at room temperature.

Stir-Fried Udon with Pork and Shrimp JAPAN

MAKES **4 SERVINGS**

TIME **40 MINUTES**

Udon noodles are generally made with softer wheat than Italian pasta, giving them a more tender texture. You can find them at Japanese markets and many supermarkets. Like Chinese noodles, they're great stir-fried. And, as in any stir-fry, you can substitute for the pork, shrimp, or vegetables if you like.

Salt and black pepper to taste

³⁄₄ pound udon noodles

¹⁄₄ cup peanut or neutral oil, like corn or grapeseed

10 scallions, trimmed and roughly chopped

¹⁄₂ pound shrimp, peeled and chopped

¹⁄₂ pound finely chopped boneless pork

10 shiitake mushrooms, stems removed and discarded (or reserved for stock), caps sliced

1 cup bean sprouts

¹⁄₂ cup chicken or vegetable stock, preferably homemade (page 160 or 162), or noodle-cooking liquid

¹⁄₄ cup good-quality soy sauce, or more to taste

¹⁄₄ cup bonito flakes, optional

1. Bring a large pot of water to a boil and add salt. Meanwhile, prepare the other ingredients. Cook the noodles in the boiling water until just tender but not at all mushy. Drain, reserving some of the cooking liquid if you have no stock. Rinse and drain again.

2. Put half the oil in a large skillet or wok, preferably nonstick, over medium-high heat. A minute later, add the scallions and cook, stirring, until they begin to wilt, less than a minute. Remove with a slotted spoon. Add the shrimp and pork and cook, stirring, until the shrimp turn pink and the pork loses its color, 3 or 4 minutes. Remove with a slotted spoon and add to the scallions.

3. Add the remaining oil to the skillet, followed by the shiitakes. When they begin to wilt, after about 5 minutes, add the bean sprouts and noodles. Turn the heat to high and toss a few times, then add the cooked ingredients and toss to blend. Add the stock and soy sauce, then taste and adjust the seasoning.

4. Serve in bowls or on plates garnished, if you like, with the bonito.

Spaetzle ALSACE ■ ▨

MAKES **4 SERVINGS**

TIME **20 MINUTES**

Spaetzle is harder to spell than make. In fact, it's one of the easiest and most impressive side dishes there is, a noodle whose dough is about as complicated as pancake batter and that can be crisped up in a pan to create a delicious accompaniment for almost any poultry or pork dish, especially braised ones.

Once you get the technique down, you've got plenty of latitude with how you flavor these fresh little dumplings. The recipe here is for plain spaetzle, though adding two or three tablespoons of an assortment of flavorings in the first step will infuse them with taste without changing the method at all. Try pureed chives, roasted and minced garlic, chopped shallots, and so on.

Salt

2 cups flour

1/2 teaspoon or more freshly ground black pepper

3 eggs

1 cup milk, more or less

2 to 4 tablespoons butter or extra virgin olive oil

Chopped fresh parsley or chives for garnish

1. Bring a large pot of water to a boil and salt it. Combine the flour with the pepper and a large pinch of salt in a bowl. Lightly beat together the eggs and milk and add the flour; stirring. If necessary, add a little more milk to make a batter about the consistency of pancake batter.

2. Scoop a tablespoon or so of batter and drop it into the water; small pieces may break off but the batter should remain largely intact and form a disk; repeat, using about one-third to one-fourth of the batter, depending on the size of your pot. When the spaetzle rise to the top, a couple of minutes later (you mave have to loosen them from the bottom, but they'll pop right up), cook another minute or so, then transfer with a slotted spoon into a bowl of ice water. Repeat until all the batter is used up.

3. Drain the spaetzle (at this point you can toss them with a bit of oil and refrigerate, covered, for up to

DRYING PASTA

a day). Heat the butter or oil in a large skillet, preferably nonstick, over medium-high heat. When it's hot, add the spaetzle, a few at a time, and quickly brown on both sides. Serve hot, garnished with the parsley or chives.

Pappardelle, Tagliatelle, or Other Fresh, Hand-Cut Pasta ITALY ■
MAKES **4 SERVINGS**
TIME **AT LEAST 1 HOUR, SOMEWHAT UNATTENDED**

This is a very rich pasta dough, as made in Emilia-Romagna. My feeling is if you're taking the trouble to make fresh pasta, it ought to be sensational. This recipe meets that qualification. If this is the first time you've made fresh pasta, allow extra time; the rolling process takes some getting used to. But the dough is very sturdy and can be worked over and over, so eventually you'll get it right. And, believe me, it will be easier each time you do it.

About 2 cups flour, or as needed

1 teaspoon salt

2 eggs

3 egg yolks

1. Combine 1 1/2 cups of the flour and the salt on a counter or large board. Make a well in the middle. Into this well, break the eggs and yolks. Beat the eggs with a fork, slowly and gradually incorporating a little of the flour at a time. When it becomes too hard to stir with the fork, use your hands. When all the flour has been mixed in, knead the dough, pushing it against the board and folding it repeatedly until it is not at all sticky and is quite stiff. Sprinkle with a little of the reserved flour and clean your hands. Cover the dough with plastic wrap or a cloth and let it rest for about 30 minutes.

(You can store the dough in the refrigerator, wrapped in plastic, until you're ready to roll it out, for up to 24 hours.)

2. Clamp a pasta machine to the counter; sprinkle your work surface lightly with flour. Cut off about one third of the dough; wrap the rest in plastic or cloth while you work. Roll the dough lightly in the flour and use your hands to flatten it into a rectangle about the width of the machine. Set the machine to its highest (that is, thickest) setting and crank the dough through. If it sticks, dust it with a little more flour. Repeat. Set the machine to its next-thinnest setting and repeat. Each time, if the pasta sticks, sprinkle it with a little more flour and, each time, put the dough through the machine twice.

3. Continue to work your way down (or up, as the case may be—each machine is numbered differently) through the numbers. If at any point the dough tears badly, bunch it together and start again (you will quickly get the hang of it). Use as much flour as you need to, but in small amounts each time.

4. Pass the dough through the machine's thinnest setting, only once. (If this fails, pass it through the next-thinnest once.) Flour the dough lightly, cover it, and set it aside. Repeat the process with the remaining dough.

5. Cut each sheet into rectangles roughly 16 inches long and as wide as the machine: trim the ends to make it neat. Put it through the machine once more, this time using the broadest (tagliatelle) cutter. Or cut by hand into broad strips (pappardelle). Cook right away or hang the strands to dry for up to a couple of hours.

6. To cook the noodles, drop them into boiling salted water; they'll be done when tender, in less than 3 (and probably less than 2) minutes. Sauce them immediately and serve.

Pizzocheri. The buckwheat noodles of the mountains of northeastern Italy, best sauced as described on page 549: substitute $1\frac{1}{2}$ cups fine buckwheat flour for $1\frac{1}{2}$ cups of the white flour; use white flour for the balance of the dough and all of the rolling and proceed as directed.

Malfatti. This translates as "badly cut," and is perfect for soups, many pasta dishes, and the lazy cook: Roll out about a quarter of the dough as thin as possible, using a machine or rolling pin, then simply cut it into random shapes. Cook as you would any other fresh pasta.

Vegetarian Ravioli ITALY ■
MAKES **30 TO 60 RAVIOLI**
TIME **AT LEAST 1 HOUR**

Every traveler to Italy's countryside tells stories about elderly couples seen out on the hillsides scavenging for greens. One of the things they do with the greens is fill pasta. One of my favorite quotes about ravioli was from a friend: "The older my grandmother gets, the bigger her ravioli." If you're unskilled, start with big ones; you will be far more successful. Remember that in Italy there have long been people—women, it's safe to guess—who specialize in handmade pasta; it is a skill and an art, and unless you practice frequently, you're not likely to get good at it. But it can be fun, and you can always choose to make cannelloni; see page 545.

About $1\frac{1}{2}$ pounds spring greens, one kind or a mixture, such as dandelion, chard, and/or spinach
Salt and black pepper to taste
$\frac{1}{2}$ cup extra virgin olive oil, divided, plus more if desired
1 garlic clove, minced

About ¹/₂ cup chopped fresh fennel fronds, sage, chervil,
　　basil, or a mixture
2 cups flour
3 eggs
4 tablespoons (¹/₂ stick) butter
¹/₄ cup extra virgin olive oil
Freshly grated Parmesan cheese

1. Make the filling first: Wash the greens well, then cook them in plenty of salted boiling water until tender, 2 to 10 minutes, depending on the green. Rinse, squeeze dry, and chop fine. Heat ¹/₄ cup olive oil in a skillet over medium heat; add the garlic and cook until it is dark golden, about 5 minutes. Sauté the greens in the oil just until coated, a minute or two. Season with salt and pepper and toss in half the herb(s); stir well and set aside to cool.

2. Combine 1¹/₂ cups of the flour and a large pinch of salt on a counter or large board. Make a well in the middle. Into this well, break the eggs. Beat the eggs with a fork, slowly and gradually incorporating a little of the flour at a time. When it becomes too hard to stir with the fork, use your hands. When all the flour has been mixed in, knead the dough, pushing it against the board and folding it repeatedly until it is not at all sticky and is quite stiff. Sprinkle with a little of the reserved flour and clean your hands. Cover the dough with plastic wrap or a cloth and let it rest for about 30 minutes. (You can store the dough in the refrigerator, wrapped in plastic, until you're ready to roll it out, for up to 24 hours.)

3. Clamp a pasta machine to the counter; sprinkle your work surface lightly with flour. Cut off about one third of the dough; wrap the rest in plastic or cloth while you work. Roll the dough lightly in the flour and use your hands to flatten it into a rectangle about the width of the machine. Set the ma-

MAKING RAVIOLI

■ make ahead　　■ serve at room temp./cold　　■ 30 minutes or less　　GRAINS　**543**

chine to its highest (that is, thickest) setting and crank the dough through. If it sticks, dust it with a little more flour. Repeat. Set the machine to its next-thinnest setting and repeat. Each time, if the pasta sticks, sprinkle it with a little more flour and, each time, put the dough through the machine twice.

4. Continue to work your way down (or up, as the case may be—each machine is numbered differently) through the numbers. If at any point the dough tears badly, bunch it together and start again (you will quickly get the hang of it). Use as much flour as you need to, but in small amounts each time. Pass the dough through the machine's thinnest setting, only once. (If this fails, pass it through the next-thinnest once.) Flour the dough lightly, cover it, and set it aside. Repeat the process with the remaining dough.

5. Cut each sheet into two or more 4-inch-wide strips. Drop heaping teaspoons of filling at about $1\frac{1}{2}$-inch intervals about 1 inch from one long edge of the strip (that is, about 3 inches from the other edge). Fold the dough over onto itself, pressing with your fingers to seal. Trim the dough with a sharp knife or fluted pastry wheel, then cut into individual ravioli. (You can prepare the ravioli to this point, dust with cornmeal, and refrigerate for up to a day or freeze for up to a week or so.)

6. Bring a large pot of salted water to a boil for the ravioli. As you cook them, 20 or 30 at a time, make the sauce: Melt the butter with $\frac{1}{4}$ cup olive oil in a small saucepan over medium-low heat; season with salt and pepper and add the remaining herb(s). Turn off the heat and pour over the ravioli when they are done (they'll rise to the surface and swell a bit); add a little more olive oil if you like. Top with plenty of cheese and serve.

Spinach-Ricotta Ravioli ITALY ■
MAKES **30 TO 60 RAVIOLI**
TIME **AT LEAST 1 HOUR**

A classic ravioli filling. Top with any tomato sauce.

2 cups flour

Salt to taste

3 eggs

1 egg yolk

$\frac{1}{2}$ cup (about 2 ounces) cooked spinach, squeezed dry and chopped

$1\frac{1}{2}$ cups ricotta, drained for a few minutes in a strainer

$\frac{1}{4}$ cup chopped fresh parsley leaves

1 teaspoon minced garlic

Small grating of nutmeg

1 cup freshly grated Parmesan cheese

1. Combine $1\frac{1}{2}$ cups of the flour and a large pinch of salt on a counter or large board. Make a well in the middle. Into this well, break the whole eggs. Beat them with a fork, slowly and gradually incorporating a little of the flour at a time. When it becomes too hard to stir with the fork, use your hands. When all the flour has been mixed in, knead the dough, pushing it against the board and folding it repeatedly until it is not at all sticky and is quite stiff. Sprinkle with a little of the reserved flour and clean your hands. Cover the dough with plastic or a cloth and let it rest for about 30 minutes. (You can store the dough in the refrigerator, wrapped in plastic, until you're ready to roll it out, for up to 24 hours.)

2. Clamp a pasta machine to the counter; sprinkle your work surface lightly with flour. Cut off about one third of the dough; wrap the rest in plastic or cloth while you work. Roll the dough lightly in the flour and use your hands to flatten it into a rectangle about the width of the machine. Set the machine to its highest (that is, thickest) setting and

crank the dough through. If it sticks, dust it with a little more flour. Repeat. Set the machine to its next-thinnest setting and repeat. Each time, if the pasta sticks, sprinkle it with a little more flour and, each time, put the dough through the machine twice.

3. Continue to work your way down (or up, as the case may be—each machine is numbered differently) through the numbers. If at any point the dough tears badly, bunch it together and start again (you will quickly get the hang of it). Use as much flour as you need to, but in small amounts each time. Pass the dough through the machine's thinnest setting, only once. (If this fails, pass it through the next-thinnest once.) Flour the dough lightly, cover it, and set it aside. Repeat the process with the remaining dough.

4. Combine the egg yolk with the spinach, ricotta, parsley, garlic, nutmeg, Parmesan, and salt to taste. Cut each sheet into two or more 4-inch-wide strips and follow the directions for the ravioli in step 5 of the preceding recipe.

5. Bring a large pot of salted water to a boil for the ravioli. Cook them for just a few minutes, until they rise to the surface. Drain, sauce, and serve immediately.

Cannelloni. Far easier to deal with: The first three steps remain the same. Cut the dough into rectangles about 6 × 8 or 6 × 10 inches. Boil the sheets a couple at a time, just for about 2 minutes, or until they are tender. Remove them with a slotted spoon and drop into a bowl of ice water. Remove from the ice water, drain, and spread on a baking sheet; drizzle with oil to prevent sticking. (You will need 8 rectangles, and this is enough dough to make 12, so you have plenty of room for error.) Generously grease a large baking pan with butter and preheat the oven to 350°F. Work with 2 or 3 of the pasta sheets at a time. Put them on a work surface, a long end facing you. Fill with a por-

tion of the ricotta mixture, then roll up the long way, enclosing the ingredients. As you finish each of the cannelloni, lay it in the baking pan. When all the rolls are made, dot with more butter and pour a cup of good-quality chicken stock, preferably homemade (page 160), or tomato sauce over the top. Sprinkle with about $1/2$ cup freshly grated Parmesan and bake until heated through, about 15 minutes.

Pinci
Handmade Pasta with Garlic and Bread Crumbs ITALY
MAKES **4 SERVINGS**
TIME **ABOUT 1 HOUR**

These are hand-rolled spaghetti from Tuscany; they're thick, like bucatini, but have no holes. They must be boiled right away, or they will stick together. I think this is a fine project for a rainy afternoon with a ten- or twelve-year-old who likes to cook. If you're not in the mood, simply make spaghetti and follow the directions for this wonderful and simple sauce.

This—as you'll quickly gather—is poor people's food, a rather meager dish. This does not prevent it from being delicious, which it is, but you might want to follow it with a meat or fish course and vegetables.

Salt and black pepper to taste

2 cups flour, plus more as needed

1 egg

$1/4$ cup plus 2 tablespoons extra virgin olive oil

Cornmeal as needed

1 tablespoon minced garlic

3 or 4 small dried red chiles

$1/2$ cup fresh bread crumbs, preferably homemade (page 580)

1. Bring a large pot of water to a boil and add salt. Mix together the flour, egg, a liberal amount of

pepper, and 2 tablespoons of the oil in a bowl, then stir in water, about $\frac{1}{4}$ cup at a time, until you have a pliable, fairly soft dough (the total amount of water will be less than a cup). Transfer to a floured board and work it with your hands, kneading the dough and adding flour as necessary until the dough is no longer sticky but still quite soft and pliable; don't make it too tough (which will happen if you keep adding flour and working it).

2. Roll out the dough about $\frac{1}{4}$ inch thick (you can do this in batches if you prefer). Cut a long piece, about 2 inches wide, then, using cornmeal for dusting, roll it into a snake. Pinch a piece off the snake and, with your hands, roll it into a—for want of a better word—worm, a section of pasta 2 or 3 inches long and $\frac{1}{4}$ inch thick. Set aside. Work quickly, using cornmeal to keep the strands separate.

3. When they're all ready, make the sauce first. Put the remaining $\frac{1}{4}$ cup oil in a large skillet over medium heat and add the garlic and chiles; when they sizzle, add the bread crumbs and a large pinch

ROLLING PINCI

of salt (there is no salt in the dough, so you will need a lot). Cook for a minute or so, until the crumbs brown a little but do not burn; keep warm over the lowest possible heat while you cook the pasta until it is tender but not mushy; it will take only a couple of minutes.

4. Drain the pasta, reserving some of the cooking liquid. Toss the pasta with the bread crumb sauce, adding as much of the reserved liquid as necessary to make the mixture moist. Serve immediately.

Pasta alla Gricia ITALY ■

MAKES **3 TO 6 SERVINGS**

TIME **30 MINUTES**

I featured this little group of recipes in my *New York Times* column and in *The Minimalist Cooks Dinner*, but it's so instructive, important, and wonderful that I felt it belonged here as well. All (well, almost all) the variations begin with bits of cured meat cooked until crisp, around which are built a number of different sauces of increasing complexity.

Most people insist that the "genuine" meat for these recipes is pancetta—salted, cured, and rolled pork belly. Pancetta is available at almost any decent Italian deli and at many specialty stores, but you can use bacon (or even better, if you can find it, guanciale, which is cured pig's jowl; see the back of the book for mail-order sources).

Pecorino Romano is the cheese of choice here, but Parmesan is also good.

> **Salt and black pepper to taste**
>
> **2 tablespoons extra virgin olive oil**
>
> **$\frac{1}{2}$ cup (about $\frac{1}{4}$ pound) minced pancetta, guanciale, or bacon**
>
> **1 pound linguine or other long pasta**
>
> **$\frac{1}{2}$ cup grated pecorino Romano cheese, or more to taste**

1. Bring a large pot of water to a boil and add salt. In a small saucepan, combine the olive oil and meat and turn the heat to medium. Cook, stirring occasionally, until the meat is nicely browned, about 10 minutes. Turn off the heat.

2. Cook the pasta in the boiling water until it is tender but not mushy. Before draining the pasta, remove about a cup of the cooking water and reserve it.

3. Toss the drained pasta with the meat and its juices; stir in the cheese. If the mixture is dry, add a little of the pasta-cooking water (or a little olive oil). Toss in lots of black pepper and serve.

Spaghetti Carbonara. You might call this pasta with bacon and eggs: While the pasta is cooking, warm a large bowl and beat 3 eggs in it. Stir in about $\frac{1}{2}$ cup freshly grated Parmesan and the pancetta and its juices. When the pasta is done, drain it and toss with the egg mixture. If the mixture is dry (unlikely), add a little reserved cooking water. Add plenty of black pepper and some more Parmesan to taste and serve.

Pasta all'Amatriciana. Step 1 is the same. Remove the pancetta with a slotted spoon and, in the juices left behind, sauté a medium onion, sliced, over medium heat, stirring occasionally, until well softened, about 10 minutes. Turn off the heat and let the mixture cool a bit. Stir in 2 cups chopped tomato (canned is fine; drain it first) and turn the heat back to medium. Cook the sauce, stirring occasionally, while you cook the pasta. When the pasta is done, drain it and toss it with the tomato sauce, the reserved pancetta, and at least $\frac{1}{2}$ cup freshly grated pecorino Romano or Parmesan cheese.

Pasta with Pepper and Cheese. The meatless version: toss cooked pasta with the oil, cheese, a lot of cracked black pepper, and enough of the reserved cooking water to thin the sauce slightly (it should be moist, not soupy).

Linguine with Garlic and Oil ITALY ■
MAKES **ABOUT 4 SERVINGS**
TIME **20 MINUTES**

Another classic, this one Roman, that simply cannot be omitted; to do so would be a huge disservice to beginners. This is a great snack, late-night meal, or starter.

For variety, toss in a couple of tablespoons of toasted fresh bread crumbs (page 580) or start with a few anchovy fillets along with the garlic and chile.

Salt to taste

$\frac{1}{2}$ cup extra virgin olive oil

2 tablespoons minced garlic

1 or more small dried red chiles or hot red pepper flakes to taste, optional

1 pound linguine, spaghetti, or other long, thin pasta

Chopped fresh parsley leaves for garnish

1. Bring a large pot of water to a boil and add salt. Combine the oil, garlic, chile if desired, and a large pinch of salt in a small skillet or saucepan over medium-low heat. Cook, shaking the pan occasionally, until the garlic turns light gold, about 5 minutes, then remove from the heat or turn it to an absolute minimum; the garlic should not brown, or at least not much.

2. Cook the pasta until it is tender but not mushy, then drain it; reserve a bit of the cooking water. Toss the pasta with the sauce, adding a little more oil or some of the cooking water if necessary. Garnish and serve.

Penne all'Arrabbiata ITALY ▨

MAKES **4 SERVINGS**

TIME **30 MINUTES**

A fast, classic pasta sauce popular not only in Rome but throughout central and southern Italy. Arrabbiata means "angry," and this sauce should be not only spicy but also strong, with the taste of garlic that has been browned, not just colored—as well as a good dose of chile.

> Salt and black pepper to taste
>
> ¼ cup extra virgin olive oil
>
> 3 garlic cloves, cut into chunks or slices
>
> 4 to 6 small dried chiles or hot red pepper flakes to taste
>
> 2 pounds plum tomatoes, cored and roughly chopped, or one 28-ounce can plum tomatoes, drained and chopped
>
> 1 pound penne, ziti, or other cut pasta
>
> Chopped fresh parsley leaves for garnish
>
> Freshly grated pecorino Romano cheese

1. Bring a large pot of water to a boil and add salt. Put the olive oil in a large skillet over medium-high heat and add the garlic and chiles. Cook, stirring occasionally, until the garlic is browned, 5 minutes or so. Turn off the heat and wait a couple of minutes.
2. If you want the dish very hot, leave some or all of the chiles in the skillet; otherwise, remove some or all of them. Turn the heat back to medium-high and add the tomatoes, along with some salt and pepper. Cook, stirring occasionally, until the mixture becomes saucy, 10 to 15 minutes. (After about 5 minutes, you can start to cook the pasta.)
3. Cook the pasta until it is tender but not mushy, then drain and sauce it. Taste and adjust the seasoning, then garnish with parsley and cheese and serve.

Pasta with Tomato and Olive Puree

ITALY ▨

MAKES **4 SERVINGS**

TIME **30 MINUTES**

A Ligurian specialty, usually made with "stamped" pasta—pasta that is rolled out and then cut with dies in special designs. You can use any cut pasta for this, though perhaps it's best with fresh pasta like malfatti (page 542).

If you have Tapenade (page 604), simply stir it into any tomato sauce to get the same effect.

> Salt and black pepper to taste
>
> ½ cup extra virgin olive oil
>
> 1 tablespoon minced garlic
>
> About 1 pound ripe fresh or canned tomatoes, peeled, seeded, drained if canned, and chopped
>
> ½ pound good-quality black olives (page 18)
>
> 3 or 4 anchovy fillets
>
> 1 pound any good-quality pasta
>
> Chopped fresh parsley leaves for garnish

1. Bring a large pot of water to a boil and add salt. Put half the olive oil in a 10- or 12-inch skillet over medium-high heat. Add the garlic and, when it sizzles, the tomatoes, along with some salt and pepper. Cook, stirring occasionally, until the tomatoes break up and the mixture becomes saucy, about 15 minutes.
2. Meanwhile, pit the olives: press on them with the broad side of a knife to break them, then remove the pit. Combine them in a small food processor with the anchovies and the remaining olive oil. Pulse the machine until you have a fairly smooth paste. Stir this paste into the tomato sauce and keep warm, stirring occasionally.
3. Cook the pasta until it is tender but not mushy. Serve with the sauce, garnished with the parsley.

CRUSHING AND PITTING OLIVES

Pasta with Mint and Parmesan ITALY ■

MAKES **4 SERVINGS**

TIME **20 MINUTES**

There is something about the sprightliness, the lightly assaultive, somehow-sweet nature of mint that is unlike any other herb. Here, softened by butter and cheese, to which it in turn lends spark, it converts a simple and basic but undeniably heavy combination into an easy but complex pasta dish that can best be described as refreshing.

Salt and black pepper to taste

1 pound cut pasta, such as ziti or penne, or long pasta, such as linguine or spaghetti

4 tablespoons ($1/2$ stick) butter, cut into pieces

About $1/2$ cup not-too-finely chopped fresh mint leaves

1 cup freshly grated Parmesan cheese

1. Bring a large pot of water to a boil and add salt. Cook the pasta until it is tender but not mushy. Drain the pasta, reserving about $1/2$ cup of the cooking water.

2. Toss the pasta in a warmed bowl with 2 or 3 tablespoons of the cooking water, the butter, mint, and half the Parmesan. Taste and adjust the seasoning, then serve, passing the remaining Parmesan at the table.

Pizzocheri with Savoy Cabbage, Potatoes, and Cheese ITALY

MAKES **4 SERVINGS**

TIME **30 TO 40 MINUTES**

If you can't find pizzocheri, a buckwheat pasta cut like fettuccine, you have two choices: make it yourself (page 542) or substitute any fettuccinelike pasta. If you can't find Taleggio (already a compromise, because when I had this dish it was made with a local Alpine cheese whose name exists only in dialect), use fontina (real fontina, if you can find it, from the Valle d'Aosta), or another fairly strong but not too hard or harsh cheese.

Salt and black pepper to taste

1 pound Savoy or other cabbage, cored and shredded

2 waxy potatoes, peeled and diced

3 tablespoons butter

5 fresh or 2 dried sage leaves

1 pound pizzocheri or other pasta

1 cup grated Taleggio, fontina, or other semisoft cheese

1 cup freshly grated Parmesan cheese

1. Bring a large pot of water to a boil and add salt. Add the cabbage and the potatoes. When they are tender, after about 10 minutes, remove them with a slotted spoon and place them in a large bowl; season with pepper and a little salt and keep warm.

2. Put the butter and sage in a small saucepan and simmer while you cook the pasta. Cook the pasta until tender but still firm. Just before the pasta is

done, remove $^1/_2$ cup of the cooking liquid and pour over the cabbage and potatoes. Drain the pasta and add it to the vegetables, along with the Taleggio and half the Parmesan.

3. Pour the butter-sage mixture over all, grind pepper over the pasta, and serve, tossing it at the table and passing the remaining Parmesan.

Spaghetti con Cipolle
Pasta with Onion Sauce ITALY ■

MAKES **4 SERVINGS**

TIME **ABOUT 30 MINUTES**

Diced onions mix well with fusilli and penne, so those are the pasta shapes most often used here, but you can use spaghetti if you prefer. Best with Spanish onions (the large yellow ones); add a handful of black olives if you like, too.

Salt to taste

2 medium to large (about 1 pound) onions, diced

$^1/_4$ cup extra virgin olive oil

1 cup any tomato sauce (see page 606, for example)

Black pepper to taste

Hot red pepper flakes to taste

1 pound penne, fusilli, or long pasta such as spaghetti

Freshly grated Parmesan cheese

1. Bring a large pot of water to a boil and add salt. Combine the onions and all but a tablespoon of the oil in a skillet with a lid. Add $^1/_2$ cup water and turn the heat to medium-high. Cover and let cook for about 15 minutes, stirring two or three times. The onions should be browning but not becoming crisp. Uncover and cook for another 5 minutes, stirring occasionally. Stir in the tomato sauce, along with some salt, pepper, and red pepper and keep warm.

2. Meanwhile, cook the pasta until it is tender but not mushy. Dress the pasta with the sauce, stir in the remaining oil, and serve with the Parmesan.

Pansotti Pasta with Walnuts ITALY ■

MAKES **4 SERVINGS**

TIME **20 MINUTES**

True pansotti are stuffed, with a mixture like this, but I rarely feel like filling pasta, and this way it makes a very fast meal and tastes just as good (it tastes even better with fresh pasta, page 541). Like Tarator or Skordalia (page 600), a terrific use of nuts as sauce.

Salt and black pepper to taste

1 thick slice Italian bread

$^1/_2$ cup milk

1 cup walnut or pecan halves

2 garlic cloves, peeled

$^1/_2$ cup freshly grated Parmesan cheese, plus more for serving

2 teaspoons fresh marjoram leaves or $^1/_2$ teaspoon dried

$^1/_2$ cup extra virgin olive oil

1 pound linguine, spaghetti, or other long pasta

1. Bring a large pot of water to a boil and add salt. Soak the bread in the milk. Combine the nuts, garlic, cheese, and marjoram in a food processor and turn the machine on. With the machine running, gradually add the oil, using just enough so that the mixture forms a very thick paste. Squeeze out the bread and add it to the mix, which will be very thick. Now add the milk the bread soaked in and enough water to make a saucy mixture. Season with salt and pepper.

2. Cook the pasta, stirring occasionally, until it is tender but not mushy. When it is ready, drain it—reserve some of the cooking water—and toss with

the sauce. If the mixture appears too thick, thin with a little of the pasta-cooking water (or more olive oil). Taste and adjust the seasoning, then serve, with more Parmesan.

Pasta with Fennel ITALY ■
MAKES 4 SERVINGS
TIME 30 MINUTES

The sweet, familiar combination of pine nuts and currants offsets the mild anise bitterness of fresh fennel here. Omit the pasta from this Sicilian sauce and you'll have a good vegetable dish.

If you can find the herb fennel (those living in southern California can find it wild, and many gardeners use it as an ornamental), use a few of the feathery parts of its stalks in place of the tops of the bulb. If you cannot, add the fennel seeds for stronger flavor.

1/4 cup currants
1/4 cup pine nuts
Salt and black pepper
1 fennel bulb, about 1 1/2 pounds
1/4 cup extra virgin olive oil
1 large onion, chopped
1 teaspoon fennel seeds, optional
1 pound bucatini or cut pasta, like penne or farfalle

1. Soak the currants in warm water to cover. Toast the pine nuts in a small dry skillet over medium heat, shaking the pan occasionally, until lightly browned, just a few minutes. Bring a large pot of water to a boil and add salt. Separate the fennel stalks and leaves from the bulb; chop the bulb. Trim the feathery leaves, mince, and set aside. Chop the stalks and put them in the boiling water.
2. Meanwhile, put the olive oil in a medium skillet or saucepan over medium heat; a minute later, add

the onion, chopped fennel bulb, and fennel seeds if you're using them. Cook, stirring occasionally, until the onion and fennel are softened, 5 to 10 minutes. Add some salt and pepper. Drain the currants and add them, along with all but a tablespoon of the pine nuts. Scoop the chopped fennel stalks from the boiling water and add them, along with about 1/2 cup of the water. Simmer while you cook the pasta.
3. When the pasta is tender but not mushy, drain it, reserving a little of the cooking water. Put it in a bowl and add the sauce, along with a little of the reserved water if necessary. Taste and adjust the seasoning, then garnish with a little of the fennel leaves and the remaining pine nuts.

Pasta with Cabbage ITALY ■
MAKES 3 TO 6 SERVINGS
TIME 30 MINUTES

Cabbage, when it begins to break down, becomes quite creamy, and that's what makes this dish somewhat unusual. This will be stronger tasting if you use plenty of black and red pepper, olive oil, and pecorino or quite mild if you start with butter, reducing the black pepper, eliminating the red, and finishing with pecorino. You can also make it far more substantial; see the variation.

Salt and black pepper to taste
1 small or 1/2 large head of green or Savoy cabbage, about 1 pound
3 tablespoons extra virgin olive oil or butter
1 tablespoon minced garlic
2 cups cored and chopped tomatoes, with the liquid (canned are fine; don't bother to drain)
1/2 teaspoon hot red pepper flakes, or to taste
1 pound spaghetti, linguine, or other long pasta

Freshly grated Parmesan or pecorino Romano cheese for garnish

1. Bring a large pot of water to a boil and add salt. Use a sharp knife to cut a cone-shaped wedge out of the bottom of the cabbage to core it. Shred it finely; it should be almost as thin as the pasta. Put the oil or butter in a large skillet and turn the heat to medium; a minute later, add the garlic and cook, stirring occasionally, until the garlic just begins to color, 3 or 4 minutes. Add the cabbage, turn the heat to medium-high, and cook, stirring occasionally, for 3 to 4 minutes, until the cabbage begins to wilt.

2. Turn the heat back to medium and add the tomato, along with some salt, black pepper, and the red pepper. Cook, stirring occasionally, until the tomato breaks up and the cabbage is tender, about 10 minutes. Taste and adjust the seasoning. Meanwhile, cook the pasta until it is tender but not mushy.

3. Drain the pasta and toss it with the sauce and the cheese; serve immediately.

Pasta with Cabbage and Sausage. Use 2 tablespoons olive oil. Cut about 1 pound fresh sausage into small pieces and cook it in the oil over medium heat, stirring occasionally, until nicely browned, about 10 minutes. Add the garlic and then proceed with the recipe.

Pasta with Broccoli Raab ITALY ■
MAKES **4 SERVINGS**
TIME **30 MINUTES**

This is a simple preparation that can serve as a side dish or main course (add some cooked sausage if you like) and can be made with any dark green, from spinach to collards to turnip or mustard greens. It needs no cheese.

Salt and black pepper to taste
1 pound broccoli raab, bottom stems trimmed
¼ cup extra virgin olive oil
3 or 4 large garlic cloves, thinly sliced, to taste
1 teaspoon hot red pepper flakes, or to taste
1 pound ziti or other cut pasta

1. Bring a large pot of water to a boil and add salt. Put the broccoli raab in the water and cook it for about 5 minutes, until tender but still bright green. Remove it from the water, leaving the water in the pot, and rinse it quickly under cold water. Bring the water back to a boil.

2. Meanwhile, heat the olive oil in a large deep skillet over low heat. Add the garlic and red pepper and cook just until the garlic begins to sizzle, less than 5 minutes. Turn off the heat.

3. Cook the pasta in the boiling water, stirring frequently. Chop the broccoli raab so that no piece is more than an inch long. Turn the heat under the skillet to medium and heat the greens with the garlic and oil. When the pasta is done, reserve about a cup of the cooking liquid and drain. Add the pasta to the skillet with the greens and toss, adding enough of the pasta-cooking liquid to keep the dish moist and saucy. Taste and add black pepper and some salt if necessary. Serve immediately.

Pasta with Anchovies and Walnuts
ITALY ■
MAKES **4 SERVINGS**
TIME **30 MINUTES**

There are several types of pasta sauce based on walnuts in northern Italy, including the one on page 550;

this is among my favorites. It also happens to be the easiest. If you like, you could throw in a tablespoon of capers, too.

½ cup walnuts, roughly chopped

Salt to taste

2 tablespoons extra virgin olive oil

1 tablespoon minced garlic

¼ pound anchovy fillets, chopped, with their oil

1 pound linguine

Minced fresh parsley leaves for garnish

1. Preheat the oven to 350°F. Place the walnuts on an ungreased baking sheet and toast in the oven until fragrant, shaking occasionally, 10 to 15 minutes. Set aside. Bring a large pot of water to a boil and add salt.
2. Meanwhile, heat the oil in a large skillet over medium heat, add the garlic, and cook, stirring, until the garlic is lightly colored, about 5 minutes. Add the anchovies, along with their oil, and cook for 1 minute, then turn off the heat.
3. Cook the pasta in the boiling water until it is tender but not mushy; drain, reserving about ½ cup of the water. Dilute the anchovy sauce with ¼ to ½ cup of the pasta-cooking water. Toss the pasta, sauce, and walnuts together, garnish with the parsley, and serve.

Pasta with Walnuts and Bread Crumbs. No anchovies: In step 2, put ¼ cup extra virgin olive oil in a skillet over medium heat. Add the garlic and ½ cup bread crumbs, preferably fresh (page 580). Cook, stirring occasionally, until the mixture is golden brown and fragrant, then stir in the walnuts. Meanwhile, cook and drain the pasta, reserving some of the cooking water. Toss the pasta with the walnut mixture, along with as much of the cooking liquid as is necessary to moisten the dish (it should not be wet). Garnish and serve.

Penne with Pumpkin or Squash ITALY ▨
MAKES **4 TO 6 SERVINGS**

TIME **30 MINUTES**

I love filled pasta, but I rarely have the time or energy to make it. So, when I became enamored of pasta con zucca—a raviolilike affair stuffed with the Italian equivalent of pumpkin—I created this alternative, which is not quite as elegant but tastes just as good. If you cannot find a small pumpkin—the only kind whose flesh is dense enough for this dish—use butternut squash. Peel either with a paring knife; their skins are too tough for vegetable peelers.

1 pound peeled and seeded pumpkin or butternut squash

Salt and black pepper to taste

2 tablespoons butter or extra virgin olive oil

1 pound penne or other cut pasta

½ teaspoon hot red pepper flakes, or more to taste

⅛ teaspoon freshly grated nutmeg, or to taste

1 teaspoon sugar, optional

½ cup freshly grated Parmesan cheese

1. Cut the squash into chunks and place in a food processor. Pulse the machine on and off until the squash appears grated. Alternatively, grate or chop the squash by hand. Bring a large pot of water to a boil for the pasta and add salt.
2. Place a large skillet over medium heat and add the butter. A minute later, add the squash, salt and pepper to taste, and about ½ cup water. Cook over medium heat, stirring occasionally and adding water about ¼ cup at a time as the mixture dries out, being careful not to make it soupy, until the squash begins to disintegrate, after 10 or 15 minutes. Begin cooking the pasta at that point. While it cooks, season the squash with the red pepper, nutmeg, sugar if necessary, and additional salt and pepper if needed.

3. When the pasta is tender, scoop out about ½ cup of the cooking water and reserve it, then drain the pasta. Toss the pasta in the skillet with the squash, adding the reserved pasta-cooking water if the mixture seems dry. Taste and add more of any seasonings you like, then toss with the Parmesan and serve.

Pasta with Fresh and Dried Mushrooms ITALY

MAKES 4 SERVINGS

TIME ABOUT 1 HOUR, LARGELY UNATTENDED

Fresh porcini make the base of an incredible pasta sauce but cost at least twenty dollars a pound, if and when you can find them. Portobellos, which are cultivated, not wild, are sold at every supermarket every day at prices ranging from four to ten dollars a pound, and they're consistent in quality. And if you cook them slowly in oil, adding a few reconstituted dried porcini as they cook—a technique popularized by Marcella Hazan—the results are wonderful.

This mushroom topping is also great with nice, soft polenta (page 529).

½ pound portobello mushrooms

3 garlic cloves

Leaves from 2 or 3 fresh thyme sprigs

½ cup extra virgin olive oil

Salt and black pepper to taste

¼ cup dried porcini, optional

3 cups peeled, seeded, and chopped tomatoes (canned are fine)

1 pound penne or other cut pasta

Freshly grated Parmesan cheese

1. Trim and clean the mushrooms; cut the caps into slices and the stems into small chunks. Combine in a medium skillet with 1 clove of the garlic, crushed and peeled, the thyme, the olive oil, and some salt and pepper. Cook over sufficiently low heat so the mixture bubbles but the mushrooms do not brown. Continue to cook, stirring occasionally, until they are quite shrunken in size and appear firm, 30 to 45 minutes. Turn off the heat and remove with a slotted spoon, leaving the oil in the skillet. (At this point you can pause for several hours before resuming cooking.)

2. Bring a large pot of water to a boil for the pasta and add salt. If you're using the porcini, soak them in hot water to cover for a few minutes so they soften, then drain, trim, and slice. Mince the remaining garlic. Turn the heat under the oil to medium and add the garlic, portobellos, and drained porcini. Cook, stirring occasionally, until the garlic begins to color, about 5 minutes; add the tomato and raise the heat to medium-high. Cook, stirring occasionally, until the tomato breaks up and becomes saucy, about 15 minutes.

3. Meanwhile, cook the pasta until tender but not mushy. Taste the sauce and adjust its seasoning. When the pasta is done, drain it, toss with the sauce, top with Parmesan, and serve.

Spaghetti with Octopus Braised in Red Wine ITALY

MAKES 4 SERVINGS

TIME 1½ HOURS, LARGELY UNATTENDED

If you love octopus, this dish will satisfy your cravings. Just be sure to allow enough time for the octopus to become fully tender. (You can also use squid, which will cook much more quickly.)

This dish employs the unusual but excellent technique of completing the cooking of the pasta in its sauce, something done throughout Italy.

1/4 cup olive oil

1 carrot, chopped

1 medium onion, chopped

1 celery stalk, chopped

Salt and black pepper to taste

2 medium octopuses, about 3/4 pound each, cleaned and
    cut into chunks

2 cups dry red wine

1 bay leaf

1 garlic clove, minced

1 pound spaghetti or linguine

16 cherry tomatoes, cut in half

1/2 cup chopped fresh basil leaves

1. Place 2 tablespoons of the olive oil in a large skillet or sauté pan over medium-high heat. Add the carrot, onion, and celery. Sprinkle with a pinch of salt and cook, stirring occasionally, until the onion becomes translucent, about 5 minutes.

2. Add the octopus along with some pepper and a little more salt. Cook, stirring, for a minute, then add the wine, bay leaf, and garlic. Cook until the octopus is tender, about an hour (check with the point of a sharp knife). Remove the octopus and cut it into bite-sized pieces, then return it to the skillet; turn the heat to a minimum.

3. Meanwhile, bring a large pot of water to a boil and add salt. Fifteen minutes before eating, begin to cook the pasta. When it is barely tender—but not nearly tender enough to eat—drain it, reserving about 1 cup of the cooking water. Add the pasta to the octopus mixture, along with half the reserved cooking water. Cook until the pasta is tender but not mushy, adding the remaining cooking water if necessary to keep the mixture from drying out.

4. Add the remaining olive oil, along with the cherry tomatoes. Cook for another minute, taste and adjust the seasoning, then stir in the basil and serve.

Pasta with Tuna Sauce ITALY ■

MAKES **4 SERVINGS**

TIME **30 MINUTES**

One of those wonderful from-the-pantry pasta dishes that can be prepared in the time it takes to boil the water and cook the pasta. Canned tuna is not only acceptable but necessary; but the ideal tuna here would be that taken from the tuna's belly, the fattiest part, and cured (preferably by your Sicilian grandmother) in great olive oil. Assuming you don't have that, buy tuna packed in olive oil from Italy or Spain. (In a serious specialty store, you might find belly tuna—probably labeled ventresca—packed in olive oil. It's dynamite.) What you're looking for is dark, soft meat that will flake nicely and add its rich flavor to the sauce.

Salt and black pepper to taste

2 tablespoons extra virgin olive oil

1 medium onion, roughly chopped

1 teaspoon hot red pepper flakes, or to taste

2 tablespoons drained capers

One 28-ounce can plum tomatoes, drained and roughly
    chopped

1 pound long pasta, like spaghetti or linguine

One or two 6-ounce cans tuna packed in olive oil

Chopped fresh parsley leaves for garnish, optional

1. Bring a large pot of water to a boil and add salt. Put the olive oil in a deep skillet or a medium saucepan over medium-high heat. Add the onion and cook, stirring occasionally, until it softens, about 5 minutes. Stir in the red pepper and capers, then the tomatoes. Cook, stirring occasionally, until the tomatoes begin to break up, 10 to 15 minutes; then lower the heat and cook for another 5 to 10 minutes.

2. Cook the pasta in the boiling water, stirring frequently, until it is tender but not mushy. Just before

it's done, stir the tuna into the tomato sauce, breaking it into flakes. Taste and adjust the seasoning, adding salt, pepper, or red pepper as necessary.

3. Drain the pasta, toss with the sauce, garnish with the parsley if you wish, and serve.

Maccheroni alla San Giovanniello
Pasta with Whole Garlic Cloves ITALY ▓

MAKES **ABOUT 4 SERVINGS**

TIME **30 MINUTES**

A deliciously strong pasta dish, taught to me (as were so many others) by my friend Andrea. See page 546 for information on guanciale. Frankly, I can barely write this recipe without rushing off to the stove.

Salt and black pepper to taste

1/3 cup extra-virgin olive oil

10 garlic cloves, peeled and lightly crushed

1/2 cup cubes or strips of guanciale, prosciutto, other salted ham, or slab bacon

6 fresh plum tomatoes or 1 1/2 cups canned (drained, liquid reserved)

1 pound cut pasta, such as ziti

1 cup roughly chopped fresh basil leaves

1 cup freshly grated pecorino Romano cheese, Parmesan cheese, or a combination

1. Bring a large pot of water to boil for the pasta and add salt. Combine the oil, garlic, and ham in a 10-inch skillet and turn the heat to medium-low. Cook slowly, stirring occasionally, until the garlic becomes deep golden, nearly brown, all over, 10 to 15 minutes.

2. Chop the plum tomatoes (or crush the canned tomatoes) and add them, along with some salt and pepper, to the skillet; stir and simmer while you cook the pasta.

3. Drain the pasta when it is done, reserving a little of the cooking water and adding it to the sauce if it appears dry (quite likely if you used fresh tomatoes). Toss the pasta with the sauce and most of the basil, along with the cheese. Mince the remaining basil, garnish the pasta, and serve.

Pasta with Ham, Peas, and Cream
ITALY ▓

MAKES **4 SERVINGS**

TIME **30 MINUTES**

A pasta dish kids love and one that became traditional with mine whenever we left them with a sitter for the evening. It's best if the ham is prosciutto, the cream thick and fresh, and the peas just shelled, but it's pretty good with supermarket ham and cream and frozen peas, and I've made it that way plenty of times.

For variety, add about a cup of sliced button mushrooms to the ham mixture.

Salt and black pepper to taste

1 cup peas, fresh or frozen

2 tablespoons butter

2 ounces ham, preferably prosciutto, roughly chopped

1/2 cup heavy cream

1 pound linguine, fettuccine, or other long pasta

1/2 cup freshly grated Parmesan cheese, or more to taste

1. Bring both a large and a small pot of water to a boil; salt them both. In the small pot, cook the peas until tender, 3 or 4 minutes. Drain and set aside. Put the butter in a medium skillet over medium heat; when it melts, add the ham and cook for about a minute. Stir in the peas, the cream, a pinch of salt, and a fair amount of black pepper. Turn the heat to low; keep warm, stirring occasionally, while you cook the pasta.

2. Cook the pasta until tender but not mushy; drain, reserving about a cup of the cooking liquid. Toss the pasta with the cream mixture; if it seems too thick, add a little of the reserved cooking water. Stir in the Parmesan, taste and adjust the seasoning, and serve.

Pasta with Duck Sauce ITALY

MAKES **4 SERVINGS**

TIME **AT LEAST 2 HOURS, LARGELY UNATTENDED**

This is a dark pasta sauce served in much of Italy, made with stewed, shredded meat. I like to make it with duck legs, though you could use rabbit, pork—cut from the ribs or shoulder—or even the dark meat of a good chicken (hardest to find). The meat must first be braised in red wine or, even simpler, cooked in its own fat as I do here. That's the only time-consuming part of the process, and it may be done a day or more in advance. (Refrigerate both meat and juices if you complete this step more than an hour or two before proceeding.) Sharp pecorino Romano is a better choice of cheese than Parmesan here, though chopped parsley also makes a good garnish.

2 duck legs

1 medium onion, chopped

Salt and black pepper to taste

1½ cups dry red wine, like Barolo or Cabernet Sauvignon

One 28-ounce can plum tomatoes, drained and roughly chopped

1 pound cut pasta, such as penne

Freshly grated pecorino Romano or Parmesan cheese or chopped fresh parsley leaves for garnish

1. Trim the visible fat from the duck legs, then lay them, skin side down, in a 10-inch skillet with a lid. Turn the heat to medium and, when the duck begins to sizzle, turn the heat to low and cover. Cook undisturbed for about an hour (check once to make sure the legs aren't burning), by which time the skin should be golden brown. Turn, then cook until the duck is very tender, at least 30 minutes more.

2. Remove the duck and set aside. Add the onion to the skillet and turn the heat to medium-high. Cook, stirring occasionally, until the onion is softened, about 5 minutes. Bring a large pot of water to a boil for the pasta and add salt.

3. Add the wine to the onion and raise the heat to high; cook until the liquid is reduced by about half, after about 5 minutes, then add the tomatoes along with some salt and pepper and cook over medium-high heat, stirring occasionally, until the mixture is saucy, about 15 minutes. Taste and adjust the seasoning. (You can prepare the dish to this point and let sit for a few hours or cover and refrigerate for up to a day before reheating and proceeding.)

4. Meanwhile, shred the duck meat from the bone and add it to the sauce as it cooks. A few minutes after adding the tomatoes, cook the pasta. When it is tender but not mushy, drain it and serve it with the sauce, along with the cheese or parsley.

Pasta with Sausage and Cream ITALY ■

MAKES **ABOUT 4 SERVINGS**

TIME **30 MINUTES**

A dish I learned from my good friend Andrea, who is originally from Rome but has collected unusual pasta dishes from all over Italy. This is clearly a peasant dish, but the presence of sausage, butter, and cream makes it special enough for guests. Use well-seasoned "Italian" sausage; it can be hot if you like. That made without casing—in patties or bulk—will save you a step.

Salt and black pepper to taste

2 tablespoons butter

$^1/_2$ pound sweet or hot Italian sausage, casings removed

$^1/_2$ cup heavy cream

1 pound ziti or other cut pasta

Freshly grated Parmesan cheese

1. Bring a large pot of water to a boil for the pasta and add salt. Put the butter in a medium skillet over medium heat. As it melts, crumble the sausage meat into it, making the bits $^1/_2$ inch or less in size. Add the cream and adjust the heat so that the mixture simmers gently.
2. Cook the pasta until it is tender but not at all mushy. Drain, reserving about a cup of the cooking water. Dress the pasta with the sauce, adding some of the reserved cooking liquid if necessary. Taste and adjust the seasoning, toss with the Parmesan, and serve.

Pasta with Sausage. This is simpler, lighter, and just as good in its own way: in step 1, replace the butter with olive oil, omit the cream, and add $^1/_2$ cup water to the sausage.

Pasta Frittata ITALY ■
MAKES **4 SERVINGS**
TIME **40 MINUTES (LESS IF YOU HAVE LEFTOVER PASTA)**

It's no secret that people eat leftover pasta, but this is a time-honored way to turn it into something else. It's so good that you might find yourself cooking extra pasta just so you have an excuse to make this.

As with any other frittata, you can add what you like here. It might be a bit of pancetta or bacon, but it can also be a bit of cooked vegetable or something as simple as minced scallion or parsley.

$^1/_4$ pound spaghetti, linguine, fettuccine, or other long pasta or about $^1/_2$ pound cooked

Salt and black pepper to taste

4 tablespoons ($^1/_2$ stick) butter or extra virgin olive oil

$^1/_4$ cup minced pancetta, bacon, or prosciutto, optional

5 eggs

1 cup freshly grated Parmesan cheese

1. If you're using cooked pasta, chop it up. Otherwise, bring a large pot of water to a boil, add salt, and cook the pasta until barely tender, somewhat short of where you would normally cook it. Drain and immediately toss it in a wide bowl with half the butter. Cool it a bit.
2. Preheat the oven to 400°F. Put the remaining butter in a large ovenproof nonstick skillet and turn the heat to medium-high. Add the meat if you're using it and cook, stirring occasionally, until it is nice and crisp, 3 to 5 minutes.
3. Combine the pasta with the remaining ingredients, along with some salt and pepper (less salt if you used meat). Pour the mixture into the skillet and immediately turn the heat to medium-low. If necessary, use a spoon to even out the top of the frittata. Cook, undisturbed, until the mixture firms up on the bottom, then transfer it to the oven. Bake until the top is just cooked, about 10 minutes. Remove and serve hot in wedges or at room temperature.

Pasta "Frittata," Sicilian Style. It's amazing how close this is to a Chinese noodle cake: Combine the cooked pasta with salt, pepper, and olive oil—no more. Cook it as you would the panfried noodle cake that forms the base for Shrimp with Crisp-Fried Noodles (page 534) and top it with Fast, Fresh Tomato Sauce (page 606) or any other good tomato sauce. Serve as a first course, side dish, or light main course.

BREADS

Probably the most misunderstood and rewarding category in the cooking world, breads take time but—usually—not a whole lot of work. I like to compare them to laundry, which was, before the invention of the washing machine, a terrible, time-consuming chore. Similarly, the creation of the food processor has turned breadmaking from a harsh daily chore into a simple labor of love.

Almost every dough can be made in the food processor. And it's not just faster—immeasurably faster—but also better, because good dough is usually moist, and dough that is too moist to be dealt with easily by hand presents no challenge to the food processor.

So, with a food processor and "instant" yeast (the kind that does not require mixing with liquid but can simply be tossed into the food processor with the flour, sold under various brand names like SAF and sometimes called "bread machine yeast"), making dough for bread is about as difficult as making pancake batter.

Furthermore, the dough's development can be hurried (put in a warm place) or retarded (refrigerate it, as long as 12 hours or even more). None of this requires any further discussion; it's as easy as the recipes make it appear.

Paratha Whole Wheat Flatbreads INDIA
MAKES **8 TO 12 FLATBREADS, ENOUGH FOR 4**

TIME **AT LEAST 1 HOUR**

These simple, flaky breads are easy to make, but there is one caveat: you must not treat them (or any Indian bread) as you would European breads, which is to say that although the dough can be prepared in advance (indeed, it's better if it rests for a while), the breads

themselves must be cooked at the last minute before serving.

Serve with any dal (page 433) and a dish like Tandoori Chicken (page 291).

1½ cups whole wheat flour

1½ cups all-purpose flour, plus more for rolling out the dough

1 teaspoon salt

About 4 tablespoons (½ stick) butter, melted, or about ¼ cup corn, grapeseed, or other neutral oil

1. Combine the flours and salt in a food processor. Turn the machine on and add ¾ cup water through the feed tube. Process for about 30 seconds, adding more water, a little at a time, until the

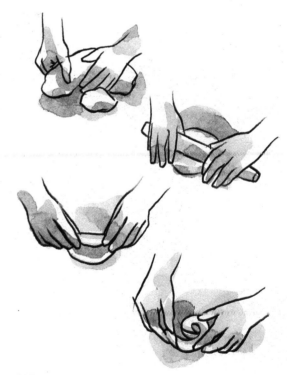

PARATHA

mixture forms a ball and is slightly sticky to the touch. If dry, add another tablespoon or two of water and process for another 10 seconds. (In the unlikely event that the mixture is too sticky, add flour, a tablespoon at a time.) Remove the dough and, using flour as necessary, shape into a ball; wrap in plastic and let rest for at least 20 minutes or up to several hours at room temperature. (Or refrigerate for up to a day or freeze for up to a week.)

2. Pinch off pieces of dough about 1½ to 2 inches in diameter; the recipe will make 8 to 12 breads. Using flour as necessary, roll each piece into a 4-inch disk and brush with butter. Roll up like a cigar, then press into a coil not unlike a cinnamon bun; set aside until you finish all the pieces.

3. Put a griddle or cast-iron or nonstick skillet over medium heat. When it's hot, press one of the coils flat, then roll it out into a disk about ¼ inch thick, or slightly thinner. Put on the griddle or pan and cook until lightly browned on one side; brush the top with butter, flip, and brown on the second side. Continue until all the breads are done, then serve.

Aloo Paratha Whole Wheat Flatbreads Stuffed with Potatoes INDIA ■ ■

MAKES 8 TO 12 STUFFED FLATBREADS, ENOUGH FOR 4 TO 6
TIME AT LEAST 1 HOUR

Not to put too fine a point on it, but this is one of my favorite foods ever. Fifteen years ago, Julie Sahni, the great Indian cook and cookbook writer (her *Classic Indian Cooking* remains the best book on the subject published in the States), showed me how to make aloo paratha. I continued to follow her recipes for years and never ate a better one until I traveled to India (and even then I may have been influenced by the

atmosphere, a truck stop near a mountaintop fort). This is essentially Julie's recipe, with a few changes I've incorporated over the years.

Cooked paratha will keep at room temperature for up to twenty-four hours and can be served without reheating or can be reheated quickly in a dry skillet or even a microwave. But there is nothing like one fresh from the skillet.

Ajwain comes from carom seeds, which look like celery seeds but taste like very strong, slightly coarse thyme.

> 1½ cups whole wheat flour
> 1½ cups all-purpose flour, plus more for rolling out the dough
> 1 teaspoon salt
> 1 teaspoon ajwain, dried thyme, or ground cumin
> 2 tablespoons corn, grapeseed, or other neutral oil, plus more for brushing the breads
> 1½ pounds baking potatoes, peeled and cut in half
> Salt and black pepper to taste
> 1 jalapeño or other hot fresh chile, stemmed, seeded, and minced
> 2 teaspoons ground coriander
> Juice of ½ small lemon
> Melted butter, optional

1. Combine the flours, salt, and ajwain in a food processor. Turn the machine on and add the 2 tablespoons of oil and ¾ cup water through the feed tube. Process for about 30 seconds, adding more water, a little at a time, until the mixture forms a ball and is slightly sticky to the touch. If dry, add another tablespoon or two of water and process for another 10 seconds. (In the unlikely event that the mixture is too sticky, add flour, a tablespoon at a time.) Remove the dough and, using flour as necessary, shape into a ball; wrap in plastic and let rest while you make the potato mixture. (Or refrigerate for up to a day or freeze for up to a week.)

2. Put the potatoes in a large saucepan and add water to cover and a large pinch of salt. Turn the heat to high, bring to a boil, and adjust the heat so the mixture simmers steadily; cook until the potatoes are tender, 15 to 20 minutes, then drain. Mash with the chile, coriander, a large pinch of salt, some pepper, and the lemon juice; taste and adjust the seasoning (you may prefer more chile; sometimes aloo paratha are quite hot).

3. Set out a bowl of flour and a small bowl of neutral oil, with a spoon or brush, on your work surface. Lightly flour your work surface and your rolling pin. Break off a piece of dough about the size of a golf ball. Toss it in the bowl of flour and then roll it in your hands to make a ball. Flatten it into a 2-inch disk, then use a floured rolling pin to roll it into a thin round, about 5 inches in diameter, dusting with flour as necessary.

4. Mound about 2 tablespoons of the filling into the center of one of the rounds of dough. Bring the edges of the round up over the top of the filling and press them together to make a pouch. Press down on the "neck" of the pouch with the palm of one hand to make a slightly rounded disk. Turn the disk in the bowl of flour and roll it out again into a round 6 to 7 inches in diameter. Pat it between your hands to brush off the excess flour. Put the paratha on a plate and cover with a sheet of plastic wrap. Continue to roll all of the remaining dough into paratha and stack them on the plate with a sheet of plastic wrap between them. You can keep the paratha stacked like this for an hour or two in the refrigerator before cooking them if necessary.

5. Heat a nonstick skillet or griddle over medium-high heat for a minute or two, then put a paratha (or two, if they'll fit) on it and cook until it darkens slightly, usually less than a minute. Flip the paratha with a spatula and cook for another 30 seconds on the second side. Use the back of a spoon or a brush to coat the top of the paratha with oil. Flip and coat the other side with oil. Continue cooking the paratha until the bottom of the bread has browned, flip, and repeat. Do this a few times until both sides of the paratha are golden brown and very crisp, 2 to 3 minutes total for each paratha. As the paratha finish, remove them from the pan and brush with melted butter if you wish if you're going to serve hot; otherwise wait until you've reheated them. (You can reheat them in a 300°F oven or by recooking them in a dry pan.)

Keema Ke Paratha Whole Wheat Flatbreads Stuffed with Lamb, Chiles, and Cilantro INDIA ■ ▨

MAKES 8 TO 12 STUFFED FLATBREADS, ENOUGH FOR 4 TO 6
TIME 1½ HOURS

When they're hot from the pan, it's hard not to fill up on paratha alone, though they're usually served in the context of a larger Indian meal. I learned this spicy, delicious lamb filling from Suvir Saran, an Indian chef and friend who lives and works in New York and whose book, written with Stephanie Lyness—*Indian Home Cooking: A Fresh Introduction to Indian Food*—is one of the best on the topic written for the American audience.

1½ cups whole wheat flour

1½ cups all-purpose flour, plus 1 tablespoon for the filling and more for rolling out the dough

1 teaspoon salt, plus more to taste

2 tablespoons corn, grapeseed, or other neutral oil, plus more for brushing the breads

1 pound ground lamb or beef

½ cup finely chopped red onion

1 small hot fresh green chile, minced

1 teaspoon minced garlic

½ teaspoon cayenne

½ teaspoon fennel seeds

½ teaspoon ajwain (page 560), dried thyme, or ground
  cumin

2 tablespoons chopped fresh cilantro leaves

½ teaspoon garam masala (page 594)

Juice of ½ lime

Melted butter, optional

1. Combine the flours and salt in a food processor. Turn the machine on and add the 2 tablespoons of the oil and ¾ cup water through the feed tube. Process for about 30 seconds, adding more water, a little at a time, until the mixture forms a ball and is slightly sticky to the touch. If dry, add another tablespoon or two of water and process for another 10 seconds. (In the unlikely event that the mixture is too sticky, add flour, a tablespoon at a time.) Remove the dough and, using flour as necessary, shape into a ball; wrap in plastic and let rest while you make the meat filling. (Or refrigerate for up to a day or freeze for up to a week.)

2. Preheat a large heavy skillet over medium-high heat for a minute or two, then add the meat to the pan. Sauté the meat in its own fat, breaking it up with a wooden spoon, until it's lost its raw red color, 5 minutes or a little more. Add the onion, chile, garlic, cayenne, fennel, and ajwain; cook, stirring frequently, until the meat is browned, about 5 minutes more. Transfer to a bowl, stir in the cilantro, garam masala, lime juice, a tablespoon of flour, and salt to taste; cool completely. (The meat filling can be made 2 or 3 days in advance and kept in the refrigerator; bring to room temperature before using.)

3. Set out a bowl of flour and a small bowl of neutral oil, with a spoon or brush, on your work surface. Lightly flour your work surface and your rolling pin. Break off a piece of dough about the size of a golf ball. Toss it in the bowl of flour and then roll it in your hands to make a ball. Flatten it into a

2-inch disk, then use a floured rolling pin to roll it into a thin round, about 5 inches in diameter, dusting with flour as necessary.

4. Mound about 2 tablespoons of the filling into the center of one of the rounds of dough. Bring the edges of the round up over the top of the filling and press them together to make a pouch. Press down on the "neck" of the pouch with the palm of one hand to make a slightly rounded disk. Turn the disk in the bowl of flour and roll it out again into a round 5 to 6 inches in diameter. Pat it between your hands to brush off the excess flour. Put the paratha on a plate and cover with a sheet of plastic wrap. Continue to roll all of the remaining dough into paratha and stack them on the plate with a sheet of plastic wrap between them. You can keep the paratha stacked like this for an hour or two in the refrigerator before cooking them if necessary.

5. Heat a nonstick skillet or griddle over medium-high heat for a minute or two, then put a paratha (or two, if they'll fit) on it and cook until it darkens slightly, usually less than a minute. Flip the paratha with a spatula and cook for another 30 seconds on the second side. Use the back of a spoon or a brush to coat the top of the paratha with oil. Flip and coat the other side with oil. Continue cooking the paratha until the bottom of the bread has browned, flip, and repeat. Do this a few times until both sides of the paratha are golden brown and very crisp, 2 to 3 minutes total for each paratha. As the paratha finish, remove them from the pan and brush with melted butter if you wish if you're going to serve hot; otherwise wait until you've reheated them. (You can reheat them in a 300°F oven or by recooking them in a dry pan.)

Naan Yeasted Flatbreads INDIA

MAKES **ABOUT 12 FLATBREADS, ENOUGH FOR 6 TO 12**

TIME **2 HOURS, LARGELY UNATTENDED**

Although there's something lost in translation between the scorching heat of a tandoor—the clay oven of northern India—and the relatively tame 500°F of a home oven, you can indeed make creditable, even delicious naan at home. With their slightly sour flavor and ultrasoft texture, they're the perfect accompaniment to dal (page 433) or any Indian meat dish.

- 1 tablespoon active dry yeast
- 2 tablespoons milk
- 2 tablespoons yogurt
- 1 tablespoon sugar
- 3½ cups unbleached all-purpose flour plus ½ cup whole wheat flour or all unbleached flour, plus flour for rolling out the dough
- 1 egg
- 2 teaspoons salt
- Oil for the bowl
- 4 tablespoons (½ stick) butter, melted, warm

1. Stir together the yeast, milk, yogurt, and sugar in a bowl and set aside.
2. Combine the flour, egg, and salt in a food processor. Turn the machine on and add the yeast mixture through the feed tube. Process for about 30 seconds, adding 1½ cups water, a little at a time, until the mixture forms a ball and is slightly sticky to the touch. If dry, add another tablespoon or two of water and process for another 10 seconds. (In the unlikely event that the mixture is too sticky, add flour, a tablespoon at a time.)
3. Turn the dough onto a floured work surface and knead by hand for a few seconds to form a smooth, round ball. Put the dough in a lightly oiled bowl and cover with plastic wrap; let rise until the dough doubles in size, 1 to 2 hours. (You can cut this rising time short if you are in a hurry, or you can let the dough rise more slowly, in the refrigerator, for up to 6 or 8 hours.)
4. Put a baking sheet (or, preferably, a baking stone) on a rack on the lowest shelf of your oven; preheat the oven to 500°F. Punch the dough down and, using as much flour as necessary to keep the dough from sticking to the board or your hands, roll it into a snake, then tear the snake into 12 equal-sized balls. Let them rest for 10 minutes covered with plastic wrap or a damp towel.
5. Using flour as necessary, roll out one of the balls into an oval roughly 6 to 8 inches long and 3 or 4 inches wide. Open the oven door, grab the dough, one hand on each end of the oval, and give it a little tug with one hand to shape it into a teardrop, then toss it onto the baking sheet or stone. Close the oven door and flip the naan after 3 minutes. The naan is ready when it's puffed, mottled, and browned around the edges, 6 to 8 minutes. You can cook as many naan as will comfortably fit at once.
6. Wrap the freshly baked naan in a kitchen towel to keep them warm and pliable. Serve as soon as possible, brushed on one side with melted butter.

Onion Kulcha INDIA

MAKES **6 STUFFED FLATBREADS**

TIME **2 HOURS, LARGELY UNATTENDED**

Kulcha are like doughier, softer paratha and are absolutely delicious. Combined with basmati rice, dal (page 433), and an Indian vegetable dish, like the cauliflower on page 451 or the eggplant on page 457, kulcha are a perfect centerpiece for a vegetarian meal. Chaat masala is a deliciously sour-tasting spice mix you can buy at Indian markets (it's possible to make it yourself, but almost no one does).

1 recipe Naan (page 563), prepared through step 3

Flour for rolling out the dough

1½ cups finely chopped red onion

¼ cup minced fresh cilantro leaves

2 teaspoons chaat masala (page 594), or to taste

½ teaspoon cayenne, or to taste

Pinch of salt

3 tablespoons butter, melted or clarified

1. Put a baking sheet (or, preferably, a baking stone) on a rack on the lowest shelf of your oven; preheat the oven to 500°F. Punch down the risen naan dough and, using as much flour as necessary to keep the dough from sticking to your hands, roll it into a snake, then tear the snake into 6 equal-sized balls. Let them rest for 10 minutes covered with plastic wrap or a damp towel.

2. While the dough is resting, chop the onion and cilantro for the filling. Combine them with the chaat masala, cayenne, and salt in a small bowl and set aside.

3. Lightly flour your work surface and your rolling pin. Flatten the balls of dough into 2-inch disks with your palm, then use the rolling pin to roll them into thick rounds, about 4 inches in diameter, dusting with flour as necessary.

4. Mound 2 heaping tablespoons of the filling into the center of one of the rounds of dough. Bring the edges of the round up over the top of the filling and press them together to make a pouch. Press down on the "neck" of the pouch with the palm of one hand to make a slightly rounded disk. Sprinkle the disk with flour on both sides and roll it out again into a round 4 to 6 inches in diameter. Put the kulcha on a plate and cover with a sheet of plastic wrap. Stuff the remaining kulcha and stack them on the plate with a sheet of plastic wrap between them.

5. Cook the rolled-out and stuffed kulcha on the pre-heated baking stone as in the naan recipe, flipping them once after 3 minutes. The kulcha are ready when they're mottled and browned around the edges, 6 to 8 minutes. You can cook as many kulcha as will comfortably fit on your baking stone at one time.

6. Wrap the freshly baked kulcha in a kitchen towel to keep them warm and pliable. Brush with melted butter on one side and serve.

Dosa Rice and Lentil Flour Crêpes INDIA

MAKES **16 TO 20 CRÊPES**

TIME **2 DAYS, LARGELY UNATTENDED**

Thin and crisp, the distinctively large and cylindrical dosa are the famous crispbreads of southern India. Made from a base of ground lentils and rice, they're delicious and, paired with a simple raita or chutney, the basis of a meal for many people.

I ate dosa with amazement throughout India, but I learned how to make them here, with help from Monica Bhide and Suvir Saran, both friends who have written wonderful books about Indian cooking.

Note that the difficult part of the dosa-making process—soaking and pureeing—can easily be by-passed if you have an industrial milling machine that can pulverize the lentils and rice into flour straight-away. And a couple of companies do just that, adding salt and fenugreek for flavor, add baking soda to give them a little puff, and sell the resulting mix through-out India and in the States. This mix makes dosa a convenience food you can fry up at the drop of a hat.

I think it's still worthwhile to give this recipe a try, but if the soaking and pureeing are going to keep you from trying dosa, by all means use the mix. Soak the lentil and rice flour in water as directed on the back of the package, and when the batter's ready, start with step 4. (You can use the mix for the uttapam on the next page as well.)

½ cup white urad dal (also sold as dhuli urad; available at
all Indian markets)

2 cups basmati rice

2 to 3 tablespoons corn, grapeseed, or other neutral oil,
as needed

Salt to taste

1. Soak the dal and rice in separate bowls in water to cover for 4 to 6 hours or overnight if you prefer.

2. Turn your oven to its lowest temperature. Drain the dal and put it in a blender with a tablespoon or two of water. Puree it to a smooth consistency, adding as little additional water as necessary, but enough to allow the machine to do its work. Transfer the puree to a large mixing bowl.

3. Drain the rice and add half of it to the blender (there's no need to clean between batches) with about ¼ cup water. Again, puree (it won't become as smooth as the dal), adding as little additional water as possible. Repeat with the remaining rice. Add the pureed rice to the dal and stir the two together; the resulting mixture should have the texture of a thick pancake batter. Cover the bowl with plastic wrap, turn the oven off, and let the batter ferment overnight in the warmed oven.

4. Preheat a large rectangular nonstick or cast-iron griddle over medium heat for a full minute before greasing it with a film of oil. Season the dosa batter with a large pinch of salt and stir to incorporate. Use a flat-bottomed measuring cup to pour ¼ cup of batter into the center of the pan, then use the bottom of the measuring cup to spread the dough across the pan into a large oval shape not much more than ⅛ inch thick; don't worry if the thickness is inconsistent. (It's the same motion a pizza maker would use—concentric circles with the bottom of the ladle—to spread tomato sauce thinly and evenly across pizza dough.)

5. Tiny bubbles will form across the surface of the dough, and the bottom will crisp and turn a deep golden brown in 3 to 5 minutes. Use a spatula to loosen the edges of the dosa, then roll it onto itself to make a cylinder and remove it from the griddle. Repeat with the remaining batter, greasing the griddle as necessary. Serve hot.

Uttapam INDIA ■
MAKES 6 TO 8 PANCAKES
TIME 30 MINUTES (WITH PREMADE DOSA BATTER)

If you're going to the trouble of making dosa—all the soaking, pureeing, and overnight resting—it's sensible to make the amount called for in the preceding recipe (plus it's not like 4 cups of rice and 1 cup of dal cost much more than half those amounts). But it's unlikely you'll have the griddle stamina or appetite to make it through all that batter. Hence, uttapam—a fancy version of dosa.

These are perfect for lunch—I usually fry a couple and eat them with whatever leftovers there are from the dosa meal the night before. And although it might be untraditional, I season them with a pinch of chaat masala (page 594), but feel free to omit it if it doesn't appeal or you don't have it on hand.

If you're using a pancake griddle, you should be able to cook two uttapam at a time; or you could have two nonstick griddles going at the same time.

¼ cup finely chopped red onion

¼ cup finely chopped fresh cilantro leaves

¼ cup finely chopped yellow or red bell pepper

1 teaspoon chaat masala, optional

Salt to taste

2 tablespoons corn, grapeseed, or other neutral oil,
or more as needed

½ recipe dosa batter (preceding recipe; leftover dough
keeps in the refrigerator for a couple days; let it come
to room temperature before cooking)

1. Stir together the red onion, cilantro, bell pepper, chaat masala if you're using it, and salt in a small bowl, taste, add more salt or chaat masala if necessary, and set aside.

2. Preheat a nonstick or cast-iron griddle over medium heat for a full minute before greasing it with a film of oil. Pour ¼ cup of the batter onto the griddle. Uttapam are usually 5- or 6-inch pancakes ¼ to ½ inch thick; if the batter is particularly thick or cold, you may need to spread it with the back of a spoon (or the measuring cup) to those dimensions.

3. After a minute or so, scatter the top of the pancake with a couple tablespoons of the onion-cilantro-pepper mix. When the bottom starts to color and crisp, 2 to 3 minutes later, flip the pancake and cook for another 4 to 5 minutes, until the second side is crisped and colored. Serve hot.

Lahmacun with Meat Turkish Meat "Pizza"
TURKEY ■ ▪

MAKES **6 TO 12 SERVINGS**

TIME **ABOUT 1 HOUR (WITH PREMADE DOUGH)**

Traditionally, these were made as small pies and rolled up after baking (the dough is not cooked crisp but left soft like a pita); you might make twelve or even more from this recipe. Now, to make them look more familiar to visitors from other parts of the world, lahmacun are often made as large pizzas, which you can do if you prefer.

> 1 recipe Pizza Dough (page 572)
> 2 tablespoons extra virgin olive oil, plus more as needed
> 1 large onion, roughly chopped
> 1 tablespoon minced garlic
> 1 pound ground lamb

> 1 teaspoon Aleppo pepper (available at Middle Eastern markets), hot paprika, or pure chile powder, like ancho or New Mexico, or to taste
> Salt and black pepper to taste
> ¼ cup pine nuts, optional
> 1 cup cored and chopped tomato, preferably fresh
> ¼ cup chopped fresh parsley leaves
> ¼ cup chopped fresh mint leaves
> 1 tablespoon fresh lemon juice
> Flour for rolling out the dough
> 2 tablespoons melted butter, optional

1. Divide the dough into as many balls as you would like; small ones are traditional, and this recipe will conveniently make 12. Cover the balls with plastic wrap and allow to rest. Preheat the oven to 450°F; put a baking stone in it if you have one, on a rack set low in the oven.

2. Put the olive oil in a large skillet over medium-high heat. A minute later, add the onion and cook, stirring occasionally, until it softens, about 5 minutes. Add the garlic and stir; add the lamb and cook, stirring to break up any clumps, until it loses its color, about 5 minutes. Add the Aleppo pepper, some salt and black pepper, and the pine nuts; stir. Add the tomato, bring to a boil, and cook, stirring occasionally, until the mixture is saucy, 5 to 10 minutes. Stir in the herbs and lemon juice, taste and adjust the seasoning, then turn off the heat. Cool for a few minutes.

3. If you have a peel and a baking stone, roll or pat out the dough on the peel, as thinly as you like, turning occasionally and sprinkling it with flour as necessary. If you are using baking sheets, oil them lightly, then press each dough ball into a flat round directly on the oiled sheets. Let the rounds sit for a few minutes; this will relax the dough and make it easier to roll out. Then roll or pat out the dough, as thin as you like, flouring or oiling your hands if

necessary. Roll out as many of the dough balls as will fit in your oven at a time.

4. Spoon a portion of the topping onto each of the pies, leaving a small border. Brush with melted butter if you wish and bake for about 10 minutes, until the crust just begins to brown. Serve hot or at room temperature, flat or rolled up.

Lahmacun with Egg. My favorite; you can omit the meat or not (just use a simple tomato sauce if you like) as you prefer: After topping the pies, carefully break an egg onto the top of each. Bake as directed.

Piadine Italian Flatbreads ITALY

MAKES **6 TO 8 SERVINGS**

TIME **1 HOUR**

I love aggressively seasoned vegetables (see Broccoli or Cauliflower with Garlic and Lemon, Two Ways, page 452, specifically the second way, with the optional anchovies and dried chile added), and piadine are one of the best ways of justifying a meal centered around them.

Piadine are griddle-cooked flatbreads from southern Italy that are sometimes folded and stuffed like calzones. But it's equally authentic, more convivial, and certainly easier to put a pile of piping hot piadine in the middle of the table surrounded by bowls of wilted kale and plates of grilled sausages or prosciutto. Have plenty of red wine on hand and let everybody help themselves.

¼ cup olive oil or, more traditionally, melted lard

¾ cup milk

½ teaspoon baking soda

4 cups flour, plus more for rolling out the dough

Large pinch of salt

1. Combine all the ingredients in a food processor and pulse on and off until they form a dough, adding a little more liquid if necessary. Turn the dough out onto a lightly floured counter and knead for 5 to 10 minutes, until smooth and resilient. You can put the dough in a bowl covered with plastic wrap and put it aside for 2 or 3 hours at this point or proceed with the recipe.

2. Preheat a cast-iron or nonstick skillet or griddle over medium heat. While the pan is heating, roll out the piadine: separate the dough into 6 or 8 roughly equal little balls, then roll them out as thin as possible and as wide as your pan will accommodate, using additional flour if necessary to keep the dough from sticking to the rolling pin or your work surface.

3. Cook the piadine in the dry pan, flipping them once or twice a minute, 3 to 5 minutes in total, until browned and spotted but not burned.

4. Cut the piadine into wedges, then put them on a baking rack to cool just for a minute or two—the wedges will steam and soften if you put them directly on a plate. Serve warm and repeat for the remaining dough (or finish the remaining dough and reheat the whole batch on the baking rack in a 200°F oven for a couple minutes).

Olive Oil Bread, with or without Olives GREECE, TURKEY ■ ▨

MAKES **2 ROUND LOAVES OR 1 HUGE ONE**

TIME **AT LEAST 3 HOURS, LARGELY UNATTENDED**

A better-keeping bread than the standard baguette or boule, largely because it contains olive oil, and an easy one to fancify, with the addition of olives and rosemary.

3 cups all-purpose or bread flour, plus more as needed

2 teaspoons instant active dry yeast, such as SAF

2 teaspoons coarse kosher or sea salt

1/3 cup extra virgin olive oil

1 tablespoon fresh rosemary leaves, optional

1 cup halved and pitted black olives, preferably oil-cured
   (but reasonably tender), optional

1. Combine the flour, yeast, and salt in a food processor. Turn the machine on and add the olive oil through the feed tube, followed by 1 cup water. Process for about 30 seconds, adding more water, a little at a time, until the mixture forms a ball and is slightly sticky to the touch. If dry, add another tablespoon or two of water and process for another 10 seconds. (In the unlikely event that the mixture is too sticky, add flour, a tablespoon at a time.)

2. Turn the dough onto a floured work surface and, by hand, knead in either the rosemary or the olives or both (or neither). Form a smooth, round dough ball, put this in a bowl, and cover with plastic wrap; let rise until the dough doubles in size, 1 to 2 hours. (You can cut this rising time short if you are in a hurry, or you can let the dough rise more slowly, in the refrigerator, for up to 6 or 8 hours.) Proceed to step 3 or wrap the dough tightly in plastic wrap and freeze for up to a month. (Defrost in a covered bowl in the refrigerator or at room temperature.)

3. When the dough is ready, form it into a ball and divide it into 2 pieces if you like or leave whole; roll each piece into a round ball. Place each ball on a lightly floured surface, sprinkle with a little flour, and cover with plastic wrap or a towel. Let rest until the dough puffs slightly, about 20 minutes.

4. Pinch the bottom of the ball(s) to seal the seam as best you can. Sprinkle all over with flour and let rise on a well-floured (or use cornmeal) peel or

baking sheet, covered, for at least an hour and preferably longer, up to 2 hours.

5. Preheat the oven to 425°F. Slash the top several times with a razor blade (you can make a pattern if you like). Put the baking sheet directly into the oven or slide the dough from the peel onto a pizza stone on a rack set low in the oven. Bake until the loaves are beginning to brown, 15 to 20 minutes, then lower the heat to 375°F. (If necessary, adjust the oven heat so the breads brown evenly.) Bake until the crust is golden brown and the internal temperature of the bread is at least 210°F, 40 to 60 minutes total. Remove and cool on a wire rack.

Olive Oil Bread with Onions and Mint. You can make this with olives, too, but omit the rosemary: In step 2, knead 1 large onion, minced, into the dough in place of or along with the olives. Add, if you like, 1 tablespoon chopped fresh mint leaves.

Semolina Bread. A standard in North Africa: Substitute 2 cups fine semolina flour for 2 cups of the white flour. Instead of forming the dough into loaves, roll or press it into large rounds (at least 10 inches in diameter), as you would pizza (page 572).

Pita MIDDLE EAST ■ ■
MAKES **6 TO 12 FLATBREADS, DEPENDING ON SIZE**
TIME **AT LEAST 2 HOURS, SOMEWHAT UNATTENDED**

Also called pide or pitta, the now-familiar flatbread of the Middle East—pocket and all—is easy to make at home. As with French or Italian Bread (page 570), you can speed up or slow down the time it takes to make these. It's best to equip your oven with a baking (pizza) stone, but they can also be baked successfully on cookie sheets. Even better is to use a heavy skillet.

3 cups all-purpose or bread flour, plus more as needed

3 tablespoons extra virgin olive oil

2 teaspoons instant active dry yeast, such as SAF

2 teaspoons coarse kosher or sea salt

$\frac{1}{2}$ teaspoon sugar

Melted butter, optional

1. Combine the flour, olive oil, yeast, salt, and sugar in a food processor. Turn the machine on and add 1 cup water through the feed tube.

2. Process for about 30 seconds, adding more water, a little at a time, until the mixture forms a ball and is slightly sticky to the touch. If dry, add another tablespoon or two of water and process for another 10 seconds. (In the unlikely event that the mixture is too sticky, add flour, a tablespoon at a time.)

3. You can simply cover the food processor bowl with plastic wrap (remove the blade first) or turn the dough onto a floured work surface and knead by hand for a few seconds to form a smooth, round dough ball. Put the dough in a bowl and cover with plastic wrap; let rise until the dough doubles in size, 1 to 2 hours. (You can cut this rising time short if you are in a hurry, or you can let the dough rise more slowly, in the refrigerator, for up to 6 or 8 hours.) Proceed to step 4 or wrap the dough tightly in plastic wrap and freeze for up to a month. (Defrost in a covered bowl in the refrigerator or at room temperature.)

4. When the dough is ready, form it into a ball and divide it into 6 or more pieces; roll each piece into a round ball. Place each ball on a lightly floured surface, sprinkle with a little flour, and cover with plastic wrap or a towel. Let rest until the balls puff slightly, about 20 minutes.

5. Roll each ball out to less than $\frac{1}{4}$-inch thickness, using flour to prevent sticking as necessary. As you work, spread the flat disks out on a floured surface

and keep them covered. When all the disks are rolled out, preheat the oven to 500°F (the disks should rest for at least 20 minutes after rolling). If you have a pizza stone, use it, on a rack set low in the oven; if you do not, lightly oil a baking sheet and put it in the oven on a rack set in the middle. Alternatively, lightly oil and wipe out a heavy skillet.

6. To bake on a stone, slide the individual disks—as many as will fit comfortably—directly into the oven, using a peel or a large spatula. Or bake 2 disks at a time on a cookie sheet. Or cook in the skillet over medium to medium-low heat, turning once, until lightly browned on both sides (this is a good method, but rather labor-intensive). Baking time will be between 5 and 10 minutes, generally only 5 or 6.

7. As the breads finish baking, remove them from the oven. If you're going to eat them fairly soon, brush with melted butter if you wish. Otherwise cool, then store in wax paper or plastic bags; reheat in a 300°F oven or a dry skillet before using.

Whole Wheat Pita. Substitute whole wheat flour for half the all-purpose flour.

Cheese-Filled Pita MIDDLE EAST ■ ■ ▨

MAKES **6 SERVINGS**

TIME **20 MINUTES (WITH PREMADE DOUGH)**

A quick street snack found in Greece, Turkey, Lebanon, and other parts of the Middle East. Great hot or at room temperature.

2 cups crumbled feta or blue cheese

4 tablespoons ($\frac{1}{2}$ stick) butter, at room temperature

4 eggs

CHEESE-FILLED PITA

1 cup snipped fresh dill

Black pepper to taste

1 recipe Pita (page 568), prepared through step 5

Lightly toasted sesame seeds (page 596), optional

1. Combine the feta, butter, eggs, and most of the dill in a bowl, along with a good sprinkling of black pepper; stir to combine. Put a portion of this filling on each of the prepared pita disks and bring the sides up to seal; do not enclose entirely (the traditional filled pita is longer than it is wide, kind of boat shaped; you can make any shape you want).

2. Bake as for pita, but for a little bit longer, perhaps 10 minutes. Sprinkle with the remaining dill and a few sesame seeds if desired and eat hot or at room temperature.

Meat-Filled Pita. Essentially rolled lahmacun; use the meat filling for Lahmacun (page 566), but proceed as directed for filling and baking pita.

French or Italian Bread ■ ▪

MAKES **4 SMALL BAGUETTES, 3 LARGER BAGUETTES, 2 ROUND LOAVES, OR 1 HUGE ROUND LOAF**

TIME **AT LEAST 3 HOURS, LARGELY UNATTENDED**

The basic European bread, which requires more patience than work. It's eminently flexible, because at any time you can refrigerate the dough and retard the process for hours, even overnight. Many people, in fact, believe that the slower you go with bread, the better. So it's not only acceptable but preferable to make the dough at night, leave it in a cool place to rise for 8 or 10 hours, then proceed with the recipe, taking all day—if you like—to finish it. So, this recipe is written as if you will proceed from start to finish, but you don't have to do so.

3 cups all-purpose or bread flour, plus more as needed

2 teaspoons instant active dry yeast, such as SAF

2 teaspoons coarse kosher or sea salt

1. Combine the flour, yeast, and salt in a food processor. Turn the machine on and add 1 cup water through the feed tube.

2. Process for about 30 seconds, adding more water, a little at a time, until the mixture forms a ball and is slightly sticky to the touch. If dry, add another tablespoon or two of water and process for another 10 seconds. (In the unlikely event that the mixture is too sticky, add flour, a tablespoon at a time.)

3. You can simply cover the food processor bowl with plastic wrap (remove the blade first) or turn the dough onto a floured work surface and knead by hand for a few seconds to form a smooth, round dough ball. Put the dough in a bowl and cover with plastic wrap; let rise until the dough doubles in size, 1 to 2 hours. (You can cut this rising time short if you are in a hurry, or you can let the

dough rise more slowly, in the refrigerator, for up to 6 or 8 hours.) Proceed to step 4 or wrap the dough tightly in plastic wrap and freeze for up to a month. (Defrost in a covered bowl in the refrigerator or at room temperature.)

4. When the dough is ready, form it into a ball and divide it into 2 or more pieces if you like; roll each piece into a round ball. Place each ball on a lightly floured surface, sprinkle with a little flour, and cover with plastic wrap or a towel. Let rest until the balls puff slightly, about 20 minutes.

5. To make baguettes, pat each piece into a rectangle, then fold it over onto itself, the long way, twice; seal the resulting seam and, using your hands, roll the dough into a long snake; use only as much flour as you need to keep the dough from sticking. Spread a large, heavy piece of canvas or cotton (you can use a large tablecloth, folded into quarters to give it extra stiffness) on a table or countertop and sprinkle it very lightly with flour. Or use baguette pans, sifting a little bit of flour into them. Place the loaf, seam side up, in a fold of the cloth (this is called a couche, or bed), or seam side down in the baguette pan. When all the loaves are formed, cover with a cloth and let rise for about 1 hour at room temperature. To make boules, shape the loaf or loaves into a round ball, pinching the bottom to seal the seam as well as you can. Sprinkle all over with flour and let rise on a well-floured (or use cornmeal) board or baking sheet, covered, for at least an hour and preferably longer, up to 2 hours.

6. Preheat the oven to 450°F. For the baguettes, sprinkle each loaf very lightly with flour and slash the top several times with a razor blade. If the dough has risen on a cloth, slide it onto floured baking sheets or gently move it onto a peel (or just a piece of wood), then slide the bread directly onto a baking stone set on a rack low in the oven. If the dough has risen in baguette pans, place them in the oven, with the rack set in the middle. For the boules, slash the top several times with a razor blade (you can make a pattern if you like). Put the baking sheet directly into the oven or slide the dough onto a pizza stone.

7. Bake until the loaves are beginning to brown, 15 to 20 minutes, then lower the heat to 375°F. (If necessary, adjust the oven heat so the breads brown evenly.) Bake until the crust is golden brown and the internal temperature of the bread is at least 210°F, 30 to 40 minutes for baguettes, 40 to 60 for boules (or longer if the boule is very large). Remove and cool on a wire rack.

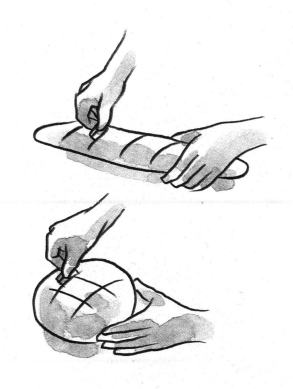

SLASHING BREAD

Bruschetta ITALY ■

MAKES **4 SERVINGS**

TIME **ABOUT 20 MINUTES**

Bruschetta is toast. Usually with olive oil. Often grilled. But no more than that—or not much more. You need coarse, crusty bread; the preceding recipe will give you the kind you want, but any peasant bread will do.

The amount of garlic you use is up to you. You might split a single clove and rub it on the slices of bread after they're toasted; or you might mash a few cloves and smear them on, which is obviously stronger.

> 8 thick slices coarse bread
>
> 1 to 4 garlic cloves, halved or peeled and crushed, to taste
>
> Extra virgin olive oil as needed
>
> Salt and black pepper to taste

1. Preheat the broiler or start a charcoal or wood fire. Broil or grill the bread until lightly browned on both sides. This may take less than a minute on a side; watch carefully so the bread doesn't burn.
2. While it's still hot, rub the bread with the garlic on one or both sides. Put it on a plate, then drizzle it with olive oil and sprinkle it with salt and pepper. Serve warm.

Pizza Dough ITALY ■

MAKES **1 LARGE OR 2 OR MORE SMALLER PIZZAS**

TIME **AT LEAST 1 HOUR**

In southern Italy, where the flatbread called pizza originated, it was traditionally kept very, very simple, topped with as little as salt, olive oil, and rosemary or a few tomato slices and a bit of fresh mozzarella. Now, of course, you see American-style pizzas on the streets of Rome.

The recipes here, then, are a bit of a throwback—very simple and very real. Even simpler if you use a food processor; you can knead the dough by hand, of course, if that's your preference, but the machine is far easier and more efficient and, in fact, does a better job, at least for most of us.

Be sure to see the recipes for Pissaladière (page 45) and Tarte Flambé (page 44), both of which are based on this dough.

> 3 cups all-purpose or bread flour, plus more as needed
>
> 2 teaspoons instant active dry yeast, such as SAF
>
> 2 teaspoons coarse kosher or sea salt, plus extra for sprinkling
>
> 2 tablespoons extra virgin olive oil

1. Combine the flour, yeast, and salt in a food processor. Turn the machine on and add 1 cup water and the oil through the feed tube.
2. Process for about 30 seconds, adding more water, a little at a time, until the mixture forms a ball and is slightly sticky to the touch. If dry, add another tablespoon or two of water and process for another 10 seconds. (In the unlikely event that the mixture is too sticky, add flour, a tablespoon at a time.)
3. Turn the dough onto a floured work surface and knead by hand for a few seconds to form a smooth, round dough ball. Put the dough in a bowl and cover with plastic wrap; let rise until the dough doubles in size, 1 to 2 hours. (You can cut this rising time short if you are in a hurry, or you can let the dough rise more slowly, in the refrigerator, for up to 6 or 8 hours.) Proceed to step 4 or wrap the dough tightly in plastic wrap and freeze for up to a month. (Defrost in a covered bowl in the refrigerator or at room temperature.)

PIZZA DOUGH

4. When the dough is ready, form it into a ball and divide it into 2 or more pieces if you like; roll each piece into a round ball. Place each ball on a lightly floured surface, sprinkle with a little flour, and cover with plastic wrap or a towel. Let rest until the balls puff slightly, about 20 minutes. Proceed as the individual pizza recipes direct.

Pizza Bianca White Pizza ITALY ■ ▨

MAKES **1 LARGE OR 2 OR MORE SMALL PIZZAS**

TIME **ABOUT 3 HOURS, LARGELY UNATTENDED, PLUS TIME TO PREHEAT THE GRILL**

In many southern Italian homes, this is daily bread, the closest thing to the prototypical pizza. I vividly re-member the first time I tasted it (in Rome)—it blew my mind. Please try it. Not only is it delicious, but it's the launching pad for making any other pizza you like (see the variations for a couple of ideas).

For this to be most successful, your oven should be equipped with a pizza stone, and you should make the dough directly on a peel. However, it's almost as good on a baking sheet, and I give directions for both.

1 recipe Pizza Dough (preceding recipe)

Flour for rolling out the dough

Extra virgin olive oil as needed

Coarse kosher or sea salt to taste

1 tablespoon or more roughly chopped fresh rosemary leaves

Several fresh rosemary sprigs, optional

1. When the dough is ready, knead it lightly, form it into a ball, and divide it into 2 balls if you like; roll each piece into a round ball and place each ball on a lightly floured surface. Sprinkle with a little more flour, cover with plastic wrap or a towel, and let rest while you preheat the oven.

2. Preheat the oven to 500°F or higher. Roll or lightly press each dough ball into a flat round, lightly flouring the work surface and the dough as neces-sary (do not use more flour than you need to). Let the rounds sit for a few minutes; this will relax the dough and make it easier to roll out. If you have a peel and baking stone, roll or pat out the dough on the peel, as thin as you like, turning occasion-ally and sprinkling it with flour as necessary. If you are using baking sheets, oil them, then press each dough ball into a flat round directly on the oiled sheets. Then roll or pat out the dough, as thin as you like, flouring or oiling your hands if necessary.

3. Top with salt and sprinkle with the rosemary—decorate with the sprigs if you like—then drizzle

with a little more olive oil, and slide the baking sheet into the oven on a rack set in the middle (or the pizza itself onto the stone, which should be set on a lower rack). Bake for 6 to 12 minutes, depending on the oven heat, until nicely browned. Serve immediately or at room temperature (these will keep for a few hours).

Margherita Pizza. Top the pies with sliced fresh tomato, extra virgin olive oil, a little mozzarella, preferably fresh, some fresh basil leaves, salt, and Parmesan cheese.

Marinara Pizza. Top the pies with sliced fresh tomatoes, thinly sliced garlic (or Fast, Fresh Tomato Sauce, page 606), extra virgin olive oil, and, if you like, a few anchovy fillets.

Sfincione Onion Pizza SICILY
MAKES **2 LARGE SHEETS**
TIME **ABOUT 2 HOURS**

What's different about this pizza is the inclusion of semolina flour in the crust and bread crumbs on the top, which makes the pie slightly crunchy. Nevertheless, the large quantity of onions (consider using a food processor to slice them) produces a distinctively sweet pizza. This is a large recipe; you can halve it or make it for a party.

2^1/2 cups all-purpose flour, plus more as needed

1^1/2 cups semolina flour

1 teaspoon salt

2 teaspoons instant active dry yeast, such as SAF

1 egg

^{1}/2 cup extra virgin olive oil, plus more for the pan

4 large onions, thinly sliced

3 or 4 ounces oil-packed anchovy fillets, drained and coarsely chopped, or salt-packed anchovies, rinsed, heads and bones removed

One 6-ounce can tomato paste

2 teaspoons black pepper

1 cup unseasoned dry bread crumbs

1. Combine the flours, salt, yeast, and egg in a food processor. Turn the machine on and add 1^1/4 cups water and 3 tablespoons of the oil through the feed tube. Process for about 30 seconds, adding more water, a tablespoon at a time, until the mixture forms a ball and is slightly sticky to the touch. If dry, add another tablespoon or two of water and process for another 10 seconds. (In the unlikely event that the mixture is too sticky, add flour, a tablespoon at a time.)

2. Turn the dough onto a floured work surface and knead by hand for a few seconds to form a smooth, round dough ball. Put the dough in a bowl and cover with plastic wrap; let rise until the dough doubles in size, 1 to 2 hours. (You can cut this rising time short if you are in a hurry, or you can let the dough rise more slowly, in the refrigerator, for up to 6 or 8 hours.) Proceed to step 4 or wrap the dough tightly in plastic wrap and freeze for up to a month. (Defrost in a covered bowl in the refrigerator or at room temperature.)

3. Heat the remaining oil in a deep, 12-inch skillet over medium heat for 1 minute. Add the onions and cook, stirring and turning occasionally, for 15 to 20 minutes, until they are soft but not caramelized. Add the anchovies, stir to combine, and cook for several minutes; add the tomato paste and pepper. Cook for another 5 minutes over low heat, stirring occasionally; remove and set aside.

4. Preheat the oven to 450°F; set a rack or racks in the center of the oven. Brush 2 large rectangular pizza pans or cookie sheets that have ^{1}/2-inch rims with

olive oil. Punch down and divide the dough into 2 pieces; roll it out on a board dusted with flour, until each is the size and shape of the pan in which it will bake. Lay out the dough in the pans and sprinkle with the bread crumbs. Bake for 10 to 12 minutes, until the bottom begins to turn pale golden.

5. Cover each crust with half of the onion mixture, leaving a $\frac{1}{2}$-inch border. Place in the oven and bake for 15 to 20 minutes, until the bottom is dark golden but not burned and the top is a richly colored caramel. Remove and cool for a few minutes before cutting.

Arepas SOUTH AMERICA

MAKES **4 SERVINGS**

TIME **40 MINUTES**

These fresh cornmeal cakes are wonderful for breakfast or as a side dish. They can be served simply with butter or topped with scrambled eggs with tomatoes and onions.

> 1 cup yellow cornmeal
>
> $\frac{1}{2}$ teaspoon salt
>
> $\frac{1}{2}$ cup grated mild Cheddar, Monterey Jack, or mozzarella cheese
>
> 1 cup milk
>
> 2 tablespoons butter, plus more for serving
>
> $\frac{1}{2}$ cup fresh or thawed frozen corn kernels
>
> 3 tablespoons corn, grapeseed, or other neutral oil

1. Put the cornmeal in a food processor or blender and grind until fine. Transfer to a large bowl and mix with the salt and cheese.
2. Heat the milk in a small saucepan over medium heat until it comes to a steady simmer. Add the butter and stir until melted. Remove from the heat

and stir into the cornmeal mixture to form a thick batter. Fold in the corn kernels.

3. Let the batter rest until it thickens into a soft dough, about 15 minutes. Form 1-inch balls from the mixture and flatten with your palm to $\frac{1}{4}$-inch-thick disks.
4. Heat the oil in a large skillet and cook the arepas, working in batches, until golden brown, about 5 minutes, then flip and cook for 3 minutes on the other side. Serve hot with butter.

Grissini ITALY ■ ▪

MAKES **ABOUT 100 BREADSTICKS**

TIME **ABOUT 1 DAY, LARGELY UNATTENDED**

In Piedmont, the home of grissini, these best-of-all breadsticks are scattered on restaurant tables, unpackaged, waiting for someone to sit down and start the inevitable and irresistible munching. They're usually quite thin, irregular in shape, and very crisp, with a faint sweetness.

You can make these stirato, or straight, by following the directions here. Or make them rubata—hand-rolled and irregular—by just rolling the strips of dough after you've cut them to make them even thinner.

Sprinkle these with toasted sesame seeds, poppy seeds, freshly grated Parmesan cheese, or sea salt before baking if you like, though it's rarely done in their homeland.

> 2 teaspoons instant active dry yeast, like SAF
>
> 1 teaspoon sugar
>
> 3 cups all-purpose flour
>
> 2 teaspoons salt
>
> 1 tablespoon extra virgin olive oil, plus more as needed
>
> 1 tablespoon lard or 2 tablespoons more olive oil
>
> $\frac{1}{2}$ cup semolina flour or cornmeal

1. Combine the yeast, sugar, all-purpose flour, and salt in a food processor; pulse once or twice. Add the oil and lard if you're using it and, again, pulse a couple of times. With the machine running, add 1 cup warm water through the feed tube. Continue to add water, a tablespoon at a time, until the mixture forms a ball. It should be a little shaggy and quite sticky.

2. Put a little oil in a bowl and transfer the dough ball to it, turning to coat well. Cover with plastic wrap and let it rise in a warm place for 1 hour. Reshape the ball, put it back in the bowl, cover again, and let rise in the refrigerator for several hours or, preferably, overnight.

3. Preheat the oven to 400°F. Lightly grease 2 baking sheets with olive oil and sprinkle very lightly with semolina flour.

4. Cut the dough into 3 pieces. On a well-floured surface, roll the first out as thin as possible into a large rectangle, about a foot long. Use a sharp knife to cut the dough into roughly $\frac{1}{4}$-inch-thick strips (slightly smaller is better than slightly bigger). You can also use a pasta machine: Roll out the dough to $\frac{1}{4}$-inch thickness by hand. Put it through the machine at the largest setting, then cut it using the fettuccine setting and cut the strips into 1-foot lengths.

5. Transfer the strips to the baking sheets, about $\frac{1}{2}$ inch apart, and brush with olive oil. Bake until crisp and golden, 10 to 20 minutes, then cool completely on wire racks. Serve immediately or store in an airtight container for up to 1 week.

Fresh Herb Grissini. Add 2 tablespoons chopped fresh rosemary, thyme, sage, or a combination to the dough mixture along with the olive oil.

Caraway Breadsticks EASTERN EUROPE ■ ■
MAKES **SEVERAL DOZEN**
TIME **ABOUT 2 HOURS, LARGELY UNATTENDED**

This Eastern European version of the breadstick is somewhat lighter and tastier than the common kind and equally crisp; the caraway flavor makes it more unusual. Like other breadsticks, these can be stored in an airtight container for a few days.

1 tablespoon sugar

1 teaspoon instant active dry yeast, like SAF

1$\frac{1}{2}$ cups flour, plus more for kneading

$\frac{1}{2}$ teaspoon salt

8 tablespoons (1 stick) cold butter, cut into chunks

$\frac{1}{2}$ cup milk, or as needed

1 small egg, lightly beaten

2 tablespoons caraway seeds, plus more as needed

2 tablespoons coarse sea salt, plus more as needed

1. Combine the sugar, yeast, flour, and salt in a food processor; pulse once or twice. Add the butter and process until the butter is combined. With the machine running, add half the milk through the feed tube. Continue to add milk, a tablespoon at a time, until the mixture forms a ball.

2. Turn the dough onto a floured work surface and knead, adding a little flour as necessary, until the dough is smooth and no longer sticky, about 10 minutes. Let it rest for about 20 minutes.

3. Cut the dough in half and roll out each piece into a long rectangle 5 inches wide and $\frac{1}{2}$ inch thick. Cut lengthwise into $\frac{1}{2}$-inch strips and lay them on a nonstick or lightly greased baking sheet, spaced at least $\frac{1}{2}$ inch apart. Brush with the beaten egg and then sprinkle on the caraway seeds and coarse salt. Cover the breadsticks with a towel and let rise for 30 to 60 minutes. Meanwhile, preheat the oven to 400°F. Bake the breadsticks until golden brown,

about 8 minutes. Serve warm or at room temperature.

Rich Bread PORTUGAL ■ ▦

MAKES **2 ROUND LOAVES OR 1 HUGE ONE**

TIME **AT LEAST 3 HOURS, LARGELY UNATTENDED**

This is not unlike the classic American "white" bread—not the stuff sold in supermarkets today but the rich, milk-laden, soft (but not mushy) loaves of much of the nineteenth and twentieth centuries. It is no more difficult to make than French or Italian bread, but it keeps much better and is better for sandwiches. (Though it isn't done in Portugal, you could even bake this in loaf pans.)

If you have some saffron, add a pinch to the flour at the beginning for a lovely color and mysterious flavor.

3 cups all-purpose or bread flour, plus more as needed

2 teaspoons instant active dry yeast, such as SAF

2 teaspoons coarse kosher or sea salt

1 tablespoon sugar

2 tablespoons cold butter

2 eggs

About 1 cup milk

Softened butter as needed

Melted butter as needed

1. Combine the flour, yeast, salt, sugar, and butter in a food processor. Pulse the machine on and off until the butter is cut throughout the flour. Add the eggs and pulse a few more times. With the machine running, slowly add ¾ cup of the milk through the feed tube.

2. Process for about 30 seconds, adding more milk if necessary, a little at a time, until the mixture forms a ball and is slightly sticky to the touch. If dry, add another tablespoon or two of milk and process for another 10 seconds. (In the unlikely event that the mixture is too sticky, add flour, a tablespoon at a time.)

3. Turn the dough onto a floured work surface and knead, adding a little flour as necessary, until the dough is smooth and no longer sticky, about 10 minutes. Form a smooth, round dough ball, put it in a bowl, and cover with plastic wrap; let rise until the dough doubles in size, 1 to 2 hours. (You can cut this rising time short if you are in a hurry, or you can let the dough rise more slowly, in the refrigerator, for up to 6 or 8 hours.) Proceed to step 4 or wrap the dough tightly in plastic wrap and freeze for up to a month. (Defrost in a covered bowl in the refrigerator or at room temperature.)

4. When the dough is ready, form it into a ball and divide it into 2 pieces if you like or leave whole; roll each piece into a round ball. Place each ball on a lightly floured surface, sprinkle with a little flour, and cover with plastic wrap or a towel. Let rest until the dough puffs slightly, about 20 minutes.

5. Pinch the bottom of the ball(s) to seal the seam as well as you can. Butter 1 or 2 casseroles or loaf pans that will comfortably hold the loaves; they should not (yet) quite fill the pans. Cover and let rise for an hour and preferably longer, up to 2 hours.

6. Preheat the oven to 350°F and set a rack in the middle. Brush the top of the loaf or loaves with melted butter, then put the casserole(s) in the oven. Bake for about 40 minutes, until the crust is golden brown and the internal temperature of the bread is at least 210°F. Remove the breads from the casseroles and cool on a wire rack; cut with a serrated knife—the bread will be rich and delicate.

Saffransbrod Sweet Rolls with Saffron

SCANDINAVIA ■ ■

MAKES **ABOUT 18 BUNS**

TIME **AT LEAST 3 HOURS, LARGELY UNATTENDED**

Scandinavia has more food celebrations than any place I've ever been, with a special food for every occasion. On St. Lucia Day—twelve days before Christmas—it's almost imperative to eat a couple of these delicious buns, but most people would happily wolf them down any other day of the year as well. Great for breakfast or as a midmorning or afternoon snack.

> 3 cups all-purpose or bread flour, plus more as needed
>
> 2 teaspoons instant active dry yeast, like SAF
>
> $1/2$ teaspoon salt
>
> Large pinch of saffron threads
>
> $3/4$ cup sugar, plus more for sprinkling
>
> 2 eggs
>
> About 1 cup milk
>
> Butter or oil as needed
>
> $1/2$ cup golden or dark raisins, optional
>
> $1/4$ cup blanched almonds, chopped

1. Combine the flour, yeast, salt, saffron, and sugar in a food processor. Pulse the machine on and off a couple of times; add 1 egg and pulse a few more times. With the machine running, slowly add $3/4$ cup of the milk through the feed tube.

2. Process for about 30 seconds, adding more milk if necessary, a little at a time, until the mixture forms a ball and is sticky to the touch. Knead the raisins if you're using them into the dough by hand (use a little flour if the dough is too sticky to handle, but no more than is necessary). Put the dough in a bowl and cover with plastic wrap; let rise until the dough nearly doubles in bulk, 1 to 2 hours.

3. When the dough is ready, divide it into 18 pieces; use lightly buttered or oiled hands to roll each piece into a round ball, pinching the seam closed as well as you can. Place the balls on a buttered baking sheet or in buttered muffin tins. Cover with plastic wrap or a towel while you preheat the oven to 400°F, with the rack set in the middle.

4. Beat the other egg and lightly brush the tops of the rolls with it; sprinkle each with sugar and a tiny bit of the chopped almonds. Bake for 10 to 15 minutes, until the top is glossy and nicely browned. Cover with a towel and let cool to room temperature. Serve within a day.

Semla Sweet Almond Buns SCANDINAVIA ■ ■

MAKES **15 TO 20 BUNS**

TIME **AT LEAST 3 HOURS, LARGELY UNATTENDED**

I thought Lent was a time of self-denial, but in Sweden it's when these absolutely delicious buns appear, filled with almond paste and whipped cream. They certainly could be served as dessert, but in Sweden people eat them as a midmorning or midafternoon snack.

> 3 cups all-purpose or bread flour, plus more as needed
>
> $1/2$ cup almonds
>
> 1 teaspoon ground cardamom
>
> 1 teaspoon ground cinnamon
>
> 2 teaspoons instant active dry yeast, like SAF
>
> Pinch of salt
>
> $1/2$ cup granulated sugar
>
> 4 tablespoons ($1/2$ stick) cold butter
>
> 4 eggs
>
> About 1 cup milk
>
> Butter or oil as needed
>
> 1 cup confectioners' sugar, more or less
>
> 1 cup heavy cream

1. Combine the flour and half the almonds in a food processor. Process until the almonds are finely

ground, then add the spices, yeast, salt, granulated sugar, and butter. Pulse the machine on and off until the butter is cut throughout the flour. Add 2 eggs and pulse a few more times. With the machine running, slowly add $1/2$ cup of the milk through the feed tube.

2. Process for about 30 seconds, adding more milk if necessary, a little at a time, until the mixture forms a ball and is quite sticky to the touch, almost too sticky to handle. Put the dough in a bowl and cover with plastic wrap; let rise until nearly doubled in bulk, 2 to 3 hours. Proceed to step 3 or wrap some or all of the dough tightly in plastic wrap and freeze for up to a month. (Defrost in a covered bowl in the refrigerator or at room temperature.)

3. Divide the dough into 15 to 20 pieces; use lightly buttered or oiled hands to roll each piece into a round ball, pinching the seam closed as well as you can. Place the balls on a buttered baking sheet or in buttered muffin tins. Cover with plastic wrap or a towel while you preheat the oven to 350°F; set the rack in the middle of the oven.

4. Separate the remaining eggs; beat the yolks and use them to brush the tops of the buns. Bake the buns for 15 to 20 minutes, until the crust is golden brown and glossy. Let cool while you prepare the filling.

5. Grind the remaining almonds in a food processor or spice or coffee grinder until as fine as possible. With an electric mixer, beat the 2 egg whites until they hold stiff peaks, then combine, by hand, with $3/4$ cup of the confectioners' sugar, the ground almonds, and 2 tablespoons of the cream. When the buns have cooled a bit, cut off the top of each one and put a bit of the almond mixture inside. In a clean bowl, using the mixer, whip the remaining cream with another tablespoon of the confectioner's sugar and put a spoonful into each of the buns; replace the tops. Sift some confectioners' sugar over all the buns and serve within a few hours.

Sweet Breakfast Buns SPAIN ■ ■
MAKES **15 TO 20 SMALL ROLLS**
TIME **AT LEAST 3 HOURS, LARGELY UNATTENDED**

Even more than the Italians, the Spanish eat sweet breads for breakfast. I like these in midafternoon— they are great with tea—but suit yourself.

These rich rolls don't keep especially well, so if twenty-four is too many for you, divide the recipe in half or freeze half the dough before baking; it will keep well for up to a month.

> 3 cups all-purpose or bread flour, plus more as needed
>
> 2 teaspoons instant active dry yeast, such as SAF
>
> 2 teaspoons coarse kosher or sea salt
>
> $3/4$ cup sugar, plus more for sprinkling
>
> 4 tablespoons ($1/2$ stick) cold butter
>
> 3 eggs
>
> About $3/4$ cup milk
>
> Softened butter as needed
>
> Melted butter as needed

1. Combine the flour, yeast, salt, sugar, and butter in a food processor. Pulse the machine on and off until the butter is cut throughout the flour. Add the eggs and pulse a few more times. With the machine running, slowly add $1/2$ cup of the milk through the feed tube.

2. Process for about 30 seconds, adding more milk if necessary, a little at a time, until the mixture forms a ball and is quite sticky to the touch, almost too sticky to handle. Put the dough in a bowl and cover with plastic wrap; let rise until nearly doubled in bulk, 2 to 3 hours. Proceed to step 3 or wrap some or all of the dough tightly in plastic wrap and freeze for up to a month. (Defrost in a covered bowl in the refrigerator or at room temperature.)

3. When the dough is ready, divide it into 15 to 20 pieces; use lightly buttered or oiled hands to roll

each piece into a round ball, pinching the seam closed as well as you can. Place the balls on a buttered baking sheet or muffin tins. Cover with plastic wrap or a towel while you preheat the oven to 350°F; set a rack in the middle of the oven.

4. Brush the tops of the rolls with melted butter, then sprinkle with sugar and put in the oven. Bake for 15 to 20 minutes, until the crust is golden brown and glossy. Serve hot, warm, or at room temperature, within a day.

Fresh Bread Crumbs ■ ■ ■

MAKES **ABOUT 2 CUPS**

TIME **10 MINUTES**

Fresh bread crumbs are superior to packaged ones in many ways. First of all, you can start with good bread. Second, you can keep them coarse, and coarse bread crumbs are almost always preferable to fine. Finally, you can season and toast them as you like.

About 1/2 loaf French or Italian bread, preferably a day or 2 old

1. Tear the bread into pieces, then grind in a food processor until coarsely chopped; you may have to do this in batches. Use immediately or store in a plastic bag.

2. To toast, put the bread crumbs on a baking sheet and place in a 350°F oven, shaking the pan occasionally, until lightly browned, about 15 minutes; these may be stored as fresh (though it makes more sense to store untoasted bread crumbs and toast just before using). Or heat 1/4 cup extra virgin olive oil in a skillet and add the bread crumbs; cook, stirring occasionally, until lightly browned, about 5 minutes. Season with salt and drain on paper towels; use immediately.

Croutons FRANCE AND ELSEWHERE ■ ■ ■

MAKES **ABOUT 2 CUPS**

TIME **20 MINUTES**

Packaged croutons may lead the way in useless foods sold at the supermarket. For the price of a box of croutons you can buy a loaf of good bread, let it get stale, and make the equivalent of five boxes of terrific croutons, without chemistry-class additives—just olive oil and salt.

Croutons, of course, are one of the many ways to use up leftover day-old bread (bread pudding, bread crumbs, and bread salad are some others), and to make really good ones you need the kind of bread that will actually get stale, not bagged, sliced sandwich loaves that just start growing mold once they're past their prime. Really, any French- or Italian-style loaf will do, though the better the bread, the better the crouton.

This is a recipe for the most basic of croutons—you could rub the torn bread with a peeled garlic clove or scatter some chopped fresh rosemary over it before it goes in the oven—but this is the place to start. Many people remove the crust from bread before making croutons; I do not.

1/2 pound good-quality bread, preferably a day or 2 old, crusts removed if you like
1/3 cup extra virgin olive oil
Salt to taste

1. Preheat the oven to 400°F. Tear or cut the bread into roughly 1-inch pieces; don't worry about making them uniform. Toss with the olive oil and place on a baking sheet.

2. Bake for about 15 minutes, until crisp and lightly colored on the outside but still tender inside. Season with salt and cool; you can make these up to a day in advance if you like.

Neater, Stovetop Croutons. These are great at the bottom of a bowl of soup; throw in some minced garlic if you like: Take 10 or so 1-inch-thick slices of baguette or other long loaf and brown lightly in enough olive oil to coat the bottom of your skillet, adding more olive oil if necessary (start with $\frac{1}{4}$ cup). Use medium-low heat and try to brown evenly and fairly slowly (it's an easy process, so your only real job is to avoid burning). Sprinkle with salt or set aside (uncovered) for up to a day before using.

Sauces and Condiments When I first learned to cook, sauces were the most intimidating aspect of cuisine. This was largely because the only sauces anyone talked about—with the exception of "spaghetti sauce"—were French. And, from a global perspective, classic French cuisine features a very unusual method of preparing sauces, often starting with stocks or even much-reduced stocks and combining flavors slowly, to build a complex, often remarkable mixture in which most of the components become unrecognizable.

Most of the rest of the world treats sauces much differently, quickly combining strong-tasting ingredients—often uncooked—to build salsas, relishes, flavored oils, pastes, and dipping sauces. Once your pantry is stocked, most of these are easily made and keep for a while (another contrast to the French model).

In truth, these have been my favorite discoveries in the course of my travels, because if you learn how to make the simplest, most basic versions of ordinary food—steamed vegetables, grilled meats, cooked grains and pasta, roasted poultry, broiled fish, and so on—these sauces can transform them into interesting, wonderful, even spectacular dishes, without much work.

Chile Oil with Szechwan Peppercorns CHINA ■ ■ ▨

MAKES **ABOUT ¹/₂ CUP**

TIME **20 MINUTES**

This is a condiment. Set it on the table and use it whenever the mood strikes. I've put it on everything from scrambled eggs to tuna salad, but I like it best on plain steamed vegetables.

> ¹/₂ cup peanut or neutral oil, like corn or grapeseed
>
> ¹/₄ cup Szechwan peppercorns (page 369)
>
> 6 small dried red chiles, or to taste
>
> 1 teaspoon salt

1. Combine all the ingredients in a very small saucepan and heat until bubbling. Adjust the heat so the mixture bubbles steadily and cook for about 5 minutes.
2. Let cool and pour into a bowl or jar; you can strain if you like, but it isn't necessary. Keep for a few days at room temperature, longer if you refrigerate.

Szechwan Salt-and-Pepper CHINA ■ ■ ▨

MAKES **2 TABLESPOONS**

TIME **10 MINUTES**

A sprinkling of this mixture works wonders on stir-fries, even steamed vegetables. It takes no time to make and can simply be set on your table and used as the whim strikes you.

> 1 tablespoon Szechwan peppercorns (page 369)
>
> 1 tablespoon coarse salt

1. Toast the peppercorns in a dry skillet over medium heat, shaking the pan occasionally, until they are fragrant, about 2 minutes.

2. Mix with the salt and grind in a coffee or spice grinder.

Ginger-Scallion Dipping Sauce

CHINA ■ ■ ▨

MAKES ¹/₄ CUP

TIME **10 MINUTES**

A popular accompaniment for White Cut Chicken (page 273), this is also good stirred into soups.

> One 1-inch piece fresh ginger, peeled and minced
>
> 2 scallions, trimmed and chopped
>
> 1 teaspoon salt, or more to taste
>
> ¹/₄ cup peanut or neutral oil, like corn or grapeseed

1. Mix the ginger, scallions, and salt together thoroughly in a heatproof bowl.
2. Place the oil in a small saucepan or skillet over high heat until smoking. Carefully pour the oil over the ginger-scallion mixture, mix well, and serve, or store, refrigerated, for up to 3 days (bring back to room temperature before serving).

Soy Dipping Sauce ASIA ■ ■ ▨

MAKES **ABOUT ¹/₃ CUP**

TIME **5 MINUTES**

So basic yet so wonderful, this sauce has literally dozens of possible permutations. Especially good with spring, summer, or egg rolls, it's also terrific with grilled fish or meats. If you have the time, let it sit for a few minutes before serving to allow the flavors to come together. Information on Asian fish sauces like nam pla is on page 500.

1 tablespoon vinegar or fresh lime juice

1 tablespoon soy sauce or nam pla

1 tablespoon water or to taste

1 rounded teaspoon peeled and minced fresh ginger, optional

$\frac{1}{4}$ teaspoon minced fresh chile or cayenne, or to taste, optional

1 teaspoon sugar, optional

Combine all the ingredients and stir to dissolve the sugar if you're using it. Taste and adjust the seasonings as necessary.

Hoisin Chili Sauce CHINA ■ ▨ ▨
MAKES **ABOUT $\frac{1}{3}$ CUP**

TIME **5 MINUTES**

This is no more than hoisin sauce spiced up. It's great with Spring Rolls (page 38) or Lumpia Rolls (page 68) and makes an acceptable substitute for Sesame-Chile Paste (page 591). Like every other bottled condiment, hoisin varies in quality: look for a jar that lists soy as the first ingredient and little more than that, sugar, chile, and spices.

As for chili sauce, look for Vietnamese chili-garlic sauce, sold at almost every Asian food store; like hoisin sauce, it keeps indefinitely in your refrigerator.

$\frac{1}{3}$ cup hoisin sauce

2 teaspoons chili sauce, plus more if desired

1. Whisk together the sauces until smooth.
2. Thin with water if the mixture seems too thick, then taste and adjust the seasoning if necessary (add more hoisin if too fiery, more chili sauce if too mild). Serve or store in the refrigerator (it will keep for more than a week).

Ginger-Chile Sauce
SOUTHEAST ASIA ■ ▨ ▨

MAKES **ABOUT 1 CUP**

TIME **20 MINUTES**

A good all-purpose fresh chile sauce, one that will keep for a couple of weeks in the refrigerator. Hot but flavorful; great for bland foods, such as Hainanese Chicken Rice (page 275).

6 to 10 fresh chiles, like jalapeños or long red chiles, stems and seeds removed

10 garlic cloves, peeled

$\frac{1}{4}$ cup peeled and roughly chopped fresh ginger

$\frac{1}{4}$ cup fresh lime juice

1 tablespoon sugar

Salt to taste

1. Combine all the ingredients except the salt in a food processor and puree, stopping the machine to scrape down the sides as necessary.
2. Taste and add salt as necessary. Serve or cover and refrigerate for up to 2 weeks; bring back to room temperature before serving.

Coconut Milk ■ ▨ ▨
MAKES **ABOUT 2 CUPS**

TIME **20 MINUTES**

Canned coconut milk is great stuff—I use it all the time. But fresh coconut milk—made from dried, unsweetened coconut, which is sold at every health food store (and many Indian, Latin, and Caribbean markets)—is cheap, easy, delicious, and pure.

You can make coconut milk thick or thin, depending on the proportions of water to coconut; this is a fairly rich blend, equivalent to canned coconut milk.

The coconut also can be reused to make a thinner milk from a second pressing.

1 cup unsweetened shredded coconut

1. Combine the coconut with 2 cups very hot water in a blender. Pulse on and off quickly, then turn on the blender and let it work for 15 seconds or so (take care that the top of the blender stays in place). Let sit for a few minutes.
2. Put through a strainer, pressing to extract as much of the liquid as possible. Discard the solids and use the milk immediately or store, covered, in the refrigerator for up to a few days.

Toasted Chile Sauce
SOUTHEAST ASIA ■ ■ ■
MAKES **ABOUT ¹/₂ CUP**
TIME **30 MINUTES**

Still fiery, but mellower than raw chile sauces (and, of course, somewhat more work). Incredible on grilled chicken. This will keep fairly well, but because of the lime juice it is definitely at its best when fresh; thus I keep the quantity small. Information on Asian fish sauces like nam pla is on page 500.

6 dried red chiles
2 tablespoons peanut or other oil
6 garlic cloves, peeled and lightly crushed
¹/₄ cup nam pla
Juice of 1 lime

1. Put the chiles in a small dry skillet and turn the heat to medium. Cook, shaking the pan occasionally, until fragrant and lightly browned, about 5 minutes. Turn off the heat and remove. Stem the chiles and, if you like, remove their seeds (this will reduce the sauce's intensity, but it will still be plenty hot).
2. Add the oil to the same skillet and turn the heat to medium. Add the garlic along with the chiles and cook, stirring occasionally, until the cloves have softened and turned golden, about 5 minutes.
3. Transfer the oil, chiles, and garlic to a food processor and process until nearly pureed, stopping to scrape the sides of the machine as necessary. Add the nam pla and lime juice and serve. (You can prepare the sauce in advance, but it's best used within a few hours, and after a couple of days it will not be nearly as nice as when fresh. Do not store longer than that.)

Tamarind Paste ■ ■ ■
MAKES **1 CUP**
TIME **20 MINUTES**

Like coconut milk, this is nearly universal, seen from Mexico to Thailand to India. For information about tamarind, see the sidebar on page 587.

1 pound tamarind pulp

1. Put the pulp in a saucepan with 1 cup water over medium heat. Cook, whisking lightly, breaking up the lumps and adding more water whenever the mixture becomes dry, until you've added a total of about 2 cups. The process will take about 10 minutes; the result will be quite thick but fairly smooth.
2. Put the tamarind through a food mill or strainer; discard the seeds and stringy material left behind. Use or cover and refrigerate for up to a week before using.

■ make ahead   ■ serve at room temp./cold   ■ 30 minutes or less   SAUCES AND CONDIMENTS   **585**

Sweet Nam Pla Dipping Sauce

THAILAND ■ ▦ ▦

MAKES ½ CUP

TIME **5 MINUTES**

The strong, unusual aroma of nam pla (Thai fish sauce, page 500) is not something that instantly appeals to many Westerners. But when you cook with it, or mix it with other flavors, its wonderful, characteristic saltiness blossoms. This incredibly simple dressing is great with seafood or mixed greens.

> 4 limes
>
> 2 tablespoons nam pla
>
> 1 tablespoon palm sugar or brown sugar

1. Grate the zest of 2 of the limes into a small bowl, then juice all 4 limes into the same bowl.
2. Whisk in the nam pla and palm sugar. Let sit for 5 minutes for the flavors to meld.

Nam Prik THAILAND ■ ▦ ▦

MAKES **ABOUT ½ CUP**

TIME **5 MINUTES**

This is an essential, basic, slightly sweet Thai sauce (the Vietnamese nuoc cham is almost identical) used as a dressing for vegetables, noodles, meats, and fish and as a dipping sauce for almost any tidbit of food. Addictive, if you ask me. (Try it with plain grilled shrimp and you'll see.)

Many people make this blazingly hot; my version is much tamer. If you add five, or even ten, small Thai chiles, you won't be breaking with tradition. See page 500 for information on Asian fish sauces like nam pla, page 185 for a description of dried shrimp.

> 2 tablespoons fresh lime juice
>
> 2 tablespoons nam pla
>
> 1 teaspoon minced garlic
>
> ¼ teaspoon minced fresh chile, cayenne, or hot red pepper flakes, or to taste
>
> 2 teaspoons sugar
>
> 1 tablespoon minced dried shrimp, optional
>
> 1 tablespoon finely shredded carrot, optional

1. Combine all the ingredients and stir; make sure the sugar dissolves.
2. Taste and adjust the seasonings as necessary (I often add more nam pla). Let rest for a few minutes before serving or cover and refrigerate for about a day (return to room temperature before using).

Peanut Sauce THAILAND ■ ▦

MAKES **2 CUPS**

TIME **35 MINUTES**

A complex, multipurpose sauce that is good enough to eat with a spoon; adjust the proportions to your taste once you get used to it. Serve it warm, with Grilled Satay (page 101), Fried Satay (page 100), Spring Rolls (page 38), or simply rice crackers, sold at many Asian and health food markets, or other crackers. See page 500 for information on Asian fish sauces like nam pla.

> 3 small dried red chiles, stemmed and seeded, or cayenne or hot red pepper flakes to taste
>
> 3 garlic cloves, peeled
>
> 2 shallots, peeled
>
> 1 lemongrass stalk, white part only (page 143), thinly sliced
>
> 2 teaspoons ground turmeric
>
> 1 tablespoon peanut or neutral oil, like corn or grapeseed

Tamarind

Tamarind is the fruit pod of a semievergreen tree native to Africa that will grow almost anywhere it's warm year-round. In most cases you won't be dealing with the pod (though you can find it if you like, it's a total hassle to deal with) but with a packaged version of its pulp (and sometimes seeds).

This is a good thing, because the pulp is easily pre-pared (page 585), used, and stored in the refrigerator for a couple months without any noticeable degradation in quality. Its simultaneously sweet and sour flavor is unmistakable and unjustifiably unheralded in this country; try the Shrimp in Tamarind Sauce (page 214) and you'll probably become a fan immediately.

---

1 cup coconut milk, homemade (page 584) or canned

1 tablespoon palm sugar or brown sugar

2 tablespoons nam pla

2 tablespoons fresh lime juice

1 teaspoon salt

1/2 cup chopped roasted peanuts or crunchy peanut butter

1. Combine the first 5 ingredients in a food processor and grind until fairly smooth; scrape down the sides of the machine once or twice if necessary.

2. Heat the oil in a saucepan over medium heat and sauté the chile-garlic mixture until fragrant, about 1 minute. Add the remaining ingredients and whisk until smooth. Simmer until the sauce thickens, about 15 minutes. This may be stored, covered and refrigerated, for up to a week; gently rewarm over very low heat or in a microwave before using.

Chinese Peanut Sauce. Simpler and leaner, this is a good last-minute addition to stir-fries: omit the lemongrass, turmeric, coconut milk, and lime juice; substitute soy sauce for the nam pla.

Khao Koor Ground and Toasted Rice

THAILAND ■ ▨ ▨

MAKES **2 TABLESPOONS**

TIME **10 MINUTES**

Who knew something so simple could be so good? Ground, toasted sticky rice is an ingredient used as a binder in some Thai dishes, but it's also sprinkled over sticky rice as a seasoning, contributing a toasty, smoky note. Unless you make Thai food with unusual frequency, I think it's best to make single-meal batches, though you could easily multiply this recipe. Use it in Laarb (page 199), or sprinkle over sticky rice any time you make it.

2 tablespoons sticky (glutinous) rice

1. Toast the sticky rice in a small sauté pan over medium heat until deeply golden and fragrant, stirring almost constantly, about 5 minutes.

2. Transfer to a spice grinder (or mortar) and grind to a powder. Use immediately or, if you're making a larger batch, store in an airtight container for a few weeks.

■ make ahead   ▨ serve at room temp./cold   ▨ 30 minutes or less   SAUCES AND CONDIMENTS   **587**

Chiles

Because chiles play a very small role in most Western European cooking (they originated in South America), they were barely known to most people living in the United States until the last generation or two. Though it's fair to say that citizens and residents of Latin descent have cooked with them for centuries—New Mexico is one of the world's chile capitals—outside the Southwest, Mexican communities elsewhere, and Asian restaurants, chiles were rare.

That's all changed. Chipotles seem to be in every fusion dish, even among fast-food chains; jalapeños are sold fresh even in supermarkets in Maine; you can buy a variety of dried chiles everywhere; and, in most of the Southwest, they are a staple.

Chile peppers—the genus *Capsicum,* and technically berries—fall into two primary categories: hot and sweet. They're also categorized by their level of heat, pungency, color, shape, scent, and flavor. The unique anatomy of a chile lends it its distinctive heat. Most people fear the seeds of a chile, and they do pack some heat (and certainly bitterness), but the real heat comes from the veins inside, which carry the hot oil, capsaicin.

To distinguish among the varying degrees of heat in chiles, a man named Wilbur Scoville developed a heat rating system in the early 1900s. Since then, other methods have been devised, but the Scoville Heat Scale is still widely used. It lists most chile varieties in order of heat, assigning each a level of "Scoville units." The hottest chiles are habanero (Scotch bonnet), followed by cayenne, jalapeño, ancho, and a host of others, and finally mild bell peppers and pimientos. Though the scale is reasonably accurate, each chile plant is different according to soil and light conditions; you can find both blazing-hot and very mild anchos, for example.

The form of the chile affects the heat as well. Fresh chiles are hotter and more biting, especially if they are not fully ripened—that is, green. Ripened and dried chiles have a more flavorful balance of spicy and hot; smoked chiles are even more aromatic and fuller in flavor.

Because of all these differences, chiles are not as interchangeable as you might think. And some—like the chipotle, which is a smoked jalapeño—are unique. Nevertheless, I would not hesitate to substitute one hot chile—especially when dried—for another. And I almost always add chiles to a dish slowly and to taste. There are times when a huge dried chile added to a dish produces less heat than a tiny one. So until you learn your way around this world, take care.

Chiles are an indispensable pantry item, and the dried ones keep for a long, long time (if they're pliable and moist when you buy them, so much the better). To control the heat of a chile—to derive more spice and flavor than fire—you should remove the seeds and scrape out at least some of the veins before cooking. And always be sure to wash your hands well after handling chiles or wear disposable rubber gloves while handling them.

Many chiles, both fresh and dried, are best when roasted (fresh) or toasted (dried) first. The goal is pretty much the same, though you have a little more flexibility with fresh chiles: to brown the skin and bring out more flavor (with fresh chiles, the roasting also enables you to remove the skin, a nice touch). Roast fresh chiles in a dry skillet, over medium heat, turning them until they blacken; or grill them over hot coals, roast in an oven (at a high temperature, say, 450°F), or broil. Toast dried chiles in a dry heavy pan (cast iron is good), over medium heat, turning them until they color slightly, just a couple of minutes (use an exhaust fan if you have one; the air can become pretty pungent). Remove and set aside for a couple of minutes to cool, then stem and seed them.

Finally, the easiest way to neutralize the heat of a chile—that is, the way to cool your mouth if you've eaten one that's too hot—is to drink a glass of milk. It may not be that appealing, but it works.

Chile/Pepper	Heat	Availability
Habanero (Scotch Bonnet)	Very hot	Fresh
Charleston Hot	Very hot	Fresh and canned
Chipotle	Very hot	Fresh, dried, and canned in adobo
Cayenne	Very hot	Fresh, dried, and powder
Tabasco	Very hot	Fresh, dried, and sauce
Chile de Árbol	Hot	Fresh and dried
Serrano (Hot)	Hot	Fresh and dried
Thai Bird	Hot	Fresh and dried
Pasilla de Oaxaca	Hot	Fresh and dried
Giant Thai	Hot	Fresh
Jalapeño	Hot	Fresh
Guajillo	Medium	Fresh and dried
Serrano (Mild)	Medium	Fresh and dried
Ancho	Medium	Fresh, dried, and powder
Poblano	Medium	Fresh and dried
Jalapeño (Mild)	Medium	Fresh
Pasilla Negro	Medium	Fresh and dried
Anaheim	Medium	Fresh and dried
Paprika	Mild	Dried and powder
New Mexico	Mild	Fresh and dried
Pimiento	Mild	Bottled
Mild Bell Pepper	Mild	Fresh

Nuoc Cham Dipping Sauce with Ginger

VIETNAM ■ ▣ ▣

MAKES **ABOUT $1/2$ CUP**

TIME **10 MINUTES**

Used widely for spring rolls, this also tastes great with plain grilled meat or chicken or spooned over lightly steamed vegetables. You can substitute soy sauce for the nuoc mam (usually called nam pla in this book and described on page 500, but in any case Southeast Asian fish sauce) if you prefer.

$1/4$ cup nuoc mam or nam pla

$1/4$ cup fresh lime juice

1 teaspoon minced garlic

1 tablespoon peeled and minced fresh ginger

2 tablespoons sugar

1 small fresh chile, preferably Thai, stemmed, seeded, and minced, or hot red pepper flakes to taste

Combine all the ingredients and stir to blend. Let sit for a few minutes before serving. This keeps well, refrigerated, for a day or two, but no longer. Bring back to room temperature before serving.

Sambal Oelek Chile-Lime Sauce

INDONESIA ■ ▣ ▣

MAKES **ABOUT $3/4$ CUP**

TIME **25 MINUTES**

Sambal is the generic name given to sauces in Indonesia, and this is the most basic. Nuts, coconut, dried shrimp, sugar, garlic, and other seasonings are often added before using this as a condiment for noodle, rice, and other dishes. If you want a really fiery sambal, leave in the chile seeds.

1 cup hot fresh chiles, preferably red, stemmed, seeded, and minced

6 garlic cloves, minced, optional

1 teaspoon fresh lime juice

1 teaspoon salt, or to taste

1 tablespoon sugar, or to taste

$1/2$ teaspoon finely grated lime zest

1. Use a mortar and pestle or a food processor to blend the chiles, garlic, lime juice, salt, and sugar into a paste. Use a spatula to transfer the mixture to a container with a lid.
2. Stir in the lime zest; add more salt if you like. Serve or cover and refrigerate; this will keep for 2 to 3 weeks. (Bring back to room temperature before serving.)

Sweet Garlic Soy Sauce

PHILIPPINES ■ ▣ ▣

MAKES $1/2$ CUP

TIME **10 MINUTES**

In Philippine cuisine, dark, fairly harsh soy sauce is favored, but it's often combined with sugar to create a syrupy dressing for vegetables. The added garlic gives this sweet and salty sauce a pleasant kick.

$1/2$ cup dark soy sauce

$2/3$ cup palm or brown sugar

2 garlic cloves, minced

1. Place the soy sauce and sugar in a saucepan and cook over low heat until slightly caramelized and thickened, about 5 minutes.
2. Remove from the heat and stir in the garlic. Cool and serve. This sauce will keep well, refrigerated, for a couple of days; bring to room temperature if

you're using it as a dipping sauce. (If you're cooking with it, you can use it directly from the refrigerator, of course.)

Sesame-Chile Paste KOREA ■ ▤ ▨

MAKES **ABOUT ¼ CUP**

TIME **15 MINUTES**

You can buy go chu jang, the excellent, slightly sweet and not-superhot Korean chile paste that is a part of Crab Soup (page 135) and many other Korean dishes, but in many places it's easier just to make this substitute, which keeps for about a month, covered, in the refrigerator. It's a good sauce for any grilled food or even raw vegetables. The best chile powder for this is not the typical Mexican chile powder but ground Korean chiles—co chu kara—which (obviously) you can buy at Korean markets (you can also buy pretoasted and ground sesame seeds). It's bright red, looks like coarse cayenne, and is not superhot. A good alternative is chile powder made from ground New Mexico chiles.

> 2 tablespoons co chu kara
>
> 2 scallions, trimmed and roughly chopped
>
> 2 teaspoons dark sesame oil
>
> 2 teaspoons toasted sesame seeds (page 596), ground
>
> 2 garlic cloves, peeled
>
> 2 tablespoons soy sauce
>
> 1 teaspoon sugar

Combine all the ingredients in a blender or food processor and blend until smooth. Use immediately or store in a tightly covered container in the refrigerator for up to a month.

Ponzu JAPAN ■ ▤

MAKES **2½ CUPS**

TIME **10 MINUTES, PLUS RESTING TIME**

This common, versatile sauce is usually served with grilled fish or vegetables or with shabu-shabu, but it turns up everywhere and can be used in many ways. It keeps indefinitely—a friend of mine insists it's best after months in the refrigerator; certainly it's no worse. You can buy yuzu juice frozen or—sometimes—fresh at Japanese specialty markets; it has a unique flavor but close enough to lemon and lime that the combination is a good substitute. You can also get bonito flakes at Japanese markets. If you are serving this as a dipping sauce at the table, garnish with finely chopped scallions or chives.

> 1 cup fresh yuzu (Japanese citrus) or ½ cup each fresh lemon and fresh lime juice
>
> 1 cup soy sauce
>
> ⅓ cup mirin or 2 tablespoons honey
>
> 1 tablespoon sugar
>
> ½ cup dried bonito flakes

1. Whisk together all the ingredients in a mixing bowl, cover, and refrigerate overnight.
2. Strain into an airtight container and refrigerate until ready to use.

Gari Pickled Ginger JAPAN ■ ▤

MAKES **4 SERVINGS**

TIME **AT LEAST 1 DAY, LARGELY UNATTENDED**

This is not the pickled ginger served at most Japanese restaurants: it's better, because it contains no preservatives or coloring. It will not turn pink, or only slightly, but it will be delicious.

You may have to play with the sugar content: some people like it far sweeter than others. Two tablespoons, the amount I use here, is the minimum.

If at all possible, use fresh young ginger for this recipe. It will be pinker, with a soft, smooth skin, not woody, like most of the ginger at the market (which is fine for other recipes and uses). Young ginger is easier to peel and slice, and the resulting pickle will have a more delicate texture.

> 1 large piece fresh ginger, about ¼ pound
> 1 tablespoon salt
> Rice vinegar as needed
> 2 tablespoons sugar

1. Peel and thinly slice the ginger, using a mandoline if you have one. Toss it with the salt and let stand for an hour. Rinse thoroughly.
2. Combine about ¼ cup rice vinegar with an equal amount of water and the sugar; heat, stirring to dissolve the sugar. Cool slightly and combine with the ginger in a nonmetal bowl. If the liquid does not cover the ginger, add more vinegar and water, again in equal parts. Cover and refrigerate.
3. You can begin eating the ginger within a day, though it will improve for several days and keep for up to a couple of weeks.

Sesame Sauce JAPAN ■ ▨ ▨
MAKES **ABOUT 1 CUP**
TIME **20 MINUTES**

Sesame seeds flavor foods from the Middle to the Far East, and this Japanese version is sublime. Spooned over grilled or broiled chicken, meat, or full-flavored fish, it produces a kind of instant teriyaki. It's also fine over lightly steamed spinach or other vegetables. Good with a little minced ginger added, too.

> ½ cup sesame seeds
> ½ cup Dashi (page 160) or good-quality chicken or vegetable stock, preferably homemade (page 159 or 162)
> 3 tablespoons soy sauce
> 2 tablespoons mirin or 1 tablespoon honey plus 1 tablespoon water
> 1 tablespoon miso, optional
> 1 tablespoon dark sesame oil

1. Toast the sesame seeds in a small dry skillet over medium heat, shaking the pan frequently until the seeds color slightly. Grind to a powder in a spice or coffee grinder (or use a mortar and pestle).
2. Whisk in the remaining ingredients; taste and adjust the seasoning and serve or cover and refrigerate for up to a day or two (stir before serving).

Hot Curry Powder INDIA ■ ▨ ▨
MAKES **ABOUT ¼ CUP**
TIME **15 MINUTES**

Curry powder may be hot, mild, or fragrant; it's usually blended to the producer's taste, and if you make it often enough, you'll find exactly what you like. Here the heat comes from a combination of black pepper and chiles. But the heat is usually moderate and well tempered by the other spices. If you like a milder, sweeter curry powder, see the next three recipes.

> 2 small dried red chiles or cayenne to taste
> 1 tablespoon black peppercorns
> 1 tablespoon coriander seeds
> 1 teaspoon cumin seeds
> 1 teaspoon fennel seeds
> 1 teaspoon ground fenugreek
> 1 tablespoon ground turmeric
> 1 tablespoon ground ginger

Curry Powder

Curry powder is a blend of dried ground spices that most of the world uses in curries and other approximations of Indian cookery. When you have "curry" in Thailand, Japan, England, or France, it's almost always spiked with curry powder. Ironically, "curry powder" is not used much in India.

Curry powder as we know it came about during the British rule of India and is a derivative of a family of spice mixtures that Indians *do* use—garam masala, which means "hot" (garam) "spice mix" (masala). The differences between the two are vague, as the constituent spices of garam masalas change from town to town throughout India, and there is no single recipe for curry powder.

In fact, for the home cook not living in India, the names are unimportant. Store-bought curry powder and store-bought garam masala can both be fine or terrible, but homemade versions of both are usually delicious and have the advantage of being customized to your taste. You can make them hot or mild or sweet or fragrant or any combination of these characteristics, and if you toast and grind your own spices, the results will be better than anything, authentic or not, that you buy at the store—no matter what it's called.

---

1. Combine the chiles, peppercorns, and seeds in a medium skillet over medium heat. Cook, shaking the pan occasionally, until lightly browned and fragrant, just a few minutes; for the last minute of cooking, add the powdered spices.
2. Cool, then grind to a fine powder in a spice or coffee grinder; add cayenne at this stage if you're using it. Store in a tightly covered opaque container for up to several months.

Milder Curry Powder INDIA ■ ■ ■
MAKES **ABOUT ¼ CUP**
TIME **15 MINUTES**

This curry still carries a bit of heat but is mild and fragrant. If I were looking for an all-purpose curry powder, this would be it.

- **1 teaspoon black peppercorns**
- **3 cloves**
- **3 seeds from white cardamom pods**
- **1 tablespoon cumin seeds**
- **1 tablespoon coriander seeds**
- **1 tablespoon fennel seeds**
- **2 teaspoons ground ginger**
- **¼ teaspoon cayenne, or to taste**
- **1 teaspoon ground fenugreek**
- **2 teaspoons ground turmeric**

1. Combine the peppercorns, cloves, and seeds in a medium skillet over medium heat. Cook, shaking the pan occasionally, until lightly browned and fragrant, just a few minutes; for the last minute of cooking, add the powdered spices.
2. Cool, then grind to a fine powder in a spice or coffee grinder. Store in a tightly covered opaque container for up to several months.

Fragrant Curry Powder INDIA ■ ■ ■
MAKES **ABOUT ¼ CUP**
TIME **15 MINUTES**

This is a sweet, mild, but very complex curry powder; you can add a bit of cayenne if you want some heat.

You can chip pieces off a whole nutmeg with the blunt edge of a heavy knife or crack the whole thing by pressing on it with a heavy skillet.

    ¼ teaspoon nutmeg pieces

    Seeds from 5 white cardamom pods

    3 cloves

    1 cinnamon stick

    1 teaspoon black peppercorns

    2 tablespoons cumin seeds

    ¼ cup coriander seeds

    2 bay leaves

    2 dried curry leaves, if available

    1 teaspoon ground fenugreek

1. Combine all the ingredients except the fenugreek in a medium skillet over medium heat. Cook, shaking the pan occasionally, until lightly browned and fragrant, just a few minutes; for the last minute of cooking, add the fenugreek.
2. Cool, then grind to a fine powder in a spice or coffee grinder. Store in a tightly covered opaque container for up to several months.

Garam Masala INDIA ■ ■ ■
MAKES **ABOUT ¼ CUP**
TIME **15 MINUTES**

Generally speaking—but not always—garam masala is milder than curry, containing little or no pepper or chile. Again, it's a matter of taste. This garam masala has a load of cardamom in it, because that's the kind I favor. It's delicious with fish.

    Seeds from 10 cardamom pods

    1 cinnamon stick

    1 teaspoon cloves

    ½ teaspoon nutmeg pieces

    1 tablespoon cumin seeds

    1 tablespoon fennel seeds

1. Combine all the ingredients in a medium skillet over medium heat. Cook, shaking the pan occasionally, until lightly browned and fragrant, just a few minutes.
2. Cool, then grind to a fine powder in a spice or coffee grinder. Store in a tightly covered opaque container for up to several months.

Chaat Masala INDIA ■ ■ ■
MAKES **ABOUT 2 TABLESPOONS**
TIME **5 MINUTES**

You can probably buy premade chaat masala more easily than you can find some of its ingredients, which may include ground pomegranate seeds and other exotica. But this is a good, simple version, contributed by my friend chef Suvir Saran. The sourness, which is its defining characteristic, is provided by the distinctive amchoor, a powder made from dried mangoes.

If you have the time, toast together in a dry skillet (as for Hot Curry Powder, page 592) whole cumin and coriander seeds, then grind them before mixing them with the other ingredients.

    2 tablespoons amchoor (dried mango powder)

    1 teaspoon ground cumin

    1 teaspoon ground black pepper

    1 teaspoon ground coriander

    1 teaspoon ground ginger

    ¼ teaspoon hing (asafetida)

    ¼ teaspoon cayenne

    Pinch of salt

Combine all the ingredients and store in a tightly covered opaque container for up to several months.

Mint Chutney with Tomato INDIA ■ ▦ ▦

MAKES **ABOUT 2 CUPS**

TIME **10 MINUTES**

Lighter than Mint Chutney with Yogurt (following recipe), and, with its fresh ginger and garam masala, spicier. I'd serve it with grilled chicken or lamb.

> 1 tablespoon peeled and minced fresh ginger
>
> 1 jalapeño or other small fresh chile, stemmed, seeded, and minced, or hot red pepper flakes to taste
>
> 1 medium or ¹⁄₂ large white onion, peeled and cut into chunks
>
> 1 large ripe tomato, cored and roughly chopped
>
> 2 teaspoons any curry powder or garam masala, preferably homemade (pages 592–594), or to taste
>
> 2 cups fresh mint leaves
>
> Salt to taste

1. Combine the first 5 ingredients in a food processor and process, pulsing the machine on and off and stopping to scrape down the sides if necessary, until the onion and tomato are roughly chopped, not pureed.
2. Add the mint leaves and pulse a few more times to combine and roughly chop the leaves. Add salt and more chile or spice mix if you like. Serve immediately or cover and refrigerate for up to a day.

Simplest Mint Chutney. Omit the tomato and the curry powder. Add a squeeze of lime if you like.

Mint Chutney with Yogurt INDIA ■ ▦ ▦

MAKES **4 SERVINGS**

TIME **10 MINUTES**

Hot enough to counter the yogurt's blandness and sweet enough to offset its sourness, complex with spice and bright and sparkling with a load of mint, this is the model mint chutney, a refreshing counterpoint to simple grilled lamb, beef, eggplant, salmon, even hamburger.

> Juice of 2 limes
>
> 1 garlic clove, peeled
>
> One 1-inch-long piece fresh ginger, peeled and roughly chopped
>
> ¹⁄₄ teaspoon cayenne, or to taste
>
> 1 cup whole-milk yogurt
>
> 1 tablespoon sugar
>
> 2 cups fresh mint leaves
>
> Salt and black pepper to taste

1. Combine the lime juice, garlic, ginger, cayenne, yogurt, and sugar in a food processor or blender and puree, stopping the machine and scraping down the sides if necessary.
2. Stir in the mint by hand, then add salt and pepper. Serve immediately or refrigerate for up to a day.

Dry Peanut Chutney INDIA ■ ■ ▦

MAKES **ABOUT 1 CUP**

TIME **15 MINUTES**

This can be served, with rice, alongside any dal (page 433) or as a condiment with spicy stewed dishes. It can also be mixed into yogurt to make a kind of Raita (page 175).

> 1 teaspoon cumin seeds
>
> 1 teaspoon coriander seeds
>
> 1 cup roasted unsalted peanuts
>
> 1 small dried red chile, or to taste
>
> Salt and black pepper to taste
>
> 1 garlic clove, peeled

1. Toast the seeds in a small dry skillet over medium heat, shaking the pan frequently, until they color slightly, just a couple of minutes. (If the peanuts are raw, you can toast them the same way.)
2. Grind all the ingredients together in a blender or food processor, stopping the machine to scrape down the sides if necessary; you are looking for a coarse grind, short of peanut butter. (If the mixture turns to peanut butter, it's not a disaster. Add a few more peanuts and make it extra-chunky; I've had this that way, too.) Serve immediately or refrigerate for up to a week (bring back to room temperature before serving).

Toasted Sesame Seeds ■ ▪ ▪

MAKES **½ CUP**

TIME **10 MINUTES**

Toasted sesame seeds are an important ingredient in a great deal of Middle Eastern and Asian cooking. You can buy sesame seeds pretoasted (especially at Korean markets), but the toasting process is nearly effortless (just make sure not to burn the seeds).

There are many colors of sesame seeds. The most common variety, which are called white but are actually pale to dark tan, sometimes with tinges of gray, are fine for almost all uses. Store sesame seeds in the refrigerator or freezer to prevent them from turning rancid—an uncommon but not impossible eventuality.

½ cup sesame seeds

Toast the sesame seeds in a small dry skillet over medium heat, shaking the pan frequently, until the seeds color slightly, less than 5 minutes. Use immediately or store in a closed container.

Avgolemono Egg-Lemon Sauce MIDDLE EAST ■

MAKES **ABOUT 1 CUP**

TIME **10 MINUTES**

Most closely associated with Greece, this is seen throughout the Eastern Mediterranean, and it remains a standard. It works equally well with whole eggs or yolks, but it is far prettier when you use yolks only. It's a simple sauce, not meant to be especially elegant, but quite flavorful. Perfect with steamed green vegetables.

4 egg yolks or 2 whole eggs

¼ cup fresh lemon juice

1 cup warm chicken or other stock, preferably homemade (pages 160–163)

Pinch of cayenne

Salt and black pepper to taste

1. Beat the egg yolks in a bowl until light and foamy (with an electric mixer, about a minute; by hand, 2 or 3). Slowly add the lemon juice, still beating. Gradually add the stock, still beating, followed by the cayenne.
2. Transfer to a small saucepan and place over low heat. Cook, stirring, until the mixture thickens slightly (it will not be superthick) and is hot, just a few minutes. Do not boil. Taste and adjust the seasoning, then use immediately.

Parsley-Onion Condiment

MIDDLE EAST ■ ▪

MAKES **ABOUT 1 CUP**

TIME **1 HOUR, LARGELY UNATTENDED**

Here's a "Why didn't I think of that?" concoction that's added to many plates—and sometimes simply set on the table as a condiment—throughout the Middle East. Fresh and delicious, it's often made with mint instead of parsley or shallot in place of onion. Serve with any grilled meat, but especially Kofte (page 355).

> 1 large white onion, finely chopped
> Salt to taste
> ¹/₂ cup chopped fresh parsley leaves

1. Sprinkle the chopped onion liberally with salt and toss in a strainer. Put the strainer over a bowl or the sink and let sit for at least 30 minutes, preferably a bit longer.
2. Rinse the onion under cold running water and combine with the parsley. Taste and add salt if necessary. Serve immediately or within several hours; do not refrigerate.

Tahini Sauce MIDDLE EAST ■ ■ ■
MAKES **ABOUT 1 CUP**
TIME **10 MINUTES**

This sauce is lovely layered with tomatoes or cucumbers. Thinned with more water, oil, or yogurt, it also makes a great salad dressing. You can buy canned or bottled tahini—ground sesame seed paste—at any Middle Eastern or health food store.

> ¹/₂ cup tahini, with a bit of its oil
> ¹/₂ cup yogurt or water
> Juice of 1 lemon, or to taste
> Salt and black pepper to taste
> ¹/₂ teaspoon minced garlic, or to taste
> ¹/₂ teaspoon ground cumin, optional

1. Combine all the ingredients in a bowl and whisk until smooth. Thin, if necessary, with a little sesame or olive oil, yogurt, or water.
2. Taste and adjust the seasoning and serve, or refrigerate, covered, for a day or two.

Thin Yogurt Sauce MIDDLE EAST ■ ■ ■
MAKES **2 CUPS**
TIME **10 MINUTES**

Serve this raitalike dressing with any Middle Eastern kebab or kofte (pages 354–356), just as a drizzle, or with any grilled meat, poultry, or fish. If you have a source for fresh yogurt, this is the place to use it.

Many times this is made with a teaspoon or more of minced garlic. Obviously, that changes its character greatly, but some people cannot live without it. Good either way.

> 2 cups good-quality whole-milk yogurt
> 2 tablespoons fresh lemon juice, or to taste
> Salt and black pepper to taste
> Pinch of cayenne
> ¹/₄ cup or more chopped fresh parsley leaves, fresh mint
>   leaves, or a combination

1. Whisk together the yogurt and lemon juice until smooth.
2. Stir in the other ingredients. Serve immediately or cover and refrigerate for up to several hours; drain excess liquid if necessary and stir again before serving.

Tabil Tunisian Spice Rub ■ ■ ■
MAKES **ABOUT ¹/₄ CUP**
TIME **15 MINUTES**

As with most spice rubs, there are nearly infinite versions of this, but all have four things in common: coriander, chile, garlic, and caraway. It's the latter that gives it a surprising flavor, one that complements meat, especially lamb, beautifully.

If you are going to use this as a spice rub on the same day you make it, by all means use fresh garlic. If

---

■ make ahead   ■ serve at room temp./cold   ■ 30 minutes or less   SAUCES AND CONDIMENTS   **597** you plan to store it for a while, use garlic powder. And of course you can substitute preground spices for fresh, but this way is better.

2 tablespoons coriander seeds

1 small dried chile

2 tablespoons caraway seeds

1 teaspoon fennel seeds, optional

1 teaspoon cumin seeds, optional

$^1/_2$ teaspoon black peppercorns

1 teaspoon minced garlic or 1 teaspoon garlic powder

1. Combine all the ingredients except the garlic in a small skillet over medium heat. Toast, shaking the skillet occasionally, until the mixture becomes fragrant, a couple of minutes.
2. Grind in a spice mill or coffee grinder until powdery. Mix in the garlic; use immediately or, if using garlic powder, store in a tightly covered container for up to several weeks.

Harissa Chile Paste NORTH AFRICA ■ ■ ■
MAKES **ABOUT $^1/_2$ CUP**
TIME **20 MINUTES**

Among the simplest and most useful all-purpose chile pastes—terrific as a condiment for grilled food, and useful by the spoonful in braised dishes—this one can be made with nothing more than dried chiles (the standard red ones, inexpensive and readily available at any Asian market, are fine), garlic, and olive oil. A bit of cumin or Tabil is a nice addition.

However—and this is a big however—harissa need not be fiery; it can be made with relatively mild chiles, like New Mexico or ancho chiles. Furthermore, whether you need the chiles or not is up to you; even if you use "mild" chiles, the sauce will be fairly hot if you do not. Obviously, some experimenting may be neces-

sary to find your tolerance level. I have eaten harissa in many different forms, and this recipe is my choice. Harissa keeps for at least a week or two, refrigerated. It will lose a bit of intensity over time, but this is not necessarily a bad thing; some would call it mellowing.

6 to 12 dried chiles, preferably New Mexico or ancho

4 garlic cloves, peeled

$^1/_2$ cup extra virgin olive oil

1 teaspoon ground cumin or Tabil (page 597)

1 teaspoon salt, or to taste

1. Soak the chiles in hot water until they soften, about 15 minutes; drain. Remove the stems and, if you like, the seeds. Put in a food processor with the garlic, olive oil, and cumin. Pulse the machine on and off, scraping down the sides if necessary, until the mixture forms a coarse paste.
2. Taste and add salt as necessary. Store in a covered jar in the refrigerator.

Preserved Lemons MOROCCO ■ ■
MAKES **1 QUART**
TIME **20 MINUTES PLUS 2 WEEKS TO CURE**

Preserved lemons are a staple of North African cuisine that are called for in two recipes in this book, Onion and Saffron Chicken (page 295) and Roast Pepper Salad with Tomatoes and Preserved Lemon (page 193). But you can add them to almost any tagine—chicken, fish, or lamb—with excellent results.

In fact, if you have a batch of these on hand, you may find yourself incorporating them into dishes that have nothing to do with their land of origin, things like Sautéed Scallops with Garlic (page 211), or as an adjunct to the fresh lemon in the meunière recipe on page 240.

I'd had mixed luck with preserving lemons over

the years and, while I can't quite account for why that was, I can say I've worked out a way around it: treat preserved lemons like a "quick" or refrigerator pickle.

The spices listed here are optional—feel free to omit them, change their quantities, or add to them to taste. They're included to round out the sweet lemony high note and salty, acidic tang that characterizes the flavor of the preserved lemons.

About ³/₄ cup kosher salt

About 3 pounds lemons, preferably unwaxed, quartered lengthwise

¹/₂ cinnamon stick

2 or 3 cloves, to taste

1 star anise

2 or 3 black peppercorns

2 cardamom pods

1 bay leaf

1. Sprinkle a ¹/₄-inch-deep layer of salt across the bottom of a sterile 1-quart canning jar. Nestle a layer of quartered lemons into the bottom of the jar, sprinkle liberally with salt, then repeat, adding the spices as you go. Stop when the jar is about three-quarters full and squeeze the remaining lemons into the jar—seeds and all—so that the fruit is completely submerged in the lemon juice–and–salt brine. (If you don't have enough lemons on hand, top the lemons off with freshly squeezed juice the following day.)

2. Set the jar out on a counter and vigorously shake it once a day for 7 to 10 days—during this time it will start to bubble a little and the dried spices will swell back to their original size. (You'll be surprised at the size of the cloves!)

3. Transfer the jar to the refrigerator and let the lemons continue to cure for another week before using them. (The lemons will keep for at least 2 months in the refrigerator, though you'll probably want to get into them sooner.) When they have cured, unscrew the lid. After a moment, they should smell sweet and citrusy. An ammonia smell means they've gone wrong somewhere along the line and should be discarded.

4. To use in stews, blanch the quartered lemons in unsalted boiling water for 10 seconds, just long enough to leach out a little of the salt. For salads or quick-cooked dishes, scrape the flesh away from the peel, discard the flesh, and blanch the peel in unsalted boiling water.

STAR ANISE

Dried Fruit and Nut Sauce with Cilantro BALKANS, MIDDLE EAST ■ ▨ ▨

MAKES **ABOUT 2 CUPS**

TIME **15 MINUTES**

You don't see much cilantro in Europe, but you find it in the southeastern part of the continent, where several cultures mingle. Regardless of this sauce's origin (it is closely related to Tarator or Skordalia; recipe follows), it is fabulous with grilled meats, especially lamb. Walnut oil is not essential here, but it really does make a difference.

½ cup prunes or dried apricots

2 garlic cloves, peeled

½ cup walnuts

2 cups fresh cilantro leaves

½ cup fresh parsley or dill leaves

½ cup chopped scallion

¼ cup fresh lemon juice or vinegar

Salt and black pepper to taste

1 cup walnut oil, more or less, or extra virgin olive oil

Cayenne to taste

1. Combine the prunes in a saucepan with ½ cup water and cook gently, covered, until softened, just 5 to 10 minutes. Drain.

2. Combine the prunes in a food processor with the garlic, walnuts, cilantro, parsley, scallion, lemon juice, salt, and pepper. Process for a few seconds, then begin adding the oil in a steady stream until you have created a thick sauce.

3. Add some cayenne, taste and adjust seasoning, and serve or cover and refrigerate for up to a few days.

Tarator or Skordalia
TURKEY OR GREECE ■ ■ ▨

MAKES **ABOUT 2 CUPS**

TIME **10 MINUTES**

A wonderful all-purpose sauce and mayonnaise substitute; use it for grilled meats, steamed vegetables, even chicken salad.

For a milder sauce, reduce the garlic to one clove and substitute paprika for the chile. And there are lots of options for the liquid; the flavors of the other ingredients are so strong that it doesn't matter all that much. Many cooks simply use a bit of olive oil and some water. Others use hazelnuts, pine nuts, or blanched almonds in place of walnuts; all are good. Be sure to see Chicken with Walnut Sauce (page 278).

1 thick slice day-old bread

About 1½ cups stock, preferably homemade
(pages 160–163), milk, or water

1 cup walnuts

3 garlic cloves, peeled

1 hot red chile, stemmed and seeded, or 1 teaspoon pure
hot chile powder

1 tablespoon fresh lemon juice, or to taste

Salt and black pepper to taste

1. Put the bread in a bowl and saturate it with some of the liquid. Wait a couple of minutes, then put the bread in a food processor with the nuts, garlic, and chile. Process until the walnuts are ground, then, with the machine running, pour in enough liquid to form a creamy sauce.

2. Add the lemon juice, salt, and pepper and serve immediately or cover and refrigerate for up to a couple of days.

French Walnut Sauce. Omit the chile and garlic. With the nuts, grind 2 ounces fresh horseradish, roughly chopped. (See cautions about horseradish, page 607.) Or finish the sauce with prepared horseradish to taste, at least 1 tablespoon.

FRENCH, ITALIAN, AND SPANISH SAUCES

Vinaigrette FRANCE ■ ▨ ▨
MAKES **ABOUT 1 CUP**

TIME **10 MINUTES**

In Western cooking, vinaigrette is the closest thing to an all-purpose sauce. I recommend making vinaigrette in a blender, where it becomes so stable that it can be prepared hours before it is needed. Once made, it can be used on everything from green salad to cold meat, vegetables, or fish dishes to anything that has been broiled or grilled, whether served hot or at room temperature.

I well remember the first time I had good vinaigrette, and it was in France. It was so far and away the best salad dressing I'd ever tasted (and at this point I was twenty-six years old, so I'd tasted at least a few, though the vast majority had come out of bottles) that I had to ask the secret. The answer—now so obvious, then a revelation—was shallots. But you can use such a wide variety of flavors in vinaigrette (see the variations) that these days the standard French variety seems almost clichéd.

> 3/4 cup extra virgin olive oil
>
> 5 tablespoons or more good-quality wine vinegar
>
> Salt and freshly ground black pepper to taste
>
> 1 heaping teaspoon Dijon mustard
>
> 1 large shallot (about 1 ounce), peeled and cut into chunks

1. Combine all the ingredients except the shallot in a blender and turn the machine on; a creamy emulsion will form within 30 seconds. Taste and add more vinegar, a teaspoon or two at a time, until the balance tastes right to you.
2. Add the shallot and turn the machine on and off a few times until the shallot is minced within the dressing. Taste, adjust the seasoning, and serve. (This is best made fresh but will keep, refrigerated, for a few days; bring back to room temperature and whisk briefly before using.)

Sauce Gribiche. Plain vinaigrette is lovely over steamed vegetables or poached or grilled fish, but gribiche surpasses it: to 1 cup vinaigrette, add 2 tablespoons chopped cornichons or gherkins, 1 teaspoon minced lemon zest, and 1 hard-cooked egg (page 338), peeled and well chopped.

Soy Vinaigrette. People love this on green salad or plain steamed vegetables: Use peanut oil or a neutral oil, like corn or grapeseed; use rice wine vinegar and add 1 to 2 tablespoons good-quality soy sauce. The shallot is optional. Taste and adjust the seasoning before serving.

Lemon Vinaigrette, Greek Style. Great on any chopped salad. Substitute lemon juice for the vinegar. Omit the mustard. Add 1 or 2 garlic cloves, minced, or to taste, or about 1/4 medium onion, minced, and 1 tablespoon chopped fresh oregano leaves to the blender; omit the shallot.

Chervil-Butter Sauce for Fish
FRANCE ■

MAKES **ABOUT 1 CUP**

TIME **15 MINUTES**

Chervil is the most fragile of common herbs, hard to find in the supermarket but beloved by chefs and gardeners; when you see it, grab it. (You can achieve something of the same effect by combining parsley and basil.)

Because this sauce contains flour, it is leaner and easier to make than Béarnaise (recipe follows), but it still has great flavor. Serve it over poached or grilled fish.

> 2 teaspoons flour
>
> Salt and freshly ground pepper, preferably white, to taste
>
> 4 tablespoons (1/2 stick) butter, cut into 4 or 5 pieces
>
> 1/2 cup finely minced fresh chervil leaves
>
> 1 teaspoon fresh lemon juice

1. In a small saucepan, whisk the flour with 1/2 cup water; season with salt and pepper. Set it over low heat and cook, stirring.

2. Add the butter one piece at a time, stirring until each bit melts before adding the next one. Keep the heat low, stir frequently, and do not let the mixture boil.

3. When all the butter has been incorporated, the sauce should be smooth and thick. Taste for salt and pepper, stir in the chervil and the lemon juice, and serve immediately.

Béarnaise Sauce FRANCE ■
MAKES **ABOUT 1 CUP**
TIME **20 MINUTES**

Yes, béarnaise is overkill, but this old-fashioned sauce has such good flavor it deserves to be made every now and then. It's best with grilled beef or fish. If you can find it, use chervil—a couple of tablespoons—in place of the tarragon.

    1 tablespoon minced shallots
    2 teaspoons minced fresh tarragon leaves or $^1/_2$ teaspoon
        dried
    Salt and freshly ground black pepper to taste
    3 tablespoons white wine or other vinegar
    2 egg yolks
    8 tablespoons (1 stick) butter, cut into pieces
    Fresh lemon juice if necessary

1. In a small saucepan, heat together the shallot, most of the tarragon, the salt, pepper, and vinegar, until most of the vinegar has evaporated, about 5 minutes. Cool.

2. Beat the egg yolks with 1 tablespoon water and stir into the vinegar mixture. Return to the stove over low heat and beat continuously with a wire whisk until thick. With the heat as low as possible, use a wooden spoon to stir in the butter a bit at a time. Add the remaining tarragon and taste; add salt and

pepper if necessary and, if the taste is not quite sharp enough, a bit of lemon juice. Use immediately.

Mayonnaise FRANCE ■ ■ ■
MAKES **1 CUP**
TIME **10 MINUTES**

An invaluable sauce that has countless uses with both fish (especially poached or fried) and vegetables, not to mention canned tuna. Make it once and, although you'll probably keep the bottle variety around, you will turn to this time and again.

For a stronger mayonnaise, use extra virgin olive oil and add a pinch or more of cayenne.

    1 egg yolk
    2 teaspoons Dijon mustard
    1 to 1$^1/_2$ cups neutral oil, like corn or grapeseed
    Salt and freshly ground black pepper to taste
    1 tablespoon fresh lemon juice

1. To make by hand, use a wire whisk to beat the yolk and mustard together in a bowl. Begin to add the oil as you beat, a little at a time, adding more as each bit is incorporated. When a thick emulsion forms—you'll know it—you can add the oil a little faster. Depending on how fast you beat, the whole process will take 2 to 5 minutes. You can add up to 1$^1/_2$ cups oil per yolk (or you can use only 1 cup oil and thin the mayonnaise a little bit with about $^1/_4$ cup hot water, beaten in).

    To make by machine, put the yolk and mustard in a blender or food processor and turn the machine on. While it's running, add the oil in a steady stream. When an emulsion forms, you can add it a little faster.

2. Add salt and pepper, then stir in the lemon juice. If the mixture is thicker than you like, thin with a little hot water, cream, sour cream, or milk.

Aïoli Provençal Garlic Mayonnaise or **All-i-Oli.** Catalan Garlic Mayonnaise. This can be pretty powerful stuff, essential for Bourride (page 137), good for cooked vegetables or potatoes: Use at least half olive oil. Add 3 or more garlic cloves to the mix, minced if you are making the mayonnaise by hand, roughly chopped if you're adding it to the blender; some people use 5, 10, or more cloves.

Sauce Verte. Green Mayonnaise, French Style. Difficult to make by hand, but easy in the food processor and wonderful over cold poached salmon or even hard-cooked eggs. Use 2 or even 3 egg yolks to start, to make a very yellow, rich mayonnaise. Once the emulsion is formed and all the olive oil has been added, add 1 fresh tarragon sprig, about 10 watercress sprigs (thick stems removed), 10 chives, and the leaves of 5 parsley stems. Process until not quite pureed but distinctively green.

Sauce Rémoulade Spicy Mayonnaise

FRANCE ■ ■ ▨

MAKES **ABOUT 1 CUP**

TIME **10 MINUTES**

Forget tartar sauce. Rémoulade is its predecessor, and it's superior in every way, the ideal sauce for grilled (and other) fish.

> 1 cup mayonnaise, preferably homemade (page 602)
>
> Salt and black pepper to taste
>
> 1 small garlic clove, minced
>
> 2 tablespoons chopped capers
>
> 2 tablespoons chopped fresh parsley leaves

> 1 teaspoon chopped fresh tarragon leaves or a pinch of dried
>
> 1 tablespoon Dijon mustard
>
> 2 anchovy fillets, minced, optional
>
> 1/4 teaspoon cayenne, or to taste

1. If you've already made the mayonnaise, combine it with all the remaining ingredients. If you're making the mayonnaise for this recipe and you're using a food processor or blender, you can save yourself some mincing by adding the garlic at the beginning and pulsing in the other solid ingredients while the sauce is still in the machine.

2. The sauce will keep well in the refrigerator for a few days, though it will lose a bit of intensity each day. To freshen it before serving, squeeze in a little lemon juice.

Rouille FRANCE ■ ▨ ▨

MAKES **ABOUT 1 CUP**

TIME **20 MINUTES**

The classic accompaniment to Bouillabaisse (page 138), this is also a great spicy mayonnaise for use almost anywhere.

> 2 small dried red chiles
>
> 1 egg yolk
>
> 1 tablespoon fresh lemon juice, or a little more
>
> 2 teaspoons Dijon mustard
>
> 2 garlic cloves, peeled
>
> 1 cup extra virgin olive oil
>
> 1/2 cup roasted red pepper (page 470), peeled and seeded, canned pimiento, drained, or, better, piquillo pepper (page 47)
>
> Salt and cayenne to taste

1. Soak the chiles in hot water to soften. Meanwhile, put the yolk, lemon juice, mustard, and garlic in a

blender or food processor and turn the machine on. While it's running, add the oil in a steady stream. When an emulsion begins to form, you can add the oil a little faster.

2. Drain the chiles and remove their seeds; add them, along with the red pepper, and continue to blend until the mixture is smooth. Add salt and cayenne if necessary (the rouille should be quite hot). Taste and add more salt or lemon juice if you like. Best served immediately, but keep it for a few hours if you must.

Tapenade Black Olive Paste FRANCE ■ ■ ■
MAKES **ABOUT 1½ CUPS**
TIME **20 MINUTES**

The key to good tapenade, not surprisingly, is good olives. I like the oil-cured kind for this, but they must not be too dried out or they become unpleasantly acrid, and no amount of olive oil can save them. So taste one before buying. (Regular canned black olives are fine too if you can't find olives in bulk.)

In Provence, considered its home, tapenade is used mostly as a spread for plain toasted bread or Crostini (page 41). But it's also great as a dip for raw vegetables, on sandwiches of any type, or as a quick spread to put on meat or fish before roasting or after grilling or broiling. It will keep, refrigerated, for about a month; always bring back to room temperature before serving.

About 1 pound black olives

¼ cup drained capers

6 to 10 anchovy fillets, or to taste, with their oil

2 garlic cloves, peeled and lightly crushed, or more to taste

About ½ cup extra virgin olive oil

Freshly ground black pepper to taste

Chopped fresh parsley leaves for garnish, optional

1. Pit the olives. If you're using oil-cured olives, you can simply squeeze out the pit; with brined olives you might have to flatten the olive with the side of a knife, which will split it and allow you to remove the pit.

2. Combine the olives, capers, anchovies, and garlic in a food processor or blender, along with some of the olive oil. Pulse the machine once or twice, then add the remaining olive oil a bit at a time, pulsing between additions. Do not keep the machine running; you want a coarse, chunky, uneven blend— what you're trying to do is mimic the kind of paste you'd get with a mortar and pestle (which you can certainly use, if you feel like it; I never would).

3. Add more olive oil if necessary to reach a nice pasty consistency; stir in the black pepper, then refrigerate or garnish if you wish and serve.

Simpler Tapenade. Milder in flavor and easier to make: omit the anchovies, garlic, and capers; add a teaspoon or so of red wine vinegar and a pinch of dried thyme (or, if you have it, herbes de Provence).

Green Tapenade. Use good green olives; the large kind from Sicily are nice, as are the small kind from southern France. Substitute canned tuna (in water or olive oil) for the anchovies, about ¼ cup. A little cumin—a teaspoon or so—is pleasant here.

Parsley Sauce ITALY ■ ■ ■
MAKES **ABOUT 2 CUPS**
TIME **30 MINUTES OR LESS**

Like the Uncooked Tomato-Mustard Sauce on page 606, this is often used to lend flavor to the ultrabland bollito misto, boiled mixed meats. But it's a perfect sauce for roasted or poached fish and can even be thinned with more olive oil to make a salad dressing.

1 cup chopped fresh parsley leaves

2 tablespoons pine nuts, toasted briefly in a dry skillet and chopped

1 hard-cooked egg (page 338), chopped

2 anchovy fillets, chopped

1 tablespoon drained capers, chopped

1 tablespoon balsamic vinegar

1 large or 2 medium shallots, minced

1 green tomato, cored, seeded, and diced

1 garlic clove, minced

Salt and black pepper to taste

About $1/2$ cup extra virgin olive oil

1. Combine all the ingredients except the olive oil. Add the oil a bit at a time to thin the mixture to a spoonable but still pasty consistency.
2. Let sit for about 30 minutes before serving if time allows. (Or cover and refrigerate for up to a day; return to room temperature before serving.)

Parsley Puree SPAIN ■ ▤ ▨

MAKES **ABOUT 1 CUP**

TIME **10 MINUTES**

Parsley puree is almost universal, but this is the Spanish version, sharp, garlicky, and great with fish or any grilled meat. There are a couple of different ways to make parsley puree, and other herbs can be used in the same way (pesto is very closely related).

1 cup roughly chopped parsley leaves (thin stems are okay)

2 garlic cloves, peeled, or to taste

$2/3$ cup extra virgin olive oil

$1/4$ cup sherry or other vinegar

Salt to taste

1. Combine the parsley in a blender or small food processor with the garlic and about half the oil.

Turn on the machine and puree, adding the remaining oil to make a smooth paste.
2. Add the vinegar and a large pinch of salt and blend for a second. Taste and adjust the seasoning, then serve or cover and refrigerate for up to a couple of days.

Cilantro Puree, Dill Puree, Basil Puree, or Mint Puree. Simply substitute the herb of your choice for the parsley.

Leaner Parsley Puree. Reduce the oil to $1/4$ cup; puree the herb with that, then drizzle in about $1/2$ cup warm water. Vinegar is unnecessary in this mix.

Anchovy Sauce ITALY ■ ▤ ▨

MAKES **ABOUT $1/2$ CUP**

TIME **30 MINUTES**

Obviously not a sauce for everyone. But in Liguria, where it seems people eat anchovies daily, it's popular. An incredibly easy sauce to spice up grilled chicken or fish—swordfish, for example—whether hot or cold.

1 tablespoon minced garlic

1 tablespoon extra virgin olive oil, or more if you're using salt-cured anchovies

6 or 8 anchovy fillets, minced, oil reserved

$1/4$ cup mild vinegar, such as white wine or rice

1 tomato (drained canned is fine), chopped

Salt and freshly ground black pepper to taste

1. Put the garlic in a small saucepan with the oil and/or anchovy oil; turn the heat to medium-low and cook just until the garlic begins to color. Add the anchovies and stir; cook for a minute over low heat.
2. Add the vinegar, raise the heat to medium, and cook until the liquid is reduced by half. Add the

tomato and cook until the sauce separates, about 10 minutes. Season, place in a bowl, and whisk with a fork for a minute or so. Serve hot or at room temperature or cover and refrigerate for up to a couple of days; rewarm before serving.

Fast, Fresh Tomato Sauce ITALY ■ ▩ ▨
MAKES **3 TO 4 CUPS**
TIME **20 MINUTES**

I love this over pasta, but it's also good used as you would salsa, hot or cold: over grilled or poached fish, meat, or poultry, or even as a dip. Be sure, one day, to try the Spanish version (page 606).

> **3 tablespoons extra virgin olive oil**
> **4 garlic cloves, sliced**
> **About 1 pound ripe fresh tomatoes (preferably peeled and seeded), chopped, or canned tomatoes, drained and chopped**
> **Salt and black pepper to taste**

1. Put the olive oil in a 10- or 12-inch skillet over medium-high heat. Add the garlic and, when the slices have colored slightly, after about 2 minutes, the tomatoes, along with some salt and pepper.
2. Cook, stirring occasionally, until the tomatoes break up and the mixture becomes saucy, about 10 minutes. Use immediately or cover and refrigerate for up to several days (reheat before serving).

Japanese Tomato Sauce with Miso. A terrific sauce for grilled fish, just shockingly good. In step 2, combine about $1/2$ cup of the cooked tomato liquid in a bowl with $1/4$ cup miso and 1 tablespoon rice vinegar and whisk to blend. Stir back into the sauce just before serving.

Uncooked Tomato-Mustard Sauce
ITALY ■ ▩
MAKES **ABOUT $1/2$ CUP**
TIME **1 HOUR, LARGELY UNATTENDED**

A simple sauce that is often served with bollito misto, the mixed boiled meat dish of central Italy, this is a great homemade replacement for ketchup. Nice with grilled meats.

> **1 medium onion, minced**
> **1 tablespoon minced garlic**
> **1 tablespoon white or wine vinegar**
> **Salt to taste**
> **1 teaspoon sugar**
> **3 tablespoons tomato paste**
> **1 tablespoon Dijon or other strong mustard**

1. Combine the first 5 ingredients in a bowl and let sit for an hour.
2. Add the tomato paste and mustard, then taste and add more salt, pepper, and vinegar if necessary. Serve immediately or cover and refrigerate; this will keep its flavor for several days.

Romesco Tomato-Nut Sauce for Fish
SPAIN ■ ▩ ▨
MAKES **ABOUT 1 CUP**
TIME **10 MINUTES**

There is no definitive source for how to make romesco, the sauce served with Zarzuela (page 270) and many other Spanish seafood dishes (you can serve it with any simple fish dish you like). I've had it cooked and uncooked, and I like it better raw, which may be due in part to the lack of hassle, but I also like the fresher flavor.

If you can find a fragrant dried chile, like a pasilla, by all means use it.

¼ cup blanched almonds or hazelnuts

2 medium or 1 large tomato, peeled, seeded, and roughly chopped

1 small dried chile or cayenne to taste

1 garlic clove, peeled, or more to taste

½ cup extra virgin olive oil, or to taste

Salt to taste

2 tablespoons sherry or other vinegar

1. Toast the nuts in a small dry skillet over medium heat, shaking the pan frequently, until they become aromatic and color slightly, less than 5 minutes.
2. Combine the tomato, chile, and garlic in a blender or small food processor and puree. Add the nuts and turn on the machine, adding the oil gradually until it is all used up. Add a pinch of salt and the vinegar, then taste and adjust the seasoning. You can make it stronger if you like, adding more chile, garlic, or vinegar. Use within a few hours.

Tomato Sauce with Garlic and Orange SPAIN ■ ▧

MAKES **ABOUT 2 CUPS**

TIME **30 MINUTES**

From the Mediterranean coast of Spain comes this distinctive sauce, whose flavors are reminiscent of bouillabaisse. Not surprisingly, it's often served on grilled fish, but it is equally good on chicken and incredible over pork. If possible, use strong-tasting oranges—Valencias are a good choice—not overly sweet ones like navels. In Spain, the oranges used for this are very acidic, even bitter.

3 tablespoons extra virgin olive oil

10 garlic cloves, peeled and lightly smashed

2 cups cored and chopped fresh or canned tomato, with liquid

Pinch of cayenne or ½ teaspoon paprika

Salt and black pepper to taste

1 orange, sliced

1. Put the oil in a 10-inch skillet or medium saucepan over medium heat. A minute later, add the garlic and cook, stirring and turning the cloves occasionally, until they are slightly browned, 5 to 10 minutes. Add the tomato and stir, then the remaining ingredients.
2. Adjust the heat so the mixture simmers steadily and cook, stirring occasionally, for about 15 minutes, until thick and quite tasty. Remove the orange (and, if you must, the garlic), and serve hot. (The sauce may be covered and refrigerated for up to a couple of days before reheating; add a bit of water if it seems too thick when you reheat.)

CENTRAL AND NORTHERN EUROPEAN SAUCES

Sharp Horseradish Sauce

EASTERN EUROPE ■ ▧ ▨

MAKES **ABOUT ½ CUP**

TIME **10 MINUTES**

Essentially prepared homemade horseradish and powerful stuff. If you want to make it in quantity, that's fine, but wear goggles (seriously). Even with small amounts, keep your hands away from your eyes until you have washed them well.

One 4- to 6-inch piece fresh horseradish

2 tablespoons white or wine vinegar, or to taste

Salt to taste

1. Peel and, using a hand grater or the fine grating disk on a food processor, finely grate the horseradish. (The food processor is easy, but there will be a lot of waste, so start with the larger amount, at least a 6-inch piece. Also, avert your eyes when you first turn on the machine.)
2. Combine the grated horseradish with the vinegar and some salt. If the mixture is thick but sharp enough, thin with a bit of water. Serve immediately or store, tightly covered, in the refrigerator. Horseradish loses potency over time, but this will stay pretty strong for days if not weeks.

FRESH AND BOTTLED HORSERADISH

Creamy Horseradish Sauce
SCANDINAVIA ■ ▨ ▨

MAKES **ABOUT 1 CUP**

TIME **10 MINUTES**

You can make horseradish sauce by blending freshly grated (or even bottled) horseradish into many dairy products: whipped cream or yogurt, for example. I like it best with sour cream, its flavor boosted with a little mustard and vinegar, though neither is essential.

1 cup sour cream

Salt and black pepper to taste

At least 2 tablespoons freshly grated horseradish or prepared horseradish to taste

1 teaspoon Dijon mustard, or to taste, optional

1 teaspoon white wine or other vinegar, or to taste, optional

1. Beat the sour cream lightly with a fork or whisk to thin it a bit. Stir in the remaining ingredients.

2. Taste and adjust the seasoning, then serve or cover and refrigerate for up to a day.

Mustard Dill Sauce SCANDINAVIA ■ ▨ ▨

MAKES **ABOUT 1 CUP**

TIME **10 MINUTES**

Practically ubiquitous in Sweden and wonderful with cold vegetables, gravlax, cold meats, and sandwiches. You can leave it fairly thick and use it as a dip or thin it as much as you like to make it a little more saucy or even as thin as a salad dressing.

$1/4$ cup strong mustard, like English or Dijon, or to taste

1 tablespoon sugar

Salt and black pepper to taste

$1/2$ cup mayonnaise, preferably homemade (page 602)

2 tablespoons snipped fresh dill

Extra virgin olive oil or heavy cream as needed

1. Put the mustard, sugar, salt, pepper, mayonnaise, and dill in a bowl and beat to blend.
2. Add the oil or cream as needed to reach the desired consistency. Taste and adjust the seasoning and serve or cover and refrigerate for up to a day.

NEW WORLD SAUCES

Chili Powder MEXICO ■ ▦ ▦

MAKES **ABOUT ¹/₂ CUP**
TIME **20 MINUTES**

To me, chili powder need not be superhot, but you can change that if you like—just add cayenne or some spicy dried chiles (most of the common dried red ones you find are pretty fiery). But it is easy enough to add heat at any stage of cooking or even at the table, whereas the warm, welcoming flavor of good chili powder is hard to come by.

When you're buying dried chiles, look for those that are not brittle; they should retain some moisture and even be a bit soft.

4 ancho or 8 dried New Mexico chiles, stemmed and
seeded, 1 dried hot chile, like chile de árbol, stemmed
and seeded, or cayenne to taste
2 tablespoons cumin seeds
2 tablespoons dried oregano, preferably from Mexico

1. Combine the whole chiles and cumin seeds in a large skillet over medium heat. Cook, shaking the pan occasionally, until lightly browned and fragrant, just a few minutes; for the last minute of cooking, add the oregano.
2. Cool, then grind in a spice or coffee grinder to a fine powder; add cayenne at this stage if you're using it (some cooks also put in a bit of garlic pow-

der). Store in a tightly covered opaque container for up to several months.

Recado Rojo Annatto Seasoning Paste

MEXICO ■ ▦
MAKES **ABOUT ¹/₂ CUP**
TIME **AT LEAST 2 HOURS, LARGELY UNATTENDED**

Classically used for Cochinita Pibil (page 351), this gorgeous, bright red paste can be smeared on any meat you're about to roast or grill. Its color belies its flavor, which is not at all hot (though you can throw a chile in there if you like).

Annatto—or achiote—is something you've probably encountered unknowingly, since it colors processed cheeses, margarine, and lipstick. The triangular, brick-colored seeds of the annatto tree have been especially important in the Yucatán peninsula and South and Central America for centuries; make sure the seeds you buy are bright red, smell earthy or musky, and taste slightly peppery. Whole seeds keep for a year or more in a tightly covered container.

¹/₂ cup annatto seeds
2 tablespoons white or cider vinegar
1 teaspoon black peppercorns
1 teaspoon chopped fresh oregano leaves or dried
**   Mexican oregano**
1 teaspoon cumin seeds
¹/₃ cinnamon stick
1 teaspoon coriander seeds
1 teaspoon salt
8 garlic cloves, peeled

1. Combine the annatto, vinegar, and 2 tablespoons water in a small saucepan over medium heat. Do not boil; turn off the heat when steam rises from the mixture. Let stand for about 2 hours.

2. Meanwhile, combine the peppercorns, oregano, cumin, cinnamon, and coriander in a small skillet and turn the heat to medium. Toast, shaking the pan occasionally, until the mixture is fragrant, 3 to 5 minutes. Turn off the heat.

3. When the annatto has soaked, combine it with its liquid, the toasted spices, the salt, and the garlic in a food processor. Pulse the machine on and off, scraping down the sides as necessary, until the mixture is pasty (add a little more water if necessary). Use immediately or cover and refrigerate for up to several days.

Salsa Fresca MEXICO ■ ■ ■
MAKES **ABOUT 2 CUPS**
TIME **10 MINUTES**

Probably the quickest salsa you can make and a fresh, delicious one for chips or simply cooked fish or chicken. Best with good fresh tomatoes, but still decent with canned (and definitely better with canned than with hard, unripe "fresh").

> 2 large ripe fresh tomatoes, cored and chopped
> 1/2 large white onion, minced
> 1/4 teaspoon minced garlic, or to taste
> 1 habanero or jalapeño chile, stemmed, seeded, and
>   minced, or to taste
> 1/4 cup chopped fresh cilantro leaves
> 1 tablespoon fresh lime juice or 1 teaspoon red wine
>   vinegar
> Salt and freshly ground black pepper

1. Combine all the ingredients, then taste and adjust the seasoning as necessary.

2. If possible, let the flavors marry for 15 minutes or so before serving, but by all means serve within a couple of hours.

Blistered Tomato Salsa MEXICO ■ ■ ■
MAKES **ABOUT 2 CUPS**
TIME **20 MINUTES**

If you can grill the tomatoes for this salsa—especially over wood—so much the better. But you can broil or even pan-grill them, and the salsa will still be good, as long as you make sure they blacken a bit. This makes a wonderful all-purpose condiment, and a great salsa for burritos and tacos; it's also fabulous used in an omelet or scrambled eggs.

> 12 plum tomatoes, cored
> 1 large white onion, chopped
> 2 garlic cloves, minced
> 1 tablespoon pure chile powder, like ancho or
>   New Mexico, or to taste
> Salt to taste
> 1 cup chopped fresh cilantro leaves

1. Grill, broil, or pan-grill the tomatoes, as close to the heat source as you can get them, until blistered and a little blackened, 5 to 10 minutes.

2. Put them in a blender, skins and all, with the onion, garlic, chile powder, and a big pinch of salt. Whiz until chunky, then stir in the cilantro by hand. This is best used right away but will retain decent flavor, covered and refrigerated, for a day or two.

Salsa Roja Cooked Red Salsa MEXICO ■ ■
MAKES **2 CUPS**
TIME **30 TO 60 MINUTES**

A standard and very useful salsa, great with anything grilled. I don't make it fiery hot—it's based on mild chiles—but you can add more of the hot ones if you like, and it's easy enough.

2 fresh or dried poblano (ancho) or other relatively mild
    chiles

2 tablespoons extra virgin olive oil

2 large onions, roughly chopped

2 celery stalks, roughly chopped

2 carrots, roughly chopped

2 tablespoons chopped garlic

2 pounds tomatoes, peeled, seeded, and chopped,
    with their liquid (canned are fine)

Salt and black pepper to taste

1 jalapeño, habanero, or chipotle chile, stemmed, seeded,
    and minced, or cayenne to taste, optional

1. Roast the chiles over a grill or in a dry skillet, turning frequently, until they are lightly charred, about 10 minutes (dried will be faster than fresh). Remove the stems and seeds (and, from the fresh, as much of the skin as you easily can) and mince.

2. Put the olive oil in a saucepan or skillet over medium-high heat. Add the chiles, onions, celery, carrots, and garlic and cook, stirring occasionally, until the onions soften, about 5 minutes. Add the tomatoes, some salt, plenty of pepper, and, if you're using it, the hot chile; adjust the heat so the mixture simmers steadily but not violently; cook, stirring occasionally, for about 20 minutes, until the mixture is saucy.

3. You may serve the salsa as is or cool and puree or strain it, then cook it again until it is somewhat reduced and thick. In any case, taste and adjust the seasonings. Serve hot or at room temperature.

Tomato-Chipotle Salsa MEXICO ■ ■ ▨
MAKES **ABOUT 2 CUPS**
TIME **30 MINUTES**

Reminiscent of canned chipotles in adobo, but obviously fresher and with an emphasis on the tomatoes

and the smokiness the chipotles bring, rather than their heat. (You can, of course, make it hotter by adding more chipotles.) It's good stirred into soups but is used primarily as a salsa for bland dishes, whose blandness will be turned around immediately.

2 tablespoons lard or neutral oil, like corn or grapeseed

1 medium white onion, chopped

Salt and black pepper to taste

2 dried chipotle chiles, or to taste

2 cups cored and chopped tomatoes, preferably fresh

Chopped fresh cilantro leaves for garnish

1. Put the lard in a medium saucepan or skillet over medium heat. When it is hot, add the onion and some salt and pepper and cook, stirring occasionally, until it begins to brown at the edges, 5 to 10 minutes. Add the chiles, tomatoes, and $1/2$ cup water and adjust the heat so the mixture simmers steadily but not violently. Cook for about 15 minutes, stirring occasionally, or until the chiles are soft and the tomatoes broken up. Taste and add more salt and pepper if necessary.

2. Cool for a few minutes (you should always take care when pureeing hot mixtures), then remove the stems from the chipotles. Put the mixture in a blender and puree. Use immediately, garnished with the cilantro, or cover and refrigerate for up to several days, garnishing only at the last minute. (Bring back to room temperature before serving.)

Habanero-Garlic Salsa MEXICO ■ ■ ▨
MAKES **ABOUT $1/4$ CUP**
TIME **20 MINUTES**

The variously colored habanero (also called Scotch bonnet, for its shape) is blisteringly hot. It also has wonderful flavor, which, I suppose, is why people tolerate it. This salsa will turn up on any grilled meat, but it's often served with Cochinita Pibil (page 351).

Care is needed when handling all chiles, but especially habaneros; do not touch your eyes or other sensitive parts of your body after touching the chiles until you wash your hands very well (some people wear gloves to handle them, and that's not a bad idea).

5 fresh habanero chiles

5 garlic cloves, peeled

1/4 cup fresh lime juice

Large pinch of salt

1. Combine the habaneros and garlic in a small skillet over medium heat. Cook, shaking the skillet occasionally, until the garlic browns all over and softens a bit and the chiles brown, about 10 minutes. (If the smoke bothers you, turn down the heat a bit or partially wrap the garlic and chiles in foil and roast in a 400°F oven for about 30 minutes.) Stem and seed the chiles (then wash your hands).

2. Combine the chiles, garlic, lime juice, and salt in a food processor and turn the machine on, stopping it to scrape down the sides as necessary. Process until the mixture is pasty. Serve or cover and refrigerate for up to a few days.

Pasilla Salsa MEXICO ■ ■ ■

MAKES **ABOUT 1 CUP**

TIME **20 MINUTES**

When dried—as you will usually find them—pasillas are often called chile negro, or black chile. They are thin, small, shriveled, and very dark. They are also earthy and not especially hot, so they yield a rich, densely flavored sauce traditionally used with lamb,

beef, and chicken. If you want some heat, soak a dried chipotle or two with the pasillas. If you can find fresh tomatillos, use them in place of the tomatoes. Slip off the papery husks and add a little water to the sauce.

3 to 5 pasilla chiles, at least 1 ounce, to taste

2 tablespoons lard or neutral oil, like corn or grapeseed

4 small tomatoes, cored and chopped

Salt and black pepper to taste

2 garlic cloves, peeled

1/2 large white onion, peeled and chunked

1. Soak the pasillas in hot water to cover until they are quite soft, about 10 minutes. Meanwhile, put the lard in a small saucepan over medium heat; a minute later, add the tomatoes, along with some salt and pepper. Cook, stirring occasionally, until soft, about 10 minutes.

2. Drain the chiles and reserve some of their soaking liquid. Remove their stems and seeds; tear each into several pieces as you do so. Combine in a blender with the tomatoes, garlic, onion, and a little of the soaking liquid. Puree, adding more liquid if necessary to allow the machine to do its work. Taste and adjust the seasoning, then serve warm or refrigerate.

Pipián Pumpkin Seed Sauce MEXICO ■ ■ ■

MAKES **ABOUT 2 CUPS**

TIME **ABOUT 30 MINUTES**

Pumpkin seeds figure heavily in much Mexican cooking. You can buy them toasted, but toasting them is an easy enough task, and they're arguably better when toasted fresh—especially in lard or oil. (If you'd like to avoid the mess—or the lard—you can also toast the seeds on a baking sheet in a 350°F oven or in a dry skillet as you would sesame seeds, page 596.)

Ancho chiles—dried poblanos—are mild and richly flavored. You can use them freely without worrying about overpowering heat.

This sauce is best served over something simple, like grilled steak or chicken.

1 cup hulled pumpkin seeds

4 tablespoons lard or neutral oil, like corn or grapeseed

2 cups chicken stock, preferably homemade (page 160), or water

3 or 4 ancho chiles, to taste

2 garlic cloves, peeled

Salt and freshly ground black pepper to taste

Fresh lime juice to taste

1. If the pumpkin seeds you have are already toasted, proceed to step 2. Otherwise, heat 3 tablespoons of the lard in a heavy skillet over medium-high heat. A minute later, add the pumpkin seeds and cook, shaking and stirring the pan constantly for a minute or two, until the seeds start to puff. (Take care not to overcook the seeds, which will make the sauce bitter; and be prepared for flying seeds popping out of the pan.) Remove the toasted seeds with a slotted spoon and cool. (Discard any blackened seeds.) Meanwhile, warm the stock and soak the chiles in it. When they have softened, after 10 to 15 minutes, remove their stems and seeds; reserve the soaking liquid.

2. Put the seeds in a food processor and process until pasty, stopping the machine and scraping down the sides if necessary. Add the garlic, chiles, and as much of the soaking liquid as you need to process until quite smooth.

3. Turn the heat under the pan back to medium and add the remaining lard or oil. Reheat the sauce with enough liquid to thin to a pleasing consistency, stirring occasionally, until it just boils and thickens slightly. Remove from the heat. Taste and add salt and pepper as needed, then stir in the lime

juice; serve hot or at room temperature. (This keeps well, covered and refrigerated, for up to 3 days; bring back to room temperature or reheat before serving and always add the lime juice at the last minute.)

Pipián with Tomatoes and Garlic. In step 2, add 2 tomatoes (preferably peeled and seeded) and 2 to 4 garlic cloves, peeled, to the mix; you will need less of the reserved liquid.

Simpler, Leaner Pipián. Omit the lard and toast the pumpkin seeds as you would sesame seeds (page 596). Omit the ancho chiles and puree the toasted seeds with chile powder to taste (about 1 tablespoon), at least $1/4$ cup chicken stock, preferably homemade (page 160), or water, and salt and pepper to taste. Reheat and add the lime juice.

Papaya and Red Onion Salsa

MEXICO ■ ▦ ▨

MAKES **ABOUT 2 CUPS**

TIME **20 MINUTES**

The best substitute for papaya here, believe it or not, is watermelon. Cantaloupe isn't bad either. Serve this with any grilled meat, poultry, or fish.

2 cups papaya in $1/2$-inch chunks

$1/2$ cup minced red onion

$1/2$ cup minced red, yellow, or green bell pepper or a combination

1 tablespoon extra virgin olive oil

2 tablespoons fresh lime juice

Salt and black pepper to taste

1 jalapeño or other fresh chile, stemmed, seeded, and minced, or hot red pepper flakes to taste

$1/4$ cup or more chopped fresh cilantro leaves

1. Combine all the ingredients. Let sit for about 5 minutes, then taste and adjust the seasoning.
2. Serve immediately or refrigerate for up to a couple of hours. (Bring back to room temperature before serving.)

Salsa Verde Green Sauce MEXICO ■ ▨ ▨
MAKES **ABOUT 2 CUPS**
TIME **15 MINUTES**

This is a sharp, spiky sauce, but not a superhot one (it's not a supergreen one, either!). Use it as a dip for chips or vegetables or as a basting sauce when roasting meat, fish, or vegetables.

> 4 poblano or ancho chiles
> 1/4 cup extra virgin olive oil
> 2 large onions, roughly chopped
> 1/2 cup chopped fresh cilantro leaves
> Juice of 1 lime
> Salt and black pepper to taste

1. Roast or toast the chiles either over a grill or in a dry skillet, turning frequently, until they are lightly charred all over, about 10 minutes (dried will be faster than fresh). Remove the stems and seeds (and, from the fresh, as much of the skin as you easily can) and mince.
2. Heat the olive oil over medium heat in a 10-inch skillet; add the onions and chiles and cook, stirring, until well softened and lightly browned, about 10 minutes. Remove from the heat and cool.
3. Puree in a blender, then stir in the cilantro and lime juice; add salt and pepper to taste. Serve at room temperature or cover and refrigerate for up to a day (bring back to room temperature before serving).

Salsa Verde with Tomatillos
MEXICO ■ ▨ ▨
MAKES **ABOUT 2 CUPS**
TIME **10 MINUTES**

A raw salsa, with nice strong flavors. Best with tomatillos, but still good with not-too-hard green tomatoes. I like to mix a little just-ripe red tomato in as well.

> 1 1/2 cups husked and chopped tomatillo or cored and chopped green tomato
> 1/2 cup cored and chopped ripe tomato
> 1 teaspoon minced garlic, or to taste
> 1/4 cup chopped fresh cilantro leaves
> Salt and black pepper to taste
> Cayenne to taste

Mix all the ingredients, taste, and adjust the seasoning. Serve immediately or cover and refrigerate for up to several hours (bring back to room temperature before serving).

Roasted Onion Salsa MEXICO ■ ▨
MAKES **ABOUT 2 CUPS**
TIME **30 MINUTES, PLUS TIME TO PREHEAT THE GRILL AND MARINATING TIME IF POSSIBLE**

Somewhere between a vegetable dish and a salsa, this is great as a topping for simple grilled fish or chicken. If you have a gas grill, you can make this almost effortlessly; it's easy, too, when you've started a charcoal fire for another purpose.

> 2 large red or white onions
> Salt and black pepper to taste
> 1/2 habanero chile, stemmed, seeded, and minced, or to taste, optional

2 tablespoons fresh orange juice

1 tablespoon fresh lime juice

1/2 cup chopped fresh cilantro leaves

1. Start a charcoal fire or preheat a gas grill or preheat the oven to 450°F. Grill the onions over not-too-high heat or roast in the oven in an aluminum-foil-lined pan, turning as necessary, until they blacken slightly and become quite soft, 15 to 30 minutes.

2. Peel and roughly chop the onions, then combine with salt and pepper, the habanero if you're using it, and the citrus juices. Marinate for several hours or serve immediately, stirring in the cilantro and adjusting the seasoning just before serving.

Cebollas Curtidas Pickled Onion Relish

MEXICO ■ ▩

MAKES **ABOUT 2 CUPS**

TIME **ABOUT 30 MINUTES, PLUS MARINATING TIME**

I saw these lovely red onions throughout the Yucatán and wondered why their color was so vivid. Turns out they're pickled in beet juice (you can omit the beets if you like; in fact they add little flavor). These are a perfect condiment for plain grilled fish.

2 large red onions

Salt and black pepper to taste

1 beet, peeled and grated or finely chopped

2 garlic cloves, peeled and lightly smashed

2 bay leaves

1 teaspoon fresh oregano leaves or 1/2 teaspoon dried

1/2 cup white vinegar

Juice of 2 limes

Juice of 2 lemons

Juice of 2 oranges

1. Peel and slice the onions; sprinkle liberally with salt and toss. Let sit while you make the pickling liquid; 30 minutes would be ideal.

2. Combine the beet, garlic, bay leaves, oregano, and vinegar in a small saucepan and add water to cover. Bring to a boil and simmer for 5 minutes. Cool slightly.

3. Rinse the onions, then put them in a bowl and strain the pickling liquid over them. Cool, then stir in the citrus juices and a few grindings of black pepper. Let rest for at least 30 minutes before serving or refrigerate for up to several days (bring back to room temperature before serving). Be sure to taste and adjust seasoning before serving.

Xec Mayan Citrus Salsa MEXICO ▩

MAKES **ABOUT 2 CUPS**

TIME **15 MINUTES**

A tiny little side condiment served with grilled chicken or fish that can make any meal sing. It's fine without any chile at all, but I like a touch.

This is a very fragile dish; make it at the last minute and serve it all at once. It will go fast, believe me.

1 orange

1 small grapefruit

1 lemon

1/2 cup chopped fresh cilantro leaves

1/2 habanero or other hot fresh chile, seeded and minced, or to taste, optional

Salt to taste

1. Cut the orange in half horizontally and section it as you would a grapefruit; do this over a bowl to capture all its juice. Remove the seeds and combine the flesh and juice in the bowl. Repeat with the grapefruit and lemon.

2. Stir in the remaining ingredients, taste and adjust the seasoning, and serve.

Adobo PUERTO RICO ■ ■ ■

MAKES **ABOUT 1 CUP**

TIME **5 MINUTES**

Adobo is an oregano-based spice mixture that, when purchased in stores, is usually made from dried ingredients—dried oregano, onion powder, and garlic powder. This fresh version is infinitely better; use it as a rub for pork, chicken, or beef.

> 2 garlic cloves, peeled
>
> 1 small onion, peeled and quartered
>
> 1 tablespoon fresh oregano or marjoram leaves
>
> 1 teaspoon salt
>
> 1 teaspoon freshly ground black pepper

1. Mince all the ingredients together by hand or combine them in a food processor and turn the machine on, stopping to scrape down the sides as necessary.
2. Use immediately or store in the refrigerator, tightly covered, for a couple of days.

Avocado "Mayonnaise" CARIBBEAN ■ ■ ■

MAKES **ABOUT 1 CUP**

TIME **20 MINUTES**

Neither mayonnaise nor guacamole, but something in between and, in some instances, better than either as a sandwich spread. Great, too, as a dip for cold shellfish. You can also thin it with heavy cream, sour cream, or yogurt and use it as a salad dressing (think of it as real Green Goddess). Make it spicy or not, as you like; I've had it both ways.

> 1 large or 2 small ripe avocados, peeled and pitted
>
> 1 habanero or other hot fresh chile, stemmed and seeded, or hot red pepper flakes, or to taste
>
> 1 garlic clove, peeled and lightly smashed
>
> 2 scallions, trimmed and roughly chopped
>
> 1 tablespoon neutral oil, like corn or grapeseed
>
> 1/4 cup chopped fresh cilantro leaves
>
> Juice of 1 lime, or to taste
>
> Salt and black pepper to taste

1. Combine all the ingredients but the lime juice, salt, and pepper in a food processor and blend until smooth.
2. Scrape into a bowl and add the lime juice, salt, and pepper to taste, then taste and adjust the seasoning. Serve or cover and refrigerate for up to 2 days.

Cilantro Salsa

SOUTH AMERICA, CARIBBEAN ■ ■ ■

MAKES **ABOUT 1 CUP**

TIME **10 MINUTES**

Killer on grilled meats, this simple herb puree is like pesto with more kick.

> 1 cup chopped fresh cilantro leaves
>
> 2 garlic cloves, peeled and lightly smashed
>
> 1 tablespoon peeled and roughly chopped fresh ginger
>
> 1 habanero or jalapeño chile, stemmed, seeded, and roughly chopped, or hot red pepper flakes to taste
>
> 1/4 cup extra virgin olive or neutral oil, like corn or grapeseed, or as needed
>
> Salt and black pepper to taste
>
> Fresh lime juice to taste

1. Combine the cilantro with the garlic, ginger, chile, and oil in a blender or small food processor. Turn on the machine and puree, adding more oil if nec-

essary to form a smooth paste and stopping the machine to scrape down the sides as needed.

2. Transfer to a bowl and add some salt and pepper, then thin with a tablespoon or two of lime juice. Taste and adjust the seasoning and serve or cover and refrigerate for up to a day (bring back to room temperature before serving).

Chimichurri SOUTH AMERICA ■ ■ ▨

MAKES **ABOUT 1 1/2 CUPS**

TIME **10 MINUTES**

Chimichurri should be quite strong; you can cut back on the garlic and/or the red pepper, but it won't be the same. Try it at least once at full strength; you'll be surprised by how much the freshness of the parsley keeps everything in perspective, especially when served with meat, which it usually is.

1 cup finely chopped (but not minced) parsley leaves, preferably flat-leaf

1/3 cup extra virgin olive oil

3 tablespoons fresh lemon juice

1 tablespoon finely chopped garlic

1 teaspoon hot red pepper flakes, or to taste

Salt to taste

1. Combine the parsley, olive oil, lemon juice, garlic, and red pepper in a bowl and stir to combine. Season to taste with salt and add more red pepper if you like (it should be quite hot).
2. Serve within a few hours; do not refrigerate.

Mojo Criollo Creole Garlic Sauce

CARIBBEAN ■ ■ ▨

MAKES **ABOUT 1 CUP**

TIME **20 MINUTES**

Powerfully delicious, this sauce is served throughout the Caribbean, often with grilled chicken but also over vegetables. Best made with the juice of sour oranges, but you won't find those here; I use a combination of orange and lime juices.

1/4 cup peeled garlic cloves

1 medium onion, peeled and cut into chunks

Salt and black pepper to taste

1/4 cup extra virgin olive or neutral oil, like corn or grapeseed

1/4 cup fresh orange juice

1/4 cup fresh lime juice

1. Combine the first 4 ingredients in a small food processor and process to a paste.
2. Put a small skillet or saucepan over medium heat and wait a minute. Add the garlic mixture and cook, stirring frequently, until it sizzles and begins to color. Add the juices and cook, stirring occasionally, for about a minute more. Serve immediately or cover and refrigerate for up to a day (reheat gently before serving).

Desserts   While it's probably true that no place in the world has developed desserts as an art form the way Western Europe and the United States have, it's equally true that the sweet tooth is a global phenomenon and there are delightful nuggets to be found everywhere. Most—thankfully, in my opinion—are not of the stature or complexity of the great French creations and are perfectly suitable for home kitchens.

FRUIT DESSERTS

Fruit is best treated simply and often is. The classic pies and tarts are rarely extravagant, and most of the fruit-based recipes here are even easier than those.

Caramelized Apples FRANCE ■ ▥

MAKES **6 TO 8 SERVINGS**

TIME **ABOUT 1 HOUR**

Not "caramel apples"—whole apples coated with candy—but caramelized: sliced apples baked in caramelized butter and sugar until lightly browned, served warm or at room temperature. If you think applesauce smells good when you make it, wait till you try this—for many, a new way to enjoy our continent's favorite fruit.

There are two ways I like to prepare this: one when I have time and one when I'm in a hurry. The preferred method—essentially a tarte tatin without the crust (if you like, top it with Sweet Tart Pastry, page 654, before baking)—is the main recipe, but it takes a while. This is good with pears (not too ripe) or Asian pears, too.

6 tablespoons (^{3}/4 stick) unsalted butter

1^1/4 cups sugar

4 to 5 pounds crisp, not-too-sweet apples, like Granny Smith, peeled, cored, and sliced

^{1}/2 teaspoon ground cinnamon, optional

1. Preheat the oven to 400°F. Combine 4 tablespoons (^{1}/2 stick) of the butter with 1 cup of the sugar and a tablespoon of water in a 10 or 12 inch nonstick ovenproof skillet and turn the heat to medium. Cook, shaking the pan occasionally (don't stir), until the sugar melts into the butter and the mixture bubbles. Turn off the heat and add the apples

in layers; about halfway through, dot with some of the remaining butter and sugar. Use the rest of the butter and sugar on top of the last layer, along with the cinnamon if you like. Put in the oven.

2. Bake, undisturbed, until the apples give up their liquid and it evaporates and the sides of the mass are dark brown and sticky looking. This will take around 45 minutes, but it could be considerably longer or shorter depending on the water content of your apples. Remove and let cool. Serve straight from the pan or—for a more attractive presentation—invert onto a plate.

Apples Cooked in Butter. Great with ice cream: Melt 4 tablespoons (^{1}/2 stick) butter in the pan; add the apples and sugar, only ^{1}/2 to ^{3}/4 cup in this instance, depending on the sweetness of your apples; add the cinnamon at this point too. Cook on top of the stove, shaking and gently turning the apples, until they are tender and lightly browned. Serve hot or warm.

Äppletorte Apple Cake SCANDINAVIA ■ ▥

MAKES **6 TO 8 SERVINGS**

TIME **ABOUT 1 HOUR**

There are probably as many apple cakes as there are varieties of apples. This one is easy, rich, and delicious, and it keeps fairly well, too. Use an apple that will soften during cooking, like Cortland, Rome, Golden Delicious, or McIntosh.

Pinch of salt

1 teaspoon baking powder

1 teaspoon ground cinnamon

2 cups flour, plus some for the pan

^{1}/2 pound (2 sticks) butter, softened, plus some for the pan

1 cup sugar, plus more for the top

3 eggs

4 cups peeled, cored, and sliced apples

Ice cream, crème fraîche, sour cream, or sweetened
   whipped cream for serving

1. Preheat the oven to 350°F. Combine the dry ingredients in a bowl. Use an electric mixer to cream the butter and sugar together, then add the eggs, one at a time, beating after each addition until the mixture is smooth. By hand, stir in the dry ingredients, stirring just to combine; do not beat. Stir in the apples.

2. Grease and flour a 9- or 10-inch springform or tube pan and pour in the batter; sprinkle liberally with sugar. Bake until a toothpick inserted in the center comes out clean, 45 minutes or a little longer. Cool on a rack, then remove from the pan and serve with the ice cream or other topping.

Apricot Meringue with Walnuts

FRANCE ■ ▪

MAKES **6 SERVINGS**

TIME **ABOUT 1 HOUR**

There are many ways to serve this simple classic, but I like to pipe the meringue into a ring on a baking sheet, then fill the center with the puree and top it with a little sour cream. The result is a surprising, rather elegant winter dessert that's not too heavy but certainly sweet enough and fun to eat.

$\frac{1}{2}$ cup walnuts, pecans, blanched almonds, or hazelnuts

4 egg whites

1 cup sugar, plus more to taste

1 teaspoon vanilla extract

1 teaspoon white vinegar

2 teaspoons cornstarch

Pinch of salt

2 cups dried apricots

2 tablespoons fruity white wine, like Gewürztraminer,
   optional

Crème fraîche or sour cream, sweetened whipped cream,
   or vanilla ice cream for serving

1. Toast the nuts in a small dry skillet over medium heat, shaking the pan frequently until they color slightly, about 5 minutes. Chop finely or grind in a food processor (do not pulverize completely; you do not want a powder).

2. Preheat the oven to 300°F. Beat the egg whites in a bowl or mixer until foamy; gradually add the sugar, vanilla, vinegar, cornstarch, and salt and beat until the whites hold quite stiff peaks. Line a baking sheet with parchment paper (or use a non-

SPREADING OR PIPING MERINGUE

stick sheet) and pipe with a pastry tube or spread the whites into a ring or other shape. Bake until firm and lightly browned, about 45 minutes.

3. Meanwhile, poach the apricots in water barely to cover, along with the wine if you're using it, until very soft, 20 minutes or more, depending on how dry they were to begin with. Drain excess cooking liquid, reserving it. Puree the apricots in a blender with sugar to taste, adding enough of the cooking liquid to allow the machine to do its work.

4. When the meringue is done and has cooled slightly, pour the apricot puree into the middle of the ring or around the meringue, and serve, with the topping of your choice.

Apricot, Cherry, or Pear Clafouti

FRANCE ■ ▧

MAKES **4 TO 6 SERVINGS**

TIME **1 HOUR**

Pronounced *cla-FOO-tee,* this is one of the most successful spontaneous desserts you can add to your repertoire, yet fancy enough for a blowout dinner party. It can be made with any ripe fruit (including berries, and even apples if you cook them) and (aside from such tasks as pitting cherries and the like) takes well under an hour to prepare.

Note that in place of the cream and milk mixture you can use half-and-half.

> Butter for the pan
> $^{1}/_{2}$ cup plus 1 tablespoon granulated sugar
> About 1 pound ripe apricots, halved and pitted,
> $1^{1}/_{4}$ pounds sweet cherries, pitted, or 3 or 4 very ripe
> pears, stemmed, peeled, halved, and cored
> 3 eggs
> 1 vanilla bean or 1 teaspoon vanilla extract
> $^{3}/_{4}$ cup flour

> $^{3}/_{4}$ cup heavy cream or yogurt
> $^{3}/_{4}$ cup milk
> Pinch of salt
> Confectioners' sugar for garnish

1. Preheat the oven to 375°F. Butter a gratin dish that will hold the fruit in one layer; sprinkle it with the tablespoon of granulated sugar, then swirl the sugar around to coat all inner surfaces. Lay the fruit in the dish, cut sides down.

2. Use a whisk to beat the eggs until foamy. Add the remaining $^{1}/_{2}$ cup granulated sugar and beat with a whisk or an electric mixer until foamy and fairly thick. Split the vanilla bean in half lengthwise and use a small sharp knife to scrape the seeds into the eggs, discarding the pod, or add the vanilla extract.

3. Add the flour and continue to beat until thick and smooth. Add the cream, milk, and salt. Pour the batter over the fruit and bake for about 20 minutes, or until the clafouti is nicely browned on top and a knife inserted into it comes out clean. Sift some confectioners' sugar over it and serve warm or at room temperature.

Baked Apricots FRANCE ▧

MAKES **4 SERVINGS**

TIME **30 MINUTES**

There is nothing quite like ripe fresh apricots, but a good one is hard to find (and dried apricots, as good as they are, will not do here). Roasting them in the oven, however, intensifies their sweetness and makes average apricots quite succulent. As a result, few fruit desserts are as simple and delicious as this one.

> 3 tablespoons unsalted butter, cut into small cubes, plus
> more for the baking dish
> 1 pound ripe fresh apricots, halved and pitted

2 tablespoons sugar

Crème fraîche or vanilla ice cream for serving

1. Preheat the oven to 400°F. Generously butter a large baking dish. Put the apricot halves, cut side up, in the dish in one layer. Sprinkle with sugar, dot with butter, and bake until tender, about 15 minutes. The apricots should be caramelized with the sugar but retain their shape.
2. Serve immediately with crème fraîche or ice cream.

Baked Figs or Apricots Stuffed with Walnuts or Almonds MIDDLE EAST ■ ■ ■

MAKES **4 SERVINGS**

TIME **30 MINUTES**

Whether seasoned with rose water or cinnamon, these are beguiling. They're best with fresh fruit that is just short of perfectly ripe, but you can use reconstituted dried fruit also. Though they will not take as much stuffing, dates are good this way too. Rose water can be found in small bottles at Middle Eastern stores.

1/2 cup sugar

1/2 cup blanched almonds or walnuts

2 tablespoons butter, 1 tablespoon chilled and

**   1 tablespoon softened**

1 teaspoon ground cinnamon or 1 tablespoon rose water

12 fresh figs or apricots, not too ripe

1 tablespoon fresh lemon juice

Sweetened yogurt or sour cream for serving, optional

1. Preheat the oven to 350°F. Combine 1/4 cup of the sugar with 1/4 cup water in a small saucepan and bring to a boil. Stir and set aside.
2. Combine the remaining 1/4 cup sugar with the nuts in a small food processor or in a spice or cof-

fee grinder and process to a powder; add the chilled butter and process to make a paste, then blend in the cinnamon. Slit open each piece of fruit; if you're using apricots, remove the pit. Stuff with a bit of the nut mixture and press to reseal.
3. Use the softened butter to grease the bottom of a dish or pan just large enough to hold the fruit; arrange the fruit so that it fits without crowding. Bake for 15 to 20 minutes, or until warm and softened. Stir the lemon juice into the sugar syrup and drizzle over the fruit. Serve the fruit warm, at room temperature, or cold, with or without yogurt or sour cream.

Stuffed Dried Dates, Figs, Apricots, or Prunes. These can be made days in advance of eating, though they will be eaten before then: Omit step 1. In step 2, omit the butter, using enough sweet wine, rose water, or orange-flower water to bind the nuts, sugar, and cinnamon. Make a slit in the side of any of the dried fruits (remove the pit if necessary) and stuff with a bit of this filling. Pinch to close.

Bananas in Coconut Milk

SOUTHEAST ASIA ■

MAKES **4 SERVINGS**

TIME **15 MINUTES**

The small "finger" bananas are perfect for this, because they're denser-fleshed than regular bananas; you can find them at many supermarkets and almost all Asian and Latin markets. Regular bananas work well too, of course, but they should not be too ripe.

1 1/2 cups thick, unsweetened coconut milk, preferably

**   homemade (page 584)**

2 tablespoons sugar, plus more to taste

Bananas and Plantains

Bananas are no longer simple. We now see many varieties—green-striped red ones with pink interiors, tiny finger bananas with orange flesh, and, if you move beyond the sweet varieties, countless subtly different plantains, or "cooking" bananas, that start out forest green or crimson red and, when fully ripe, are blacker than you'd ever want an "eating" banana to be.

Bananas, it should be noted, are "full-service" plants in the tropical regions where they're grown—their leaves are used like corn husks to wrap foods for cooking, and the flower, which has a pleasantly bitter, astringent flavor, is added to stews or salads or recruited as a garnish.

Our familiar big yellow bananas are bred for export and, like many fruits and vegetables designed for transport and long shelf life, they are insipid compared to some of their cousins. Don't hesitate to experiment with other varieties that you see, because they'll often be sweeter and more full flavored. "Cooking" and "eating" distinctions between plantains and bananas aside, both are great (if not better) cooked.

One distinctive thing about plantains versus bananas that is very real: plantains require a special technique to peel, even when very ripe; see page 472.

---

¹/₂ teaspoon salt, plus more to taste

7 or 8 finger bananas or 3 regular bananas

1. Put the coconut milk, sugar, and salt in a medium saucepan over low heat. Cook, stirring occasionally, until the sugar and salt are dissolved, just a few minutes. Meanwhile, peel the bananas and cut into 1-inch chunks. Add the bananas to the saucepan and cook until heated through, about 3 minutes. Do not let the bananas get mushy.
2. Spoon into individual bowls and serve warm.

Bananas in Tapioca Coconut Milk. Bring 2 cups water to a boil over high heat in a medium saucepan. Add ¹/₄ cup tapioca pearls and cook, stirring occasionally, until translucent, about 15 minutes. Stir in the coconut milk, sugar, and salt. Add the bananas and proceed as directed.

Baked Plantains
CARIBBEAN, CENTRAL AMERICA ■
MAKES **4 SERVINGS**
TIME **ABOUT 30 MINUTES**

Plantains just get riper and riper, sweeter and sweeter, until they rot. They should be good and black for this dish, which is great served with vanilla ice cream.

2 large plantains
¹/₄ cup brown sugar
Pinch of ground allspice
¹/₄ teaspoon ground cinnamon
2 tablespoons butter

1. Preheat the oven to 400°F. Don't peel the plantains, but cut off their ends, then split them in half the long way. Make a few gashes in their flesh. Mix together the sugar, allspice, and cinnamon and push into those gashes. Dot with butter, pushing some of the butter into the slits as well.

■ make ahead   ■ serve at room temp./cold   ▩ 30 minutes or less

DESSERTS   **623**

2. Put the plantains in a baking dish that will hold them comfortably. Bake until the tops are bubbly, about 20 minutes; you can run them under the broiler if you'd like, to brown them a bit. Let cool a little before serving.

Berry Pudding SCANDINAVIA ■ ▓

MAKES **6 TO 8 SERVINGS**

TIME **30 MINUTES, PLUS CHILLING TIME**

Berries are a big deal in Scandinavia. The farther north you go, the more precious they become. They are not only enjoyed fresh and preserved; they are celebrated, almost worshiped.

This Jell-O-like dessert is a beaut.

1 cup blueberries

1 cup raspberries

1 cup blackberries

³/₄ cup sugar, plus more to taste

Juice of ¹/₂ lemon, more or less

One ¹/₄-ounce envelope unflavored gelatin

1¹/₂ cups heavy cream

³/₄ cup sour cream

1. Combine the fruit with the sugar and about 1 cup water in a medium saucepan over medium-low heat. Bring to a gentle boil and simmer for about 10 minutes, until the mixture is mostly liquid and the berries are soft. Put through a medium-fine strainer, pushing to extract as much juice as possible. You will have about 1 quart; add a bit more water if necessary. Cool the liquid (if you are in a hurry, put it in a container and place the container in a bath of ice water). Add the lemon juice, taste, and stir in more sugar or lemon juice if you like.

2. Put ¹/₄ cup water in a small saucepan and sprinkle the gelatin onto it. Cook over low heat, stirring,

until dissolved; stir it into the fruit juice and pour the mixture into individual bowls or one large one. Chill until firm.

3. When you're ready to serve, whip the cream until it holds soft peaks; beat in about ¹/₄ cup sugar—the mixture should be sweet, but only just so. Stir in the sour cream and a bit more sugar if you like. Serve the pudding with the cream.

Simple Fruit Soup

CENTRAL/EASTERN EUROPE ■ ▓

MAKES **4 SERVINGS**

TIME **20 MINUTES, PLUS CHILLING TIME**

Made with soft berries, this is straightforward, easy, and delicious; it also has beautiful color. I like it best with blueberries, because they need no straining. If you use raspberries or other berries with seeds, force the soup through a fine strainer instead of pureeing it in the blender to remove them.

This is great not only as a dessert but also for breakfast or as a snack.

1 quart blueberries, raspberries, strawberries, huckleberries, or a combination, picked over and trimmed as necessary, washed, and, if necessary, sliced

¹/₂ cup sugar, plus more if needed

1 lemon, washed and thinly sliced

1 teaspoon ground cinnamon, plus more if needed

1 cup yogurt or sour cream, plus more for garnish

1. Combine the berries, sugar, lemon, cinnamon, and 1 quart water in a medium saucepan and turn the heat to medium. Cook, stirring occasionally, until the blueberries fall apart, 10 to 15 minutes.

2. Cool the mixture at least until tepid (to avoid burning yourself), then puree in a blender. Taste and add more sugar or cinnamon if necessary.

Chill, then stir in the yogurt. Serve cold, garnished with more yogurt.

Stewed Cherries on Bread TURKEY

MAKES **4 SERVINGS**

TIME **45 MINUTES**

Sound like just about the least appealing dessert you've ever encountered? That's exactly what I thought when I was offered it in Istanbul. But you know what? I crave it. Whenever you have good cherries, sweet or sour, this is worth considering. And the most difficult part is pitting the cherries.

> 1½ pounds fresh cherries, sour or sweet
> Sugar to taste
> Juice of ½ lemon, or to taste
> Four ¾-inch-thick slices good French or Italian bread
>   (if the bread is small, use 8 or even 12 slices)
> Butter as needed
> Sweetened whipped cream for serving, optional

1. Pit the cherries over a bowl to catch as much of the juice as you can. Combine the cherries and juice in a saucepan with ¼ cup sugar and 1 cup water. Bring to a boil, then simmer until the cherries are tender, about 15 minutes. Taste and add more sugar if necessary, along with lemon juice to taste. Cool for 15 minutes or so.

2. Put the bread on a baking sheet and dot with butter; sprinkle lightly with sugar. Run under the broiler (or use a toaster oven) until the butter and sugar both melt.

3. Divide the bread among 4 plates. Spoon some of the cherry juice over each piece and let soak in for a few minutes. Top with the cherries and, if you like, some whipped cream.

Date or Fig and Walnut Balls

MIDDLE EAST ■ ■ ■

MAKES **ABOUT 12**

TIME **20 MINUTES**

When I was a kid, these were always sold in candy shops, and I loved them. They were considered far too exotic to make at home; or at least no one would consider doing such a thing. Years later I learned how. Turns out, of course, they couldn't be easier, and now they are a wintertime staple in my house.

> 1 cup dried figs or dates (preferably Medjool), trimmed
>   and/or pitted
> 2 tablespoons cold butter, optional
> 1 cup walnuts
> Sweetened or unsweetened shredded coconut or
>   confectioners' sugar for dredging

1. Combine the fruit and butter in a small food processor. (If you are not using the butter, which is not essential, just start with the figs or dates alone.) Process until quite smooth, stopping the machine to scrape down the sides if necessary. Add the walnuts and pulse to blend; you don't want to process the walnuts to a powder, but they should be finely chopped.

2. Use your hands to form into small balls. Roll in coconut or sugar to coat. Stored in the refrigerator, these keep for a few days.

Figs Poached in Wine FRANCE ■ ■

MAKES **4 SERVINGS**

TIME **20 MINUTES, PLUS CHILLING TIME**

You can poach dried figs, of course, but fresh ones achieve a kind of swollen, bursting tenderness that is sublimely sensual. Green figs, not quite fully ripe, are best for this purpose, but the more common Black Mission figs—also not quite ripe—are almost as good.

16 figs, preferably fresh

2 cups fruity red wine, preferably Burgundy (Pinot Noir)

$1/2$ cup sugar, or to taste

Grated or julienned zest of 1 orange

1. Gently wash the figs. Put the wine and sugar in a saucepan or skillet with a lid; the pan should be broad enough to hold the figs in one layer. Bring to a boil, then adjust the heat so the mixture simmers. Add the figs, cover, and cook gently for about 5 minutes. Transfer the figs to a shallow bowl.
2. Reduce the cooking liquid over high heat until syrupy, about 10 minutes. Stir in the orange zest and pour over the figs. Chill, then serve, spooning some of the sauce over the figs as you do so.

Pears "Poached" with Butter and Cream FRANCE ■ ▩
MAKES **4 SERVINGS**
TIME **45 MINUTES**

More luxurious than the following recipe and great served hot, with a little sour cream or crème fraîche.

4 tablespoons ($1/2$ stick) butter

4 not quite fully ripe pears, preferably Bosc, peeled, quartered, and cored

$1/4$ cup sugar, or to taste

$1/3$ cup heavy cream

$1/2$ teaspoon ground cinnamon

1. Preheat the oven to 425°F. Put the butter in an ovenproof skillet over medium heat. When the butter foam subsides, add the pears and sugar;

cook, turning the pears occasionally and allowing them to brown a bit, until quite soft, 15 to 20 minutes (longer if the pears were not nearly ripe).
2. Add the cream and cinnamon and continue to cook, stirring constantly, until the cream thickens a bit, about a minute. Put the skillet in the oven and cook until the mixture browns on top, 5 to 10 minutes. Serve hot or at room temperature.

Caramelized Pears Poached in Red Wine FRANCE ■ ▩
MAKES **4 SERVINGS**
TIME **AT LEAST 1 HOUR**

A light, appealing dessert that is a French classic. You may simply serve the pears after poaching them but the browning is a very nice touch. Pinot Noir is the ideal wine for this, but any fruity, not-too-tannic red will do.

4 small, not quite fully ripe pears, preferably Bosc, peeled

2 cups fruity red wine

1 cup sugar

1 cinnamon stick

1. Use a spoon or melon baller to remove the core from the blossom end of the pears, but leave the stem on. Combine the pears, wine, $3/4$ cup sugar, and the cinnamon in a broad saucepan with a lid and bring to a boil over medium-high heat.
2. Cover the pan and let simmer, turning the pears occasionally, until they are very tender but not mushy, at least 30 minutes and possibly as long as an hour.
3. Preheat the broiler and place the rack about 4 inches from the heat source. Transfer the pears to a baking sheet, preferably nonstick; arrange them flat side down. Turn the heat to high and reduce the liquid until syrupy, about 15 minutes.

4. Sprinkle the pears with the remaining sugar and broil carefully until lightly browned. Transfer to a plate and pour the liquid over them; serve at room temperature.

Multifruit Soup

CENTRAL/EASTERN EUROPE ■ ▨

MAKES **4 SERVINGS**

TIME **40 MINUTES**

This is often served as an appetizer, but most people are going to find it more appropriate for dessert. The fruit can be varied, but cherries really make the best base. For wine, use Gewürztraminer or Riesling, preferably from Germany and at least slightly sweet (if the wine is very sweet, reduce the sugar).

> **3 cups sweet or sour cherries, pitted, juice reserved**
>
> **2 cups fruity white wine**
>
> **1 teaspoon minced lemon zest**
>
> **½ cup sugar, or to taste**
>
> **1 apple, peeled, cored, and diced**
>
> **1 pear, peeled, cored, and diced**
>
> **1 ripe peach, peeled, pitted, and diced**
>
> **2 plums, peeled, pitted, and diced**
>
> **Pinch of black pepper**
>
> **Fresh lemon juice to taste**
>
> **Chopped fresh mint leaves for garnish, optional**
>
> **About 1 cup sour cream for garnish, optional**

1. Combine 2 cups of the cherries with 2 cups water in a medium saucepan with a lid; bring to a boil, then cover and adjust the heat so the mixture simmers steadily. Cook for about 15 minutes, or until the cherries are very soft. Cool (if you're in a hurry, put the pan in a larger pan of cold water), then force through a strainer.

2. Return the juice to the pan and add all the remaining ingredients except the lemon juice and garnishes. Simmer until the diced fruit is soft, about 15 minutes, then taste and add more sugar or lemon juice if necessary. Chill and serve cold, garnished with mint and/or sour cream as desired.

Macerated Dried Fruits and Nuts

MIDDLE EAST ■ ▨

MAKES **6 TO 8 SERVINGS**

TIME **12 TO 24 HOURS, LARGELY UNATTENDED**

I have been making this winter fruit salad from the time I first started looking at cookbooks and well remember the original Claudia Roden recipe (in her wonderful classic *A Book of Middle Eastern Food*). My version, honed by experience and travel, is a little different.

If you use water, you will probably need to add a bit of sugar; start with ½ cup and see how that tastes.

This recipe produces a lovely syrup of its own, but you can serve it with yogurt or fresh or sour cream if you like.

If you're in a hurry, you may cook the mixture, gently, until the fruit softens. The texture will be mushier, the fruits less distinctive, but the taste will still be great.

> **2 pounds assorted dried fruits: apricots, pears, peaches, prunes, raisins, cherries, etc., in any combination**
>
> **½ pound blanched almonds, halved or slivered, optional**
>
> **2 tablespoons pine nuts**
>
> **2 cups fresh orange juice, 1 cup grape juice plus 1 cup water, or all water**
>
> **1 teaspoon ground cinnamon, 1 tablespoon rose water, 1 tablespoon orange-flower water, or 1 tablespoon anise liqueur, like raki, ouzo, or Pernod**

■ make ahead   ▨ serve at room temp./cold   ▨ 30 minutes or less

DESSERTS **627**

1. Mix all the ingredients together; add more water if necessary, enough to cover the fruit by an inch or two. Cover and put aside (if your house is very warm, refrigerate).
2. Stir every few hours, for 12 to 24 hours. Serve when the fruits are tender.

NUT DESSERTS

We underestimate and underutilize nuts, mostly preferring them as a snack food. But they have several major attributes in desserts. For one, their keeping powers are phenomenal, so they are almost always of good quality and "fresh," whether recently harvested or not. Two, they have distinctive flavors that are brought out by cooking, especially with sugar. And three, they have incomparable crunch.

Baklava Phyllo and Walnut Cake
GREECE, TURKEY ■ ▨
MAKES **ABOUT 50 SERVINGS**
TIME **AT LEAST 2 HOURS, PLUS RESTING TIME**

If you ask me, baklava is a two-person job, and even at that it's a difficult one. I curse and fret during the production, but in reality there is no way to make such a huge quantity of dessert in such a reliable manner. And this is among the most wonderful, foolproof, impressive, and delicious desserts on the planet.

A lasagne pan is about the right size; if you need to buy a pan, look for one that measures about 16 × 10 × 2 inches. You will also need a 1-inch brush (paintbrushes, bought at the hardware store, are cheaper than and identical to so-called pastry brushes).

BAKLAVA

Phyllo

Phyllo, which means "leaf" in Greek, is a very thin, delicate sheet of pastry found in Greek and Near and Middle Eastern cuisine. (Warka and brik are North African versions of phyllo; strudel is its German cousin.)

Phyllo is most often used to wrap savory and sweet fillings in packets or to create a crunchy layer for pastries. While you can make phyllo at home, almost everyone uses the frozen phyllo sold at supermarkets. (Making phyllo is a laborious and difficult process, and though the store-bought stuff is not nearly as good—for one thing, it includes margarine or oil instead of butter—it's good enough.)

There are just a few tips you need to know to use phyllo successfully:

1. Buy phyllo frozen and store it in the refrigerator if you plan on using it within a week. Otherwise, it will keep in your freezer for up to a year.
2. Phyllo dries out quickly, so when you begin working with it, keep all of it except the sheet you are currently using covered with a damp towel. (Store any leftover sheets, refrigerated, in an airtight container.)
3. Phyllo sheets are large; allow plenty of work space; use a pizza wheel to cut the pastry if you have one.
4. When brushing phyllo layers with butter or oil, use a light touch.
5. Patch any holes with phyllo scraps brushed lightly with butter or oil.
6. Always cook until deep golden brown and crisp.

Two possible variations (there are dozens, but these are the simplest): substitute hazelnuts, almonds, or unsalted pistachios (the best, but the most expensive) for the walnuts, and add about 2 tablespoons orange-flower water or rose water to the syrup after cooking it.

With thanks to Virginia Christy and her brother Sem.

1 cup honey

3 cups plus 7 tablespoons sugar

2 teaspoons fresh lemon juice

6 cups (about 1½ pounds) walnuts

2 teaspoons ground cinnamon

1 pound (4 sticks) butter, melted

2 pounds phyllo dough

1. Combine the honey, 3 cups sugar, and the lemon juice with 2½ cups water and bring to a boil. Stir to melt the sugar and chill. (This can be done hours, days, even weeks in advance.)

2. Chop the nuts (the food processor makes quick work of this: be sure to pulse, not blend—you don't want puree). Combine with the 7 tablespoons sugar and the cinnamon.

3. Brush the pan's bottom with butter; lay 7 sheets of phyllo on it, the narrow way, overlapping slightly and with alternating ends hanging over the edges. Brush the phyllo with butter and sprinkle with about ¼ cup of the nut mixture. Fold over the ends; if you overlap and alternate in a coordinated fashion, the ends will meet or overlap and you will completely cover the filling. Brush with butter and sprinkle with nuts, then repeat with 7 more sheets. Repeat until only 10 or 11 sheets remain, and do these sheets in the same manner, but only buttering them (you will have used up the nuts by now).

4. Refrigerate for about an hour, longer if you prefer. Preheat the oven to 300°F. Score the top of the sheets, first lengthwise, then widthwise, and finally diagonally, to make about 50 triangles. Bake for about 1 hour, until golden brown.

5. Cool slightly, then cut through your score marks, using a sharp, thin-bladed knife. Pour the cold syrup over all, tilting the pan so it spreads all over. Cool to room temperature, then serve. This keeps well, covered and at room temperature, for several days.

Coconut Sorbet SOUTHEAST ASIA ■ ▩

MAKES **4 SERVINGS**

TIME **5 MINUTES, PLUS FREEZING TIME**

Like most sorbet recipes, this one is infinitely easier to make if you have an ice cream machine. The key is to serve it as soon as you can after making it—it does not keep well and in fact is best the day it is made—and, if necessary, "warming" it slightly in the refrigerator before serving.

> **Two 12- to 14-ounce cans coconut milk (about 3 cups),**
> **or homemade coconut milk (page 584)**
> **$3/4$ to 1 cup sugar, to taste**
> **1 teaspoon vanilla extract**

1. Combine the coconut milk with $3/4$ cup sugar and taste; add more sugar if you like. Add the vanilla and stir.
2. Freeze in an ice cream machine according to the manufacturer's instructions or spread in a roasting pan or on a baking sheet and freeze, stirring once every 30 minutes or so until it achieves the desired consistency (figure at least 2 hours using this method).
3. Serve as soon as possible after making or freeze and let "warm" in the refrigerator for 30 minutes before serving.

Coconut Macaroons FRANCE ■ ▩

MAKES **ABOUT 2 DOZEN**

TIME **ABOUT 45 MINUTES, PLUS COOLING TIME**

This is the best use of leftover egg whites you'll find. Generally, one egg white will support one cup of shredded coconut or ground nuts, but I like to be safe and use an extra egg white. You can combine nuts and coconut or use any of them alone.

> **4 egg whites**
> **$1^1/2$ cups superfine or confectioners' sugar**
> **3 cups unsweetened shredded coconut**
> **1 teaspoon vanilla or almond extract**
> **Pinch of salt**

1. Preheat the oven to 325°F. Use an electric mixer to beat the whites until foamy. Gradually add the sugar until the mixture is stiff. Fold in the remaining ingredients.
2. Use a pastry bag, a resealable plastic bag with a corner cut out, a spoon, or wet hands to form small mounds from tablespoons (or a little more) of the meringue mixture and place on a nonstick baking sheet or a baking sheet lined with wax paper. You can space them quite closely since they will not rise.
3. Bake until light brown, 15 to 20 minutes. Remove the baking sheet and cool on a rack for at least 30 minutes before eating. These keep well in a covered container for up to 3 days.

Walnut or Almond Macaroons. Toast $2^1/2$ cups walnuts or blanched almonds in a skillet over medium heat, shaking the pan frequently until they become fragrant, about 5 minutes. Grind to a powder (you can use granulated sugar in this case, grinding it with the nuts) in a food processor. Then proceed as directed, substituting nuts for the coconut.

Almendrados. The famous Spanish version, always made with almonds, sometimes with egg yolks: Follow the preceding variation, using almonds and adding 1 teaspoon finely grated lemon zest. After putting the cookies on the sheet, sprinkle their tops with some sliced blanched almonds and bake as directed.

Coconut Macaroons, Caribbean Style. In step 1, substitute dark rum for the vanilla extract and add 1 teaspoon peeled and grated fresh ginger with the coconut mixture.

Linzertorte AUSTRIA ■ ▧
MAKES **ABOUT 8 SERVINGS**
TIME **ABOUT 1 1/2 HOURS**

Linzertorte is really a big jam-topped cookie, and, for the amount of work—it's pretty simple—is one of the most impressive desserts around. You can make individual cookies if you prefer.

Red currant or raspberry jam is traditional, but you can use any jam you like as long as it is of high quality. If it is not already seedless, strain it to remove the seeds.

1 cup walnuts or blanched almonds

1 1/2 cups flour

Pinch of salt

1/2 cup granulated sugar

1/4 teaspoon ground cinnamon

Zest of 1 lemon

8 tablespoons (1 stick) butter, cut into chunks

2 egg yolks

1 tablespoon fresh lemon juice, or more as needed

1 to 1 1/2 cups any jam, strained if seeded

Confectioners' sugar for dusting

1. Preheat the oven to 375°F. Toast the nuts in a medium skillet over medium heat, shaking the pan frequently until they brown slightly and become aromatic, 2 or 3 minutes.
2. When the nuts are cool, grind them to a powder in a food processor. Add the flour, salt, granulated sugar, cinnamon, and lemon zest and pulse to blend and mince the zest. Add the butter and process just until the mixture is crumbly, about 10 seconds.
3. Transfer the mixture to a bowl and stir in the egg yolks. Add the lemon juice. If 1 tablespoon does not allow you to gather the mixture into a ball, add a little more. Wrap the ball in plastic or wax paper, flatten into a small disk, and freeze the dough for 10 minutes or refrigerate for 30 minutes.
4. Roll out about two thirds of the dough, keeping the remainder wrapped in plastic. Place the dough in an 8- or 9-inch tart pan. Prick the crust all over with a fork. Bake for 12 minutes, or just until it begins to darken. Cool for a few minutes; meanwhile, roll out the remaining dough and cut it into strips.
5. Spread the jam on the crust, then top with the lattice strips. Bake for another 30 minutes or so, until the crust is brown. Remove and cool. Sprinkle with a little confectioners' sugar before serving at room temperature.

Kabak Tatlisi Pumpkin and Walnuts
TURKEY ■ ▧
MAKES **6 OR MORE SERVINGS**
TIME **30 MINUTES, PLUS CHILLING TIME**

Most of our pumpkins—which are grown more for decoration than for eating—are too watery for this wonderful Turkish dessert. If you can get a small, firm pumpkin, that will do the job just fine. If not, go with winter squash, like butternut, which has firm flesh and is easy to peel.

> **3 pounds pumpkin or winter squash, like butternut, peeled, seeded, strings removed, and cut into slices or chunks**
> **1 cup sugar**
> **1 cup chopped walnuts**
> **Sweetened whipped cream, crème fraîche, or sour cream for serving, optional**

1. Combine the pumpkin and sugar with about 1 cup water in a wide skillet or flameproof casserole with a lid. Cover, turn on the heat, and adjust so the mixture simmers steadily. Cook until the pumpkin is very tender, about 20 minutes.
2. Uncover and adjust the heat so the mixture bubbles; cook until the liquid is syrupy. Transfer the pumpkin to a serving platter and pour the syrup over it. Refrigerate until cold, then sprinkle with the walnuts and serve, with the garnish if you like.

Walnut Tart FRANCE ■ ▨
MAKES **8 SERVINGS**
TIME **30 MINUTES (WITH A PREMADE CRUST), PLUS CHILLING TIME**

For nut lovers, there is no better dessert than a walnut tart, and one of the great things about it is that you can always find high-quality walnuts—no searching for a ripe peach or waiting for strawberry season. The recipe is so common that it is claimed by nearly every region of France and is found in varying forms in other parts of Europe as well; everyone, it seems, has his or her own version. This, of course, is my favorite; if you can find honey made from lavender, it's even better.

> **1 unbaked Sweet Tart Pastry (page 654) shell in a 9-inch tart pan**
> **Butter for the dish**
> **1¼ cups sugar**
> **8 tablespoons (1 stick) butter**
> **½ cup heavy cream**
> **¼ cup honey**
> **2 cups roughly chopped walnuts (you should have large chunks)**

1. Preheat the oven to 400°F. Tear off a piece of foil twice as large as the crust. Fold it in half and smear it with butter; lay the buttered side onto the crust. Weight the foil with a pile of dried beans or rice (these can be reused for the same purpose), pie weights, or a tight-fitting skillet or saucepan—anything that will sit flat on the surface. Bake for 12 minutes, then remove the foil and continue to bake at 350°F, until the crust is a beautiful shade of brown. Remove and let cool on a rack while you prepare the filling (turn off the oven).
2. Put the sugar and 1 tablespoon water in a heavy 6- or 8-inch saucepan or deep skillet over medium heat. Cook, gently shaking the pan occasionally, until the sugar melts and turns light golden, about 10 minutes. Turn the heat to low, then carefully add the butter and cream—the mixture will bubble up—and cook, stirring, until the butter melts and the mixture is uniform. Stir in the honey and the walnuts, cool a bit, then spread on the crust. Refrigerate for about an hour before serving.

Tarta de Almendras Almond Cake SPAIN ■ ▨
MAKES **4 SERVINGS**
TIME **1 HOUR**

An ironic creation, in that it is usually said to originate in Santiago de Compostela, the capital of Galicia, in northwestern Spain—where almonds do not grow. Nevertheless, it's a wonderful, not-too-sweet dessert, most definitely for grown-ups. I like this in a springform pan, but it can be made in two layers if you prefer.

Butter for the pan
Flour for the pan
2 cups blanched almonds
6 eggs
1 cup granulated sugar
1/2 teaspoon ground cinnamon
Zest of 1 lemon, grated or minced
Confectioners' sugar for dusting

1. Preheat the oven to 350°F. Grease an 8- or 9-inch springform pan very well with butter, then dust with flour, shaking off the excess.

2. Grind the almonds to a powder in a food processor or spice mill. Beat the eggs and granulated sugar together, preferably in a stand mixer, until thick and light in color (if you are doing this by hand, it will take a good 10 minutes or more). Stir in the cinnamon, lemon zest, and almonds. Pour into the prepared pan.

3. Bake for 30 to 45 minutes, or until a toothpick inserted in the center comes out clean. Cool on a rack, then remove the sides of the pan. Dust the top with confectioners' sugar and serve.

CREAMY, EGGY DESSERTS

These are the luxurious desserts many people love the most, and the fact that this section is relatively large attests to their universal appeal.

CUSTARDS

The only tricky part about making egg-thickened custards, like flan and crème brûlée, is the baking. I'm not a fan of unnecessary fussing, but here a water bath, which promotes even cooking, is worthwhile. And you must always remember that custard is done when still quite jiggly in the center. The first time you make a custard you will, like everyone else, overcook it a bit. But when the sides are set and the center is still looking a bit underdone, it is ready.

A word about the composition of the custard itself: Heavy cream produces that rich, luxurious custard that you get at the best restaurants. But half-and-half (which, relatively speaking, is practically skim milk) yields a smooth, rich custard that doesn't make you feel like you've eaten a pint of ice cream, and even straight milk makes a fine, light custard. The choice is yours, obviously.

Flan SPAIN ■ ▨

MAKES **4 SERVINGS**
TIME **ABOUT 45 MINUTES**

The classic custard of Spain, widely made throughout Latin America, is like crème brûlée, but upside down and lighter. Like any custard, it must not be overcooked. The center must be quite jiggly when you remove it from the oven—for beginners, this is a leap of faith, but it's the only way to keep the custard smooth.

2 cups milk, cream, or a mixture
1 cinnamon stick or 1/2 teaspoon ground cinnamon
1 cup sugar
2 eggs
2 egg yolks
Pinch of salt

1. Preheat the oven to 300°F and bring a kettle of water to a boil. Put the milk in a small saucepan with the cinnamon over medium heat. Cook just until it begins to steam, about 10 minutes, then cool a bit.

2. Meanwhile, combine ½ cup of the sugar and ¼ cup water in a small heavy saucepan over low heat. Cook, shaking the pan occasionally (it's best not to stir), until the sugar liquefies and turns clear, then golden brown, about 15 minutes. Remove from the heat and immediately pour the caramel into the bottom of a flat ovenproof bowl or gratin dish, or 4 individual ramekins.

3. Beat the eggs and yolks with the salt and remaining ½ cup sugar until pale yellow and fairly thick. Remove the cinnamon stick (if you used it) and gradually add the milk to the egg mixture, stirring constantly. Pour the mixture into the prepared bowl or ramekins and place in a baking pan, adding hot water to within about 1 inch of the top.

4. Bake for about 40 (for the ramekins) to 50 (for the bowl) minutes, or until the center is barely set. (It's best to start checking after 30 minutes or so, to avoid overcooking.) Serve warm or at room temperature or cover and refrigerate for a day or so. You can serve by spooning from the bowl, or in the ramekins. Or you can unmold by putting the cups in a bowlful of hot water for 30 seconds or so, then inverting; spoon any melted caramel on top of the custards.

Vanilla Flan. Substitute 1 vanilla bean, split lengthwise, for the cinnamon stick or add 1 teaspoon vanilla extract to the steamed milk after it cools a bit.

Coconut Flan. Substitute homemade (page 584) or canned coconut milk for the milk or cream.

Pumpkin Flan. This makes 6 to 8 flans, and is best with calabaza—Caribbean pumpkin—if you can find it, butternut squash or a not-too-stringy pumpkin if not: Steam or poach about 2 cups peeled and cubed pumpkin or squash until very tender, about 20 min-

utes. Cool, then puree with some of the milk after it has cooled. Increase the sugar to 1½ cups, still divided in half (increase the water for the caramel slightly). Increase the eggs to 3 eggs and 3 yolks and proceed as directed.

Flan de Naranja Orange Custard SPAIN ■ ■
MAKES **4 SERVINGS**
TIME **ABOUT 1 HOUR, PLUS COOLING TIME**

If you are one of those people who think flan is too heavy, or you like a little acidity in your desserts, or you simply want a change from ordinary flan, this is for you.

> 1 cup sugar
>
> 3 eggs
>
> 3 egg yolks
>
> 2 cups fresh orange juice
>
> Grated zest of 1 orange

1. Preheat the oven to 350°F and bring a kettle of water to a boil. Combine ½ cup of the sugar and ¼ cup water in a small heavy saucepan over low heat. Cook, shaking the pan occasionally (it's best not to stir), until the sugar liquefies and turns clear, then golden brown, about 15 minutes. Remove from the heat and immediately pour the caramel into the bottom of a flat ovenproof bowl or gratin dish, or 4 individual ramekins.

2. Beat the eggs and yolks with the remaining ½ cup sugar until pale yellow and fairly thick. Gradually add the orange juice to the egg mixture, stirring constantly. Stir in the zest and pour the mixture into the prepared bowl or ramekins and place in a baking pan, adding hot water to within about 1 inch of the top.

3. Bake for about 40 (for the ramekins) to 50 (for the bowl) minutes, or until the center is barely set. (It's best to start checking after 30 minutes or so, to avoid overcooking.) Serve warm or at room temperature or cover and refrigerate for a day or so; you can serve by spooning from the bowl, or in the ramekins. Or you can unmold by putting the cups in a bowlful of hot water for 30 seconds or so, then inverting; spoon any melted caramel on top of the custards.

Crème Brûlée FRANCE ■ ▧

MAKES **4 SERVINGS**

TIME **ABOUT 1 HOUR, PLUS COOLING TIME**

Crème brûlée may seem mysterious, but it is actually quite straightforward and simple. Just remember two things: One, like almost all custards, this one is done before it appears to be; remove it from the oven when it is still jiggly. And two, brûlée means "burnt," not browned. It's important that some of the topping blacken; the best tastes of campfire-toasted marshmallows.

Chefs, and many devoted home cooks, use a propane torch to melt and brown the sugar in the final step. If you have one lying around, give it a shot—just hold the flame so it touches the sugar, which will react quickly. Move the flame around so it touches all of the sugar; when the melted sugar begins to blacken, it's done.

2 cups heavy cream, light cream, or half-and-half

1 vanilla bean, split lengthwise, or 1 teaspoon vanilla extract

5 egg yolks

½ cup sugar, plus more for the top

1. Preheat the oven to 325°F. Bring a kettle of water to a boil. Combine the cream and vanilla bean and cook over low heat just until hot to the touch (an instant-read thermometer will read 120 degrees or so). Let sit for a few minutes, then discard the vanilla bean. (If you're using vanilla extract, add it now.)

2. Beat the yolks and sugar together until light. Stir about a quarter of the cream into this mixture, then pour the sugar-egg mixture into the cream and stir. Pour into four 6-ounce ramekins and place the ramekins in a baking dish or roasting pan; fill the dish with boiling water halfway up the side of the dishes. Bake for about 30 minutes (start checking after 20), or until the center is barely set. Cool or wrap tightly and chill for up to a couple of days.

3. When you're ready to serve, set up a broiler so that the tops of the ramekins will be no more than 3 inches from the heat source; 2 inches is better. (If your broiler is in your oven, it may be helpful to rest a broiling pan or even a casserole upside down on the rack to achieve the proper height.) Do not preheat the broiler. Cover the top of each custard with a thin layer of sugar—about a teaspoon each is right. Turn on the broiler and put the ramekins under the heat; arrange them so that the heat hits the tops of all of them evenly. (If necessary, brown in batches; it takes only a couple of minutes anyway.) Cook until the sugar melts and blackens a bit, about 5 minutes, then remove. Serve within an hour.

Crema Catalana SPAIN. Replace the vanilla bean with the grated zest of a lemon and a cinnamon stick (or 1 teaspoon ground cinnamon). Remove the cinnamon stick before adding the yolks to the cream.

Buttermilk Panna Cotta Cooked Cream

ITALY ■ ▨

MAKES **4 TO 6 SERVINGS**

TIME **ABOUT 30 MINUTES, PLUS CHILLING TIME**

Panna cotta is a no-brainer, sweetened cream thickened with gelatin. It has long been made with whatever dairy is around, and I think it's far better when a certain amount of the cream is replaced by buttermilk. The result is more complex and not so stultifyingly rich.

> 1$\frac{1}{2}$ cups buttermilk
>
> One $\frac{1}{4}$-ounce envelope unflavored gelatin
>
> 1 vanilla bean
>
> 1$\frac{1}{2}$ cups heavy cream
>
> $\frac{1}{2}$ cup sugar

1. Put $\frac{1}{2}$ cup of the buttermilk in a medium saucepan with a lid and sprinkle the gelatin over it; let sit for 5 minutes. Turn the heat to low and cook, stirring, until the gelatin dissolves completely.

2. Cut the vanilla bean in half lengthwise. Scrape out the seeds and add both seeds and pod to the pot along with all the remaining ingredients. Cook over medium heat, stirring, until steam arises from the pot, 5 to 10 minutes. Turn off the heat, cover, and steep for 15 to 30 minutes.

3. Remove the vanilla pod and pour the mixture into 4 large or 6 small custard cups. Chill until set, about 4 hours. Serve in the cups or dip the cups in hot water for about 10 seconds each, then invert onto plates. Serve within 24 hours of making it.

Blancmange ENGLAND. Popular in England though clearly French in origin, blancmange (pronounced, in England at least, "blahmanj") is a subtly flavored custard made in the manner of panna cotta: Substitute whole milk for the buttermilk and $\frac{1}{2}$ teaspoon almond extract for the vanilla bean. Grind 1 cup lightly toasted blanched almonds with the whole milk in a food processor until finely chopped but not pureed. Transfer the mixture to a fine-mesh strainer lined with a triple thickness of cheesecloth and squeeze out the milk. Discard the solids. Proceed as directed, adding the almond extract in step 1 and skipping the steeping in step 2.

Tembleque CARIBBEAN. Tembleque is a popular Caribbean custard traditionally made with coconut milk and cornstarch. But it's easier and better when made with gelatin à la panna cotta. Substitute 3 cups coconut milk (either homemade, page 584, or canned) for the buttermilk and cream and omit the vanilla bean (or substitute a dash of orange-flower water for the vanilla). Dissolve the gelatin in $\frac{1}{2}$ cup coconut milk, as directed in step 1, combine it with the remainder of the coconut milk (omit the orange-flower water), and skip the steeping and proceed to step 3. Garnish the unmolded custards with a dusting of ground cinnamon just before serving.

Arroz con Leche

Rice Pudding with Cinnamon SPAIN ■ ▨

MAKES **4 SERVINGS**

TIME **ABOUT 2$\frac{1}{2}$ HOURS, LARGELY UNATTENDED**

It seems every country that grows rice makes rice pudding, and almost every experienced cook has his or her own technique. After years of playing with it, this is the one I like best, and it works well with the variations of most cuisines.

In many cases rice pudding is simply milk bound by rice; often the amount of rice is well under 10 percent of the total. I prefer this recipe with just $\frac{1}{4}$ cup, no more. The result is a thick milk custard with a recognizable but understated rice presence. If you want a dense and slightly chewier mixture, use the larger amount of rice.

Other possible additions to rice pudding: a strip of lemon zest, a pinch of saffron threads, or a teaspoon of ground cardamom added at the beginning; a couple of tablespoons of raisins and/or slivered pistachios stirred in at the end. See the variations, and the following recipes, too—this group of recipes is unending.

¹⁄₄ to ¹⁄₃ cup rice
¹⁄₃ to ¹⁄₂ cup sugar, to taste
Small pinch of salt
1 quart whole milk
1 cinnamon stick
Ground cinnamon for garnish

1. Preheat the oven to 325°F. Combine the first 5 ingredients in a 3- or 4-quart casserole (an ovenproof saucepan will do), stir a couple of times, and place in the oven. Cook for 30 minutes, then stir. Cook for 30 minutes more, then stir; at this point the milk will have developed a filmy cream-colored skin, and the rice will have begun to swell. Stir the filmy skin back into the liquid.

2. Cook for 30 minutes more. The skin will have re-developed, a little darker this time, and the kernels of rice will have swollen a little more. Cook for another 30 minutes, then stir. Now the pudding is almost done. Return the mixture to the oven and begin to check the pudding every 10 minutes, stirring gently each time you check.

3. The pudding may be done 10, 20, or 30 minutes later. Invariably, it is done before you believe it is. When the mixture is silky, creamy, and thick, the rice suspended perfectly in a rich custard, it is overcooked; when it cools, it will become too hard (though still quite good to eat). You must make a

leap of faith and remove the custard from the oven when the rice kernels are very swollen and the mixture is thick but still quite fluid. As it cools, it will thicken considerably. While it's cooling, remove the cinnamon stick.

4. Serve warm, at room temperature, or cold, garnished with a bit of ground cinnamon.

Rice Pudding, Middle Eastern Style. The cinnamon is optional. When the rice pudding is done, stir in 1 tablespoon rose water or orange-flower water; taste and add more if you like.

Rice Pudding, Galician Style. Closely related to crème brûlée (page 635): When you're ready to serve the pudding, set up a broiler so that the top of the casserole will be no more than 3 inches from the heat source; 2 inches is better. Cover the top of the custard with a thin layer of sugar—a tablespoon or two. (You may also divide the custard into small bowls or ramekins before proceeding.) Turn on the broiler and put the casserole or ramekins under the heat; rotate it so that the heat hits all parts of the top evenly. Cook until the sugar melts and blackens a bit, about 5 minutes, then remove. Serve within an hour.

Soupy Rice Pudding. An interesting and soothing Scandinavian tradition: Double the amount of milk; reduce the sugar to ¹⁄₄ cup. Do not bake, but cook, covered, over low heat, stirring occasionally, until the rice is very tender, about 1 hour. Serve warm, in bowls, with fresh, whipped, or sour cream.

Coconut Rice Pudding, Jamaican Style. This is good with some minced crystallized or peeled fresh ginger in it: substitute homemade (page 584) or canned coconut milk for all or some of the milk.

Kheer Rice Pudding INDIA ■ ■

MAKES **6 TO 8 SERVINGS**

TIME **2 TO 3 HOURS**

A recipe from my friend Sumana Chatterjee, whose family lives in Calcutta. The ingredient list, obviously, could not be shorter, but don't be deceived: this is a labor-intensive dish, best made on a cool day (we made it on a hot one and lost about five pounds each) when you are going to be in the kitchen for a long time.

Having said that, it is wonderful stuff, creamy and delicious, representative of the scores of different milk desserts made throughout India.

2 quarts whole milk

2 cardamom pods

$^3/_8$ to $^1/_2$ cup rice

$^3/_8$ to $^1/_2$ cup sugar, to taste

1. Combine the milk and cardamom in a heavy pot and bring to a boil over medium heat. As the mixture warms, begin to stir it with a wooden spoon. Be patient and do not cook too quickly or the milk will burn on the bottom; you want the mixture simmering, but not really boiling. You don't have to stir constantly, but you must stir frequently.

2. When the quantity of milk has reduced by half, an hour or so later, stir in the rice. Continue to cook and stir until the rice is very soft and the milk further reduced, 30 minutes or so. Stir in the sugar and cook for another 10 or 15 minutes, still stirring.

3. When the pudding is done, pour it into a bowl and refrigerate (or you can serve it warm or at room temperature). The skin that forms on it and that left behind in the pot are the prime parts.

Zerde Saffron-Rice Pudding

TURKEY ■ ■

MAKES **6 OR MORE SERVINGS**

TIME **ABOUT 1 HOUR, SOMEWHAT UNATTENDED**

A lovely yellow rice pudding, with the exotic flavor of saffron; interestingly, it's dairy free. Use cinnamon or cardamom in addition to (or in place of) the rose water (available in small bottles at Middle Eastern stores) if you like.

$^1/_2$ cup short-grain rice

Tiny pinch of salt

$^3/_4$ cup sugar

Large pinch of saffron threads

1 tablespoon rose water, or to taste

2 tablespoons currants or raisins, optional

2 tablespoons roughly chopped blanched almonds, optional

2 tablespoons roughly chopped unsalted pistachios, or more to taste

1. Combine the rice and salt with 6 cups water in a medium saucepan with a lid; bring to a boil, then partially cover and adjust the heat so the mixture simmers steadily. Cook for about 30 minutes, stirring occasionally, then add the sugar and saffron. Uncover and continue to simmer for at least another 30 minutes, or until the mixture is fairly thick. (It will thicken more upon standing, and it should be a little loose when you eat it.)

2. Stir in the rose water and cool; this is good warm, at room temperature, or cold. Just before serving, garnish with the currants or raisins and the almonds if you're using them, plus the pistachios.

Steamed Coconut Custard THAILAND ■ ▨

MAKES **4 SERVINGS**

TIME **45 MINUTES**

Palm sugar, or jaggery, is dark, unrefined sugar made from a variety of sources, including the sap of the palm tree. It can be chunky and must be broken up; dark brown sugar is a nearly perfect substitute.

This dish is great with slices of ripe fresh mango.

4 eggs

1/2 cup palm or brown sugar

1 cup thick coconut milk, preferably homemade (page 584)

3 cups steamed Sticky Rice (page 508)

1. Bring 2 inches of water to a steady simmer in the bottom of a large steamer. Whisk the eggs in a large bowl just until beaten. Whisk in the sugar until the mixture is smooth, then add the coconut milk and whisk again until well blended.
2. Pour the mixture into a 9-inch cake pan or similar container, cover with plastic wrap, and place in the steamer. Steam until the custard is barely set, still jiggling slightly, about 20 minutes. Remove and cool to room temperature.
3. To serve, place a portion of sticky rice in a bowl and spoon a bit of the cooled custard over it.

Sweet Sticky Rice with Mangoes

SOUTHEAST ASIA ▨

MAKES **4 SERVINGS**

TIME **20 MINUTES (WITH PREPARED RICE)**

A quicker, easier version of the preceding coconut milk pudding, this simple dessert is popular at food markets throughout Southeast Asia. Great with mangoes or any other ripe tropical fruit.

1 1/2 cups coconut milk, homemade (page 584) or canned

3 tablespoons sugar

1/2 teaspoon salt, or more to taste

About 4 cups freshly cooked Sticky Rice (page 508)

4 ripe mangoes, peeled, pitted, and sliced (page 119)

1. Put the coconut milk, sugar, and salt in a medium saucepan over low heat. Cook, stirring occasionally until the sugar and salt are dissolved, just a few minutes.
2. Pour half the coconut milk mixture over the warm sticky rice and stir well to combine. Transfer the sweetened rice to individual serving bowls and top with the remaining coconut milk mixture. Add the mangoes and serve.

Sweet Rice Flour Dumplings

SOUTHEAST ASIA, CHINA ■ ▨

MAKES **4 SERVINGS**

TIME **45 MINUTES**

These sticky, sweet dumplings, which are easier to produce than most savory dumplings, are served at New Year's festivities throughout East and Southeast Asia. Palm sugar and glutinous rice flour can be found at most Asian markets.

2 cups glutinous rice flour, plus more as needed

1/2 teaspoon salt

Three 1/2-inch slices peeled fresh ginger

1/3 cup palm or brown sugar, chilled

1/2 cup unsweetened shredded coconut, optional

1. Mix the flour and salt in a large mixing bowl. Slowly stir in 3/4 cup hot water until a dough forms. Transfer the dough to a floured work surface and knead until stiff, about 5 minutes. Or combine the flour and salt in a food processor

and, with the machine running, add water until a dough ball forms, then knead by hand for about 30 seconds.

2. Combine the ginger with 5 cups water in a large pot and bring to a boil; adjust the heat so the mixture simmers steadily but not violently. Meanwhile, form the dough into 2-inch balls, using as much flour as you need to keep the mixture from sticking. Using your thumbs, make an indentation in the center of each ball. Fill each indentation with $1/2$ teaspoon palm sugar and seal the balls shut. Gently roll the filled dumplings into balls again.

3. Put the balls into the water one at a time and cook, stirring occasionally to keep the balls from sticking to each other, until they float to the surface, about 4 minutes. Remove with a slotted spoon, roll in the shredded coconut if you like, and serve warm or at room temperature, with some of the ginger broth spooned over them if desired.

Sweet Rice Flour Dumplings with Sesame. Omit the palm sugar and shredded coconut. Using a spice grinder or food processor, grind together 2 tablespoons toasted black sesame seeds (page 596) with 3 tablespoons sugar. Stir in 3 teaspoons corn, grapeseed, or other neutral oil until a stiff paste is formed. Use this as the filling and proceed as directed, serving the dumplings with the ginger broth.

Sweet Rice Flour Dumplings with Peanuts, Hong Kong Style. Omit the palm sugar. Mix $1/4$ cup unsweetened shredded coconut with $1/4$ cup chopped roasted peanuts and 3 tablespoons sugar. Roll the dough into 1-inch balls and cook, unfilled, until they float to the surface, about 5 minutes. Remove with a slotted spoon and toss with the coconut-peanut mixture.

Basbousa Semolina Pudding MIDDLE EAST
MAKES **6 TO 8 SERVINGS**

TIME **1 HOUR**

Something between pudding and cake, basbousa is popular throughout the Middle East. It's always drenched in sugar syrup and often topped with fresh whipped cream. Rose water (sold in small bottles at Middle Eastern stores; it keeps indefinitely) is an odd ingredient, a lovely flavor that can quickly become overpowering. Use it judiciously.

> 2$1/2$ cups plus 1 tablespoon sugar
>
> Juice of $1/2$ lemon
>
> 1 teaspoon rose water, or to taste, optional
>
> 8 tablespoons (1 stick) butter, plus more for the pan
>
> $1/2$ cup blanched almonds, very finely chopped or ground in a food processor
>
> $1/2$ cup whole-milk yogurt
>
> 1$1/4$ cups semolina (coarse durum flour)
>
> 1 teaspoon baking powder
>
> 1$1/2$ teaspoons vanilla extract
>
> 1 cup heavy cream, preferably not ultrapasteurized

1. Put 1$1/2$ cups of the sugar, the lemon juice, and $1/2$ cup water in a saucepan and bring to a boil. Simmer until the mixture is thick and syrupy, about 5 minutes. Stir in the rose water if you're using it. Remove from the heat; when it has cooled, refrigerate until ready to use it.

2. Preheat the oven to 375°F. Place half the butter in a skillet over medium-high heat. When the butter foam subsides, add the almonds. Cook, stirring constantly, until they are lightly browned, about 5 minutes.

3. Beat the yogurt and 1 cup of the remaining sugar together in a large bowl. Add the almonds and the butter they were cooked in, the semolina, baking powder, and 1 teaspoon of the vanilla extract, and beat until thoroughly blended. Grease a 9-inch

square baking pan and add the batter. Cook for about 30 minutes, until the cake is lightly browned. Whip the cream until it holds soft peaks, then whip 1 minute more, incorporating the remaining 1 tablespoon sugar and ½ teaspoon vanilla.

4. Pour the syrup over the basbousa and cut it as you would brownies. Put it back in the oven and bake for 3 minutes more. Melt the remaining 4 tablespoons (½ stick) butter and pour it over the basbousa. Let rest for a few minutes, then serve warm with the whipped cream.

Seffa Sweet Couscous with Almond Milk
NORTH AFRICA
MAKES **4 SERVINGS**
TIME **1 HOUR, LARGELY UNATTENDED**

Not unlike rice pudding, this couscous dessert is found throughout the Middle East and North Africa. Scent it with a few drops of rose water (available at Middle Eastern stores) or orange-flower water in place of the cinnamon if you like.

Until recently, the topping for seffa was a thick sugar syrup, like that used on basbousa (preceding recipe). But more and more you see it without syrup or with a substitute like almond milk, which is very good.

> 1 cup whole milk
> ½ cup blanched almonds, very finely chopped or ground in a food processor
> 4 tablespoons (½ stick) butter
> 1½ cups couscous
> Salt to taste
> ¼ cup raisins, optional
> ¼ cup chopped dried apricots, optional
> ¼ cup chopped dates, optional

> ¼ cup sugar or honey, or to taste
> ½ teaspoon ground cinnamon, or to taste

1. Combine the milk and almonds in a saucepan with a lid and bring just to a boil over medium-high heat. Turn off the heat, cover, and let sit while you proceed with the recipe.

2. Put 2 tablespoons of the butter in a medium saucepan with a lid and turn the heat to medium-low. When it melts, add the couscous and cook, stirring, until it is coated with butter, about 1 minute. Add 2¼ cups water and a pinch of salt. Bring to a boil, then turn the heat down to its minimum. Cover and cook until all the liquid is absorbed, 7 to 12 minutes. If you're using the dried fruit, soak the raisins and apricots in warm water to cover while the couscous cooks.

3. Pour the couscous into a large serving bowl and stir in the remaining butter with a fork, along with the drained dried fruit and the dates if you're using them, fluffing the couscous and breaking up any lumps. Add the sugar and cinnamon, then stir; taste and adjust the seasoning as necessary. Strain the almond milk, pour it over the couscous, and serve.

Ginger Ice Cream SOUTHEAST ASIA ■ ▨
MAKES **ABOUT 1 PINT**
TIME **20 MINUTES, PLUS CHILLING AND FREEZING TIME**

The French brought ice cream to Asia, but it took the Asians to make it with ginger. I like it with a double dose, both fresh and candied.

Even when made with milk, this is extremely rich ice cream, the best I know how to make. If you would like something a little lighter, add another cup of milk, half-and-half, or cream after making the custard.

2 ounces fresh ginger, peeled and roughly chopped

2 cups milk or half-and-half

6 egg yolks

$1/2$ cup sugar

$1/2$ cup minced candied (crystallized) ginger

1. Combine the ginger and milk in a saucepan over medium-high heat and bring just to a boil, stirring. Cover and let sit for about 10 minutes. Meanwhile, with a whisk or an electric mixer, beat the yolks and sugar together until thick and slightly lightened in color.

2. Strain the milk, then stir about $1/2$ cup of it into the yolk mixture and beat. Stir the warmed egg mixture back into the milk and return to the pan. Heat, stirring constantly, until thick, 10 minutes longer. The mixture is ready when it thickly coats the back of a spoon and a line drawn with your finger remains intact.

3. Cool in the refrigerator, then stir in the candied ginger and freeze in an ice cream machine according to the manufacturer's directions.

Green Tea Ice Cream JAPAN. Omit the ginger and heat the milk with 1 tablespoon green tea powder (matcha).

Gelato Affogato al Caffè
Ice Cream "Drowned" with Espresso ITALY ▪

MAKES **4 SERVINGS**

TIME **10 MINUTES**

This is quite possibly the simplest dessert "recipe" imaginable: vanilla ice cream doused with coffee. The dessert probably originated in Turin, an important city for both coffee and ice cream, and is served in bars there all over town.

1 pint vanilla ice cream

1 cup freshly brewed strong coffee, preferably espresso

1. Put the ice cream in 4 bowls and take them to the table.

2. Pour over each of them a portion of the still-hot coffee and serve.

Vanilla Soufflé FRANCE

MAKES **4 TO 6 SERVINGS**

TIME **1 $1/4$ HOURS, LARGELY UNATTENDED**

Soufflés are far easier than most of us have been led to believe, and, surprisingly, they're quite flexible; with the exception of whisking and folding in the egg whites, they can be prepared several hours in advance.

You may, of course, make the soufflé with vanilla extract instead of a vanilla bean. The difference is real but subtle.

$1 1/2$ cups milk

$1/2$ cup granulated sugar, plus more as needed

1 vanilla bean

4 tablespoons ($1/2$ stick) butter

$1/3$ cup flour

4 eggs, separated

Pinch of salt

Confectioners' sugar for dusting

1. Put the milk in a small saucepan and cook over medium heat until steam rises, about 10 minutes. Stir in the granulated sugar to dissolve, then turn off the heat. Split the vanilla bean lengthwise and scrape the seeds into the milk. Add the pod as well, cover, and steep for about 15 minutes. Remove the pod and discard. Meanwhile, use a bit of the butter to grease a 2-quart soufflé or other deep baking dish. Sprinkle the dish with granulated sugar and

invert it to remove excess sugar. (Hold off on this step if you're going to delay baking the soufflés until later.)

2. Put the remaining butter in another small saucepan over medium-low heat. When the foam subsides, stir in the flour and cook, stirring, until the mixture darkens, about 3 minutes. Turn the heat to low and whisk in the milk, a bit at a time, until the mixture is thick. Let cool for a few minutes, then beat in the egg yolks. (You can prepare this base a few hours in advance of baking; cover tightly and refrigerate; bring back to room temperature before continuing.)

3. About an hour before you're ready to serve, preheat the oven to 375°F. Use an electric or hand mixer or whisk to beat the egg whites with the salt until quite stiff. Stir about a third into the sauce to lighten it, then fold in the remaining whites, using a rubber spatula or your hand. Transfer to the prepared dish and bake until the top is brown, the sides are firm, and the center is still quite moist, about 30 minutes. Dust with confectioners' sugar and serve immediately.

Chocolate Soufflé. Omit the vanilla or not, as you prefer, and add 4 ounces good bittersweet chocolate (like Valrhona, for example), chopped, to the milk as it heats, stirring so the chocolate dissolves.

Sirniki Fried Cheesecakes RUSSIA

MAKES **4 SERVINGS**

TIME **AT LEAST 2 HOURS, LARGELY UNATTENDED**

A classic Russian dessert that I like to serve for breakfast, which is convenient because the dough—or batter; actually it's somewhere in between—can rest overnight (or longer). Serve with sour cream and jam.

1 pint cottage cheese
½ cup sour cream or yogurt
3 egg yolks
3 tablespoons granulated sugar
½ cup flour
Tiny pinch of salt
Butter for frying
Confectioners' sugar, optional
Sour cream for serving
Jam for serving

1. Squeeze the cottage cheese in a towel until quite dry; combine in a bowl or food processor with the sour cream, yolks, granulated sugar, flour, and salt and blend until smooth. Cover and refrigerate for at least 2 hours and up to 24 hours.

2. Preheat a griddle or large skillet over medium-low heat for a couple of minutes; at the same time, preheat the oven to 200°F. Add about 2 tablespoons butter and, when it is hot, begin to shape the dough into 3-inch patties, ½ to 1 inch thick. Add as many patties as will fit comfortably in the pan, then cook until lightly browned on the bottom, 3 to 5 minutes. Turn and cook until the second side is brown, another 3 to 5 minutes. Keep the finished cakes warm in the oven while you cook the remainder, adding butter as needed, until they are done; dust with confectioners' sugar if you like and serve immediately, with sour cream and jam.

CAKES, TARTS, AND COOKIES

What we think of as pastry—flour, usually combined with butter and sweeteners, often leavened with eggs or chemicals like baking soda or powder—is (like yeasted bread) largely a European phenomenon. It is omnipresent throughout Europe—and, in fact, well into Russia and the non-European parts of the

Mediterranean as well. Here is a selection of my favorites.

Braided Coffee Cake with Cardamom SCANDINAVIA ■ ■

MAKES **8 OR MORE SERVINGS**

TIME **SEVERAL HOURS, LARGELY UNATTENDED**

This is what I think of as real coffee cake—not extraordinarily sweet and for some people not even a dessert. If you want it more cakelike, double the sugar in the dough and consider adding a couple more tablespoons of butter. But this is wonderful with a cup of coffee in the afternoon or toasted, with a little butter, in the morning.

With the food processor, this dough becomes quite quick to make; just keep the processing to a minimum. You want to avoid building up the gluten in the flour so it doesn't become tough.

BRAIDING COFFEE CAKE

If you don't feel like braiding the dough (it really is fun, though, and takes only a few extra minutes), by all means bake this in a loaf pan.

3 cups flour, plus more for rolling the dough

1 1/2 teaspoons instant active dry yeast, like SAF

Pinch of salt

1/2 cup plus 2 tablespoons sugar

1 teaspoon ground cardamom

8 tablespoons (1 stick) butter, plus more as needed

3 egg yolks

1/2 to 1 cup milk, as needed

1/2 cup walnuts, pecans, or almonds

1 teaspoon ground cinnamon

1. Combine the flour, yeast, salt, 1/2 cup sugar, and the cardamom in a food processor and pulse to combine. Add 6 tablespoons of the butter and the egg yolks and pulse again until well combined. With the machine running, drizzle about half the milk through the feed tube. Process just until a dough ball forms, adding a little more milk if necessary, then stop. Knead a little by hand, until the dough is smooth (add a little flour if necessary), then form the mixture into a ball and place it in a buttered bowl. Cover with plastic wrap and let rise in a warm place until about doubled in bulk, 1 to 2 hours.

2. When the dough is ready, cut it into 3 pieces. On a floured board, roll each piece into a long rope just over a foot long. Braid the pieces, pinching both ends to seal. Put on a buttered cookie sheet, cover with plastic wrap, and let rise again for about an hour.

3. Preheat the oven to 375°F. Chop the nuts and combine with the remaining 2 tablespoons butter (you can do this in a small food processor, but be careful not to pulverize the nuts) and the cinnamon. Brush the dough with a little milk and sprinkle the nut mixture over it.

4. Bake for 25 to 35 minutes, or until a toothpick inserted in the center comes out clean. Cool, then slice and serve.

Kulich Russian Easter Bread. This is a bit more elaborate: In step 1, substitute a large pinch of saffron threads for the cardamom and add 1 tablespoon rum. When kneading by hand, add 2 tablespoons raisins, 2 tablespoons diced candied fruit, and 2 tablespoons slivered blanched almonds. To be strictly traditional, you would bake the cake in a coffee can or other cylindrical mold, and you can if you like (just make sure the mold is very well buttered). In step 3, omit the topping, but when the cake comes out of the oven, brush it with melted butter and sprinkle with granulated or confectioners' sugar.

Sugared Crêpes FRANCE

MAKES **6 TO 8 SERVINGS**

TIME **40 MINUTES**

Between the omelet and the pancake lies the crêpe, an almost pastalike thin wrapper usually served as a snack or dessert. (Not always, though; see Buckwheat Crêpes, page 86.) They are universal but most closely associated with France and are sometimes made with chestnut flour (which, if you can find it, is a nice change). Fill them with cooked berries or other fruit, with fresh ricotta mixed with a little sugar, with chocolate sauce, or with anything else you like—ice cream, whipped cream, and so on.

There was a time when you needed a special crêpe pan—one reserved strictly for this purpose—but a six- or eight-inch nonstick skillet is the perfect vessel.

1 cup flour

Pinch of salt

1 tablespoon sugar, plus sugar for sprinkling

1¼ cups milk

2 eggs

2 tablespoons melted and cooled butter, plus butter for cooking

Fresh lemon juice for sprinkling

1. Whisk together the first 6 ingredients until smooth; you can do this in a blender. If time allows, let rest in the refrigerator for an hour or up to 24 hours.
2. Put a 6- or 8-inch skillet over medium heat and wait a couple of minutes; add a small pat of butter. Stir the batter with a large spoon or ladle; add a couple of tablespoons of the batter to the skillet. Swirl it around so that it forms a thin layer on the bottom of the pan, then pour the excess batter back into that which remains.
3. When the top of the crêpe is dry, after about a minute, turn and cook the other side for 15 to 30 seconds. (The crêpe should brown only very slightly and not become at all crisp.) Bear in mind that the first crêpe almost never works, even for professionals, so discard it if necessary; there is plenty of batter.
4. Sprinkle with sugar and a few drops of lemon juice and roll up. Keep warm in a low oven or, better

ROLLING CRÊPES

still, eat on the spot. Repeat the process, adding butter to the skillet and adjusting the heat as needed, until all the batter is used up.

Crêpes Suzette. The best-known French version: Add a tablespoon of grated lemon or orange zest to the batter. Melt 4 tablespoons ($^1/_2$ stick) butter with $^1/_4$ cup sugar, 1 tablespoon grated or minced orange zest, and 1 tablespoon Grand Marnier or other orange-flavored liqueur. As the crêpes are done, fold their sides in, then their bottom up, and arrange on a plate (keep warm in a low oven). Just before serving, pour the sauce over all.

Coconut Crêpes SOUTHEAST ASIA. In step 1, substitute coconut milk, homemade (page 584) or canned, for the milk and proceed as directed. Make a sauce from 1 cup coconut milk and 3 tablespoons sugar and drizzle it over the crêpes before serving.

Plattar Swedish Pancakes ▪
MAKES **4 SERVINGS**
TIME **30 MINUTES**

Where to put a recipe like this? The Swedes eat these pancakes as dessert, but my guess is that 90 percent of Americans who make them will consume them before noon, as breakfast or a brunch dish. Though I'm in that 90 percent, these are undeniably sweet enough for postmeal status.

There is a special pan for these, with small depressions, so you can make your pancakes the appropriate size. But using a tablespoon works almost as well.

Serve them with confectioners' sugar, applesauce, lingonberry preserves or any other jam, ice cream, sour cream, yogurt, or whipped cream. Or try an assortment.

3 eggs
2 tablespoons granulated sugar
Pinch of salt
1 cup milk
$^3/_4$ cup flour
2 tablespoons melted butter, optional, plus some for cooking
Confectioners' sugar for dusting

1. Separate the eggs and beat the yolks in a medium bowl with the granulated sugar and salt. Add the milk and flour alternately, stirring gently after each addition, to form a thin, smooth batter; do not overbeat. Stir in the melted butter if you're using it. The batter can be refrigerated at this point for up to a day.
2. When you're ready to cook, beat the egg whites until they hold stiff peaks; gently stir them into the batter. Don't worry about fully incorporating them.
3. Preheat a cast-iron or nonstick skillet or griddle over medium-high heat; when a drop of water skips across it before evaporating, it's ready. Melt a little butter in the pan and, using a tablespoon, scoop up a bit of the batter and put it in the pan. Cook as many pancakes at once as will fit comfortably, turning them after a couple of minutes, when they are brown. Total cooking time is less than 5 minutes per pancake.
4. Serve immediately, ideally straight from the pan, sprinkled with confectioners' sugar.

Lekach Honey Cake EASTERN EUROPE ■ ▪
MAKES **1 LOAF, ENOUGH FOR 8 OR MORE**
TIME **ABOUT 1 HOUR**

Rich, dark, and sweet, honey cake was originally a kind of pound cake made by people who could not afford refined sugar or flour (many old honey cake recipes use rye flour, not exactly what we think of as dessert). This is a light, more modern (at least twentieth-century) recipe, quite succulent.

Some people stir raisins (about ½ cup) and/or chopped almonds or walnuts (also about ½ cup) into the batter just before baking. Others cut the loaves in half after baking and add a layer of jam, then reassemble. Personally, I like my honey cake plain.

2 tablespoons butter, plus butter for the pan

Zest of 1 orange, minced

1½ cups all-purpose flour

½ cup rye or whole wheat flour

1 teaspoon baking soda

½ teaspoon ground cinnamon

Pinch of salt

Pinch of ground allspice

Pinch of freshly grated nutmeg

Pinch of ground cloves

Pinch of ground ginger

2 eggs

½ cup sugar

½ cup honey

½ cup brewed coffee

1. Preheat the oven to 350°F. Grease a loaf pan (if you double the recipe, you can use a tube pan). Combine the butter and zest in a small saucepan over medium heat; cook until the butter sizzles, then turn off the heat. Combine the dry ingredients in a large bowl.

2. Beat together the eggs and sugar until the mixture is light and thick; beat in the honey and coffee, followed by the butter/orange zest mixture. Add this mixture to the dry ingredients, stirring just to combine; do not beat any longer. Pour into the prepared loaf pan and bake for 30 to 45 minutes, or until a toothpick inserted into the center of the loaf comes out clean. Cool and serve.

Galette de Pérouges Sweet "Pizza"

FRANCE ■ ■

MAKES **ABOUT 6 SERVINGS**

TIME **ABOUT 2 HOURS, LARGELY UNATTENDED**

Served on the street in the medieval city of Pérouges, not far from Lyons, this sweet, crisp pastry, preferably served hot, makes a fantastic snack or a surprising dessert. Serve, if you like, with crème fraîche, whipped cream, or sour cream and cut-up fruit.

1 teaspoon instant active dry yeast, like SAF

2 cups flour, plus more for sprinkling

Pinch of salt

¼ cup plus 1 tablespoon sugar

8 tablespoons (1 stick) cold unsalted butter, cut into
    chunks

1 egg

Zest of 1 lemon

8 tablespoons (1 stick) unsalted butter, softened

1. Combine the yeast, flour, salt, 1 tablespoon sugar, cold butter, egg, and lemon zest in a food processor. Turn the machine on, let it run for a second until the mixture is blended, then let the machine run while you add ¼ cup water through the feed tube, a little at a time, until the mixture forms a ball and is slightly sticky to the touch. If dry, add another tablespoon or two of water and process for another 10 seconds. (In the unlikely event that the mixture is too sticky, add flour, a tablespoon at a time.)

2. Turn the dough onto a very lightly floured work surface and knead by hand for a few seconds to form a smooth, round dough ball. Place in a bowl, cover with plastic wrap or a damp cloth, and let rise in a warm, draft-free spot until the dough just about doubles in size, or at least 1 hour. (You can also let the dough rise more slowly, in the refrigerator, for as long as 6 or 8 hours.)

3. Preheat the oven to at least 500°F (600°F is better if your oven goes that high) with a pizza stone in place if you have one. Knead the dough lightly and place it on a very lightly floured surface; sprinkle it with a little more flour and cover with plastic wrap or a towel. Let it rest while the oven heats.

4. Pat or roll out the dough as thinly as possible to a diameter of 12 inches, using a little more flour if necessary. The process will be easier if you allow the dough to rest occasionally between rollings. If you have a pizza stone in your oven, place the dough on a floured peel or a long-handled board; if you do not, lay the dough on a lightly buttered baking sheet.

5. Spread the dough with the softened butter and sprinkle it with the remaining sugar. Bake until the crust is nicely crisp and the sugar lightly caramelizes, about 10 minutes; if the galette is browning unevenly, rotate it back to front about halfway through cooking time. Serve hot or at room temperature, but within the hour.

Kolackys Fruit-Filled Cookies

EASTERN EUROPE ■ ▥

MAKES **4 SERVINGS**

TIME **1 HOUR, PLUS CHILLING TIME FOR DOUGH**

This is all about the dough: there is none better. My earliest appreciation for it came from a cookie my grandmother made. I could never get over how delicious they were, but it was only years later that I realized they were a variation on the standard kolacky. These are most easily filled with thick preserves, or you can make your own fillings from stewed dried or fresh fruit as long as the mixture is thick.

Some people add enough flour to make a stiff dough, but it's really preferable to leave the dough sticky, which translates to tenderness, and refrigerate it for a few hours, which makes it easier to handle. If you're in a hurry, however, make the dough a little stiffer and roll it out right away.

These are fun to make with kids, as the ultimate shape really doesn't matter.

½ pound (2 sticks) butter, slightly softened

½ pound cream cheese, slightly softened

Tiny pinch of salt

2 cups flour, plus more as needed

An assortment of thick preserves, like apricot, raspberry, and orange

2 egg whites, lightly beaten

Sugar as needed

1. In a bowl, using a wooden spoon or your hands, or in an electric mixer, combine the butter and cream

KOLACKYS

cheese; stir in the salt. Gradually add the flour, making a sticky dough. Sprinkle the outside of the dough with flour, wrap in plastic, and refrigerate for at least 1 hour and up to 24 hours.

2. Preheat the oven to 350°F. Working with about a quarter of the dough at a time, roll it out to less than $1/4$-inch thickness ($3/16$ is about right), using flour as necessary to prevent sticking. Cut into 2-inch squares and put a dollop of one of the preserves in the center of each square or spread it across the diagonal, stopping short of the edges. Roll up and seal, or fold into triangles, or, if you spread the filling on the diagonal, bring up the corners and pinch across the center.

3. Brush each finished cookie with egg white and sprinkle with sugar, then put on a greased or nonstick cookie sheet and bake for 10 to 15 minutes, or until very lightly browned. Cool and serve within a day.

Madeleines FRANCE

MAKES ABOUT A DOZEN

TIME 2 HOURS OR MORE, LARGELY UNATTENDED

Madeleines are a classic French sweet, a delightful spongy cookie in a convenient bite size. The longer the batter is chilled, the greater the chance that you will have the signature madeleine hump. Serve warm, please.

$3/4$ cup flour

Tiny pinch of salt

$1/4$ cup almonds, unblanched and finely ground, optional

3 eggs

$1/2$ cup sugar

1 teaspoon vanilla extract or orange-flower water

5 tablespoons unsalted butter, gently melted and cooled,
    plus butter for the pan

1. Mix together the flour and salt, along with the almonds if you're using them.

2. Use an electric mixer (preferably a stand mixer; this will take a while) to beat the eggs and sugar together until very thick and at least doubled in volume; the mixture should form a ribbon when you lift the beater blade(s) from it. Stir in the vanilla.

3. Gently and gradually, fold the flour or flour-and-almond mixture into the egg-and-sugar mixture. Gently stir in the melted butter. Cover and refrigerate for about an hour.

4. Preheat the oven to 375°F. Generously butter a madeleine tin. Drop rounded teaspoonfuls of the batter into the molds. Bake for 11 to 15 minutes, until the madeleines are golden and springy to the touch. Rap the pan against the counter; the madeleines should loosen and will be easy to remove. Serve immediately; these are really best warm.

Honey Madeleines. Add 1 tablespoon honey to the egg-and-sugar mix.

Lemon Madeleines. Add the grated zest from 1 lemon along with 2 tablespoons fresh lemon juice to the egg-and-sugar mix.

Génoise Buttery Sponge Cake FRANCE ■

MAKES ONE 8- TO 9-INCH CAKE

TIME ABOUT 1 HOUR, PLUS COOLING TIME

The basic cake of the French pastry repertoire is génoise, used as the foundation for dozens of cakes and other desserts. While it is essentially sponge cake made with butter, it's rarely eaten plain or on its own. Rather, it might be moistened with liqueur or sweet or fortified wine (Grand Marnier, Sauternes, or Oloroso sherry, for example) and served with a little whipped cream or used as a building block for other desserts like Trifle (page 651).

1 cup cake flour, plus flour for the pan

$^1/_4$ teaspoon salt

4 tablespoons ($^1/_2$ stick) butter, melted, plus butter for the
pan and the paper

5 eggs

$^1/_2$ cup sugar

1 teaspoon vanilla extract

1. Preheat the oven to 350°F. Mix the flour and salt together. Butter the bottom and sides of a 9-inch round cake pan; cover the bottom with a circle of wax or parchment paper, butter the paper, and sift a little flour over the whole pan; invert and tap out excess flour.

2. Use an electric mixer to beat the eggs until doubled in volume and very thick and light, at least 5 minutes. Add half the sugar and beat for another 5 minutes or so, gradually adding the remaining sugar, until nearly tripled in volume. (When you remove the whisk from the eggs, a ribbon of egg will fall from the beaters and hold its shape on top of the mixture for a few seconds. It's a very satisfying sight.) Beat in the vanilla.

3. Use a rubber spatula to fold the flour-salt mixture into this batter, a third at a time, gently but thoroughly. Finally, and very gently, fold in the melted butter. Turn the batter into the cake pan and bake for 25 to 30 minutes, until the cake is just firm and slightly springy.

4. Remove the cake from the oven and let it rest for a couple of minutes. Run a knife around the edge, cover the pan with a rack, and invert the rack and pan. Cool, then store, covered with wax paper and at room temperature, for no more than a day, or wrap well in plastic and freeze for up to a week.

Crème Pâtissière Pastry Cream
FRANCE ■ ▩ ▨
MAKES **ABOUT 3 CUPS**
TIME **20 MINUTES**

An elementary ingredient of French pastry. The pastry cream will be predictably richer if you use heavy cream (preferably *not* ultrapasteurized) but is equally delicious with half-and-half or whole milk.

$^2/_3$ cup sugar

2 tablespoons flour

2 tablespoons cornstarch

Pinch of salt

3 or 4 egg yolks

2 cups cream, half-and-half, or whole milk

1 vanilla bean or 2 teaspoons vanilla extract

2 tablespoons unsalted butter, softened

1. In a small saucepan, combine the sugar with the flour, cornstarch, and salt. Mix together the yolks and cream. If you're using a vanilla bean, split it and scrape out the seeds; stir them into the cream mixture.

2. Stir the cream-egg mixture into the sugar-cornstarch mixture over medium heat; at first, whisk occasionally to eliminate lumps. Then stir almost constantly until the mixture boils and thickens, about 10 minutes. Continue to cook until the mixture coats the back of a spoon; when you draw your finger through this coating, the resulting line will hold its shape.

3. Stir in the butter (and vanilla extract if you're using it) and set aside. Cool the pastry cream for a few minutes, then proceed with your recipe or refrigerate, with plastic wrap directly on the surface to prevent a skin from forming.

Trifle ENGLAND ■ ■

MAKES **6 TO 8 SERVINGS**

TIME **20 MINUTES (WITH PREMADE GÉNOISE AND PASTRY CREAM), PLUS CHILLING TIME**

Trifles are anything but trifles: they take a good deal of work to put together, they're about as caloric as desserts get, and, in the right serving vessel—like a large glass dish with tall, straight sides that reveals the tempting layers of cake, cream, fruit—they're absolute showstoppers.

In England, one is often wowed by the guiltless and masterful employment of loads of cream in many desserts. Trifles are a showcase for the British love of cream—in this case both whipped and pastry.

> 3 cups strawberries, hulled and sliced
>
> 3 tablespoons sugar
>
> Pinch of salt
>
> ¼ cup Grand Marnier or Oloroso sherry
>
> ½ recipe Génoise (page 649; leftover cake from a day or two before is perfect)
>
> 1 recipe Crème Pâtissière (preceding recipe)
>
> 1 cup heavy cream
>
> 1 teaspoon vanilla extract
>
> ½ cup chopped pistachios or walnuts
>
> Fresh mint leaves for garnish, optional

1. Toss the sliced strawberries with the sugar, salt, and liqueur and let the mixture sit for 10 minutes.
2. Cut the génoise into ladyfinger-sized pieces and nestle them tightly in one layer across the bottom of your serving vessel. Drain the liquid from the macerated strawberries and pour it over the layer of génoise.
3. Top the génoise with a thick layer of pastry cream, then top the pastry cream with the strawberries, reserving a few to garnish the top of the trifle.
4. Beat the cream and vanilla together with a whisk or hand mixer until the cream holds soft peaks. Spread the whipped cream on top of the strawberries.
5. Sprinkle the chopped nuts and reserved strawberries over the whipped cream and chill the trifle for 1 to 3 hours. Garnish with mint leaves just before serving if desired.

Sand Cake SCANDINAVIA ■ ■

MAKES **ONE 8- OR 9-INCH CAKE**

TIME **ABOUT 1¼ HOURS**

A delicious buttery northern European specialty whose name derives from its rough texture.

For the best possible flavor, toast and grind fresh spices. If you have whole cardamom, remove the seeds from the pods by crushing the pods lightly with the side of a knife (discard the hulls). Then combine them with a bit of cinnamon stick and a small piece of nutmeg in a small dry skillet and toast over medium heat, shaking the pan frequently until the mixture is aromatic. Grind well, then combine with the ginger.

> ½ pound (2 sticks) unsalted butter, at room temperature, plus a little butter for the pan
>
> ½ cup fresh bread crumbs, preferably homemade (page 580)
>
> 1¾ cups flour
>
> ¼ cup cornstarch
>
> 2 teaspoons baking powder
>
> ¼ teaspoon salt
>
> 2 teaspoons ground cardamom
>
> ½ teaspoon ground ginger
>
> ½ teaspoon ground cinnamon
>
> ¼ teaspoon freshly grated nutmeg
>
> 1 cup granulated sugar
>
> 4 eggs
>
> 1 teaspoon vanilla extract

Whipped cream or confectioners' sugar for serving,
optional

1. Preheat the oven to 350°F. Smear the bottom, sides, and cone of an 8- or 9-inch tube pan with butter and sprinkle with bread crumbs; invert the pan over the sink to remove excess crumbs. Set aside.
2. Mix together the flour, cornstarch, baking powder, salt, and spices and set aside. Using an electric mixer, cream the butter with the granulated sugar until light and fluffy, 5 minutes or so. Add the eggs one at a time, continuing to beat. Add the vanilla and beat for another 30 seconds.
3. Remove the bowl from the mixer and add the dry ingredients all at once; mix, by hand, until they are well incorporated but no longer. Pour and scrape the batter into the prepared pan; rap the pan sharply against the counter to eliminate any lingering pockets of air. Bake for 45 minutes before checking; the cake is done when it is golden brown and a toothpick inserted in its center comes out clean.
4. Remove the cake from the oven and let it rest for a couple of minutes. Run a knife around the edge, cover the pan with a rack, and invert the rack and pan. Cool before serving plain, with whipped cream, or sprinkled with confectioners' sugar if desired.

Paskha Crustless Easter Cheesecake RUSSIA ■ ■
MAKES **8 OR MORE SERVINGS**
TIME **ABOUT 1 HOUR, LARGELY UNATTENDED, PLUS CHILLING TIME**

Traditionally paskha is not cooked but put in a special pyramid-shaped mold, weighted, and drained in the fridge for a day or so. But given people's concerns about raw eggs, and since baking is a legitimate alternative, I make a baked version, which is just as good (and actually keeps longer).

12 tablespoons (1 1/2 sticks) butter
3/4 cup sugar
1 pound farmer cheese or full-fat small-curd cottage cheese
1/2 cup sour cream
4 eggs, separated
1 teaspoon vanilla or almond extract
2 tablespoons potato starch or cornstarch
1/2 cup golden raisins, optional
1/2 cup slivered almonds

1. Preheat the oven to 350°F. Use some of the butter to liberally grease an 8-inch cake pan. Line the bottom with wax paper and butter that too.
2. Put the remaining butter in a food processor along with all but a tablespoon of the sugar and the farmer cheese and sour cream; process until very, very smooth; there should be no lumps at all. Add the egg yolks, vanilla, and potato starch and once again process until very smooth.
3. Whisk the egg whites until foamy, then add the remaining sugar; continue to whisk until they hold soft peaks. Fold in the cheese mixture, along with the raisins if you're using them. Pour into the cake pan and bake for 45 to 50 minutes, or until just firm.
4. Cool, then unmold. Toast the almonds in a small dry skillet over medium heat, shaking the pan frequently until they color slightly. Press the almonds into the top of the paskha, chill, and serve.

Tuiles or Mandelflarn "Tiles" or Broomstick Cookies FRANCE, SWEDEN ■ ■ ■
MAKES **ABOUT 2 DOZEN**
TIME **30 MINUTES**

Tuiles are better known, but the same cookies are popular in Sweden. You can make them without almonds, but unless you have allergies I don't know why you would. Great alone or with ice cream or fruit.

- **8 tablespoons (1 stick) unsalted butter, plus butter for the cookie sheets**
- **³/₄ cup almonds, very finely chopped or ground in a food processor**
- **¹/₂ cup sugar**
- **¹/₄ cup flour, plus flour for the cookie sheets**
- **Pinch of salt**
- **2 tablespoons heavy cream**

1. Preheat the oven to 375°F. Melt the butter in a small heavy pan over medium-low heat. When it foams, add all the remaining ingredients and stir to blend. Let sit for a few minutes until the batter thickens a bit. Grease and flour one or more cookie sheets (unless they are nonstick—very useful here—in which case just rub with a tiny bit of butter).
2. Drop teaspoonfuls of the batter onto the sheets, allowing lots of room between cookies—these spread like mad. Figure about 6 cookies per sheet. Bake for 5 to 7 minutes, or until lightly browned. Use the thinnest spatula you have to carefully re-

move the cookies from the baking sheet; drape the hot cookies around the handle of a broomstick propped between 2 chairs or set up a similar arrangement (you can also use a rolling pin or other cylinder). Cool, then eat within a day.

Torrijas Castellanas
Spanish "French" Toast ■
MAKES **4 SERVINGS**
TIME **20 MINUTES**

If you're tempted to replace the butter or heavy cream in this recipe, don't; just make plain old pain perdu, or French toast. But if you're ready for the creamiest, most custardy French toast you've ever tried, give these babies a go. This recipe comes courtesy of Jose Andres, a Washington, D.C.–based Spanish chef and good friend.

- **3 eggs**
- **1 cup milk**
- **1 cup heavy cream**
- **Pinch of salt**
- **¹/₄ cup ground cinnamon**
- **¹/₄ cup sugar**
- **4 thick slices brioche or good-quality bread (8 slices if the loaf is small)**
- **8 tablespoons (1 stick) butter**
- **2 tablespoons extra virgin olive oil**

1. Combine the eggs, milk, cream, and salt in a wide shallow bowl. Combine the cinnamon and sugar on a plate.
2. Soak a piece or two of bread in the egg mixture (do not crowd) while you put the butter and oil in a large skillet over medium-high heat. Turn the bread in the egg mixture so it soaks well; when the butter melts and its foam subsides, add the soaked

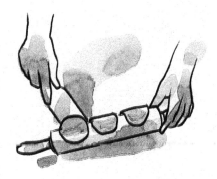

TUILES

bread, again without crowding (it's likely that you'll have to cook two batches).

3. Brown the bread nicely on both sides, for a total of 6 to 10 minutes, then transfer each piece in turn to the cinnamon sugar mixture; turn to coat both sides evenly and serve hot.

Sweet Tart Pastry FRANCE ■ ▪

MAKES **ENOUGH FOR ONE 8- TO 10-INCH TART**
TIME **20 MINUTES, PLUS RESTING TIME**

A richer, sweeter pastry than that used for most American pies (though it can be employed successfully for same). The food processor makes quick work of it, and if you chill the dough before rolling, you should have little trouble handling it, even on your first try.

1¹/₂ cups flour, plus more for rolling

Pinch of salt

2 tablespoons sugar

10 tablespoons (1¹/₄ sticks) frozen or cold butter, cut into chunks

1 egg

PRESSING PASTRY INTO A TART PAN

1. Combine the flour, salt, and sugar in a food processor and pulse once or twice. Add the butter all at once; process until the mixture is uniform, about 10 seconds (do not overprocess). Add the egg and process for another few seconds.

2. Put the mixture in a bowl and add 3 tablespoons ice water; mix with your hands until you can form the dough into a ball, adding another tablespoon or two of ice water if necessary (if you overdo it and the mixture becomes sodden, add a little more flour). Form into a ball, wrap in plastic, and freeze for 10 minutes or refrigerate for at least 30 minutes. (You can refrigerate for up to a couple of days or freeze for up to a couple of weeks.)

3. Sprinkle a countertop with flour and put the dough on it; sprinkle with flour. Use a rolling pin to roll with light pressure, from the center out. If the dough is sticky, add a little flour (if it continues to become sticky, and it's taking you more than a few minutes to roll it out, refrigerate or freeze again). Roll, adding flour and rotating and turning the dough as needed; use ragged edges of dough to repair any tears, adding a drop of water while you press the patch into place.

4. When the diameter of the dough is about 2 inches greater than that of your tart pan, drape it over the rolling pin and move it into the pan. Press the dough firmly into the pan all over. Refrigerate for about an hour before filling (if you're in a hurry, freeze for 30 minutes or so).

Tarte Vaudoise Cream Tart FRANCE ■ ▪

MAKES **ABOUT 8 SERVINGS**
TIME **ABOUT 1¹/₂ HOURS, LARGELY UNATTENDED**

If you want to impress your guests with minimalism, here's the ticket: a crust with a little sweetened cream on it. Ridiculously simple but—like a simple sugar cookie—enormously enjoyable. And be assured that this and the variation are traditional recipes.

This is best with good, thick heavy cream, not ultrapasteurized. It's worth a trip to a nearby farm or farmers' market if that's possible.

1 Sweet Tart Pastry (page 654)
$1/2$ cup sugar
$1 1/2$ cups heavy or sour cream
1 teaspoon ground cinnamon

1. Preheat the oven to 450°F. After refrigerating the dough, prick it all over with a fork. Combine the sugar and cream and spread the mixture over the bottom of the dough. Sprinkle with cinnamon.
2. Bake until the crust is golden brown, 10 to 15 minutes; cool completely before serving.

Tarte au Sucre. Use $1/2$ cup brown sugar creamed with 1 egg and 2 tablespoons butter. Omit the cream and cinnamon and proceed as directed.

Churros Fresh Sugar Crullers SPAIN
MAKES **ABOUT 2 DOZEN CHURROS**
TIME **1 $1/2$ HOURS**

In the world of fresh pastry, few things are quicker than churros, the crisp, crullerlike strips of fried dough that are still popular in Spain, where they originated, but perhaps even more so in Mexico. In fact, there are few breakfast or last-minute late-night snacks that can match a batch of churros.

Churros served at restaurants can be awful because they're fried in stale oil and made in advance. But make them fresh once, for breakfast or dessert (ideally, you'll serve them with Chocolate Español, page 665, or Mexican Hot Chocolate, page 664) and you will have a reliable addition to your repertoire.

Olive, corn, or grapeseed oil for frying
1 teaspoon ground cinnamon
$1/2$ cup plus 1 tablespoon sugar
8 tablespoons (1 stick) butter
$1/4$ teaspoon salt
1 cup flour
3 eggs

1. Put at least 2 inches of oil into a large saucepan or deep skillet and heat to about 350°F. Mix the cinnamon and $1/2$ cup sugar together on a large plate.
2. Combine the remaining sugar, butter, salt, and 1 cup water in a saucepan over high heat and bring to a boil. Turn the heat to low and add the flour all at once. Stir constantly until the mixture forms a ball, about 30 seconds. Remove from the heat and beat in the eggs one at a time, stirring until smooth after each addition.
3. Spoon the dough into a pastry bag with a large star tip (or you can simply drop spoonfuls of the batter into the oil). Press strips of dough about 4 inches long into the hot oil. Cook as many as will fit comfortably at once, turning as they brown, for a total of 5 to 10 minutes each.
4. Remove the churros from the oil and drain them on paper towels, then immediately roll them in the cinnamon-sugar mixture. Serve hot or at least warm.

Loukoumades Honey and Cinnamon Fritters
GREECE ■ ■
MAKES **24 TO 30**
TIME **3 HOURS, LARGELY UNATTENDED**

Loukoumades are served across Greece and Cyprus, with a wide range of garnishes. I've suggested honey and cinnamon because they're a simple, delicious, and authentic combination. But you could add a sprinkling of chopped pistachios or a dusting of confectioners' sugar or even substitute the syrup used in making Baklava (page 628) for the honey.

1 teaspoon instant active dry yeast, like SAF

2 tablespoons sugar

3 1/2 cups flour, plus more as needed

1 1/2 teaspoons salt

1 cup water or milk

Oil or butter for the bowl

Corn, grapeseed, or other neutral oil for deep-frying

1/2 cup honey, more or less, gently warmed

1 tablespoon ground cinnamon, or more to taste

1. Combine the yeast, 1 tablespoon of the sugar, the flour, and salt in a food processor and pulse once or twice. Turn the machine on and add the liquid, a little at a time, through the feed tube, until the mixture forms a ball and is slightly sticky to the touch. If dry, add another tablespoon or two of water and process for another 10 seconds. (In the unlikely event that the mixture is too sticky, add flour, a tablespoon at a time.)

2. Turn the dough onto a floured work surface and knead by hand for a few seconds to form a smooth, round dough ball. Put the dough in a lightly oiled or buttered bowl and cover with plastic wrap; let rise until the dough doubles in size, 1 to 2 hours.

3. Put at least 2 inches (more is better) of oil in a large deep saucepan; the narrower the saucepan, the less oil you'll need, but the more oil you use, the more fritters you can cook at the same time. Heat the oil over medium-high heat to about 350°F (a pinch of the batter will sizzle immediately).

4. Punch the dough down in the bowl, then moisten or flour your hands and shape tablespoon-sized pieces of the batter into little balls. Keep a piece of plastic wrap draped over the shaped fritters. Fry in batches, without crowding, until nicely browned,

turning as necessary; total cooking time will be less than 7 to 10 minutes. Drain on paper towels. Serve hot or at room temperature, drizzled with the honey and sprinkled with a mixture of the cinnamon and the remaining tablespoon of sugar.

Ossi dei Morti Chewy Sugar Cookies ITALY ■ ▓

MAKES **ABOUT 2 DOZEN**

TIME **30 MINUTES, PLUS TIME TO REST OVERNIGHT**

"Bones of the Dead"—long-lasting cookies that will keep for about a month in an airtight container. They're easy, sweet, and great with a cup of espresso. Flavor with vanilla, almond, cinnamon, or nothing at all.

3 eggs

2 cups confectioners' sugar

2 cups flour, plus more if needed

1 teaspoon baking powder

1 teaspoon vanilla or almond extract or 1/2 teaspoon ground cinnamon, optional

1. Combine the eggs and sugar in the bowl of an electric mixer and start the machine slowly; when the sugar has been incorporated, turn up the speed and beat until very light in color, 5 minutes or more. In a bowl, combine the flour, baking powder, and cinnamon if you're using it and gradually add to the batter, with the machine again working slowly. If the dough is still sticky, add another tablespoon or two of flour. (If your machine stalls, start kneading by hand.) Add the vanilla if you're using it.

2. On a lightly floured surface, roll the dough into logs about 1 1/2 inches thick; cut into 1 1/2-inch pieces and place on greased cookie sheets. (If you don't have enough cookie sheets, just refrigerate the logs and cut the dough the next day.) Cover

the dough with a towel or plastic wrap and refrigerate overnight, or at least 12 hours.

3. Preheat the oven to 350°F. Bake the cookies for about 15 minutes, until they are lightly browned; cool before serving.

Orange-Nut Biscotti ITALY ■ ▩

MAKES **3 TO 4 DOZEN**

TIME **ABOUT 1¼ HOURS**

The familiar zwiebacklike cookie originated not at Starbucks but in Italy, where it is nowhere near as popular as it is in the States. Still, it's nice to have a bunch around, and they keep far better than regular cookies, up to a week in an airtight container. Increase the sugar to a cup if you like your biscotti sweet.

These may be made, of course, without nuts, with lemon instead of orange, or with added ingredients like raisins or even chocolate chips.

1 cup almonds or hazelnuts

¾ cup sugar

2 cups flour

Pinch of salt

1 teaspoon baking powder

3 eggs

1 teaspoon vanilla or almond extract

Zest of 1 orange

1 to 2 tablespoons milk, if necessary

Flour for the pans

1. Preheat the oven to 375°F. Toast the nuts in a dry skillet over medium heat, shaking the pan frequently until they color slightly and become fragrant, 3 or 4 minutes.

2. Combine the sugar, flour, salt, and baking powder in a food processor; pulse to blend. Add the eggs,

vanilla, and zest and process until the mixture forms a dough ball; if necessary, add a tablespoon or two of milk. Add the toasted nuts and pulse a few times; you don't want to pulverize the nuts, just chop them lightly (and it's okay if some remain whole) and integrate them into the dough.

3. Butter 2 baking sheets and dust them with flour; invert the sheets and tap them to remove excess flour. Divide the dough in half and shape each half into a 2-inch-wide log. Place each log onto one of the baking sheets.

4. Bake until the loaves are golden and beginning to crack on top, about 30 minutes; remove the logs from the oven. Lower the oven temperature to 250°F. When the loaves are cool enough to handle, use a serrated knife to cut each on the diagonal into ½-inch-thick slices. Put the slices on the sheets, return to the oven, and leave them there until they dry out, 15 to 20 minutes, turning once. Cool on wire racks.

Olive Oil Cookies with Orange and Cinnamon SPAIN ■ ▩

MAKES **2 DOZEN COOKIES**

TIME **40 MINUTES**

These can be produced, if you like, with lard or (more likely) butter, but this is an ancient recipe from southern Spain and probably was originally made with olive oil. Terrific with sherry or coffee.

2 cups flour

½ teaspoon baking powder

Pinch of salt

½ cup granulated sugar

1 teaspoon ground cinnamon

1 egg

½ cup extra virgin olive oil, plus oil for the cookie sheets

Grated zest of 1 orange or lemon, plus some of its juice if needed

¼ cup Grand Marnier or other orange liqueur

Confectioners' sugar for garnish

1. Preheat the oven to 375°F. Combine the dry ingredients. Beat the egg with the olive oil, orange zest, and liqueur. Gently stir the liquid mix into the dry one, just until well combined; if the mixture is stiff, add a little orange juice.

2. Drop by rounded teaspoonfuls onto a lightly oiled cookie sheet and bake for 15 to 20 minutes, or until lightly browned. Cool for a couple of minutes, then transfer the cookies to a rack to cool further. Store in a covered tin for up to 3 days; sprinkle with confectioners' sugar just before serving.

Beverages We have adopted many of the alcohol-based traditions of the rest of the world (see pages 669–672), but our repertoire of other drinks is sadly restricted compared to that of many countries. The idea of drinking salty limeade or nonsweet yogurt drinks may seem unusual, but these and many of the other beverages in this chapter—especially the fruit-based ones—are far more refreshing (and healthier) than the supersweet drinks many Americans regularly consume.

FRUIT-BASED DRINKS

Straight fruit, blended with ice, sugar, often lime, and sometimes salt, makes some of the world's simplest and most refreshing beverages. Lemonade is the most familiar example of this to most of us, but throughout the world almost every fruit is used to make a drink of some type.

Sugar Syrup ■ ■ ▩

MAKES **1 CUP**

TIME **10 MINUTES**

A basic ingredient in mixed drinks and elsewhere; convenient and elegant for iced tea, too.

1 cup sugar

1. Combine the sugar with 1 cup water in a small saucepan over medium heat. Cook, stirring occasionally, until the sugar dissolves, about 5 minutes. Cool.
2. Cover and refrigerate; it will keep indefinitely.

Salty Limeade INDIA ■ ■ ▩

MAKES **8 SERVINGS**

TIME **30 MINUTES**

Limeade is popular throughout Asia and often served salty. It will take some experimentation on your part to determine whether you like it really salty—in which case you should reduce the sugar substantially—or sweet, like lemonade. You might be surprised; salty limeade is usually considered more refreshing (and makes a good substitute for sports

drinks). You can omit the salt entirely to make standard limeade.

1 cup fresh lime juice, pulp and rinds reserved

1 teaspoon salt, or to taste

1 cup Sugar Syrup (preceding recipe), or to taste

1. Bring 6 cups water to a boil. Remove from the heat and add the lime pulp and rinds. Cover and steep for 10 minutes, then strain and combine with the lime juice and salt. (You can serve at this point or refrigerate the lime mixture and sugar syrup until you're ready to serve, up to a couple of days.)
2. Add sugar syrup to taste and serve over ice.

Ginger Ale ASIA ■ ■

MAKES **ABOUT 2 CUPS SYRUP, ENOUGH FOR ABOUT 16**

TIME **35 MINUTES**

Add sparkling water and ice to this easily made syrup to produce the best ginger ale you've ever tasted. Incredible with rum, the syrup is also a quick way to add ginger flavor to stir-fries and other dishes.

¾ cup fresh ginger, sliced or roughly chopped (don't bother to peel)

1 cup sugar

Sparkling water

Lemon or lime wedges for garnish

1. Place the ginger, sugar, and 2 cups water in a saucepan; bring to a boil. Lower the heat and simmer for 10 minutes, then remove from the heat and let cool.
2. Strain the syrup and store, refrigerated, for up to 2 weeks. To serve, combine 2 tablespoons (more or

less according to taste) syrup in a glass with ice, sparkling water, and a wedge of fresh lemon or lime.

Pineappleade SOUTHEAST ASIA ■ ▣ ▨
MAKES **1 QUART, ENOUGH FOR 4**
TIME **20 MINUTES**

Great at a barbecue, with or without rum.

  1 pineapple, peeled and cut into chunks
  ¹/₂ cup fresh lime juice, or to taste
  1 cup Sugar Syrup (page 660), or to taste
  Chopped fresh mint leaves for garnish

1. Put the pineapple in a blender with water to cover (you may need to do this in batches). Puree; strain, pressing on the solids to extract as much juice as possible.
2. Combine the pineapple juice with enough water (or sparkling water) to make 1 quart. Add lime juice and sugar syrup to taste. Chill and serve, garnished with mint.

Avocado or Fruit Shake
SOUTHEAST ASIA, MEXICO ■ ▨
MAKES **2 SERVINGS**
TIME **10 MINUTES**

Shakes like this one are produced just about everywhere soft fruit is grown; sometimes they're very sweet and sometimes not. You must play with the recipe a bit to find out where your own taste lies. For fruit shake ideas, see the variations.

  1 medium to large avocado, quite ripe
  1¹/₂ cups milk or sweetened condensed milk
  1 tablespoon sugar, or to taste
  Ice cubes

1. Cut the avocado in half, remove the pit, scoop out the pulp, and place it in a blender with the milk, sugar, and ice cubes. Blend until smooth and frothy.
2. Taste and add more sugar if you like. Serve immediately.

Banana Shake. Really great with a tiny bit of vanilla extract added: substitute 1 or 2 ripe bananas for the avocado.

Mango Shake. I like this with a squeeze of lime: substitute the pulp of 1 or 2 mangoes for the avocado.

Cantaloupe Horchata MEXICO ■ ▨ ▨
MAKES **4 OR MORE SERVINGS**
TIME **10 MINUTES**

The unusual thing about many Mexican fruit drinks is that the seeds are included; they're blended, so you don't realize this until you watch them being made, but this is the reason for their wonderfully intense flavors. This procedure works well for cantaloupe, honeydew, watermelon, or other melon.

  1 very ripe cantaloupe, 2 pounds or more
  About ¹/₄ cup fresh lime juice, to taste
  About ¹/₄ cup sugar, to taste

1. Cut the cantaloupe in half; scoop the flesh, seeds, and liquid into a blender. Add a couple tablespoons each of lime juice and sugar, along with 2

cups water. Blend until very smooth, adding a little more water if necessary.

2. Taste and add more lime juice or sugar if you like. Serve immediately, over ice, or refrigerate for up to a couple of hours before serving.

Watermelon Cooler INDIA ▨ ▪

MAKES **4 SERVINGS**

TIME **20 MINUTES**

I like this one quite sweet, but you can eliminate the sugar entirely if you prefer. Add a little vodka if you're in the mood.

> **4 cups seeded or seedless watermelon, cut into chunks**
> **1/2 cup milk**
> **1/4 cup sugar, or to taste**
> **1 cup ice cubes, preferably crushed**
> **1 tablespoon fresh lime juice, or to taste**
> **1/4 cup chopped fresh mint leaves, plus mint for garnish**

1. Combine the watermelon, milk, and sugar in a blender with the ice. (If you have a small blender, work in 2 batches.) Blend until pureed but not entirely smooth.

2. Add the lime juice and mint, along with more sugar if you like. Serve over ice, garnished with more mint.

DAIRY-BASED DRINKS

Dairy is even more important in the Middle East and India than it is in most of Europe and the United States. Especially in India, it's a major source of protein, but throughout the band from Greece through India yogurt is eaten daily by almost everyone. And one of its primary forms is as a drink.

Ayran Yogurt "Milk" TURKEY ▨ ▪

MAKES **2 LARGE OR 4 SMALL GLASSES**

TIME **10 MINUTES**

A popular drink throughout the Middle East, ayran is a refreshing protein-packed beverage for a hot day. In some places sugar is added instead of salt; try it either way. The amount of water you add will depend on the thickness of your yogurt; very thick yogurt will take almost an equal amount of water, and very thin yogurt may need only 1/2 cup or so.

> **2 cups good-quality plain yogurt**
> **Salt or sugar to taste**
> **2 tablespoons chopped fresh mint leaves**

1. Whisk together the yogurt and salt or sugar with enough water (or sparkling water) to achieve a milky consistency. (You can also use a blender if you prefer.)

2. Add the mint and serve over ice.

Piyush. This is the Indian version: In step 1, honey is sometimes substituted, and a large pinch of saffron threads is added. In step 2, eliminate the mint and add about 1/4 cup chopped unsalted pistachios. Let sit for a little while before serving so the saffron colors the drink nicely.

Lassi Namkeen Savory Yogurt Shake INDIA ▨ ▪

MAKES **2 TO 4 SERVINGS**

TIME **10 MINUTES**

If you like ayran (preceding recipe), the slightly savory yogurt drink of Turkey, you might try this, the even more unusual yogurt beverage of India. Like many beverages, it comes with a variety of health claims, but regardless of those, it's refreshing and—

obviously—protein packed. I have had this with a clove of garlic included and with so much black pepper—probably around 2 teaspoons for this quantity—that I was stunned. This version is relatively tame.

    2 cups yogurt, preferably whole-milk
    ½ teaspoon salt, or to taste
    ¼ teaspoon black pepper, or to taste
    1 teaspoon ground cumin, or to taste
    Pinch of cayenne
    1 cup ice cubes

Combine all the ingredients in a blender with 1 cup cold water. Blend until smooth and serve.

Mint Lassi. Add about ¼ cup fresh mint leaves and a small piece—maybe ½ inch or so, peeled—of fresh ginger.

Lassi Meethi Sweet Yogurt Shake INDIA ■ ■
MAKES **4 SERVINGS**
TIME **10 MINUTES**

While Lassi Namkeen (preceding recipe) is an acquired taste for most people, this is instantly appealing. Be sure to try the fruit variation.

    2 cups whole-milk yogurt
    ½ teaspoon ground cardamom, or to taste
    2 tablespoons sugar, or to taste
    Pinch of salt
    1 cup ice cubes

Combine all the ingredients in a blender with 1 cup cold water. Blend until smooth and serve.

Mango (or Other Fruit) Lassi. Add 1 cup pulp of mango, peach, or other fruit to the mix.

Almond Milk ITALY ■ ▦ ▩
MAKES **4 SERVINGS**
TIME **20 MINUTES**

An ancient and delicious dairy substitute, useful in baking but also good as a straight cold drink.

    ½ pound blanched almonds, very finely chopped or
        ground in a food processor
    1½ tablespoons almond extract, optional
    Sugar to taste, optional

1. Combine the almonds and 1 quart water in a blender or food processor; blend until the mixture is as smooth as it will get. Let sit for 10 to 20 minutes.
2. Strain through a fine-mesh strainer, lined with cheesecloth if necessary; taste and add the almond extract and sugar if you like. Refrigerate for up to 3 days.

Horchata Chilled Rice Drink MEXICO ■ ■
MAKES **4 SERVINGS**
TIME **45 MINUTES, PLUS SOAKING TIME**

Horchata (which can be used to describe any sweet drink, but has come to mean, by default, this one) is sold all over Mexico (and throughout southern California). It's an addictive, deliciously creamy drink that contains no dairy but is based on ground rice. Traditionally it's made in a mortar and pestle; you'll be glad you live in the age of blenders.

1 1/2 cups long-grain rice

Two 4-inch cinnamon sticks

1 lime, zest cut into large pieces and juice reserved

1/2 cup sugar, or more to taste

1. Put the rice, cinnamon sticks, and lime zest into a large bowl. Pour 1 quart warm water over the mixture and let it sit overnight. If the weather is hot, cover the bowl and refrigerate.

2. Remove the cinnamon sticks and zest from the mixture and pour the rice and soaking liquid into a blender. (Work in batches if necessary.) Blend, pouring in an additional 2 cups water with the machine running, until just about smooth. Pour the mixture through a strainer and discard the solids.

3. Stir in the sugar until dissolved, adding more to taste. Chill, season to taste with the reserved lime juice, and serve.

Almond Horchata. Add 1 cup blanched almonds to the blender in step 2.

TEA, COFFEE, AND INFUSIONS

With coffee we have plenty of experience. But even with "regular" tea, we have a lot to learn, and when it comes to the arena of fruit and herb teas, the rest of the world is light-years ahead. Here is a small sampling.

Remember, hot infusions like these can be only as good as the water with which they're made. If your tap water tastes like chlorine or other foreign substances, either filter it or use bottled water.

Mexican Hot Chocolate ▪

MAKES **2 SERVINGS**

TIME **20 MINUTES**

Make sure you don't skip the last part of this classic—the wonderful frothiness is one of the two things that make Mexican hot chocolate special (the cinnamon is the other). For a great dessert, serve this with Churros (page 655).

The chocolate sold in Mexican stores for hot chocolate already contains cinnamon and sugar, so you can just melt it with some milk and beat until frothy. You can actually make it with water if you like, and it isn't half bad.

1 disk (about 3 ounces) Mexican chocolate or 4 ounces
   semisweet chocolate

2 cups milk

1/2 teaspoon ground cinnamon, or to taste, optional (you
   won't need it if you're using Mexican chocolate)

1 vanilla bean, split lengthwise, or 1 teaspoon vanilla
   extract, optional

1. Chop the chocolate if necessary and combine it with the milk and cinnamon if you're using it in a saucepan. Scrape the seeds from the vanilla bean and add the pod and seeds or the vanilla extract if you're using it. Simmer, stirring, until the chocolate is melted.

2. Remove the pan from the heat. Using a molinillo (a Mexican chocolate beater), a wire whisk, an immersion blender, or an electric mixer, beat the chocolate mixture well until frothy. You can also put the mixture in a blender and (carefully!) pulse until frothy. Reheat if necessary and serve immediately.

Chocolate Español Spanish Hot Chocolate ■

MAKES **4 SERVINGS**

TIME **10 MINUTES**

Montezuma introduced Cortés to chocolate in the sixteenth century, and the Spaniards immediately began messing around with it. The original Mexican beverage (preceding recipe) was tweaked to suit the tastes of the Spaniards, and their associated versions of hot chocolate remain different to this day.

Spanish hot chocolate is incredibly rich and thick—almost like loose pudding—and perfect for dunking Churros (page 655). Some people use cornstarch (or eggs) to thicken their chocolate, but I prefer the natural thickness that comes from melting chocolate into milk.

¹/₂ pound good-quality semisweet or bittersweet
    chocolate

1 quart milk

2 tablespoons sugar

1 teaspoon ground cinnamon

1. Put the chocolate, milk, and sugar in a heavy saucepan over low heat. Whisk slowly until the chocolate melts and the sugar dissolves.
2. When the mixture is smooth and steamy, transfer to mugs, top with a dusting of cinnamon, and serve.

Agua de Jamaica Hibiscus Iced Tea MEXICO ■

MAKES **4 SERVINGS**

TIME **30 MINUTES, LARGELY UNATTENDED, PLUS**
    CHILLING TIME

Make this mysterious and delicious herbal iced tea in advance, because it's best cold. You can buy dried hi-biscus (known as jamaica) flowers at almost any Mexican market.

1 cup dried hibiscus flowers

About ¹/₄ cup sugar or honey, to taste

1. Combine the hibiscus with 1 quart water in a small saucepan and bring to a boil. Cover, turn off the heat, and let stand for about 30 minutes.
2. Strain, then stir in sugar to taste. Refrigerate to chill and serve over ice.

Salabat Ginger Tea SOUTHEAST ASIA ■ ■ ■

MAKES **4 SERVINGS**

TIME **15 MINUTES**

It's long been believed that ginger is a digestive aid, but this drink would be popular in any case. If you like ginger ale or candied ginger, you owe it to yourself to try this.

¹/₂ cup fresh ginger, rinsed and chopped or sliced
    (don't bother to peel)

¹/₂ cup brown sugar

1. In a small saucepan, combine the ginger and 1 quart water. Bring to a boil, then lower the heat and simmer for 10 minutes.
2. Strain, then add the sugar and stir until it is completely dissolved. Taste and adjust the seasoning (you can add more water if it is too strong or, of course, more sugar). Serve hot or iced.

Lemongrass-Ginger Tea

SOUTHEAST ASIA ■ ■ ■

MAKES **4 SERVINGS**

TIME **15 MINUTES**

Health claims aside, this is delicious, hot or iced, sweetened or not. You can make another interesting tea by omitting the lemongrass and serving the brew with milk instead of lime juice.

> **1 tablespoon black tea, optional**
> **10 nickel-sized slices fresh ginger (don't bother to peel)**
> **2 lemongrass stalks, trimmed (page 143) and roughly chopped**
> **Sugar to taste, optional**
> **2 tablespoons fresh lime juice, or to taste**

1. In a small pot with a lid, combine 1 quart water with the tea if you're using it, the ginger, and the lemongrass. Turn the heat to medium and heat until steam rises from the surface. Turn off the heat and cover; steep for 5 minutes.
2. Strain, then return to the pan and reheat gently. Add sugar, then lime juice to taste. Serve immediately or refrigerate and serve cold.

Iced Lemongrass Tea SOUTHEAST ASIA ■ ■

MAKES **4 SERVINGS**

TIME **20 MINUTES, PLUS CHILLING TIME**

Like most iced teas from Asia, this has no caffeine and is not a true tea—more an herbal infusion. Because of the natural sweetness of lemongrass, it needs less sugar than most other iced beverages.

> **1 1/2 cups lemongrass stalks, trimmed (page 143) and cut into 1-inch lengths**

> **1/4 cup sugar, or to taste**
> **Lime wedges for serving**

1. Combine the lemongrass with 1 quart water in a saucepan with a lid over medium heat; cook until it steams, then turn the heat to a minimum, cover, and steep for 10 minutes. Add the sugar and stir until it dissolves.
2. Cool, then place the mixture in a blender and (carefully if it's still hot) blend for about 1 minute, until the lemongrass pieces are chopped up; they will not become pureed—lemongrass is simply too tough. Strain into a pitcher and chill. Serve over ice, with lime wedges.

Iced Coffee, Vietnamese Style ■ ■

MAKES **4 SERVINGS**

TIME **20 MINUTES**

You must use strong coffee for this, and it must be finely ground; the drip should be agonizingly slow. This can be served hot, too, of course, and it's good. But to me it's the best iced coffee in the world.

> **1/4 cup Thai or Vietnamese ground coffee beans or espresso beans, as fine as possible**
> **Sweetened condensed milk to taste**

1. Use a drip cone with a coffee filter; place the coffee in the filter. Bring 2 cups water to a boil and pour over the coffee. (You may also bring the water to a boil in a saucepan and stir in the coffee, then strain.)
2. Put about 1/2 inch sweetened condensed milk in the bottom of 4 glasses; fill with ice and add coffee. Stir, then add more milk to taste if you like.

Cha Yen Thai Iced Tea ■ ▨

MAKES **4 SERVINGS**

TIME **15 MINUTES**

In Thailand, this refreshing drink is served at many stands in little plastic bags with straws so you can drink it on the go, but Thai iced tea has soared in popularity at Thai restaurants across America—and for good reason. Thai tea leaves, which can be found at most Asian groceries, combine black tea leaves, star anise, orange flowers, vanilla, cloves, and cinnamon. This blend gives the tea its distinctive taste and orange color, but the technique and style of the drink will work with any good black tea, or you can use black tea with added herbs, in the style of chai (page 668).

> 1¼ cups Thai tea leaves or any black tea leaves mixed with any or all of the spices mentioned above
>
> ¼ cup sweetened condensed milk or fresh milk to taste
>
> Sugar to taste
>
> Milk to taste

1. Bring 6 cups water to a boil. Put the tea leaves in a heatproof pitcher and pour in the hot water. Allow the tea to steep for about 5 minutes.
2. Divide the sweetened condensed milk among 4 glasses. Carefully strain the hot tea into the glasses and stir well, adding sugar and milk to taste. Add ice cubes to chill and serve.

Hot Thai Tea. Omit the ice and substitute teacups for the glasses.

Cha Dum Yen. Thai Tea without Milk. Omit the sweetened condensed milk and milk.

Cinnamon Tea KOREA ■ ▨

MAKES **4 SERVINGS**

TIME **20 MINUTES, PLUS CHILLING TIME**

Though this is traditionally and usually made with persimmon, I find the flavor of cinnamon so overwhelming (and the availability of persimmon so limited) that I do away with it. An unusual but super meal ender, always served ice cold.

> 5 cinnamon sticks
>
> ½ cup sugar, or to taste
>
> 1 teaspoon pine nuts, lightly toasted (see Toasted Sesame Seeds, page 596)

1. Combine the cinnamon with 1 quart water and the sugar in a saucepan. Bring to a boil, turn the heat to low, and simmer for about 20 minutes. Cool, then chill.
2. To serve, fish out the cinnamon sticks and pour into cups or glasses. Garnish with the pine nuts.

Roasted Barley Tea KOREA ■ ▨ ▨

MAKES **1 QUART**

TIME **30 MINUTES**

Most people find the distinctive flavor of this tea, which is served hot or cold, instantly appealing. Theoretically, it is a digestive aid, but in any case it's a great alternative to soft drinks or sweet tea.

> ¼ cup whole (not pearl) barley

1. Put the barley in a skillet over medium heat; toast for about 10 minutes, shaking the pan occasionally, until browned and fragrant. Meanwhile, bring 1 quart water to a boil.

2. Add the barley to the water; cover, turn the heat to very low, and simmer for 15 minutes. Strain and serve hot, at room temperature, or chilled. You can add sugar or honey if you like, but it isn't necessary.

Masala Chai Spiced Tea INDIA ▪

MAKES **4 SERVINGS**

TIME **15 MINUTES**

One of the national beverages of India, chai—often called masala chai—is simply sweetened tea with milk and spices. Which spices? Ah, there's the question. I like a simple, minimal mix; other people use complicated spice mixtures; many would eliminate the fennel and use a mixture of cloves, cinnamon, and ginger.

5 tablespoons black tea, preferably Assam

4 teaspoons sugar, or to taste

About 1/3 cup whole milk

5 green cardamom pods, lightly crushed

1 tablespoon fennel seeds

Pinch of black pepper

1. Brew the tea as usual, using 1 quart hot water and allowing to steep for 3 to 5 minutes. Strain. This may be done as far in advance as you like.
2. Reheat the tea slowly and over low heat with the remaining ingredients. When it is very hot, strain again; taste and adjust the seasoning and serve immediately.

Cardamom-Scented Tea ENGLAND ▪

MAKES **4 SERVINGS**

TIME **10 MINUTES**

This is a gentler version of the preceding Indian Masala Chai, perhaps better suited to the palates of Western Europe. Yet it remains exotic and delicious, as does cardamom-spiced coffee (still consumed in the Middle East). Wonderful iced.

4 rounded teaspoons Assam, Keemun, or other black tea (English or Irish Breakfast is okay)

1 teaspoon ground cardamom

Fresh lemon juice or milk as desired

1. Boil 3 cups water, then brew the tea in the hot water with the cardamom in a pot for 4 to 5 minutes.
2. Strain into cups and serve with lemon juice or milk.

Sbiten Spiced Honey Drink RUSSIA ▪ ▪ ▪

MAKES **4 SERVINGS**

TIME **30 MINUTES**

This groglike drink has been popular in Russia for centuries. It's usually prepared without alcohol, but it's pretty good with it, too—just add 1/2 to 3/4 cup vodka or brandy during the last couple of minutes of simmering.

It's not often served cold in Russia, but I like it that way, as a kind of spicy, odd relation of Masala Chai (page 668).

1/2 cup sugar

1/2 cup honey

2 cloves

4 cardamom pods

Several slices fresh ginger

1 cinnamon stick

1 teaspoon minced lemon zest

1 tablespoon chopped fresh mint leaves

1. Combine all the ingredients with 1 quart water in a saucepan with a lid over medium heat; bring almost to a boil.
2. Cover and turn off the heat; steep for 15 to 20 minutes. Strain, then reheat and serve (or refrigerate, covered, for a couple of days and reheat or serve cold).

Tea with Jam RUSSIA ■
MAKES **4 SERVINGS**
TIME **10 MINUTES**

Tea is usually served black in Russia, with preserves. You can add milk or cream if you like. Also completely optional, but not inappropriate, is a bit of vodka, brandy, or rum.

5 rounded teaspoons (or tea bags) of good black tea, like
    Assam, Darjeeling, or Keemun (or English Breakfast
    tea)

Fruit preserves, such as strawberry, raspberry, cherry,
    lingonberry, or black currant

Sugar, optional

Small wedges or thin slices of lemon, optional

1. Bring a kettle of water to a boil. Heat a teapot by rinsing it with a little of the hot water. Combine 1 quart water and the tea in the teapot and steep for 3 to 5 minutes.
2. Strain the tea into preheated cups and stir in the preserves, usually a couple of tablespoons per cup. Add sugar to taste and a piece of lemon if you like; serve.

ALCOHOLIC BEVERAGES

There was a time when beverages with alcohol were considered food, and people depended on them for nourishment (they are, after all, a convenient way to preserve and consume carbohydrates). This is hardly appropriate in the contemporary world, but some of the older drinks remain interesting. Here are a few, along with some current classics.

Glögg SCANDINAVIA ■
MAKES **2 QUARTS, ENOUGH FOR ABOUT 8**
TIME **25 MINUTES, PLUS TIME TO CHILL OVERNIGHT**

Traditionally served at Christmas parties in Sweden and elsewhere, this is powerful stuff, as you can see by its ingredients. Nevertheless, it goes down easily, so be careful. The wine and port should be decent but obviously need not be fantastic; most of their flavors will be overwhelmed.

One 750-ml bottle dry and fruity red wine, like Pinot Noir
    or Zinfandel

One 750-ml bottle port

Half 750-ml bottle cognac, brandy, rum, or vodka

Zest of 1 orange

10 cardamom pods

2 cinnamon sticks

10 cloves

5 slices fresh ginger

Sugar to taste

1 cup raisins, optional

1 cup blanched almonds, optional

1. Combine the wine, port, spirit, orange zest, and spices in a saucepan, along with 2 cups water; bring to a boil. Reduce the heat and simmer for

about 5 minutes. Cool, cover, and refrigerate overnight, at least 12 hours.

2. Strain the mixture, then reheat (do not boil) and add sugar. Add the raisins and almonds (you might put a teaspoonful in each glass if you're using these) and serve hot.

Fruit-Infused Vodka RUSSIA ■ ▪

MAKES ONE 750-ML BOTTLE

TIME 20 MINUTES, PLUS AT LEAST 5 DAYS TO INFUSE

You might call this pickled fruit, but more people will discard the fruit and drink the vodka than the other way around. You could, of course, eat the one and drink the other.

One 750-ml bottle high-quality vodka

4 cups cut-up fruit, such as strawberries, raspberries, passion fruit, pears, peaches, blackberries, or watermelon

¹/₂ cup sugar or honey

Handful of fresh mint leaves

1. Combine all the ingredients in a large bowl, jar, or plastic container and seal tightly. Refrigerate for at least 5 days, preferably a couple of weeks; taste periodically and you will know when it is ready.

2. Strain and store the vodka in the refrigerator or freezer.

Spiced Vodka RUSSIA ■ ▪

MAKES ONE 750-ML BOTTLE

TIME 5 MINUTES, PLUS AT LEAST 12 HOURS TO INFUSE

Contrary to what you might believe, Absolut and

Stolichnaya did not invent flavored vodka; it's been around forever, and you can make your own.

1 tablespoon aniseeds, 2 tablespoons caraway seeds, 1 tablespoon coriander seeds, zest of 1 lemon or orange, or 30 peppercorns, lightly crushed or ground

One 750-ml bottle good-quality vodka

1. Put one of the flavoring ingredients in the vodka. Let sit, tasting every 12 hours, until the mixture achieves the intensity you like. This may take as little as 12 or as many as 72 hours.

2. Strain and store, preferably in the freezer.

Classic Daiquiri CARIBBEAN ■ ▪

MAKES 2 STRONG SERVINGS

TIME 10 MINUTES

The real thing, not the frozen kind, an elegant and delicious drink, especially when made with good aged dark rum.

³/₄ cup rum

2 teaspoons Sugar Syrup (page 660) or superfine sugar to taste

1 tablespoon fresh lime juice, or to taste

Cracked ice as needed

2 lime wedges for garnish

1. Combine the first 4 ingredients in a cocktail shaker; shake well, then taste and add more sugar or lime if you like.

2. Strain into a martini or cocktail glass and garnish with the lime.

Cuba Libre Rum and Coke CUBA ■ ▧

MAKES **1 SERVING**

TIME **3 MINUTES**

The classic rum drink of the fifties. To make a Dark and Stormy, use dark rum and ginger ale.

> 1½ ounces good-quality rum
> ½ cup Coca-Cola, or to taste
> Zest and juice of ½ lime
> 1 slice lime for garnish

1. Fill a tall glass with ice cubes. Pour over them the rum, Coke, and lime juice; stir in the zest.
2. Garnish with the slice of lime.

Margarita MEXICO ■ ▧

MAKES **4 SERVINGS**

TIME **10 MINUTES**

The influx of great-quality tequilas into this country over the last decade has gently nudged my concept of what a margarita should be ever further away from the sweet blender drinks that bars and American Mexican restaurants pass off as "margaritas."

These days a long pour of good tequila, a dash of orange liqueur, and a quarter of a lime over ice is how I make them. The following recipe has a little more padding, but is still a vehicle for the flavor of tequila, so I advise buying the best you can (it should be 100 percent agave). If the salt-rimmed glass doesn't appeal to you (or a guest), omit the first step.

> Coarse salt, preferably kosher
> ¾ cup tequila, preferably 100 percent agave silver or
>   blanco
> Scant ¼ cup Grand Marnier or other orange liqueur

> ¼ cup fresh lime juice
> Lime wedges for garnish

1. Fill a saucer wider than your margarita glasses with a layer of salt. Moisten the rims of the glasses with a lime wedge, then invert the glasses into the coarse salt to coat the rims with a thin layer of salt.
2. Combine the tequila, Grand Marnier, and lime juice in a large cocktail shaker or pitcher with plenty of ice and vigorously shake or stir to combine and chill.
3. Add ice to the prepared glasses and strain the margarita over it. Garnish each drink with a wedge of lime and serve at once.

The Easy Margarita for One. Combine in a glass, over ice, ¼ cup good tequila; 1 tablespoon orange liqueur, or to taste; and the juice of ½ lime, or to taste.

Mojito CUBA ■ ▧

MAKES **1 SERVING**

TIME **10 MINUTES**

I have had more bad mojitos in the last couple of years—since they became popular—than I had had in my entire life previously. This is the real thing and a fantastic cocktail. There should be enough mint to chew on.

> About 2 tablespoons Sugar Syrup (page 660), or to taste
> 1½ ounces good-quality dark rum
> 2 tablespoons fresh lime juice, or to taste
> ¼ cup chopped fresh mint leaves, or more

1. Combine all the ingredients over ice in a glass. Alternatively, combine all the ingredients except

---

the mint in a blender with some crushed ice. Blend.

2. Taste and adjust the seasoning, then serve.

Sangria SPAIN ■ ▣

MAKES **4 SERVINGS**

TIME **20 MINUTES, PLUS AT LEAST 2 HOURS' CHILLING TIME**

The original sangria is this: good red wine, spiced with lemon juice, served with a piece of lemon over ice, with a splash of soda. That sangria has become more complicated, and a cliché of America's Spanish restaurants, does not detract from its basic appeal; it's as good a way as exists to spice up insipid red wine.

Of course, the better the wine you start with, the better the sangria; decent but inexpensive (red) Zinfandel, wine from the south of France, and Rioja are all good.

¼ cup Sugar Syrup (page 660)

One 750-ml bottle fruity, full-bodied red wine

3 tablespoons cognac, brandy, or Grand Marnier, optional

Juice of 1 lemon

1 orange, sliced

1 lemon, sliced

1 apple, sliced

1 peach, sliced

Sparkling water, optional

1. Combine all the ingredients in a pitcher and refrigerate for at least 2 hours, preferably overnight.

2. Serve with ice cubes and, if you like, sparkling water.

White Sangria with Peaches SPAIN ■ ▣

MAKES **6 OR MORE SERVINGS**

TIME **20 MINUTES, PLUS AT LEAST 2 HOURS' CHILLING TIME**

A great alternative to red wine sangria and perfect for the summertime. This is a good place to use canned peaches.

One 750-ml bottle not-too-dry white wine, like Gewürztraminer or Riesling

¼ cup Grand Marnier or other orange liqueur

1 lime, peeled and sliced

1 orange, peeled and sliced

1 cup sliced ripe fresh or canned peaches

½ cup Sugar Syrup (page 660), or to taste

Sparkling water

1. In a large pitcher, combine the wine, Grand Marnier, lime, orange, and peaches. Cover and refrigerate for at least 2 hours, preferably overnight.

2. Add the sugar syrup to taste. Serve in glasses with ice cubes and sparkling water.

Menus Here are a few ideas for ways to assemble some of the many dishes scattered throughout the book according to their regional traditions. But please don't take them too literally. In almost every instance you can "trade" recipes from one menu to another, as if you were in a restaurant, and still be reasonably authentic.

CHINESE MENUS

The oily sauces, MSG, and fortune cookies of American take-out joints serving "Chinese" food are as representative of that country's great cuisine as pizza is of that of Italy—probably better defined as American food.

But even recently, when we've seen better Chinese food here, because most Chinese immigrants come to the United States from places like Hong Kong and Taiwan, most of us have been exposed to only a sliver of real Chinese cuisine—the food that those immigrants have brought from the major cities of eastern and southern China. Central and northern Chinese culinary traditions, most notably Szechwan, are only now beginning to make inroads. Here are a few typical menus for Chinese home-style meals; each would serve about six, except for the Chinese Banquet menu, which could easily feed many more.

A SIU MAY MENU

Siu may, which literally means "roasted flavor," is the name for the savory-sweet meats you see hanging in the windows of urban Chinese restaurants.

Egg Flower Soup (page 115)
Roast Duck (page 325), Soy-Poached Chicken
    (page 274), or Barbecued Pork (page 373), served
    on Basic Long-Grain Rice (page 506)

Sliced oranges
Tea

A WINTERTIME HOME-STYLE MENU

Cream-Style Corn Soup (page 141) or West Lake
    Beef Soup (page 145)
Basic Long-Grain Rice (page 506)
Braised Whole Fish in Hot-and-Sour Sauce
    (page 260), Sea Bass or Other Fillets Wrapped in
    Bean Curd (page 228), or Stir-Fried Shrimp with
    Cabbage and Black Beans (page 213)
Quick-Braised Root Vegetables with Hoisin
    (page 499) or Stir-Fried Potatoes with Chiles
    (page 473)
Sliced oranges
Tea

A SPRINGTIME MENU

Chicken and Watercress Soup (page 140)
Basic Long-Grain Rice (page 506)
Stir-Fried Pork with Asparagus (page 370), Soy-
    Poached Chicken (page 274), White Cut Chicken
    (page 273), or Steamed Dungeness Crab with
    Ginger (page 224)
Gai Lan (Chinese Mustard Greens) with Oyster Sauce
    (page 463) or Snow Peas with Ginger (page 470)
Seasonal fruit
Tea

A MENU FOR WARM WEATHER

Spicy Cold Celery (page 17)

Minced Shrimp in Lettuce Wrappers (page 213)

Basic Long-Grain Rice (page 506)

Drunken Chicken (page 273) or Lemon Chicken (page 314)

Gai Lan (Chinese Mustard Greens) with Oyster Sauce (page 463) or Snow Peas with Ginger (page 470)

Sliced watermelon or other seasonal fruit

Tea

A CHINESE BANQUET

Cold Cut Beef Shank (page 39) and Soy-Poached Chicken (page 274)

West Lake Beef Soup (page 145)

Stir-Fried Chicken with Walnuts (page 311) or Stir-Fried Spicy Shredded Beef (page 368)

Drunken Shrimp (page 212) or Shrimp with Peas and Ham (page 214)

Tea-Smoked Duck or Chicken (page 327) or Roast Duck (page 325)

Steamed Crabs with Soy Dipping Sauce (page 225)

Whole Steamed Sea Bass or Other Fish (page 261)

Egg Noodles with Spring Onions (page 536) or Fried Rice (page 506)

Sweet Rice Flour Dumplings (page 639)

Tea

JAPANESE MENUS

Most Americans associate Japanese food with raw fish, rice, and soy sauce. These are all important aspects of the Japanese diet, but the cuisine is quite diverse, especially considering that it comes from a small island nation that existed in almost total cultural isolation for centuries. During that period, Japanese cuisine developed a personality based largely on a foundation of many foods that originated in China, like soy sauce, rice, and tofu.

Like all island nations, Japan has long depended on fish. Fresh seafood is grilled, fried, and steamed or served cold (or just barely warmed) with rice (sushi) or alone (sashimi). (Since sushi and sashimi are traditionally viewed as special-occasion foods—largely because raw fish tastes best when it's from fish that's exceptionally fresh, and that's never been easy to come by—it is not generally made at home, so I haven't included recipes for it.)

Many Japanese recipes are well within the grasp of the non-Japanese home cook: tempura and other Japanese-style foods, teriyaki (a technique, not a bottled sauce), noodle dishes and soups, steamed dishes, and stews, many of which are based on dashi. And even though very little meat was eaten in Japan until it opened its borders to trade in the middle of the last century, it has created a sophisticated and delicious range of beef and pork dishes—many of which owe a debt to Korean and Chinese cooking.

Home cooking in Japan usually means rice, pickles, miso soup, and green tea (sencha) accompanied by one or more "main courses," a salad, and fruit for dessert. The first two of the following menus reflect that, the third is a little more elaborate—what you might be served as a guest in a Japanese household—and the final is an homage to a meal at a yakitori bar: a meal to go with plenty of beer or sake.

A WINTERTIME HOME-STYLE MENU

Clam Soup (page 136)

Beef Stew with Winter Squash (page 377), Domburi: Rice Soup with Chicken or Tofu and Egg (page 124), or Halibut Simmered in Soy and Sake (page 253)

Rice

Pickles, like homemade Oshinko: Pickled Cabbage (page 444), Gari: Pickled Ginger (page 591), and Kimchi (page 444), or a variety of purchased pickles

Sencha

Oranges

A WARM-WEATHER HOME-STYLE MEAL

Hiyashi Somen: Cold Noodles with Dipping Sauce
(page 534) or Cucumber Seaweed Soup (page 120)
Cold Spinach with Sesame (page 184) or Green
Beans with Sesame-Miso Dressing (page 190)
Soy-Glazed Flounder or Other Fillets (page 232)
Basic Short-Grain Rice (page 507)
Fresh peaches or other seasonal fruit

A JAPANESE-STYLE DINNER FOR GUESTS

Negima: Beef-Scallion Rolls (page 102)
Octopus "Confit" (page 51) or Miso-Broiled
Scallops (page 210)
Asparagus Salad with Soy-Mustard Dressing (page
190) or Seaweed Salad with Cucumber, without
the chicken or shrimp (page 200)
or
Tempura: Batter-Fried Fish and Vegetables
(page 91)
Miso Soup with Tofu (page 122)
Sencha
Seasonal fruit or Green Tea Ice Cream (page 642)

A YAKITORI-STYLE MEAL

Serve these together or as you cook them; this is
Japanese bar food, meant to be served informally. Accompany it with beer or sake poured from large bottles, honoring the Japanese custom of always keeping
your companions' glasses full and never pouring for
yourself.

Edamame (page 433)
Pickles, like homemade Oshinko: Pickled Cabbage
(page 444), Gari: Pickled Ginger (page 591), and
Kimchi (page 444), or a variety of purchased
pickles
Sautéed Peppers with Miso (page 78)
Yakitori: Grilled Chicken on Skewers (page 319)
Salt-Grilled (Broiled) Fish (page 259)
Grilled or Broiled Eggplant with Sweet Miso (page 457)

KOREAN MENUS

Korean food is among the world's most strongly flavored—fiery, garlicky, peppery, sweet, and deeply
pungent, often all at once. But outside of Kimchi
(page 444)—which you either love or hate—most
Korean dishes are enjoyed by even picky eaters, at
least those who can tolerate a bit of chile.

Korean meals are traditionally served with a number of panchan, little side dishes shared at the table. In
Korea, daily meals are often served with as many as
five panchan and ceremonial or celebratory meals
with seven or more. You can obviously omit them
from the following menus, but they do add considerable charm, and many are easy and quick. Conclude
the following menus with fresh fruit and Roasted Barley Tea (page 667).

A VEGETARIAN MENU

Panchan: Kimchi (page 444) and Kong Namul: Bean
Sprout Salad (page 182)
Basic Short-Grain Rice (page 507)
Seaweed Soup (page 155)
Pajon: Crisp Vegetable Pancake (page 80) or Potato
Pancakes with Scallions and Kimchi (page 474)

A MENU FOR WINTER

A selection of panchan, like Kimchi (page 444), Kong
Namul: Bean Sprout Salad (page 182), and/or
Sweet Dried Anchovies (page 52)
Basic Short-Grain Rice (page 507)
Sesame Spareribs (page 392)
Sweet-and-Spicy Broiled Mackerel or Other Fillets
(page 234)
Beef Stew with Bean Paste (page 376)

A WARM-WEATHER MEAL

A selection of panchan, like Kimchi (page 444), Kong
Namul: Bean Sprout Salad (page 182), and/or
Sweet Dried Anchovies (page 52)
Clam Cakes (page 83)

Naengmyon: Cold Buckwheat Noodle Soup
(page 149)
Grilled Chicken with Sesame (page 290)

AN EASY MEAL FOR WEEKNIGHTS
Serve this stew communally, in the center of the table, as is the custom in Korea.

A selectin of panchan, like Kimchi (page 444), Kong
Namul: Bean Sprout Salad (page 182), and/or
Sweet Dried Anchovies (page 52)
Basic Short-Grain Rice (page 507)
Spicy Pork and Tofu Stew (page 398)

A FORMAL DINNER
A selection of panchan, like Kimchi (page 444), Kong
Namul: Bean Sprout Salad (page 182), and/or
Sweet Dried Anchovies (page 52)
Basic Short-Grain Rice (page 507)
Crab Soup, Korean Style (page 135)
Gogi-Jun: Meat and Tofu Pancakes (page 51)
Kalbi Jim: Braised Short Ribs (page 388)

THAI MENUS
Most Thai dishes are simultaneously sweet (from sugar or coconut milk), sour (lime juice or tamarind), salty (fish sauce or simply salt), and hot (Thai chiles), though the combination rarely tastes as cacophonous as it may sound. Mild (and again, sweet) Sticky Rice (page 508), served at almost every sit-down meal, helps to temper the highly seasoned cuisine.

A few thoughts that might hearten the cautious cook to give Thai food a shot: the Thai use far less cilantro than you think; consecotaleophobics (yes, there's a word for those who fear chopsticks) can rest easy—meals in Thailand are served with forks and spoons; and you can easily (and traditionally) regulate the heat and salinity of Thai food by serving a little bowl of Nam Prik (page 586)—fish sauce mixed with chiles and lime—and adding it by the spoonful to dishes at the table as you eat, everyone adding as much or little as they like.

The streets of Bangkok and other major Thai cities are filled with food carts and street vendors who sell snacks and one-dish lunches. Don't let the curbside kitchen fool you: many Thai dishes require advance preparation. But once you have everything measured, cleaned, and ready—which you can take care of a few hours in advance—the "cooking" part is superfast.

A GRILL PARTY
Cha Yen: Thai Iced Tea (page 667) or Iced
Lemongrass Tea (page 666)
Skewered Chicken Thighs with Peanut Sauce
(page 321) or Spicy Grilled Chicken (page 288)
Shrimp on Lemongrass Skewers (page 215) or
Miang Gung: Green Leaf Wraps (page 33)
Sliced fresh pineapple or melon

A WINTERTIME HOME-STYLE MEAL
Dom Yam Gai: Chicken and Coconut Soup (page 142)
Sticky Rice (page 508) with Khao Koor (page 587)
Oranges

A SPRINGTIME HOME-STYLE MEAL
Beef Salad with Mint (page 203)
Ginger Chicken (page 313) with Sticky Rice
(page 508)
Steamed Coconut Custard (page 639) or Bananas in
Coconut Milk (page 622)

A MEAL FOR WARM WEATHER
Som Tum: Green Papaya Salad (page 174)
Stir-Fried Squid with Basil and Garlic (page 221) or
Steamed Shrimp with Lemongrass-Coconut Sauce
(page 216)
Sweet Sticky Rice with Mangoes (page 639)

VIETNAMESE MENUS

Vietnam's cuisine is defined by the country's location—at the crossroads of China, Southeast Asia, and Indonesia—and the time it spent under French colonial rule. Like their Thai neighbors, the Vietnamese use fish sauce and lime juice liberally. But their food is generally not very spicy; instead, they add loads of aromatic herbs—especially cilantro, basil, and mint—that add a scintillating freshness to their food. Take Pho Bo (page 152), for example, which has become a well-known dish in the States for good reason: it's one of the world's best soup recipes. And although the Vietnamese traditionally eat it for breakfast, I think Pho Bo's subtle broth, chewy noodles, and thin slices of meat are good eating at any time of day.

A STREET FOOD PARTY

A Saigon-style street food menu that's perfect for a crowd. Serve with plenty of cold beer.

Lemongrass "Hamburgers" (page 350)
Goi Cuon: Rice Paper Spring Rolls (page 38)
Green Mango Salad with Meat (page 203)
Green Papaya Salad with Shrimp (page 198)

ONE-DISH MEAL (BREAKFAST, LUNCH, OR DINNER)

Pho Bo: Meat and Noodle Soup with Herbs (page 152) or Quicker Pho with Meatballs (page 152)

A HOME-STYLE DINNER

Accompany this and the following menu with Basic Long-Grain Rice (page 506), good bread, or rice paper sheets (soften the rice paper as you would for Goi Cuon, page 38) to wrap the food as you eat.

Hot and Sour Fish Soup (page 136)
Grilled Lemongrass Beef (page 349)
Stir-Fried Vegetables with Nam Pla (page 499)
Fresh seasonal fruit

A DINNER PARTY

Chicken Salad with Vietnamese Seasonings (page 201)
Beef Tenderloin in Caramelized Sugar (page 359)
Sweet Black Pepper Halibut or Other Fish Steaks, Vietnamese Style (page 252)
Tofu Salad with Peanut Sauce (page 195)
Bananas in Coconut Milk (page 622)

MENUS FROM GREECE, TURKEY, AND THE EASTERN MEDITERRANEAN

To me (neither Greek nor Turkish), it doesn't matter much where the eastern Mediterranean dishes in this book came from, because most are now ubiquitous throughout the area. I've used one country or the other's name for dishes—arbitrarily, sometimes, or because the dish is better known by that name in the States—but there are some, like Skordalia/Tarator, where I've stayed out of the fracas.

Besides, the names, origins, and lore of the classics of the eastern Mediterranean are less interesting to me than the seemingly infinite combinations cooks there have coaxed from a relatively limited palette of ingredients. The following three menus are loose generalizations of meals that you might have in Greece, Turkey, or the Middle East, based on the foods I've eaten throughout the region.

A SEAFOOD DINNER

Taramasalata: Fish Roe Puree (page 24)
Olive Oil Bread, with or without Olives (page 567)
Grilled Octopus (page 49) or Grilled Squid with Vinaigrette (page 50)
Cold Lemony Greens (page 180)
Loukoumades (page 655)

A CLASSIC MEAL

A lavish spread that requires a bit of work, but almost all in advance, so you can finish the bulk of the hustle-bustle before your guests arrive. Serve with an earthy, spicy red wine like a Côtes-du-Rhône or a Primitivo (Zinfandel).

> Pita, store bought or made from the recipe on page 568
> Imam Bayildi: Stuffed Eggplants (page 30)
> Chicken Salad with Tarator (page 201)
> Grilled Lamb Skewers with Bay Leaves (page 357)
> Baklava: Phyllo and Walnut Cake (page 628)

A MIDDLE EASTERN DINNER

Soak the chickpeas, fruits, and nuts overnight, and the next day you can turn this impressive-looking menu around for lunch or dinner in about forty-five minutes. Muslim law forbids the consumption of alcohol, so you'll have to drum up your own pairing here (I'd go with rosé) or try the Ayran: Yogurt "Milk" on page 662.

> Pita, store bought or made from the recipe on page 568
> Tomato and Onion Salad (page 183)
> Falafel (page 42)
> Macerated Dried Fruits and Nuts (page 627)

NORTH AFRICAN MENUS

The cooking of the southern Mediterranean, collectively known as "North Africa," is marked by the emphatic use of fragrant spices like cumin, cinnamon, cloves, and saffron in both savory and sweet dishes. Couscous is ubiquitous, but the best-known dish is probably the tagine, a spiced stew, traditionally cooked and served in a tagine, an earthenware serving dish with a conical lid. The great cookbook writer Paula Wolfert, who lived in Morocco for years, neatly sums up North African–style entertaining: "Arab hospitality is legendary—an embarrassment of riches,

total satisfaction, abundance as an end in itself and a point of pride for the host."

If you want to take a stab at "abundance as an end in itself," you can prepare all the dishes in any of the following three "dinner party" menus to serve 10 to 12 people family style, with fresh bread as an accompaniment. Otherwise, prepare just the salad, one of the main courses, and the couscous. Conclude any of the following menus with either fresh seasonal fruit or Seffa (page 641).

A SUMMERTIME DINNER PARTY

> Roast Pepper Salad with Tomatoes and Preserved Lemon (page 193)
> Brik: Egg in Pastry (page 74), Chicken with Green Olives (page 298), or Fish Tagine (page 239)
> Couscous (page 526)

A WINTERTIME DINNER PARTY

> Beet Salad with Cumin (page 179) and/or Orange and Walnut Salad (page 174)
> Chicken B'stilla (page 322) or Lamb Tagine with Prunes (page 407)
> Couscous with Vegetables (page 527)

A SPRINGTIME DINNER PARTY

> Leek Salad (page 169)
> Choua: Steamed Lamb Shoulder (page 408) or Baked Whole Fish with Dates (page 264)
> Couscous (page 526)

A SIMPLE MEAL FOR A WINTER NIGHT

> Houria: Spicy Carrot Salad (page 191)
> Braised Lamb with Honey and Almonds (page 406)
> Couscous (page 526)

A SPRINGTIME WEEKNIGHT MEAL

> Grilled Eggplant Salad (page 191)
> Chicken and Lentil Tagine (page 284)

CENTRAL AND EASTERN EUROPEAN MENUS

Because of the relatively harsh climate of Central and Eastern Europe, the cooking of its regions traditionally drew on a limited roster of ingredients—beets, horseradish, button mushrooms, kasha and other grains, tame-tasting freshwater fish like carp or catfish—that seem quite one-dimensional to the modern palate. But the ingredients of the New World—especially potatoes and peppers (in the form of paprika)—had an impact, as did time and contact with the more sophisticated cuisines to the west and south. Now the cuisine is diverse and delicious; not expansive and not world beating, but well worth considering, especially in the colder months. The following menus focus on the key flavorings of the regions and could be accompanied successfully by beer or white wine.

A MENU FOR COMPANY

Make the breadsticks and linzertorte as far as two days in advance and the beet salad the day before. All that's left is to cook the lamb or fish and eat. Add the Cabbage Soup with Thyme and Apples (page 106), if you've got the time, appetite, and inclination.

Caraway Breadsticks (page 576)
Breaded Lamb Cutlets (page 364) or Poached Fillets
   in Caraway Sauce (page 249)
Pkhali: Beets with Walnut-Garlic Sauce (page 443)
Linzertorte (page 631)

AN OLD-FASHIONED VEGETARIAN MENU

A menu culled from the legacy of rich vegetarian dishes that resourceful cooks in this part of the world came up with when money or meat was in short supply.

Mushroom Caviar (page 76) with toast
Kapusniak: Sauerkraut Vegetable Stew made with
   vegetable stock (page 114)
Sirniki: Fried Cheesecakes (page 643)

A SUMMER MENU

Though cold windswept plains are what come to mind when we think of this part of the world, summer comes here too. Make some Fruit-Infused Vodka (page 670) to go with the nuts and serve a light red wine with the steak.

Roasted Walnuts (page 28)
Simple Vegetarian Borscht (page 116)
Fleica: Grilled Steak with Garlic with rye bread
   (page 346)
Kolackys (page 648)

A WEEKNIGHT DINNER

Everyday ingredients—cucumbers, chicken, and berries—combine with a little paprika and sour cream for an easy weeknight dinner.

Cucumber Salad, European Style (page 169)
Roast Chicken with Paprika (page 277)
Kasha (page 528) or plain, boiled new potatoes
Simple Fruit Soup (page 624)

FRENCH MENUS

Except among old-fashioned food snobs, France is no longer proclaimed as the sole source of the world's great cooking; though it led the pack for a couple of hundred years, many other cuisines (including American) are now of equal importance to most home cooks.

Which doesn't at all detract from French food: it is, in all of its many forms (few countries have as many distinctive regional cuisines), among the most enjoyable to cook and to eat, with its accent on fairly strong and almost always familiar flavors.

A PARIS BISTRO MENU

Serve the main course with French fries or plain boiled potatoes.

Green Salad with Vinaigrette, Roquefort, and Walnuts
(page 165), Salade Lyonnaise (page 202), or
Steamed Asparagus with Sauce Gribiche
(page 429)
Grilled Steak with Roquefort Sauce (page 347) or
Skate with Brown Butter (page 267)
Crème Brûlée (page 635) or Caramelized Apples
(page 619)

A PROVENÇAL FEAST

Tapenade: Black Olive Paste (page 604)
Eggplant Caviar (page 31)
Pissaladière: Onion Pizza (page 45)
Ratatouille (page 501) with grilled or broiled
sausages
Sautéed Scallops with Garlic (page 211) or Bourride:
Fish Stew with Aïoli (page 137) or Bouillabaisse
(page 138)
Provence-Style Chicken (page 306)
Apricot, Cherry, or Pear Clafouti (page 621)

A NORTHERN MENU

Ham and Cheese Crêpes (page 87)
Cod Poached in Cider (page 247) or Pork Chops with
Prunes and Cream (page 362)
Pears "Poached" with Butter and Cream (page 626)

A SIMPLE SOUTHWESTERN MENU

Green Salad with Oil and Vinegar (page 165)
Crisp-Braised Duck Legs with Aromatic Vegetables
(page 331), Beef Braised with Sweet White Wine
(page 384), or Lamb Shanks with Lentils (page 416)
Walnut Tart (page 632) or Figs Poached in Wine
(page 625)

SPANISH MENUS

Spanish food bears the imprint of so many people—
Greeks, Romans, and Jews, to name a few—who have
either occupied the Iberian Peninsula or fled there for
refuge at some point in history.

None, however, were more influential than the
North Africans, or Moors, who ruled Spain for seven
centuries. Some Moorish culinary legacies, like the
emphatic use of cumin, the cultivation of rice, and
the ubiquity of almonds, strike us today as innately
Spanish. Those Arab-African touches, matched with a
native love of garlic and a very un-Moorish reverence
for pork, are among the characteristics that distinguish Spanish cooking from that of its neighbors.

PAELLA AND SANGRIA

This is a perfect menu for a cool spring or beginning-
of-fall night. Serve the Almendrados with an Oloroso
or Amontillado sherry.

Sangria (page 672)
Salt Cod Salad (page 198)
Paella de Setas y Pollo: Mushroom and Chicken
Paella (page 520)
Almendrados (page 631)

A SIMPLE DINNER

Queso Frito: Fried Cheese (page 85)
Sea Bass or Other Fillets in Saffron Sauce (page 241)
or Cod with Chickpeas and Sherry (page 242)
Sautéed Piquillo Peppers (page 471)
Tarta de Almendras: Almond Cake (page 632)

A TAPAS-STYLE DINNER

Augment the dishes you cook for a tapas party with as
many store-bought items as you can, like good bread
with olive oil for dunking, olives (Spanish if they have
them, marinated as on page 17 if it's not too much
trouble), prosciutto or jamón Serrano, a wedge of
manchego, and sliced chorizo, and have a ready-made
dessert like flan in the fridge to pull out at the end of
the night. For a party of four to six, pick two or more
dishes from each of the following lists, grouped by
how much (or really, how little) time it takes to throw
them together.

ITALIAN MENUS

At this point, at least in the United States, Italian food is the most popular "foreign" food—it's the most widely eaten in restaurants and the most often cooked at home. (Why the quotes around *foreign*? Because in a real way, "American" cooking is mostly Italian at this point. But that's another story.)

This is with good reason: the flavors are simple and straightforward, as is the preparation. When you simply grill, or poach something, adding a few basic flavors like lemon, garlic, or olive oil, that's Italian. And it needn't get much more complicated than that.

Bread of some form or another (simple pizza is considered bread) is served at almost every meal in much of Italy. In addition, because food is often served at room temperature (contorni, or vegetable dishes, may accompany the main course or be served after it but are often room temperature), it is a natural for entertaining.

MEXICAN MENUS

Packaged salsa outsells ketchup. Make-your-own taco nights are a tradition in the homes of many of our country's non-Mexicans. Burritos, fajitas, and tacos are fast-food staples. But there are huge differences between Mexican-American and Mexican food.

In recent years we've seen more and more authentic regional Mexican cuisine in the States; not surprisingly, it appears most in the Southwest, but even in the Northeast you can find real Mexican food without much difficulty. The cuisine is essentially Native American, with very strong Spanish influences—like the culture in general. In many ways, it's remained unchanged for centuries: corn is elementary in many dishes, sweet or spicy chiles are an essential seasoning, cilantro and onions are ubiquitous.

Accompany the following menus with beer (with or without lime wedges), red wine, margaritas (page 671), or nonalcoholic Mexican drinks like horchata (page 663) or the avocado shake on page 661. If you're feeling particularly ambitious, serve Flan de Naranja (page 634) or Churros (page 655) for dessert. Otherwise, serve ice cream or fresh fruit, like papaya, banana, or mango, dressed with a sprinkling of sugar and a squeeze of lime.

A SIMPLE MEAL FOR COOL WEATHER
Caldo Cantina: Chicken-Rice Soup (page 138)
Pork and Posole with Chipotles (page 155)
Refried Beans (page 438)

A MORE ELABORATE MEAL
Queso Fundido: Melted Cheese (page 84) with flour or corn tortillas
Stewed Lamb Shanks with Mushrooms and Pasilla Chile Sauce (page 414) or Almendrado de Pollo: Chicken in Almond Mole (page 301)
Arroz a la Mexicana: Mexican Rice (page 517)

A WARM-WEATHER HOME-STYLE MEAL
Cucumber, Jicama, and Fruit Salad (page 178) or Roasted Corn and Black Bean Salad (page 195)
Lime-Cooked Fish with Crisp Garlic (page 237) with tortillas or Arroz a la Mexicana: Mexican Rice (page 517)

AN INFORMAL MEAL
Tortilla chips with Salsa Roja: Cooked Red Salsa (page 610) and/or Papaya and Red Onion Salsa (page 613)
Sopa de Aguacate: Avocado Soup (page 118)
Fish Tacos (page 238) or Empanadas (page 48)

A SUMMERTIME DINNER PARTY
Blistered Tomato Salsa (page 610) with tortilla chips
Ceviche: Marinated Scallops (page 21)
Rice with Vegetables (page 517) or Black Beans with Garlic and Cumin (page 438) with Basic Long-Grain Rice (page 506)
Pollo con Salsa Verde: Chicken in Green Sauce (page 302), Cochinita Pibil: Yucatecan Pit-Roasted Pork (page 351), or Garlic Shrimp, Yucatecan Style (page 219)

Sources

Increasingly, you can buy everything you need for international cooking at a supermarket (and some of the best supermarkets in this country are in areas you'd least expect to find them, like the so-called Rust Belt and the Southwest). Furthermore, virtually every metropolitan area with a six-figure population has Asian and Mexican markets. But if you find yourself unable to find something (or just prefer to shop online), there are mail-order options galore. These are some of the best.

However—and this is important—Internet offerings change all the time. And though sometimes you can find better things cheaper online, sometimes worse things are more expensive. Furthermore, Internet stores push luxury items, and—to me—foie gras and caviar are not exactly essential ingredients.

I prefer to shop in stores (the exception: I usually buy spices at Penzey's online; but I have years of experience with that company and trust it). When forced to shop online, I usually Google what I want, rather than go to any specific site. When you do this, you'll quickly find that you can buy dried porcini, for example, for $50 a pound including shipping or $100 a pound including shipping. Quick comparisons like these can save you a ton of money.

The sources that follow are the ones with which I've had experience; there are dozens more. But, as I said, this is a constantly changing world. And, ultimately, I like to see my food before I buy it.

penzeys.com is the only site I go to regularly. It is the source (and, no, I don't take money from this company) for dried herbs and spices. It has esoteric items, like horseradish powder, but—more important—its spices and herbs are fresh, and you can buy them in small or large quantities. Either way, the prices are extremely competitive.

amazon.com/gourmet is up and coming. Many of the offerings come from other sources, like Dean & Deluca, Niman Ranch, and ethnicgrocer.com, but amazon is the clearinghouse. Especially notable is the cheese selection, and you can also buy various dried mushrooms, beans and chiles, herbs and spices, and luxury items like foie gras, truffles, and caviar; there are anchovies, smoked salmon and other preserved seafood, chorizo and other sausage, and prosciutto and Serrano hams. The variety is incredible.

ethnicgrocer.com is a good general source. Look for dried chiles as well as piquillo peppers; dried mushrooms in abundance; a good variety of Asian ingredients, like seaweed, mirin, panko, Shaoxing wine, dried shrimp, palm sugar, rice noodles, and more;

and Indian staples, like asafetida powder and garam masala.

igourmet.com has a good list: cheese, pancetta, salami, prosciutto, sardines, specialty meats, chiles, dried beans, and vinegars.

importfood.com stocks Asian ingredients like black vinegar, sesame seeds, hoisin sauce, oyster sauce, star anise, curry paste, dried shrimp, fish sauce, galangal, lemongrass, lime leaves, palm sugar, rice noodles, tamarind paste, and Thai basil seeds. Good, unusual cookware, too (and a great place to buy a mortar and pestle).

quickspice.com is another good source of Asian ingredients like miso paste, mirin, bonito shavings ($3.49 for $4/5$ ounce), panko bread crumbs, sesame seeds, hoisin sauce, curry paste, fish sauce, and tamarind paste ($2.35 for 16 ounces).

chefshop.com has a broad selection. It's a good place to look for olive oils, pastas, rice, beans, and dried mushrooms; bonito flakes, fermented black beans, star anise, and palm sugar; and dried chiles, cornichons, and tahini.

tienda.com is probably the best online source for Spanish ingredients, worth a look.

Recipe Guide

	MAKE AHEAD	ROOM TEMP/ COLD	30 MIN OR LESS	PAGE
APPETIZERS AND SNACKS				
Almonds, Spicy Fried	■	■	■	28
Anchovies, Crisp Dried	■	■	■	52
Anchovies, Fresh Marinated (Boquerones)	■	■		24
Anchovies, Sweet Dried	■	■	■	52
Artichoke Hearts, Fried (Carciofi Fritti)			■	71
Bean Dip, Red or Black	■	■	■	29
Bean Dip, White	■	■	■	19
Beef "Jerky," Grilled	■	■		40
Beef Shank, Cold Cut	■	■		39
Beef, Marinated (Carne Cruda)		■	■	25
Beet Caviar	■	■		32
Brandade de Morue	■			56
Celery, Spicy Cold	■	■		17
Cheese and Chile Quesadillas			■	103
Cheese Dip, Herbed	■	■		20
Cheese Mantecaos	■	■	■	35
Cheese, Fried (Queso Frito)			■	85
Cheese, Melted (Queso Fundido)			■	84
Chickpea Pancake, Ligurian (Farinata Genovese)	■			42
Chickpeas, Crunchy (Channa)	■	■	■	28
Chorizo and Bread (Migas)			■	99
Chorizo in Red Wine	■		■	70
Clam Cakes			■	83
Clams with Garlic, Hardshell			■	99
Crostini	■	■	■	41
Crostini with Beans and Greens	■	■	■	41
Egg Custard, Savory (Chawan Mushi)	■	■		53
Egg in Pastry (Brik)			■	74
Eggplant Caviar	■	■		31
Eggplant Fritters			■	88
Eggplants, Stuffed (Imam Bayildi)	■	■		30
Eggs, Pocket (Hou Bao Daan)			■	73
Eggs, Shrimp Deviled	■	■	■	34
Eggs, Tea	■	■		34
Empanadas	■	■		48
Falafel	■	■		42
Fish "Sandwiches," Panfried	■	■		57
Fish or Shrimp Cakes (Tod Mun)			■	83
Fish Roe Puree (Taramasalata)	■	■		24
Gefilte Fish	■	■		36
Gougères	■	■	■	69
Green Chiles, Fried			■	77
Green Leaf Wraps (Miang Gung)	■	■	■	33

	MAKE AHEAD	ROOM TEMP/ COLD	30 MIN OR LESS	PAGE
Guacamole	■	■	■	22
Ham and Cheese Puffs			■	86
Herring, Pickled	■	■		37
Hummus	■	■	■	19
Liver Pâté, Calf or Chicken (Pashtet)	■	■		39
Lotus Root Fries (Nadroo Korma)			■	71
Lumpia Rolls			■	68
Meat and Tofu Pancakes (Gogi-Jun)	■	■		51
Meat Samosas		■		65
Meatballs (Polpette)	■	■	■	53
Meatballs, Almond	■	■	■	54
Meatballs, Raw (Cig Kofte)	■	■		26
Mock Ceviche	■	■	■	35
Mushroom Caviar	■		■	76
Mushrooms and Eggs			■	74
Mushrooms with Herbs and Butter	■		■	55
Mushrooms with Sherry	■		■	54
Mushrooms, Grilled, and Bacon			■	75
Octopus "Confit"	■	■		51
Octopus and Potatoes, Warm	■			50
Octopus, Grilled	■	■		49
Olives, Marinated	■	■		17
Peanuts, Fried	■	■	■	27
Pepper Spread with Walnuts and Garlic, Roast	■	■		32
Peppers, Sautéed, with Miso			■	78
Piquillo Peppers and Anchovies, Canapés with	■	■	■	48
Piquillo Peppers Stuffed with Fish	■		■	46
Piquillo Peppers with Shiitakes and Spinach	■	■	■	48
"Pizza," Alsatian (Tarte Flambé)	■			44
Pizza, Onion (Pissaladière)	■	■		45

	MAKE AHEAD	ROOM TEMP/ COLD	30 MIN OR LESS	PAGE
Plantain Chips (Platanitos)		■	■	22
Pork Buns, Steamed Barbecued (Char Siu Bao)	■			79
Pork, Piquillo, and Cheese Canapés	■	■	■	47
Pork-Filled Tortillas, Fried (Taquitos)	■			69
Portobello Spread	■	■		18
Rice Balls, Fried (Supplì)	■	■	■	43
Salmon, Salt- and Sugar-Cured (Gravlax)	■	■		23
Sardines or Smelts, Broiled ("Grilled")			■	96
Satay, Fried			■	100
Scallops, Marinated (Ceviche)	■	■	■	21
Shrimp with Garlic			■	98
Shrimp, Crisp-Fried (Rebozados)			■	92
Spinach Pancakes			■	82
Spinach, Sautéed, with Sesame	■	■	■	33
Spring Rolls, Rice Paper (Goi Cuon)	■	■		38
Squid, Grilled Baby			■	97
Walnuts, Roasted	■	■	■	28
Warm Olive Oil Bath (Bagna Cauda)	■		■	56
Wontons, Fried			■	63
Yogurt Cheese	■	■		20
Zucchini Custard (Flan de Courgettes)	■	■		44

SOUPS

	MAKE AHEAD	ROOM TEMP/ COLD	30 MIN OR LESS	PAGE
Almond Soup	■	■		118
Avocado Soup (Sopa de Aguacate)	■		■	118
Beef Soup, West Lake			■	145
Borscht with Meat	■			148
Borscht, Simple Vegetarian	■	■		116
Buckwheat Noodle Soup, Cold (Naengmyon)			■	149

	MAKE AHEAD	ROOM TEMP/ COLD	30 MIN OR LESS	PAGE
Caldo Gallego	■			144
Carrot Soup, Creamy (Potage Crécy)	■	■		111
Carrot, Spinach, and Rice Stew	■			107
Chicken and Coconut Soup (Dom Yam Gai)	■			142
Chicken and Egg Soup			■	142
Chicken and Watercress Soup			■	140
Chicken Soup with Chipotle Paste	■		■	139
Chicken-Rice Soup (Caldo Cantina)	■			138
Chickpea and Pasta Soup	■		■	129
Chickpeas in Their Own Broth, with Fried Bread Crumbs			■	128
Cilantro and Garlic Soup			■	121
Clam Soup			■	136
Coconut Milk Soup	■			121
Congee, or Rice Porridge (Jook)	■			123
Consommé	■		■	161
Corn Soup, Cream-Style			■	141
Crab Soup, Korean Style			■	135
Cucumber Seaweed Soup	■	■	■	120
Dumpling Soup (Mandoo Kuk)			■	154
Egg Flower Soup			■	115
Fish Soup, West Lake			■	134
Gazpacho, Basic Red	■	■	■	117
Gazpacho, Ignacio Blanco's Roasted Vegetable	■	■		117
Green Bean Soup with Mint	■	■		120
Lemon Soup			■	114
Lentil Soup with Sorrel (Potage de Lentilles à l'Oseille)	■			108
Mango Soup, Savory Cold (Sopa Fria de Mango)	■	■		119
Miso Soup with Tofu			■	122
Mushroom-Barley Soup	■			112
Mussel Soup			■	134
Onion Soup	■			109

	MAKE AHEAD	ROOM TEMP/ COLD	30 MIN OR LESS	PAGE
Oxtail Soup (Gori Gom Tang)	■			151
Passatelli			■	126
Peanut Soup			■	132
Plantain Soup	■			133
Ramadan Soup (Harira)	■			153
Rice Soup with Chicken or Tofu and Egg (Domburi)			■	124
Sauerkraut Soup (Shchi)	■			147
Spinach and Chickpea Soup	■			127
Squash and Chickpea Soup, Mediterranean	■			130
Tomato-Potato Soup, Creamy (Potage Crème de Tomates et de Pommes de Terre)	■			110
Vegetable Soup with Basil (Soupe au Pistou)	■			111
Vegetable Soup, Spicy (Mulligatawny)	■			115

SALADS

	MAKE AHEAD	ROOM TEMP/ COLD	30 MIN OR LESS	PAGE
Arborio Rice Salad		■	■	188
Artichoke Hearts and Parmesan, Salad of		■	■	167
Asparagus Salad with Soy-Mustard Dressing	■	■	■	190
Bean and Tuna Salad	■	■	■	189
Bean Sprout Salad (Kong Namul)	■	■	■	182
Beef Salad with Mint		■		203
Beef, Grilled, Salad (Neua Nam Tok)			■	202
Beet Salad with Cumin	■	■		179
Beet Salad with Horseradish	■	■		178
Beets, Pickled	■	■		179
Bitter Greens with Sour Cream Dressing		■	■	176
Bulgur and Tomato Salad with Nuts (Batrik)	■	■		186
Cabbage and Beet Salad	■	■	■	168
Caesar Salad		■	■	167
Carrot Salad, Spicy (Houria)	■	■	■	191

	MAKE AHEAD	ROOM TEMP/ COLD	30 MIN OR LESS	PAGE
Chicken and Cucumber Salad	■	■	■	182
Chicken Salad with Tarator	■	■	■	201
Chicken Salad with Vietnamese Seasonings		■	■	201
Chicken, Minced, "Salad" (Laarb)	■	■		199
Chickpea Salad	■	■		179
Chickpea Salad with Ginger	■	■	■	180
Corn, Roasted, and Black Bean Salad	■	■	■	195
Cucumber Salad, European Style	■	■	■	169
Cucumber, Jicama, and Fruit Salad	■	■		178
Eggplant and Yogurt Salad	■	■		192
Eggplant Salad with Mustard-Miso Dressing	■	■	■	185
Eggplant Salad with Sesame Dressing, Cold	■	■		186
Eggplant Salad, Grilled	■	■		191
Fennel and Cucumber Salad		■	■	181
Fennel and Orange Salad		■	■	173
Fish Salad with Horseradish Dressing	■	■	■	197
Garlic Bread Salad with Tomatoes		■	■	181
Ginger Cucumber Salad	■	■		177
Green Beans with Sesame-Miso Dressing	■	■	■	190
Green Mango Salad with Meat		■	■	203
Green Papaya Salad (Som Tum)		■	■	174
Green Papaya Salad with Shrimp		■	■	198
Green Salad with Oil and Vinegar		■	■	165
Green Salad with Vinaigrette, Roquefort, and Walnuts		■	■	165
Greens, Cold Lemony	■	■	■	180
Leek Salad	■	■	■	169
Mushrooms, Marinated	■	■		176
Orange and Walnut Salad		■	■	174
Potato Salad with Mustard Vinaigrette	■	■		194
Pressed Tofu Salad	■	■		185
Radish Salad	■	■	■	172
Raita	■	■	■	175
Roast Pepper Salad with Tomatoes and Preserved Lemon	■	■		193
Roasted Pepper, Anchovy, and Caper Salad	■	■		194
Salade Niçoise	■	■	■	196
Salade Olivier	■	■		199
Salade Lyonnaise		■	■	202
Salt Cod Salad		■		198
Sauerkraut Salad	■	■	■	168
Seafood Salad, Mediterranean-Style	■	■		197
Seaweed Salad with Cucumber and Chicken or Shrimp		■	■	200
Spinach and Dried Shrimp Salad	■	■	■	185
Spinach with Sesame, Cold	■	■	■	184
Tabbouleh	■	■		187
Tofu Salad with Peanut Sauce			■	195
Tomato and Onion Salad	■	■	■	183
Tomato and Tapenade Salad		■	■	184
Tomato Salad with Ginger		■	■	173
Tomato Salad, Fresh		■	■	172
Vegetable Salad with Horseradish, Mixed		■	■	188

FISH

	MAKE AHEAD	ROOM TEMP/ COLD	30 MIN OR LESS	PAGE
Catfish or Other Fillets with Rice			■	249
Catfish, Roast, or Other Fillets with Sauerkraut and Bacon			■	247
Clams in Sherry Sauce			■	207
Clams with Black Bean Sauce, Stir-Fried			■	206

	MAKE AHEAD	ROOM TEMP/COLD	30 MIN OR LESS	PAGE
Shrimp, Chipotle			■	219
Shrimp, Drunken			■	212
Shrimp, Garlic, Yucatecan Style			■	219
Shrimp, Minced, in Lettuce Wrappers			■	213
Shrimp, Steamed, with Lemongrass Coconut Sauce	■	■		216
Skate with Brown Butter			■	267
Squid in Red Wine Sauce	■			222
Squid with Basil and Garlic, Stir-Fried			■	221
Swordfish Rémoulade, Grilled	■	■	■	256
Swordfish, Pan-Seared, with Tomatoes, Olives, and Capers			■	257
Swordfish, Seared, with Lemongrass, Tamarind, and Fried Garlic			■	253
Tuna with Miso-Chile Sauce			■	254
Tuna with Onions and Lemon, Roast	■	■	■	258

POULTRY

	MAKE AHEAD	ROOM TEMP/COLD	30 MIN OR LESS	PAGE
Chicken Adobo	■			282
Chicken and Lentil Tagine	■			284
Chicken and Sausage in Vinegar			■	316
Chicken Biryani	■	■		292
Chicken Breasts with Sage			■	308
Chicken Escabeche	■	■		294
Chicken Teriyaki	■	■	■	317
Chicken Thighs, Skewered, with Peanut Sauce			■	321
Chicken Under a Brick (Pollo al Mattone)	■	■		276
Chicken with Citrus Sauce			■	316
Chicken with Rice (Arroz con Pollo)	■			293
Chicken with Walnut Sauce	■	■		278
Chicken, Braised Chestnut	■			279

	MAKE AHEAD	ROOM TEMP/COLD	30 MIN OR LESS	PAGE
Chicken, Drunken	■	■		273
Chicken, Fried, Caribbean Style	■	■		309
Chicken, Fried, Creole		■		309
Chicken, Fried, Parsi Style	■	■		310
Chicken, Ginger			■	313
Chicken, Grilled, in Chipotle Sauce	■	■		289
Chicken, Grilled, Spicy	■	■		288
Chicken, Grilled, with Sesame	■	■		290
Chicken, Kung Pao			■	312
Chicken, Peanut			■	313
Chicken, Soy-Poached	■	■		274
Chicken, Stir-Fried, with Creamed Corn			■	312
Chicken, Stir-Fried, with Walnuts			■	311
Chicken, Two-Way	■	■		289
Chicken, White Cut	■	■		273
Duck Confit	■			330
Duck Legs, Crisp-Braised, with Aromatic Vegetables	■			331
Duck or Chicken, Tea-Smoked	■	■		327
Duck, Pan-Roasted, with Olives	■			331
Duck, Roast	■	■		325
Eggs, Hard-Cooked	■	■	■	338
Eggs, Poached	■		■	337
Eggs, Spicy Scrambled (Akoori)			■	338
Goose, Braised, with White Wine and Coffee	■			333
Omelette aux Fines Herbes			■	343
Rabbit or Chicken Stew (Stifado)	■			336
Tortilla		■		341

MEAT

	MAKE AHEAD	ROOM TEMP/COLD	30 MIN OR LESS	PAGE
Beef and Onions Stewed in Beer (Carbonnade)	■			385
Beef Braised with Sweet White Wine	■			384

	MAKE AHEAD	ROOM TEMP/ COLD	30 MIN OR LESS	PAGE
Beef Daube	■			384
Beef Stew with Bacon, Red Wine, and Mushrooms (Boeuf Bourguignon)	■			383
Beef Stew with Bean Paste	■			376
Beef Stew with Cinnamon	■			382
Beef Stew with Dried Mushrooms	■			380
Beef Stew with Prunes	■			378
Beef Stew with Winter Squash	■			377
Beef Stew, Sour, with Horseradish	■			379
Beef Stroganoff, Real			■	381
Beef Tenderloin in Caramelized Sugar			■	359
Beef Tenderloin, Poached			■	387
Beef, Stir-Fried Curry			■	369
Beef, Stir-Fried Spicy Shredded			■	368
Bigos	■			403
Bistecca alla Fiorentina			■	346
Cholent	■			380
Escabeche, Grilled, with Pork	■	■		350
Flank Steak, Stuffed (Matambre)	■			372
Ham and Cheese Sandwich, Grilled (Sandwich Cubano)			■	363
"Hamburgers," Lemongrass			■	350
Kofte with Bulgur		■		426
Kofte, Panfried, with Potatoes	■	■		425
Lamb "Burgers" (Grilled Meat Kofte)			■	355
Lamb Chops with Sherry	■			413
Lamb Chops, Grilled, with Mint Chutney			■	352
Lamb Shanks Cooked in Yogurt	■			414
Lamb Shanks with Lentils	■			416
Lamb Shanks with Potatoes	■			415
Lamb Shanks, Stewed, with Mushrooms and Pasilla Chile Sauce	■			414
Lamb Skewers, Grilled, with Bay Leaves			■	357
Lamb Stew with Mushrooms	■			410
Lamb Tagine with Prunes	■			407
Lamb, Braised, with Egg-Lemon Sauce	■			409
Lamb, Braised, with Honey and Almonds	■			406
Liver with Garlic, Sage, and White Wine			■	367
Liver, Fried, with Egg			■	367
Meat Hash (Pytt i Panna)			■	421
Osso Buco	■			419
Oxtail with Capers	■			389
Oxtail, Braised (Rabo de Toro)	■			389
Plantain and Meat Casserole	■	■		420
Pork and Beans Asturian Style (Fabada)	■			401
Pork and Lamb, Baeckoffe of	■			399
Pork and Shrimp, Minced, in Coconut Milk			■	423
Pork and Tofu Stew, Spicy	■			398
Pork Chops, "Deviled"			■	362
Pork Cutlets, Breaded (Tonkatsu)			■	361
Pork Vindaloo	■			399
Pork with Red Wine and Coriander	■			395
Pork, Barbecued	■			373
Pork, Braised, with Coconut Milk	■			397
Pork, Ground, Simmered Tofu with (Ma Po Tofu)			■	423
Pork, Jerked	■			352
Pork, Roast (Lechon Asado)	■	■		375
Pork, Shredded	■			396
Pork, Stir-Fried, in Garlic Sauce			■	370

	MAKE AHEAD	ROOM TEMP/ COLD	30 MIN OR LESS	PAGE
Pork, Yucatan Pit-Roasted (Cochinita Pibil)	■	■		351
Ribs, Braised, with Spicy Adobo	■			394
Sausage and Beans	■		■	401
Sausage and Orange with Bay Leaves			■	374
Sausage Patties, Fresh	■		■	421
Short Ribs, Braised (Kalbi Jim)	■			388
Skirt Steak, Grilled, with Sauce au Chien		■	■	348
Smoked Meats, Sauerkraut with (A Grand Choucroute)	■			404
Spareribs, 12345	■			391
Spareribs, Braised, with Cabbage, Roman Style	■			393
Spareribs, Braised, with Cabbage, Root Vegetables, and Caraway	■			392
Steak au Poivre			■	360
Steak Teriyaki			■	360
Steak, Grilled, with Roquefort Sauce			■	347
Tenderloin with Miso			■	348
Veal Paprikas			■	366
Veal Rolled with Mushrooms (Involtini di Vitello)				365
Veal Shanks with Cherries	■			418
Veal Stew with Dill and Sour Cream	■			416

VEGETABLES

	MAKE AHEAD	ROOM TEMP/ COLD	30 MIN OR LESS	PAGE
Artichokes with White Wine and Lemon	■	■		428
Asparagus with Eggs and Parmesan			■	430
Asparagus, Steamed, with Sauce Gribiche		■	■	429
Baby Artichokes, Stewed, with Fava Beans and Peas	■	■		428
Beans, Black, with Garlic and Cumin	■			438
Beans, Black, with Soy	■	■		432
Beans, Spicy Red (Rajma)	■			437

	MAKE AHEAD	ROOM TEMP/ COLD	30 MIN OR LESS	PAGE
Beans, Spicy, Goan Style (Feijoada)	■			436
Beans, White, Mashed	■	■		440
Beans, White, with Chicken Stock and Tomatoes, Aromatic	■			442
Beans, White, with Garlic	■	■		441
Beets with Walnut-Garlic Sauce (Pkhali)	■	■	■	443
Beets, Roasted	■	■		442
Black-Eyed Peas with Coconut Milk	■			434
Broccoli or Cauliflower with Garlic and Lemon, Two Ways	■	■	■	452
Cabbage Pie	■	■		449
Cabbage, Pickled (Oshinko)	■	■		444
Cabbage, Stuffed	■			445
Carrots, Curried			■	451
Carrots, Glazed			■	450
Cauliflower, Curried	■	■	■	451
Cauliflower, Curried Sautéed (Gobi Taktakin)	■	■	■	452
Chickpea Dumplings in Yogurt Sauce	■			435
Chickpeas or Other Legumes, Cooked	■	■		431
Collards, Kale, or Other Dark Greens Cooked in Yogurt	■	■	■	463
Corn, Pan-Grilled, with Chiles			■	454
Cucumber or Other Vegetables, Lightly Pickled	■	■	■	455
Dal with Coconut	■			434
Edamame			■	433
Eggplant Pie (Torta di Melanzane)	■	■		459
Eggplant with Sweet Miso	■	■		457
Eggplant, Sautéed	■	■		456
Endives, Braised	■			462
Escarole with Olive Oil, Anchovies, and Pepper	■	■	■	462
Grape Leaves, Stuffed	■	■		446

	MAKE AHEAD	ROOM TEMP/ COLD	30 MIN OR LESS	PAGE
Green Beans with Yogurt and Dill	■	■		461
Green Beans, Pears, and Ham			■	460
Hijiki with Shiitakes and Beans			■	485
Kale or Collards, Flash-Cooked, with Lemon Juice	■	■	■	464
Kimchi	■	■		444
Leek Pie (Torta di Porri)	■	■		466
Leeks in Red Wine	■	■		466
Leeks Vinaigrette	■	■	■	464
Leeks, Braised, with Olive Oil and Rice	■	■		465
Lentils or Other Legumes, Slow-Cooked (Dal)	■			433
Lentils with Bulgur	■	■		440
Mushrooms Poached in Sour Cream			■	467
Mustard Greens, Chinese (Gai Lan) with Oyster Sauce			■	463
Nori Snacks			■	485
Olives, Braised, with Tomatoes	■	■		468
Onions, Sweet and Sour	■	■		469
Peperonata	■	■		471
Piquillo Peppers, Sautéed	■	■	■	471
Plantains in Coconut Milk (Ndizi wa Nazi)			■	472
Plantains, Sautéed Ripe (Platanos Maduros)			■	472
Potato "Nik," Helen Art's	■	■		479
Potato and Horseradish Gratin	■			482
Potato and Tomato Pie (Torta di Patate e Pomodori)	■	■		494
Potato Croquettes with Meat	■			475
Potato Dumplings	■		■	479
Potatoes, Caramelized			■	482
Potatoes, Home-Fried, with Onion and Amchoor	■	■		477
Potatoes, Mashed, with Anchovies			■	480
Potatoes, Mashed, with Mushrooms and Onions	■			480
Potatoes, Panfried Spicy, with Eggplant	■	■		476
Potatoes, Peasant-Style			■	477
Potatoes, Stir-Fried, with Chiles			■	473
Radicchio with Bacon	■	■		461
Radicchio, Grilled	■	■	■	462
Red Peppers, Roasted	■	■		470
Root Vegetables, Quick-Braised, with Hoisin			■	499
Snow Peas with Ginger			■	470
Spinach Croquettes	■	■	■	487
Spinach Gratin	■	■		489
Spinach Pie, Cheese and (Spanakopita)	■	■		488
Spinach with Coconut Milk			■	487
Spinach with Hing (Haaq)			■	487
Spinach with Raisins and Pine Nuts	■	■	■	489
Spinach, Creamed			■	490
Tofu with Black Beans			■	492
Tomatoes or Peppers, Stuffed Roasted	■	■		492
Tomatoes Provençal	■	■	■	494
Tomatoes, Faster Roasted	■	■		493
Turnips, Glazed			■	496
Vegetables, Stir-Fried, with Nam Pla			■	499
Watercress, Stir-Fried, with Bean Sauce			■	496
Yam in Mirin			■	498
Zucchini with Dill and Mint	■	■		498

GRAINS

	MAKE AHEAD	ROOM TEMP/ COLD	30 MIN OR LESS	PAGE
Barley with Dried Mushrooms			■	524
Bread, French or Italian	■	■		570
Bread, Olive Oil, with or without Olives	■	■		567

	MAKE AHEAD	ROOM TEMP/ COLD	30 MIN OR LESS	PAGE
Bread, Rich	■	■		577
Breadsticks, Caraway	■	■		576
Bruschetta			■	572
Buns, Sweet Almond (Semla)	■	■		578
Buns, Sweet Breakfast	■	■		579
Couscous			■	526
Farro Salad	■	■		527
Flatbreads, Whole Wheat, Stuffed with Lamb, Chiles, and Cilantro (Keema Ke Paratha)	■	■		561
Flatbreads, Whole Wheat, Stuffed with Potatoes (Aloo Paratha)	■	■		560
Grissini	■	■		575
Kasha			■	528
Kimchi-Rice "Stew"			■	512
Linguine with Garlic and Oil			■	547
Lo Mein, Beef			■	535
Noodles, Cold, with Dipping Sauce (Hiyashi Somen)		■	■	534
Noodles, Cold, with Sesame Sauce	■	■	■	532
Noodles, Curried Rice, with Pork or Chicken and Shrimp ("Singapore" Noodles)			■	538
Noodles, Egg, with Spring Onions			■	536
Noodles, Glass, with Vegetables and Meat (Chop Chae)	■	■		539
Noodles, Spicy Cold	■	■	■	533
Pad Thai			■	536
Paella, The Original			■	519
Pasta alla Gricia			■	546
Pasta Frittata		■		558
Pasta with Anchovies and Walnuts			■	552
Pasta with Broccoli Raab			■	552
Pasta with Cabbage			■	551
Pasta with Fennel			■	551
Pasta with Ham, Peas, and Cream			■	556
Pasta with Mint and Parmesan			■	549
Pasta with Onion Sauce (Spaghetti con Cippole)			■	550
Pasta with Sausage and Cream			■	557
Pasta with Tomato and Olive Puree				548
Pasta with Tuna Sauce			■	555
Pasta with Walnuts (Pansotti)			■	550
Pasta with Whole Garlic Cloves (Maccheroni alla San Giovanniello)			■	556
Penne all'Arrabbiata			■	548
Penne with Pumpkin or Squash			■	553
Pita	■	■		568
Pita, Cheese-Filled	■	■	■	569
Pizza Bianca	■	■		573
"Pizza," Turkish Meat (Lahmacun)	■	■		566
Ravioli, Spinach-Ricotta	■			544
Ravioli, Vegetarian	■			542
Rice Balls (Onigiri)	■	■	■	511
Rice with Cheese (Ris in Cagnon)			■	523
Rice with Onions, Garlic, and Herbs			■	518
Rice with Umeboshi			■	507
Rice with Vegetables			■	517
Rice, Basic Long-Grain			■	506
Rice, Basic Short-Grain				507
Rice, Basmati, with Shiso			■	510
Rice, Coconut			■	516
Rice, Fragrant Coconut Milk (Nasi Lemak)			■	515
Rice, Fried			■	506
Rice, Yellow			■	518
Rice, Yellow, with Chorizo			■	519
Rolls, Sweet, with Saffron (Saffransbrod)	■	■		578

	MAKE AHEAD	ROOM TEMP/ COLD	30 MIN OR LESS	PAGE
Sambal Ikan Billis		■	■	515
Soba Noodles, Cold, with Dipping Sauce	■	■	■	533
Spaetzle	■	■		540
Tamales		■		531
Uttapam			■	565

SAUCES AND CONDIMENTS

	MAKE AHEAD	ROOM TEMP/ COLD	30 MIN OR LESS	PAGE
Adobo	■	■	■	616
Anchovy Sauce	■	■	■	605
Annatto Seasoning Paste (Recado Rojo)	■	■		609
Béarnaise Sauce			■	602
Black Olive Paste (Tapenade)	■	■		604
Chaat Masala	■	■	■	594
Chervil-Butter Sauce for Fish			■	601
Chile Oil with Szechwan Peppercorns	■	■	■	583
Chile Paste (Harissa)	■	■	■	598
Chile Sauce, Toasted	■	■	■	585
Chile-Lime Sauce (Sambal Oelek)	■	■	■	590
Chili Powder	■	■	■	609
Chimichurri	■	■	■	617
Chutney, Dry Peanut	■	■	■	595
Chutney, Mint, with Tomato	■	■	■	595
Chutney, Mint, with Yogurt	■	■	■	595
Coconut Milk	■	■	■	584
Curry Powder, Fragrant	■	■	■	593
Curry Powder, Hot	■	■	■	592
Curry Powder, Milder	■	■	■	593
Dipping Sauce with Ginger (Nuoc Cham)	■	■	■	590
Dipping Sauce, Ginger-Scallion	■	■	■	583
Dipping Sauce, Soy	■	■	■	583
Dipping Sauce, Sweet Nam Pla	■	■	■	586
Dried Fruit and Nut Sauce with Cilantro	■	■	■	599

	MAKE AHEAD	ROOM TEMP/ COLD	30 MIN OR LESS	PAGE
Egg-Lemon Sauce (Avgolemono)			■	596
Garam Masala	■	■	■	594
Garlic Sauce, Creole (Mojo Criollo)	■	■	■	617
Garlic Soy Sauce, Sweet	■	■	■	590
Ginger, Pickled (Gari)	■	■		591
Ginger-Chile Sauce	■	■	■	584
Green Sauce (Salsa Verde)	■		■	614
Hoisin Chili Sauce	■	■	■	584
Horseradish Sauce, Creamy	■	■		608
Horseradish Sauce, Sharp	■	■	■	607
Lemons, Preserved	■	■		598
Mayonnaise	■	■	■	602
"Mayonnaise," Avocado	■	■	■	616
Mayonnaise, Spicy (Sauce Rémoulade)	■	■	■	603
Mustard Dill Sauce	■	■		608
Nam Prik	■	■	■	586
Onion Relish, Pickled (Cebollas Curtidas)	■	■		615
Parsley Puree	■	■	■	605
Parsley Sauce	■	■	■	604
Parsley-Onion Condiment	■			596
Peanut Sauce	■	■		586
Ponzu	■	■		591
Pumpkin Seed Sauce (Pipián)	■	■	■	612
Rice, Ground and Toasted (Khao Koor)	■	■	■	587
Rouille	■	■	■	603
Salsa Fresca	■	■	■	610
Salsa Verde with Tomatillos	■	■	■	614
Salsa, Blistered Tomato	■	■	■	610
Salsa, Cilantro	■	■	■	616
Salsa, Cooked Red (Salsa Roja)	■	■		610
Salsa, Habanero-Garlic	■		■	611
Salsa, Mayan Citrus (Xec)			■	615
Salsa, Papaya and Red Onion	■	■		613
Salsa, Pasilla	■	■	■	612

	MAKE AHEAD	ROOM TEMP/ COLD	30 MIN OR LESS	PAGE
Salsa, Roasted Onion	■	■		614
Salsa, Tomato-Chipotle	■	■	■	611
Sesame Sauce	■	■	■	592
Sesame Seeds, Toasted	■	■	■	596
Sesame-Chile Paste	■	■	■	591
Spice Rub, Tunisian (Tabil)	■	■	■	597
Szechwan Salt-and-Pepper	■	■	■	583
Tahini Sauce	■	■	■	597
Tamarind Paste	■	■	■	585
Tarator or Skordalia	■	■	■	600
Tomato Sauce with Garlic and Orange	■		■	607
Tomato Sauce, Fast Fresh	■	■	■	606
Tomato-Mustard Sauce, Uncooked	■	■		606
Tomato-Nut Sauce for Fish (Romesco)	■	■	■	606
Vinaigrette	■	■	■	600
Yogurt Sauce, Thin	■	■	■	597

DESSERTS

	MAKE AHEAD	ROOM TEMP/ COLD	30 MIN OR LESS	PAGE
Almond Cake (Tarta de Almendras)	■	■		632
Apple Cake (Äppletorte)	■	■		619
Apples, Caramelized	■	■		619
Apricot Meringue with Walnuts	■	■		620
Apricot, Cherry, or Pear Clafouti	■	■		621
Apricots, Baked			■	621
Bananas in Coconut Milk			■	622
Berry Pudding	■	■		624
Cheesecake, Crustless Easter (Paskha)	■	■		652
Coconut Custard, Steamed	■	■		639
Coconut Macaroons	■	■		630
Coconut Sorbet	■	■		630
Coffee Cake, Braided, with Cardamom	■	■		644
Cream Tart (Tarte Vaudoise)	■	■		654
Cream, Cooked (Buttermilk Panna Cotta)	■	■		636

	MAKE AHEAD	ROOM TEMP/ COLD	30 MIN OR LESS	PAGE
Crème Brûlée	■	■		635
Date or Fig and Walnut Balls	■	■	■	625
Dried Fruits and Nuts, Macerated	■	■		627
Figs or Apricots, Baked, Stuffed with Walnuts or Almonds	■	■	■	622
Figs Poached in Wine	■	■		625
Flan	■	■		633
"French" Toast, Spanish (Torrijas Castellanas)			■	653
Fruit Soup, Simple	■	■		624
Fruit-Filled Cookies (Kolackys)	■	■		648
Ginger Ice Cream	■	■		641
Honey and Cinnamon Fritters (Loukoumades)	■	■		655
Honey Cake (Lekach)	■	■		646
Ice Cream "Drowned" with Espresso (Gelato Affogato al Caffè)			■	642
Linzertorte	■	■		631
Multifruit Soup	■	■		627
Olive Oil Cookies with Orange and Cinnamon	■	■		657
Orange Custard (Flan de Naranja)	■	■		634
Orange-Nut Biscotti	■	■		657
Pancakes, Swedish (Plattar)			■	646
Pastry Cream (Crème Pâtissière)	■	■	■	650
Pears "Poached" with Butter and Cream	■	■		626
Pears, Caramelized, Poached in Red Wine	■	■		626
Phyllo and Walnut Cake (Baklava)	■	■		628
Plantains, Baked			■	623
Pumpkin and Walnuts (Kabak Tatlisi)	■	■		631
Rice Pudding (Kheer)	■	■		638
Rice Pudding with Cinnamon (Arroz con Leche)	■	■		636
Rice, Sweet Sticky, with Mangoes			■	639

	MAKE AHEAD	ROOM TEMP/ COLD	30 MIN OR LESS	PAGE
Saffron-Rice Pudding (Zerde)	■	■		638
Sand Cake	■	■		651
Sponge Cake, Buttery (Génoise)	■			649
Sugar Cookies, Chewy (Ossi dei Morti)	■	■		656
Sweet "Pizza" (Galette de Perouges)	■	■		647
Sweet Rice Flour Dumplings	■	■		639
"Tiles" or Broomstick Cookies (Tuiles or Mandelflarn)	■	■	■	652
Trifle	■	■		651
Walnut Tart	■	■		632

BEVERAGES

	MAKE AHEAD	ROOM TEMP/ COLD	30 MIN OR LESS	PAGE
Almond Milk	■	■	■	663
Avocado or Fruit Shake		■	■	661
Cantaloupe Horchata	■	■	■	661
Daiquiri, Classic		■	■	670
Ginger Ale	■	■		660
Glögg	■			669
Honey Drink, Spiced (Sbiten)	■	■	■	668
Hot Chocolate, Mexican			■	664
Hot Chocolate, Spanish (Chocolate Español)		■		665
Iced Coffee, Vietnamese Style		■	■	666

	MAKE AHEAD	ROOM TEMP/ COLD	30 MIN OR LESS	PAGE
Iced Tea, Hibiscus (Agua de Jamaica)		■		665
Iced Tea, Lemongrass	■	■		666
Iced Tea, Thai (Cha Yen)		■	■	667
Lemongrass-Ginger Tea	■	■		666
Limeade, Salty	■	■	■	660
Margarita		■	■	671
Mojito		■	■	671
Pineappleade	■	■	■	661
Rice Drink, Chilled (Horchata)	■	■		663
Rum and Coke (Cuba Libre)		■	■	671
Sangria	■	■		672
Sangria, White, with Peaches	■	■		672
Tea with Jam			■	669
Tea, Cardamom-Scented			■	668
Tea, Cinnamon	■	■		667
Tea, Ginger (Salabat)	■	■	■	665
Tea, Roasted Barley	■	■	■	667
Tea, Spiced (Masala Chai)			■	668
Vodka, Fruit-Infused	■	■		670
Vodka, Spiced	■	■		670
Watermelon Cooler		■	■	662
Yogurt "Milk" (Ayran)		■	■	662
Yogurt Shake, Savory (Lassi Namkeen)		■	■	662
Yogurt Shake, Sweet (Lassi Meethi)		■	■	663

Recipes by Cuisine

SOUTHEAST ASIA

JAPAN AND KOREA

CARIBBEAN AND SOUTH AMERICA

FRANCE

Index

NOTE: Recipe titles in *italics* indicate that the ingredient they are listed under is suggested as a substitute.

Bacon (*cont'd*)

potato salad with mustard vinaigrette and, 194

quiche lorraine, 467

radicchio with, 461

rice porridge (jook) with, 123–24

roast fish fillets with sauerkraut and, 247–48

salade lyonnaise, 202

sautéed scallops with shallots and, 212

zucchini tart with, 77

Baeckoffe of pork and lamb, 399–400

Bagna cauda (warm olive oil bath), 56

Baklava (phyllo and walnut cake), 628–30

Balsamic vinegar, 170, 171

Bamboo shoot-mushroom sauce, braised whole fish in, 261

Banana(s), 623. See also Plantain(s)

banana-coconut raita, 176

in coconut milk, 622–23

green, in coconut milk, 472–73

shake, 661

in tapioca coconut milk, 623

Banana leaves

fish and coconut chutney steamed in (patra ni machhi), 231

fish fillets steamed in, 230–31

Bare-bones risotto, 522

Barley

cholent, 380–81

with dried mushrooms, 524–25

mushroom-barley soup, 112–13

rice and beans, Korean style, 511–12

roasted barley tea, 667–68

salad, 527–28

vegetarian tsimmes, 502

Basbousa (semolina pudding), 640–41

Basil, 13

fresh tomato salad with, 172

puree, 605

rice with onions, garlic, and herbs, 518

Thai, 10, 221

vegetable soup with (soupe au pistou), 111–12

Basmati rice, 505

with shiso, 510

Bass. *See also* Black bass; Black sea bass; Sea bass; Striped bass

baked in foil, 246

with rice, 249–50

shallow-fried, with ginger sauce, 259–60

Batrik (bulgur and tomato salad with nuts), 186–87

Batter-fried fish and vegetables (tempura), 91–92

Batter-fried vegetables (pakoras), 90–91

Bay leaves, 12–13

grilled lamb skewers with, 357

potatoes with, 481

roast duck with Marsala and, 329–30

sausage and orange with, 374–75

Bean(s), 6, 11, 13, 15, 430–31, 460. See also specific colors and types

basic cooked, 431–32

black, with garlic and cumin, 438

black, with soy, 432–33

black, tofu with, 492

black bean and roasted corn salad, 195

and cheese empanadas, 49

with coconut milk, 434–35

coconut rice and beans, 516

crostini with greens and, 41

fava, stewed baby artichokes with peas and, 428

fava bean soup, 130–31

fresh tomato and green bean salad, 172

green, garlic bread salad with tomatoes and, 181

green, with garlic and lemon, 452–53

green, in mixed vegetable curry (subz miloni), 500–501

green, with sesame-miso dressing, 190

green, with sweet sesame dressing, 190

green, with yogurt and dill, 461

green beans, pears, and ham, 460–61

green bean soup with mint, 120

green bean and tuna salad, 189

green papaya salad (som tum), 174–75

hijiki with shiitakes and, 485

meaty bean stew from the Pyrenees (garbure), 402–3

and nut filling for stuffed vegetables, 449

pork, bean, and sauerkraut soup (jota), 146–47

pork and, Asturian style (fabada), 401–2

red, spicy (rajma), 437

red or black bean dip, 29–30

refried beans, 438–39

rice and, Korean style, 511–12

and salami salad, 189

sausage and, 401

spicy, Goan style (feijoada), 436–37

tofu salad with peanut sauce, 195–96

and tuna salad, 189

vegetables with dried shrimp and coconut milk, 502–3

vegetable soup with basil, 111–12

vegetarian samosas, 66

with walnut-garlic sauce, 443

white, aromatic, with chicken stock and tomatoes, 442

white, with garlic, 441

white, mashed, 440–41

white bean dip, 19

Bean curd. *See also* Tofu

fish fillets wrapped in, 228

Bean curd noodles, 537

Bean paste, beef stew with, 376

Bean sauce, stir-fried watercress with, 496–97

Bean sprout(s)

how to grow, 183

salad (kong namul), 182–83

Bean thread noodles, 537

Béarnaise sauce, 602

Beef, 26, 346, 377. See also Short ribs; Steak

chilaquiles with meat, 342

Beef appetizers and snacks

beef-scallion rolls (negima), 102

carpaccio, 26

cold cut beef shank, 39

grilled beef "jerky," 40

grilled satay, 101

marinated beef (carne cruda), 25–26

steak pajon, 81

Beef, grilled

beef skewers with bay leaves, 357

with fenugreek cream, 353

Buckwheat (*cont'd*)
  pizzocheri, 542
  pizzocheri with Savoy cabbage,
    potatoes, and cheese, 549–50
Bulgur, 186, 525
  kofte with, 426
  lentils with, 440
  pilaf, with chickpeas, 526
  pilaf, with meat, 525–26
  raw meatballs (cig kofte), 26–27
  tabbouleh, 187–88
  and tomato salad, with nuts (batrik),
    186–87
Buns
  mantou, 80
  steamed barbecued pork buns
    (char siu bao), 79–80
  sweet almond buns (semla), 578–79
  sweet breakfast buns, 579–80
  sweet rolls with saffron, 578
Buñuelos (yucca fritters), 87–88
Butter
  apples cooked in, 619
  brown, skate with, 267
  chervil-butter sauce for fish, 601–2
  clarified, 241
  dal with cream and, 433
  pears "poached" with cream and, 626
  quick baked fish with, 264
Buttermilk panna cotta, 636
Butternut squash. *See* Winter squash

Cabbage, 107, 443. *See also* Sauerkraut
  and beet salad, 168
  braised, with apples or chestnuts, 445
  braised spareribs with root vegetables,
    caraway, and, 392–93
  braised spareribs with, Roman style,
    393–94
  breaded pork cutlets with (tonkatsu),
    361–62
  brown cabbage soup, 106
  caldo gallego, 144–45
  fresh, bigos with, 404
  grand borscht, 149
  kimchi, 444–45
  lightly pickled, 455

  lion's head (meatballs in broth), 157–58
  meaty bean stew from the Pyrenees
    (garbure), 402–3
  pasta with sausage and, 159, 552
  pasta with, 551–52
  pickled (oshinko), 444
  pie, 449–50
  and potato soup, 106
  sauerkraut soup with (shchi), 147–48
  and sausage soup, 158–59
  savory pancakes (okonomiyaki), 81–82
  Savoy, pizzocheri with potatoes, cheese,
    and, 549–50
  soup, with thyme and apples, 106–7
  in sour cream, 468
  stir-fried shrimp with black beans and,
    213
  stuffed, 445–46
  vegetarian samosas, 66
Cake(s), sweet
  almond, 632–33
  apple (äppletorte), 619–20
  braided coffee cake with cardamom,
    644–45
  buttery sponge cake (génoise), 649–50
  fried cheesecakes (sirniki), 643
  honey (lekach), 646–47
  phyllo and walnut (baklava), 628–30
  sand cake, 651–52
  trifle, 651
Cakes, savory. *See also* Croquettes;
    Pancake(s)
  clam, 83
  cornmeal (arepas), 575
  fish or shrimp (tod mun), 83–84
  shrimp, Indian style, 84
Caldo cantina (chicken-rice soup),
    138–39
Caldo gallego, 144–45
Calf liver. *See* Liver
Canapés
  with piquillo peppers and anchovies, 48
  pork, piquillo, and cheese, 47
Cannelloni, 545
Canola oil, 93
Cantaloupe horchata, 661–62
Capers, 6, 13
  grilled eggplant salad with, 192

  oxtail with, 389–90
  pan-seared swordfish with tomatoes,
    olives, and, 257
  rémoulade sauce, 603
  roasted pepper, anchovy, and caper
    salad, 194
  Russian sauce, poached fish with,
    251–52
  veal with, 367
Caramel
  beef tenderloin in caramelized sugar,
    359–60
  sauce, fish fillets poached in, 232
  sweet black pepper fish, Vietnamese
    style, 252–53
Caramelized apples, 619
Caramelized onions, lentils and rice with,
    439
Caramelized pears poached in red wine,
    626–27
Caramelized potatoes, 482
Caraway
  braised spareribs with cabbage, root
    vegetables, and, 392–93
  cabbage and potato soup with, 106
  caraway breadsticks, 576–77
  sauce, poached fish fillets in, 249
Carbonnade (beef and onions stewed in
    beer), 385–86
Carciofi fritti (fried artichoke hearts), 71
Cardamom, 10–11
  braided coffee cake with, 644–45
  cardamom-scented tea, 668
Cardini, Caesar, 167
Carne cruda (marinated beef), 25–26
Carom seeds, 560
Carp
  gefilte fish, 36–37
  grilled or broiled with lime, 262–63
  poached, with Russian sauce, 251–52
  with raisin almond sauce, 268–69
  roast with sauerkraut and bacon,
    247–48
  whole baked, with dates or almonds,
    264
  whole braised, in hot-and-sour sauce,
    260–61
Carpaccio, 25, 26

coconut custard, steamed, 639
coconut flan, 634
coconut rice, 516
coconut rice pudding Jamaican-style, 637
coconut sorbet, 630
cold mango soup, sweet or savory, 119–20
dal with coconut, 434
fragrant coconut milk rice (nasi lemak), 515
lemongrass-coconut sauce, steamed shrimp with, 216
minced pork and shrimp in, 423–24
mulligatawny with, 116
plantains in (ndizi wa nazi), 472–73
red-braised chicken with, 282
soup, 121
soup, with clams and shrimp, 121
spinach with, 487
sticky rice with nam pla and, 508
stir-fried chicken in, 371
stir-fried pork in, 371
sweet coconut rice, 516–17
sweet sticky rice with mangoes, 639
tembleque, 636
vegetables with dried shrimp and, 502–3
Cod. *See also* Black cod; Salt cod
baked, with dried mushroom sauce, 251
bouillabaisse, 138
with chickpeas and sherry, 242
choucroute de poissons, 270
cod potato patties, 315–16
escabeche, 235–36
fish salad with horseradish dressing, 197–98
grilled, rémoulade, 256–57
grilled fillets, coastal-style, 268
Jamaican codfish curry (run down), 239
piquillo peppers stuffed with fish, 46–47
poached in cider, 247
Coffee
braised goose with white wine and, 333–34

ice cream "drowned" with espresso, 642
iced, Vietnamese style, 666
Coffee cake, braided, with cardamom, 644–45
Collards
cold lemony greens, 180–81
cooked in yogurt, 463–64
croquettes, 487–88
flash-cooked, with lemon juice, 464
with garlic and lemon, 452–53
with oyster sauce, 463
pasta with, 552
with raisins and pine nuts, 489
Conch
ceviche, 21–22
Condiments, 582–617. *See also* Dipping sauce; Relish; Salsa; Sauce(s)
adobo, 616
annatto seasoning paste (recado rojo), 609–10
chaat masala, 594
chile oil with Szechwan peppercorns, 583
chile paste (harissa), 191, 598
chili powder, 609
chutney, dry peanut, 595–96
chutney, mint, 595
curry powder, 592–94
garam masala, 594
gremolata, osso buco with, 419–20
ground and toasted rice (khao koor), 587
parsley-onion condiment, 596–97
pickled ginger (gari), 591–92
preserved lemons, 598–99
salmoriglio, skewered swordfish chunks with, 257–58
sambal oelek, nasi lemak with, 515
sesame-chile paste, 591
sesame seeds, toasted, 596
sweet garlic soy sauce, 590–91
Szechwan salt-and-pepper, 583
tamarind paste, 585
Tunisian spice rub (tabil), 597–98
Confit, duck, 330
"Confit," octopus, 51
Congee (rice porridge), 123–24
Conpoy (dried scallops)
jook with, 124

Consommé, 161
borscht, 116
Jerez style, 115
Cooked cream (buttermilk panna cotta), 636
Cookies
almendrados, 631
chewy sugar cookies (ossi dei morti), 656–57
coconut macaroons, 630
coconut macaroons, Caribbean style, 631
fruit-filled (kolackys), 648–49
madeleines, 649
olive oil, with orange and cinnamon, 657–58
orange-nut biscotti, 657
"tiles" or broomstick cookies, 652–53
walnut or almond macaroons, 630
Cooking oil, 93. *See also* Oil; *specific types*
Cooking techniques, 1–2
Coq au vin, 307
Coriander, 11, 12
pork with red wine and, 395
Corn, 454. *See also* Cornmeal; Polenta; Posole
ajiaco (creamy chicken soup with vegetables), 140
arepas (cornmeal cakes), 575
creamed, stir-fried chicken or beef with, 312–13
fresh, polenta with, 530
fresh corn fritters, 89–90
grilled, 454–55
grilled, with cream and cheese, 455
pan-grilled, with chiles, 454
roasted corn and black bean salad, 195
soup, cream-style, 141–42
Cornichons, 13
poached fish with Russian sauce, 251–52
sauce gribiche, 601
veal stew with pickles, 417
Cornish game hen, marinated and grilled, 334
Cornmeal, 6. *See also* Polenta
cakes (arepas), 575
empanadas, 48–49

steamed, with black beans, 262
steamed, Italian style, 262
steamed in its own juice, with cilantro
    sauce, 263–64
Flageolet beans, 13, 430
    hijiki with shiitakes and, 485
    mashed, 440–41
Flan, 633–34
    de courgettes (zucchini custard), 44
    de naranja (orange custard), 634–35
    vanilla, coconut, or pumpkin, 634
Flatbreads. *See also* Pizza
    onion kulcha, 563–64
    Italian (piadine), 567
    pita, 568–69
        cheese-filled, 569–70
        meat-filled, 570
        whole wheat, 569
    Turkish "pizza" (lahmacun), with meat
        or egg, 566–67
    whole wheat (paratha), 559–60
        stuffed with lamb, chiles, and cilantro
            (keema ke paratha), 561–62
        stuffed with potatoes (aloo
            paratha), 560–61
    yeasted (naan), 563
Flautas, chicken, 324
Fleica (grilled steak with garlic), 346–47
Flounder
    escabeche, 235–36
    fish and coconut chutney steamed in
        banana leaves (patra ni machhi),
        231
    lime-cooked, with crisp garlic, 237
    soy-glazed, 232–33
    West Lake fish soup, 134
Flour, 6
Foo foo (mashed plantains), 473
French bread, 570–71
French cooking, 4–5, 12, 679
French menus, 679–80
French pantry items, 12–13
"French" toast, Spanish (torrijas
    castellanas), 653–54
French walnut sauce, 600
Fried almonds, spicy, 28
Fried artichoke hearts, 71
Fried cheese (queso frito), 85–86

Fried cheesecakes (sirniki), 643
Fried chicken, 308–11
Fried fish, spicy (amritsari), 94–95
Fried green chiles, 77
Fried peanuts, 27–28
Fried rice, 506–7
    Malaysian style (nasi goreng), 507
    with pineapple, 507
    vegetarian, 507
    yang chow, 507
Fried rice balls (supplì), 43–44
Fried satay, 100
Frikadeller (Danish meatballs), 101–2
Frittata, pasta, 558
Fritters
    batter-fried fish and vegetables
        (tempura), 91–92
    batter-fried vegetables (pakoras), 90–91
    black-eyed pea, 87
    eggplant, 88–89
    falafel, 42–43
    fresh corn, 89–90
    fresh sugar crullers (churros), 655
    honey and cinnamon (loukoumades),
        655–56
    lightly fried fish and vegetables (fritto
        misto), 94
    salt cod (bacalaitos), 90
    shrimp, Spanish or Indian, 90
    split pea or chickpea (phulouri), 87
    yucca (buñuelos), 87–88
Fritto misto (lightly fried fish and
    vegetables), 94
Fromage blanc, 13
    Alsatian "pizza" (tarte flambé), 45
Fruit. *See also specific fruits*
    beverages, 660–62
    cucumber, jicama, and fruit salad,
        178
    desserts, 619–28
    dried, 12
        beef daube with, 384
        dried fruit and nut sauce with
            cilantro, 599–600
        macerated dried fruits and nuts,
            627–28
    fresh, lamb tagine with, 408
    fruit salad "salsa," 178

Fruit-filled cookies (kolackys), 648–49
Fruit preserves. *See* Jam

Gai lan with oyster sauce, 463
Galangal, 9
Galette de Pérouges (sweet "pizza"),
    647–48
Garam masala, 11, 594
Garbanzos. *See* Chickpea(s)
Garbure (meaty bean stew from the
    Pyrenees), 402–3
Gari (pickled ginger), 591–92
Garlic, 14
    almond garlic sauce, chicken with,
        297–98
    and artichokes, squid with, 222–23
    black bean and garlic spareribs, 391–92
    black beans with cumin and, 438
    braised lamb with lemon and, 408–9
    and bread soup ("boiled water"), 127
    broccoli or cauliflower with lemon and,
        452–53
    chicken in garlic sour cream, 305–6
    and cilantro soup, 121–22
    crisp, lime-cooked fish with, 237
    fried, seared swordfish with
        lemongrass, tamarind, and, 253–54
    garlic bread salad with tomatoes, 181
    garlic crostini, 41
    garlic duck and rice, 327–28
    garlic-fried shrimp, Indian style, 218
    garlic shrimp, Yucatecan style, 219
    garlic-tomato soup, 127
    "grilled" mackerel with rosemary and,
        266–67
    grilled steak with (fleica), 346–47
    habanero-garlic salsa, 611–12
    handmade pasta with bread crumbs
        and (pinci), 545–46
    hardshell clams with, 99
    lamb stew with vinegar and, 410–11
    and lime soup, 127
    linguine with oil and, 547
    liver with sage, white wine, and,
        367–68
    mayonnaise. *See* Aïoli
    pasta with whole garlic cloves, 556

Garlic (*cont'd*)
  pipián with tomatoes and, 613
  poached sausage with, 422
  rice with cheese and, 524
  rice with onions, herbs, and, 518
  roast pepper spread with walnuts and,
    32–33
  roast pork and, with milk, 401
  roasted vegetable gazpacho, Ignacio
    Blanco's, 117–18
  sauce, Creole (mojo criollo), 617
  sauce, stir-fried pork in, 370
  sautéed scallops with, 211–12
  shrimp with tomatoes, chiles, and, 99
  shrimp with, 98
  spicy scrambled eggs (akoori), 338
  stir-fried squid with basil and, 221–22
  sweet garlic soy sauce, 590–91
    soy barbecued chicken, 288
  tomato sauce with orange and, 607
  veal with, 367
  walnut-garlic sauce, beets with
    (pkhali), 443
  warm olive oil bath (bagna cauda), 56
  white beans with, 441
Gazpacho
  basic red, 117
  roasted vegetable, Ignacio Blanco's,
    117–18
Gefilte fish, 36–37
Gelato affogato al caffè (ice cream
  "drowned" with espresso), 642
Génoise (buttery sponge cake), 649–50
Ghee, 241
Ginger, 8, 9
  chickpea salad with, 180
  crab with, Chinese style, 226
  dipping sauce with (nuoc cham), 590
  ginger ale, 660–61
  ginger chicken, 313
  ginger-chile sauce, 584
  ginger cucumber salad, 177
  ginger-scallion dipping sauce, 583
  ice cream, 641–42
  lemongrass-ginger tea, 666
  pickled (gari), 591–92
  sauce, shallow-fried small fish with,
    259–60

  snow peas with, 470
  steamed Dungeness crab or lobster
    with, 224
  tea (salabat), 665
  tomato salad with, 173
Glass (mung bean) noodles
  dumpling soup (mandoo kuk), 154
  with vegetables and meat (chop chae),
    539–40
Glögg, 669–70
Gnocchi, 478–79
  potato puffs, 481–82
Gobi taktakin (curried sautéed
  cauliflower), 452
Go chu jang, 8, 135, 234
Gogi-jun (meat and tofu pancakes), 51–52
Goi cuon (rice paper spring rolls), 38–39
Golden rice pilaf, 514
Goose
  bigos, 403–4
  braised, with white wine and coffee,
    333–34
  confit, in garbure (meaty bean stew
    from the Pyrenees), 402–3
  roast, with sauerkraut, 332–33
Gorgonzola. *See* Blue cheese
Gori gom tang (oxtail soup), 151
Goshtaba (lamb meatballs simmered in
  milk), 424
Gougères, 69–70
Grains, 504–81. *See also* Bread(s);
  Breadsticks; Noodles; Pasta; *specific
  grains*
  about, 504
Grape leaves, stuffed, 446–47
Grapeseed oil, 93, 187
Gratin(s)
  crustless vegetable pie, 460
  Jansson's temptation, 96
  onion or shallot, 469–70
  potato and Gruyère, 483
  potato and horseradish, 482–83
  spinach, 489–90
"Gratin," polenta, 530
Gravlax (salt- and sugar-cured salmon),
  23–24
Greek menus, 677–78
Greek pantry items, 11–12

Green bean(s), 460
  baked eggs "flamenco," 340–41
  and fresh tomato salad, 172
  garlic bread salad with tomatoes and,
    181
  with garlic and lemon, 452–53
  green beans, pears, and ham, 460–61
  mixed vegetable curry (subz miloni),
    500–501
  with sesame-miso dressing, 190
  soup, with mint, 120
  with sweet sesame dressing, 190
  and tuna salad, 189
  with walnut-garlic sauce, 443
  with yogurt and dill, 461
Green chiles, fried, 77
Green leaf wraps (miang gung),
  33–34
Green mayonnaise, French style
  (sauce verte), 603
Green papaya
  salad (som tum), 174–75
  salad, with shrimp, 198–99
Green peppers. *See also* Peppers
  stir-fried lamb with black beans and,
    371–72
Green rice (arroz verde), 517
Greens, 177, 461–64. *See also* Green
  salad(s); *specific greens*
  about, 166, 177, 461
  bitter, with sour cream dressing, 176
  cold lemony greens, 180–81
  cooked in yogurt, 463–64
  croquettes, 487–88
  crostini with beans and, 41
  with garlic and lemon, 452–53
  pasta with, 552
  vegetarian ravioli, 542–44
  with walnut-garlic sauce, 443
Green salad(s), 202–3. *See also* Greens;
  specific greens
  bitter greens with sour cream dressing,
    176
  Caesar salad, 167
  with lemon, 165
  with nut oil, 165
  with oil and vinegar, 165
  salade lyonnaise, 202

with vinaigrette, Roquefort, and
walnuts, 165
Green salsa. *See* Salsa: verde
Green sauce
chicken in, 302
shrimp in, 220
Green tea ice cream, 642
Gremolata, osso buco with, 419–20
Gribiche sauce, 601
steamed asparagus with, 429
Grissini, 575–76
Groundnut stew with chicken (nketia
fla), 296
Grouper
in almond sauce, 243
baked whole, with dates or almonds,
264
broiled, with olives, 265–66
with chiles and tomatoes, 228–29
fish couscous, 265
fish tacos, 238–39
fish tagine, 239–40
meunière, 240
miso-broiled, 211
pan-cooked with "killed" onions, 237–38
in paprika sour cream, 248–49
poached, in caraway sauce, 249
poached in caramel sauce, 232
quick-braised, in black bean sauce,
227–28
in red sauce, 230
roasted, coastal-style, 267–68
roast with sauerkraut and bacon, 247–48
simmered in soy and sake, 253
steamed, with hard-cooked egg sauce,
250–51
steamed in banana leaves, 230–31
steamed in its own juice, with cilantro
sauce, 263–64
whole, in spicy tomato sauce, 229
whole braised, in hot-and-sour sauce,
260–61
whole steamed, 261–62
wrapped in bean curd or rice paper,
228
zarzuela, 270–71
Gruyère and potato gratin, 483
Guacamole, 22

Guanciale
pasta alla gricia, 546–47
pasta with whole garlic cloves, 556
Gyoza, 59, 64
dumpling soup, 154
vegetarian, 64

Haaq (spinach with hing), 487
Habanero chiles, 589, 611
habanero-garlic salsa, 611–12
jerked pork, 352
Haddock
piquillo peppers stuffed with fish,
46–47
smoked, choucroute de poissons, 270
Hainanese chicken rice, 275–76
Halibut
baked, with dried mushroom sauce,
251
braised in red wine, 256
fish salad with horseradish dressing,
197–98
fish tacos, 238–39
fish tagine, 239–40
grilled fillets, coastal-style, 268
pan-cooked, with "killed" onions, 237–38
in paprika sour cream, 248–49
red fish stew, fast and spicy, 269–70
in red sauce, 230
with rice, 249–50
simmered in soy and sake, 253
steamed in banana leaves, 230–31
sweet black pepper halibut, Vietnamese
style, 252–53
with vegetables, 255–56
wrapped in bean curd or rice paper, 228
zarzuela, 270–71
Ham, 144–45, 340–41. *See also* Prosciutto
braised endives with, 462
and cheese crêpes, 87
and cheese puffs, 86
and cheese sandwich, grilled (sandwich
Cubano), 363
fried rice with, 506–7
green beans, pears, and, 460–61
omelet, 344
pasta with peas, cream, and, 556–57

pasta with whole garlic cloves, 556
shrimp with peas and, 214
"Hamburgers," lemongrass, 350
Haricots verts. *See also* Green bean(s)
tofu salad with peanut sauce, 195–96
Harira (Ramadan soup), 153–54
Harissa (chile paste), 191, 598
Hasenpfeffer (civet of rabbit), 335
Hash, meat (pytt i panna), 421
Hazan, Marcella, 554
Hazelnut oil
green salad with, 165
sauerkraut salad with, 168–69
Hazelnuts, 29
apricot meringue with, 620–21
baklava, 628–30
chicken with nuts and raisins, 296–97
nutty zarzuela, 271
orange-nut biscotti, 657
romesco (tomato-nut sauce for fish),
606–7
tarator, 600
Herbs. *See also specific herbs*
and butter or oil, mushrooms with, 55
fish quenelles with, 95–96
fresh herb grissini, 576
green mayonnaise, French style (sauce
verte), 603
grilled or roast lamb with, 358–59
herbed cheese dip, 20–21
herb purees, 605
meat and noodle soup with (pho bo),
152
mixed-herb pancakes, 83
omelette aux fines herbes, 343–44
rice with onions, garlic, and, 518
soft polenta with, 529–30
Herring
panfried fish "sandwiches," 57–58
pickled, 37
Hibiscus iced tea (agua de jamaica), 665
Hijiki, 484
with shiitakes and beans, 485
Hing, 10, 435
chaat masala, 594
spinach with (haaq), 487
Hiyashi somen (cold noodles with
dipping sauce), 534

Mail order ingredients sources, 330, 484, 683–84

Mako, *grilled, rémoulade,* 256–57

Malanga, 88

Malfatti, 542

Malt vinegar, 171

Mamaliga, 529

Mandelflarn, 652–53

Mandoo, 59, 64

Mandoo kuk (dumpling soup), 154

Mango(es), 120
  cold savory mango soup, 119–20
  cold sweet mango soup, 120
  green mango salad with meat, 203–4
  green mango salad with smoked fish, 204
  lassi, 663
  shake, 661
  sweet sticky rice with, 639
  tropical spring rolls, 39

Mango powder. *See* Amchoor

Mantecaos, cheese, 35
  ham and cheese puffs, 86

Manti (lamb-filled dumplings), 65

Ma po tofu (simmered tofu with ground pork), 423

Margarita, 671

Margherita pizza, 574

Marinara pizza, 574

Marinated mushrooms, 176–77

Mariquitas de yucca (yucca chips), 23

Marjoram, 13

Marsala, roast duck with bay leaves and, 329–30

Martin, Marie, 44, 76

Masala chai, 668

Masala winter squash, 497

Matambre (stuffed flank steak), 372–73

Matzo ball soup, 126–27

Mayonnaise, 602–3
  garlic. *See* Aïoli
  green, French style (sauce verte), 603
  mustard dill sauce, 608–9
  rouille, 603–4
  spicy (rémoulade), 603
  grilled fish with, 256–57

"Mayonnaise," avocado, 616

Meat, 345–426. *See also* Meatball(s); *specific meats*

about, 345; cooking methods, 346, 359, 368, 372, 376; grilled, 346–59; grinding, 355; ground, 420–26; pan-cooked, 359–68; raw meat, 26; roasted, 372–76; stews and braises, 376–420; stir-fries, 368–72

Meatball(s). *See also* Kofte
  in broth (lion's head), 157–58
  lamb, simmered in milk (goshtaba), 424
  pearl balls, 158
  pho with, quicker, 152–53
  polpette, 53–54
    and orzo, in broth, 156–57
  prune-stuffed, in yogurt sauce (alubukhara kofta), 424–25
  raw (cig kofte), 26–27
  soup, with lemon (kofte in broth), 157
  Swedish or Danish, 101–2

Mediterranean squash and chickpea soup, 130

Mediterranean-style seafood salad, 197

Mei Kuei Lu Chiew, 212, 274

Melon. *See also* Bitter melon
  cantaloupe horchata, 661–62
  watermelon cooler, 662

Melted cheese (queso fundido), 84

Menu suggestions, 673–82

Meringue, apricot, with nuts, 620–21

Mexican cheeses, 85

Mexican cooking, 14–15, 682

Mexican hot chocolate, 664

Mexican menus, 682

Mexican pantry items, 15

Mexican radish salad, 172

Mexican rice, 517

Miang gung (green leaf wraps), 33–34

Middle Eastern menus, 677–78

Middle Eastern pantry items, 11–12

Migas (chorizo and bread), 100

Milk
  lamb meatballs simmered in (goshtaba), 424
  roast pork or chicken with, 400–401
  roast pork and garlic with, 401

Milk, almond, 663
  sweet couscous with (seffa), 641

"Milk," yogurt (ayran), 662

Mint, 9
  beef salad with, 203
  chicken breasts with, 308
  chutney, 595
    grilled lamb chops with, 352–53
  cucumber-mint raita, 175
  green bean soup with, 120
  mint lassi, 663
  mint-onion condiment, 596–97
  mojito, 671–72
  olive oil bread with onions and, 568
  pasta with Parmesan and, 549
  puree, 605
  zucchini with dill and, 498

Mirin, 8, 210–11
  quick salted vegetables with soy and, 455
  yam in, 498

Miso, 8, 123, 210
  beef stew with, 376
  beef tenderloin with, 348–49
  Japanese tomato sauce with, 606
  miso-broiled fish fillets, 211
  miso-broiled scallops, 210–11
  miso-chile sauce, tuna with, 254–55
  mustard-miso dressing, eggplant salad with, 185–86
  rice balls with, 511
  sauce, black cod or mackerel in, 233–34
  sautéed peppers with, 78
  sesame-miso dressing, green beans with, 190
  soup, 122–23
  spicy pork and tofu stew with, 398–99
  sweet, eggplant with, 457

Mititei (fresh sausages), 422–23

Mixed vegetables. *See* Vegetables: mixed

Miyuk. *See* Wakame

Mojito, 671–72

Mojo criollo (Creole garlic sauce), 617

Mole
  almond, chicken in, 301–2
  sauce, chicken with, 300–301

Monkfish
  in almond sauce, 243
  with artichokes, 245–46
  bouillabaisse, 138
  braised in red wine, 256
  grilled, rémoulade, 256–57

Monkfish (*cont'd*)
grilled fillets, coastal-style, 268
miso-broiled, 211
red fish stew, fast and spicy, 269–70
in saffron sauce, 241–42
zarzuela, 270–71
Mulligatawny (spicy vegetable soup),
115–16
Multifruit soup, 502
Mung bean noodles. *See* Glass noodles
Mushroom(s), 6, 8, 112
and bacon, 75–76
beef stew with bacon, red wine, and
(boeuf bourguignon), 383
caviar, 76
and chicken paella, 520
cod poached in cider with, 247
and cranberry chicken, 304–5
with cream, 55
dried, barley with, 524–25
dried, beef stew with, 380
dried mushroom sauce, baked fish
fillets with, 251
and eggs, 74–75
fresh and dried, pasta with, 554
with herbs and butter or oil, 55
kasha with, 529
lamb stew with olives and, 411
lamb stew with, 410
marinated, 176–77
mashed potatoes with onions and,
480–81
mushroom-bamboo shoot sauce,
braised whole fish in, 261
mushroom-barley soup, 112–13
mushroom-potato soup, 113
mushroom sherry chicken, 299–300
poached in sour cream, 467–68
portobello spread, 18
rice with meat and, 512
with sherry, 54–55
shiitakes, piquillo peppers with spinach
and, 48
shiitakes and beans, hijiki with, 485
stewed lamb shanks with pasilla chile
sauce and, 414–15
stir-fried noodles with chives and, 536
veal rolled with, 365–66

Mussel(s), 206, 208
bouillabaisse, 138
cod poached in cider with, 247
with linguiça, 210
red fish stew, fast and spicy, 269–70
rice pilaf with, 514
seafood pajon, 81
soup, 134–35
steamed, 209
zarzuela, 270–71
Mustard
"deviled" pork chops, 362
mustard-cream sauce, halibut with
vegetables with, 256
mustard dill sauce, 608–9
cabbage and beet salad with, 168
mustard-miso dressing, eggplant salad
with, 185–86
rémoulade sauce, 603
grilled swordfish with, 256–57
soy-mustard dressing, asparagus salad
with, 190
tomato tart, 76–77
uncooked tomato-mustard sauce, 606
vinaigrette, potato salad with, 194
Mustard greens
Chinese, with oyster sauce, 463
cold lemony greens, 180–81
pasta with, 552

Naan (yeasted flatbreads), 563
Nadroo korma (lotus root fries), 71
Naengmyon (cold buckwheat noodle
soup), 149–50
Nam pla, 500
sticky rice with coconut milk and, 508
stir-fried vegetables with, 499–500
sweet nam pla dipping sauce, 586
Nam prik, 586
Napa cabbage, 443. *See also* Cabbage
Nasi goreng (fried rice, Malaysian style),
507
Nasi lemak (fragrant coconut milk rice),
515
Navarin of lamb, 411–12
Ndizi wa nazi (plantains in coconut
milk), 472–73

Negima (beef-scallion rolls), 102
Neua nam tok (grilled beef salad), 202–3
"Nik," potato, Helen Art's, 479–80
Nketia fla (groundnut stew with
chicken), 296
Noodles, 531–41. *See also* Pasta
about, 9, 531–32, 537
beef lo mein, 535–36
cold:
with dipping sauce (hiyashi somen),
534
with sesame sauce, 532
soba noodles with dipping sauce,
533–34
spicy, 533
cold buckwheat noodle soup
(naengmyon), 149–50
crisp-fried, shrimp with, 534–35
curry soup noodles, 125
dumpling soup with (mandoo kuk), 154
egg noodles, fresh, 63
egg noodles with spring onions, 536
fresh, dough for, 62
glass noodles with vegetables and meat
(chop chae), 539–40
meat and noodle soup with herbs
(pho bo), 152
pad thai, 536–38
pho with meatballs, 152–53
Ramadan soup (harira), 153–54
"Singapore" noodles (curried rice
noodles with pork or chicken and
shrimp), 538–39
spaetzle, 540–41
stir-fried, with chives and mushrooms,
536
stir-fried udon with pork and shrimp,
540
vegetarian tsimmes, 502
vermicelli pilaf, 514
Nori, 8, 484
cucumber seaweed soup, 120–21
nori snacks, 485–86
rice balls (onigiri), 511
North African menus, 678
North African pantry items, 11–12
Nuoc cham (dipping sauce with ginger),
586, 590

barley with dried mushrooms, 524–25
beef stew with dried mushrooms, 380
civet of rabbit (hasenpfeffer), 335
kasha with mushrooms, 529
lamb stew with, 410
mushroom-barley soup, 112–13
mushroom and chicken paella, 520
mushrooms with herbs and butter, 55
pasta with fresh and dried mushrooms, 554
sauerkraut vegetable stew (kapusniak), 114
Porgies, shallow-fried, with ginger sauce, 259–60
Pork, 393. *See also* Bacon; Chorizo; Ham; Sausage; Spareribs
chilaquiles with meat, 342
stuffed tofu, 491–92
tacos, 324
tamales, 531
Pork appetizers and snacks
empanadas, 48–49
fried pork-filled tortillas (taquitos), 69
fried satay, 100
grilled satay, 101
lumpia rolls, 68–69
pork, piquillo, and cheese canapés, 47
pork and cheese puffs, 86
pork-scallion rolls, 102
rice paper spring rolls (goi cuon), 38–39
steamed barbecued pork buns (char siu bao), 79–80
Pork, grilled
chops in chipotle sauce, 289
escabeche, 350–51
jerked pork, 352
lemongrass "hamburgers," 350
lemongrass pork, 349
pork skewers with bay leaves, 357
ribs with spicy adobo, 394
with sauce au chien, 348
tenderloin with miso, 348–49
Pork, ground
almond meatballs, 54
fresh sausage patties, 421–22
fresh sausages (mititei), 422–23
fried wontons, 63
green mango salad with meat, 203–4

lemongrass "hamburgers," 350
lion's head (meatballs in broth), 157–58
lion's head pie, 158
meatballs (polpette), 53–54
meat-filled pelmeni, vareniki, or pierogi, 61–62
meat hash (pytt i panna), 421
meat samosas, 65–66
minced pork and shrimp in coconut milk, 423–24
pearl balls, 158
plantain and meat casserole, 420–21
poached sausage with garlic, 422
potato croquettes with, 475–76
pot stickers (wor teep) or mandoo, 63–64
prune-stuffed meatballs in yogurt sauce, 424–25
quicker pho with meatballs, 152–53
rice and beans, Korean style, 511–12
rice with mushrooms and meat, 512
rice pilaf with meat, 514–15
savory egg custard (chawan-mushi), 53
simmered tofu with (ma po tofu), 423
steamed chicken cups, 321–22
Swedish or Danish meatballs, 101–2
veal rolls with, 365–66
Pork, noodle and rice dishes
cold noodles with sesame sauce and pork, 532
curried rice noodles with pork and shrimp, 538–39
fried rice with barbecued pork, 506–7
pork lo mein, 535–36
spicy cold noodles with barbecued pork, 533
udon with pork and shrimp, 540
Pork, pan-cooked
breaded pork cutlets (tonkatsu), 361–62
chops with prunes and cream, 362–63
crisp pork cutlets (Wiener schnitzel), 364–65
cutlets rolled with mushrooms, 365–66
"deviled" chops, 362
in caramelized sugar, 359
pork paprikás, 366–67
teriyaki, 360

Pork, roasted
barbecued pork, 373
lechon asado, 375–76
with orange and bay leaves, 374–75
with prunes and apricots, 374
sandwich Cubano (grilled ham and cheese sandwich), 363
Yucatecan pit-roasted pork (cochinita pibil), 351–52
Pork, in salads
green mango salad with meat, 203–4
minced pork "salad" (laarb), 199–200
Pork, soups with
hot and sour soup, 145–46
jook with tea eggs and pork, 124
lion's head (meatballs in broth), 157–58
miso soup with pork, 122–23
pho with meatballs, 152–53
pork, bean, and sauerkraut (jota), 146–47
pork and posole with chipotles, 155–56
posole with pumpkin seeds, 156
Pork stews and braises
12345 spareribs, 391
baeckoffe of pork and lamb, 399–400
with bean paste, 376
bigos, 403–4
black bean and garlic spareribs, 391–92
braised ribs with spicy adobo, 394
with capers, 389–90
cholent, 380–81
chops with sherry, 413–14
with cinnamon, 382–83
with coconut milk, 397
with dill and sour cream, 416–17
with dried mushrooms, 380
with garlic and lemon, 408–9
with mushrooms, 410
with mushrooms and pasilla chile sauce, 414–15
with orange, 395–96
pilaf with cinnamon, 412–13
pork and beans, 401
pork and beans Asturian style (fabada), 401–2
pork vindaloo, 399
with potatoes, 415–16
with prunes, 378–79

Galician style, 637
kheer, 638
Middle Eastern style, 637
saffron-rice (zerde), 638
soupy, 637
rutabaga, 495–96
semolina (basbousa), 640–41
Puffs
ham and cheese, 86
potato, 481–82
Pumpkin. *See also* Winter squash
flan, 634
penne with, 553–54
and walnut dessert (kabak tatlisi),
631–32
Pumpkin seeds (pepitas), 15
chicken in green sauce, 302
chicken with mole sauce, 300–301
pipián (pumpkin seed sauce), 612–13
posole with, 156
Puree
eggplant, braised lamb in (hunkar
begendi), 405–6
fish roe (taramasalata), 24–25
herb purees, 605
olive (tapenade), 604
pasta with tomato and olive puree, 548
tomato and tapenade salad, 184
Pytt i panna (meat hash), 421

Quail
deep-fried, 334–35
marinated and grilled, 334
Quenelles, fish, with herbs, 95–96
Quesadillas, cheese and chile, 103–4
Queso fresco, 13
Queso frito (fried cheese), 85–86
Queso fundido (melted cheese), 84
Quiche Lorraine, 467
Quinces, lamb tagine with, 408

Rabbit
civet of (hasenpfeffer), 335
stew (stifado), 336–37
sweet and sour, 336
Rabo de toro (braised oxtail), 389

Radicchio, 177
with bacon, 461
grilled, 462
with olive oil, anchovies, and pepper,
462–63
Radish(es), 495. *See also* Daikon
curried, 451–52
curried sautéed, 452
glazed, 450–51, 496
lightly pickled, 455
mixed pickled vegetables, 444
quick-braised root vegetables with
hoisin, 499
salad, 172
Raisins. *See also* Currants
chicken with nuts and, 296–97
couscous with butter or oil, pine nuts,
and, 526
escarole with olive oil, pepper, and, 463
macerated dried fruits and nuts,
627–28
pilaf with pine nuts and, 514
raisin almond sauce, fish with, 268–69
spinach with pine nuts and, 489
Raita
banana-coconut, 176
basic, 175
beet, 176
chickpea, 176
cucumber-mint, 175
mixed-vegetable, 175
potato, 176
tomato, 175
Rajma (spicy red beans), 437
Ramadan soup (harira), 153–54
Ramps, *vinaigrette,* 464–65
Raspberries
berry pudding, 624
simple fruit soup, 624–25
Ratatouille, 501
Rau ram, 201
Ravioli, 59
spinach-ricotta, 544–45
vegetarian, 542–44
Rebozados (crisp-fried shrimp or
vegetables), 92
Recado rojo (annatto seasoning paste),
218, 609–10

pit-roasted pork (cochinita pibil),
351–52
shrimp or ribs in annatto sauce,
218–19
Red beans
bean and nut filling for stuffed
vegetables, 449
with coconut, 434
with coconut milk, 434–35
coconut rice and beans, 516
with garlic and cumin, 438
red bean dip, 29–30
refried beans, 438–39
rice and beans, Korean style, 511–12
slow-cooked, 433
spicy (rajma), 437
spicy beans, Goan style (feijoada),
436–37
with walnut-garlic sauce, 443
Red-braised chicken, 282
Red cabbage, 443. *See also* Cabbage
braised, with apples, 445
Red-cooked chicken, 280–81
Red fish stew, fast and spicy, 269–70
Red lentils with rice, 513
Red peppers. *See also* Peppers
basic red gazpacho, 117
grilled, 470–71
roasted, 470–71
roast pepper spread with walnuts and
garlic, 32–33
rouille, 603–4
Red sauce, fish fillets or shrimp in, 230
Red snapper
in almond sauce, 243
with artichokes, 245–46
baked, with dried mushroom sauce, 251
broiled, with olives, 265–66
with chiles and tomatoes, 228–29
choucroute de poissons, 270
crisp-fried, in spicy tomato sauce,
234–35
fish couscous, 265
fish salad with horseradish dressing,
197–98
fish stew with aïoli (bourride), 137
fish tacos, 238–39
fish tagine, 239–40

Salad(s) (cont'd)
eggplant, cold, with sesame dressing, 186
eggplant, grilled, sautéed, or roasted, 191–92
eggplant, with mustard-miso dressing, 185–86
eggplant, roasted, 192
eggplant, sautéed, 192
eggplant and yogurt, 192–93
farro or barley, 527–28
fennel and cucumber, 181–82
fennel and orange, 173
fish, with horseradish dressing, 197–98
fresh tomato, 172
fresh tomato, spicy, 172–73
fresh tomato and green bean, 172
garlic bread salad with tomatoes, 181
ginger cucumber, 177
green, with oil and vinegar or lemon, 165
green, with vinaigrette, Roquefort, and walnuts, 165
green beans with sesame-miso or sweet sesame dressing, 190
green bean and tuna, 189
green mango, with meat, 203–4
green mango, with smoked fish, 204
green papaya (som tum), 174–75
green papaya, with shrimp, 198–99
leek, 169
leek and olive, 169
marinated mushrooms, 176–77
minced chicken "salad" (laarb), 199–200
mixed vegetable, with horseradish, 188
orange, artichoke, and olive, 174
orange, fennel, and olive, 173–74
orange, red onion, and rosemary, 174
orange and walnut, 174
pickled beets, 179
potato, with mustard vinaigrette, 194
pressed tofu salad, 185
radish, 172
raita, 175–76
roasted corn and black bean, 195
roasted pepper, anchovy, and caper, 194
roast pepper, with tomatoes and preserved lemon, 193–94

salade lyonnaise, 202
salade niçoise, 196–97
salade Olivier, 199
salt cod, 198
sauerkraut, 168–69
seafood, Mediterranean-style, 197
seaweed, with cucumber and chicken or shrimp, 200–201
spinach and dried shrimp, 185
tabbouleh, 187–88
tofu, with peanut sauce, 195–96
tomato, with ginger, 173
tomato and onion, 183
tomato and tapenade, 184
walnut chicken salad, 278
Salade lyonnaise, 202
Salade niçoise, 196–97
Salade Olivier, 199
Salami and bean salad, 189
Salbutes, chicken, 324
Salmon, 236
choucroute de poissons, 270
crisp-skin fillets, with chimichurri sauce, 236–37
grilled, rémoulade, 256–57
miso-broiled, 211
potato croquettes with, 475–76
in rice "sandwiches," 511
salmon deviled eggs, 34
salt- and sugar-cured (gravlax), 23–24
teriyaki, 255
Salmoriglio, skewered swordfish chunks with, 257–58
Salsa
blistered tomato, 610
cilantro, 616–17
grilled crab with, 227
grilled or roast lamb with, 359
citrus, Mayan (xec), 615–16
fresca, 610
fruit salad "salsa," 178
habanero-garlic, 611–12
papaya and red onion, 613–14
pasilla, 612
roasted onion, 614–15
roja (cooked red salsa), 610–11
tomato-chipotle, 611

chicken, turkey, or pork chops with, 289
verde (green sauce), 614
verde, chicken in, 302
verde, with tomatillos, 614
Salt-and-pepper, Szechwan, 583
Salt cod, 56, 245
bacalao with eggplant, 244
Basque style (bacalao a la vizcaina), 243–44
brandade de morue, 56–57
stuffed piquillos with, 47
fried, in tomato sauce, 245
fritters (bacalaitos), 90
salad, 198
in tomato sauce, 244–45
Salt-grilled (broiled) fish, 259
Salty limeade, 660
Sambal ikan billis, 515–16
Sambal oelek (chile-lime sauce), 590
Samosas, 59
meat, 64–65
potato-and-pea, 66
vegetarian, 66
Sand cake, 651–52
Sandwich Cubano (grilled ham and cheese), 363
"Sandwiches"
fish, panfried, 57–58
rice, 511
Sangria, 672
white, with peaches, 672
Saran, Suvir, 561, 564, 594
Sardines, fresh
broiled or grilled, 96–97
panfried fish "sandwiches," 57–58
Satay
fried, 100
grilled, 101
Sauce(s), 582–617. See also Condiments; Dipping sauce; Pasta; Relish; Salsa; Vinaigrette
about, 582
aïoli, 603
almond, fish fillets in, 243
almond garlic, chicken with, 297–98
anchovy, 605–6
annatto, shrimp or ribs in, 218–19

avgolemono (egg-lemon), 596
avocado "mayonnaise," 616
béarnaise, 602
black bean, quick-braised fish fillets in, 227–28
black bean, stir-fried clams or crabs in, 206–7
caramel, fish fillets poached in, 232
caraway, poached fish fillets in, 249
chervil-butter, for fish, 601–2
au chien, grilled skirt steak with, 348
chile, chicken with, 301
chile-lime (sambal oelek), 590
chimichurri, 617
chipotle, chicken, turkey, or pork chops in, 289
cilantro, fish steamed in its own juice with, 263–64
cilantro, quick baked fish in, 264
citrus, chicken with, 316
dried fruit and nut, with cilantro, 599–600
dried mushroom, baked fish fillets with, 251
fenugreek cream, marinated lamb "popsicles" with, 353
garlic, Creole (mojo criollo), 617
garlic, stir-fried pork in, 370
ginger, shallow-fried small fish with, 259–60
ginger chile, 584
green, chicken in, 302
green, shrimp in, 220
gribiche, 601
hard-cooked egg, steamed fish fillets with, 250–51
herb purees, 605
hoisin chili sauce, 584
horseradish, creamy or sharp, 607–8
hot-and-sour, braised whole fish in, 260–61
lemon, braised lamb with, 410
lemongrass-coconut, steamed shrimp with, 216
mayonnaise, 602–3
mayonnaise, green, French style (sauce verte), 603

miso, black cod or mackerel fillets in, 233–34
miso-chile, tuna with, 254–55
mole, almond, chicken in, 301–2
mole, chicken with, 300–301
mushroom-bamboo shoot, braised whole fish in, 261
mustard-cream, halibut with vegetables with, 256
mustard dill, 608–9
nam prik, 586
parsley, 604–5
pasilla chile, stewed lamb shanks with mushrooms and, 414–15
peanut, 586–87
ponzu, 591
pumpkin seed (pipián), 612–13
raisin almond, fish with, 268–69
red, fish fillets or shrimp in, 230
red wine, squid in, 222
rémoulade, 603
Roquefort, grilled steak with, 347–48
rouille, 603–4
Russian, poached fish with, 251–52
saffron, fish fillets in, 241–42
sesame, 592
sherry, clams in, 207–8
spinach, cheese or tofu with (saag paneer), 486
spinach, spicy, 486–87
sweet-and-sour, braised whole fish in, 261
tahini, 597
tamarind, shrimp in, 214–15
tapenade, 604
toasted chile, 585
tomato:
    fast, fresh, 606
    with garlic and orange, 607
    kofte with yogurt and, 356
    with miso, Japanese, 606
    salt cod in, 244–45
tomato, spicy:
    crisp-fried fish fillets or shrimp in, 234–35
    hard-cooked eggs in, 338–39
    mixed vegetables with, 339
    whole fish in, 229

tomato-mustard, uncooked, 606
tomato-nut, for fish (romesco), 606–7
walnut (tarator, skordalia), 600
    chicken with, 278
    chicken salad with, 201
walnut, French, 600
walnut-garlic, beets with (pkhali), 443
yogurt:
    chickpea dumplings in, 435–36
    prune-stuffed meatballs in (alubukhara kofta), 424–25
    thin, 597
Sauerkraut, 483
    bigos (hunter's stew), 403–4
    braised in wine, 483
    fish with (choucroute de poissons), 270
    pork, bean, and sauerkraut soup (jota), 146–47
    roast fish fillets with bacon and, 247–48
    roast goose with, 332–33
    salad, 168–69
    sauerkraut vegetable stew (kapusniak), 114
    with smoked meats (grand choucroute), 404
    soup (shchi), 147–48
Sausage. See also Chorizo
    and beans, 401
    bigos (hunter's stew), 403–4
    and cabbage soup, 158–59
    chicken and, in vinegar, 316–17
    Chinese:
        flavorful sticky rice (yau mei faan), 508–9
        fried rice with, 506–7
        shrimp with peas and, 214
    fresh sausage patties, 421–22
    fresh sausages (mititei), 422–23
    linguiça, mussels with, 210
    meaty bean stew from the Pyrenees (garbure), 402–3
    and orange, with bay leaves, 374–75
    pasta with cabbage and, 159, 552
    pasta with cream and, 557–58
    pasta with, 558
    poached, with garlic, 422
    pork and beans Asturian style (fabada), 401–2

with dill and mint, 498
pie, 459–60
vegetables with dried shrimp and
coconut milk, 502–3
Supplì (fried rice balls), 43–44
Swedish meatballs (kottbullar), 101–2
Swedish pancakes (plattar), 646
Sweet almond buns (semla), 578–79
Sweet-and-sour dishes
12345 spareribs, 391
braised pork, 398
braised whole fish in sweet-and-sour
sauce, 261
rabbit or chicken, 336
sweet and sour onions, 469
Sweet breakfast buns, 579–80
Sweet potatoes
beef stew with, 377–78
Cuban (boniato), in yucca fritters
(buñuelos), 87–88
masala sweet potatoes, 497
potato pancakes with scallions and
kimchi, 474–75
potato puffs, 481–82
vegetarian tsimmes, 502
with white wine and lemon, 428–29
yam in mirin, 498
Sweet rolls with saffron, 578
Sweet tart pastry, 654
Swiss chard
braised, with olive oil and rice, 465–66
croquettes, 487–88
fish stew with aïoli (bourride), 137
with raisins and pine nuts, 489
vegetarian ravioli filling, 542–44
Swordfish
grilled, rémoulade, 256–57
Mediterranean-style seafood salad, 197
pan-cooked, with "killed" onions, 237–38
pan-seared, with tomatoes, olives, and
capers, 257
with salmoriglio, 257–58
seared, with lemongrass, tamarind, and
fried garlic, 253–54
simmered in soy and sake, 253
sweet-and-spicy broiled, 234
sweet black pepper swordfish,
Vietnamese style, 252–53

Syrup, sugar, for beverages, 660
Szechwan pepper, 9, 369
chile oil with, 583
cold cut beef shank, 39
Szechwan salt-and-pepper, 583

Tabak maaz (fried lamb ribs), 103
Tabil (Tunisian spice rub), 597–98
Tacos
chicken, 323–24
fish, 238–39
shredded pork, 324
Tagine
chicken and chickpea, with vanilla,
285
chicken and lentil, 284–85
fish or chicken, 239–40
lamb, with fresh fruit, 408
lamb, with prunes, 407–8
Tagliatelle dough, 541–42
Tahini, 12, 187
baba ghanoush, 31
cold noodles with sesame sauce, 532
hummus, 19
sauce, 597
tomato and onion salad with, 183
Tamale pie, 396–97
Tamales, 531
Tamarind, 10, 214, 587
paste, to make, 585
sauce, shrimp in, 214–15
seared swordfish with lemongrass, fried
garlic, and, 253–54
Tandoori chicken, 291
Tandoori raan (grilled or roast lamb with
spices), 354
Tapenade, 604
pasta with tomato and olive puree, 548
tomato and tapenade salad, 184
Tapioca coconut milk, bananas in, 623
Taquitos (fried pork-filled tortillas), 69
Taramasalata (fish roe puree), 24–25
Tarator (walnut sauce), 600
chicken salad with, 201, 278
chicken with, 278
Tarhana (pasta grattata), 126
Taro, 88

Tarragon
rémoulade sauce, 603
roast chicken with, 277
Tart(s). *See also* Pie(s), savory
about savory tarts, 459
cream tart (tarte vaudoise), 654–55
savory tart pastry, 458–59
sweet tart pastry, 654
tarte au sucre, 655
tomato, 76–77
walnut, 632
zucchini, with bacon, 77
Tarta de almendras (almond cake),
632–33
Tarte flambé (Alsatian "pizza"), 44–45
Tarte au sucre, 655
Tarte aux tomates, Marie Martin's, 76–77
Tarte vaudoise (cream tart), 654–55
Tea, 664
cardamom-scented, 668
cinnamon, 667
ginger (salabat), 665
green tea ice cream, 642
hibiscus, iced (agua de jamaica), 665
with jam, 669
lemongrass, iced, 666
lemongrass-ginger, 666
roasted barley, 667–68
spiced (masala chai), 668
Thai, hot or iced (cha yen, cha dum
yen), 667
Tea eggs, 34–35
jook with pork and, 124
Tea-smoked duck or chicken, 327
Teem ding tenh cho, 171
Tembleque, 636
Tempura (batter-fried fish and
vegetables), 91–92
Teriyaki
chicken, 317–18
salmon, 255
steak, chicken, pork, or shrimp, 360
Thai barbecued chicken, 288
Thai basil, 10, 221
Thai chiles, 10, 589
Thai menus, 676
Thai tea, 667
Thai pantry items, 9–10

Whole wheat pita, 569
Wiener schnitzel (crisp veal cutlets),
    364–65
Wild mushrooms. *See also* Porcini
    mushrooms
    with herbs and butter, 55
    mushrooms and eggs, 74–75
    stewed lamb shanks with pasilla chile
        sauce and, 414–15
Wine, 13. *See also* Mirin; Red wine;
        Sherry; White wine
    Chinese, 9, 212, 274
Wine vinegar, 170, 171
Winter squash, 497
    beef stew with, 377–78
    couscous with vegetables, 527
    flan, 634
    in mirin, 498
    masala winter squash, 497
    Mediterranean squash and chickpea
        soup, 130
    penne with, 553–54
    pumpkin and walnut dessert (kabak
        tatlisi), 631–32
    soup, Laotian-style, 130
    with white wine and lemon, 428–29
Witloof. *See* Belgian endive
Wolfert, Paula, 678
Wolffish, in saffron sauce, 241–42
Wontons, 59
    fried, 63
    wonton soup, 63
Wood ear mushrooms, 8
Wor teep (pot stickers), 59, 63–64
Wrappers
    for Chinese dumplings, 62

for egg rolls, 62
lettuce, minced shrimp in, 213–14
for lumpia rolls, 68
for vareniki, pelmeni, or pierogi, 58–59

Xec (Mayan citrus salsa), 615–16

Yakitori, chicken, 319–20
Yams. *See also* Sweet potatoes
    yam in mirin, 498
Yang chow fried rice, 507
Yard-long beans, 196
    green papaya salad (som tum), 174–75
    tofu salad with peanut sauce, 195–96
Yau mei faan (flavorful sticky rice), 508–9
Yeast, 559
Yeasted flatbreads (naan), 563
Yellow coconut rice, 516
Yellow rice, 518–19
    with chorizo, 519
Yogurt, 13
    chicken with rice and (chicken korma
        pulao), 293
    collards or kale cooked in, 463–64
    eggplant with peppers and, 457
    and eggplant salad, 192–93
    fruit lassi, 663
    green beans with dill and, 461
    kofte with tomato sauce and, 356
    lamb kebabs with peppers and, 356–57
    lamb shanks cooked in, 414
    "milk" (ayran), 662
    mint chutney, grilled lamb chops with,
        352–53

mint chutney with, 595
mint lassi, 663
piyush, 662
raita, 175–76
sauce:
    chickpea dumplings in, 435–36
    prune-stuffed meatballs in
        (alubukhara kofta), 424–25
    thin, 597
shake, savory (lassi namkeen), 662–63
shake, sweet (lassi meethi), 663
yogurt cheese, 20
yogurt chickpea salad, 180
Yucca, 473
    ajiaco (creamy chicken soup) with, 140
    chips, 23
    fritters (buñuelos), 87–88
Yuzu, in ponzu, 591

Zarzuela, 270–71
Zerde (saffron-rice pudding), 638
Zucchini, 498
    couscous with vegetables, 527
    custard (flan de courgettes), 44
    with dill and mint, 498
    fritters, 89
    lightly pickled, 455
    pie, 459–60
    ratatouille, 501
    roasted vegetable gazpacho, Ignacio
        Blanco's, 117–18
    tart, with bacon, 77
    *vegetables with dried shrimp and
        coconut milk,* 502–3